THE QUICKWAY CROSSWORD DICTIONARY

The Quickway

CROSSWORD DICTIONARY

Compiled by

COLONEL H. W. HILL
C.M.G., D.S.O.

and revised by his son

FREDERICK WARNE

LONDON

First published by Frederick Warne & Co Ltd, London 1953

This edition published by Frederick Warne (Publishers) Ltd, London 1977

Revised edition © Frederick Warne & Co Ltd 1977

Third Reprint 1984

ISBN 0 7232 2019 0

Printed and bound in Great Britain by
William Clowes Limited,
Beccles and London

D7346.584

CONTENTS

THE CROSSWORD CURE

To The Times *Crossword Editor*

O nameless coiner of the cryptic clue,
  O master of delusive definition,
Embracing in your panoramic view
  A world of miscellaneous erudition,
Once more I pay the homage due
  To your wise conduct of your Inquisition,
Bringing a daily boon and breathing space
To the tired runners in a mad world's race.

You leave no fruitful avenues unexplored
  That minister to innocent hilarity,
But never strike a harsh or jarring chord,
  Or find a virtue in unveiled vulgarity.
Rumour and gossip are by you ignored;
  You season ridicule with kindly charity,
Yet on occasion with unerring eyes
Transfix malicious folly as it flies.

You jog my memory with your mental jerks;
  To you, in fine, I owe a double debt
For while the old machinery still works
  And shows no sign of breaking down as yet—
Thanks to the stimulus of your quips and quirks—
  You teach me to remember, and forget.
For Hell's most grisly gangsters have no power
To crash the gate that guards the Crossword hour.

C. L. GRAVES

The above poem, which appeared in *The Times* of July 23, 1941, is reproduced by the kind permission of the author's son.

PREFACE

This Dictionary has been specially compiled to meet the exacting needs of modern crossword enthusiasts. All the distinctive features of *The Quickway Key*—of which over 100,000 copies have been sold—have been retained; but notable additions have been made. These include a far greater number of CLUE words, a wide range of synonyms, and a complete vocabulary of the Eight-Letter Words.

The distinctive features are:

1. All CLUE words having the same number of letters are grouped together.
2. Every line begins with a possible CLUE word.
3. All CLUE words are printed in capital letters.
4. Classification code letters, such as **ar** = architecture, **md** = medicine, etc. are placed at the extreme right-hand edges of the lines, on the basis of the equivalents. A detailed list is given on page xi.
5. A very wide range of the latest words has been recorded, of which few may be found in any other one dictionary. Words in brackets indicate, not synonyms or equivalents, but areas in which the word in question is to be encountered.
6. Participles and past tenses of verbs have frequently been recorded, especially when in the passive they form adjectival phrases.

These distinctive features materially reduce the time that has to be spent in the search for interesting clues.

A large number of dictionaries have been consulted; these include *The Shorter Oxford Dictionary, The Century, Chambers's, Nuttall's, Webster's Collegiate Dictionary;* also etymological and classical dictionaries, Roget's *Thesaurus* and Nuttall's *Synonyms and Antonyms.* Clue words have been taken from encyclopaedias, *The Statesman's Year Book,* Dr. Brewer's *Reader's Handbook,* and authoritative books on Glass, China, Pewter, Curios, etc.

Words such as **CRITH, HELITE, CHENAR, LIBIDO, ZYGOTE,** etc., have been collected from scientific books and reports dealing with Modern Chemistry, Electricity, Physics, Zoology, Botany, Engineering, Physiology, etc., also from books on Theosophy and New Thought. Store catalogues and the special catalogues referring to wireless apparatus, tools, seeds, drapery, and other trades have been ransacked. A wide range of terms dealing with sports and pastimes has been included, as for example: **SCRUM, CAPPED, STANCE, DORMY, ROQUET, BURNED, GOLD, HYPE, OXER, CRAPS.**

Australian, South African, Canadian, Indian, American, and foreign words, such as **COOEE, TREK, MUSH, BHYLE, PRONTO, DUCE, TCHEKA,** are represented.

The mythological names include many Greek, Roman, Norse, Egyptian, Chaldean, and Hindu Gods.

Nearly all English words have in the course of centuries passed through many variations in their spellings. For example, in Murray's *New English Dictionary* the spelling of the word 'POWDER' has between the thirteenth and seventeenth centuries passed through the following variations, *poudre, pudre, puder, powdre, powdir, powdyr, pouder, powdere, poudire, pouldre, pulder, poulder, powlder;* and to these might be added the Scots variations of *pouther* and *powther.* A number of variations in spelling have been collected, but the range of variations recorded in different dictionaries is so large that those now given should not be regarded as exhaustive.

The selection of suitable definitions or synonyms for the words of three or four letters seldom presents any difficulty; in fact, these short words often have so many

PREFACE

completely different meanings that more than one line is required to indicate possible clue solutions. For example, **BOX** may refer to a receptacle, a shrub, a driver's seat, a box at the theatre, an affair of fisticuffs, or to some occult nautical rite in which a compass is involved.

The longer words are usually more definite in their meanings; but **BESTED** and **WORSTED** may in some cases be synonymous terms, whilst **CLEAVE** may imply either 'adhere to' or 'split asunder.' Crossword setters, however, have a somewhat similar outlook to that master of the English language, Humpty Dumpty, who declared that: 'When *I* use a word, it means just what I choose it to mean—neither more nor less.' And further, being bound by no inhibition of compunction in splitting up words to suit the nefarious purpose, the setter may insist that **BOOKS-HOP** is a voluminous dance in spite of any exact or meritorious definition while evolving his uncanny mystification.

Similarly, there are those who insist upon providing a clue such as 'five o'clock disappointment' for 'no tea' (spelt 'NO-T' i.e. 'NOT'), or 'up to his neck in the sea' for the philosopher Seneca ('SE-NECK-A').

This particular aspect of crosswords has been delightfully epitomized in the sonnet commemorating the 5,000th Crossword in *The Times*, reproduced on the facing page by the kind permission of its author.

The various items enumerated under the heading GENERAL INFORMATION will frequently be found of special value in elucidating clues without the necessity of delving into a selection of reference books.

The compiler wishes to express his thanks to those numerous correspondents who so kindly forwarded valuable suggestions. It is his hope that this new volume will be found to fulfil the multifarious requirements of earnest crossword solvers and setters and so enhance the pleasures of the crossword hour.

H. W. HILL

Publisher's Note

In 1976 a second revision was undertaken by Rowland Hill and March Laumer. Many modern words and terms were added, while obsolete words were omitted. This crossword dictionary remains, however, substantially that compiled during the years 1920–1951 by Col. H. W. Hill.

CROSSWORD MISCELLANY

TO THE EDITOR OF THE TIMES

Sir,

Much have I travelled in another life,
Taken the golden road to Samarkand,
Rolled down to Rio, wandered down the Strand
(Bananaless), asked after Laban's wife.
I swore, "I will not cease from mental strife
Nor shall my pencil slumber in my hand
Till I have re-discovered Penguinland
And found a cricketer's Malayan knife."

In vain; the tangled clues still tantalize
And synonyms elude, like runic rhymes.
So would-be solvers with lack-lustre eyes,
Confronted with the anagram for limes,
Look at each other with a wild surmise
Silent, upon a crossword in The Times.

Your faithfully,
ELTON EDE

---

50 YEARS AGO

From the Manchester Guardian Weekly, December 12, 1924

The world is a puzzling place, but man is not to be deterred from the delights of additional and self-inflicted bewilderment. At one time he found his pleasure in the manipulation of bits and pieces in a jig-saw. Then came the more intellectual diversion of acrostics. Now we are asked to revel in an import from America called 'cross words.' The acrostic in its time must have done valuable work for the Bible Society, since the more obscure names of the Old Testament have a knack of beginning and ending with the vowels that otherwise defy the puzzle-maker, while they are also fairly hard to remember. The new pastime must be a great comfort to the salesmen of dictionaries, glossaries, and the like, and the old complaint that the average man's vocabulary is limited to some five or six hundred words out of the treasury that is open to him may be dissipated by the present quest of verbal oddities. The complete 'cross word' enthusiast is led up hills of chemistry into dales of botany, he must even put his nose to the English grammar and be quite sure where the species 'adverb' begins and ends. The thing beneath the word need not excite him; it is the raiment of letters that he seeks, and he must be sure to get them in their proper order. The young lady who thought that to write was human but to spell divine might profit by the new pastime, but people who are more deeply interested in things than in words will wonder, like the charity boy confronted with the alphabet, whether it is worth going through so much to learn so little. However, the nominalists appear to be a large, happy, and busy faction, but this only increases one's fears as to the fate of a family in which there should be a lonely realist railing at all this quest of the shy noun or dim elusive epithet. May not the result of such a clash become upon occasion – cross words?

Within that decade the first edition of this book—in pocket diary format, with a pencil—was already in evidence, especially among those travelling to and from the City. Later editions were enlarged to the present size.

Cryptic

March 5, 1976.

Sir, — Returning home from my local **hammam** I was somewhat **esurient** and so visited our **spence** and set the table complete with **ortolan** but my fear was **adipose**, so I stopped eating and performed a quick **antiphon** with my wife, before retiring to bed.

All the words in bold appeared in this week's crossword puzzles, and if they are known and understood by your average reader I will eat my **zucchetta**.

W. L. Fraser,
Glasgow

Crosswords Keep Man Young at 110

Britain's oldest living person, Mr Alfred Harrow, notches up his 110th birthday on 21st November 1976. Even in recent years he has kept a wonderfully alert mind doing crosswords. . . . 'I have to keep my mind alert,' he says.

Evening Standard

CATEGORY CLASSIFICATION

ac	acoustics	**lw**	law
ae	aeronautics	**ma**	mathematics
ag	agriculture	**md**	medicine
am	automation	**me**	measurements
ar	architecture	**ml**	metallurgy
as	astronomy	**mn**	mining
au	automobiles	**mt**	meteorology
ba	bacteriology	**mu**	music
bc	biochemistry	**nc**	nuclear (physics)
bd	building	**nm**	numismatics, coins
bl	biology	**nt**	nautical
br	brewing	**nv**	navigation
bt	botany	**oc**	oceanography
ce	civil engineering	**pb**	plumbing
ch	chemistry	**pc**	psychology, psychiatry
ck	cookery	**pg**	photography
cn	cinema	**pl**	physiology
cp	computers	**pm**	pharmaceutics
cr	carpentry	**pp**	paper
cy	cytology	**pr**	printing
ec	ecology	**ps**	physics
eg	engineering	**pt**	paints, painting
el	electrical, electronics	**rd**	radar
fd	foundry	**rl**	religion
fr	forestry	**ro**	radio
gl	geology	**rw**	railways
gn	genetics	**sp**	space
gp	geophysics	**sv**	surveying
gs	glass	**tc**	telecommunications
hd	heraldry	**to**	tools
hr	horology	**tv**	television
hy	hydraulics	**tx**	textiles
jn	joinery	**vt**	veterinary
le	leather-working	**wv**	weaving
lt	light	**zo**	zoology

Note: Language and nationality abbreviations are found closer to the definition, within parenthesis, but not in bold type, which is reserved for the above classifications.

Sc. = Scottish	Gr. = Greek	Ind. = Indian
Fr. = French	It. = Italian	Jew. = Jewish
Rus. = Russian	Lat. = Latin	Sp. = Spanish
Scand. = Scandinavian	Turk. = Turkish	Aust. = Australian, etc.

Various literary abbreviations are also given:

obs. = obsolete	Shak. = Shakespeare	Spens. = Spenser

A B a Hebrew month
A D a short advertisement
A E one (Sc.)
A H ! exclamation of satisfaction
A I South American three-toed sloth   zo
A L 'the' in Arabic
A M part of verb 'be'
A N if, ornate box
A P son of (Welsh)
A S Roman pound   me
A S an integer; Roman bronze   nm
A T preposition of place
A X axe   to
A Y yes; yea; more so

B A the soul (Egypt)   rl
B E exist
B I bisexual
B O sacred tree of Buddha   bt
B Y preposition of agent

C A' ca' canny (Sc.)
C O company

D O ditto; act; perform
D O 1st note   mu
D Y lake-bottom plant detritus   ec

E A Chaldean fish god   rl
E A an inlet; drainage canal in Fens
E E eye (Sc.)
E H ! exclamation
E L 'the' in Spanish (masc. sing.)
'E M them
E M printing unit of space   me
E N half the width of an em   me
E X late; out of

F A 4th note   mu
F O Chinese Buddha   rl
F U Chinese prefecture
F Y ! fie; denoting disgust

G E Mother-Earth (Gr.)
G O proceed; depart; fare

H A ! exclamation
H E male pronoun
H I !
H O ! } exclamation

I D fish (carp) also ide   zo
I F supposing that
I L 'the' in Italian
I'M I am
I N within, inside
I O triumphal cry
I O beloved of Jupiter
I S being, existing
I T personality; sex appeal

J O a sweetheart (Sc.)

K A jackdaw (Sc.)   zo
K A ethereal double (Egypt)
K O knock out
K Y kye; kine; cattle (Sc.)
L A 'the' (Fr., It., Sp.: fem.); 6th note   mu
L E 'the' (Fr., masc.)
L I Chinese mile (1.6 km)   me
L O 'the' (It., masc.); behold

M A goddess of Right (Egypt)   rl
M E 1st-person pronoun
M I 3rd note   mu
M O (half-a-mo); medical Officer   md
M P a legislator; a politician
M S abbr. for Mrs or Miss
M Y of me

N O negative reply

O D magnetic force
O F preposition of possession
O G King of Basan
O H ! exclamation
O K all correct
O N preposition of location
O P a short work; opus
O R alternatively; heraldic gold
O S bone; mouth   md
O X a male of cattle   zo

P A Maori fort
P H acid/alkaline content value   me
P I mixed type (printing)

R A hawk-headed sun-god (Egypt)   rl
R E concerning
R E ra, 2nd note   mu
R H rhesus blood type

S I 7th note   mu
S O thus, therefore, then, 7th note   mu
S T street; saint (abbreviation)

T A thanks
T I tree-lily (Polynesia)   bt
T M measure of glucose in man   md
T O preposition of direction
T V (television)

U G disgust; a surfeit
U P preposition, adverb of direction
U R of the Chaldees
U S objective of 'we'
U T 1st note   mu

V A go on   mu
V E brother of Odin   rl
V O a creek

W E plural pronoun
W O ! whoa! stop

Y A ! exclamation
Y E you; the (obs.)

Z O Image (Jap.)

A

AAH the Moon-God of Egypt   rl
AAM 30–35 gallons (136–159 litres), Dutch liquid   me
ABA Eastern camel-hair fabric
ABB yarn for the warp
ABC a railway guide; alphabet
ABP abbr. for Archbishop
ABU father (Arabic)
ABY atone; pay penalty; retribution
ACE aviator; particle; (cards)
ACT deed in writing; do; perform   lw
ADD join; tag; annex; append; tot
ADO stir; fuss; commotion; hubbub
ADS. advertisements
ADZ adze   to
AFT abaft; astern   nt
AGA Turkish officer; agha
AGE era; period; epoch; senility
AGO past; gone
AHA! exclamation of discovery
AID succour; help; subsidy; assistant
AIK oak (Sc.)   bt
AIL suffer; pain; peak; pine
AIM object; direct; intend; purpose
AIN own (Sc.)
AIR mien; ventilate; display; tune
AIT river or lake islet; eyot
AKE ache (obs.)
ALA wing or side petal of blossom   bt
ALB white linen clerical vestment   rl
ALE mead; beer
ALK resin from turpentine tree
ALL entirely; whole
ALP pasture land
ALS also (Sc.)
ALT high notes in the scale   mu
AMA holy wine or vessel   rl
AMP electrical unit (abb. for ampère)   me
ANA miscellaneous facts; Celtic goddess
ANA equal parts   md
AND the ampersand; &   pr
ANE one (Sc.)
ANN annat (Sc.)   lw
ANT emmet; pismire; termite   zo
ANU Celtic goddess; Babylonian sea-god
ANY some (in questions, negatives)
APE imitate; copy; mimic; monkey   zo
APT appropriate; pertinent; prone
ARC bow; luminous bridge
ARE hectare (2.5 acres)   me
ARG abbreviation for chemical silver
ARK chest; coffer; place of refuge   rl
ARM equip; limb; estuary
ARN elder tree   bt
ART skill; dexterity; craft
ARY any (Sc.)
ASA gum; Norse God   bt, rl
ASE Peer Gynt's mother

ASH cinder; forest tree; wood   bt
ASK interrogate; invite; sue
ASP poisonous snake (Cleopatra)   zo
ASS moke; burro; donkey   zo
ATE Goddess of Mischief
AUF fool; oaf; simpleton
AUK flightless sea-bird; garefowl   zo
AVA kava; Hawaiian palm-lily drink
AVE prayer; hail   rl
AWA' away (Sc.)
AWE reverential veneration
AWL the cobbler's tool; bradawl   to
AWN beard in chaff   bt
AXE to cut down; hatchet   tl
AYE yea; for ever
AZO azobenzene derivative   ch

B

BAA to bleat
BAB fishing bob
BAC ferry; brewing tub
BAD depraved; detrimental; evil; baneful
BAG sack; wallet; pouch; steal
BAH! a derogatory exclamation
BAM bamboozle; hoax
BAN muslin; bar; interdict; outlaw
BAP small soft bread loaf (Scotland)
BAR ban; prohibit; hinder; stop; ingot
BAT spree; batsman; vampire
BAY mill-dam; bark; laurel   bt
BBC (broadcasting)
BED couch; berth; layer; plant
BEE emblem of the French Empire; insect   zo
BEG crave; implore; entreat; petition
BEL Baal; a Babylonian God   rl
BEN (Big Ben); mountain; within (Sc.)
BEN winged seed of ben-tree
BET lay; wager; stake; gamble; pledge
BEY or **BEG** a Turkish title
BIB feeder; sip; tipple; whiting pout   zo
BID order; charge; direct; offer; invite
BIG huge; swollen; pregnant; barley   bt
BIN a receptacle for wine, corn, etc.
BIS encore   mu
BIT (horse's bit); piece; fragment   to
BOA snake; fur collar   zo
BOB style of hairdressing
BOB sled, sleigh; shilling (5 pence)   nm
BOG sog; morass; swamp; marsh
BOK a South African deer   zo
BOM boma; boa; snake   zo
BOO cry down; decry; hoot; execrate
BOT the larva of the bot-fly   zo
BOW arc; bob; bend; a tie; prow   nt
BOX (theatre); (compass); driver's seat
BOX case; chest; encase; shrub   bt
BOX cuff; buffet; spar; fight
BOY lad; page; stripling; Champagne
BOZ Charles Dickens

BRA woman's garment
BUB yeast; strong drink; boy (USA)
BUD sprout; blossom; graft **bt**
BUG insect; bedbug; bugbear; secret mike **zo**
BUM bailiff; loafer; backside
BUN style of coiffure; a confection
BUR burr; rough edge; chestnut shell **bt**
BUS an omnibus
BUT yet; except; nevertheless; unless
BUY purchase; bribe; corrupt
BYE (cricket); (golf); (tournament draw)

C

CAB cabriolet; 3 pints (1.7 litres) (Heb.) **me**
CAD a vulgarian
CAM (machinery)
CAN able to; preserve (food); pannikin
CAP to out-do; (hunt collection)
CAR vehicle
CAT tackle; whip; puss; mouser **zo**
CAW also kaw
CAY kay; key; shoal; reef; islet
CEE a shape of spring
CID Spanish chief; poem
CIG cigarette, fag
CIT citizen
CLY to steal
COB pony; male swan; spider **zo**
COB a head; spike of maize; nut **bt, ck**
COB harbour; clay; basket; dollar **nm**
COD pod; husk; deceive; codfish **zo**
C.O.D. cash on delivery
COG toothed wheel; small boat **nt**
COG coax; wheedle; cheat; wooden bowl
COL mountain pass; neck
CON study; memorize; steer; a knock; swindle
COO (dove)
COP hill; head; tuft
COP policeman; arrest
COR heart
COS lettuce **bt**
COT cottage; crib; small boat **nt**
COW browbeat; intimidate; depress **zo**
COX coxswain **nt**
COY shy; bashful; demure; diffident
COZ cousin
CRI the crackle of pewter
CRU proposed int'n'l monetary unit
CRU yield; produce; grape-juice (Fr.) **ck**
CRY sob; yell; bawl; blazon
CUB enclosure for cattle; young animal **zo**
CUD food for re-chewing
CUE (billiards); (acting)
CUP to bleed; a beverage
CUR mongrel; pariah; dog **zo**
CUT incision; gash; wound; channel
CUT chop; sever; carve; avoid; shorten

CWM steep rounded hollow (Welsh)
CWT a hundredweight (50 kg) **me**

D

DAB fish; expert **zo**
DAD a blow; to thrash; to scatter; father
DAG shred; cut
DAG dagger; pistol
DAH dhar; Burmese curved knife
DAK post; bungalow (Ind.) **ar**
DAL lentil **bt**
DAM Indian coin; barrier **nm**
DAN tub; a title
DAP to fish with a may-fly
DAR dace **zo**
DAW dawn; jackdaw **zo**
DAY epoch; era; time
DEB a debutante
DEE die (Sc.)
DEN cave; haunt; snuggery
DEW an aqueous precipitation
DEY Turkish title; bey; dairymaid
DIB dip; make holes
DID diddled; performed
DIE stamp; (dice); perish
DIG appreciate, like (slang)
DIG delve; scoop; excavate
DIK trouble
DIM obscure; vague; tarnish
DIN clamour, row; paper size; film **pt, me**
DIP dop; duck; douse; souse
DIS to fail; Pluto; the underworld
DIT a ditty (Spens.)
DIV evil spirit (Persian) **rl**
DOD clip; poll; lop
DOE female of fallow-deer, hare, rabbit **zo**
DOG follow; trail; track; canine **zo**
DOL pain intensity unit
DOM a Portuguese title
DON put on; assume; a Spanish title
DOP to dip; duck
DOP Cape brandy
DOR befool; mock; mockery; bedim
DOR dorr; dung-beetle; drone **zo**
DOT dowry; point; stop; speck
DOW fit and able
DRY sere; parch; desiccate
DUB to name; substitute sound **cn**
DUB to smooth; rub; confer knighthood
DUD worthless; defective
DUE owing; proper; becoming
DUG udder; nudged; exhumed; excavated
DUN mound; drab colour; gloomy
DUN to cure fish; to demand payment
DUO song in two parts **mu**
DUO microcopying film process
DUP to open
DUX a leader

DWT a pennyweight — me
DYE colour; tinge; stain

E

EAN to produce
EAR plough or till; lug; heed
EAT chew; consume; devour; erode
EAU -de-Cologne
EBB recede; wane; subside
ECU five-franc piece — nm
EEL snake-like fish — zo
EEN eyes (Sc.)
E'EN even
E'ER ever
EFT a newt; forthwith (obs.) — zo
EGG incite; impel; stimulate — zo
EGO the self-conscious subject
EIK eke; add; addition (Sc.)
EKE increase; likewise; in addition
ELD old age; olden times; decrepitude
ELF sprite; gnome; imp; pixy; fairy
ELK wapiti; the whooper swan — zo
ELL 45 inches (114 cm) (cloth) — me
ELM stately tree — bt
EMU Australian bird, cassowary type — zo
END kill; close; conclude; terminate
ENE once (Sc.)
ENG durable dark Burmese wood — fr
ENS entity
EON eternity; perfection; an age; aeon
EOS Dawn Goddess — rl
ERA age; period; epoch; cycle
ERE before; sooner than
ERF small garden in S. Africa
ERG unit of work — me
ERN sea eagle — zo
ERR offend; sin; wander; trespass
ERS vetch — bt
ESS the letter 'S'
ETC et cetera, and so forth
EVE evening; the day before an event
EWE a female sheep — zo
EYE observe; watch; view; bud — bt

F

FAD whim; craze; crochet; hobby
FAG knot; end; cigarette
FAG drudge; fatigue; a bore
FAM the hand (slang)
FAN a votary; agitate; inflame
FAP drunk; fuddled (Shak.)
FAR distant; remote; buck-wheat — bt, ck
FAT printing term; vat; obese
FAW gypsy
FAY fairy; elf; fit closely
FAY fey; to clean out
FEB a short month
FED ate; subsisted; supplied
FEE remuneration; pay; reward; toll

FEN marsh lands; (Chinese) money — nm
FET get; fetch (obs.)
FEU tenure; to rent, lease
FEW scant; rare; scarce
FEY fay; spiritual exaltation; fated
FEZ cap with tassel
FIB petty falsehood
FID a wedge — nt
FIE! exclamation of disgust
FIG excrescence; tobacco; a fruit — bt
FIL (Iraq), (Jordan) — nm
FIN an organ of locomotion — zo
FIR a cone-bearing tree — bt
FIT appropriate; qualified; spasm — md
FIX quandary; dilemma; hitch; tie
FLU influenza — md
FLY vehicle; sly; observant; abscond
FLY printing term; flee; decamp; insect — me
FOB watch pocket; impose; delude
FOE antagonist; opponent; enemy
FOG moss; rank grass; thick mist — bt
FOH Buddha (Chinese)
FOO Chinese department
FOP a dandy; a nut; beau; coxcomb
FOR on this account
FOU tipsy; full; a bushel (Sc.) — me
FOX deceive; to stain; reynard — zo
FOY parting feast; assistance boat — nv
FRA brother; (Fra Anselmo) (It.) — rl
FRO from; away; back
FRY cook; swarm; smolt (fish) — zo, ck
FUB fat man; cheat
FUD hare's tail — zo
FUG frowsty warmth
FUM Chinese phoenix
FUN merriment; jollification
FUR incrustation; a pelt — zo

G

GAB talk; a hook
GAD gauntlet spike; wedge — to
GAD rod; goad; to rove
GAE go (Sc.)
GAG a wheeze; to silence
GAL unit of gravity; girl — me
GAM gossip; talk; school of whales — zo
GAM mouth; leg
GAP fissure; rift; cranny; chink
GAR to compel (Sc.); a marine fish — zo
GAS to gab; ether; gasoline — ch
GAT pistol; a strait; a gap
GAY gey; lively; merry; homosexual
GED pike or luce — zo
GEE turn; go faster
GEL viscous, colloidal
GEM jewel; treasure; a leaf-bud — bt
GEN detailed information; manna (Heb.)
GEO gio; creek; voe; vae; firth; frith
GET obtain, breed; divorce (Jewish) — rl

GEY	gay; fairly; rather (Sc.)	
GIB	a cat; the Rock	zo
GID	sheep-disease; sturdy	
GIE	give (Sc.)	
GIF	if (Sc.)	
GIG	whirl; cloth machine; vehicle	
GIM	neat	
GIN	machine; snare; schnapps	
GIN	native woman (Australia)	
GIP	clean herrings	
GNU	buffalo (S. Africa)	zo
GOA	Tibetan antelope	zo
GOB	mouthful; refuse coal	
GOB	worked out mine	
GOD	Deity; idol; image	
GOG	and Magog	
GOT	seized; procured; achieved	
GOY	gentile, Christian (Jew.)	
GRU	ice	
GUE	Shetland violin	mu
GUG	inclined mine road	mn
GUM	stick; mucilage; resin	bt
GUN	a revolver or pistol	
GUP	idle chatter; rumour	
GUT	narrow channel; intestine	md
GUY	rope; effigy; burlesque; man	nt
GYM	gymnastics	
GYN	timber-loading device	fr
GYP	college servant; bedmaker	

H

HAD	befooled; caught; kept; owned	
HAE	have (Sc.)	
HAG	parasite fish; virago; beldam	zo
HAH!	exclamation	
HAM	Noah's second son	
HAM	a heavy actor; amateur radio operator	
HAN	plural of have (Spens.)	
HAP	chance; luck; accident; fortuity	
HAS	owns; possesses; acquires	
HAT	dignity of Cardinal; bonnet	
HAW	hawthorn berry	bt
HAW	hedge; boundary	
HAY	cut grass; hedge; fence	
HEL	Goddess of Death (Scand.)	
HEM	a cough; to sew; to edge	
HEN	a fowl	zo
HEP	hip; berry of the dog-rose	bt
HER	of a female	
HET	hot and bothered	
HET	heterosexual	
HEW	chop; hack; fell; cut	
HEY!	exclamation to call attention	
HIC!	a small hiccup	
HID	secreted; cached; concealed	
HIE	a cry; to hasten	
HIM	objective of 'he'	
HIN	6 quarts (6.8 litres) (Heb.)	me
HIP	rafter; berry; hep	ar, bt
HIP-hurray		

HIS	belonging to him	
HIT	strike; success; computer-made answer	
HOA!	ahoy	
HOB	part of grate; hub	
HOB	a rustic; a fairy	
HOD	(for bricks); a coal-scuttle	
HOE	a promontory; to weed	to
HOG	scrubbing broom; boar; pig	zo
HOG	to cut hair; bend	
HOO!	hold! stop!	
HOP	small dance; plant	bt
HOT	violent; acrid; fervid; ardent	
HOW	glen; dell; low hill	
HOX	to hamstring	
HOY	small ship	nt
HOY!	ahoy; hoa!	
HUB	hilt; a boss; a centre	
HUB	mark on quoits	
HUE	and cry; tint	
HUG	embrace; enfold; clasp	
HUH!	exclamation	
HUM	wordless singing; homosexual	
HUN	Tartar; savage nomadic Asiatic race	
HUP!	a horse hastener	
HUT	hovel; shed; cabin; cot	
HUX	method of fishing	
HYP	depression; hip	

I

IBO	native of East Nigeria	
ICE	to cover with sugar	
ICH	(Ich Dien) Prince of Wales' motto	
ICY	frigid; cold; chilling; frosty	
IDE	kind of carp	zo
IDO	artificial language	
ILK	clan, category	
ILL	ailing; evil; badly; sick	
IMP	extend; strengthen; graft; sprite	
INK	writing, printing fluid	
INN	caravanserai; tavern; hostelry	
ION	electrically charged particle	el
I.O.U.	a note of hand	
IRE	rage; fury; resentment; passion	
IRK	weary; trouble; distress	
ISE	I shall (Sc.)	
ISH	exit; issue (Sc.)	
ISM	ideological prejudice	
ITS	belonging to it	
IVY	a creeper sacred to Bacchus	bt

J

JAB	prod; poke; stab; a thrust	
JAD	a quarrying cut	
JAG	a notch; a binge; to stab	
JAH	Jehovah	
JAK	bread-fruit tree	bt
JAM	child's garment; squeeze; a conserve	
JAP	Japanese	
JAR	discord; jolt; jangle; gallipot	

JAT Indo-Aryan
JAW lecture; the mouth; to splash   md
JAY bird; nitwit   zo
JEE to move; to budge (Sc.)
JET spray; black variety of lignite   mn
JEU a game (Fr.)
JEW Hebrew, Israeli
JIB to balk; to shy; a sail   nt
JIG tune; dance; mechanical guide   to
JOB stab; profession; work
JOE a sweetheart (Sc.)
JOG rog; push; nudge; remind; trot
JOT an iota; a tittle; to note
JOW to toll; a stroke of a bell (Sc.)
JOY rapture; ecstasy; bliss; glee
JUD a mass of coal
JUG incarcerate; a ewer; to stew
JUR earth-nut   bt
JUT protrude; project; to collide

K

KAA The Rock Python   zo
KAE jackdaw (Sc.)   zo
KAF fountain conferring immortality
KAM crooked (Shak.)
KAT Egyptian weight   me
KAW caw
KAY shoal; cay; key; reef
KEA parrot that kills sheep (NZ)   zo
KEB ewe; sheep louse   zo
KEF drugged stupor
KEG small cask or barrel
KEN know; recognise; knowledge
KEP shaft-hoist stop; to catch (Sc.)
KET carrion; matted wool; a fleece (Sc.)
KEV 1,000 Electron-Volts   me
KEX fool's parsley; dried stalks   bt
KEY quay; cay; crib; wedge; clamp   me
KID faggot; bundle of sticks
KID tub; deceive; hoax; young goat   zo
KIF Indian hemp
KIN relationship; affinity; kindred
KIP 1000-lb (454-kg) force unit; nap   eg
KIP small untanned hide   le
KIT tub; bottle; violin; gear   mu
KOA acacia (Sandwich Islands)   bt
KOB water antelope   zo
KOP hill (S. Africa)
KRI Hebrew marginal direction
KRU Kroo; a Liberian
KYA native hut (S. Africa)
KYE kine (Sc.)   zo

L

LAC dye; shellac; transparent resin   nm
LAD youngster; stripling; boy
LAG convict; dawdle; loiter; dally
LAM to thrash; weaving device
LAP fold; wrap; polish; circuit; drink

LAR Roman Household God   rl
LAR white-handed gibbon   zo
LAT inscribed pillar (India)
LAT Latvian money   nm
LAV a word (Gypsy)
LAW an allowance; edict; statute; canon
LAX slack; loose; remiss
LAY lea; ballad; exorcise; put
LAY non-clerical; laic; inexpert
LAZ las, Black Sea Turks
LBW leg before wicket
LEA measure of yarn; meadow   me
LEA lay; open land; pasture
LED induced; helped; conducted
LEE sheltered; lea; meadow
LEG lower limb; stage, tack in sailing   nv
LEI plural of **LEU**; garland   nm
LEK bird courtship; coin   zo
LEO lion; 5th sign of Zodiac
LET (tennis); permit; allow; lease; hire
LET hindrance; prevent; delay
LEU Romanian money   nm
LEW luke-warm; tepid
LEX an enactment   lw
LEV ⎫
LEY ⎬ Bulgarian money   nm
LEY lea; pasture; common pewter
LIB ad lib.
LID top; cover; coverlet
LIE falsehood; rest; recline; repose
LIN a waterfall; to cease
LIP touch the edge; rim; mouth
LIS litigation   lw
LIS fleur-de-lis; heraldic lily   bt, hd
LIT lighted; kindled; ignited
LOB clumsy; (cricket); worm   zo
LOG record; tree-trunk   nt
LOG ¼ pint (0.4 litres) (Hebrew)   me
LOO toilet; card game
LOP truncate; amputate; dock
LOT to catalogue; fate; portion
LOW base; vile; abject; depressed
LOW bellow; moo; to flame; to blaze (Sc.)
LOY narrow spade
LSD money, (Libra; Solidus; Denarius)
LSD hallucination drug   md
LUD King Lud
LUE to sift
LUG ear; tug; haul; drag
LUM chimney (Sc.)
LUX unit of light   me
LUZ a legendary bone
LYE alkaline solution   ch
LYM dog on leash   zo

M

MAB the queen of the fairies
MAC son of (Sc.)
MAD crazy; demented; raving; insane
MAG chatter; steal; magpie   zo

MAG halfpenny   nm
MAM Madame; ma'am
MAN employee; husband; mankind   nt
MAO The Peacock   zo
MAP delineate; chart; draw
MAR spoil; deface; impair; disfigure
MAT dull surface; weave; interlace; twist
MAW craw; crop stomach
MAX a kind of gin
MAY have permission, possibility
MAY hawthorn blossom; 5th month   bt
MEL honey
MEN humanity
MET Metropolitan; a bushel (36 litres)   me
MEV Million Electron-Volts   me
MEW sea-gull; moult   zo
MEW cage; confine; a cat-call
MHO electrical unit of conductivity   me
MID central; amid; middle
MIL one-thousandth of an inch (2.5 cm)   me
MIM prim; demure; precise
MIR Russian commune
MIX blend; combine; jumble; mingle
MNA mina; 50 shekels   nm
MOA extinct bird, emu type (NZ)   zo
MOB cap; rabble; populace; crowd
MOD assembly; meeting
MOD modern; Gaelic choral contest   mu
MOE mow; grimace; mop
MOG move away
MON Cambodian language
MOO cow noise
MOP swab; a hiring-fair; a grimace
MOR type of humus layer   fr
MOT bon mot; witticism
MOW stack; heap; pile of hay; cut down
MOW facial expression; moe
MRS mistress
MUD mire; sludge; slime
MUG fool; face; cup
MUM silence; a special brew of beer
MUN man (dialect)
MUX to spoil; a mess
MYA shellfish   zo

N

NAB seize; nap; grab; a knoll
NAE none (Sc.)
NAF unfashionable; unsuitable
NAG harass; pester; horse   zo
NAM distraint (obs.)   lw
NAP doze, forty winks
NAP a card game; a racing tip
NAY contrariwise
N.C.O. non-commissioned officer
NEB beak; nose; nib; a point
NEE born (Fr.)
NEF silver model ship; cadenas; casket
NEK a pass (S. Africa); a col

NEO new style
NEP catmint; knot in cotton fibre   bt
NET neat; nett; snare; capture
NEW novel; recent; fresh; modern
NIB beak; point; neb
NIL nihil; zero; nothing
NIM steal; margosa oil
NIP squeeze; pinch; sip; a dram
NIS not so; imp; hobgoblin; mix
NIT insect's egg   zo
NIX water elf; nothing
NOB aristocrat; knave at cribbage; head
NOD bow; beck; drowse
NOG small pot; tree nail
NOG wooden brick; peg; noggin; ale
NOM de plume
NOR logic
NOT negating adverb
NOW at this time
NOX illumination measurement unit   lt, me
NOX Nyx; personification of night
NOY unit of perceived noisiness   ac, me
NUB shove; hang; knob; gist
NUN a religeuse; a sister   rl
NUR knot in wood
NUT a dandy; screwed bolt end   bt
NUT boss on anchor   nt
NUX (vomica)   md, bt
NYE brood of pheasants   zo
NYS none is (Spens.)
NYX Goddess of Night, daughter of Chaos

O

OAF changeling; fool; dolt; idiot
OAK outer door   bt
OAR to row; an oarsman   nt
OAT a grain; a pan-pipe   bt, mu
OBI oby; magic; a fetish (West Indies)
OBI Japanese sash
OCA potato (S. Amer.); palm-leaf book (Sri Lanka)
OCH! oh! or ah! (Sc. & Ir.)
ODD singular; peculiar; quaint; droll
ODE poem or song set to music
ODO Bishop of Bayeux, A.D. 1066
O'ER poetical over
OES O's; circlets
OFF away; gone
OFT often; frequently; repeatedly
OHM electrical resistance   me
OHO! exclamation
OIL anoint; lubricate; a lubricant
OKE Turkish weight, 2¾ lb (1.2 kg)   me
OLD antique; archaic; pristine; aged
OLM a blind lizard   zo
ONE individual; unity; undivided
OOF money
OOM Uncle (Cape Dutch)
OPE open

OPS Goddess of Wealth; wife of Saturn
OPT to choose; elect; pick
ORB globe; circle
ORC whale; grampus; an ogre   zo
ORD edge; beginning
ORE mineral-bearing earth; coin (Scand.)
              nm, mn
ORT a bit; refuse; a crumb
OUR three-quarters of an hour
OUT without; beyond; get out!
OVA eggs   zo
OWE run up an account
OWL night bird; to smuggle   zo
OWN possess; admit; concede
OXO organic compound radical   ch
OZS ounces

P

PAD cushion; stuff; paw   zo
PAH! exclamation of disgust
PAH stockade (New Zealand)
PAL staunch friend; palooka; mate
PAM knave of clubs at loo (card game)
PAN forest god; small pool
PAP conical hill; nipple
PAR equality; (golf)
PAR parr; young salmon   zo
PAS pace, ballet step
PAT dab; tap; rap; caress; aptly
PAU bustard (S. Africa)   zo
PAW pad; handle roughly
PAX era of peace
PAX kiss of peace; an osculatory   rl
PAY to cover with pitch; stipend; wages
PEA (thimble-rigging)   bt
PED pack-saddle; basket
PED small pack-saddle; pedal   mu
PEG short drink; spigot; spile
PEN pound; enclosure; mountain; indite
PEN female swan; quill   zo
PEP energy; drive (USA)
PER by
PES hind-limb podium   zo
PET temper; fondle; a favourite   zo
PEW a seat in church   rl
PIA arrowroot (Polynesian)   bt
PIE magpie; pye   zo
PIE prayer-book; pi; mixed print
PIG earthen vessel; to guzzle; hog; iron   zo
PIN half a firkin; transfix   me
PIN peg; nail; to fasten
PIP to black-ball; chirp; a depression
PIP disease of fowls; melancholy   bt
PIT set; match; mine; abyss
PIU more (It.)   mu
PIX holy box; coin box; pyx
PLY fold; layer; bias   nt
POA a genus of grass   bt
POD husk; to swell   bt
POD a shoal of whales or seals   zo

POE or parson-bird (New Zealand)   zo
POH! exclamation
POI Polynesian taro paste   ck
POM Pomeranian dog; Englishman in
     Australia   zo
POP burst; explode; pawn
POT to shoot; tankard; mug
POW poll; head (Sc.)
POX a disease   md
POY balancing-pole; a grant
POZ positive; certain
PRO for; professional
PRY peer; snoop; examine
PUB public-house
PUD paw; pad; pudding   zo
PUG dog; fox or monkey; pugilist   zo
PUN a form of humour; a paronomasia
PUP to whelp; young dog or seal   zo
PUR purr; curr; (owl or cat noise)
PUS discharge from infection   md
PUT to steer; bud; game at cards; rustic
PUT wanton woman; signal of distress
PUY volcanic formation
PYA Burmese money   nm
PYE rule for determining Easter date   rl
PYE pie; magpie   zo
PYX pix; holy box; coin box at the Mint

Q

QUA as (Latin)
QUI who (Latin)
QUO whither (Latin); status quo: as it is

R

RAD radical; afraid (Sc.)
RAD unit of radiation dose   me
RAG a famous club; to torment; garment
RAI one-third acre (Siam)   me
RAJ power (India)
RAM engine; prow; butt; cram   zo
RAN raced; scurried; flowed; melted
RAP snatch; tap
RAP counterfeit Irish halfpenny   nm
RAS vizier (Abyssinia)
RAT to desert; a rodent   zo
RAW bleak; crude; uncooked
RAX reach; strain (Sc.)
RAY part of flower; a beam   bt
RAY the skate; sheep scab   zo
RED to disentangle; revolutionary
REE hen-bird of ruff   zo
REE riddle; tipsy; Portuguese coin   nm
REF referee
REH saline efflorescence (India)
REI Portuguese money of account   nm
REM ionizing radiation dosage
REN the kidney   md
REP debauchee; rip
REP fabric; repetition; repertory (theatre)

RES	a thing; a point	lw
RET	to rot flax; hemp or jute	
REV	to speed up; Reverend	rl
REV	to increase revolutions, accelerate	
REV	revise, revision; revert, reverse	
REX	a king	
RIA	inlet of the sea	
RIB	bone; watercress; petiole	bt
RID	to free; clear; expel; destroy	
RIE	rye	bt
RIG	wanton; manipulate	nt, zo
RIM	brim; border; edge	
RIO	ounce (28 grams) (Japan); a tael	me
RIP	fish-basket; tear; rend; a Lothario	
RIT	strike; tear (Sc.)	
ROB	rook; fleece; strip; fruit syrup	
ROC	fabulous bird; rok	zo
ROD	twig; wand; 5½ yd (5 metres)	me
ROE	of fish; deer	zo
ROG	to jog; to shake	
ROK	roc; fabulous bird	zo
ROM	gipsy; a Romany	
RON	King Arthur's ebony spear	
ROO	a kangaroo	zo
ROT	to decay; putrefy; nonsense	
ROW	line; brawl; a dreadful din; (oars)	
ROY	a king (obs.)	
RUA	storage pit (New Zealand)	
RUB	chafe; abrade; dilemma	
RUC	rok; roc; a fabulous bird	zo
RUD	rub; polish; flush; ochre	
RUE	lament; regret; suffer; sorrow	
RUE	herb of grace	bt
RUG	mat; coverlet; a drink; shaggy dog	
RUM	grog; queer; quaint; odd; fantastic	
RUN	hurry; speed; propel; tour; demand	
RUT	wheel track; groove; desire	
RYE	rie; (whisky)	bt
RYE	a bird disease	

S

SAB	sob (Sc.)	
SAC	bag, often fluid-containing	md
SAD	sorry; downcast; gloomy; dismal	
SAE	so (Sc.)	
SAG	droop; settle; bend; sink	
SAI	Brazilian monkey	zo
SAL	Indian timber tree	bt
SAL	salt	ch
SAM	together; to collect; to curdle	
SAP	undermine; juice; a worker	bt
SAT	seated; perched; settled	
SAW	a saying; an adage; seen	to
SAX	a knife; slate-cutter's hammer	to
SAY	tell; declare; utter; allege	
SEA	basin; an ocean; wave surge	rl
SEC	dry (flavour)	
SED	(fish-hook); a fillet	
SEE	watch; descry; heed; a throne	rl
SEG	sedge; a bullock	bt, zo

SEL	self (Sc.)	
SEN	(Japanese) (Indonesian)	nm
SEP	sepal; leaf	bt
SET	a twist; squared block; firm; fixed	
SET	group; clique	cn
SET	Egyptian deity of darkness	
SEW	stitch; baste	
SEX	gender	
SHA	shapo; wild sheep	zo
SHE	feminine pronoun	
SHY	coy; bashful; diffident; wary	
SIB	akin to; also syb	
SIC	as written	
SIK	to seek (Sc.)	
SIL	ochre pigment	
SIM	a Simeonite; low churchman	rl
SIN	transgress; wickedness; iniquity	
SIP	sup	
SIR	sire; master	
SIS	girl; sweetheart	
SIT	brood; incubate; rest; repose	
SIX	sax (Sc.)	
SKI	(winter sport)	
SKY	to loft; heavens; the weather	
SLY	artful; wily; astute; fly	
SNY	upward curve	
SOB	cry; blubber; weep; snivel	
SOC	privilege; sac	lw
SOD	turf; sward; lawn; grass	
SOG	a bog; morass; marsh; to saturate	
SOL	old French halfpenny (Peru)	nm
SOL	the sun; gold; 5th note	mu
SON	offspring; a disciple	
SOP	to soak; to steep; a bribe	
SOS	help!	
SOT	drunkard	
SOU	French mite; sol	nm
SOW	disseminate; plant; broadcast	zo
SOX	haberdashery	
SOY	bean, sauce; oriental footwear	bt, ck
SPA	spring; health resort; hydro	
SPY	espy; behold; detect; observe	
STY	(in eye); pig-pen	md
SUB	subaltern; substitute	
SUE	prosecute; plead	lw
SUG	a kind of worm	zo
SUM	add; total; amount; aggregate	
SUN	Phoebus Apollo; Sol; Helios	
SUP	to take supper	
SYB	sib; akin to	
SYN	syne; since (Sc.)	

T

TAB	flap; tally; check	
TAD	street boy (USA)	
TAG	catchword; touch; label; game	
TAI	Japanese bream	zo
TAJ	Mahal; headdress (Ind.)	
TAN	to beat; brown colour	
TAP	rap; pat; knock; broach	

TAP cock; faucet; screw — to
TAR sailor; pitch; bitumen; incite — nt
TAT needlework; pony
TAT native cloth
TAU bug; toad-fish — zo
TAU Egyptian or St Anthony's cross — rl
TAW a marble; game
TAX accuse; strain; tariff; levy
TEA beverage; bohea — bt, ck
TEC teck; detective
TED spread
TEE (golf); Chinese umbrella
TEG deer; sheep; tag — zo
TEN a net drawn up
TER thrice
TEW gear; iron chain; scourge
THE definite article
THO' though
THY of thee
TIB a courtesan
TIC nervous twitch; spasm — md
TIE dead-heat; bind; link; unite
TIG a game; a cup
TIN can; preserve; receptacle; money — mn
TIP gratuity; vails; cant; tilt; incline
TIR shooting contest (Fr.)
'TIS it is
TIT small bird; pony — zo
TOD 28 lb of wool — me
TOD bush; fox — bt, zo
TOE extremity
TOG to dress; a garment
TOK a nesting place of capercaillies — zo
TOL take away
TOM male cat — zo
TON fashion; 20 cwt (1 tonne) — me
TOO more than enough
TOP a toy; vertex; zenith; acme; excel
TOR rocky hill
TOT to add; child — me
TOW flax; hemp; haul — bt
TOY to trifle; plaything
TRY 3 points at Rugby football
TRY test; essay; attempt; endeavour
TUB basin, container; a boat — nt
TUG haul; tow; lug — nt
TUI parson-bird (NZ) — zo
TUN barrel; large cask — me
TUP ram; to butt; hammer — zo
TUR Caucasian goat — zo
TUT! deprecating exclamation
TUT piece work; a hassock
TWA two (Sc.)
TWO a pair; brace; couple; deuce
TYE ore washing buddle; tie
TYG tall china cup
TYR a son of Odin — rl

U

UDA purplish brown glaze
UDO Japanese vegetable — bt

UDO universal language
UGH! exclamation of disgust
ULE gum (Mexico) — bt
ULT ultimo
UMA wife of Siva — rl
UNA cat-boat having a centreboard — nt
UNO United Nations Organisation
URE practice; wont; work; exercise
URE wild ox; aurochs — zo
URF stunted child (Sc.)
URN jar; vase; receptacle
URY hazy (Sc.)
USE usage; avail; employ; apply; usury
UTA American lizard — zo
UTU blood-money; requital (NZ)
UVA a bunch — bt

V

VAC vacation
V.A.D. war worker
VAE voe; gio; creek; firth; frith; fiord
VAG peat (Sc.)
VAN fan; forefront; vehicle; vane
VAS blood vessel — md
VAT fat; vessel; tank; value-added tax
VET horse doctor; examine
VEX plague; harass; fret; chafe
VIA by way of
VIE strive; contend; contest
VIM force
VIS power
VIZ namely
VLY vlei; pool (S. Africa)
VOE vae; geo; gio; fiord; estuary; firth
VOL two wings conjoined at base — hd
VOR navigational ranging system — nv
VOW pledge; dedicate; consecrate; oath
VOX voice; song part — mu
VUG rock cavity (Cornish)
VUM vow (Amer.)

W

WAD Manganese ore; mass of paper — mn
WAE woe (Sc.)
WAG vibrate; wit; jester; humorist
WAN pale; sickly; languid
WAP whop; a bundle; swat; wrap
WAR strife; enmity; discord; contend
WAS past of 'be' (sing.)
WAT hare; drunken (Sc.) — zo
WAX increase; grow; beeswax
WAY route; passage; track; usage
WEB a textile fabric; cobweb
WED a pledge; to marry
WEE diminutive
WEN (London); tumour; wart — md
WET humid; moist; watery; drench
WEY various weights, salt, corn, &c. — me
WHO which person?

WHY for what reason?
WIG vallancy; toupee; periwig; peruke
WIG berate; scold; lecture; upbraid
WIN gain; procure; acquire; achieved
WIS know (obs.)
WIT wag; humour; reason; facetiousness
WOE affliction; sorrow; grief; anguish
WON to dwell; an abode (Korea)   nm
WON earned; got; swayed; persuaded
WOO to court
WOP whop; whip; Italian
WOT know
WOW event; sound change
WOX waxed (Spens.)
WRY awry; askew; crooked; distorted
WYE a person (Sc.)
WYE Y-branched pipe   pb

Y

YAB jabber (Sc.)
YAH! exclamation of derision
YAK Tibetan ox   zo
YAM sweet potato   bt, ck
YAP yell; cry; bark
YAW deviate   nt
YEA ay; aye; yes; truly; verily

YEN a gold or silver Japanese coin   nm
YEP yeh; yes (Amer.)
YES yea; aye; ay
YET a gate (Sc.)
YET still; further; besides; however
YEW wood for the bow   bt
YEX hiccough
YID a Jew
YIP pert forward girl (Sc.)
YOD phonetic sound 'y'
YON yonder
YOU 2nd-person pronoun
YOW ewe (Sc.)   zo
YUG an age of the world (Hind.)

Z

ZAK Kashmir raft
ZAX slate cutter; sax   to
ZEA maize   bt
ZED or **ZEE**, the letter Z
ZEL cymbal   mu
ZHO zobo; hybrid yak and cow   zo
ZIP liveliness; a ping; a fastening
ZOO zoological gardens
ZUZ an ancient Jewish coin   nm

A

ABBA	Chaldean or Coptic divine; father	rl
ABBE	French abbot; priest	rl
ABED	in bed	
ABER	river mouth (Celtic)	
ABET	aid; incite; favour; countenance	
ABIB	1st month of the Jewish year	
ABLE	skilful; adroit; expert; competent	
ABLY	masterly; powerfully; cleverly	
A-BOX	opposite bracing of yards	nt
ABUT	meet; adjoin; rest; terminate	
ABYE	aby; atone; pay the penalty (obs.)	
ACER	the maple-tree	bt
ACHE	pain; pang; agony; anguish	
ACID	sour; tart; bitter; vitriolic	
ACME	zenith; apex; pinnacle; pitch	
ACNE	a skin disease	md
ACOP	atop; on high (obs.)	
ACOR	acidity	md
ACOY	accoy; to soothe (obs.)	
ACRE	4840 square yards (hectare); 4 roods	me
ACTA	proceedings in a court	lw
ACYL	carboxylic acid radical	ch
ADAM	the first man; a gaoler	
ADAR	12th month of the Jewish year	
ADIT	opening or passage; entrance	
ADRY	athirst	
ADZE	adz; a mattock	to
AEON	an age; era; cycle; period; eon	
AERY	eyry; ayry; an eagle's nest	zo
AERY	ethereal; visionary	
AFAR	away; distant; remote; aloof	
AFER	the South-West wind	
AFFY	to betroth; trust; confide (obs.)	
AGAR	ploughman of playing fields, Eton	
AGED	elderly; ancient; antiquated	
AGEE	awry; askew; asquint; ajee	
AGEN	again	
AGHA	aga; Turkish Officer; ruler	
AGIO	premium; discount; brokerage	
AGNI	Hindu fire-god and protector	
AGOG	astir; eager; excited	
AGON	sardine-like Alpine fish	ck
AGUA	South American toad	zo
AGUE	malarial fever; chilliness	md
AHEM!	exclamation	
AHOY!	exclamation (nautical)	nt
AIDE	helper; assistant; coadjutor	
AINE	elder son; cadet	
AIN'T	(are not)	
AINU	aboriginal (Jap.)	
AIRA	hair-grass	bt
AIRE	an altar; Irish freeman	
AIRT	direction; quarter (Sc.)	
AIRY	blythe; breezy; ethereal; spacious	
AJAR	slightly opened	
AJEE	agee; ajar; askew	
AJOG	jogging along	
AKEE	West Indian fruit tree	bt

AKIN	sib; agnate; similar; related	
ALAR	winged, pertaining to wings	
ALAS	alack; welladay	
ALBE	albeit; even though	
ALCA	sea-auk genus	zo
ALEE	on the lee-side	nt
ALEW	halloo (obs.)	
ALFA	esparto grass	bt
ALGA	seaweed	bt
ALLA	in the manner of	me
ALLY	alley; a marble of real alabaster	
ALLY	unite; marry; confederate; friend	
ALMA	or **ALME,** Egyptian dancing girl	
ALMS	oblations; gifts; bounty	
ALOD	allod; freehold	
ALOE	a large genus of bitter herbs	bt
ALOW	below; ablaze (Sc.)	nt
ALPS	European mountains	
ALSO	in like manner; further	
ALTO	male voice of highest pitch	mu
ALUM	mordant mineral salt	ch
AMAH	ayah; Indian nurse	
AMBE	ancient surgical instrument	md
AMBO	high reading desk	
AMEN	Egyptian deity of the dead	rl
AMIA	bow-fin or mud-fish (N. Amer.)	zo
AMIC	ammoniac	ch
AMID	betwixt; between; amongst	
AMIN	ammoniate	ch
AMIR	Ameer; Emir	
AMMA	a truss; Syrian abbess	rl
AMMO	ammunition	
AMOK	amuck; frenzy (Malay)	
AMOR	Roman cupid; Eros	
AMOY	language (Formosa)	
AMYL	a tar product	ch
ANAK	a giant of Palestine	
ANAL	of the anus	zo
ANER	male ant	zo
ANEW	again; freshly; repeatedly	
ANIL	the indigo plant	bt
ANKH	life symbol (Egypt)	
ANNA	16 annas to the rupee	nm
ANOA	wild ox of Celebes	zo
ANON	at once; then again	
ANSA	decorated vase-handle	
ANTA	a pilaster	
ANTE	a stake at poker	
ANUS	excremental opening	zo
APAY	to satisfy; to repay (obs.)	
APED	copied; imitated; mimicked	
APER	an impersonator	
APEX	acme; zenith; pinnacle; point	
APIS	sacred bull (Egypt)	
APOD	fish without ventral fins	zo
APSE	polygonal recess	rl
AQUA	water; solution	rl
ARAB	Saracen; Moor	
ARAF	Mohammedan purgatory	
ARAK	oriental palm sap spirit; areca nut	bt
ARAR	North African timber tree	bt

ARBA covered wagon (Tartar)		
ARCA chest or coffer	rl	
ARCH roguish; cunning; shrewd		
AREA yard; enclosure; region; district		
ARES Mars, the God of War		
ARGO the Argonauts' ship	nt	
ARIA air; tune; melody	mu	
ARID dry; parched; sterile; barren		
ARIL outer seed cover	bt	
ARMS armorial emblems		
ARMY host; array; throng; force		
AROW successively; in a row		
'ARRY jovial Cockney name		
ARSE backside; tail of block	nt	
ARTS crafts; guiles		
ARTY spuriously aesthetic		
ARUM lily genus	bt	
ARYL aromatic hydrocarbon radical	ch	
ASAR eskar; gravel ridges		
ASCI bags of spores	bt	
ASHY ashen; wan; pallid; hueless		
ASIA largest continent		
ATKA type of mackerel	zo	
ATLI a Norse king (Atle)		
ATOM jot; tittle; whit; particle		
ATOP acop; on top (obs.)		
AULA a hall; a court		
AULD old (Sc.)		
AUNT (Aunt Sally)		
AURA a zephyr; emanation	nm	
AUTO da fe; autocar		
AVAL an endorsement on a bill		
AVEL an awn of barley	bt	
AVER avouch; confirm; authenticate		
AVES birds collectively	zo	
AVID eager; greedy; voracious		
AVON river (Celt.)		
AVOW own; aver; admit; confess		
AWAY afar; distant; abroad; absent		
AWED inspired by reverence; cowed		
AWNY bearded	bt	
AWRY askew; oblique; crooked		
AXAL axial (obs.)		
AXED discharged; sacked; cut down		
AXIL angle between branch and trunk	bt	
AXIN cochineal ointment		
AXIS the chital; Indian spotted deer	zo	
AXLE axis; spindle; shaft		
AXON nerve-cell impulse-carrying process		
	zo	
AYAH amah; Indian nurse		
AYES supporting votes		
AYRY eyry; eyrie; an eagle's nest	zo	
AZAN polychrome microanalytical		
AZER native of Central Asia		
AZOL developer	pt	

B

BAAL Phoenician god; false god; idol		
BAAS the boss; master (Cape Dutch)		

BABA Patriarch of Alexandria; a cake		
BABE infant; suckling		
BABU Hindu clerk		
BACK help; support; wager; retreat		
BADE (bid); commanded		
BAFF biff; smite; buff		
BAFT abaft; an oriental fabric		
BAHT Thai monetary unit	nm	
BAIL (cricket); hoop-handle; surety	lw	
BAIT worry; badger; a lure; refreshment		
BAKE harden; parch		
BALD bare; hairless; prosaic; unadorned		
BALE bane; harm; misery; bundle		
BALK bauk; impede; refuse; timber		
BALL party; rout; globe; bullet		
BALM salve; unguent; fragrance		
BANC bench (obs.)	lw	
BAND bond; unite; a troupe; a coterie		
BANE poison; ruin; sheep-rot		
BANI Romanian monetary unit	nm	
BANG explosion; a fringe of hair		
BANG bhang; the assassin's drug		
BANG a drink: beer, cider, nutmeg, ginger		
BANK bench of rowers; deposit		
BANT adopt a slimming diet		
BARB to shave; (fish-hook); horse	zo	
BARD wandering minstrel; a poet		
BARE naked; nude; exposed; bleak		
BARK cortex; yelp; yap; a ship	bt, nt	
BARM yeast; ferment; leaven		
BARN granary; store; out-building		
BART baronet		
BARU fluffy fibre	bt	
BASE basis; abject; vile; sordid		
BASH smite; baff; biff; wallop; buffet		
BASK luxuriate; revel		
BASS (ale); low; deep; grave	mu	
BASS American linden tree; perch	zo	
BAST bass; fibre of that tree	bt	
BAST cat-heated Egyptian goddess		
BATE abate; decrease; lessen; curtail		
BATH 6 gallons (27 litres), Jewish liquid	me	
BAUD telegraphic transmission speed unit	tc	
BAUK balk; beam; ridge; hinder		
BAWD whore; hare	zo	
BAWL howl; yawl; yell; shout		
BAWN fort; cattle-pen		
BAYA the Indian weaver bird	zo	
BAYS laurels of distinction	bt	
BEAD bubble; globule; a moulding		
BEAK magistrate; prow; bill; mandible		
BEAM rafter; ray; shine; emit; smile		
BEAM radio directional system; width	nt	
BEAN leguminous plant	bt	
BEAR carry; uphold; suffer; produce	zo	
BEAT spent; exhausted; batter; throb		
BEAT a policeman's perambulation		
BEAU fop; dandy; gallant; coxcomb		
BECK beckon; a small stream		
BEEF grumble (USA); strength		
BEEN the vina; Indian guitar	mu	

13

BEEP telephonic signal		
BEER ale; lager; swipes		
BEET the beetroot	bt	
BEIN comfortable; well-found (Sc.)		
BEJA tribe (Africa)		
BELL model of soundness; to bellow		
BELT zone; girdle; band; thrash		
BEMA judge's seat; pulpit	rl	
BEND deflect; stoop; incline; a spree		
BEND diagonal band on a shield	hd	
BENE the oil-plant	bt	
BENT curved; crooked; withered grass		
BERE bear; barley (Sc.)	bt	
BERG mountain; iceberg		
BERM a ledge; slanting bank		
BEST worst; defeat; overcome		
BETA ray; function	nc	
BEVY swarm; flock; throng		
BHEL Bengal quince	bt	
BHIL a Dravidian race (India)		
BIAS prejudice; prepossession		
BICE pale blue or green		
BIDE await; tarry; stay; dwell		
BIER a conveyance for the dead		
BIFF baff; buff; smite; crash		
BIGA two-horsed Roman chariot		
BIGG bere; a kind of barley (Sc.)		
BIKE bicycle; wasp's nest; a swarm	zo	
BIKH aconitine (Hindu)		
BILE bitter liver secretion	md	
BILE ill-humour		
BILK balk; cheat; deceive; thwart		
BILL fondle; account; placard; poster		
BIND tie; fasten; restrain; secure		
BINE hop-stems; etc.	bt	
BING a heap of corn or alum		
BINK bench; bank; shelf (Sc.)		
BINT a girl (Arabic)		
BION plant capable of separate life	bt	
BIOS yeast-growth promoter	ch	
BIRD (get the bird); a fowl	zo	
BIRK the birch-tree	bt	
BIRL spin; whirl (Sc.)		
BIRR impetus; violent thrust; a whirr		
BIRT the turbot	zo	
BISE cold dry wind (Swiss)		
BISK bisque; soup; pottery		
BITE a nibble; etch; nip; grip; grasp		
BITT (to bitt a cable)	nt	
BLAB divulge; disclose; tell tales		
BLAD fragment; lump; stain; batter (Sc.)		
BLAE blue (Sc.)		
BLAY } a river fish; the bleak	zo	
BLEY }		
BLEA inner bark of tree	bt	
BLEB transparent blister; bubble	md	
BLED past tense of bleed		
BLEE complexion; colour		
BLET spot on decayed fruit; to rot	bt	
BLEW sounded; puffed; panted		
BLIP radar reflection spot	rd	

BLOB viscous globule		
BLOC political/economic grouping		
BLOT blur; mar; tarnish; erase		
BLOW sound; puff; pant		
BLUB sob; cry; blubber		
BLUE navy; cobalt; ultramarine; glum		
BLUE azure; sapphire; (Oxford)		
BLUR dim; sully; obscure; blot		
BOAR male hog	zo	
BOAT craft; bark; skiff; vessel	nt	
BOCK light beer		
BODE portend; presage; augur		
BODY corpse; carcass; substance		
BOER Africander		
BOGY bogey; bugbear; hobgoblin		
BOIL seethe; rage; fume		
BOKO nasal organ (slang)		
BOLD brave; valiant; daring; doughty		
BOLE a tree-trunk; recess	bt	
BOLL pod; capsule	bt	
BOLO Filipino knife		
BOLT abscond; gulp; missile; fasten; sift		
BOMA boa; anaconda	zo	
BOMB petard; block-buster		
BOND link; band; contract; (bricks)		
BONE to steal; os	md	
BONT many coloured (S. Africa)		
BONY full of bones; strong; stout		
BOOB booby; dunce; blockhead		
BOOH! a derisive interjection		
BOOK tome; volume; manual		
BOOM boost; resound; barrier	nt	
BOON benefit; merry; jovial		
BOOR clodhopper; lout; lubber		
BOOT gain; to eject; luggage recess		
BORA cold Adriatic wind		
BORD coal face (mining)		
BORE tidal wave; tire; calibre; drill		
BORN née; begotten		
BORT diamond dust		
BOSA a Persian liquor		
BOSH tosh; inane chatter; bunkum		
BOSK bosket; thicket; grove		
BOSS foreman; stud; protuberance		
BOTE compensation; reparation	lw	
BOTH all of two		
BOTS botts; the larvae of the botfly	zo	
BOUD insect in grain; weevil	zo	
BOUN to dress; prepare; set out (Sc.)		
BOUT contest; conflict; turn		
BOWK large iron barrel; kibble	mn	
BOWL beaker; goblet; (cricket)		
BOWS the fore-end of a ship	nt	
BRAD small nail		
BRAE steep hill (Sc.)		
BRAG boast; vaunt; a game of cards		
BRAN refuse of grain	bt	
BRAT urchin; gamin; child		
BRAW fine; brave; showy (Sc.)		
BRAY braise; pound; clamour; blare		
BRED reared; raised; nurtured		

BREE eyebrow; liquor	
BREN sub-machine gun	
BRER brother; (brer-rabbit)	
BRET a fish of the turbot kind	zo
BREW concoct; devise; plot	
BRIE a cream cheese	
BRIG two-masted square-rigged ship	nt
BRIM verge; marge; border; to coast	
BRIN a fan-stick	
BRIO vivacity	mu
BRIT whitebait, etc.	zo
BROB a wooden wedge	
BROC pewter wine measure	
BROG an awl; to pierce	to
BROW rim; edge; brink; forehead	
BUBO the eagle owl	zo
BUCK talk; jump; deer; dollar	nm, zo
BUDE a gas burner	
BUFF baff; biff; strike; yellow	
BUFF pliant leather; the bare skin	
BUHL brass and tortoiseshell inlay	
BUHR burr-stone; a millstone	mn
BULB (electric); corm; tuber	bt
BULK mass; volume; magnitude	
BULL (papal); (Irish); walrus; moose	zo
BUMP thump; the call of the bittern	zo
BUND league; embankment; quay	
BUNG barrel-stopper; large cork	
BUNK depart; sleeping berth	nt
BUNT butt; part of a sail	nt
BUOY cheer; sustain; float	nt
BURG bury; borough; burgh	
BURK burke; murder; smother; hush up	
BURL a knot in thread or wood	
BURN a brook; parch; char; glow	
BURR rough edge; the burdock	bt
BURT flat-fish, turbot type	zo
BURY burgh; clump of trees; inter	
BUSH thimble; (bearings); a shrub	bt
BUSK to act in the street	
BUSS to kiss; a fishing boat	nt
BUST bosom; sculpture; broken	
BUSY sedulous; officious; industrious	
BUTT thrust; a mound	
BUZZ rumour; a whispered report	
BYRE a cow-house	
BYTE data-counting unit	cp

C

CABA cabas; work-basket; pannier	
CADE cask of herrings; pet lamb	zo
CADI kadi; Turkish judge	
CAER camp; fort (Celt.)	
CAFE coffee-house; restaurant	
CAGE crib; cabin; confine; mew	
CAIC Turkish skiff	nt
CAID alcayde; Arab judge	
CAIN kain; rent in kind; a weasel	zo
CAKE solidify; harden; a tablet	

CAKY encrusted	
CALF part of leg; (Golden)	zo
CALK caulk; spike; calkin	nt
CALL dub; term; summon; visit	
CALM still; unflurried; peaceful	
CALP shale bed (Irish)	mn
CALX chalk or lime	mn
CAMA South African hartebeest	zo
CAME arrived; reached; attained	
CAMP encamp; pitch a tent	
CAMP exaggeratedly stylized	
CAMP temporary outdoor dwelling place	
CANE rattan; bamboo; beat	bt
CANG Chinese pillory	
CANT incline; thieves' patter; hypocrisy	
CANY made of cane	
CAPA Spanish cloak	
CAPE capa; cope; headland; ness	
CARD woolcomb; personality; game	
CARE tend; concern; worry; heed	
CARK care; trouble; fret; anxiety	
CARL churl; clown	
CARP cavil; censure; goldfish	zo
CARR reclaimed bog land	
CART van; wagon; transport	
CASE box; enclose; plight; lawsuit	lw
CASH specie; money; small Chinese coin	nm
CASK casque; helmet; barrel; tub; cade	
CAST mien; shed; toss; mould; tint	
CATE dainty food	
CAUF live fish box	
CAUK sulphate of baryta	mn
CAUL net; membrane	md
CAVE cavern; grotto; den; beware!	
CAVY genus of rodents; guinea-pig	zo
CAWK heavy spar	mn
CEDE yield; relinquish; apportion; forego	
CEIL ciel; roof; ceiling	
CELL cavity; dungeon; nucleus	el
CELO unit of acceleration	me
CELT Kelt; early Aryan	
CENT 10 cents make one dime	nm
CERE to wax; to wrap in cerecloth	
CERT alleged certainty; a snip	
CESS sess; to tax; a local rate	
CEST cestus; a belt or girdle	
CHAC Central American rain gods	
CHAD shad; a fish; sea-bream	zo
CHAI gipsy girl	
CHAL gipsy man	
CHAM King of Tartary; Mogul khan	
CHAP jaw; cleft; fellow; guy; chapman	
CHAR a lake fish; to scorch; to burn	zo
CHAT talk; gossip; warbler; wheatear	zo
CHAW chew; masticate; champ	
CHAY shay; chaise; open carriage	
CHEF expert cook	
CHEW ruminate; munch	
CHIC charmingly correct	
CHID scolded; rated; rebuked	

CHIG to chew; a quid; chaw		
CHIN part of face		
CHIP fruit basket; cut; to chaff; stake		
CHIT pert child; note; memo; voucher		
CHOP the jaw; veer; vary; change		
CHOU ornamental ribbon		
CHOW Chinese dog	zo	
CHOY Indian madder	bt	
CHUB the cheven; a freshwater carp	zo	
CHUG a fussy engine noise		
CHUM pal; palooka; buddy; messmate		
CHUT a peevish cry		
CIEL ceil; plaster; wainscot		
CIMA cyma; ogee moulding of cornice		
CIRC prehistoric stone circle		
CIRE polished silk fabric (Fr.)		
CIRL a species of bunting	zo	
CIST cyst; stone chest; tomb		
CITE quote; summon; adduce	lw	
CITY cathedral town		
CIVE chive; onion	bt	
CLAD garbed; dressed; clothed		
CLAG clog; bemire (Sc.)		
CLAM bivalve shellfish; to clog	zo	
CLAN family; coterie; clique; set		
CLAP beak of hawk; applaud; cheer	zo	
CLAW tear; scratch; lacerate; talon		
CLAY alumina	mn	
CLEF key	mu	
CLEG horse-fly		
CLEM to starve		
CLEW clue; trace; brail; truss	nt	
CLIO Muse of History; molluscs	zo	
CLIP cut; trim; prune; curtail; embrace		
CLOD sod; turf; lump; yokel; rustic		
CLOG obstruct; hamper; trammel		
CLOT curdle; thicken; coagulate	md	
CLOU the essential point		
CLOY glut; pall; satiate; surfeit		
CLUB cudgel; bludgeon; combine; set		
CLUE clew; hint; guide; ball of string		
COAK a dowel-pin; metal bush		
COAL mineral fuel	mn	
COAT cover; lay; spread; vesture		
COAX cajole; allure; wheedle		
COCA the cocaine plant (Peru)	bt	
COCH coach (Spens.)		
COCK rooster; cockerel; chanticleer	zo	
COCK haycock; chief; arrow-notch		
COCO coconut palm	bt	
CODA finale	mu	
CODE digest of laws or rules; cipher		
CO-ED mixed school		
COFF to buy (Sc.)		
COFT bought (Sc.)		
COHO acronym: coherent oscillator	rd	
COIF headdress; Judge's black cap	lw	
COIL trouble; bustle; curl; wind		
COIN counterfeit; invent; quoin; wedge		
COIR cordage; coconut fibre	nv	
COIX a grass; Job's tears	bt	

COKE slang for cocaine		
COLD icy; polar; gelid; passionless		
COLE kale; cabbages generally	bt	
COLL fondle; embrace		
COLT young horse; camel or ass	zo	
COLT gun; young cricketer		
COMA stupor; drowsiness	md	
COMA tuft of follicles; (comet)	bt	
COMB cock's comb; crest; wave; (bees)		
COMB combe; coomb; dell; valley		
COME reach; attain; ensue; arrive		
COMS malt-dust		
COND to navigate	nt	
CONE (fir-cone)	bt	
CONK the nose		
CONN con; cond; steer; navigate	nt	
CONS arguments against; cf. pros		
CONY coney; hyrax; rock-rabbit	zo	
COOF silly coon (Sc.)		
COOK cuckoo-noise; chef; falsify		
COOL calm; collected; allay; indifferent		
COOM soot; axle dirt; coal-dust		
COON nigger; sly fellow; raccoon	zo	
CO-OP co-operative stores		
COOP hen-coop; cask; cage; confine		
COOT the ankle (Sc.); a water-fowl	zo	
COPE vie; contend; struggle; cloak	rl	
COPT Egyptian Christian		
COPY model; ape; mimic; transcribe		
CORB iron coal basket;		
CORF alms-basket		
CORD line; rope; braid; cut wood	me	
CORE centre; heart; kernel		
CORK a stopper; bung	bt	
CORM a kind of bulb	bt	
CORN preserve; an excrescence; grain	bt	
COSE to make one's self cosy (Sc.)		
COSH to slug; to smite; cosy		
COSS about 1¼ miles (2.8 km) (Indian)	me	
COST price; charge; outlay; detriment		
COSY tea-pot cover; cozy; snug		
COTE sheepfold; pass by; outstrip		
COUP exploit; stroke; barter; overturn		
COVE bay; bight; harbour; a fellow		
COWL a monk's hood; chimney-pot		
COXA the hip-joint	md	
COXY cocksure; bumptious		
COZE to chat; a talk		
COZY cosy; snug; comfortable		
CRAB bitter apple; peevish person	bt	
CRAB a portable winch; crustacean	zo	
CRAG ragged rock		
CRAM ram; stuff; glut; study		
CRAN about 750 herrings	me	
CRAW maw; crop; fowl's stomach		
CRAX S. American bird; curassow	zo	
CREE to soften grain		
CREW mob; gang; crowd; crowed	nt	
CREX the white bullace	bt	
CRIB manger; cot; coop; copy		
CRIS creese; Malay knife; kris		

CROP reap; an ox-hide; whip; craw
CROW brag; vaunt; crowbar; croak   zo
CROY embankment; fish-trap
CRUP the buttocks; brittle
CRUT a dwarf; shaggy oak-bark   bt
CRUX the crucial point
CUBE the third power
CUCA coca; cocaine shrub   bt
CUFF sleeve-end; buffet; slap; a stroke
CUIR leather
CULL pick; pluck; choose
CULM coal-dust; corn or grass stalk   bt
CULT ritual; worship; system; ism
CURB check; restraint; kerb
CURD coagulated milk
CURE remedy; antidote; panacea; heal
CURE care of souls, priest (Fr.)   rl
CURL wind; wave; ringlet; ripple
CURR purr; snore like a barn-owl
CURT abrupt; terse; brief; laconic
CUSK burbot, an eel-like fish   zo
CUSP a kink in a curve
CUSS a curse; cross-grained fellow
CUTE shrewd; clever; adroit; chic
CWYM rounded valley
CYAR the ear-hole   pl
CYMA moulding of a cornice; ogee
CYME young; shoot; inflorescence   bt
CYST water-bag; bladder; growth   pl
CZAR Tsar; Tzar (Rus.)

D

DACE small river fish; dare; dart   zo
DADA anarchic artistic non-style
DADE hold child by leading-strings
DADO decorative skirting
DAFF to play the fool (Sc.)
DAFT idiotic; absurd; ridiculous
DAGO a Southern European
DAIL Irish Parliament
DAIS raised platform; a canopy
DAKS sports trousers
DALE vale; valley; dingle
DALI Brazilian timber-tree   bt
DALL incised tile; cow-dung fuel
DALT a foster-child
DAME the wife of a baronet
DAMN doom; condemn; ruin
DAMP dank; humid; depress; discourage
DANE great dane dog   zo
DANG elegant form of damn
DANK moist; clammy; humid; damp
DANT soft or fine coal   pl
DARE defy; venture; challenge; presume
DARG a day's work; a task (Sc.)
DARI Indian millet   bt
DARK ebon; murky; Cimmerian
DARN to mend by stitching
DART rush; run; hurl; a missile
DASH throw; onset; elan; frustrate
DATA accepted inferences; premises

DATE period; epoch; age; a fruit   bt
DAUB smear; sully; smirch; plaster
DAUD dawd; thump; knock; a lump (Sc.)
DAUK a flaw in timber
DAUR to dare (Sc.)
DAUW Burchell's zebra   zo
DAVY safety-lamp; affidavit
DAWK dak; mail carried by relays (India)
DAWM a fortieth of a rupee, Indian   nm
DAWN cock-crow; dayspring; gleam
DAZE stun; amaze; astound; confuse
D-DAY invasion day
DEAD exactly; directly; defunct; late
DEAF heedless; inattentive; (no kernel)
DEAL pinewood; allot; treat; bargain
DEAN guild president; church dignitary   rl
DEAR beloved; costly; expensive
DEBT liability; arrears; obligation
DECK adorn; array; (cards)   nt
DEED feat; exploit; document   lw
DEEM opine; judge; imagine; believe
DEEP the ocean; profound; recondite
DEER a solid-horned ungulate   zo
DEEV evil spirit (Persia)
DEFT dextrous; adroit; handy; skilful
DEFT flout; spurn; brave; dare
DEIL the devil; scrat; Old Scratch (Sc.)
DELE delete; erase; efface; obliterate
DELF delftware; pottery; a drain
DELL dale; dene; dingle; vale
DEME Greek township; tribal division
DEMY a size of paper
DENE dell; dune; sandhill
DENT niche; notch; dint; indentation
DENY contradict; gainsay; refute
DERM the skin   md
DERN durn; secret; dreadful; gatepost
DERV diesel oil
DESK writing table; a lectern
DEVA a benign spirit (Hindu)   rl
DEVI the wife of Siva (Hindu)   rl
DEWY spangled with dew
DHAI midwife, wet-nurse (Hindu)
DHAK East Indian timber-tree   bt
DHAL pulse porridge (Ind.)   ck
DHAR Burmese curved knife
DHOW Arab ship   nt
DIAD divalent atom   ch
DIAL (telephone); face; indicator disc
DICE sometimes loaded
DICK sworn declaration; detective   lw
DIDO antic; caper; queen of Carthage
DIEB North African jackal   zo
DIED perished; expired; departed
DIES (dies non); (screw-taps)   to
DIET assembly; viands; sustenance
DIGS lodgings
DIKA West African mango   bt
DIKE ditch; rine; rhine; mortarless wall
DILL medicinal herb; condiment   bt, ck
DIME a ten-cent piece (USA)   nm
DINE give a dinner to; eat

DING ring; urge; enforce; dash		
DINK braw; neat; trim (Sc.)		
DINT dent; power; blow; stroke		
DIOL dihydric alcohol	ch	
DIRE awful; disastrous; calamitous		
DIRK dagger; poniard (Sc.); dark (obs.)		
DIRL to tingle; vibrate (Sc.)		
DIRT mud; mire; dust; muck; grime; soil		
DISA S. African orchid	bt	
DISC disk; record; flat round plate		
DISH a culinary conception; frustrate		
DISK disc; any flat round growth	bt	
DISS an Algerian grass	bt	
DIVA a prima donna	mu	
DIVE plunge; descend; a gambling hell		
DOAB alluvial land (India)		
DOCK curtail; lessen; deduct; a weed	bt	
DODD cut off; clip; poll; a mound		
DODO extinct bird (Mauritius)	zo	
DOER agent; executive; performer		
DOFF daff; take off; divest		
DOGE Venetian magistrate		
DOHL pulse; (dried peas)	bt	
DOIT Dutch or Scotch half-farthing	nm	
DOKE a dint; a dimple		
DOLE an allowance; dispense; pain; grief		
DOLL to dress up; a toy		
DOLT dunce; booby; dullard		
DOME a cupola; round roof		
DONE ended; finished; transacted		
DONG Vietnamese monetary unit	nm	
DON'T prelude to a prohibition		
DOOB an Indian grass	bt	
DOOD camel or dromedary	zo	
DOOK a bung; a bathe (Sc.)		
DOOL dole; gloom; sorrow (Sc.)		
DOOM kismet; condemn; judgment		
DOOR portal; entrance; access; egress		
DOPE drug; narcotic; doctor; varnish		
DORA Defence of the Realm Act		
DORN the thorn-back skate	zo	
DORP burg; town; village		
DORR the dor-beetle	zo	
DORY golden coloured fish; skiff	zo, nt	
DOSE draught; drench; physic		
DOSS a shake-down; a hassock		
DOST thou doest		
DOTE love tenderly; talk trash		
DOTH a poetical 'do'		
DOTY decayed; half-rotten		
DOUC a highly coloured monkey	zo	
DOUM the doom-palm	bt	
DOUP weaving half-heald	tx	
DOUR stern; grim; relentless; obstinate		
DOUT extinguish		
DOVE emblem of peace	zo	
DOWF dull; heavy; spiritless (Sc.)		
DOWN fluff; pasture; hill; prone		
DOXY loose woman; moll		
DOZE nap; slumber; forty-winks		
DOZY drowsy; sleepy; dreamy		

DRAB khaki colour; a cloth; a trull		
DRAD dread; dreaded (Spens.)		
DRAG a hunt; a vehicle; haul; pull		
DRAM drachm; a tot of spirits	me	
DRAT a mild expletive		
DRAW limn; allure; attract; (chimney)		
DRAY strong cart for heavy goods		
DREE endure; bear; suffer (Sc.)		
DREW drafted; depicted; extracted		
DREY a squirrel's nest	zo	
DRIB purloin small pieces; inveigle		
DRIP ooze; dribble; trickle; percolate		
DROP globule; bead; sink; quit		
DROW trow; troll; cave elf (Shetland)		
DRUB maul; thrash; beat; pound		
DRUG drudge; a narcotic	md	
DRUM ridge of hills; tambour	mu	
DUAD union of two		
DUAL twofold		
DUAN a division of a poem; a canto		
DUCE leader, dictator (Italian)		
DUCK cloth; dive; dip; underplay; bird	zo	
DUCT tube; canal; pipe; conduit		
DUDE a dandy; fop; nut		
DUDS clothing; rags		
DUEL single combat		
DUET composition for two voices	mu	
DUFF low-calory fine-grain coal	mn	
DUFF muff; a pudding; refurbish		
DUKE (strawberry leaves); peer		
DUKW amphibious army vehicle		
DULE woe (Sc.)		
DULL benumb; blunt; abate; stolid		
DULY properly; regularly; exactly		
DUMA Russian Parliament		
DUMB mute; inarticulate; soundless		
DUMP unload; rubbish-heap		
DUNE dene; sandy waste		
DUNG manure; compost; soil		
DUNT staggering affection; heavy blow		
DUPE gull; delude; outwit; hoodwink		
DURA an Indian grass	bt	
DURE endure; harden; severe		
DURN dern; a door-post		
DUSE deuce; demon; evil spirit		
DUSH to throw down (Sc.)		
DUSK eventide; twilight; eve		
DUST pulverulence; a disturbance		
DUTY obligation; excise; tariff		
DWAM swoon; qualm; faint (Sc.)		
DYAD cf. monad	ch	
DYAK a native of Borneo		
DYED stained; tinted; tinged		
DYER dye-worker		
DYKE dike; ditch; fosse		
DYNE the unit of force	me	

E

EACH both; every one	
EARL jarl; lord; peer	

EARN win; gain; merit; acquire
EASE allay; still; assuage; relief
EAST a cardinal point
EASY facile; affluent; flowing
EBON of ebony; black
ECAD habitat-adapted plant form   bt
ECHE to eke out; augment (Sc.)
ECHO repeat; resound; reverberate
ECRU pale yellowish brown
EDAM spherical Dutch cheese
EDDA Scandinavian saga
EDDY ripple; swirl; vortex
EDEN garden of delight
EDGE brink; fringe; zest; sharpness
EDGY on edge; nervous
EDIT revise; annote; amend
EGAD a refined expletive
EGAL equal (Shak.)
EGER eagre; bore; tidal wave
EGIS aegis; a shield
EIGH exclamation of surprise
EILD dry; not giving milk (Sc.)
EIRE Republic of Ireland
EJOO the sago palm   bt
EKED existed on small pittance
ELAN dash; impetuosity; vivacity
ELIA Charles Lamb
ELMO Elmo's fire; electrical flame
ELMY abounding with elms   bt
ELSE other; otherwise; besides
ELUL 12th month of the Jewish year
EMIR amir; Eastern title
EMIT vent; eject; exhale; discharge
EMYS terrapin genus   zo
ENEW drive back; pursue (obs.)
ENOW enough; just now; soon (Sc.)
ENSA forces entertainment organisation
ENTE heraldic engraftment
ENVY ill-will; malice; covet; grudge
EOAN dawning; eastern
EPHA ephah; Hebrew bushel   me
EPEE foil; rapier (Fr.)
EPIC heroic; lofty; a rhapsody
EPOS epic poem; Homeric narrative
ERGO therefore
ERIC eriach; blood-money (Irish Law)
ERIN the Green Isle
ERNE the sea-eagle   zo
EROS God of Love; Cupid
ERSE the Gaelic language
ERSH stubble   bt
ERST formerly; whilom
ESOX the pike   zo
ESPY discover; observe; perceive; notice
ESSE mere existence
ETCH engrave; draw; cropped ground
ETEM chemical fungicide   ch
ETNA small spirit stove
ETON a returnable note
ETUI needle case; container; etwee
EUGE bravo; well done

EUGH obsolete form of yew   bt
EVEN level; uniform; steady; impartial
EVER aye; always; eternally
EVET eft; newt; ewft   zo
EVIL harm; malice; baneful; malign
EVOE a Bacchanalian cry
EWER pitcher; jug with handle
EWFT eft; newt; evet (obs.)   zo
EWRY scullery
EXAM examination
EXES expenses
EXIT way out; a stage departure
EXON an officer; Yeoman of the Guard
EXUL an exile (Spens.)
EYAS nyas; young hawk   zo
EYED observed; watched; espied
EYER a watcher
EYNE eyes (Sc.)
EYOT ait; river or lake islet
EYRA S. American cat   zo
EYRE journey; circuit; court   lw
EYRY eyrie; ayry; eagle's nest   zo

F

FAAM Indian orchid   bt
FAAP the garfish   zo
FABA broad Windsor bean; purée   bt, ck
FACE defy; dare; surface; confront; dial
FACT incident; actuality; occurrence
FACY impudent
FADE wither; dwindle; insipid
FAEX dregs
FAIK to abate; to excuse (Sc.)
FAIL wane; flag; decline; neglect
FAIN willingly; gladly; readily
FAIR market; just; equitable; blond
FAIX by my faith
FAKE a cable coil; counterfeit
FALA old madrigal   mu
FALL autumn; the Fall; drop; cascade
FALX a membrane   md
FAMA the goddess of rumour
FAME renown; repute; lustre; celebrity
FANE vane; temple; church   rl
FANG tooth; claw; talon
FANK sheepfold (Sc.)
FARD face-paint
FARE manage; victuals; passenger
FARL Scottish oatcake   ck
FARM ferm; till; cultivate; lease
FARO card game; sour beer   ck
FART passing of wind; flatus
FASH to bother; trouble; annoy (Sc.)
FAST firm; rapid; fleet; dissolute
FATA Morgana; a mirage
FATE kismet; doom; destiny; lot
FAUN woodland deity; Pan
FAUX pas
FAVA faba; bean purée   ck
FAWN cringe; a colour; fallow-deer   zo

FAZE disconcert; worry		
FEAL faithful; constant; loyal		
FEAR awe; alarm; dread; anxiety		
FEAT exploit; deed; trick		
FECK efficacy; strength (Sc.)		
FEED cater; sustain; provender		
FEEL sense; touch; experience		
FEER or **FERE,** companion		
FEET paws; hoofs		
FELL hew; cut; tumbled; barren hill		
FELL cruel; deadly; spirited; skin		
FELO de se; suicide	lw	
FELT fabric; sensed; handled; touched		
FEME a woman		
FEND parry; ward off; make shift		
FEOD feud; fief (obs.)		
FERM a farm; abode; lodging (Spens.)		
FERN vascular cryptogamous plant	bt	
FESS fesse; broad heraldic band	hd	
FETE gala; festival; carnival; holiday		
FEUD clan warfare; strife; a fief		
FIAR freeholder, not a life-renter	lw	
FIAT decree; command; ukase		
FICO a snap of the fingers; a fig	bt	
FIEF land held on feudal tenure	lw	
FIFE a variety of flute	mu	
FIKE fidget; trivial detail		
FIKY fussy (Sc.)		
FILE list; dossier; artful dodger	to	
FILL sate; glut; replenish		
FILM thin skin; scum; thread; pellicle		
FIND discover; discovery; decide		
FINE forfeit; delicate; tenuous; exact		
FINN a Finlander		
FIRE discharge; kindle; ignite; blaze		
FIRK whip; beat; rouse (Sc.)		
FIRM fast; tight; compact; a company		
FIRN neve; granular glacier snow		
FISC state treasury; revenue; purse		
FISH to angle; search by sweeping		
FISK to frisk; to move briskly (obs.)		
FIST neif; the clenched hand; to punch		
FIST calligraphy		
FITT fitte; fytte; song (obs.)		
FITZ son of		
FIVE the pentad		
FIZZ hiss; champagne		
FLAG banner; ensign; to signal	nt	
FLAG droop; weary; a stone; a plant	bt	
FLAK anti-aircraft gunfire (German)		
FLAM whim; fancy; falsehood; impose		
FLAN open tart		
FLAP flop; wave; vibrate; flutter		
FLAT smooth; level; insipid; residence		
FLAW blemish; defect; crevice; a gust		
FLAX linum; the linen plant	bt	
FLAY skin; excoriate; strip; criticise		
FLEA pulex irritans	zo	
FLED ran; bolted; retreated		
FLEE escape; abscond; decamp		
FLEW fled; the chap of a hound		

FLEX to bend; an electric lead		
FLEY flay; frighten; cause to fly		
FLIP a joy ride; (egg-flip)		
FLIT fly; dart; flicker; migrate		
FLIX fur; beaver-down	zo	
FLOE an icefield		
FLOG lash; thrash; scourge; whip		
FLOP flap; a failure; a fiasco		
FLOT stratified ore	mn	
FLOW run; emanate; abound; circulate		
FLUE smoke pipe; light down; fluff		
FLUX flow; mutation; change; (soldering)		
FOAL colt or filly	zo	
FOAM spume; froth; spray; rage		
FÖHN warm mtn. wind (N. Alpine)		
FOIE liver (Fr.)		
FOIL track of game; baffle; outwit		
FOIL thin metal; fencing rapier		
FOIN a thrust with spear or sword		
FOLD lap; wrap; furl; double; envelop		
FOLK kindred; relations; people		
FOND loving, attached; archive unit	pr	
FONE foes (Spens.)		
FONT fount; source; spring; type	pr, rl	
FOOD viands; victuals; rations		
FOOL gull; beguile; hoodwink; ninny		
FOOT pay; discharge; settle	me	
FORD wade; a river crossing		
FORE a warning cry at golf		
FORK branch; divide; divaricate		
FORM bench; formula; mould; fashion		
FORM bed of hare; mode; ceremony		
FORS force; fortitude; fortune (Ruskin)		
FORT keep; citadel; fastness		
FOSS ditch or moat		
FOUD magistrate or bailiff (Orkney)		
FOUL noisome; ribald; unfair; sullied		
FOUR 4		
FOWL poultry	zo	
FOXY sly; wily; sour; a colour		
FOZY spongy (Sc.)		
FRAB to worry		
FRAP to bind; to strike		
FRAU a German married woman		
FRAY rub; brush; quarrel; skirmish		
FREE rid; loose; clear; informal		
FRET fray; fume; chafe; abrade; grieve		
FRIT glass material; a wheat-fly	zo	
FRIZ frizz; to curl; to crisp		
FROE woodcutter's cleaver	to	
FROG a batrachian; horse's foot	zo	
FROG cloak or coat button or tassel		
FROM preposition of source		
FROW tool for lathe splitting	to	
FROW a loose woman; a slut		
FUAR feuar; landholder (Sc.)		
FUEL combustibles		
FUFF puff; a burst of anger (Sc.)		
FUGH exclamation of abhorrence		
FULL replete; copious; ample; thicken		
FUME smoke; vapour; exhalation; reek		

FUMY vaporous; fumous; fussy
FUND reserve; store; supply; capital
FUNG mythical Chinese pheasant   zo
FUNK terror; fear; shirk; touchwood
FUOR decayed-rafter strengthener   cr
FURL fold; roll; stow; wrap
FURY frenzy; rage; turbulence; shrew
FUSE } melt; liquefy; blend;
FUZE } quickmatch; a timing device
FUSS ado; stir; fume; fidget; fret
FUST shaft of column; musty smell
FUZZ fluff; light particles; police
FYKE bagnet for fishing
FYRD pre-Conquest Saxon military array

G

GABY a simpleton; nitwit
GADE gaid; gad; goad; graver   to
GAEL Celtic
GAFF low theatre; a hook; a spar   nt
GAGE a pledge; stake; wager; plum   bt
GAID gade; gad; spike on gauntlet   to
GAIN get; win; acquire; profit
GAIR gore (Sc.)
GAIT walk; bearing; step; pace
GAIT pasturage; charge; sheaf of corn   bt
GALA festival; festivity; pomp; show
GALE high wind; rent; a bog plant   bt
GALL vex; torment; provoke; rancour
GALL bile; malignity; glass scum
GALT gault; clay; marl; brick-earth
GAMB leg; shank
GAME lame; plucky; dauntless; pastime
GAMP an umbrella
GAMY high in flavour
GANG crew; band; horde; coterie   hd
GANT to yawn (Sc.)
GAOL jail; prison; objective
GAPE stare; to yawn
GARB dress; costume; heraldic sheaf
GARE greedy (Sc.); beware; look out
GARI Indian carriage
GASH slash; score; slit; wound
GASP pant; puff
GAST to terrify (Shak.)
GATA tropical Atlantic shark   zo
GAUB an Indian tree; guy-rope   bt, nt
GAUD a gewgaw; showy ornament; gawd
GAUL old France
GAUM to smear; to daub
GAUN going (Sc.)
GAUP gawp; gape
GAUR a wild Indian ox   zo
GAVE presented; granted; yielded
GAWD gaud; a piece of finery
GAWK gowk; simpleton; a cuckoo   zo
GAWN small tub; a ladle
GAZE stare; view; regard; contemplate
GEAL to congeal; pert. to earth
GEAN wild cherry   bt

GEAR tackle; harness; dress; mechanism
GEAT hole for metal casting
GECK dupe; mock; simpleton
GEDD the pike   zo
GEED went faster
GEEZ archaic Semitic dialect
GEGG a hoax; a trick (Sc.)
GELD gold; tribute; castrate; spay
GELT geld; gilt; money; emasculated
GENA the cheek   md
GENE heredity factor   md
GENS Roman clan
GENT a would-be gentleman
GENU nerve-tract bend
GERM ovule; nucleus; a bacillus   md
GEST an exploit; feat; bearing
GEUM avens and herb-bennet genus   bt
GHAT Indian mountain; landing-stair
GHEE Indian oil or butter
GIBE jibe; sneer; deride; taunt   nt
GIFT boon; bounty; gratuity; faculty
GILD guild; trade's union; add lustre
GILL a flirt; a ravine; ground ivy   bt
GILL breathing organ; ¼ pint   zo, me
GILT gilded; aureate; a young sow   zo
GIMP smart; spruce; a trimming
GING gang or company
GINN jinn; djinn; demon; spirit
GIRD bind; reproach; gibe; spasm
GIRL young roe-buck; young woman   zo
GIRN grin; snarl (Sc.)
GIRO payment transfer system
GIRR a hoop (Sc.)
GIRT tightly moored; bound   nt
GIST essential point; pith
GITE bed or an abode (Fr.)
GIVE yield; confer; grant; present
GIZZ phiz; face (Sc.)
GLAD (eye); joyous; elated; delectable
GLEE hilarity; merriment; mirth
GLEE squint; part song   mu
GLEG clever; apt; sharp (Sc.)
GLEN vale; dale; dell; dingle; valley
GLEY to squint; to glance (Sc.)
GLIB voluble; fluent; ready; facile
GLIM a light; a glimmer
GLOW fervour; shine; burn; gleam
GLUE cement; an adhesive
GLUM grum; crestfallen; downcast
GLUT surfeit; surplus; cloy; satiate
G-MAN gun-man; bandit
GNAR knar; yarr; snarl
GNAT insect   zo
GNAW bite; corrode; erode; champ
GOAD spur; rouse; incite; an ankus
GOAF worked out mine; slag
GOAL end; aim; ambition; object
GOAN Indian; East African Indian
GOAT Capricornus; horned animal   zo
GOBO sound-absorbing panel   cn
GO-BY evasion

GOBY fish having nests of seaweed   zo
GODS lofty theatrical supporters
GOEL an avenger of blood (Heb.)
GOER a mover; a go-between
GOLA a cyma; cyme; a moulding
GOLD or; money wealth; bull at archery
GOLF goff; gowf
GOME black cart-grease
GOND native Indian tribe
GONE hied; wended; fared; left; parted
GONE group of 4 nuclei or cells   cy
GONG prelude to a meal; medal (slang)
GOOD weal; virtuous; upright; proper
GOOF simpleton; silly cuckoo
GOOR coarse sugar from the date-palm
GORE clotted blood; wedge of cloth
GORM sheen; shine of varnish
GORY sanguinary; ensanguined
GOSH an ejaculation
GOTH Teutonic barbarian
GOUL } howl;
GOWL } yowl
GOUM native Algerian soldier (Fr.)
GOUT a drop; taste; relish
GOUT paroxysmal form of arthritis   md
GOWD gold (Sc.)
GOWF golf; goff
GOWK gouk; simpleton; oaf; cuckoo   zo
GOWN robe; garment
GRAB snatch; seize; grip; a card game
GRAB two-masted vessel (Malabar)   nt
GRAF German title; a count
GRAM Indian corn; weight   bt, me
GRAM misery
GRAY grey; ash-coloured
GREE a step; degree; goodwill
GREW thrived; raised; progressed
GREY gray; a neutral tint
GRID lines on a map   el
GRIG sand-eel; grasshopper; cricket   zo
GRIM stern; dire; hideous; grisly
GRIN girn; smirk; a snare
GRIP clutch; handbag; small ditch
GRIT endurance; courage; sand
GROG rum and water
GROS silken fabric
GROT a grotto
GROW wax; develop; expand; raise
GRUB caterpillar; food; (cricket)   zo
GRUM glum; surly; morose; guttural
GUAG space left by mineral extraction   mn
GUAN Brazilian game bird   zo
GUDE good (Sc.)
GUFA Tigris ferry boat   nt
GUHR loose earth found in rocks   mn
GUIB the harnessed antelope   zo
GULF chasm; abyss; bight; bay
GULL beguile; hoax; deceive; sea-bird   zo
GULP gasp; swallow; choke
GULY coloured red in heraldry   hd
GUNK semi-solid material from synthesis

GURU Hindu teacher
GUSH rush; spout; stream; an outburst
GUST squall; burst of passion; relish
GUY'S Guy's Hospital
GYAL gayal; East Indian ox   zo
GYBE gibe; sneer   nt
GYLE to ferment; a brew
GYNE queen ant   zo
GYRA embroidered border
GYRE a circular motion
GYRO a gyroscope
GYTE crazy; mad; a child (Sc.)
GYVE fetter; shackle; handcuff; bond

H

HAAF deep-sea fishing ground (Shetland)
HAAR harr; a cold sea mist
HACK notch; gash; kick; chopper   to
HACK literary drudge; sorry; jade (horse)   zo
HADE slope of mineral vein or fault
HADJ or **HAJJ,** a pilgrimage to Mecca
HAEM iron pigment in haemoglobin   md
HAET or **HAIT,** a whit (Sc.)
HAFT heft; hilt; handle; to haggle
HA-HA haw-haw; sunken fence; laughter
HAIK hyke; haick; an Arab wrap
HAIL health; greeting; frozen rain
HAIN save; preserve; spare (Sc.)
HAIR jot; iota; quality; character
HAKA native dance (New Zealand)
HAKE a pot-hook; loiter; sea fish   zo
HALD hold (Sc.)
HALE haul; drag; healthy; robust
HALF a moiety; a half-back; partial
HALL manor house; a college
HALM haum; haulm; corn-stalk; stubble
HALO a saintly hat-band
HALT to stop; to limp; crippled; waver
HAME bar for trace attachment
HAND manual labour; assistance
HAND proffer; (cards); 4 in (horses)   me
HANG suspend; hover; slope; drift
HANK skein; coil; hoop; ring
HARD firm; compact; arduous
HARE to speed; puss   zo
HARK hear; listen; attend
HARL fibres of flax; troll for fish   bt
HARM hurt; scathe; wrong; injury
HARN coarse linen fabric (Sc.)   tx
HARO an appeal (Channel Islands)   lw
HARP reiterate; Lyra   mu
HARR haar; a storm; an eagre
HART male red-deer   zo
HASH chop; mangle; mince; a jumble
HASP clasp or fastening
HAST (thou) havest
HATE abhor; loathe; enmity; odium
HATH has
HAUL tug; pull; drag; draw; heave

HAUM halm; haulm; stubble   bt
HAVE own; possess; hold; contain
HAWK rapacious bird or person   zo
HAWK intentional cough; to peddle
HAWK plasterer's mortar board   to
HAWM to lounge about
HAZE fog; mist; pall; miasma; to bully
HAZY vague; obscure; indistinct; murky
HEAD (bowls); acme; top; steer
HEAL cure; remedy; assuage; compose
HEAP pile; mound; amass; collect
HEAR heed; hark; try judicially   lw
HEAT rage; passion; ardour; excite
HEBE an Olympian cup-bearer
HECK fish-weir; a rack; river bend
HEED mind; mark; obey; regard; caution
HEEL (cock-spurs); low fellow; twerp
HEFT hilt; handle; heaved
HEIR inheritor; offspring
HELD grasped; adhered; restrained
HELE to conceal; to hide (obs.)
HELL Hades, Gehenna; gambling house
HELM tiller; steering gear; steer   nt
HELM helmet; crown; top; guide; direct
HELP aid; abet; back; second; relieve
HEMP rope-fibre; a plant   bt
HEND to seize; to apprehend (obs.)
HERA (Juno), wife of Zeus
HERB a simple; an annual plant   bt
HERD drove; rabble; tend; collect
HERE at this place
HERL harl; barb of feather
HERN heron (obs.)   zo
HERO a priestess of Aphrodite
HERR German gent
HERS also **HERN** of her
HEST behest; command (Shak.)
HEWN cut; felled; chiselled
HICK bucolic; country cousin (USA)
HIDE about 100 acres (41 hectares)   me
HIDE a skin; pelt; secrete; cache
HIED set off
HI-FI high-fidelity sound
HIGH eminent; lofty; arrogant; shrill
HIKE to carry; to ramble
HILA the eyes of beans   bt
HILL to earth up plants
HILT haft; heft; handle
HIND a rustic; backward; a deer   zo
HINK a reaping hook   to
HINT imply; insinuate; innuendo
HIRE rent; charter; lease; salary
HISK to breathe with difficulty
HISS also **HISH** and **HIZZ**
HIST! hush!
HIVE to collect; store up; a skep
HOAR hoary; rime; venerable
HOAX gammon; spoof; dupe; delude
HOBO a tramp; a vagrant (USA)
HOCK Rhenish wine; a joint, the hough
HOED weeded

HOER manipulator of a hoe
HOGG hog; a two-year old sheep   zo
HOIK hike; an upward turn
HOIT to leap; to caper
HOLD grasp; contain; keep   nt
HOLE cavity; lair; burrow; pierce
HOLM evergreen oak; holly   bt
HOLM flat land; an islet
HOLT woodland; a copse; a burrow
HOLY sanctified; consecrated; divine
HOME habitat; seat; institution
HOMO homosexual
HOMY homelike
HONE to pine; to moan; a whetstone
HONG Chinese factory
HONK to hoot
HOOD cowl; cover; to blind
HOOF pad the hoof; to walk
HOOK promontory; snare; sickle   to
HOOK to bend; to decamp; to steal
HOOP a whoop; a band; a toy
HOOT honk; boo; decry; execrate
HOPE expect; anticipate; confidence
HOPS beer flavouring   bt
HORN cornucopia; drinking cup   mu
HORS out of; beyond; hors-de-combat
HOSE stockings; hosiery; to sprinkle
HOSH courtyard of Arab house
HOST multitude; consecrated water   rl
HOUR always passing
HOVA a Malagasi
HOVE to heave; to raise; to loiter
HOWE how; hollow; glen; dell (Sc.)
HOWK dig; burrow; extract (Sc.)
HOWL gowl; yowl; wail; yell; squall
HOYA genus of climbing plants   bt
HUCK a German trout   zo
HUED coloured; tinted
HUEL a wheal; a Cornish mine
HUER fish-scout watching for shoals
HUFF swell; bluster; anger; (draughts)
HUGE vast; colossal; gigantic; immense
HUIA New Zealand starling   zo
HULK old ship   nt
HULL husk; pod; to pierce; ship   bt, nt
HUMP hillock; to carry; depression
HUNG dangled; draped; hovered
HUNK chunk; lump; large slice
HUNT pursue; hound; search; chase
HURL cast; pitch; fling; whirl
HURT pain; offend; mar; an injury
HUSH quiet; calm; still; silence
HUSK hull; rind; coating   bt
HUSO the great sturgeon   zo
HUTU native of Rwanda (Africa)
HWAN (Korea)   nm
HWYC emotional fervour, intonation (Welsh)
HYKE haik; loose Arab garment
HYMN panegyric; paean; song of praise   mu
HYPE a wrestling throw
HYPO sodium thiosulphate   ch

I

IBEX chamois; mountain wild goat   zo
IBID in the same place (Latin)
IBIS a wading bird, sacred in Egypt   zo
ICED frozen; congealed
ICON also **IKON,** sacred picture; image
IDEA notion; fantasy; conceit
IDEM the same
IDES Roman date
IDLE inert; lazy; futile; inactive
IDLY indolently
IDOL hero; pet; image
IDYL idyll; pastoral poem
ILEX evergreen oak   bt
ILKA each (Sc.)
IMAM ⎱ Mohammedan priest;
IMAN ⎰ Mohammedan prince
IMPI Zulu regiment
INBY inbye; inwards (Sc.)
INCA ancient king or prince of Peru
INCA an Indian of Peru
INCH creep forward; isle (Sc.)   me
INKY black; blotted
INLY inward; secret
INRO Japanese comfit box
INTO preposition of direction
IOTA a jot; tittle; whit; particle
IRIS Rainbow Goddess, messenger of Zeus
IRON golf club; metal; to smoothe   mn
IRON gyve; fetter; strength
ISCA excrescence on oak or hazel   bt
ISIS Moon Goddess; mother of Horus
ISLE ait; eyot; islet
ITCH constant teasing desire   md
ITEM detail; entry; innuendo
ITER canal or duct   zo
ITIS undiagnosed disease   md
IWIS ywis; certainly
IXIA South African iridaceous plants   bt
IZBA log hut (Rus.)

J

JACA the bread-fruit tree   bt
JACK knave at cards; national flag
JACK various appliances; (bowls); pike   zo
JADE sorry nag; mean woman   zo
JADE to fatigue; to become tired   mn
JAIL gaol; to imprison
JAIN Indian religious sect
JAMB a door-post; to wedge; stick
JANE jean; twilled cloth; Genoese   nm
JANN jinn; Moslem demon
JANT jaunt; ramble
JAPE jibe; joke; jest; quip
JARL earl (Norse)
JAUP to bespatter (Sc.)
JAWY with jaws
JAZZ rag-time music   mu
JEAN jane; twilled cloth
JEEP American general purposes vehicle

JEER mock; scoff; taunt; deride
JEFF dicing with quadrats; circus rope
JEHU a coachman
JERK yerk; jolt; pluck; twitch
JESS a leg-strap in falconry
JEST jape; quirk; raillery; banter
JHOW Indian grass   bt
JIFF a jiffy; a moment
JILL a flirt; Jack's girl friend
JILT deceive; delude; to discard
JIMP neat; slender; elegant (Sc.)
JINK a sharp turn; to dodge
JINN ginn; djinn; Moslem demon
JINX bad joss
JIVE jazz dance (swing)
JOCK a Scotsman
JOEY small kangaroo   zo
JOEY small drinking glass; 4d. piece   nm
JOHN a variety of pink   bt
JOIN link together; associate
JOKE jest; banter; witticism
JOLE jowl; jaw; jolt
JOLT jar; jog; jerk; shake
JOSH to rag; ridicule
JOSS Chinese idol; luck
JOUK jook; duck; dodge; bow (Sc.)
JOVE Jupiter; alchemist's tin
JOWL dewlap; the cheek
JUBA negro dance
JUBE rood-loft   rl
JUDO advanced form of Jap. wrestling
JUDY Mr. Punch's wife
JUGA leaflets in a pinnate leaf   bt
JU-JU West African black magic
JUKE a head movement
JULY seventh month
JUMP leap; skip; bound; purloin
JUNE sixth month
JUNK scrap-metal; trask; Chinese ship
JUNO Queen of Heaven
JURY twelve persons; makeshift   lw
JUST true; exact; impartial; barely
JUTE sack and twine fibre   bt

K

KADI cadi; Moslem judge
KAGO Japanese palanquin
KAGU crane of New Caledonia   zo
KAIF keif; drugged stupor
KAIL a ninepin
KAIN cain; tribute in kind
KAKA New Zealand parrot   zo
KAKI the Chinese date-plum   bt
KALA time; destiny; death (Sanskrit)
KALE kail; colewort; curly cabbage   bt
KALI prickly saltwort or glasswort   bt
KALI wife of Siva; goddess of destruction
KAMA Hindu cupid
KAME glacier-outwash mound

KAMI Japanese god or title	
KANA Japanese handwriting	
KANG Chinese water-jar	
KANS Indian sugar-cane grass	bt
KAON 1 of class of mesons	
KART midget racing car	
KATA Tibetan cloth or scarf	
KAVA ava; Polynesian drink; plant	bt
KECK to retch; dried hemlock	bt
KEEK to peep (Sc.)	
KEEL ruddle; flat-bottomed barge	nt
KEEN lamentation; acute; eager; sharp	
KEEP stronghold; provender; retain	
KEIF kaif; drugged stupor	
KEIR bleaching-vat	
KELK a blow; to beat; large stone	
KELL caul; cobweb; film; network	
KELP kilp; seaweed; wrack	
KELT Celt; salmon; woollen cloth	tx, zo
KEMB to comb	
KEMP coarse rough hairs of wool	
KENT pole; pike; bugle with keys	mu
KEPT held; stored; retained; endured	
KERB curb; edge of pavement	
KERF a saw-cut; a swath	
KERN quern; a hand-mill; to granulate	
KERN or **KIRN** Irish foot-soldier	
KETA a caviare fish	zo
KHAN Eastern inn; caravanserai; ruler	
KHEL a clan (Afghanistan)	
KHUD Indian ravine	
KIBE chilblain	md
KIBY affected with chilblains	
KICK resist; rebel; spurn; boot; punt	
KIEF keif; kef; stupor; drowsiness	
KIER keir; bleaching-vat	
KILL slay; destroy; despatch; consume	
KILN furnace; oven	
KILO 2.205 lb	me
KILP kelp; calcined ashes of seaweed	
KILT a philibeg; pleated skirt; tuck up	
KIND class; type; genus; benign; gentle	
KINE cows	zo
KING monarch; sovereign; ruler; a card	
KINK bend; knot; curl; loop; whim	
KINO a mixture of gums; catechu	
KIPE basket for catching fish	
KIRI knobkerrie; Kaffir throwing stick	·
KIRK a church (Sc.)	rl
KIRN kern; last sheaf; harvest image	
KISH wicker turf basket; impure graphite	
KISS buss; touch gently; (billiards)	
KIST chest; coffer	
KITE accommodation bill; a toy; a bird	zo
KITH kindred; acquaintances; friends	
KIVE a mashing vat	
KIWI apteryx, NZ flightless bird	zo
KNAB to bite; to gnaw	
KNAG knot in wood; peg; a wart	
KNAP to snap; a swelling; a hillock	
KNAR gnar; snarl; growl; a knarl	

KNEE a genuflection	
KNEW understood; perceived	
KNIT draw together; weave; wrinkle	
KNOB a bunch; boss; door-handle	
KNOP knob; tufted top; button	
KNOT knag; small sandpiper; (speed)	zo
KNOW comprehend; discern; approve	
KNUB knob; a small lump	
KNUR knar; gnarl; wooden ball	
KNUT a nut; a dandy	
KOBA kob; African water antelope	zo
KOEL Indian cuckoo	zo
KOFF Dutch sailing vessel	nt
KOHL black antimony eye pigment	
KOLA African nut tree; a beverage	bt
KOTH volcanic mud (S. America)	mn
KOTO Japanese stringed instrument	mu
KRIS creese; Malay dagger	
KROO an African race	
KUDU a large African antelope	zo
KUNA Panamanian Indian	
KURD native of Kurdistan	
KVAS rye beer (Rus.)	ck
KYAT (Burma) monetary unit	nm
KYLE narrow strait or sound (Sc.)	

L

LACE tie; fasten; beat; intermix	
LACK want; need; deficiency	
LACY lace-like texture	
LADE load; burden; ladle; bale	
LADY a gentlewoman	
LAIC a layman	
LAID deposited; ribbed; prostrate	
LAIN rested; reclined; reposed	
LAIR den; form; burrow; quagmire	
LAIS a courtesan	
LAKE mere; pool; crimson colour	pt
LAKH lac; 100,000 rupees	nm
LAKY resembling a lake	
LAMA Tibetan priest	
LAMB to yean	zo
LAME halt; crippled; feeble; imperfect	
LAME gold- or silver-threaded material	
LAMP lantern; to shine	
LANA the genipap tree of Demerara	bt
LAND realm; tract; debark; (fish)	
LANE narrow way; passage; by-road	
LANG long (Sc.)	
LANK lax; loose; languid; drooping; thin	
LANX Roman platter	
LAPP a Laplander	
LARD bacon fat; smear; flatter	
LARK frolic; prank; spree; skylark	zo
LASH whip; scourge; satirize; a stripe	
LASS girl; a sweetheart	
LAST final; boot-maker's anvil	to
LAST continue; endure; a cargo	
LATE overdue; past; recent; deceased	

LATH a narrow strip of wood
LAUD extol; praise; eulogy; panegyric
LAVA plutonic rock matter   mn
LAVE to wash; bathe; bath
LAWN fine linen or cambric; sward
LAZE to idle
LAZY inert; torpid; slothful; sluggish
LEAD surpass; guide; precede; plummet
LEAF thin plate; lamina; page of book
LEAK ooze; drip; percolate; rift
LEAL loyal; true; faithful
LEAN rest; rely; depend; incline; lank
LEAP clear; spring; caper; frisk
LEAR to learn; learning (Spens.)
LEAT watercourse to a mill
LEDA beloved of Zeus; disguised as swan   rl
LEEK an emblem of Wales   bt, hd
LEER ogle; smirk
LEES the dregs
LEET court of record; list of candidates   lw
LEFT sinister; abandoned; bequeathed
LEHR glass annealing oven
LEND advance; loan; furnish; grant
LENE unaspirated
LENO a fabric like muslin   tx
LENS optical glass
LENT loaned; inclined; a fast   rl
LESS smaller; inferior; minor
LEST for fear that
LETO mother of Apollo and Artemis
LETT Baltic tribe
LEUD Frankish vassal
LEVY tribute; exact; muster; impose
LEWD licentious
LIAR an economiser of the truth
LIAS argillaceous limestone   mn
LICE insect carriers of typhus   zo
LICH or **LYCH** dead body; corpse
LICK to lap; defeat; overcome
LIDO a bathing pool
LIED stated falsely; German ballad
LIEF gladly; willingly; beloved
LIEN right of retention   lw
LIEU place; stead
LIFE vitality; duration; memoir
LIFT exalt; raise; elevate; steal
LIKE prefer; enjoy; cognate; match
LILT cheerful song or air; ditty   mu
LILY fleur-de-lis   bt
LIMB edge; border; an imp; branch   ht
LIME to ensnare; citrous fruit   bt
LIMN to paint; draw; illuminate
LIMP walk lamely; slack; flaccid
LIMY glutinous; viscous
LINE ancestry; business; the Equator
LING sea-fish; common heather   zo, bt
LINK torch; nexus; tie; connect
LINK (missing); 7.92 in (20 cm)   me
LINN pool; waterfall
LINO linoleum
LINT surgical linen; loose fibre dust   md

LINY streaky; wrinkled
LION Hercules killed Nemean lion   zo
LIPP a crimson fish   zo
LIRA Italian silver coin   nm
LIRE the plural of lira   nm
LIRK a fold; to hang in creases (Sc.)
LISP make th of s
LIST enlist; register; roll; elect; wish
LITH joint; segment
LIVE exist; survive; active; alive; dwell
LOAD lade; cumber; charge; incubus
LOAF lounge; dawdle; (bread)
LOAM rich mould
LOAN lend; advance; imprest
LOBE projecting part; a cotyledon   bt
LOCH lake; arm of the sea
LOCK close; seal; bolt; hug; ringlet
LOCO locomotive
LODE vein in ore; drain; open ditch
LOFT upper room; to glide
LOGE a box in a theatre
LOIN area of animal body
LOKE grassy road (East Anglia)
LOKI Norse spirit of evil or mischief
LOLL sprawl; lounge
LOMA lobe; fringe
LOMP the lump fish   zo
LONE isolated; solitary; secluded
LONG prolix; lengthy; crave; aspire
LONK north-Engl. mountain wool   tx
LOOF the palm of the hand
LOOK scan; gaze; peer; seem; mien
LOOM machine; approach menacingly
LOON rascal; Great Northern Diver   zo
LOOP bight; bend; loophole
LOOS laus; praise (Spens.)
LOOT booty; plunder; sack; ransack
LOPE run with easy strides
LOPH molar cusp crest   zo
LORD dominate; master; ruler; a peer
LORE wisdom; erudition; doctrine
LORN forlorn; lost; forsaken; undone
LORY Australian parrot   zo
LOSE mislay; waste; squander; fail
LOSS defeat; reverse; deprivation
LOST missing; astray; vicious; dreamy
LOTE lotus; water-lily   bt
LOTH averse; unwilling; allergic
LOTO lotto; a game
LOUD stentorian; clamorous; noisy
LOUP loop; to leap
LOUR scowl; frown; glower
LOUT boor; clod; booby; yokel
LOVE adore; affection; courtship
LOWN sheltered; tranquil (Sc.)
LUAU traditional roast-pig feast (Hawaii)   ck
LUCE full grown pike   zo
LUCK hap; fate; hazard; fortune; chance
LUDO a game
LUES poison; plague; disease
LUFF the weather-gauge   nt

LUGE toboggan		**MAST** beech-nuts, etc.	nt
LULL calm; assuage; an interim		**MATE** comrade; checkmate; tea plant	
LUMP chunk; projection; hunk		**MATH** a mowing	
LUNA the moon; heraldic argent	hd	**MATT** roughened	
LUNE half-moon shape		**MAUD** shepherd's woollen plaid (Sc.)	
LUNG respiratory organ	md	**MAUL** mall; hammer; to molest	to
LUNT a light; a slow-match		**MAWK** a maggot	zo
LURE entice; decoy; bait		**MAXI** larger than standard	
LURK skulk; lie in wait		**MAYA** language; Hindu mythology	
LUSH juicy; luscious; succulent; watery		**MAZE** daze; bewilder; a labyrinth	
LUSK a sluggard; to laze		**MAZY** winding; intricate	
LUST desire; cupidity; covet		**MEAD** spiced ale; meadow; field	
LUTE tenacious composition; guitar	mu	**MEAL** a repast; ground grain	
LUXE luxuriousness (Fr.)		**MEAN** middle; average; intend; signify	
LYAM leam; dog-leash		**MEAT** food; flesh	
LYME a coarse grass	bt	**MEDE** a native of Media	
LYNX sharp-eyed cat	zo	**MEED** reward; recompense; guerdon	
LYON Heraldic Court (Sc.)	hd	**MEEK** mild; lowly; pacific; unassuming	
LYRA a constellation		**MEER** mere; pool; lake (obs.)	
LYRA brain psalterium in mammals	zo	**MEET** fit; proper; encounter; join	
LYRE early form of harp	mu	**MELT** fuse; thaw; soften; dissolve	
LYSE make undergo lysis		**MEMO** memorandum; note; jotting	
		MEND repair; patch; amend; correct	
		MENU bill of fare	
M		**MERE** pool; lake; marsh; boundary	
		MERE unmixed; simply; alone; only	
MA'AM marm; madame		**MERI** Maori war club	
MAAR a crater		**MERK** an old Scots silver coin	nm
MACE staff of authority; spice	bt	**MERV** silk dress material	
MACH supersonic speed		**MESA** broad; flat; rocky; tableland (Sp.)	
MACK or **MAIK** make (Sc.)		**MESH** ensnare; net-work; brewery grains	
MADE formed; fashioned; compelled		**MESS** muddle; jumble; dish of food; eat	
MAGE a magician		**META** Roman racing pylon	
MAGI wise men of the East		**METE** measure; limit; boundary	
MAID lass; lassie; damsel		**MEUM** and tuum (liturgical me or thee)	rl
MAIL the post; chain-armour		**MEWL** to squall	
MAIM cripple; mutilate; disable		**MEWS** stables; cages for hawks	
MAIN at dice or cockfighting; essential		**MEZE** hors d'oeuvres (Turk.)	
MAIN the ocean; might; power; pipe		**MIAN** Ind. title of respect	
MAKE do; gain; form; cause; reach		**MIAU** a cat-call	
MAKI a Malagasy lemur	zo	**MICA** a silicate used as glass	mn
MAKO Australasian shark	zo	**MICE** small rodents	zo
MALA maxilla lobe in insects	zo	**MICH** lie hid; skulk; sneak; play truant	
MALE masculine		**MICO** vegetable butter or solid oil	bt
MALL hammer; to bruise; public walk		**MIDA** the larva of the bean-fly	zo
MALM calcareous loam	mn	**MIEN** air; bearing; deportment; aspect	
MALT steeped grain		**MIFF** annoyance; resentment	
MAMA mamma; mammy		**MIKE** shirk; loiter; microphone	
MANA magical influence (Maori)		**MILD** suave; bland; placid; soothing	
MANE neck hair on lions, horses	zo	**MILE** 1760 yards (1.609 km)	me
MANX curtailed		**MILK** cat-lap	
MANY sundry; divers; manifold		**MILL** grind; factory; fight	nm
MARC oil-cake refuse		**MILO** the strong man of Crotona	
MARE female horse	zo	**MILT** the spleen; roe; spawn	zo
MARK (letters of); brand; stigma	nm	**MIME** mimic; ape; copy; a farce	
MARL mixture of clay, sand and lime		**MINA** 50 shekels; Indian bird	zo
MARM ma'am; madame		**MIND** mark; heed; dislike; intention	
MARS God of War; a planet		**MINE** pit; colliery; sap; weaken	
MART market; bazaar; emporium		**MING** Chinese porcelain; dynasty	
MASH mix; crush; knead; compound		**MINI** compact size	
MASK veil; cloak; revel; disguise; visor		**MINK** furry animal, weasel type	zo
MASS bulk; size; whole; heap	rl		

MINO Japanese raincoat
MINT coin factory; unused, fresh   nm
MINT aromatic plant; to invent   bt
MINX pert selfish girl; she-puppy   zo
MINY subterraneous
MIRE mud; ooze; slime
MIRK murk; gloom; dark
MIRY muddy; marshy; soggy
MISE cost; expense; a treaty   lw
MISS fail; want; need; spinster
MIST fog; haze; obscurity
MISY mysy; impure iron ore   mn
MITE widow's donation; insect   nm, zo
MITT mitten; a covering for the wrist
MITY full of insects   zo
MIXT mixed; mingled; blended
MOAN bewail; lament; deplore
MOAT protective ditch
MOCK taunt; flaunt; deride; imitate
MOCO the rock cavy   zo
MODE style; form; way; vogue
MODI methods; (modus)
MODS first B.A. examination, Oxford
MOFF Caucasian silk fabric
MOHO earth crust/mantle boundary
MOHR West African gazelle   zo
MOIL toil; soil; daub
MOKE ass; donkey; burro   zo
MOKO Maori tattooing
MOLD mould
MOLE jetty; a blemish; artificial harbour
MOLE the gentleman in velveteens   zo
MOLL courtesan; gangster's sweetheart
MOLT melt; moult (obs.)
MOLY a countercharm; garlic   bt
MOME a dullard; buffoon
MONK an ink-stain in printing; friar   rl
MONO single transmission path   el
MOOD disposition; humour; temper; vein
MOON wander aimlessly; a satellite
MOOP to nibble; to browse (Sc.)
MOOR fasten; berth; heath; (Othello)
MOOT an assembly; debate; discuss
MOPE to be dull and listless
MOPS a pug-dog   zo
MOPY downcast; dejected; sad
MORA finger game; tree; short syllable   bt
MORE additional; further; again
MORN morning; tomorrow
MORT death tune; a quantity
MOSS a cryptogamic plant   bt
MOST more than more
MOTE mite; particle; speck; blemish
MOTE moot; assembly; to debate (obs.)
MOTH large-winged insect   zo
MOUE a pout; a grimace (Fr.)
MOUL mool; mouldy (Sc.)
MOVE stir; shift; budge; propose
MOWN scythed; cut
MOXA a cauterizer   bt, md
MOYA volcanic mud   mn

MOZE to raise the nap on cloth
MUCH plenteous; greatly; largely
MUCK refuse; dirt
MUFF a duffer; hand-warmer
MUID hogshead; dry measure for corn
MUIR moor (Sc.)
MULE slipper; machine; a hybrid   zo
MULL snuff-box; headland; mistake
MULL to heat wine, punch; to ponder, err
MULL cotton book-cover   pr
MULT multure; fee for grinding corn
MUMM to mask; act; masquerade
MUMP nibble; grin; deceive; beg
MUON heaviest known lepton   nc
MURE immure; a wall
MURK mirk; darkness; obscurity
MUSA banana genus   bt
MUSE meditate; ponder; contemplate
MUSH pulp; travel by dog-sled
MUSK a scent; a deer   zo
MUSS a mess; scramble; disarrange
MUST obliged; necessitated
MUST mould; unfermented grapejuice
MUST elephant frenzy
MUTE dumb; still; a sordine   mu
MUTT a fool
MUXY gloomy; dirty
MYNA the Indian starling   zo
MYTH legend; fable; invention
MYXA beak extremities   zo

N

NABK a plant in the crown of thorns   bt
NAGA sacred Hindu snakes   zo
NAIB Indian law officer
NAIF naive; artless; ingenuous
NAIK Indian corporal
NAIL to spike; secure; $2\frac{1}{4}$ inches (57 mm)   me
NAJA venomous snake; a cobra   zo
NAME call; term; nominate; renown
NANA benteak skill
NAND logic
NAOS a shrine (Greek)
NAPE the back of the neck
NAPO (ne plus); finish
NAPU the musk-deer of Java   zo
NARD spikenard; an unguent   bt
NARE nostril   zo
NARK police spy; a squealer
NATE buttock   md
NAVE (wheel); hub; main aisle   rl
NAVY fleet of ships   nt
NAZE cape; mull; headland; ness
NAZI German national socialist
NEAL anneal; to temper
NEAP lowest tide
NEAR nigh; close; stingy; miserly
NEAT trim; tidy; simple; cattle   zo
NECK col; an isthmus
NEED want; lack; require; poverty

NEEM margosa oil
NEEP a turnip — bt
NE'ER never
NEMO nobody
NEON a gas — ch
NEPE flannel footwear
NERO a tyrant
NESH soft; crumbly; tender
NESS naze; cape; promontory
NEST abode; resort
NETT without discount
NEUM neume; a musical phrase — mu
NEVE glacial snow; firn
NEWS tidings; word; report; advice
NEWT an eft; amphibian — zo
NEXT close to; bordering
NIAS nyas; eyas; a young hawk — zo
NIBS His Nibs
NICE precise; fine; finical; pleasant
NICK notch; reckoning; winning throw
NIDE a brood of pheasants — zo
NIGH near; impending; almost
NIKE Greek goddess of victory
NILE reactivity unit — nc
NILL unwilling; incandescent sparks
NINE one over the eight
NIPA Indian palm tree; toddy — bt
NISI prius; unless previously — lw
NIXY nixie; malignant water-spirit
NIZY dunce; simpleton
NOCK the notch of an arrow
NODE knot; knob; intersection
NODE plot of play; principal difficulty
NOEL Xmas; Yule
NOES opposition votes
NOIL a knot of combed wool
NOLL
NOUL } the head; poll; the crown
NOWL
NOMA mouth gangrene — md
NOME tract of land in Egypt or Greece
NONE not one
NOOK cranny; corner; recess; arbour
NOON mid-day; height; meridional
NOPE American negation
NORM rule; model; standard
NORN one of the three Norse fates
NOSE sagacity; scent; pry; projection
NOSY nosey; inquisitive
NOTE heed; mark; record; letter; fame
NOUN a substantive
NOUS talent, sharp wit, intellect
NOUT neat; cattle (Sc.) — zo
NOVA a new star
NOWT cattle (Sc.)
NOWY knotted — hd
NUDE bare; naked; undraped; stark
NULL void; invalid; nugatory
NUMB torpid; deadened; paralyzed
NUNG a bale of cloves
NURL to mill; to indent

NYAS nias; eyas; young hawk — zo

O

OAKS a race for fillies at Epsom
OAKY hard; tough; strong
OAST hop-kiln
OATH vow; pledge; curse; expletive
OBEX a barrier; an obstacle
OBEY heed; mind; comply; submit
OBIT R. C. funeral service — rl
OBOE the hautboy — mu
OBOL Charon's ferry fee over Styx — nm
OBUS projectile (Fr.)
ODAL udal; absolute tenure in land — lw
ODDS chances; probabilities
ODIC odylic force
ODIN Norse father of heaven
ODYL magnetic force
OFFA King of Mercia
OGAM ogham; ancient Irish writing
OGEE a double curve in architecture
OGLE side glance; leer; smicker
OGPU Soviet police
OGRE monster; giant
OILY greasy; unctuous; oleaginous
OKAY perfectly correct
OKRA gumbo vegetable; mallow — bt, ck
OKTA ⅛ of sky area — mt
OLEO oleomargarine; oleograph
OLID evil-smelling
OLIO mess; medley; mixture; stew
OLLA olio; jar; urn; cooking pot
OLPE Grecian jug
OMAR Khayyam, the tentmaker
OMEN sign; portent; presage; augury
OMER a Hebrew unit of capacity — me
OMIT miss; skip; exclude; neglect
ONCE also onst
ONDE fabric using shades for effect — tx
ONDY wavy — hd
ONER singular; a single; an adept
ONLY sole; alone; singly; barely; but
ONST once
ONUS burden; load; responsibility
ONTO on to
ONYM species or zoological group — zo
ONYX agate streaked with chalcedony
OOFY wealthy; opulent; plutocratic
OOID egg-shaped
OOZE slime; mire; exude; leak; drip
OOZY viscous; slimy
OPAH the king-fish or sunfish — zo
OPAL iridescent precious stone — mn
OPEN overt; candid; undo; begin; start
O-PIP observing station
OPUS a composition; a work — mu
ORAL by word of mouth
ORCA the whale genus — zo
ORFE a gold fish; ide — zo

ORGY drunken revelry; orge	
ORLE fillet under an ovolo	ar
ORRA odd; worthless (Sc.)	
ORYX antelope; legendary unicorn	zo
OTIC a medicine for the ears	md
OTTI attar; an essential oil; perfume	
OUCH a jewel socket	
OURS also **OURN**	
OUSE bark for tanning	
OUST evict; eject; expel; dislodge	
OUZO aniseed spirits (Gr.)	
OVAL elliptical	
OVEN kiln	
OVER (cricket); above; besides; very	
OVUM egg, female reproductive cell	md, zo
OWED due; outstanding; indebted	
OWRE the wild ox	zo
OWSE tan vat liquor	
OXEN kine; cattle; neat	zo
OXER a stiff fence	
OYER judicial authority to hold courts	lw
OYES } the call of the public crier	
OYEZ }	

P

PACA South American rodent	zo
PACE rate; speed; step; walk; peace	
PACK stow; crowd; bale; load; (cards)	
PACO the alpaca; Peruvian sheep	zo
PACT bond; agreement; contract	
PAFF piff-paff; jargon	
PAGE buttons; bell-hop; to paginate	
PAID requited; defrayed; settled; met	
PAIK a beating (Sc.)	
PAIL bucket	
PAIN vex; fret; rack; torment; injure	
PAIR two; twain; brace; couple	
PAIS a jury list	lw
PALA South African antelope	zo
PALE wan; sallow; paling; district	
PALE a vertical division	hd
PALI Buddhist sacred language	rl
PALL mantle; cloak; cloy; sate; surfeit	
PALM to conceal; a token of victory	bt
PALP jointed feeler	zo
PALT rubbish (Dutch)	
PALY ashen; divided vertically	hd
PAND narrow curtain over a bed (Sc.)	
PANE window glass; a patch	
PANG throe; paroxysm; to cram	
PANT gasp; puff; blow; palpitate	
PAPA Greek parish priest; a bishop	rl
PARA paragraph; Turkish copper	nm
PARA Brazilian rubber	bt
PARD the leopard; a partner	zo
PARE cut; peel; skive; lessen; diminish	
PARK train of artillery; an enclosure	
PARR young salmon	zo
PART sever; allot; parcel; divide; quit	

PASS exceed; overstep; ignore; enact	
PAST gone; done; over; former; bygone	
PATE top of head; pie, patty, meat paste	
PATH way; track; trail; route; access	
PAUL, PAWL a check stop	nt
PAUW the South African bustard	zo
PAVE smooth; prepare; facilitate	
PAVE the cobbled roads of France	
PAVO peacock; southern constellation	zo
PAWK trick; a cunning device (Sc.)	
PAWN pledge; hypothecate; a chessman	
PAYA Honduran Indian	
PAYE pay as you earn	
PEAK top; acme; apex; zenith	
PEAL clang; echo; resound; thunder	
PEAN paean; song of triumph	
PEAR a fruity	bt
PEAT turf used for fuel	
PEBA armadillo; the black tatou	zo
PECH also **PEGH** to pant (Sc.)	
PECK strike with beak; 2 gal. (9 litres)	me
PEEK to peep (Sc.)	
PEEL skin; pare; rind; bark; flay	
PEEL a shovel; a fort; to pillage	
PEEN the back of a hammer-head	
PEEP a sly look; the cry of a chicken	
PEER to peep; to appear; a nobleman	
PEKE a Pekinese dog	zo
PELA white wax from a scale-insect	
PELF money; riches; filthy lucre	
PELL skin; hide; parchment	
PELT raw hide; throw; rain heavily	
PEND hang; impend; an enclosure	
PENT enclosed; confined; shut up	
PEON day-labourer; bondsman; police	
PEON foot-soldier; serf (Mex.); messenger	
PEPO a fruit of the gourd type	bt
PERI fairy excluded from paradise	
PERK smarten up; trim; spruce	
PERM a permanent wave	
PERN the honey-buzzard	zo
PERT saucy; forward; impertinent	
PESO (Philippines); dollar	nm
PEST plague; pestilence; scourge	
PHEW! exclamation of exertion	
PHIZ face; visage; physiognomy	
PHON a decibel; unit of loudness	me
PHOT unit of illumination	me
PIAL spinal chord membrane	md
PIAT anti-tank gun	
PICA magpie; size of type	pr
PICA depraved appetite	md
PICE Indian (Nepalese)	nm
PICK cull; select; choice; peck	to
PICT early Scottish race	
PIDE unleavened bread (Turk.)	ck
PIED spotted	
PIER jetty; mole; pillar	
PIET the magpie; dipper; water-ousel	zo
PIKA small rodent; guinea-pig type	zo
PIKE peak; a turnpike; a weapon; fish	zo

PILA	pillar-shaped structure	zo
PILE	nap; heap; mass; stake	el
PILL	to rod; plunder; blackball	md
PIMP	a pander	
PINE	to wilt; pine-apple; fir-tree	bt
PING	the noise of a bullet	
PINK	to pierce; to knock; a flower	bt
PINT	measure of capacity; 4 gills (0.5 l)	me
PINY	full of pines	bt
PIPE	exchequer roll; long tube; calumet	
PIPE	to call; cask; bosun's whistle	mu
PIPI	pods for tanning	
PIPY	tubular	
PIRN	reel; bobbin; thread on a reel	
PISE	rammed clay	
PISH!	exclamation of contempt	
PITH	quintessence; gist; marrow	bt
PITY	ruth; condolence; compassion	
PIXY	pixie; a small fairy	
PIZE	term used in execration	
PLAN	plot; scheme; design; sketch	
PLAP	plop; plash; splash	
PLAT	to plait; piece of ground; dish	
PLAX	flat platelike structure	zo
PLAY	act; romp; game; frolic; farce	
PLEA	excuse; prayer; claim; argument	
PLED	pleaded; argued; disputed	
PLIM	to swell	
PLOD	jog along; toil; moil; drudge	
PLOP	to fall into water	
PLOT	plan; concoct; outline; allotment	
PLOW	a plough	
PLOY	employment; a frolic (Sc.)	
PLUG	a stopple; stop; plod	
PLUM	£100,000; a fruit	bt
PLUS	in addition; more	
PNYX	Athenian meeting place	
POCK	a pustule	md
POCO	little; rather (It.)	md
POEM	ode; lyric; elegy	
POET	bard; balladmonger	
POGO	a pastime	
POKE	bag; bonnet; nudge; prod	
POKY	small; cramped; confined; stupid	
POLE	a mast; 5½ yd (5 m); Polish man	me
POLK	to dance the polka	
POLL	clip; lop; election; head; parrot	zo
POLO	ball game	
POLT	a blow; a hard knock; a club	
POME	an apple; a ball of dominion	bt
POMP	pageantry; ceremony; display	
POND	pool; mere; to ponder	
PONE	bread made from Indian corn	ck
PONE	who cuts dealt cards	
PONK	a nocturnal spirit (Shak.)	
PONS	medical link or bridge	md
PONY	£25; nag; tit; palfrey	zo
POOD	Russian weight, 36 lb (16 kg)	me
POOH!	exclamation of contempt	
POOL	mere; pond; tarn; merge; combine	
POON	East Indian tree; wood for spars	bt

POOP	nincompoop; stern of ship	nt
POOR	scant; meagre; sterile; needy	
POPE	the Bishop of Rome	rl
PORE	con; study; small orifice	md
PORK	swine flesh	
PORN	pornography	
PORT	bagpipe music; mien; bearing	mu
PORT	wine; haven; entry; larboard	nt
PORY	porous; pervious	
POSE	puzzle; nonplus; feign; a posture	
POSH	very superior	
POST	size of paper; mail; station; record	
POSY	motto or verse; nosegay	bt
POTT	size of hand-cut paper	pp
POUF	pouffe; large cushion; gauze	
POUR	rush; gush; flow; emit; stream	
POUT	to register pique; whiting	zo
PRAD	a horse (slang)	
PRAM	perambulator; Baltic boat	nt
PRAY	beg; crave; implore; entreat	
PREE	to prove; to taste (Sc.)	
PREP	preparation; preparatory	
PREX	college president (USA)	
PREY	despoil; pillage; devour; quarry	
PRIG	pilfer; a coxcomb; a fop	
PRIM	formal; precise; privet shrub	bt
PROA	Malay sailing canoe	nt
PROD	goad; poke; nudge; prick	
PROG	proctor	
PROM	promenade concert	mu
PROP	support; uphold; buttress	
PROS	arguments for; cf. cons	
PROW	the cutwater	nt
PROX	proximo	
PRYS	price (Spens.)	
PSHA!	pshaw	
PTAH	Egyptian God, the Creator	
PUCE	flea-colour	
PUCK	ice hockey ball; an imp	
PUDU	a small deer of the Andes	zo
PUFF	fuff; pant; blow; flatter; a whiff	
PUGH!	interjection of disgust	
PUJA	Hindu ritual; obeisance	
PUKE	to vomit	
PUKU	Central African antelope	zo
PULE	to whine; to cry	
PULK	Laplander's sledge	
PULL	draw; drag; haul; pluck; pick	
PULP	any soft uniform mass	
PULS	Afghan monetary unit	nm
PULU	Hawaiian tree-fern fibre	bt
PUMA	Peruvian lion	zo
PUMP	raise water; interrogate	
PUMY	pumice-stone	mn
PUNA	Andean plateau	
PUNK	tinder; dud; worthless	
PUNT	gamble; kick; flat-boat	nt
PUNY	tiny; weak; petty; Lilliputian	
PUPA	also **PUPE** a chrysalis	zo
PURE	chaste; unsullied; unmixed; neat	
PURL	knit; flow; ripple; mulled ale	

PURR curr; (a cat or pigeon noise)
PUSH a gang; urge; jostle; press
PUSS hare or cat   zo
PUTT an endeavour to hole the ball
PUXI North Amer. edible caterpillar   zo
PYES calendar for calculating Easter   rl
PYIC discharging pus   md
PYRE a funeral pile
PYRO pyrogallic acid   ch

Q

QUAB quob; tremble (obs.)
QUAD quadrangle; quadruped; prison   zo
QUAG quagmire; morass; swamp
QUAT a nonentity; a twerp
QUAY wharf; landing place
QUEY a young cow or heifer (Sc.)   zo
QUIB quip; jibe; jest
QUID £1; a chew of tobacco   nm
QUIN a kind of scallop   zo
QUIP sally; retort; taunt; quirk
QUIT leave; desert; retire; release
QUIZ puzzle; chaff; ridicule; an enquiry
QUOB quab; tremble
QUOD prison
QUOP quap; throb

R

RAAD South African parliament
RABI the grain crop of Hindustan
RACA a term of contempt
RACE run; compete; tribe; nation
RACE flavour; root; rapid; current
RACH dog; pointer or setter   zo
RACK torture; stretch; anguish; harass
RACK a grating; wrack; cloud; to amble
RACY spirited; piquant; pungent
RAFF riff-raff; rabble; rubbish
RAFT a floating framework   nt
RAGE rave; fume; fury; storm; craze
RAGG ragstone; siliceous sandstone   mn
RAGI species of millet   bt
RAHU the dark planet in Hindu Myth
RAID foray; inroad; invasion; irruption
RAIL fence; scold; genus of birds   bt
RAIN pitter-patter; a downpour
RAIS Arab chief, captain
RAJA rajah
RAKE roué; inclination; gardening   to
RAKI Levant; aniseed brandy
RALE rattling sound in the lungs   md
RAMA heroic incarnation of Vishnu   rl
RAMI appendage ends in collembola   zo
RAMP a slope; a swindle; climb; spring
RANA amphibian genus, frogs, etc.   zo
RANA a Rajput prince or chief
RAND mountain; S. African monetary unit   nm
RAND edge; border; margin; inner sole
RANG past tense of ring

RANI ranee; the wife of a rajah
RANK row; grade; range; foul; musty
RANT rave; orate; spout; declaim
RAPE land division in Sussex; oil-seed   bt
RAPE ravish; violate; outrage
RAPT enthralled; absorbed; fascinated
RARE choice; unusual; precious; raw
RASE raze; erase; expunge; level
RASH hasty; headlong; to slice   md
RASP to file; abrade; raspberry   to, bt
RATA a New Zealand ironwood tree   bt
RATE scold; assess; appraise; speed
RATH Burmese state carriage
RATH rathe; early; soon; Irish fort
RAVE rant; fume; storm; drive
RAZE rase; gut; demolish; overthrow
READ peruse; decipher; study; erudite
REAL true; genuine; a Spanish coin   nm
REAM to enlarge; to froth; 20 quires
REAN rine; rone; rune; a ditch
REAP gain; crop; gather; harvest
REAR raise; breed; erect; end; behind
RECK to care for; regard; heed
REDD to tidy; to arrange; to clear
REDE counsel; advise; advice
REED rush; aquatic grass
REED to thatch; a pipe   mu
REEF rocky ledge; shoal; lode   nt
REEK smoke; vapour; fume; stink
REEL sway; whirl; totter; a bobbin
REEM the unicorn of the Bible   zo
REFT bereft; left destitute
REIM riem; raw-hide thong (S. Africa)
REIN govern; restrain; check; curb
REIS Brazilian or Portuguese money   nm
RELY depend; lean; confide; trust
REND rip; tear; sunder; sever; rupture
RENT hire; let; lease; schism; tear
REPP ribbed fabric
RESP a sheep disease
REST repose; lean; recline; respite
RETE a plexus; network of vessels   md
REUS a defendant; debtor   lw
REVE dream; reverie (obs.)
RHEA the South American ostrich   zo
RHEA Hellenic nature-goddess   rl
RHEA the ramie plant or fibre   bt
RHOM parallelogram brick
RHUS cashew-nut genus   bt
RIAL ryal (Iran); English gold   nm
RICE a wedding cereal   bt
RICH opulent; wealthy; fertile; luscious
RICK stack; wrench; sprain
RIDE domineer; control; a district
RIEL (Cambodia)   nm
RIEM reim; leather rope (S. Africa)
RIFE ryfe; prevalent; current; abundant
RIFF a moroccan
RIFT fissure; cleft; gap; split; chink
RIGA deal; balsam; hemp from Riga   bt
RILE vex; anger; provoke; irritate

RILL rivulet; brook; streamlet
RIMA narrow cleft — pl
RIME hoar-frost; rhyme; poem
RIND peel; bark; external cover — bt
RINE rind; to touch
RINE rone; rune; rean; water-course
RING encircle; hoop; arena; combine
RINK a sheet of ice
RIOT orgy; broil; uproar; tumult
RIPE mature; ready; mellow; fit
RIPT ripped; torn
RISE soar; mount; tower; rebel
RISK chance; hazard; peril; speculate
RISP to rasp; branch of green stalks — bt
RITE form; usage; observance
RIVA rift; cleft
RIVE a bank; tear; rend; pierce
RIVO a drinking cry (Shak.)
RIXY quarrelsome; the sea-swallow — zo
ROAD route; thoroughfare; highway
ROAM rove; ramble; meander; saunter
ROAN a colour; sheepskin binding
ROAR yell; shout; bellow; howl
ROBE clothe; invest; drape; dress
ROCK a distaff; oscillate; sweetmeat
RODE travelled; a raid; a roadstead
ROER elephant gun
ROIL rile; to stir up; to vex
ROIN royne; whisper; mutter
ROKE reek; smoke; mist
ROKY foggy
ROLE part; function; character
ROLL reel; lurch; enfold; scroll
ROME Catholicism
ROMP sport; frisk; caper; gambol
RONE rine; rune; rean; gutter
RONG rung; tolled (obs.)
RONT runt; stunted; a stump
ROOD The Cross — rl
ROOD a quarter of an acre — me
ROOF cover; canopy; shelter
ROOK cheat; defraud; fleece; castle — zo
ROOL to ruffle; to raggle
ROOM chamber; stead; space; scope
ROOM roum; a deep-blue dye
ROON rim; border (Sc.)
ROOP to roar; hoarseness (obs.)
ROOT fix; implant; origin; radix — bt
ROPE tie; secure; bind; tether
ROPY stringy; viscous; adhesive
ROSE arose; colour; a spray — bt
ROSS the refuse of plants (Sc.)
ROSY roseate; blooming; blushing
ROTA roster; R.C. court — rl
ROTE mechanical repetition
ROTI the joint (Fr.)
ROTL a 12 oz (350 g) Arab weight — me
ROUE rake; debauchee; libertine
ROUM room; a deep-blue dye
ROUP a fowl disease; an auction (Sc.)
ROUT vanquish; defeat; disorder

ROUT social fuction; soirée
ROUX sauce of melted butter, flour — ck
ROVE roam; ramble; stray; range
RUBE a rustic (USA)
RUBY a size of type; a gem — mn
RUCK wrinkle; fold; crease
RUDD freshwater fish; the red-eye — zo
RUDE boorish; churlish; rough; raw
RUED regretted; repented
RUFF a frill; to trump; a bird — zo
RUGA fold; corrugation
RUIN wreck; demolish; subvert
RUKH the jungle (India)
RULE control; sway; precept; custom
RUMP the Parliament of 1648
RUNE incised writing of the Norsemen
RUNG a ladder step; tolled
RUNN low-lying land in India
RUNT ront; dwarf; stump; a pigeon — zo
RUSA Indian deer, the sambar — zo
RUSA Indian grass; (geranium oil) — bt
RUSE wile; trick; artifice; stratagem
RUSH dash; fly; career; sally; a reed — bt
RUSK a biscuit
RUSS a Russian
RUST fust; must; corrosion
RUTA genus of plants; rue — bt
RUTH mercy; pity; sorrow; misery
RYAL rial; rose-noble, old English — nm
RYKE to reach (Sc.)
RYND iron millstone support
RYOT Indian cultivator
RYPE the Norwegian ptarmigan — zo
RYVE rive; to pierce (Spens.)

S

SACK wine; garment; pillage; pouch
SADR the lote-bush — bt
SAFE sure; secure; reliable; certain
SAGA heroic Norse legends
SAGE a Solomon; genus salvia — bt
SAGO edible palm pith — bt
SAGY seasoned with sage
SAIC Levantine ketch — nt
SAID stated; declared; alleged
SAIL cruise; glide; depart — nt
SAIN to consecrate (Sc.)
SAIR to serve; to satisfy; sore (Sc.)
SAKE cause; regard; reason
SAKI Japanese beer from rice — ck
SAKI South American monkey genus — zo
SALE auction; market; vendition
SALP swimming tunicate — zo
SALT mariner; wit; pungent; salacious
SALT sodium chloride — ch
SAME ditto; identical; exactly similar
SAMP porridge made from Indian corn
SAND grit; force of character — mn
SANE rational; sound; normal; lucid
SANG chanted; blood red — hd

SANK	foundered; subsided; dug	
SANS	without (Shak.)	
SAPO	the toad-fish	zo
SARD	a precious stone; agate	mn
SARI	Indian garment; scarf	
SARK	a shirt or chemise	
SARN	a pavement	
SASH	window frame; a scarf	
SASS	impudence; sauce	
SATE	cloy; glut; gratify; surfeit	
SATI	suttee; self-immolation (India)	
SAUL	Indian tree; an oratorio	bt, mu
SAUT	salt (Sc.)	
SAVE	except; rescue; to husband; retain	
SAWN	cut with a saw	
SAXE	a kind of paper; light blue	
SCAB	a blackleg; a sore	md
SCAD	horse-mackerel	zo
SCAN	view; examine; scrutinize	
SCAR	mark; blemish; steep rock	
SCAT	a tax; scare away; be off!	
SCAW	skaw; a promontory	
SCON	scun; skim; skip	
SCOT	a Scotsman; a tax	
SCOW	flat-bottomed boat	nt
SCRY	descry; espy	
SCUD	rack; wrack; hasten; bustle	
SCUG	skug; shelter; expiate	
SCUM	dross; froth; refuse; scoria	
SCUN	scon; skim	
SCUP	a swing; the porgy fish	zo
SCUR	graze; jerk; a stunted horn (Sc.)	
SCUT	a short tail	
SCYE	armhole of a garment	
SEAH	Jewish dry measure, 14 pt	me
SEAL	fasten; a pinniped	zo
SEAM	joint; vein; stratum	
SEAN	seine; a drag-net	
SEAR	burn; scorch; a pawl; dry; sere	
SEAT	chair; site; residence; abode	
SEAX	Celtic sword	
SECT	faction; schism; party	
SEED	germ; embryo; progeny	bt, zo
SEEK	try; ask; hunt; search; court	
SEEL	to close the eyelids; good fortune	
SEEM	appear; look; pretend	
SEEN	observed; regarded; perceived	
SEEP	to ooze; to trickle; to sipe	
SEER	augur; prophet; soothsayer	
SEER	Indian kilogram	me
SEGO	an American plant	bt
SEID	a descendant of Mohammed	
SEIL	sile; strain; a sieve (Sc.)	
SELF	particular; simple; selfishness	
SELL	vend; barter; hawk; betray	
SEME	heraldic printing design detail	⎧ pr
SEME	strewn with stars, etc.	⎩ hd
SEMI	demi; hemi; a prefix	
SEND	transmit; propel; eject	
SENS	since (Spens.)	
SENT	forwarded; despatched; flung	

SEPS	reptile genus; lizards	zo
SEPT	a clan in Ireland	
SERA	a lock of any kind; pl. of serum	md
SERB	native of Serbia	
SERE	sear; withered; parched; dry	
SERE	succession of plant communities	bt
SERF	thrall; villein; slave; helot	
SESS	cess; tax	
SETA	bristle; prickle	
SETT	squared block; packing piece	
SETT	badger's home; (mining)	
SEVE	wine's distinctive bouquet (Fr.)	
SEWN	stitched	
SEXT	musical interval	mu
SHAD	a fish of the herring type	zo
SHAG	tobacco; green cormorant	zo
SHAG	coarse hair; roughen; deform	
SHAH	Persian monarch	
SHAM	deceive; substitute	
SHAN	Burmese borderer	
SHAW	a grove; a thicket	
SHAY	chaise; a vehicle	
SHEA	African butter-tree	bt
SHED	emit; diffuse; cot; shack	
SHET	free from; be rid of	
SHEW	show; exhibit; parade	
SHIM	brake-plate; to wedge up; packing tool	
SHIN	to climb; tramp; trudge	
SHIP	to export; seagoing vessel	nt
SHIR	shirr; to pucker	
SHOD	provided with shoes	
SHOE	footwear	
SHOG	shake; jog; a shock	
SHOO!	begone; scare away	
SHOP	emporium; store; imprison	
SHOT	a reckoning; a marksman; missile	
SHOW	flaunt; blazon; expound; pomp	
SHUG	to shrug; to crawl	
SHUN	avoid; evade; eschew; elude	
SHUT	bar; lock; close; slam; secure	
SIAL	granitic earth shell	gl
SICE	the six at dice	
SICE	syce; groom (India)	
SICK	to incite; poorly; ailing; disgusted	
SIDA	genus of mallows	bt
SIDE	verge; border; cause; behalf	
SIDI	Afr. Moslem title of respect	
SIDY	aloof and pretentious	
SIFT	separate; examine; sort	
SIGH	mourn; repine; lament	
SIGN	beckon; endorse; emblem; portent	
SIKE	syke; Arctic stream	
SIKH	a Punjab soldier	
SILE	a sieve; a colander	
SILK	cocoon thread; Queen's Counsel	tx, lw
SILL	doorstep; window frame	
SILO	fodder storage; ensilage	
SILT	sediment; ooze; percolate	
SIMA	basaltic earth shell	gl
SIMP	a simpleton; a mutt	
SIND	or **SYND** to rinse (Sc.)	

SINE syne; since; then (Sc.)
SING relate in verse; chant; squeal
SINK flag; droop; subside; founder
SINN Fein
SIPE to ooze; to seep; to percolate
SIRE Your Majesty; progenitor
SIST summon; delay; stay (Sc.)   lw
SITE location; place; position; spot
SIUM the water parsnip   bt
SIVA the Destroyer in Hindu religion   rl
SIZE glue; varnish; bulk; volume
SIZY sticky; viscous
SKAT a card game
SKAW scaw; a promontory
SKEE ski; a winter sport
SKEG stump; branch; wild plum   bt
SKEP beehive; wicker basket
SKEW or **SKUE** awry; oblique; a squint
SKID heavy timber; drag shoe; side-slip
SKIM graze; touch; skirt; brush
SKIN peel; pare; flay; hide; pelt
SKIO or **SKEO** a hut in the Orkneys
SKIP skipper; large tub; omit; leap
SKIT a lampoon; burlesque
SKOT unit of low-intensity lighting
SKUA the pirate gull   zo
SKUG a squirrel   zo
SKUG scug; shelter; expiate
SKYE terrier   zo
SKYR curds (Iceland)
SLAB chunk; block; thick; mud
SLAE sloe (Sc.); blackthorn   bt
SLAG scoria; debris; mine waste
SLAM bang; shut with violence; (cards)
SLAP spank; a cleft; a gap in a fence
SLAT strip; lath; slate; sharp blow
SLAV a Slavonic Aryan
SLAW sliced cabbage used as salad
SLAY kill; destroy; despatch; murder
SLED sledge; sleigh
SLEW slue; to twist; turn round; killed
SLEY the reed of a weaver's loom
SLIC Selecting Listing in Combination
SLID slipped; skidded; glided; tripped
SLIM slight; slender; lithe; crafty
SLIP trip; fall; scion; twig; cutting
SLIT rip; rend; tear; slash; sever
SLOB muddy ground
SLOE slae; blackthorn   bt
SLOG smite; swipe; work doggedly
SLOP a policeman; a mess; a spill
SLOT track of deer; slit; groove
SLOW tardy; dilatory; dull; inactive
SLUB to twist whilst spinning
SLUD sludge; ooze; mud
SLUE slew; to revolve
SLUG sluggard; a pellet   zo
SLUM a purlieu; squalid neighbourhood
SLUR stigma; stain; aspersion; sully   mu
SLUT a slattern; a jade
SMEE widgeon; pintail   zo

SMEW migratory sea duck   zo
SMIT to infect; a stain; infection
SMOG smoky fog
SMUG self-satisfied; to confiscate
SMUR fine misty rain; to drizzle (Sc.)
SMUT soot; a plant disease
SNAG projecting stump; an obstacle
SNAP bite; nip; snip; crack; break
SNAP a snap-shot; a photo; a game
SNAR to snarl (Spens.)
SNEB snib; snub; check; reprimand
SNEE a large knife (Dutch)
SNIG to cut; an eel   zo
SNIP clip; piece; snippet; a certainty
SNOB shoemaker; tuft-hunter
SNOD neat; trim; sleek (Sc.)
SNOW (cocaine)
SNUB snib; check; slight
SNUG cosy; compact; sheltered
SOAK steep; drench; saturate
SOAP to flatter
SOAR rise; mount; tower; aspire
SOCK plough-share; hose
SODA an alkali   ch
SOFA couch; divan; ottoman
SOFI or **SUFI** religious Persian; dervish   rl
SOFT pliable; plastic; yielding; dulcet
SOHO a sportsman's halloo (Shak.)
SOIL loam; stain; sully; tarnish
SOKE soc; privilege; (East Anglian)   lw
SOLA hat-plant; sponge-wood; pith   bt
SOLD retailed; peddled; taken in
SOLE only; unique; solitary
SOLI the plural of solo   mu
SOLO a card game   mu
SOMA an intoxicating drink   ck
SOMA animal body   zo
SOME distinctive (American)
SONE unit of loudness   ac
SONG lay; carol; ballad; lullaby   mu
SOON anon; early; willingly; lief
SOOP to sweep (Sc.)
SOOT sout; grime
SOPH sophomore; a student
SORA Carolina rail   zo
SORB mountain ash; service tree   bt
SORE raw; tender; grievous; painful
SORI fern spore-cases   bt
SORN to cadge board and lodgings
SORT arrange; classify; kind; race
SORY sulphate of iron   ch
SO-SO indifferent; moderate
SOSS a mess; a puddle; plump
SOUK bazaar; Eastern market
SOUL spirit; fervour; essence
SOUM sowm; pasturage (Sc.)
SOUP broth; consommé
SOUR tart; acid; rancid; caustic; bitter
SOUT soot; grime (obs.)
SOWL to pull by the ears (Shak.)
SOWN disseminated; scattered; strewn

SOYA Japanese bean	bt
SPAE spay; foretell; divine	
SPAM spiced ham	
SPAN a yoke; to bridge; wholly	me
SPAR to box; rafter; pole	nt, mn
SPAT the spawn of shellfish; a slap	zo
SPAY to render unfertile; geld	
SPEC speculation	
SPED fled; hurried; hastened	
SPER to bolt; to shut (obs.)	
SPET to spit (obs.)	
SPEW spue; vomit	
SPIE a keen glance; spy (obs.)	
SPIN turn; twist; twirl; prolong	
SPIT a shoal; an iron prong	
SPIV felonious speculating parasite	
SPOT blot; stain; patch; mark; site	
SPRY alert; brisk; nimble; lively	
SPUD narrow spade; potato	bt
SPUE spew; eject; vomit	
SPUN whirled; woven; extended	
SPUR goad; urge; impel; prick	
STAB pierce; spear; gore; thrust	
STAG a colt; an ox	zo
STAM to confound; confusion	
STAR an asterisk; a heavenly body	
STAW to stand still; a surfeit (Sc.)	
STAY stop; check; curb; tarry; abide	lw
STEM dam; hold; resist; stock; stalk	bt
STEN a tommy-gun	
STEP pace; tread; rung; stage	
STET let it stand (Latin)	
STEW ragout; simmer; fishpond	
STIE to ascend (Spens.)	
STIR spur; stimulate; tumult; prison	
STOA covered colonnade	ar
STOB stub; stump; wedge	
STOG to stir up mud	
STOP block; impede; cease; desist	
STOT young ox; steer	zo
STOW pack; arrange; place	
STUB stump; to extirpate; a counterfoil	
STUD knob; nail; breeding place	
STUG a thorn (Sc.)	
STUM unfermented wine; must	
STUN bewilder; amaze; dumbfound	
STYE an inflamed eyelid	md
STYX river in Hades; (see **Obol**)	
SUCH sich; so; like; similar	
SUCK imbibe; absorb; engulf	
SUDD⎫ flood debris, Nile	
SUDD⎭ dense mat of aquatic vegetation	
SUDS soapsuds	nt
SUED entreated; prosecuted; high and dry	
SUER a plaintiff	lw
SUET fatty tissue	
SUEZ canal; (Lesseps, the engineer)	
SUFI Islamic mystic; Moslem sect	
SUIT gratify; beseem; action; case	
SULK glower; be sullen	
SUMA Nicaraguan Indian	

SUMP pit; morass	
SUNG chanted	
SUNK immersed; engulfed; dug	
SUNN Indian plant; its fibre	bt
SUPE a supernumerary; a toady	
SURA a chapter of the Koran	
SURA the sap of the coco-palm	bt
SURD an irrational number	
SURE certain; secure; reliable; safe	
SURF foaming waters	
SWAB swob; mop up	
SWAD pod; podgy person; clump	
SWAG plunder; festoon; sag	
SWAM swim (past tense)	
SWAN the Swan of Avon, Shakespeare	zo
SWAP swop; a blow; a stroke; to barter	
SWAT a fly-killer; a smart blow	
SWAY rock; roll; reel; influence; power	
SWIG gulp down; pulley gear	
SWIM float; overflow; be dizzy	
SWIN sea river or channel	
SWOB swab; mop	
SWOP swap; exchange; barter	
SWOT swat; an earnest student	
SWUM swim (past participle)	
SYBO cibol; onion	bt
SYCE sice; chauffeur; groom (India)	
SYKE sike; rill; rivulet (Sc.)	
SYNE sine; since (Sc.)	

T

TAAL Cape Dutch	
TABU taboo; ban; veto; prohibit	
TACE be silent	mu
TACK a nail; hard food; hasten	nt
TACO fried tortilla/salad dish (Mex.)	ck
TACT diplomacy; finesse	
TAEL money of account	nm
TAEL Chinese ounce	me
TA'EN taken	
TAFT a plumbing joint	
TAHA African weaver-bird	zo
TAHR Himalayan goat	zo
TAIC Indo-Chinese; their language	
TAIL extremity; queue; trail; entail	
TAIN mirror silver	
TAIT tate; fibre; lock of hair (Sc.)	
TAKE grasp; seize; adopt; carry	
TALC mica	mn
TALE story; fable; narration	
TALK parley; prate; palaver	
TALL towering; elevated	
TAME docile; dull; insipid; domesticate	
TAMP pack earth round a mine	
TANA Indian police station	
TANE ta'en; taken	
TANG point; twang; seaweed; flavour	
TANK cistern; reservoir	
TANT small scarlet spider	zo
TAPA Polynesian fibre cloth	

TAPE to bind; ribbon; to measure
TAPU tabu; taboo; bar; veto
TARA old Irish Convocation
TARA an edible New Zealand fern   bt
TARE gross weight; a weed   bt
TARN mountain pool; a marsh
TARO edible plant of the arum type   bt
TART sharp; bitter; pungent; small pie
TASH Indian silk fabric with gold thread
TASK toil; drudgery; labour
TASS a drinking-cup; a heap
TASS pouch; thigh-armour
TA-TA good-bye; a short walk
TATE a London Picture Gallery
TATH cattle dung; to manure
TATU tatou; peba; armadillo   zo
TAUT tense; strained; stressed
TAWA N. Zealand hardwood
TAWS tawse; a leather strap (Sc.)
TAXI motor-cab; move on runway   ae
TAYO apronlike garment (S. America)
TEAK hardwood tree; the wood   bt
TEAL small waterfowl; a duck   zo
TEAM side; group; draught animals   zo
TEAN sorrow; vex; tease (Sc.)
TEAR rip; rend; lacerate; (sob)
TEAT a nipple
TECK detective
TEDE tead; torch; flambeau
TEED (golf)
TEEM swarm; to abound; be prolific
TEEM pour molten glass   gs
TEEN grief; affliction; allot (obs.)
TEER to stir; to sieve
TEFF Abyssinian cereal grass   bt
TEIL the lime tree   bt
TEIL part of book, volume of series
TELA weblike tissue   zo
TELD told (Spens.)
TELL recite; divulge; blab; reckon
TEND incline; verge; mind; nurture
TENT lint; probe; a pavilion
TENT sacramental wine   rl
TERM dub; entitle; phrase; period
TERN threefold; sea-bird; gull-type   zo
TERN a prize in a lottery
TEST refining vessel; essay; assay
TEST attest; proof; ordeal; criterion
TETE head; head-dress (Fr.)
TETT a plait (obs.)
TETT theme; subject; thesis; treatise
THAI (Siamese); language
THAN conjunction of comparison
THAR goat-antelope of Nepal   zo
THAT demons. adj.; pronoun
THAW run; fuse; melt; liquefy
THEA the tea plant   bt
THEE objective of thou
THEM objective of they
THEN adverb of past time
THEW muscle; sinew; strength

THEY Kipling's pronoun
THIG to beg; to beseech; to sorn
THIN lean; fine; lank; spare; sparse
THIS demons. adj.; pronoun
THOR the God of Thunder   rl
THOU treat with familiarity
THRO, THRU through
THUD a dull sound
THUG Indian strangler or poisoner
THUS frankincense; a form of resin   bt
TIAO Chinese money of account   nm
TIBU Saharan tribe
TICE entice; a decoy
TICK credit; bed fabric; mark; insect   zo
TIDE season; course; current
TIDY neat; spruce; trim; orderly
TIED united; constrained; fastened
TIER row; rank; mountain range
TIFF also **TIFT** quarrel; peevishness
TIFF quaff; a short drink; adorn
TIGE the shaft of a column   ar
TIKE tyke; dog; cur; Yorkshireman   zo
TIKI Maori charm or amulet
TILE roofing material; a hat
TILL cash drawer; cultivate
TILT tent; a covering; a hood
TILT to hammer; incline; lean; slant
TIME era; epoch; term; spell; date
TINE point of antler; spike; to enclose
TING, TINK ring; tinkle
TINT hue; dye; stain; tinge
TINY pygmy; wee; puny; minute
TIRE tyre; iron hoop; attire; headdress
TIRE weary; harass; vex; fatigue
TIRL quiver; vibrate; twirl (Sc.)
TIRO tyro; novice; beginner
TIRR tear; strip off (Sc.)
TITI South Amer. squirrel monkey   zo
TIVY with speed; tantivy
TOAD an amphibious batrachian   zo
TOAT handle of bench plane   cr
TOBY beer-mug; Punch's pet dog   zo
TOCO toko; punishment
TO-DO ado; bustle; excitement
TODY green humming bird   zo
TOED of obliquely fastened timber   cr
TOED trod; toed the line
TOFF fop; dandy; swell
TOFT grove; messuage   lw
TOGA Roman raiment
TOGE a robe (Shak.)
TOGS ceremonial garments
TOHO a dog-call
TOIL moil; snare; travail; pains; strive
TOIT a cushion
TOKO toco; a drubbing
TOLA Indian weight; 180 grains troy
TOLD narrated; related; recounted
TOLE toll; entice; attract
TOLL tribute; (funeral bell); telephone
TOLT old English writ   lw

TOLU oleo-resin; balsam	bt	
TOMB grave; sepulchre; mausoleum		
TOME book; volume; work		
TONE cadence; inflection; tint		
TONG the tongue of a buckle (Spens.)		
TONK a mighty smite		
TONY a simpleton; genteel; posh		
TOOK grabbed; gained; captured		
TOOL cat's-paw; drive a coach		
TOOM empty; rubbish-heap		
TOON Indian cedar	bt	
TOOT a wastrel; the devil; honk		
TOPE shark known as the penny-dog	zo	
TOPE Buddhist monument		
TOPE clump of trees; to booze		
TORE dead winter grass	bt	
TORE rent; split; a torus; a moulding		
TORI mouldings at the base of columns		
TORN lacerated; ript		
TORR unit of low pressure	ps	
TORT redress of wrongs	lw	
TORY a Conservative		
TOSE to tease (obs.)		
TOSH bosh; twaddle; boloney		
TOSS pitch; hurl; cast; throw; lob		
TOST flung; writhed		
TOSY teased; soft (obs.)		
TOTE to carry; totalisator		
TOTY Ind. odd-job man		
TOUR trip; round; jaunt; ramble		
TOUT paid agent; tipster; to pout		
TOWN a city; London		
TOWY like tow; hempen		
TOZE to pluck; pull by the ears		
TRAM a beam; tramcar		
TRAP a gin; igneous rock	mn	
TRAP adorn; drape; ambush; ensnare		
TRAY salver; trez; third		
TREE the Cross; to chase up a tree	bt	
TREK travel by ox-wagons (S. Africa)		
TRET a trade allowance		
TREY a three at cards or dice		
TREZ third; the third tine of antler		
TRIG trim; tight; secure; a dandy		
TRIG wedge; skid; boundary line		
TRIM neat; tidy; clip; adjust; Corporal		
TRIO composition in three parts	mu	
TRIP tour; err; slip; stumble; dance		
TROD trampled; walked		
TRON ancient beam balance (Sc.)		
TROT to run; an old woman (Shak.)		
TROW to trust; believe; suppose		
TROY weights used for gold, etc.	me	
TRUE loyal; staunch; straight; exact		
TRUG hod for mortar; gardening basket		
TSAR Czar; Ksar; Tzar; Zsar		
TSUN Chinese inch	me	
TUAN title of respect (China and Malay)		
TUBA bass trumpet; transmitter	mu	
TUBE pipe; telescope; Underground		
TUCK rapier; fold; net; pull; thrust		

TUCK beat of drum; food; to cram		
TUFA inexpensive cheroot		
TUFA calcareous deposit	mn	
TUFF volcanic rock-debris	mn	
TUFT knot; bunch; clump; tuffet		
TULE Californian bulrush	bt	
TUMP hillock; to earth up		
TUNA the prickly pear	bt	
TUNA the great tunny fish	zo	
TUNE air; melody; strain; harmony		
TURF sod; sward; earth; peat; racing		
TURK Ottoman		
TURM a troop (obs.)		
TURN spin; bend; divert; curdle; hinge		
TURR three-stringed Burmese violin	mu	
TUSH! pshaw; tusk (Shak.)		
TUSK pointed tooth; sea-fish cod type	zo	
TUTU short ballet skirt; shrub (NZ)	bt	
TUUM (meum and teum); thine (Latin)		
TUZA tucan; Mexican pouched rat	zo	
TWAL twelve (Sc.)		
'TWAS it was		
TWAY twain; two (Sc.)		
TWEE precious, overly cute		
TWIG observe; understand; sprig	bt	
TWIN double; duplex		
TWIT taunt; ridicule; upbraid; ass		
TYKE tike; Yorkshireman; dog; cur	zo	
TYMP mouth of blast furnace's hearth		
TYNE anxiety; disappear; perish (obs.)		
TYPE kind; sort; class; species; emblem		
TYPO a compositor		
TYRE tire; attire; dress		
TYRO tiro; novice; recruit; neophyte		
TZAR Tsar; Czar; Ksar; Zsar (Rus.)		

U

UDAL odal; freehold estate	lw	
UGLY hideous; unsightly; hateful		
ULEX furze genus	bt	
ULNA an arm-bone	md	
UMBO boss of a shield; a knob		
UMBO the point of a bivalve shell	zo	
UNAU S. American two-toed sloth	zo	
UNBE undo; destroy (obs.)		
UNCO uncommon (Sc.)		
UNDE wavy	hd	
UNDO open; untie; nullify		
UNIO genus of freshwater mussels	zo	
UNIT a standard quantity	me	
UNTO preposition of direction		
UPAS the deadly antiar tree	bt	
UPBY further up (Sc.)		
UPON on		
URAO American soda	mn	
URDE pointed, variated	hd	
URDU a language much used in India		
UREA a crystalline compound	md	
URGE push; drive; impel; incite; spur		

URIA a genus of sea-birds, guillemots	zo		**VILL** villa; suburban seat	
URIC an acid	md		**VINA** East Indian banjo	mu
URIM and Thummim			**VINE** climbing plant	bt
URRY blue clay near a coal seam	mn		**VINT** Russian card game; to make wine	
URSA a constellation			**VINY** producing grapes or vines	
URUS the European wild ox	zo		**VIOL** antique violin	mu
URVA an ichneumon (India)	zo		**VIRE** crossbow-bolt; heraldic amulet	hd
USED habituated; employed; worn			**VISA** vise; stamp; permit; authorization	
USER consumer; frequenter; expender			**VISE** official endorsement	
USUS act, right of making use of something			**VIVA** Italian applause; (viva-voce)	
UTAS⎫ a festivity;			**VIVE** French applause	
UTIS ⎭ a period			**VIVO** lively; with animation	mu
UVAE grapes, raisins, etc.	bt		**VLEI** artificial lake (S. Africa)	
UVEA part of the iris of the eye	md		**VOCE** the voice; (sotto-voce)	
			VOID null; invalid; empty; vacant; emit	
			VOLA rapid series of notes	mu

V

			VOLE a grand slam	
VADE fade (Shak.)			**VOLE** genus of rodents, water-rats, etc.	zo
VAIL veil; tip; gratuity; submission			**VOLT** electrical unit	me
VAIN empty; conceited; unavailing			**VOLT** a turn; sudden leap; (fencing)	
VAIR heraldic fur	hd		**VOTE** suffrage; ballot; elect; poll	
VAKE to be vacant (Sc.)			**VOYA** anchor cable	nt
VALE dale; valley; recede; farewell			**VRIL** force	
VALI provincial governor (Turk.)			**VULN** to wound (heraldic)	hd
VAMP boot-uppers; to patch				
VAMP cinema character; to strum	mu			
VANE weathercock; flag; blade; fane				
VANG peak steadying brace	nt			

W

VARA S. Amer. yd of 33 in (84 cm)	me		**WADD** manganese ore	mn
VARE a wand of authority			**WADE** to ford	
VARI monkey (Madagascar)	zo		**WADI**⎫ often dry river bed (Arab.)	
VARY alter; change; alternate; differ			**WADY**⎭	
VASE urn			**WAFD** Egyptian nationalist party	
VAST huge; spacious; colossal			**WAFF** yaff; to bark; weak; paltry (Sc.)	
VEAL dinner for prodigal son; calf flesh	ck		**WAFT** float; convey; beckon; ventilate	
VEDA sacred Hindu books	rl		**WAGE** pay; hire; stipend; salary	
VEER vary; turn; shift			**WAIF** a stray; vagabond; ownerless	
VEGA Cuban tobacco-field; a star			**WAIL** cry; weep; deplore; plaint	
VEIL mask; cloak; screen; cover			**WAIN** wagon; constellation	
VEIN lode; seam; ledge; mood; humour			**WAIR** a plank	
VELD veldt (South Africa)			**WAIT** bide; tarry; linger; serve; minister	
VELE veil (Spens.)			**WAKA** Maori canoe	
VELL rennet; to cut turf			**WAKE** funeral vigil; rouse; trail; wash	
VELO speed of 1 ft (30 cm) per sec.	me		**WALD** weld; mignonette (Sc.)	bt
VENA a vein	md		**WALE** weal; raised streak; ridge; bruise	
VEND sell; hawk; peddle			**WALK** hike; saunter; gait; career; beat	
VENT utter; discharge; orifice; sale			**WALL** dividing construction	bd
VERB part of speech			**WALT** cranky; tottering	
VERT the greenery of the forest	lw		**WALY** beautiful; alas! (Sc.)	
VERT convert; pervert; heraldic green	hd		**WAME** the belly (Sc.)	
VERY a signal light			**WAND** rod; twig; staff; baton	
VEST endow; endue; clothe; a garment			**WANE** ebb; fail; decline; droop	
VETO ban; forbid; taboo; embargo			**WANG** cheek-bone; shoe-lace	
VETU lozenge	hd		**WANT** need; crave; wish; penury	
VIAL phial; ampulla			**WAPP** shroud-tightener; yachting	nt
VICE vise; a screw-press	to		**WARD** fend; repel; custody; a minor	
VICE iniquity; defect; sin; in place of			**WARE** a caution; goods; seaweed	bt
VIDE see (Latin)			**WARK** bulwark; work (obs.)	
VIED contested; competed; strove			**WARM** ardent; fervid; keen; zealous	
VIEW eye; scan; survey; vista; prospect			**WARN** caution; admonish; notify	
VILE base; ignoble; paltry; cheap			**WARP** twist; haul; carpet thread base	nt, tx

WART a verruca; an excrescence	md	**WILE** ruse; stratagem; dodge; chicanery	
WARY canny; cautious; vigilant		**WILL** wish; desire; bequeath; testament	
WASE straw head-pad		**WILT** to droop; to wither	
WASH wake; lave; rinse; cleanse		**WILY** sly; artful; crafty; insidious	
WASP stinging insect	zo	**WIND** coil; twist; turn; breeze; blow	
WAST preterite of 'to be'		**WINE** fermented fruit juice	
WATT unit of work	me	**WING** to fly; to wound	
WAUL wawl; caterwaul		**WINK** to nictitate	
WAVE sway; beckon; brandish; ripple		**WINY** having the flavour of wine	
WAVE swell; billow; comber; roller		**WIPE** rub; clean; handkerchief	
WAVY curly; sinuous; billowy		**WIRE** bind; snare; telegram	
WAWE a wave (Spens.)		**WIRY** flexible and strong	
WAWL waul; to howl; caterwaul		**WISE** sagacious; sage; sapient; method	
WAXY pliant; yielding; wrathful		**WISH** will; want; desire; behest	
WEAK frail; insipid; watery; fragile		**WISP** (of snipe); small broom; a whisk	
WEAL prosperity; state; wale; stripe		**WISS** to wish (Sc.)	
WEAN alienate; detach		**WIST** knew	
WEAR bear; don; sport; impair		**WITE** to blame; to reproach (Spens.)	
WEED a cigar; to root out; eradicate	bt	**WITH** withe; a twig; in company	
WEEK 7 days		**WIVE** to marry	
WEEL fish-trap; whirlpool; well (Sc.)		**WOAD** plant yielding a blue dye	bt
WEEM underground abode (Sc.)		**WOLD** wood; a down; a weald	
WEEN to think; consider; guess; judge		**WOLF** devour; wild canine	zo
WEEP sob; bewail; lament		**WOMB** uterus	
WEFT threads crossing warp; waif	tx	**WONT** habit; custom; practice; use	
WEIR wear; a dam across a river		**WOOD** timber; grove; forest	bt
WEKA Maori hen	zo	**WOOF** the weft	
WELD join together; mignonette	bt	**WOOL** fleece; a staple product	
WELK wither; shrivel; wrinkle		**WOOM** beaver fur	
WELL fount; source; origin; hale		**WOON** governor of a Burmese province	
WELT shoe-edging; to flog		**WORD** term; news; advice; pledge	
WEND wander; a Slavonic race		**WORE** bore; sported; donned; lasted	
WENT left; departed; decamped		**WORK** toil; operate; endeavour	
WEPT cried; lamented; sobbed		**WORM** a groveller; to insinuate	zo
WERE } past of 'to be'		**WORN** rather the worse for wear	
WERT }		**WORT** malt after mashing; a plant	bt
WEST cardinal direction		**WOVE** intertwined; matted; knitted	
WHAP whop; whip; defeat		**WOWF** crazy (Sc.)	
WHAT interrogative		**WRAP** wind; swathe; enfold; muffle	
WHEN adverb of time		**WREN** member of WRNS; a bird	zo
WHET sharpen; heighten; rouse		**WRIT** summons; formal document	lw
WHEW! exclamation of exertion		**WULL** will (Spens.)	
WHEY skimmed milk		**WYND** a lane; narrow alley	
WHID to whisk; a lie; a quarrel (Sc.)			
WHIG Liberal; sour whey			
WHIM caprice; crotchet; notion			
WHIN doleritic igneous rock	gl	**X**	
WHIN gorse; furse	bt	**XEMA** genus of gulls	zo
WHIP quirt; flog; driver; coachman		**XMAS** Noel; Yule	
WHIR whirl; spin; twirl		**X-RAY** Roentgen ray	md
WHIT jot; iota; speck; scintilla		**XYST** gymnasium	
WHIZ whizz; a noise			
WHOA! exclamation to halt			
WHOM objective of who		**Y**	
WHOP whap; whip; defeat			
WHOT hot (Spens.)		**YAFF** waff; to bark (Sc.)	
WHUR a noise		**YALD** yauld; active; supple (Sc.)	
WICK (candle); creek; quick; alive		**YAMA** Hindu Pluto	
WIDE spacious; rife; distant; (cricket)		**YANK** an American; to heave	
WIFE spouse		**YAPP** limp leather binding	
WILD rash; disorderly; savage		**YARD** 36 in (91 cm); enclosed area	me
		YARD (Scotland); a spar; a court	nt

YARE dexterous; quick; prompt	
YARN spun thread; sailor's story	
YARR to snarl; the spurrey plant	bt
YAUD a jade (Sc.)	
YAUP yelp; hungry; blue titmouse	zo
YAWL yowl; howl; fishing-boat	nt
YAWN gape	
YAWS a form of scurvy	md
YEAH yes (USA)	
YEAN yeen; to lamb	
YEAR 12 months	
YEEN yean; to produce; to lamb	
YEGG hobo; cracksman; safe-breaker	
YELD barren, not giving milk	
YELK yolk	
YELL bawl; scream; screech	
YELP yap; cry of pain; bark	
YERK jerk; rouse; excite	
YEST yeast	
YETI abominable snowman	zo
YETT yate; a gate (Sc.)	
YILL ale (Sc.)	
YITE the yellow bunting	zo
YLEM theoretical neutron substance	nc
YMIR the Frost Giant (Scand.)	
YOGA Hindu philosophy	
YOGI ascetic yoga practitioner (Ind.)	
YO-HO exclamation	
YOIT the yellow bunting	zo
YOKE team together; enslave; restrain	
YOKO Japanese wood block	
YOLK, YOLKY, YELK wool oil	
YOND beyond; yonder; mad (Spens.)	
YOOP an onomatopoetic sob	
YORE in olden time	
YOUR of you	
YOWL howl; yawl; gowl; bawl	
YO-YO a toy; a bandalore	
YUAN (China)	nm
YUCK to itch; the itch	
YUGA one of the Hindu ages of the world	
YULE Xmas; Noel	
YUNX the wryneck bird	zo
Y-WIS i'wis; truly	

YURT a Siberian house or tent	

Z

ZAIM Turkish military chief	
ZANY buffoon; merry-andrew; mimic	
ZARF zurf; metal coffee-cup holder	
ZATI an Indian parrot	zo
ZAWN cavern	mn
Z-BAR building fixture	
ZEAL fervour; intensity; enthusiasm	
ZEBU humped domestic ox (India)	zo
ZEIN zeine; a protein found in maize	bt
ZEND a Persian dialect	
ZEPP zeppelin; airship	
ZERO cipher; naught; nothing	
ZEST peel-flavouring; gusto; relish	
ZETA the Greek Z	
ZETA sexton's room over porch	rl
ZEUS Olympian deity	
ZIMB Abyssinian tse-tse fly	zo
ZINC a metallic element	ch
ZING pep (USA)	
ZION a hill in Jerusalem	
ZOAR a place of refuge	
ZOBO zhobo; dsomo; hybrid yak-cow	
ZOEA crustaceans in a larval stage	zo
ZOIC pertaining to life	
ZOID zoospore	bt
ZOLA Borax hardener	ch
ZOLL German toll or custom-duty	
ZONA zone; belt	
ZONA patch; strip; area	zo
ZONE belt; girdle; district	
ZOOM aerobatic manoeuvre	
ZOON the product of a fertilized ovum	
ZOOP extraneous noise	ac
ZOOT fashionable; gaudy	
ZSAR Czar; Ksar; Tsar; Tzar (Rus.)	
ZULU African nation	
ZUNA Angola sheep	zo
ZUNI Mexican Indians	
ZUPA Serbian village confederation	
ZURF zarf; metal coffee-pot holder	
ZYME a ferment; a disease germ	md

A

AAZIZ Queen of Sheba; also Balkis
ABACA Manila hemp   bt
ABACI counting frames
ABACI crowns of columns
ABACK aft; behind; backwards
ABAFT aft; astern   nt
ABASE lower; reduce; disgrace
ABASH awe; confound; disconcert
ABASK basking in the sun
ABATE wane; diminish; lessen
ABBEY a monastery   rl
ABBOT the head of an abbey   rl
ABCEE an abc; an alphabet
ABEAM abreast; on the beam   nt
ABEAR to bear; endure; tolerate
ABELE the hoary poplar   bt
ABHAL the fruit of the cypress   bt
ABHOR hate; loathe; abominate; detest
ABIDE lodge; tarry; tolerate; sojourn
ABIES the fir genus   bt
ABLEN a freshwater fish; the bleak   zo
ABLER more competent; more expert
ABLET ablen; the bleak   zo
ABODE house; dwelling; home; lived
ABOHM electro-magnetic unit   me
ABOIL on the boil; boiling
ABOMA boa-constrictor (S. Amer.)   zo
A-BOMB nuclear weapon
ABORT to miscarry; sterile; break off
ABOUT almost; around; anent; near
ABOVE aloft; over; before; exceeding
ABRAY rouse; startle; waken (obs.)
ABRIN toxic protein   ch
ABUSE misuse; defame; traduce; revile
ABUZZ buzzing; humming
ABYSM⎫ chasm; bottomless pit;
ABYSS⎭ gulf; gorge; gap; fissure
ACARI mites and ticks   zo
ACCRA Caribbean batter fritters   ck
ACERA bubble-shell genus   zo
ACERB sour; bitter; acid; harsh
ACHAR acid pickles; salt relishes (Pers.)
ACHED pained; sorrowed; grieved
ACHOR dandruff   md
ACINI granulations; berries   md, bt
ACKEE Jamaican fruit   bt
ACLIS spiked club; javelin
ACOCK jaunty; defiantly
ACOLD chilly
ACONE insects' coneless compound eyes   zo
ACORN oak seed; cord-end   bt
ACRED lavishly landed
ACRID sour; pungent; bitter; mordant
ACRON head of embryonic insect   zo
ACTED performed; simulated; deputized
ACTIN muscle protein   bl
ACTON padded jerkin
ACTOR player; trouper; histrion
ACUTE keen; sharp; astute; poignant

ADAGE proverb; dictum; maxim; saw
ADAPT adjust; accommodate
ADAYS nowadays
ADDAX African antelope   zo
ADDED affixed; subjoined; appended
ADDER viper; snake; basilisk; asp   zo
ADDLE confuse; putrid; muddled
ADEEM to revoke a legacy   lw
ADEPS fatty tissue   md
ADEPT adroit; expert; proficient
ADIEU farewell; goodbye
ADIOS farewell (Sp.)
AD-LIB extemporise freely   mu
ADMAN advertising pundit
ADMIT acknowledge; concede; own
ADMIX infuse; blend; mingle
ADOBE sun dried brick
ADOBO braised stew (Philippines)   ck
ADOPT accept; assume; espouse; father
ADORE worship; revere; idolize; love
ADORN decorate; deck; enrich; garnish
ADOWN downward
ADOXY a tolerant belief
ADSUM (present at a roll-call)
ADULT a grown-up; mature; ripe
ADUST incinerated; pulverized
ADYTA chancels   rl
AEGER sick; ill   md
AEGIS Minerva's shield; protection
AERIE eyrie; eagle's nest   zo
AESOP a fabulist
AFEAR affear; to terrify (obs.)
AFFIX add; fasten; subjoin; attach
AFIRE aflame; blazing
AFLAT level with the ground
AFOAM foaming
AFOOT astir; happening
AFORE previously; before
AFOUL entangled; in collision with
AFRIC African
AFRIT afreet; evil demon; jinn (Arab)
AFTER later; in imitation of
AGAIN anew; afresh; moreover
AGAIT astir; afoot (Sc.)
AGAMA genus of lizards; saurians   zo
AGAMI game bird, edible when young (S. America)   zo, ck
AGAPE staring; a love feast
AGATE a quartz; ruby type   mn
AGATE type printing measure   pr
AGATY like an agate
AGAVE American aloe   bt
AGAVE daughter of Cadmus
AGAVE succulent cactus; drink; peyote drug
AGAZE gazing
AGENT doer; factor; deputy; proxy
AGGER a mound; rampart
AGILE nimble; spry; alert; brisk
AGIST pasture rate   lw
AGLEE⎫ asquint; askew; awry;
AGLEY⎭ off the line (Sc.)

AGLET a pendant; braided tag
AGLOW glowing; gleaming; shining
AGNEL French gold coin (lamb)   nm
AGNUS Dei; pascal lamb   zo
AGONE ago; past; since; a line
AGONY pangs; anguish; torment; throe
AGOOD in earnest
AGORA Grecian market
AGRAS sweet Algerian drink
AGREE accede; engage; conform; concur
AGRIN grinning
AGROM an Indian tongue disease   md
AGUED fevered; shivering
AHEAD leading; onward; in front
AHEAP trembling with fear
AHIGH on high
AHOLD close to the wind   nt
AHULL hove to   nt
AIDED abetted; seconded; succoured
AIDER helper; assistant; acolyte
AIERY aerie; eyrie; eagle's nest   zo
AIGRE eagre; bore; high tidal wave
AILED afflicted; peaked; pined
AIMED directed; pointed; trained
AIMER purposeful person
AIRED ventilated; spread abroad
AIRER dryer; ventilator
AISLE passage; walk   rl
AITCH (h); aitch-bone
AJUGA bugle genus of plants   bt
AKALI Sikh fanatic
AKELA Kipling's lone wolf   zo
ALACK alas; lackaday; woe is me
ALAND landed
ALANT heraldic mastiff   hd
ALARM fear; scare; dismay; a tocsin
ALARY alar; having wings   zo
ALATE winged; of late; lately
ALBIN an opaque white mineral   mn
ALBUM book for photos or stamps
ALCES the elk   zo
ALDER a tree   bt
ALERT wary; watchful; vigilant
ALGAE the seaweeds   bt
ALGID cold; chilly   md
ALGIN seaweed extract for iodine
ALGOL a star; computer term
ALGOR unusual coldness   md
ALGUM almug; sandal-wood   bt
ALIAS otherwise; an assumed name
ALIBI elsewhere
ALIEN strange; exotic; remote; foreign
ALIGN \ adjust; rectify; arrange;
ALINE / regulate; conform
ALIKE similar; analogous; equal
ALISH resembling beer
ALITE ground clinker from sintering   ch
ALIVE vital; quick; alert; brisk
ALKYD glyptal resins; polyesters
ALKYL aliphatic radicals   ch
ALLAH Moslem word for the Deity   rl

ALLAY lull; calm; relieve; repress
ALLEY large marble; taw; passage
ALL-IN (policy) comprehensive
ALL-IN exhausted
ALLIS the allice shad; a fish   zo
ALLOD freehold estate
ALLOO halloo
ALLOT distribute; apportion; assign
ALLOW admit; own; concede; grant
ALLOY a base admixture
ALLYL organic radicle   ch
ALMAH \ an Egyptian
ALMEH / dancing girl
ALMRY almonry; cupboard
ALMUG algum; sandal-wood   bt
ALOED \ tinctured with aloes;
ALOID } resembling aloes;   md
ALOIN / bitter aloe extract
ALOES bitter purgative drug   bt
ALOFT above; overhead; skyward
ALONE only; sole; single; isolated
ALONG by; beside; together
ALOOF apart; away; distant
ALOSE allis; shad-fish   zo
ALOUD audibly; loudly; clamorously
ALPEN Alpine
ALPHA the first or beginning
ALPIA bird-seed   bt
ALTAR shrine; sanctuary   rl
ALTER vary; change; turn; transform
ALULA bastard wing   zo
ALURE cloister; gallery (obs.)
ALUTA leather treated with alum
ALWAY ever; always; regularly
AMAIN forcibly; suddenly; violently
AMASS heap; gather; accumulate; pile
AMATE subdue; daunt; stupefy (obs.)
AMATI violin (Cremona)   mu
AMAZE daze; astound; perplex
AMBER fossilized resin   mn
AMBIT precinct; extent; compass
AMBLE dawdle; saunter; stroll
AMBON lectern; pulpit   rl
AMBRY alms-box; niche; almonry   rl
AMEER \ Afghan king;
AMERE / emir; prince
AMEND emend; better; rectify; correct
AMENT a catkin   bt
AMICE pilgrim's cloak; linen gown
AMICT amice; cape or hood   rl
AMIDE \ an ammonia compound
AMINE /   ch
AMISS wrong; faulty; erroneously
AMITY friendship; fellowship; harmony
AMMON Tibetan sheep   zo
AMONG emong; amidst; amongst
AMORT halfdead; dejected; spiritless
AMOUR an affair; a love intrigue
AMOVE stir up; to affect
AMPLE ointment-box; wide; capacious
AMPLY plentifully; bountifully

AMPUL ample; oil-jar; flask
AMSEL } blackbird   zo
AMZEL }
AMUCK madly; in murderous frenzy
AMUSE entertain; cheer; charm; divert
ANANA the pineapple   bt
ANCLE also **ANKLE**
ANCON the elbow; a console   md
ANEAL anele; to anoint   rl
ANEAR near; nigh
ANELE extreme unction   rl
ANENT concerning
ANGEL divine messenger; fish   zo, nm
ANGER ire; rage; choler; passion
ANGLE a corner; to entice; to fish
ANGOR acute pain or anxiety
ANGRY irate; wroth; piqued; riled
ANIGH nigh; near by
ANILE old womanish; imbecile
ANIMA female part of male personality   pc
ANIME resin; fiery   bt
ANION electro-negative ion
ANISE plant furnishing aniseed   bt
ANISO unequal
ANKER European liquid measure   me
ANKLE also **ANCLE**   md
ANKUS elephant goad
ANNAL a Mass   rl
ANNAT an Ecclesiastical levy   rl
ANNET the kittiwake   zo
ANNEX add; append; join; unite
ANNOY badger; worry; affront; molest
ANNUL cancel; quash; revoke
ANODE positive electrical pole
ANOMY lawlessness; a miracle
ANONA custard-apple genus   bt
ANTIC fantastic; prank; lark; caper
ANTRE a cave; a cavern
ANURA batrachians   zo
ANVIL ossicle, ear bone for sound   zo, md
ANVIL blacksmith's forge block
ANZAC Australian, NZ, Army Corps
AORTA the great artery   md
APACE rapidly; swiftly; at speed
APART aloof; asunder; separately
APEAK } anchor aweigh   nt
APEEK } or atrip
APERT open; public (obs.)
APERY monkey-house   zo
APHID } green-fly;   zo
APHIS } ant-cows   zo
APIAN relating to bees   zo
APING copying; mimicking; imitating
APISH ape-like   zo
APIUM the celery genus   bt
APODA eels, etc.   zo
APODE limbless creature   zo
APOOP astern   nt
APORT to port   nt
APPAL scare; daunt; shock; astound
APPAY apay; to satisfy (obs.)

APPLE the award of Paris   bt
APPLY bestow; use; employ; refer
APPUI } support; reciprocal action
APPUY }
APRIL 4th month
APRON short cassock; protective garment   rl
APRON wedge; lathe; sea defence   to
APRON aircraft parking area
APRON lead sheet dam slope
APSIS extreme point in an orbit
APTLY fittingly; appositely; apropos
ARABA Turkish ox-cart
ARABY Arabia
ARACK arrack; fermented palm juice
ARBOR tree genus; bower   bt
ARBOR spindle; axis
ARDEA the heron genus   zo
ARDES 5½ bushels, Egyptian   me
ARDIL fibre from groundnuts   bt
AREAD } to divine;
AREDE } counsel; explain;
AREED } interpret; solve
AREAL (area); superficial
AREAR in the rear; to raise; uplift
ARECA betel-nut palm   bt
AREFY dry up; shrivel; wither
ARENA ring; stage; battlefield
ARENG the sago palm   bt
ARETE knife-edge mountain ridge (Swiss)
ARGAL crude tartar   ch
ARGIL potter's earth   mn
ARGOL argal; crude tartar   ch
ARGON a light gas   ch
ARGOT slang; jargon (Fr.)
ARGUE plead; dispute; reason; debate
ARGUS watchful; a pheasant   zo
ARIAN heretic sect (Christian)   rl
ARIEL a sprite; a gazelle   zo
ARIES the Ram of the Zodiac
ARIOT riotously; uproariously
ARISE ascend; soar; emerge; rebel
ARLES earnest money on engagement
ARMED equipped; protected
ARMET medieval helmet
ARMIL insignia of royalty
ARNEE Indian buffalo
ARNOT pig-nut; earth-nut   bt
AROAR uproariously; ariot
AROID a plant allied to the arum   bt
AROMA scent; perfume; fragrance; odour
AROSE got up; began; sprang; revolted
ARRAH Indian lentil   bt
ARRAH Irish expletive
ARRAS tapestry; hangings
ARRAY range; marshal; deck; hosts
ARRET decree; arrest   lw
ARRIS sharp edge; arete
ARROW bolt; shaft; dart; reed
ARSIS vocal inflection; emphasis
ARSON fire-raising; pyromania   lw
ARTEL a Russian guild

ARYAN Indo-European	
ASADO Argentine barbecue	ck
ASCII dwellers on the equator	
ASCOT fashionable race meeting	
ASCUS spore case	bt
ASDIC submarine-detector	nt
ASHEN wan; pale; hueless; pallid	
ASHES results of cricket on the hearth	
ASHET a serving dish (Sc.)	
ASHUR Assyrian god	
ASIAN Asiatic	
ASIDE apart; away; aloof; laterally	
ASKED invited; demanded; requested	
ASKER a newt; petitioner; suitor	zo
ASKEW awry; aslant; askance; oblique	
ASOAK sodden	
ASPEN the trembling poplar	bt
ASPER a small silver Turkish coin	nm
ASPIC savoury meat jelly; sap	ck
ASPIC 12 pounder cannon; lavender	bt
ASSAI enough; very	mu
ASSAY essay; test; try; analysis	
ASSER rafter; thin lath	
ASSES mokes; donkeys; burros	
ASSET a possession	
ASSOT besot; infatuate (Spens.)	
ASTAY a cable direction	nt
ASTEL a dam; a splinter	
ASTER flowering plant	bt
ASTIR alert; awake; agog; excited	
ASTON astun; astonished (obs.)	
ASWAY swinging; oscillating	
ASWIM afloat	
ATAXY functional disorder	md
ATCHI Caucasian ibex	zo
ATILT on edge; slanting	
ATIMY dishonour; disgrace	
ATLAS a Titan; a moth	zo
ATMAN the Buddhist ego	
ATOLL coral island	
ATOMY atom; skeleton; a pygmy	
ATONE expiate; satisfy; propitiate	
ATONY debility; off colour	md
ATRIP anchor clear; aweigh	nt
ATTAR otto; fragrant rose oil	
ATTIC Athenian; (salt); garret; loft	
ATTLE refuse from mines; rubbish	
AUBIN Canterbury gallop	
AUDIT examine accounts	
AUGER a drill	to
AUGET explosive charge for mines	
AUGHT zero; ought; naught; 0	
AUGUR seer; soothsayer; portend	
AULAE Roman halls or courts	
AULIC (royal court)	
AUMIL amildar; Indian tax collector	
AUNTY auntie	
AURAL (exhalation); (ear)	
AURIC golden	
AURIN golden red dye	ch
AURUM gold; chemical element	ch

AUXIN growth-affecting substance	ch
AVAIL benefit; help; suffice; use	
AVAST stop; stay; cease	nt
AVENS the herb bennet	bt
AVERT avoid; divert; forfend; parry	
AVETE greetings, welcome	
AVGAS aviation spirit	ae
AVIAN bird-like	zo
AVINE pertaining to birds	
AVION aeroplane (French)	
AVISO a dispatch boat (Sp.)	nt
AVOID shun; elude; forsake; eschew	
AVOUE French lawyer; advocate	lw
AWAIT tarry; bide; stay; pause	
AWAKE alert; ready; alive; vigilant	
AWARD give; grant; adjudge; prize	
AWARE mindful; conscious	
AWASH nearly submerged	nt
AWAVE waving; fluttering	
AWEEK per week	
AWFUL dire; dread; fearful; imposing	
AWHIR whirring; spinning	
AWING on the wing; flying; cowing	
AWNED bearded like barley	bt
AWNER grain separator	
AWOKE bestirred; roused; incited	
AWORK at work	
AXIAL } on the same axis	
AXILE }	
AXIOM truism; assumed truth	
AXION brain/spinal cord	
AXITE a propellant	
AXLED having a spindle	
AXOID axoidean	
AYELP yelping; howling	
AZIDE hydrazoic acid salt	ch
AZOIC devoid of life	
AZOTE nitrogen	ch
AZOTH the alchemist cure-all; panacea	
AZOXY potash/nitro-affected	ch
AZTEC extinct Mexican-Indian	
AZURE } sky-blue; the sky;	
AZURN } the vault of heaven	
AZURY blue; cerulean	
AZUSA missile tracking system	ro
AZYME unleavened bread	

B

BABEL tower; din; jargon; clamour	
BABOO babu; Indian clerk	
BABUL gum-arabic tree	
BACCA a berry	bt
BACCY bacco; tobacco	bt
BACON something to be saved	
BADGE sign; mark; emblem; token	
BADLY corruptly; wickedly; imperfectly	
BAFFY an old golf club	
BAGEL hard glazed doughnut roll (Jew.)	ck

BAGGY loose fitting; bulging
BAHAR 3½ cwt (197 kg), East Indian — me
BAIRN a child (Sc.)
BAIZE bayze; a coarse cloth
BAJAN bejan; a freshman (Sc.)
BAKAL oriental shopkeeper
BAKED parched; hardened; dried up
BAKER bread/pastry maker — ck
BALAS orange ruby — mn
BALED in bundles — ae
BALER a bowl; scoop
BALKY apt to stop suddenly
BALMY fragrant; soothing
BALOO the Bear — as
BALSA Peruvian raft; a tree — bt
BALUN balance/unbalance transformer — tc
BAMBI faun — zo
BANAK American tree — bt
BANAL commonplace; trivial; trite
BANAT Hungarian division
BANCO bench; bank money — lw
BANDY ice hockey; crooked; dispute
BANJO job an octaroon would like — mu
BANNS public notice of marriage — lw, rl
BANNY a minnow — zo
BANTU Negroid African tribe
BARBE war-horse armour
BARBE nun's kerchief
BARED naked; unadorned; stripped
BARET a biretta; cardinal's cap — rl
BARGE shove; jostle — nt
BARIA baryta — mn
BARIC pert. to weight/barium; barometric
BARKY of bark
BARMY (yeast); crazy; insane
BARON (of beef); a title
BARRY divided by horizontal bars — hd
BARYE unit of pressure dynes — me
BASAL basic; fundamental
BASED founded on
BASEL tanned skin; basil
BASIC basal; fundamental — ch
BASIL chisel edge; leather; a herb — bt
BASIN pond; dock; reservoir; bowl
BASIS ground work; first principle
BASON a basin
BASSE bass; fish like a perch — zo
BASSO a bass singer
BASTA stop! enough (It.) — mu
BASTE cook; sew; stitch; thrash
BASTO ace of clubs
BATAK language
BATCH lot; quantity; amount; crowd
BATED restrained; repressed; reduced
BATEY gold and silver embroidery
BATHE immerse
BATIK method of dyeing (Ind.) — tx
BATON staff; wand; sceptre; rod — mu
BATTA Indian grant
BATTY bat-like; dotty
BAUGE cloth; drugget

BAULK beam; (billiards); thwart
BAVIN faggot of brushwood
BAWDY lewd; immoral
BAYED recessed; howled like a dog
BAYOU channel, outlet of river/lake
BAZAR bazaar; mart; souk; exchange
BEACH shore; strand; sands; margin
BEADS a rosary — rl
BEADY small and bright
BE-ALL sum and substance; ultimate
BEAMY shining; radiant; broad
BEANO jamboree; beanfeast; spree
BEARD defy; oppose; confront
BEAST brute; ruffian; animal — zo
BEAUX gallants (Fr.)
BEBOP dissonant jazz — mu
BECHE drill extractor — to
BECKE of microscope juncture light — lt
BEDAD! Irish interjection
BEDEL beadle (obs.)
BEDEW sprinkle; moisten
BEDIM obscure; cloud; darken
BEECH a forest tree — bt
BEEFY stolid; powerful
BEELD shelter (Sc.)
BEELE pickaxe — to
BEERY maudlin; fuddled
BEFIT suit; become
BEFOG confuse; obfuscate
BEFUR cover with fur or scale
BEGAD! exclamation of surprise
BEGAN started; initiated; originated
BEGAT bred; sired; engendered
BEGEM bejewel
BEGET produce; generate
BEGIN start; initiate; commence
BEGOT procreated; gave rise to
BEGUM Indian native princess
BEGUN originated; opened
BEHEN sea lavender — bt
BEIGE fabric; yellowish grey
BEING existence; actuality
BEISA oryx; unicorn — zo
BEJAN bajan; freshman (Sc.)
BEKAH half shekel (Hebrew) — nm
BEKER S. African cup
BELAY fasten; hold — nt
BELCH eructate; discharge; emit
BELEE on the lee side
BELGA Belgian currency
BELIE falsify; contradict; slander
BELIT rekindled; illuminated
BELLE a beauteous damsel
BELLY stomach; abdomen
BELOW under; beneath; in Hades
BEMAD madden
BENCH seat; form; court; tribunal
BENDY divided into bends — hd
BENET to ensnare; an exorcist
BENJY a straw hat
BENNE bene; an oil plant — bt

BENTH ground ivy	bt	**BITCH** female dog; wolf; disagreeable	
BENTY covered with dry grass		woman	
BEPAT pat or tap repeatedly		**BITER** nibbler; cheat	
BERET Basque cap		**BITTS** a cable attachment	nt
BEROB rob; plunder; pillage		**BITTY** incomplete; fragmentary	
BEROE luminous medusa	zo	**BIXIN** annatto	ch
BERRY mound; barrow; fruit	bt	**BLACK** ebon; inky; dusky; sombre	
BERTH bed; post; situation	nt	**BLADE** roisterer; (knife); (oar)	bt
BERYL a gem	mn	**BLAES** hardened shale	mn
BERYX perch-like sea fish	zo	**BLAIN** blister; blotch	md
BESAN Indian lentil flour	ck	**BLAME** chide; rebuke; reproach	
BESET assail; encircle; surround		**BLAND** soft; suave; mild; benign	
BESIT besiege		**BLANK** lacuna; vacant; void	
BESOM a broom		**BLARE** blazon; proclaim; clangour	
BESOT assot; get fuddled		**BLASE** cloyed; surfeited (Fr.)	
BETEL nut of the areca palm	bt	**BLASE** immune to novelty or impressions	
BETON a kind of concrete		**BLASH** watery stuff (Sc.)	
BETSO a small Venetian coin	nm	**BLAST** gust; outbreak; shrivel	
BETTY flask; jemmy; sweet pastry	ck	**BLATE** shy; bashful (Sc.)	
BEVEL slant; to incline	to	**BLAZE** (horse); flame; proclaim	
BEWET to wet; to moisten		**BLAZE** a mark on trees	
BEWIG to don a wig		**BLEAK** drear; desolate; river-fish	zo
BEWIT leather strap in falconry		**BLEAR** dim; rheumy; watery	
BEZAN Bengal cotton cloth		**BLEAT** the cry of a sheep	
BEZEL basil; setting; groove		**BLECK** coal-fish	zo
BEZIL bezel		**BLEED** exude; secrete; impoverish	
BHANG hashish; Indian hemp	bt	**BLEEP** radio signal	
BHYLE Indian ox	zo	**BLEND** mix; unite; knead; coalesce	
BIBBS wooden brackets	nt	**BLENT** blended; amalgamated	
BIBLE The Scriptures		**BLESS** laud; exalt; praise; extol	
BIDDY a fowl; a chicken	zo	**BLEST** endowed with blessings	
BIDET sitz bath; pack-pony	zo	**BLIMP** small airship; (Colonel)	
BIDON about 5 qt (5.6 litres)	me	**BLIND** ruse; feint; cover; issueless	
BIDRI Indian metal-ware		**BLINK** glance; flicker; ignore	
BIELD shelter; protection		**BLIRT** blore; squall; gust	nt
BIFER twice-yearly flowering/fruiting	bt	**BLISS** ecstasy; rapture; felicity	
BIFID two-clefted		**BLITE** the plant Good King Henry	bt
BIGHT cove; bay; coil; loop	nt	**BLIVE** soon; speedily (Sc.)	
BIGLY ostentatiously		**BLOAT** blote; dry by smoke; dilate	
BIGOT zealot; fanatic; dogmatist		**BLOCK** bar; obstruct; a mass	nt
BIJOU small; pretty; gem; trinket		**BLOKE** a fellow; a man	
BILBO Spanish rapier		**BLOND** fair; flaxen	
BILGE bulging part of a cask	nt	**BLOOD** cruor; gore; kindred; lineage	
BILIN bile	md	**BLOOM** bud; blossom; prime; thrive	bt
BILLY Australian cooking can, goat (male)		**BLOOP** sound-track joint thud	cn
	zo	**BLORE** blirt; violent gust	
BINAC Binary Automatic Computer		**BLOTE** bloat; dry by smoke	
BINAL twin, double		**BLOWN** winded; trumpeted	
BINGE a carousal		**BLOWY** breezy; gusty; windy	
BINGO brandy; gambling pastime		**BLUED** tempered; squandered	
BINNY a Nile fish	zo	**BLUER** more blue; gloomier	
BIOME largest land community area	ec	**BLUES** Royal Horse Guards	mu
BIOTA a region's fauna/flora	ec	**BLUEY** blanket; bundle (Australia)	
BIPED two-footed animal	zo	**BLUFF** sheer; brusque; spoof	
BIPOD (c.f. tripod)		**BLUNT** blont; dull; abrupt	
BIRCH to flog; forest tree	bt	**BLURB** recommendation; description (bk.	
BIRLE to carouse (Sc.)		cover)	
BIRSE bristle; to bruise		**BLURT** utter hastily	
BIRSY stubbly		**BLUSH** flush; colour; redden	
BIRTH genesis; nativity; origin		**BOARD** embark; victuals; council	
BISON American buffalo	zo	**BOAST** brag; crow; vaunt	

BOBBY policeman		**BOURN** bourne; stream; bound; border	
BOCAL glass beaker		**BOUSE** boose; booze; bowze; swill	
BOCHE a Hun		**BOUSY** tipsy; drunken; crapulous	
BODED portended; presaged; augured		**BOVEY** a kind of coal	mn
BODGE botch; mess up; fail		**BOWED** bent; curved; subdued	
BODHI Buddhist sacred tree	bt	**BOWEL** intestine	md
BODLE farthing (Sc.)	nm	**BOWER** arbour; shelter; anchor	nt
BOGEY (golf); hobgoblin; ghost		**BOWER** the knave at eucre	
BOGGY soggy; swampy; marshy		**BOWET** young hawk	zo
BOGIE four-wheeled truck		**BOWIE** a large knife	
BOGLE bugbear; scarecrow		**BOWLS** skittles; a game	
BOGUS sham; spurious; false		**BOWSE** to heave; bouse	nt
BOHEA inferior tea	bt	**BOXED** crated	
BOIAR boyar; Russian nobleman		**BOXEN** made of boxwood	
BOITE night-club, disco		**BOXER** a pugilist	
BOLAR pertaining to clay		**BOX-IN** surrounding type with rule	pr
BOLAS S. American missile		**BOXTY** Halloween dish (Irish)	ck
BOLIN bowline	nt	**BOX-UP** mistake; error	
BOLUS large pill	md	**BOYAR** boiar; Russian nobleman	
BONCE marble game; head (slang)		**BOYAU** ditch; trench (Fr.)	
BONED seized; stole; purloined		**BOYER** Flemish sloop	nt
BONES bobbins	mu	**BRACE** pair; couple; stiffen	to
BONGO African antelope	zo	**BRACH** bitch-hound	zo
BONNE French nurse		**BRACK** a flaw in cloth	
BONNY bonnie; ore pocket		**BRACT** specialized leaf	bt
BONUS award; premium; subsidy		**BRAID** brede; broid; weave; entwine	
BONZE Buddhist priest	rl	**BRAIL** (falconry); to furl	nt
BOOBY looby; dunce; simpleton		**BRAIN** cerebellum; intellect	
BOODY to sulk; to mope		**BRAIT** rough diamond	mn
BOOED hooted; noisily objected		**BRAKE** thicket; harrow; wagonette	
BOOER vociferous interrupter		**BRAKY** overgrown with ferns	bt
BOOPS humpbacked whale	zo	**BRAND** brond; stigma; mark; torch	
BOORT (diamond polishing)		**BRANK** buckwheat	bt
BOOSE booze; drink; swill		**BRANK** bridle for scolds	
BOOST boom; push; eulogize		**BRANT** a goose	zo
BOOSY boozy; tipsy; fuddled		**BRASH** hasty; brittle; loose rock	
BOOTH market stall		**BRASS** money; impudence; effrontery	
BOOTS last joined; shoe cleaner		**BRAST** burst (Spens.)	
BOOTY loot; spoil; plunder		**BRAUL** striped cloth	
BORAK banter; chaff (Australia)		**BRAVE** to dare; heroic; valiant	
BORAX tincal; borate of soda	ch	**BRAVO** well done!; an assassin	
BORED drilled; wearied		**BRAWL** wrangle; bicker; quarrel	
BOREE French peasants' dance		**BRAWN** muscular strength	
BORER an insect; seaworm	zo	**BRAXY** splenetic sheep disease	
BORIC boracic	ch	**BRAZE** to solder	
BORNE narrow-minded; carried		**BREAD** food; fare; aliment	
BORON a non-metallic element	ch	**BREAK** interval; smash; shatter	
BOSCH wood, bush (S. Afr.)		**BREAM** a fish; to clean	zo
BOSKY busky; shady; thickly wooded		**BREED** beget; race; progeny	
BOSOM breast; confidential		**BREEM** ⎫ stern; fiery (Spens.);	
BOSON bo'sun; boatswain	nt	**BREME** ⎬ clear; raging; celebrated	
BOSSY dictatorial; domineering		**BREER** ⎫	
BOTCH to patch; worthless		**BRERE** ⎬ to sprout (Sc.)	
BOTHY hut; cottage (Sc.)		**BRENT** lofty; smooth; a goose	zo
BOTTS larvae; worms	zo	**BREST** breast	
BOUCH to bush; to debouch		**BREVE** a long note	mu
BOUGH branch; limb; offshoot	bt	**BRIAR** a pipe; wild rose	bt
BOULE (buhl) boule work		**BRIBE** suborn; graft; an inducement	bt
BOULE Greek Parliament; roulette		**BRICK** a stout-hearted fellow	
BOUND limit; pale; leap; spring		**BRIDE** banned but beloved	
BOURG a town; burgh; borough		**BRIEF** short; concise; a writ	lw

BRIER briar; wild rose — bt
BRILL prill; type of turbot — zo
BRINE salt water; the sea; tears
BRING fetch; convoy; produce
BRINK brim; brow; verge; marge
BRINY the sea; salty
BRISK agile; alert; nimble
BRITE over-ripe
BRIZA totter-grass — bt
BRIZE the gadfly — zo
BROAD wide; spacious; liberal
BROCH early stone hut
BROCK badger; a brocket — zo
BROGH burgh (Sc.)
BROGH prehistoric stone fort (Scand.)
BROID braid; to interweave
BROIL brawl; quarrel; affray
BROKE ruined; penniless
BROMA prepared chocolate
BROME a grass — bt
BROND brand
BRONX a cocktail
BROOD incubate; progeny; meditate
BROOK beck; rill; tolerate; allow
BROOL a deep murmur
BROOM a besom; a shrub — bt
BROSE Scotch porridge
BROTH soup; a decoction
BROWN tan; ecru; russet; sorrel
BRUIN a bear — zo
BRUIT to noise abroad; a rumour
BRUME fog; mist; vapour
BRUNT shock; impulse
BRUSH skirmish; scrap; sweep
BRUTE savage; senseless; rough
BUCCO puff-bird genus — zo
BUCHU African medicinal plant — bt
BUCKO a bully (USA)
BUDDY a partner; blooming
BUDGE lambskin fur; pompous; to stir
BUFFO comic actor
BUFFS a famous regiment
BUFFY buff colour
BUGGY a gig; a vehicle
BUGLE jet bead; horn — mu
BUGLE genus of flowering plants — bt
BUILD erect; construct; raise
BUILT fabricated; established
BUIST to mark sheep or cattle (Sc.)
BULBY bulbous
BULGE swell; belly
BULGY protuberant
BULKY vast; massive; voluminous
BULLA Papal seal; a mollusc — zo
BULLY hector; intimidate; splendid
BULSE a bag of diamonds
BUMBO rumbo; a drink
BUMPY uneven
BUNCH set; lot; lump; batch
BUNIA Indian trader or banker
BUNKO bunco; a trick; swindle

BUNNY a rabbit — zo
BUNTY wheat disease
BURAN blizzard (Central Asia)
BURGH town; borough
BURIN engraving tool — to
BURKE murder; hush up
BURLY stout; lusty; portly
BURNT charred; parched; tanned
BURRO donkey; moke — zo
BURRY having burs; prickly — bt
BURSA a sac; a pouch — md
BURSE purse; bourse
BURST split; exploded; rent asunder
BUSBY bearskin headdress
BUSES vehicles
BUSHY overgrown; bosky
BUSKY bosky; woody; shady
BUTTE hill with flat top; ridge
BUTTS rifle range
BUTTY mining partner; deputy; barge
BUTYL butter extract — ch
BUXOM comely; lively; jolly
BUYER purchaser; shopper
BUZZY muzzy; dazed
BWANA master; boss (Swahili)
BYARD miner's hauling strap
BY-END subsidiary aim
BY-LAW bye-law
BYOUS extraordinary (Sc.)
BY-WAY by-path

C

CAABA Kaaba; shrine in Mecca — rl
CABAL clique; junto; set
CABAS rush-basket
CABBY a cab-driver
CABER pole; tree-trunk (Sc.)
CABIN hut; shed; room in ship — nt
CABIR nature worship (Lemnos)
CABLE wire; 100 fathoms — me, nt
CABOB or **KEBAB** dish of meat — ck
CABRE aero-stunt
CACAO the chocolate-tree — bt
CACHE a hide; secret store
CADDY (golf); a tea-caddy
CADET younger son; trainee
CADGE peddle; sponge
CADGY frolicsome; wanton
CADRE nucleus; framework
CAGED captive; mewed
CAGEY cautious; irritable; secretive
CAGOT Pyrenees pariah race
CA-IRA 'on with it' (Fr.)
CAIRD tinker; gipsy
CAIRN heap of stones; terrier — zo
CAKED clotted; plastered
CALID hot; fiery; ardent; glowing

CALIF Caliph; Kalif	
CALIN a Chinese alloy	
CALIX calyx; cup	bt
CALLA bog-arum	bt
CALLE caul; callet; network cap	
CALMY calm; quiet; pacific	
CALPA Kalpa; a day of Brahma	rl
CALVE give birth	zo
CALYX flower's outer whorl, calix	bt
CAMAN shinty stick (Sc.)	
CAMEL a Bactrian; caisson	zo
CAMEO opposite to intaglio	
CAMPO Savanna (Brazil)	
CAMIS chemise; loose garment	
CANAL channel; duct; waterway	
CANDY a sweetmeat; to crystallize	
CANED thrashed; tanned	
CANEY with unduly narrow growth rings	fr
CANNA arrowroot	bt
CANNY shrewd; cautious; knowing	
CANOE a dugout	nt
CANON precept; rule	rl
CANTO a division of a poem	
CANTY cheerful; talkative	
CAPEL caple; composite stone	zo, mn
CAPER dance; gambol; a plant	bt
CAPER Dutch privateer	nt
CAPLE capel; capul; a horse	zo
CAPOC kapok; Indian cotton	bt
CAPON fish; letter; fowl	zo
CAPOT to win all tricks at piquet	
CAPRA she-goat	zo
CAPUL caple	zo
CAPUT distal-end swelling; head	md
CARAT a weight	me
CARED heeded; recked; minded	
CARET the mark ∧	
CAREX sedge; reed; grass	bt
CARGO load; freight	nt
CARIB a Caribbean	
CARLE rude strong man	
CARNY blarney; flattery	
CAROB locust or algaroba tree	bt
CAROL lay; ditty; warble; hymn	
CAROM cannon in French billiards	
CARRY convey; urge; accomplish	
CARSE low-lying land	
CARTE (fencing); card	
CARUS unconsciousness	
CARVE cut; hack; slice; engrave	
CARVY caraway plant	bt
CASAL belonging to a case (grammar)	
CASCO Manila barge	nt
CASED boxed; packed; enveloped	
CASSE broken paper	
CASTE class; rank; lineage	
CATCH latch; clutch; ensnare	
CATER provide food, etc.	
CATES viands; dainties	
CATTY feline; spiteful	
CAULD dam; weir (Sc.)	

CAULK make water-tight	nt
CAUSE reason; object; source	
CAVED collapsed; fallen	
CAVIE hen-coop or cage	
CAVIL carp; censure; criticize	
CAVIN covered approach	
CAWED crowed	
CAWKY of baryta; of barium oxide	ch
CAXON hairy wig	
CEASE cesse; end; stop; desist	
CEBUS S. American monkey	zo
CEDAR a Lebanon tree	bt
CEDED granted; allotted; yielded	
CELLA central body of temple	
CELLO violincello	mu
CENSE burn incense	
CENTO a medley	mu
CEORL churl; a freeman	
CERED covered with wax	
CERES harvest goddess	rl
CERGE altar candle	rl
CERIC wax-like	
CERIN a constituent of wax	ch
CERTY certainly (Sc.)	
CETIC (spermaceti)	zo
CETYL a radical in spermaceti	
CHACK the toss of a horse's head	
CHAFE rub; heat; vex; gall	
CHAFF husks; deride; raillery	
CHAFT chaps; the jaw (Sc.)	
CHAIN fetter; 22 yd (20 m)	me
CHAIR seat; professorship	
CHAKO shako; a headdress	
CHALK to record; white soft rock	mn
CHAMA large oyster	zo
CHAMP (horses); chew; crunch	
CHAMP potato dish (N. Ire.)	
CHANK species of conch-shell	zo
CHANT intone; carol	mu
CHAOS anarchy; disorder; confusion	
CHAPE the catch of a buckle	
CHAPS the jaws; chops	
CHAPS cowboy breeches	
CHARD vegetable with edible leaves, stalk	bt
CHARE chore; daily work	
CHARE narrow street or court	
CHARK char; charcoal	
CHARM spell; allure; amulet	
CHARM nuclear behaviour	
CHARR char; (trout)	zo
CHART sea-map	nt
CHARY frugal; circumspect; wary	
CHASE pursue; hunt; follow; race	
CHASE engrave; frame; type-case	
CHASM gap; cleft; rift; abyss	
CHAUS Ind./Afr. wild cat	zo
CHEAP mean; common; paltry	
CHEAT dupe; fraud; swindle	
CHECK curb; stay; bridle; tally	
CHEEK insolence; sauce	

CHEEP pipe; chirp; churr
CHEER gaiety; hearten; encourage
CHELA lobster claw   zo
CHELA a Buddhist disciple
CHENG Chinese reed instrument   mu
CHERI darling (masc., Fr.)
CHERT flint; hornstone   nt
CHESS a matey game
CHEST coffer; coffin; breast
CHEVY chivy; chase; scamper
CHIAN of Chios
CHICA orange-red dye; liquor
CHICH a dwarf pea; lentil
CHICK to sprout; child; chicken   zo
CHICK bamboo screen
CHIDE scold; rebuke; reprove
CHIEF boss; head; prime; principal
CHIEL child; lad (Sc.)
CHILD babe; nursling; offspring
CHILI pod of cayenne pepper   bt
CHILL cold; frigid; depress
CHIMB edge of cask
CHIME harmonize; strike; agree
CHINA porcelain; Celestial Empire
CHINE cleft; ravine; backbone   md
CHINK gap; rift; cranny; clink
CHIPS a carpenter
CHIRK chirp; cheep; cheerful
CHIRM bird noises
CHIRP chirr; chirl; to trill; bird call
CHIRT to squeeze
CHIVE a type of onion   bt
CHIVY chevy; chase; pursue
CHOCK wedge; block; a log
CHODE scolded; rated; upbraided
CHOIR the chancel   rl
CHOKE gag; stifle; burke; strangle
CHOKY prison (slang)
CHOPS chaps; the jaws
CHORD harmonious sound   mu
CHORE chare; household toil
CHOSE selected; picked; culled
CHOUT blackmail; extortion (Hindu)
CHUBB patent lock; a safe
CHUCK jerk; throw; cluck; instrument   to
CHUET a pie of minced meat
CHUFF, SHUFF cracked bricks; clown; boor
CHUMP lump of wood; blockhead
CHUNK thick slice
CHURL ceorl; freeman; clodhopper
CHURN foam; jostle; agitate
CHURR chirp; chirk
CHUTE waterfall; sloping channel
CHYAK tease; chaff (Australia)
CHYLE milky fluid   md
CHYME partially digested food   md
CHYND cleft to the chine (obs.)
CIBOL variety of onion; shallot   bt
CICER chick-pea   bt
CIDER cyder; fermented apple-juice

CIGAR a Havana
CILIA filaments; eye-lashes   md
CIMAR cymar; simar; scarf
CIMEX bed-bug   zo
CINCH girth; a certainty
CIRCA about, approximately (Latin)
CIRCE a glamorous Syren
CIRRI tendrils; clouds
CISCO American char   zo
CISSY effeminate youth
CITAL summons; accusation   lw
CITED quoted; adduced; mentioned
CIVET cat; perfume; fur
CIVIC municipal; corporate
CIVIL polite; courteous; suave
CIVVY a civilian
CLACK click; clink; clatter; prate
CLAES clothes (Sc.)
CLAIK the barnacle goose   zo
CLAIM right; privilege; usurp
CLAMP clump; fasten   to
CLAMS pincers; vice   to
CLANG clank; clash
CLANK clatter; clangour
CLARE a nun of St. Clare   rl
CLARO mild in taste (cigars)
CLARY sweet-herb   bt
CLASH jar; differ; contend; collide
CLASP hasp; catch; grip
CLASS set; grade; category
CLATS slops; (mud wall) (Sc.)
CLAUT rake; scratch (Sc.)
CLAVA club-shaped swelling; fungi   zo, bt
CLAVE clove; cleft; clung
CLEAN immaculate; pure; scour
CLEAR pellucid; serene; free
CLEAT a wedge; slat   nt
CLEEK golf club; hook; peg
CLEFT clift; split; rift; cranny
CLEPE to name; (yclept)
CLERK scribe; scrivener; recorder
CLEVE a cliff; a valley
CLEVY draught-iron of a plough
CLICK klick; tick; a latch
CLIDE, CLITE burweed   bt
CLIFF crag; headland; precipice
CLIFT cleft; fissure; breach
CLIMB scale; ascend; surmount
CLIME region; place; climate
CLINE ecological life assessment   bt, zo
CLING hold; cleave; embrace
CLINK prison; chink; jingle
CLINT a hard rock   mn
CLOAK cover; pretext; mask
CLOAM earthenware
CLOCK chronometer; horologe
CLOFF cleft; a weight allowance
CLONE plant stock; pure line   bt
CLONE asexually produced individual   zo
CLOOM cloam; clay
CLOOP pop! (interjection)

CLOOT cloven hoof (Sc.)		
CLOSE estop; end; grapple	rl	
CLOSH skittles		
CLOTH woven fabric; the clergy	rl	
CLOUD haze; vapour; obscure		
CLOUR to knock; a bump		
CLOUT dish-cloth; nail; buffet		
CLOVE a spice; a weight	bt, me	
CLOWN jester; fool; buffoon; dunce		
CLUCK the call of a hen		
CLUMP cluster; group; patch		
CLUNG clasped; adhered; held		
CLUNK a gurgle		
CLUNY pillow-lace		
CNIDA stinging thread; jellyfish	zo	
COACH teach; trainer; vehicle		
CO-ACT co-operate; aid; abet		
CO-AID helper; assistant		
COALY resembling coal		
COARB bishop or abbot	rl	
COAST shore; strand; seaside		
COATI American racoon	zo	
COBBY stout; brisk		
COBLE fishing boat	nt	
COBRA hamadryad	zo	
COCKY conceited		
COCOA a beverage	bt	
COCUS green ebony	bt	
CODAN carrier-operated-device-anti-noise		
CODED in code; in cipher		
CODEX ancient manuscript		
CODLE coddle; pamper; caress		
CODON triplet DNA bases fixing genetic codes		
COGUE wooden milk bowl (Sc.)		
COIGN corner-stone; quoin; wedge		
COKED converted into coke		
COLIC flatulence	md	
COLIN American partridge	zo	
COLLY coal-smut		
COLON punctuation; money	md	
COLOR colour; hue; tint; pigment		
COLZA cabbage; rape oil	bt	
COMBE coomb; wooded valley		
COMBO small jazz/dance band		
COMER an arrival		
COMET card game; nebulous body		
COMFY comfortable		
COMIC droll; farcical; ludicrous		
COMMA a butterfly; punctuation mark	zo	
COMPO plaster; stucco; soldier's ration		
COMPT to count (obs.)		
COMUS God of Revelry; a masque		
CONCH shell; trumpet	mu	
CONED tapering		
CONES fine flour		
CONEY cony; bunny	zo	
CONGA dance (Afro-Cuban)	mu	
CONGE leave; dismissal (Fr.)		
CONGO black tea	bt	
CONIA hemlock	bt	

CONIC conical; tapering		
CONIN conine; hemlock	bt	
CONNE conn; con; study; steer		
CONTO money of account (Portugal)		
COOED made love		
COOEE cooey; Australian bush-call		
COOKY a cook; a small cake	ck	
COOLY coolie (Hindu)		
COOMB 4 bushels; wooded valley	me	
CO-OPT to elect		
COPAL a resin; a varnish	rl	
COPEC kopeck; a Russian copper	nm	
COPED vied; contended; overcame		
COPER dealer		
COPOS lassitude		
COPRA dried coconut kernels	bt	
COPSE coppice; grove; thicket		
COPSY covered with undergrowth		
CORAL lobster roe	zo	
CORAL marine growth reef	bt, mn	
CORED centre removed, bored		
CORER fruit/earth-sample cutting device		
CORGI small breed of dog (Wales)	zo	
CORKY lively; skittish		
CORNO French horn	mu	
CORNU a horn	zo	
CORNY horny; (humour) trite (slang)		
CORPS staff; contingent; troops		
CORSE a corpse (obs.)		
CORVE tram used in mines	mn	
COSEY cosy; snug; teapot-cover		
COSTS expenses	lw	
COTTA a surplice	rl	
COUCH sofa; divan; squat; grass	bt	
COUGH tussis; a cold	md	
COULD was able (past of can)		
COUNT compute; number; reckon		
COUPE closed car		
COURB to stoop; bent (obs.)		
COURT woo; invite; homage; tribunal		
COUTH familiar; agreeable		
COVED arched over		
COVEN a muster of witches		
COVER wrap; cloak; shroud; invest		
COVET desire; hanker after		
COVEY a brood; a bevy	zo	
COVIN collusive fraudulence	lw	
COWAN uninitiated mason		
COWED daunted; overawed; abashed		
COWER fawn; quail; cringe; shrink		
COWLE written agreement (Ang.-Ind.)		
COWRY small shell used as money		
COYLY bashfully; demurely; shyly		
COYPU nutria; S. American rodent	zo	
COXAE hip-joints	md	
COZEN cheat; deceive; sponge		
CRACK gap; rift; rent; crevice		
CRAFT skill; dexterity; guile; vessel	nt	
CRAIG crag; the neck (Sc.)		
CRAKE the corncrake	zo	
CRAME booth; covered stall		

CRAMP a spasm; hinder; impede		
CRANE hoisting machine; wader	zo	
CRANK handle; bend; twist; quirk		
CRAPE transparent gauze; to curl		
CRAPS a dice game		
CRAPY resembling crape		
CRARE trading vessel	nt	
CRASH coarse cloth; shatter; smash		
CRASS gross; dense; stupid		
CRATE hamper; packing case		
CRAVE beg; yearn; implore		
CRAWL fish-pen; creep; abase		
CRAZE mania; insane passion; fad		
CRAZY mad; idiotic; rickety		
CREAK grate		
CREAM to mantle; top of milk		
CRECK the corncrake	zo	
CREDO the creed	rl	
CREED belief; tenet; dogma		
CREEK bay; cove inlet; bight		
CREEL fish-basket		
CREEP crawl; cringe; grovel		
CREME cream-like substance	ck	
CRENA a furrow; a notch		
CREPE wrinkled fabric; rubber; pancake	ck	
CREPT crawled; fawned; glided		
CRESS watercress, etc.	bt	
CREST top; apex; summit; device		
CREUX the reverse of relief		
CREWE cruse; earthenware pot		
CRICK cramp; spasm; convulsion		
CRIED wept; sobbed; lamented		
CRIER proclaimer; howler		
CRIES yells; shrieks; shouts		
CRIME felony; enormity; misdeed		
CRIMP corrugate; decoy		
CRINE shrink; shrivel (Sc.)		
CRISP curl; brittle; friable		
CRITH unit weight of a gas	me	
CROAK grumble; complain; die		
CROAT (Yugoslavian)		
CROCK soot; jar; pitcher; shard		
CROFT a small farm; a pasture		
CROMA crome; a quaver	mu	
CROME cromb; crook; hook		
CRONE old woman; a ewe	zo	
CRONY familiar friend		
CROOK crome; bend; crosier	rl	
CROOL to mutter		
CROOM a pitchfork	to	
CROON low moan		
CROPE a finial; the top		
CRORE 100 lacs of rupees	nm	
CROSS crusty; sullen; thwart		
CROUD Welsh violin	mu	
CROUP rump; throat disease	md	
CROUT pickled cabbage	ck	
CROWD mob; throng; herd; swarm		
CROWN diadem; garland; 5/- (25p)	nm	
CROZE cooper's tool; groove	to	
CRUDE raw; tough; immature		

CRUEL fell; dire; brutal; inhuman		
CRUET eucharistic flagon	rl	
CRUMB soft part of a loaf	ck	
CRUMP crooked; wrinkled; a bang		
CRUNT a blow on the head (Sc.)		
CRUOR coagulated blood; gore	md	
CRUSE vial; small bottle		
CRUSH squeeze; subdue; pulverize		
CRUST incrustation; coating		
CRWTH Welsh violin	mu	
CRYPT vault; tomb; catacomb		
CUBAN a native of Cuba		
CUBEB dried pepper-berry	bt, ck	
CUBED raised to third power		
CUBIC volumetric	me	
CUBIT length of 18 or 22 in (45 or 55 cm)		
	me	
CUDDY cabin; rent; donkey	zo	
CUFIC an Arabic script		
CUISH cuisse; thigh-armour		
CULCH rubbish		
CULET lower facet of a diamond		
CULEX a gnat genus	zo	
CULLY silly dupe; to deceive		
CUMIN cummin; caraway	bt	
CUPEL assaying vessel		
CUPID Eros; the god of love		
CURCH a kerchief		
CURDY coagulated		
CURED healed; remedied; preserved		
CURER a fish-drier		
CURIA Senate house; court		
CURIE unit of radiation	me	
CURIO rare bric-à-brac		
CURLY wavy; sinuous; twisty		
CURRE golden-eye duck	zo	
CURRY to dress leather; thrash		
CURRY Indian spiced dish	ck	
CURSE anathema; execrate; maledict		
CURST tormented; plagued		
CURVE turn; bend; inflect		
CUSEC cubic flow per second	me	
CUSHY easy and well-paid		
CUTCH catechu; couch grass	bt	
CUTER more cunning; sharper		
CUT-IN football; motoring		
CUTIS true skin	md	
CUTTO cuttoe; large knife	to	
CUTTY short; curtailed; clay pipe		
CUVEE blend of wine (Fr.)		
CYCAD a palm	bt	
CYCLE period; age; era; circle		
CYMRY Cymric; Welsh		
CYNIC misanthrope; captious; morose		
CZECH Bohemian		

D

DACHA weekend villa (Rus.)		
DADDY dadda; papa; father		
DAGON Philistine Fish-God	rl	

DAILY diurnal; quotidian
DAIRI Mikado's palace
DAIRY milkshop; creamery
DAISY sometimes ox-eyed   bt
DAKER corncrake; crake   zo
DAKIR daker; dicker; half-a-score
DALAI Lama; Tibetan Priest-King   rl
DALER a dalesman
DALLY sport; wanton; toy; dawdle
DAMAN coney; Syrian hyrax   zo
DAMAR dammar; resin   bt
DAMON and Pythias
DAMPS exhalations
DAMPY dejected; moist; humid
DANCE hop; caper; prance; pirouette
DANDY fop; beau; swell; coxcomb
DANTY broken coal   mn
DARAF elastance unit   el
DARBY plasterer's float   to
DARCY permeability coefficients unit
DARED braved; ventured; presumed
DARIC gold coin of Darius   nm
DARKY darkey; negro; lantern
DAROO sycamore   bt
DASHY showy; ostentatious; gaudy
DATED of an era
DATUM something given
DAUBE braised meat in wine (Fr.)   ck
DAUBY sticky; viscous; glutinous
DAUNT cow; appal; scare; intimidate
DAVIT usually davits   nt
DAYAK Dyak; Malay race
DAZED mazed; dazzled; bewildered
DEADS ore débris
DEALT (cards); trafficked; traded
DEARN mournful; lonely; solitary
DEARY a dear
DEATH demise; decease
DEAVE to deafen (Sc.)
DEBAG remove trousers forcibly
DEBAR ban; deny; prevent; stop
DEBEL to conquer; subdue
DEBIT due; arrears; liability
DEBUG de-programme   cp
DEBUS get off a bus
DEBUT first appearance
DECAD decade; a group of ten
DECAY rot; wane; decline
DECEM ten; (a prefix)
DECOR scheme of decoration
DECOY lure; ensnare; inveigle
DECRY censure; vilify; disparage
DEDAL daedal; intricate
DEEDY illustrious; active
DEFER delay; adjourn; postpone
DEIFY idolize; apotheosize
DEIGN condescend; vouchsafe
DEISM belief in a god
DEIST a free-thinking believer
DEITY divinity; providence
DEKKO reconnoitring look (Ind.)

DEKLE deckle; ragged
DELAY dally; retard; impede
DELFT glazed earthenware (from Holland)
DELPH delf; pottery
DELTA river mouth; alluvial deposit
DELVE dig; scoop; excavate
DEMIT release; resign
DEMOB demobilize
DEMON imp; goblin; devil; troll
DEMOS the proletariat
DEMPT deemed; judged (Spens.)
DEMUR pause; object; waver
DENAY deny; denial (obs.)
DENIM twilled cotton goods
DENSE compact; close; solid
DEPOT depository; storehouse
DEPTH profundity; abyss
DERAY to disarrange
DERBY a race; a hat
DERIC pertaining to skin
DERMA lobster-skin   zo
DERRY a prejudice (Australia)
DETER prevent; restrain; dissuade
DEUCE the Devil; (cards); (tennis)
DEVIL imp; to drudge; Lucifer
DEWAN Indian fiscal officer
DEWED bedewed
DHOBI Indian washerman
DHOLE Indian wild dog   zo
DHOTI loin cloth (Hindu)
DIAMB 2-iambi verse foot
DIANA moon-goddess; Artemis   r
DIARY journal; chronicle; record
DIAZO reproduction process paper   p.
DICED cut in cubes; bookbinding decoration
DICER dice-player
DICHT to wipe (Sc.)
DICKY seat; apron; shirt-front
DICTA pronouncements
DIDOT typographical measurement
DIDST (thou) did
DIDUS the dodo genus   ze
DIENE unsaturated hydrocarbons
DIGHT adorned; arrayed
DIGIT finger; toe; integer
DIGUE water-advance-prevention seawall
DIKED banked; ditched
DILLY native bag (Australia)
DILLY diligence; the daffodil   b
DILSH inferior coal layer   m
DIMER 2-like-molecule-based species   c
DIMLY obscurely; vaguely
DINAR (Iran, Jordan, Yugoslavia)   nn
DINED postprandially replete
DINER restaurant car
DINEX chemical insecticide
DINGO Australian dog
DINGY dull; sullied; squalid
DINIC dizzy; vertiginous
DINKY elegant
DIODE thermionic valve; a circuit

DIOTA two-handled jar		**DORTY** pettish; delicate (Sc.)	
DIPUS the jerboa	zo	**DOSED** physicked; drenched	
DIPPY a little insane		**DOSEH** religious ceremony (Cairo)	
DIRGE elegy; requiem; lament		**DOSEL** dossal; tapestry	rl
DIRTY foul; sordid; mean; paltry		**DOSER** dossel; coloured cloths	
DISCO recorded-music dancehall, discotheque		**DOTAL** referring to a dowry	
		DOTED loved; drivelled	
DISME a tithe; a tenth; a dime		**DOTTY** barmy; silly; deranged	
DITAL guitar tuning key	mu	**DOUAR** dowar; Arab camp	
DITCH moat; trench; rine; drain		**DOUAY** a Bible edition	
DITTO the same again		**DOUBT** distrust; indecision; demur	
DITTY refrain; sonnet; ode; lilt		**DOUCE** dulce; sweet	
DIVAN council; saloon; sofa; couch		**DOUGH** money; the kneadful	
DIVED plunged; fathomed; explored		**DOURA** millet	bt
DIVER a sea-bird	zo	**DOUSE** dowse; slacken suddenly; drench	
DIVES the rich man in the Bible		**DOVER** doze; slumber; a powder	md
DIVOT a piece of turf		**DOWDY** slovenly; untidy; slatternly	
DIVVY share; divide		**DOWEL** a wooden pin	
DIXIE camp-kettle; Southern USA		**DOWER** dowry; dot; bequest	
DIZEN to dress gaudily		**DOWLE** fluff; down fibre	
DJINN genie; demon; afrit		**DOWNY** filamentous; knowing	
DO-ALL factotum		**DOWRY** dower; dot; endowment	
DOBBY a dotard; part of a loom		**DOWSE** lower; close; put out	nt
DOBOS choc. torte with caramel topping	ck	**DOYEN** senior member	
DODDY hornless cow	zo	**DOZED** snoozed; drowsed; slumbered	
DODGE evade; avoid; shuffle		**DOZEN** apostolic number	
DODGY artful; tricky		**DOZER** nap taker	
DOGAL (doge of Venice)		**DOZER** earth-moving tractor blade	
DOGGO concealed		**DRACO** a constellation	
DOGGY fond of dogs		**DRAFF** dregs; residue	
DOGMA tenet; doctrine; maxim		**DRAFT** outline; sketch; prepare	
DOGRA a Kashmiri		**DRAIL** to trail; to draggle	
DOILT crazy; daft (Sc.)		**DRAIN** empty; tap; a gutter	
DOILY ornamented napkin		**DRAKE** male duck	zo
DOING performing; swindling		**DRAMA** histrionic art; play	
DOLCE softly	mu	**DRANK** quaffed; caroused; imbibed	
DOLED bestowed sparingly		**DRANT** to drone; to drawl	
DOLLY camera carriage	tv	**DRAPE** cover; array; deck	
DOLMA rice-filled leaf	ck	**DRAWL** lag; drag; drone	
DOLOR dolour; grief; sorrow		**DRAWN** hauled; sketched; eviscerated	
DOMAL relating to a house		**DREAD** awe; fear; apprehension	
DOMED vaulted		**DREAM** reverie; hallucination	
DONAH coster's sweetheart		**DREAR** bleak; dismal; gloomy	
DONAT donet; grammar-book; primer		**DREGS** less; draff; sediment	
DONEE the recipient		**DRENT** drenched (obs.)	
DONGA S. African ravine		**DRESS** garb; guise; apparel	
DONNA donya; a lady don (Sp.)		**DREST** attired; arrayed	
DONOR giver; bestower		**DREUL** drool; dribble	
DONYA Spanish lady		**DRIED** aerified; parched; desiccated	
DOOLE dole; gloom (obs.)		**DRIER** desiccator; dryer	
DOOLY Indian litter		**DRIFT** wander; aim; intention	to
DOORN S. African briar	bt	**DRILL** cloth; ape; bore	zo, to
DOPED drugged; covered with varnish		**DRILY** dryly; sarcastically	
DOPER dauber; horse-coper		**D-RING** 'D'-shaped ring	to
DOPEY slow-witted; dull		**DRINK** potion; draught; absorb	
DORAN missile-tracking system	rd	**DRIVE** urge; impel; coerce	
DOREE dory; golden-yellow fish	zo	**DROIL** ca' canny; drudgery	
DORIC Greek architecture	ar	**DROIT** right; title	
DORMY unbeatable at golf		**DROLL** odd; rummy; whimsical	
DORSE Baltic cod; coal-fish	zo	**DROME** racecourse; aerodrome	
DORSE reverse side		**DRONE** idler; hum; dawdle; bee	

DRONE	bagpipes tone; male bee	mu, zo
DROOK	to drench; to duck (Sc.)	
DROOL	dreul; slaver; drivel	
DROOP	sag; fade; wilt; languish	
DROPS	small doses; gouts	md
DROSS	scum; dregs; scoria	
DROUK	drook; to duck (Sc.)	
DROVE	(cattle); forced; actuated	
DROWN	swamp; flood; deluge	
DRUID	bard	
DRUNK	crapulous; tipsy; quaffed	
DRUPE	a stone fruit	bt
DRUSE	mining cavity; a sect	mn, rl
DRUSY	having cavities	mn
DRUXY	partly decayed timber	
DRYAD	wood-nymph	
DRYAS	mountain avens	bt
DRYER	drier	
DRYLY	drily; insipidly; aridly	
DSOMO	zhomo; a hybrid	zo
DUCAL	with strawberry leaves; duke's	
DUCAT	Italian gold or silver	nm
DUCHY	a dukedom; duke's holiday	
DUDDY	ragged; in tatters	
DUKEY	wheeled platform; inclined-road train	
DULCE	douce; sweeten; soothe	
DULIA	angel adoration (RC)	rl
DULLY	stupidly; inertly; languidly	
DULSE	edible seaweed	bt
DUMBA	fat-tailed sheep	zo
DUMMY	declarer's mute partner	
DUMPS	low spirits; dejection	
DUMPY	short and thick	
DUNCE	dolt; dullard; booby	
DUNCH	punch; jolt; to gore	
DUNNE	the knot-sandpiper	zo
DUNNY	deaf; dull of apprehension	
DUOMO	Italian cathedral	rl
DUPED	deluded; gulled; hoaxed	
DUPER	trickster; dodger; sharper	
DUPLE	double; twofold	
DUPPY	W. Indian ghost	
DURED	endured (obs.)	
DURGA	wife of Siva	rl
DURGY	undersized; dwarf	
DURIO	Malay tree; (durian fruit)	bt
DUROY	corduroy; figured serge	
DURRA	molasses/sugar-source sorghum grass	bt
DURRA	semi-tropical grain sorghum	bt
DURST	dared	
DURUM	hard wheat for pasta	bt, ck
DUSKY	swarthy; shady; dark; dim	
DUSTY	powdery	
DUTCH	a coster's wife; courage; treat	
DUVET	eiderdown	
DWALE	heretic; heraldic sable	hd
DWALE	the deadly nightshade	bt
DWALM	dwaum; swoon; sicken	
DWAMY	faint; languid; sickly (Sc.)	
DWANG	a crowbar	to

DWARF	imp; pygmy; midget; stunted	
DWELL	abide; reside; linger	
DWELT	stayed; tarried; sojourned	
DWINE	to pine; to fade	
DYING	moribund; expiring; demise	
DYNAM	the unit of work	me

E

EAGER	keen; ardent; avid; zealous	
EAGLE	(golf); 10 dollar gold piece	nm
EAGLE	lectern; standard; erne; bird	zo
EAGRE	aigre; tidal wave; bore	
EARED	having lugs	
EARLY	rathe; forward; betimes	
EARST	erst; formerly	
EARTH	world; soil; humus	
EASED	allayed; soothed; assuaged	
EASEL	canvas carrier	
EASLE	hot ashes (Sc.)	
EATEN	masticated; corroded	
EATER	consumer; devourer	
EAVES	overhanging roof-edges	a
EBBED	waned; receded; declined	
EBLIS	a djinn; evil spirit	
EBONY	black wood	b
ECLAT	splendour; brilliance	
ECTAL	ectad; outer; external	
EDDER	top binding of a hedge	
EDGED	keen; bordered; fringed	
EDICT	ukase; decree; order	
EDIFY	uplift; enlighten; instruct	
EDILE	Roman magistrate	
EDUCE	elicit; draw; extract	
EDUCT	deduction	
EERIE	eirie; uncanny; weird	
EGEST	throw out; eject; cast	
EGGAR	egger; silkworm moth	z
EGGED	incited; urged; impelled	
EGGER	an egg collector	
EGRET	aigrette; heron	z
EIDER	sea-duck	z
EIGHT	twice four	
EIGNE	eldest son; first born	
EIGNE	entailed and inalienable	lv
EIKON	ikon; likeness	
EIRIE	eerie; weird; unaccountable	
EISEL	vinegar	ch
EJECT	evict; expel; oust; emit	
EKING	prolonging	
ELAIN	clarified oil or fat	
ELAND	antelope (S. Africa)	z
ELAPS	venomous coral snake	z
ELATE	exult; rouse; animate	
ELBOW	jostle; nudge; a bend	
ELCHI	Turkish envoy	
ELDER	older; ancestor	b
ELECT	cull; select; chosen	
ELEGY	dirge; threnody; lament	
ELEMI	resin; chewing gum	b

ELEOT species of apple	bt	
ELERS designer of china-ware		
ELEVE pupil (Fr.)		
ELFIN small elf; puckish; pixy		
ELGIN (marbles)		
ELIDE contract; curtail		
ELITE the elect; very select		
ELMEN made of elm	bt	
ELOGE funeral oration		
ELOGY panegyric; eulogy; encomium		
ELOIN banish; remove (obs.)		
ELOPE run away; abscond; decamp		
ELOPS herring genus	zo	
ELSIN an awl (Sc.)	to	
ELSSE missile-tracking system	el	
ELUDE evade; baffle; escape		
ELUTE cleanse; purify by washing		
ELVAN Cornish rock; elvish	mn	
ELVAS prune; plum (Port.)	bt	
ELVER young eel	zo	
EMAGE area of text block in square ems		
EMBAR prevent; bar; shut; stop		
EMBAY to shelter; to landlock		
EMBED imbed; set firmly		
EMBER glowing fuel		
EMBOG engulf		
EMBOW to arch; to vault		
EMBOX encase; pack		
EMBUS to put in a bus		
EMEER Ameer; Emir		
EMEND amend; rectify; correct		
EMERY carborundum	mn	
EMMER bucket; pail (S. Africa)		
EMMET an ant; a pismire	zo	
EMMEW enmew; immew; confine		
EMOTE register emotion		
EMPTY void; vacant; vacuous; inane		
EMURE immure (obs.)		
ENACT ordain; decree; authorize		
ENATE growing out		
ENDED finished; concluded; ceased		
ENDER a finale; a cropper		
END-ON abutting		
ENDOR home of a witch		
ENDOW endue; indue; endew		
ENDUE to invest; provide		
ENEID epic poem		
ENEMA a clyster; rectal spray	md	
ENEMY foe; rival; antagonist		
ENGLE Angle; early English		
ENJOY relish; appreciate		
ENMEW emmew; immew; confine		
ENNUI weariness; boredom (Fr.)		
ENODE jointless; knotless		
ENORM enormous (obs.)		
ENROL list; enlist; chronicle		
ENSKY to place in the sky (Shak.)		
ENSOR levers net	tx	
ENSUE pursue; result; follow		
ENTAL internal		
ENTER invade; record; insert		

ENTRY adit; inlet; portal; note		
ENURE inure; accustom		
ENVOI ⎫ diplomatic agent; legate;		
ENVOY ⎭ postscript		
ENZYM a ferment; yeast	ch	
EOLIC Eolian; Aeolian		
EOLUS God of the Winds		
EOSIN red dye or ink	ch	
EPACT moon's age at new year		
EPHAH Hebrew bushel	me	
EPHOD vestment; surplice	rl	
EPHOR Greek magistrate		
EPOCH era; cycle; remarkable period		
EPODE part of an ode		
EPOPT an Eleusinian initiate		
EPOXY oxygen fixed to 2 different atoms		
EPSOM salts	md	
EPURE large working plan (Fr.)		
EQUAL peer; competent; equable		
EQUES Roman Knight		
EQUIP rig; arm; accoutre; array		
EQUUS the horse genus	zo	
ERASE blot; delete; cancel; efface		
ERATO Muse of lyric poetry		
ERECT build; upright; vertical		
ERGOT parasitical fungus	bt	
ERICA the heath genus	bt	
ERICK a blood-fine (Irish)	lw	
ERODE eat away; corrode; consume		
EROSE gnawed-looking (of leaves)	bt	
ERRED strayed; sinned; wandered		
ERROR mistake; fault; fallacy		
ERUCA the salad plant; a larva	bt, zo	
ERUPT eject; eruct; burst forth		
ERVUM the lentil		
ESCOT scot; an ancient tax		
ESCAR ⎫		
ESKAR ⎬ glacial gravel ridge		
ESKER ⎭		
ESSAY assay; attempt; trial; paper		
ESTER ethereal salt	ch	
ESTOC short cavalry sword (Fr.)		
ESTOP stop; bar; impede	lw	
ETAPE stage point, esp. cycle races		
ETERN eternal; endless		
ETHAL (spermaceti)	ch	
ETHER upper air; volatile gas	ch	
ETHIC ethical; moral		
ETHOS guiding spirit of a group or nation		
ETHYL alcohol radical	ch	
ETTLE intend; guess (Sc.)		
ETUDE a composition (Fr.)	mu	
ETWEE etui; pocket-case		
EUPAD (antiseptic)	ch	
EURUS the East wind	mt	
EUSOL (antiseptic)	ch	
EVADE elude; avoid; foil; dodge		
EVENS fifty-fifty		
EVENT incident; outcome; occurrence		
EVERT turn inside out		
EVERY all; each		

EVICT eject; dislodge; dispossess	
EVITE evade; avoid; shun	
EVOKE arouse; excite; summon	
EWEST near (Sc.)	
EWHOW alas! (Sc.)	
EXACT precise; extort; mulct	
EXALT raise; extol; magnify	
EXCEL outvie; surpass; exceed	
EXEAT a short leave	
EXEME exempt (Sc.)	
EXERT strive; try; endeavour	
EXIES ecstasy; hysterics (Sc.)	
EXILE refugee; banish; proscribe	
EXINE outer pollen-grain wall layer	bt
EXIST be; live; endure; last	
EXITE limb-lobe in arthropoda	zo
EX-LEX outlaw	lw
EXODE dramatic climax	
EXPEL eject; dislodge; oust	
EXTOL exalt; laud; glorify	
EXTRA supernumerary; additional	
EXUDE ooze; percolate; sweat	
EXULT crow; gloat; triumph	
EYING watching; observing	
EYRIE aerie; eagle's nest	

F

FABLE myth; legend; allegory	
FACED defied; confronted; covered	
FACER a blow	
FACET small polished surface	
FACIA control panel; shop name-board	
FADDY crotchety; particular	
FADGE suit; prosper; burden	
FAERY fairy	
FAGIN beech mast; a Jew (Dickens)	bt
FAGOT faggot; bundle of sticks; bassoon	mu
FAGUS the beech tree	bt
FAHAM Indian orchid	bt
FAINT swoon; dim; indistinct	
FAIRY faery; peri; elf; pixie	
FAITH tenet; dogma; belief	
FAKED spurious; counterfeit	
FAKER forger; cheat; swindler	
FAKIR monkish mendicant; magician	
FALSE sham; erroneous; untrue	
FAMED illustrious; renowned	
FANAL lighthouse; beacon	
FANAM Madras money of account	nm
FANCY pugilism; whim; idea; caprice	
FANGO radio-active mud	md
FANON napkin; scarf	rl
FARAD unit of electrical capacity	
FARCI stuffed, filled	ck
FARED fed; travelled; prospered	
FARCE comedy; travesty; parody	
FARCE, FARSI forcemeat	ck
FARCY glanders; equine malady	
FARLE oatcake (Sc.)	
FARSE a Bible extract	rl

FARSI Parsi (Persian) language	
FASTI Roman calendar of festivals	
FATAL lethal; baneful; ruinous	
FATED doomed; destined	
FATES Clotho, Lachesis & Atropos	
FATLY obesely; grossly	
FATTY adipose; pudgy; plump	
FAULT blemish; tennis; earth-crust break	g
FAUNA animal life	z
FAUST a drama by Goethe	
FAVUS scalp disease	m
FEAST banquet; carousel; delight	
FEAZE unravel	
FECIT he (or she) made it (art)	
FED-UP disgruntled; browned off	
FEEZE to twist; worry	
FEIGN pretend; simulate; assume	
FEINT stratagem; artifice; trick	
FELID one of the cat tribe	z
FELIS the cat tribe	z
FELIX the cartoon cat	
FELLY felloe; part of rim of wheel	
FELON criminal; miscreant; outlaw	
FEMUR thigh bone	m
FENCE receiver of stolen goods	
FENDY shifty	
FENKS finks; blubber refuse	
FENNY marshy; swamp; boggy	
FEOFF a fief; grant of land	lv
FERAE wild animals	z
FERAL wild; deadly; funereal	
FERLY fearful; a wonder	
FERMI very small length unit	n
FERNY fernlike, covered with fern	b
FERRY river transport	
FESSE heraldic band	h
FESTA saint's-day carnival (It.)	
FETAL also **FOETAL** embryonic	m
FETCH trick; ghost; bring; carry	
FETED honoured; lionized	
FETID noxious; stinking; noisome	
FETOR offensive odour	
FETUS an embryo; the young	m
FETWA a judgment (Arab)	lv
FEUAR a lease-holder (Sc.)	
FEVER ferment; passion; ardour	m
FEWER rather less	
FIARS the prices of grain (Sc.)	
FIBRE staple; filament; strand	
FICHE chit, official note form	
FICHU small lace or muslin shawl	
FICUS the fig	b
FIDGE to fidget; to be eager (Sc.)	
FIELD glebe; (cricket); (racing)	
FIEND imp; demon; monster; wretch	
FIERI facias; a writ	lv
FIERY ardent; fierce; igneous	
FIFED fluted	m
FIFER fife-player	
FIFTH ordinal of 5	
FIFTY L	

FIGHT fray; brawl; combat; contest		
FILAR threadlike; filamentous		
FILCH steal; pilfer; purloin		
FILED smooth; polished		
FILER one who files; artful		
FILLY girl; foal	zo	
FILMY diaphanous		
FILTH dirt; muck; impurity		
FINAL last; ultimate; terminal		
FINCH a passerine	zo	
FINED mulcted; amersed		
FINER refiner; keener; smaller		
FINIS the end; conclusion		
FINOS merino wool		
FIORD) rock-bound inlet;		
FIRTH) river mouth;		
FJORD) frith; arm of the sea		
FIRED discharged; kindled; sacked		
FIRER an incendiary; igniter		
FIRRY full of pines	bt	
FIRST chief; premier; primeval		
FISHY questionable; unreliable		
FISTY left-handed person (Sc.)		
FITCH pole-cat; fur-brush	zo	
FITCH vetch; chick-pea	bt	
FITLY aptly; properly; seemly		
FITTE fytte; ballad		
FIVER £5 bank note	nm	
FIVES horse disease; a ball-game		
FIXED secured; placed; settled		
FLACK) to flap; to flick; (Sc.);		
FLAFF) to flutter; to pant		
FLAIL a threshing implement	to	
FLAIR natural aptitude		
FLAKE hurdle; hanging platform		
FLAKE scale; lamina; to peel off		
FLAKY fissile		
FLAME ardour; blaze; flare		
FLAMY lambent		
FLANG miner's pick	to	
FLANK side; border; touch		
FLARE a signal light; glare		
FLARE flame; dress spread		
FLARY flaming; flickering		
FLASH glint; sparkle; showy		
FLASK ampulla; vial; phial		
FLAWN custard; pancake		
FLAWY defective; gusty		
FLAXY light in colour		
FLEAD pork fat for lard		
FLEAK a small lock		
FLEAM surgical knife	md	
FLECK dapple; speckle; variegate		
FLECK the flounder	zo	
FLEER to mock; to flout		
FLEET a creek; swift; flotilla	nt	
FLESH mankind; to accustom		
FLEWS bloodhound's chaps		
FLICK flip; fleece; wound		
FLIER flyer; aeronaut		
FLIES back-stage appliances		

FLIMP watch-snatching (slang)		
FLING hurl; dance; escapade		
FLINT variety of quartz	mn	
FLIPE to fold back (Sc.)		
FLIRT philander; coquet; flip		
FLISK a comb; frisk; caper		
FLITE flyte; scold; brawl (Sc.)		
FLOAT waft; drift; raft; buoy		
FLOCK wool; swarm; herd	zo	
FLONG stereotyping paper		
FLOOD spate; downpour; deluge		
FLOOK fluke		
FLOOR to stump; nonplus		
FLORA flowers collectively	bt	
FLORY fleury; boat	nd, nt	
FLOSS silky substance; slag		
FLOTA Spanish fleet	nt	
FLOUR meal		
FLOUT scoff; mock; taunt; jeer		
FLOWN swollen with insolence		
FLUEY fluffy; downy		
FLUFF nap; down; lint		
FLUID liquid; unsettled; gaseous		
FLUKE parasite worm; (whale)	zo	
FLUKE (anchor); fortunate shot	nt	
FLUKY accidentally good		
FLUME a water-chute		
FLUMP plump down		
FLUNG tossed; hurled; pitched		
FLUOR calcium spar	mn	
FLUSH blush; poker term; level, even margin	pr	
FLUTE kind of boat; wind instrument	mu, nt	
FLUTY flutelike		
FLYER flier; aviator		
FLYTE flite; scold; brawl (obs.)		
FOAMY frothy; spumy		
FOCAL converging		
FOCUS point of convergence		
FOEHN a hot wind in the Alps	mt	
FOGEY old-fashioned person		
FOGGY obscure; hazy; indistinct		
FOGLE silk handkerchief (slang)		
FOISM Chinese Buddhism	rl	
FOIST impose; thrust; palm		
FOLIC acid in vitamin-B complex	md	
FOLIO a sheet of paper		
FOLLY inanity; absurdity; fatuity		
FOMES absorbent substance		
FONDU colour blending in calico		
FOOTS refuse; sediment		
FORAY raid; inroad; sally; invasion		
FORBY adjacent		
FORCE power; energy; army; coerce		
FORDO undo; ruin; destroy		
FOREL heavy parchment book cover	pr	
FORET a drill	to	
FORGE smithy; falsify; fabricate		
FORGO renounce; go without		
FORKY branching		
FORME bed of type	pr	

FORTE outstanding skill; loud	mu
FORTH forward; onward; ahead	
FORTY two score	
FORUM tribunal; court; market-place	
FORUM open discussion; public-speaking	
FOSSA Malagasy civet cat	zo
FOSSE ditch; moat; canal	
FOUAT } an onion (Sc.);	
FOUET } the house-leek	bt
FOUND to cast; establish; start	
FOUNT spring; well; source; type	pr
FOUTH fowth; abundance (Sc.)	
FOVEA pit; a pock-mark	md
FOXED baffled; deluded; yellow damp stain	
FOYER lobby; fire-grate	
FRACK freck; eager; bold; hale	
FRAIL weak; infirm; rush-basket	
FRAME fashion; concoct; mood	
FRAME a game of snooker	
FRANC 100 centimes	nm
FRANK candid; open; gannet	zo
FRASS excrement; manure	zo
FRATE friar	rl
FRATI friars; brethren	rl
FRAUD guilt; imposture; deception	
FREAK monstrosity; quirk; vagary	
FRECK frack; eager; hale (Sc.)	
FREED emancipated; exempted	
FREER deliverer; more lavish	
FREET friet; superstition (Sc.)	
FREMD strange; a stranger (Sc.)	
FRESH novel; recent; unsalted	
FRETT ore refuse	
FREYA wife of Odin	rl
FRIAR frier; frate; wandering monk	rl
FRIED simmered	
FRILL ruffle; border; mannerism	
FRISK romp; search; flisk	
FRITH firth; forest; peace	
FRITO crisp tortilla chip (Mex.)	
FRITZ a German	
FRIZZ to curl; to crisp	
FROCK smock; costume	
FROND fern leaf	bt
FRONS part of skull	md
FRONT van; face; assurance	
FRORE flory; frozen (Spens.)	
FROST rime; iciness; a failure	
FROTH spume; foam; effervesce	
FROWN glower; scowl	
FROWY rank; musty	
FROZE became ice	
FRUIT produce; crop; issue	bt
FRUMP a joke; dowdy woman	
FRUSH brittle; broken; thrush	
FRYER a frying pan	
FUBBY } fat and squat;	
FUBSY } chubby	
FUCUS dye; disguise; seaweed	bt
FUDER large wine cask (Moselle)	ck
FUDGE fake; nonsense; sweetmeat	ck

FUERO statute; charter (Sp.)	lw
FUFFY fluffy; soft; downy	
FUGAL like a fugue	mu
FUGIE a runaway; a coward (Sc.)	
FUGLE to act as ringleader	
FUGUE } polyphonic composition	mu
FUGUE } escape from sanity	pc
FULLY amply; entirely; completely	
FUMET bone/veg. essence for sauce; deer dung	mh
FUMID smoky; vaporous	
FUNDI a West African grain	bt
FUNGI mushrooms; toadstools, etc.	bt
FUNIS umbilical cord	md
FUNKY nervous; timid; cowardly	
FUNNY droll; comical; boat	nt
FURCA forked structure	zo
FUROR wave of enthusiasm	
FURRY incrusted	
FURZE gorse; whin	
FURZY whinny	
FUSED melted; merged; blended	
FUSEE vesuvian; firelock fuzee	
FUSIL fusible; a musket	
FUSSY fidgety; bustling	
FUSTY musty; rank; mouldy	
FUZED provided with a fuze	
FUZEE fusee	nt
FUZZY woolly; shaggy; blurred	
FYTTE fitte; song; ballad	

G

GABEL excise duty; salt tax (Fr. obs.)	
GABLE roof/window construction	ar
GADGE instrument of torture	
GADUS the cod genus	zo
GAFFE a social solecism	
GAGED pledged; pawned; engaged	
GAGER gauger	
GAILY gayly; blithely; lively	
GAIZE friable sandstone	be
GALAH Australian cockatoo	zo
GALBE elegant sweep; contour	ar
GALEA helmet-shaped	bt
GALLY like gall; scare; daze	
GALON scalloped-edge narrow lace	tx
GALOP lively round dance	
GAMBA a viol	mu
GAMBE leg (often animal)	zo
GAMED gambled; hazarded; wagered	
GAMIC sexual	
GAMIN urchin (Fr.)	
GAMMA kind of radioactive ray	
GAMUT range; scope	me
GANCH Turkish form of execution	
GANIL limestone	mn
GANJA Indian drink made of hemp	
GANZA a wild goose	zo
GAPED wide open; yawned	
GAPPY crannied	
GARNI vegetables added to a dish	ck

GARRY Indian carriage		
GARTH fish-weir; yard; garden		
GARUM fish sauce		
GASSY gaseous; aerated		
GATED confined		
GAUCY gawsy; buxom; jolly (Sc.)		
GAUDY garish; tawdry; flashy		
GAUGE estimate; measure	to	
GAULT clay	mn	
GAUMY dauby; smeary		
GAUNT lean; lanky; emaciated		
GAUSS unit of magnetic intensity	me	
GAUZE transparent fabric		
GAUZY filmy		
GAVEL mason's hammer; mallet	to	
GAVEL sheaf of corn		
GAVOT gavotte; a dance		
GAWKY awkward; ungainly; clumsy		
GAYAL wild ox	zo	
GAYER merrier; brighter		
GAZED looked intently		
GAZEL gazelle	zo	
GAZER starer; rubber-neck		
GAZON turf (Fr.)		
GEACH a thief; to steal (slang)		
GECKO lizard	zo	
GECOM automatic computer code		
GEESE plural of goose	zo	
GEEST alluvial deposit		
GEIST mental drive		
GELID cold; freezing		
GEMEL twin; coupled vessels/bottles		
GEMMA leaf-bud	bt	
GEMMY glittering		
GEMOT moot; assembly (obs.)		
GENET civet-cat fur		
GENIE jinee; Arabian sprite		
GENII men of ingenuity		
GENIO ingenious person (It.)		
GENOA a cake		
GENOM gamete nucleus chromosome content	gn	
GENRE specialty; type of painting	pt	
GENRO Japanese elder statesmen		
GENTY graceful (Sc.)		
GENUS group of a species	zo	
GENYS lower jaw in vertebrates	zo	
GEODE crystalline cavity	mn	
GEOID the figure of the earth		
GERAH twentieth of a shekel	nm	
GERBE sheaf; firework (Fr.)		
GESSO stucco; plaster		
GESTE generous action		
GET-UP style of dress		
GHAUT Indian mountain pass		
GHAZI Arab fanatic; conqueror		
GHOST spook; spectre; phantom		
GHOUL a gruesome fiend		
GHYLL goyal; ravine; gully		
GIANT Cyclops; colossus; huge		
GIBBE a worn-out animal (Shak.)		

GIBED jibed; taunted; jeered	nt	
GIBEL Prussian carp	zo	
GIBER scoffer; joker; derider		
GIBUS an opera hat		
GIDDY dizzy; fickle; mutable		
GIGOT jigot; leg of mutton (Fr.)		
GIGUE lively tune	mu	
GILLY gillie; keeper (Sc.)		
GILPY a tom-boy (Sc.)		
GIPSY gypsy; zingaro		
GIRTH girdle; thong; cinch		
GISMO gadget, thing (slang)		
GIUST joust (Spens.)		
GIVEN presented; conceded		
GIVER bestower; donor; granter		
GIVES gyves; fetters; bonds		
GLACE polished; sugar-surfaced		
GLADE woodland avenue		
GLAIK trick (Sc.)		
GLAIR white of egg; varnish		
GLAND a secretory organ	md	
GLARE glower; frown; glitter		
GLARY dazzling; lustrous		
GLASS mirror; telescope; tumbler		
GLAUM to grasp eagerly (Sc.)		
GLAUR glower (Sc.)		
GLAUX sea milkwort	bt	
GLAVE glaive; kind of halbert		
GLAZE lustre; burnish; (windows)		
GLAZY shiny; filmy		
GLEAD glede; buzzard; kite	zo	
GLEAM ray; beam; glimmer; shine		
GLEAN cull; collect; harvest		
GLEBA spore-bearing tissue in truffles	bt	
GLEBE sod; church land	rl	
GLEBY turfy; cloddy		
GLEDE glead; buzzard; kite	zo	
GLEED glowing ember		
GLEEK three-handed card game		
GLEET ooze (Sc.); inflammation	md	
GLIDE slide; slip; skim; flow		
GLIFF glift; an alarm (Sc.)		
GLINT gleam; a flash		
GLISK a glimpse (Sc.)		
GLIST glimmer; mica	mn	
GLOAM to darken		
GLOAT exult; crow; revel		
GLOBE orb; sphere; ball; earth		
GLOBY spherical		
GLOME globular head of flowers	bt	
GLOOM sadness; depression; darkness		
GLORY exult; honour; renown		
GLOSS comment; polish; veil		
GLOUT to be sulky		
GLOVE gauntlet; mitten		
GLOZE wheedle; flattery; adulation		
GLUED stuck together; adhered		
GLUER a user of mucilage		
GLUEY adhesive; viscous; glutinous		
GLUGG, GLÖGG mulled wine (Scand.)	ck	
GLUME husks	bt	

GLYPH vertical fluting	
GNARL snarl; growl; grumble	
GNARR a knot in wood; a snag	
GNASH to grind the teeth	
GNOME dwarf; a maxim	
GOBBO okra; a fruit	bt
GODET small glass reel	tx
GODET gore/gusset to make a dress flare	
GODLY holy; pious; devout	rl
GOETY black magic	
GOFER gauffre; wafer	
GOING wending; faring; elapsing	
GOLDY goldfinch	zo
GOLLY exclamation	
GONAD reproductive gland	pl
GONAL forming a gonad	zo
GONER irretrievably lost	
GOODS chattels; effects	
GOODY a sweet	
GOOSE tailor's iron; poultry bird	to, zo
GORAL Indian antelope	zo
GORED (bull-fighting); (tailoring)	
GORGE gulch; defile; gulp; cram	
GORSE whin	bt
GORSY abounding in gorse	
GOUDA a Dutch cheese	
GOUGE scoop; circular chisel	to
GOURA a pigeon genus	zo
GOURD drinking cup; (cucumber)	bt
GOUTY swollen; boggy	md
GOWAN a daisy	bt
GOYAL ghyll; kloof; combe	
GRAAL Holy Grail; sacred cup	rl
GRACE adorn; embellish; favour	
GRADE step; rank; slope; degree	
GRAFF graft; ditch; moat	
GRAFT intrigue; swindle; engraft	
GRAIL Holy Grail; sacred cup	rl
GRAIN corn; seed; grist	bt, me
GRAIP dung-fork	to
GRAMA pasture land (USA)	
GRAME gram; misery	
GRAND lordly; 1,000 dollars	nm
GRANT cede; confer; gift; largess	
GRAPE fruit of the vine	bt
GRAPH a diagram	
GRAPY like a grape	
GRASP clasp; clutch; hold; scope	
GRASS herbage; pasture; to turf	bt
GRATE abrade; rasp; jar; fireplace	
GRAVE solemn; engrave; tomb	
GRAVY meat juice	
GRAZE skim; browse; touch lightly	
GREAT eminent; bulky; huge	
GREBE web-footed bird	zo
GRECE grize; steps; staircase	
GREED voracity; avidity; gluttony	
GREEK Attic; Doric; Hellenic	
GREEN raw; fresh; inexperienced	
GREEN verdant; (village); (golf)	
GREES grece; steps; stairway	

GREET cry; weep; lament (Sc.); hail	
GREIT greet; weep; cry	
GREYS cavalry regiment	
GRIAS species of pear	bt
GRICE young wild boar	zo
GRIDE gryde; grate; pierce	
GRIEF woe; anguish; mishap	
GRIKE limestone-rock fissure	gl
GRILL broil; grid-iron; question	
GRIME dirt; soil; sully; befoul	
GRIMY filthy; smutty; unclean	
GRIND abrade; pulverize; sharpen	
GRIPE grasp; squeeze; ditch	
GRIST corn; provision	
GRITS coarse oatmeal (Sc.)	
GRIZE grece; grees; staircase	
GROAN moan; complain; grumble	
GROAT Joey; fourpenny piece	nm
GROCK a kindly clown	
GROIN sea-wall; side of body	mc
GROOM syce; equerry; bridegroom	
GROPE search by feeling	
GROSS coarse; 12 dozen	me
GROUP clump; cluster; arrange	
GROUT coarse meal; mortar	
GROVE wood; thicket; spinney	
GROWL snarl; grumble; complain	
GROWN raised; waxed; extended	
GRUEL thin porridge	
GRUFF surly; rude; churlish	
GRUNT snort like a pig	
GRYDE gride; grate	
GUACO plant; snake-bite antidote	bt
GUANA American lizard	ze
GUANO sea-fowl's manure	
GUARD shield; watch; bulwark	
GUAVA pear-shaped fruit	bt
GUESS surmise; conjecture; divine	
GUEST visitor; lodger	
GUIDE pilot; signpost; control	
GUILD trade's union; fraternity	
GUILE craft; duplicity; cunning	
GUILT proof or sense of wrong	lw
GUIRD Cuban instrument	mu
GUISE garb; aspect; manner	
GULAR (throat)	
GULCH gully; gorge; ravine	
GULES heraldic red	he
GULFY full of whirlpools	
GULLY water-worn channel; (cricket)	
GUMBO a stew; okra soup	
GUMMY viscous, sticky	
GUNGE market, granary (Ind.)	
GUNNY Bengal sacking	
GURGE whirlpool (obs.)	
GURRY fish-offal; Ind. fortress	
GUSTO zest; relish; enjoyment	
GUSTY squally; stormy; puffy	
GUTTA Doric ornament; drop	a
GUTTY old type golf ball	
GUYED mocked; ridiculed; derided	

GUYOT submarine mountain	
GYALL gayal; jungle bull	zo
GYBED (a sailing manoeuvre)	nt
GYGIS tern genus (water birds)	zo
GYPSY gipsy; zingaro	
GYRAL revolving; whirling	
GYRON heraldic device	hd
GYRUS convolution of the brain	md
GYVES bonds; fetters; shackles	

H

HABIT dress; usage; wont; custom	
HABLE habile; able (Spens.)	
HADES the abode of the dead	
HADJI pilgrim (Arab); hajji	
HAFIZ knowledge of the Koran	
HAICK Arab wrap	
HAIKH an Armenian	
HAILY apt to hail; icy	
HAIRY vairy; furry	
HAJIB Moslem court chamberlain	
HAJJI hadji; pilgrim (Arab)	
HAKIM wise man; physician (Arab)	
HALED hauled; dragged along	
HALFA esparto grass	bt
HALLO! hello! hillo!	
HALMA a game	
HALVA ground sesame sweetmeat	
HALVE bisect; divide	
HAMAL porter, male servant (Turk.)	
HANAP pewter goblet	
HANCE haunch	ar
HANCH to snap	
HANDY near; dexterous; adroit	
HANIF orthodox Moslem	
HANKY handkerchief	
HANSA a league (German)	
HAPLY perchance; peradventure	
HAPPY joyous; lucky; opportune	
HARAS stud; breeding establishment	
HARDS hurds; refuse of flax	
HARDY bold; intrepid; robust	
HARED sprinted; sped; ran	
HAREM seraglio; zenana	
HARLE harl; flax-fibre	
HARPE spinelike insect structure	zo
HARPY fabulous monster; vulture	zo
HARPY golden eagle; extortioner	zo
HARRY harass; ravage; raid	
HARSH raucous; strident; caustic	
HASTE alacrity; speed; hustle	
HASTY swift; reckless; headlong	
HATCH to plot; doorway; to shade	
HATED loathed; abominated	
HATER abhorrer; detester	
HATHI wild Indian elephants	zo
HATTO bishop eaten by rats	
HAULM halm; stubble	bt
HAUNT frequent; importune; resort	
HAURL harl; rough-cast	

HAUSA Northern Nigerian	
HAVAS news-agency	
HAVEN port; refuge; asylum	
HAVER to drivel; blather	
HAVOC waste; carnage; devastation	
HAWSE part of ship's bows	nt
HAZED bullied; punished	
HAZEL a colour; nut-tree	bt
HAZRI Indian breakfast	
HEADS or tails; latrines	nt
HEADY rash; hasty; wilful	
HEADY intoxicating	
HEALD warp guide in a loom	
HEAPY in piles	
HEARD listened to; tried	lw
HEART core; centre; spirit	
HEATH shrubs; common land	bt
HEAVE to raise; push; haul	nt
HEAVY weighty, serious	
HEDGE lay off; enclose; fence	
HEFTY heavy; strong; powerful	
HEIGH! exclamation	
HEKIM judge (Arab.)	
HELIO a heliograph	
HELIX screwthread form; snail	zo
HELLO! hallo! hillo! hollo!	
HELOT Spartan slave; serf	
HELVE axe-handle; haft	
HEMAL haemal; (blood)	md
HE-MAN butch; virile	
HEMPY like hemp	
HENCE henceforth; away; therefore	
HENCH chimney shaft side	bd
HENNA a dye; a shrub	bt
HENRY electrical induction unit	me
HEPAR a sulphur compound	ch
HERBY herbaceous; herbous	
HEROD a tyrant	
HERON a wading bird	zo
HERSE a portcullis	
HERTZ unit of electrical frequency	me
HERUT political party (Israel)	
HET-UP hot and bothered, aroused	
HEVEA rubber-tree	
HEWED axed; hacked; fashioned	
HEWER cutter; sculptor; miner	
HIDER one who conceals	
HIGHT hecht; to command; to call	
HIKED tramped	
HIKER rambler; pedestrian	
HILCH to hobble; a limp (Sc.)	
HILLY undulating	
HILUM the eye of a bean	bt
HINDI Indian dialect	
HINDU devotee of Ind. religion	
HINGE depend; turn; hang	
HINNY whinny; a mule	zo
HIPPO the river-horse	zo
HIRED chartered; leased; rented	
HIRER an employer of labour	
HITCH fasten; catch; obstacle; knot	

HITHE hythe; haven; port
HIVED stored; gathered
HIVER an apiarist
HIVES the croup; nettle-rash   md
HOARD amass; garner; save; secrete
HOARY venerable; ancient; silvery
HOAST a cough; to cough
HOBBY recreation; horse; falcon   zo
HOBIT mortar; short gun
HOCUS to cheat; to drug
HODGE a rustic
HOGAN strong liquor
HOIST hoise; heave; elevate
HOLEY holed; riddled
HOLLY an evergreen   bt
HOMER homing pigeon   zo
HOMER guide signal arrangement
HONED whetted; sharpened
HONEY sweetness
HOOCH fire-water
HOOEY, HOO-HA balderdash
HOOKA hookah; Turkish pipe
HOOKY full of barbs
HOOLY carefully; softly (Sc.)
HOOSH a stew; a mixture
HOOVE a cattle disease   vt
HOPED desired; anticipated
HOPPO Chinese overseer
HOPPY flavoured with hops
HORAL horary; hourly
HORDE clan; throng; gang; crew
HORNY callous
HORSE steed; palfrey; nag; cob   zo
HORSE cavalry; flogging frame
HORSY horsey; equine
HORUS son of Osiris (Egypt)
HOSED drenched; watered
HOTEL inn; tavern; hostel
HOTLY eagerly; ardently; fervidly
HOUGH hamstring; the ham
HOUND pursue; chase; hunting dog   zo
HOURI a nymph of paradise; peri
HOUSE mansion; domicile; lineage
HOVEL shelter; hut; cabin; shed
HOVER hang; vacillate; wave
HOWDY a midwife (Sc.); howdie
HOWEL cooper's tool   to
HOWFF houff; a haunt; resort (Sc.)
HOWSO howsoever; although
HUBBY husband
HUFFY petulant; irritable
HULCH hunch; bump; bunch
HULKY unwieldy; clumsy
HULLO! hallo!
HULLY husky
HUMAN mortal; cosmic; rational
HUMET abbreviated fesse   hd
HUMIC wet; dank; mouldy
HUMID damp; moist
HUMPH! exclamation of dissatisfaction
HUMPY Australian native hut

HUMUS rich soil
HUNCH presentiment; hump; lump
HUNKS miser; niggard
HUNYA fighting rams   zo
HURDS hards; flax refuse
HURLY confusion; flurry
HURRY hasten; expedite; speed
HURST a grove; a wood
HUSKY Canadian sled-dog   zo
HUSKY hoarse; raucous; guttural
HUSSY housewife; brazen girl
HUTCH coop; chest; bin
HUTIA West Indian hog-rat   zo
HUZZA also hurra
HYADS hyades; cluster of stars
HYDRA water monster; source of trouble
HYDRO a spa; a hotel
HYENA hyen; a carnivore   zo
HYLEG ruling planet in horoscope
HYLIC materialistic
HYMEN God of Marriage   rl
HYMEN maidenhead; vaginal membrane   pl
HYOID tongue-bone   md
HYPHA a fungus filament
HYRAX rock-rabbit; cony   zo
HYSON green tea (China)   bt
HYTHE hithe; haven; port

I

ICENI Ancient British tribe
ICHOR a god's blood; a fluid   md
ICIER colder
ICILY frigidly; frostily
ICING a sugar-coating
ICKER an ear of corn (Sc.)   bt
ICTIC abrupt; sudden
ICTUS a stroke; accentuation
IDEAL Utopian; fanciful; visionary
IDIOM peculiarity of phraseology
IDIOT Gothamite; Bedlamite; moron
IDIST Ido linguist
IDLED slacked
IDLER drone; lounger; trifler
IDOLA fantasies; apparitions
IDOSE monosaccharide
IDRIS mythical Welsh giant; (water)
IDYLL pastoral poem
IGLOO Eskimo snow-hut
ILEAC colicky; iliac   md
ILEUM (intestine)   md
ILEUS intestinal obstruction, colic   md
ILIAC pertaining to loins
ILIAD epic poem; (siege of Troy)
ILIUM part of hip-bone   md
ILLAM gem-bearing Sri L. gravel   gl
IMAGE ikon; idol; copy; likeness
IMAGO perfect state of insect   zo
IMAUM imam; Islamic priest
IMBAR embar; exclude
IMBAT cool Near-Eastern wind   mt

IMBED embed	
IMBER the great northern diver	zo
IMBOW to arch	
IMBUE dye; steep; stain; permeate	
IMIDE acid anhydride compound	ch
IMMEW emmew; to confine	
IMMIT inject	
IMMIX to mingle	
IMPEL urge; drive; incite; actuate	
IMPEN to pen; to write	
IMPLY mean; hint; signify; involve	
IMPUT input; charge	
INAJA Brazilian palm	bt
INANE fatuous; empty; void; vapid	
INAPT unfit; inapposite; clumsy	
INARM to encircle	
INBYE mine direction	mn
INCOG incognito; disguised	
INCUR contract; gain; acquire	
INCUS ear-bone like an anvil	md
INCUT inset; side note let into text	pr
INDEX pointer; forefinger; exponent	
INDRA Hindu God of Rain	
INDRI babakoto; large lemur	zo
INDUE endue; invest; endow	
INEPT inane; futile; pointless	
INERM without prickles	bt
INERT slack; dull; torpid; inactive	
INEYE to graft	
INFER deduce; gather; surmise	
INFIX implant; ingraft; instil	
INGLE fireside	
INGOT a mass of metal	mn
INION the nape of the neck; occiput	md, pl
INKER recording device	
INKLE broad linen tape	
INKOS Zulu chief	
INLAW c.f. outlaw	
INLAY (buhl); tesselate	
INLET bay; bight; creek; entrance	
INNER interior (next to a bull)	
INPUT c.f. output; charge	
INSET an insertion; implant	
INTER bury; inhume; entomb	
INULA herb	bt
INURE enure; harden; toughen; train	
INURN bury; entomb	
INUUS Barbary ape	zo
INVAR an alloy of nickel and steel	
INWIT intuition; conscience	
IODAL } containing iodine	ch
IODIC }	
IONIC (Ionia)	
IRADE Turkish written decree	lw
IRAQI, IRAKI dwellers in Iraq	
IRATE wroth; ireful; angry; incensed	
IRENE Roman goddess of peace	
IRIAN relating to the iris	md
IRISH Hibernian	
IRITE an iridium compound	mn
IRKED bored; wearied; jaded	

IROKO African utility timber	fr
IRONE smell constituent of violets	ch
IRONS gyves; golf clubs	nt
IRONY satire; sarcasm; mockery	
ISIAC referring to Isis	
ISLAM (Mohammedanism)	rl
ISLET isle; eyot; atoll	
ISSUE egress; vent; outcome; result	
ISTLE } aloe fibre	bt
IXTLE }	
ITCHY scratchy; desirous; uneasy	
IULUS julus; catkin; wireworm	bt, zo
IVIED ivyed; covered with ivy	
IVORY dentine	zo
IVRIT modernised Hebrew (language)	
IXION wheel-bound king; (Hell)	
IZARD Pyrenean ibex or chamois	zo

J

JABOT lace frill; neck ruffle	
JACKS wooden wedges	
JADED weary; tired; fagged; exhausted	
JADOO artificial silk	
JAFFA orange	
JAGER the great skua; pirate gull	zo
JAGGY uneven; serrated; notched	
JALAP a cathartic root	bt, md
JAMBE a piece of leg armour	
JAMBU rose-apple tree	bt
JAMES a flunkey	
JAMMY smothered in jam	
JANTU Indian water-raising device	
JANTY jaunty; airy; showy	
JANUS god of doorways	
JAPAN varnish; lacquer; enamel	
JARDE tumour on a horse's leg	
JASEY worsted wig	
JASPE veined jaspar	mn
JAUNT trip; outing; excursion	
JAWED talked; lectured	
JEANS overalls; denim trousers	tx
JEDGE gauge; dean's warrant (Sc.)	
JEHAD Islamic Holy War	
JELLY gelatin; aspic	
JEMMY gemmy; spruce; lever	to
JENNY spinning machine; billiard shot	
JERID Turkish javelin	
JERKY spasmodic; convulsive; irregular	
JERKY beef biltong	ck
JERRY a German	
JESSE candlestick; stained window	rl
JETTY jut; projection; a pier	nt
JEWEL gem; trinket	
JEWRY Judaea; the Jews	
JHEEL Indian marsh	
JHOOM jungle cultivation	
JIBED gibed; sneered; taunted	nt
JIFFY a moment; an instant	
JIMMY jemmy; a lever	to
JIMPY, JINTY slender; elegant (Sc.)	

JINGO ultra-militarist		
JINKS high jinks; merry-making		
JIPPO jupon; vest		
JOCKO a chimpanzee	zo	
JODEL yodel; Tyrolese singing	mu	
JOINT splice; seam; united; concerted		
JOIST floor beam		
JOKED bantered; rallied		
JOKER jester; wag; humorist; a card		
JOLLY a marine; mirthful; a boat	nt	
JONAH bad luck bringer		
JORAM⎫ drinking bowl or its contents		
JORUM⎭		
JORIA East Indian wool	tx	
JOTUN Norse giant		
JOUGS iron neck-ring; pillory		
JOULE electrical unit of work	me	
JOUST giust; tilt; encounter; a tourney		
JUDAS traitor; spy-hole; tree	bt	
JUDGE decide; arbiter; critic	lw	
JUGAL malar; (cheek-bone)	pl	
JUGUM pair of opposite leaves	bt	
JUICE sap; fluid extract; petrol		
JUICY succulent; moist; lush		
JULAP⎫ sweet medicine;		
JULEP⎭ mixed liquor	md	
JULIS a wrasse; a small fish	zo	
JULUS iulus; catkin; wire-worm	zo, bt	
JUMBO elephant; locomotive	zo	
JUMPY nervous; nervy		
JUNCO North American snow-bird	zo	
JUNTA Spanish Grand Council; cabal		
JUNTO coterie; clique; faction		
JUPON jippo; surcoat; petticoat		
JURAL legal; lawful		
JURAT an alderman; (affidavit)	lw	
JUROR a juryman		
JUSSI Manila textile fabric	tx	
JUTES invaders from Jutland		
JUTTY a jetty		
JUXTA sclerotized support in lepidoptera		

K

KAABA caaba; sacred stone at Mecca		
KAAMA hartebeest; S. Afr. antelope	zo	
KABOB, KEBAB meat on skewer	ck	
KADIR (cup for pig-sticking)		
KAFIR Kaffir		
KALAN sea otter of North Pacific	zo	
KALIF Calif; Caliph		
KALPA calpa; a day of Brahma	rl	
KAMES glacial deposits	mn	
KAMIS Eastern tunic		
KANDY candy; S. Indian weight	me	
KANEH caneh; 6 cubits (Hebrew)	me	
KANYA Afr. shea tree; its butter		
KAPOK fibre of silk-cotton tree		
KAPUR Indonesian wood	fr	
KARMA destiny based on each incarnation		
KAROB 24th part of a grain	me	

KAROO South African plateau		
KARRI dense Australian wood; tree	fr	
KARST limestone caves (Yugoslavia)		
KASHA dress material		
KASHA cracked-buckwheat meal (Rus.)	ck	
KASSU catechu made from betel-nut	bt	
KAURI New Zealand fir tree	bt	
KAYAK, KAIAK Eskimo sealskin canoe		
KAYLE ninepin; skittle		
KEBAB meat dish (Turk.)	ck	
KECKS fool's parsley	bt	
KEDGE small anchor	nt	
KEDGE kidge; brisk; lively		
KEDGY cadgy; happy; merry; wanton		
KEEPS permanent possession		
KEESH carburet of iron	mn	
KEEVE vat; fermenting tub		
KEFIR fermented milk		
KELAT short springy Asian wool	tx	
KELLY top pipe of drill string	mn	
KELPY malignant water-sprite (Sc.)		
KELTY a penalty drink (Sc.)		
KEMPS the plantain		
KERNE Irish foot-soldier; boor		
KETCH two-masted vessel	nt	
KETEN colourless gas	ch	
KEVEL belaying pin	nt	
KEVEL young gazelle	zo	
KEYED wedged		
KEYER frequency-change device	tc	
KHAKI olive-drab; army uniform colour		
KHEDA elephant enclosure		
KHMER people and language (Cambodia)		
KIANG Tibetan wild horse	zo	
KIBED chapped with cold		
KIDDY youngster		
KIDEL kiddle; fish-trap		
KIDGE kedge; brisk; pot-bellied		
KILEY kyley; boomerang		
KILIM woven carpet without pile (Turk.)		
KINGS two Biblical books		
KININ plant hormone; quinine	bc	
KINKY crotchety; entangled		
KINSH stone-mason's lever	to	
KIOSK covered stall		
KITTY pool; kitten	zo	
KLANG complex musical tone	mu	
KLICK click		
KLOOF S. African ravine		
KNACK skill; dexterity; faculty		
KNARL gnarl; a knot in wood		
KNAUR swollen tree-trunk outgrowth	bt	
KNAVE rascal; rogue; caitiff		
KNEAD mix; blend; incorporate		
KNEED baggy		
KNEEL bend knee, submit		
KNELL toll; ring; sound		
KNEPH an Egyptian deity		
KNIFE to stab; to lance	to	
KNOCK rap; beat; buffet		
KNOLL knell; hillock; mound		

KNOSP ornamental flower-bud
KNOTE (rope-making)
KNOUD the grey gurnard　　zo
KNOUT Russian whip
KNOWN understood; recognized
KNUBS waste silk
KNURL knob; milled edge
KNURR knot in wood
KOALA Australian bear　　zo
KOBIL cobble; small boat　　nt
KOFTE, KOFTA meat rissole　　ck
KOKOB venomous serpent　　zo
KOKRA wood used for flutes　　bt
KONDO bronze-gilt finish
KOPEC kopek; Russian farthing　　nm
KOPJE S. African hill
KORAN Moslem Bible　　rl
KOTOW kow-tow; make obeisance
KRAAL native village
KRAIT venomous snake　　zo
KRANG kreng; whale flesh
KRILL plankton; whale food　　bt, zo
KRONE Scandinavian coin　　nm
KRUPP a gun
KUDOS credit; prestige; fame
KUFIC early Arab alphabet
KUKRI Gurkha knife
KULAK Russian peasant proprietor
KUNDA lawyer-vine　　bt
KUTCH cutch; catechu　　bt
KVASS Russian beer
KWELA tin whistle (African)
KYACK American pack saddle
KYLEY kiley; boomerang
KYLIN Chinese or Japanese dragon
KYLIX Greek drinking vessel
KYLOE Hebridean cattle　　zo
KYOTO Japanese pottery
KYPOO extract of catechu
KYRIE (Mass)　　rl, mu

L

LABEL an adhesive stamp　　hd
LABEL dripstone; codicil
LABIS cochlear; eucharistic spoon　　rl
LACED stiffened; twined
LACET lace-work
LACIS filet lace; network
LADAS a classic runner
LADED burdened; loaded
LADEN freighted
LADIN Swiss Latin
LADLE scoop; bale; dole
LAGAN ligan (flotsam)　　lw
LAGER beer
LAINE woollen fabric
LAIRD Scottish landowner
LAITY laymen
LAKIN ladykin; small damsel
LAMED crippled

LAMIA sorceress; witch
LAMMY sailor's quilted jumper
LANCE lancet; spear; pierce
LANCH launch
LANDE sterile tract (Fr.)
LANKY lean; tall; gaunt
LAPEL part of a coat
LAPIS stone; (calico-printing)　　mn
LAPSE slip; slide; indiscretion
LARCH genus of trees　　bt
LARDY full of lard
LARES Roman household gods
LARGE massive; bulky; copious
LARGO slowly　　mu
LARKY sportive; frolicsome
LARRY lorry; truck
LARRY mortar-mixing tool　　to
LARUM alarm
LARUS aquatic bird　　zo
LARVA caterpillar; grub; maggot　　zo
LASER resin; searing ray　　md
LASSO rope with running noose
LATCH catch; fasten
LATER tardier; more recent
LATEX sap; untreated rubber　　bt
LATHE county division; machine　　to
LATHI bamboo cudgel
LATHY thin; long and slender
LATIN Roman
LAUGH deride; guffaw
LAURA a hermitage
LAUTA royal Inca badge
LAVED washed; bathed
LAVER brazen washing basin
LAVER edible seaweed　　bt
LAXLY loosely; slackly; remissly
LAY-BY halting place beside road
LAYER seam; stratum; bed; hen　　zo
LAZAR leper
LAZED tranquillized
LEACH to wash by percolation
LEADY leaden
LEAFY leavy; full of leaves
LEAKY not watertight; tattling
LEANT inclined; reposed; trusted
LEAPT jumped; sprang
LEARN acquire; hear; memorize
LEARY old mine-shaft
LEASE let; hire; tenure
LEASH three; bind; thong
LEAST smallest; minutest
LEAVE forsake; quit; depart
LEAVY leafy
LEDGE shelf; ridge; layer
LEDGY full of ridges
LEECH blood-sucker; doctor　　zo
LEECH edge of a sail　　nt
LEERY sly
LEGAL lawful; licit; proper
LEGER a race; light; small
LEGGY lanky

LEMAN lover; gallant; paramour
LEMMA grass glume; subsidiary theorem   bt, ma
LEMMA summary preceding a tome
LEMON citrus fruit; the answer   bt, ck
LEMUR ghost; nocturnal monkey   zo
LENCA Honduran Indian
LENTO slowly   mu
LEPER lazar   md
LEPID jocose; pleasant
LEPIS a scale   zo
LEPRA leprosy   md
LEPTA (Greece)   nm
LESTE dry African South wind   mt
LETCH to separate by percolation
LETHE the river of oblivion
LET-IN admission; note added to text
LET-UP an alleviation
LEVAN polymerized grass fructose   ch
LEVEE embankment; reception
LEVEL raze; plane; even; flush
LEVER a jemmy; prise   to
LEWIS a grip for masonry
LIANA tropical climbing plant   bt
LIANE woody jungle climber   bt
LIANG Chinese ounce   me
LIART liard; lyart; dapple-grey
LIBEL slander; defame; traduce   lw
LIBER bast; inner bark; a book
LIBRA the Balance (Zodiac)
LICIT lawful; permissible
LIDAR cloud pattern detector   mt
LIEGE one bound by oath
LIFER prisoner sentenced for life
LIGAN lagan; (flotsam)   lw
LIGHT kindle; illume; buoyant
LIGNE watch-movement measure unit   hr
LIKED enjoyed; relished
LIKEN to compare
LIKIN Chinese transport duty
LILAC a colour; a shrub   bt
LIMBO hell; paradise of fools
LIMED cemented; ensnared; treated
LIMEN threshold   pc
LIMER fibre brush for limewashing
LIMIT restraint; bound; border
LIMMA a semitone   mu
LINCH ledge; projection; cliff
LINED care-worn; with lines
LINEN flax cloth; underwear
LINER a shim; a vessel; layer of paint   nt
LINGO speech; language
LINGO jacquard harness weight   wv
LINGY active; limber; heathery
LININ (cell nucleus)
LINKS (cuff); golf course
LIPID living-tissue fat/wax   ch
LIPPY half-a-gallon (Sc.)   me
LISLE thread
LISSE warp threads in tapestry
LISTS the combat-ground

LITAS Lithuanian currency unit   nm
LITHE ⎫ lythe; active; supple; pliant;
LITHY ⎭ pliable; easily bent; limber
LITHO a lithograph
LITRE nearly $1\frac{3}{4}$ pints   me
LIVED dwelt; abode; survived
LIVEN enliven; animate; vivify
LIVER internal organ   md
LIVID ghastly pale
LIVRE old French franc   nm
LLAMA Peruvian camel   zo
LLANO S. American plain
LOACH loche; a river-fish   zo
LOAMY soil
LOATH reluctant; unwilling
LOBAR, LOBED lobate   bt, md
LOBBY passage; to seek votes
LOCAL an inn; topical; regional
LOCHE a loach; a river-fish   zo
LOCUM locum tenens; a deputy
LOCUS locality
LODAR special loran system, radar   nv
LODGE reside; sojourn; deposit
LOESS alluvial deposits
LOFTY stately; imposing; towering
LOGAN poised rock; a berry   bt
LOGGE miller's thumb; small fish   zo
LOGIA oracles; dicta
LOGIC reasoning; dialectics
LOGIE sham jewels
LOGON provision for new group to be added
LOGOS the Divine Word
LOKAL tavern, club, assembly place
LOKUM Turkish delight (sweetmeat)   ck
LOLLY lollipop; a lump; money
LOLOS aboriginal race (China)
LOOFA luffa; flesh-brush   bt
LOONY mad; lunatic
LOOPY kinky; dotty
LOOSE liberate; slack; vague; lax
LOPED ran with easy strides
LORAN radio-navigation system   nt
LORDS cricket ground
LORIS Cingalese monkey   zo
LORRY larry; truck; vehicle
LORUM mandibular plates in hemiptera   zo
LOSER also ran; (billiards)
LOSSY of energy-dissipating equipment
LOTIC of running water   ec
LOTTO a game
LOTUS lotos; water lily   bt
LOUGH loch; an arm of the sea
LOUIS obsolete French gold coin   nm
LOUSE parasitic insect   zo
LOUSY mean; louse infested
LOVAT a tweed
LOVED adored; liked; esteemed
LOVER a Romeo; admirer; swain
LOWER depress; degrade; frown
LOWLY meek; humble; modest
LOXIA cross-bill birds   zo

LOYAL leal; true; devoted
LUBRA black woman (Australia)
LUCID clear; limpid; sane; pure
LUCKY fortunate; auspicious
LUCRE gain; profit; wealth
LUGER automatic pistol
LUMEN unit of luminous flux   me
LUMPY coagulated
LUNAR of the moon
LUNCH luncheon
LUNGE, LONGE thrust; (equitation)
LUNIK artificial moon satellite
LUPIN a flower   bt
LUPPA cloth of gold or silver
LUPUS skin disease   md
LURCH stagger; sway; roll; toss
LURED enticed; decoyed; inveigled
LURID glowing; sensational
LUSHY tipsy
LUSTY robust; vigorous; sturdy
LUSUS a freak; an exception
LUTED sealed with luting
LUTER lute-player   mu
LYART liart; liard; dapple-grey
LYASE double-bonding enzyme
LYCEE French school
LYING mendacious; recumbent
LYMPH a fluid; vaccine   md
LYNCH mob law; kill
LYRIC a short poem; tuneful
LYRID meteor from Lyra
LYRIE Manx shearwater gull   zo
LYSIN disintegratory antibody   md
LYSIS recovery   md
LYSSA hydrophobia; rabies
LYTHE the pollack   zo
LYTHE lithe; flexible; agile
LYTIC pertaining to lysis   md
LYTTA rod of tongue cartilage   zo

M

MACAW parrot; palm   zo, bt
MACER a court usher   lw
MACHE materials for papier maché
MACLE double crystal   mn
MACON French wine
MADAM madame
MADGE leaden hammer; magpie   zo
MADIA the tar-weed; oil-plant   bt
MADID moist; wet; damp
MADLY deliriously; insanely
MAFIA Sicilian secret society
MAFIC non-felsic material in igneous rock
MAGAR Indian crocodile   zo
MAGAS stringed-instrument bridge   mu
MAGIC witchery; sorcery; charm
MAGMA plutonic rock   mn
MAGOG legendary figure; giant
MAGOT Barbary ape   zo

MAHDI Moslem prophet (dervish)   rl
MAHWA butter-tree   bt
MAIZE Indian corn   bt
MAJOR a rank; greater
MAKER creator; manufacturer
MAKWA Chinese jacket   md
MALAR cheek-bone
MALAX soften by kneading/diluting
MALAY of Malaysia
MALIC (apples)   bt
MALIK village headman (Ind.)
MALTY malt-flavoured
MAMBA S. African snake   zo
MAMBO dance   mu
MAMMA mother
MAMMY negro nurse
MANAL pertaining to the hand
MANEB chemical fungicide   ch
MANED having a mane
MANEH mina; 50 shekels   nm
MANES ghosts; departed souls
MANET stage direction 'remain'
MANGA covering for a cross
MANGE parasitic disease   md
MANGO a fruit   bt
MANGY scabrous
MANIA frenzy; delirium; craziness
MANIS the scaly ant-eater   zo
MANLY hardy; intrepid; bold
MANNA food; a form of sap   bt
MANOR freehold estate
MANSE the minister's house (Sc.)
MANTA ox-ray; a sea-fish   zo
MANUS the hand   md
MANUS fore-limb podium   zo
MAORI native race (N. Zealand)
MAPLE sugar-tree   bt
MAQUI Chilian evergreen shrub   bt
MARAH bitterness (Hebrew)
MARAY moray; muray; eel-like fish   zo
MARCH border; advance; walk
MARDY spoilt; naughty
MARGE brink; brim; verge; edge
MARIA lunar seas   as
MARID powerful jinn
MARLY clay-like
MARRY unite; wed; espouse; join
MARSH bog; swamp; fen; morass
MASAI African tribe
MASER micro-wave amplifier   el
MASHY mashie; a golf club
MASON stone-worker
MASSA master
MASSE a billiard stroke
MASSY massive; bulky
MASTY full of beech-mast   bt
MATCH suit; tally; agree; lucifer
MATED (chess); married; matched
MATER mother
MATEY friendly
MATIN morning

MATTE crude black copper	mn	**MIASM** miasma; effluvia	md
MATZO thin unleavened Passover bread	ck	**MICHE** hide; skulk; pilfer	
MAULS marsh mallow	bt	**MICKY** Irish lad; young bull	zo
MAUND an Eastern weight	me	**MIDAS** had a golden touch	
MAUVE a mallow colour		**MIDDY** a midshipman	nt
MAVIS the thrush	zo	**MIDGE** dwarf; gnat	zo
MAWKY crotchety; maudlin		**MID-ON** (cricket)	
MAXIM gun; adage; saw; precept		**MIDST** among; middle	
MAYAN native of Honduras		**MIGHT** force; power; main	
MAYBE perhaps		**MILCH** giving milk	
MAYOR town chief		**MILER** a mile runner	
MAZDA Supreme Deity (Zend-Avesta)		**MILKY** lacteal; lactic	
MAZED bewildered; dazed; astounded		**MIMED** mimicked; acted	
MAZER goblet; bowl		**MIMIC** ape; copy; mime; mock	
MEALY farinaceous		**MINCE** chop fine; palliate	
MEANS mode; agency; method; wealth		**MINED** dug; undermined	
MEANT signified; purposed		**MINER** sapper	
MEASE a group of 500	me	**MINIE** old type rifle	
MEATY fleshy		**MINIM** dwarf; single drop; note	mu
MEBOS salted apricots (S. Africa)		**MINIM** down-stroke of pen	
MECCA desired objective		**MINIM** 2 crotchets or ½ semi-breve	mu
MEDAL decoration		**MINOR** petty; lesser; small	mu
MEDIA agencies		**MINOS** King of Crete	
MEDIC clover, lucerne, etc	bt	**MINUS** less; lacking; wanting	
MEDOC a red French wine		**MIRED** bogged; unit of colour temperature	
MEINY a retinue (Shak.)			me
MELEE fray; brawl; scuffle; mixture		**MIRTH** glee; gaiety; hilarity	
MELES badger genus	zo	**MIRZA** a Persian title	
MELIC lyric; a grass	bt	**MIS-DO** err; sin; trespass	
MELLA honey mixtures	ck	**MISER** skinflint; hoarder; niggard	
MELON a gourd	bt	**MISLE** mizzle; rain in small drops	
MENSA tooth biting surface	md	**MISLY** drizzly	
MERCY pity; lenity; clemency; grace		**MISSY** sentimental; namby-pamby	
MERGE coalesce; immerse; submerge		**MISTY** dim; obscure; cloudy	
MERIT desert; worth; credit; earn		**MITRA** Persian sun-god	rl
MERLE the blackbird	zo	**MITRE** angle of 45 degrees; cap	lw
MERON posterior of certain insects	zo	**MITTS** mittens	
MEROS triglyph channel surfaces	ar	**MIXED** blended; mingled; confused	
MERRY the English wild cherry	bt	**MIXEN** midden	
MERRY gay; blithe; jocund; lively		**MIXER** a good companion	
MESAL mesial; median; central		**MIX-UP** mêlée; scuffle; brawl; muddle	
MESHY netted; reticulated		**MIZZY** bog; swamp; quagmire	
MESNE intermediate	lw	**MNEME** effect of memory persistence	pc
MESON cosmic ray constituent		**MOBBY** fermented fruit juice	
MESSY mussy; muddled; disordered		**MOBLE** wrap the head in a hood	
METAL bullion; courage; ore		**MOBUS** motor-bus	
METAL broken stone for roads		**MOCHA** agate	mn
METED measured; apportioned		**MOCHA** chocolate/coffee mixture	ck
METEL thorn apple	bt	**MOCHE** packet of spun silk	
METER a measuring instrument		**MODAL** moody; (logic)	
METIC alien; foreign resident		**MODEL** example; pattern; copy	
METIF octaroon		**MODER** matrix of astrolobe	
METIS American half-breed		**MODUS** style; a method	lw
METOL 4-methylaminophenol	ch, pg	**MOGUL** a Mongolian	
METRA a measuring instrument		**MOHUR** Indian gold coin	nm
METRE (verse); 39.37 inches	me	**MOIRE** watered silk	
METRO underground railway (Fr.)		**MOIST** dank; clammy; humid	
MEUTE mew; cage for hawks		**MOLAR** grinding; a tooth	
MEWED (cats); moulted; confined		**MOLER** diatomaceous earth	bd
MEZZO middle	mu	**MOLLY** the wagtail bird	zo
MIAOW miaul; caterwaul		**MOLTO** very; much	mu

MOMUS God of Ridicule		rl
MONAD primitive organism		zo
MONAL a pheasant		zo
MONDE society (Fr.)		
MONEL an alloy		
MONEY cash; coin; currency; wealth		
MONGO (Mongolia)		nm
MONOX the crowberry		bt
MONTE gambling game like Faro		
MONTH lunar cycle		
MOOCH slouch; loiter		
MOODY sullen; morose; glum; captious		
MOOED lowed		
MOOLA mollah; Moslem judge		lw
MOONY dreamy		
MOORY sterile; boggy		
MOOSE the elk		zo
MOPED pined; motorised bicycle		
MOPPY tipsy; fuddled		
MOPSY mopsey; untidy woman		
MOPUS a mope; drone; money		
MORAL ethical; virtuous; meaning		
MORAT mulberry juice		
MORAY maray; fish of eel-type		zo
MOREL cherry; nightshade		bt
MORIL morel; mushroom		bt
MORMO bugbear		
MORNE blunt head of a lance		
MORON childish imbecile		
MORSE signalling; the walrus		zo
MORUS mulberry		bt
MOSES a law-giver		
MOSEY saunter; walk slowly (Amer.)		
MOSSY cryptogamous		bt
MOTED dusty		
MOTEL motorists' hotel		
MOTET sacred melody		mu
MOTHY moth-eaten		
MOTIF theme; feature		mu
MOTIF repeated pattern in art, music		
MOTOR automobile; engine		eg
MOTTO pithy maxim; slogan		
MOUCH mooch; skulk; slouch		
MOULD blight; create; shape; form		
MOULT to cast feathers		
MOUND knoll; tumulus; hillock		
MOUNT climb; scale; ascend; tower		
MOURN bewail; lament; deplore		
MOUSE small rodent		zo
MOUSY mouselike; quiet		
MOUTH opening; orifice; declaim		
MOVED shifted; budged; roused		
MOVER proposer		
MOWED scythed; cut		
MOWER a mowing machine		
MOYEN means; influence		
MPRET Albanian ruler		
MUCIC an acid		ch
MUCID musty; mouldy; slimy		
MUCIN viscous proteins/carbohydrates		
MUCKY dirty; filthy; muddy		

MUCOR mould; fungus		bt
MUCRO stiff sharp point		bt
MUCUS slime		md
MUDAR madar; medicinal herb		bt
MUDDY turbid; impure; obscure		
MUDIR Eastern Governor		
MUFTI Moslem priest or lawyer		
MUFTI civilian clothing		
MUGGY damp and warm		
MUGIL the mullet fish		zo
MULCH mulsh; litter; manure		
MULCT fine; penalize		lw
MULEY mooly; hornless		
MULGA Australian acacia		bt
MULLA mullah; fanatic		
MULSE mulled wine		
MULSH mulch; litter; manure		
MUMMY bituminous drug; (Egypt)		
MUMPS epidemic parotitis		md
MUNCH chew; crunch; masticate		
MUNGO shoddy; inferior cloth		
MURAL fixed to a wall		
MURAY cf. moray; murry		zo
MURED immured; pent		
MUREX Tyrian dye; molluscs		zo
MURID Moslem disciple		
MURKY lurid; dark; lowering		
MURRA fluorspar		mn
MURRE razorbill or guillemot		zo
MURRY also **MORAY**; eel-like fish		zo
MUSAL pert. to poetry/Muses		
MUSCA fly genus		zo
MUSCI the mosses		bt
MUSED pondered; contemplated		
MUSER ruminator		
MUSET a gap in a fence (Fr.)		
MUSHY pulpy		
MUSIC melody; harmony		mu
MUSKY fragrant like musk		
MUSSY messy; disordered		
MUSTY mucid; fusty; mouldy		
MUTCH a woman's cap (Sc.)		
MUTED muffled; pianissimo		mu
MUTIC lacking defensive parts		zo
MUTON smallest mutable gene element		gn
MUZZY dazed; confused		
MYALL Australian hard-wood tree		bt
MYOID like muscle		md
MYOMA muscle-fibre tumour		md
MYOPE myops; short-sighted person		
MYOPY myopia; short-sight		md
MYRRH scented resin		bt
MYSIS the opossum shrimp		zo
MYXON fish of mullet family		zo

N

NABAM chemical fungicide		
NABEE aconite poison		md
NABIT crushed candy		
NABOB nawab; wealthy individual		

NACRE mother-of-pearl		**NEXUS** interconnecting cluster of ideas	
NADIR opposite to zenith		**NICER** more pleasant; more exact	
NAEVE a birthmark	md	**NICHE** nook; corner; recess	
NAGGY querulous; quarrelsome		**NICOL** (polarizing light)	
NAGOR Senegal antelope	zo	**NIDGE** to dress stones	
NAIAD water-nymph		**NIDOR** the smell of cooking	
NAIVE artless; ingenuous; candid		**NIDUS** nest; a breeding place	md
NAKED stark; open; bare; denuded		**NIECE** daughter of brother or sister	
NAKER a kettle-drum	mu	**NIFFY** smelly	
NAKIR examiner of the dead (Koran)		**NIFTY** classy; stylish	
NAMED yclept; specified; dubbed		**NIGHT** darkness; obscurity	
NAMER nominator		**NIHIL** nil; zero; nothing	
NANDU rhea; American ostrich	zo	**NIKAU** New Zealand palm	bt
NANNY nurse; goat	zo	**NINNY** simpleton; nitwit; palooka	
NAPOO (ne plus); finished		**NINON** dress material	
NAPPE mountain-chain structure	gl	**NINTH** ordinal number	
NAPPY) drowsy; a dish		**NIOBE** a weeper	
NAPPY) napkin; baby's diaper		**NIPPY** a waitress; alert; parsimonous	
NARES nostrils	md	**NISAN** Jewish April	
NARIS nostril	md	**NISUS** an effort; an endeavour	
NARRE near (Spens.)		**NITID** gleaming; shining	
NASAL an errhine	md	**NITON** gaseous element	ch
NASIL conflict-inhibiting social signal		**NITRE** saltpetre	ch
NASTY foul; loathsome; ribald		**NITTY** full of nits; lice eggs	zo
NATAL nascent; initial		**NIVAL** nivose; niveous; snowy	
NATCH notch; the rump		**NIXIE** water-elf	
NATTE interlaced ornamentation		**NIZAM** Indian prince	
NATTY neat; spruce; trig		**NOBBY** smart; ornate	
NAVAL nautical; maritime; marine		**NOBEL** invented dynamite; prize	
NAVEL the centre	md	**NOBLE** patrician; obsolete gold coin	nm
NAVEW wild turnip	bt	**NOBLY** grandly; splendidly	
NAVVY excavator; canal digger		**NODAL** knotty	mu
NAWAB nabob; Eastern ruler		**NODDY** fool; sea-mew	zo
NAZIR Indian bailiff		**NODUS** knotty point	
NEATH beneath		**NOHOW** in no way	
NEBBY saucy (Sc.)		**NOILS** wool-combings	
NEBEL the Jew's harp	mu	**NOINT** anoint (Shak.)	
NEDDY donkey; moke; burro	zo	**NOISE** din; clamour; uproar	
NEEDS perforce; necessarily		**NOISY** blatant; vociferous; riotous	
NEEDY poor; indigent; penniless		**NOKES** a boob	
NEELE neeld; needle; sharp point		**NOMAD** a wanderer; vagrant	
NEESE neeze; sneeze		**NOMEN** name (Latin)	
NEGRE nigger-colour (Fr.)		**NOMIC** customary	
NEGRO black (African)		**NOMOS** Greek province	
NEGUS Abyssinian King		**NONCE** the present	
NEGUS a drink; hot punch		**NONES** (Roman calendar)	
NEIGH to whinny		**NONET** piece for 9 singers	mu
NEIST next		**NOOPS** the cloudberry	bt
NEMPT named; yclept (Spens.)		**NOOSE** loop; lasso; lariat	
NEPER power ratio unit	me	**NOPAL** Mexican cactus	bt
NERVE brace; pluck; hardihood	md	**NORIA** Persian water-wheel	
NERVY vigorous; nervous; fearful		**NORMA** a rule; a model	
NESKI Arabic script		**NORNS** Scandinavian Fates	
NETTY meshy; reticulated		**NORSE** Viking; early Scandinavian	
NEUME a musical phrase	mu	**NORTH** septentrion (Shak.)	
NEVEL to punch (Sc.)		**NOSED** snooped	
NEVER not at any time		**NOSEY** inquisitive	
NEWEL finial of a staircase		**NOTAL** dorsal; of the back	md
NEWLY recently; freshly		**NOTCH** natch; dent; nick; incision	
NEWSY chatty; gossipy		**NOTED** famous; recorded; remarked	
NEXUS connecting link; bond	lw	**NOTUM** back of a bug	zo

NOTUS southerly wind
NOVEL recent; new; book of fiction
NOWAY in no manner; nohow
NOWED tied in a knot; coiled — hd
NOWEL foundry loam
NOYAU almond cordial
NUCHA nape of the neck — md
NUDGE jog; jostle; elbow
NULLO a game
NUQUE nape — md
NURSE tend; sickbed attendant
NUTTY nut-like; -flavoured — ck
NYALA African antelope — zo
NYLON artificial fibre — tx
NYMPH maiden
NYULA parasite insect — zo

O

OAKEN made of oak — bt
OAKUM picked tarred rope — nt
OARED rowed; oar-bearing — nt
OASIS fertile spot in desert
OATEN made of oats — ck
OAVES dolts; changelings
OBANG old Japanese gold coin — nm
OBEAH obi; West African magic
OBESE abnormally fat; corpulent
OBOLE weight of 10 or 12 g — me
OCCUR happen; befall; chance
OCEAN main; the deep
OCHRE ocher; yellow pigment
OCHRY yellowish-brown
OCREA armoured shin-guard — zo, bt
OCTAD series of eight
OCTAN happening every 8 days
OCTET group of eight — mu
OCTYL organic radical — ch
OCUBA vegetable wax — bt
ODDLY queerly; quaintly
ODEON \ ancient Grecian
ODEUM / music hall
ODIUM obloquy; hatred; enmity
ODOUR scent; fragrance; perfume
ODYLE mesmerism
OFBIT devil's bit; a scabious — bt
OFFAL edible entrails; garbage
OFFER bid; tender; proposal
OFTEN oft; frequently; repeatedly
OGHAM Irish alphabet
OGIVE pointed arch
OGLED leered
OGLER voyeur
OILED lubricated
OILER oilcan; oilman
OKAPI animal related to giraffe — zo
OLDEN ancient; aged; antique
OLDER more elderly
OLEIC an acid — ch
OLEIN oleic glycerine ester — ch
OLENT fragrant

OLEON olein; fatty oil — ch
OLEUM fuming sulphuric acid — ch
OLIVE emblem of peace — bt
OLLAM Irish doctor
OLOGY theory in general
OMAHA a Sioux Indian of Nebraska
OMATI a Mexican Indian
OMBRE a card game
OMBRE colour-shaded woven stripes — tx
OMEGA last letter of Greek alphabet
OMLAH N. Ind. court officers
OMRAH Moslem court lord
ONCER he did not do it again
ONION a shallot — bt
ON-OFF control and keying electron
ONSET assault; attack; storm
ONTAL pert. to reality/noumena
ONYMY group nomenclature
OOMPH magnetic personality
OOPAK black tea
OOZED seeped; percolated
OPERA works — mu
OPHIC pertaining to snakes, serpents — zo
OPINE suppose; surmise; ween
OPIUM a narcotic — bt
OPSIN rhodopsin protein — bc
OPTED chosen; elected
OPTIC optical; the eye — md
ORACH a kind of spinach — bt
ORALE Papal veil — rl
ORANG an ape — zo
ORANT worshipper
ORATE spout; declaim; harangue
ORBED globular; spherical
ORBIT ambit; heavenly path; circuit
ORBIT the eye-socket — md
ORCIN purple dye — bt
ORDER bid; decree; enact; ukase
OREAD mountain nymph
ORGAL argal; crude tartar — ch
ORGAN medium; means — mu
ORIBI South African antelope — zo
ORIEL mullioned window
ORION a constellation
ORIYA (Orissa, India) language
ORLON artificial textile fabric
ORLOP a ship's deck — nt
ORMER ear-shell — zo
ORNIS avifauna; a bird — zo
ORPIN yellow pigment
ORRIS gold or silver lace
ORRIS astringent root — bt
ORTYX American quail — zo
ORVAL the herb clary — bt
ORYZA grass genus; rice — bt
OSCAN early Italic tribe
OSCAR film award
OSHAC gum-plant — bt
OSIER a willow — bt
OSMIC (osmium) — bt
OSONE oxidation product of osazone — ch

OSRAM osmium and wolfram	ch
OTARY genus of seals	zo
OTHER different	
OTTAR attar; aromatic oil	
OTTER fishing device	zo
OUBIT a hairy caterpillar	zo
OUGHT aught; nought; a cipher	
OUIJA planchette	
OUNCE snow-leopard	me, zo
OUNDY wavy; scalloped	
OUPHE oaf; dolt; idiot (Shak.)	
OUSEL ouzel; blackbird	zo
OUTBY out of doors (Sc.)	
OUTDO exceed; surpass; eclipse	
OUTED ejected; thrown out; sacked	
OUTER exterior; external; outside	
OUTRE odd; bizarre; strange	
OUZEL ousel; blackbird	zo
OVARY seed-vessel	pl
OVATE oval; egg-shaped	
OVERT open to view; apparent	
OVINE sheep-like	zo
OVISM ovum germ theory	gn
OVOID oval; oviform	
OVOLO a moulding	
OVULE small seed	bt
OWCHE ouch; jewel socket	
OWING due; outstanding	
OWLER smuggler of wool	
OWLET young owl	
OWNED admitted; confessed; allowed	
OWNER the captain	nt
OWSEN oxen	zo
OWSER tan vat liquor	
OX-BOT bot-fly	zo
OXBOW part of yoke	
OX-EYE daisy; marguerite	bt
OX-FLY bot-fly	zo
OXIDE oxygen compound	ch
OXIME aldehyde/ketone compound	ch
OXINE metal analysis reagent	ch
OXLIP species of primrose	bt
OXTER armpit; to hug (Sc.)	
OZENA an ulcer	md
OZONE condensed oxygen	ch

P

PAAUW African bustard	zo
PACED stepped; walked; hurried	
PACER speed-maker	
PADAR coarse flour or meal	
PADDY Irishman; temper; rice	bt
PADMA lotus	bt
PADRA black tea (China)	bt
PADRE army chaplain	rl
PAEAN chant of praise, joy, triumph	
PAEON a poetical foot	
PAGAN paynim; heathen; idolator	
PAGED found by the bell-hop	

PAGLE paigle; cowslip	bt
PAGUS county division (obs.)	
PAINS meticulous care	
PAINT limn; depict; portray	
PAIRK a park; a field (Sc.)	
PALAS Punjab bean	bt
PALAY ivory-tree	bt
PALEA inner husk; chaff	bt
PALED blanched; encompassed	
PALES Goddess of cattle	
PALKI palanquin	
PALMY flourishing; thriving	
PALPI jointed feelers	zo
PALSY paralysis; benumb	md
PANAX ginseng; medicinal plant	bt
PANCH thick mat; fender	nt
PANDA bear-cat	zo
PANDY a slap on the open hand	
PANED variegated; glazed	
PANEL list; board; schedule	lw
PANIC fear; fright; terror; alarm	
PANSY flower; effeminate man	bt
PANTS undershorts	
PAPAL popish; pontifical	rl
PAPAW a fruit tree	bt
PAPER journal; sheet; essay	
PAPPY succulent; juicy; easy	
PARCH dry; scorch; shrivel	
PARDI } perdy; pardieu;	
PARDY } in truth (Spens.)	
PARED cut; shaved	
PARER trimmer	
PAREU Polynesian wrap	
PARGE to apply plaster; whitewash	
PARKA Alaskan fur coat with hood	
PARKY cold; chilly	
PAROL oral; by word of mouth	
PARRY avert; evade; prevent	
PARSE analyse grammatically	
PARSI Parsee; Indo-Persian	
PARTI eligible suitor	
PARTS abilities; talents	
PARTY set; clique; cabal; faction	
PASCH Passover (Hebrew); Easter	
PASEO leisurely stroll, promenade (Sp.)	
PASHA pacha; Turkish governor	
PASHM under-fur of Cashmere goat	
PASSE faded; out of date (Fr.)	
PASSE 17 to 36 at roulette	
PASTE to stick; an adhesive	
PASTY glutinous; patty; a pie	
PATCH cobble; botch; mend	
PATED with a head	
PATEN patin; eucharistic plate	rl
PATER father	
PATIO courtyard	
PATLY aptly; fitly; apropos	
PATTE sash-band (Fr.)	
PATTY a small pie	ck
PAUSE halt; delay; tarry; hesitate	
PAVAN paven; pavin; a dance (Sp.)	

PAVED tesselated		
PAVER pavier; pavement layer		
PAVID timid		
PAVON lance pennon		
PAWED fingered; scraped		
PAWKY sly; crafty; shrewd		
PAYED coated with pitch		
PAYEE the receiver		
PAYER rewarder; liquidator		
PAYNE decorative floral printing style	pr
PAYSE paise; peise; poise		
PEACE harmony; concord; repose		
PEACH to divulge	bt
PEAKY sickly		
PEARL a gem; a size of type	pr
PEASE peas as pudding		
PEATY like peat		
PEAVY lumberman's hook	to
PECAN American nut	bt
PECUL Chinese weight, 133 lb (60 kg)	me
PEDAL to cycle	mu
PEDUM shepherd's crook		
PEERY peg-top		
PEGGY a warbler	zo
PEINE (squeeze to death)		
PEKAN the fisher-marten	zo
PEKOE black tea (China)	bt
PELLS records; rolls of parchment		
PELMA sole of foot	md
PELTA light shield or buckler		
PENAL punitive; disciplinary		
PENCE pennies; (Peter)	nm
PENIS male reproductive organ; phallus	pl
PENNA a feather	zo
PENNY a denarius	nm
PEONY piony; a plant	zo
PERCH pole; 5½ yd (5 m)	me, bt
PERDU lost (Fr.); hidden; ambush		
PERIL risk; hazard; danger; jeopardy		
PERKY smart; lively; brisk		
PERMO lustre; dress fabric	tx
PERRY fermented pear juice		
PERSE dark blue; a cloth		
PESKY irksome; trying; vexatious		
PETAL a flower-leaf	bt
PETAR petard; firework (Shak.)		
PETER blue flag; (Cards); (out)		
PETIT mignon; petty; trivial		
PETRE saltpetre	ch
PETTY trivial; mean		
PEWIT pewet; peewit; lapwing	zo
PHARE pharos; lighthouse; beacon		
PHARO faro; a game of chance		
PHASE appearance; aspect; guise		
PHEON the broad arrow		
PHIAL vial; ampulla; small flask		
PHLOX a plant	bt
PHOCA the seal genus	zo
PHONE to telephone		
PHOTO photograph; snapshot		
PHREN the mind; head	pl

PHYLA classifications		
PHYMA tubercle	md
PIANO softly; keyboard	mu
PICEA spruce genus	bt
PICOT little lace loop		
PICRA powdered aloes	md
PICUL pecul; Chinese weight	me
PICUS woodpecker	zo
PIDAN preserved duck egg	ck
PI-DOG Indian pariah dog	zo
PIECE unite; bit; part; scrap		
PIEND peen; hammer-point		
PIENO all performing	mu
PIETA holy picture	rl
PIETY holiness; sanctity		
PIEZE pressure unit	me
PIGMY pygmy; dwarf; midget		
PIKED pointed; sharp; spiked		
PIKER a tramp		
PILAR hairy; hirsute		
PILAU } pillau; pilaff; pilav	ck
PILAW } a savoury stew (rice)	ck
PILCH fur or flannel gown		
PILED amassed; heaped; erected		
PILER gatherer		
PILOT guide; steer; direct	nt
PILUM heavy javelin		
PILUS a botanical hair	bt
PINCH squeeze; take	me
PINED languished; drooped		
PINIC an acid	ch
PINKY small boat; dinghy	nt
PINNA wing-like structure	zo
PINNA bone in ear/nose	md
PINNY pinafore		
PINTA tropical Amer. skin disease	md
PINTO spotted American bean; piebald horse	zo
PIN-UP cut-out romantic wall picture		
PIONY peony; a flowering plant	bt
PIOUS devout; godly; religious		
PIPAL pipul; sacred fig-tree	bt
PIPED hollow		
PIPER (bagpipes)	mu
PIPIT tit-lark	zo
PIQUE vexation		
PISTE track; footprint; ski-way		
PITCH toss; hurl; locate; tar		
PITHY terse; concise; laconic		
PITON iron spike for ropes (climbing)		
PITOT tube recording air speed		
PIVOT hinge; axle; axis; centre		
PIXIE pixy; a fairy; elf		
PIZZA Italian savoury 'pie'	ck
PLACE site; scene; post; assign		
PLAGE spectroheliogram spot	as
PLAGE continental seaside resort		
PLAID a tartan; a maud		
PLAIN prairie; obvious; simple		
PLAIT weave; twine; braid		
PLANE level; flat; a tree	to, bt

PLANK sawn timber; lay down
PLANT inculcate; sow; machinery   bt
PLASH plesh; pool; weave; splash
PLASM mould or matrix
PLATE silver-ware; to overlay
PLATO Greek philosopher
PLATT ore dump
PLAZA public square; market-place
PLEAD argue; reason; entreat
PLEAT fold
PLEBS common people; proletariat
PLEON abdominal region in crustacea   zo
PLESH plash; splash
PLICA a hair disease   md
PLIED folded; carried on
PLUCK animal offal; pick; cull
PLUCK valour; daring; mettle; courage
PLUFF to puff
PLUMB vertical; to fathom level
PLUME feather; crest; to pride
PLUMP stout; chubby; corpulent
PLUMY feathered
PLUSH a material
PLYER transport worker
PMEST formula: personality: matter:
  energy: space: time   me
POACH (eggs); (game)
POCKY pitted
PODEX anal region   zo
PODGE a fat man; a puddle
PODGY short and fat; pudgy
POESY poetry; a posy
POGGE armed bull-head fish   zo
POILU French soldier; unshaven
POIND distrain   lw
POINT aim; tip; apex; sharpen
POISE paise; payse; peise; weigh
POKAL a drinking-cup
POKED thrust; jabbed; prodded
POKER (cards); the pochard duck   zo
POLAR opposite
POLEY polled; without horns
POLIO infantile paralysis   md
POLJE large limestone depression   gl
POLKA a dance (Polish)   mu
POLLY parrot   zo
POLYP many-limbed animal   zo
PONGO African ape   zo
POOJA Hindu ritual; obeisance
POORT col or pass (S. Africa)
POPPY (opium)   bt
PORCH portico; entrance; stoa
PORED examined diligently
PORER student
PORGY porgie; a sea-fish   zo
PORKY fat
PORTA transverse fissure; liver   md
PORTE Ottoman government centre
POSED perplexed; masqueraded
POSER an attitudiniser
POSIT to affirm; postulate

POSSE power; force of constables
POTCH thrust (Spens.)
POTIN Roman coin-metal
POTTO West African sloth   zo
POTTY petty; small; dotty
POUCE cortex particles in flax-roughing
POUCH bag; wallet; sack; steal
POULP a cephalopod   zo
POULT a young bird   zo
POUND pen; to crush   zo, me, nm
POUZE refuse of crushed apples
POWAN Loch Lomond fish   zo
POWER force; faculty; control   zo
POYOU armadillo   zo
PRAAM a barge   nt
PRADO Art Gallery, Madrid
PRAHU Malay boat
PRANG a crash landing; destroy
PRANK prink; bedizen; caper; frolic
PRASE green quartz   mn
PRATE babble; chatter; jabber
PRAWN a crustacean   zo
PREDY ready for action   nt
PREEN to clean the feathers
PRESS crush; urge; crowd; hurry
PREST at hand; ready money; to loan
PREXY college president (USA)
PRICE cost; charge; rate; reward
PRICK perforate; mark; penis   pl
PRIDE arrogance; hauteur; conceit
PRIED peeped; spied; snooped
PRIER pryer; a nosey Parker
PRILL brill; a fish   zo
PRIMA first; leading
PRIMA repeated, resumption mark   pr
PRIME chief; principal; zenith
PRIMO leading part   mu
PRIMY blooming
PRINK prank; to dress up
PRINT stamp; brand; impress
PRIOR previous; earlier; c.f. abbot   rl
PRISE to lever
PRISM refracting glass
PRIVY private
PRIZE esteem; reward; booty
PROBE scrutinize; examine; prove
PROEM preface
PRONE face downwards; apt to
PRONG the tine of a fork
PROOF test; ordeal; impenetrable
PROPS theatrical properties
PRORE the prow of a ship   nt
PROSE non verse writing
PROSY prolix; tedious; vapid
PROUD vain; imperious; stately
PROVE evince; verify; examine
PROWL prey; stalk; rove; slink
PROXY substitute; deputy; agent
PRUDE person of intolerant modesty
PRUNE dried plum
PRUNT applied glass badge mass   gs

PRYAN felspathic clay mn
PRYER prier; snooper
PSALM sacred song
PSHAW! belittling exclamation
PSOAS tenderloin md
PSORA the itch md
PTERE an alate organ; a wing zo
PUBIC of genital/loin region pl
PUBIS pelvic bones md
PUDGY podgy; fat; fleshy
PUFFY tumid; swollen; bombastic
PUGIL a pinch of
PUKKA veritable; genuine (Hindu)
PULED whined
PULER a whimperer
PULEX the flea zo
PULKA Lapland sledge
PULPY soft; succulent
PULSE a lentil; to throb md, bt
PUMPS evening shoes
PUNCH pummel; pierce; horse zo
PUNIC Carthaginian; faithless
PUNKA punkah; Indian fan
PUNTO fencing; Cuban dance
PUNTY glass blower's iron to
PUPAL in the chrysalis state zo
PUPIL scholar; tyro; alumnus
PUPPY a whelp
PUREE thick soup; strained pulp
PURER cleaner; more chaste
PURGE cleanse; absolve; shrive
PURIM Jewish feast
PURRE the dunlin bird zo
PURSE to wrinkle; money-bag
PURSY fat and asthmatic
PUSSY willow catkin; tame cat bt, zo
PUTID putrid; worthless
PUTOO nut-meal
PUTTI chubby Baroque child image art
PUTTY cement with linseed oil
PUT-UP preconcerted
PUTZI Chinese game
PYGAL related to backsides
PYGMY pigmy; midget; Lilliputian
PYLON gateway; turning mark; tower
PYOID pus-like md
PYRAL (funeral pyre)
PYRAN cyclic carbon/oxygen compound ch
PYRUS apple or pear genus bt
PYXIS pyx; sacred box rl

QUAKY unstable; shaky; trembling
QUALE having independent existence
QUALM scruple; pang; throe
QUANT punt or jumping pole
QUARK hypothetical sub-atomic entity
QUARL a segment of fireclay
QUARL jellyfish zo
QUART (cards); 2 pints (1.13 litres) me
QUASH nullify; annul; override
QUASI as it were; virtually
QUASS kvass; Russian beer
QUEAN a saucy girl (obs.)
QUEEN (cards); (chess)
QUEER odd; rummy; curious; strange
QUEET an ankle; a gaiter (Sc.)
QUELL suppress; crush; quench
QUERK to throttle; to grunt
QUERL to twirl; a coil
QUERN primitive stone handmill
QUERY question; dispute; ask
QUEST search; pursuit; inquiry
QUEUE a hopeful tail
QUICK fleet; agile; brisk; alive
QUIET still; calm; lull; pacify
QUIFF a curly lock
QUI-HI Anglo-Indian
QUILL a feather; a pen zo
QUILP a hideous dwarf
QUILT twilt; counterpane
QUINA quinine md
QUINS a quintuplet
QUINT sequence of five
QUIPO \ mnemonic Inca language;
QUIPU / coloured and knotted cords
QUIRE choir; 24 sheets me
QUIRK twist; subterfuge; evasion
QUIRT riding whip
QUITE fully; exactly; entirely
QUITS acquittance; clear of debt
QUOAD as far as
QUOIF coif; headdress
QUOIN wedge
QUOIT discus
QUOOK quaked (Spens.)
QUOTA share; portion; allotment
QUOTE cite; mention; adduce
QUOTH spake; said; remarked
QURAN Koran

Q

Q-BOAT disguised, armed ship nt
QUACK charlatan; humbug; empiric; cry
QUADS quadruplets
QUAFF gulp; swallow; drink deep
QUAID quelled (Spens.)
QUAIL cower; flinch; small bird zo
QUAIR quire; a book me
QUAKE tremble; quiver; rock

R

RABBI Jewish teacher
RABID furious; violent
RABOT marble-polisher
RACED ran; hurried; competed
RACER that races; competes
RACON remote-object identifying beacon
RADAR radio-location
RADGE rodge; grey duck; gadwall zo

RADII plural of radius	
RADIO a radio-telegram; wireless	
RADIX (logarithms); a root	bt
RADON radioactive element	ch
RAFFE three-cornered sail	nt
RAFTY damp; musty	
RAGED raved; fumed; stormed	
RAINY showery	
RAISE erect; uplift; exalt; breed	
RAJAH Indian prince	
RAKED enfiladed; searched; combed	
RAKER ransacker; scraper	
RAKER inclined tubular scaffolding	bd
RALLY banter; recover; (tennis)	
RALPH a mischievous raven	zo
RAMAL branching	
RAMED framed on the stocks	nt
RAMEX hernia	md
RAMIE ramee; rope fibre	nt
RAMIE Chinese grass for banknotes, textiles	tx
RAMMY strongly scented	
RAMUS branch; twig; spray	bt
RANCE a rocket trough	
RANDY sexually rampant	
RANDY a virago; a romp; a beggar	
RANEE rani; Indian queen	
RANGE array; align; tier; scope	
RANGY long-limbed and slender	
RANTY boisterous; vociferous	
RAPED violated; outraged	
RAPHE seam; rib; partition	
RAPID fast; fleet; swift; hasty	
RAPIN devouring animal	he
RARER scarcer; more uncommon	
RASED | erased; effaced;	
RAZED | demolished; blotted out	
RASPY rough; scratchy; abrasive	
RASSE small civet	zo
RATAL rate value	
RATAN rattan; a cane	zo
RATCH pawl; ratchet; rack	
RATED valued; scolded; chid	
RATEL honey-badger	zo
RATER assessor; (yachting)	
RATHE early; quickly; rapidly	
RATIO proportion; rate; quota	
RATTY irascible; irate; angry	
RAVED raged; ranted; drivelled	
RAVEL entangle; untwist	
RAVEN large crow-like bird	zo
RAVER a maniac	
RAVIN raven; prey; plunder; rapine	
RAWLY unskilfully; immaturely	
RAYAH non-Mohammedan Turk	
RAYED shone; arrayed	
RAYON artificial silk	
RAZEE to cut down; prune	nt
RAZOR shaving device	
REACH expanse; stretch; scope	
REACT recoil; resist; repeat	

READY prompt; alert; willing	
REALM kingdom; domain	
REAMY novelty yarn	tx
RE-ARM re-equip	
REAST to dry by smoke	
REATA riata; lariat; lasso	
REAVE to bereave; ravage	
REBEC Moorish fiddle	mu
REBEL revolt; rise; insurgent	
REBID (auction)	
REBUS a pictorial puzzle	
REBUT confute; disprove; rebuff	
RECAP redescribe briefly	
RECCE reconnaisance	
RECIF reef or bar (S. Africa)	
RECTO right-hand page	
RECUR reappear; revert; resort	
REDAN earthwork; redoubt	
REDIA large stage in trematoda	zo
REDLY blushingly	
REDUX re-appearance; return	
REEDY a thin tone	
REEFY full of rocks	
REEKY smoky; vaporous	
REESK rank grass; waste land (Sc.)	
REEST resist; arrest; stop (Sc.)	
REEVE steward; sheriff; rope	
REEVE the female ruff; a bird	zo
REFEL refute; disprove (Shak.)	
REFER submit; relate; advert	
REFIT repair; re-equip	
REGAL royal; kingly; princely	
REGET regain; recover	
REGIE government monopoly	
REGMA botanical capsule	bt
REICH German realm	
REIFY to materialize	
REIGN rule; govern; control	
REIST reest; to baulk; arrest	
REIVE reave; to ravage	
RELAI chain of inns	
RELAX abate; slacken; loosen	
RELAY team race; pass on	
RELET to offer on hire again	
RELIC memento; souvenir; keepsake	
RELIT rekindled	
REMAN get a fresh crew	
REMEX a flight feather	zo
REMIT replace; diminish; re-lease	
RENAL (kidneys)	md
RENES the kidneys	md
RENEW renovate; refurbish; restore	
RENIN kidney enzyme	
RENTE annuity from French funds	
REPAY refund; recompense; avenge	
REPEL repulse; parry; withstand	
REPET repeat; the same again	md
REPLY echo; answer; respond	
REPOT transplant	
RESAW saw again; revisualized	
RESET reprint with alterations; adjust	

RESIN rosin		
RESOL synthetic resin	ch
RESOW to sow again	
RESTY indolent; restive	
RETCH reach; strain	
RETEX to annul	
RETRO backwards	
RETRY try again	
REVEL feast; carouse; luxuriate	
REVET (revetment)	
REVIE outdo; retort	
REVUE variety entertainment	mu
REWET part of a wheel-lock	
REWIN regain	
RHEIC (rhubarb)	bt
RHEIN chrysophanic acid	ch
RHEMA word, verb (Gr.)	
RHEUM watery mucous discharge	md
RHINE rine; a ditch	
RHINO money	zo
RHOMB a rhombohedron	
RHONE eaves gutter	
RHUMB vertical circle; (compass)	
RHYME rime; poetry; metre	
RHYNE Russian hemp	bt
RIANT laughing; smiling (Fr.)	
RIATA reata; lariat; lasso	
RIBES currant genus	bt
RICER machine for mincing food	ck
RICIN castor bean albumin	ch
RIDER horseman; added clause	
RIDGE ledge; crest; weal	
RIDGY furrowed	
RIFLE ransack; strip; to groove	
RIGEL a star in Orion	
RIGHT due; equity; privilege	
RIGID staunch; unbending; strict	
RIGOL a diadem; crown; coronet	
RIGOR rigour; rigidity	md
RIGOR shivering, chill (of death)	md
RILED angered; annoyed	
RILLE lunar valley	
RIMED frosted	
RIMER an enlarging tool	to
RINGE heather whisk	
RINSE lave; clean; wash	
RIOJA Spanish wine	
RIPEN mature; develop; perfect	
RIPER further advanced	
RIPON a spur	
RISEL support for a vine	
RISEN ascended; mounted; revolted	
RISER rebel; stair-board	
RISHI poet; Vedic seer	
RISKY hazardous; speculative	
RISSA kittiwake genus	zo
RITHE small stream	
RITZY luxurious	
RIVAL vie; emulate; match; equal	
RIVEL to wrinkle; shrivel	
RIVEN rived; rent; split	

RIVER stream; torrent; tributary		
RIVET clinch; fasten	
RIYAL Sudanese coin	nm
RIZOM heat of corn or oats	bt
ROACH part of sail; a fish	nt, zo
ROAST parch; chaff outrageously	
ROBED garbed; attired; arrayed	
ROBIN sometimes round	zo
ROBLE Californian white oak	bt
ROBOT an automaton	
ROCKY stony; shaky; unsteady	
ROCTA ancient violin	mu
RODEO cattle round-up	
RODGE radge; grey duck; gadwall	zo
ROGER a ram; a rogue	zo
ROGUE knave; scamp; rascal; caitiff	
ROHAN red-wood mahogany tree	bt
ROIST to bluster; to swagger	
ROKER thornback ray; skate	zo
ROMAL kerchief; raw hide whip	
ROMAN type of type	
ROMEO a lover	
ROMIC a phonetic notation	
ROMPU heraldic fracture	hd
ROMPY rampageous	
RONDE round-hand type (Fr.)	
RONDE circular dance	
RONDO music in several strains	mu
RONIN Japanese outcast	
ROODY coarse; luxuriant	
ROOFY having roofs	
ROOKY inhabited by rooks; newcomer	
ROOMY spacious	
ROOPY roupy; hoarse	
ROOSE to extol (Sc.)	
ROOST a fowl support; to perch	
ROOTY radical; bread (India)	
ROPED tied; lashed; bound	
ROQUE a form of croquet (Fr.)	
RORAL dewy; roscid	
RORIC moist with dew	
RORTY exuberant; rampageous	
ROSET a red colour; rosin	
ROSIN resin	bt
ROTAL according to roster	
ROTON quantum of rotational energy	ps
ROTOR a machine; airfoil	
ROUGE (Eton wall game); make-up	
ROUGH rugged; crude; coarse	
ROUND convex; rotund; period; tour	
ROUPY roupy; hoarse	
ROUSE carouse; disturb; awaken	
ROUST rouse; stir up; incite	
ROUSY noisy; riotous	
ROUTE way; course; itinerary	
ROUTH plentiful; abundant (Sc.)	
ROVED roamed; wandered; rambled	
ROVER nomad; pirate; (croquet)	
ROWAN mountain ash	bt
ROWDY ruffian; rough; boisterous	
ROWED sculled; upbraided	

ROWEL part of a spur
ROWEN second hay crop
ROWER oarsman
ROYAL regal; superb; august
ROYLE to rile; to salt fish
ROYNE to bite; to gnaw; whisper
RUBIA madder genus — bt
RUBLE rouble; Russian silver coin — nm
RUBUS bramble genus — bt
RUCHE plaited trimming
RUDAS a hag; virago (Sc.)
RUDDY rubicund; red
RUDER coarser; cruder
RUDGE a partridge — zo
RUFFE ruff; freshwater perch — zo
RUGBY (football); (school)
RUING regretting; lamenting
RULED lined; governed; decided
RULER monarch; regent; dictator
RUMAL romal; shawl (Hindu)
RUMBA Cuban dance
RUMBO rum punch
RUMEN paunch of ruminant
RUMEX sorrel genus — bt
RUMMY odd; queer; card game
RUNCH crunch; the wild charlock — bt
RUNER bard
RUNIC Ancient Scandinavian script
RUN-IN the finish in racing
RUNNY liquid
RUN-ON process of continuing unbroken — pr
RUN-UP gold band, binding — pr
RUPEE 16 annas — nm
RUPIA skin disease — md
RURAL Arcadian; sylvan; pastoral
RUSHY full of rushes
RUSMA rhusma; a depilatory — md
RUSTY corroded; out of practice
RUTAL ⎫ derived from rue — bt
RUTIC ⎭
RUTTY uneven; furrowed; grooved
RUVID rough
RYBAT in- or outband — bd
RYPER ptarmigans (Scand.) — zo

S

SABAL a fan palm genus — bt
SABIN unit of acoustic absorption — ac
SABLE antelope; marten; fur — zo
SABLE black; dusky; sombre — hd
SABOT wooden shoe
SABRA native of Israel
SABRE also **SABER** cavalry sword
SACRE saker; falcon; cannon — zo
SADDA abbreviated Zendavesta
SADHU Hindu ascetic
SADLY gloomily; dismally; mournfully
SAFER surer; more secure
SAGAN Jewish priest

SAGER wiser; cleverer
SAGRA beetle genus — zo
SAGUM Roman cloak
SAHIB a white man; gentleman (India)
SAIGA puff-nosed antelope — zo
SAILY like a sail — nt
SAINT to canonize — rl
SAITH (says)
SAIVA votary of Siva — rl
SAJOU American monkey — zo
SAKER sacre; hawk; old gun — zo
SAKIA Persian water-wheel
SALAD mixed cold dish — ck
SALAL evergreen shrub — bt
SALDA a bug genus — zo
SALEP salop; dried orchis root — bt
SALIC (Salic Law)
SALIN saline; a salt — ch
SALIX willow genus — bt
SALLE salon; hall (Fr.)
SALLE paper-sorting room — pr
SALLY bell-rope tufting; outburst; wit
SALLY a stone-fly; a wren — zo
SALMI hashed game
SALMO salmon genus — zo
SALON saloon; hall
SALOP salep; dried orchis root — bt
SALPA genus of sea-squirts — zo
SALSE volcanic mud
SALTS saline draughts — md
SALTY witty; briny; saline
SALVE save; rescue; heal; a remedy
SALVO an exception; a volley
SAMBA dance (S. America) — mu
SAMBO a negro
SAMIA silkworm genus — zo
SAMMY American Tommy
SANDY yellowish red
SANER less idiotic; more normal
SANSA tambourine — mu
SAPID savoury; affected; palatable
SAPOR flavour; taste
SAPPY juicy; succulent; weak
SARDA mackerel; tunny genus — zo
SAROH Indian guitar — mu
SAROS an astronomical cycle
SARSE a fine sieve
SARUM Salisbury; (rotten borough)
SASIA pigmy woodpeckers (Ind.) — zo
SASIN antelope; Indian blackbuck — zo
SASSE Dutch weir with flood-gates
SATAN clootie; Devil; Lucifer
SATED replete; surfeited; cloyed
SATIN glossy fabric
SATIS enough (Latin)
SATYR goat-like sylvan deity
SAUCE impudence; a condiment; relish
SAUCH, SAUGH the willow (Sc.) — bt
SAUCY pert; bold; malapert; flippant
SAUDI gold sovereign (Arabia) — nm
SAULT a rapid (Canadian)

SAUNA Finnish steam-bath	
SAURY skipper-fish	zo
SAUTE fried in fat	ck
SAVED rescued; freed; redeemed; kept	
SAVER a hoarder; an economist	
SAVIN evergreen conifer	bt
SAVOR savour; taste; odour; relish	
SAVOY curly cabbage	bt
SAVVY commonsense; nous; gumption	
SAWED cut with a saw; sawn	
SAWNY or **SAWNEY** a Scotsman	
SAXIN saccharin	ch
SAXON of Saxony	
SAYER a speaker; an assayer	
SAYON medieval peasant's jacket	
SAY-SO a dictum	
SCAFF food of any kind (Sc.); scoff	
SCAIL skail; scatter; disperse (Sc.)	
SCALA a surgical instrument	md
SCALD the dodder-plant; a burn	bt
SCALD skald; Scandinavian bard	
SCALE climb; balance; flake; lamina	
SCALL leprosy; a scab; mean	md
SCALP token of victory; trophy	
SCALY encrusted; shabby; mean	
SCAMP rogue; knave; stint	
SCANT to stint; scarcely sufficient	
SCAPE leafless peduncle bearing flowers	bt
SCAPE shaft of column; a fault	
SCAPE stem; escape; miss	
SCARD shard; sherd; fragment	
SCARE alarm; appal; dismay; daunt	
SCARF neckerchief; a carpenter's joint	
SCARF cormorant; scart; skart	zo
SCARP heraldic scarf; rampart slope	
SCART to scratch; scrape; a niggard	
SCARY timid; frightened; windy	
SCATE skate; a fish	zo
SCATH scathe; damage; injury; harm	
SCATT scat; tax (Shetland Is.)	
SCAUD scald; scold (Sc.)	
SCAUP a sea-duck	zo
SCAUR river bank; rocky cliffs; scar	
SCELP skelp; iron for gun-barrels	
SCENA stage of an ancient theatre	
SCEND ascend; to heave upwards	
SCENE show; pageant; sight; view	
SCENT perfume; odour; redolence; trail	
SCHUT cattle-pound (South Africa)	
SCION offshoot; branch; descendant	
SCISE to cut (obs.)	
SCOAT scote; to scotch; to wedge	
SCOBS shavings; sawdust; dross	
SCOBY or **SCOBBY** the chaffinch	zo
SCOFF (food); sneer; mock; deride	
SCOLD rate; upbraid; censure; chide	
SCOMM a buffoon (obs.)	
SCONE coronation stone; a confection	
SCOON skim along the water	
SCOOP dig; hollow; excavate; a ladle	
SCOOT decamp; bolt; run	

SCOPA stiff hairs of moths	zo
SCOPE room; space; liberty; object	
SCOPS screech-owl	zo
SCORE record; mark; furrow; scratch	
SCORN spurn; scout; disdain; deride	
SCOTE a scotch; a wedge; a prop	
SCOTS Scottish	
SCOUP to run; to scamper (Sc.)	
SCOUR scrub; scrape; purge	
SCOUT contemn; spurn; reconnoitre	
SCOUT the guillemot; razor-bill	zo
SCOVE to tamp; to poise	
SCOVY smeared; blotched	
SCOWL frown; lower; glower	
SCRAB crab-apple; to scratch; scrape	bt
SCRAG to throttle; odd lean bit	
SCRAM! clear off! get out!	
SCRAM emergency plant shutdown	nc
SCRAN skran; scraps of food	
SCRAP bit; atom; particle; tussle	
SCRAT a devil; a goblin; monster	
SCRAW a turf; a sod (Irish)	
SCRAY sea-swallow	zo
SCREE steep stony slope	
SCREW twist; distort; force; old horse	
SCRIM strong muslin lining for walls	
SCRIP wallet; purse; satchel	
SCRIP (receipt for) share certificates	
SCROD to shed; young codfish	zo
SCROG stunted bush; thicket	
SCRUB underwood; clean; scour	bt
SCRUM (football)	
SCUBA underwater breathing apparatus	
SCUDO Italian silver dollar	nm
SCUFF scurf; a scale; to shuffle	
SCUFT the nape of the neck	
SCULK skulk; lurk; slink	
SCULL an oar; a cockboat; to row	nt
SCULL skua-gull; a shoal of fish	zo
SCULP to carve; to engrave; to flay	
SCURF dandruff; scum; bull-trout	zo
SCUSE excuse me	
SCUTE a shield; scale of fish	zo
SEAMY dark; sordid; nasty	
SEA-OX the walrus	zo
SEAVE a wick made of a rush	
SEAVY overgrown with rushes	bt
SEBAT 5th month of the Jewish year	
SEBUM sebaceous gland excretion	zo
SECCO a fresco; unaccompanied	mu
SEDAN carrying chair; a disaster	
SEDGE flock of herons; reeds; grass	zo, bt
SEDGY overgrown with sedge or rushes	
SEEDY shabby; run to seed; unwell	
SEGNO repetition	mu
SEINE large fishing net	
SEISM an earthquake	
SEITY personality; selfhood	
SEIZE grasp; clutch; grapple; impound	
SEKOS Greek sanctuary	
SELAH a pause in the Psalms	

SELVA tropical rainforest (Brazil)	
SEMEN fluid containing spermatozoa	zo
SEMIC pertaining to a sign	
SEMIS Roman bronze coin, half an as	nm
SENAL a landmark (South America)	
SENCH to cause to founder	
SENEX S. American hawk; a swift	zo
SENNA dried cassia leaves	md
SENOR Spanish title of address	
SENSE perceive; wisdom; reason	
SENZA without	mu
SEPAL calyx segment	bt
SEPIA genus of cuttlefish; pigment	zo
SEPIC done in sepia	
SEPOY native Indian soldier	
SERAC glacial ice	
SERAI caravanserai; a Persian inn	
SERGE twilled fabric	
SERIC Chinese; silken	
SERIF short cross-line in typography	pr
SERIN song-bird; canary	zo
SERON bale of exotic produce	
SEROW Asiatic goat	zo
SERRA a saw; sierra; mountain ridge	
SERRY to crowd together	
SERUM antibody for inoculation	md
SERVE do; act; suit; aid; obey; attend	
SERVO braking system	au
SESHA Serpent-King (Hindu)	rl
SESIA clear-wing moths	zo
SESSA hurry! (Shak.)	
SETON a dressing	md
SETAE bristles; cat's whiskers	bt, zo
SET-TO an affray	
SET-UP scheme; plot	
SEVEN cardinal number	
SEVER cut; part; sunder; detach	
SEWED stitched; threaded	
SEWEL a scarecrow	
SEWEN sewin; salmon type	zo
SEWER drain	
SEXTE sixth hour service	rl
SEXTO a size of book	
S'FOOT an imprecation	
SHACK a shed; to tramp; a vagabond	
SHADE hue; tint; veil; cover; screen	
SHADY shadowy; obscure; doubtful	
SHAFT arrow; missile; handle; pit	
SHAHI Persian copper coin	nm
SHAKE jar; jolt; agitate; quiver; dance	
SHAKO chako; military cap	
SHAKY tottering; unstable; loose	
SHALE shaly clay; husk	mn
SHALL future auxiliary verb	
SHALM ⎱ type of oboe	mu
SHAWM ⎰	
SHALT future auxiliary verb	
SHALY laminated and friable	
SHAMA Indian song-bird; cereal	zo
SHAME abash; mortify; infamy	
SHAND shame; base coin; worthless	

SHANK (golf); the tibia	pl
SHAPE mould; fashion; form; image	
SHAPO wild sheep of Tibet	zo
SHAPS chaps; cowboy breeches	
SHARD sherd; fragment; wing case	zo
SHARE quota; part; portion; divide	
SHARK a cheat; artful greedy fellow	zo
SHARN cow-dung (Sc.)	
SHARP fine; thin; keen; caustic	mu
SHAVE pare; clip; shear; skim; graze	
SHAWL a wrap	
SHEAF a bundle; a collection	
SHEAL to shell; to husk	
SHEAL shiel; shepherd's hut	
SHEAR clip; cut; fleece; strip	
SHEEN gloss; lustre; shine; polish	
SHEEP a woolly ruminant	zo
SHEER absolute; precipitous; turn aside	
SHEET a bed-cloth; wide expanse; rope	tx
SHEIK Arab chief	
SHELF ledge; shoal; sandbank	
SHELL case; husk; projectile; bombard	
SHEND to disgrace (Spens.)	
SHEOL pit; Hades (Heb.)	rl
SHERD shard; fragment; scard	
SHETH part of plough	
SHEVA (Hebrew vowel point)	
SHEWN displayed; revealed; taught	
SHIAH Mohammedan sect	
SHIED (coconuts); (horses)	
SHIEL shieling; shelter for sheep (Sc.)	
SHIER shyer; more bashful	
SHIFT chemise; vary; alter; trick; wile	
SHIKO prostrate veneration (Burma)	
SHILY shyly; coyly; timidly	
SHINE radiate; glitter; flash; gloss	
SHINY the East; gleaming	
SHIRE county; draught-horse	zo
SHIRK evade; avoid; neglect; malinger	
SHIRL to slide	
SHIRR to pucker; to wrinkle	
SHIRT a blouse; distinctive garment	
SHIST schist; crystalline rock	mn
SHIVE a slice; a wooden bung	
SHOAD fragments of ore	mn
SHOAL swarm; throng; bank; bar	
SHOAT young hog	zo
SHOCK stouk; sheaf; onset; to disgust	
SHOER a farrier; blacksmith	
SHOLA a wood, a thicket (Ind.)	
SHOLE ground plank	
SHONE radiated; sparkled; flashed	
SHOOK cask staves; trembled; quaked	
SHOOL beg; grimace; shovel (Sc.)	
SHOON shoes	
SHOOT emit; dart; fire; sprout	bt
SHORE prop; brace; strand; beach	
SHORL tourmaline	mn
SHORN shaven; fleeced; clipped	
SHORT terse; abrupt; laconic; pithy	
SHOTT, CHOTT seasonal salt lake	

SHOUT cry; cheer; call; bellow
SHOVE jostle; push; press; elbow
SHOWN presented; paraded; revealed
SHOWY gay; garish; loud; gaudy
SHRAB shrub; a drink (Arab)
SHRED scrap; tatter; atom; piece
SHREW vixen; virago; scold   zo
SHROF Indian money-lender
SHROW shrew; small dormouse   zo
SHRUB a cordial; dwarf tree   bt
SHRUG to draw up; contract
SHUCK a husk; shell or pod   bt
SHUNT divert; electrical device
SHYLY shily; coyly; bashfully
SIBBE sib; akin
SIBYL prophetess; witch; sorceress
SICCA newly coined; a rupee   nm
SIDED flattened; biased
SIDER partisan; protagonist
SIDLE to go crabwise
SIEGE besiege; invest; a throne
SIELD ceiled; plastered (Spens.)
SIEUR title of respect (Fr.)
SIEVE to sift; to strain; a temse
SIGHT see; view; observe; scene
SIGIL signature; occult mark
SIGMA a Greek letter; reactor circuit
SILAL high-silica cast iron   ml
SILEX silica   mn
SILKY silken
SILLY inane; inept; unwise; stupid
SILVA sylva; forest trees   bt
SIMAR cymar; cimar; scarf; loose dress
SIMIA genus of apes   zo
SINAL pertaining to sinus
SINCE after; subsequently; because
SINEW a tendon   md
SINGE sear; burn; scorch
SINIC Seric; Chinese
SINTO shinto; ancestor-worship (Jap.)   rl
SINUS a cavity; a bay; nasal duct   pl
SIOUX Dakota Indian
SIPED oozed; exuded; percolated
SIRED fathered; generated
SIREN syren; seducer; hooter
SIRIH betel-leaf (Malay)   bt
SIRUP sorop; syrup
SISAL fibrous plant, (ropemaking)   bt
SISON stone parsley   bt
SISSY sweetheart; a weakling
SITED placed, situate
SIT-IN demonstration by occupying premises
SITTA the nut-hatch   zo
SIVAN Jewish month
SIXTH ordinal number
SIXTY cardinal number
SIZAR a rationed student
SIZED graded; glued
SIZEL scissel; metal clipping
SIZER sizing machine

SKAIL scail; disperse; scatter; empty; spill
SKAIN skein; coil of yarn
SKALD scald; Scandinavian bard
SKARN silicate-gangue mineral   gl
SKATE scate; the ray; a roller-skate   zo
SKEAN skene; a dagger; a dirk (Sc.)
SKEEL a milking-pail; a tub (Sc.)
SKEET the pollack; a long scoop   zo
SKEIN tangle; wild geese flying   zo
SKELP a blow; a large portion (Sc.)
SKELP tube-steel strip   ml
SKENE skean; dagger; dirk (Sc.)
SKIED skyed; lofted; elevated
SKIER a lofted shot at cricket
SKIER one who travels on skis
SKIES the firmament
SKIFF a light boat; to skim   nt
SKILL knack; address; art; facility
SKIMP stint; scamp; scanty
SKINK African lizard; a shin-bone   zo
SKIRL a shrill cry or sound
SKIRR scurry; hasten; scour
SKIRT hem; border; skim; edge
SKITE skyte; to glide or slip (Sc.)
SKITE the yellow bunting   zo
SKIVE pare; split; shirk (slang)
SKOAL Hail! a toast! (Scand.)
SKRAN scran; scraps; rubbish; refuse
SKULK lurk; slink; cower; sneak
SKULL the sconce; the noddle
SKYEY skiey; ethereal
SKYTE skite; glide; slip (Sc.)
SLACK lax; loose; lazy; sluggish
SLACK shallow dell; small coal
SLADE valley; spade; Art School
SLAIE weaver's reed
SLAIN killed; despatched; murdered
SLAKE quench; extinguish; allay
SLANG argot; to scold; to abuse
SLANT tilt; list; lean; slope
SLASH cut; gash; slit; swipe
SLATE reprimand; slang   mn
SLATT slat; a lath
SLATY like slate
SLAVE serf; thrall; drudge; menial
SLEEK smooth; soft; glossy; silken
SLEEP doze; slumber; nap; siesta
SLEET snow mingled with rain
SLEPT drowsed; slumbered; rested
SLICE fire-shovel; cut; sever; piece
SLICK plausible; easily done; ore   mn
SLICY apt to slice
SLIDE glide; skid; grace notes   mu
SLIER slyer; more crafty
S'LIFE an imprecation
SLILY slyly; artfully; astutely
SLIME mire; sludge; ooze; mud
SLIMY viscid; viscous; clammy
SLING a drink; hurl; hang; cast
SLINK untimely beast; skulk; lurk

SLIPE	slype; mining skip	
SLIPO	men's bathing trunks	
SLIPS	(theatre); (shipbuilding)	
SLISH	slice; slash; cut	
SLIVE	to slide; to skulk	
SLOAM	clay between coal-beds	mn
SLOAT	slot; bar; bolt	
SLOID, SLOYD	handicrafts	
SLOOM	to slumber; to sleep	
SLOOP	a warship	nt
SLOPE	slant; shelve; grade; a ramp	
SLOPS	ready-made clothes	
SLOSH	slush; sludge; sentimentality	
SLOTH	torpor; tree bear; laziness	zo
SLOYD	sloid; Swedish manual training	
SLUED	turned round; tipsy	
SLUGS	half-roasted ore	
SLUMP	collapse; sudden fall; marsh	
SLUNG	flung; thrown; suspended; cast	
SLUNK	lurked; cowered; skulked	
SLUSH	slosh; sludge; mire; bathos	
SLYLY	slily; astutely; craftily	
SLYNE	face of a jointed rock	
SLYPE	narrow passage	
SMACK	slap; flavour; spice; dash	nt
SMALL	tiny; petty; trivial; minute	
SMALT	blue glass; blue pigment	
SMART	rankle; pungent; trim; witty	
SMASH	crash; crack; disrupt; ruin	
SMEAR	daub; plaster; sully; begrime	
SMELL	scent; aroma; odour; perfume	
SMELT	stank; melt ore; small fish	zo
SMIFT	a fuse	
SMILE	smirk; grin; simper	
SMIRK	an affected smile	
SMITE	hit; buffet; knock; chasten	
SMITH	a metal worker; blacksmith	
SMOCK	a chemise; pastoral garment	
SMOKE	fume; reek; exhale; vapour	
SMOKY	steamy; vaporous	
SMOLT	young river salmon	zo
SMOOT	journeyman printer; smout	
SMORE	smother (Sc.)	
SMOTE	struck; blasted; slew	
SMOUT	smowt; speckled trout	zo
SMUCK	a crowd of jellyfishes	zo
SNACK	hasty light repast; a share	
SNAIL	spiral cam; mollusc	zo
SNAKE	serpent; reptile	zo
SNAKY	sly; cunning; serpentine	
SNAPE	to bevel	
SNARE	gin; net; toil; wile; trap	
SNARL	gnarl; gird at; entangle	
SNARY	insidious; complicated	
SNASH	insolence; abusive language (Sc.)	
SNATH	curved handle of a scythe	
SNEAD	snath; snathe; sned	
SNEAK	lurk; slink; skulk; blab	
SNEAP	check; rebuke; nip	
SNECK	snick; cut; a latch	
SNEER	gibe; mock; jeer; scoff	

SNELL	keen; sharp; severe (Sc.)	
SNICK	a notch; nick; (cricket)	
SNIDE	spurious; dishonest; counterfeit	
SNIFF	to smell; inhale; scent; snuff	
SNIFT	snort; sniff	
SNIPE	to shoot from ambush; bird	zo
SNIRT	a smothered laugh; snigger	
SNOEK	S. African fish; barracouta	zo
SNOOD	hairnet; a fillet	
SNOOK	lurk; snoop; derisive action	
SNOOL	to cringe; a sniveller (Sc.)	
SNOOP	to pry	
SNORE	loud breathing during sleep	
SNORT	loud exhalation through nostrils	
SNOUK	snook; lurk; snoop	
SNOUT	nose; nozzle; proboscis	
SNOWY	pure; unblemished; niveous	
SNUFF	sniff; (tobacco)	
SOAPY	unctuous; emollient; flattering	
SOAVE	sweetly	mu
SOBER	staid; sedate; steady; grave	
SOBOL	the Russian sable	zo
SOCKS	a drubbing; foot covers	
SOCLE	plinth	
SODDY	covered with sod; turfy	
SOFAR	underwater navigation system	
SOFTA	Moslem student	
SOGER	a shirker	
SOGGY	boggy; marshy; wet; saturated	
SOKEN	socage district	
SOKOL	Czech organisation	
SOLAH	solar; sola; sponge-wood	bt
SOLAR	sunshine parlour; solarium	
SOLDO	Italian copper coin	nm
SOLED	(boots)	
SOLEN	razor-fish genus	
SOL-FA	(singing)	mu
SOLID	hard; dense; stout; stable	
SOLON	wise legislator; wiseacre	zo
SOLUM	piece of ground; soil	
SOLUS	alone; sole right, agreement	lw
SOLVE	elucidate; unravel; interpret	
SOMAJ	a Hindu society	
SONDE	upper atmospheric probe	
SONIC	relating to sound	
SONNY	term of endearment	
SONSY	soncy; buxom; jolly; cordial	
SONTY	sanctity (Shak.)	
SOOJA	soya bean	bt
SOOTE	sweetly (Spens.)	
SOOTH	truth; reality; true; indeed	
SOOTY	begrimed	
SOPHA	a sofa; seat of a king	
SOPHI	Persian king	
SOPOR	deep sleep; moral lethargy	
SOPPY	moist; wet; silly	
SOPRA	above	mu
SORAL	pertaining to sorus	
SORBO	porous rubber	
SORDA	damped with a mute	mu
SORDE	lips/teeth crust during fever	me

SOREL a buck of the third year   zo
SORER more grieved; tenderer
SOREX a genus including shrew-mice   zo
SORRA not; never (Irish)
SORRY sad; dejected; regretful; abject
SORUS cluster of capsules on ferns   bt
SOUGH low moan; whine; drain
SOUND probe; fathom; hale; valid
SOUPY like soup
SOUSE pickle; sauce; douse; swoop
SOUTH the Southern regions
SOWAR Indian cavalryman
SOWED strewn; spread; cast
SOWER propagator; disseminator
SOWLE to pull by the ears (Shak.)
SOWTH to whistle softly (Sc.)
SPACE extent; capacity; duration
SPADE (cards); gelding; dig   to
SPADO spade; eunuch; a sword
SPAER a diviner (Sc.)
SPAHI Algerian cavalryman
SPAKE discoursed; declared; told
SPALE spail; a splinter (Sc.)
SPALL break; split; clip
SPALT a flux; brittle
SPANE spean; to wean (Sc.)
SPANG a spangle; to leap; to hurl
SPANK a blow; a slap
SPARE save; hoard; store; frugal
SPARK to flash; bright lad
SPASM tic; throe; twitch; paroxysm
SPATE spait; a sudden flood
SPAVE to geld; to spay
SPAWL to spit; to slaver
SPAWN offspring; ova; sperm   zo
SPEAK express; declare; talk
SPEAR a lance; to pierce
SPEAR male descent (cf. **DISTAFF**)
SPECS spectacles
SPECK stain; blemish; blubber; lard
SPEED haste; urge; celerity; rate
SPEER speir; to ask (Sc.)
SPELD chip; splinter
SPELK rod; switch
SPELL charm; cantrip; period
SPELT spelled; German wheat   bt
SPEND lavish; disburse; exhaust
SPENT consumed, worn, wasted
SPERM spawn; semen   zo
SPEWY wet; boggy
SPHEX the wasp genus   zo
SPICA spur; spike; bandage   md
SPICE to season; flavour; relish
SPICK spike; nail; tidy; fresh
SPICY aromatic; piquant; racy   ck
SPIED observed; beheld
SPIES secret agents
SPIKE large nail; lavender   bt
SPIKY spiny; sharp; pointed
SPILE spigot; peg
SPILL upset; shed; effuse; lighter

SPILT diffused; scattered; dropped
SPINE spina; spike; back-bone   md
SPINK chaffinch; primrose   zo, bt
SPINY thorny; spiky; difficult
SPIRE steeple; a curl; sedge   bt
SPIRT spurt; spout; gush; jet
SPIRY spiral
SPITE gall; pique; hatred; malice
SPITZ Pomeranian dog   zo
SPIZA a finch genus   zo
SPLAT part of a chair-back
SPLAY wide; to slant; to slope
SPLIT divulge; rent; cleave
SPODE china-ware
SPOIL mar; booty; snake's skin   zo
SPOKE orated; spouted; said
SPOLE spool; a small wheel
SPOOF hoax; humbug; bamboozle
SPOOK phantom; ghost; spectre
SPOOL spole; small wheel
SPOOM to scud down wind   nt
SPOON ladle; to court
SPOOR track or trail of an animal
SPORE reproductive cell   bt
SPORT play; gambol; romp; frolic
SPOSH slush
SPOTS a leopard   zo
SPOUT pawn; gush; issue; nozzle
SPRAG a check-stop; young salmon   zo
SPRAT small sea-fish   zo
SPRAY foam; sprig; diffuse
SPREE a carousal
SPRIG shoot; twig; a brad
SPRIT a sprout; boom; spar   nt
SPROD a second year salmon   zo
SPRUE a disease   md
SPUME froth; spray
SPUMY foaming
SPUNK pluck; courage; tinder; semen
SPURN scorn; scout; slight; disdain
SPURT spout; sprint; rush; speed
SQUAB clumsy; curt; unfledged; coy
SQUAD band; gang; crew; bevy
SQUAT crouch; cower; dumpy; stocky
SQUAW American Indian woman
SQUIB firework; skit; lampoon
SQUID cuttlefish; a calamary   zo
SRUTI Hindu tradition
STACK to pile; chimney; (cards)
STADE stadium; arena   me
STAFF rod; pole; stick; personnel
STAGE produce; present; platform
STAGY theatrical; histrionic
STAID steady; grave; sedate
STAIN sully; taint; tarnish; soil
STAIR a step; a stairway
STAKE picket; wager; risk; hazard
STALE musty; vapid; effete; trite
STALK hunt; strut; stride   bt
STALL (flying); stop; halt; booth
STAMP impress; brand; mark; type

STAND provide; stay; stall; rostrum	
STANG wooden pole; to throb	
STANK stunk; smelt	
STARE gape; gaze; the starling	zo
STARK rigid; still; sheer; bare	
STARR Jewish deed or bond	
START evoke; rouse; shrink; wince	
STATE aver; avow; plight; phase	
STAVE avert; fend; burst	mu
STEAD bedstead; use; help	
STEAK thick slice of meat	ck
STEAL filch; purloin; pilfer; creep	
STEAM vapour; fume; reek	
STEAN steen; crockery	
STEED warhorse; palfrey; mount	zo
STEEK stitch; pierce; shut (Sc.)	
STEEL brace; nerve; vigour; blade	
STEEP imbue; dip; soak; excessive	
STEER guide; pilot; bullock	zo
STEIN earthenware beer tankard (Ger.)	
STELA) inscribed column; tablet;	
STELE) sap system	
STEND leap; walk with long strides	
STENT to stint; restrain; limit	
STERE cubic metre	nt
STERN dour; grim; rigorous	nt
STEVE to stow	
STICA Saxon farthing	nm
STICH stave; a verse	mu
STICH a row of trees	
STICK stab; fix; attach; adhere	
STIED penned like pigs	
STIFF stark; rigid; prim; starchy	
STILB unit of luminance	me
STILE the gnomon of a sundial	
STILL not sparkling; calm; distil	
STILP to go on crutches (Sc.)	
STILT a pole; a snipe	zo
STIME styme; a glimmer; ray (Sc.)	
STIMY stymie; (golf)	
STING prick; wound; hurt; afflict	
STINK stench; odour; smell	
STINT allotted task; limit; scrimp	
STINT sandpiper; dunlin	zo
STIPA the feather grasses	bt
STIPE stalk; stem	bt
STIRK young ox or cow	zo
STIRP line of descent	
STIVE to stew	
STIVY stuffy; close	
STOAK to stop; to choke	me
STOAT ermine; weasel	zo
STOCK cravat; store; garner; fund	
STOCK ski-stick; log	
STOEP stoop; verandah (S. Africa)	
STOIC a disciple of Zeno	
STOKE replenish; refuel	
STOLA Roman lady's dress	
STOLE peculated; plagarised	rl
STOLE a stolon; a sucker	bt
STOMA breathing pore	bt

STOMP stamp; stump	
STONE boulder; pelt; 14 lb (6.3 kg)	me
STONY hard; flinty; obdurate; broke	
STOOD allowed; brooked; bore	
STOOK stouk; 12 sheaves	bt
STOOL a seat without a back; ramify	
STOOM stum; renew fermentation	
STOOP flagon; condescend; yield	
STOOR stour; dust; commotion	
STOPE mining ledge; to excavate	
STORE hoard; garner; stock; supply	
STORK infant conveyor	zo
STORM fume; rage; scold; turmoil	
STORY narrative; recital; account	
STOSH fish-offal; pomace	
STOUK stook; sheaves of corn	bt
STOUP stoop; flagon; tankard	
STOUR stoor; tumult; paroxysm	
STOUT resolute; robust; a drink	
STOVE oven; kiln; to heat	
STOWN stolen (Sc.)	
STRAD a Stradivarius violin	mu
STRAE straw (Sc.)	bt
STRAP a strop; chastise; beat	
STRAW strae (Sc.); valueless trifle	
STRAY err; rove; wander; deviate	
STREW scatter; spread; broadcast	
STRIA stripe; streak; small channel	
STRIG stalk; footstalk	bt
STRIP peel; divest; dismantle; shred	
STRIX screech-owl	zo
STROB measure of angular velocity	
STROP strap; sharpen; a rope	me
STROW strew; scatter	
STRUB to rob	
STRUM thrum	mu
STRUT support; brace; walk; swagger	
STUCK set; fixed; adhered; stabbed	
STUDY con; scan; reflect; learning; den	
STUFA jet of steam	
STUFF cram; pack; cloth; fabric	
STULL cross-timber in a mine	me
STULM shaft used to drain a mine	me
STULP a stump	
STUMP log; block; stub; nonplus	
STUNG pricked; afflicted; had	
STUNK stank; smelt	
STUNT to dwarf; check; exploit	
STUPA Buddhist monument; a dagoba	
STUPE hot bandage; fomentation	me
STURT strife; wrath; vexation	
STYCA Saxon half-farthing	nm
STYLE pen; dub; entitle; vogue	
STYLO a pen; a stylograph	
STYME stime; stimie (golf)	
SUAGE to assuage (Milton)	
SUAVE bland; pleasant; polite	
SUBAH province; viceroyship (Ind.)	
SUDAK the pike-perch	ze
SUDRA the lowest Hindu caste	
SUEDE unglazed leather	

SUENT neat and tidy	
SUETY of suet fat	ck
SUFIC Islamic mysticism	rl
SUGAR flattery	
SUING legal prosecution	lw
SUINT lanoline	
SUIST self-seeker	
SUITE retinue; series; train	
SULKS grumpiness	
SULKY light vehicle; sullen; morose	
SULLY soil; taint; stain; defame	
SUMAC sumach; plant used in dyeing	bt
SUMPH dunce; blockhead (Sc.)	
SUNNA Moslem traditions	lw, rl
SUNNI orthodox Moslem; member of sect	
	rl
SUNNY bright; brilliant; unclouded	
SUN-UP sunrise; dawn; cock-crow	
SUPER a supernumerary; special	
SURAH Indian silk; chapter of Koran	rl, tx
SURAL (calf of the leg)	md
SURAT coarse Indian cotton	tx
SURER more certain; safer	
SURFY covered with surf	
SURGE roll; swell; heave; a billow	
SURGY swirling; towering; surfy	
SURLY churlish; morose; crusty; gruff	
SURMA Ind. eyeshadow	
SURRA Eastern horse disease	
SURYA Hindu sun-god	rl
SUSHI bean-curd rice dish (Jap.)	ck
SUTOR a cobbler	
SUTRA (Brahminical ritual)	rl
SWACK active; nimble; to gulp (Sc.)	
SWAGE assuage; soften; mitigate	to
SWAGE drill-bit shaping tool	to
SWAIN a peasant; a country lover	
SWALE shady spot; a vale; melt; sweal	
SWAMI religious instructor (Hindu)	
SWAMP flood; inundate; fen; slough	
SWANG swamp; greensward	
SWANK brag; swagger	
SWAPE handle; oar; sconce	
SWARD turf; bacon rind	
SWARE testified; deposed; cursed	
SWARF to faint; to swoon; grit	
SWARM throng; teem; cluster; bevy	
SWART swarthy; tawny; dusky	
SWASH dash, splash, with flourish	pr
SWATH swathe; the sweep of a scythe	
SWATS new ale (Sc.)	
SWAZI (Swaziland)	
SWEAL scorch; melt; gutter; swale	
SWEAR affirm; vow; vouch; blaspheme	
SWEAT exude; ooze; perspire; toil	
SWEDE a turnip	bt
SWEEP (chimney); brush; lottery	
SWEEP a bend; scope; curve; oar	nt
SWEER sweir; lazy; reluctant (Sc.)	
SWEET luscious; honeyed; dulcet	
SWELL expand; dilate; amplify; bulge	

SWELT to swelter (Spens.)	
SWEPT brushed; scoured; scrubbed	
SWIFT fleet; quick; sudden; prompt	zo
SWILL boose; quaff; wash; rinse	
SWINE pig	zo
SWING sway; vibrate; dangle; hang	
SWINK labour; to toil; to drudge	
SWIPE smite; slog; steal	
SWIRE a col; a hollow between 2 hills	
SWIRL whirl; gyrate; eddy	
SWISH to birch; thrash	
SWISS Helvetian	
SWITH quickly; away! begone!	
SWOON to faint	
SWOOP rush; stoop; descent	
SWORD hanger; rapier; cutlass; blade	
SWORE sworn; sware; testified	
SWORN under oath; affirmed	
SWOTE sweetly (Spens.)	
SWUNG rocked; vacillated; dangled	
SYCEE silver in small ingots (China)	
SYKER surely (Spens.)	
SYLPH an airy fairy; (Pope)	
SYLVA silva; forest trees	
SYNOD ecclesiastical Council	rl
SYREN siren; enticer; hooter	
SYRUP sirup; sirop; sweetened liquid	
SYTHE scythe (obs.)	

T

TABAC snuff-colour	
TABBY brindled; watered silk; a cat	zo
TABES emaciation; atrophy	md
TABID consumptive; phthisical	md
TABLE index; list; schedule; board	
TABOO ban; bar; prohibit; interdict	
TABOR camp; laager; small drum	mu
TACAN navigation system	nt
TACCA tropical plant genus	bt
TACET be silent!	mu
TACHE a catch; stain; freckle; loop	
TACIT silent; implicit; inferred	
TACKY viscous; gummy; sticky	
TAFFY a Welshman; toffy; blarney	
TAFIA Malay rum	
TAGAL Filipino	
TAGMA region of metameric animal	zo
TAHLI Hindu gold ornament	
TAIGA coniferous region (Siberia)	
TAILS evening dress (for men)	
TAINT stain; tarnish; sully; defile	
TAIPO taepo; vicious animal (NZ)	zo
TAKEN seized; captured; won; assumed	
TAKER grasper; acceptor	
TALBE air/sea rescue system	ro
TALES equals in kind; (jurors)	lw
TALLY agree; correspond; match	
TALMA loose cloak	
TALON claw; concave; moulding	
TALPA the mole genus; a wen	zo, md

TALUK Indian subdistrict
TALUS sloping mound; earthwork; ankle
  bone **md**
TAMBU tamboo; taboo; ostracism
TAMED docile; domesticated; curbed
TAMER subjugator; subduer
TAMIL a Dravidian language (Sri Lanka)
TAMIN glazed worsted stuff
TAMIS tammy; straining cloth
TAMMY tamis; a tam-o'-shanter
TAMUS black bryony **bt**
TANGO Argentine dance
TANGY piquant; sharp in taste
TANIA African farinaceous tuber **bt**
TANKA Canton boat population
TANNA tana; Indian police station
TANSY Easter cake; bitter herb **bt, ck**
TANTO so; so much **mu**
TANTY Hindu loom
TAPED measured; sized up
TAPEN made of tape
TAPER wax-candle; slender and conical
TAPET tapestry; tapis
TAPIR related to pig (South America) **zo**
TAPIS tapestry; carpet (Fr.)
TAPIS hidden; under consideration
TAPPA tapa; fibre for mats **bt**
TARDO slowly **mu**
TARDY late; sluggish; dilatory
TARED tare allowance recorded
TARFA tamarisk; (exudes manna) **bt**
TARGE target; shield or buckler
TARIN the siskin **zo**
TAROC) card game in which there are
TAROT) 78 cards in the pack
TARRY stay; linger; sojourn; loiter
TARSE the tarsus; foot; ankle **md**
TARSI feet of insects **zo**
TARUS projection between roof surfaces
TARVE a curve; a bend
TASSE thigh armour
TASSO Italian poet; 16th Century
TASTE savour; smack; experience
TASTY piquant; savoury; appetising
TATAR native of Tartary
TATOU tatu; peba; armadillo **zo**
TAT-TA goodbye; a stroll
TATTA Indian screen: of cuscus grass
TATTY tattered; worn out
TAUNI deride; revile; high-masted **nt**
TAWED treated with alum
TAWER a leather-dresser
TAWIE tame (Sc.)
TAWNY fulvous; fulvid; tanned
TAWSE taws; leather strap (Sc.)
TAXED burdened; accused
TAXEL N. American badger **zo**
TAXER inspector of taxes
TAXIN yew extract **bt**
TAXIS classification; manipulation
TAXIS organism movement toward stimulus

TAXUS yew genus **bt**
TAZZA bowl
TEACH coach; edify; instruct
TEASE vex; annoy; plague; harass
TECHY tetchy; touchy; testy; petulant
TEDDY a bear **zo**
TEENS thirteen to nineteen
TEENY wee; tiny; minute
TEETH dentures
TE-HEE titter; snigger
TEIAN Ionian, (Anacreon)
TEINT colour; tinge; tint; hue
TELAR web-like; woven; spun
TELEX teleprinter exchange
TELIC final; conclusive
TELUM last abdominal somite in insects **zo**
TEMPE amusement park in Thessaly
TEMPO (cards); relative rapidity **mu**
TEMPT allure; lure; decoy; entice
TEMSE sieve; to sift
TENCH a fish **zo**
TENET rigid doctrine; dogma; belief
TENNE an orange-brown colour
TENON mortise projection
TENOR purport; trend; course **mu**
TENSE taut; tight; intent; strained
TENTH a tithe; ordinal number
TENTY attentive; alert
TEPAL a perianth leaf **b**
TEPEE Sioux tent
TEPID, TEPOR lukewarm; moderate
TERCE about 42 gal (191 litres) **me**
TEREK a sandpiper **zo**
TERES a muscle **me**
TERFA edible fruit-body of terferia **b**
TERMA terminal lamina of brain **me**
TERNE inferior tin-plate
TERRA earth
TERRY a fabric
TERSE abrupt
TESLA magnetic-flux density **me**
TESTA husk; integument **b**
TESTY techy; fretful; irritable
TEUCH teugh; tough (Sc.)
TEWEL chimney flue
THANE, THEGN Anglo-Saxon title
THANK express gratitude
THARM twisted gut
THAWY inclined to thaw
THECA seed or spore case **b**
THEFT larceny; robbery; pilfering
THEIC tea-pot devotee
THEIN tea **b**
THEIR of them
THEMA subject for discussion
THEME melodic/topical motif repeated **m**
THERE at that place
THERM thermal unit of gas **m**
THESE pl. of this
THETA a Greek letter
THEWY muscular; strong

THICK dense; solid; stupid; friendly		
THIEF pickpocket; an Autolycus		
THIGH upper part of leg	pl	
THILK the same		
THILL shaft of a cart; fire-clay		
THINE thy		
THING object; article; entity		
THING Scandinavian Parliament		
THINK deem; muse; cogitate		
THIRD ordinal number		
THIRL to cut through workings	mn	
THIRL a restriction; to pierce		
THOFT a rowing bench		
THOLE pin for an oar; to suffer	nt	
THONG lash of whip; strap		
THORN prickle; spine	bt	
THORP homestead; hamlet; dorp		
THOSE pl. of that		
THOTH Egyptian god of wisdom		
THOUS African jackal genus	zo	
THOWL thole; pin for an oar	nt	
THRAP to fasten		
THRAW to wrench; to twist (Sc.)		
THREE brace and a half; a leash		
THREW flung; hurled; projected		
THRID to thread		
THROB beat; palpitate; quiver		
THROE pang; agony; anguish		
THROW cast; toss; fell; pitch		
THRUM yarn; fringe; to strum	mu	
THULE Ultima Thule		
THUMB finger clumsily		
THUMP bang; whack; pommel		
THURL thirl; passage in a mine		
THUYA arbor vitae	bt	
THYME a genus of plants	bt	
THYMY fragrant		
TIARA ornamental head-dress		
TIBBY cat		
TIBET heavy goat-hair fabric		
TIBIA the large shinbone	md	
TICAL Siamese rupee	nm	
TICED enticed; decoyed		
TIDAL of tides		
TIDED surmounted		
TIDDY the wren	zo	
TIE-IN tubular scaffolding, interior grip		
TIFFY an artificer		
TIGER diminutive groom; jungle cat	zo	
TIGHT taut; tense; close; compact		
TIKUL Indian tree	bt	
TILDE diacritical mark: ~		
TILED tessellated		
TILER tyler; Masonic doorkeeper		
TILIA lime-tree	bt	
TILKA Hindu caste mark		
TILTH cultivation		
TIMED measured, finite		
TIMER time-fixed, -ing device		
TIMES the newspaper		
TIMID shy; fearful; diffident		

TIMON Athenian misanthrope		
TINEA moth genus; ringworm	zo, md	
TINED pronged		
TINGE hue; tint; stain; dye		
TINGI Brazilian soap-tree	bt	
TINNY like tin; sharp in sound		
TINTY crudely tinted		
TIPSY tight; drunk; fuddled		
TIRAZ Moorish silk fabric		
TIRED weary; harassed; attired		
T'IRON a webbed bar		
TISIC consumptive (Shak.)		
TISRI Hebrew month		
TITAN giant; Cyclops; Goliath		
TITHE a tenth; a tax	rl	
TITLE claim; right; due; name		
TITRE quantity of antibody	ba	
TITUP tittup; skip; canter		
TIVER ochre sheep dye		
TIZZY a sixpence	nm	
TOADY a sycophant		
TOAST scorch; health proposal		
TOBAS S. American native race		
TOBIT Apocryphal book		
TODAY this day		
TODDE 28 lb weight (obs.)	me	
TODDY a cordial		
TOE-IN front-wheels adjustment	au	
TOFFY toffee; taffy		
TOGED arrayed in a toga		
TOGUE mackinaw; lake-trout	zo	
TOILE twill; linen-silk mixture	tx	
TOILS a snare		
TOISE old French linear unit	me	
TOKAY Hungarian wine		
TOKEN sign; symbol; mark; badge		
TOMAN Persian gold coin	nm	
TOMIN a weight of 12 grains	me	
TOMMY Atkins; soldier; lever	to	
TONAL accented; harmonious		
TONDO circular relief sculpture		
TONED moderated; shaded; tinted		
TONGA Eastern cart		
TONIC bracing; key-note	md, mu	
TONKA tree whose seeds contain coumarin	bt	
TONUS state of persistent excitation	zo	
TOOTH prong; fang; tusk	bt	
TOPAU rhinoceros-bird	zo	
TOPAZ a gem	mn	
TOPEE sun helmet		
TOPER toss-pot; sot; tippler		
TOPET crested titmouse	zo	
TOPHI ear cartilage nodules	zo	
TOPIA Roman mural decoration		
TOPIC theme; subject; a remedy	md	
TOPOS cliché description		
TOQUE woman's twisted silk turban	tx	
TORAH the Mosaic law	lw	
TORAN Buddhist porch	rl	
TORCH flambeau; link; fire-brand		

TORIC type of lens	
TORII lap, gateway	ar
TORSE heraldic wreath	hd
TORSK a cod	zo
TORSO body trunk	md
TORUS an architectural moulding	ar
TOSSY contemptuous	
TOSYL toluene/sulphonyl compound	ch
TOTAL all; sum; whole; gross	
TOTED carried; borne; transported	
TOTEM superstitious symbol	
TOUCH handle; concern; effect	
TOUGH tenacious; coriaceous	
TOUSE tousle; haul; tease	
TOUSY disarranged	
TOWED hauled; dragged; tugged	
TOWEL an altar cloth	rl
TOWER soar; mount; turret	
TOWNY a townsman	
TOXIC toxicological	
TOXIN poison; virus	md
TOYED dallied; sported	
TOYER trifler	
TRACE vestige; trail; follow	
TRACK spoor; pathway; race-course	
TRACT region; pamphlet; homily	
TRADE barter; traffic; craft	
TRAIK to wander (Sc.)	
TRAIL haul; tow; track; follow	
TRAIN drill; school; retinue	
TRAIT characteristic	
TRAMA agaric-gill hyphae	bt
TRAMP hike; trudge; vagrant; hobo	
TRANK skin for glove cutting	
TRANT to hawk; to peddle	
TRAPA the water-chestnut	bt
TRAPE traipse; tramp	
TRAPS luggage	
TRASH poor whites (USA)	
TRASS volcanic earth	mn
TRAVE beam; wooden frame	
TRAWL a drag-net	
TREAD trample; step; press	
TREAT doctor; manage; deal	
TREED cornered	
TREEN wooden	
TREND tend; incline; lean	
TRESS ringlet; lock of hair	
TREST a beam; a stool (Sc.)	
TREWS Scottish trousers	tx
TRIAD a trinity	mu
TRIAL test; ordeal; case	lw
TRIAS sandstone	mn
TRIBE clan; race; class; order	
TRICE an instant; to haul	nt
TRICK dupe; cheat; artifice	
TRIED essayed; attempted	lw
TRIER experimentalist	
TRIES (Rugby football, 3 points)	
TRILL warble; quaver; shake	mu
TRINE triple; threefold; a triad	

TRINE favourable planet aspect	
TRIOR an examiner	lw
TRIPE offal, rubbish	
TRIST sorrowful; sad	
TRITE hackneyed; obvious; worn	
TROCO a ball game	
TROIC Trojan	
TROKE exchange; small wares (Sc.)	
TROLL to fish; sing; cave-elf	
TRONA Egyptian soda	m
TRONC distribution of pooled tips	
TRONE steelyard; a drain	m
TROOP throng; crowd; cluster	
TROPE a metaphor; figure of speech	
TROTH to plight; confidence; faith	
TROUT fish of Salmo genus	zo
TROVE treasure trove	
TRUCE lull; respite; armistice	
TRUCK a wheel; barter; a vehicle	
TRUCK wagon; mast-head	n
TRUER more worthy of belief	
TRULL vagrant; a drab	
TRULY verily; exactly; veritably	
TRUMP (the last trump); to ruff	
TRUMP a trumpet; Jew's harp	m
TRUNK torso; butt; stem; saratoga	
TRUSS bind; fasten	me
TRUST credit; reliance; merger	
TRUTH probity; fact; candour	
TRYMA a stone fruit; a drupe	b
TRY-ON a bluff	
TRYST rendezvous; (Lutheran carol)	
TSUBA Japanese sword hilt	
TUBAL tubar; tubular; hollow	
TUBBY fat; obese; dull	
TUBED piped	
TUBER bulbous growth	b
TUCAN Mexican pouched rat	zo
TUCUM S. American palm	b
TUDEH political party (Iran)	
TUDOR a royal house	
TUFTY feathery	
TUILE tuille; armour plates	
TUISM a curious theory	
TULIP showy flower	b
TULLE a delicate fabric	
TUMBA instrument S. Domingo	m
TUMID swollen; bombastic	
TUMPY lumpy; uneven	
TUNED attuned; harmonized; adapted	
TUNER sound adjuster	mu, r
TUNIC surcoat; a membrane	m
TUNNY large fish, mackerel type	z
TUQUE toque; Canadian knitted cap	
TURBA chorus of the people in opera	
TURBO whelk and winkle genus	z
TURCO Algerian soldier	
TURFY swardy; grassy; cespitose	
TURPS turpentine	
TUSKY with long teeth	
TUSSE wall-face projecting stone	b

UTOR coach; instruct; guardian
UTSI native of Burundi (Africa)
UTTI all in   **mu**
UTTY impure oxide of zinc   **ch**
UZZY tuft; tuffet; cluster
WAIN a couple; brace; pair
WAIT species of shad   **zo**
WANG tang; flavour
WANK twang; a nasal note   **mu**
WEAK pinch; twist; twitch
WEED twilled cloth   **tx**
WEEN between; twixt
WEER twier; blast-furnace
WERE it were
WERP nasty nitwit
WICE twofold; doubly; encore
WILL, TWEEL woven fabric
WILT a quilt (Sc.)
WINE entwine; wind; cord; string
WINK twinkle; twitter; chirp
WIRE to gleam; twist; twirl
WIRK a twitch (Sc.)
WIRL whirl; rotate; revolve
WIST writhe; hunger; (tobacco)
WITE mountain linnet   **zo**
WIXT betwixt; between
WO-ON doing 2 jobs at once   **pr**
WO-UP printing, processing twin series **pr**
WYER tweer; blast furnace; jet
YCHE Greek goddess of fortune
YING fastening; shackling
YLER tiler; Masonic doorkeeper
YLER tight-line gorge system   **fr**
YPAL typical; representative
YPED typewritten; given a classification **pr**
YPHA bulrush   **bt**
YPIC emblematic; symbolic
YRED wheeled, pneumatic
YTHE tithe; a tenth; church tax   **rl**

U

U-BOAT a submarine   **nt**
UDDER mammary gland   **zo**
UGRIC Finns, Magyars, Turks, etc.
UHLAN Prussian cavalryman
UHURU freedom (Swahili)
UKASE Russian decree
ULCER open sore   **md**
ULEMA Turkish hierarchy
ULMIC (elm exudations)   **bt**
ULMIN humus; a brown pigment
ULMUS elm genus   **bt**
ULNAD toward the ulna   **md**
ULNAR (forearm bone)   **md**
ULOID like a scar   **md**
ULTOR anode   **el**
ULTRA extreme
UMBEL inflorescence flower   **bt**
UMBER brown pigment   **zo**
UMBRA a shadow

UMBRE umber; the grayling   **zo**
UMIAK Eskimo boat   **nt**
UNAPT inept; irrevelant
UNARM disarm
UNARY consisting of 1 component   **ch**
UNBAR open; permit
UNBAY to open up
UNBED arouse
UNBID uninvited; spontaneous
UNBIT not bitten
UNBOW to unbend
UNBOX uncase; unpack
UNCAP unhat; uncover
UNCLE pawnbroker
UNCLE oom; Sam; Tom; Remus
UNCUS hook or claw   **zo**
UNCUT untrimmed; book before guillotine process
UNDAM release
UNDER below; lower; subject to
UNDID untied; nullified
UNDUE excessive; inordinate
UNFIT unqualified; improper
UNFIX detach; undo; loosen
UNGUM unstick
UNHAT uncover; uncap
UNIAT Russian Christian   **rl**
UNIFY unite; combine
UNION coalition; guild; league
UNITE join; concert; bind
UNITY concord; harmony; accord
UNKED unkid; strange; ugly
UNLAP unfold
UNLAY untwist; unravel
UNLED without guidance
UNLET vacant; tenantless
UNMAN dishearten; unnerve
UNMEW release from confinement
UNNUN unfrock
UNODE a geometric conception
UNOIL free from oil
UNPAY make undone
UNPEN release
UNRIG dismantle
UNRIP rip open
UNSAY retract; disavow
UNSET unmounted; runny; sticky
UNSEX geld
UNSON disinherit
UNTAX remove a tax
UNTIE undo; unbind; unknot
UNTIL till
UNTIN uncan
UNWEB unweave; unravel
UNWED unmarried
UNZIP undo patent fastening
UP-END tilt
UPHER rough scaffolding pole   **bd**
UPLAY to hoard
UPPER superior; higher
UPRUN run up; ascend

UPSEE after the manner of		
UPSET capsize; overturn; disconcert		
UPUPA hoopoe genus	zo	
URATE (uric acid)	ch	
URBAN of the city		
UREDO fungus genus		
UREIC pertaining to urea		
URENA Indian mallow	bt	
URGED pleaded; drove; impelled		
URGER inciter; prompter; agitator		
URIAL Asiatic wild sheep	zo	
URILE cormorant	zo	
URINE liquid body waste	md	
URITE tail of insect	zo	
URMAN Siberian forest land		
URNAL urn-shaped		
URNED (cremated)		
URSON Canadian porcupine	zo	
URSUS the bear genus	zo	
URUBU American turkey-buzzard	zo	
URVED curved upward		
USAGE habit; wont; custom		
USHAS Hindu aurora		
USHER herald; introduce; precede		
USING applying; employing		
USUAL normal; ordinary; habitual		
USURP arrogate; assume; seize		
USURY usure; exorbitant; interest		
UTTER declare; enunciate; total		
UVULA (soft palate)	md	
UZBEG, UZBEK Turkish Tatar		

V

VAGAL of the vagus nerves		
VAGUE dim; indistict; indefinite		
VAGUS a cranial nerve	md	
VAILS tip; gratuity; backsheesh		
VAIRE } charged with heraldic fur	hd	
VAIRY }		
VAKIL Indian attorney	lw	
VALED lowered; receded		
VALES vails; pourboire; douceur		
VALET gentleman's gentleman		
VALID cogent; substantial; strong		
VALSE waltz		
VALUE worth; price; cost; utility		
VALVE mechanical device		
VAMPS short hose		
VANED having vanes or blades		
VANIR three Norse deities		
VAPID insipid; feeble; jejune		
VAPOR vapour; miasma; steam		
VAREC seaweed; kelp	bt	
VARIA miscellany		
VARIX uneven dilation	md	
VARUS pigeon-toed	md	
VASAL (blood-vessel)	md	
VASTY spacious; immense; boundless		
VATIC prophetic; oracular		
VAULT leap; cell; tomb; crypt		

VAUNT boast; exult; swagger		
VEALY calflike; immature		
VEDAS Hindu sacred writings		
VEDIC according to the Vedas		
VEERY American thrush	z	
VEHME German secret society		
VEINY full of veins		
VELAR cupola or dome	a	
VELDT grass lands (S. Africa)		
VELIA water-bugs	z	
VELUM soft palate	m	
VENAL mercenary; corrupt; sordid		
VENEW } a thrust or hit in fencing		
VENEY }		
VENGE avenge (Shak.)		
VENOM virus; poison; rancour; gall		
VENUE location of an event		
VENUS Aphrodite		
VEREY signal light		
VERGE edge; staff; mace	
VERSE poetry; stanza; stich; stave		
VERSO left-hand page		
VERST Russian: ⅔ of a mile (1 km)	m	
VERTU virtu; rarity in art		
VERVE energy; vigour; inspiration		
VESPA wasp genus	z	
VESTA goddess of the hearth		
VESTA match; lucifer; taper		
VETCH ers; the tare	b
VEXED troubled; bothered; piqued		
VEXER provoker; annoyer		
VEXIL a banner; a petal	b
VIAND food		
VIBEX a blood spot	m
VICAR parish parson	
VIDEO recorded television film		
VIEWY visionary; speculative		
VIFDA vivda; dried meat		
VIGIA charted rock (Sp.)		
VIGIL watch; wake; eve		
VILER more degraded		
VILLA country residence		
VILLI small fibres	md, b
VIMEN slender shoot	b
VINCA periwinkle	b
VINED with tendrils		
VINIC alcoholic		
VINYL plastic fibre		
VIOLA plant genus	mu, b
VIPER adder; asp	z
VIREO American song-birds	z
VIRGO (Zodiac); a constellation		
VIRID green		
VIRTU vertu; rarity in art		
VIRUS poison; venom; toxin	m
VIRUS transmitter of infection	m
VISIE a searching glance (Sc.)		
VISIT frequent; call; drop in		
VISON American mink	z
VISOR } movable part of a helmet;		
VIZOR } a mask		

VISTA view; scene; prospect	
VITAL essential; animate; living	
VITEX verbena	bt
VITIS the vine	bt
VITTA a headband; garland	
VITTA stripe; oil cavity	bt
VIURE heraldic ribbon (Fr.)	hd
VIVAT (applause)	
VIVDA vifda; dried meat	
VIVES a disease of horses	vt
VIVID intense; brilliant; graphic	
VIZEN scold; shrew; termagant	zo
VIZIR vizier; vezir; minister (Turkish)	
VLACH a Wallachian	
VOCAL articulate	
VODAS echo-suppression device	tc
VODER synthetic-speech device	ac
VODKA Russian drink	
VOGAD telephony	
VOGIE vain; merry (Sc.)	
VOGUE fashion; mode; practice	
VOICE express; declare; utter	
VOILE gauzy material	
VOLAR (palm of the hand)	md
VOLEE rapid phrase	mu
VOLET part of triptych	
VOLTA an old dance; repeat	mu
VOLTE old dances; turns	
VOLTI turn over	mu
VOLVA hypha sheath in agarics	
VOLVE ponder; turn over (obs.)	
VOMER ploughshare; nose-bone	md
VOMIT spew; eject; disgorge	
VOTED polled; balloted	
VOTER elector	
VOUCH guarantee; affirm; aver	
VOWED swore; pledged; dedicated	
VOWEL open speech sound	
VOWER devotee	
VROUW woman; wife (Dutch)	
VUGGY full of cavities	
VULGO vernacular; popular style	
VULVA female genital opening	zo
VYING striving; competing	

W

WACKE basalt; trap-rock	mn
WADDY Australian war club	
WADED forded	
WADER long-legged bird	zo
WADEX word/author index for computers	
WAFER crisp cake	
WAGED pledged; conducted	
WAGEL black gull	zo
WAGER bet; hazard; stake; gamble	
WAGES stipend; remuneration	
WAGON wain; lorry; truck	
WAHOO cascara sagrada	md, bt
WAIST bodice; corsage	
WAITS Yule minstrels	

WAIVE remit; forego; relinquish	
WAKED kept vigil; stimulated	
WAKEN awaken; excite; animate	
WALAN amboyna tree	bt
WALED striped	
WALER Australian horse	zo
WALTY unstable	nt
WALTZ valse	
WANDY wandlike; flexible	
WANED ebbed; decreased; declined	
WANLY sickly; languidly	
WANTY a loading strap	
WARES merchandise; commodities	
WARTY excrescent	
WASHY watery; thin; feeble	
WASTE dissipate; squander; fritter	
WATCH guard; tend; mark	nt
WATER irrigate; moisten; sprinkle	
WAVED fluctuated; brandished	
WAVER sway; totter; vacillate	
WAVEY the snow-goose	
WAXED cered; grew; increased	
WAXEN ceruminous	
WAZIR vizier	
WEALD wold; woodland	
WEARY jaded; spent; fatigue; tire	
WEAVE plait; mat; entwine; interlace	
WEBBY filmy; reticulated	
WEBER magnetic flux	me
WEDGE coign; a scotch	
WEEDS widow's mourning apparel	
WEEDY weak and lanky	bt
WEELY wicker fish trap	
WEEPY lacrimose; oozy	
WEIGH balance; ponder; (anchor)	nt
WEIRD eerie; uncanny: supernatural	
WEISM excessive use of 'we'	
WELCH Welsh; Cymric	
WELSH Cymric; abscond	
WENCH maid; damsel	
WENNY (sebaceous cyst)	md
WERSH tasteless; unsalted (Sc.)	
WHACK thwack; defeat; smite	
WHALE the orc; a cetacean	zo
WHALL wall-eye	
WHAME the burrel-fly	zo
WHANG bang; whack; leather thong	
WHARE Maori hut	
WHARF quay; dock; pier	
WHAUP curlew	zo
WHEAL wale; weal	
WHEAL mine (Cornish)	mn
WHEAT a cereal	bt
WHEEL turn; revolve; whirl	
WHEEN a small quantity (Sc.)	
WHEFT a knotted flag	
WHELK a gasteropod	zo
WHELM overwhelm	
WHELP puppy; cub; pup; to litter	
WHERE the place concerned	
WHICH the item concerned	

WHIFF puff; outrigger boat	nt	**WORLD** universe; globe; earth	
WHIFT a breath; a snatch; glimpse		**WORMY** vermigerous	zo
WHILE pass the time		**WORRY** fret; chafe; fidget; badger	
WHILK the scoter; sea duck	zo	**WORSE** comparative of bad	
WHINE whimper; snivel; cry		**WORST** best; defeat; conquer	
WHIPT scourged; thrashed		**WORTH** value; cost; merit; desert	
WHIRL twirl; spin; gyrate; eddy		**WOTAN** Odin; Woden	rl
WHISK a brush; stir; hasten; rush		**WOULD** conditional auxil. verb	
WHIST keep silence; (cards)		**WOUND** harm; hurt; lacerate	
WHITE pale; wan; pallid; chalky		**WOVEN** plaited; interlaced	
WHIZZ whiz		**WRACK** ruin; seaweed	b
WHOLE entire; intact; total		**WRANG** wrung; twisted and squeezed	
WHOOP a shout of joy		**WRAPT** wrapped; hidden; enveloped	
WHOOT hoot		**WRATH** ire; rage; fury; passion	
WHORL convolution; spiral		**WRAUL** wrawl; to caterwaul	
WHORT whurt; whortleberry	bt	**WREAK** avenge; inflict; indulge	
WHOSE the owner of item concerned		**WRECK** ruin; blight; shatter	
WHOSO he who		**WREST** twist; wrench; strain	
WICKY mountain ash	bt	**WRICK** to sprain	
WIDDY widow; withy; withe	bt	**WRIER** more contorted	
WIDEN extend; enlarge		**WRING** extort; wrest; writhe	
WIDER broader; more remote		**WRIST** hand/arm joint	p
WIDOW to bereave		**WRITE** indite; scrawl; scribble	
WIDTH span; amplitude; beam		**WRONG** injure; falsify; error; tort	
WIELD control; exert; ply; brandish		**WROTE** inscribed; penned; engrossed	
WIERY wet; moist; miry (obs.)		**WROTH** wrathful; angry; furious	
WIGAN stiff canvas	tx	**WRUNG** tormented; racked	
WIGHT a creature; strong; nimble		**WRYLY** distorted; askew	
WILED beguiled; hoaxed; cheated			
WILLY wool cleaning machine			
WINCE flinch; blench; shrink		**X**	
WINCH hoisting machine			
WINDY timid; nervous; bombastic		**XEBEC** Algerian pirate ship	n
WINED drank wine		**XENIA** pollen effect on young plant	b
WINGY rapid		**XENON** a gas	c
WINZE ventilating shaft; a curse		**XERES** sherry	
WIPED rubbed; mopped; cleansed		**XERIC** adapted to dry conditions	e
WIPER mechanical device		**X-MARK** face-mark	c
WIRED telegraphed; snared		**XYLEM** woody tissue	
WISER sager; more expedient		**XYLIC** benzoic acid	c
WISPY flocculent; nebulous		**XYLOL** aromatic fluid	
WITAN Witanagemote (Anglo-Saxon)		**XYLYL** xylene	c
WITCH hag; crone; sibyl			
WITHE willow twig	bt		
WITHY species of willow	bt	**Y**	
WITTY droll; facetious; humorous			
WIVES spouses		**YACCA** Jamaican tree	b
WIZEN shrivelled; dried up		**YACHT** pleasure ship	n
WODEN Odin; Wotan	rl	**YACOU** guan; a game bird	zo
WOMAN female human		**YAGER** Jaeger; light infantry	
WOMBY capacious (Shak.)		**YAHOO** hooligan	
WOMEN pl. of woman		**YAMEN** ⎫ mandarin's house;	
WONGA Australian pigeon	zo	**YAMUN** ⎭ Chinese office	
WOODY sylvan; ligneous		**YAPOK** S. American water-opossum	zo
WOOED courted		**YAPON** evergreen shrub; cassine	b
WOOER a lover; a swain		**YAQUI** Mexican Indians	
WOOFY dense; close in texture		**YASHT** Zend-Avesta prayer book	
WOOLD to twist; dyer's weed	bt	**YAWED** out of course	n
WOONT the mole	zo	**YAWEY** (tropical disease)	m
WOOTZ Bengal steel		**YEARN** crave; hanker; desire	
WORDY verbose; prolix; garrulous		**YEAST** leaven; balm; ferment	

YELEK a long vest (Turk.)
YERBA Paraguay tea   bt
YESTY yeasty
YEWEN made of yew   bt
YEXED hiccupped
YIELD submit; render; supply
YODEL yodle; Tyrolese singing
YOGIN Hindu philosopher
YOICK to encourage
YOJAN about 5 miles (8 km) (E. Ind.)   me
YOKED coupled; linked; paired
YOKEL rustic; churl; clodhopper
YOLKY egg-yolk consistency
YORKY slate with curved cleave
YOUNG boyish; juvenile; recent
YOURS of you
YOUTH lad; stripling; heyday
YRNEH unit of reciprocal inductance   el
YUCCA lily genus   bt
YUCKY itchy
YULAN Chinese magnolia   bt
YULOH aft-oar for sculling   nt

Z

ZABRA Spanish coasting vessel   nt
ZAMBO cross-bred Indian
ZAMIA a palm genus   bt
ZANJE irrigation canal (S. America)
ZANTE satin-wood   bt
ZAYAT Burmese inn
ZEBEC xebec; Algerian ship   nt
ZEBRA an ungulate   zo
ZEBUS Abyssinian tsetse-fly   zo
ZEINE the gluten of maize   bt
ZEMNI the blind mole-rat   zo
ZENER semi-conductor current

ZERDA African fox   zo
ZHOBO ⎫
ZHOMO ⎬ hybrid, yak and cow
ZIARA Moslem shrine
ZIBET Asiatic civet   zo
ZIMBA Am. Indian and Eskimo game
ZIMBI cowry used as money   zo
ZINCO zincograph
ZINEB chemical fungicide
ZINKE old type of cornet   mu
ZINKY zincy; partly zinc
ZIRAM chemical fungicide
ZIZEL marmot; ground-squirrel   zo
ZLOTY Polish money   nm
ZOAEA ⎫
ZOOEA ⎬ larval crustacean   zo
ZOCCO ⎫
ZOCLE ⎬ square base
ZOEAL early crustacean life   zo
ZOFRA Moorish carpet
ZOGAN Japanese inlay work
ZOHAR sacred Jewish book   rl
ZOISM theory of life origin
ZOIST a believer in zoism
ZONAL zonic
ZONAR like a girdle
ZONDA the dry wind of the Andes
ZOOID polyp; polypide   zo
ZOOKS gadzooks
ZOPPO occasional syncopation   mu
ZORIL African skunk   zo
ZORRA American skunk   zo
ZORRO S. American fox-wolf   zo
ZUPAN Serbian rural council
ZYGAL like an 'H'
ZYGON connecting bar
ZYMIC relating to fermentation
ZYMIN ex-enzyme   zo

A

ABACOT bycoket; hat of state (15th cent.)
ABACUS a counting device
ABALYN synthetic resin; lacquer
ABASED humbled; debased; sunk
ABASIA inco-ordination in walking   md
ABATED mitigated; subsided
ABATER reducer; assuager
ABATIS abattis; obstacles
ABATTE heavy meat-flattening knife   ck
ABBACY office of abbot   rl
ABBATE a title   rl
ABBESS head of nuns' abbey   rl
ABDALS Moslem fanatics (Pers.)
ABDEST Mohammedan rite
ABDIEL the faithful seraph
ABDUCE separate; retract
ABDUCT remove; kidnap
ABIDED abode; sojourned; tarried
ABIDER dweller; settler
ABIENT avoidance reflex   pc
ABJECT servile; base; ignoble
ABJURE renounce; recant; repudiate
ABKARI ⎫
ABKARY ⎭ Persian excise duty on wine
ABLAUT (vowel change)
ABLAZE flaming; excited
ABLEST most competent; cleverest
ABLINS perhaps
ABLOOM thriving
ABLUSH blushing; flushing
ABOARD afloat; inside   nt
ABORAL remote from the mouth
ABOUND flow; team; swarm
ABRADE scrape; grate
ABRAYD to awaken (Spens.)
ABROAD apart; far; widely
ABROOK endure
ABRUPT steep; hasty; brusque; curt
ABSENT away; left; distracted
ABSORB engulf; consume; swallow
ABSURD irrational; asinine
ABUSED reviled; violated; traduced
ABUSER reviler; slanderer
ACACIA flowering shrub   bt
ACACIO acajou; cashew nut   bt
ACADIA Nova Scotia
ACAJOU gum; acacio   bt
ACARUS insect genus   zo
ACATES food
ACCEDE assent; agree; comply
ACCEND kindle (obs.)
ACCENT tone; stress; cadence
ACCEPT take; receive; admit
ACCESS entry; approach; fit
ACCITE to cite
ACCLOY to cloy; satiate; surfeit
ACCOIL to collect (Spens.)
ACCORD concede; deign; tally
ACCOST confront; hail; greet

ACCOUB edible thistle   ck
ACCREW ⎫ to result in; inure; proceed;
ACCRUE ⎭ accumulate
ACCUSE charge; cite; censure
ACEDIA torpor; fish   md, zo
ACERIC (maple)   bt
ACETAL plastic; cosmetic base   ch
ACETIC an acid   ch
ACETYL radical of acetic acid   ch
ACHENE seeded fruit   bt
ACHING continued pain; sorrowing
ACHIRA edible canna   ck
ACICLE bristle; sharp crystal   bt, mn
ACIDIC containing acid   ch
ACINUS berry   bt
ACK-ACK anti-aircraft
ACLIDE spiked club
ACMITE pyroxene rock   mn
ACNODE in double point tangents   ma
ACOPIC curative of fatigue   md
ACORIA morbid appetite for food   md
ACORUS sweet flag   bt
ACQUIT absolve; release; exonerate
ACRACY anarchy
ACRISY poor judgment
ACRITA sponges   zo
ACROSS athwart; transversely
ACTING performing; pretending
ACTION deed; feat; gesture   lw
ACTIVE agile; alert; nimble; busy
ACTUAL real; true; genuine; positive
ACUATE pointed
ACUITY sharpness
ACULEI prickles   bt, zo
ACUMEN keenness of perception
ADAGIO leisurely   mu
ADAMIC pertaining to Adam
ADDEEM judge
ADDICT accustom; habituate; devote
ADDING totting; summing
ADDLED deranged; rotten
ADDUCE allege; assign; advance; cite
ADDUCT product of molecular reaction   ch
ADENIA enlargement of glands   md
ADHERE cohere; cling; cleave
ADIENT tending to expose to stimulus
ADIEUS or **ADIEUX** farewells
ADIPIC fatty; adipose
ADJECT to add to
ADJOIN abut; annex; touch; unite
ADJURE exhort; urge; beg; pray
ADJUST arrange; trim; rectify; fit
ADMASS common consumers; the masses
ADMIRE esteem; prize; revere; respect
ADNATE joined to another organ
ADNEXA appendages, close structures   zo
ADNOUN an adjective
ADONAI lord (Hebrew)
ADONIC species of short verse
ADONIS bird's eye; pheasant's eye   bt
ADONIS youth loved by Venus

ADOORS at the door
ADORAL adjacent to the mouth   zo
ADORED worshipped; idolized; beloved
ADORER admirer; lover; venerator
ADREAD fearful; apprehensive
ADRIFT afloat; distracted; loose
ADROIT expert; skilful; masterly
ADSORB to condense a gas
ADVENE accede
ADVENT arrival; approach; coming   rl
ADVERT to notice; to regard
ADVICE counsel; warning; tidings; rede
ADVIEW to view (Spens.)
ADVISE urge; recommend; inform
ADVISO news; intelligence
ADYTUM chancel   rl
ADZUKI red Japanese bean   ck
AECIAL spore-producing part of fungi bt
AEDILE Roman magistrate
AENEID epic poem
AEOLIC Greek dialect
AEOLUS god of the winds
AERATE expose to air action
AERIAL etherial; empyreal; airy
AERIFY aerate
AEROBE an organic growth   md
AEROSE coppery; brassy
AERUGO verdigris; patina; rust
AETHER ether   ch
AFEARD affrighted
AFFAIR incident; concern; skirmish
AFFEAR to terrify
AFFECT assume; feign; influence
AFFEER settle a price   lw
AFFINE similar curves of variables ma
AFFIRM vouch; ratify; endorse; allege
AFFLUX to flow
AFFORD produce; impart; confer; spare
AFFRAY onset; brawl; strife; fracas
AFFRET effray; broil; startle; frighten
AFFUSE sprinkle; pour upon
AFGHAN of Afghanistan
AFIELD in the open
AFLAME blazing; afire
AFLOAT at sea; unfixed
AFOCAL without focal length   pg
AFRAID timid; fearful; anxious
AFREET evil spirit (Arab.)
AFRESH anew; again
AFRONT in front (obs.)
AFRIDI (Afghan.)
AFTERS sweet or dessert course   ck
AGALMA impression of a seal
AGAMAE cryptogamic plants   bt
AGAMIC asexual
AGARIC fungus; mushroom   bt
AGAZED thunder-struck; amazed
AGEING maturing; mellowing
AGENCY intervention; mediation
AGENDA items of business
AGHAST appalled; astounded

AGNAIL a whitlow   md
AGNAME nickname
AGNATE (relationship) akin; allied
AGNISE acknowledge; confess
AGNOSY ignorance
AGOING current
AGONIC zero declination
AGOUTA Haitian rat   zo
AGOUTI } guinea-pig;
AGOUTY } S. American rodent   zo
AGRAFA Greek cheese   ck
AGRAIL narrow-gauge railway
AGREED reconciled; concerted; tallied
AGUISE to dress (Spens.)
AGUISH shivering; chilly   md
AHIMSA sacredness of life (Hindu, Jain)
AIDANT assisting
AIDFUL helpful; co-operative
AIDING assisting; succouring
AIGLET aglet; pendant; young eagle   zo
AIGRET aigrette; plume
AILING sick; unwell; indisposed
AIMING pointing; endeavouring
AINHUM chronic Negro disease causing digit loss
AIR-ACE super-airman
AIR-BED inflated mattress
AIRDOX coal-mining process using air
AIR-DRY dry to parity with atmosphere
AIR-GUN air-operated weapon
AIRILY buoyantly; gaily
AIRING stroll; ventilation
AIR-LOG linear travel recorder
AIRMAN aeronaut
AIR-SAC air-cell
AIRWAY flying lane; airline
AISLED having aisles   ar
AKIMBO arched; bent arms
ALALIA loss of speech   md
ALARUM alarm clock; alarm
ALATED alate; winged   bt
ALBATA an alloy
ALBEDO light reflective power
ALBEIT although
ALBERT a watch chain
ALBIAN cretaceous rock stage   gl
ALBINO abnormally white
ALBION England (Morte D'Arthur)
ALBITE (felspar)   mn
ALBUGO eye-trouble; fungus   bt, md
ALCADE } judge; magistrate (Spain)
ALCAID }
ALCAIC poetic metre
ALCEDO } kingfisher
ALCYON }   zo
ALCLAD an aluminium alloy
ALCOVE a bower; arbour; recess
ALDERN made of alder
ALDINE 16th century books by Aldus
ALDRIN naphthalene insecticide   ch
ALECTO a Fury

ALEGAR sour ale	
ALEGER lively; cheerful	
ALERCE cedar wood	bt
ALETTE pilaster	ar
ALEVIN salmon fry	zo
ALEXIA inability to read	md
ALEXIN defensive protein	md
ALGATE always; nevertheless	
ALGOID (seaweeds)	bt
ALGOUS (algoid)	bt
ALIBLE nourishing	
ALIGHT descend; ignited; flaming	
ALINED, ALIGNED brought into line	
ALIPED having winged feet	
ALKALI opposite to acid	ch
ALKANE methane series	ch
ALKENE ethylene series	ch
ALLEGE also alegge; assert; maintain	
ALLELE alternative form of gene	gn
ALLICE Severn shad; fish	zo
ALLIED united; related; cognate; akin	
ALLIES affinities; associates	
ALL-OUT top speed	
ALLUDE refer; imply; hint; insinuate	
ALLURE tempt; decoy; seduce; cajole	
ALMAIN German; dance (obs.)	
ALMIRA storage furniture (Ind.)	
ALMNER almoner; dispenser	
ALMOIN alms; alms-chest (tenure)	
ALMOND dessert nut	bt
ALMOST well-nigh; nearly	
ALMUCE amice or furred hood	
ALNAGE measuring by the ell	me
ALNICO permanent magnet alloy	
ALOGIA mental deficiency speech defect	
ALPACA llama; Peruvian sheep	
ALPHUS leprosy; psoriasis	md
ALPINE of the Alps	
ALPINI Italian mountain troops	
ALPIST bird-seed	bt
ALSIKE Swedish clover	bt
ALTERN alternate	
ALTHEA rose of Sharon	bt
ALUDEL distilling apparatus	ch
ALUMNA a woman graduate	
ALUMNI collegiates; pupils; scholars	
ALVINE pert. to belly, intestines	md
ALWAYS age; evermore; eternally	
AMADOU dried fungus; tinder	
AMATOL explosive	ah
AMAZED astounded, nonplussed	
AMAZIA mammary non-development	md
AMAZON female warrior; virago; shrew	
AMBAGE circumlocution; subterfuge	
AMBERY amber-like	
AMBLED at an easy pace; strolled	
AMBLER saunterer	
AMBURY ⎫ a disease in turnips	
ANBURY ⎭	bt
AMBUSH troops in waiting	
AMELIA congenital limb absence	md

AMENDE ⎫ reparation (Fr.) recompense;	
AMENDS ⎭ compensation; apology	
AMENED ratified	
AMENIA amenorrhoea	
AMENTA catkins	bt
AMERCE to fine arbitrarily	
AMIDIN starch solution	ch
AMIDOL developing agent	pg
AMINOL an explosive	ch
AMNION embryonic habitat	md, zo
AMNOIS membrane	md
AMOEBA protozoa	zo
AMOMUM cardamom; aromatic shrub	
AMORAL non-moral	
AMORCE toy detonator; percussion cap	
AMORET sweetheart; love knot	
AMORPH animal decoration	ar
AMOUNT sum; total; aggregate; attain	
AMPERE unit of current intensity	el, me
AMPLER more copious; fuller; richer	
AMREET water of immortality	
AMRITA nectar; ambrosia	
AMULET charm; talisman; safeguard	
AMURCA olive-oil extract	
AMUSED diverted; beguiled; enlivened	
AMYLIC, AMYLUM starch	ch
AMYOUS lacking muscle	
AMYTAL hypnotic barbiturate	pm
ANABAS tree climbing fish	zo
ANADEM garland; chaplet	
ANALET précis of an analysis	
ANANAS pineapple	bt
ANANYM name written backwards	
ANATTO ⎫ orange-red dye used for cheeses	
ANOTTO ⎭	
ANCHOR often dropped; (sheet)	nt
ANCOME a boil; a whitlow	md
ANCONA a fowl	zo
ANDEAN (Andes)	
ANDRON men's meeting room (Gr.)	
ANELED anointed (extreme unction)	
ANEPIA loss of power of speech	md
ANERGY failure of energy; immunity	
ANESIS tuning to lower pitch	mu
ANESIS abatement of symptoms	md
ANGARY angaria; war-rights	
ANGINA quinsy	md
ANGLED fished; schemed	
ANGLER the fishing frog	zo
ANGLES early East Anglican settlers	
ANGORA ⎫ cloth; mohair;	tx
ANGORA ⎭ cat; goat; rabbit	zo
ANHIMA horned screamer bird	zo
ANICUT dam for irrigation (Ind.)	
ANIGHT at night	
ANILIC pert. to anil, indigo	
ANIMAL creature; beast; carnal	zo
ANIMUS malice; bias; animosity	
ANKLED having ankles	
ANKLET ornament or fetter	
ANLACE dagger	

ANNALS historical records
ANNATE ⎱ first fruits **rl**
ANNATS ⎰
ANNEAL to temper
ANNEXE an addition
ANNONA year's produce
ANNUAL yearly
ANODAL genetic spiral upward **bt**
ANODIC anodal; positively polar
ANOINT anele; consecrate
ANOLIS lizard genus (Amer.) **zo**
ANONYM pseudonym
ANOPIA defective vision
ANORAK hooded windproofer
ANOTIA absence of ears
ANOURA frog genus **zo**
ANOXIA deficiency of oxygen **md**
ANSATE handled
ANSWER respond; reply; fulfil; refute
ANT-COW an aphis **zo**
ANTHEM song of praise **mu**
ANTHER part of stamen **bt**
ANTHUS meadow pipit
ANTIAR upas tree **bt**
ANTLER a horn **zo**
ANTLIA proboscis of insects **zo**
ANTRUM cavity; cave; den **md**
ANUBIS jackal-headed Egyptian deity
ANURAL tailless **zo**
ANURIA absence of urine secretion **md**
ANYHOW in any case
ANYWAY anyhow
AONIAN (Muses)
AORIST a past tense (Greek)
AORTAL ⎱ arterial **md**
AORTIC ⎰
AOSMIC free from odour
APACHE Parisian assassin; Red Indian
APATHY torpor; lethargy; dullness
APEDOM apishness
APEPSY poor digestion **md**
APERCU a précis; a summary
APHONY loss of voice; dumbness **md**
APHTHA thrush disease **md**
APIARY (bees)
APICAL topmost
APICES culminations; highest points
APIECE to each
APINCH pinching
APLITE quartz-feldspar microgranite **gl**
APLOMB self-possession; poise
APLOME garnet **mn**
APNOEA breath cessation **md**
APODAL ⎱ footless **zo**
APODEL ⎰ without feet or fins **zo**
APOGEE furthest point; apex
APONIA painlessness
APORIA rhetorical doubt
APOSIA absence of thirst feeling **md**
APOZEM a decoction **bt**
APPEAL entreat; implore; invoke **lw**

APPEAR seem; emerge; dawn; look
APPEND add; fasten; subjoin
APPORT object produced by medium
APPOSE to seal; superimpose
APTERA wingless insects **zo**
APTOTE indeclinable noun
APULSE pulsing
AQUILA lectern; eagle **rl, zo**
AQUILO N., N-E. wind (Lat.)
ARABIC language; race
ARABIN gum arabic **bt**
ARABIS rock-cress **bt**
ARABLE tillable; cultivable
ARAISE to raise from the dead
ARANGO cornelian **mn**
ARBOUR bower; recess; retreat; spindle
ARBUTE strawberry tree **bt**
ARCADE arched gallery
ARCADY pastoral district; (Sir Philip Sidney)
ARCANA mysteries
ARCANE secret
ARCATE shaped like a bow
ARCHED vaulted; concave
ARCHER a bowman; Zodiac sign
ARCHIL violet dye **bt**
ARCHLY roguishly; merrily; shrewdly
ARCHON Greek magistrate
ARCING electrical leakage; diversion **el**
ARCTIC northern; boreal; cold
ARDENT fiery; fervent; intense
ARDOUR warmth; heat; passion; zeal
AREOLA ⎱ cell nucleus; small area; **md**
AREOLE ⎰ interstitial space **bt**
ARETTE entrust (Spens.)
ARGALA adjutant bird (Hindu) **zo**
ARGALI wild sheep of Asia **zo**
ARGAND (burner); (diagram)
ARGEMA optical ulcer **md**
ARGENT silver **hd**
ARGIVE (Argos); Greek
ARGOSY richly laden vessel
ARGUED reasoned; implied; mooted
ARGUER disputed; debated; pleaded
ARGUFY wrangle
ARGUTE subtle; ingenious
ARIDAS East African taffeta **tx**
ARIGHT rightly
ARIOSE ⎱ melodious song-like
ARIOSO ⎰ recitation **mu**
ARISEN appeared; cropped up
ARISTA beard of corn **bt**
ARKITE Noachian
ARMADA fleet; flotilla **nt**
ARMING preparing for war
ARMLET band; creek; (armour)
ARMORY armoury; heraldry
ARMOUR defensive arms
ARMPIT the axilla **md**
ARMURE embossed-appearing cloth **tx**
ARNAUT Albanian mountaineer

ARNICA a plant genus   bt
AROINT } begone!
AROYNT }
AROUND about; encompassing
AROURA 100 square feet (Egyptian)   me
AROUSE excite; stir; provoke
ARPENT 100 square perches   me
ARRACH plant; the orache   bt
ARRACK fermented toddy
ARRANT errant; unmitigated
ARREAR backward
ARRECT erect; intent; alert
ARREST stem; curb; detain; capture
ARRIDE to please; to laugh at
ARRIVE reach; attain; land; come
ARROBA Spanish 25 lb (11 kg) weight   me
ARROWY like an arrow
ARROYO ravine; gully (Sp.)
ARSHIN 30 in (76 cm) (Rus.)   me
ARSINE poison gas   ch
ARTERY blood vessel   md
ARTFUL sly; wily; subtle; astute
ARTIST painter; master; adept
ARUNDO reed genus   bt
ASCEND climb; scale; mount
ASCENT rise; elevation; eminence
ASCIAN equator dweller
ASEITY self-origination
ASGARD abode of Norse gods
ASHAKE ashiver; aquake
ASHAME to feel shame (obs.)
ASHERY ash-heap
ASHIER more ashen; paler
ASHLAR } hewn stones   ar
ASHLER }
ASHORE stranded; aground
ASH-PAN dust-pan
ASH-PIT fire-refuse tip
ASITIA off one's oats   md
ASKANT askance; obliquely
ASKARI African soldier
ASKING requesting; begging; inviting
ASLAKE to slake; to mitigate
ASLANT sloping; askew; awry
ASLEEP dormant; slumbering
ASLOPE obliquely; aslant; atilt
ASNORT snorting
ASONIA inability to distinguish pitch
ASPECT outlook; mien; bearing; view
ASPICK lavender; asp   zo, bt
ASPIRE crave; soar; yearn; aim
ASPORT remove feloniously
ASPOUT spouting
ASQUAT squatting
ASSAIL attack; defame; asperse
ASSART to grub up trees, etc.
ASSARY ancient Roman coin   nm
ASSENT concur; agree; accord
ASSERT declare; maintain; allege; aver
ASSESS compute; tax; rate; value
ASSETS possessions; effects

ASSIGN allot; appoint; adduce
ASSIST aid; help; succour; abet
ASSIZE to assess   lw
ASSOIL to pardon; to soil
ASSORT group; arrange; classify
ASSUME feign; sham; arrogate
ASSURE aver; guarantee; warrant
ASTARE staring
ASTART suddenly
ASTERN aft; abaft   nt
ASTERT astart; suddenly (Spens.)
ASTHMA breathing disorder   md
ASTRAL starry; stellar; sidereal
ASTRAY erring; wandering; missing
ASTRUT puffed up (obs.)
ASTUTE artful; subtle; wily
ASWARM swarming
ASWING asway
ASWOON in a swoon
ASYLUM a sanctuary; refuge
ATABAL Moorish drum   mu
ATAMAN Cossack chief
ATAVIC inherent; hereditary
ATAVUS remote ancestor
ATAXIA paralysis   md
ATAXIC irregular   md
ATHENE goddess of wisdom and war   rl
AT-HOME a reception
ATHROB throbbing
ATHYMY melancholy
ATKINS British private soldier
ATOCIA female sterility   md
ATOMIC minute
ATONAL lacking tone   mu
ATONED reconciled; propitiated
ATONER an expiator
ATONIC unaccented; debilitated   md
ATOPIC displaced; allergic
ATRIAL pertaining to atrium
ATRIUM Roman hall
ATROUS jet black
ATTACH annex; adhere; cement
ATTACK storm; charge; assail; impugn
ATTAIN acquire; achieve; reach; grasp
ATTASK to task
ATTEND serve; guard; hearken; heed
ATTENT intention; attentive (Spens.)
ATTEST ratify; confirm; endorse
ATTIRE garb; rig; accoutre; outfit
ATTORN transfer homage   lw
ATTRAP array; adorn
ATTUNE harmonize; accord; adapt
ATWAIN in sunder
ATWEEN between
ATWIXT betwixt
ATYPIC unclassified; unusual   md
AUBADE dawn; concert; morning song
AUBURN carroty; Titian
AUDILE (mental image of sound)
AUDION wireless amplifier
AUGEAN foul; arduous and toilsome

AUGITE volcanic rock   mn
AUGURY omen; portent; sign; presage
AUGUST majestic; venerable; imposing
AULETE flautist   mu
AUMBRY ambry; cupboard   rl
AUMUCE amice; furred hood
AUNTIE aunty; prude
AURATE having ears; gilded
AUREAT gilded; golden; auric
AUREUS Roman gold coin   nm
AURIFY change into gold
AURIGA a constellation; the Charioteer
AURINE dye-acid
AURIST ear specialist   md
AURORA goddess of dawn; northern lights
AUROUS golden; aureate
AUSPEX seer; diviner; prophet
AUSSIE an Australian
AUSTER South wind
AUSTIN Augustine
AUTHOR writer; creator; cause; agent
AUTISM self-absorption
AUTUMN the fall
AVALON a western fairy isle
AVANCE avens; herb bennet   bt
AVANTI forward (It.)
AVATAR incarnation of Brahma   rl
AVAUNT begone; to boast
AVENER } master of the Horse in feudal
AVENOR } times
AVENGE vindicate; retaliate; visit
AVENUE entry; access; approach
AVERSE loath; allergic; reluctant
AVIARY a large bird-cage   zo
AVIATE to fly
AVIDIN protein in egg   ch
AVIDLY voraciously; greedily; eagerly
AVISED hue; complexion
AVITAL hereditary; ancestral
AVOCAT advocate (Fr.)   lw
AVOCET } wading birds   zo
AVOSET }
AVOUCH maintain; guarantee
AVOURE confession; justification (Spens.)
AVOWAL frank admission; confession
AVOWED openly declared; owned
AVOWEE (advowson)   lw
AVOWRY (replevin)   lw
AVULSE to grab
AWAKEN rouse; stir up; kindle
AWASTE wasting
AWATCH watching; alert
AWEARY tired; faded; spent
AWEIGH atrip; apeak   nt
AWHEEL cycling
AWHILE sometime; briefly; soon
AWNING tilt; canopy; baldequin
AWRACK wrecked
AXENIC free from parasites   md
AXICLE sheave; pulley wheel
AXILLA armpit   md

AXUNGE hog's lard; wheel-grease
AYE-AYE squirrel-like lemur   zo
AZALEA plant, rhododendron type   bt
AZARIN brilliant crimson dye   ch
AZAZEL Satan's standard-bearer
AZMURE cloth with embossed appearance   tx
AZONAL recent formation (soil)
AZONIC not local
AZOTIC lifeless
AZRAEL destroying angel
AZURED colour of azure
AZURIN blue dye   ch
AZYGOS occurring singly

B

BAAING bleating
BAALIM false gods (Baal)
BABBIT Babbit metal
BABBLE chatter; prattle; drivel
BABIES infants; twins; triplets
BABISH infantile; foolish
BABLAH acacia-rind   bt
BABOON type of primate   zo
BACKED retired; aided; abetted
BACKER supporter; partisan
BACKET coal-box
BADGER pester; annoy; bait; tool   zo
BADIAN tree with anise-flavoured fruit   bt
BAFFLE balk; thwart; acoustics
BAFTAS cotton; muslin
BAGFUL contents; capacity of a bag   me
BAGGED stolen; shot
BAGGIT salmon after spawning   zo
BAGMAN commercial traveller
BAGNIO bath-house
BAGWIG an 18th century wig
BAILED released on security   lw
BAILEE (trustee)   lw
BAILER one who stands bail
BAILEY a prison; castle wall
BAILIE alderman (Sc.)   lw
BAILOR bailee
BAITED badgered; lured; enticed
BAJREE Indian grass   bt
BAKERY bake-house
BAKING cooking
BALAAM unimportant newsprint
BALASS a ruby   mn
BALATA rubberlike gum   bt
BALBOA coin of Panama   nm
BALDER less hirsute
BALDLY inelegantly; plainly
BALDUR son of Odin (mistletoe)   rl
BALEEN whalebone   zo
BALING bundling; emptying
BALIZE a sea-mark   tv
BALKAN of S.E. Europe

BALKED refused; frustrated
BALKER fish-spotter
BALKIS Queen of Sheba; also Aaziz
BALLAD epic song
BALLED clogged
BALLET art dance
BALLOT vote; ticket; to elect
BALSAM aromatic balm — bt
BALTIC shipping exchange
BAMBOO tree-like grass — bt
BAMMIE Caribbean cassava cake — ck
BANANA tropical fruit — bt
BANATE) Hungarian territorial
BANNAT) divisions (military)
BANCOR monetary unit — nm
BANDED united; bound
BANDIT outlaw; brigand; footpad
BANDLE 2 ft (60 cm) (Irish) — me
BANDOG watch-dog — zo
BANGED with hair cut square
BANGHY Ind. porter's shoulder-yoke
BANGLE bracelet; armlet; ring
BANGUE bhang; a narcotic
BANG-UP slap-up; stylish
BANIAN Hindu caste; fig-tree — bt
BANISH exile; expel; eject
BANKED (road construction)
BANKER fishing-boat — nt
BANKER mason's bench; card game
BANKET auriferous rock (Transvaal) — gl
BANNED barred; tabooed; vetoed
BANNER petal; flag; standard — bt
BANTAM carved work; small — zo
BANTER twit; rally; deride; bandy
BANYAN Indian fig; banian — bt
BANZAI! Japanese hurrah
BAOBAB African tree — bt
BARBED bearded; hooked; pointed
BARBEL carp — zo
BARBER hairdresser
BARBET bird; dog — zo
BARCOO grass (Australia) — bt
BARDIC poetic; epic
BAREGE fabric
BARELY only just
BAREST bleakest; baldest; plainest
BARGED charged into; shoved
BARGEE bargeman
BARING uncovering; unsheathing
BARISH rather bare
BARIUM metallic element — ch
BARKED grazed (shins); helped
BARKEN to become like bark
BARKER shop-tout
BARLEY a cereal — bt
BARMAN pot-man; bar-tender
BARNED stored
BARNEY humbug; prize fight
BARONY a baron's holding
BARQUE three-masted ship — nt
BARRAS resin — bt

BARRED banned; excluded; ostracized
BARREL 36 gal (163.6 litres) cask — me
BARREN bare; sterile; unfertile
BARRET beret; cap — rl
BARROW mound; tumulus; truck
BARSAC white wine (Fr.)
BARTER trade; exchange; traffic
BARTON domain lands; farmhouse
BARYON heavy subatomic particle — ps
BARYTA barium oxide — ch
BASALT igneous rock — mn
BASELY spuriously; corruptly
BASHAW pasha (Turkish)
BASIAL osculatory
BASIFY make into a salifiable salt
BASING founding; establishing
BASKED warmed by the sun
BASKET pannier; creal; punnet; trug
BASNET helmet; bassinet
BASQUE Biscayan
BASSET outcrop; (cards); hound — zo
BASTED (sewing) — ck
BASTON heraldic baton — hd
BASUTO African
BASYLE radicle — ch
BATATA sweet potato — bt
BATEAU light boat — nt
BATHED laved; suffused
BATHER swimmer
BATHIC pertaining to sea depths
BATHOS anti-climax; bombast
BATING except; abating; deducting
BATLET linen-beater
BATMAN an officer's servant
BATOON baston; bar; staff; truncheon
BATTED (cricket)
BATTEL Oxford kitchen account
BATTEN grow fat; a lath
BATTER culinary mixture; smite
BATTLE war; strive; contest; fight
BATTON batten; a slat
BATTUE a beat; slaughter
BAUBEE, BAWBEE halfpenny (Sc.)
BAUBLE) showy finery; gee-gaw;
BAUBLE) jester's wand
BAVIAN poetaster; baboon
BAWSON)
BAWSIN) a badger — zo
BAWLED clamoured; shouted; yelled
BAWLER a howler
BAWLEY Thames fishing-boat — nt
BAWTIE a hare; a dog — zo
BAXTER (prints)
BAYARD a famous steed
BAYARD a very perfect knight
BAYEUX famous for its tapestry
BAYING in full cry
BAYRAM Mohammedan festival
BAY-RUM hair lotion
BAZAAR mart; emporium; exchange
BEACHY pebbly (of shoreline) — gl

BEACON signal-fire; lighthouse
BEADED strung together
BEADLE parish officer; servitor
BEAGLE a hound; jammer — ro, zo
BEAKED sharp-pointed
BEAKER a cup; glass vessel
BEAMED (antlers); smiled
BEARER a carrier; (funerals)
BEATEN defeated; hackneyed
BEATER striker; (game)
BEAUNE a French wine
BEAUTY grace; comeliness; fairness
BEAVER a hat; fur — zo
BECALL miscall; vituperate
BECALM still; pacify; soothe
BECAME grew into; graced
BECKED nodded; signed
BECKET an eye in a knot — nt
BECKON call; wave; signal; invite
BECOME suit; befit; grace; adorn
BECURL to curl
BEDASH bespatter
BEDAUB smear; befoul; stain; paint
BED-BUG cimex — zo
BEDDED planted out
BEDDER millstone; a plant — bt
BEDECK array; gild; adorn
BED-KEY bedstead tightener — to
BEDLAM mad-house; uproar
BEDRAL a beadle
BEDRID bedridden
BEDROP sprinkle; to speckle
BEDUCK to plunge under water
BEDUIN a Bedouin Arab
BEDUST cover with dust
BEENAH marriage (Sri Lanka)
BEEPER remote controlled aircraft
BEETLE maul; heavy mallet — zo
BEEVES oxen; kine — zo
BEFALL betide; happen; chance
BEFANA Epiphany present; a fairy
BEFOAM bespatter with foam
BEFOOL dupe; hoodwink; hoax
BEFORE prior to; formerly; above
BEFOUL defoul; defile; sully
BEGAUM princess (E. Indies)
BEGGAR ruin; surpass; pauper
BEGGED entreated; cadged
BEGIFT to make a presentation
BEGILD gild
BEGILT gilt
BEGIRD enclose; encircle; environ
BEGNAW to corrode
BEGONE! go away; avaunt!
BEHALF benefit; interest; advantage
BEHAVE act; comport; demean
BEHEAD decapitate; execute
BEHELD saw; surveyed; contemplated
BEHEST command; mandate; order
BEHIND abaft; following; buttocks — pl
BEHOLD regard; discern; look

BEHOOF profit; advantage; benefit
BEHOTE promised; vowed (Spens.)
BEHOVE befit; suit; beseem
BEHOWL to howl at (Shak.)
BEHUNG draped
BEJANT bejan; freshman (Sc.)
BEJUCO a cane — bt
BEKISS kiss intensively; osculate
BELACE adorn with lace; beat
BELAMY good friend (Spens.)
BELATE delay; retard; hinder
BELAUD overpraise; bepuff
BELDAM a hag; beldame
BELFRY bat habitat; bell-tower
BELGIC Belgian
BELIAL a low and profligate devil
BELIED falsified; counterfeited
BELIEF faith; creed; dogma; tenet
BELIER a confidence-man
BELIKE likely; perhaps; maybe
BELIVE speedily; ere long (Sc.)
BELLED bellowed
BELLIS the daisy — bt
BELLOW lead colic — md
BELLOW roar; bawl; clamour
BELOCK to fasten; to lock
BELONE garfish — zo
BELONG to appertain
BELTED girt; zoned; girdled
BELUGA sturgeon; dolphin — zo
BEMASK to conceal
BEMAUL wound; disfigure; bruise
BEMBEX genus of sand-wasps — zo
BEMIRE bedaub; soil; besmirch
BEMOAN lament; bewail; mourn
BEMOCK deride; jeer; flout
BEMOIL bemire; bedraggle
BEMUSE daze; bewilder
BENDER spree; a stretcher
BENGAL fabric; (Lancer)
BENIGN kindly; amiable; friendly
BENITO navigation system — nv
BENNET herb — bt
BEN-NUT oil-nut of horse-radish tree — bt
BENSHI banshee; Irish fairy
BENUMB stupefy; deaden; blunt
BENZOL benzene — ch
BEPELT pelt vigorously
BEPITY to sympathize
BEPUFF belaud; overpraise
BERATE rate; scold; chide; reprove
BERBER Moroccans of Atlas mountains
BERBER a Barbary language
BEREAN extinct Scottish sect
BEREFT stripped; deprived; destitute
BERLIN a vehicle; wool
BERTHA Hun gun
BESANT } Byzantine gold; — nm
BEZANT } gold heraldic circlet — hd
BESEEM behove; befit; suit; become
BESEEN comely

BESIDE near; close to; alongside
BESIGH to sigh
BESING celebrate in song
BESMUT begrime; blacken
BESOIL defile; besmirch
BESORT to fit; to become
BESPAT spat upon
BESPED helped on
BESPIT to spit upon
BESPOT to mark with spots
BESTED overwhelmed; worsted
BESTIR hasten; rouse; strive; labour
BESTOW confer; grant; give; award
BESTUD to stud
BETAIL curtail
BETAKE remove or repair to
BETEEM produce; shed
BETHEL a chapel
BETIDE befall; happen; chance
BETIME betide; befall
BETISE stupid act (Fr.)
BETONY a plant   bt
BETOOK went away; left
BETORN torn to pieces
BETOSS agitate violently
BETRAP ensnare
BETRAY divulge; reveal; entrap
BETRIM arrange; to deck
BETTED wagered
BETTER superior; amend; rectify
BETTOR punter; wagerer
BEVIES flocks; crowds
BEVILE heraldic device   hd
BEWAIL moan; lament; grieve; deplore
BEWARE achtung! heed; mind
BEWEEP bewail
BEWEPT disfigured by weeping
BEWRAP envelope; enclose
BEWRAY betray; accuse
BEWTER bittern   zo
BEYLIK a Bey's province
BEYOND over; past; farther
BEZANT besant; Dutch ship   nt
BEZOAR a stony concretion
BHARAL wild sheep (Tibet)   zo
BHISTI Indian water-carrier
BIACID of a base   ch
BIASED prejudiced
BIAZAL having two optical axes
BIBBER wine-bibber; toper
BIBLUS papyrus; paper-reed   bt
BICEPS a muscle   md
BICKER bowl; quarrel; nipple
BICORN having 2 horns
BIDALE a benefit
BIDDED (auction)
BIDDER tenderer
BIDENT two-pronged
BIDING pausing; awaiting
BIDOUS lasting 2 days
BIFFED coshed; bashed

BIFFIN apple-pie; dried apple
BIFLEX double curve
BIFOIL two blade plant   ht
BIFOLD two-fold; double
BIFORM having two shapes
BI-FUEL propelled with two fuels
BIGAMY plural marriage
BIG-END crank end of connecting rod
BIGGEN ⎤ child's cap;
BIGGIN ⎦ small wooden bowl
BIGGER larger; greater; bulkier
BIGRID double-control-grid thermionic   el
BIG-WIG important person
BIKING cycling
BIKINI minimum two-piece garment
BILDAR Ind. camp servant
BILGED broad-bottomed
BILGED fractured in the bilge
BILKED defrauded
BILKER an absconder
BILLED advertised
BILLET a log; note; lodgings; ticket
BILLIE tin can; billy; male goat   zo
BILLON an alloy
BILLOT gold or silver bar
BILLOW roll; heave; surge; swell
BIMANA bimane; two-handed
BINARY double; mathematical system   ma
BINATE double; in pairs
BINDER a bandage
BINGHI Australian aborigine
BINODE 2-electrode thermionic tube   el
BINOUS binate; double
BIOPSY tissue examination   md
BIOSIS life distinguishing organisms   zo
BIOTIC biological   md
BIOTIN B vitamin
BIPACK two-film colour photography
BIPONT bipontine   pr
BIRDED snared
BIRDER bird catcher
BIRDIE one under bogey at golf
BIREME cf. trireme   nt
BIRKEN made of birch-wood
BIRKIE lively lad (Sc.)
BIRLER a carouser
BIRSLE to scorch; to toast (Sc.)
BISECT to halve
BISHOP a drink; dress   rl
BISHOP horse-faking
BISLEY (rifle shooting)
BISMAR Orkney steel-yard
BISQUE croquet handicap; glazeless firing
BISQUE lobster soup   ck
BISSON blind; blinding (Shak.)
BISTRE, BISTER brown pigment; sombre
BISTRO small eating house (Fr.)
BITING mordant; champing
BITTED (horse's bit)   nt
BITTEN tricked; corroded
BITTER acrimonious; sour; tart

BITTLE flat club; beetle	
BITTOR the bittern	zo
BIURET urea product	ch
BIZARD carnation	
BLADED having a blade	
BLAGUE blarney; swagger	
BLAMED reproached; censured	
BLANCH bleach; whiten; fade	
BLARED trumpeted; pealed	
BLASHY watery	
BLAZED proclaimed; (trees)	
BLAZER bright coloured sports jacket	
BLAZON, BLASON to display; blare	
BLEACH blanch; whiten	
BLEAKY bleak; cheerless	
BLEARY blear-eyed	
BLEBBY bubbly; blistered	
BLENCH blink; shrink; flinch	
BLENDE an ore of zinc	mn
BLENNY fish	zo
BLEWIT mushroom	bt
BLEYME inflammation	
BLIGHT mildew; wither; shrivel	
BLINDS camouflage	
BLINKS chickweed	bt
BLINKY blink-eyed	
BLITHE merry; gay; vivacious; joyous	
BLONDE silk lace; fair lady	
BLOODY sanguinary	
BLOOMY blooming	
BLOSME bloom (Spens.)	
BLOTCH a blemish; pustule	
BLOTTO fuddled	
BLOUSE loose outer garment	
BLOW-BY piston-leakage gas	au
BLOWED blasted; confounded	
BLOWER a whale; telephone; voice pipe	
BLOWSE see blouse	
BLOWTH bloom; blossoms	
BLOWZE coarse woman	
BLOWZY fat; tawdry; unkempt	
BLUELY, BLUISH of blue colour	
BLUEST most blue; gloomiest	
BLUFFY rather bluff	
BLUING tempering steel	
BLUISM (blue-stocking)	
BLUNGE (clay mixing)	
BOATEL botel; boating hotel afloat	
BOATER straw hat	
BOBBED (hair); (winter sports)	
BOBBIN spool; reel	
BOBBLE pobble; ripple	
BOBWIG wig of short hair	
BOCAGE boscage; leafy underwood	bt
BODEGA wine-shop (Sp.)	
BODGER pedlar; botcher	
BODICE woman's upper body garment	
BODIED embodied	
BODIES organizations	
BODILY corporeally	
BODING an omen; portending	

BODKIN dagger; needle for tape	
BODKIN three people crowded up	
BOFFIN back-room scientist	
BOGGLE to waver; to dissemble	
BOGLET a small bog	
BOG-OAK near-fossil wood	bt
BOG-ORE porous limonite found in marshes	mn
BOILED seethed	
BOILER hot water heater	
BOIOBI green snake	zo
BOLARY clay-like	
BOLDEN to make bold; embolden	
BOLDER more daring; saucier	
BOLDLY confidently; valiantly	
BOLERO Spanish dance; rhythm	mu
BOLIDE meteor	
BOLLED podded;	
BOLLEN swollen	
BOLTED barred; swallowed	
BOLTER bran-machine	
BOMBAX cotton-tree	bt
BOMBED blitzed	
BOMBIC, BOMBYX silkworm	zo
BON-BON sugar-plum; Xmas cracker	
BONDED (warehoused)	
BONDER binding stone or brick	
BONGAR poisonous Indian snake	
BONGOS Conga twin drums	mu
BONING levelling; removing bones	
BONITO (tunny)(Sp.)	zo
BON-MOT witticism	
BONNET cap; (sail)	nt
BONNIE blithe; fair; joyous; pretty	
BONTEN woollen stuff	
BON-TON chic; good style	
BONXIE skua-gull	zo
BONZER lucky strike (Aust.)	
BOODLE money; marigold; loot	bt
BOOHOO weep aloud	
BOOING noisily disapproving; hooting	
BOOKED entered; recorded	
BOOKIE bookmaker	
BOOMED advertised; resounded	
BOOMER kangaroo	zo
BOOPIC ox-eyed	
BOOSED, BOOZED drank, swilled	
BOOTED sacked	
BOOTEE short boot	
BOOTES constellation	
BO-PEEP hide and seek	
BORAGE a plant	bt
BORATE boric oxide	ch
BORCER rock-drill	to
BORDAR cottage	
BORDEL bawdy-house	
BORDER margin; boundary; edge	
BOREAL of North wind	
BOREAS the North wind	
BOREEN Irish lane or track	
BORING tedious; drilling	

BORLEY bawley; Thames barge	nt
BORROW copy; assume; feign	
BORZOI Russian hound	zo
BOSCHE a Hun; German soldier	
BOSKET a grove; small wood	bt
BOSSED controlled; dominated	
BOSSET rudimentary antler	zo
BOSTAL hill road	
BOSTON a dance	
BOTANY Australian wool	bt
BOTCHY ill-done; clumsy	
BOT-FLY gad-fly	zo
BOTHER pother; pester; worry	
BOTHIE a house; a hut (Sc.)	
BOTONE heraldic budding	hd
BO-TREE sacred tree; pipal	bt
BOTTLE bundle of hay	
BOTTOM basis; foot; foundation	
BOUCAN dried meat	
BOUCHE metal plug	
BOUCLE tube of woven cloth	
BOUFFE farcical (Fr.)	
BOUGHT purchased; bribed	md
BOUGIE instrument; form of music	
BOULET sloping pastern	
BOUNCE dog-fish; rebound	zo
BOUNDS (out of bounds)	
BOUNTY gift; reward; liberality	
BOURNE destination	
BOURSE exchange; money market	
BOUTON axon arborization end	cy
BOVATE peasant holding (20 acres; 8 hectares)	
BOVINE dull; stupid	
BOVRIL an extract of beef	
BOW-BOY Cupid; Eros	
BOW-CAP an extreme bow of airship	
BOW-DYE scarlet	
BOWELS entrails	pl
BOWERY shady; (New York)	
BOWESS a young hawk	zo
BOWFIN mudfish (N. Amer.)	zo
BOWING fiddling; submitting	
BOWLED (cricket); (bowls)	
BOW-LEG a crooked leg	
BOWLER a hat; cricketer	
BOWMAN archer	
BOW-NET lobster-pot	
BOW-OAR No. 1 of a racing crew	
BOW-PEN a drawing instument	
BOW-SAW narrow saw	to
BOWSIE cleat	nt
BOW-TIE male neckwear	tx
BOW-WOW jocular word for dog	zo
BOWYER bowman (obs.)	
BOXCAR data converter; goods truck	cp
BOX-DAM surrounding coffer-dam	ce
BOX-DAY day for lodging papers	lw
BOXING pugilism	
BOYISH youthful; puerile; young	
BOYUNA serpent	zo

BRACED supported; propped	
BRACER pick-me-up	
BRAGLY braggingly; boastfully (Spens.)	
BRAHMA lock	
BRAINY intellectual; clever	
BRAIRD germination	bt
BRAISE to stew	
BRAIZE red pandora fish	zo
BRAKED put on the brake	
BRANCH limb; bough; off-shoot	
BRANDY cognac	
BRANKS scold's bridle	
BRANKY showy (Sc.)	
BRANNY like bran	
BRASEN } made of brass;	
BRAZEN } impudent	
BRASHY fragmentary	
BRASIL } Brazil wood;	bt
BRAZIL } sappan tree	
BRASSE perch	zo
BRASSY brassie; a golf club	
BRAVED dared; defied; challenged	
BRAVER nobler; more daring	
BRAWLY bravely; excellently	
BRAWNY hefty; lusty; sturdy; robust	
BRAYED ground in a mortar	
BRAYER (printing) roller	to
BRAYLE hawk leash	
BRAZED soldered	
BREACH rupture; crack; rift; quarrel	
BREAST a torus; bosom; oppose; stem	
BREATH aroma; pause; exhalation	
BREECH the hinder part of a gun	
BREEKS trousers	
BREESE breeze	
BREEZE gad-fly; cinders	zo
BREEZY gusty; windy; hearty	
BREGMA part of skull	md
BREHON Irish judge	lw
BRETON of Brittany	
BREVET a patent; nominal rank	
BREWED plotted; concocted	
BREWER a brewster; maltster	
BRIBED seduced; hired	
BRIBER a corrupter	
BRICKY of brick	
BRIDAL nuptial; conjugal	
BRIDGE card game; span; surmount	
BRIDLE curb; control; restrain; check	
BRIERY set with brambles	
BRIGHT vivid; shining; gay; merry	
BRIGUE intrigue; cabal; strife	
BRILLS eye-lashes (horse)	
BRIONY bryony; a plant	bt
BRIQUE red-haired Negro half-caste	
BRISKY brisk; effervescing	
BRITON ancient British inhabitant	
BROACH hint; suggest; tap	to
BROADS waterways	
BROCHE brocade; embroider	
BROGAN leather shoe	

BROGUE shoe; Irish accent		**BULGAR** Bulgarian	
BROKEN fractured; snapped; smashed		**BULGED** protruded	
BROKER dealer		**BULGER** a golf club	
BROLLY umbrella		**BULGUR** cracked wheat (Levant)	
BROMAL oily fluid	ch	**BULIMY** morbid appetite; voracity	md
BROMIC containing bromine	ch	**BULKED** in bulk	
BRONCO unbroken horse (Amer.)	zo	**BULKER** street thief	
BRONZE an alloy of copper and tin		**BULLED** (Stock Exchange)	
BRONZY bronze-like		**BULLER** torrential turmoil	
BROOCH (a painting); ornamental clasp		**BULLET** projectile; slug	
BROODY pensive; hen		**BUMKIN** short broom	nt
BROOKY abounding with streams		**BUMMED** hummed	
BROOMY full of broom		**BUMMEL** meander; cycle seat	
BROUGH town; burgh; borough		**BUMMER** camp follower; loafer	
BROWNY of a brown colour		**BUMMLE** to blunder; an idler	
BROWSE nibble; crop; feed		**BUMPED** thumped	
BRUANG Malayan bear	zo	**BUMPER** buffer; full; generous	
BRUCIA a poison	md	**BUNCHY** clustered; tufty	
BRUISE batter; crush; contuse; wale		**BUNDLE** parcel; package; packet; roll	
BRUMAL (wintry)		**BUNGED** closed up	
BRUMBY unbroken horse	zo	**BUNGLE** miss; fail; botch	
BRUNCH combined breakfast-lunch	ck	**BUNION** a swelling	md
BRUSHY rough; shaggy		**BUNKED** decamped	
BRUTAL inhuman; ruthless; savage		**BUNKER** (golf); (coal); bin; crib	
BRUTUS a kind of wig		**BUNKUM** blather; nonsense	
BRUZZE V-shaped woodturning tool	to	**BUNSEN** gas burner	ch
BRYONY briony; a plant	bt	**BUNTED** butted	
BUBBLE gurgle; cheat		**BUNTER** mottled sandstone	mn
BUBBLY champagne; effervescent		**BUNYIP** Australian monster	
BUCCAL (cheek)	md	**BUOYED** sustained; upheld	
BUCCAN dried meat		**BURBLE** confusion; trouble	
BUCKED bleached; exhilarated		**BURBOT** eel-pout; fish	zo
BUCKET pail; ride furiously		**BURDEN** chorus; incubus; load; onus	
BUCKIE large whelk	zo	**BUREAU** office; department	
BUCKLE brooch; clasp; wrinkle		**BURGEE** pennant; flag; coal	mn
BUCKRA white man		**BURGLE** rob premises	
BUDDED grafted		**BURGOO** savoury mess	ck
BUDDHA founder of religion	rl	**BURHEL** Asiatic goat	zo
BUDDLE (ore-washing)		**BURIAL** interment	
BUDGER a stirrer; a mover		**BURIED** interred; inhumed	
BUDGET package; batch; (finance)		**BURKED** hushed up; smothered; hesitated	
BUDLET a little bud	bt	**BURLAP** coarse canvas	
BUDZAT ne'er-do-well (Ind.)		**BURLED** with knots removed	
BUFFED buffeted; polished		**BURLER** cloth-dresser	
BUFFEL an American duck	zo	**BURMAN** native of Burma	
BUFFER concussion-force deadener; foolish		**BURNED** (bowls); scorched; charred	
fellow		**BURNER** flame controller	
BUFFET cuff; smite; sideboard		**BURNET** plant; moth	bt, zo
BUGEYE wide-angle	cn	**BURN-UP** reactor fuel-rod consumption	nc
BUGGER active sodomite		**BURRED** roughened	
BUG-KEY faster transmission key	tc	**BURROW** tunnel; mine; excavate	
BUGLER horn blower	mu	**BURSAL, BURSAE** cavity	md
BUGLET a small glass bead		**BURSAR** treasurer; cashier; (college)	
BUGONG a moth	zo	**BURSCH** German student	
BUKSHA Yemeni coin	nm	**BURTON** a tackle	nt
BUKSHI tip; percentage (India)		**BURYAT** Central Asian Turkmens	
BULBAR } bulbous; bulbiform;		**BUS-BAR** metallic rod link; contact	el
BULBED } bulby; bulbaceous	bt	**BUSHED** lost in the bush	
BULBIL bud developing into a plant	bt	**BUSHEL** 8 gallons (36 litres)	me
BULBUL nightingale; Turkish sweet	zo	**BUSIED** actively employed	
BULBUS a corm; a bulb	bt	**BUSIES** detectives (slang)	

BUSILY diligently; assiduously
BUSKED wearing a busk; corseted
BUSKER tragedian; street actor
BUSKIN kind of boot; cothurnus
BUSMEN transport workers
BUSSED kissed; osculated
BUSTED gone bust (slang); bankrupt
BUSTER frolic; a roisterer
BUSTLE stuffed pad; stir; tumult
BUST-UP violent quarrel
BUTANE a paraffin   ch
BUTLER house steward
BUTTED rammed; bunted
BUTTER to flatter
BUTTON to fasten
BUXINE (alkaloid)   ch
BUYING bribing; corrupting
BUZZED spread abroad; bruited
BUZZER tatler; tell-tale
BY-BLOW illegitimate child
BYE-BYE (golf); adieu
BYE-LAW subsidiary law
BY-FORM a variant
BYGONE past; of yore
BY-LANE side road
BYLINA Russian poem; song
BYNAME nickname
BY-PASS a shunt; avoidance road
BY-PAST past; gone by
BY-PATH hidden path
BY-PLAY significant acting in dumb show
BY-PLOT subsidiary plot
BY-ROAD secondary road
BY-ROOM small ante-chamber
BYSSUS fine linen cloth
BYSSUS a tuft of filaments   zo
BY-TIME leisure time
BY-VIEW self-interest
BY-WALK by-path
BY-WIPE a sarcastic allusion
BY-WORD taunt; saw; adage; maxim
BY-WORK by-time work
BYZANT bezant; coin   nm

C

CABALA Jewish traditional doctrine
CABANA beach house; shack
CABANE pyramidal strut system   ae
CABBLE smash into small pieces
CABECA Indian silk
CABIRI ancient Semitic divinities
CABLED telegraphed
CABLET tow-rope
CABMAN cabby
CABRIE } prong-horn antelope   zo
CABRIT }
CABURN spun-yarn
CACHED hidden; concealed
CACHET a seal; distinctive stamp
CACHOU a sweetmeat

CACKLE titter; snigger; chatter
CACOON bean   bt
CACTAL (cactus)
CACTUS prickly plant   bt
CADANE Turkish carpet
CADDIE caddy (golf); messenger
CADDIS tape; a worm   zo
CADENT falling; dropping
CADGED sponged; begged; importuned
CADGER huckster; beggar; mendicant
CADION chemical detection reagent   ch
CADMIA sulphide of cadmium   ch
CAECUM a blind sac   md
CAESAR an autocrat
CAFARD Algerian desert melancolia
CAFFRE Caffrarian
CAFTAN kaftan; Persian vest
CAGING confining; mewing; penning
CAGMAG meat unfit for food
CAHIER book; report; an issue
CAHOOT partnership
CAIMAN alligator (S. Amer.)   zo
CAIQUE a Turkish skiff   nt
CAKING coagulating; clotting
CAJOLE coax; wheedle; beguile
CALADE (manege ground)
CALASH vehicle; hood
CALCAR glass furnace
CALCED wearing shoes; shod
CALCIC containing calcium   ch
CALICO cotton cloth
CALIGO dimness of sight   md
CALIPH Calif; Khalif; Islamic chief   rl
CALKED caulked
CALKER }
CALKIN } part of horseshoe
CALLED left cards; dubbed
CALLER fresh; visitor
CALLET a scold
CALLID skilled; expert; shrewd
CALL-IN transfer control: main to sub
CALLOW unfledged; inexperienced
CALL-UP military induction
CALLUS hardened skin   md
CALMED quiescent; lulled; allayed
CALMLY sedately; serenely; placidly
CALORY caloric; thermal unit   me
CALPAC Eastern cap
CALTHA king-cup   bt
CALVER caller; fresh; cool
CALVES pl. of calf   zo
CALYON wall construction stone   bd
CAMAIL chain-mail
CAMASS lily (edible bulbs)   bt
CAMATA acorns   bt
CAMBER convexity; to arch; dock
CAMERA judge's room   lw
CAMESE, CAMISE, CAMISO Arab shirt
CAMION motor truck, waggon
CAMLET fabric

CAMPER who lives temporarily rough	
CAMPOS Savannah (Brazil)	
CAMPUS college grounds	
CANAPÉ cocktail delicacy	
CANARD a hoax; rumour	
CANARY wine; bird; dance	zo
CANCAN a dance	
CANCEL quash; annul; blot	
CANCER the Crab (Zodiac)	md
CANDID frank; honest; sincere	
CANDIE 500 lb (226 kg) (Ind.)	me
CANDLE light; taper	
CANGUE Chinese criminal yoke	
CANINE doggy	
CANING thrashing	
CANKER corrode; infect	md
CANNED preserved; drunk	
CANNEL bituminous coal	mn
CANNON (artillery); (billiards)	
CANNOT unable to	
CANOPY awning; tilt; firmament	
CANTAB Cambridge (degree)	
CANTAR about 1 cwt (50 kg) (Syrian)	me
CANTED atilt	
CANTER a horse pace	
CANTHI corners of the eye	md
CANTLE (saddle); fragment	
CANTON Swiss province	
CANTOR a precentor	rl
CANTUS chant	mu
CANUCK Canadian	
CANVAS sails in general	nt
CANYON deep ravine; gulch	
CAPFUL filling a cap	
CAPIAS writ	lw
CAPITE royal tenant, feudal	lw
CAPIVI balsam; copaiva	md
CAPLIN small smelt	zo
CAP-NUT end-sealed nut	eg
CAPOTE long cloak (Fr.)	
CAPPED (international); (hunting)	
CAPRIC acid	ch
CAPRID goaty	
CAPRIN an acid found in butter	
CAPTOR capturer	
CARACK cargo-boat	nt
CARACT mark; sign; character	
CARAFE glass water-jug	
CARANX mackerel	zo
CARAPA crab-wood tree (S. Amer.)	bt
CARBOL (carbolic)	ch
CARBON charcoal	ch
CARBOY glass jar	
CARBRO carbon/bromide printing	pg
CARCEL French luminous-flux unit	lt
CARDED combed (wool)	
CARDOL cashew-nut oil	ck
CAREEN to heel over	
CAREER rush; progress; race; life	
CARESS fondle; wheedle; embrace; hug	
CARFAX cross-roads	
CARFOX carfax; four-forked	
CARICA paw-paw tree	bt
CARIES decay	md
CARINA keel-like structure	bt, zo
CARING tending; feeling	
CARKED worried; perplexed	
CARLOT churl; peasant	
CARMAN van driver	
CARMEN carriers; an opera	
CARNAL fleshy; sensual	
CARNET motor passport	
CARNEY horse-disease	
CARNOT thermal-efficiency unit	eg
CARPAL of the wrist	pl
CARPED cavilled; grumbled	
CARPEL seed vessel	bt
CARPER censurer; critic	
CARPET floor fabric	
CARPUS the wrist	md
CARRAT carat	me
CARREL cross-bow arrow; quarry	
CARROT orange vegetable	bt
CARTED removed	
CARTEL price fixers' ring	
CARTER wagoner	
CARTON (bulls-eye); pasteboard box	
CARVED hewn; chiselled; engraved	
CARVEL jellyfish; caravel	nt, zo
CARVEN cut; sliced; shaped	
CARVER sculptor; a knife	
CASABA yellow winter melon	
CASEIC (cheese)	ch
CASEIN milk protein	
CASERN barracks	
CASEUM caseine	ch
CASHED converted into specie	
CASHEW tropical nut	bt
CASHOO catechu; an astringent	bt
CASING boxing; packing; wrapping	
CASINO saloon; gaming-house	
CASKET jewel case; reliquary	
CASQUE a helmet; morion	
CASSIA plant; cinnamon	bt
CASTER cruet; small wheel	
CASTLE citadel; fortress; stronghold	ar
CASTOR beaver genus	zo
CASTOR a hat; plant	bt
CAST-UP vomit; job content	pr
CASUAL accidental; fortuitous	
CASULA a chasuble	rl
CATCHY deceptive; infectious	
CATENA a chain; a series	
CATENA doctrinal writings	
CATGUT cord; violin string	zo
CATHAY China; (Marco Polo)	
CATION electro-positive element cathode	el
CATKIN pendulous inflorescence	bt
CAT-LAP tame tipple	
CATLOG catalogue	
CATNAP forty winks; doze	
CATNIP mint; catmint	bt

CATSUP a relish; ketchup	ck	
CATTED anchor housed		
CATTLE kine; oxen	zo	
CAUCUS political organization		
CAUDAL tail-bearing	zo	
CAUDEX palm-stem	bt	
CAUDLE hot spiced wine		
CAUGHT trapped; entangled		
CAUKED / **CAWKED** water-tight	nt	
CAUKER (caulking oakum); **CAWKER** a dram; a tall story	nt	
CAULIS stem	bt	
CAUSAL producing; resulting		
CAUSED occasioned; created; effected		
CAUSER instigator; prime mover		
CAUSEY pavée; causeway (obs.)		
CAUTEL craft; wariness (obs.)		
CAUTER searing-iron		
CAVASS kavass; Turkish policeman		
CAVEAT a warning	lw	
CAVERN cave; grotto; den		
CAVIAR fish-roe of the sturgeon	zo	
CAVIES guinea-pig	zo	
CAVING giving way		
CAVITY void; pocket; vacuum		
CAVORT prance; buck; leap		
CAWASS attendant (Arab)		
CAXTON a book in black letter		
CAYMAN alligator; caiman	zo	
CAYUSE Wild West bronco; nag	zo	
CEASED stopped; desisted; terminated		
CECILS rissoles		
CECITY blindness	md	
CEDARN made of cedar-wood; **CEDARY** of cedar colour	bt	
CEDING yielding; resigning		
CEDRAT citron	bt	
CEDULA S. American mortgage	lw	
CELERY crisp vegetable	bt	
CELIAC coeliac; abdominal	md	
CELLAR vault		
CELLED honeycombed; alveolate		
CELTIC Keltic		
CEMENT cohere; unite; attach		
CENSED redolent with incense		
CENSER tray for burning incense	rl	
CENSOR critic; inspector; carper		
CENSUS official enumeration		
CENTAL 100 lb (45 kg)	me	
CENTRE also center; middle; midst		
CEPOLA snake-fish	zo	
CERAGO pollen	bt	
CERATE an ointment	md	
CERCAL caudal, of the tail		
CEREAL grain; corn	bt	
CEREUS a cactus genus	bt	
CERINE an ore of cerium	mn	
CERING covering with wax		
CERIPH serif	pr	

CERISE cherry-colour		
CERITE cerium silicate	ch	
CERIUM metallic element	ch	
CERMET metal-ceramic alloy	ml	
CEROON seroon; a bale		
CERRIS the bitter oak	bt	
CERTES in sooth; **CERTIE** certainly (Sc.)	ch	
CERUSE white-lead		
CERVIX neck of womb	md	
CERVUS the stag genus	zo	
CESSED taxed		
CESSIO an assignment	lw	
CESTUI a beneficiary	lw	
CESTUS a girdle; boxing glove		
CESURA metrical pause; **CESURE** an interruption		
CETINE spermaceti	zo	
CHABUK Eastern ship	nt	
CHACMA baboon	zo	
CHAFED fretted by rubbing; galled		
CHAFER a beetle; cockchafer	zo	
CHAFFY light; worthless; jovial		
CHAGAN a Khan		
CHAISE vehicle; shay		
CHALET Swiss cottage		
CHALKA Zulu king		
CHALKY of chalk, pasty		
CHANCE happen; betide; fortune		
CHANCY hazardous; risky; fortuitous		
CHANGE alter; vary; shift; veer		
CHANTY sailor's song	nt	
CHAPEL a printer's association	rl	
CHAPPY cleft; chinky		
CHARET a chariot (Spens.)		
CHARGE command; bid; trust; ward		
CHARON ferryman of the Styx		
CHARRY like charcoal		
CHASED followed; tracked; engraved		
CHASER hunter; pursuer	to	
CHASMY gaping; yawning		
CHASSE a liqueur; dance step		
CHASTE pure; incorrupt; virtuous		
CHATON the head of a ring (Fr.)		
CHATTA umbrella (Ind.)		
CHATTY talkative; gossipy		
CHAWED / **CHEWED** gnawed; crunched		
CHECKY checkered		
CHEEKY insolent; impudent		
CHEERY buoyant; merry; blithe		
CHEESE milk product		
CHEESY chic		
CHEKOA porcelain-clay	mn	
CHENAR, CHINAR oriental plane tree	bt	
CHEQUE a draft		
CHERRY ruddy; a fruit tree	bt	
CHERTY flinty		
CHERUB angel; child		
CHERUP chirp; to urge		
CHESIL gravel; shingle	mn	

CHESTY low pitched	
CHEVAL a frame	
CHEVEN chevin; chub	zo
CHEVET an apse	ar
CHEWET chough; chatterer	zo
CHIASM (optic nerve)	md
CHIAUS chouse; a cheat (obs.)	
CHICHA liquor from maize (S. Amer.)	ck
CHICHI 'precious'; over-decorated	
CHICLE chewing gum	bt
CHICLY fashionably; modishly	
CHICOT jester to Henri III	
CHILDE chylde; nobleman's son	
CHILLI cayenne pepper	bt
CHILLY bleak; frigid	
CHIMED struck; accorded	
CHIMER bishop's robe	rl
CHINCH grain insect; bed-bug; cimex	zo
CHINED cleft to the back-bone	
CHINEE a Chinaman	
CHINKY gaping; chappy	
CHINSE to caulk	nt
CHINTZ floral cotton cloth	tx
CHIPPY off colour	
CHIRAL pertaining to the hand	pl
CHIRPY chatty; cheerful; cheery	
CHISEL to cheat	to
CHISIL chesil; gravel	mn
CHITAL spotted deer	zo
CHITIN horny material	zo
CHITON a mollusc; Greek tunic	zo
CHITTY childish; infantile	
CHIVES onion-like salad plant	bt, ck
CHIVVY hasten; nag; pester	
CHOICE select; dainty; option; election	
CHOKED stifled; throttled; suppressed	
CHOKER a tie; a neckerchief	
CHOKEY prison	
CHOKRA office boy (Ind.)	
CHOLER anger; ire; spleen; rage	
CHOLIC (bile); bilious	md
CHOOSE pick; elect; adopt; prefer	
CHOOSY pernickety; fastidious	
CHOPIN quart (Sc.)	me
CHOPPY irregular	
CHORAL chanted	
CHOREA St. Vitus' dance	me
CHOREE trochee	
CHORIA external membranes	bt
CHORIC (chorus)	
CHORUS group of voices	mu
CHOSEN elected; selected; picked	
CHOUAN Breton guerilla	
CHOUGH a crow	zo
CHOUSE to cheat; a trick	
CHOWRY fly-whisk (Ind.)	
CHRISM Holy oil	rl
CHROMA purity of colour; scale (Gr.)	
CHROME metal	ch
CHUBBY plump; buxom	
CHUFFY puffy; surly	

CHUKKA period of play at polo	
CHUMMY sociable; matey	
CHUNAM lime; stucco (Ind.)	mn
CHURCH temple; kirk	rl
CHURLY churlish; surly; sullen	
CHUTNY chutney; fruity pickle	ck
CHYLDE churlish; surley; sullen	
CHYMIC chemical	ch
CHYPRE a perfume	
CICADA } a chirping insect	zo
CICALA }	
CICELY a genus of plants; myrrh	bt
CICERO a fount of type	
CICUTA hemlock; cow-bane	bt
CIGALE cigala; cicada	zo
CIERGE wax candle	rl
CILERY carving; carved foliage	ar
CILICE hair-cloth	
CILIUM whip-like plant structure	bt
CIMBEX the saw-fly	zo
CIMBIA a fillet	ar
CIMIER crest of helmet (Fr.)	
CIMISE bed-bug; cimex	zo
CIMNEL simnel; Saffron cake	
CINDER ember; ash	
CINEMA kinema; movies; talkies	
CINGLE surcingle; girth; cinch	
CINQUE (cards or dice); (ports)	
CINTRE centering	ar
CIPHER zero; dot; nought; device	
CIPPUS funereal column	
CIRCAR district (Hindu)	
CIRCLE ring; compass; circuit; set	
CIRCUS round place	
CIRRUS tendril; cloud	bt
CISLEU a Jewish month	
CISSUS wild vine	bt
CISTED in a cyst; entombed	
CISTIC cystic	md
CISTIL pewter box	
CISTUS rock-rose	bt
CITESS citizeness	
CITHER zither (guitar)	mu
CITIED with many cities	
CITING quoting; summoning	
CITOLE a dulcimer; psaltery	mu
CITRIC (lemons)	ch
CITRIL song bird; a finch	zo
CITRIN vitamin P	
CITRON a fruit; lemon	bt
CITRUL the pumpkin	bt
CITRUS plant genus	bt
CIVICS science of citizenship	
CIVISM good citizenship	
CIVIES mufti; civilian clothes	
CLAGGY sticky; cloggy; cledgy	
CLAMMY dank; viscous; sticky	
CLAQUE hired applause	
CLARET a wine; a colour	ck
CLARTY miry; muddy	
CLASSY superior; high-toned	

CLATCH botch; daub	
CLAUSE paragraph; proviso; condition	
CLAVER gossip (Sc.)	
CLAVES Cuban percussion	mu
CLAVIS a translation; a key	
CLAVUS toga stripe; corn	md
CLAWED torn; scratched; lacerated	
CLAYES hurdles; wattles	
CLAYEY like clay; cledgy	
CLEATS herb coltsfoot; hooks	bt
CLEAVE cling; cohere; split; rend	
CLECHE a cross voided	hd
CLEDGE fuller's earth	mn
CLEDGY clayey; tenacious	
CLENCH clinch; secure; fasten; grapple	
CLERGY the cloth; priesthood	rl
CLERIC clerical; a clerk; church officer	
CLEUCH clough (Sc.); ravine	
CLEVER able; adroit; gifted; dexterous	
CLEVIS draught-iron of plough	
CLEWED coiled; trussed	nt
CLICHE artist's proof; trite phrase	
CLIENT customer; dependant	
CLIFFY ⎫ craggy; broken	
CLIFTY ⎭	
CLIMAX acme; zenith; height; top	
CLINCH clench; clutch; catch; grasp	
CLINGY adhesive; sticky	
CLINIC (bedside); hospital	md
CLIONE 'whales' food'; small fish	zo
CLIQUE coterie; junto; cabal; set	
CLOACA a sewer; reproductive canal	zo
CLOCHE bell-glass; (hat)	
CLOCHE protective glass cover for plants	
CLODDY clodly; earthy; gross; boorish	
CLOGGY adhesive; clingy	
CLOKED cloaked; concealed	
CLONIC convulsive	
CLONUS a spasm	md
CLOSED united; grappled; shut	
CLOSER closure; tighter	
CLOSET small room; wardrobe	ar
CLOTHE attire; drape; invest; robe	
CLOTTY curdy	
CLOUDY dim; overcast; gloomy; murky	
CLOUGH ravine; cleft; chine	
CLOUGH trade allowance	
CLOVEN cleft; split asunder	
CLOVER trifolium	bt
CLOYED satiated; cumbered; surfeited	
CLUMPS a numskull; nitwit; dullard	
CLUMPY massive; shapeless	
CLUMSY awkward; heavy-handed	
CLUNCH marl; clay	mn
CLUPEA sprat genus	zo
CLUTCH (of eggs); grasp; clench; grip	
COACHY a coachman	
COAGEL gel made by coagulation	md
COAITA S. American monkey; coati	zo
COALED stoked	
CO-ALLY fellow-helper; partner	

COARSE crude; impure; rough; rude	
COATED spread; covered	
COATEE coat with short tails	
COAXED persuaded; allured; seduced	
COAXER cajoler; flatterer; wheedler	
COBALT element; blue	mn
COBBLE a stone; to repair	mn
COBCAL sandal	
COBNUT hazel-nut	bt
COBRES S. American indigo	bt
COBRIC cobra-type	zo
COBURG a twilled fabric	tx
COBWEB flimsy fly-trap; spider's web	
COCCUS seed-vessel; microbe	md, bt
COCCYX terminal bone of spine	md
COCHIN a fowl	zo
COCKAL the game of knuckle-bones	
COCKED erect; inebriated	
COCKER to pamper; a spaniel	zo
COCKER famous for his arithmetic	
COCKET customs seal; a certificate	
COCKLE a weed	bt
COCKLE shellfish; to pucker	zo
COCKSY bumptious; conceited	
COCK-UP extend above normal level	
COCK-UP obvious mistake	
COCOON insect case	zo
CODBER pillow-slip	
CODDED in a pod; hoaxed	
CODDER a gatherer of peas	
CODDLE indulge; pamper; humour	
CODGER an eccentric old man	
CODIFY digest; regulate	
CODING putting into cipher	
CODIST summarist; arranger	
CODLIN an apple	bt
COELOM the body cavity	md
COERCE force; impel; constrain	
COEVAL contemporaneous	
COFFEE beverage from Ethiopian berry	bt
COFFER panel; chest	ar
COFFIN a printing frame	
COFFLE a slave gang	
COGENT potent; urgent; forcible	
COGGED toothed; cheated	
COGGIE small bowl	
COGGLE small boat	nt
COGNAC brandy	ck
COHEIR joint heir	
COHERE cleave; unite; join; stick	
COHORN obsolete trench-mortar	
COHORT tenth part of a legion	
COHUNE palm	bt
COIGNE enforced billeting (Irish)	
COILED spiral; wound	
COINED invented; minted	
COINER counterfeiter; inventor	
COITUS sexual intercourse	
CO-JOIN join together; unite	
COKING taking cocaine	
COLDER chillier	

COLDLY frigidly
COLLAR neckband; part of clothing
COLLED embraced; hugged
COLLET collar; setting of a jewel
COLLIE colley; sheep-dog   **zo**
COLLOP a slice of meat   **ck**
COLLUM lowest part of stem   **bt**
COLMAR pear   **bt**
COLMEY the coal-fish   **zo**
COLONY a settlement
COLOUR tint; hue; dye; shade
COLTER ploughshare
COLUGO flying lemur   **zo**
COLUMN pillar; file; row; line
COLURE intersecting celestial circle   **as**
COMARB abbot; coarb   **rl**
COMART an agreement
COMATE comose; hairy; hirsute
COMBAT contest; war; resist; oppose
COMBED brushed, carded, straightened
COMBER foaming billow
COMEDO a blackhead   **md**
COMEDY a play
COMELY seemly; graceful; shapely
COMFIT sweetmeat; confit   **ck**
COMFRY comfrey; wild plant   **bt**
COMING approach; future; expected
COMITY courtesy; civility
COMMIS waiter's assistant; deputy
COMMIT entrust; enact; consign
COMMIX to mix; mingle
COMMON public; ordinary; usual
COMOPT ciné-film with optical soundtrack
COMOSE hairy; downy; comate
COMPEL coerce; oblige; make
COMPLY agree; submit; yield; conform
COMPOT a preserve   **ck**
CONCHA ear-cavity; conch   **md**
CONCHY conscientious objector
CONCUR agree; harmonize; help
CONDED \ navigated; steered;
CONNED / memorized; studied
CONDER pilot; fish-scout
CONDOR vulture   **zo**
CONFAB pow-wow; conference
CONFER bestow; grant; consult
CONFIT comfit; sweetmeat
CONFIX fasten; attach; append
CONGEE conjee; dismissal; farewell
CONGER eel   **zo**
CONGOU black tea   **bt**
CONICS geometry of the cone
CONIES \ rabbits; pikas;
CONEYS / hyrax genus   **zo**
CONIIN conin; hemlock extract   **md**
CONIMA gum resin   **bt**
CONINE an alkaloid   **ch**
CONIUM hemlock   **bt**
CONJEE congee; rice-water
CONKED petered out
CONKER chestnut   **bt**

CON-MAN trickster; swindler
CONNER an inspector; look-out   **md**
CONOID pineal gland; a paraboloid   **pl**
CONSOL long-range navigational system
CONSOL Brit. funded gov't security
CONSUL a government official
CONTRA against; opposite
CONVEX protuberant
CONVEY carry; transport; transfer
CONVOY escort; guard; protect
CONYZA fleabane   **bt**
COOEED (Australian bush call)
COOING and billing
COOKED done to a turn
COOKER cooking-range
COOKIE super-heavy bomb; a bun
COOLED calmed; allayed; moderated
COOLER a drink; colder
COOLIE labourer (China)
COOLLY calmly; placidly; impudently
COOMBE combe; deep valley
COONTY arrowroot (Florida)   **bt**
COOPED cabined and confined
COOPER a mixed drink; cask-maker
COOTIE feathered legs (Sc.)
COPANG Japanese gold coin   **nm**
COPECK 1/100th part of rouble   **nm**
COPIED transcribed; aped
COPIER copyer; scribe; plagiarist
COPIES reduplications; imitations
COPING top course of a wall; striving
COPPED caught; run in
COPPER a policeman; a penny   **nm**
COPPIN ball of thread
COPTIC (Egyptian Christianity)
COPULA a link
COQUET to flirt
CORBAN, KURBAN gift; ceremony
CORBEL stone bracket   **ar**
CORBIE a raven; carrion crow   **zo**
CORCLE embryo seed   **bt**
CORCUR purple dye
CORDED ribbed; furrowed
CORDON a ribbon of honour; a guard
COREAN or **KOREAN**
CORING boring; drilling
CORIUM true skin   **md**
CORKED sealed (bottle)
CORKER a poser; a finisher
CORKIR red or purple lichen dye
CORMUS stem   **bt**
CORNEA eye-membrane   **md**
CORNED preserved; granulated; salted
CORNEL dog-wood   **bt**
CORNER bend; angle; nook; cranny
CORNET an officer; trumpet   **mu**
CORNUA horns   **zo**
CORODY an allowance; a pension
CORONA a halo; a crown; a cigar
COROZO vegetable ivory   **bt**
CORPSE carcass; corse; remains

CORPUS a body; association	md
CORRAL cattle-pen; to round up	
CORRIE a hollow; a valley (Sc.)	
CORSAC, CORSAK Central Asian fox	zo
CORSET a bodice; stays	
CORTES Spanish Parliament	
CORTEX treebark; covering	bt
CORVEE forced levy (pre-1789 Fr.)	
CORVEE recruitment for road service	
CORVET curvet; leap; frolic	
CORVUS a crow	zo
CORVUS grappling iron	
CORYMB a panicle; a raceme	bt
CORYZA snuffly cold	md
COSHED bashed; slugged	
COSHER to pamper; to chat	
COSIER a botcher; cozier; cobbler	
COSILY snugly	
COSINE sine of complement of angle	ma
COSMIC cosmical; orderly	
COSMOS universe; order	
COSSAS Indian Muslims	rl
COSSET a pet lamb; to pet	zo
COSTAL (rib)	md
CO-STAR actors cast together	
COSTER costermonger; apple-seller	
COSTLY dear; sumptuous; rich	
COTEAU divide between valleys	
COTISE a bendlet	hd
COTTAR a cottager; cotter	
COTTER wedge; pin	
COTTON to harmonize; attract; plant	bt
COTYLA a sucker	zo
COTYLE bone-cavity; cup	md
COUCAL cuckoo	zo
COUGAR puma	zo
COULEE ravine; couloir	
COUPED bartered for; cut off	
COUPEE an antic; a salute	
COUPER a dealer	
COUPLE pair; brace; connect	
COUPON a voucher	
COURAP disease (E. Ind.)	md
COURSE circuit; orbit; progress; series	
COUSIN a Kinsman	
COUTER £1 (slang)	nm
COUTIL strong cotton fabric	
COVENT a convent	rl
COVERT concealed; secret; thicket	
COVESS female cove or chap	
COVING (fireplace); (jutting out)	
COWAGE a leguminous plant	bt
COWARD craven; dastard; recreant	
COW-BOY cattle herder	
COWDIE cowrie-pine	bt
COWING intimidating; browbeating	
COWISH like a cow	
COWLED hooded	
COW-MAN cow-herd	
COWPEA herb, source of black-eye peas	
COW-POX cow-teat disease	md

COWRIE sea-shell; cowry	zo
COYISH coy; rather reserved	
COYOTE prairie wolf	zo
COYPOU coypu; rodent (S. Amer.)	zo
COZIER tramp; cosier	
CRABBY perplexing; peevish	
CRABER water-vole	zo
CRABRO hornet genus	zo
CRADLE crib; a frame; to compose	
CRAFTY artful; deceitful; cunning	
CRAGGE the neck	
CRAGGY rugged; rough; jagged	
CRAMBO a game; a rhyme	
CRAMPY affected with cramp	
CRANCH crunch; chew	
CRANED with neck out-stretched	
CRANIA skulls (cranium)	md
CRANKY eccentric; crotchet	
CRANNY chink; fissure; cleft; rift	
CRANSE boom iron to take stay-sails	nt
CRANTS funeral garlands	
CRAPED curled	
CRASIS temperament	mc
CRATCH hay-rack; manger	
CRATED boxed; encased	
CRATER bomb-hole	
CRAVAT necktie	
CRAVED entreated; desired	
CRAVEN coward; recreant; dastard	
CRAVER beggar; an addict	
CRAYER small trading ship	nt
CRAYON chalk pencil	
CRAZED decrepit; loony; deranged	
CREACH } foray (Sc.);	
CREAGH } booty; raid	
CREAKY crepitative	
CREAMY like cream	
CREANT forming; creative	
CREASE Malay dagger; creese	
CREASE (cricket); a fold	
CREASY crumpled	
CREATE cause; fashion; invent	
CRECHE a day-nursery	
CREDIT trust; loan; merit; belief	
CREEKY winding	
CREEPY, CREEPS eerie; horrific	
CREESE Malay dagger; crease	
CREESH grease (Sc.)	
CREMOR creamy juice	
CRENEL loophole or notch	
CRENIC acid	ch
CREOLE West Indian half-breed	
CREPON crepe fabric	
CRESOL tar product	ch
CRESOL resin/plastic phenols	ch
CRESSY like water-cress	bt
CRESTA the ice-run at St. Moritz	
CRETIC a metric foot	
CRETIN deformed; idiot; moron	
CREVET goldsmith; crucible	
CREWEL embroidery	

CRIKEY exclamation of surprise	**CULTUR** Kultur; German culture	
CRIMED charged with	**CULTUS** a cult	
CRIMPY frizzy, waved	**CULVER** pigeon; wood-pigeon	zo
CRINAL comate; hirsute, hairy	**CUMBER** hamper; impede; clog	
CRINGE fawn; stoop; cower	**CUMBLY** harsh woollen cloth (Ind.)	
CRISES decisive moments	**CUMMER** kimmer; godmother; gossip	
CRISIS emergency; turning point	**CUMMIN, CUMIN** spice seed; anti-colic	
CRISPY curled; brittle	**CUNEAL** wedge-shaped	
CRISTA a crest	**CUPFUL** filling a cup	me
CRITIC arbiter; reviewer; judge	**CUP-MAN** boon companion	
CROAKY harsh; guttural	**CUPOLA** dome; furnace	
CROATS Croatia (Yugoslavia)	**CUPPED** bled; hollowed	
CROCUS the saffron	bt	**CUPPER** cup-bearer	
CRONET horse-hoof hair	**CUPRIC** (copper)	ch
CROOKS tubular devices	mu	**CUP-TIE** annual football competition	
CROPPY crop-eared	**CUPULA** acorn-cup	bt
CROSSE lacrosse stick	**CUPULE** filbert-husk; cupula	bt
CROTCH a crutch; a fork	**CURACY** curate's job	rl
CROTON oil plant	bt	**CURARA** \ arrow poison used by South	
CROUCH cringe; stoop; cower	**CURARE** } American Indians	
CROUPY affected with croup	md	**CURARI** /	
CROUSE lively; pert (Sc.)	**CURATE** assistant to parish priest	
CROWDY gruel (Sc.)	**CURBED** restrained; held back	
CROWED exulted; boasted	**CURCAS** a nut	bt
CRUCKS tree trunk framework	ar	**CURDLE** coagulate; congeal	
CRUDER rougher; coarser; harsher	**CURFEW** time to rake out the fires	
CRUISE ocean travel	**CURIET** cuirass (Spens.)	
CRUIVE fish trap	**CURING** preserving; healing; remedying	
CRUMBY in crumbs; crummy	**CURLED** rippled; waved; twisted	
CRUMMY cow with crumpled horn	zo	**CURLER** (ice); (hair)	
CRUNCH cranch; munch; bite	**CURLEW** the whaup	zo
CRURAL leggy	**CURRED** purred; cooed	
CRUSET crucible; crevet	**CURRIE** quarry (obs.); Indian stew	ck
CRUSIE lamp with rush wick (Sc.)	**CURSED** anathematized; tormented	
CRUSTA engraved gem; a shell	**CURSER** vituperator	
CRUSTY surly; peevish; morose; crabby	**CURSOR** a slide-rule adjunct	
CRUTCH to support	**CURSUS** a course; curriculum	
CRYING notorious; outcry; clamour	**CURTAL** docked; curt	
CUBAGE solid content	**CURTER** more brusque; terser	
CUBICA shallon cloth	**CURTLY** concisely; shortly; briefly	
CUBING raising to third power	**CURTSY** curtesy; an obeisance	
CUBISM modern artistic geometry	**CURULE** Roman chair	
CUBIST geometrical daubist	**CURVED** arched; bent; bowed	
CUBOID (cubical)	**CURVET** corvet; leap; frolic	
CUBSHA Indian drug	**CUSCUS** fibre; North African dish	bt, ck
CUCKOO migratory bird; simpleton	zo	**CUSCUS** flying squirrel	zo
CUDDIE a donkey; a silly ass	zo	**CUSHAT** ring dove	zo
CUDDLE hug; embrace; fondle	**CUSPID** a canine tooth	md
CUDGEL bludgeon; club; batter	**CUSSED** cursed (slang)	
CUE-BID (Contract bridge)	**CUSTOM** habit; usage; wont; tax	
CUE-OWL scops-owl; a migrant owl	zo	**CUSTOS** a keeper	
CUERPO querpo; undress; partial array	**CUTCHA** temporary (Ind.)	
CUISSE thigh-armour	**CUTEST** most cunning; slyest	
CUITER fondle; pamper	**CUTLER** a dealer in knives	
CULDEE order of monks	rl	**CUTLET** meat sliced with bone; chop	ck
CULLED picked; gathered	**CUT-OFF** paper process	
CULLER a selector	**CUT-OFF** temporary fuel cessation	eg
CULLET scrap-glass	**CUT-OUT** automatic process stoppage	
CULLIS broth; jelly; gutter; groove	ck	**CUTTER** a tailor; seagoing vessel	nt
CULMEN summit; highest point	**CUTTER** author's abbreviation marks	
CULTCH oyster-spawn	zo	system	

CUTTLE squid — zo
CUTTOE large knife (US)
CYANIN colouring of rose/cornflower — bt
CYCLED repeated sequence of operations
CYCLIC periodic; epic
CYCLUS a bicycle or tricycle
CYESIS pregnancy
CYGNET young swan — zo
CYGNUS swan genus — zo
CYMBAL metal clashing instrument — mu
CYMENE (camphor) — md
CYMOID having a waving profile
CYMOSE) (inflorescence definite — bt
CYMOUS) or centrifugal)
CYMRIC Welsh
CYNARA artichoke genus — bt
CYNICS Athenian philosophical sect
CYNOID dog-like
CYPHEL flowering shrub — bt
CYPHER cipher; naught; a nonentity
CY-PRES near — lw
CYPRIS shrimp species — zo
CYPRUS black fabric — tx
CYSTIC, CYSTIS bladder — md
CYTASE an enzyme — md
CYTOID cell-like
CYTULA fertilised ovum; zygote — zo

D

DABBED pecked; patted
DABBER an inking ball
DABBLE mix; meddle; sprinkle
DABOIA venomous snake — zo
DABREY latex collection tray — fr
DACKER to saunter; to lounge (Sc.)
DACOIT pirate; robber (Burma)
DACRON polyester fibre
DACTYL finger or toe
DADDLE walk totteringly
DAEDAL intricate; mazy; complex
DAEMON friendly spirit
DAFTLY idiotically; crazily
DAGGED cut into slips
DAGGER dirk; stiletto; poniard
DAGGLE bedraggle; defile; sully
DAGOBA Buddhist shrine — rl
DAGOES Spaniards and Italians
DAHLIA a flower genus — bt
DAIKER to adorn; to deck
DAIKON Japanese radish — bt
DAIMIO Japanese noble
DAINTY choice; exquisite; tasty; chic
DAKOIT pirate; robber; dacoit
DALILA Delilah; a betrayer
DALLOP a tuft of grass; a lump
DALTON $\frac{1}{16}$ of oxygen atom mass
DAMAGE mar; hurt; impair; injury
DAMASK linen fabric — tx
DAMIER large-squared pattern

DAMINE like a fallow deer
DAMMAR resin; damar — b
DAMMED embanked; confined
DAMNED condemned; doomed
DAMPED moderated; deadened
DAMPEN moisten; discourage; depress
DAMPER (food); a regulator
DAMPER printing roller (lithography) — p
DAMPLY unenthusiastically
DAMSEL lass; maiden; girl
DAMSON small plum — b
DANCED capered; frisked; hopped
DANCER a ballerina; Pavlova; Salome
DANDER saunter; anger
DANDIE terrier — z
DANDLE pet; fondle; caress
DANGER risk; peril; hazard; jeopardy
DANGLE to fondle; swing; suspend
DANIEL a wise judge
DANISH of Denmark
DANITE (Mormon sect)
DANTON to daunt; to subdue (Sc.)
DAPHNE evergreens — b
DAPPED fished with a mayfly
DAPPER neat; nimble; sprightly
DAPPLE to variegate with spots
DARGER day-worker
DARING lark snaring; audacious
DARKEN darkle; cloud
DARKEN obscure; perplex
DARKER blacker; duskier
DARKEY, DARKIE negro
DARKLE to grow dark
DARKLY opaquely; mysteriously
DARNED repaired; mended
DARNEL rye grass; tares — b
DARNER a darning machine
DARTED sprang out; shot; flew
DARTER Brazilian pelican — z
DARTLE spring-out
DARTRE skin-disease; herpes — m
DARWAN doorkeeper (Ind.)
DASHED cast; sped; rushed; shattered
DASHER plunger
DASSIE badger; hyrax — z
DATARY papal officer
DATING reckoning; beginning
DATION act of giving
DATIVE a case
DATURA thorn-apple —
DAUBED smeared; plastered
DAUBER inferior painter
DAUBRY the work of a dauber
DAUCUS the carrot —
DAUNER dander; perambulate
DAVINA volcanic substance — m
DAWDLE lag; dally; idle; trifle
DAWISH like a jackdaw
DAWNED began to appear
DAY-BED a sofa
DAY-BOY non-resident schoolboy

DAY-FLY an ephemeral insect   zo
DAZING mazing; stunning
DAZZLE daze; confuse; bewilder
DEACON church official   rl
DEADEN benumb; blunt; obtund
DEADLY fatal; mortal; baneful; lethal
DEAFEN confuse; stun
DEAFLY unhearingly
DEALER vendor; monger; trader
DEARER costlier; fonder
DEARIE term of endearment
DEARLY expensively
DEARTH scarcity; lack; shortage
DEASIL opp. to widdershins
DEBARK disembark; land
DEBASE degrade; lower; humble
DEBATE dispute; contest; argue
DEBLAI cf. remblai; excavated soil
DEBOSH debauch (obs.)
DEBOUT to expel
DEBRIS bits and pieces
DEBTED indebted; owed
DEBTEE the lender   lw
DEBTOR the borrower
DEBUNK expose; unmask; reveal
DECADE ten of
DECAMP abscond; bolt; fly
DECANI deans   rl
DECANT to pour gently
DECARE 1000 sq. metres   me
DECEIT guile; fraud; chicanery
DECENT proper; seemly; suitable
DECERN to judge; to decree
DECIDE settle; determine; resolve
DECILE aspect   as
DECIMA a tenth   mu
DECIME a tenth of a franc   nm
DECKED adorned; arrayed; layered   nt
DECKER adorner   nt
DECKLE paper gauge
DECKLE paper-making frame; paper edge
DECOCT to boil; to devise; digest
DECODE decipher
DECREE ordain; ukase; fiat; edict
DECREW to decrease (Spens.)
DECURY squad of ten (Roman)
DEDANS gallery (tennis)
DEDUCE infer; gather; conclude
DEDUCT bate; subtract; withdraw
DEEDED conveyed by deed   lw
DEEMED believed; determined; judged
DEEPEN darken; dredge; make obscure
DEEPER further down
DEEPLY profoundly
DEFACE disfigure; injure; sully
DEFAME asperse; vilify; traduce
DEFEAT rout; frustrate; overwhelm
DEFECT flaw; blemish; fault
DEFEND ward; protect; guard
DEFIED challenged; braved
DEFIER scorner; ignorer; spurner

DEFILE violate; taint; vitiate; a gorge
DEFINE specify; explain; limit
DEFLEX bend down
DEFLUX a discharge   md
DEFORM distort; deface; spoil
DEFRAY pay; meet; liquidate; bear
DEFTLY deffly (Spens.); adroitly
DEGAGE unconstrained (Fr.)
DEGRAS sheepskin fat   ch
DEGREE grade; rank; class; order
DEGUST to taste
DEHORN remove horns from cattle
DEHORS irrelevant (Fr.)
DEHORT dissuade
DE-ICER anti-wing-ice device
DEIFIC divine; godlike
DEJECT cast down; depress; dishearten
DELATE to sneak; to inform
DELETE erase; obliterate; efface
DELIAC, DELIAN (of Delas) a vase
DELICE, DELUCE fleur-de-lis
DELICT an offence; crime   lw
DELOUL fast Arabian riding camel   zo
DELUDE dupe; beguile; trick; cozen
DELUGE flood; cataclysm; inundate
DELVED dug; excavated; searched
DELVER a digger
DEMAIN demesne; an estate
DEMAND query; claim; require; exact
DEMEAN behave; lower; degrade
DEMENT madden; derange
DEMISE a death; to bequeath
DEMODE old fashioned
DEMOTH prepare stored arms (war)
DEMURE modest; grave; discreet
DENARY ten
DENGUE a fever   md
DENIAL dementi; refutation; refusal
DENIED refused; contradicted; refuted
DENIER disowner; silk; nylon
DENNET light two-wheeled carriage
DENOTE signify; imply; indicate
DENSER more compact; thicker; closer
DENTAL of teeth
DENTED, DINTED notched; concussed
DENTEL, DENTIL dog toothed   ar
DENTEX sea perch   zo
DENTIN, DENTINE tooth ivory
DENUDE strip; bare; divest
DEODAR sacred tree
DEPART start; vanish; retire; die
DEPEND rely; hang; hinge; rest
DEPICT sketch; limn; portray; draw
DEPLOY open; expand; extend; unfold
DEPONE to testify under oath   lw
DEPORT banish; expel; behave
DEPOSE oust; divest of office; depone
DEPUTE delegate; authorize; charge
DEPUTY envoy; proxy; agent
DERAIL upset; leave rail track
DERAIN vindicate; prove; justify

DERATE reduce
DERBIO a green sea-fish   zo
DERHAM dirhem; Moroccan coin   nm
DERIDE ridicule; mock; lampoon; scorn
DERIVE obtain; draw; trace; receive
DERMAL dermic; relating to skin   pl
DERMIS skin   pl
DERNED darned; damned
DERNLY secretly
DERRIS plant insecticide
DESCRY to espy; detect; discern
DESERT quit; abandon; forsake; merit
DESERT a Sahara; fruit, etc.   ck
DESIGN plan; devise; concoct; scheme
DESINE denote (Spens.)
DESIRE covet; crave; want; passion
DESIST stay; stop; forbear; pause
DESMAN musk-rat   zo
DESMID river-weed   bt
DESPOT dictator; tyrant; autocrat
DETACH sever; divide; part; disengage
DETAIL delineate; recount; relate; item
DETAIN retain; keep; hold; confine
DETECT discover; reveal; unmask
DETENT a check-stop
DETEST hate; abhor; loathe
DETORT to pervert   lw
DETOUR deviation; circumambulation
DETUNE adjust resonant circuit   ro
DEUCED devilish; confounded
DEUNME Jew turned Moslem   rl
DEVALL cease; a stop (Sc.)
DEVICE gadget; ruse; artifice; emblem
DEVISE scheme; plan; bequeath   lw
DEVOID lacking; vacant; empty
DEVOIR politeness; duty
DEVOTE dedicate; give; resign
DEVOUR gorge; gobble; consume
DEVOUT pious; saintly; sincere
DEWANI a dewan's office
DEWING bedewing
DEWITT to lynch
DEWLAP pendulous neck-flesh
DEXTER on the right-hand side
DHANUK member of low Indian caste
DHARMA law of Buddha   rl
DHOBIE Indian washerman
DHOOLY Indian litter
DHURRA millet   bt
DIADEM crown; coronet; tiara
DIAMYL (amyl)   ch
DIAPER a napkin
DIARCH with 2 xylem strands   bt
DIATOM a seaweed   bt
DIAXON with 2 axes, in sponges   zo
DIBBED (gardening)
DIBBER pointed tool   to
DIBBLE dibber; to make holes
DICAST dikast; Athenian judge
DICING gaming

DICKER ten; to barter
DICKY bird; ass; unwell   zo
DICKEY false shirt-front; back-seat
DICTUM maxim
DICTUM precept; award   lw
DIDDER to shiver
DIDDLE cheat; totter; dodder
DIESEL heavy oil engine
DIESIS printing mark
DIETED, DIETAL, DIETER food regime
DIFFER deviate; vary; wrangle
DIGAMY second marriage
DIGENY sexual reproduction
DIGEST peptonise; summary of ideas/plot   lw
DIGGED delved; dug
DIGGER Australian
DIGLOT bi-lingual
DIGRAM a digraph
DIKAST dicast; Athenian judge
DIK-DIK S. African antelope   zo
DIKING ditching
DIKKAH tribune in a mosque
DIKKOP bustard (S. African)   zo
DIKTAT enforced settlement
DILATE amplify; expand; enlarge
DILOGY double-entendre
DILUTE water; thin; attenuate
DIMITY figured cloth
DIMMED obscured; clouded; dulled
DIMMER more indistinct; fainter
DIMOUT partial black-out
DIMPLE cheek depression
DIMWIT fool
DIN-DIN Indian cymbals   mu
DINDLE ⎫ to tingle (Sc.);
DINNLE ⎭ a thrill
DINFUL clamorous; noisy
DINGED hurled; enforced; urged
DINGES what's its name (S. African)
DINGHY dingey; boat   nt
DINGLE dell; dale; vale; glen
DINGUS gadget; contraption
DINKUM honest; genuine (Australia)
DINNED persistently repeated
DINNER principal meal
DIODON globe fish genus   zo
DIONYM name containing 2 terms
DIOTIC affecting both ears   md
DIOXAN wax/resin solvent   ch
DIPLEX simultaneous transmission
DIPLOE skull tissue   md
DIPNOI fish with lungs and gills   zo
DIPODY two-footed   pl
DIPOLE type of radio aerial   el, ro
DIPPED immersed; doused; soused
DIPPER water ousel; ladle   zo
DIP-ROD oil gauge   me
DIPSAS serpent   zo
DIPYRE a silicate of alumina   mn
DIRDUM uproar; a scolding (Sc.)

DIRECT straight; bid; order; address
DIREST most calamitous; cruellest
DIRHAM } ancient oriental weight;   **me**
DIRHEM } silver coin (Morocco)   **nm**
DIRKED stabbed
DIRZEE Indian needlewoman
DISARM render harmless
DISBAR to expel   **lw**
DISBUD remove buds
DISCAL (disc)
DISCUS quoit; (Greek Games)
DISCUS flower centre   **bt**
DISEUR (diseuse) raconteur (Fr.)
DISHED frustrated
DISMAL dull; doleful; lugubrious
DISMAN unman
DISMAY appal; scare; daunt; alarm
DISOWN deny; disclaim; reject; ignore
DISPEL banish; scatter; dismiss
DISTAL terminal; furthest from axis   **bt**
DISTIL vaporize; drip; emanate
DISUSE desuetude; neglect
DITHER didder; tremble; quake
DITION dominion; rule; power
DITONE an interval   **mu**
DITTAY an indictment (Sc.)   **lw**
DITTOS a mono-coloured suit
DIURNA insects; ephemerae   **zo**
DIVALI Feast of Lanterns (Hindu)
DIVERS diverse; different; sundry
DIVERT distract; amuse; relax; deflect
DIVEST devest; strip; denude; bare
DIVIDE sever; sunder; cleave; share
DIVINE predict; augur; angelic; sacred
DIVING plunging; penetrating; swooping
DIVOTO solemnly   **mu**
DIZAIN poem in ten stanzas
DIZOIC with 2 sporozoites   **zo**
DJIBBA Eastern garment
DOABLE practical
DOBBIE a dotard; a brownie
DOBBIN old horse   **zo**
DOCENT teaching
DOCILE pliant; amenable; compliant
DOCITY docility
DOCKED cut short; moved into harbour   **nt**
DOCKER dock-labourer; stevedore
DOCKET doquet; a summary   **lw**
DOCTOR a fish; medico; to falsify   **zo**
DODDED hornless   **bt**
DODDER parasitic plant; didder; shake
DODDLE a pollard   **bt, zo**
DODGED evaded; quibbled; avoided
DODGER trickster; shifter; evader
DODINE chemical fungicide
DODKIN a doit   **nm**
DODMAN a snail   **zo**
DOFFED removed; took off
DOFFER carding mechanism
DOGANA custom-house (It.)
DOGATE dignity of doge (Venice)

DOG-BEE a drone   **zo**
DOG-BOX enclosure for dogs
DOG-EAR broken/damaged book corner
DOG-FOX renard   **zo**
DOGGAR ironstone   **mn**
DOGGED sullen; obstinate; determined
DOGGER fishing boat   **nt**
DOG-MAD rabid; crazy; insane
DOILED doilt; crazy (Sc.)
DOINGS multifarious activities
DOITED crazy; stupid
DOLENT full of woe (obs.)
DOLING distributing
DOLIUM molluscs   **zo**
DOLLAR 100 cents   **nm**
DOLLED prinked up
DOLLOP viscous mass
DOLMAN hussar's jacket
DOLMEN stone table; cromlech
DOLOSE fraudulent; deceitful
DOLOUR anguish; sorrow; pain
DOMAIN demesne; dominion; sway   **lw**
DOM-BOC Saxon book
DOMETT shroud fabric
DOMIFY (horoscope)
DOMINO priest's cape; cloak
DOMITE variety of trachyte   **mn**
DONARY a gift   **rl**
DONATE present; give
DONJON the keep
DONKEY burro; moke; ass   **zo**
DONSIE perverse (Sc.)
DONZEL budding knight; a page
DOOCOT dovecote (Sc.)
DOODLE a simpleton; a trifler; drawing
DOOLIE Indian litter
DOOMED destined; condemned
DOPING doctoring; varnishing
DOPPER Dutch baptist
DORADO constellation; a dolphin   **as, zo**
DORBIE the dunlin   **zo**
DORCAS charitable society
DORIAN Doric decoration   **ar**
DORING lark-catching
DORISM Doricism
DORMER window in the roof   **ar**
DORMIE dormy; unbeatable at golf
DORMIN hormone controlling dormancy   **bt**
DORNIC figured linen
DORSAL back fin   **pl**
DORSEL fabric; pannier
DORTER dormitory   **rl**
DOSAGE, DOSING taking medicine
DOSSAL, DOSSEL altar cloth   **rl**
DOSSIL pledget; slug   **md**
DOTAGE senility
DOTANT a dotard
DOTARD imbecile; driveller
DOTERY drivel
DOTING madly fond

DOTISH daft; imbecile; demented	
DOTTED stippled	
DOTTER birds'-eyes graining brush	pt
DOTTLE pipe-ash	
DOUANE custom-house (Fr.)	
DOUBLE dual; twofold; duplicate	
DOUCHE shower-bath	
DOUGHY soft consistency like dough	ck
DOUKAR dabchick	zo
DOURLY grimly; sternly; obstinately	
DOUSED extinguished;	
DOUTED struck;	
DOWSED drenched	
DOUTER extinguisher	
DOWERY dowry; dot	
DOWLAS coarse cloth	tx
DOWNED floored	
DOWSER water-diviner	
DOYLEY lace mat; a doily	
DOZING somnolent; drowsy	
DRABBY sluttish	
DRACHM drachma; a dram	nm
DRAFFY dreggy; waste; worthless	
DRAFTS draughts; a game	
DRAGEE sweetmeat	ck
DRAGON monstrous saurian	zo
DRAPED dressed; robed; clothed	
DRAPER haberdasher	
DRAPET coverlet	
DRAPPY a wee drop (Sc.)	
DRAWEE (Bill of Exchange)	
DRAWER pot-man; an attraction	
DRAZEL a slut	
DREAMT imagined; fancied	
DREAMY fanciful; visionary	
DREARY dismal; lonely; dull; gloomy	
DREDGE a drag-net; to sprinkle	
DREGGY (dregs); muddy	
DREICH tiresome (Sc.)	
DRENCH (tenure); soak; imbrue	lw
DRESSY dapper; dandified	
DRIEST very dry	
DRIFTY (snow-drifts)	
DRIVEL twaddle; prate; balderdash	
DRIVEN urged; compelled; overworked	
DRIVER a golf club	
DROGER a coaster; drogher	nt
DROGUE sea anchor; sleeve target	nt
DROLLY droll; laughable	
DROMIC (race course)	
DROMON medieval warship	nt
DROMOS Greek race-course	
DRONED buzzed; drawled; idled	
DRONGO king crow	zo
DROPAX a depilatory	
DROP-IN computer error; visit	
DROPSY fluid-collection disease	md
DROSKY Russian vehicle	
DROSSY impute; foul; worthless	
DROUGE harpoon drag	
DROUMY troubled; muddy	

DROUTH dryness; thirst	
DROVER cattle-driver	
DROWSE nap; slumber; doze	
DROWSY lethargic; comatose; soporific	
DRUDGE menial; scullion; toil; slave	
DRUIDS a sacred order	
DRUMLY turbid; muddy	
DRUPEL a stone-fruit; a drupe	bt
DRUSED crystalline	
DRUSES Moslem sect	rl
DRY-BOB non-rower (Eton)	
DRY-FLY (fishing)	
DRYING parching; desiccating	
DRYISH somewhat sarcastic	
DRYITE fossil wood	mn
DRY-ROT wood decay	
DRY-RUB nettoyage à sec	
DUALIN an explosive	ch
DUBASH interpreter; guide (Ind.)	
DUBBED styled; greased	
DUBBER Indian bottle; dupper	
DUBBIN a leather grease; dubbing	
DUCKED bobbed; immersed	
DUCKER a plunger; bird	zo
DUDDER to shake; to deafen	
DUDEEN Irish clay pipe	
DUELLO duelling (It.)	
DUENNA chaperone	
DUETTO a duet	mu
DUFFED stole cattle (Australia)	
DUFFEL coarse cloth with thick nap	
DUFFLE	
DUFFER a pedlar; muff; stupid person	
DUGONG sea-cow; halicore; manatee	zo
DUG-OUT canoe; shelter	
DUG-OUT retired officer	
DUIKER duyker; cormorant	zo
DUKERY seat of a duke	
DUKKER to tell fortunes	
DULCET melodious; honeyed	
DULCIN super-sweet crystalline chemical	
DULLED blunted; assuaged; softened	
DULLER more listless	
DUMBLY silently; mutely	
DUM-DUM soft-nosed bullet	
DUMOSE abounding with bushes	
DUMOUS and briars	
DUMPED unloaded; deposited; heaped	
DUMPLE to cook a dumpling	
DUN-COW species of ray	zo
DUNDER dregs; lees	
DUNITE olivine igneous rock	g
DUNKER tunker; baptist	
DUNLIN sandpiper	zo
DUNLOP a cheese; a tyre	
DUNNED importuned	
DUNNER debt-collector	
DUPERY duping; chicanery	
DUPING gulling; deceiving	
DUPION double cocoon	zo
DUPLET electrons bonding atoms	

DUPLEX two-fold paper; double   **pp**
DUPLEX double photography emulsion paper
DUPPER Indian bottle; dubber
DURAIN type of coal   **mn**
DURANT glazed fabric
DURATE harsh to the ear   **mu**
DURBAR audience; festival
DURDEN a thicket; a copse
DURDUM dirdum; an uproar
DURENE a tetramethylbenzene   **ch**
DURESS restraint; imprisonment
DURGAH Moslem saint's shrine (Ind.)   **rl**
DURGAN dwarf
DURHAM breed of cattle   **zo**
DURIAN Malay fruit   **bt**
DURING throughout; pending
DURION see durian   **bt**
DURITY hardness; firmness
DURRIE Indian cotton fabric
DUSKEN to grow dark
DUSKLY duskily; gloomily
DUSTER a cloth
DUST-UP quarrel
DUTIED taxed
DUTIES obligations; excises
DUYKER duiker; African antelope   **zo**
DYADIC (two)   **ch**
DYEING colouring; staining
DYNAMO energy converter   **el**
DYNAST a ruler; dynasty
DYNODE valve   **el**
DYVOUR a bankrupt (Sc.)   **lw**
DZEREN ⎫
DZERON ⎬ Mongolian antelope   **zo**
       ⎭

E

EADISH aftermath; second crop
EAGLET a young eagle   **zo**
EAR-BOB an earring
EAR-CAP ear-muff
EARFUL a diatribe
EARING ploughing; rope   **nt**
EARLAP tip of ear   **md**
EARNED merited; won; deserved
EARNER wage taker; breadwinner
EARTHY material; gross; unrefined
EAR-WAX cerumen
EAR-WIG informer; insect   **zo**
EASIER more tranquil; more pliant
EASILY tranquilly; calmly
EASING relieving; calming; soothing
EASSEL easterly (Sc.)
EASTER Christian festival   **rl**
EATAGE cattle food
EATING eroding; devouring
EBBING waning; declining; subsiding
ECARTE card game

ECBOLE a digression
ECESIS unviable-species invasion   **bl**
ECHARD non-usable soil water   **bt**
ECHOED repeated; resounded
ECHOES reverberations
ECLAIR a confection
ECLEGM oil and syrup   **md**
ECTYPE a cast; a copy   **ar**
ECURIE stable (Fr.)
ECZEMA a skin disease   **md**
EDDIED swirled; rippled
EDDISH eadish; aftermath
EDDOES W. Indian potatoes   **bt**
EDENIC (Eden)
EDGING border; frill; rim
EDIBLE eatable; esculent
EDITED revised; emended
EDITOR corrector; reviser; annotator
EDUCED extracted; elicited; derived
EEL-POT an eel-trap
EERILY weirdly; uncannily
EFFACE erase; expunge; delete
EFFECT achieve; cause; create
EFFEIR effere; affair (Sc.)
EFFETE spent; worn; barren; abortive
EFFIGY image; statue; figure; likeness
EFFLUX flow; effusion; discharge
EFFORM to shape
EFFORT essay; trial; striving; strain
EFFRAY affray (Sc.)
EFFUSE emanate; issue; pour; spill
EGENCE exigence
EGERAN garnet   **mn**
EGERIA spiritual adviser
EGG-CUP boiled-egg server
EGGERY nesting-place
EGGING inciting
EGGLER an egg-dealer
EGG-NOG a drink; egg and rum
EGOISM conceit; vanity; self-praise
EGOIST egotist; not an altruist
EGOITY identity; personality
EGRESS exit; outlet; emergence
EGROIT a sour cherry   **bt**
EIDENT diligent (Sc.)
EIDOLA apparitions
EIFFEL tower, 985 ft (300 metres) high
EIGHTH an interval   **mu**
EIGHTS (boat-racing)
EIGHTY four-score
EIRACK young hen (Sc.)   **zo**
EITHER one of two
EKEING eking; adding; stretching
ELAEIS African oil palm   **bt**
ELAINE the lily-maid of Astolat
ELANCE throw out; launch
ELANET insectivorous kite   **zo**
ELAPSE intervene; pass; slip
ELATED exalted; proud; excited
ELATER click-beetle genus   **zo**
ELATOR a rouser

ELCHEE eltchi; Turkish ambassador
ELDEST oldest
ELDING fuel (dial.)
ELEGIT writ   lw
ELEMIN oil from resin
ELENCH a disproof; a refutation
ELEVEN a cricket team
ELEVON hinged wing-control surface   ae
ELFISH puckish; impish; mischievous
ELICIT deduce; evoke; extract
ELIDED cut off a syllable
ELISOR (jury selection)   lw
ELIXIR a cordial; quintessence
ELK-NUT oil-nut   bt
ELLECK red gurnet   zo
ELLOPS snake or fish (obs.)   zo
ELODES sweating sickness   md
ELOHIM the Creator (Hebrew)
ELOIGN to carry away
ELOPED bolted; absconded; disappeared
ELTCHI elchee; Turkish ambassador
ELUDED evaded; dodged; foiled
ELVANS felspar veins   mn
ELVISH elfish; elf-like; tricksy
ELWAND an ellwand   me
ELYSEE French president's residence
ELYTRA chitinized forewings in coleoptera
EMBACE ⎫ to degrade (obs.);
EMBASE ⎭ depreciate; debase
EMBALE to pack; to bundle
EMBALL encircle; ensphere
EMBALM perfume; to preserve
EMBANK confine by banks
EMBARK imbark; start; enter; launch
EMBERS live cinders
EMBLEM badge; token; device; symbol
EMBODY imbody; incorporate; include
EMBOIL imboil; boil with anger (Spens.)
EMBOLY pushing or growing in   zo
EMBOSS conceal; cover
EMBRUE imbrue; soak; drench; steep
EMBRYO germ; nucleus; rudiment
EMERGE emanate; appear; issue
EMESIS vomiting   md
EMETIC causing vomiting   md
EMETIN an emetic   md
EMEUTE riot; disorder; insurrection
EMIGRE French royalist abroad
EMMESH immesh; enmesh; entrap
EMPALE impale; to enclose
EMPARK to enclose; to fence
EMPASM a deodorant powder
EMPAWN pawn; impawn; pledge
EMPERY empire; power
EMPIRE rule; sway; dominion
EMPLOY use; engross; occupy
EMPUSA ⎫ spectre or goblin
EMPUSE ⎭ sent by Hecate
EMUCID mouldy
ENABLE allow; permit; empower
ENAMEL durable paint

ENCAGE to coop; emmew; incage
ENCAMP camp; pitch; settle
ENCASE incase; enclose
ENCASH pay in cash
ENCAVE to cache
ENCODE prepare for algebraic/
     computer handling   cp
ENCOPE an incision   md
ENCORE call for repeat (theatre)
ENCYST put in a bag
END-ALL finish; conclusion
ENDEAR captivate; charm; win
ENDING finale; closing; finis
ENDITE phyllopodium lobe in crustacea   zo
ENDIVE species of chicory   bt
ENDOSS endorse; sanction; ratify
ENDRIN chemical insecticide
END-SAC coelomic vesicle in arthropoda
ENDUED indued; endowed; supplied
ENDURE abide; brook; tolerate
ENECIA fever   md
ENERGY vigour; power; intensity
ENFACE superscribe
ENFEST infest
ENFOLD infold; wrap up
ENFORM to fashion; to mould
ENFREE to release
ENGAGE contend; agree; promise
ENGAOL to put in prison; enjail
ENGILD to gild; brighten
ENGINE machine; device; method
ENGIRD surround; encircle
ENGLUT to swallow; to fill
ENGLYN 4-line stanza (Welsh)
ENGOBE ceramic technique
ENGORE to gore; to wound
ENGRAM essence of memory   md
ENGULF ingulf; overwhelm
ENHALO surround with a halo
ENIGMA puzzle; riddle; mystery; rebus
ENISLE isolate
ENJAIL imprison; incarcerate
ENJOIN bid; direct; command
ENKOMO small Cuban drum   mu
ENLACE enfold; entwine
ENLARD to baste
ENLINK to connect; concatenate
ENLIST engage; enroll; secure
ENLOCK lock up
ENMESH emmesh; entrap
ENMITY animus; hatred; aversion
ENMURE to immure; imprison
ENNEAD group of nine
ENNUYE bored (Fr.)
ENODAL without knobs
ENOSIS political union (Gr.)
ENOUGH ample; adequate; sufficient
ENRACE to enroot; implant
ENRAGE incense; infuriate; madden
ENRAIL entrain
ENRANK place in order

ENRAPT in an ecstasy
ENRICH fertilize; endow; adorn
ENRING encircle; surround
ENROBE invest; attire; array
ENROLL enlist
ENROOT enrace; implant
ENSATE sword-shaped   bt
ENSEAL seal up; impress
ENSEAM to sew up
ENSEAR to cauterize
ENSIGN an officer; a flag
ENSILE store in a pit
ENSPAN to yoke up (S. Africa)
ENSUED followed; resulted; accrued
ENSURE insure; assure; secure; fix
ENTAIL leave; bequeath; involve   lw
ENTAME to tame; domesticate
ENTENT intention; design
ENTERA intestines   md
ENTICE seduce; allure; decoy; cajole
ENTIRE (stout); complete; perfect
ENTITY being; essence; existence
ENTOIL to ensnare
ENTOMB bury; inter; inhume
ENTRAP inveigle; ensnare; entangle
ENTREE freedom of access; a dish
ENTUNE chant; sing
ENURED inured; hardened   lw
ENVIED grudged; coveted
ENVIER rival
ENWALL inwall; enclose
ENWIND entwine; enlace
ENWOMB to bury; make pregnant
ENWRAP envelop; engross; perplex
ENZONE to girdle; surround
ENZYME (fermentation); leavened bread
EOCENE a geological period
EOLIAN Aeolian; Eolic
EOLITH prehistoric flint implement
EOSTRE Saxon goddess; (Easter)
EOTHEN from the East
EOZOIC } rock containing fossilized
EOZOON } foraminifera   mn
EPACME vigorous period in a life-history
EPARCH Greek governor
EPAULE part of bastion   ar
EPEIRA genus of spiders   zo
EPHEBE young Athenian
EPHORI Spartan magistrates
EPIGEE perigee; astronomical point
EPIZOA parasites   zo
EPODIC lyric
EPONYM name derived from a person
EPOPEE epic poem
EPULIS gum disease   md
EQUANT imaginary circle
EQUATE to equalize; to average
EQUINE horsey
EQUITY impartial justice
ERASED expunged; cancelled; deleted
ERASER a scraper; a mark remover

ERBIUM rare metal
EREBUS darkness; son of Chaos
EREMIC pertaining to sandy desert
ERENOW before this time
ERGATE sterile female ant, worker   zo
ERIACH a fine; blood-money (Irish)   lw
ERINGO eryngo; sea-holly   bt
ERINYS one of the Furies
ERLANG unit of telephone traffic flow
ERMINE the stoat's winter coat
ERODED corroded; eaten; consumed
EROTIC amatory
ERRAND mission; charge; message
ERRANT roving; rambling; wandering
ERRATA errors; mistakes
ERRING straying; mistaking
ERSATZ German reserve; a substitute
ERYNGO sea-holly genus   bt
ESCAPE shun; evade; elude; flee
ESCARP steep slope
ESCARS gravel ridges
ESCHAR burnt wounds; scab   md
ESCHEW to shun; avoid; miss
ESCORT protect; guard; convoy
ESCROL heraldic scroll   hd
ESCROW deed; escrol   lw
ESCUDO Portugese coin   nm
ESKIMO an Innuit; arctic dweller
ESLOIN eloign; to carry away
ESNECY privilege of choice   lw
ESODIC afferent, carrying towards
ESPADA bull-fighting sword
ESPIAL spying; discovery; notice
ESPIED discovered unexpectedly
ESPIER a spy; a watcher
ESPRIT wit; sprightliness
ESSENE ascetic Hebrew   rl
ESSERA skin eruption   md
ESSOIN excuse for absence   lw
ESTAIN French pewter
ESTATE condition; rank; property
ESTEEM deem; consider; value
ESTRAY to stray; a stray
ETALON an interferometer   lt
ETCHED engraved; corroded by acid
ETCHER an engraver   pr
ETERNE eternal (obs.)
ETHANE odourless paraffin gas   ch
ETHICS moral science
ETHION chemical insecticide   ch
ETHIOP an Ethiopian
ETHNIC racial; ethnological
ETNEAN (Etna)
ETYMON derivation; meaning
ETYPIC unique
EUCAIN drug similar to cocaine   md
EUCHRE card game
EUCLID a geometer
EUCONE of insect compound eyes   zo
EULITE an orthopyroxene   mn
EULOGY panegyric; encomium

EUNOMY good government
EUNUCH emasculated man
EUONYM a suitable name
EUPION vegetable oil   bt
EUPODA beetles   zo
EUREKA Found! (Archimedes)
EURITE a granite   mn
EUTAXY regularity
EUTONY pleasantness of word sound
EVADED eluded; dodged; avoided
EVADER sidestepper of law, tax, etc.
EVANID faint; evanescent
EVENER leveller
EVENLY smoothly; fairly; uniformly
EVILLY wickedly; maliciously
EVINCE display; show; exhibit
EVIPAN soporific injection   md
EVOKED roused; inflamed; elicited
EVOLVE unfold; unroll; develop
EXAMEN a disquisition; an enquiry
EXARCH a title; viceroy; Gr. bishop   rl
EXCEED cap; outdo; surpass; transcend
EXCEPT bar; ban; exclude; omit
EXCERN to sweat
EXCESS surplus; glut; balance
EXCIDE to cut off
EXCISE duty; impost; tax; (Walpole)
EXCITE wake; rouse; incite; kindle
EXCUSE acquit; pardon; exempt
EXCUSS to decipher; shake off
EXCUSS to seize and detain   lw
EXEDRA a hall; a recess
EXEMPT free; released; immune
EXEQUY funeral rites
EXEUNT all quit the stage
EXHALE emit; reek; emanate; breathe
EXHORT urge; encourage; counsel
EXHUME unearth; disinter; resurrect
EXILED banished; outlawed
EXILIC (Jewish) exile
EXITUS yearly rent; issue   lw
EXODIC (Exodus); migratory
EXODUS departure
EXOGEN a class of plant   bt
EXOMIS Greek sleeveless tunic
EXOTIC not native; extraneous; foreign
EXPAND spread; dilate; swell; extend
EXPECT hope; await; forecast
EXPEND disburse; consume; exert
EXPERT apt; adroit; skilful; able
EXPIRE end; die; stop; finish
EXPIRY conclusion; extinction
EXPORT ship; produce; send; carry
EXPOSE an exposure; reveal; unmask
EXPUGN take by assault; conquer
EXSECT to cut away; cut out
EXSERT to protrude
EXSULE apterous life-cycle form in
    hemiptera   zo
EXTANT existent; current
EXTASY ecstasy; rapture; trance

EXTEND stretch; reach; expand
EXTENT amount; scope; range; field
EXTERN day-boy
EXTERN not inherent; external
EXTINE (pollen grain)   b
EXTORT exact; extract; wrench; elicit
EXUDED sweated; oozed; percolated
EXUVIA cast-off skins, shells   z
EYALET Turkish province; a vilayet
EYE-CUP (used for eye lotion)   m
EYEFUL a glance
EYEING watching
EYELET loop-hole
EYELID eye skin cover   p
EYEPIT eye socket   p
EYRANT bird of prey on nest   z

F

FABIAN policy of patiently waiting
FABLED fabricated; fictional
FABLER an Aesop; parable teller
FABRIC structure; texture; web
FACADE front view; face
FACIAL frontal   m
FACIES external appearance; the face
FACILE easy; dexterous; pliant
FACING confronting; opposing
FACTOR broker; middleman
FACTOR agent or manager of estate
FACTUM memorandum; deed; point of
    controversy   lw
FACULA sun-spot
FADDLE to trifle; to play
FADGED suited; prospered
FADING diminishing; withering   r
FAECES human excrement
FAERIE fairy; fairyland; (Spens.)
FAFFLE to stammer
FAG-END butt (cigarette)
FAGGED tired
FAGGOT fagot; bundle of sticks
FAIKES shaly sandstone   m
FAILED miscarried; declined
FAILLE nun's veiling
FAINTY feeble; languid
FAIRER more equitable
FAIRLY moderately; passably
FAITOR rogue; impostor; evil-doer
FAKEER Indian beggar
FAKING forging; doctoring
FALCON hawk; cannon   z
FALLAL finery; streamer
FALLEN sunk; lapsed; ebbed
FALLOW untilled; idle; dormant
FALSER more fallacious
FALTER totter; waver; vacillate
FALUNS miocene deposits
FAMBLE the hand (slang)

FAMILY household; race; lineage
FAMINE dearth; scarcity; starvation
FAMISH starve; exhaust; hunger
FAMOUS renowned; eminent
FANGED toothed; taloned
FANGLE a contraption; novelty
FANGOT a quantity of wares
FANNED inflamed
FANNEL, FANION flag; banner; splint
FANNER winnower
FANTAN Chinese gambling game
FANTOM phantom; spook; ghost
FAQUIR religious mendicant
FARCIN glanders; farcy
FARDEL a bundle; burden; load
FARFEL kosher dumplings; dough grains ck
FARINA pollen; flour   bt, ck
FARING experiencing; feeding
FARMED leased
FARMER tiller; cultivator
FARROW litter of pigs
FASCES Roman badge
FASCIA a band; name-board
FASHED vexed; worried (Sc.)
FASTED abstained from food
FASTEN bind; secure; tie; latch
FASTER quicker; speedier
FASTLY firmly
FAT-HEN goose-foot   bt
FATHER adopt; beget; sire
FATHOM 6 ft (1.8 m); comprehend   nt
FATTED fattened
FATTEN grow plump
FATTER more obese
FAUCAL throaty; guttural
FAUCES (mouth)   md
FAUCET a tap; fosset
FAULTY defective; blameworthy
FAUNAL relating to animals   zo
FAUNUS Pan
FAUTOR a supporter
FAVOSE honeycombed; cellular
FAVOUR gift; patronize; bias
FAWNER sycophant; clinger; parasite
FAYING fitting closely   nt
FEALTY fidelity; loyalty; homage
FEARED apprehended; dreaded
FEATLY neatly; dexterously; adroitly
FEAZED untwisted; unravelled
FECIAL Roman priest; fetial   rl
FECKLY effectually
FECULA (plants); starch   bt
FECUND prolific; fertile; fruitful
FEDARY a confederate
FEDORA trilby hat (USA)
FEEBLE faint; frail; weak
FEEBLY languidly
FEEDER a bib; a channel
FEEING hiring; recompensing
FEELER organ of animals, plants
FEELER tentative suggestion

FELINE catty; spiteful   zo
FELLAH an Egyptian peasant
FELLER wood-cutter
FELLIC (bile)   md
FELLOE felly; rim of wheel
FELLOW peer; mate; equal
FELONY crime; misdemeanour   lw
FELTED covered with felt
FELTER to mat together
FELTRE cuirass
FEMALE feminine
FENCED equivocated
FENCER hedger; prevaricator
FENDER protective bar   nt
FENIAN an Irish conspirator
FEN-MAN fen-lander
FENNEC African fox   zo
FENNEL vegetable   bt, ck
FENSON chemical insecticide
FEODAL feudal
FERASH lowly servant (Ind.)
FERBAM chemical fungicide   ch
FERIAE Roman holidays
FERIAL (holidays)
FERINE wild; savage; untamed; fierce
FERITY wildness
FERRET silk ribbon; polecat   zo
FERRIC (iron)   ch
FERULA fennel   bt
FERULE a rod; cane
FERVID fervent; eager; ardent
FESCUE a pointer; a grass   bt
FESTAL joyous; gay
FESTER rankle; rot; putrefy
FETIAL fecial; Roman priest   rl
FETISH fetich; charm; amulet; talisman
FETTER manacle; shackle; bond; gyve
FETTLE good condition; fitness
FEUDAL vassal-lord polity
FIACRE French cab
FIANCE betrothed man
FIASCO total failure, breakdown; flask
FIBBER a liar
FIBRED having fibres
FIBRID synthetic fibrous bonding particle
FIBRIL small fibre; slender thread
FIBRIN gluten; clot formative   md, bt
FIBULA ancient brooch; leg bone   md
FICKLE volatile; mercurial; unstable
FICTOR a modeller
FIDDLE a railing; violin; ruse   mu
FIDGET fret; chafe; worry
FIERCE savage; cruel; violent
FIESTA carnival, bullfight (Sp.)
FIGARO a schemer; French newspaper
FIGGED all dressed up
FIGURE reckon; digit; diagram
FIJIAN (Fiji Islands)
FIKERY fuss (Sc.)
FILAGO cudweed   bt
FILFOT fylfot; a swastika

FILIAL as a son
FILING particle; (documents)
FILLED replete
FILLER (Hungary)   nm
FILLET hair-ribbon; boneless fish/meat
FILLET band; plain lines on book; tool   to
FILL-IN shadow technique   pg
FILLIP to flip; an incitement
FILOSE thread-like
FILTER strain; percolate
FILTHY foul; dirty; corrupt
FILTRE coffee-brewing method (Fr.)   ck
FIMBLE hemp   bt
FINALE climax; conclusion; finis
FINDER discoverer
FINDON dried haddock   ck
FINEER (fraudulent credit)
FINELY excellently; delicately
FINERY splendour; trappings; fallals
FINEST keenest; sharpest; purest
FINGER digit; pilfer; touch
FINIAL a pinnacle   ar
FINING refining
FINISH end; terminate; accomplish
FINITE limited; restricted
FINLET small fin   zo
FINNAN findon haddock   zo
FINNED bearing fins
FINNER fin-back whale; torqual   zo
FINNIC Finnish
FINNOC white trout   zo
FIORIN bent-grass   bt
FIRING igniting; kindling; expelling
FIRKIN 9 imperial gallons   me
FIRLOT a quarter boll   me
FIRMAN Ottoman decree; licence (Turk.)
FIRMED confirmed; established
FIRMLY steadily; compactly
FISCAL treasurer; monetary   lw
FISHED strengthened   nt
FISHER weasel; black fox   zo
FISHES alternate pl. of fish   zo
FISSLE rustle; whistle (Sc.)
FISTED struck with the fist
FISTIC (boxing); pugilistic
FITCHE\
FITCHY⟩ pointed   hd
FITFUL irregular; unreliable
FITTED apt; seemly; adjusted
FITTER an artificer; more seemly
FIXING deciding; settling
FIXITY permanence; fastness
FIXIVE gummy; adhesive; glutinous
FIXURE stability; firmness (Shak.)
FIZGIG fisgig; a flirt; damp squib
FIZZED hissed; effervesced
FIZZER a fast one
FIZZLE a fiasco; splutter
FLABBY tabid; flaccid; lax
FLACON scent-bottle; small flask (Fr.)
FLAGGY drooping; languishing

FLAGON a flask
FLAKED peeled off
FLAMBÉ ignited brandy dish; uneven
     pottery glaze   ck
FLAMED glazed; excited
FLAMEN Roman official of rites
FLANCH a flange
FLANGE projecting rim
FLANKS sore back (horse)
FLARED burnt unsteadily
FLASHE a sluice
FLASHY gaudy; impulsive; vapid
FLATLY positively; plainly
FLATTY a policeman (slang)
FLATUS puff of wind
FLAUNT vaunt; parade; display
FLAVIN yellow dye
FLAWED defective
FLAXEN pale yellow
FLAYED skinned
FLAYER skinner
FLECHE arrow; slender spire
FLEDGE grow feathers
FLEDGY feathery; downy
FLEECE to strip; plunder
FLEECH flatter; coax (Sc.)
FLEECY woolly; flocculent   tx
FLENCH⟩ to cut up the blubber of a
FLENSE⟩ whale
FLESHY carnal; corporeal
FLETCH to feather an arrow
FLEURY (fleur-de-lis)
FLEWED deep-mouthed
FLEXED bent
FLEXOR muscle   md
FLICKS movies
FLIGHT retreat; exodus; rout
FLIMSY frail; trivial; weak
FLINCH wince; blench; quail
FLINTY obdurate; hard; miserly
FLISKY frisky (Sc.)
FLITCH a side of bacon
FLITTY flighty; unstable
FLOATS (paddle-wheels)
FLOATY buoyant; light
FLOCCI woolly filaments
FLOCKS waste wool   tx
FLOCKY downy
FLOPPY flaccid; drooping
FLORAL flowery
FLORAN tin ore   mn
FLORET flowerlet; decoration for spacing
     pr
FLORID ornate; meretricious
FLORIN once coined at Florence   nm
FLOSSY silky
FLOURY like flour
FLOUSE⟩ to turn the edge of a tool;
FLOUSH⟩ to splash (Sc.)
FLOWER blow; bloom; blossom   bt
FLUATE fluoride   ch

FLUCAN clay	mn	**FOREDO** to destroy; undo; overpower	
FLUENT flowing; voluble; fluid		**FOREGO** yield; resign; relinquish	
FLUFFY downy; fluey		**FOREST** woodland; grove; boscage	
FLUING of splayed window jambs	bd	**FORFEX** scissors	to
FLUKED was fortunate		**FORGAT** forgot	
FLUNKY a lackey; snob		**FORGED** fabricated; spurious; welded	
FLURRY agitation; bustle; perturb		**FORGER** falsifier; hammerman	
FLUSHY reddish		**FORGET** overlook; slight	
FLUTED channelled; grooved	ar, mu	**FORGOT** neglected	
FLUTER flutist; flautist	mu	**FORINT** Hungarian currency	nm
FLUXED melted; purged		**FORKED** bifurcated	
FLYING aviation; fleeing; soaring		**FORLAY** to ambush; lie in wait for	
FLYMAN cabman		**FORMAL** precise; exact; stiff; set	
FLY-NET mosquito curtain		**FORMAT** style; book/paper production size	
FLY-NUT winged nut		**FORMED** arranged; moulded; shaped	
FOAMED spumed; frothed		**FORMER** prior; previous; bygone	
FOBBED imposed on; tricked		**FORMIC** (acid)	ch
FOCILE a bone (arm or leg)	pl	**FORMYL** organic radical	ch
FOCOSO spiritedly	mu	**FORNIX** (shell); (brain)	md
FO'C'SLE forecastle; bows	nt	**FORPET** ⎫ a fourth part;	
FODDER a weight; animal food	me	**FORPIT** ⎭ a quarter (Sc.)	
FOEMAN foe; antagonist; enemy		**FORREL** forel; parchment	
FOETOR a stench; offensive odour		**FORRIT** forward (Sc.)	
FOETUS life in embryo	md	**FORROW** not with calf (Sc.)	zo
FOG-BOW white rainbow		**FORSAY** forbid; renounce	
FOGGED blurred; overcast		**FORTED** guarded; castellated	
FOGRAM antiquated; a fogey		**FOSSIL** petrified	mn
FOIBLE faible; weak point; defect		**FOSTER** cherish; nourish; encourage	
FOILED baffled; thwarted; balked		**FOTHER** leak-stopping	nt
FOILER a frustrator		**FOTMAL** 70 lb (31.7 kg) of lead	me
FOISON plenty; autumn		**FOUDRE** large storage/transport wine cask	
FOLDED doubled; wrapped; furled		**FOUGHT** strove; contended; warred	
FOLDER paper jacket		**FOULED** polluted; sullied	
FOLIAR (leaves); laminar		**FOULLY** scurvily; unfairly; basely	
FOLIER goldsmith's foil		**FOURBE** a cheat; trickster	
FOLIOT goblin		**FOURTH** ordinal number	
FOLIUM thin geological stratum		**FOWLER** bird-shooter	
FOLKSY imitation rustic		**FOX-BAT** flying fox	zo
FOLLIA (composition)	mu	**FOXING** deceiving; duping; deluding	
FOLLOW succeed; chase; pursue; heed		**FOXISH** cunning; sly; shrewd	
FOMENT fan; excite; stimulate		**FOYBLE** part of sword-blade	
FONDER tenderer; sillier		**FRACAS** an uproar; brawl; riot	
FONDLE pet; caress; dandle		**FRACID** overripe; rotten	
FONDLY affectionately; foolishly		**FRAGOR** a crash	
FONDUE melted-cheese/wine dish (Swiss)		**FRAISE** defence of pointed stakes	
	ck	**FRAMED** constructed; devised	
FONDUS calico-printing		**FRAMER** contriver; frame-maker	
FONTAL primary; baptismal		**FRANCO** free of expense	nt
FOOLED duped; hoodwinked; hoaxed		**FRANZY** crotchety (dial.)	
FOOLEN (embankment)		**FRAPPE** chilled with ice (Fr.)	
FOOTED walked; paid; kicked		**FRATCH** a quarrel; a brawl (dial.)	
FOOTER football (slang)		**FRATER** refectory; brother; friar	rl
FOOTLE twaddle; bunkum		**FRAYED** worn; chafed; fretted	
FOOZLE bungle; mishit		**FRAZIL** anchor-ice; spicular ice	
FORAGE fodder; search; pillage		**FREELY** unimpeded; willingly; readily	
FORBID ban; inhibit; taboo; veto		**FREEZE** chill; numb; congeal	
FORBYE besides; hard by		**FRENCH** Gallic	
FORCED unnatural; compulsory		**FRENUM** a ligament	pl
FORCER compeller		**FRENZY** delirium; madness; fury	
FORDED crossed by wading		**FRESCO** drink; paint	
FORE-BY besides (Sc.)		**FRESCO** coolness; wall painting	

FRETTE a strengthening band	
FRETTY ornate	
FRIARY monastery	rl
FRIDAY (Robinson Crusoe); assistant	
FRIDGE ice-box	
FRIEND ally; chum; intimate	
FRIEZE rough stuff; decorative border	ar
FRIGGA wife of Odin	rl
FRIGHT alarm; dismay; panic; dread	
FRIGID icy; cold; formal	
FRILLY fluted; overdressed	pg
FRINGE border; edge	
FRINGY adorned with fringes	
FRISKY gay; lively; sportive	
FRIVOL to trifle	
FRIZEL (flint-lock)	
FROGGY abounding in frogs	
FROISE pancake; fraise	
FROLIC romp; gambol; play; lark	
FRONDE political party (Fr.) 17th c.	
FROSTY chilling; wintry	
FROTHY empty; unsubstantial; foamy	
FROUZY rank; musty; rancid	
FROWER a cleaver	to
FROWST stuffy and hot	
FROWSY frowzy; unkempt; disorderly	
FROZEN froren; frosty; iced	
FRUGAL thrifty; saving; parsimonious	
FRUITY fruitful; luscious	
FRUMPY dowdy	
FRUTEX a shrub	bt
FRYING cooking with fat	
FUCATE painted; a sham	
FUCOID a fossil seaweed	mn
FUDDLE muddle; inebriate	
FUDGED cheated; faked; bungled	
FUFFED puffed	
FUGATO like a fugue	mu
FUGILE ear trouble	md
FUGUES memoryless wandering	pc
FUHRER Hitler-type dictator; leader	
FULANI tribe (South Sahara)	
FULFIL meet; effect; satisfy	
FULGID fulgent; flashing; steaming	
FULGOR splendour	
FULHAM a die loaded at one	
FULLAM corner to throw high	
FULLAN	
FULICA coot genus	zo
FULLED scoured and thickened	
FULLER hammer	to
FULMAR sea-fowl; the petrel	zo
FULVID tawny; yellow	
FUMADO smoked pilchard (Sp.)	
FUMAGE chimney tax; hearth money	
FUMBLE grope; bungle; stammer	
FUMILY sulkily; smokily	
FUMING ammonia process	pg
FUMMEL funnel; mule	zo
FUMOUS (fumes); vaporous	
FUNDED endowed	

FUNDUS back part	
FUNEST doleful; lamentable	
FUNGAL, FUNGIN (fungi) mushrooms	bt
FUNGIA genus of corals	zo
FUNGUS plant	bt
FUNKED played the coward	
FUNKIA a lily genus	bt
FUNNEL fummel; smoke-stack	
FURFUR dandruff	md
FURIES avenging deities	
FURLED closely rolled	
FURORE outburst of excitement; anger	
FURROW rut; groove; seam; corrugate	
FURZEN furzy; whinny	bt
FUSAIN friable coal	mn
FUSEAU macroconidium of dermato-phytes	bt
FUSING liquefaction	
FUSION melting; amalgamation	
FUSOID wide-middled and end-tapered	bt
FUSSED worried; fretted; fidgeted	
FUSTED mouldy; rancid; malodorous	
FUSTET shrub; the sumac	bt
FUSTIC tropical American tree	bt
FUSURE smelting; fusion	
FUTILE bootless; vain; useless	
FUTTAH rat-proof raised	
FUTTER store-house (N.Z.)	
FUTURE hereafter; prospective	
FUZZED ground to powder	
FUZZLE intoxicate; fuddle	

G

GABBED talked; prattled	
GABBLE jabber; prate; chatter	
GABBRO (felspar)	mn
GABION basket for earthworks	ce
GABLED having gables	bd
GABLET small gable	
GABOON African mahogany-like wood	fr
GADDED wandered about	
GADDER a gadabout; a rover	
GADFLY horse-fly	zo
GADGET a cunning device; contraption	
GADINE gadean; cod-type	zo
GADOID codfish type	zo
GAELIC Scottish-Highland dialect	
GAFFED (fishing)	
GAFFER rustic; foreman	
GAFFLE spur (cock-fight)	
GAGGED silenced; joked	
GAGGER an interpolator	to
GAGGLE a flock of geese	zo
GAGMAN joke-writer; comic	
GAIETY gayety; merriment; vivacity	
GAINED acquired; reached; won	
GAINER winner, beneficiary	
GAINLY comely; conveniently	
GAINST against	

GAITED having a distinctive walk
GAITER gamash
GALAGE galosh; golosh
GALAGO lemur (Madagascar)   zo
GALAXY Milky Way; brilliant assembly
GALBAN a gum used in medicine   bt
GALEAS galley   nt
GALEGA goat's rue   bt
GALENA lead sulphide   ch
GALIOT brigantine   nt
GALIUM bed-straw genus   bt
GALLED chagrined; fretted; vexed
GALLET stone splinter
GALLEY ship; boat; cook-house   nt
GALLIC French; an acid   ch
GALLIO insouciance personified
GALLON 4 quarts (4.5 litres)   me
GALLOP a dance; speed
GALLOW to terrify
GALLUP poll; voting system
GALOON galloon; silk fabric
GALOOT lout
GALORE golore; in abundance
GALOSH galage; overshoe
GAMASH gaiters
GAMBET a bird; red-shank   zo
GAMBIT move in chess
GAMBLE stake; hazard; risk; wager
GAMBOL frolic; romp; caper
GAMELY pluckily
GAMETE egg cell   zo
GAMGEE absorbent wool/gauze   tx
GAMING gambling
GAMMER old woman
GAMMON (bacon); hoax; cozen
GAMONT gamete-bearing individual   zo
GANDER a glance (USA)
GANESA Hindu elephant god
GANGER foreman; overman
GANGUE veinstone   mn
GANNET solan goose   zo
GANOID sturgeon type of fish   zo
GANOIN fish dermis secretion   zo
GANTRY travelling crane
GAOLED imprisoned; incarcerated
GAOLER jailer; prison warder
GAPING yawning; staring; gazing
GARAGE motor shed; repair shop
GARBED clothed
GARBLE separate; pervert; misquote
GARCON waiter (Fr.)
GARDEN a pleasance
GARDON roach; ide (Fr.)   zo
GARGET throat inflammation
GARGIL goose disease
GARGLE a mouth wash
GARGOL swine disease
GARIAL gavial; crocodile   zo
GARISH gaudy; ornate; florid
GARLIC genus of plants   bt
GARNER to store; collect; hoard

GARNET carbuncle; precious stone   mn
GAROUS garum, a fish sauce
GARRAN horse; galloway (Sc.)   zo
GARRET loft; attic
GARRON (see garran)
GARROT a tourniquet; execution   md
GARROT ocean duck   zo
GARRYA flowering evergreen   bt
GARTER stocking supporter
GARUDA Hindu demi-god
GARVIE the sprat   zo
GAS-BAG a blimp; airship; chatterbox
GASCON of Gascony
GASHED severely wounded
GASHLY ghastly; frightful
GASIFY convert into gas
GAS-JET a burner; flame
GASKET } cord for lashing   nt
GASKIN } sails to yards
GAS-MAN gas company employee
GASPED panted; blew; puffed
GASPER cigarette; fag (slang)
GASSED poisoned by gas
GAS-TAR coal-tar
GASTER hymenoptera abdomen   zo
GATEAU cake (Fr.)
GATHER assemble; muster; fold
GATING a university restriction
GATING use of electronic circuit   el
GATTEN dogwood   bt
GAUCHE boorish; clumsy (Fr.)
GAUCHE bad-mannered (Fr.)
GAUCHO cow-boy; shepherd (S. Amer.)
GAUGED measured; estimated
GAUGER excise officer
GAUPUS a silly person
GAVAGE forced bird-feeding   vt
GAVIAL garial; crocodile (Asia)   zo
GAWPUS a silly person
GAYEST liveliest; merriest; blithest
GAY-YOU fishing boat (Annam.)
GAZEBO summer house; balcony
GAZING viewing; gaping; regarding
GAZOON Hogg's body
GEARED harnessed
GEBBIE the stomach (Sc.)
GEEZER man in charge; elder
GEIGER radio-activity counter
GEISHA mousmee; Jap dancing girl
GELDED castrated; enfeebled
GELERT Llewellyn's faithful hound   zo
GEMARA (Talmud) (Heb.)   rl
GEMINI Castor and Pollux; (Zodiac)
GEMMAE leaf-buds   bt
GEMMAN gentleman
GEMMED jewelled; budded
GEMMHO inverse meg-ohm   me
GEMOTE meeting; gemot
GENDER to beget; sex; character
GENERA plural of genus
GENEVA gin; hollands

GENIAL hearty; kindly; cordial		
GENIUS adept; gift; talent; djinn		
GENNET jennet; small Spanish horse	zo	
GENOME gamete nucleus chromosome content		
GENTLE larva of fly; tender; mild	zo	
GENTLY tenderly; gradually		
GENTOO a Hindu; a penguin	zo	
GENTRY 'the nobs'; 'the upper ten'		
GENUAL (knee)	pl	
GEODIC (crystalline cavity)	mn	
GEOGEN environmental factor		
GEOMYS rodents (USA)	zo	
GEORGE a jewel	nm	
GERANT gerent; manager		
GERBIL a rodent	zo	
GERMAN related to; germane; teutonic		
GERMEN an ovary;	bt	
GERMIN a germ		
GERUND verbal noun		
GERVAO West Indian shrub	bt	
GERVAS plant (W. Indies)	bt	
GESTIC legendary		
GETTER a sire		
GEW-GAW bauble; trinket; gaud		
GEYSER hot spring		
GHARRY gharri; Indian cart		
GHAZAL a form of Persian verse;		
GHAZEL gazelle	zo	
GHEBER Zoroastrian		
GHEBRE also Guebre	rl	
GHETTO Jewish quarter		
GHURKA Gurkha; native of Nepal		
GHURRY clock; time interval (Ind.)		
GIAOUR unbeliever (Turk)		
GIBBER jabber; gabble; babble		
GIBBET the gallows; to hang		
GIBBON an ape	zo	
GIB-CAT wornout cat		
GIBING scoffing; jibing	nt	
GIBLET internal part of a fowl		
GIFTED intellectual; able; talented		
GIGGIT to move rapidly (USA)		
GIGGLE snigger; titter; cackle		
GIGLET a giddy girl; a wanton		
GIGLOT		
GIGMAN would-be gent		
GIGOLO dancing partner; kept man		
GILDED gilt		
GILDER a guilder		
GILLIE attendant; game-keeper (Sc.)		
GILPEY boisterous boy or girl (Sc.)		
GILPIN the coal-fish	zo	
GIMBAL (compass)	nt	
GIMLET a boring tool	to	
GIMMAL (machinery)	zo	
GIMMER 2-year-old ewe		
GIMPED crenate	bt	
GINETE Spanish trooper		
GINGAL Indian musket; swivel gun		
GINGER sandy; reddish	bt	

GINGKO Chinese yew; maiden-hair tree		
GINKGO	bt	
GINGLE jingle; Irish car		
GINNED snared; (cotton)		
GINNET a nag; a jennet	zo	
GIRDED reproached; braced; surrounded		
GIRDER a cross-beam		
GIRDLE belt; zone; enclosure		
GIRKIN gherkin	bt	
GIRNEL granary; meal-chest		
GITANA Spanish gipsy woman		
GITANO Spanish gipsy man		
GIUSTO in time; regular	mu	
GIVING yielding; allowing		
GIZZEN to wither; leaky		
GLACIS gentle slope; parapet		
GLADLY with pleasure; joyously		
GLAGOL Slavonic alphabet		
GLAIRY viscous		
GLAIVE broadsword or falchion		
GLANCE glimpse; look; ricochet		
GLARED stared; glowered; frowned		
GLASSY, GLAZED vitrified		
GLAZER polisher; calico-smoother		
GLEAMY casting rays of light		
GLEDGE cunning look; to squint		
GLEETY limpid; ichorous		
GLIBLY volubly; oily tongued		
GLIDED skimmed; skated		
GLIDER engineless aeroplane		
GLIOMA nervous-tissue disease	md	
GLOBAL globular; world-wide		
GLOBIN (haemoglobin)	md	
GLOMUS capillary-mass glomeruli	zo	
GLOOMY dim; dismal; obscure		
GLORIA a hymn; halo	rl	
GLOSSY smooth; sheeny; bright		
GLOVED wearing gloves		
GLOVER glove-maker		
GLOWED flushed; shone; gleamed		
GLOWER scowl; frown; glare		
GLOZED palliated; wheedled		
GLOZER flatterer; sycophant		
GLUCIC (glucose)	ch	
GLUING cementing; uniting		
GLUISH (glue); sticky; viscous		
GLUMAL of the husk	bt	
GLUMLY sulkily; sullenly		
GLUMPS the sulks		
GLUTEN (wheat); glutin	bt	
GLYCIN gelatin-sugar	ch	
GLYCOL a liquid	ch	
GNARLY knotted; crabbed; gnarled		
GNARRY		
GNAWED fretted; tormented		
GNAWER a rodent; masticator	zo	
GNEISS laminated granite	mn	
GNETUM plant (E. Indies)	bt	
GNOMIC didactic		
GNOMON sundial; shadow-caster		
GNOSIS esoteric knowledge		

GOADED impelled; spurred; stung	**GOUSTY** dreary (Sc.)
GOALIE goalkeeper (football)	**GOVERN** rule; sway; control; restrain
GOANNA iguana (Australia) **zo**	**GOWANS** dandelion **bt**
GOATEE a beard	**GOWNED** robed; arrayed
GO-BANG a game	**GOWPEN** a handful (Sc.)
GOBBET lump; swallow; mouthful	**GRABEN** land-subsidence structure **gl**
GOBBIN coal refuse	**GRACED** virtuous; chaste
GOBBLE to swallow; bolt; (turkey)	**GRACES** the Greek Charities
GOBLET tumbler; glass cup; rummer	**GRADED** classified; arranged
GOBLIN sprite; gnome; spectre	**GRADIN** raised step or seat
GO-CART two-wheeled cart	**GRADUS** dictionary of prosody
GO-DOWN warehouse	**GRAFIN** German count
GODSON protegée	**GRAINS** malt husks; prongs; harpoons
GODWIT bird of passage **zo**	**GRAINY** granulated
GOETIC (black magic)	**GRAITH** accoutrements; equipment (Sc.)
GOFFER to plait; to crimp	**GRAKLE** starling **zo**
GOGGLE to roll the eyes	**GRAMME** weight (Fr.) **me**
GOGLET porous vase	**GRANGE** farmers' union; farm-house
GOIDEL Celtic; Gael	**GRANNY** knot **nt**
GOITER ⎫ a tumour; bronchocele **md**	**GRANTH** Sikh Scriptures **rl**
GOITRE ⎭	**GRANUM** pigment globule **bt**
GOLDEN gilt; excellent; auric	**GRAPPA** strong spirit from wine
GOLFER golf player	**GRASSY** green
GOLIAS medieval nom de plume	**GRATER** kitchen implement; shredder
GOLLAR to scold; speak loudly	**GRATHE** to repair coal-mine plant **mn**
GOLORE abundance; galore	**GRATIN** brown crust; oven-toasted/cheese
GOLOSH overshoe	**GRATIS** without payment
GOMMER soup ingredient	**GRAVED** cleaned; chiselled; cut **nt**
GOMUTI ⎫ sago palm; black fibre **bt**	**GRAVEL** disease **md**
GOMUTO ⎭	**GRAVEL** embarrass; puzzle
GONGED prelude to a fine	**GRAVEN** engraved; carved
GONION angle (of lower jaw) **md**	**GRAVER** (engraver); more sedate **to**
GOODLY fair; comely; seemly	**GRAVES** white wine (Fr.)
GOOGLY a strange delivery	**GRAVES** melted tallow
GOOGOL 10 to the 100th power **el**	**GRAVID** pregnant
GOORAL Asiatic goat **zo**	**GRAZED** scratched; brushed
GOOROO Hindoo teacher; guru **rl**	**GRAZER** browser
GOPHER American rodent **zo**	**GREASE** lubricate; bribe
GOPHER timber used for the Ark **bt**	**GREASY** unctuous; sebaceous; slippery
GOPURA Hindu temple tower	**GREATS** final exam. in classics, Ox. B.A.
GORAMY gourami; fish **ar, zo**	**GREAVE** leg armour; greeve
GORGED glutted; stuffed **hd**	**GREECE** ⎫ flight of steps; staircase; a
GORGET throat armour; lady's ruff	**GREESE** ⎬ degree
GORGET instrument **md**	**GRIECE** ⎭
GORGIO gipsy term for a non-gipsy	**GREEDY** eager; voracious; grasping
GORGON ugly monster	**GREENS** vegetables **bt**
GORHEN hen grouse **zo**	**GREENY** greenish
GORIER more blood-stained	**GREEVE** greave; steward; a reeve
GORING a pricking; puncture	**GREGAL** gregarious
GOSHEN land of plenty	**GRIDED** grated; pierced
GOSPEL glad tidings; (new testament)	**GRIEVE** greeve; sadden; lament
GOSSAN ⎫ ferruginous rock **mn**	**GRIFFE** horizontal frame knives **wv**
GOZZAN ⎭	**GRILLE** iron grating
GOSSIP chatter; boon companion	**GRILSE** young salmon **zo**
GOTHIC rude; barbarous	**GRIMED** begrimed; foul
GOTTEN got; acquired	**GRIMLY** fiercely; dourly
GOUDIE ⎫ goldfinch (Sc.); a jewel; gold	**GRINGO** Yankee in S. America
GOWDIE ⎭ lace **zo**	**GRIPED** furrowed; trenched
GOUGED scooped out	**GRIPER** extortioner; oppressor
GOURDE coin (Haiti) **nm**	**GRIPPE** influenza (Fr.)
GOURDY swelling (horse) **vt**	**GRISLY** grim; ferocious; fierce; dire

GRISON weasel (S. Amer.)	zo	**GUNNEL** ship's side; gunwale	nt
GRITER teasel spade	to	**GUNNER** artillery-man	
GRITTY sandy		**GUN-SHY** fearful of firearms	
GRIVET Abyssinian monkey	zo	**GUNTER** emergency sail, instrument	nt
GRIZEL meek patient wife		**GUNYAH** Australian native hut	
GROATS hulled oats		**GURGLE** purl; ripple; murmur	
GROCER provisioner		**GURHKA** a native of Nepal	
GROGGY tipsy; staggering		**GURJUN** Indian balsam	bt
GROMEL gromil; gromwell; a plant	bt	**GURLET** type of pickaxe	bd
GROMET a rope ring	nt	**GURLEY** cylinder fall speed	el, me
GROOVE furrow; rut; cutting		**GURNET** fish; gurnard	zo
GROPED searched; picked; sought		**GURRAH** Indian earthen jar	
GROSER gooseberry	bt	**GUSHED** rushed; spurted; spouted	
GROSZY Polish coin	nm	**GUSHER** oil-well	
GROTTO cavern; cave		**GUSSET** an insertion	
GROUND earth; clod; domain; cause		**GUTNIK** swallowable transistor radio	
GROUSE complaint	zo	**GUTTAE** Doric ornamentation	ar
GROUTS coarse meal		**GUTTED** plundered; eviscerated	
GROUTY thick; muddy; sulky		**GUTTEE** bedewed	hd
GROVEL crawl; cringe; fawn		**GUTTER** trough, drainage	
GROWER husbandman		**GUTTER** inner margins of book	pr
GROWTH increase; progress		**GUTTLE** to guzzle	
GROYNE sea wall		**GUZZLE** swill; swallow greedily	
GRUBBY grimy; dirty		**GYBING** jibing	nt
GRUDGE envy; covet; enmity; dislike		**GYMNIC** gymnastic (obs.)	
GRU-GRU edible insect	zo	**GYPSEY** gipsy	
GRUMLY morosely; surlily		**GYPSUM** lime sulphate	ch
GRUMPH grunt (Sc.)		**GYRATE** spiral; revolve; spin	
GRUMPY surly; sullen; churlish		**GYROSE** like a crook	bt
GRUNDY (Mrs.)			
GRYFON griffin (obs.)			
GUACHE style of painting		**H**	
GUANIN (GUANO) bird excrement			
GUDDLE to tickle trout (Sc.)		**HABBLE** perplex; stutter (Sc.)	
GUEBRE Gueber; Parsee fire-worshipper		**HABOOB** Sudan line-squall	mt
GUELPH German medieval faction		**HACHEL** a sloven (Sc.)	
GUENON African monkey	zo	**HACKED** mangled; hired; kicked	
GUFFAW boisterous laugh		**HACKEE** chipmunk; American squirrel	zo
GUGGLE to gurgle		**HACKET** kittiwake	zo
GUIDED regulated; instructed; steered		**HACKLE** cock's neck feathers	
GUIDER a director; leader; pilot		**HACKLE** fly (angling); comb	
GUIDON flag; signal (Fr.)		**HACKLY** rough	
GUILED beguiled; treacherous		**HADDIE** haddock (Sc.)	
GUILLS corn marigold	bt	**HADDIN** a holding; residence (Sc.)	
GUILTY criminal; culpable; sinful		**HADING** geological fault	mn
GUINEA fowl; worm; pig	nm, zo	**HADITH** Moslem oral tradition	rl
GUISER mummer		**HADRON** elementary particle class	nc
GUITAR type of lute	mu	**HAEMAD** on same side as heart	pl
GULDEN florin	nm	**HAEMAL, HAEMIC** relating to blood	md
GULLED duped; tricked; hoaxed		**HAEMIN** hydrochloride of haematin	ch
GULLER a cheat; impostor		**HAFFET** the temples (Sc.)	
GULLET throat	md	**HAFFLE** to lie; prevaricate	
GULLEY large knife (Sc.); earth cleft		**HAFTED** handled	
GULOSE aldohexose monosaccharide	ch	**HAGBUT** arquebuse; hackbut	
GULPED swallowed; bolted		**HAGDEN** shearwater gull	zo
GUMLAC resinous matter		**HAGEEN** dromedary; camel	zo
GUMMED stuck; cemented		**HAGGED** ugly; lean; haggish	
GUNITE fine cement concrete	eg	**HAGGIS** Scottish dish	ck
GUNMAN armed bandit		**HAGGLE** to mangle; higgle; bargain	
GUNMEN desperadoes		**HAGLET** shearwater gull	zo
GUNNEL a blenny; butterfish	zo	**HAIDUK** Hungarian yeoman	

HAIGHA a king's messenger
HAILED greeted; came from
HAIQUE Arab wrap
HAIRDO hairstyle; coiffure
HAIRED hairy; hirsute; comate
HAIRST harvest (Sc.)
HAKEEM physician (Arabic)
HALFER fallow deer   zo
HALIDE compound of halogen and other radical
HALING hauling
HALION skipper fish   zo
HALLAN a partition (Sc.)
HALLEL Passover hymn   rl
HALLOA hallo!
HALLOO a hunting cry
HALLOW to reverence
HALLUX hind toe of bird   zo
HALOED sainted
HALOID (salt)   ch
HALSED embraced by the neck
HALSER hawser   nt
HALTED limped; hesitated; stopped
HALTER rope; cord
HALVED bisected; fifty-fifty
HALVES moieties
HAMATE set with hooks
HAMBLE mutilate the foot
HAMITE fossil; native (E. Africa)
HAMLET cluster of cottages
HAMMAL Turkish porter
HAMMAM Turkish bath
HAMMER forge; a gavel   to
HAMOSE } hooked
HAMOUS }   bt
HAMPER basket; impede; embarrass
HANDED served; conducted; led on
HANDLE touch; feel; manipulate
HANGAR aircraft shed
HANGED dangled; depended
HANGER broadsword; wood on hill-side
HANGER the sword of Damocles
HANJAR Persian dagger
HANKED skeined; jibbed   nt
HANKER desire; crave; yearn; want
HANSEL earnest penny; handsel
HANSOM a cab
HANTLE considerable number (Sc.)
HAPPEN occur; betide; chance; befall
HAPTIC pert. to sense of touch
HARASS annoy; tire; vex; worry
HARDEN nerve; steal; brace; inure
HARDER stiffer; firmer
HARDLY barely; scarcely; narrowly
HARD-UP impecunious; indigent
HARELD sea-duck   zo
HARIER a harrier   zo
HARING speeding
HARISH like a hare
HARKED listened; hurried
HARKEN hearken; listen; attend

HARLED covered with rough-cast
HARLOT strumpet; moll; trollop
HARMAN policeman; a copper
HARMED damaged; injured
HARMEL Syrian rue   bt
HARPED iterated; dwelt   mu
HARPER lyrist; harpist   mu
HARRIS a tweed
HARROW lacerate; tear
HARTAL Indian boycott
HASHED chopped, mixed
HASLET roasting meat, pig's fry
HASTED hastened; hurried
HASTEN hurry; speed; despatch; urge
HAT-BOX for hat transport
HATHOR goddess of love (Egypt)
HATING detesting; loathing; abhorring
HAT-PEG place to hang hat
HAT-PIN woman's hat fixer
HATRED odium; enmity; rancour
HATTED wearing a hat
HATTER independent miner (Australia)
HAULED dragged; tugged; towed
HAULER haulier; carter
HAUNCH part of an arch
HAUSSA West African race
HAUTIN sea-fish in fresh water   zo
HAUYNE a silicate   mn
HAVANA (cigar)
HAVERS twaddle; empty talk
HAVING holding; possessing
HAWHAW sunk fence; guffaw
HAWKED peddled; streaked
HAWKER pedlar; retailer; falconer
HAWKEY } dark cow with white streaked
HAWKIE } face (Sc.)   zo
HAWSER halser; cable   nt
HAY-BOX cooking method
HAYMOW hay in barn
HAYSEL hay-makers' festival
HAZARD risk; chance; peril; jeopardy
HAZILY obscurely; foggily; mistily
HAZING bullyng; brutal horse-play
HEADED (cask); (football)
HEADER (brick); (diving)
HEAD-ON directly, straight
HEALED cured; remedied
HEALER doctor; restorer
HEALTH soundness; hygiene; haleness
HEAPED massed; accumulated; piled
HEARER one of an audience
HEARSE funeral car
HEARTH fireplace; fireside; home
HEARTY robust; sincere; cordial
HEATED agitated; excited; hectic
HEATER warmer
HEATHY heathery   bt
HEAUME heavy helmet
HEAVED hoisted; dilated; panted
HEAVEN Elysium; Paradise; bliss
HEAVER a lever; strong man

HEAVES disease (horse); broken wind	vt	**HESPER** evening star	
HEBREW a Jew		**HESVAN** Heshvan; Jewish month	
HECATE goddess of witchcraft		**HETMAN** Cossack chief	
HECKLE to comb; to question		**HEWING** hacking; shaping	
HECTIC feverish; heated; hot		**HEXADE** series of six	
HECTOR to bully; bluster; vaunt		**HEXANE** paraffin	ch
HEDDLE heald shaft in handloom	wv	**HEXODE** a thermionic valve	
HEDERA ivy	bt	**HEXOSE** monosaccharide subgroup, a sugar	ch
HEDGED skulked; (betting)		**HEYDAY** frolic; period of vigour	
HEDGER a trimmer of fences		**HIATUS** a chasm; gap; lacuna	
HEEDED attended; noticed		**HICCUP** hiccough	
HEE-HAW to bray		**HIDAGE** a tax	lw
HEELED armed; equipped; leant		**HIDDEN** latent; covert; recondite	
HEELER hanger-on (USA)		**HIDING** a beating; screening; masking	
HEGIRA } Mohammed's flight from		**HIEING** going along; hiking	
HEJIRA } Mecca to Medina, A.D. 622		**HIEMAL** wintry; hyemal	
HEIFER young cow	zo	**HIGGLE** to bargain; haggle	
HEIGHT altitude; acme; zenith		**HIGHER** superior; nobler	
HELIAC heliacal; (sun)		**HIGHLY** eminently; loftily	
HELION virago; shrew; hell-cat		**HI-JACK** kidnap; rob	
HELITE an amalgam	ch	**HIJRAH** Hegira; flight from Mecca	
HELIUM a gaseous element	ch	**HIKING** walking; foot-slogging	
HELLAS ancient Greece		**HILARY** Law Court session; Oxford term	
HELLER German copper coin	nm	**HILLED** earthed up	
HELMED with a helmet; directed		**HILSAH** fish (Ganges)	zo
HELMET part of retort; head armour		**HILTED** hafted; helved	
HELOMA corn on foot	md	**HINDEE** North Indian tongue	
HELPED prevented; aided; succoured		**HINDER** delay	
HELPER assistant; abettor; ally		**HINGED** depended on	
HELVED having a handle; hafted		**HINTED** implied	
HELVIN mineral	mn	**HINTER** suggester	
HEMINA about 10 oz (283 g)	me	**HIPPED** melancholic; roof	ar
HEMMED bordered; enclosed		**HIPPIC** horsy; equine	
HEMMER a stitcher; a sewer		**HIPPUS** clonic spasm of iris	md
HEMPEN made of hemp	bt	**HIRCIN** mutton suet	
HENBIT dead nettle	bt	**HIRCUS** the goat	zo
HENISM philosophical belief		**HIRING** bribing; engaging	
HEPTAD series of seven		**HIRMOI** } hymns; ode (Greek church)	
HERALD harbinger; crier; proclaim		**HIRMOS** }	
HERBAL book describing plants		**HIRSEL** } flock of sheep (Sc.); a throng	
HERDED tended; massed		**HIRSLE** } to slide	
HERDIC a cab (USA)		**HISPID** bristly	
HEREAT at this point		**HISSED** hizzed	
HEREBY by this		**HISSER** disapprover	
HEREIN in this		**HITCHY** catchy	
HEREOF of this		**HITHER** to this place	
HEREON on this		**HITTER** smiter; slogger; striker	
HERESY schism; heterodoxy; recusancy		**HIVING** storing; clustering	
HERETO in addition		**HOARSE** guttural; husky; raucous	
HERIFF burweed	bt	**HOAXED** tricked; gulled; gammoned	
HERIOT a fine	lw	**HOAXEE** the victim	
HERMAE sculptured busts		**HOAXER** practical joker	
HERMES Mercury (Greek) the messenger	rl	**HOAZIN** (S. Amer.) pheasant	z
HERMIT anchorite; recluse		**HOBBLE** halt; limp; shackle; clog	
HERNIA rupture	md	**HOBJOB** an odd job	
HEROES demi-gods		**HOBNOB** to be familiar; associate; chat	
HEROIC bold; intrepid; valiant		**HOCKEY** an outdoor game	
HEROIN a drug	md	**HOCKLE** to mow; hamstring	
HERPES skin disease; shingles	md	**HODDEN** grey cloth	
HERREN gentlemen (Ger.)		**HODMAN** mason's labourer	
HERSED in harrow form	hd		

HOEING weeding	
HOGGED clipped; bent	
HOGGER (whole)	
HOGGET young sheep; colt or boar	zo
HOGGIN sand and gravel mixture	
HOGPEN hogsty	
HOG-PIT waste paper stock pit	pp
HOGSTY pig pen	
HOIDEN hoyden; a romp; rude; rustic	
HOLARD whole of soil water	bt
HOLDER a tenant	
HOLD-UP robbery under arms	
HOLIER more sacred	
HOLILY piously	
HOLISM evolution	
HOLLER, HOLLOA shout (distress)	
HOLLOW empty; vacant; void; cavity	
HOLMIA oxide of holmium	ch
HOLMIC (holmium)	ch
HOMAGE fealty; devotion; loyalty	
HOMELY plain; simple; domestic	
HOMILY sermon; address; discourse	
HOMING (pigeons); aerial navigation	ae
HOMINY boiled maize	
HONEST fair; just; trusty; sincere	
HONING whetting	
HONKED (cry of wild geese)	
HONOUR exalt; dignify; fame; renown	
HOODED cowled; cloaked	
HOODIE carrion-crow (Sc.)	zo
HOODOO voodoo; witchcraft; (W. Indies)	
HOOFED ungulate	
HOOKAH water smoking pipe, narghile (Turk.)	
HOOKED (golf); hamate	
HOOKER fishng boat	nt
HOOKUM command, instructions (Ind.)	
HOOK-UP radio connections	
HOOPED encircled; whooped	
HOOPER (tubs); a cooper	
HOOP-LA game at fairs	
HOOPOE } crested birds, horn-bill type	zo
HOOPOO }	
HOOTCH hooch; firewater (USA)	
HOOTED honked	
HOOTER a siren	
HOOVEN (cattle-disease)	
HOOVER dust-removing appliance	
HOOVES pl. of hoof	
HOPDOG pale tussock moth	zo
HOP-FLY plant louse	zo
HOPING desiring; trusting	
HOPPED danced; bounced	
HOPPER wooden trough; hop-picker	
HOPPER young locust	zo
HOPPET hand-basket	
HORARY hourly; book	rl
HORNED with horns; butted	
HORNER dealer in horns; sand-eel	zo
HORNET stinging insect	zo
HORNIE the devil; old Nick	

HORRID horrific; terrible; dreadful	
HORROR terror; panic; alarm; dismay	
HORSED mounted	
HOSIER dealer in stockings	
HOSTEL an inn; lodging house	
HOT-BED earth-bed; breeding place	bt
HOT-DOG sausage sandwich	
HOT-POT peppery stew	
HOT-ROD supercharged car	
HOTTER more ardent	
HOUDAH howdah; seat on an elephant	
HOUDAN breed of fowls	zo
HOUNDS (mast head)	nt
HOURLY horary	
HOUSED resided; sheltered; stored	
HOUSEL the Eucharist	rl
HOUSTY a sore throat (dial.)	
HOWDAH houdah; seat on an elephant	
HOWDIE midwife (Sc.)	
HOWKER hooker; vessel (Dutch)	nt
HOWLED yowled; cried; lamented	
HOWLER (monkey); grievous error	zo
HOWLET (owlet)	zo
HOYDEN hoiden; tomboy; romp	
HRAMSA garlic-flavoured cheese (Scot.)	
HUBBLE an uproar; hubbub	
HUBBLY rowdy	
HUBBUB disorder; noise; uproar; din	
HUCKLE the hip; a haunch	
HUDDLE crowd; confuse; jumble	
HUDDUP get up!	
HUFFED blustered; (draughts)	
HUFFER a bully; blusterer	
HUGELY enormously; immensely	
HULLED pierced; husked	
HULLER hulling machine	
HUMANE kind; benign; merciful	
HUMBLE degrade; abash; meek; lowly	
HUMBLY unobtrusively	
HUMBUG quackery; charlatan	
HUMECT, HUMIFY } to moisten; to	
HUMEFY } dampen	
HUMERI bones of the upper arm	md
HUMETE abbreviated fesse	hd
HUMHUM coarse cloth (Ind.)	
HUMIAN philosophy of David Hume	
HUMINE black ground powder; humus	
HUMITE limestone	mn
HUMMED buzzed; droned	
HUMMEL hornless; awnless	
HUMMER a sledge-runner	
HUMMIE small bulge	
HUMMUZ chick-pea/garlic purée (Mid. East)	ck
HUMOUR indulge; pamper	md
HUMOUS mouldy	
HUMPED shouldered; hunchback	
HUMPER meat-porter; carrier	
HUNGER hanker; desire; crave	
HUNGRY ravenous; famishing	
HUNKER to squat down; old fogey	

HUNNIC Hunnish
HUNTED searched; sought; hounded
HUNTER chaser; stalker   zo
HURBUR burdock   bt
HURDLE wattle fence
HURLED flung; heaved; slung; cast
HURLER a thrower; pitcher
HURLEY shinty; (hockey)
HURRAH } shout of triumph
HURRAY }
HURTER a buffer plank
HURTLE to whirl; to crash
HUSHED quietened; calmed; stilled
HUSKED hulled
HUSKER a remover of husks
HUSSAR light cavalryman
HUSSIF (housewife); a holdall
HUSTLE bustle; jostle; elbow; rush
HUTTED in huts
HUZOOR Indian title of respect
HYADES 5 stars in Taurus   as
HYAENA hyena   zo
HYBRID cross-bred; mongrel
HYDRIA Grecian water-vase
HYDRIC (hydrogen)   ch
HYDRID hydrogen compound   ch
HYDROA itching skin disease   md
HYDRON dry/rigid, wet/soft plastic
HYDRUS constellation; water-snake   as, zo
HYEMAL hiemal; wintry
HYETAL (rainfall)
HYGEIA Goddess of Health
HYKSOS Egyptian dynasty
HYLISM materialism
HYMNAL collection of hymns
HYMNED celebrated in song
HYMNIC of hymns
HYPHAE fungoid filaments   bt
HYPHEN word-join stroke
HYPNUM a moss genus   bt
HYSSOP aromatic herb   bt

I

IAMBIC rhythmic
IAMBUS Greek satiric metre
IATRIC medicinal   md
IBERIS candytuft   bt
IBEXES wild goats (Alps)   zo
IBIDEM in the same place
ICARUS an early aeronaut
ICE-AGE period of icing over
ICE-AXE ice-breaking, -cutting device
ICE-CAP earth ice layer
ICE-MAN ice deliverer
ICE-SAW ice-cutting device
ICICLE frozen water stalactite
ICIEST frostiest
ICONIC illustrative
IDEATE to fancy
IDIASM a peculiarity

IDIOCY lunacy; demenentia; craziness
IDLING nothing doing
IDOLUM }
IDOLON } mental picture
I'FAITH indeed; truly; verily
IGNAVY laziness, idleness
IGNITE kindle; inflame; fire
IGNORE disregard; overlook; skip
IGUANA lizard; a saurian   z
ILEXES holm-oaks   b
ILL-GOT ill-gotten
ILLISH somewhat unwell
ILLITE monoclinic clay mineral   m
ILLUDE to deceive; delude
ILLUME illumine; brighten
ILL-USE mistreat
IMAGED imagined; fancied
IMBALM embalm
IMBAND form into band
IMBANK embank
IMBARK embark; board
IMBIBE absorb; assimilate; drink
IMBODY embody; incorporate
IMBOIL emboil; burn with anger
IMBREX pantile; curved roof-tile
IMBRUE to moisten; to drench
IMBUED dyed; inspired; steeped
IMMANE huge; savage (Shak.)
IMMASK to cover
IMMESH entangle; enmesh
IMMUNE secure against attack
IMMURE enclose; incarcerate; confine
IMPACT shock; stroke; collision
IMPAGE horizontal part of door-frame   b
IMPAIR mar; injure; harm; vitiate
IMPALA South African antelope   z
IMPALE transfix
IMPALM to grasp
IMPARK enclose
IMPARL to hold mutual discourse
IMPARL parley
IMPART bestow; confer; divulge
IMPAVE to pave
IMPAWN to pledge
IMPEDE obstruct; hinder; thwart
IMPEND threaten; hover; approach
IMPEST infect with plague
IMPING ekeing; extending; grafting
IMPISH puckish; mischievous
IMPLEX complicated
IMPONE to stake, to wager
IMPORT imply; purport; gist; drift
IMPOSE lay; inflict; charge; dictate
IMPOST a tax; a duty; a cess
IMPUGN attack; contradict; question
IMPURE unclean; sullied; tarnished
IMPUTE charge; ascribe; imply
INARCH to graft
INBAND header stone   b
INBOND brick-laying   b
INBORN innate; inherent; congenital

INBRED natural; inborn	**INHOUR** reactivity unit	nc
INCAGE encage; confine	**INHUME** to inter; to bury; entomb	
INCARN to incarnate	**INJECT** interpolate; insert	
INCASE encase; enclose; enshrine	**INJURE** harm; hurt; mar; impair	
INCASK to put in a cask	**INJURY** ill; detriment; wrong	
INCAST a bonus; thrown in	**INK-BAG** (cuttle-fish)	zo
INCAVO incised part of an intaglio	**INKING** marking with ink	
INCEPT to begin; to commence	**INKNIT** to knit in	
INCEST prohibited co-habitation	**INKNOT** to knot	
INCHED advanced by inches	**INKOSI** Zulu chief, king	
INCISE engrave; scribe	**INK-POT** ink container	
INCITE stir; goad; foment; rouse	**INK-SAC** (cuttle-fish)	zo
INCLIP to grasp; enclose; surround	**INLACE** to lace	
INCOME revenue; annual receipts	**INLAID** fitted flush to surface	
INCONY delicate; fine; pretty (Shak.)	**INLAND** remote from the sea	
INCULT uncultivated	**INLIER** geological formation	
INCUSE to stamp	**INLINE** white-relieved black-letter print	pr
INCUSS incuse; forge	**INLOCK** enlock	
INDABA native council	**INMATE** resident; guest; denizen	
INDART to rush in (Shak.)	**INMOST** innermost; deepest	
INDEED really; truly; verily; actually	**INNATE** inherent; congenital; inborn	
INDENE liquid coal-tar hydrocarbon ch	**INNING** harvest grain	
INDENT to notch; order	**INNUIT** an Eskimo	
INDIAN of India, aboriginal Amer.	**INRAIL** enclose with rails	
INDICT to charge in writing lw	**INROAD** raid; foray; incursion	
INDIGN unworthy	**INROLL** enroll (obs.)	
INDIGO a blue dye bt	**INRUSH** invasion; irruption	
INDITE endite; write; pen; dictate	**INSANE** mad; crazy; deranged	
INDIUM metallic element ch	**INSEAM** mark with a seam	
INDOLE benzpyrrole ch	**INSECT** mean; contemptible	
INDOOR within the house	**INSECT** six-legged invertebrate	zo
INDUCE urge; actuate; incite	**INSERT** inject; introduce; infix	
INDUCT introduce; install; initiate	**INSHIP** embark; to ship	
INDUED endued; invested with	**INSIDE** inner; internal; interior	
INDUNA Zulu chief	**INSIST** maintain; demand; urge	
INEUNT a cusp	**INSOLE** inner sole	
INFALL an inroad	**INSPAN** to yoke	
INFAME defame	**INSTAL** install; induct; invest	
INFAMY shame; obloquy; disgrace	**INSTAR** adorn with stars	
INFANT babe; suckling; minor	**INSTEP** part of the foot	pl
INFECT corrupt; vitiate; taint	**INSTIL** infuse; ingraft; implant	
INFEFF, INFEFT (land transfer) lw	**INSTOP** make fast; to stop	
INFELT heart-felt	**INSULT** abuse; affront; ridicule	
INFEST enfest; overrun; throng; beset	**INSURE** ensure; assure; guarantee	
INFIMA end species in classification list	**INTACT** inviolate; integral; scatheless	
INFIRM frail; weak; decrepit	**INTAKE** inlet of a pipe	
INFLOW that which flows in	**INTEND** mean; purpose; contemplate	
INFLUX importation in abundance	**INTENT** set; bent; eager; attentive	
INFOLD enfold; embrace	**INTERN** confine; segregate	
INFORM tell; notify; apprize	**INTIMA** innermost organ layer	zo
INFULA Roman priestly badge	**INTIME** private; home-like	
INFUSE instil; inculcate; steep	**INTINE** inner coat of pollen grain	bt
INGATE aperture in a mould	**INTOED** with toes turned in	
INGEST absorb; swallow	**INTOMB** entomb; bury; inter	
IN-GOAL rugby football	**INTONE** to chant	
INGULF engulf; overwhelm	**INTORT** to twist; to wreathe; to wind	
INHALE breathe in	**INTRAP** entrap (obs.)	
INHAUL (a rope) nt	**INTUSE** a bruise (Spens.)	md
INHERE to be innate	**INULIN** vegetable base (elecampane)	bt, ck
INHIVE to hive	**INUNCT** anoint	
INHOOP to confine	**INURED** hardened; accustomed	lw

INVADE raid; infringe; assault; violate		
INVENT devise; contrive; create; make		
INVERT reverse; upset; overturn		
INVEST indue; bedeck; array; beset		
INVITE ask; bid; call; request; solicit		
INVOKE adjure; conjure; implicate		
INWALL enclose; enwall		
INWARD inside; inner; internal		
INWICK curling cannon		
INWITH within (Sc.)		
INWORK work within		
INWORN inwrought		
INWRAP to perplex; enwrap		
INYALA nyala; bushbuck	zo	
IODATE (iodic acid)	ch	
IODIDE salt of hydriodic acid	ch	
IODINE medicinal element	ch	
IODISM morbid state		
IODIZE treat with iodine		
IOLITE a translucent silicate	mn	
IONIAN (Ionia)	ar	
IONISM Ionic architecture		
IONIUM (radium)	ch	
IONIZE convert into ions	ps	
IONONE terpene compound	ch	
IRANIC from Iran		
IREFUL angry; wroth; incensed		
IRENIC pacific		
IRIDAL prismatic; iridian		
IRIDIN active principle of iris		
IRISED like a rainbow		
IRITIC (iritis); inflamed	md	
IRITIS (eye disease)	md	
IRKING irksome; tedious; wearying		
IRONED in irons; smoothed		
IRONER a laundry operative		
IRONIC satirical; sarcastic		
IRRUPT to interrupt; invade		
ISABEL brownish yellow		
ISAGON equi-angular figure		
ISATIC woad-like	bt	
ISATIN an indigo product	ch	
ISATIS plant providing woad dye	bt	
ISLAND isle; to insulate		
ISOBAR line of equal barometric press.		
ISODIA Jewish sacred feast	rl	
ISOGON an isagon		
ISOHEL sunshine comparison map	mt	
ISOLUX same-light-intensity line	lt	
ISOMER (similar substance)	ch	
ISONYM paronym		
ISOPIC contemporaneously formed	gl	
ISOPOD (crustaceans)	zo	
ISRAEL Jacob and his offspring		
ISSUED distributed; emitted; emerged		
ISSUER publisher; utterer		
ITALIC Italian; semi cursive script	pr	
ITCHED wanted to; craved; hankered		
ITSELF reflexive pronoun		
IVIGAR sea-urchin	zo	
IZZARD the letter Z		

J

JABBED poked; prodded		
JABBER much talk; prattle; gabble		
JABBLE rough sea; splash (Sc.)		
JABIRI Brazilian stork	zo
JACANA wading bird	zo
JACENT lying at length		
JACKAL dog-like animal	zo
JACKED lifted with a jack		
JACKET cover; jerkin; coat		
JADERY tricks of a jade		
JADISH vicious; unchaste		
JAEGER gull; huntsman (Ger.)	zo
JAGGED notched; ragged; serrated		
JAGGER brass wheel; pastry		
JAGHIR a reward (Hindu)		
JAGUAR American leopard	zo
JAILED gaoled; incarcerated		
JAILER \ gaoler; warder		
JAILOR /		
JALEBI saffron batter sweetmeat (Ind.)	cl
JAMBEE a cane; walking-stick		
JAMBOK sjambok; hide whip		
JAMBUL Indian evergreen	bt
JAMMED crushed; squeezed		
JAMPAN sedan chair (Ind.)		
JANGLE wrangle; clash; bicker		
JANKER log-transporter (Sc.)		
JARGON nonsense; gibberish; palaver		
JAROOL Indian blood-wood	bt
JARRAH tree (W. Australia)	bt
JARRED wrangled; grated		
JARVEY jaunty driver (Irish)		
JASHER lost Hebrew book	rl
JASMIN climbing shrub	bt
JASPER quartz	mn
JATAKA nativity (Buddha)	rl
JAUNCE to jolt; a jaunt (Shak.)		
JAUNTY airy; sprightly; finical		
JAW-BOX a sink (Sc.)		
JAWING scolding		
JEAMES a flunkey		
JEERED mocked; derided; taunted		
JEERER scoffer; sneerer		
JEJUNE void of interest; meagre		
JENNET gennet; small Spanish horse	zo
JERBOA a jumping rodent	zo
JEREED jerid; blunt javelin		
JERKED twitched; flipped; jolted		
JERKER underhand thrower		
JERKIN a coat; jacket		
JERKIN a hawk; gyrfalcon	zo
JERQUE examine ship's papers		
JERSEY cow; knitted garment	zo
JERVIN alkaloid (hellebore)	cl
JESSED heraldic ornamentation	hd
JESTED joked; made merry; quizzed		
JESTER joker; buffoon; wag; fool		
JESUIT an intriguer		
JETSAM goods thrown overboard	lw

JETSOM jetson; jetsam
JETTEE projection   ar
JETTON metal counter
JEWESS female Jew
JEWISH Hebrew
JEZAIL Afghan rifle
JIBBAH jubbah; Eastern garment   tx
JIBBED refused to go; baulked
JIBBER restive horse   zo
JIBING sneering; quizzing; taunting
JIBOYA boa-constrictor   zo
JIFFEY an instant
JIGGED danced
JIGGER liquid measure; mechanical device
JIGGER gold club; insect: chigger
JIGGLE wriggle; joggle; jolt
JIGJOG jolting
JIG-SAW fret-saw; a puzzle
JILLET a flirt; a wanton
JILTED discarded
JIMSON thorn-apple   bt
JINGAL Eastern cannon
JINGLE Irish covered car; tinkle; rhyme
JINKER dodged; eluded; turned sharply
JINKER timber-cart (Australia)
JINNEE djinn; jinn; genie
JITTER instability; fear   el
JOBBER stockbroker; book stocker/dealer
JOB-LOT odds and ends
JOCKEY to cheat; rider of races
JOCOSE facetious; humorous; waggish
JOCUND sportive; merry; cheerful
JOGGED travelled slowly; shook
JOGGER jostler
JOGGLE a notch; to jar; to shake
JOHNNY gay spark
JOINED united; coupled; connected
JOINER a carpenter
JOKING jesting; bantering; rallying
JOLTED jogged; shook; jounced
JOLTER hustler
JORDAN a river; chamber pot (Shak.)
JOSEPH riding habit; unsized paper   pr
JOSKIN yokel; clown
JOSSER a fellow; a chap; a palooka
JOSTLE hustle; elbow; joggle; justle
JOTTED noted; recorded
JOTTER memorandum book
JOUNCE to jolt; shake
JOVIAL genial; convivial; blithe
JOVIAN (Jupiter) of Jove
JOWDER, JOWTER fish hawker
JOWLER hunting dog   zo
JOYFUL happy; pleased; glad; blithe
JOYOUS gay; airy; merry; jocund
JUBATE maned; having a fringe
JUBBAH Eastern garment   tx
JUDAIC Jewish; Hebrew; Israelitish
JUDDER jar and shudder
JUDEAN native of Judea
JUDGED considered; sentenced

JUDGER a judge; umpire; arbitrator
JUDICA Passion Sunday   rl
JUGATE coupled; yoked   bt
JUGFUL filling a jug   me
JUGGED (hare); imprisoned
JUGGLE conjure; shuffle; swindle
JUG-JUG meat in aspic; nightingale's song
JUICER machine for extracting fruit juice
JUJUBE shrub; lozenge   bt
JULIAN calendar; system
JUMART hybrid animal (Fr.)   zo
JUMBAL crisp sweet cake
JUMBLE confuse; mix; muddle
JUMBUK a sheep (Australia)   zo
JUMENT a mare   zo
JUMPED bounded; grabbed; sprang
JUMPER chisel   to
JUMPER religious sect; over-blouse   rl
JUNCUS plants (rush)   bt
JUNGLE the rukh
JUNGLY jungli; unsophisticated
JUNIOR younger; a son
JUNIUS anonymous writer
JUNKER Prussian landowner, aristocrat
JUNKET a sweetmeat; to feast; regale   ck
JUPATI palm yielding raffia fibre   bt
JURANT swearing
JURIST a lawyer   lw
JUSTER more equitable
JUSTLE jostle; nudge; elbow
JUSTLY fairly; impartially; rightly
JUTTED projected; protruded
JUZAIL Afghan heavy rifle
JYMOLD gimmal; gimbal

K

KABAKA former ruler of Buganda (Uganda)
KABALA Moslem Holy of Holies   rl
KABOOK iron-stone (Sri Lanka)   mn
KABUKI realistic dramatic art (Jap.)
KABYLE Algerian Berber
KACHIN Burmese borderer
KAFFIR a Kafir
KAFILA caravan; train of camels
KAFTAN robe (Turk.)   tx
KAISER German emperor
KAKAPO New Zealand parrot   zo
KALIUM potassium   ch
KALMIA American laurel   bt
KALONG Malay fox-bat   zo
KALPIS Grecian water-vase
KAMEES kamis; Eastern garment
KAMELA } orange dye (E. Indies)   bt
KAMILA
KAMERA camera; private room; secret
KAMSIN a hot wind of the Sahara
KANAKA South Sea Islander
KANTEN a seaweed   bt
KANUCK a Canadian

139

KAOLIN China clay		**KHILIM** reversible rug (Turkey)	tx
KARAKA NZ food tree	bt	**KIBBLE** cudgel; hand-mill; hound	zo
KARATE open-handed fighting (Jap.)		**KIBBLE** iron-ore bucket; coal measure	me
KARMIC relating to Karma		**KICKED** hacked; objected; punted	
KAROSS skin blanket (S. Africa)	tx	**KICKER** footballer; thrill-giver	
KARROO tableland (S. Africa)		**KICKUP** small dance	
KARYON cell-nucleus	bl	**KIDDER** a corn cornerer; a carpet	tx
KASBAH Arab town, fort (N. Africa)		**KIDDER** forestaller; huckster	
KATION cation	el	**KIDDLE** weir	
KATIPO Austral. venomous spider	zo	**KIDDOW** guillemot	zo
KAVASS Turkish constable		**KID-FOX** young fox	zo
KAYSER wave-number unit	ps	**KIDNAP** abduct; capture; steal	
KAYMAK clotted cream (Turk.)		**KIDNEY** kind; humour	md
KEBBIE a cudgel (Sc.)		**KIEKIE** a New Zealand shrub	bt
KEBLAH, KIBLAH towards Mecca		**KIKUYU** tribe (Kenya)	
KECKLE cackle; (rope protection)		**KILERG** 1,000 ergs	me
KECKSY dried stalks	bt	**KILHIG** tree-pushing pole	fr
KEDDAH kheda; elephant trap		**KILLAS** slate	mr
KEDGED warped; towed into dock	nt	**KILLED** fascinated; neutralized	
KEDGER a kedge; small anchor	nt	**KILLER** whale	zo
KEEKER mine inspector (Sc.)		**KILLOW** a black earth	mr
KEELED carinated; navigated		**KILLUT** Indian robe of honour	tx
KEELER tub; bargee	nt	**KILTED** wearing Scots kilt	
KEELIE kestrel; street Arab (Sc.)	zo	**KILTIE** kilted soldier	
KEENER professional mourner		**KIMMER** woman neighbour	
KEENLY sharply; acutely; astutely		**KIMONO** Japanese robe	tx
KEEPER guard-ring; warden		**KINASE** activator of true enzymes	bc
KEEVED tubbed		**KINATE** salt	ch
KELKEL dried sole	ck	**KINCOB** Indian thread work	tx
KELOID of scar tissue	md	**KINDER** more benevolent	
KELPIE water spirit		**KINDLE** provoke; animate; ignite	
KELSON keelson; inner keel	nt	**KINDLY** congenial; benevolent	
KELTIC Celtic		**KINEMA** cinema; the movies; talkies	
KELTIE kittiwake gull	zo	**KINETY** structure unit in protozoa	zo
KELVIN thermo-dynamic temperature	me	**KINGLY** regal; imperial; august	
KENCHI ivory carving tool	to	**KINKED** snarled; twisted	
KENNED recognized; knew		**KINKLE** a kink	
KENNEL channel; gutter; a haunt		**KIPPER** a salmon after spawning	zo
KENTLE 100 lb (45 kg); quintal	me	**KIPPER** smoked herring	ch
KENYTE fine-grained igneous rock	gl	**KIRBEH** Arab water-skin	
KERION hair disease	md	**KIRKIN** (church attendance)	
KERITE insulating material		**KIRPAN** Sikh 3 foot (0.9m) knife	
KERMES crimson dye; cochineal	zo	**KIRSCH** wild cherry liqueur	ch
KERMIS kermess; Dutch fair		**KIRTLE** a gown; a mantle	tx
KERNED letter with projecting face	pr	**KIRTLE** weight of flax	me
KERNEL nucleus; heart of nut	bt	**KISHKA** Yid./Polish sausage	ck
KERRIA Japanese rose	bt	**KISMET** fate; destiny	
KERRIE knob-kerrie		**KISSED** bussed; (billiards)	
KERSEY woollen cloth	tx	**KISSER** mouth (slang)	
KESLOP (rennet)		**KIT-BAG** army barracks bag	
KETENE acetone-based compound	ch	**KITTEN** baby cat	zo
KETONE acetone	ch	**KITTLE** ticklish; intractable (Sc.)	
KETOSE ketonic monosaccharide	ch	**KITTLY** ticklish; sensitive	
KETTLE water-boiling pot		**KLAXON** a motor horn	
KEUPER sandstone	mn	**KLEPHT** Greek bandit	
KEYAGE quayage		**KNACKY** cunning	
KEYING signals by modulation	el	**KNAGGY** knotty; rough in temper	
KEY-MEN the indispensables		**KNARRY** knotty; rugged	
KEY-PIN key-pivot		**KNAWEL** a plant	bt
KEY-WAY longitudinal key-slot cut	eg	**KNICKS** knickers	
KHALIF Calif; Caliph; Moslem leader	rl	**KNIFED** stabbed	

KNIGHT a chess-man; a paladin
KNITCH faggot (dial.)
KNOBBY knotty; stubborn
KNOTTY intricate; difficult
KNOWER an erudite man
KOBALT cobalt ch
KOBANG old Japanese gold coin nm
KOBOLD goblin; gnome
KOODOO antelope (S. Africa); kudu zo
KOPECK Russian farthing nm
KOREAN Corean
KORKIR corkir; purple dye bt
KORUNA crown (Czech) nm
KOSHER of food: ritually prepared (Jew.)
KOSMOS Cosmos; opposite to chaos
KOTWAL Indian police officer
KOUSSO plant (Abys.) bt
KOWHAI Maori trees bt
KOW-TOW salutation (China)
KOZUKA knife beside a sword (Jap.)
KRAKEN sea monster (Danish)
KRANTZ rocky summit (S. Africa)
KRASIS Eucharistic wine with water rl
KREESE creese; Malay dagger
K-THIBH (Hebrew Scriptures)
KUKANG lemur or loris (Malay) zo
KULICH Orthodox Easter cake (Rus.) ck
KULTUR education; German culture
KUMBAR Indian coarse wood bt
KUMBUK E. Indian tree bt
KUMISS koumiss; drink (Tartar) ck
KUMMEL a liqueur ck
KUNKUR Indian limestone
KURKEE coarse blanket
KURUSH (Turkey) small coin nm
KUSKUS cuskus bean stew; Indian fibre bt
KUTTAR short Indian dagger
KYBOSH insurmountable obstruction
KYLOES Highland cattle zo

L

LAAGER Boer wagon encampment
LABEFY impair; weaken
LABIAL (lips) pl
LABILE unstable; liable to err
LABIUM a lip bt, pl
LABOUR toil; drudge; industry
LABRET lip ornament
LABRUM upper lip pl
LACCIC (a resinous dye) ch
LAC-DYE (dye); shellac
LACHES negligence lw
LACING twining; beating; intermixing tx
LACKED short of; needed; wanted
LACKER one in want
LACKEY flunkey; footman; attendant
LACMUS litmus; lichen-dye ch
LACTIC acid, milk, products, yogurt ch, ck
LACUNA a void; gap; blank; hiatus

LADDER rent in stockings; climbing aid
LADDIE youngster; lad; boy
LA-DI-DA affected manner
LADIES gentlewomen
LADING freight; cargo; burden
LADINO Spanish dialect
LADLED spooned; dispensed
LAGENA amphora; vase
LAG-END the bitter end
LAGGED loitered; apprehended
LAGGEN barrel projection (Sc.)
LAGGER laggard; loafer; idler
LAGOON lake; bayou
LAGUNE lagoon; pool
LAICAL (laity)
LAID-IN note of inclusion of extra item pr
LAIDLY loathly; clumsy (dial.)
LAID-ON available, made ready for use
LAID-UP ill; out of action
LAITHE pollack fish zo
LAKIST (Lake school of poetry)
LALLAN Lowland (Sc.)
LAMBED yeaned
LAMBIE small lamb (Sc.) zo
LAMELY haltingly
LAMENT deplore; wail; a jeremiad
LAMINA thin plate
LAMING crippling; disabling
LAMISH somewhat lame
LAMMAS 1st August
LAMMED thrashed; drubbed
LAMMER amber (Sc.)
LAMMIE quilted jumper; lammy
LAMPAS swelling in horse's palate vt
LAMPIC (alcohol) ch
LANARY wool store
LANATE woolly tx
LANCED cut open; pierced
LANCER a cavalry-man
LANCET a cutting instrument md
LANCET window ar
LANDAU a carriage
LANDED disembarked; owning estates
LANDER a miner
LANGET coarse Dutch lace tx
LANGUE tongue (linguistics)
LANGUR Indian monkey zo
LANKLY laxly; languidly
LANNER hawk; falcon zo
LANUGO prenatal hair in mammals zo
LAPDOG small pet dog zo
LAPFUL load in one's lap
LAPPED gem cutting; racing
LAPPEL lapel; folded flap
LAPPER folder
LAPPET loose flap; a lobe
LAPSED slipped; became void; sank
LARDED smeared with lard ck
LARDER storehouse
LARDON slice of bacon ck
LARGER bigger; wider; greater; bulkier

LARIAT lasso; rope with noose	
LAROID pertaining to gulls	zo
LARRUP to beat; to flog	
LARVAE caterpillars; grubs; maggots	zo
LARVAL (larva)	zo
LARYNX throat; vocal cord	pl
LASCAR East Indian sailor	
LASHED secured; scourged	
LASHER rope; pool below a weir	
LASHES thongs; eye-lashes; whip strokes	
LASKET loop line in a sail	nt
LASQUE flat diamond	mn
LASSIE damsel; maid; lass; collie dog	zo
LASTED endured; remained; continued	
LASTER bootmaker; cobbler	
LASTLY ultimately; finally; endwise	
LATEEN triangular sail	nt
LATELY recently; latterly	
LATENT dormant; concealed; potential	
LATEST most up-to-date	
LATHEN made of laths	
LATHER soapy froth; foam	
LATISH somewhat late	
LATRIA highest kind of worship	rl
LATTEN sheet brass	
LATTER modern; recent; previous	
LAUDED praised; extolled; magnified	
LAUDER eulogist; ecomiast; panegyrist	
LAUNCE a balance; an eel	zo
LAUNCH hurl; inaugurate; start	
LAUREL the bay-tree	bt
LAURIN an extract from laurel	ck
LAVABO ritualistic washing	rl
LAVAGE washing	md
LAVING bathing	
LAVISH squander; dissipate; luxurious	
LAVOLT medieval dance; lavolta	
LAW-DAY day of open court	lw
LAWFUL legal; legitimate; rightful	
LAWING litigation; tavern-bill	lw
LAWYER solicitor; counsel; advocate	
LAXIST amoral philanderer	
LAXITY slackness; latitude; neglect	
LAY-DAY a lading day	
LAYING placing; betting; imputing	
LAYMAN not a cleric; unprofessional	
LAY-OFF dismissal (industrial)	
LAY-OUT set-out; plan	
LAZILY slothfully; drowsily; supinely	
LAZING idling	
LAZULI blue spar	mn
LEADED set in lead	
LEADEN heavy; dull	
LEADER head; chief; guide; director	
LEAD-IN wire connecting an aerial	
LEAFED having leaves	bt
LEAGUE combine; union; cabal	
LEAKED oozed; percolated	
LEALTY loyalty; fidelity	
LEAMER dog on leam	zo
LEANED relied; leant; inclined	
LEANER thinner; skimpier	
LEANLY lankly; slenderly; scantily	
LEAN-TO a shed beside a wall	ar
LEAPED sprang; skipped; gambolled	
LEAPER jumper; vaulter; chaser	zo
LEASED let out	
LEASER gleaner	
LEAVED interleaved	bt
LEAVEN yeast; balm; ferment; imbue	
LEAVER a forsaker; quitter; deserter	
LECTIN antibody-like substance	bc
LECTOR reader	rl
LEDGER scaffold; account book	ar
LEERED ogled; gloated	
LEEWAY arrears of work	nt
LEGACY bequest; gift; devise	lw
LEGATE ambassador; envoy; delegate	
LEGATO smoothly	mu
LEG-BYE (cricket)	
LEGEND myth; fable; fiction; caption	
LEGGED dashed off	
LEGION host; multitude; horde; army	
LEGIST skilled in law; jurist	lw
LEGUME seed vessel; pod; vegetable	bt
LEIGER a resident ambassador (Shak.)	
LEIPOA Australian game-bird	zo
LENDER loaner	
LENGTH extent; duration; reach	
LENIFY assuage; mollify	
LENITY clemency; leniency	
LENTEN (Lent); sparing; during fast	rl
LENTIC of standing water	ec
LENTIL a bean; pulse	bt
LENTOR slowness; tenacity; viscosity	
LENVOY postscript	
LEONID a meteor from Leo	
LEPCHA native of Sikkim	
LEPTON hundredth of a drachma	nm
LEPTON nuclear particle	
LEPTUS larval form of acarina	zo
LESION injury; wound	md
LESSEE (lease); tenant	lw
LESSEN reduce; mitigate; decrease	
LESSER lower; minor; inferior	
LESSON task; precept; warning	
LESSOR lease holder	lw
LETHAL fatal; deadly; mortal	
LET-OFF a reprieve	
LET-OUT release	
LETTER note; epistle; missive	
LETTIC Lettish; (Latvia)	
LEUCOL coal-tar product	
LEVADE horse dressage movement	
LEVANT to decamp; eastern	
LEVIED mustered; taxed	
LEVITE Jewish tribe; priest	rl
LEVITY frivolity; flippancy; giddiness	
LEVURE flour/water paste sealing for lids	
LEVYNE zeolite	mn
LEWDLY lustfully	
LEYDEN electrical jar	el

.IABLE accountable; likely; obnoxious		**LINTIE** linnet; a song-bird (Sc.)	zo
.IAISE to form a liaison		**LINVAR** linear variometer resolver	el
.IBANT sipping		**LIONEL, LIONET** young lion	
.IBATE to make a libation		**LIPASE** enzyme	ch
.IBIDO life force; sexual urge		**LIPLET** little lip	
.IBYAN (N. Africa)		**LIPOIC** an acid regulating oxidation	ch
.ICHEN flowerless plant	bt	**LIPOID** fatty; sebaceous	md
.ICHEN skin disease	md	**LIPOMA** a fatty tumour	md
.ICKED lapped; lammed; defeated		**LIPPED** labiate; (golf)	
.ICTOR Roman officer		**LIPPEN** to rely; to trust (Sc.)	
.IDDED having lids		**LIPPER** a rippling; surface roughness	
.IEDER German ballads		**LIPPIE** quarter of a peck (Sc.)	me
.IENAL of the spleen	zo	**LIQUID** fluid; fluent; melting; dulcet	
.IERNE cross-rib	ar	**LIQUOR** spirits; drink	
.IFTED elevated; stole; upraised		**LISBON** a Portuguese wine	
.IFTER a thief; raiser		**LISPED** couldn't pronounce 's' sounds	
.IGAND outlying ion	ch	**LISPER** person who lisps	
.IGASE catalysing enzyme		**LISSOM** lithe; agile; pliant; supple	
.IGATE to tie up	md	**LISTED** enlisted; canted over; chose	
.IGGER beadspread; night-line		**LISTEL** fillet	ar
.IGHTS (ancient); (Northern); offal		**LISTEN** hark; attend; eavesdrop	
.IGNIN wood-fibre		**LISTER** arranger; recorder	
.IGNUM hardwood	bt	**LITANY** solemn supplication	rl
.IGULA, LIGULE grass; petal	bt	**LITCHI** fruit (China)	bt
.IGURE precious stone	mn	**LITHER** lazy; worthless; smooth	
.IKELY probable; credible; pleasing		**LITHIA** oxide of lithium	md
.IKING love; fondness; regard		**LITHIC** (stone)	md
.ILIED adorned with lilies		**LITMUS** dye from lichen	ch
.ILITH Adam's first wife		**LITTER** scatter; the newborn; bedding	zo
.ILTED sung rhythmically		**LITTLE** tiny; pygmy; brief; trivial	
.IMBEC a still; a distilling vessel		**LITUUS** augur's staff	
.IMBED with limbs		**LIVEDO** blueness of skin from congestion	
.IMBER flexible; pliant; supple		**LIVELY** joyful; active; vigorous; quick	
.IMBIC bordering; marginal	pr	**LIVERY** uniform; costume	tx
.IMBUS limbo; paradise of fools		**LIVERY** writ of possession	lw
.IMING snaring; treating with lime		**LIVING** livelihood; animate	rl
.IMMER mongrel; idler; jade	zo	**LIZARD** saurian reptile	zo
.IMNED painted; illuminated		**LLANOS** plains of South America	
.IMNER artist; delineator		**LOADED** laden; filled; cumbered	
.IMOUS muddy; slimy; sticky		**LOADER** one of the gun's crew	
.IMPED walked with disability		**LOAFED** lounged	
.IMPER a lame man		**LOAFER** idler; vagrant; flaneur; drone	
.IMPET univalve mollusc	zo	**LOANED** lent; advanced; borrowed	
.IMPID clear; pellucid; pure		**LOATHE** hate; detest; abhor	
.INAGE (cost per line) advert rate	pr	**LOAVES** of bread	ck
.INDEN lime tree	bt	**LOBATE** (lobes)	
.INEAL in a direct line		**LOBBED** pitched; gently threw	
.INEAR slender; rectilinear		**LOBOLA** wife-purchase (S. Africa)	
.INE-UP show of unity		**LOBOSE** lobate	bt
.INGAM sacred symbol (Hindu)	rl	**LOBULE** small lobe	
.INGEL waxed thread (Sc.)		**LOCALE** a locality (Fr.)	
.INGER lag; loiter; dawdle; tarry		**LOCATE** fix; place; settle; find	
.INGET ⎫		**LOCHAN** a pond; a loch (Sc.)	
.INGOT ⎭ an ingot		**LOCKED** grappled; embraced; clasped	
.INHAY farm shed		**LOCKER** a cupboard; a drawer	
.INING aligning; inner cover		**LOCKET** an ornament; a fastening	
.INKED connected; united; coupled		**LOCK-UP** jail-cell, garage with lock	
.INNET bird; lintie	zo	**LOCULI** cells	bt
.INSEY mixed wool and linen cloth		**LOCUST** acacia tree; insect	bt, zo
.INTEL the top of a door		**LODGED** deposited; dwelt; harboured	
.INTER cotton fibre		**LODGER** temporary resident	

LODORE a cataract
LOFTED skied
LOFTER (golf)
LOGGAN rocking stone; logan
LOGGAT \ medieval ninepin;
LOGGET / heavy wooden pole
LOGGED recorded — nt
LOGGER lumberman
LOGGIA gallery or arcade (Italian) — ar
LOG-HUT log-cabin — ar
LOG-LOG logarithm of a logarithm
LOGMAN woodman; logger
LOHOCK syrup — md
LOIMIC (plague) — md
LOITER linger; dawdle; delay; tarry
LOLIGO cuttle-fish; squid — zo
LOLIUM genus of grass — bt
LOLLED hung out; reclined
LOLLER lounger; flaneur
LOLLOP to lounge
LOMENT a type of legume — bt
LONELY solitary; remote; forlorn
LONGAN Chinese fruit tree — bt
LONGED craved; desired
LONGER more extensive; taller
LOOFAH sponge; skeleton; gourd — bt
LOOKED examined; observed; glanced
LOOKER onlooker; spectator
LOOK-IN hasty visit; glance
LOOMED rose to view
LOOPED encircled
LOOPER a caterpillar — zo
LOOSED set free
LOOSEN slacken; release; untie; relax
LOOTED ransacked
LOOTER plunderer; pillager; despoiler
LOP-EAR a lop-eared rabbit — zo
LOPING running easily
LOPPED trimmed; truncated
LOPPER to curdle; trimmer; a cutting
LOQUAT Chinese fruit — bt
LORATE thong-shaped
LORCHA junk-rigged Chinese ship — nt
LORDED domineered
LORDLY noble; magnificent; arrogant
LORICA a cuirass
LORING learning (Spens.)
LORIOT golden oriole — zo
LOSING mislaying; squandering; failing
LOSSES casualties; damages; privations
LOTION a wash
LOUDER noisier; more stentorian
LOUDLY uproariously; clamorously
LOUNGE loll; loaf; recline; idle
LOURED frowned; scowled
LOUSED infested with lice
LOUVER louvre; ventilator
LOUVRE open turret (Fr.) — ar
LOVAGE genus of herb; angelica type — bt
LOVELY beauteous; delectable
LOVING adoring; liking; esteeming

LOWERY gloomy; overcast; murky
LOWEST most debased; deepest
LOWING bellowing; mooing
LUBBER heavy, clumsy fellow
LUBRIC slippery; lewd
LUCAMA fruit (Chile) — bt
LUCENT bright; shining; clear
LUCINA Diana or Juno
LUCKIE elderly woman (Sc.)
LUCUMO Etruscan title
LUETIC pestilential — md
LUFFER (see Louvre); open turret — ar
LUGGED tugged; hauled; dragged
LUGGER small sailing ship — nt
LUGGIE vase with ears
LULLED soothed; assuaged; calmed
LUMBAL, LUMBAR vertebrae — md
LUMBER junk; rubbish; trash; refuse
LUMERG unit of luminous energy — lt, me
LUMPED heaped up
LUMPER stevedore
LUMPIA oriental egg roll — ck
LUNACY mania; dementia; craziness
LUNARY lunar; moonwort fern — bt
LUNATE like a crescent-moon
LUNGED thrust
LUNKAH Indian cheroot
LUNULA \ crescent-like; lunate
LUNULE /
LUPINE wolf-like; wolfish
LUPINE lupin; a fodder plant — bt
LURING enticing; inveigling; decoying
LURKED hid; laid in wait
LURKER skulker
LUSIAD Portuguese epic poem
LUSTED eagerly desired
LUSTIC lusty; vigorous
LUSTRA periods of five years
LUSTRE Roman purification ceremony
LUSTRE gloss; splendour; glory
LUTEAL of the corpus luteum — zo
LUTEIN egg yellow — ck
LUTINE (Lloyd's bell)
LUTING a composition; clay
LUTIST lute player — mu
LUTOSE miry
LUXATE dislocate
LUXURY epicurism; voluptuousness
LUZULA a rush genus — bt
LYCEUM lecture hall
LYCHEE Chinese dessert fruit — ck
LYDIAN effeminate
LYDITE black slate; touchstone — mn
LYMPHY (lymph) — md
LYRATE lyre-shaped
LYRISM playing the lyre — mu
LYRIST lyrical writer
LYSINE diamino-caproic acid — ch

M

MABOLA Philippine tree — fr

MACACO a tropical tree	bt		**MANANA** tomorrow (Spanish)	
MACHAN platform for tiger-shooting			**MANCHE** sleeve; the channel (Fr.)	hd
MACIES emaciation; wasting	md		**MANCHU** former ruling class in China	
MACKLE macule; a blur in printing			**MANDOM** humanity	
MACLED spotted			**MANEGE** riding school; equitation	
MACRON a mark showing long vowel			**MANFUL** virile; courageous; bold	
MACULA sun-spot; a spot on skin	md		**MANGAL** charcoal brazier (Turk.)	
MACULE mackle; a blotch; stain			**MANGER** a trough	
MADCAP hair-brained; frolicsome			**MANGLE** mutilate; to calender	
MADDEN enrage; infuriate			**MANIAC** madman; lunatic; fiend	
MADDER a plant; a red dye	bt		**MANILA** Manilla cheroot	
MADMAN maniac; bedlamite			**MANIOC** tapioca; cassava	bt
MADRAS bright kerchief; cotton fabric	tx		**MANISM** belief in nature cult	
MAENAD a frenzied woman			**MANITO** Great Spirit (American Ind.)	rl
MAFFIA mafia; Sicilian secret society			**MANJAK** Barbados asphalt	
MAGGOT worm; grub; larva; a whim	zo		**MANNAN** anhydride of mannose	ch
MAGIAN Wise Men of the East			**MANNED** provided a crew	
MAGILP megilp; painters' varnish			**MANNER** behaviour; style; deportment	
MAGISM Persian philosophy			**MANQUE** 1 to 18 in roulette; missed career	
MAGNET lodestone; attraction; lure			**MANTEL** a beam; mantel-shelf	
MAGNON spin-wave energy quantum	nc		**MANTIC** inspired; prophetic; vatic	
MAGNUM 2 quart (2.2 litres) bottle	me		**MANTID** pertaining to mantis	zo
MAGNOX magnesium alloy	ch		**MANTIS** a praying insect	zo
MAGPIE (target shooting)	zo		**MANTLE** cloak; hood; covering; suffuse	
MAGUEY Mexican aloe	bt		**MANTON** Spanish shawl	
MAGYAR Hungarian			**MANTRA** a Vedic hymn	
MAHOUN mahound; evil spirit (Arabic)			**MANTUA** lady's cloak or gown	
MAHOUT elephant driver			**MANUAL** handbook; organ key-board	mu
MAHSIR mahseer; an Indian fish	zo		**MANURE** compost; fertilizer; dressing	
MAIDAN Indian parade ground; a plain			**MANWAY** underground ladderway	mn
MAIDEN lass; damsel; virgin; guillotine			**MAOISM** } follower of Mao Tse Tung	
MAILED posted; clad in armour			**MAOIST** }	
MAIMED crippled; disabled; mutilated			**MAPPED** charted; drew; delineated	
MAINLY chiefly; principally; largely			**MAQUIS** French Resistance Force	
MAINOR stolen goods; theft	lw		**MAQUIS** rough scrub in Corsica	bt
MAJLIS parliament of Iran, Turkey			**MARAUD** raid; plunder; pillage	
MAJOON narcotic drug mixture (Hindu)			**MARBLE** decorative stone; ball	mn
MAKE-UP fiction; facial embellishment			**MARBLY** like marble	
MAKING forcing; compelling; reaching			**MARCEL** a hair wave; style of coiffure	
MALADY ailment; disorder; complaint			**MARCID** wasting	
MALAGA a Spanish wine			**MARCOR** marasmus	
MALATE a salt of malic acid	ch		**MARGAY** American tiger-cat	zo
MALAWI native of E. Africa			**MARGED** bordered; edged	
MALAXE to rub, knead plaster			**MARGIN** verge; brim; brink; reserve	
MALEIC obtained from malic acid	ch		**MARGOT** fish (perch)	zo
MALGRE maugre; in spite of			**MARIAN** (Mary)	
MALICE spite; rancour; malevolence			**MARIET** violet campanula	bt
MALIGN defame; slander; traduce			**MARINA** yacht-mooring basin	nt
MALISM pessimistic belief			**MARINE** nautical; naval; maritime	nt
MALKIN scarecrow; mawkin			**MARISH** a marsh; swamp	
MALLEE Australian tree	bt		**MARIST** sect, follower of Virgin Mary	
MALLET maul; beetle; hammer			**MARKED** unmistakable; notable	
MALLOW plant	bt		**MARKER** recorder	
MALTED converted to malt	br		**MARKET** mart; emporium; sale; vend	
MALTHA petroleum			**MARMOT** desert rodent	zo
MAMMAL young-suckling animal	zo		**MAROON** claret-colour; firework	
MAMMEE West Indian fruit	bt		**MAROON** runaway negro slave	
MAMMER stammer; hesitate; hover			**MARQUE** accredited; boundary; model	
MAMMET puppet; scarecrow			**MARRAM** sand dune; bent grass	bt
MAMMON god of riches; wealth			**MARRED** disfigured; impaired	
MANAGE contrive; control; regulate			**MARRER** spoiler; bungler; botcher	

MARRON chestnut (Fr.)	bt
MARROT guillemot	zo
MARROW medulla; essence; pith	
MARSHY boggy; fenny; paludal	
MARTEN (weasel)	zo
MARTIN swallow	zo
MARTYR victim; sacrifice; persecute	
MARVEL wonder; prodigy; miracle	
MARVER iron or stone block	
MARVER glass blower's table	gs
MASCLE heraldic lozenge	hd
MASCON moon high-gravity region	as
MASCOT charm; talisman; halidom	
MASHAQ Persian goatskin water-bag	
MASHED bruised; pulped; kneaded	
MASHER fop; dandy; lady-killer	
MASHIE a golf-club	
MASJID masjed; a mosque	
MASKED disguised; cloaked; screened	
MASKER masquerader; mummer	
MASLIN rye-bread	ck
MASORA Hebrew traditions	
MASQUE mask; a play; revel	
MASSED collected; heaped; lumped	
MASSES the proletariat	
MASSIF central mountain-mass	
MASTAX gizzard in rotifera	zo
MASTED having masts	nt
MASTEL maple tree	bt
MASTER maestro; tutor; teacher	
MASTIC resin	bt
MASTIC liquorice-like flavour	ck
MATHES may-weed	bt
MATICO Peruvian astringent plant	bt
MATIES herring; a wrasse	zo
MATING pairing; check-mating	zo
MATINS morning service	rl
MATRIX original die; mould; cavity	
MATRON head nurse; dame	
MATTED entangled; interlaced	
MATTER signify; import; stuff; affair	
MATURE ripen; mellow; full grown	
MAUDIT one pursued by bad luck	
MAUGRE in spite of	
MAULED hammered; mangled; bruised	
MAUMAU Kenyan nationalists	
MAUNDY Thursday before Good Friday	
MAUSER rifle	
MAWMET maumet; mammet; puppet	
MAXIMA highest or top limits	
MAXIXE dance (Brazil)	mu
MAY-BUG cockchafer	zo
MAYDAY verbal distress call	tc
MAY-DEW spring	
MAY-FLY a species of ephemera	zo
MAYHAP perhaps	
MAYHEM criminal mutilation	lw
MAYING gathering may	
MAZARD skull; cherry	bt
MAZDAH supreme deity (Zend Avesta)	rl
MAZILY confusedly; distractedly	

MAZING bewildering; perplexing	
MAZOUT petroleum extract	ch
MEABLE easily penetrable	
MEADOW mead; lea; sward; field	
MEAGER } thin; skinny; lean; gaunt	
MEAGRE } lank; mean; emaciated	
MEAKER a minnow	zo
MEALER (out-boarder)	
MEALIE maize	bt
MEANLY ignobly; basely; sordidly	
MEASLY stingy; miserly; meagre	
MEATHE mead; a liquor	ck
MEATUS passage in the body	p
MEDDLE muddle; intrude; interfere	
MEDIAD, MESIAD toward median axis	
MEDIAL average; mean; mediocre	
MEDIAN traversal; a Mede	as
MEDICK lucerne or clover	bt
MEDICO doctor or student	md
MEDISM Grecian treachery	
MEDIUM moderate; means; psychic	
MEDIUS the middle finger	p
MEDLAR fruit	bt
MEDLEY farrago; jumble; olio	mu
MEDUSA jellyfish; a gorgon	zo
MEEKEN to humble; to abase	
MEEKLY lowly; submissively	
MEETLY fitly; suitably; correctly	
MEGASS bagasse; cane refuse	
MEGERG million ergs	me
MEGGER insulation recorder	
MEGILP magilp; linseed-oil and varnish	
MEGOHM a million ohms	me
MEGRIM neuralgic pain; migraine	me
MEGRIM flat fish; witch/lemon sole	zo
MEHARI racing dromedary; camel	zo
MEHTAR Ind. house-servant, groom	
MELINE canary-yellow	
MELLAY mêlée; affray; broil; brawl	
MELLEY scuffle; contest; conflict	
MELLIT a horse-scab	vt, zo
MELLOW mature; ripe; genial; soften	
MELODY air; tune; descant; theme	mu
MELTED molten; dissolved; relaxed	
MELTER liquefier	
MELTON woollen cloth	tx
MEMBER part; limb; component	
MEMNON desert crier	
MEMOIR life; biography; journal	
MEMORY remembrance; recollection	
MENACE threat; alarm; intimidate	
MENAGE housekeeping; household	
MENALD speckled	
MENDED restored; rectified; improved	
MENDER repairer; restorer	
MENHIR obelisk; long grave stone	
MENIAL slave; flunkey; lackey; servile	
MENINX a brain-membrane	p
MENNAD the minnow	zo
MENSAL monthly	

MENSES menstruation	pl	**MIDWAY** halfway	
MENTAL intellectual; psychical		**MIFFED** ruffled; annoyed	
MENTOR guide; monitor; counsellor		**MIGHTY** puissant; potent; dynamic	
MENURA lyre-bird	zo	**MIGNON** dainty; pretty	
MERCER a dealer in silks or money		**MIHRAB** mosque niche facing Mecca	rl
MERELY simply; solely; only; purely		**MIKADO** Emperor of Japan	
MERESE wine-glass stem flange		**MILADY** my lady	
MERGED sunk; absorbed; immersed		**MILDEN** to mollify	
MERGER an amalgamation		**MILDER** calmer; softer; gentler	
MERINO sheep; wool	zo	**MILDEW** mould; blight; rust; must	bt
MERISM development of like members	bt	**MILDLY** leniently; placidly; suavely	
MERKIN false hair; a mop		**MILIEU** environment	
MERLIN falcon; small hawk	zo	**MILIUM** millet grass	bt
MERLON projecting part of battlement	ar	**MILKED** emptied, taken advantage of	
MERMAN cf. mermaid		**MILKEN** milk-like	
MERONT phase in neosporidia	zo	**MILKER** cow-man	
MEROPS bird; bee-eater	zo	**MILLED** ground; struggled; levigated	
MERULA thrush; blackbird	zo	**MILLER** one who grinds corn	
MESAIL vizor of helmet		**MILLET** grain	
MESCAL Mexican drink		**MILORD** my lord	
MESETA tableland (S. Amer.)		**MILSEY** milk strainer	
MESHED reticulated; engaged		**MILTER** male fish	zo
MESIAL } middle;		**MIMBAR** pulpit in a mosque	
MESIAN } median		**MIMING** mimicking; aping; acting	
MESJID masjid; a mosque; prayers	rl	**MIMOSA** plant genus	bt
MESLIN maslin; mixed grain	bt	**MINCED** affected; abbreviated	
MESODE part of an ode		**MINCER** mincing machine	
MESPOT Mesopotamia		**MINDED** heeded; noted; objected	
MESSED mussed; confused; ate together		**MINDER** care-taker	
MESSIN a mongrel (Sc.)	zo	**MINGLE** blend; mix; join; jumble	
MESTEE half-caste; octaroon		**MINIFY** diminish; depreciate	
METAGE measurement	me	**MINIMA** the lowest	
METEOR aerolite; shooting star		**MINING** burrowing; sapping	
METHAM chemical insecticide, weedkiller		**MINION** a favourite; sycophant	
METHER vessel for mead; band (Turk.)	mu	**MINISH** diminish; reduce; minify	
METHOD order; system; process		**MINIUM** vermilion	
METHYL spirit	ch	**MINNIE** trench mortar	
METIER role (Fr.); profession		**MINNOW** meaker; mennad	zo
METING measuring		**MINOAN** Cretan	
METOPE forehead; (frieze)	ar	**MINTED** coined; stamped; invented	
METRIC decimal		**MINTER** inventor; creator	
METTLE courage; ardour; pluck		**MINTON** china ware	
MEWING caterwauling; confining		**MINUET** a dance	mu
MEWLED yowled; squalled		**MINUTE** small; tiny; minikin; record	
MEWLER a crying child		**MIOSIS** rhetorical understatement	
MIASMA bad air; exhalation		**MIOTIC** eye-pupil contractor	zo
MICHED concealed; played truant		**MIRAGE** optical illusion	
MICHER skulker; beggar; pilferer		**MIRING** muddying	
MICKLE muckle; great; much		**MIRROR** exemplar; reflector	
MICMAC an American Indian		**MISCUE** (billiards)	
MICRON millionth part of metre	me	**MISDID** erred; blundered	
MID-AGE middle time of life		**MISERE** (solo whist, no tricks)	
MID-AIR up in the air		**MISERY** distress; woe; grief; anguish	
MIDDAY noon; meridian		**MISFIT** square peg in round hole	
MIDDEN dunghill		**MISGET** obtain unjustly	
MIDDLE centre; intermediate; medial		**MISHAP** accident; ill chance	
MIDGET sand-fly; dwarf	zo	**MISHMI** vegetable drug	md
MID-LEG (cricket)		**MISHNA** the text of the Talmud	rl
MID-OFF (cricket)		**MISKEN** to ignore; be unaware (Sc.)	
MIDRIB largest leaf vein	bt	**MISKIN** a little bagpipe	mu
MID-SEA at sea	nt	**MISLAY** misplace; lose	

MISLED (mislead); deluded; deceived	
MISSAL Mass-book	rl
MISSAY say wrongly; slander	
MISSED failed; wanted; needed	
MISSEE view erroneously	
MISSEL thrush; storm cock	zo
MIS-SET to arrange unfitly	
MISSIS missus; mistress	
MISTER ordinary title for man	
MISTLE missel-thrush	zo
MISUSE abuse; profane; misapply	
MITHAN Indian ox; gayal	zo
MITHRA sun-god (Pers.)	rl
MITRAL like a mitre; somewhat conical	
MITRED wearing mitre	
MITTEN a boxing glove (fingerless)	
MIURUS dactylic hexameter	
MIXING mingling; jumbling	
MIZZEN a sail	nt
MIZZLE fine rain; to drizzle; decamp	
MIZZLY misty	
MNESIC pertaining to memory	pc
MOANED lamented; bewailed; deplored	
MOATED surrounded with a ditch	
MOBBED thronged; set about	
MOBCAP a frilly cap	
MOBILE volatile; mercurial; motile	
MOB/LAW lynch-law	lw
MOCKED derided; jeered; aped	
MOCKER scorner; scoffer; taunter	
MOCK-UP a non-working model	
MODENA crimson	pt
MODERN present; current; up-to-date	
MODEST chaste; unassuming; diffident	
MODIFY alter; change; vary; moderate	
MODISH stylish; fashionable; chic	
MODIST a follower of fashion	
MODIUS 2 gallons (Roman)	me
MODOCS Oregon Indian tribe	
MODULE model; proportion	ar
MODULE unit in multi-stage rocket	
MOFFLE bungle	
MOHAIR hair of the Angora goat	
MOHAWK ruffian; N. Amer. Indian	
MOHOLE penetration of earth's crust	
MOIDER to toil; confuse; spend (Sc.)	
MOIETY a half; a share	
MOILED drudged; toiled; soiled	
MOIRAE the Fates	
MOLEGH) Phoenician god, Semitic	rl
MOLOCH) deity; Australian lizard	zo
MOLEST vex; harry; worry; pester	
MOLINE mill-stone rynd	
MOLLAH) judge;	
MOOLAH) Moslem teacher;	rl
MULLAH) fanatic	
MOLTEN melted; liquefied; fused	
MOMENT instant; trice; import	
MONDAY Solomon Grundy's birthday	
MONERA simple protozoans	zo
MONGER deal; to deal in	
MONGOL native of Mongolia	
MONIAL nun	
MONIED rich; opulent	
MONIES coins; means; specie	
MONISM a doctrine	
MONIST believer in monism	
MONKEY a primate; bandar; rhesus	z
MONKEY £500; pile-driver; meddle	
MONODY a dirge	m
MONOID (versification)	
MONOSY abnormal condition	
MONTEM Eton custom of money-raising	
MONTON ore (Sp.)	m
MONTRE organ stop; ceramic	m
MOO-COW pet word for cow	z
MOOING lowing	
MOONED wandered aimlessly	
MOONER listless lounger	
MOONET little moon	
MOORUK Bennett's cassowary	z
MOORVA fibre; bowstring-hemp	
MOOTED debated; discussed	
MOOTER disputer	
MOPING languishing	
MOPISH gloomy; spiritless; despondent	
MOPOKE Australian owl	z
MOPPED swabbed	
MOPPET) puppet	
MOPSEY)	
MORALE courageous endurance	
MORASS bog; fen; swamp; quagmire	
MORBID diseased; vitiated; sickly	
MOREEN watered woollen fabric	
MORGAY shark; dog-fish	z
MORGEN about 2 acres (0.8 hectare)	m
MORGUE mortuary (Fr.)	
MORIAN a Moor; Moroccan	
MORION open helmet	
MORKIN dead beast	
MORLOP jasper	m
MORMON member of sect Utah	h
MORNED blunted	
MORONE a deep crimson colour	
MOROSE sullen; surly; churlish	
MORRIS folk dance style	
MORROW the next day	
MORSAL pert. to cutting edge	
MORSED signalled by Morse	
MORSEL titbit; piece; fragment	
MORTAL human; deadly; fatal	
MORTAR trench weapon; cement	
MORULA button-scurvy	m
MOSAIC law; inlaid ornamentation	
MOSLEM Muslim; Mohammedan	
MOSQUE temple; mesjid	
MOSTIC maulstick	
MOSTLY chiefly; mainly	
MOTHER (liquors); dam; generatrix	
MOTILE mobile; capable of movement	
MOTION proposal; action; impulse	
MOTIVE spur; incentive; reason	

MOTLEY mixed; clown's costume
MOT-MOT American bird   zo
MOTORY giving motion
MOTTLE to stain
MOUJIK muzhik; Russian peasant
MOULDY fusty; musty; rusty
MOULIN glacial crevasse; hand-mill   ck
MOUNTY the rise of a hawk
MOUSED bound with spun-yarn   nt
MOUSER capable cat   zo
MOUSSE culinary confection
MOUTAN tree-peony   bt
MOUTHY ranting; bombastic
MOUTON sheep; ancient French coin   nm, zo
MOVIES moving pictures
MOVING stirring; budging; touching
MOWING grass cutting
MOZING raising nap (cloth)   tx
MUCAGO mucilage, mucus
MUCATE ⎫
MUCITE ⎬ mucic acid   ch
MUCHLY rather much
MUCKED muddled; dirtied; spread dung
MUCKER a failure; a fall
MUCKLE much (Sc.)
MUCOID resembling mucus   md
MUCOUS mucoid; slimy; viscous   md, ps
MUDDLE confuse; chaos; derange
MUD-PIE child's inedible confection
MUFFED fumbled and failed
MUFFIN a winter's delicacy
MUFFLE (furnace); deaden; shroud
MUGGED crammed up; beaten up
MUGGER Indian crocodile   zo
MUGUET lily of the valley   bt
MULIER wife   lw
MULISH obstinate
MULLAH (see Mollah); teacher (Moslem)   rl
MULLED heated; dispirited
MULLEN mullein plant   bt
MULLER a miller (Sc.)
MULLER heating vessel; pestle
MULLET genus of fish   zo
MULLET a star; a rowel   hd
MULLEY mooly; a cow; hornless   zo
MULTUM adulterant used in brewing
MUMBLE mutter; chew
MUMMER masquerader; actor; histrion
MUMPED nibbled; grinned; chewed
MUMPER a beggar
MUNDIC iron pyrites   mn
MUNDIL a turban
MUNSHI Eastern teacher
MURAGE money for town repairs (Fr.)
MURDER kill; assassinate; slaughter
MURINE (mice)   zo
MURING immuring; walling up
MURMUR whisper; complain; repine
MURPHY potato (Irish)   bt
MURREN a murrain (obs.)   gl
MURREY dark red

MUSANG East Indian coffee-rat   zo
MUSCAL (mosses)   bt
MUSCAT a grape; a wine   bt
MUSCLE thew; sinew   pl
MUSEUM collection/treasure repository
MUSHED sledded (Alaska)
MUSHER snow traveller (Canada)
MUSING ruminating; reflecting
MUSIVE mosaic
MUSKEG swamp; marsh (Canada)
MUSKET hawk; smooth-bore gun   zo
MUSK-OX N. American arctic ox   zo
MUSLIM Moslem; Mohammedan
MUSLIN soft cotton fabric   tx
MUSMON moufflon; European sheep   zo
MUSNUD Persian throne of state
MUSSAL Indian torch
MUSSED messed; disarranged
MUSSEL a shellfish   zo
MUSTAC small tufted monkey   zo
MUSTEE mestee; an octaroon
MUSTER parade; assemble; rally
MUTAGE (checking fermentation)
MUTATE to change
MUTELY dumbly; silently
MUTING the dung of birds; silencing
MUTINY riot; sedition; revolt
MUTISM dumbness; speechlessness
MUTIVE tending to alter
MUTTER murmur; grumble; maunder
MUTTON proverbially dead
MUTUAL reciprocal; correlative
MUTULE projection   ar
MUTUUM loan contract   lw
MUZHIK moujik; Russian peasant
MUZZLE curb; restrain
MUZZLE snout; mouth
MYCOID fungus-like
MYELIC pertaining to spinal cord
MYELIN fatty material round nerve   zo
MYELON spinal cord   pl
MYGALE shrew mouse   zo
MYOGEN water-soluble muscle albumin   ch
MYOPIA near-sightedness   md
MYOPIC short-sighted; purblind   md
MYOSIN ⎫
MYOSIS ⎬ disease of the eye   md
MYOTIC ⎭
MYRIAD countless; innumerable
MYRTLE genus of shrub   bt
MYRTUS wax-myrtle; bay-berry   bt
MYSELF reflexive pronoun
MYSTIC occult; recondite; enigmatic
MYTHIC legendary; fictitious; fanciful
MYTHUS a myth; a fable
MYXINE hag-fish   zo
MYXOID mucoid   pl
MYXOMA a tumour   md

N

NABBED grabbed; arrested

NABKET snuff; small cake (Sc.)	ck
NAEVUS birth-mark	md
NAGANA tse-tse fly disease	md
NAGARI Sanskrit script	
NAGGED scolded; upbraided; pestered	
NAGGER a fault-finder	
NAHOOR sheep (Nepal)	zo
NAIANT (swimming)	hd, zo
NAILED caught; secured; exposed	
NAILER nail-maker	
NAKONG water-koodoo (S. Africa)	zo
NAMELY viz., specifically	
NAMING christening; nominating	
NANDOO S. American ostrich	zo
NANISM dwarfishness	
NANKIN nankeen; cotton cloth	tx
NANNAR Chaldean moon-god	rl
NANOID dwarf; pigmy	
NAPALM inflammable oil/soap gel	ch
NAPERY household linen	tx
NAPKIN serviette	tx
NAPPAL soaprock	mn
NAPPED dozed; slumbered	
NARDOO Australian plant	bt
NARDUS mat-grass	bt
NARGIL coconut tree; hubble-bubble	bt
NARIAL ⎫ nasal	md
NARINE ⎭	
NARROW strait; close; contracted	
NARWAL sea-unicorn; whale	zo
NASARD organ stop	mu
NASION part of nose	md
NASUTE captious; critical	
NATANT swimming; naiant	hd
NATION people; race; country	
NATIVE aboriginal; intrinsic; congenital	
NATRIX genus of snakes	zo
NATRON carbonate of soda	ch
NATTER to nag (dial.)	
NATTES surface decoration	ar
NATURE universe; species; quality	
NAUGHT 0; zero; nought; nothing	me
NAUSEA sea-sickness; disgust; qualm	
NAUTCH dancing girl; a dance	
NAUTIC nautical; naval; maritime	nt
NAZARD 3-f organ pitch	mu
NEANIC of adolescent period	zo
NEAPED aground at low tide	
NEARBY adjacent; nigh; at hand	
NEARED approached; drew nigh	
NEARER more adjacent	
NEARLY closely; all but; almost	
NEATLY smartly; featly; dexterously	
NEBBUK (crown of thorns)	bt
NEB-NEB acacia pods	bt
NEBRIS fawn-skin worn by Bacchus	
NEBULA heavy cloud; mist	
NEBULE nebula; mist; fog	
NEBULY wavy	
NECKED embraced; hugged; beheaded	
NECRON dead plant material	bt

NECTAR ambrosia; honey	cl
NEED-BE a necessity	
NEEDED wanted; lacked; necessitated	
NEEDER requirer	
NEEDLE critical	to
NEEDLY thorny	
NEESED, NEEZED sneezed	
NEGATE deny; mollify	
NEKTON swimming water organisms	bt, zo
NEMEAN (lion killed by Hercules)	
NEPALI language (Nepal)	
NEPHEW sibling's male child	
NEREID sea-nymph	
NEREUS sea-god	
NERINE Guernsey lily	b
NERITE mollusc	z
NERIUM oleander	b
NEROLI oil from orange flowers	
NERVAL nervous; sinewy	
NERVED fortified; plucky; courageous	
NESHEN to soften	
NESHKI Arabic script	
NESSUS a Centaur	
NESTED built a nest	
NESTLE snuggle; rest; cherish	
NESTOR genus of parrots (NZ)	zo
NETHER lower; under	
NETRUM minute spindle	cy
NETTED reticulated; gained; trapped	
NETTLE to irritate; fret	b
NEURAD dorsal	zo
NEURAL (nerves)	me
NEURIC nervous	
NEURON nerve cell	me
NEUTER neutral; non-partisan	
NEWING yeast; barm	
NEWISH somewhat novel	
NEW-SAD recently bereaved (Shak.)	
NEWTON gravity force	me
NIACIN nicotinic acid; B Vitamin	cl
NIBBED complete with nib	
NIBBLE bite; gnaw	
NICELY exactly; accurately; adroitly	
NICENE creed (Asia)	
NICEST daintiest; choicest	
NICETY precision; delicacy	
NICHED in a niche or recess	
NICHER neigh; snigger	
NICKED notched; stolen	
NICKEL 5 cent piece	nm, cl
NICKER a cheat; woodpecker	z
NIDDER shiver; molest	
NIDGED nudged (stone-cutting)	
NIDGET a fool	
NID-NOD nod repeatedly	
NIDOSE olfactory	
NIELLO engraving; ornamentation	
NIFFLE pilfer; steal	
NIGGER negro	
NIGGLE trifle; to be finicky	
NIGHLY nearly; adjacent	

NIGRIC black
NILGAI Indian antelope — zo
NIMBLE agile; lively; swift
NIMBLY alertly; briskly; quickly
NIMBUS a halo; rain cloud — mt
NIMROD a mighty hunter
NINETY cardinal number
NINGAL Nannar's wife
NIPPED pinched; compressed; gripped
NIPPER tooth (horse); boy (slang)
NIPPLE teat; dug; pap; mamilla
NIPPON Japan
NIPTER feet-washing ceremony — rl
NIRLES herpes; shingles — md
NITRIC (nitre) — ch
NITRON reagent for nitric acid — ch
NITTER bot-fly — zo
NITWIT numskull
NIVOSE 4th French month (Revol.)
NO-BALL (cricket)
NOBBLE dope; doctor; get at — vt
NOBLER more illustrious
NOBODY a nonentity
NOCAKE parched corn — ck
NOCENT hurtful; mischievous
NOCTUA large moth genus — zo
NODDED bowed; acknowledged
NODDER a drowsy person
NODDLE the head
NODOSE knotted
NODULE small knot
NOESIS pure knowledge
NOETIC intellectual
NOGGIN small cup; ¼ pint (0.14 litres) — me
NO-GOOD useless
NOISED reported; rumoured
NOMIAL a single term in algebra
NOMISM moral law as basis of conduct
NONAGE immature; minority
NONANE paraffin hydrocarbon — ch
NONARY group of nine
NON-COM an NCO
NON-CON not content
NON-EGO (metaphysics)
NONIUS a graduating instrument
NONOSE monosaccharide group — ch
NOODLE simpleton; form of pasta — ck
NOOSED snared; caught; lassooed
NORDIC Scandinavian
NORITE coarse-grained igneous rock — gl
NORMAL regular; perpendicular
NORMAN of Normandy
NORROY king at arms — hd
NOSEAN a silicate — mn
NO-SIDE end of a game of Rugby
NOSING projection; snooping — ar
NOSISM speaking of self as regal 'we'
NOSTOC genus of seaweed — bt
NOTARY a court official — lw
NOTICE see; remark; heed; intimation
NOTIFY warn; advise; apprise

NOTING recording; registering
NOTION idea; belief; theory; concept
NOTOUR notorious (Sc.)
NOUGAT a sweetmeat — ck
NOUGHT 0; naught; zero; a cypher
NOUNAL (noun)
NOUSLE to nurse; nuzzle
NOVENA nine days' devotion — rl
NOVENE by nines
NOVICE tyro; neophyte; probationer
NOWAYS in no way
NOWISE nohow
NOWYED heraldic branches — hd
NOYADE execution by drowning (Fr.)
NOZZLE snout; projecting mouthpiece
NUANCE a subtle distinction
NUBBIN stunted maize — bt
NUBBLE punch; small lump
NUBBLY bumpy; knotty
NUBIAN of Nubia
NUBILE marriageable
NUCHAL (nape of neck) — md
NUCLEI cell-centres; cores; kernels
NUCULE a little nut
NUDELY barely; nakedly
NUDGED jogged; poked; pushed
NUDISM, NUDIST naked sun-worship
NUDITY nakedness
NUGGAR mugger; alligator — zo
NUGGET a lump of gold — mn
NULLAH watercourse; ravine (Ind.)
NUMBED torpid; paralyzed; dazed
NUMBER count; compute; figure
NUMBLY in a frozen manner
NUMNAH saddle cloth — tx
NUNCIO Papal representative
NUNCLE mine uncle (Shak.)
NUNOME mesh fabric — tx
NUPHAR water-lily — bt
NURLED milled like a coin — nm
NURSED fostered; encouraged
NURSER tender; cherisher
NUTANT nodding
NUT-MEG an aromatic kernel — bt, ck
NUT-OIL paint ingredient — bt
NUTRIA the fur of the coypu — zo
NUTTER a nut-gatherer
NUZZER a presentation (India)
NUZZLE nousle; fondle
NYANZA African lake
NYLGAU nilgai; an Indian antelope — zo
NYMPHA pupa; chrysalis — zo

O

OAFISH idiotic; dull; doltish
OARAGE rowing
OARING sculling
OARIUM an ovary; ovarium — bt
OARLAP a distinctive rabbit — zo
OBDUCE draw over

OBECHE W. Afr. satinwood, Niger.
whitewood   bt, fr
OBELUS mark (†); obelisk
OBERON king of the fairies
OBEYED complied; yielded
OBEYER heeder; minder
OBIISM West Indian witchcraft   rl
OBITER incidentally
OBJECT protest; demur; goal; intent
OBJURE to swear
OBLATE communion wafer   rl
OBLIGE compel; bind; favour; serve
OBLONG longer than broad
OBOIST oboe-player   mu
OBOLUS Charon's ferry fee   nm
OBSESS besiege; beset; haunt
OBTAIN get; win; acquire; attain
OBTECT of pupae unable to move   zo
OBTEST to beseech; supplicate
OBTUND deaden; blunt
OBTUSE dull; stolid; stupid
OBVERT turn toward; to face
OCCAMY silvery alloy
OCCULT mystic; hidden; obscure
OCCUPY fill; possess; inhabit
OCELLI peacock's 'eyes'
OCELOT American leopard   zo
OCHREA cup-shaped plant structure   bt
O'CLOCK an indefinite time
OCRACY government
OCTANE petrol purification figure   ch
OCTANS constellation (South Pole)   as
OCTANT measuring instrument   mu
OCTAVE ottava; consisting of eight   mu
OCTAVO (eight leaves to the sheet)   pr
OCTILE octant; eighth of a circle
OCTODE a thermionic valve   ps
OCTOSE monosaccharide group   ch
OCTROI monopoly, trade privilege (Fr.)
OCULAR visible
ODDITY singularity; strangeness
ODIOUS hateful; detested; obnoxious
ODYLIC mesmeric
OECIST founder of Greek colony
OEDEMA localized dropsy   md
OEUVRE complete works: artist, writer
OFF-DAY unlucky occasion; free day
OFFEND affront; insult; trespass
OFFICE post; function; bureau   rl
OFFING outer sea; future   nt
OFFISH haughty; snobbish
OFF-LAP strata conformation   gl
OFFSET counter-balance
OFFSET rubber-to-paper process   pr
OGAMIC ancient Irish script
OGDOAD group of 8
OGHAMS ancient Irish alphabet
OGIVAL arched   ar
OGLING an amorous advance
OGRESS a monstrous lady
OGRISH ogreish

OIDIUM fungus; vine-mildew   bt
OIL-BAG oil gland   pl
OIL-CAN oil applier
OILERY oilman's stock
OIL-GAS inflammable gas   ch
OILING lubricating
OIL-MAN oil-dealer
OIL-NUT butternut   bt
OIL-RIG boring apparatus for oil
OLDEST most senile; eldest
OLDISH somewhat ancient
OLEATE (oleic acid)   ch
OLEFIN ethylene hydrocarbon   ch
OLEINE liquid fat
OLEOSE oily; oleic   ps
OLERON ancient code of sea laws   nt
OLIVER small tilt-hammer; (Roland)
OLIVET mock pearl
OLIVIL gum from the olive tree
OLLAMH ancient Irish doctor   md
OMASAL (cow's stomach)   zo
OMASUM ruminant's third stomach
OMBROS madder
OMELET omelette; beaten eggs   ck
OMENED predicted; augured; presaged
OMNIFY to render universal
OMNIUM (Stock Exchange)
ONAGER wild ass; ghorkhar   zo
ONCOME deluge; approach
ONCOST extraneous mining charges   mn
ONDINE undine; water-spirit
ONDING fall of rain or snow
ONE-MAN soloist
ONE-WAY (traffic); single route
ONEYER (of uncertain origin)
ONFALL storm; attack; assault
ONFLOW gush; stream
ON-LINE part of main computer operation
ONRUSH onset; charge
ON-SIDE (football)
ONWARD forward; advancing
ONYMAL (technical group name)   zo
OOCYST cyst round gametes in protozoa   zo
OODLES quantities; heaps
OOGAMY union of un-like-sized gametes   bl
OOGENY embryonic development
OOIDAL egg-shaped
OOLITE a limestone   mn
OOLITH spherical concretion   gl
OOLOGY the study of birds' eggs
OOLONG oulong; tea
OOMIAK Eskimo boat   nt
OORIAL wild sheep (India)   zo
OOTYPE oviduct section   zo
OOZING exuding; seeping; percolating
OPAQUE impermeable to light
OPENED undid; disclosed; revealed
OPENER beginner; cutter
OPENLY publicly; above-board
OPERON genes together in chromosome   gn
OPHITE porphyry   mn

OPHITE gnostic serpent-worshipper	rl	
OPIANE narcotine	ch	
OPIATE a sedative medicine	md	
OPINED supposed; thought; fancied		
OPPOSE prevent; hinder; combat		
OPPUGN oppose; obstruct; resist		
OPTANT volunteer		
OPTICS science of light and vision		
OPTIME almost a wrangler		
OPTING choosing; co-opting		
OPTION choice; wish; selection		
ORACHE genus of plants; spinach	bt	
ORACLE wiseacre; ambiguous response		
ORALLY by word of mouth		
ORANGE Citrus aurantium	bt	
ORATED harangued; prated; spouted		
ORATOR declaimer; spell-binder		
ORBATE bereaved; fatherless		
ORBITA eye-sockets	pl	
ORCHIC of the testis	zo	
ORCHID orchis	bt	
ORCHIL archil; purple dye; a lichen	bt	
ORCINE lichen dye		
ORDAIN prescribe; enjoin; appoint		
ORDEAL test; trial; assay; scrutiny		
ORDURE excrement		
OREIDE imitation gold		
OREXIS appetite	md	
ORGASM sexual climax	md	
OR-GATE pulse circuit	el	
ORGEAT liquor (barley)	br	
ORGIES revels; carousals		
ORIENT eastern; the east		
ORIGAN marjoram (herb)	bt, ck	
ORIGIN fount; spring; source; root		
ORIHON continued folded uncut sheet	pr	
ORIOLE a bird species	zo	
ORISON prayer; supplication	rl	
ORMULU, ORMOLU gilt brass		
ORMUZD (Magian system)		
ORNATE florid; embellished		
ORNERY ordinary; mean; low		
OROIDE alloy; oreide	mn	
OROTIC vitamin B-13; growth acid	ch	
ORPHAN who has lost a parent		
ORPHIC (Orpheus)		
ORPINE a yellow plant	bt	
ORRERY model of solar system		
ORRICE dried iris root	bt	
ORTIVE rising; eastern		
OSCINE of a sub-order of birds	zo	
OSCULE small mouth		
OSELLA Doge's medal (Venice)		
OSIERY osier-bed	bt	
OSIRIS greatest Egyptian god	rl	
OSMIUM metallic element	mn	
OSMOLE unit of osmolic pressure	me	
OSMOSE (diffusion of fluids)		
OSOPHY belief or doctrine		
OSPREY sea-hawk; an egret plume	zo	
OSSEIN bone-cartilage	pl	

OSSIFY to become bone		
OSTEAL pertaining to bone		
OSTENT portent; show; appearance		
OSTIUM an opening; mouth of river		
OSTLER stableman; groom		
OSTMEN Danish settlers in Ireland		
OSTREA oyster	zo	
OTALGY earache	md	
OTARIA genus of seals	zo	
OTIANT idle; resting		
OTIOSE at ease; lazy; idle		
OTITIS ear-trouble	md	
OTTAVA an octave	mu	
OUSTED deposed; ejected; thrown out		
OUSTER ejection; dispossession		
OUTAGE electrical failure		
OUTASK ask for the last time		
OUTBAR to shut out		
OUTBID offer more		
OUTBYE out of doors (Sc.)		
OUTCRY hue; clamour; tumult; bruit		
OUTDID excelled; surpassed; exceeded		
OUTFIT equipment; clothing		
OUTING expedition; trip; holiday		
OUTJET project		
OUTLAW brigand; bandit; proscribe		
OUTLAY expense; disbursement		
OUTLET exit; vent; loophole		
OUTLIE excel in lying		
OUTMAN outnumber		
OUTPUT production		
OUTRUN outstrip; beat; surpass		
OUTSET start; beginning; opening		
OUTSIT sit longer than		
OUTSUM outnumber		
OUTTOP over-reach		
OUTVIE surpass; out-rival; eclipse		
OUTWIT dupe; overreach; circumvent		
OVALLY elliptically		
OVERBY adjacent		
OVERDO carry too far		
OVERGO exceed		
OVIBOS musk-ox; buffalo-cow	zo	
OVISAC (ovary)	zo	
OVULAR embryonic	bt	
OWLERY haunt of owls	zo	
OWLING smuggling; especially wool		
OWLISH not very wise		
OWNING possessing; conceding		
OXALIC an acid	ch	
OXALIS wood sorrel	bt	
OXALYL bivalent acid radical	ch	
OXBIRD the dunlin	zo	
OXEOTE rod-shaped	zo	
OX-EYED having large eyes		
OXFORD (blue); (shoe)		
OXGALL cleaning/painting agent		
OXGANG a bovate; about 15 ac. (6 ha) of		
OXGATE land; amount that could be		
OXLAND cultivated with one ox		
OXHEAD block-head; dolt (Shak.)		

OX-HEEL the setter-wort   bt
OX-HIDE leather
OXTAIL soup ingredient
OXYGEN non-metallic element   ch
OXYGON a triangle with 2 acute angles
OXYMEL honey and vinegar
OYSTER ostrea   zo
OZALID copy of engineering drawing
OZOENA chronic atrophic rhinitis   md
OZONIC of ozone

P

PACIFY calm; appease; reconcile
PACING setting the pace
PACKED crowded; compressed
PACKER stower
PACKET parcel; bale; a vessel   nt
PADANG a field (Malay)
PADDED travelled slowly; (cell)
PADDER foot-pad; highwayman
PADDLE also pattle
PADNAG ambling horse   zo
PADUAN (Padua); the pavan   mu
PAELLA Span. rice-shellfish dish   ck
PAGING marking pages; name-calling
PAGODA pagode; temple; (Ind. coin)   nm
PAID-UP shares or capital   lw
PAIGLE cowslip   bt
PAINED hurt; distressed; grieved
PAINIM (see Paynim); pagan
PAIRED coupled; yoked; mated; (voting)
PAKEHA white man (Maori)
PALACE (Crystal)
PALAMA toe-webbing   zo
PALATE roof of mouth; taste; relish   pl
PALELY wanly; ashy; pallidly
PALING a fence; blanching
PALISH wan
PALKEE palanquin (Ind.)
PALLAH African antelope   zo
PALLAS Athene, goddess of wisdom   rl
PALLED cloaked
PALLET palette; small bed
PALLID pale; sallow; cadaverous
PALLOR pallidness
PALMAR (hand)
PALMED concealed; handled
PALMER pilgrim
PALMUS palpitation; twitching   md
PALOLO edible worm   zo
PALPAL ⎫ (antennae-like feelers)   zo
PALPED ⎬   zo
PALPUS feeler of an insect   zo
PALTER dodge; shuffle; prevaricate
PALTRY mean; petty; despicable
PAMPAS treeless plains (S. Amer.)   bt
PAMPER indulge; coddle; humour
PANADA bread pulp   ck
PANAMA hat
PANARY store-house for bread; pantry

PANDER a procurer
PANDIT pundit; a learned man
PANDUR robber; Austrian soldier
PANFRY cook in frying pan   ck
PANFUL filling a pan   ck
PANGED emotionally upset
PANISC Pan as a satyr
PANMUG crockery; butter-pan
PANNED yielded   mn
PANNEL rustic saddle
PANNER a nagger; faultfinder
PANNUS birthmark; a dressing   md
PANSER belly-armour (obs.)
PANTED gasped; blew; palpitated
PANTER a snare; panther   zo
PANTON a special kind of horseshoe
PANTRY food storage closet
PANZER armoured corps (Ger.)
PAPACY (Pope); popery   rl
PAPAIN digestive enzyme   md
PAPAYA large sub-tropical fruit; pawpaw   bt
PAPERY resembling paper
PAPISH papist
PAPISM Popery
PAPIST Roman Catholic
PAPPUS hairy tuft   bt
PAPUAN from New Guinea
PAPULA pimple   md
PAPYRI scrolls of papyrus (Egypt)
PARADE show; display; flaunt
PARAMO wind-swept desert in Andes
PARANG heavy Malay knife
PARAPH a flourish to a signature
PARCAE the Fates
PARCEL packet; bundle; piece; share
PARDON remit; condone; forgive
PARDON mercy
PAREIL an equal
PARENT author; producer; cause
PAREVE made without animal products   ck
PARFAY! by or in faith!
PARGET rough plaster; gypsum
PARIAH outcast; mongrel   zo
PARIAN (marble); (porcelain)
PARINE pertaining to titmouse
PARING rind; shaving; reducing
PARISH a county subdivision
PARITY equality; parage
PARKED (left); enclosed; assembled   au
PARKER park-keeper; (nosey)
PARKIN perkin; Lancashire cake   ck
PARLAY expand; exploit
PARLEY confer; discuss; talk
PARODY travesty; burlesque; caricature
PAROLE word of honour
PAROUS with borne offspring
PARRAL ⎫ collar to prevent spars from
PARREL ⎬ slipping from the mast   nt
PARROT to repeat by rote   zo
PARSEC interstellar distance unit   me

PARSED analysed grammatically	
PARSEE Persian living in India	
PARSON vicar; clergyman	rl
PARTAN crab (Sc.)	zo
PARTED left; broke; separated	
PARTER distributor; sharer	
PARTIM in part	
PARTLY not altogether	
PARURE set of jewels	
PARVIS court; portico	rl
PASSED ignored; spent; elapsed	
PASSEE faded (Fr.)	
PASSER a passer-by	
PASSIM here and there	
PASTED basted; gummed	
PASTEL crayon; chalk drawing	
PASTIL medicated lozenge	md
PASTOR shepherd; starling	rl, zo
PASTRY confiserie	
PATCHY unequal	
PATENT spreading; open; copyright	lw
PATERA shallow circular dish	
PATHAN Afghan	
PATHIC (diseases)	md
PATHOS deep emotion	
PATINA glow given by age	
PATINE paten; eucharistic plate	rl
PATOIS dialect (Fr.)	
PATROL mobile armed guard	
PATRON friend; helper; protector	
PATTED tapped	
PATTEN a clog	
PATTER high speed talk	
PATTLE a paddle	
PAUNCH the belly	
PAUPER indigent person	
PAUSAL ceasing; pausing	
PAUSED hesitated; halted; tarried	
PAUSER a deliberator; a demurrer	
PAVAGE paving cost	
PAVANE stately dirge; pavan	mu
PAVIER ⎫ paver; pavement layer	
PAVIOR ⎭	
PAVING surfacing	
PAVISE great shield	
PAWING flattering; scrapping; handling	
PAWNED pledged; risked; hazarded	
PAWNEE N. American Indian tribe	
PAWNEE pawnbroker	
PAWNER a borrower on security	
PAWPAW papaw; a tropical fruit	bt
PAWWAW powwow; a palaver	
PAXWAX tendon; faxwax	zo
PAY-DAY day when wages paid	
PAYING gainful; punishing; tarring	
PAYNIM painim; infidel; heathen	
PAY-OFF payment; denouement	nt
PAYOLA bribe to mention on media	
PEACHY like a peach	
PEACOD pea-pod	bt
PEAHEN a peafowl	zo

PEAKED looked ill; pointed	nt
PEALED resounded; reverberated	
PEANUT the ground-nut	bt
PEA-ORE oxide of iron	mn
PEA-POD pea seed envelope	bt
PEARLY transparent; translucent	
PEBBLE a stone; an agate	mn
PEBBLY shingly	
PECKED stumbled	
PECKER woodpecker; courage	zo
PECTEN bivalve genus; scallop	zo
PECTEN eye membrane of a bird	zo
PECTIC congealing; gelatinizing	
PECTIN (apple jelly)	
PECTUS insect sclerite; vertebrate breast	zo
PEDALE altar foot-cloth	rl
PEDANT schoolmaster; precise person	
PEDATE divided like a foot	bt
PEDDLE to sell retail; to trifle	
PEDION single-plane crystal	
PEDLAR ⎫ hawker; vendor; bagman	
PEDLER ⎭	
PEECED imperfect (Spens.)	
PEELED stripped; skinned; pillaged	
PEELER policeman (Sir Robert Peel)	
PEENGE whimper (Sc.)	
PEEPED chirped; glimpsed; snooped	
PEEPER (chicken); the eye	zo
PEEPUL sacred tree; Indian bo-tree	bt
PEERER a peeping Tom	
PEERIE peg-top (Sc.)	
PEEVED annoyed; fretful	
PEEWIT green plover; lapwing	zo
PEGGED fixed; toiled	
PEG-LEG wooden leg	
PEG-TOP a spinning top	
PELAGE animal fur	zo
PELIKE double-handled Greek vase	
PELION and Ossa, mountains	
PELLET small ball or shot	
PELMET curtain housing	
PELOTA a Basque ball game	
PELTER rainstorm; shower of missiles	
PELTRY skins with fur on them	
PELVIC (pelvis)	pl
PELVIS a bony cavity	pl
PENCIL light rays; small brush	
PENDED held up; balanced	
PENFUL contents of a pen	
PENIAL pertaining to penis	pl
PENMAN scribe; author; clerk	
PENNAL freshman (Ger.); student	
PENNED wrote; indited; enclosed	
PENNER writer; scribe	
PENNON pennant; flag; streamer	nt
PENSEE thought (Fr.)	
PENSUM an imposition; examination	
PENTAD set of five	
PENT-UP confined; mewed	
PENULT last but one	
PENURY need; want; indigence	

PEOPLE mob; rabble; populace; nation		**PHONEY** specious; sham; bogus	
PEPITA nugget of gold (Sp.)		**PHONIC** phonetic	
PEPLIS water-purslane	bt	**PHONON** quantum of thermal energy	me,p
PEPLUM ⎱ robe worn by		**PHOSSY** caused by phosphorus	
PEPLUS ⎰ Greek women	tx	**PHOTON** unit of light energy	me
PEPPER pelt with shot	bt	**PHRASE** idiom; diction; style	
PEPSIN (gastric juice)	md	**PHYLON** ⎱ biological group	
PEPTIC digestive		**PHYLUM** ⎰	
PERDIE! pardieu!		**PHYSIC** dose; drug; medicine	bt, md
PERDUE perdu; hidden; concealed		**PHYTIC** of a cereal acid	ch
PERIOD age; era; term; epoch; stage		**PHYTON** bud	
PERISH die; wither; expire; pass		**PIACLE** sin, crime	
PERKED smartened up		**PIAFFE** a horse gait (Sp.)	
PERKIN perry; see parkin		**PIAZZA** square; market place (It.)	
PERMIT let; grant; sanction; tolerate		**PICARD** high shoe (Fr.)	
PERNIS honey-buzzard	zo	**PICENE** coal-tar hydrocarbon	ch
PERONE fibula		**PICKED** chose; culled; pilfered	
PERRON external stairway		**PICKER** selector; collector	
PERSIC Persian		**PICKET** sharp stake; guard	
PERSON individual; party; someone		**PICKLE** preserve	
PERSUE a track (Spens.)		**PICK/UP** (motoring)	ro
PERTLY impudently; saucily		**PICNIC** alfresco meal	
PERUKE a periwig; a vallancy		**PICRIC** trinitro-phenol; lyddite	ch
PERUSE read; scrutinize; observe		**PIDGIN** Chinese English	
PESADE an equine evolution		**PIECED** mended; joined; augmented	
PESETA Spanish money	nm	**PIECER** patcher	
PESHWA Mahratta chief		**PIEDOG** a pariah; pye-dog	zo
PESTER vex; worry; harass; nettle		**PIELED** peeled; bare; bald (Shak.)	
PESTLE a pulveriser		**PIEMAN** (Simple Simon)	
PETARD explosive machine; bomb		**PIERCE** drill; bore; perforate	
PETARY a peat-bog		**PIERID** belonging to certain butterfly group	
PETITE small (Fr.)		**PIFFLE** nonsense; worthless talk	
PETREL sea-bird	zo	**PIGEON** sometimes a gull	zo
PETROL gasoline	ch	**PIGGIN** small bowl	
PETTED fondled; caressed; indulged		**PIGNON** pine seed	bt
PETTLE indulge (Sc.)		**PIGNUT** ground nut	bt
PEWTER an alloy of tin and lead		**PIG-STY** pig enclosure	
PEYOTE cactus; source of mescalin	bt	**PILAFF** rice dish	ck
PEZIZA cup-shaped fungi	bt	**PILARY** hairy; comate	p
PHANIC visible; obvious		**PILEUM** top of head in birds	zo
PHAROS lighthouse		**PILE-UP** crash (motoring)	
PHASEL French bean	bt	**PILEUS** mushroom cap	bt
PHASIS a phase		**PILFER** purloin; filch; peculate	
PHASMA leaf insects, etc.	zo	**PILING** amassing; stacking; heaping	
PHATIC of speech as mood implement		**PILLAR** post; column; support	
PHEESE to beat; to worry (Sc.)		**PILLED** black-balled	
PHENIC carbolic	ch	**PILLOW** a block; bearing	n
PHENIX fabulous bird; phoenix	zo	**PILOSE** ⎱ hairy; comate	
PHENOL carbolic acid		**PILOUS** ⎰	
PHENYL an organic radicle	ch	**PILULA** ⎱ a small pill	me
PHINOC sea trout	zo	**PILULE** ⎰	
PHLEGM calmness; indifference		**PI-MODE** multicavity magnetron operation	
PHLEME lancet	md	**PIMPLE** a pustule	me
PHLEUM cat's-tail grass, etc.	bt	**PIMPLY** having pimples	
PHLOEM bast tissue	bt	**PINANG** betel nut	b
PHOBIA morbid fear or aversion	md	**PINARD** red Algerian wine	ch
PHOBOS a satellite of Mars		**PINCOP** weft in power loom	
PHOCAL (seal)	zo	**PINDAR** Greek poet	
PHOEBE the moon-goddess	rl	**PINDER** pinner; impounder	
PHOLAS stone-boring molluscs	zo	**PINEAL** like a pine cone	b
PHONED telephoned		**PINENE** terpene	ch

PINERY hothouse	bt
PINGED whistled by	
PINGLE dawdle	
PINING languishing; desiring	
PINION feather; wheel; to shackle	
PINITE (iolite)	mn
PINKED pierced; pricked; stabbed	
PINNED transfixed	
PINNER pinmaker; pinder	
PINNET pinnacle (Sc.)	
PINOLE meal of sorts (USA)	
PINTLE iron bolt	nt
PINXIT he painted it	
PIONED full of peonies (Shak.)	
PIONER a pioneer (Shak.)	
PIPAGE pipe-distribution	
PIPING boiling; shrill; feeble	
PIPKIN boiler; small pot	
PIPPED pilled; just defeated	
PIPPIN apple	bt
PIQUED offended; irritated	
PIQUET card game; picket	
PIRACY buccaneering; (copyright)	
PIRATE freebooter; corsair; picaroon	
PIRNIE night cap (Sc.)	
PISANG plantain; banana	bt
PISCES the fishes (Zodiac sign)	
PISTIL part of flower	bt
PISTOL a fire-arm	
PISTON part of engine	au
PITAKA Buddhist scriptures	rl
PITCHY black; dark; tarry	
PITHED central nervous system destroyed	
PITHOS round Greek vase	
PITIED commiserated	
PITIER a compassionate party	
PITMAN a miner	
PITSAW large saw	to
PITTED pock-marked; matched	
PLACED invested; ascribed; put	
PLACER auriferous gravel	
PLACET Latin affirmation; 'so be it'	
PLACID serene; calm; even; tranquil	
PLAGAL (Gregorian music)	mu
PLAGUE pest; contagion; pester	
PLAGUY vexatious; harassing	
PLAICE plaise; fish	zo
PLAINT lamentation; dirge; wail	lw
PLAISE plaice	zo
PLANCH to cover with planks	
PLANED smoothed; (aeroplane)	
PLANER planing machine	to
PLANET a celestial body	
PLANISH to hammer smooth	
PLANTA vertebrate foot sole	zo
PLAQUE an ornament	
PLAQUE destructive coating on teeth	md
PLASHY sloppy	
PLASMA quartz; congealed blood	md
PLATAN plane tree	bt
PLATED overlaid; armoured	

PLATEN the roller of a typewriter	
PLATER race-horse	zo
PLATEY flat	
PLAYED sported; trifled; acted	
PLAYER professional cricketer	mu
PLEACH interweave	
PLEASE like; prefer; delight; oblige	
PLEDGE security; plight; pawn; toast	
PLEIAD a star	as
PLEION flat platelike structure	zo
PLENTY abundance; profusion	
PLENUM space; a full assembly	
PLEUGH plough (Sc.)	
PLEURA (lungs)	md
PLEVIN assurance	lw
PLEXOR hammer used with pleximeter	
PLEXUS nerve centre	md
PLIANT flexible; limber; lithe; facile	
PLIERS plyers	to
PLIGHT promise; dilemma; predicament	
PLINTH pedestal	ar
PLISSE pleated/woven cloth with shirred effect	tx
PLONGE superior slope of parapet	
PLOUGH plow; furrow; to pluck	
PLOVER bird	zo
PLOWED ploughed	
PLUCKY courageous; brave; bold	
PLUFFY puffy (Sc.)	
PLUG-IN connect to source	el, ro
PLUMAE stiff feathers	zo
PLUMED took pride in	
PLUMPY plump; fat; burly	
PLUNGE dip; dive; sink; souse	
PLURAL more than one	
PLUSHY like plush	tx
PLUTUS the god of wealth	
PLYERS pliers	to
PLYING folding; touting; urging	
PNEUMA breath; spirit	
POACHY set and soft	
POCKED pitted	
POCKET pouch; cavity; a poke	
PODERE country estate, farm (It.)	
PODGER tightening wrench for tubular coupling	
PODIAL stalk-like	bt
PODITE lobster's limb	zo
PODIUM pedestal; balcony; stylobate	
PODZOL leached subpolar strata	gl
POETIC lyrical; metrical	
POETRY poesy; verse	
POGROM plunder and massacre (Rus.)	
POINTE tip of toes (ballet)	
POISED suspended in equilibrium	
POISER a balancer	
POISON taint; venom; pest; bane	
POKING thrusting	
POLACK a Pole	
POLDER reclaimed, drained land in Holland	
POLICE constabulary	
POLICY statesmanship; strategy; plan	

POLING scaffolding; punting		
POLISH furbish; burnish; lustre		
POLITE courtly; urbane; civil		
POLITY the constitution		
POLLAM jurisdiction of Ind. chief	lw	
POLLAN a salmon-type of Irish fish	zo	
POLLED cropped; lopped; voted		
POLLEN flower seed; fine bran	bt	
POLLER voter; tree-trimmer		
POLLEX thumb	md	
POLLUX twin brother of Castor		
POLONY sausage	ck	
POLYAD polygamous element	ch	
POLYPE polyp; aquatic animal	zo	
POMACE crushed fruit		
POMADE perfumed hair unguent		
POMELO a citrus fruit; shaddock	bt	
POMMEL part of saddle; belabour		
POMONA goddess of fruit		
POM-POM quick-firing gun		
POMPON ornament; a tuft		
PONCHO cloak (S. America)		
PONDER weigh; meditate; ruminate		
PONENT western		
PONGEE soft woven silk		
PONGYI Buddhist priest (Burma)		
PONTAC claret		
PONTEE pontil	gs, to	
PONTIC (Black Sea)		
PONTIL glass-maker's iron rod	to	
PONTON lighter; pontoon		
POODLE curly-haired dog	zo	
POOGYE nose-flute (Ind.)	mu	
POOLED shared; amalgamated		
POOLER leather worker	le	
POONAC pulp refuse		
POOPED overtaken by a wave		
POORER more impecunious; inferior		
POORLY indisposed		
POPERY Roman Catholicism		
POPGUN an air gun of sorts		
POPISH of Catholics; denigratory		
POPLAR genus of trees; abele	bt	
POPLIN silk stuff (Fr.)		
POPPED pawned; proposed; exploded		
POPPER a pistol; maize-popper		
POPPET puppet; head of a lathe		
POPPLE to bob about		
PORGIE bream fish	zo	
PORING sweating; brooding, studying		
PORISM corollary		
PORITE a species of coral	mn	
PORKER young pig	zo	
PORKET porker	zo	
POROID having obvious pores	bt	
PORRON wine bottle with descending spout		
POROSE of pore-pierced cell walls	bt	
POROUS porose; interstitial limestone	gl	
PORRET small onion; leek	bt	
PORTAL gate; entry; entrance		
PORTED conveyed	nt	
PORTER door-keeper; carrier		

PORTLY burly; stout; imposing		
POSEDA a Spanish inn		
POSEUR poser; an affected person		
POSING feigning; puzzling; posturing		
POSNET small bowl		
POSSET a bedtime drink	ck	
POSSUM opossum	zo	
POSTAL (order); (Union)		
POSTEA record of subsequent events		
POSTED set; stationed; hastened		
POSTER bill; placard; advertisement		
POSTIL marginal note; a homily		
POT-ALE distillery refuse	br	
POTALE grain refuse	br	
POTASH alkali; potass	ch	
POTATO murphy; a tuber	bt	
POTBOY a junior tapster		
POTEEN home-made spirits (Irish)	ck	
POTENT efficacious; powerful; cogent		
POTHER bother; bristle; fuss; ado		
POTION dose; draught; philter		
POT-LID a cover		
POTMAN barman; general factotum		
POTTAH lease (Ind.)		
POTTED preserved; abbreviated		
POTTER clay-worker		
POTTLE 4 pints (2.2 litres); a tankard	me
POTTLE a small basket for fruit		
POUDRE powdered (Fr.)		
POUFFE a cushion (Fr.)		
POULPE octopus; poulp	zo	
POUNCE suddenly snatch; seize		
POUNCE claw of a bird of prey	zo	
POUNCE fine blotting powder		
POURED uttered; flowed; gushed		
POURER the lady of the tea-pot		
POUSSE bitters added to a drink		
POUTED registered displeasure		
POUTER } pigeon having an inflated		
POWTER } breast	zo	
POWDER crush; pulverize; sprinkle		
POW-WOW incantation; conference		
PRAISE laud; extol; eulogize; encomium		
PRANCE to bound; to spring		
PRANZO meal (It.)	ck	
PRATED orated; gabbled; talked		
PRATER a chatter-box		
PRAXIS use; practice; an example		
PRAYED supplicated; craved; besought		
PRAYER petition; entreaty; orison		
PREACH teach; exhort; declare		
PRECIS prayers		
PRECIS summary; abstract		
PRECUT uniformity of size, shape		
PREDAL rapacious; voracious; ravenous		
PREFAB a prefabricated house	a
PREFER pick; select; choose; promote		
PREFIX appoint beforehand		
PREPAY pay in advance		
PRESEE foresee; anticipate; foretell		
PRESES chairman (Sc.)		
PRESTO quickly; (conjuror) (It.)	mu

PRETER a prefix; beyond
PRETOR praetor; Roman judge
PRETTY neat; comely; pleasing; canning
PRETTY the fairway of a golf course
PRE-WAR from before a war
PREYED ravened; ravaged; despoiled
PREYER a plunderer; freebooter
PRICED appraised; valued
PRICEY expensive
PRIDED plumed; arrogated
PRIEST pastor; divine; minister   rl
PRIMAL primary; main; first; original
PRIMER detonator
PRIMER prayer-book; type of type
PRIMET privet (dialect)   bt
PRIMLY precisely; formally; demurely
PRIMUS bishop (Sc.); first   rl
PRINCE sovereign; lord; ruler
PRIORY monastery   rl
PRISED prized; levered
PRISMY prismatic
PRISON jail; gaol; quod; restrain
PRIVET genus of shrub; primet   bt
PRIZED valued; esteemed
PRIZER an appraiser
PROBAN flameproof fabric finish   ch, tx
PROBUD reproductive bodies in cyclo-
   myaria
PROCES law-suit (Fr.)   lw
PROFIT gain; benefit; advantage
PROJET a proposal; draft
PROKER a poker (dial.)
PROLAN mammal pregnancy hormone   pl
PROLEG a caterpillar's leg   zo
PROLIX long-winded; verbose
PROMPT urge; incite; quick; apt
PRONTO precipitately
PROPED pseudo-leg   zo
PROPEL hurl; cast; throw; impel
PROPER correct; accurate; seemly
PROSED conversed in lengthy periods
PROSER tedious speaker
PROSIT! here's luck! a toast!
PROTEA S. African flowering shrubs   bt
PROTON electrical nucleus
PROVED tested; verified; established
PROVEN proved; justified
PROVER demonstrator; assayer
PROXAN chemical herbicide
PRUINA powdery bloom on plant surfaces
PRUNED trimmed; clipped; lopped
PRUNUS genus of trees and shrubs   bt
PRUTAH Israeli coin   nm
PRYING peeping; curious; inquisitive
PSEUDO false; spurious
PSORIC (psora); itchy   md
PSYCHE maiden beloved by Cupid
PTERIC of wing or shoulder   zo
PTERIS fern genus   bt
PTERNA heel-pad in birds   zo
PTERON Greek portico
PTISAN barley water; tisane   ck

PTOSIS (fallen eyelid)   md
PTYXIS leaf-folding in bud   bt
PUBLIC open; common; general
PUCKER wrinkle; crease; furrow
PUDDER tumult; pother
PUDDLE muddy pool; (iron)
PUDDLY dirty; foul
PUDEUR sexual modesty (Fr.)
PUEBLO S. American town or village
PUFFED fuffed; blown
PUFFER globe-fish   zo
PUFFIN bird; an auk   zo
PUG-DOG a lap-dog   zo
PUGREE Indian hat scarf
PUISNE inferior in rank
PUKKHA pucka; real (Ind.)
PULING whimpering; whining
PULLED drawn; hauled; extracted
PULLER hauler; an attraction
PULLET young hen   zo
PULLEY grooved wheel; tackle
PULL-IN, PULL-UP roadside halt
PULL-ON boxing gloves
PULPED, PULPER mashed, machine-
   shredded
PULPIT rostrum; ambo   rl
PULQUE a Mexican beverage   ck
PULSAR space radio-energy source   as
PULSED throbbed; vibrated
PULTUN native infantry regiment (Ind.)
PULVIL scented powder
PULWAR Ganges boat
PUMELO pomelo; shaddock; fruit
PUMICE spongy lava   mn
PUMPED exhausted; interrogated
PUMPER cross-examiner; pump man
PUNCHI Kashmiri people
PUNCHY fat; stocky
PUNCTO point (fencing); punctilio
PUNDIT savant; wiseacre
PUNICA pomegranate   bt
PUNIER weaker; feebler
PUNISH correct; chasten; scourge
PUNKAH fan (Ind.)
PUNNER a ram; maul   to
PUNNET basket for fruit
PUNTED betted; kicked
PUNTER gambler
PUPATE become a pupa   zo
PUPOID like a chrysalis   zo
PUPPED whelped; littered
PUPPET doll; marionette; pawn
PURANA sacred Sanskrit books   rl
PURDAH curtain; seclusion
PURELY simply; clearly; really
PUREST without blemish
PURFLE embroider
PURFLY wrinkled
PURGED cleared; purified; shriven
PURGER an aperient; laxative
PURIFY cleanse; clean
PURINE uric acid compound   ch

PURISM precision; nicety; exactness
PURIST stickler for style
PURITY chastity; fineness; simplicity
PURLED curled; swirled; knitted
PURLER a fall; a cropper
PURLIN a roof timber
PURPLE a cardinalate — rl
PURRED curred, (cats or pigeons)
PURSED contracted; wrinkled
PURSER paymaster — nt
PURSUE follow; track; chase; practise
PURVEY sell; cater; retail; procure
PUSHED urged; impelled; jostled
PUSHER type of plane; thruster
PUSHTU Afghan tongue
PUSULE small plant vacuole — bt
PUTEAL well-curb
PUTELI Ganges boat
PUTLOG short board; putlock
PUTRID corrupt; rotten; decaying
PUTSCH German revolt
PUTTED endeavoured to hole out
PUTTEE cloth legging; puttie (Ind.)
PUTTER a golf club
PUTTOO goat's-wool cloth — tx
PUZZLE bewilder; enigma; problem
PYCNID (fungus' spores) — bt
PYCNON a semi-tone — mu
PYEDOG piedog; a pariah — zo
PYEMIA blood-poisoning — md
PYEMIC septicaemic — md
PYGARG antelope (Herodotus) — zo
PYGARG osprey or sea-eagle — zo
PYKNIC fat (of persons) — md
PYLOME opening in sarcodina — zo
PYOSIS formation of pus — md
PYRENE fruit stone — bt
PYRENE tar product — ch
PYRITE pyrites — mn
PYROLA wintergreen — md
PYRONE heterocyclic compound — ch
PYROPE garnet — mn
PYTHIA Delphic oracle priestess
PYTHON serpent slain by Apollo — zo
PYURIA pus in urine — md

Q

QUADRA square frame or border
QUAERE enquire; seek (Latin)
QUAGGA extinct zebra (S. Africa) — zo
QUAGGY boggy; marshy
QUAHOG clam (N. America) — zo
QUAICH }
QUAIGH } drinking cup; tassie (Sc.)
QUAINT droll; fantastic; curious; odd
QUAKED shook; quivered; rocked
QUAKER a Friend
QUARRY pit; prey; victim; an arrow
QUARTE guard (fencing)
QUARTO a size of book — pr

QUARTZ silica — mn
QUASAR far-space radio-energy source — as
QUATCH squat; flat (Shak.)
QUAVER quiver; tremble; vibrate — mu
QUAYED having a wharf
QUBBAH domed tomb (Arabic)
QUEASY squeamish; fastidious
QUEEST ring-dove — zo
QUEINT quaint (Spens.)
QUELCH squelch
QUELEA weaver-bird — zo
QUENCH extinguish; slake
QUERRY an equerry; groom
QUESAL } resplendent trogon;
QUEZAL } brilliant green bird — zo
QUEUED lined up
QUHILK whilk; which (Sc.)
QUICHE cheese-egg-meat flan — ck
QUIDAM somebody (Latin)
QUIHYE Anglo-Indian (Bengal)
QUIJAL badge of Guatemala
QUILCH couch grass — bt
QUILLS clerk
QUINCE fruit — bt
QUINIC (quinine) — md
QUINOA Mexican oats — bt
QUINOL reducing agent — pg
QUINSY tonsilitis — md
QUINTA villa in Madeira
QUINZE card game
QUIRED in quires; sang in harmony — pr
QUIRKY evasive; artful; illusive
QUITCH couch grass — bt
QUIVER case for arrows; vibrate
QUORUM a valid executive — lw
QUOTED referred; repeated; mentioned
QUOTER a citer
QUOTHA forsooth
QUOTUM share; proportion

R

RABATE beat down; an abatement
RABATO turned-down collar; rebato
RABBAN super-rabbi
RABBET a groove in a plank
RABBIN Jewish lawyer or rabbi
RABBIT timid breeder and burrower — zo
RABBLE the mob; iron puddling bar
RABIES madness — md
RACEME a cluster — bt
RACHIS backbone; spine — bt, zo
RACIAL ethnic; colour judgement
RACILY piquantly; spicily; pungently
RACING contesting; competing
RACISM superiority theory
RACKED strained; wrestled; ambled
RACKER a torturer; storer
RACKET snow-shoe; clamour; (tennis)
RACKLE rattle; crackle

RADDLE twist; red ochre	
RADIAL like a ray	
RADIAN an angle of 57.3 degrees	
RADISH plant	bt
RADIUM metal	mn
RADIUS bone of forearm	md, bt
RADOUB refitting of a ship	nt
RADULA mollusc's tongue	zo
RAFALE burst of fire; squall	
RAFFED swept; huddled together	
RAFFEE, RAFFIE schooner sail	nt
RAFFIA palm fibre	bt
RAFFLE sweepstake; draw; lottery	
RAFTER roof-timber; lumberman	
RAGBAG odd scraps of fabric	tx
RAG DAY students' carnival	
RAGGED jagged; uneven; torn	
RAGGEE Indian millet	bt
RAGGLE notch irregularly	
RAGING wroth; rabid; furious	
RAGLAN loose overcoat style	tx
RAGLET narrow masonry groove	ar, pb
RAGMAN rag-picker	
RAGOUT stew; a spicy mixture	ck
RAG-TAG riff-raff	
RAGULY jagged	hd
RAIBLE rabble (Sc.)	
RAIDER invader; plunderer	
RAILER scoffer; sneerer	
RAILEX postal express service	
RAISER producer	
RAISIN a dried grape	bt, ck
RAJPUT Royal Hindu	
RAKERY debauchery	
RAKING inclining; enfilading	
RAKISH dissolute; licentious	
RALLUS water-rails, etc.	zo
RAMAGE boughs of tree	bt
RAMARK non-directional radio beacon	nv
RAMBLE excursion; stroll; roam	
RAM-CAT tom-cat	zo
RAMEAL branching	bt
RAMENT bristle-shaped leaflet	bt
RAMIFY branch; divide; sub-divide	
RAMISM system of logic	
RAMJET open duct combustion	ae
RAMMED butted; crammed	
RAMMEL refuse wood	
RAMMER sand-packing hand tool	to
RAMOON mulberry (W. Indies)	bt
RAMOUS, RAMOSE branched	
RAMPED bounded; sprang	
RAMPER race-course rough	
RAMROD gun-bore stuffer	
RAMSON hedgerow garlic	bt
RAMULE small branch	bt
RANCHO ranch; stock farm; ranche	
RANCID sour; musty; fetid	
RANDAN a row boat	nt
RANDLE plate rack	
RANDOM casual; haphazard; fortuitous	

RANGED extended; disposed	
RANGER park-keeper; rover	
RANGIA a bivalve genus	zo
RANINE frog-like	zo
RANKER fouler; officer from the ranks	
RANKLE fester; burn; smoulder	
RANKLY rampantly; excessively	
RANSOM a fine for redemption	
RANTAN clatter of pots and pans	
RANTER spouter; boisterous preacher	
RANULA frog-tongue	md
RAPHIA raffia; palm fibre	bt
RAPHIS crystal in plant cell	bt
RAPIDO with rapidity; express	mu
RAPIER a thrusting sword	
RAPINE pillage; spoliation; plunder	
RAPING ravishing; violating	
RAPPED tapped; struck	
RAPPEE snuff	
RAPPEL call to arms	
RAPPEN Swiss centime (coin)	nm
RAPPER knocker; arouser	
RAPTOR a ravisher; a hawk	zo
RAPTUS trance, seizure	
RAREFY attenuate	
RARELY seldom; infrequently	
RAREST sparsest; thinnest; scarcest	
RARITY scarcity; fewness; tenuity	
RASANT flanking; raking	
RASCAL rogue; scamp; knave; caitiff	
RASHER thin slice; hastier	
RASHLY audaciously; recklessly	
RASING razing; levelling	
RASION rasure; an erasure	
RASPED filed; abraded; grated	
RASPER scraper; stiff fence	
RASTER cathode ray projector	tv
RASURE an erasure	
RATANY Peruvian shrub	bt
RATEEN ratteen; woollen fabric	
RATHER sooner; preferably; slightly	
RATIFY confirm; endorse; approve	
RATINE rough-surface dress fabric	tx
RATING tonnage; class; seaman	nt
RATION share; quota; portion	
RATITE flat-breasted	zo
RATLIN (shrouds)	nt
RATOON sugarcane sprout	bt
RAT-PIT no such thing	
RATTAN drum-beat; basketry	bt
RAT-TAT postman's knock	
RATTED deserted; informed upon	
RATTEN stealing non-unionists' tools	
RATTER rat-catcher	
RATTLE chatter; vibrate; a herb	bt
RAUCID raucous; hoarse	
RAUCLE rough; fearless (Sc.)	
RAVAGE spoil; lay waste; ransack	
RAVINE gulch; gulley; gorge; defile	
RAVING delirious; raging; frenzied	
RAVISH rape; violate; delight	

RAWISH somewhat raw	**REDBUD** Judas tree	bt
RAYING radiating; shining	**REDCAP** goldfinch	zo
RAY-OIL ray-fish oil	zo	**REDDED** tidied; arranged (Sc.)	
RAZING overthrowing; rasing	**REDDEN** blush	
RAZURE rasure; an erasure	**REDDLE** raddle; red chalk	
RAZZIA a foray (Algerian); police raid	**RED-DOG** low-grade flour	ck
READER proof corrector; reading book	**REDEEM** ransom; free; retrieve	
REALIA 3-dimensional exhibits	**RED-EYE** rudd; carp	zo
REALLY truly; verily; actually	**RED-GUM** eucalyptus	bt
REALTY real estate	lw	**RED-HOT** extreme	
REAMED frothed; enlarged; edged	**RED-LAC** Japanese wax-tree	bt
REAMED rotatory cutter	to	**RED-OAK** N. American oak	bt
REAPED acquired; cropped; obtained	**REDOUT** fort	
REAPER harvester; a machine	**REDOWA** Bohemian dance	mu
REARED erected; educated	**REDRAW** redraft; copy	
REARER an up-bringer	**RED-TOP** kind of grass	bt
REASON argue; intelligence; motive	**REDUCE** degrade; curtail; abridge	
REASTY rancid; rotting	**REDUCT** a diminution in size	
REAVED bereaved; robbed	**REDUIT** redoubt; redout	
REAVER reiver; freebooter	**RED-WUD** stark mad (Sc.)	
REAVOW avow again	**REEBOK** rhebok; S. African antelope	zo
RE-BACK to repair spine of book	pr	**RE-ECHO** repeat; reverberate	
REBATE blunt; abatement; a rabbet	**REECHY** smoke-stained	
REBATE freestone; discount	mn	**REEDED** covered with reeds	
REBATO a ruff; rabato	**REEDEN** (reeds)	
REBECK Moorish violin	mu	**RE-EDIT** compile new edition	
REBIND refasten	**REEFER** wind-jacket; drugged cigarette	nt
REBITE engraving; acid process	pr	**REEFER** refrigerated ship	nt
REBOIL seethe again	**REEKED** exhaled; fumed; smelt	
REBORE worn-cylinder treatment	au	**REELED** staggered; span; swayed	
REBORN re-incarnated	**REELER** the grasshopper warbler	zo
REBUFF snub; repel; repulse	**REFAIT** a drawn game (Fr.)	
REBUKE upbraid; reprove; chide	**REFILL** replenish; film cassette	pg
REBURY inter again	**RE-FIND** retrieve	
RECALL revoke; rescind; retract	**REFINE** clarify; purify; cleanse	
RECANT adjure; renounce; deny	**REFLET** iridescent glaze	
RECAST compute again	**REFLEX** reactive; introspective	
RECEDE ebb; retire; withdraw	**REFLOW** re-issue	
RECENT modern; late; new; novel	**REFLUX** ebb; return; redound	
RECEPT extraneous idea	**REFOLD** replicate	
RECESS niche; alcove; nook	**REFORM** amend; remodel; better	
RECIPE prescription; formula	ck	**REFUEL** take in more fuel	
RECITE tell; relate; repeat; recount	**REFUGE** security; sanctuary; asylum	
RECKED regarded; heeded	**REFUND** repay; return; restore	
RECKON deem; calculate; estimate	**REFUSE** veto; decline; deny; trash	
RECOAL refuel	**REFUTE** disprove; confute	
RECOCT re-cooked; to vamp up	**REGAIN** retrieve; recover; recapture	
RECOIL kick; rebound; shrink	**REGALE** feast; entertain; gratify	
RECOIN remint	nm	**REGALO** a gift; a sumptuous repast	
RECORD enter; note; achievement	**REGARD** note; watch; repute	
RECORD a gramophone disc	**REGENT** ruling; a ruler during minority	
RECOUP indemnify; make good	**REGIME** diet; system; administration	
RECTOR academic leader; vicar	rl	**REGINA** a queen	
RECUIL ⎫ recoil (Spens.)	**REGION** province; tract; vicinity	
RECULE ⎭	**REGIUS** ⎫ appointed by the Crown	
RECUMB to repose	**REGIUM** ⎭	
RECURE recover	**REGIVE** restore	
RECUSE reject	lw	**REGLET** flat moulding	
RECTUM section of intestine above anus	**REGLET** spacing block	pr
RECTUS equal-width muscle	zo	**REGLOW** to recalesce; rekindle	
REDACT to reduce; to edit	pr	**REGNAL** during the reign of	

REGNUM badge of loyalty
REGRET rue; deplore; remorse
REGULA book of rules
REHASH discuss again; rearrange
REHEAD head again
RE-HEAL to heal again
REIGLE a channel or guide
REINED curbed
REITER German trooper
REIVER reaver; robber; freebooter
REJECT jilt; spurn; discard; repudiate
REJOIN reunite
REJOLT a new shock
RELAID (carpets)
RELAIS a rampart walk   ro
RELAND land again
RELATE tell; recite; narrate; report
RELENT relax; yield; soften
RELICT a widow (obs.)
RELIED depended on; confided
RELIEF aid; redress; alleviation
RELIER a trusting person
RELISH appreciate; zest; gusto; taste
RELIVE revive
RELOAD recharge; refill
RELUCT to resist (obs.)
RELUME to rekindle
REMADE (golf balls); refashioned
REMAIN persist; tarry; stop; survive
REMAKE revamp
REMAND send back to custody
REMARK also re-mark; say; comment
REMBLE remove (dial.)
REMEDY cure; panacea
REMIGE large wing contour feather   zo
REMIND call to remembrance
REMISE release; give back   lw
REMISS slack; dilatory; negligent
REMORA a sucking fish   zo
REMORD strike with remorse (obs.)
REMOTE far; distant; secluded; slight
REMOVE dislodge; transport; eject
REMPLI heraldic colouring   hd
RENAME rechristen
RENARD Reynard, a fox   zo
RENATE renewed; born again
RENDER return; assign; supply; restore
RENEGE to revoke (cards)
RENNET enzyme for cheesemaking   ck
RENNIN gastric juice ferment   md
RENOWN fame; eminence; repute
RENTAL rent-roll; schedule
RENTED endowed; leased
RENTER lease-holder
RENTES French Government securities
RENULE small kidney   md
RENVOY return; dismissal (obs.)
RE-OPEN restart
REPACE retrace one's steps
REPAID requited; rewarded; liquidated
REPAIR patch; mend; restore; wend

REPAND bent back
RE-PART share; divide again
REPAST a meal; victuals; food
REPEAL annul; rescind; nullify
REPEAT iterate; renew; echo
REPENT creeping; rue; regret; deplore
REPINE fret; complain; murmur
RE-PLAN re-design; re-arrange
REPLUM a botanical structure   bt
REPONE re-appoint   lw
REPORT rumour; relate; bang
REPOSE lie; recline; rest; respite
REPOUR re-issue
REPPED ribbed
REPUGN oppose (Shak.)
REPUTE reputation; renown; regard
REQUIT requited; repaid (Spens.)
RESAIL put to sea again
RESALE a second sale
RESCUE save; redeem; release
RESEAT repair a seat
RESEAU a network
RESECT cut off   md, sv
RESEDA mignonette genus   bt
RESELL revend
RESENT dislike; repel; resist; hate
RESIDE live; dwell; lodge; sojourn
RESIGN also re-sign; forgo; yield
RESILE recede; start back
RESINY resinous; rosiny
RESIST oppose; thwart; withstand
RESORB swallow up
RESORT recourse; assemble; haunt
RESTED reposed; quieted; desisted
RESTEM force back; recheck
RESTIO plant genus   bt
RESULT ensue; outcome; sequel; end
RESUME renew; summarize; synopsis
RETAIL hawk; peddle; recount
RETAIN hold; keep; reserve; detain
RETAKE recapture
RETARD clog; hinder; impede; check
RETENE coal-tar constituent   ch
RETENT retained; held back
RE-TEST try again
RETINA a network of optic nerves   pl
RETINE cancer cell growth inhibitor   md
RETIRE recede; withdraw; shrink
RETOLD already narrated
RETOOK regained; recaptured
RETORT rejoinder; distilling vessel
RETOSE reticulated   bt
RETOSS throw again
RETOUR return (Sc.)
RETRAD backward
RETRAL posterior; retrorse
RETREE paper refuse; wastage
RETRIM embellish; smarten up
RETUND to dull; to blunt
RETURN also re-turn; restore; recur
RETUSE blunt

REUTER news agency
REVALE of cornices completed in position
REVAMP renovate; remake
REVEAL disclose; divulge; unveil
REVERB reverberate (Shak.)
REVERE adore; venerate; honour
REVERS revere; lapel
REVERT return; reverse; relapse
REVERY reverie; dream; trance
REVEST revert; clothe again (obs.)
REVIEW survey; inspect; critique
REVILE asperse; traduce; defame
REVISE reconsider; improve; correct
REVIVE rouse; invigorate; quicken
REVOKE annul; cancel; quash
REVOLT rebel; nauseate; mutiny
REVVED rotated at speed
REWARD guerdon; repay; premium
REWOOD afforest
REWORD change the phraseology
REXISM ⎫ Anti-Communist Belgian party
REXIST ⎭
RHAGON form of sponge
RHAPIS genus of Chinese palms   bt
RHESUS bandar; Indian monkey   zo
RHEUMY watery; rheumatic   md
RHEXIA genus of flowering plants   bt
RHEXIS rupture of bodily structure   md
RHINAE shark genus   zo
RHINAL nasal   md
RHIZIC radical; root-like   bt
RHUSMA a depilatory   ch
RHYMED harmonized
RHYMER versifier
RHYMIC almost poetic
RHYSSA ichneumon flies   zo
RHYTHM cadence; metre; symmetry
RHYTON Greek vase
RIALTO a bridge in Venice
RIANCY gaiety; laughter
RIBALD coarse; rude; gross; lewd
RIBAND a ribbon
RIBBED ridged; furrowed
RIBBON riband; strip
RIBIBE rebec; old woman (obs.)   mu
RIBLET rudimentary rib
RIBOSE pentose sugar in vitamin B-2   ch
RICCIA a plant genus   bt
RICHEN enrich; enhance
RICHER wealthier
RICHES abundance; affluence
RICHLY opulently; sumptuously
RICKED piled; sprained
RICKER thin round timber   fr
RICKLE small pile or rick (Sc.)
RICTAL gaping
RICTUS open mouth
RIDDEL altar-curtain   rl
RIDDEN p. part. of ride
RIDDER a remover
RIDDLE sieve; enigma; rebus

RIDEAU curtain (Fr.)
RIDGED ribbed; furrowed
RIDGEL ⎫ riglan; riggot; defective male   zo
RIDGIL ⎭
RIDING county sub-division
RIEVER reaver; robber; pirate
RIFELY abundantly
RIFFLE engraving tool   to
RIFLED pillaged; grooved
RIFLER robber; freebooter; plunderer
RIFTED cleft; split
RIGGED (the market)   nt
RIGGER an air-mechanic   nt
RIGGLE sand-eel   zo
RIGLET (see reglet); flat piece of wood
RIGOUR rigidity; austerity; harshness
RIG-OUT complete outfit; uniform
RILING annoying; irritating
RILLED trilled; flowed
RILLET rivulet; stream
RIMIST writer of doggerel
RIMLET thin rim
RIMMED bordered; edged
RIMMER pastry cutter
RIMMON Syrian god   rl
RIMOSE ⎫ gnarled
RIMOUS ⎭
RIMPLE wrinkle; rumple
RIMSAW   to
RIMULA fossil limpets   mn
RINDED peeled
RINDLE gutter; runnel; rine
RINGED encircled
RINGER expert shearer (Australia)
RINKED roller-skated
RINSED laved; cleansed; cleared
RINSER a washer
RIOTED brawled; luxuriated
RIOTER disturber of the peace
RIPECK ⎫
REPECK ⎬ punt pole for mooring
RYPECK ⎭
RIPELY maturely
RIPEST mellowest
RIPPED torn; rent
RIPPER foghorn; cutter   to
RIPPLE flax-comb; small wave
RIPPLY rippling
RIPPON a spur from Ripon
RIPRAP broken stone used for walls
RIPSAW a ripper   to
RISALA troop of native cavalry
RISBAN defended ground
RISING insurrection; towering
RISKED chanced
RISKER gambler; venturer
RISLEY an acrobat
RISQUE indelicate; audacious (Fr.)
RITELY with due rites
RITTER a knight (Ger.)
RITUAL rite; ceremony

RIVAGE the coast; shore; bank	**ROOMER** lodger	
RIVERY riparian	**ROOPIT** hoarse; roopy; roupy	
RIVINA the pokeweed genus	bt	**ROOTED** rootled; deep-set	
RIVING splitting; rending	**ROOTER** grubber	
RIVOSE tabby; furrowed	**ROOTLE** rookle; poke about like a pig	
RIZZER dry in the sun (Sc.)	**ROPERY** rope walk	
RIZZER a red currant (Sc.)	bt	**ROPING** lassoing	
RIZZLE to creep; frizzle (dial.)	**ROQUET** (croquet)	
ROAMED ranged; rambled	**ROSARY** a chaplet; string of beads	
ROAMER nomad; vagrant; stroller	**ROSCID** dewy; roric	
ROARED bawled; guffawed	**ROSEAL** rose-like	
ROARER broken-winded horse	zo	**ROSERY** a rose garden	
ROBALO a fish (USA)	zo	**ROSIED** adorned with roses	
ROBBED stole; despoiled; purloined	**ROSING** sprinkling	
ROBBER brigand; bandit; burglar	**ROSINY** resiny	
ROBBIN spun-yarn	**ROSSER** policeman (slang)	
ROBERD chaffinch	zo	**ROSTEL** embryo root; radicle	bt
ROBING attiring; dressing	**ROSTER** duty list; roll of names	
ROB-ROY a canoe	nt	**ROSULA** small rose	bt
ROBUST sturdy; vigorous; hale; hearty	**ROTARY** rotatory	
ROCCUS striped bass fish	zo	**ROTATE** spin; whirl; twirl; revolve	
ROCHEA a plant genus	bt	**ROTCHE** little auk	zo
ROCHET fish; the roach	zo	**ROT-GUT** bad liquor	
ROCHET bishop's surplice	rl	**ROTHER** roaring; lowing (Shak.)	
ROCKED reeled; tottered	**ROTTED** disintegrated; decayed	
ROCKEL a woman's cloak	**ROTTEN** corrupt; rank; moribund	
ROCKER mining cradle	**ROTTER** a pestilent person	
ROCKET Stephenson's locomotive 1829	**ROTULA** knee-cap	md
ROCKET firework; jet transport	**ROTUND** round; spherical	
ROCKIE rock-linnet	zo	**ROTURE** plebeian rank (Fr.)	
ROCOCO florid style	**ROUBLE** 100 kopecks (Russian)	nm
RODDIN rowan-tree (Sc.)	bt	**ROUCOU** a dye (anotto)	
RODENT gnawing	**ROUGED** powdered	
RODING evening flight	**ROUGET** swine-fever	
ROGGAN logan; rocking stone	**ROUNCE** a pulley; card game	
ROGGLE shake (dial.)	**ROUNCY** a nag; a hack	zo
ROILED riled; vexed	**ROUSED** ruffled; agitated; provoked	
ROINEK Boer name for British soldier	**ROUSER** a stimulator; inciter	
ROLAND legendary hero	**ROUTED** fled in disorder; defeated	
ROLLED trundled; rotated; turned	**ROUTER** sash-plane	to
ROLLER wave; blue crow; a sect	zo	**ROUTLE** grub up; rootle	
ROLL-IN hockey	**ROVERY** roving; nomadism	
ROMAGE tumult (Shak.)	**ROVING** rambling; ranging	
ROMAIC modern Greek	**ROWING** sculling	
ROMANT exaggerate; romance	**ROYENA** ebony	bt
ROMANY gipsy; gipsy language	**RUBACE** rock crystal	mn
ROMERO pilot-fish	zo	**RUBATO** change of rhythm	mu
ROMIST papist	**RUBBED** wiped; scoured; chafed; galled	
ROMPED frolicked; gambolled; sported	**RUBBER** coagulated latex	
ROMPER garment	**RUBBLE** undressed stone	
RONDEL short poem	**RUBBLY** broken	
RONDLE bastion turret	**RUBIAN** madder colour	
RONION } mangy animal; leprous lounger	**RUBIED** red as a ruby	
RONYON }	zo	**RUBIFY** to redden	
ROOFED covered	**RUBIGO** mildew; rust	bt
ROOFER tiler	**RUBINE** crimson dye; rubin	
ROOKED cheated	**RUB-OFF** incidental harm	
ROOKER swindler	**RUBRIC** a heading in red	rl
ROOKIE recruit	**RUCKLE** wrinkle; pucker	
ROOKLE rootle	**RUDDER** boat guiding device	nt
ROOMED lodged	**RUDDLE** red chalk or ochre	

RUDDOC robin redbreast   zo
RUDDOC kind of apple; gold coin   bt. nm
RUDELY boorishly; insolently
RUDEST most savage; crudest
RUEFUL mournful; sad; melancholy
RUELLE a coterie
RUFFED trumped
RUFFER comb for flax
RUFFIN freshwater perch   zo
RUFFLE a pleated border; disorder
RUFOUS ruddy; florid
RUGATE wrinkled; furrowed
RUGGED ragged; harsh; austere
RUGGER Rugby football
RUGINE surgeon's rasp   to
RUGOSA corals   mn
RUGOSE }
RUGOUS } wrinkled; rugate
RUINED wrecked; destroyed; beggared
RUINER demolisher
RULING governing; ascendant
RULLEY a dray
RUMBLE carriage-seat; reverberate
RUM-BUD grog-blossom
RUMKIN tailless fowl   zo
RUMMER drinking glass
RUMOUR report; bruit; hearsay
RUMPLE rimple; crumple; pucker
RUMPUS uproar; disturbance
RUM-TUM Thames sculling boat
RUNDLE a ladder-rung; a spoke
RUNKLE wrinkle
RUNLET, RUNNEL rivulet   nt
RUN-MAN naval deserter   nt
RUNNER racer; messenger
RUNNET rennet
RUN-OFF experimental, production-line method
RUN-OUT cricket; experiment
RUNRIG land tenure (Sc.)
RUNWAY track; airfield take-off path
RUPIAH (Indonesia)   nm
RUPPIA a grass genus   bt
RUSCUS butcher's broom   bt
RUSHED dashed; flew; ran; plunged
RUSHEN of rushes   bt
RUSHER impetuous person; thruster
RUSINE of E. Ind. maned deer   zo
RUSSEL woollen fabric; fox   zo
RUSSET homespun, apple   bt, tx
RUSSIA leather
RUSTED oxidized
RUSTIC rural; bucolic; pastoral
RUSTLE quiver; whisper
RUSTRE heraldic lozenge   hd
RUSURE earth-slide
RUTELA beetle genus   zo
RUTILE an oxide of titanium   ch
RUTTED grooved; furrowed
RUTTER a chart; trooper
RUTTLE gurgle; rattle (dial.)

RYPECK ripeck; repeck; punt-pole

S

SABALO the tarpon
SABEAN zabian
SABIAN star worshipper
SABINE plant; the savin   b
SABLED darkened; furred
SACBUT sackbut; stringed instrument   m
SACCOS Oriental vestment   rl, t
SACCUS pouchlike structure   z
SACHEL satchel
SACHEM Red Indian chief
SACHET scent bag
SACKED plundered; dismissed
SACKER sack-filling machine
SACRAL (pelvic arch)   F
SACRED holy; divine; consecrated
SACRUM a pelvis bone   b
SADDEN to grieve; depress
SADDLE burden; clog; encumber
SADDLE earth formation
SADINA sort of sardine   z
SADISM lustful cruelty
SADIST torturer; tormentor
SAETER Norwegian mountain hut
SAFARI caravan
SAFARI expedition
SAFELY securely; surely; reliably
SAFEST surest
SAFETY security; protection; safeguard
SAGELY wisely; sagaciously
SAGENE fishing net; a network
SAGENE 7ft (2.1 m) Russian   m
SAGEST wisest
SAGGAR sagger; fire-clay pot
SAGGED drooped; bent
SAGGER clay retort for stoneware
SAGINA pink genus   b
SAGOIN S. American monkey   z
SAGUIN capuchin monkey   z
SAHARA a desert
SAILED cruised   n
SAILOR A.B.; tar; seaman   n
SAIRLY sorely (Sc.)
SAITHE cod; ling, etc.   z
SAJENE sagene; 7ft (2.1 m) (Russian)   m
SAKIEH Persian water-wheel
SALAAM salutation (India)
SALAMI spiced sausage (It.)   c
SALARY pay; wages; stipend
SALIAN (Mars); salic
SALIFY to salten; add salt   ch, c
SALINA salt-marsh (Sp.)
SALINE salty; briny
SALITE to season with salt   c
SALITE monoclinic pyroxene   m
SALIVA spittle   m
SALLAL a fruit   b
SALLET light helmet

SALLIE } hired mourner (Sc.)		
SALUIE }		
SALLOW yellow; a willow	bt	
SALMIS ragout; salmi; a hash	ck	
SALMON highly prized fish	zo	
SALOON meeting room		
SALOOP a decoction of sassafras	bt, ck	
SALTED preserved		
SALTEN to preserve; made of salt		
SALTER salt-seller		
SALTIE a dab	zo	
SALTUS a mental jump		
SALUKI hunting dog (Iran)	zo	
SALUTE hail; greet; accost		
SALVED soothed; rescued		
SALVER a tray		
SALVIA sage	bt	
SALVOR a salvage expert		
SAMARA winged fruit	bt	
SAMARE old-fashioned jacket		
SAMBAL hot red-pepper paste	ck	
SAMBOO } sambar; Indian elk	zo	
SAMBUR }		
SAMELY monotonous; unvaried		
SAMIAN of Samos		
SAMIEL the simoon; hot wind		
SAMIOT native of Samos		
SAMITE silk		
SAMLET a parr; salmon	zo	
SAMOAN native of Samoa		
SAMPAN sanpan; Chinese boat	nt	
SAMPLE try; taste; specimen		
SAMSHU rice spirit (China)	ck	
AMYDA West Indian birch	bt	
ANCHO negro guitar	mu	
ANDAL a Barbary vessel; footwear	nt	
ANDIX } red lead;		
ANDYX } vermilion		
ANELY rationally		
ANEST most intelligent; soundest		
ANGAR stone breastwork		
ANGHA Buddhist church		
ANIES discharge from ulcer	md	
ANIFY to restore to health		
ANITY wisdom; normality; lucidity		
ANJAK division of a vilayet (Turk.)		
ANNOP } a brave;		
ANNUP } American Indian		
ANTIR } Eastern dulcimer	mu	
ANTUR }		
ANTON Dervish priest	rl	
APELE silky-grained Afr. hardwood	fr	
APFUL juicy		
APIUM gum-tree	bt	
APOTA sapodilla	bt	
APOUR flavour		
APPED undermined		
APPER Royal Engineer		
APPHO Greek poetess		
AP-ROT dry rot		
APYGA digger-wasps	zo	

SARCEL pinion of a hawk's wing	zo	
SARCEN } Stonehenge sandstone;	mn	
SARSEN } tin-worker		
SARDEL herring type of fish	zo	
SARGUS fish of mullet type	zo	
SARLAK sarlac; the yak	zo	
SARONG Eastern skirt		
SARSEN large sandstone boulder		
SARSIA jellyfish	zo	
SARTOR one who dresses		
SASHES window-framings; scarves		
SASINE seizin (Sc.)	lw	
SASTRA sacred book (Hindu)	rl	
SATANG Thailand coin	nm	
SATARA lustred woollen cloth		
SATEEN fabric		
SATINE a hard wood	bt	
SATING satisfying; cloying		
SATINY glossy		
SATIRE irony; sarcasm; lampoon		
SATIVE sown		
SATRAP Persian provincial governor		
SATURN planet; god of agriculture		
SAUCER a piece of china-ware		
SAUGER American pike	zo	
SAUMER white wine		
SAUREL the horse-mackerel	zo	
SAURIA reptile genus	zo	
SAURUS lizard-fish genus	zo	
SAVAGE barbaric; ferocious; brutal		
SAVANT a scientist; professor		
SAVATE French boxing		
SAVINE medicinal shrub; red cedar	bt	
SAVING husbanding; excepting		
SAVORY aromatic pot-herb	bt	
SAVOUR taste; flavour; odour		
SAVVEY nous; commonsense		
SAWDER flattery		
SAW-CUT groove, binder's sewing mark	pr	
SAW-FLY plant-harmful insect	zo	
SAW-NEB sawbill	zo	
SAWNEY Sandy		
SAWNEY complete yarn breakage	tx	
SAW-PIT sawing location		
SAW-SET tool for wrenching	to	
SAWYER plank-cutter		
SAXONY flannel	tx	
SAYING saw; dictum; adage; proverb		
SAYNAY a lamprey	zo	
SBIRRO Italian policeman		
S'BLOOD an imprecation		
SCABBY rough; itchy; leprous		
SCAEAN western (gate of Troy)		
SCAITH harm; damage (Sc.)		
SCALAR magnitude without direction		
SCALER climber		
SCALER instrument to register a count	to	
SCALES a balance; octaves	mu	
SCALMA a horse disease		
SCAMEL bar-tailed godwit	zo	
SCAMPI prawns (It.)	ck, zo	

SCANTY meagre; niggardly; chary		
SCAPHA (helix of ear)	md	
SCAPUS shaft of column		
SCARAB beetle; gem	zo	
SCARCE rare; infrequent; uncommon		
SCARED affrightened; panic-stricken		
SCARPH to scarf	cr	
SCARRY scarred; disfigured		
SCARUS parrot fish	zo	
SCATCH a horse-bit	vt	
SCATHE injury; damage		
SCATHY dangerous; mischievous (Sc.)		
SCATTY showery; crazy		
SCAURY gull (Shetlands)	zo	
SCAZON imperfect rhythm		
SCELIO parasite insects	zo	
SCENIC dramatic; theatrical		
SCHANS Zulu fort		
SCHEIK sheik (Arabic)		
SCHELM a rascal (Boer)		
SCHEMA scheme; synopsis		
SCHEME plan; plot; intrigue; devise		
SCHEMY cunningly devised		
SCHENE 7½ miles (12 km) (Egyptian)	me	
SCHISM a split; discord; dissent		
SCHIST slatey rock	mn	
SCHOOL train; educate; academy		
SCHORL tourmaline	mn	
SCHOUT Dutch colonial official		
SCHUSS unimpeded downhill ski run		
SCIARA gnats and midges	zo	
SCIATH Irish wicker shield		
SCIENT knowing		
SCILLA hyacinth	bt	
SCLATE slate (obs.)		
SCLAVE a Slav; Slavonian		
SCLERA hard coating	md	
SCLERE skeletal structure	zo	
SCOBBY chaffinch	zo	
SCOGIE a drudge (Sc.)		
SCOLEX a worm	zo	
SCOLIA burrowing insects	zo	
SCOLUS thornlike process in larvae	zo	
SCONCE skull; bulwark		
SCONCE to fine; candle-stick		
SCOPIC visual		
SCOPUS genus of wading birds	zo	
SCORCH singe; char; parch; scar		
SCORED registered; scratched		
SCORER recorder		
SCORIA dross	mn	
SCORSE exchange (Sc.)		
SCORZA variety of epidote	mn	
SCOTCH to cut; wedge		
SCOTER a sea-duck	zo	
SCOTIA Scotland; a concave moulding		
SCOUSE meat and vegetable broth		
SCOUTH scope (Sc.)		
SCOVAN tin lode (Cornish)		
SCOVED smeared (dial.)		
SCOVEL oven-mop		

SCRAMB ⎱ scrape together (dial.);	
SCRAMP ⎰ snatch	
SCRAPE grate; abrade; rasp; difficulty	
SCRAWL hasty writing	
SCRAWM to scratch (dial.)	
SCREAK a screech; scream	
SCREAM cry; yell; squall; shriek	
SCREED tiresome harangue; a shred	
SCREEN shroud; cloak; hide; sieve	t
SCREES stony debris	
SCREWY nefarious; underhand; exacting	
SCRIBE writer; notary; scrivener	
SCRIKE shriek (Spens.)	
SCRIME to fence	
SCRIMP to stint	
SCRINE a shrine (Spens.)	
SCRIPT handwriting; typescript	
SCRIVE scribe; engrave	
SCROBE groove in mandible	z
SCROLL roll; list; register; flourish	
SCROOP to grate; to crack	
SCRUFF of neck	
SCRUNT miser (Sc.)	
SCRUTO theatrical trap	
SCRUZE squeeze (Spens.)	
SCUFFY shabby; seedy	
SCULPT to sculpture; carve	
SCULSH rubbish; lollypops	
SCUMMY covered with scum	
SCURFF bull-trout	z
SCURFY leprous	m
SCURRY skurry; a race; scamper	
SCURVY vile; shabby; vitamin lack	m
SCUTCH to beat; to comb	
SCUTUM Roman shield	
SCUTUM middle notum sclerite in insec	
SCYLLA six-headed monster; (Charybdis)	
SCYTHE a reaping implement	
S'DEATH an imprecation	
SDEIGN disdain (Spens.)	
SEA-APE sea-otter	
SEA-BAR tern	z
SEA-BAT flying fish	z
SEA-BOY sailor lad	i
SEA-BUN sea-urchin	
SEA-CAP a sponge	z
SEA-CAT cat-fish	z
SEA-COB a gull	z
SEA-COW manatee; walrus	z
SEA-DOG common seal	z
SEA-EAR a mollusc; ormer shell	z
SEA-EEL conger	z
SEA-EGG sea-urchin	z
SEA-FAN a polyp	z
SEA-FIR another polyp	z
SEA-FOX thrasher shark	z
SEA-GOD Neptune	
SEA-HEN guillemot	z
SEA-HOG porpoise	z
SEALED ratified; confirmed; shut	
SEALER seal hunter; vessel	i

SEAMAN A.B.; tar; sailor	nt	**SEIZIN**	possession	lw
SEA-MAT polyzoa	zo	**SEISIN**		lw
SEA-MAW sea-mew	zo	**SEIZOR** bailiff		lw
SEAMED united by sewing; lined	tx	**SEJANT** sitting up		hd
SEAMER seamster		**SEJOIN** separate (obs.)		
SEA-MEW a gull	zo	**SELDOM** rarely; hardly ever		
SEA-MUD ooze		**SELECT** cull; pick; choose; prefer		
SEANCE spiritualistic session		**SELENE** Greek Moon-goddess		rl
SEA-ORB globe fish	zo	**SELION** a ridge of land		
SEA-OWL lump fish	zo	**SELJUK** Turkish warrior; dynasty; art		
SEA-PAD star-fish	zo	**SELLER** vendor; hawker; retailer		
SEA-PEA beach-pea	bt	**SELVES** individualities		
SEA-PEN quill zoophyte	zo	**SEMBLE** to dissemble (obs.)		
SEA-PIE a seafowl	zo	**SEMELE** genus of bivalves		zo
SEA-PIG the dugong	zo	**SEMESE** half-eaten		
SEA-RAT herring-king; a fish	zo	**SEMITA** (sea-urchins)		zo
SEARCE to sift; a sieve (Sc.)		**SEMITE** descendant of Shem		
SEARCH scrutiny; seek; inquire; quest		**SEMMIT** undershirt (Sc.)		
SEARED cauterized; burnt; scorched		**SEMOLA** semolina flour		ck
SEA-ROD a polyp	zo	**SEMPLE** simple (Sc.)		
SEASON time; period; flavour		**SEMPRE** in the same style		mu
SEATED sited; established		**SENARY** six of		
SEA-WAY steerage way	nv	**SENATE** assembly; council		
SEBATE a fatty compound	ch	**SENDAL** thin linen		
SECALE plant	bt	**SENDER** transmitter; despatcher		
SECANT (geometrical); cutting	nv	**SEND-UP** compliment; ridiculing		
SECEDE withdraw; segregate		**SENEGA** snake-root; an antidote		bt
SECERN secrete; discriminate		**SENHOR** Portuguese signor		
SECESH secessionist (USA)		**SENILE** aged; doting; tottering; infirm		
SECKEL variety of pear	bt	**SENIOR** elder; older; higher; superior		
SECOHM electrical unit	me	**SENNET** trumpet call (Shak.)		
SECOND support; assist; inferior	me	**SENNIT** braided cord; plaited straw		
SECRET covert; occult; privy; cryptic		**SENORA** lady (Spanish)		
SECTOR an area; a cutting; a zone		**SENSED** perceived; felt		
SECUND unilateral		**SENSOR** small-variation detection device		
SECURE get; obtain; safe; firm		**SENTRY** sentinel; watchman; guardian		
SEDATE staid; placid; serene; calm		**SEPAWN** maize-meal		ck
SEDENT inactive; quiet; torpid		**SEPHEN** sting-ray		zo
SEDGED flagged	bt	**SEPIUM** cuttle-bone		zo
SEDILE seat in chancel	rl	**SEPMAG** 1-magnetic-soundtrack film		cn
SEDUCE decoy; tempt; entice; inveigle		**SEPOPT** 1-optical-soundtrack film		cn
SEEDED tournament-placed		**SEPSIN** a ptomaine		md
SEEDER seed-drill	to	**SEPSIS** (blood poison); putrefaction		md
SEEING observing; viewing; watching		**SEPTAL** partitional (Irish)		
SEEKER inquirer; searcher		**SEPTAN** weekly		
SEELDE seldom (Spens.)		**SEPTET** party of seven; orchestra		mu
SEEMED befitted; appeared		**SEPTIC** rotten; putrid		md
SEEMER pretentious person; pretender		**SEPTON** (putrefaction)		
SEEMLY proper; becoming; decorous		**SEPTUM** a partition		bt
SEEPED oozed; percolated		**SEQUEL** consequence; upshot; result		
SEE-SAW teeter-totter; unbalance		**SEQUIN** a spangle; Venetian		nm
SEETHE to boil; to soak		**SERAIL** seraglio; harem; seray; palace		
SEGGAN sedge (Sc.)	bt	**SERANG** Lascar boatswain		nt
SEGGAR fire-clay pot; sagger		**SERAPE** zarafe; Mexican blanket		tx
SEGHOL Hebrew vowel point		**SERAPH** six-winged angel		rl
SEICHE change of water level (Fr.)		**SERDAB** secret chamber (Egypt)		
SEINER net-fisherman	nt	**SEREIN** rain from a cloudless sky		
SEISED possessed of		**SERENA** damp evening air		
SEISON a parasite genus	zo	**SERENE** calm; placid; tranquil; clear		
SEIZED lashed; grasped; stuck fast		**SERIAL** a periodical		pr
SEIZER grasper; snatcher; thief		**SERIAN** Chinese; Seric		pr

SERICA beetle genus	zo		**SHARER** participator	
SERIES sequence; succession; order			**SHARPY** oysterman's boat	nt
SERINE acid from protein hydrolysis	ch		**SHAVED** swindled	
SERIPH serif in printing			**SHAVER** a sharp dealer; a barber	
SERMON address; homily; discourse			**SHAVIE** a trick; a prank (Sc.)	
SEROON package of drugs	me		**SHAYAK** coarse cloth (Tripoli)	tx
SEROSA chorium; connective-tissue			**SHEAFY** (sheaves)	
membrane	pl		**SHEARS** sheers	to
SEROUS watery; thin	md		**SHEATH** scabbard	
SERPET basket (obs.)			**SHEAVE** pulley-wheel	
SERULA red-breasted merganser	zo		**SHEENY** bright; showy; a Jew	
SERVAL small African leopard	zo		**SHEERS** shears; a hoisting appliance	nt
SERVED ministered; acted; obeyed			**SHEIKH** Arab chief; scheik	
SERVER salver; waiter			**SHEKEL** Jewish half-crown	me, nm
SESAME plant having oily seeds	bt		**SHELFY** shelvy; shallow	
SESBAN a marsh plant	bt		**SHELLY** abounding with shells	
SESELI saxifrage	bt		**SHELLY** of shell-shake timber	fr
SESTET sextet	mu		**SHELTA** beggars' cant	
SESTON tiny plankton organisms	oc, zo		**SHELTY** Shetland pony	zo
SET-OFF compensation, insulation	pr		**SHELVE** put aside; to incline	
SETOSE			**SHELVY** sloping shallow	
SETOUS } bristly			**SHE-OAK** Australian shrub	bt
SET-OUT display			**SHEPPY** sheep-cote	
SETTEE sofa; Mediterranean ship	nt		**SHERIF** shereef; Arab title	
SETTER sporting dog	zo		**SHERRY** a wine from Xeres (Jerez)	ck
SETTLE wooden seat; colonize; pay			**SHEUCH** } ditch; drain;	
SETULE small bristle	bt		**SHEUGH** } trench; furrow (Sc.)	
SEVERE harsh; cruel; rigorous; plain			**SHEWEL** scarecrow	
SEVERY part of vaulted ceiling	ar		**SHICER** welsher (Australia)	
SEVRES porcelain (Fr.)			**SHIELD** shelter; cover; screen; guard	
SEWAGE drainage			**SHIFTY** tricky; fertile in resources	
SEWING needlework			**SHIING** skiing; a winter sport	
SEXFID six-cleft	bt		**SHIISM** Moslem schism	
SEXTAN recurring every sixth day			**SHIITE** believer in Shiism	
SEXTET six voices; orchestra	mu		**SHIKAR** big game hunting (Ind.)	
SEXTIC of the 6th degree			**SHIMMY** chemise; a dance	
SEXTON gravedigger	rl		**SHINDY** trouble; quarrel; spree	
SEXUAL of sex			**SHINER** £1; a boot-black	
SHABBY threadbare; paltry; beggarly			**SHINNY** } bandy ball;	
SHADED screened; obscured			**SHINTY** } West Highland hockey	
SHADOW umbrage			**SHINTO** Japanese ancestor worship	
SHADUF Nile water-raising device			**SHIPOV** small sturgeon	zo
SHAGGY rugged; rough; uneven			**SHIPPO** Japanese enamel	
SHAHPU Tibetan wild sheep	zo		**SHIPPY** ship-shape	nt
SHAIRL Cashmere cloth	tx		**SHIRAZ** a Persian drink	
SHAIRN cow-dung (Sc.)	zo		**SHIRES** the Shires; midland counties	
SHAKAL jackal	zo		**SHIRTY** indignant; wroth; angry	
SHAKEN jarred; agitated; moved			**SHIVER** tremble; quiver; slate	mn
SHAKER religious sect	rl		**SHOALY** shallow; shelfy	
SHALLI Indian cotton stuff	tx		**SHODDY** coarse cloth	tx
SHALOT (garlic); shallot	bt		**SHODER** goldbeater's packet	
SHAMAH shama; Indian song-bird	zo		**SHOFAR** ram's horn trumpet (Heb.)	mu
SHAMAL Mesopotamian summer wind	mt		**SHOGUN** Japanese C. in C.	
SHAMAN animist; wizard (Siberia)			**SHOOED** drove away	
SHAMED abashed; disgraced			**SHOPPY** commercial	
SHAMMY shamoy; chamois-leather	zo		**SHORAN** short-range navigation	nv, rd
SHANNY blenny fish	zo		**SHORED** propped; buttressed; braced	
SHANTY hut; hovel; shack; sea chant			**SHORER** a support	
SHAPED moulded; formed; regulated			**SHORTS** bran; pants	
SHAPER metal-planing machine	to		**SHOUGH** shaggy dog	zo
SHARED partook; divided			**SHOULD** conditional auxil. verb	

SHOVED obtruded; pushed; jostled
SHOVEL clergyman's hat; spade   **to**
SHOVER pusher
SHOWER distribute liberally; rain
SHRANK contracted; recoiled
SHREWD astute; cunning; wise; canny
SHRIEK cry; scream; yell; screech
SHRIFT confession; absolution   **rl**
SHRIKE butcher-bird   **zo**
SHRILL high; sharp; piping
SHRIMP a pink dwarf   **zo**
SHRINE tomb; reliquary
SHRINK shrivel; wrinkle
SHRITE missel thrush; bird   **zo**
SHRIVE to absolve   **rl**
SHROFF Indian banker
SHROUD winding sheet   **nt**
SHROVE Tuesday; absolved
SHRUFF dross   **tx**
SHRUNK contracted
SHUCKS! nonsense!
SHUFTI look! (Arab.)
SHUNIS herb; Scotch lovage   **bt**
SHYING throwing; starting
SIALIC derivative of neuraminic acid   **bc, ch**
SICCAN such (Sc.)
SICCAR } sure (Sc.);
SICKER } certain
SICKEN to disgust; to languish
SICKLE reaping hook   **to**
SICKLY faint; unhealthy; morbid
SICSAC crocodile bird   **zo**
SICYOS gourds   **bt**
SIDDHA } Buddhist who has attained
SIDDHI } perfection   **rl**
SIDDOW soft; pulpy (dial.)
SIDING parallel set of rails
SIDLED moved furtively
SIEMEN unit of electrical conductance   **me**
SIENNA yellow paint   **pt**
SIERRA mountain range
SIESTA nap; forty winks; doze
SIFAKA a lemur   **zo**
SIFFLE to whistle
SIFTED winnowed; bolted
SIFTER scrutinizer; separatist
SIGHED lamented; mourned
SIGHER repiner
SIGLUM seal; mark; initials
SIGNAL eminent; a sign
SIGNED signified; endorsed
SIGNER one who subscribes
SIGNET a seal
SIGNOR Mr. in Italian
SILAGE ensilage; stored fodder
SILANE silicon hydride   **ch**
SILENE bladder-campion   **bt**
SILENT mute; dumb; taciturn
SILICA flint; quartz; etc.   **mn**
SILKED repaired with silk backings (bks.)
SILKEN delicate; tender

SILLER silver; money (Sc.)
SILLON a mound in a moat
SILPHA carrion beetles   **zo**
SILTED oozed; choked with debris
SILURE cat-fish   **zo**
SILVAN woody; rustic
SILVER money; bright   **nm**
SIMBIL African stork   **zo**
SIMIAL } ape-like;
SIMIAN } monkey-like   **zo**
SIMILE parable; comparison
SIMKIN champagne (Ind.)
SIMMER a gentle boil; stew   **ck**
SIMNEL sweet fruit cake   **ck**
SIMONY buying preferment   **rl**
SIMOOM simoon   **mt**
SIMOON hot suffocating desert wind   **mt**
SIMORG } fabulous Persian bird   **zo**
SUMURG }
SIMOUS snub-nosed; concave
SIMPAI Sumatra monkey   **zo**
SIMPER silly affected smile
SIMPLE naive; artless; frank; ingenuous
SIMPLY merely; only; barely; solely
SIMSON groundsel   **bt**
SINAIC (Mount Sinai)
SINDON a wrapper; winding sheet
SINEWY strong; vigorous; muscular
SINFUL wrong; iniquitous; depraved
SINGED scorched; slightly burnt
SINGER warbler; songster   **mu**
SINGLE choose; select; alone; celibate
SINGLY uniquely; individually
SINIAN Chinese rock formation   **mn**
SINISM Chinese custom
SINKER a plummet
SINNED erred; transgressed
SINNER transgressor
SINNET sennet; braided cordage   **nt**
SINTER a siliceous deposit   **mn**
SINTOC cinnamon bark   **bt**
SIOUAN Sioux; American Indian tribe
SIPAHI sepoy; colonial soldier
SIPHON syphon
SIPING percolating; oozing; leaking
SIPPED tasted
SIPPER drinker of small draughts
SIPPET small sop
SIPPLE to sup in sips
SIRCAR sirkar; Hindu clerk
SIRDAR Egyptian commander
SIRENE a pitchpipe   **mu**
SIRING begetting
SIRIUS the Dog Star   **as**
SIRRAH sir; sirree
SIRUPY like syrup; syrupy   **ck**
SISKIN bird; a finch   **zo**
SISSOO Indian timber-tree   **bt**
SISTED summoned (Sc.)   **lw**
SISTER nun; nurse
SITTER painter's patient model

SIWASH N. American Indian; Alaskan dog	**SLIVER** continuous fibre strand	tx
SIZING size; weak glue; grading	**SLOGAN** war-cry (Sc.); curt phrase	
SIZZLE fry	**SLOKEN** quench; slocken	
SKATER one who skates	**SLOPED** decamped; at an angle	
SKATHE scathe; injury; harm; damage	**SLOPPY** maudlin; slipshod	
SKEARY scary; scared	**SLOSHY**⎫ muddy; boggy;	
SKEELY skilful (Sc.)	**SLUSHY**⎭ watery; miry	
SKELIC pertaining to skeleton	pl	**SLOUCH** a clown; depress; hang down
SKELLY to squint (Sc.)	**SLOUGH** deep mud; morass; swamp	
SKERRY rocky island	**SLOUGH** a cast skin	
SKETCH limn; portray; outline; draught	**SLOVAK** Slav of Slovakia	
SKEWER to impale	**SLOVEN** slattern; slut	
SKILLY thin gruel	**SLOVEN** splintered timber stump	fr
SKILTS trews (Sc.)	**SLOWER** not so fast	
SKIMPY scanty; meagre	**SLOWLY** gradually; tardily; sluggishly	
SKINNY emaciated; lean; lank	**SLUDGE** mire; wet refuse	
SKITTY water-rail	zo	**SLUDGY** muddy
SKIVED sliced; split	**SLUGGA** subterranean cavity	
SKIVER split sheep-skin	**SLUICE** floodgate; wash	
SKIVIE askew (Sc.)	**SLUICY** streaming	
SKLENT to slant; to split (Sc.)	**SLUING** turning round	
SKRYER a diviner	**SLUMPY** marshy	
SKURRY or **SCURRY** (Sc.)	**SLURRY** to smear; to dirty	
SKYISH ethereal	**SLUSHY** swampy; muddy; miry	
SLABBY viscous; thick; sloppy	**SLUTCH** sediment; muck; mire	
SLACKS women's trousers	**SLYEST** sliest; most artful	
SLAGGY (slag); scoriaceous	**SMALLS** exams; underwear	
SLAKED quenched	**SMALTO** glass, enamel, mosaic fragment	
SLANGY colloquial	**SMARMY** oily; ingratiating	
SLAP-UP posh; lavish	**SMARTY** over-bright youth	
SLASHY muddy (Sc.)	**SMATCH** taste; tincture (Shak.)	
SLATCH fair weather	nt	**SMEARY** bedaubed; adhesive; glutinous
SLATED abused; upbraided; chided	**SMEATH** aquatic bird; smew	zo
SLATER a wood louse	zo	**SMEECH**⎫ smell of burning (dial.)
SLAVED drudged	**SMITCH**⎭	
SLAVER dribble; slave ship	nt	**SMELLY** odoriferous
SLAVEY serving wench	**SMIDDY** a smithy (Sc.); forget	
SLAVIC Slavonic	**SMIGHT** smite (Spens.)	
SLAYER murderer; killer	**SMILAX** sarsaparilla plant	bt, ck
SLEAVE unwrought silk; floss	**SMILED** grinned; simpered	
SLEAZY, SLEEZY flimsy; worn out	**SMILET** a little smile	
SLEDGE heavy hammer; sled	to	**SMIRCH** depreciate; foul
SLEEKY of smooth appearance	**SMIRKY** smart	
SLEEPY soporous; drowsy; somnolent	**SMITER** slogger	
SLEETY wet and cold	**SMITHY** also **SMIDDY**; (dial.) workshop	
SLEEVE drogue; arm cover	**SMOKED** ridiculed; fumed; reeked	
SLEIGH sled; sledge	**SMOKER** a tobacco addict	
SLEUTH detective; bloodhound	zo	**SMOOTH** level; flatten; suave; bland
SLEWED swung askew; tipsy	**SMOUCH** smack; to kiss	
SLICED (golf); chopped; pared	**SMOUSE** pedlar (S. Africa)	
SLICER cutter	**SMUDGE** stain; blot	
SLIDER a moveable part	**SMUDGY** stained; smeary	
SLIEST slyest; most artful; most crafty	**SMUGLY** primly; neatly; complacently	
SLIGHT scorn; ignore; disdain	**SMURRY** misty (Sc.)	
SLIMSY flimsy; frail	**SMUTCH** to blacken	
SLINKY lean; furtive	**SMUTTY** sooty	
SLIP-ON easily put on (clothing)	**SNABBY** chaffinch (Sc.)	zo
SLIPPY nimble; unstable	**SNACOT** pipe-fish	zo
SLIP-UP error; mistake	**SNAGGY** full of snags	
SLITHY lithe and slimy	**SNAKED** coiled; crept	nt
SLIVER to cut; a splinter	**SNAPED** bevelled	

SNAPPY abrupt; noticeable style	**SOLION** audio signal detector	el
SNARED netted; caught	**SOLITO** in the usual manner	mu
SNARER trapper	**SOLIVE** joist; cross-timber	ar
SNATCH grab; seize; grasp; fragment	**SOLLAR** } upper gallery;	
SNATHE scythe-handle	to	**SOLLER** } garret	
SNEEZE exhale violently	**SO-LONG** good-bye	
SNIFFY disdainful	**SOLUTE** loose; cheerful	
SNIFTY having a luscious smell	**SOLVED** removed; resolved	
SNIPER concealed marksman	**SOLVER** elucidator; interpreter	
SNIPPY fragmentary; stingy	**SOMALI** native (Somalia)	
SNITCH nose	**SOMALO** Somali currency	nm
SNIVEL snuffle; blubber; whine	**SOMBRE** dismal; gloomy; lugubrious	
SNOBBY snobbish	**SOMITE** body segment	zo
SNOOTY conceited snob	**SOMNUS** sleep personified	
SNOOZE a nap; doze; siesta; drowse	**SONANT** sounding; resonant	
SNOTTY midshipman	nt	**SONATA** instrumental piece	mu
SNOUTY protuberant	**SONCIE** buxom; lucky	
SNUBBY somewhat snub; rather blunt	**SONERI** cloth of gold (Ind.)	tx
SNUDGE sneak; miser	**SONICS** study of mechanical vibrations	eg
SNUFFY irritable; peevish	**SONNET** a poem of 14 lines	
SNUGLY cosily; comfortably	**SONSIE** good natured (Sc.)	
SOAKED sodden; drenched; steeped	**SONTAG** knitted cap	
SOAKER confirmed toper	**SOODRA** Hindu caste	
SOAKER watertightness plug in roof	pb	**SOOJEE** } specially fine flour;	
SOAPED lathered; shampooed	**SOUJEE** } sujee (Ind.)	
SOARED aspired; towered; ascended	**SOONER** earlier; more readily	
SOBBED wept; cried	**SOORMA** an antimony cosmetic	
SOBEIT if it be so	lw	**SOOSOO** river dolphin	zo
SOBOLE budding/rooting stem	bt	**SOOTHE** calm; pacific; lull; palliate	
SOCAGE tenure of land by service	**SOPHIC** teaching wisdom; wise	
SOCCER association football	**SOPITE** to quash	
SOCIAL genial; civic; civil; festive	**SOPPED** very wet; sogged	
SOCKED biffed; whanged; coshed	**SOPPER** wet feeder	
SOCKET a cavity	**SORAGE** phase of hawk's life	zo
SOCMAN tenant by socage	lw	**SORBET** water-ice; sherbet	
SODAIC containing soda	**SORBIC** (sorbin); vitaminc acid	bt, ck
SODDED turfed; grassed	bt	**SORBIN** mountain ash	bt
SODDEN soaked; wet; drenched	**SORDES** dregs; filth	
SODION sodium ion	ch	**SORDET** a mute for an instrument	mu
SODIUM metallic element	ch	**SORDID** base; vile; ignoble; foul	
SODOKU rat-bite fever	md	**SORDOR** dregs; filth; sordes	
SO-EVER indefinite suffix	**SORELY** grievously; deeply; sadly	
SOFFET small sofa	**SOREST** most grievous	
SOFFIT ceiling	ar	**SORNER** gate-crasher; uninvited guest	
SOFISM form of Moslem belief	rl	**SOROSE** clustered	bt
SOFTEN enervate; relent; alleviate	**SORREL** colour; buck	bt, zo
SOFTER tenderer; milder	**SORROW** woe; distress; affliction	
SOFTLY pliably; quietly; dulcetly	**SORTED** grouped; suited	
SOGGED saturated; sopped	**SORTER** classifier; arranger	
SOIGNÉ well-decorated; carefully dressed	**SORTIE** sally; raid	
SOILED tarnished; smirched	**SOSSLE** dabble	
SOIREE evening party (Fr.)	**SOTHIC** dog-star	as
SOLACE consolation; cheer; relief	**SOTNIA** Cossack troop	
SOLAND the gannet	zo	**SOTTED** besotted	
SOLANO hot Mediterranean wind	mt	**SOUARI** butter-nut tree of Guyana	bt
SOLDER fusible metallic cement	**SOUCAR** Hindu banker/usurer	
SOLEIL worsted dress fabric	tx	**SOUGHT** quested; hunted; tried	
SOLELY singly; alone; solitarily	**SOULED** full of feeling	
SOLEMN august; grave; staid; serious	**SOUPER** (a convert)	
SOLERA cask; blending of sherry vintages	**SOUPLE** flail arm	
SOLEUS a leg muscle	pl	**SOUPLE** sericin-content yarn/fabric	tx

SOURCE fount; cause; spring; origin
SOURER more acid
SOURLY tartly; bitterly
SOUSED }
SOWSED } pickled; rushed; struck
SOUTAR }
SOUTER } a cobbler; shoemaker
SOWTER }
SOVIET Russian council committee
SOVRAN sovereign; monarch (obs.)
SOWANS } flummery from
SOWENS } oat husks   ck
SOW-BUG a millipede   zo
SOWING disseminating; propagating
SOZZLE sossle; muddle
SOZZLY sloppy
SPACED extended
SPACER distance piece
SPADED dug
SPADIX a spike   bt
SPAHEE Algerian cavalryman
SPALAX mole-rats   zo
SPANDY wholly; completely
SPARED saved; refrained; withheld
SPARER economiser
SPARES spare parts; duplicates
SPARGE to sprinkle
SPARKE battle-axe (Spens.)
SPARKS radio operator   nt
SPARRE bolt; bar (Spens.)
SPARRY (spar); (crystalline)   mn
SPARSE scanty; meagre; thin
SPARTH halberd; mace
SPARVE hedge-sparrow   zo
SPATHE flower sheath   bt
SPAVIN a swollen joint   md, vt
SPECIE bullion; coin; cash   nm
SPECKY speckled
SPEECH harangue; oration; palaver
SPEEDY prompt; fast; rapid; hasty
SPEISE cobalt/lead smelting product   mt
SPEISS metallic dross   mn
SPELIN form of Esperanto
SPENCE buttery; pantry
SPETCH strip of hide
SPEWED spat; vomited
SPHENE titanite   mn
SPHERE globe; orb; ball; domain
SPHERY spherical; round
SPHINX the Guinea baboon   zo
SPICAL spiky   bt
SPICED seasoned
SPICER spice-merchant
SPIDER a weaver of webs   zo
SPIFFY spruce; smart (slang)
SPIGHT spite (Spens.)
SPIGOT spile; peg for a cask
SPIKED pointed; put out of action
SPILTH anything spilt
SPILUS birth-mark; a naevus   md
SPINAL (back-bone)   md

SPINED thorny
SPINEL (corundum)   mn
SPINET form of harpsicord   mu
SPINNY a small copse
SPIRAL cork-screw; winding
SPIRED having a spire; sprouted
SPIRIC like an anchor-ring   nt
SPIRIT zeal; soul; essence; spook
SPITAL hospital (obs.)
SPITED thwarted; vexed
SPLASH spatter; splurge; a sensation
SPLEEN anger; melancholy   md
SPLICE to marry; a junction
SPLINE flexible ruler
SPLINT splent   md
SPLORE a jollification (Sc.)
SPOFFY officious
SPOKEN told; articulated
SPONGE cadge; cake; marine creature   ck, zo
SPONGY absorbent
SPOOKY eerie; ghostly
SPOONY weak-minded; amorous
SPOSHY slushy
SPOT-ON accurately placed
SPOTTY speckled
SPOUSE husband or wife
SPRACK sprightly; alert
SPRAID chapped with cold
SPRAIN strain; ridge; wrench
SPRANG jumped; leapt; bounded; tea
SPRAWL lounge; spread; straggle
SPREAD open; broadcast; scatter
SPRENT sprinkled
SPRING well; fount; rise; emanate
SPRINT also sprent; a spurt
SPRITE elf; fay; pixy; fairy; hobgoblin
SPRONG sprung (Spens.)
SPROUT bud; germinate; shoot; spire
SPRUCE fir-tree; neat; trim; finical   bt
SPRUIT water-course (S. Africa)
SPRUNG tipsy; bent
SPRUNT leap; sprout
SPRYER more vigorous
SPUDDY chubby; podgy
SPULYE to spoil (Sc.)
SPUNGE sponge
SPUNKY mettlesome; spirited
SPURGE a plant   bt
SPURNE to spur (Spens.)
SPURRY pink weed   bt
SPYING detecting; discerning
SPYISM spy-craft; espionage
SQUAIL a disc or counter
SQUALL blast; gust; yell; squeal
SQUAMA } a bract;   bt
SQUAME } a scale   zo
SQUARE fair; just; bribe; adjust; straight
SQUASH a gourd; a game; crush   bt
SQUAWK harsh utterance of protest
SQUEAK small creaking sound
SQUEAL to inform

SQUILL hyacinth; shrimp — bt, zo
SQUINT a strabismus; glance — md
SQUIRE escort; gallant
SQUIRM writhe; twist; wriggle
SQUIRT syringe; spout; eject
STABLE durable; fixed; constant
STABLY firmly; steadfastly; securely
STACTE myrrh — bt
STADDA comb-cutting saw — to
STADIA a range-finder
STAGED performed; produced
STAGER old hand
STAGEY melodramatic
STAITH coaling stage; staithe
STAKED (a claim); wagered
STALAG prisoners-of-war camp (Ger.)
STALER less fresh; older
STAMEN stamina — bt
STAMIN harsh woollen stuff — tx
STANCE position (golf); attitude; station
STANCH staunch; firm; stop the flow
STANZA verse of poem
STAPES ear-bones — md
STAPLE mart; raw material; chief
STARCH to stiffen; rigid
STARED gazed; glared; gaped
STAREE one who is stared at
STARER beholder
STARRY stellate
STARVE famish; lack; deprive
STASIS stagnation — md
STATED settled; regular; asserted
STATER ancient Greek gold coin — nm
STATHE landing stage
STATIC motionless; in equilibrium
STATOR cf. rotor; circuit holder
STATUA an image (obs.)
STATUE image; figurine
STATUS rank; standing; position
STAVED burst; delayed
STAVES (staff); rods; sticks
STAXIS haemorrhage — md
STAY-IN sit-in demonstration
STAYNE deface; stain (Spens.)
STAYRE a stair (Spens.)
STEADY equable; regular; uniform
STEAMY vaporous; humid
STEARE a steer; an ox (Spens.) — zo
STEBOY! go seek (dog talk)
STEEDY steady (Spens.)
STEELY hard; firm; obdurate
STEELY of glassy barley grains — br
STEEPY precipitous
STEEVE to stow; pack closely
STEGMA small silica-filled cell — bt
STEMMA pedigree; family tree
STENCH fetor; odour; effluvium
STEPPE Russian plain land
STEREO stereotype
STERIC (atomic arrangement) — ch
STEROL solid alcohol — ch

STERVE starve (Spens.)
STEVEN a clamour (Spens.)
STEWED simmered; seethed
STHENE unit of force
STIBIC (antimony) — ch
STICKY gummy; adhesive; viscid
STIDDY a forge; smiddy; smithy
STIFLE suffocate; choke; smother
STIGMA } brand; mark; tarnish;
STIGME } a dot; disgrace
STILAR (sundial stile)
STILLY calm; tranquil; silent
STILTY stilted; high-hat
STIMIE stimy (golf)
STINGO strong ale
STINGY near; close; mean; parsimonious
STINTY stinted; limited
STIPEL stipule — bt
STIPES stalk; stipe; stem — bt
STIRPS progenitor; ancestor
STITCH sew; a twinge
STITHY anvil; forge
STIVER Dutch halfpenny coin — nm
STOCKY sturdy; thick-set; robust
STODGE to cram
STODGY heavy; indigestible; starchy — ck
STOKED fuelled
STOKER furnace operator
STOLEN filched; purloined; taken
STOLID obtuse; phlegmatic
STOLON a runner — bt
STONED lapidated
STONER wall builder
STOOGE a butt; foil; dummy
STOORY dusty
STORAX resinous balsam — bt
STORED garnered; treasured
STORER hoarder; stocker
STORES an emporium; warehouse
STOREY (building); a floor
STORGE natural affection (Greek)
STORMY wild; rough; tempestuous
STOUND moment; mishap (Spens.)
STOVED dried; baked — ck
STOVER fodder for cattle
STOWED packed; placed
STOWER stevedore; packer
STRAFE punish (Ger.); attack fiercely
STRAIK } a stroke (Sc.)
STRAKE } tire of wheel
STRAIN exert; race; filter — mu
STRAIT narrow; distress; dilemma
STRAKE (wheel); planging — nt
STRAND shore; beach; thread; fibre
STRASS flint glass
STRATA layers; beds
STRATH valley (Sc.)
STRAWY straw-like
STREAK stripe; line; run naked
STREAM flow; pour; brook; burn
STREET roadway; avenue; terrace

STRENE race; strain (obs.)	
STRESS accent; force; urgency; tension	
STREWN strewed; scattered	
STRIAE stripes; streaks	
STRICH see strick (obs.)	
STRICK screech-owl; flax	zo
STRIDE stalk; step; gait	
STRIFE discord; conflict; quarrel	
STRIGA bristle; stripe	bt
STRIKE buffet; clash; lock-out	
STRING cord; twine; series	
STRIPE band; line; stroke	
STRIPY streaky	
STRIVE vie; compete; attempt	
STROAM to stroll; to roam (dial.)	
STROBE waveform enlargement	el
STRODE straddled; bestrode	
STROKE blow; knock; caress	
STROLL ramble; rove; stray	
STROMA tissue	md
STROMB a gasteropod	zo
STROND strand; beach (Shak.)	
STRONG puissant; bold; lusty	
STROOK struck (obs.)	
STROUP spout; nozzle (Sc.)	
STROUT strunt; to strut (obs.)	
STROVE vied; toiled; tried; attempted	
STRUCK smote; hit; collided; revolted	
STRUMA goitre; scrofula	md
STRUNG threaded; filed	
STUBBY stocky; blunt; truncated	
STUCCO plaster facing	ar
STUDIO atelier; broadcasting chamber	
STUFFY close; fusty; musty; angry	
STUGGY thick-set; stumpy (dial.)	
STUMER worthless cheque	
STUMPS (cricket)	
STUMPY stubby; short and thick	
STUPID witless; dull; idiotic; asinine	
STUPOR torpor; coma; lethargy	
STURDY robust; stalwart; vigorous	
STYING penning	
STYLAR pillar-like; pointed	
STYLED designated	
STYLET small pointed bristle	bt
STYLET dagger; poniard	md
STYLUS pen; style; needle (discs)	
STYMIE (golf); stimy	
STYRAX gum plants; storax	bt
STYTHE after-damp	
SUABLE liable to be sued	lw
SUBDUE quell; overpower; tame	
SUBFEU (subinfeudation)	lw
SUBITO quickly	mu
SUBLET underlet	lw
SUBMIT yield; capitulate; acquiesce	
SUBORN to bribe; commit perjury	
SUBSET subscriber's telephone apparatus	
SUBSET part of maths 'set'	ma
SUBTIL subtle; crafty	
SUBTLE subtile; sly; crafty; clever	

SUBTLY slyly; artfully; astutely	
SUBULA sharp-pointed organ prolongation	
SUBURB outskirt; neighbourhood	
SUBWAY underground passage; metro	
SUCCIN amber	
SUCCUS juice	bt
SUCKED absorbed; imbibed	
SUCKEN mill district (Sc.)	
SUCKER ⎫ a fish; a shoot; suction pad	bt, zo
SUCKER ⎭ gullible person	
SUCKET sweetmeat	
SUCKLE to wet-nurse	
SUDARY a sweat-cloth	
SUDDEN abrupt; quick; rapid; fleet	
SUDDER chief; supreme (Ind.)	
SUEING prosecuting; entreating	
SUFFER brook; endure; allow; undergo	
SUFFIX an affix	
SUFISM Moslem doctrine	rl
SUGARY sweet; honeyed; dulcet	
SUIDAE pigs, hogs; etc.	zo
SUITED contented; dressed	
SUITOR wooer; admirer; litigant	
SUIVEZ follow the soloist	mu
SUKAMA native of Tanzania	
SULCUS furrow; groove	
SULLEN morose; sulky	
SULTAN a fowl; a Turkish ruler	zo
SULTRY stuffy; oppressive; stifling	
SUMACH plant used in tanning	bt
SUMMED counted; added	
SUMMER season of year	
SUMMIT top; acme; zenith; vertex	
SUMMON bid; cite; invoke; prosecute	
SUMPIT poisoned dart (Borneo)	
SUNBOW rainbow	
SUNDAE ice-cream	
SUNDAY Christian holy day	
SUNDER sleave; sever; disrupt; part	
SUN-DEW a bog plant	bt
SUN-DOG a parhelion; mock sun	as
SUNDRY several; various; manifold	
SUN-GOD Phoebus; Apollo; Re or Ra	rl
SUN-HAT solar topee	
SUNKEN submerged; engulfed	
SUNKET an idler; food (Sc.)	
SUNLIT illuminated by sun	
SUNNED exposed to sun	
SUNSET sundown	
SUN-TAN brown skin from sun	
SUPAWN Indian porridge	ck
SUPERB magnificent; splendid	
SUPINE indolent; torpid; inert	
SUPPER evening meal	ck
SUPPLE lithe; pliant; flexible	
SUPPLY provide; furnish; grant	
SURBED (stone-laying)	
SURCLE little shoot; sucker	bt
SURELY certainly; positively	
SUREST safest; most certain	
SURETE crim. investigation service (Fr.)	

SURETY bond; guarantee; pledge	
SURGED billowed	
SURREY a fowl; carriage (Amer.)	zo
SURTAX an impost	
SURVEY see; review; look; observe	
SUSLIK marmot; ground squirrel	zo
SUTILE wound stitching	md
SUTLER camp follower; caterer	
SUTTEE self-immolation	
SUTTLE neat; (tare and tret)	
SUTURE stitching thread	md, bt
SVELTE lissom; slender	
SWADDY militia-man (slang)	
SWAGED mitigated; forged; burnt	
SWAGGY bending	
SWALED wasted; consumed	
SWAMPY marshy; spongy	
SWANKY swipes; boastful	
SWANNY swan-like	
SWARAJ home-rule (India)	
SWARDY grassy	
SWARMY oleaginous; unctuous	
SWARTH tawny; apparition	
SWARVE to swerve	
SWASHY over-ripe	
SWATCH a sample of cloth	tx
SWATHE to bind; a bandage	
SWATHY like a scythe-cut	
SWAYED vacillated; tottered; wielded	
SWEATY laborious	
SWEENY emaciation; atrophy	md
SWEEPS jeweller's dust/debris	
SWEEPY strutting; wavy	
SWERVE deviate; turn aside	
SWINGE to belabour; chastise	
SWIPED lashed out; slogged	
SWIPER a smiter	
SWIPES small beer	
SWIPEY fuddled	
SWIRLY curly	
SWITCH twig; whip; bypass; shunt	
SWIVEL to turn; revolve	
SWOUND to swoon (obs.)	
SYCITE fig-stone	mn
SYCOMA tumour	md
SYLVAN rustic; rural; woodland	
SYMBAL cymbal	mu
SYMBOL token; sign; badge; emblem	
SYNDAW a plant	bt
SYNDIC magistrate; Andorran council	
SYNEMA column of filaments	bt
SYNEPY interjunction	
SYNTAX grammatical sequence	
SYNTOL syntagmatic organisation lang.	
SYPHER to join flush	
SYPHON siphon	
SYRIAC relating to Syria;	
SYRIAN the language	
SYRINX vocal organ in birds; fistula	
SYRINX Pan's pipes	mu
SYRTIC like a quicksand	

SYRTIS quicksand	
SYRUPY sirupy; sugary	ck
SYSTEM rule; method; order; plan	
SYZYGY astronomical conjunction	as

T

TABARD herald's coat;	hd
TABERD a tunic	
TABBED having tabs; tagged	
TABEFY to emaciate	
TABLED catalogued; boarded	
TABLER boarder	
TABLES (back-gammon)	
TABLET flat monument	md
TABOUR tabor; drum	mu
TABRET small tabour or drum	mu
TABULA calcareous partition in corals	
TACKED attached; stitched	
TACKER he who tacks	
TACKET hob-nail (Sc.)	
TACKLE gear; implements; grapple	
TACTIC tactical; mode of operation	
TACTUS sense of touch	
TAENIA tape-worm; a fillet	zo
TAG-END fag-end	
TAGGED tabbed; touched; fastened	
TAGGER thin iron/tin sheet	ml
TAGGER an appendage	
TAGLIA a hoisting device	
TAG-RAG and bobtail	
TAGUAN Malayan flying squirrel	zo
TAHONA ore crusher (Sp.)	
TAIGLE entangle; delay; tarry	
TAILED docked; followed	
TAILOR clothes maker	
TAILYE entail (Sc.)	lw
TAISCH 'second sight'; apparition (Sc.)	
TAJACU Mexican wild pig; peccary	zo
TAKE-IN a hoax	
TAKE-UP tailoring	
TAKING alluring; attractive; winning	
TALBOT unit of luminous energy	lt, me
TALBOT sporting dog	zo
TALCKY containing talc	mn
TALENT genius; aptitude	nm, me
TALIAN Bohemian dance	mu
TALION retaliation	lw
TALKED discoursed; prated; spoke	
TALKER chatterbox; gossip	
TALLAT	
TALLET a hay-loft (dial.)	
TALLOT	
TALLER sturdier; bolder; higher	
TALLOW hard candle fat	
TALMUD Hebrew Bible	rl
TALWEG deep valley (Ger.)	
TAMALE Mexican corn meal-roll	ck
TAMANU gamboge tree (E. Ind.)	bt
TAMARA mixed spice	ck
TAMBAC alloy; also aloes-wood	mn, bt

TAMBOO taboo; tambu		
TAMBOR globe-fish	zo	
TAMELY meekly; submissively		
TAMEST flattest; dullest		
TAMINE ⎫ worsted stuff;		
TAMINY ⎭ tamise; tammy		
TAMING domesticating		
TAMKIN tampion		
TAMMUZ Syrian sun-god	rl	
TAMPAN South Afr. venomous tick	zo	
TAMPED packed with earth		
TAMPER meddle; interfere		
TAMPIN turning pins		
TAMPIN boxwood pipe plug	pb	
TAMPOE an E. Indian fruit	bt	
TAMPON surgical plug	md	
TAN-BED bark bed		
TANDEM one behind the other		
TANGED banged; twanged; flavoured		
TANGLE Orcadian water-spirit		
TANGLE mat; twist; involve; jumble		
TANGLY complicated; intricate		
TANGUM Tibetan piebald horse	zo	
TANIST land owner (Irish)		
TANITE a cement		
TANJIB ⎫ figured muslin (Ind.)		
TANZIB ⎭		
TANKED stored; fuddled		
TANKER oil-carrying ship	nt	
TANKIA boat population, Canton		
TANNED browned off; leathered		
TANNER sixpence; leather worker	nm	
TANNIC an acid	ch	
TANNIN an astringent	ch	
TANNOY amplified; loud speaker		
TANREC ⎫ insect eater	zo	
TENREC ⎭ (Madagascar)		
TANTRA Sanskrit holy book	rl	
TAN-VAT tub used in tanning	le	
TAOISM Chinese religion	rl	
TAOIST Chinese religionist	rl	
TAO-TAI Chinese official		
TAPETI Brazilian hare	zo	
TAPING binding; measuring		
TAPPED screw-threaded; rapped		
TAPPER rapper		
TAPPET (motor valves); small lever	au	
TAPPIT crested		
TARGET aim; butt; mark; objective		
TARGUM Bible in Chaldee	rl	
TARIFF tax; impost; schedule		
TARING recording tare allowance		
TARMAC road material		
TARNAL eternal or infernal		
TARPAN wild horse (Asia)	zo	
TARPON ⎫ the Jew-fish	zo	
TARPUM ⎭		
TARRED macadamised; asphalted		
TARSAL (tarsus); (the ankle)		
TARSEL hawk; tiercel	zo	
TARSIA marquetry		

TARSUS instep; ankle		pl
TARTAN chequered fabric; ship		nt
TARTAR argol		ch
TARTLY sharply; pungently; acidly		
TASCAL informer's reward		
TASKED employed; burdened		
TASKER taskmaster; overseer		
TASLET tasset; thigh armour		
TASSEL a pendant		
TASSET thigh armour		
TASSIE drinking cup (Sc.)		
TASTED experienced; savoured		
TASTER food/wine sampler		
TATLER a gossip; sandpiper		zo
TATTED lace making		tx
TATTER a rag		tx
TATTIE Indian trellis; tatta		
TATTLE prattle; gossip; babble		
TATTOO pageant; beat of drum		
TAUGHT imparted; tutored; coached		
TAURUS a sign of the Zodiac; the Bull		as
TAUTEN stretch; strain		
TAUTER tighter		
TAUTOG N. American black-fish		zo
TAVERN inn; hostel; caravanserai		
TAVERT fuddled; muddled (Sc.)		
TAWDRY gaudy; garish		
TAWERY white leather factory		
TAWING leather dressing		
TAWPIE taupie (Sc.)		
TAWTOG tautog		zo
TAXEME linguistic selection		
TAXIED (aeroplane on ground)		
TAXINE alkaloid mixture		ch
TAXING accusing; straining; costing		
TCHEKA Soviet secret police		
TCHICK a click		
TEA-BAG tea sachet; tisane		
TEA-CUP tea-drinking vessel		
TEAGLE a tackle; a hoist		
TEAGUE an Irishman		
TEAMED associated conjointly		
TEA-POT tea-making vessel		
TEA-POY small table		
TEARER render; ripper		
TEASED combed; tantalized		
TEASEL ⎫ plant with burs used		
TEAZEL ⎬ for raising nap		bt
TEAZLE ⎭ on cloth		
TEASER a puzzler; aggravator		
TEA-SET dishes for tea service		
TEATHE (manure)		
TEA-URN a samovar		
TEBBAD Centr. Asian simoon		
TEBETH Jewish month		
TECTUM covering/roofing structure		ze
TEDDED spread (new-mown hay)		
TEDDER a tether; hay-maker		
TEDDER machine to loosen windrows		ag
TE DEUM thanksgiving		
TEDIUM boredom; ennui; monotony		

TEEING (golf)	**TESTED** proved; assayed	
TEEMED full of life; in myriads	**TESTER** canopy; Henry VIII shilling	
TEEMER a producer	**TETANY** muscle spasm; lock-jaw	md
TEEPEE wigwam (N. Amer.)	**TETCHY** testy; peevish	
TEE-TEE S. Amer. squirrel monkey	zo	**TETHER** tie; fasten; stake	
TEETER see-saw (USA)	**TETRAD** group of four	
TEETHE to grow teeth	**TETRAO** capercaille	zo
TEGMEN inner seed coat	bt	**TETRYL** yellow detonating compound	ch
TEGULA sub-title	pr	**TETTER** a rash	md
TEINDS tithes (Sc.)	**TETTIX** cicada; tree-cricket	zo
TELARY web-like	**TEUTON** ancient German	
TELEDU stinkard; Malayan badger	zo	**TEWHIT** peewit; lapwing	zo
TELEGA Russian springless cart	**TEXTUS** authoritative version	
TELESM amulet; charm	**THAIRM** catgut (Sc.)	
TELLER bank cashier; tale-bearer	**THALER** German dollar	nm
TELLUS Goddess of Earth (Roman)	rl	**THALIA** comic Muse	
TELSON tail segment	zo	**THANKS** an expression of gratitude	
TELEGU dialect (S. India)	**THATCH** roof with straw	
TEMOIN column of earth	ce	**THAWED** melted	
TEMPER anger; passion; spleen; tantrum	**THEAVE** ewe of the 1st year	zo
TEMPER mitigate; alleviate; anneal	**THEBAN** of Thebes	
TEMPLE Inns of court; place of worship	rl	**THECAL** sac-like	bt
TEMPLE fane; part of head	**THECLA** hair-streak butterflies	zo
TENACE (bridge)	**THEINE** tea alkaloid	ch
TENANT lease-holder	lw	**THEIRS** of them	
TENDED cared for; contributed	**THEISM** belief in God	
TENDER mild; lenient; offer	nt	**THEIST** a believer in God	
TENDON a ligament	md	**THEMIS** goddess of law	
TENNER £10 note	**THENAL** (palm or sole)	md
TENNIS net/ball game	**THENAR** palm or sole	md
TENORA Catalan instrument	mu	**THENCE** for that reason	
TENREC hedgehog genus (Madagascar)	zo	**THEODY** hymn in praise of God	rl
TENSED keyed up; taut; stretched	**THEORY** speculation; hypothesis	
TENSER under greater strain	**THESIS** a theme; a dissertation; essay	
TENSON ⎫ tournament of song	**THETIC** dogmatic (thesis)	
TENZON ⎭	**THETIS** sea-nymph; the sea	
TENSOR muscle	md	**THEWED** trained; muscular	
TENTED probed	**THIBET** heavy woollen fabric	tx
TENTER machine attendant	**THIBLE** a dibble	
TENTER female cardroom operative	tx	**THIEVE** filch; pilfer; purloin; rob	
TENUIS voiceless stop consonant	**THINLY** scantily; sparsely	
TENURE possession; holding	**THIRAM** chemical fungicide	
TENUTO sustained	mu	**THIRDS** widows' rights	lw
TEPARY hardy Amer. bean	bt	**THIRST** crave; yearn; hanker; desire	
TEPEFY to warm	**THIRTY** cardinal number	
TERAPH Hebrew household god	**THOLUS** dome; cupola (Greek)	
TERBIC containing terbium	ch	**THORAH** the Pentateuch	
TERCEL male falcon	zo	**THORAL** nuptial	
TERCET triplet	mu	**THORAX** (chest)	md
TEREDO boring worm; ship-worm	zo	**THORON** thorium emanation	nc
TERETE cylindrical	**THORNY** spiny; prickly; sharp	
TERGAL dorsal	**THORPE** a homestead	
TERGUM the back	**THOUGH** notwithstanding	
TERMED terminated; designated	**THOWEL** thole-pin	nt
TERMER ⎫ holder of an estate for a	**THRALL** a slave; slavery	
TERMOR ⎭ term of years	**THRASH** drub; castigate	
TERMES white ant genus	zo	**THRAVE** two stooks (Iceland)	
TERMLY term by term	**THRAWN** twisted (Sc.)	
TERREL a spherical magnet	**THREAD** cord; filament; drift; gist	
TERRET territ; harness pad ring	**THREAP** ⎫ contradict; urge;	
TERROR awe; dismay; dread; panic	**THREEP** ⎭ insist on (Sc.)	

THREAT menace; intimidation
THRENE a lament (Gr.)
THRESH thrash; drub; maul; trounce
THRICE three times; very
THRIFT frugality; economy
THRIFT the sea-pink   bt
THRILL excite; rouse; electrify
THRIPS corn-bugs   zo
THRIST thirst (Spens.)
THRIVE wax; prosper; flourish
THROAT the fauces   md
THRONE sovereign power and dignity
THRONG crowd; flock; congregate
THROVE thrived
THROWN cast; propelled; flung
THRUSH horse disease   vt, zo
THRUST lunge; tilt; stab
THUSLY as follows
THWACK belabour; whack; thump
THWART balk; frustrate; obstruct
THYITE pale green clay   mn
THYMOL oil of thyme   md
THYMUS a gland   md
THYRSE panicle   bt
TIBIAL bone; flute   pl, mu
TICING enticing; decoying; luring
TICKED speckled; clicked; beat
TICKEN bed ticking; cloth
TICKER a watch
TICKET voucher; coupon; pass
TICKEY coin (S. Africa)   nm
TICKLE gratify; divert; amuse
TICKLY ticklish; risky; difficult
TIC-TAC bookie's signalling system
TID-BIT tit-bit
TIDDER to fondle
TIDDLE to potter; to trifle
TIDIED cleared up; shipshape
TIDIER neater
TIDILY methodically
TIED-UP busy; ready for binding in cover
TIEING binding; confining
TIE-PIN ornament for a cravat
TIERCE 42-gallon (190-litre) cask   me
TIERCE 5-f organ pitch   mu
TIE-ROD connecting rod
TIE-WIG court-wig
TIFFIN Indian lunch
TIGHTS combined stockings and pantee   tx
TIKKER electrical make and break device
TILERY tilework; tile factory
TILING roofing
TILLED cultivated; ploughed
TILLER helm; drawer; till
TILMUS floccillation   md
TILTED covered with awning; aslant
TILTER tent-pegger
TIMBAL tymbal; kettledrum   mu
TIMBER wood
TIMBRE resonance; tone; quality
TIMELY opportune; punctual; apropos

TIMING clocking
TIMIST timekeeper   m
TINCAL crude borax   m
TIN-CAN food container
TINDAL Lascar bo'sun's mate
TINDER touchwood
TINEID (small moths)   z
TINGAL, TINKAL crude borax   m
TINGED tinkled; imbued; flavoured
TINGIS an insect genus   z
TINGLE thrill; small nail
TINGUY Brazilian soap-tree   b
TINIER much smaller
TINKED tinged; tinkled; rubbish man
TINKER bungler; a fish   z
TINKLE make bell-like sound
TINMAN a manufacturer; tinker
TINNED preserved
TINNER tin miner
TIN-POT inferior
TINSEL finery; glittering; gaudy
TINTED tinged; imbued
TINTER colourist
TIP-CAT a children's game
TIP-OFF secret information
TIPPED overturned; (racing)
TIPPET garment; small cape   t
TIPPLE drink
TIP-TOE walk on the toes
TIP-TOP first class
TIPULA insect genus; daddy-longlegs   z
TIRADE diatribe; invective; harangue
TIRING dressing; wearying
TIRLED vibrated; twisted
TIRRET handcuff; manacle; fetter
TIRRIT terror (Shak.)   z
TIRWIT lapwing   z
TISANE herbal drink   c
TISSUE web; fabric; series   m
TIT-BIT tid-bit
TITELY quickly
TITHED taxed
TITHER tithe collector
TITLED yclept; inscribed; named
TITLER stickle-back   z
TITLER lettering screen   c
TI/TREE the manuka   b
TITTER giggle; snigger; laugh
TITTLE an iota; small particle
TITTUP canter
TMESIS rhetorical intersection
TOBINE twilled silk   t
TOCHER dowry (Sc.)
TOCSIN an alarm; poisonous serum   z
TODDLE saunter
TOE-CAP boot-tip
TOFFEE chewy confection
TOFORE before; heretofore
TOGGED arrayed
TOGGLE wooden pin   n
TOILED moiled; strove

TOILER labourer; worker; striver	**TORQUE** twisting force	
TOILET dress; attire; washroom	**TORQUE** collar; necklace	
TOISON a fleece	**TORRID** sultry; scorching; fiery	
TOLEDO sword-blade	**TORSEL** twisted scroll	
TOLLED annulled; (bells)	lw	**TORULA** yeast plant	bt
TOLLER toll-gatherer	**TOSSED** thrown; pitched	
TOLLER bell-ringer	**TOSSER** pitcher	
TOL-LOL goodish	**TOSS-UP** an even chance	
TOLSEY toll-booth; mart	**T'OTHER** the other	
TOLTEC early Mexican	**TOTING** carrying; humping	
TOLTER to flounder (dial.)	**TOTTED** added up	
TOLUIC (benzene)	ch	**TOTTER** topple; reel; rock; stagger	
TOLUOL methylbenzene	ch	**TOTTIE** a small tot	
TOMAND Arabian grain	me	**TOUCAN** S. American bird	zo
TOMATO red fruit-vegetable	bt	**TOUCHÉ** a palpable hit (fencing)	
TOMAUN Persian gold coin	nm	**TOUCHY** testy; irascible; petulant	
TOMBAC, TOMBAK a copper alloy	**TOUPEE** } a tuft; a curl; lock of	
TOMBED buried	**TOUPET** } false hair	
TOMBIC like a tomb	**TOURED** journeyed	
TOMBOC Javanese weapon	**TOUSED** hauled; torn; rumpled	
TOMBOY a romping girl; hoyden	**TOUSER** a teaser; a worrit	
TOM-CAT male feline	zo	**TOUSLE** to rumple; ruffle; derange	
TOMCOD a fish	zo	**TOUTED** canvassed	
TOMIAL } cutting edge	**TOUTER** a tout	
TOMIUM } of a bird's bill	zo	**TOUTIE** petulant (Sc.)	
TOMPON inking pad	**TOWAGE** haulage	
TOMPOT blenny fish	zo	**TOWARD** apt; docile; tractable	
TOM-TIT blue tit	zo	**TOWERY** lofty	
TOMTOM Hindu drum; tumtum	**TOWHEE** American marsh robin	zo
TONAME nickname; byname	**TOWING** dragging; drawing	
TONGAN native of Tonga	**TOW-NET** water-fauna sample net	oc
TONGUE language; speech; scold	**TOWSER** a dog	zo
TONING intoning	rl	**TOXOID** detoxidified toxin	md
TONING tinting	**TOY-DOG** miniature dog	zo
TONISH stylish; having 'ton'	**TOYFUL** trifling	
TONITE an explosive	ch	**TOYING** dallying; trifling	
TONSIL throat appendage	pl	**TOYISH** playful; wanton	
TOOART Australian eucalyptus	bt	**TOY-MAN** a dealer in playthings	
TOOLED ornamented; drove	**TRABAL** beamy	ar
TOOTED hooted	**TRABEA** Roman consular robe	
TOOTER a piper	**TRACED** trailed; drawn; limned	
TOOTHY with teeth too apparent	**TRACER** investigator; (bullet)	
TOOTLE play on the flute	mu	**TRADED** bartered; vended; sold	
TOO-TOO quite so; super	**TRADER** merchant; trafficker	
TOPAZA humming birds	zo	**TRAGIC** shocking; calamitous	
TOP-DOG leader; victor	**TRAGUS** (ear portal)	md
TOPFUL brimming	**TRANCE** coma; rapture; ecstasy	
TOP-HAT topper	**TRANKA** juggler's box	
TOPHET place of torment (Hebrew)	**TRAPAN** to ensnare; stratagem	
TOPHUS (gout)	md	**TRAPES** a slut; a tramp	
TOPMAE insect labrum surface	zo	**TRAPPY** treacherous	
TOPMAN top sawyer	nt	**TRASHY** rubbishy; worthless	
TOPPED surpassed; filled up; (golf)	**TRAUMA** a wound; shock	pc, md
TOPPER high hat	**TRAVEL** tour; trip; journey; move	
TOPPLE fall; tumble; collapse; totter	**TRAVIS** stable partition	
TORERO bull-fighter on foot	**TREATY** pact; covenant; alliance	
TOROID a symmetrical geometrical fig.	**TREBLE** triple; threefold	mu
TOROSE } swelling; protuberant	**TREBLY** triply	
TOROUS }	**TREFLE** trefoil	
TORPID inert; numb; lethargic	**TREMEX** an insect genus	zo
TORPOR apathy; dullness; dormancy	**TREMIE** underwater-concrete funnel	ce

181

TREMOR shock; vibration	**TRYGON** sting-ray	zo
TRENCH cut; furrow; ditch	**TRYING** irksome; difficult; arduous	
TREPAN (skull cutting) md	**TRY-OUT** preliminary trial	
TREPAN a cheat; ensnare; trapan	**TSAMBA** black barley (Tibet)	bt
TREPID quaking; trembling	**TSETSE** deadly fly (S. Africa)	zo
TRESSY curly	**TSONGA** language (Mozambique)	
TRIACT having three rays	**TSWANA** language (Africa)	
TRIAGE sorting	**T-TOTUM** teetotum	
TRIBAL clannish	**TUAREG** tribe (Sahara)	
TRICAR motor-tricycle	**TUBAGE** inserting a tube	
TRICKY intricate; difficult	**TUBBED** bathed	
TRICON on-course signal system nv	**TUBFUL** the contents of a barrel	
TRICOT knitted fabric tx	**TUB-GIG** Welsh car	
TRIFID three-cleft bt	**TUBING** piping	
TRIFLE a sweet; gewgaw; dally ck	**TUBULE** small tube	
TRIGLA gurnards zo	**TUCHUN** Chinese military governor	
TRIGLY dandified	**TUCKED** stuffed; folded; pleated	
TRIGON ancient harp; triangle mu	**TUCKER** bib; frilling	
TRILBY a hat	**TUCKET** trumpet-call	mu
TRIMER 3-molecule substance ch	**TUCK-IN** large meal; picnic	
TRIMLY neatly; compactly	**TUFFET** Miss Muffet's seat; grass	
TRINAL three-fold	**TUFTED** tufty	
TRINGA sandpiper genus zo	**TUFTER** a stag-hound	zo
TRIODE thermionic valve ro	**TUGGED** lugged	
TRIOSE simplest monosaccharide ch	**TUGGER** a heaver	
TRIPLE treble	**TUILLE** thigh armour	
TRIPLY threefold	**TULWAR** Eastern sabre	
TRIPOD three-legged stool or stand	**TUMBAK** coarse Persian tobacco	
TRIPOS Cambridge examination	**TUMBLE** trip; stumble; somersault	
TRIPUS 1 of Weberian vesicles zo	**TUMBLY** uneven; unstable	
TRISTE sad; sorrowful; gloomy mu	**TUMEFY** to swell; distend; inflate	
TRITON one of Neptune's trumpeters	**TUMOUR** morbid swelling	md
TRITON genus of molluscs zo	**TUMPED** hilled (gardening)	
TRITOR tooth masticatory surface zo	**TUM-TUM** W. Indian food; tomtom	ck
TRITYL triphenylmethyl group ch	**TUMULI** ancient mounds	
TRIUNE Trinity rl	**TUMULT** uproar; hubbub; turmoil	
TRIVET trevet; small hob	**TUNDRA** frozen Arctic plain	
TRIVIA trivial matters	**TUNDUN** a toy; a bull-roarer	
TROCAR surgical instrument md	**TUNE-IN** find station on waveband	
TROCHE a lozenge; tabloid	**TUNGUS** Turanian tribe	
TROGGS clothes (Sc.)	**TUNING** syntonizing	ro
TROGON Central American bird zo	**TUNKER** dunker; baptist	
TROIKA Russian 3-horsed sleigh	**TUNNED** casked	
TROJAN a champion; a plucky fellow	**TUNNEL** funnel; passage; burrow	
TROLLY small truck	**TUPAIA** tree-shrew (Malay)	zo
TROPHI (insect's mouth) zo	**TUPELO** gum-tree	bt
TROPHY prize; laurels	**TUPPED** butted; rammed	
TROPIC (Cancer and Capricorn)	**TURACO** Afr. plantain-eating bird	zo
TROPPO excessively mu	**TURBAN** oriental head-dress	
TROTYL explosive ch	**TURBID** muddy; cloudy; confused	
TROUGH groove; trench; furrow	**TURBOT, TURBIT** a flat-fish	zo
TROUPE a company	**TURDUS** the thrush	zo
TROVER (finding) lw	**TUREEN** a receptacle for soup	
TROWED trusted; believed	**TURFED** sodded; kicked out	
TROWEL garden implement to	**TURFEN** (turf); covered with sward	
TRUANT vagrant; vagabond; shirker	**TURGID** bloated; tumid; bombastic	
TRUDGE tramp; plod; march	**TURGOR** fullness	md
TRUEST exactest; most veracious	**TURION** runner; underground shoot	bt
TRUISM axiom; platitude	**TURKEY** straight talk; poultry	ck, zo
TRUITE crackled (porcelain)	**TURKIS** turquoise	mn
TRUSTY reliable; staunch; faithful	**TURMUT** turnip (dial.)	bt

TURNED hinged; applied (lathe)
TURNER lathe-worker; pigeon zo
TURN-IN part exchange deal
TURNIP old-fashioned watch; root bt
TURN-UP an altercation
TURNUS swallow-tail butterfly zo
TURREL tool used by coopers to
TURRET minaret; cupola; pinnacle
TURTLE marine tortoise zo
TURVES plural of turf; sods
TUSCAN a classic order of architecture ar
TUSKAR peat cutter
TUSKED tusky; toothy
TUSKER elephant zo
TUSSAC a tussock
TUSSAH wild silkworm fabric tx
TUSSER tussore silk
TUSSIS a cough md
TUSSLE scuffle; wrestle; contend
TUTRIX female guardian
TUTSAN a plant bt
TU-WHIT
TU-WHOO } owlish; night calls
TUXEDO dinner jacket (USA)
TUYERE a pipe; twyer
TWAITE species of shad zo
TWAITE arable land
TWEENY maid; small cigar
TWELVE a dozen
TWENTY a score
TWICER compositor and pressman
TWIGGY abounding in shoots
TWILLY cotton-cleaning machine tx
TWINED twisted; meandered tx
TWINER climbing plant bt
TWINGE pang; twitch; spasm
TWITCH twinge; jerk
TWITTY yarns with twisted portions tx
TWO-PLY of 2 layers (wood, wool, etc.) tx
T'WOULD it would
TWO-WAY (a switch)
TYBURN (executions); (Marble Arch)
TYCOON Japanese prince
TYLOTE sponge-spicule zo
TYMBAL kettledrum; timbal mu
TYMPAN printing frame
TYPHON evil genius (Egypt)
TYPHUS gaol fever md
TYPIFY exemplify; symbolize
TYPIST typewriter user
TYRANT autocrat; despot
TYRIAN purple
TYRITE a mineral mn
TYSTIE the black guillemot zo
TZETZE Abyssinian guitar

U

UAKARI S. American monkeys zo
UBERTY fruitfulness
UBIETY local relation
UBIQUE everywhere
UDMURT native of Central Asia
UGLIFY to make hideous
UGLILY in an ungainly manner
UGRIAN Ugro-Finnic
UGSOME hideous; gruesome
UIGITE a silicate of aluminium mn
ULITIS gum inflammation md
ULLAGE lack of fullness in a cask
ULLING ullage
ULMOUS (elm exudation) bt
ULNARE cuneiform bone md
ULOSIS cicatrisation md
ULSTER overcoat
ULTIMO last; in last month
ULTION revenge
UMBERY of umber colour pt
UMBLES entrails of deer zo
UMBRAL shady; darksome
UMBRIL umbrel; helmet vizor
UMLAUT vowel inflection
UMPIRE arbiter; referee; judge
UNABLE powerless; impotent
UNAWED undismayed; undaunted
UNBANK (stoking)
UNBEAR to unharness; ungear
UNBEND to relax; undo; unknot nt
UNBENT relaxed; untied
UNBIAS to free from prejudice
UNBIND release; unfetter
UNBITT (release cable) nt
UNBOLT unfasten; unbar
UNBONE remove the bones
UNBORN non-existent; uncreated
UNBRED rude; underbred
UNBURY disinter; exhume
UNCAGE to free
UNCALM to disturb; agitate
UNCAMP dislodge
UNCAPE unhood
UNCART unload
UNCASE unpack; display; unsheath
UNCATE hooked
UNCIAL a script used in ancient MSS.
UNCLAD naked; berserk
UNCLEW unwind
UNCLOG unhamper
UNCOCK (shooting); (hay-making)
UNCOIF remove cap
UNCOIL unwind
UNCOIN withdraw from currency
UNCOLT unhorse (Shak.)
UNCORD unbind
UNCORK open
UNCOWL unveil
UNCURL untwist
UNDATE wavy; undose
UNDEAF to free from deafness
UNDEAN deprive of that office rl
UNDECK divest of ornaments
UNDERN 9 a.m.; the third hour

UNDIES underclothes	**UNIBLE**) unifiable	
UNDINE water-nymph	**UNIFIC**)	
UNDOCK to leave dock	nt	**UNIOLA** American grass genus	bt
UNDOER subversionary agent	**UNIPED** single-footed	
UNDONE untied; awaiting performance	**UNIPOD** single support camera mount	pg
UNDOSE undulated; undate; wavy	**UNIQUE** peculiar; sole; unexampled	
UNDRAW draw aside	**UNISEX** for either, or both sexes together	
UNDUKE deprive of duke's rank	**UNISON** harmony; concord; accord	
UNDULL sharpen; whet	**UNITAL** unique; singular	
UNDULY excessively; improperly	**UNITED** combined; coalesced	
UNEASE mental unrest; anxiety	**UNITER** joiner; merger	
UNEASY restive; disturbed	**UNJUST** biased; partial	
UNEATH uneasily (Spens.)	**UNKARD**) uncouth; ugly;	
UNEDGE blunt	**UNKETH**) strange (dial.)	
UNEVEN rugged; rough; odd	**UNKENT** unknown	
UNEYED unnoticed; unobserved	**UNKEPT** discarded; rejected	
UNFACE expose	**UNKIND** cruel; harsh; unfriendly	
UNFAIR dishonest; foul; partial	**UNKING** dethrone	
UNFAST insecure	**UNKNIT** unravel	
UNFEED without fee	**UNKNOT** untie; unfasten	n
UNFELT unimpressed; callous	**UNLACE** loose; loosen	
UNFILE remove from a file	**UNLADE** disburden; unload	
UNFINE shabby	**UNLAID** not allayed; untwisted	
UNFIRM weak; unstable	**UNLASH** let loose; unbind; untie	
UNFIST to release; unhand	**UNLEAD** remove lead	p
UNFOLD open; expand; reveal	**UNLEAL** unloyal	
UNFOOL restore from folly; unhoax	**UNLENT** not loaned	
UNFORM to destroy	**UNLESS** if not; except	
UNFREE not free; tied; restricted	**UNLICH** unlike (Spens.)	
UNFURL display; unroll	**UNLIKE** dissimilar; heterogeneous	
UNGAIN ungainly; clumsy (obs.)	**UNLIME** extract the lime	
UNGEAR to unharness; unbear	**UNLINE** remove the lining	
UNGILD remove the gilding	**UNLINK** unfasten	
UNGILL release from a gill-net	**UNLIVE** kill; dull; not electrified	
UNGILT not gilt	**UNLOAD** relieve; lighten; unburden	
UNGIRD unbind	**UNLOCK** unfasten	
UNGIRT unconfined	**UNLORD** deprive of that dignity	
UNGLUE ungum; unstick	**UNLOVE** cease to love	
UNGOWN disrobe	**UNLUTE** unglue	
UNGUAL having claws, nails, etc.	**UNMADE** not manufactured	
UNGUIS claw; hoof	zo	**UNMAKE** destroy; dismantle	
UNGULA instrument	md	**UNMASK** expose; denounce; reveal	
UNGULA section of a cylinder	**UNMEET** unworthy; unbecoming	
UNGYVE unfetter	**UNMIRY** not muddy	
UNHAIR deprive of hair	**UNMIXT** pure; unalloyed; sheer	
UNHAND let go; release	**UNMOOR** to weigh anchor	n
UNHANG take off the line	**UNNAIL** extract the nails	
UNHASP unfasten	**UNNEST** eject; evict	
UNHEAD behead; decapitate	**UNNETH** uneath; not easily (Spens.)	
UNHEAL) to uncover (Spens.)	**UNOWED** not due	
UNHELE)	**UNPACK** disburden	
UNHELM (helmet)	**UNPAID** still owing; outstanding	
UNHEWN rough	**UNPICK** unravel; unknit	
UNHIVE deprive of habitation	**UNPRAY** revoke a prayer	
UNHOLD release	**UNPROP** remove a support	
UNHOLY impious; profane; ungodly	**UNPURE** impure; adulterated	
UNHOOK disconnect	**UNQUIT** not discharged	
UNHUNG unhanged	**UNREAD** not perused; ignorant	
UNHURT scatheless	**UNREAL** fantastic; visionary; illusory	
UNHUSK to shell	**UNREIN** slacken the rein	
UNIATE Greek Catholic sect	rl	**UNRENT** untorn; unripped	

UNREST disquiet; unease; fidgetiness
UNRIPE immature; crude; green
UNROBE undress
UNROLL open out; uncoil; evolve
UNROOF untile
UNROOT extirpate; eradicate
UNROPE untie; unlash
UNRUDE civil; complaisant
UNRULY riotous; turbulent
UNSAFE risky; hazardous; insecure
UNSAID unspoken
UNSEAM rip; cleave; unpick
UNSEAT unhorse
UNSEEL to open the eyes
UNSEEN invisible
UNSELF eliminate personality
UNSENT not despatched
UNSEWN unstitched
UNSHED retained; kept
UNSHIP remove; unload   nt
UNSHOD barefoot
UNSHOT not discharged
UNSHUT open
UNSOFT not softly (Spens.)
UNSOLD not purchased
UNSOUL materialize; deaden
UNSOWN not propagated
UNSPAR remove spars
UNSPED undone
UNSPIN unravel
UNSTEP remove (a mast)   nt
UNSTOP release
UNSUNG forgotten, neglected
UNSURE uncertain
UNTACK disjoin
UNTAME wild; undomesticated
UNTELL never to narrate
UNTENT uncover
UNTIDY slovenly; disorderly
UNTIED undone; unloosed
UNTILE unroof
UNTOLD uncounted; numberless
UNTOMB exhume
UNTORN unrent
UNTRIM disarray
UNTROD little frequented
UNTRUE false; fallacious; spurious
UNTUCK unfold
UNTUNE to disorder
UNTURN untwist; unscrew
UNUSED new; unaccustomed
UNVEIL uncover; reveal; unmask
UNVOTE out-vote
UNWARM chillsome
UNWARY rash; incautious; indiscreet
UNWELL ailing; sick; indisposed
UNWEPT not lamented
UNWILY lacking in craft
UNWIND uncoil; disentangle
UNWISE indiscreet; imprudent
UNWISH wish not to be (Shak.)

UNWOOF unweave
UNWORK undo
UNWORN unimpaired
UNWRAP unfold; uncloak
UNYOKE separate; disjoin
UPBEAR sustain; elevate
UPBEAT unaccentuated rhythm   mu
UPBIND confine
UPCAST uptoss
UPCAST upward strata displacement   gl
UPCOIL to coil
UPDATE bring into line; modernise
UPFILL to fill
UPFLOW upgush
UPGAZE look upwards
UPGROW develop; evolve
UPGUSH upflow
UPHAND lift
UPHEAP pile up; amass
UPHILL toilsome; arduous; strenuous
UPHOLD advocate; maintain; champion
UPHROE awning support   nt
UPKEEP maintenance
UPLAND highland
UPLEAN to incline towards
UPLIFT upheaval; exaltation
UP-LINE line to London (railway)
UPLOCK lock up
UPLOOK raise the eyes
UPMAKE column/page print arranging   pr
UPMOST topmost
UP-PILE accumulate; upheap
UPPING swan marking
UPPISH bumptious
UP-PROP to shore; support
UPREAR to raise
UPRISE ascend; revolt
UPRIST up-risen; uprose
UPROAR riot; hubbub; turmoil
UPROLL furl
UPROOT eradicate; extirpate
UPROSE stood up; rebelled
UPRUSH surging up
UPSEEK seek
UPSEES after the manner of
UPSEND throw up
UPSHOT outcome; issue; result
UPSIDE topside
UPSOAR zoom
UPSTAY sustain; support
UPSWAY swing up
UPTAKE mental agility
UPTEAR rend
UPTILT incline; tip
UPTOSS pitch
UPTOWN city centre (if north)
UPTURN overturn; overthrow
UPWARD ascending; uphill
UPWAYS upward
UPWELL upspring; gush
UPWIND to wind up

URACIL pyrimidine; nucleic acid	ch	**VALING** receding; lowering	
URAEUM tail-end of bird	zo	**VALISE** portmanteau; holdall	
URAEUS serpent emblem (Egypt)		**VALKYR** a Valkyrie; Walkyr	
URANIA Muse of astronomy		**VALLAR** (rampart)	
URANIC (uranium); celestial		**VALLEY** dale; vale; dell; glen; dingle	
URANIN yellow dye	ch	**VALLUM** Roman rampart	
URANUS a planet; father of Saturn		**VALOUR** heroism; courage; prowess	
URANYL chemical radical		**VALUED** esteemed; prized; treasured	
URATES urine salts	md	**VALUER** appraiser	
URBANE courteous; polite; affable		**VALVED** having valves	
URCEUS single-handed jug; urn		**VAMOSE** vamoose; to clear out	
URCHIN hedgehog; brat; gamin	zo	**VAMPED** improvised; patched; repaired	
UREASE enzyme	ch	**VAMPER** a pianist; siren	mu
UREIDE acid derivative of urea	ch	**VANDAL** barbarian; destroyer	
URETER duct that carries urine	md	**VANISH** fade; disappear; depart	
URETIC a medicine	md	**VANITY** conceit; egotism; futility	
URGENT pressing; imperative		**VAN-MAN** pantechnicon worker	
URGING impelling; inciting		**VANNER** light cart horse	zo
URNING consigning to an urn		**VAPORS** vapours; nervous dejection	me
URONIC of sugar oxidation compound	ch	**VAPOUR** steam; reek; fume; to boast	
UROPOD abdominal limb	zo	**VARIED** diverse; motley; altered	
URSINE bear-like	zo	**VARIER** an inconsistent person	
URTICA nettle genus	bt	**VARLET** scoundrel; rascal; knave	
URVANT turned up	hd	**VARMIN** vermin; varmint	zo
USABLE employable; applicable		**VARSAL** universal	
USAGER a religionist	rl	**VARUNA** The Creator (Hindu Myth)	r
USANCE usury		**VASSAL** retainer; dependant; bondman	
USEFUL helpful; beneficial		**VASTER** on a grander scale	
USTION combustion		**VASTLY** spaciously; widely; immensely	
USURER money-lender; a Shylock		**VASTUS** a thigh muscle	me
USWARD towards us		**VAT-DYE** oxidation of textiles	t
UTERUS womb		**VATTED** mellow	
UTGARD abode of Loki (Scand.)		**VAUDOO** voodoo; witchcraft (Afr.)	
UTMOST extreme; farthest		**VAULTY** arched	
UTOPIA a political romance		**VAWARD** vanward; in the van	
UVEOUS grape-like	md	**VEADER** Jewish intercalary month	
UVULAR (uvula)	md	**VECTOR** (direction and magnitude)	
		VEDDAH native Cingalese	
		VEDUTA painting of recognizable scene	
		VEERED changed course; shifted	n

V

VACANT void; empty; inane		**VEHMIC** (vehmgericht)	
VACATE quit; leave; annul; rescind		**VEILED** concealed; shrouded; glozed	
VACHER cow-keeper		**VEINED** streaked; variegated; venose	
VACUNA Roman goddess of horticulture		**VELARY** a sail or awning	
VACUUM void; vacuity; emptiness		**VELATE** enveloped; veiled	b
VADIUM surety (Sc.)	lw	**VELETA** waltz	m
VAGARY whim; crotchet; fancy		**VELITE** lightly armed Roman soldier	
VAGINA sexual passage in female	zo	**VELLED** removed turf	
VAGOUS wandering; erratic		**VELLET** velvet (Spens.)	
VAGUER more indefinite; dimmer		**VELLON** Spanish money of account	
VAIDIC Vedic; (philosophical)		**VELLUM** parchment from calf-skin	
VAILED submitted; tipped		**VELLUS** downy foetal hair	z
VAILER a yielder		**VELOCE** very quick	m
VAINER more conceited; falser		**VELOUR** velvet	
VAINLY ineffectually; proudly		**VELURE** velvet; smoothing pad	
VAISYA (Hindu caste)		**VELVET** soft silky stuff	
VAKASS Armenian clerical vestment		**VENDED** sold; peddled; hawked	
VAKEEL Indian attorney	lw	**VENDEE** the buyer; purchaser	
VALETE farewell		**VENDER** \\ the seller	
VALGUS knock-kneed man; club-foot		**VENDOR** / the seller	
VALINE amino acid	ch	**VENDUE** an auction; roup	

VENEER coating; layer; cover
VENERY sport; hunting
VENEUR head-keeper
VENGER an avenger (Spens.)
VENIAL excusable; pardonable
VENITE 95th Psalm
VENNEL an alley-way (Sc.)
VENOSE } veined
VENOUS }
VENTED poured forth; uttered; emitted
VENTER the abdomen md
VENTIL (cornet valve) mu
VENULE blood vessel in chordata zo
VERBAL oral; by word of mouth
VERDOY charged with heraldic flowers hd
VERDUN antique rapier (Fr.)
VERGED sloped; inclined; bordered on
VERGEE about half acre me
VERGER church caretaker rl
VERIFY confirm; authenticate; identify
VERILY truly; really; certainly
VERITÉ realism, film documentary technique cn
VERITY actuality; fact; reality
VERMES worms zo
VERMIL vermilion
VERMIN noxious animal; rabble zo
VERMIS main part of cerebellum zo
VERNAL springlike
VERREL ferrule; see virole
VERREY vaire; furry hd
VERSAL universal (Shak.)
VERSED skilled; familiar; accomplished
VERSER versifier; poetaster
VERSET prelude mu
VERSUS against; opposing
VERTEX top; apex; acme; zenith
VERVET South African monkey zo
VESICA a bladder; a sac md
VESPER evening star, Venus as
VESSEL receptacle; utensil nt
VESTAL chaste
VESTED fixed; legalized; established
VESTRY sacristy rl
VETCHY (vetch) bt
VETOED prohibited; banned; forbidden
VETTED carefully examined
VETUST ancient
VEXING annoying; tormenting; trying
VIABLE capable of existence
VIANDS food; provisions
VIATIC (journey)
VIATOR wayfarer
VIBRIO spiral bacillus zo
VICARY a vicarage rl
VICTIM a dupe; martyr; sacrifice
VICTOR conqueror; winner; champion
VICUNA the wild llama zo
VIDAME French noble
VIDUAL widowed
VIELLE antique viol (Fr.) mu

VIEWED beheld; surveyed; scanned
VIEWER examiner; inspector
VIEWLY striking
VIGOUR force; energy; manliness
VIHARA Buddhist temple
VIKING Norse sea-rover
VILELY basely; ignobly; malignantly
VILEST lowest; abject
VILIFY defame; traduce; disparage
VILLUS hair; wool md
VILNED wounded beast hd
VINAGE wine doctoring
VINERY grape house
VINNEY a blue Dorset cheese
VINOSE, VINOUS wine
VINTED turned into wine
VINTRY wine shop; bodega; bistro
VIOLAN violet blue mn
VIOLET a colour; flower bt
VIOLIN fiddle; a kit mu
VIRAGO a termagant; vixen; shrew
VIRENT verdant; green; fresh
VIRGIN maiden; damsel; spinster
VIRILE manly; robust; masculine
VIROLE ferrule; hoop hd
VIROSE } poisonous
VIROUS }
VIRTUE integrity; probity; goodness
VISAED endorsed (passport)
VISAGE face; aspect; countenance
VISCID sticky; glutinous; tenacious
VISCIN mistletoe fruit substance bt
VISCUM mistletoe bt
VISCUS an entrail md
VISHNU The Preserver (Hindu God)
VISIER } wizier; Turkish minister
VIZIER }
VISION sight; spectre; ghost; dream
VISIVE visual
VISUAL visible; perceptible
VITALS essential organs
VITRIC glassy
VIVACE lively mu
VIVARY small zoo; vivarium zo
VIVERS victuals (Sc.)
VIVIFY animate; enliven; quicken
VIZARD mask; visor
VOCULE a feeble cry
VOICED said; declared; uttered
VOICER spokesman
VOIDED evacuated; quitted; left
VOIDER shallow basket
VOLANT flying; nimble; active hd
VOLATA rapid phrase mu
VOLENT exercising will power
VOLERY flight of birds
VOLLEY salvo; shower; storm
VOLUME book; tome; bulk; mass
VOLUTE spiral scroll
VOLVOX freshwater algae bt
VOMICA an abscess in the lungs md

VOMITO yellow fever	md	
VOODOO ⎫ witchcraft, vaudoo		
VOUDOU ⎭ (Haiti and West Indies)	rl	
VORAGO whirlpool; vortex; gulf		
VORANT devouring	hd	
VORTEX whirlpool; whirlwind		
VOTARY a fan; devotee; zealot		
VOTING electing; polling		
VOTIVE vowed; devoted		
VOULGE ancient form of pike (Fr.)		
VOWING pledging; promising		
VOYAGE trip; cruise; passage		
VOYANT seer with psychic vision		
VULCAN god of fire		
VULGAR coarse; ordinary; vernacular		

W

WABBLE wobble; stand unsteadily	
WABBLY insecure; unstable	
WADDED stuffed; filled	
WADDIE Australian war club	
WADDLE walk like a duck	
WADING fording	
WADMAL thick woollen cloth	
WADSET a mortgage	lw
WAEFUL woeful; sorrowful	
WAFERY wafer-like	
WAFFLE a cake; a gauffre	
WAFTED floated; waved; beckoned	
WAFTER a fan	
WAGGED shook; vibrated; swayed	
WAGGEL great gull	zo
WAGGLE vibrate; oscillate	
WAGGON wagon; dray	
WAGING betting; venturing; conducting	
WAG-WIT a would-be wit	
WAHABI Puritan Moslem	rl
WAHINE Maori woman	
WAILED bemoaned; lamented	
WAILER howler; weeper	
WAITED attended; tarried; lingered	
WAITER attendant; servitor; garçon	
WAIVED relinquished; forwent	
WAIVER yielder; renouncer	
WAKING arousing; stimulating	
WALING chastising	
WALING trench-timbering plank	ce
WALKED perambulated; strolled	
WALKER hiker; pedestrian	
WALKYR Valkyr; a Valkyrie	
WALLAH a fellow (Ind.)	
WALLED enclosed	
WALLER a wall-builder	
WALLET purse; scrip; pouch	
WALLOP to boil; to beat; beer	br
WALLOW welter; grovel; flounder	
WALNUT commonest European nut	bt
WALRUS the morse; sea-horse	zo
WAMBLE to be queasy	
WAMMUS knitted jacket (USA)	tx

WAMPEE a Chinese fruit	
WAMPUM beads used as cash (N. A. Ind.)	
WANDER stroll; stray; roam	
WANDLE supple; nimble (dial.)	
WANDOO Australian white gum	b
WANGLE get by craft	
WANING declining; ebbing; paling	
WANION bad luck (Sc.)	
WANKLE weak; unstable	
WANNED made pale	
WANTED needed; lacked; desired	
WANTER a requirer; craver	
WANTON sportive; frolicsome; frisky	
WAPITI stag; American elk	z
WAPPER gudgeon	z
WAPPET yelping cur	z
WARBLE cattle tumour; quaver; sing	
WAR-CRY slogan	
WARDED guarded; fended; parried	
WARDEN ⎫ keeper; guardian; protector;	
WARDER ⎭ curator; custodian; turnkey	
WARELY warily (Spens.)	
WARIER more cautious	
WARILY cautiously; carefully; cannily	
WARMAN warrior; man-at-arms	
WARMER hotter; keener	
WARMLY earnestly; ardently; zealously	
WARMTH heat; enthusiasm; fervency	
WARNED cautioned; notified; apprised	
WARNER an admonisher	
WARPED distorted; perverted; biased	
WARPER a weaver; a twister	t
WARRAY to ravage by war (Spens.)	
WARREN rabbit burrows; enclosure	
WAR-TAX tax to help war	
WARTED verrucose	b
WASABI Jap. horseradish	c
WASHED laved; absterged; purged	
WASHER metal ring	
WASH-IN increase in angle of incidence	
WASH-UP cleaning dishes	
WASTED frittered; squandered	
WASTEL a fine sort of bread	
WASTER a cudgel; spendthrift	
WATERY aqueous; dilute; thin; insipid	
WATTLE fowl's gills	z
WATTLE an acacia; a hurdle	b
WAUCHT ⎫ a deep draught;	
WAUGHT ⎭ to quaff (Sc.)	
WAULED ⎫	
WAWLED ⎭ caterwauled	
WAVERY unsteady; tremulous	
WAVING undulating; swaying	
WAVURE procrastination	
WAX-END cobbler's thread	
WAXIER more irate	
WAXING growing; increasing; rising	
WAYLAY to ambush	
WAYOUT advanced; unusual	
WEAKEN impair; enfeeble; enervate	
WEAKER more dilute; thinner; feebler	

WEAKLY delicately; infirmly; frailly
WEALTH riches; opulence; abundance
WEANED alienated; withdrawn
WEAPON sometimes blunt
WEARER bearer; waster
WEASEL explosive carnivore   zo
WEAVER bird; see webster   zo
WEAZEN wizened; sharp; shrivelled
WEBBED arachnoid; woven
WEB-EYE a disease of the cornea   md
WEB-FED of printing paper by reel   pr
WEDDED married; espoused; spliced
WEDELN S-course downhill ski technique
WEDGED scotched; compressed; ceramics
WEEDED hoed; eradicated; purged
WEEDER garden tool   to
WEEKLY hebdomadary; a periodical
WEENED imagined; thought
WEEPER Niobe; a monkey   zo
WEEVER sting-fish   zo
WEEVIL a beetle   zo
WEIGHT onus; incubus; load; burden
WELDED united
WELDER Irish sub-tenant
WELKIN sky, clouds
WELLED poured forth; spouted; gushed
WELTED edged; bordered
WELTER wallow; flounder; heavy
WENDED journeyed; wandered
WENDIC a Sorabian
WESAND ⎫
WEZAND ⎬ weazand; wind-pipe
WESTER to turn westward
WET-BOB Eton aquatic sportsman
WETHER a castrated ram   zo
WETTER damper; more showery
WHALER whale-boat   nt
WHALLY having greenish-white eyes
WHATEN ⎫
WHATNA ⎬ what kind of (Sc.)
WHATSO of whatever kind
WHEELY circular
WHEEZE puff; blow; ancient joke
WHEEZY asthmatic
WHELKY rounded; protuberant
WHENAS when; whereas (Shak.)
WHENCE wherefrom
WHERRY a liquor; sailing boat   nt
WHEUGH! exclamation of surprise
WHEWER the widgeon; duck   zo
WHEYEY whey-like
WHILED beguiled
WHILES meanwhile
WHILLY to cajole; to wheedle
WHILOM formerly
WHILST while
WHIMSY fad; caprice; fancy; crotchet
WHINED whimpered
WHINER sniveller
WHINGE to whine (Sc.)
WHINNY (horse); (gorse)

WHIPPY flexible; springy
WHIRRY to hurry off (Sc.)
WHISHT! hush!
WHISKY a light gig
WHITEN blanch; bleach; turn pale
WHITER purer; brighter
WHITES flannel trousers (cricket)   tx
WHOLLY entirely; fully; utterly
WHOMSO every one whom
WHYDAH ⎫
WHIDAH ⎬ African weaver bird   zo
WICKED evil; sinful; ungodly; nefarious
WICKEN mountain ash   bt
WICKER pliant twig; osier   bt
WICKET small gate; (cricket)
WICOPY American basswood   bt
WIDELY spaciously; extensively; rifely
WIDEST broadest; remotest
WIELDY manageable
WIFELY wively
WIGEON widgeon; duck   zo
WIGGED berated; reproved; chid
WIGGLE wriggle; waggle
WIGWAG flag-wag; twist
WIGWAM Indian tent (Amer.)
WILDER bewilder
WILDLY fiercely; recklessly; savagely
WILFUL wanton; perverse; obdurate
WILIER craftier; slyer
WILILY artfully; cunningly; insiduously
WILING beguiling; deceiving
WILLED resolved; bequeathed   lw
WILLER one who wills
WILLET North American snipe   zo
WILLOW a cricket bat tree   bt
WILTED drooped; withered
WIMBLE to drill; gimlet   to
WIMBLE nimble; active
WIMPLE a headdress; to ripple
WINCED flinched; quailed
WINCER a shrinker
WINCEY winsey; a fabric   tx
WINDED blew; blown; caught scent
WINDER to fan; to winnow; a key
WINDLE a spindle; reel
WINDOW lattice; casement
WIND-UP alarm; trepidation
WINERY where wine is bottled/stored
WINGED alate; rapid; wounded
WINGER (football)
WINKED twinkled; flickered; acquiesced
WINKER horse's blinker
WINKLE periwinkle   bt, zo
WINNER victor; conqueror; champion
WINNOW sift; examine; fan
WINSEY wincey; twilled cotton
WINTER hyemal
WINTLE stagger; writhe (Sc.)
WINTRY icy; frosty; cheerless
WIPING deterging; rubbing
WIRIER capable of greater strain

WIRILY vigorously; tenaciously
WIRING circuits; telegraphing
WISARD ⎫ conjuror; sorcerer;
WIZARD ⎭ necromancer; marabout
WISDOM sagacity; knowledge
WISELY sagely; sensibly; sapiently
WISEST most learned and judicious
WISHED listed; wanted; longed for
WISHER desirer; yearner
WISKET a basket
WISTLY earnestly; attentively
WITHAL together with; likewise
WITHED bound with a withe
WITHER fade; pine; languish
WITHIN not exceeding; indoors
WITH-IT up to date; aware of trends
WITTED alert; wise
WITWAL popinjay; woodpecker   zo
WIVELY wifely
WIVERN wyvern; winged dragon   hd
WIZIER vizier; visier; minister (Turk.)
WOBBLE wabble; oscillate; vibrate
WOBBLY unstable; unsteady
WOEFUL waeful; tragic; grievous
WOLFER voracious feeder
WOLVES predacious animals   zo
WOMBAT burrowing marsupial   zo
WONDER marvel; miracle; prodigy; awe
WONING a dwelling
WONTED accustomed; usual
WONTON 'Chinese ravioli', cooked in soup
                                                    ck
WOODED afforested; timbered   fr
WOODEN clumsy; impassive
WOODIE the gallows (Sc.)
WOOFER base loudspeaker   ac
WOOING courting; courtship
WOOLLY lanate   tx
WORDED expressed; phrased
WORKED moiled; strove; slaved
WORKER hand; toiler; operative
WORK-UP rehearsal; exercise
WORMED crept; insinuated; crawled
WORMUL a wornil   zo
WORNIL cow-maggot   zo
WORREL lizard (Egypt)   zo
WORRIT an annoyance
WORSEN to defeat; to deteriorate
WORSER far worse
WORTHY exemplary; noble; meritorious
WOUNDY excessive; injurious
WOU-WOU silver gibbon; wow-wow (Java)
WOWSER kill-joy; fanatical Puritan
WRAITH apparition; ghost; spectre
WRASSE prickly fish   zo
WRATHY apt to wrath; choleric
WREATH festoon; garland; chaplet
WRENCH strain; sprain; twist   to
WRETCH villain; vagabond; miscreant
WRIEST most distorted
WRIGHT an artificer; mechanic

WRITER scribe; author; scribbler
WRITHE squirm; wriggle; contort
WUTHER to low (dial.)
WUZZLE to jumble (USA)
WYVERN wivern; heraldic dragon   hd

X

XANADU Kubla Khan's country
XANGTI Zeus (Chinese)
XENIAL genial; friendly
XENIUM gift; picture of still life
XENOPS tree-creeper birds (S. Amer.)   zo
XERXES Persian King; Ahasuerus
X-GUIDE transmission line
XOANON primitive Greek statue
X-RAYED (Rontgen rays)   md
XYLENE a benzene derivative   ch
XYLITE asbestos   mn
XYLOID like wood
XYLOMA internally spore-forming body   bt
XYLOSE wood sugar   ch
XYSTER a bone scraper   md
XYSTOS ⎫ covered portico used by
XYSTUS ⎭ athletes (Greek)

Y

YABBER speech (Australian)
YAFFLE the green woodpecker   zo
YAGGER pedlar; hawker (Sc.)
YAHVEH Jahveh; Jehovah   rl
YAKSKA Hindu gnome
YAMMER whine; blather; grumble
YANKED heaved
YANKEE Northern American
YANKEE a specially large jib   nt
YANKER a big lie (Sc.)
YAOURT Turkish fermented milk
YAPOCK S. Amer. water-opossum   zo
YAPPED yelped
YAPPER a yapping dog   zo
YARDED confined
YARNED related; narrated
YARPHA peaty soil (Shetland)
YARRAH Australian red gum tree   bt
YARROW the milfoil   bt
YARYAN soda-recovery method   pp
YAUPED yelped (USA)   bt
YAUPON holly (used as tea)
YAWING deviating from course   nt
YAWLED howled; cried
YAWNED gaped; oscitated
YCLEPT by name of; called
YEANED, YEENED brought forth
YEARLY annual
YEASTY turbid; frothy; foamy
YELLED bawled; howled; screamed
YELLOW cowardly
YELPED yauped; yapped; barked

YELPER yapper
YEMENI native of Yemen
YENITE a silicate of iron — mn
YEOMAN a beefeater; a farmer — nt
YERKED jerked
YER-NUT pig-nut — bt
YES-MAN sycophant
YESTER previous; last
YEXING hiccuping
YOGISM a Hindu philosophy
YOICKS! a hunting cry
YOJANA about 5 miles (8 km) Indian — me
YOKING coupling; linking
YOLKED having a yolk
YONDER over there
YONKER a stripling
YORKER (cricket)
YORUBA tribe (South Sahara)
YOUTHY young; callow
YOU-UNS you, you ones
YOWLED howled; yelled
YOWLEY yellow bunting — zo
Y-TRACK reversing lines for trains
YTTRIA oxide of yttrium — ch
YTTRIC containing yttrium — ch
YUCKER American woodpecker — zo

Z

ZABIAN Sabian; non-Christian gnostic
ZABISM Sabianism
ZABRUS beetle genus — zo
ZACCAB Yucatan wall plaster
ZACCHO the base of a pedestal
ZAFFER ⎫
ZAFFRE ⎬ cobalt ore — mn
ZAMITE fossil-plant — bt
ZANDER sander; pike-perch — zo
ZANIES clowns; buffoons
ZANTHA knitted fabric
ZAPOTE plums (Mexico) — bt
ZARAPE serape; Mexican blanket — tx
ZAREBA zeraba; zariba; fortified camp
ZARNEC orpiment — mn
ZEALOT fanatic; bigot; partisan
ZEATIN adenine derivative — bc
ZEBECK Algerian pirate-ship — nt
ZECHIN sequin; Venetian gold — nm
ZEEKOE hippopotamus (S. Africa) — zo
ZEETAK red-coral (S. Africa)

ZEMZEM sacred fountain at Mecca
ZENANA women's quarter (Ind.)
ZENDIK Eastern heretic; magician
ZENITH acme; apex; climax; summit
ZEPHYR the west wind; soft breeze
ZEREBA zareba; thornbush stockade
ZEUGMA grammatical conjunction
ZIAMET Turkish military district
ZICSAC sicsac; crocodile bird — zo
ZIG-ZAG tortuous
ZILLAH Indian district
ZIMONE (gluten)
ZINCKY like zinc
ZINGEL perch; Danube fish — zo
ZINNIA a flower — bt
ZIPPED whizzed
ZIPPER zip-fastener
ZIRCON a silicate — mn
ZITHER the cithern — mu
ZIVOLA yellow-hammer — zo
ZODIAC a heavenly girdle; the ecliptic
ZOETIC vital
ZOMBIE moron; drugged person
ZONARY ⎫
ZONOID ⎬ resembling a girdle
ZONATE belted
ZONING area allocation; planning
ZONNAR girdle worn in the Levant
ZONULE zonula; small zone
ZONURE lizard covered with spikes — zo
ZOONAL embryonic — zo
ZOONIC zoological — zo
ZOOSIS animal-parasite-caused disease
ZOO-ZOO wood-pigeon — zo
ZOSTER shingles — md
ZOUAVE Algerian soldier
ZOUNDS 'God's wounds'
ZUFOLO zuffolo; flageolet — mu
ZUMATE ⎫
ZYMATE ⎬ a salt of zymic acid — ch
ZUNIAN Pueblo-Indian
ZYGITE an oarsman in a trireme
ZYGOMA the cheek-bone — md
ZYGOSE (fertilization) — bt
ZYGOTE a spore; a germ-cell — bt, zo
ZYMASE a ferment; an enzyme
ZYMITE priest using leavened bread — rl
ZYMOID like a ferment; yeasty — ch, ck
ZYMOME insoluble gluten
ZYTHUM ancient type of beer — br

A

AARONIC (Jewish priest-hood) rl
ABACIST an accountant
ABACTOR cattle thief; rustler
ABADDON Apollyon; bottomless pit
ABALONE mother-of-pearl
ABANDON joie-de-vivre; forsake; quit
ABASHED shamed; embarrassed
ABASING degrading; humbling
ABATING mitigating; stopping
ABATTIS military obstacles
ABATURE beast tracks
ABAXIAL oblique rays pg
ABBOZZO preliminary sketch
ABB-WOOL warp-yarn
ABDOMEN the belly md
ABDUCED abducted; separated
ABETTED incited; aided; assisted
ABETTER an abettor; instigator lw
ABEYANT in abeyance
ABIDING residence; lasting; durable
ABIETIC (conifers) bt
ABIETIN (resin)
ABIGAIL serving-girl; Hebe; waitress
ABIGEAT cattle theft lw
ABILITY legal power; wealth; talent
ABIOSIS absence of life
ABJUDGE deprive by law lw
ABJURED recanted; repudiated
ABJURER forswearer
ABLATOR heat-protection material; instrument md
ABLEPSY blindness md
ABLINGS aiblins; perhaps
ABLUENT detergent
ABOLISH destroy; extirpate; annul
ABRADED scraped; worn away
ABRAXAS Gnostic god; amulet
ABREAST side by side
ABRIDGE curtail; epitomize; summarize
ABROACH tapped; afoot; astir
ABSCESS boil; ulcer md
ABSCIND cut off
ABSCISS a geometric line
ABSCOND decamp; bolt; quit; levant
ABSENCE lack; want; deficiency
ABSIDAL apse-like
ABSINTH liqueur; wormwood
ABSOLVE release; exonerate; shrive
ABSTAIN refrain; desist; avoid
ABUSING perverting; violating
ABUSION deception; disparagement
ABUSIVE ribald; reviling; calumnious
ABUTTAL the boundary of lands
ABUTTED contiguous; bordered on
ABUTTER neighbour lw
ABYSMAL fathomless; profound
ABYSSAL bottomless
ACADEMY also academe; institution
ACADIAN Nova Scotian
ACALEPH jellyfish zo

ACANTHA prickly plant bt
ACAPNIA loss of CO_2 in blood md
ACARDIA heart-less
ACARINA mites; ticks zo
ACCABLE overwhelm; crush (obs.)
ACCEDED assented; succeeded
ACCEDER one who concurs
ACCIDIE sloth; torpor (obs.)
ACCLAIM applaud; applause; proclaim
ACCOAST (low flying)
ACCOLLE collared hd
ACCOMPT account
ACCOUNT deem; reckon; recital; bill
ACCOURT to court (Spens.)
ACCRETE grow together
ACCRUED resulted; accumulated
ACCURSE curse; condemn; execrate
ACCURST accursed; damned; diabolical
ACCUSAL an accusation; indictment
ACCUSED defendant; arraigned lw
ACCUSER plaintiff lw
ACERATE (aceric acid) ch
ACERBIC sour; caustic; astringent
ACEROLA Amer. cherry-like fruit bt
ACEROSE acerous; prickly bt
ACETARY acid pulp
ACETATE (vinegar) ch
ACETIFY acidify ch
ACETONE liquid ketone ch
ACETOUS also acetose; sour
ACHAEAN of Archaia (Greek)
ACHAENE seeded fruit bt
ACHATES a true friend
ACHERON river of woe
ACHIEVE perform; perfect; attain
ACHIOTE red colouring matter from seeds ck
ACHOLIA lack of bile md
ACHTUNG beware!; look out! (Ger.)
ACICULA spiked crystals
ACIDIZE to add acid
ACIDITY sourness; tartness
ACIDOID potentially acid (soil)
ACIFORM needle-shaped
ACINOUS acinose; granular
ACK-EMMA a.m. (signalling)
ACLINIC no magnetic dip
ACOLOGY the healing art md
ACOLYTE also acolyth; assistant rl
ACONITE plant genus; monkshood bt
ACONTIA free threads of anthozea zo
ACOUCHY guinea pig; agouti zo
ACQUEST acquisition lw
ACQUIRE get; gain; procure; win
ACRASIA inability of self-restraint pc
ACRATIA impotence
ACREAGE area in acres
ACRISIA therapeutic uncertainty md
ACROBAT a tumbler; funambulist
ACROGEN (club-moss); (tree-fern) bt
ACRONIC non-cosmical (astronomy)
ACRONYM word composed of initials

ACRONYX ingrowing nail
ACROTER pinnacle　　　　　　　ar
ACROTIC superficial　　　　　　md
ACRYLIC acid, resins for plastics　ch
ACTABLE performable
ACTAMER substance stopping bacteria growth
ACTINIA (sea-anemones)　　　　zo
ACTINIC chemical ray action (solar)
ACTRESS a lady of parts
ACTUARY statistical expert; registrar
ACTUATE impel; urge; instigate; incite
ACULEUS sting; prickle　　　　zo, bt
ACUSHLA darling (Irish)
ACUTELY keenly; intensely; poignantly
ACYESIS sterility of female
ADACTYL fingerless
ADAGIAL proverbial
ADAMANT the diamond　　　　　mn
ADAMITE a nudist
ADAPTED conformed; attuned; adjusted
ADAPTER adaptor; a fitment
ADAXIAL axis-face of leaf　　　　bt
ADDENDA appendix; augmented matter
ADDIBLE addable
ADDLING going rotten; confusing
ADDRESS skill; accost; speech; (golf)
ADDUCED cited; brt. forward; alleged
ADDUCER a deducer
ADDULCE to sweeten
ADENINE purine derivative　　　ch
ADENOID growth in nasal pharynx　md
ADENOMA glandular tumour　　　md
ADENOSE
ADENOUS} glandular　　　　　md
ADHERED stuck; clung; held; cleaved
ADHERER partisan; ally; parasite
ADHIBIT attach; administer
ADIPOMA morbid obesity　　　　md
ADIPOSE fatty; adipous; sebaceous
ADIPSIA never thirsty　　　　　md
ADJOINT united; connected
ADJOURN suspend; postpone; defer
ADJUDGE condemn; decree; ordain
ADJUNCT a concomitant
ADJURED charged on oath
ADJURER adjuror
ADJUTOR a helper; colleague; ally
ADMIRAL also ammiral　　　　　nt
ADMIRED wondered; appreciated
ADMIRER a lover; adorer
ADMIXED adulterated; infused
ADOLODE distillation tester
ADONAIS Shelley's elegy on Keats
ADONIZE adonise; beautify
ADOPTED appropriated; fathered
ADORING worshipping; idolizing
ADORNED embellished; decked
ADORSED back to back　　　　　hd
ADRENAL (kidneys)　　　　　　md
ADULATE flatter; cajole; belaud
ADULLAM (a cave of refuge)

ADUSTED sunburnt; parched
ADVANCE to extoll; loan; promote
ADVENED acceded
ADVENER an assentor
ADVERSE contrary; hostile; inimical
ADVISED notified; informed; apprised
ADVISOR adviser; counsellor
ADVOWEE a patron of a benefice　rl
ADYNAMY weakness　　　　　md
AEOLIAN aerial　　　　　　　mu
AEOLIST wind-bag
AEONIAN eternal
AERATED gassy
AERATOR soda-water machine
AEROBAT an aerial stunter
AEROBIA bacteria　　　　　　md
AEROBIC microbial　　　　　　md
AEROBUS passenger plane
AEROGEL gel containing gas
AEROSOL sprayed mist　　　　ch
AETATIS at the age of
AFFABLE benign; gracious; sociable
AFFABLY cordially; courteously
AFFICHE notice; placard
AFFINAL akin; related
AFFINED united; allied; related
AFFININ insecticide from Mex. plant
AFFIXED attached; appended; annexed
AFFLICT distress; torment; chasten
AFFORCE reinforce
AFFRONT insult; outrage; abuse
AFFUSED sprinkled
AFFYING betrothing
AFGHANI native (Afghanistan)　　nm
AFLAUNT flaunting
AFRICAN of Africa
AGAINST opposite; counter; despite
AGALAXY lack of milk　　　　md
AGAMIST matrimonial objector
AGAMOUS cryptogamic
AGATINE like agate　　　　　mn
AGATIZE turn into agate
AGELESS timeless
AGELONG ancient; antiquated
AGENDUM a business item
AGEUSIA loss of taste　　　　md
AGGRACE to favour
AGGRATE to gratify
AGGRESS encroach; assault; intrude
AGGROUP group together
AGILELY quickly; actively
AGILITY nimbleness; readiness
AGISTER
AGISTOR} grazing controller
AGITATE ruffle; perturb; confuse
AGITATO spasmodic　　　　　mu
AGNAMED known as
AGNATIC akin
AGNOMEN added surname
AGNOSIA perceptionlessness　　md
AGONISM a competition
AGONIST a contestant

AGONIZE agonise; torture; suffer
AGRAFFE clasp for armour; a hook
AGROUND stranded
AGYNOUS non-reproductive   bt
AHRIMAN evil spirit (Persian)
AIBLINS ablings; perhaps
AIDANCE help; succour; bounty
AIDLESS unsupported; unbacked; solo
AIGULET aglet; pendant
AILANTO tree of Heaven   bt
AILERON wing lateral-control   ae
AILETTE armoured epaulet
AILMENT malady; complaint; disorder
AIMLESS pointless; random; haphazard
AIR BASE strategic air supply point
AIR-BATH nudity for health
AIR-BONE hollow bone
AIR-BUMP sudden jolt during flight   ae
AIRCAST sow seed from the air
AIR-CORE cable   tc
AIR-FLUE hot air distributor
AIRFOIL aileron
AIR-FUEL gas-liquid ratio   eg
AIR GLOW atmospheric luminosity
AIRHEAD airport (forward supply)   ae
AIR-HOLE ventilator
AIRLESS stuffy
AIRLIFT aerial transportation
AIRLINE flight transport company
AIR-LOCK pump flow stoppage
AIR MAIL post carried by air
AIR MARK par avion
AIRPARK fleet of aeroplanes
AIRPORT aeroplane landing area
AIR-PUMP vacuum maker
AIR RAID attack by aeroplanes
AIR-SACS quill vesicles   zo
AIR-SHED a hangar
AIRSHIP dirigible; zeppelin
AIRWAYS airlines
AJACINE cycactonine acid ester   ch
AJUTAGE vent pipe
AKINETE oil/food storage cell   bt
ALAMEDA shaded promenade
A-LA-MODE stylish
A-LA-MORT till death
ALANINE amino acid   md
ALANTIN starch   bt
ALARMED shocked; appalled; daunted
ALASKAN (Alaska)
ALASTOR Nemesis
ALBERIA shield without arms   hd
ALBITIC (felspar)   ch
ALBORAK Mahomet's mount to heaven
ALBUMEN white of egg
ALBUMIN (endosperm)   md
ALCAICS Alcaic verse
ALCALDE judge
ALCANNA henna   bt
ALCAYDE Spanish governor; judge
ALCAZAR Moorish palace
ALCHEMY alchymy; medieval chemistry

ALCOHOL pure wine spirit   ch
ALCYONE star in Pleiades
ALECOST costmary; ale flavouring   bt
ALE-GILL medicated liquor
ALEHOOF ground ivy   bt
ALEMBIC distilling retort
ALENGTH full length
ALERTER brisker; more wakeful
ALERTLY vigilantly; actively; warily
ALETUDE fatness; bulkiness
ALEURON albuminoid   bt
ALE-WIFE kind of skad; mackerel   zo
ALFALFA lucerne grass   bt
ALGAROT antimony emetic   md
ALGATES by all means; always
ALGEBAR the constellation, Orion
ALGEBRA number-properties investigation
ALGESIA sensitiveness to pain
ALGIFIC producing cold
ALHENNA henna; alkenna; orange dye
ALICANT Spanish wine
ALIDADE surveyor's sight rule   sv
ALIENEE transferee
ALIENER a parter
ALIFORM wing-like
ALIGNED adjusted; regulated; aimed
ALIMENT nutriment; sustenance; food
ALIMONY maintenance   lw
ALIQUOT integral factor
ALKANET henna dye   bt
ALKORAN alcoran; the Koran   rl
ALLAYED quieted; alleviated; pacified
ALLEGED averred; asserted; declared
ALLEGRO gaily   mu
ALLERGY distaste; repugnance
ALLETTE building wing; buttress   ar
ALL-GOOD a plant   bt
ALL-HAIL a greeting
ALL-HEAL a panacea; valerian, etc.
ALLOBAR non-natural-isotope form of
  element   nc
ALLONGE added leaf; lunge
ALLONYM assumed name, pseudonym
ALLOWED abated; authorized
ALLOXAN cyclic ureide   ch
ALLOYED debased; tempered
ALL-PASS phase-shift for any frequency
ALLSEED flax   bt
ALL-TIME unprecedented occurrence
ALLUDED suggested; insinuated; hinted
ALLURED enticed; inveigled; decoyed
ALLUVIA waterborne deposit
ALL-WATT induction motor   el
ALL-WAVE multi-wave   ro
ALL-WISE of infinite wisdom
ALLYING betrothing; leaguing
ALMADIE bark canoe
ALMANAC calendar
ALMOIGN charitable endowment
ALMONER giver of alms
ALMONRY almsgiving place; cupboard
ALMS-BOX charity receptacle

ALMS-FEE Peter's pence
ALMSMAN receiver of alms
ALNAGER wool inspector
ALODIUM freehold   lw
ALOETIC purgative   md
ALOGISM illogical statement
ALONGST along with
ALP-HORN Swiss cow-horn   mu
ALREADY before; previously
ALSIRAT bridge to paradise
ALTERED modified; transmuted
ALTERNE sudden plant-life change   bt
ALTHAEA hollyhock genus   bt
ALTHING Iceland Parliament
ALT-HORN saxhorn   mu
ALTRICE bird hatching immature young
ALTROSE glucose stereoisomer   ch
ALUMINA aluminium clay   mn
ALUMINE oxide of aluminium
ALUMING impregnating with alum
ALUMISH resembling alum
ALUMNUS college student
ALUNITE alum-stone   mn
ALVEARY hive; ear cavity   pl
ALVEATE to hollow out
ALVEOLA small cavity   bt
ALVEOLE tooth socket   pl
ALYSSUM a rock plant   bt
AMALGAM mercury alloy   ch
AMANDIN (almonds)   bt
AMANOUS lacking hands
AMARANT amaranth; a fadeless flower
AMASSED heaped; collected
AMATEUR not a professional
AMATIVE loving; lovesome
AMATORY ardent; erotic; passionate
AMAZING astounding; bewildering
AMAZONE riding habit
AMBAGES circumlocution; subterfuge
AMBARIE covered howdah
AMBETTI speck-containing glass
AMBIENT encompassing; enfolding
AMBITAL pertaining to skeletal parts
AMBITUS outer edge
AMBLING at an easy gait; sauntering
AMBOYNA a decorative wood   bt
AMBREIN (ambergris)
AMBROID moulded amber
AMBSACE, AMESACE double-ace (dice)
AMBULET small ambulance
AMELLUS purple star-wort   bt
AMENAGE domesticate; manage
AMENDED emended; ameliorated
AMENING ratifying; sanctioning
AMENITY pleasantness; agreeableness
AMENTAL bearing catkins   bt
AMENTIA imbecility   md
AMENTUM a catkin   bt
AMERCED fined
AMHARIC language (Ethiopia)
AMIABLE lovable; benign; winsome
AMIABLY kindly; charmingly

AMIDINE wheat extract
AMILDAR Indian official
AMMETER ampere meter   el
AMMONAL an explosive   ch
AMMONIA pungent gas   ch
AMNESIA loss of memory   md
AMNESTY pardon; absolution; oblivion
AMOEBAN pertaining to amoeba
AMONGST amid; between
AMORIST philanderer
AMOROSA, AMOROSI sweethearts;
   gallants
AMOROSO tenderly   mu
AMOROUS amative; passionate
AMORPHA indigo   bt
AMOTION deprivation   lw
AMPASSY ampersand, the &
AMPHORA two-handled wine jar
AMPLEST most lavish; most copious
AMPLIFY expand; enlarge; augment
AMPOULE } glass container for hypo-
AMPULLA } dermic dose   md
AMUSING entertaining; droll; ludicrous
AMUSIVE amusing
AMUTTER muttering
AMYLASE starch-hydrolysing enzyme   ch
AMYLENE (amyl)   ch
AMYLINE starch cellulose
AMYLOID starchy   bt, ch
AMYLOSE starch constituent   ch
ANABION anabolism-dominated organism
ANACARD cashew-nut   bt
ANAEMIA general debility   md
ANAEMIC bloodless   md
ANAGOGE } mystical
ANAGOGY } interpretation
ANAGRAM letter puzzle
ANALECT anthology
ANALGIA analgesia
ANALOGY similarity; likeness
ANALYSE examine critically
ANALYST a resolver
ANANICE absolute necessity
ANAPEST poetic metre
ANAPHIA loss of sense of touch
ANAPSID having roofed skull   zo
ANARCHY chaos; disorder; violence
ANATASE titanium oxide   ch
ANATOMY a skeleton; dissection   md
ANATRON glass scum
ANAUDIA loss of voice
ANAXIAL asymmetrical   zo
ANCHOVY a small fish   zo
ANCHUSA alkanet, red dye
ANCIENT antique; pristine ensign
ANCONES ornamental brackets
ANCORAL like an anchor; hooked
ANCRESS } female anchorite
ANKRESS }
ANDANTE rather slow   mu
ANDARAC a red pigment
ANDIRON endiron; fire-dog

ANDRASE male-producing enzyme/hormone
ANDROID automaton; robot
ANDVARI a dwarf (Norse myth.)
ANELACE anlace; a broad dagger
ANELING annointing with oil   rl
ANEMONE anemony; windflower   bt, zo
ANEROID a kind of barometer
ANESONE white anise liqueur
ANETHOL oil of anise   bt
ANEURIA lack of nervous energy
ANEURIN B-group vitamin
ANGARIA war rights
ANGELIC seraphic; cherubic; heavenly
ANGELOT ancient lute; cheese   nm
ANGELUS a prayer
ANGERED exasperated; enraged; roused
ANGERLY angrily; wrathfully
ANGEVIN of Anjou
ANGIOID like blood/lymph vessel
ANGIOMA dilated-blood-vessel tumour   md
ANGLICE in English
ANGLIFY to anglicize
ANGLING hopeful occupation
ANGLIST expert in English
ANGRILY wrathfully; irately
ANGUINE snake-like
ANGUISH agony; distress; rack; pang
ANGULAR sharp cornered
ANIDIAN shapeless
ANILINE indigo derivative   ch
ANILITY dotage; senility; imbecility
ANIMATE actuate; vivify; excite
ANIMISM) religious theory that the soul
ANIMIST)   is the vital principle
ANISEED the seed of the anise   bt
ANNATES first fruits   rl, lw
ANNATTO annotto; a reddish dye   bt
ANNELID worm   zo
ANNEXED affixed; subjoined; attached
ANNOYED harassed; pestered; molested
ANNOYER an irritator; teaser
ANNUENT nodding
ANNUITY a yearly payment
ANNULAR ring-like
ANNULET small fillet round a column
ANNULUS ring; ring-shaped formation
ANODERM skinless   bt
ANODISE dyeing aluminium
ANODONT a freshwater mussel   zo
ANODYNE pain-killer; opiate; sedative
ANOESIA idiocy   pc
ANOESIS effortless reception of impressions   pc
ANOETIC pertaining to anoesis   pc
ANOLINI ravioli   ck
ANOLYTE portion of electrolyte   el
ANOMALY irregularity; eccentricity
ANOPSIA blindness; squint   md
ANOREXY lack of appetite   md
ANORMAL abnormal
ANOSMIA loss of smell power   md

ANOTHER one more
ANSATED with a handle
ANTACID a corrective   md
ANTAPEX point opposite to apex   as
ANT-BEAR American ant-eater   zo
ANTE-ACT an act preceding
ANTEFIX ornamental tiling
ANT-EGGS the pupae of ants   zo
ANTENNA a feeler   ro, zo
ANT-HILL a formicary   zo
ANTHOID flower-like   bt
ANTHONY saint; piglet   rl
ANTHRAX wool-sorter's disease   md
ANTICAL stem/leaf upper surface   bt
ANTICER anti-icing means   ae
ANTICLY oddly; fantastically; quaintly
ANTICOR animal disease
ANTICUM a front porch
ANTI-GAS for combating gas
ANTIGEN cause of antibodies   md
ANTILOG anti-logarithm
ANTIPYR formalin   ch
ANTIQUA printing type   pr
ANTIQUE archaic; old; ancient
ANTI-RED anti-communist
ANTISAG preventing sagging   ar
ANT-LIKE industrious
ANT-LION a neuropterous insect   zo
ANTONYM the opposite of a synonym
ANVILED forged; wrought by a smith
ANXIETY concern; disquiet; uneasiness
ANXIOUS troubled; apprehensive
ANYBODY person unspecified
ANYWAYS anyhow
ANYWHEN any old time
ANYWISE somehow
APAGOGE) progressive argument;
APAGOGY) reductio ad absurdum
APANAGE natural attribute; perquisite
APANDRY male impotence
APATITE lime phosphate   mn
APAUMEE open hand   hd
APE-HOOD apishness
APELIKE imitative; simian
APELLES finished painter
APEPSIA poor digestion   md
APERTOR eye-opener; muscle   md
APETALY absence of petals   bt
APHACIA lenslessness of eye   md
APHAGIA inability to swallow, feed   md, zo
APHAKIA lenslessness of eye   md
APHASIA temporary dumbness   md
APHELIA plural of aphelion
APHEMIA loss of speech   md
APHESIS) vowel elision
APHETIC)
APHIDES plant-lice; ants' milchcows   zo
APHONIA loss of voice   md
APHONIC speechless
APHORIA sterility
APHOTIC able to grow without light   bt

APHRITE carbonate of lime	mn
APHTHAE ulceration of the mouth	md
APHYLLY absence of leaves	bt
APICIAN epicurean; gastronomic	
APIECES in pieces (obs.)	
APINOID clean	md
APISHLY monkey-like	
APITPAT palpitating	
APLANAT lens lacking spherical aberration	
APLASIA defective structural growth	md
APOCOPE elision; verbal curtailment	
APOCYTE cell-less protoplasm	bt
APODOUS apodal, footless	
APOGAMY sex function loss	bt
APOGEAN culminating; climactic	
APOGENY, APOGYNY sterility	bt
APOLOGY excuse; explanation; plea	
APOLUNE point in moon satellite orbit	as
APOPLEX apoplexy (obs.)	
APOSTIL marginal note; postscript	
APOSTLE a divine messenger	
APOTOME } mathematical difference;	
APOTOMY } a major semitone	mu
APPAREL equipment; attire; vesture	
APPEACH impeach; censure (obs.)	
APPEASE pacify; assuage; placate	
APPERIL peril (Shak.)	
APPLAUD praise; commend; extol	
APPLIED referred; exercised; used	
APPOINT nominate; prescribe; enjoin	
APPOSED placed side by side	
APPOSER an examiner; questioner	
APPRISE inform; acquaint; warn	
APPRIZE appreciate; appraise	
APPROOF sanction; praise; trial	
APPROVE ratify; assent; encourage	
APPULSE rapprochement	
APRICOT abricock	bt
APRICOT brandy; fruit	bt
APRONED wearing an apron	
APROPOS pertinent; opportune; timely	
APROTIC high-dielectric solvent	ch
APSIDAL absidal; apse	
APSIDES perigee and apogee	
APTERAL wingless	zo
APTERYX kiwi-bird (New Zealand)	zo
APTHOUS (thrush); ulcerous	md
APTNESS suitability; felicity	
APTOTIC indeclinable	
APYREXY absence of fever	md
APYROUS unchanged by heat	
AQUARIA (aquariums)	zo
AQUASOL sulphonated castor oil	ch
AQUATIC in/of water	
AQUEOUS watery; humid; damp	
AQUIFER water-containing soil	gl
AQUILON the north wind	
ARABIAN of Arabia	
ARABINE gum arabic	bt
ARABISM Arab idiom	
ARABIST Arabic expert	

ARACHIS peanut genus	bt
ARAMAIC Syriac; Aramite	
ARAMEAN Chaldaic; Chaldean	
ARATION ploughing	
ARBITER umpire; judge; referee	
ARBLAST crossbow	
ARBORED arboured	
ARBORET shrub	bt
ARBUTUS an evergreen	bt
ARCADED having arcades	
ARCADIA pastoral country	
ARCADIA (Sir Philip Sidney)	
ARCANUM a mystery; a secret	
ARCHAIC Noachian; antiquated	
ARCHERY a pastime	
ARCHEUS vital principle in alchemy	
ARCH-FOE Satan	
ARCHING curved; vaulting	
ARCHLET small arch	
ARCHWAY gateway, gatehouse	
ARC-LAMP carbon-pole-bridge lamp	
ARCTOID like a bear	
ARCUATE bow-shaped	
ARDENCY passion; warmth; fire	
ARDUOUS laborious; toilsome	
AREFIED withered; arid; parched	
ARENOSE sandy; arenaceous	
AREOLAR areolic; cell nucleus	bt
ARGHOOL Arab reed pipe	mu
ARGOTIC slangy	
ARGUING discussing; debating	
ARGYRIA silver poisoning	md
ARGYROL silver antiseptic	
ARICINA } alkaloid drug	md
ARICINE }	
ARIDITY dryness; aridness; sterility	
ARIETTA ariette; air	mu
ARIGHTS correctly	
ARILLED having a husk	bt
ARILLUS seed coating	bt
ARIPPLE aglinting	
ARISING emerging; originating	
ARMHOLE clothing aperture for arm	tx
ARMIGER an esquire; armour-bearer	
ARMILLA antique bracelet	
ARMLESS lacking arms	
ARMOIRE cupboard; aumbry	
ARMORIC Breton dialect	
ARMOURY arsenal; magazine	
ARNOTTO annatto; orange dye	bt
AROUSAL awakening; uprising	
AROUSED excited; provoked	
ARRAIGN accuse; summon	lw
ARRANGE group; classify; dispose	
ARRAYED marshalled; equipped	
ARREARS payments overdue	
ARRIDED pleased; gratified; scorned	
ARRIERE rear; back; remote (Fr.)	
ARRIVAL advent; coming; newcomer	
ARRYISH festive; jovial	
ARSENAL armoury; depository	

ARSENIC a metallic element — ch
ARTICLE essay; paper; indenture
ARTISAN artizan; workman; operative
ARTISTE a fine performer
ARTLESS simple; ingenuous; naive
ARTSMAN a craftsman
ARUSPEX soothsayer; seer; diviner
ASARONE form of camphor
ASBOLIN oil from soot
ASCARID parasite worm — zo
ASCESIS self-discipline — rl
ASCETIC austere; rigid; abstemious
ASCIANS equator dwellers
ASCIDIA molluscs — zo
ASCITES peritoneal fluid collection — md
ASCITIC dropsical — md
ASCRIBE attribute; assign; impute
ASEPSIS sterilization — md
ASEPTIC sterilized
ASEXUAL algamic; sexless
ASHAMED abashed; confused
ASH-CAKE pastry cooked in ashes
ASH-FIRE chemical operations fire
ASH-HEAP tip for ashes
ASHIVER atremble
ASH-TRAY cigarette butt tray
ASH-WORT a weed — bt
ASIARCH Asiatic Proconsul
ASIATIC of Asia
ASINEGO a dolt; asinico
ASININE ass-like; idiotic; obstinate
ASKANCE obliquely; aslant; awry
ASPERGE sprinkle
ASPERSE slander; vilify; traduce
ASPHALT bitumen — mn
ASPHYXY suffocation — md
ASPIRED soared; aimed high; yearned
ASPIRER aspirant; competitor
ASPIRIN a drug — md
ASPRAWL sprawling
ASPREAD scattered
ASPROUT sprouting
ASQUINT obliquely; askew
ASSAGAI assegai; spear
ASSAPAN flying squirrel (N. Amer.) — zo
ASSAULT onset; attack; storm; assail
ASSAYED tested; tried; endeavoured
ASSAYER metallurgist; analyst
ASSEGAI assegay; Zulu spear
ASSEVER asseverate; allege; aver
ASS-HEAD blockhead
ASSIEGE to besiege
ASSIZER inspector of weights
ASSIZES Courts of jurisdiction — lw
ASSIZOR juror — lw
ASSUAGE allay; pacify; mollify; quell
ASSUMED usurped; feigned; implied
ASSUMER an arrogant person
ASSURED pledged; guaranteed
ASSURER) underwriter;
ASSUROR) insurer — lw

ASSWAGE assuage (obs.)
ASTABLE free-running, self-sustaining — r
ASTASIA inability to keep erect — m
ASTATIC unstable; lacking polarity
ASTEISM refined irony
ASTERIA (sapphire) — m
ASTERID star-fish — z
ASTHORE darling; acushla (Irish)
ASTONED astonished; confounded
ASTOUND amaze; daze; stupefy
ASTRAEA Goddess of Justice
ASTRAND stranded
ASTRICT restrict; bind
ASTRIDE astraddle
ASTRITE star-stone — m
ASTROID star-shaped
ASTYLAR without columns
ASUDDEN suddenly
ASUNDER apart; divided; divergent
ATACTIC of randomly arranged polyme
constituents — c
ATAGHAN Turkish dagger
ATARAXY impassiveness; coolness
A-TAUNTO tidy and shipshape — n
ATAVISM reversion to type
ATEBRIN anti-malarial drug — m
ATEKNIA childlessness
ATELENE amorphous; imperfect
ATELIER studio; sculptor's workshop
ATHALIA saw-fly — z
ATHANOR alchemist's furnace
ATHEISE atheize
ATHEISM disbelief
ATHEIST a nullifidian
ATHIRST eager; dry; thirsty
ATHLETE athleta; a contestant
ATHRILL thrilling
ATHRONG crowded
ATHWART across; askew; aslant
ATHYRIA absence of thyroid gland — m
ATOBOMB atomic bomb
ATOKOUS lacking offspring
ATOMATE covered by small particles — b
ATOMISM atomic theory
ATOMIST atomic theorist
ATOMIZE vaporize
ATONING expiating; reconciling
ATRESIA failure of opening development
ATROPAL not inverted; upturned — b
ATROPHY wasting away — m
ATROPIA bella-donna — m
ATROPIN deadly nightshade — b
ATTABOY a panegyric (USA)
ATTACHE junior member of embassy; cas
ATTAGAS a pheasant — z
ATTAINT corrupt; convicted
ATTELET ornamental meat skewer — c
ATTEMPT try; aim; endeavour; effort
ATTICAL classical
ATTINGE touch
ATTIRED garbed; dressed; arrayed
ATTRACT draw; allure; charm; decoy

ATTRIST to sadden	**AVOIDER** dodger; shunner	
ATTRITE worn by friction; penitent	**AVOWANT** defendant in replevin	lw
ATTUNED in harmony	**AVOWING** owning; admitting; averring	
AUBERGE an inn (Fr.)	**AWAITED** eagerly expected; tarried	
AUCTION roup; vendue	**AWAKING** rousing; bestirring	
AUDIBLE able to be heard	**AWARDED** bestowed; granted; allotted	
AUDIBLY spoken clearly	**AWARDER** a judge; donor; giver	lw
AUDIENT listening; attentive	**AWAVING** fluttering	
AUDITED examined; checked	**AWELESS** without fear	
AUDITOR examiner; accountant	**AWESOME** full of awe; fearsome	
AUGITIC (augite); (pyroxene) mn	**AWFULLY** dreadfully; portentously	
AUGMENT amplify; increase; enhance	**AWKWARD** clumsy; ungainly; inapt	
AUGURAL soothsaying; ominous	**AWL-BIRD** woodpecker	zo
AUGURED portended; foretold	**AWL-WORT** an aquatic plant	bt
AURALLY (ear)	**AWNLESS** beardless	bt
AURATED aureate; golden	**AXIALLY** from pole to pole	
AUREATE gilded	**AXIFORM** like a spindle or aborr	
AUREITY the property of gold	**AXILLAR** a feather	zo, bt
AURELIA a chrysalis zo	**AXLE-BOX** automobile part	au
AUREOLA aureole	**AXLE-PIN** linch-pin	
AUREOLE golden halo	**AXOLOTL** larval salamander	zo
AURICLE external ear md	**AZALINE** emulsion-sensitizing dye mixture	
AURIFIC gold bearing	**AZAROLE** medlar	bt
AURITED having ears	**AZELAIC** rancid-fat acid	ch
AUROCHS urus; wild ox; Eur. bison zo	**AZILIAN** pre-Neolithic	
AURORAL (dawn); eoan	**AZIMUTH** zenith	
AUSLAUT final syllable/word sound	**AZOTITE** nitrous acid	ch
AUSONIA Italy	**AZOTIZE** to nitrogenise	
AUSPICE augury; omen; portent	**AZOTOUS** nitrous	
AUSTERE severely simple; ascetic	**AZTECAN** Aztec	
AUSTRAL southern	**AZULEJO** bright-coloured Iberian tile	
AUTARCH autocrat; tyrant	**AZUREAN** sky-blue	
AUTARKY national self-sufficiency	**AZURINE** azure	
AUTOBUS omnibus	**AZURITE** copper carbonate	mn
AUTOCAR motor car	**AZYGOUS** not in pairs	
AUTONYM true name	**AZYMITE** Armenian churchman	rl
AUTOPSY post-mortem exam. md	**AZYMOUS** unleavened; unfermented	
AUTOSET quick-levelling in surveying		
AUTO-VAC vacuum au		
AUXESIS hyperbole	**B**	
AUXETIC amplifying		
AVAILED answered the purpose; helped	**BAALISM** idolatry	
AVARICE greed; rapacity; cupidity	**BAALITE** worshipper of Baal	
AVENAGE barley-corn rent lw	**BABBLED** chattered; jabbered	
AVENGED retaliated; revenged	**BABBLER** tropical thrush	zo
AVENGER vindicator	**BABIISM** Persian religion	
AVENOUS lacking veins md	**BABUINA** female baboon	
AVERAGE mean; moderate; ordinary	**BABYISH** infantile	
AVERNUS infernal regions	**BABYISM** infancy	
AVERRED affirmed; alleged; stated	**BACCARA** baccarat	
AVERTED warded off; prevented	**BACCARE** stand back!	
AVERTER preventer; diverter	**BACCATE** berry-shaped; pulpy	bt
AVIATED flew; planed	**BACCHIC** roistering; carousing	
AVIATOR aeroplane pilot	**BACCHUS** the god of Wine	
AVICIDE killing of birds	**BACILLI** bacteria; microbes	md
AVICULA kind of pearl oyster	**BACK-CUT** tree-felling cut	fr
AVIDITY greed; voracity; eagerness	**BACKING** aiding; abetting; retiring	
AVIETTE a glider	**BACK-LOG** delayed work	
AVIFORM bird-shaped	**BACK-OUT** reversal of missile drill	
AVOCADO alligator-pear bt	**BACK-SAW** thick-backed saw	cr
AVODIRE African hard-wood bt	**BACKSET** an eddy	
AVOIDED eschewed; annulled; eluded	**BACTRIS** peach-palm	bt
	BADDISH rather bad	

BADIAGA small sponge
BADIANE bandian; aniseed — bt
BADNESS depravity; evil; wickedness
BAFFLED foiled; checked; bewildered
BAFFLER thwarter; confounder
BAGASSE refuse sugar stalks
BAGGAGE luggage; belongings; traps
BAGGALA 2-masted Arab vessel
BAGGING bag-cloth; pouching
BAGPIPE has 3 drones and a chanter
BAHADUR Indian title
BAILAGE ancient export duty
BAILIFF land steward; overseer — lw
BAILING confining; releasing
BAILLIE a baliff (Sc.)
BAITING victuals; badgering; harassing
BAKE-OUT electrode/valve pre-heating — el
BALANCE poise; weigh; surplus
BALANUS crustacean; acorn-shell — zo
BALCONY hanging porch — bd
BALDEST barest; plainest
BALDING loss of hair
BALDISH somewhat bald
BALDRIC baudric; shoulder-belt
BALEFUL evil; noxious; pernicious
BALISTA large Roman catapult
BALKING baulking; swerving; shying
BALLADE a form of poetry
BALLAST filling; discretion; stability
BALL-BOY (tennis)
BALLING becoming clogged
BALLIUM bulwark
BALLOON anything inflated and empty
BALMIER sweeter; milder
BALMILY soothingly; fragrantly
BALMING assuaging; embalming
BALNEAL pertaining to bathing
BALNEUM a bath — ch
BALONEY nonsense, something not to be
  believed
BALSAMY fragrant; aromatic
BAMBINO a child (It.)
BAMMING hoaxing; cheating
BANABAN Micronesian language
BANBURY a cake
BANDAGE ligament; ligature
BANDANA silk handkerchief
BANDBOX hat box, new-clothes box
BANDEAU brow-band
BANDIAN badiane; aniseed — bt
BANDIED discussed; tossed; agitated
BANDING uniting together
BANDLET bandelet; a flat moulding
BANDORE ancient kind of lute — mu
BANDROL banderole; small flag
BAND-SAW saw over wheels — to
BANEFUL baleful; deadly; venomous
BANGING overwhelming; clattering
BANGLED with bangles
BANK-BAR mine-shaft lining — mn
BANKING relying — ae
BANKSIA dwarf yellow climbing rose — bt

BANNING cursing; proscribing; barring
BANNOCK oaten-cake — ck
BANQUET feast; regalement — ck
BANSHEE ghost (Irish)
BANTENG Malayan wild ox
BANTERY raillery
BANTING reducing the diet; slimming
BANTING wild ox (East Ind.)
BANYULS Pyrenean wine
BAPTISM immersion at christening — r
BAPTIST member of Protestant sect
BAPTIZE christen
BARACAN camel-hair cloth
BARBARY a Saracen country (N. Africa)
BARBATE bearded; awned — b
BAR-BELL dumb-bell
BARBING shaving; trimming; piercing
BARBOLA modern gesso
BARBULE small beard — b
BARDISH bardic; (poetry)
BARDISM the lore of bards
BARDLET bardling; poetaster
BARGAIN chaffer; haggle; compact
BARGING shoving; elbowing; jostling
BARILLA raw seaweed alkali
BAR-IRON malleable iron in bars
BARK-BED tanner's hot-bed
BARKERY tan-house
BARKHAN lone crescentic sandhill — g
BARKING peeling; (shins)
BARK-PIT tan-vat
BARMAID Hebe; tavern server
BARMIER flightier; more crazy
BARMKIN outer castle ward
BARNABY the apostle, Barnabas
BARNAGH large whelk — z
BARNING storing; garnering
BARN-OWL screech owl — z
BARONET bart
BAROQUE rococo; whimsical; odd
BARRACE lists (tournament)
BARRACK (booing)
BARRAGE embankment; dam
BARRAGE (artillery fire)
BARRENS elevated plateaux
BARRICO small keg (Sp.)
BARRIER hindrance; embargo; obstacle
BARRING excluding; banning
BARRULY heraldic division — h
BAR-SHOE special horseshoe
BAR-SHOT double connected shot
BARTRAM the plant pellitory — b
BARWOOD red dye-wood — b
BARYTES barium sulphate — ck
BARYTIC (baryta)
BASBLEU blue stocking
BASCULE balanced drawbridge
BASE-BOX metal-plate measurement unit
                                              — r
BASENET bascinet; basnet; a helmet
BASENJI Congo barkless dog — z
BASHFUL strikingly modest; shy

BASHING coshing; slugging		
BASHLYK Russian hood		
BASILAR serving as a basis		
BASILIC basilican style		
BASINED in a basin		
BASINET basnet; round helmet		
BASKING luxuriating; revelling		
BASLARD a small dagger		
BASSOCK fibre mat		
BASSOON bass oboe	mu
BASTARD spurious; base-born; natural		
BASTILE castle on wheels		
BASTING coarse stitching		
BASTION an out-work		
BATABLE debatable; controversial		
BATATAS sweet potatoes	bt
BAT-BOAT sea-plane		
BATEFUL contentious; disputable		
BATH BUN a comestible	ck
BATHING giving/having a bath		
BATHMAN beach attendant		
BATH-MAT thick bathroom carpet		
BATHYAL pert. to deep-sea zone		
BATISTE cambric		
BATSMAN a cricketer		
BATTELS provisions (Oxford)		
BATTERY (artillery)	el
BATTING quilting; (cricket)		
BATTISH bat-like		
BATTLED battlemented; fought		
BATTLER resident at Oxford		
BATTURE raised sea/river bed		
BAUDRIC shoulder sash		
BAULKED shied; balked; jibbed		
BAUSOND badger-like	zo
BAUXITE (aluminium)	mn
BAWCOCK fine fellow		
BAWDILY lewdly; obscenely		
BAWDKIN baldachin; canopy	rl
BAWLING shouting; clamouring		
BAYONET a weapon of offence		
BAY-SALT evaporated sea-water		
BAY-TREE the laurel	bt
BAYWOOD mahogany	bt
BAY-YARN woollen yarn		
BAZIGAR nomadic Ind. gypsy		
BAZOOKA anti-tank gun		
BEACHED on the beach		
BEADING narrow moulding		
BEADMAN an almsman		
BEAKING (cock-fighting)		
BEAMILY broad on the beam		
BEAMING radiant; gleaming; bright		
BEAN-FLY a garden pest	zo
BEARDED awned; defied; opposed		
BEARDIE the whitethroat bird	zo
BEARING (magnetic); (rein)		
BEARISH uncouth; boorish; rude		
BEAR-PIT enclosure for bears		
BEASTLY brutal; sensual; bestial		
BEATIFY (saint-hood); canonize		

BEATING chastisement; battering		
BEATNIK latter-day Bohemian		
BEAUISH foppish		
BEBEERU greenheart tree	bt
BECAUSE owing to		
BECHARM captivate; fascinate		
BECKING nodding; bowing		
BECLOUD obscure; darken; bedim		
BEDDING planting out		
BEDEAUX piece-work system		
BEDELRY beadlery		
BEDEMAN beadman		
BEDEVIL bewitch		
BEDEWED covered with dew; affused		
BEDEWER a sprinkler		
BEDFAST bed-ridden		
BED-GOWN night gown		
BEDIGHT adorned		
BEDIZEN gaudily attired		
BED-MATE bed-fellow		
BEDOUIN nomadic Arab		
BED-POST bedstead support		
BED-REST recuperation		
BED-ROCK basic stratum	gl
BEDROOM sleeping apartment		
BEDROPT besprinkled; bedewed		
BEDSIDE clinic		
BED-SORE sore from bed-lying	md
BED-TICK cotton cloth		
BEDTIME time to sleep		
BEDWARD to bed		
BEDWARF to belittle; to dwarf		
BEDWORK easy toil		
BEE-BIRD fly-catcher	zo
BEECHEN of beech		
BEEF-TEA meat-extract drink		
BEE-GLUE beeswax		
BEE-HIVE home for bees		
BEE-LINE straight line		
BEE-MOTH wax-moth	zo
BEESWAX product of hives		
BEET-BUG agricultural pest	zo
BEET-FLY a dipterous insect	zo
BEETLED jutted out; smote		
BEE-TREE American linden	bt
BEFFANA befana; Epiphany fairy		
BEGGARY mendicancy; indigence		
BEGGING soliciting; craving; imploring		
BEGHARD beguine; religious order	rl
BEGLOOM sadden		
BEGONIA elephant's ear plant	bt
BEGORED gory; ensanguined		
BEGRIME (grime); sully; foul		
BEGROAN lament; complain		
BEGUARD a beghard; lay mendicant		
BEGUILE pass pleasantly; amuse		
BEGUILE deceive; delude; trick		
BEGUILE soothe (obs.)		
BEGUINE beghard; (religious order)		
BEHAVED acted with propriety		
BEHENIC of bean oil acid	ch

BEHONEY sweeten
BEHOOVE to be necessary
BEHOVED was necessary; befitted
BEINKED smudged
BEJEWEL set with gems
BEKNAVE to call a knave
BEKNOWN known
BELACED adorned with lace
BELATED overdue; retarded
BELAYED fastened; held   nt
BELCHED eructated
BELCHER coloured kerchief
BELDAME old hag
BELEPER infect with leprosy
BELGARD kind regard (obs.)
BELGIAN of Belgium
BELIBEL libel; traduce; slander
BELIEVE credit; opine; accept
BELL-HOP page boy
BELLIED dilated
BELLING full and ripe; bellowing
BELL-JAR vacuum enclosure
BELL-MAN town crier
BELLONA goddess of War
BELLOWS (organ); wind producer
BELOVED dear; darling
BELTANE May Day fire festival
BELTING beating; a belt
BELYING calumniating; counterfeiting
BEMAZED astounded; stupefied; dazed
BEMIRED soiled; besmirched
BEMOUTH to mouth; declaim
BEMUSED dazed; bewildered; confused
BENCHED seated
BENCHER (inns of court)   lw
BENDING curving; flexing; inclining
BENDLET small heraldic bend   hd
BENEATH inferior; subordinate; under
BENEFIC favourable (astrol.)
BENEFIT boon; profit; gain; enrich
BENELUX Belgium, Netherlands and
   Luxemburg
BENGALI of Bengal
BENIGHT obscure; cloud
BENISON benediction
BENOTED amply annotated
BENTEAK Nana-wood   bt
BENTHOS ocean-bed organisms   zo
BENZENE benzine   ch
BENZOIN resinous incense   ht
BENZOLE tar product   ch
BENZOYL benzoic acid   ch
BEPAINT paint; daub; smear
BEPATCH patch; cobble; mend
BEPEARL adorn with pearls
BEPINCH marked with pinches
BEPLUME feather
BEPROSE discuss tediously
BEQUEST legacy; inheritance
BEQUOTE quote frequently
BERATED scolded; nagged; chided

BEREAVE deprive; divest; despoil
BERGYLT red sea-fish   zo
BERHYME to lampoon in verse
BERLINE berlin; a vehicle
BERSERK Norse warrior; in a fury
BERTHED moored; situated   nt
BERTHON collapsible boat   nt
BERTRAM bastard pellitory   bt
BESAINT beatify; canonize   rl
BESAYLE great-grandfather   lw
BESEECH implore; entreat; crave
BESHAME put to shame
BESHINE light up; illuminate
BESHMET grape pulp
BESHONE sparkled; glittered
BESHREW curse; execrate
BESIDES except; save; moreover
BESIEGE beset; invest; beleaguer
BESLAVE enthral; enslave
BESLIME to soil; besmirch; defile
BESMEAR to daub; dirty; begrime
BESMOKE blacken with smoke
BESNUFF foul with snuff
BESOGNO besonio; a beggar; Besonian
BESPATE spit upon
BESPEAK stipulate; betoken; order
BESPEED help along
BESPICE to season; to drug
BESPIRT to asperse; sprinkle
BESPOKE ordered
BESPOUT orate; declaim; harangue
BESPUTT besputter
BESTAIN mark with spots
BESTEAD avail; help; relieve
BESTIAL brutal; live-stock (Sc.)
BESTICK to stick; prick
BESTILL to quiet
BESTING worsting; winning
BEST MAN groomsman
BESTORM assail
BESTREW scatter; spread
BESTRID stepped across
BESTUCK transfixed
BETAINE beet alkaloid   ch
BETAKEN departed; applied
BETHANK thank effusively
BETHINK recall to mind
BETHRAL enslave; captivate
BETHUMB crease
BETHUMP belabour; pommel
BETIDED happened; befell
BETIMES early; soon
BETITLE give a name to
BETOKEN indicate; foreshow
BETREAD step on
BETROTH affiance; plight
BETTING wagering; staking
BETTONG kangaroo rat
BETULIN birch camphor
BETUTOR instruct
BETWEEN amid

BETWIXT amidst
BEWARED took care; heeded; minded
BEWITCH fascinate; enchant; charm
BEZIQUE card game
BHANDAR store; library (Hindu)
BHISTEE water-carrier (India)
BIALATE with 2 wings
BIARCHY rule by 2 persons
BIASING prejudicing; influencing
BIAXIAL with two axes
BIBBING tippling
BIB-COCK down-curving draw-off tap   **eg**
BIBELOT small work of art
BIBLIST a faithful one
BI-CABLE multi-line aerial ropeway   **ce**
BICHORD doubly strung   **mu**
BICKERN pointed anvil   **to**
BICOLOR having 2 colours
BICONIC double-cone-shaped   **bt**
BICYCLE bike; 2 wheeler
BIDDERY metal alloy
BIDDING enjoining; directing
BIFFINS dried apples
BIFIDLY cleft
BIFILAR double-threaded
BIFOCAL type of spectacles
BIFROST Rainbow Bridge (Norse)
BIGELOW flexible sailing boom   **nv**
BIGENER cross-breed
BIGGEST largest; greatest
BIGGISH somewhat massive
BIG-HORN wild sheep   **zo**
BIGNESS of a size; bulkiness
BIGOTED dogmatic; intolerant
BIGOTRY zealotry; fanaticism
BILBOES bars and shackles
BILGING pumping   **nt**
BILIARY, BILIOUS (bile)   **md**
BILKING defrauding; eluding
BILLING love-making
BILLION a large number
BILL-MAN hedger; pruning hook
BILLOWY roughish
BILOBED double-lobed
BILTONG dried meat (S. Africa)
BIMANAL two-handed
BIMETAL of 2 different metals   **el**
BINDERY bookbinding
BINDING obligatory; a fillet
BINDWEB (nervous system)   **md**
BINNING (wine)
BINOCLE double-telescope
BINOTIC binaural
BIOCIDE plant-life-destroying substance
BIOGENY life origin science
BIOLITH rock from living organisms   **gl**
BIOLOGY science of life
BIOMASS population living weight   **ec**
BIONICS study of organism design principles
BIORGAN physiological organ

BIOTAXY } grouping of organisms   **zo**
BIOTICS }
BIOTINE (alumina)   **mn**
BIOTITE magnesia mica   **mn**
BIOTOMY vivisection
BIOTOPE uniform habitat
BIOTYPE uniform genetic make-up
BIPEDAL having two feet
BIPLANE 2-winged aeroplane
BIPOLAR with two poles
BIPRISM obtuse-angle prism   **pg**
BIRCHED flogged
BIRCHEN of birch
BIRDEYE bird's eye
BIRDING snaring
BIRDMAN fowler
BIRETTA clerical cap   **rl**
BIRLING whirling; spinning
BIRLINN Gaelic barge
BIRYANI type of pilaw (India)
BISCUIT thin dry cake
BISMITE bismuth-ochre   **mn**
BISMUTH a metal   **ch**
BISSEXT (leap year)
BISTORT snake-weed   **bt**
BITLESS no bit
BITTERN also bittour   **zo**
BITTERN brine
BITTERS spirituous liquor
BITTING (horse)
BITTOCK small bit
BITTOUR the bittern   **zo**
BITUMED bituminous
BITUMEN asphalt; pitch   **mn**
BIVALVE a mollusc   **zo**
BIVIOUS two ways
BIVOUAC tentless camp
BIZARRE fantastic; whimsical; strange
BIZONAL under dual control
BLABBED babbled; told; revealed
BLABBER sneak; tell-tale; prattler
BLACKED inked; obscured
BLACKEN darken; defame; decry
BLACKER darker; more sullen
BLACKEY a negro
BLACKLY sombrely
BLADDER urine collection organ   **md**
BLADING fitting a blade to
BLAMING censuring; reproaching
BLANDLY mildly; benign; affably
BLANKET the mullein   **bt**
BLANKLY vacantly
BLARING strident
BLARNEY whimsical flattery
BLARNEY yellow Irish cheese   **ck**
BLASTED withered; blighted; ruined
BLASTER froth-blower; golf
BLATANT obtrusively vulgar
BLATHER } also blether,
BLATTER } to babble
BLAWORT harebell   **bt**

BLAZING flaming; proclaiming
BLEAKER more exposed; barer
BLEAKLY cheerlessly; drearily
BLEEDER haemophiliac   md
BLEMISH defect
BLENDED mingled; blent; mixed
BLENDER a mixer
BLESBOK S. African antelope   zo
BLESSED extolled; glorified; adored
BLETHER blather
BLETTED decayed
BLEWART the germander speedwell   bt
BLEWITS mushrooms   bt
BLIGHTY England (soldiers' slang)
BLINDED shuttered; deceived
BLINDER more obtuse; a blinker
BLINDLY ignorantly; heedlessly
BLINKED twinkled; flickered; connived
BLISTER protective hull   nt
BLOATED swollen; distended
BLOATER smoked herring   zo
BLOBBER blubber   zo
BLOCKED obstructed; stopped; jammed
BLOMARY a forge
BLONDIN tight-rope walker
BLOODED (fox-hunting)
BLOOMED flowered; blossomed; throve
BLOOMER an error
BLOSSOM bloom; bud; flower   bt
BLOTCHY patchy; smeary
BLOTING drying by smoke
BLOTTED stained; sullied
BLOTTER a blotting pad
BLOWFLY blue-bottle   zo
BLOW-GUN blow-pipe
BLOWING puffing; disclosing
BLOW-OUT a spread; banquet
BLOWZED frowsy
BLUBBER wail; (whale)
BLUCHER a booting
BLUE-CAP tit-mouse; a Scot (Shak.)   zo
BLUE-CAT Siberian cat   zo
BLUE-EYE honey-eater bird   zo
BLUE-GUM eucalyptus   bt
BLUEING a metal finish; expanding
BLUE-JAY North American jay   zo
BLUFFED concealed; spoofed
BLUFFER a deceiver
BLUFFLY bluntly; frankly; openly
BLUNDER gross mistake; howler
BLUNGER clay-mixer
BLUNTED took the edge off; dulled
BLUNTER more outspoken
BLUNTLY stolidly; obtusely
BLURRED dimmed; obscured
BLURTED uttered abruptly
BLUSHED flushed; coloured
BLUSHET a damsel
BLUSTER turbulence; swagger; storm
BOARDED lodged; embarked   nt
BOARDER paying guest

BOARISH swinish; brutal
BOASTED vaunted; bragged; blustered
BOASTER a broad chisel   to
BOAT-CAR canal trolley
BOAT-FLY water-boatman   zo
BOATFUL ship-load   nt
BOATING an aquatic pastime
BOATMAN a rower; an oarsman
BOBADIL a swaggering captain
BOBBERY rampageous; uproar (Ind.)
BOBBING cheating; curtseying
BOBBING (winter sports); angling
BOBBISH hearty; energetic; uppish
BOB-SLED bob-sleigh
BOBSTAY bowsprit stay   nt
BOBTAIL rabble; caudal abbreviation
BOCLAND feudal freehold   lw
BODEFUL ominous
BOG-BEAN marsh plant   b
BOGGARD } bugbear; scarecrow
BOGGART } hobgoblin; spectre
BOGGLED hesitated; vacillated
BOGGLER a waverer; demurrer; doubter
BOG-LAND fen; marsh; swamp
BOG-MOSS sphagnum   b
BOG-RUSH a sedge   b
BOGYISM dreadfulness
BOILING enraged; seething
BOLDEST bravest; most valiant
BOLETIC fungoid extract   b
BOLETUS fungus genus   b
BOLIVAR Venezuelan currency unit
BOLLARD mooring post   nt
BOLLING a pollard; a lopped tree   b
BOLOGNA sausage   c
BOLONEY phoney palaver
BOLSTER to support; prop; pillow
BOLTING sifting; swallowing
BOMBARD to attack with artillery
BOMBAST fustian; rodomontade
BOMBING blitzing
BOMBOUS rounded, convex
BONANZA stroke of luck
BONASUS bison or wild ox   zo
BONDAGE captivity; thraldom; helotry
BONDING (Customs); (bricklaying)
BONDMAN villein; peon
BONE-ACE card game
BONE-ASH burnt bones
BONE-BED strata with fossils
BONETTA tunny fish   ze
BONFIRE a beacon
BONNILY handsomely
BOOKFUL theoretical
BOOKING reserving; buying
BOOKISH studious
BOOKLET brochure; pamphlet
BOOKMAN scholar
BOOMING in demand; resounding
BOOMKIN short boom   n
BOONDER Rhesus monkey   zo

BOORISH mannerless; clumsy; lubberly
BOOSING tippling; bousing
BOOSTED advertised; eulogized
BOOSTER electrical device
BOOTIED laden with booty
BOOTING foot-wear; sacking
BOOTLEG sell prohibited goods
BOOZING boosing; toping
BORACIC a boron derivative   ch
BORAZON boron/nitrogen compound   ch
BORDAGE feudal tenure
BORDMAN feudal tenant
BORDURE heraldic border   hd
BOREDOM ennui; tedium; dullness
BORNEOL camphor-yielding chemical   ch
BORNITE erubiscite; copper ore   mn
BOROUGH electoral division
BORSTAL a reformatory
BOSCAGE undergrowth
BOSHBOK bush-buck   zo
BOSKAGE woody thicket
BOSOMED embraced
BOSQUET an arbour
BOSSAGE (projecting stones)
BOSSING controlling
BOSSISM political dictatorship
BOSWELL a biographer
BOTANIC botanical; floral
BOTARGO special sausage   ck
BOTARGO grey-mullet roe   ck
BOTCHED bungled; patched
BOTCHER incompetent worker
BOTTINE small boot
BOTTLED inebriated
BOTTLER one who puts liquids in bottles
BOTTONY heraldic cross   hd
BOUCHET a pear   bt
BOUCHON hollow watch plug   hr
BOUDOIR a lady's private room
BOUILLI boiled meat
BOULDER bowlder; a large rock
BOULIMY morbid appetite   md
BOULTER fishing line
BOULTIN convex moulding
BOUNCED rebounded; bluffed
BOUNCER chucker-out; bad cheque
BOUNDED sprang; limited; bordered
BOUNDEN obligatory
BOUNDER inconsiderate ass
BOUQUET nosegay   bt
BOURBON Kentucky corn whisky
BOURDON bass stop   mu
BOURDON mule; pilgrim's staff
BOURLAW local jurisprudence
BOURREE lively dance (Fr., Sp.)
BOW-BACK crooked; hog-back
BOW-BENT bent as a bow
BOW-HAND left hand (archery)
BOWLDER a boulder
BOWLESS no bow
BOWLINE a rope; a non-slip knot   nt

BOWLING (bowls); (cricket); trundling
BOW-SHOT about 80 yards (73 m)
BOX-CALF tanned calfskin
BOX-COAT heavy coat
BOXHAUL a luffing turn   nt
BOX-IRON heater receptacle
BOX-KITE scientific kite
BOX-LOOM multiple-shuttle-box loom   tx
BOX-SLIP boxwood planing face   cr
BOX-TOOL single-point lathe cutter   eg
BOXWOOD odiferous shrub; its wood
BOYCOTT ostracize; refuse to do business with
BOYHOOD puerility
BRABBLE squabble; a quarrel; broil
BRACCIA plural of braccio
BRACCIO Italian cubit   me
BRACING fortifying; invigorating   nt
BRACKEN brake-fern   bt
BRACKET brace; corbel; a support
BRACTED (irregular leaf)   bt
BRADAWL boring tool   to
BRAGGED boasted; blustered
BRAHMAN ⎫
BRAHMIN ⎬ Hindu priest   rl
BRAIDED plaited; embroidered
BRAILED trussed   nt
BRAILLE raised letters
BRAINED brainy; bashed
BRAISED stewed
BRAKING retarding
BRAMBLE brier-bush   bt
BRAMBLY thorny; prickly
BRANCHY spreading; ramifying
BRANDED marked; disgraced
BRANDLE waver; shake
BRANGLE wrangle; a brawl
BRANLIN striped worm   zo
BRAN-NEW brand-new
BRANTLE a dance
BRASIER ⎫
BRAZIER ⎬ brass-worker; charcoal pan
BRASERO ⎭
BRASSET casque or helmet
BRASSIE a golf club
BRASSIE small fish   zo
BRATTLE clatter
BRAVADO arrogant bluster
BRAVELY gallantly; daringly
BRAVERY valour; heroism
BRAVEST most courageous
BRAVING defying; daring
BRAVOES hired assassins
BRAVURA florid   mu
BRAWLED wrangled; quarrelled
BRAWLER rowdy ruffian
BRAWNER boar-meat   zo
BRAYING clamour; pounding
BRAZIER brasier
BRAZING soldering
BREACHY unruly

BREADTH broadness; beaminess
BREAKER small water cask
BREAKER wave; circuit stop   el
BREAK-IN interruption; burglary
BREAK-UP disrupt; disillusion
BREAMED cleaned of barnacles   nt
BREATHE respire; exhale; express
BRECCIA conglomerate   mn
BREEDER begetter; sire
BREVIER a size of type   pr
BREVIUM uranium   ch
BREVITY terseness; conciseness
BREWAGE a brew   br
BREWERY brewhouse   br
BREWING plotting; hatching
BRIABOT angler-fish   zo
BRIBERY palm-oil; graft
BRIBING suborning
BRIBRIS Costa Rican Indian
BRICKED blocked completely
BRICKLE brittle
BRICOLE rebound; bounce
BRIDGED spanned; traversed
BRIDLED curbed; checked
BRIDLER controller
BRIDOON snaffle bit
BRIEFED instructed   lw
BRIEFER shorter; more concise
BRIEFLY curtly; pithily; in short
BRIERED set with briars
BRIGADE subdivision of army
BRIGAND bandit; outlaw; freebooter   to
BRIMFUL almost overflowing
BRIMMED edged
BRIMMER a hat; a full glass
BRINDLE streaky-brown
BRINING salting
BRINISH salty; brackish
BRINJAL egg-plant (Indian)   bt
BRIOCHE light cake (Fr.)
BRISKER sharper; quicker; sprier
BRISKET breast
BRISKLY vivaciously
BRISTLE a stiff hair
BRISTLY rough and prickly
BRISTOL (glass); (china)
BRISURE rampart deviation
BRITISH of Britain
BRITTLE easily broken; fragile
BRITZKA, BRITSKA Polish carriage
BROADEN enlarge; extend; amplify
BROADER wider; more liberal
BROADLY tolerantly; spaciously
BROCADE woven silk
BROCAGE brokerage; brokery
BROCARD maxim or canon
BROCKED black and white
BROCKET young red deer   zo
BRODKIN a buskin; brodekin
BROIDER embroider
BROILED grilled

BROILER grid-iron; brawler
BROKAGE brokerage
BROKERY brokerage
BROKING bargaining; negotiating
BROMATE a salt of bromic acid   ch
BROMIDE a sedative   ch
BROMINE a liquid element   ch
BROMISM state after overdose   md
BROMOIL oil pigment prints   pt
BRONCHO unbroken horse   zo
BRONZED tanned
BROODED cherished; meditated
BROOKED allowed; enjoyed; endured
BROOMED swept
BROTHEL bawdy-house
BROTHER kinsman; comrade; friar
BROUGHT conducted; led; fetched
BROWNED bronzed; tanned
BROWNER more sunburnt
BROWNIE elf; young guide
BROWSED pastured; grazed
BRUCHUS pea-beetle   zo
BRUCINE nux vomica   bt
BRUCITE hydrate of magnesia   ch
BRUISED injured; contused; pounded
BRUISER a boxer
BRUITED rumoured; noised abroad
BRULZIE broil; quarrel
BRUMMER large fly (S. Africa)   zo
BRUMOUS foggy; wintry
BRUNION nectarine   bt
BRUSHED swept; grazed
BRUSQUE abrupt; gruff; blunt
BRUSTLE rustle; bully
BRUTIFY brutalize
BRUTISH bestial; savage
BRUTISM animalism
BRUXISM teeth-grinding   md
BRYOZOA incrustations   zo
BUBALIS antelope genus   zo
BUBALUS buffalo   zo
BUBBLED gurgled; burbled
BUBBLER a cheat
BUBONIC plague   md
BUBULUM neat's-foot   ch
BUCCATE with protruding cheeks   md
BUCCULA double chin
BUCEROS rhinoceros horn-bill   zo
BUCHITE clay/shale fusion rock   gl
BUCKEEN Irish squireen
BUCKEYE horse-chestnut   bt
BUCKING boasting; soaking
BUCKISH foppish; gay; dashing
BUCKLED bent; fastened
BUCKLER round shield
BUCKRAM stiffened cloth
BUCKSAW frame-saw   to
BUCOLIC Arcadian; pastoral; rural
BUDDING germinating; blossoming
BUDGERO Bengal boat   nt
BUDGING shifting; stirring

BUDLESS barren; sterile	bt	**BURGAGE** tenure in socage	
BUFFALO cattle-like animal	zo	**BURGEON** to bud; germinate	
BUFFING polishing		**BURGESS** borough freeman	
BUFFOON a merry-andrew; jester		**BURGHAL** of a borough	
BUGBEAR bugaboo; hobgoblin; bogey		**BURGHER** inhabitant	
BUGLOSS borage	bt	**BURGLAR** house-breaker; cracksman	
BUGWORT a plant	bt	**BURGLED** stole at night	
BUHL-SAW spaced-back frame-saw	to	**BURIDDA** Ital. fish stew	ck
BUILDED built; erected; raised		**BURKING** smothering; concealing	
BUILDER constructor		**BURLACE** a variety of grape	bt
BUILD-UP favourable publicity		**BURLIER** more robust; sturdier	
BUILT-UP urban area		**BURLING** removing knots	
BUIRDLY stalwart; burly (Sc.)		**BURMESE** (Burma)	
BUKSHEE paymaster (Indian)		**BURNING** vehement; ardent; fervent	
BULBING bulging		**BURNISH** polish; furbish; brighten	
BULBLET small bulb	bt	**BURNOUS** Arab attire	
BULBOUS bulb-shaped	bt	**BURNOUT** excess-voltage change	el
BULBULE small bulb		**BUR-REED** a plant	bt
BULCHIN bull-calf	zo	**BURRELL** pear; russet cloth	bt
BULGING protuberant; distended		**BURRHEL** wild sheep of Tibet	zo
BULIMTA insatiable appetite	md	**BURRING** raising a ridge	
BULKIER more massive		**BURROCK** small weir	
BULKING looming large; blending		**BURSARY** treasury	
BULLACE wild-plum	bt	**BURTHEN** burden	
BULLARY (papal bulls)		**BUR-WEED** a plant	bt
BULLATE blistered		**BURYING** burial; concealing; sepulture	
BULL-BAT night-hawk	zo	**BUSH-CAT** the serval	zo
BULL-BEE stag-beetle	zo	**BUSHIDO** Japaese code of chivalry	
BULLDOG college police	zo	**BUSHING** detachable lining	
BULL-FLY gadfly	zo	**BUSHMAN** aborigine	
BULLIED blustered; hazed; (hockey)		**BUSH-TIT** long tailed titmouse	zo
BULLIES browbeaters; hectors		**BUSKING** cruising; preparing	
BULLING boosting		**BUSSING** kissing heartily	
BULLION uncoined metal		**BUS-STOP** here by request	
BULLISH obstinate; mulish		**BUSTARD** a bird	zo
BULLOCK steer	zo	**BUSTLED** hastened; fussed	
BULL-PUP young bulldog	zo	**BUSTLER** booster; hustler	
BULRUSH the reed-mace	bt	**BUSY-BEE** socially active person	
BULWARK ship's side		**BUSYING** meddling; interfering	
BUMBAZE bamboozle		**BUTANOL** an alcohol	ch
BUMBOAT provision boat	nt	**BUTCHER** murder; slay; slaughter	
BUMICKY masonry repair cement		**BUTLERY** pantry	
BUMMALO Bombay duck (dried fish)		**BUTMENT** an abutment	
BUMMING humming		**BUTT-END** fag-end	
BUMMOCK ale		**BUTTERY** store-room	
BUMPING thumping; jarring; knocking		**BUTTING** ramming; abutting	
BUMPKIN short boom; rustic; swain		**BUTTOCK** stern	
BUNCHED clustered; concentrated		**BUTTONS** a page; tansy	bt
BUNDLED wrapped		**BUTTONY** adorned with buttons	
BUNGLED failed; mismanaged		**BUTYRIC** rancid	ch
BUNGLER muff; botcher		**BUVETTE** refreshment bar	
BUNKAGE coaling charge	nt	**BUXEOUS** (box-tree)	bt
BUNKING decamping; bolting		**BUXOMLY** gaily; pliably	
BUNTING bird; fabric	zo	**BUYABLE** on sale	
BUOYAGE placing buoys	nt	**BUZZARD** rapacious bird	zo
BUOYANT light; floating		**BUZZ-SAW** circular saw	to
BUOYING sustaining		**BY-AND-BY** presently	
BUPHAGA beef-eater bird	zo	**BYE-ROAD** secondary road	
BURDASH fringed sash		**BY-GOING** passing by	
BURDOCK dock with prickly head	bt	**BYNEMPT** by name	
BURETTE graduated glass tube; phial		**BYOUSLY** outlandishly	

BY-PLACE a quiet spot
BYRONIC cynical
BYSSINE of flax
BYSSOID fringed
BY-THING a minor detail
BYWONER squatter (S. Africa)

C

CABARET tavern; inn; wine-shop
CABARET variety entertainment
CABBAGE to purloin; vegetable — bt
CABBALA rabbinic mysticism
CABBLED fragmented
CABEIRI deities of Semitic origin
CABESSE Indian silk
CAB-FARE money for taxi ride
CABINED confined; cribbed
CABINET chamber; ministry
CABINET a show case
CABIRIC (nature worship)
CABLING telegraphing
CABOOSE ship's galley — nt
CAB-RANK row of cars for hire
CA'CANNY work in slow time
CACHEXY morbid state — md
CACIQUE cazique; Mexican chieftain
CACKLED clacked
CACKLER a noisy fowl — zo
CACODYL oily compound — ch
CACOEPY false pronunciation
CACOLET mule-chair
CACONYM wrongly derived name
CADAVER corpse; dead body
CADDICE caddis-worm — zo
CADDISH on the boundary line
CADENAS condiment casket
CADENCE modulated flow; tone
CADENCY regularity of movement
CADENUS Dean Swift
CADENZA a flourish — mu
CADGING hawking; sponging; sorning
CADMEAN (Cadmus)
CADMIUM a metal — ch
CADRANS (jewel cutting) — to
CAESIUM a metal — ch
CAESURA poetic pause
CAFENET Turkish inn
CAFFEIC (coffee)
CAFFEIN vegetable alkaloid — md
CAINITE (Cain); a Gnostic
CAISSON tumbril — eg
CAITIFF knave; miscreant; churl
CAJEPUT cajuput; oil yielding tree — bt
CAJOLED coaxed; inveigled
CAJOLER a wheedler; beguiler
CAJUPUT pungent oil — bt
CALABER squirrel-fur
CALAMAR cuttle-fish — zo
CALAMUS dragon's blood palm — bt
CALAMUS antique pen

CALANDO diminuendo — mu
CALCIFY turn to lime
CALCINE pulverize by heat
CALCITE calc-spar — mn
CALCIUM a metallic element — ch
CALCULI gall-stones — md
CALDERA lava collapse crater — gl
CALDRON cauldron; boiler; kettle
CALECHE a vehicle; calash (Fr.)
CALENDS first of month
CALIBAN a tempestuous monster
CALIBER) diameter of bore gauge
CALIBRE) capacity; faculty; talent
CALICHE sodium nitrate — ch
CALICLE small cup — bt
CALIPEE turtle fat
CALIPER measuring instrument — to
CALIVER a musket
CALKING stopping seams — nt
CALLANT a lad (Sc.)
CALL-BOY prompter's attendant
CALLIER photographic ratio — pg
CALLING vocation; profession; trade
CALLOUS insensitive; hard; obdurate
CALLUNA heather — bt
CALMANT a sedative — md
CALMING tranquillizing
CALMUCK Kalmuck; Mongolian
CALOMEL mercuric chloride — md
CALORIC heating
CALORIE unit of heat — me
CALOTTE skull-cap
CALOYER Greek monk — rl
CALPACK felt cap (Turk)
CALTRAP) spiked obstacle for use
CALTROP) against cavalry
CALUMBA climbing plant — bt
CALUMET Indian peace-pipe
CALUMNY slander; aspersion; obloquy
CALVARY the place of skulls — rl
CALVING bringing forth
CALYCLE coral-polype — zo
CALYPSO sea nymph; (Odysseus) — bt
CAMAIEU cameo; a monochrome
CAMBIAL pertaining to cambium
CAMBISM art of exchange
CAMBIST banker; financier
CAMBIUM cellular tissue
CAMBLET camel-hair cloth
CAMBOGE gamboge — bt
CAMBREL meat-hook
CAMBRIC white linen
CAMBUCA pastoral staff — rl
CAMELOT King Arthur's Court
CAMELRY camel corps
CAMORRA secret society (It.)
CAMPANA an anemone — bt
CAMPHOR aromatic laurel — bt
CAMPING encamping; struggling
CAMPION plant — bt
CAMWOOD a red wood — bt

CANAKIN small can
CANASTA two-pack card game
CAN-BUOY conical buoy
CANDELA luminous intensity   me
CANDENT incandescent; glowing
CANDIED sugary
CANDIFY preserve in sugar
CANDOCK yellow water-lily   bt
CANDOUR frankness; openness
CANELLA West Indian tree   bt
CANHOOK cask-hook
CANKERY cankered
CANNERY factory
CANNIER more pawky (Sc.)
CANNING preserving; tinning
CANNULA surgical tube   md
CANONIC canonical   rl
CANONRY canon's benefice   rl
CANOPIC (Canopic case)
CANOPUS star in Argo
CANTATA narrative poem   mu
CANTEEN cooking tin
CANTHAL pertaining to canthus
CANTHUS corner of the eye   mu
CANTING hypocritical; sanctimonious
CANTION a song (Spens.)
CANTLET fragment; cantle; a cutting
CANTOON cotton material
CANTRED hundred; county division
CANTRIP a witch's spell
CANVASS discuss; lobby
CANZONE song or melody   mu
CAPABLE efficient; able
CAPABLY competently; skilfully
CAP-A-PIE from head to foot
CAP-CASE travelling case
CAPELIN small smelt   zo
CAPERED frolicked; frisked; bounded
CAPERER a dancer
CAP-IRON cutting-iron stiffener   cr
CAPITAL money; main; excellent
CAPITAN Turkish naval officer
CAPITOL Roman temple
CAPORAL shag tobacco
CAPOTED won all tricks at piquet
CAPOUCH monk's cowl   rl
CAPPING topping; (hunt subscription)
CAPRATE a salt   ch
CAPRICE whim; vagary; humour
CAPRINE like a goat
CAPRINO goat-milk cheese (Argentina)
CAPROIC goatish
CAPRONE flavouring oil
CAPSIZE upset; overturn
CAPSTAN windlass   nt
CAPSULA seed-vessel; a cap   bt
CAPSULE soluble envelope   md
CAPTAIN leader; chief; master   nt
CAPTION certificate; title; arrest
CAPTIVE prisoner
CAPTURE take; apprehend; catch

CAPUCHE a Capuchin's hood   rl
CAPULET father of Romeo's Juliet
CAPULIN Mexican cherry   bt
CARACAL Persian lynx   zo
CARACOL spiral shell; an evolution
CARACUL Bukhara sheep   zo
CARAMEL a sweetmeat; caromel
CARANNA aromatic resin (Amazon)   bt
CARAVAN house on wheels
CARAVEL four-masted ship   nt
CARAWAY seed; plant; spice   bt
CARBIDE carburet   ch
CARBINE short rifle
CARCAKE pancake
CARCASE body; bomb; framework
CARCASS a fire-work; shell arch
CARDECU French quarter-crown   nm
CARDIAC (heart); cordial   md
CARDING combing flax
CARDOON artichoke   bt
CARDUUS thistle genus   bt
CAREFUL meticulous; heedful; wary
CARGOES argosies
CARIAMA bird of prey   zo
CARIBOU Arctic reindeer (N. Amer.)   zo
CARIOLE light cart
CARIOUS decayed
CARITAS love of God and neighbour   rl
CARKING anxious
CARLINE a witch; thistle genus   bt
CARLISM (Don Carlos)
CARLIST Spanish Royalist
CARLOCK isinglass
CARMINE a pigment
CARNAGE slaughter; butchery
CARNIFY turn to flesh
CARNOSE, CARNOUS fleshy; meatlike
CAROCHE coach (Fr.)
CAROLUS sovereign of Charles I   nm
CAROSSE sheepskin or fur rug (SA)
CAROTID arterial   md
CAROTIN carrot pigment, vitamin   md
CAROUSE revel; feast; tipple
CAR PARK parking area
CARPING captious; cavilling; objecting
CARPORT open garage
CARRACK armed trading ship
CARRIED borne; upheld; transported
CARRIER transporter; conveyor
CARRION putrid meat
CARROTY rufous
CAR-SHED carriage depot
CARTAGE conveyance
CARTING transporting
CARTOON topical sketch
CARVING slicing; cutting; engraving
CARVIST hawk on hand   zo
CARVONE caraway oil ketone   ch
CARYOTA fish-tail palms   bt
CASCADE waterfall; collar
CASCARA a laxative   md

CASEASE casein-decomposing enzyme	
CASEATE (cheese)	ch
CASE-LAW (a precedent)	lw
CASEMAN compositor	
CASEOUS like cheese	ck
CASHIER discharge with ignominy	
CASHING (cheques)	
CASSADA tapioca	bt, ck
CASSAVA tapioca	bt, ck
CASSINO casino, card game	
CASSIUS (purple)	
CASSOCK a vestment	rl
CASSONE bridal chest (It.)	
CASTING rejecting; pitching	
CASTLED (chess)	
CASTLET small castle	
CAST-OFF laid aside	
CASTRAL (camp)	
CASUIST a quibbler; sophist	
CATALAN Catalonian	
CATALLO hybrid; buffalo and cow	zo
CATALOG university calendar (USA)	
CATALPA Shawnee-wood	bt
CATAPAN Byzantine governor	
CATARRH (inflammation)	md
CATASTA slave-block	
CATAWBA Ohio grape	bt
CAT-BIRD American thrush	zo
CAT-BOAT boat with mast in bow	
CAT-CALL derisive yell	
CATCHER (base-ball)	
CATCHES songs; (fish)	
CATCHUP ketchup sauce	ck
CATECHU an astringent	md
CATERAN freebooter (Sc.)	
CATERED provided with food, etc.	
CATERER purveyor	
CAT-EYED (night vision)	
CAT-FALL anchor rope	nt
CAT-FISH wolf-fish; nurse-hound	zo
CATHEAD anchor rest	
CATHECT to direct feelings	pc
CATHODE negative electrode	
CAT-HOLE hawser hole	nt
CATHOOD c.f. spinsterhood	
CATLIKE feline character	
CATLING small cat; cat-gut	zo
CAT-MINT a species of Nepeta	bt
CAT-SALT rough salt	
CAT'S-EYE a quartz	mn
CAT'S-PAW a dupe; a ripple	
CATTALO hybrid; buffalo and cow	zo
CATTISH spiteful	
CATWALK narrow plank bridge	nt
CATWHIN needle-gorse	bt
CAUDATE with a tail	
CAULINE stalky	bt
CAULKED rendered watertight	
CAULKER a dram; a whopper	
CAULOME all organs of a shoot	bt
CAUSING resulting in; occasioning	

CAUSTIC corrosive; mordant	
CAUTERY a searer	md
CAUTION care; heed; warning	
CAVALRY horse-soldiers	
CAVEMAN a troglodyte	
CAVETTO hollow moulding	
CAVIARE sturgeon's roe	ze
CAYENNE red pepper	bt
CAZIQUE cacique; West Ind. chief	
CEASING desisting; ending; stopping	
CEBIDAE class of monkeys	ze
CEDARED lots of cedars	
CEDILLA 'c' like 's'	
CEDRATE the citron	bt
CEDRELA a tropical cedar	bt
CEDRINE (cedar)	
CEILING (aeroplane height)	ae
CELADON green porcelain	
CELLASE apricot-kernel enzyme	ch
CELLIST violoncellist	mu
CELL-SAP cell fluid constituents	cy
CELLULE small cell	
CELSIUS (centigrade thermometer)	
CEMBALO Italian stringed instrument	
CENACLE supper-room	
CENSING burning incense	
CENSION assessment	
CENSUAL (census)	
CENSURE blame; rebuke; chide	
CENTAGE percentage	
CENTAUR mythological horse-man	
CENTAVO Portuguese halfpenny	nm
CENTIME hundredth part of a franc	nm
CENTNER foreign cwt	m
CENTRAL mediate; middlemost	
CENTRED concentrated	
CENTRIC central	
CENTRON neuron	z
CENTURY centenary; hundred	
CERAMIC (pottery)	
CERASIN plum-gum	bt
CERATED waxed	
CEREALS breakfast food	
CEREOUS, CERESIN wax	
CEROTIC beeswax extract	
CERTAIN assured; infallible; undeniable	
CERTIFY avouch; attest; witness	
CERULIN indigo	
CERUMEN ear-wax	md
CERUSED white leaded	
CERVINE (stags)	
CESIOUS bluish-grey	
CESSING taxing	
CESSION relinquishment; surrender	
CESS-PIT midden	
CESTOID tape-worm	md
CETACEA whales, etc.	z
CHABLIS white wine	
CHABOUK Eastern whip	
CHACONE slow dance	mu
CHAFERY welding furnace	

HAFFED bantered; scoffed; derided
HAFFER haggle; bargain
HAFING fretting; fuming; rubbing
HAGRIN vexation; irritation
HAINED fettered; measured
HAIRED carried in triumph
HALAZA the base of an ovule   bt
HALDEE Chaldean
HALDER 96 bushels   me
HALICE communion cup; goblet   rl
HALKED scored; recorded
HALLIS fine silk
HALONE an internal secretion   md
HAMADE invitation to a parley
HAMBER room; closet; hall; cavity
HAMFER groove; polish
HAMLET camlet; camel-hair
HAMOIS leather   zo
HAMPAC Indian tree; champak   bt
HAMPED crunched; chewed; bit
HANCED happened; befell; risked
HANCEL clergy's area of church
HANDOO prepared opium
HANGED altered; varied; shifted
HANGER exchanger; shifter
HANNEL canal; duct; strait; gutter
HANSON song (Fr.)   mu
HANTED (horse-coping); intoned
HANTER a precentor   rl
HANTER (bagpipes)   mu
HANTRY chapel for mass   rl
HAOTIC confused; disordered
HAPATI unleavened bread (India)
HAPEAU a hat (Fr.)
HAPLET garland; wreath; coronal
HAPMAN pedlar; hawker
HAPNET ⎫ pewter salt-cellar
HAPNUT ⎭
HAPPED seamed; cleft; cracked
HAPPIE ghost (Sc.)
HAPTER a decretal epistle   rl
HARACT a character (Shak.)
HARADE dramatic enigma
HARGED loaded; accused
HARGER platter; war horse   zo
HARILY stingily; warily; reluctantly
HARING drudgery
HARIOT state carriage
HARISM miraculous power
HARITY benevolence; alms
HARLEY night-watchman
HARLIE pointed beard
HARMED enchanted; fascinated
HARMER a siren; beguiler
HARNEL mortuary
HARPOY Indian bedstead
HARQUI dried beef (Peru)
HARRED scorched; seared; burnt
HARTED tabulated; recorded   nt
HARTER right; privilege; hire
HASING engraving; pursuing; hunting

CHASSIS frame-work
CHASTEN correct; punish; humble
CHATEAU country seat
CHATTAH Indian umbrella
CHATTED gossiped; prattled
CHATTEL movable property   lw
CHATTER talk; prate; tattle
CHAUVIN French patriot
CHAWING chewing; munching
CHAYOTE custard marrow   ck
CHEAPEN belittle; depreciate
CHEAPER not so dear
CHEAPLY inexpensively
CHEATED bobbed; duped; gulled
CHEATER trickster; swindler
CHECHIA Arab skull-cap
CHECKED restrained; hindered; verified
CHECKER chess board; to variegate
CHEDDAR a cheese
CHEEKED sauced; was impertinent
CHEEPED chirped
CHEEPER young game bird   zo
CHEERED applauded; enlivened
CHEERER vociferous supporter
CHEERIO convivial salutation
CHEETAH hunting leopard   zo
CHELATE (claw)   zo
CHELONE tortoise; shell flower   bt, zo
CHELSEA china
CHEMISE shift; smock; slip
CHEMISM chemical action   ch
CHEMIST chymist; pharmacist; druggist
CHEMOSH a Moabite god
CHENILE fluffy cord
CHEQUER checker; diversify
CHERISH to foster; harbour; treasure
CHERMES kermes; a crimson dye
CHEROOT Burmese or Manila cigar
CHERVIL culinary herb   bt
CHESNUT a hoary jest   bt
CHESSEL a cheese mould or vat
CHESTED boxed
CHESTON a species of plum   bt
CHETNIK Yugoslav guerrilla
CHEVIED chased; pursued; hunted
CHEVIOT sheep bred on the Cheviots   zo
CHEVRON zigzag badge
CHEWING chawing; munching
CHIANTI Italian red wine
CHIASMA nerve intersection   md
CHIBOUK Turkish pipe
CHICANE trick; artifice; (cards)
CHICKED sprouted; vegetated
CHICKEN a child   zo
CHICORY (often mixed with coffee)   bt
CHIDDEN reproved; censured; rebuked
CHIDING rating; scolding; blaming
CHIEFLY principally; mainly; mostly
CHIEFRY rent; chief's lands
CHIFFON gauzy material
CHIFFRE denoting harmony (Fr.)   mu

CHIGGER chigoe; West Indian flea	zo
CHIGNON a coiffure	
CHIKARA an Indian antelope	zo
CHIKARA Indian guitar	mu
CHILDED having a child (Shak.)	
CHILDLY childishly	
CHILEAN Chilian; native of Chile	
CHILIAD a thousand years	
CHILLED discouraged; depressed	
CHILLER an iceberg or wet blanket	
CHILLUM hookah	
CHILOMA camel's lip	zo
CHIMERA mythical monster; illusion	zo
CHIMERE bishop's robe	rl
CHIMNEY funnel; smoke-stack	
CHINCHA S. American rodent	zo
CHINDIT Burmese guerilla	
CHINESE Sinesian	
CHINGLE shingle; gravel	mn
CHINING cutting the backbone	
CHINKED jingled; clinked	
CHINOOK N. American Indian tribe	
CHINSED caulked	
CHINTHE Burmese leogriff	
CHINWAG chatty conversation	
CHIPAXE light axe	to
CHIP-HAT hat made of palm leaves	
CHIP-LOG log-line attachment	nv
CHIPPED chaffed; chopped	
CHIPPER lively; twitter	
CHIRPED bird song	
CHIRPER grasshopper	zo
CHIRRUP bird noise	
CHISLEU a Jewish month	
CHISLEY gravelly	
CHITTER shiver with cold	
CHITWAH panda; red bear-cat	zo
CHLORAL a narcotic	md
CHLORIC chlorine derivative	ch
CHLORID chloride	ch
CHOBDAR servant to a rajah	
CHOCTAW (skating); a tribe	
CHOIRED in chorus	mu
CHOKING stifling; strangling	
CHOLEIC (bile)	md
CHOLERA deadly infectious disease	md
CHOLINE B vitamin; organic base	md
CHOLTRY caravanserai; Eastern inn	
CHOOSER a picker; a selector	
CHOPINE clog or patten	
CHOPPED cut; minced; changed	
CHOPPER cleaver	to
CHORALE choral composition	mu
CHORDAL of chords	eg
CHORDED strung	mu
CHOREUS a trochee	
CHORION a membrane	bt
CHORIST chorister	rl
CHOROID eye-membrane	md
CHORTLE chuckle noisily; exult	
CHOWDER dish of clams	ck

CHOWTER grumble; croak	
CHRISOM baptismal cloth	
CHROMAX iron-based alloys	n
CHROMIC of chromium	c
CHROMYL chrome radical	c
CHRONIC long continuing; inveterate	
CHUCKED pitched; tossed; thrown	
CHUCKIE a chicken	z
CHUCKLE exult; crow	
CHUDDAH chudder; cloak or cloth (Ind.)	
CHUKKUR chukka; period of play (polo)	
CHUMMED roomed together	
CHUPATI unleavened bread (Ind.)	
CHURCHY pious; ritualistic	
CHURNED agitated; jostled; upset	
CHURRED made deep whirring sound	
CHURRUS Indian resin	
CHUTNEE chutney	
CHYAZIC (hydro-cyanic)	c
CHYMIFY to digest	c
CHYMIST chemist; pharmacist	
CIBORIA canopies	
CICHLID Tanganyika fish	z
CICONIA storks	z
CIDARIS sea-urchins	
CILIARY (eyelashes)	m
CILIATE with hairs	
CIMBRIC a language	
CIMELIA stored treasures	
CIMETER scimitar	
CINDERY full of cinders; ashy	
CINEOLE eucalyptole	c
CINEREA nerve tissue	m
CIPOLIN green marble	m
CIRCEAN fatefully fascinating	
CIRCLED went round	
CIRCLER circlet; small ring	
CIRCLET an orb; a ring	
CIRCUIT tour; revolution; journey	
CIRRATE curly	
CIRROSE | with tendrils;	
CIRROUS | with curls	
CISSING retreat of paint from surface	
CISSOID geometric curve	
CISTERN wine-cooler	
CITABLE quotable	
CITADEL keep; stronghold; fortress	
CITATOR a summoner	
CITHARA Greek lyre	m
CITHERN guitar	m
CITIZEN burgher; burgess; resident	
CITRATE lemon salts	c
CITRENE oil of lemons	
CITRINE a yellow	
CITTERN cithern; zither	m
CIVILLY courteously; politely	
CIVVIES mufti; civilian clothes	
CLABBER thicken	
CLACHAN small village (Sc.)	
CLACKED clucked; clicked; jabbered	
CLACKER clack-valve	

CLADODE leaflike branch **bt**
CLAIMED demanded; insisted; usurped
CLAIMER claimant; appellant
CLAMANT crying; insistent
CLAMBER climb; scramble
CLAMMED clogged; smeared
CLAMOUR din; uproar; hubbub
CLAMPED clumped; held down
CLAMPER iron patch
CLANGED clashed; pranged
CLANKED clinked; clanged
CLAP-NET bird fowler's net
CLAPPED applauded; shut
CLAPPER tongue of a bell
CLAQUER claqueur; hired applauder
CLARAIN fine coal
CLARIFY make clear; strain; purify
CLARION a shrill trumpet **mu**
CLARITY clearness; distinctness
CLARKIA a flowering annual **bt**
CLASHED clattered; opposed
CLASHEE Ind. sailor; tent-erector
CLASPED grasped; gripped
CLASPER tendril; embracer **bt**
CLASSED ranked; grouped; ranged
CLASSER classificationist
CLASSIC first rate; standard; masterly
CLASSIS assembly or convention **rl**
CLASTIC fragmental; brittle
CLATTER clash; rattle; crash
CLAUGHT to snatch; catch (Sc.)
CLAVATE club-shaped
CLAVIER keyboard **mu**
CLAWING scratching; fawning
CLAYING puddling; purifying
CLAYISH clay-like
CLAY-PIT marl-pit
CLEANED purified; washed; scoured
CLEANER dirt remover
CLEANLY spotlessly; adroitly
CLEANSE clear; purge; elutriate
CLEAN-UP a purge; cartoon technique
CLEARED acquitted; absolved
CLEARER more obvious; less opaque
CLEARLY distinctly; patently
CLEAVED split; parted; adhered
CLEAVER butcher's chopper
CLEDDYO Celtic sword
CLEMENT merciful; lenient; mild
CLEMMED starved; hungered
CLEPING naming (obs.)
CLERISY the clergy **rl**
CLERKLY learnedly; scholarly
CLEWING coiling; securing **nt**
CLICKED found favour; ticked
CLICKER cobbler; compositor
CLICKET knocker; door-latch
CLIMATE clime; weather
CLIMBED scaled; swarmed; ascended
CLIMBER a creeper; mountaineer **bt**
CLINKED clanked; jingled

CLINKER slag; (ship design)
CLINOID like a bed
CLIPPED shorn; pared; snipped; docked
CLIPPER schooner; cutter; trimmer
CLIPPIE bus-conductress **nt**
CLITTER clatter
CLIVERS goose-grass **bt**
CLIVITY slope; incline
CLOAKED disguised; concealed; hidden
CLOBBER clothing; cobbler's paste
CLOCKED timed; clucked
CLOCKER time-keeper; a hen **zo**
CLODDED clotted; mired
CLOGGED congested; coalesced
CLOGGER clog-maker
CLOISON partition (Fr.)
CLOOTIE cloven hoof; the Devil
CLOSELY intimately; accurately
CLOSEST nearest; densest
CLOSE-UP (movies)
CLOSING conclusion; sealing; clogging
CLOSURE also cloture; enclosure
CLOT-BUR the burdock **bt**
CLOTHED attired; arrayed; draped
CLOTHES apparel
CLOTTED curdled
CLOTTER to coagulate
CLOTURE closure; conclusion
CLOUDED obscured; blended; dimmed
CLOUTED patched; buffeted
CLOVATE inverse taper
CLOWNED played the fool
CLUBBED coshed; bludgeoned
CLUBBER clubbist; club member
CLUB-LAW might is right
CLUB-MAN member of clubs
CLUCKED clocked; cackled
CLUMBER a spaniel **zo**
CLUMPED in clusters; mustered
CLUMPER to form clumps
CLUNIAC Benedictine monk **rl**
CLUSTER bunch; clump; assembly
CLUTTER confused mass
CLYPEAL like a shield; scutate
CLYPEUS insect's forehead **zo**
CLYSMIC cleansing
CLYSTER an injection **md**
COACHED tutored; trained
COACTED compelled; concentrated
COAGENT an associate; colleague
COAKING dowelling
COAL-BED stratum of coal
COAL-GAS extraction from coal
COALING taking on coal fuel **nt**
COALISE form a coalition
COALITE a form of fuel
COAL-PIT mine
COAL-TAR extraction from bituminous coal
COAL-TIT a passerine bird **zo**
COAMING raised border **nt**

CO-ANNEX join jointly
COARSEN roughen
COARSER cruder; rougher; ruder
COASTAL littoral
COASTED free-wheeled   nt
COASTER decanter stand
COASTER small ship   nt
COATING layer; covering
CO-AXIAL having common axis
COAXING cajoling; wheedling
COBBING pulling the ears
COBBLED mended; tinkered; patched
COBBLER shoe repairer; botcher
COBIRON andiron; firedog
COBLOAF crusty loaf
COB-SWAN male swan   zo
COB-WALL mud-wall
COBWORK log-house construction   ar
COCAINE drug   md
COCALON large cocoon   zo
COCHLEA ear-cavity   md
COCINIC cocoa extract   ch
COCKADE hat badge
COCKEYE imperfect vision; a squint
COCKING strutting; (trigger)
COCKLED puckered; wrinkled
COCKLER cockle merchant
COCKNEY true Londoner
COCKPIT cock-fighting arena
COCK-SHY a target; Aunt Sally
COCONUT cocoa-nut   bt
COCOTTE light o' love (Fr.)
COCTILE baked
COCTION digestion; cooking
CODDING hoaxing
CODDLED pampered; simmered
CODEINE an alkaloid from opium   bt
CODFISH esteemed food fish   zo
CODICES manuscript books
CODICIL supplement to a will   lw
CODILLA coarse hemp   bt
CODILLE card-term at ombre
CODLING young cod   zo
CODLING codlin apple   bt
COELEBS bachelor
COELIAC abdominal   md
COENURE young tape-worm   zo
COEQUAL a peer; a compeer
COERCED concussed; compelled
COEXIST be coeval
COGENCE convincing power; force
COGENCY urgency; potency
COGGERY trickery
COGGING cheating
COGNATE related; allied; akin; sib
COGNIZE to be aware of; recognize
COG-WOOD a Jamaican tree   bt
COHABIT live together
COHERED adhered; cleaved; coalesced
COHERER early form of detector   ro
COHIBIT restrain; hinder; prevent

COIFFED (hairdressing)
COIGNED billeted (Irish)
COILING entangling; winding up
COINAGE money; specie
COINING minting; counterfeiting
COJUROR witness to credibility   lv
COLA-NUT the kola-nut   b
COLD-CUT dissolving lacquers without hea
COLDEST iciest; frostiest
COLDISH chillsome
COLD-PIG cold douche
COLIBRI species of humming-bird   z
COLICKY with pains
COLITIS colic; colonic infection   m
COLLAGE real objects on art forms   b
COLLARD cole-wort
COLLATE collect and compare
COLLAUD unite in praising
COLLECT a prayer; assemble; amass
COLLEEN Irish girl
COLLEGE academy; seminary; guild
COLLIDE crash; encounter; clash
COLLIED begrimed; coal-black (Shak.)
COLLIER miner; vessel   n
COLLING embracing; necking
COLLOID gelatinous
COLLUDE act in collusion; connive
COLOBUS a monkey genus   z
COLONEL highest regimental rank
COLOSSI gigantic statues
COLOURS (army); (awards)
COLOURY coloured
COLTISH frisky
COLUBER a snake genus   z
COLUMBA holy vessel; (Iona)
COLUMEL a small column
COMBINE unite; blend; coalesce
COMBING breaking into foam
COMBUST astrological term   a
COMETIC (comets)
COMFORT console; solace; ease; cheer
COMFREY a plant   b
COMICAL droll; diverting; farcical
COMITIA assemblies
COMMAND govern; rule; enjoin; decree
COMMARK a frontier
COMMEND laud; praise; eulogize
COMMENT remark; note; criticize
COMMERE a gossip
COMMODE chest of drawers
COMMONS food; fare; non-nobility   c
COMMOVE agitate
COMMUNE converse; discourse
COMMUNE a self-sufficient group sharin
    family tasks
COMMUTE exchange; replace; barter
COMPACT united; a treaty; close
COMPANY party; group; society
COMPARE liken; assimilate
COMPART to divide
COMPASS to encircle; scope; limit   n

COMPEAR appear in court (Sc.) lw
COMPEER equal; comrade; associate
COMPEND compendium; epitome
COMPERE the leader of a troupe
COMPETE strive; emulate; rival
COMPILE combine; arrange; amass
COMPLEX intricate; complicated
COMPLEX mental inhibition pc
COMPLIN evening service rl
COMPLOT conspiracy
COMPORT behave; agree; tally
COMPOSE create; calm; pacify
COMPOST a mixture
COMPOTE dish; fruit (Fr.)
COMPTER counter (obs.)
COMPUTE reckon; count; rate
COMRADE pal; mate; associate
COMTISM Positivism
COMTIST disciple of Comte
CONACRE sublet (Irish)
CONATUS volition; effort; impulse
CONCAVE hollow; scooped
CONCEAL cloak; disguise; screen
CONCEDE yield; allow; grant
CONCEIT vanity; egotism; notion
CONCENT harmony; concord of sounds
CONCEPT general notion; fancy
CONCERN trouble; regard; firm
CONCERT devise; concoct mu
CONCISE terse; pithy; laconic
CONCOCT plot; hatch; brew
CONCORD harmony; amity; union
CONCREW to concrete (obs.)
CONCUPY a concubine (Shak.)
CONCUSS coerce; overawe; stun
CONDEMN doom; convict; blame
CONDIGN deserved; merited
CONDING navigating nt
CONDITE to pickle; to preserve
CONDOLE console; sympathize
CONDONE pardon; overlook; forgive
CONDUCE lead to; tend; promote
CONDUCT guide; escort; deportment
CONDUIT passage; pipe; channel
CONDYLE knuckle md
CONEINE coniine; hemlock bt
CONFECT a sweetmeat; to prepare ck
CONFESS admit; own; disclose; avow
CONFEST confessed
CONFIDE rely; trust; depend
CONFINE limit; boundary; restrain
CONFIRM ratify; endorse; establish
CONFLUX confluence; a crowd
CONFORM comply; tally; adapt
CONFUSE confound; derange; perplex
CONFUTE disprove; refute
CONGEAL coagulate; benumb
CONGEED took leave
CONGEST to swell; accumulate
CONGIES vitamin-rich rice-cookery water
CONGREE to agree (obs.)

CONGRUE congree; agree; harmonize
CONGRUE to accord (obs.)
CONICAL conic; tapering
CONIFER pine; fir; etc. bt
CONIINE conine; hemlock bt
CONJECT conjecture; guess (obs.)
CONJOIN unite; link; fasten
CONJURE invoke; juggle
CONJURY conjuring; legerdemain
CONNATE congenital; innate; inherent
CONNECT couple; conjoin; hyphenate
CONNING steering; studying nt
CONNIVE permit; wink at; abet
CONNOTE imply a sequence
CONQUER overpower; vanquish
CONSENT concur; agree; assent
CONSIGN despatch; send; transmit
CONSIST subsist; make up of
CONSOLE comfort; pier table
CONSOLS funds
CONSORT compeer; fraternize
CONSTAT certificate of a record
CONSULT deliberate; confer
CONSUME devour; waste; expend
CONSUTE like stitching
CONTACT touch; juncture; taction
CONTAIN include; embody; comprise
CONTEMN despise; disregard; scorn
CONTEND strive; cope; vie; argue
CONTENT volume; satisfy; mollify
CONTEST struggle; contend; dispute
CONTEXT texture; firm; extract
CONTORT writhe; distort; twist
CONTOUR outline; height line; profile
CONTROL direct; sway; mastery
CONTUND contuse; bruise
CONTUSE bruise; crush
CONVENE assemble; muster; summon
CONVENT a nunnery rl
CONVERT change; alter; transform
CONVICT sentence; felon; lag
CONVIVE boon companion; a guest
CONVOKE convene; gather; summon
COOKERY cuisine
COOKING concocting; manipulating
COOLEST most impudent
COOLING moderating
COOLISH somewhat cool
COONCAN card game
COONTIE arrowroot bt
COOPERY barrel production
COOPING confining; penning
CO-OPTED elected
COPAIBA copaiva; balsam bt
COPEPOD minute water organism zo
CO-PILOT assistant aviator
COPIOUS abundant; plenteous; ample
COPLAND angular piece of land
COPPERY like copper
COPPICE spinney
COPPING catching; arresting

COPULAR linking	**COSHERY** billeting (Irish)
COPYCAT apeing others' ideas	**COSHING** bashing; slugging
COPYING aping; transcribing	**COSIEST** snuggest; coziest
COPYISM copyist's work	**COSMISM** a philosophy
COPYIST plagiarist; imitator	**COSMIST** a secularist
COQUITO palm with edible sap/seeds bt	**COSSACK** Russian cavalryman
CORACLE ancient British boat nt	**COSTARD** apple bt
CORANTO dance; newsletter	**COSTATE** ribbed
CORBEAU raven-black	**COSTEAN** (prospecting)
CORBEIL sculptured basket	**COSTING** accounting
CORCASS Irish salt marsh	**COSTIVE** obstructive; constipated
CORCULE an embryo bt	**COSTREL** pilgrim's bottle
CORDAGE rope	**COSTUME** dress; uniform; livery
CORDATE heart-shaped bt	**COTERIE** social circle
CORDIAL cocktail; hearty; ardent	**COT-FOLK** cottars (Sc.)
CORDING cordage; binding	**COTHURN** buskin
CORDITE a propellant	**COTIDAL** contemporaneous tides
CORE-BOX sand-moulding container fd	**COTINGA** chattering birds zo
CORINNE gazelle zo	**COTLAND** cottage land
CORINTH a currant bt	**COTTAGE** cot; lodge; hut
CO-RIVAL competitor	**COTTICE** heraldic barulet hd
CORKAGE an imposition at hotels	**COTTIER** Irish tenant
CORKING stopping	**COTTOID** fish genus; miller's thumb zo
CORK-LEG artificial limb	**COTTONY** downy; nappy
CORNAGE (land tenure)	**COT-TOWN** town of cottages
CORN-COB spike of maize bt	**COUCHED** expressed; reclined
CORNEAL (eye-membrane) md	**COUCHEE** soirée; evening reception (Fr.)
CORN-FLY destructive insect zo	**COUGHER** one having a tussis
CORNICE ledge; a top moulding	**COULDST** (could)
CORNINE quinine type bt	**COULEUR** colour (Fr.)
CORNING preserving; granulating	**COULOIR** dredge; mountain cleft
CORNISH (Cornwall)	**COULOMB** electrical unit of quantity el
CORNIST cornet blower mu	**COULTER** fore-end of plough
CORN-LAW regulating corn trade lw	**COUNCIL** ministry; assembly; diet
CORN-OIL maize oil ck	**COUNSEL** advice; barrister lw
CORN-RIG strip of growing corn	**COUNTED** reckoned; relied; numbered
CORNUAL horny	**COUNTER** contrary; adverse; opposed
CORNUTE horny	**COUNTRY** region; nation; state
CORN-VAN winnowing machine	**COUPLED** paired; bracketed; joined
COROLLA floral whorl bt	**COUPLER** connector
CORONAL circlet; wreath	**COUPLET** two lines; a pair
CORONER an inquirer lw	**COURAGE** pluck; valour; heroism
CORONET a moth; tiara zo	**COURANT** a disseminator
CORONIS elision; contraction	**COURIER** messenger; runner; dragoman
CORRECT O.K.; exact; precise; true	**COURLAN** S. American crane zo
CORRODE gnaw; rust; canker	**COURSED** hunted; pursued; chased
CORRODY allowance; pension	**COURSER** war-horse; plover zo
CORRUPT putrid; depraved; bribe	**COURSES** some sails n
CORSAGE part of a dress	**COURTED** wooed; invited; solicited
CORSAIR pirate; pirate ship nt	**COURTER** a wooer; swain
CORSITE diorite mn	**COURTLY** elegant; urbane; debonair
CORSLET sleeveless armour	**COUTEAU** long knife
CORSNED an ordeal	**COUTHIE** kindly; friendly (Sc.)
CORTEGE procession	**COUVADE** a curious custom
CORTILE courtyard	**COVELET** small bay
CORUBIN aluminium oxide ch	**COVERED** enveloped; veiled; spread
CORVINE like a crow	**COVERTS** certain feathers zo
CORYDON a rustic lover	**COVER-UP** boxing; concealment
CORYLUS hazel bt	**COVETED** longed for; desired
CORYPHA fan-palm bt	**COW-BANE** water-hemlock bt
COSAQUE cracker; bon-bon (Fr.)	**COW-BIRD** American cuckoo zo

COW-CALF female calf	zo	**CREDENT** credulous; trusting	
COWERED cringed; shrank; crouched		**CREEING** softening grain	
COWHAGE a bean (Hindu)		**CREEPER** crawler; ski-aid; cricket	
COW-HEEL ox-foot stewed to a jelly		**CREEPIE** a cutty-stool (Sc.)	
COWHERD a cow tender		**CREMATE** reduce to ashes; incinerate	
COWHIDE leather		**CREMONA** a violin	mu
COW-ITCH cowhage	bt	**CRENATE** notched	bt
COWLICK a lock of hair		**CRENAUX** loop-holes	
COWLIKE ruminant; placid		**CREOSOL** (phenol)	ch
COWLING hood	ae	**CREPANE** wound due to brushing	
COWSLIP paigle	bt	**CRESSET** beacon; torch	
COW-TREE moraceous tree	bt	**CRESTED** surmounted	
COW-WEED herb	bt	**CRETIFY** impregnate with lime	
COXCOMB conceited fellow; dandy		**CRETISM** a falsehood	
COYNESS shyness; bashfulness		**CRETOSE** chalky	
COZENED deceived; gulled		**CREVICE** fissure; rift; breach	
COZENER white collar bandit		**CREWELS** embroidery	
CRABBED morose; surly; disparaged		**CRIBBED** confined; plagiarized	
CRABITE fossil crab		**CRIBBLE** coarse sieve; a temse	
CRAB-OIL carap-oil	bt	**CRICKED** sprained	
CRACKED crazy; snapped; split; broke		**CRICKET** a low stool; an insect	zo
CRACKER cosaque; biscuit; firework		**CRICOID** ring-shaped	
CRACKLE glazed fissures in china		**CRIMINE** \ an interjection	
CRACK-UP breakdown; crash	pc	**CRIMINI** / of surprise	
CRACOWE pointed shoe		**CRIMING** charging; accusing	
CRADLED nurtured		**CRIMPED** plaited; shanghied	
CRAGGED rugged; jagged		**CRIMPER** corrugating machine	
CRAKING cawing		**CRIMPLE** shrink; curl	
CRAMBUS grass moth	zo	**CRIMSON** cramesy	
CRAMESY crimson		**CRINGED** cowered; fawned	
CRAMMED stuffed; studied		**CRINGER** a yes-man; sycophant	
CRAMMER intensive teacher		**CRINGLE** eyelet in sail	nt
CRAMPED confined; cabined		**CRINITE** hairy; a fossil	
CRAMPON mountaineering spike		**CRINKLE** crankle; wrinkle; crimp	
CRANAGE crane dues		**CRINOID** fossilized sea-lily	mn
CRANIAL skull	zo	**CRINOSE** crinite; pilose; hairy	
CRANING stretching the neck		**CRIPPLE** disable; impair; hobble	
CRANIUM a skull	md	**CRISPED** frizzled; made brittle	
CRANKED bent; turned; wound		**CRISPER** curler; more friable	
CRANKLE crinkle; wrinkle; a turn		**CRISPIN** the cobblers' saint	
CRANNOG lake dwelling		**CRISPLY** briskly	
CRAPING curling		**CRIZZEL** \ roughness on glass	
CRAPNEL grapnel; hook		**CRIZZLE** / making it cloudy	
CRAPPIE N. Amer. sunfish	zo	**CROAKED** died; grumbled; decried	
CRASHED smashed; shattered; fell		**CROAKER** a fish; a pessimist	zo
CRASHER uninvited guest		**CROCHET** fancy-work	
CRATING boxing; encasing		**CROCKED** blackened; broken down	
CRAUNCH crunch; gnaw		**CROCKET** pinnacle adornment	ar
CRAVING longing; yearning; desiring		**CROESUS** a wealthy man	
CRAWLED crept; (swimming)		**CROFTER** small farmer	
CRAWLER a reptile; a baby's overall		**CROODLE** lie snug; cower	
CRAZIER madder		**CROOKED** tortuous; awry; bent	
CRAZILY daftly; distractedly		**CROONED** moaned; lamented	
CRAZING weakening; breaking	ar	**CROONER** sentimental singer	
CREAKED grated		**CROPFUL** satiated	
CREAMED mantled; foamed		**CROPPED** mowed; reaped; cut	
CREANCE hawk-leash line		**CROPPER** printing machine; heavy fall	
CREASED folded; wrinkled; rugate		**CROQUET** up to date pall-mall	
CREATED originated; produced		**CROSIER** crozier; bishop's crook	rl
CREATIN muscular constituent	md	**CROSLET** crossed cross	hd
CREATOR maker; originator; inventor		**CROSSED** thwarted; interbred	

CROSSLY peevishly; testily; petulantly
CROTALO Turkish cymbal   mu
CROTTLE lichen dye
CROUTON chopped fried bread
CROWBAR lever; jemmy   to
CROWDED huddled; thronged
CROWDER Welsh fiddler   mu
CROWDIE porridge (Sc.)
CROWGER striped wrasse, fish   zo
CROWING exulting; rejoicing; boasting
CROWNED honoured; completed
CROWNER coroner
CROWNET coronet (Shak.)
CROW-TOE the buttercup   bt
CROZIER crosier; pastoral staff   rl
CRUCIAL cross-like; critical; decisive
CRUCIAN goldfish; crusian   zo
CRUCIFY mortify
CRUCITE red iron ore   mn
CRUDELY unpolished; roughly
CRUDEST rawest; coarsest
CRUDITY rawness; immaturity
CRUELER more brutal; harsher
CRUELTY savagery; barbarity
CRUISED sailed
CRUISER rover   nt
CRUISIE primitive lamp
CRULLER a cake   ck
CRUMBED fragmented
CRUMBLE pulverize; disintegrate
CRUMBLY friable
CRUMPED blasted; blown up
CRUMPET an indigestible comestible
CRUMPLE wrinkle; crunkle; ruffle
CRUNKLE crumple; crimp; crinkle
CRUORIN haemoglobin   md
CRUPPER saddle-strap
CRUSADE idealistic campaign
CRUSADO Portuguese coin   nm
CRUSHED overwhelmed; compressed
CRUSHER pulverizer
CRUSIAN crucian; carp; goldfish   zo
CRUSTED encrusted; incrusted
CRY-BABY a weakling
CRYOGEN a freezing mixture
CRYPTIC hidden; occult; secret
CRYPTON krypton; a gas   ch
CRYSTAL (Palace); (fortune-telling)   mn
CRYSTIC pertaining to ice
CTENOID comb-shaped
CUBBING whelping; hunting
CUBBISH ill-mannered
CUBEBIN cubeb extract   md
CUBICAL cubic
CUBICLE little bedroom
CUBITAL about 20 inches (50 cm)
CUBITED measured in cubits
CUBITUS a cubit   me
CUCKOLD husband of loose wife
CUCULUS cuckoo   zo
CUDBEAR a lichen; a purple dye   bt

CUDDLED hugged; fondled; caressed
CUDWEED a plant   b
CUE BALL (billiards)
CUFFING scuffling; buffeting
CUINAGE tin stamping
CUIRASS breastplate
CUISINE cookery
CUITTLE cajole; curry (Sc.)
CUL-DE-SAC dead-end
CULETTE hip-armour
CULICID mosquito   ze
CULLIED duped; gulled; hoaxed
CULLING selecting; gathering; picking
CULLION bulbous root   b
CULPRIT delinquent; offender
CULTIST a pedant; dilettante
CULTURE refinement; education
CULVERT small bridge
CUMBENT recumbent; lying down
CUMDACH precious-book receptacle
CUMQUAT kumquat; Chinese fruit   b
CUMSHAW gift; tip; present (Ind.)
CUMULUS a heap; a large cloud
CUNEATE wedge-shaped
CUNNING crafty; sly; wily; astute
CUP-FEED seed drill system   a
CUP-GALL an oak-gall   b
CUP-MOSS a lichen   b
CUPPING blood-letting
CUPRITE oxide of copper   m
CUP-ROSE poppy   b
CUPROUS copper compound   c
CURABLE remedial
CURACAO orange liqueur
CURATOR custodian; keeper; warden
CURBING repressing; restraining
CURCUMA (arrowroot, etc.)   b
CURDING coagulating
CURDLED congealed; thrilled
CURE-ALL panacea
CURETTE surgical scraper   m
CURIOSA collection of exotic objects
CURIOSO virtuoso; a collector
CURIOUS rum; prying; unusual; queer
CURLING a pastime; coiling; bending
CURRACH curragh; coracle
CURRANT ribes; a dried raisin   b
CURRENT accepted; present; tide; flow
CURRIED groomed
CURRIER leather-dresser
CURRING purring; cooing
CURRISH snarling; spiteful; quarrelsome
CURSING swearing; execrating
CURSIVE flowing; running
CURSORY hasty; superficial; transient
CURTAIL abridge; contract; shorten
CURTAIN theatrical drapery
CURTANA sword of mercy, (Coron.)
CURTATE reduced; abbreviated
CURT-AXE short broad-sword
CURTEST bluntest; briefest; shortest

CURVATE bent; curved
CURVING turning; inflecting
CURVITY regular bend
CUSHION pad; hassock; pouffe
CUSSING swearing (slang)
CUSTARD baked milk pudding   ck
CUSTODE a watchman; custodian
CUSTODY care; imprisonment; duress
CUSTOMS duties on merchandise
CUSTREL buckler-bearer; a costrel
CUT-AWAY (tailoring)
CUT-BACK decrease production (industrial)
CUT-DOWN reduce; cheapen
CUTICLE outer-skin   md
CUTLASS short broad sword   nt
CUTLERY edged tools
CUTTING satirical; sardonic; sarcastic
CUT-WORK type of embroidery
CUT-WORM caterpillar pest   zo
CUVETTE crucible; trench; cunette
CYANATE cyanide   ch
CYANIDE poison   ch
CYANINE cyanite   ch
CYANITE, KYANITE silicate of aluminium   mn
CYCLING bicycle sport
CYCLIST bicycle rider
CYCLOID geometric curve
CYCLONE tornado; hurricane; typhoon
CYCLOPS one-eyed Sicilian giant
CYCLORN a cycle horn
CYMBALO the dulcimer   mu
CYNICAL disparaging; ironical
CYPERUS a sedge   bt
CYPRESS funereal tree   bt
CYPRIAN licentious; (Cyprus)
CYPRINE (cypress); funereal   bt
CYPRIOT courtesan; (Cyprus)
CYSTINE calculus growth   md
CYSTOID } cystlike   md
CYSTOSE }   md
CYSTOMA tumour   md
CYTIDIN nucleic acid   ch
CYTISUS the broom genus   bt
CYTITIS dermatitis   md
CZARDAS Hungarian dance   mu
CZARINA Tsarina
CZARISM despotism

D

DABBING tapping; patting
DABBLED sprinkled; meddled; trifled
DABBLER dilettante; trifler
DABSTER an expert; adept
DACOITY dakoity; brigandage
DADAISM art movement
DADDLED tottered
DADDOCK the heart of a rotten tree
DAFTEST silliest; maddest; craziest

DAGGING wool clotted with dung, earth
DAGGING cutting into strips
DAGGLED befouled; smirched
DAG-LOCK hanging lock of wool
DAGONET King Arthur's fool
DAGWOOD dog-wood; sandwich   bt
DAHLINE dahlia starch   bt
DAKOITY dacoity
DALLIED trifled; dawdled; sported
DALLIER a trifler; flaneur
DALRIAD an Ulster Scot
DAMAGED marred; injured; hurt
DAMBROD a draught-board (Sc.)
DAMMING embanking
DAMNIFY to injure
DAMNING conclusive; condemning
DAMOSEL damozel; damsel
DAMPING discouraging   ro
DAMPISH moist; dank; humid
DANAKIL nomad fisher tribe
DANCING capering; pirouetting
DANDIFY smarten; beautify
DANDLED fondled
DANELAW Danelagh; Danish England
DANGLED suspended; swung; hung
DANGLER hanger-on
DANKISH damp and dark
DANSKER a Dane (Shak.)
DANTEAN sombre (Dante)
DANTIST a Dante scholar
DAPHNAL (laurels)   bt
DAPHNIA water-fleas   zo
DAPHNIN bay-extract   bt
DAPIFER meat-bearer; royal steward
DAPPING may-fly fishing
DAPPLED variegated
DAPSONE sulphone leprosy specific   pm
DARBIES handcuffs
DARCALL long-tailed duck   zo
DARCOCK water-rail   zo
DARIOLE rich cake
DARKEST most secret; blackest
DARKISH gloomy
DARLING beloved; dear; pet; idol
DARNING mending
DARREIN (benefice)   rl
DARTARS sheep ulcers
DARTING casting; sprinting
DASHING rushing; impetuous; spirited
DASHPOT snubber   el
DASTARD poltroon; coward; craven
DASYPUS armadillo genus   zo
DASYURE Australian cat   zo
DATABLE assignable to a period
DATARIA (papal chancery)   rl
DATISCA hemp   bt
DATIVAL (dative)
DAUBERY poor painting
DAUBING daubery; smearing
DAUNTED discouraged; cowed
DAUPHIN king's eldest son (Fr.)

DAWDLED lagged; dallied; tarried
DAWDLER time-waster; laggard
DAWNING day-break; day-spring
DAY-BOOK daily register
DAY-COAL (upper stratum) mn
DAY-GIRL non-resident schoolgirl
DAY-LILY the hemerocallis bt
DAY-MAID dairy-maid; daily girl
DAY-PEEP dawn
DAY'S-MAN umpire
DAY-STAR the morning star
DAYSURE a wolf genus zo
DAY-TIME not night
DAZZLED dazed; bewildered; confused
DAZOMET chemical fungicide
DEAD-END cul-de-sac
DEAD-EYE three-eyed naval block nt
DEADISH rather moribund; decaying
DEAD MEN empty bottles
DEADPAN expressionless (facial)
DEAD-PAY (pay drawn; death concealed)
DEAD-SET determined effort
DEAD-TOP arboreal disease bt
DEAF-AID hearing device
DEAF-NUT (no kernel) bt
DEALATE divest of wings
DEALING negotiating; (cards)
DEANERY dean's premises rl
DEAREST most expensive; costliest
DEARNLY secretly; grievously
DEASIUL, DEASOIL opposite widder-
 shins
DEATHLY mortal; deadly; destructive
DEBACLE a rout; collapse; stampede
DEBASED adulterated; degraded
DEBASER contaminator
DEBATED deliberated; disputed
DEBATER arguer; controversialist
DEBAUCH carouse; corrupt; deprave
DEBITED charged with
DEBITOR debtor (Shak.)
DEBOUCH come into the open
DECADAL in tens
DECADIC pert. to decimal system
DECAGON ten-sided figure
DECALIN hydrogenized naphthalene pro-
 duct
DECANAL (deanery) rl
DECAPOD having ten limbs; (lobster) zo
DECARCH commander over 10
DECAYED rotted; degenerated; wasted
DECAYER source of decay
DECEASE perish; die; expire; demise
DECEIVE beguile; mislead; overreach
DECENCY propriety; decorum
DECHARM disenchant
DECIARE tenth of an are (Fr.) me
DECIBEL unit of noise me
DECIDED resolute; firm; unwavering
DECIDER final heat
DECIMAL a tenth

DECKING ornament; embellishment
DECKLED with edges uncut
DECKLET record, set of IBM cards cp
DECLAIM orate; harangue; rant; spout
DECLARE avouch; assert; proclaim
DECLINE refuse; decay; wane; languish
DECODED deciphered
DECODER info. locater/fetcher/solver
DECORUM seemliness; decency
DECOYED allured; snared; inveigled
DECREED ordered; resolved; enacted
DECREET anounce court judgment
DECRIAL clamorous censure
DECRIED disparaged; traduced
DECRIER vilifier
DECROWD (slum clearance)
DECROWN discrown; dethrone
DECUMAN main gate; tenth; principal
DECUPLE tenfold
DECURVE straighten
DEDIMUS judicial commission lw
DEDUCED inferred; concluded; reasoned
DEEDFUL manful; doughty
DEEDILY valiantly
DEEDING conveying by deed lw
DEEMING opining; considering
DEEPEST most profound; lowest
DEEP-FRY cooking method ck
DEEP-SEA in deep ocean
DEERITE iron/manganese hydrous silicate
DEFACED disfigured; mutilated
DEFACER spoiler
DEFAMED libelled; vilified
DEFAMER detractor; slandered
DEFAULT to fail; failure; lapse
DEFENCE plea; excuse; protection
DEFIANT provocative; contumacious
DEFICIT shortage
DEFILED polluted; vitiated
DEFILER contaminator; seducer
DEFINED accurately described; limited
DEFINER a clarifier e
DEFLATE release the air
DEFLECT divert; turn aside
DEFORCE resist lw
DEFRAUD trick; cheat; deceive
DEFUNCT deceased
DEFYING challenging; flouting
DEGAUSS antimagnetic device
DEGLAZE to clear thick gravy
DEGRADE lower; humble; debase
DEHISCE to gape
DEICIDE a god-destroyer
DE-ICING removing ice
DEICTIC clearly proving
DEIFIED exalted; idolized
DEIFORM godlike
DEIGNED condescended; vouchsafed
DEISTIC freethinking
DELAINE all-wool dress fabric tx
DELATED gave information; squealed

DELATOR accuser; informer; relator
DELAYED procrastinated; deferred
DELAYER a cunctator; procrastinator
DELEBLE delible; erasable
DELENDA things to be erased
DELETED expunged; effaced
DELIGHT charm; ravish; joy; ecstasy
DELILAH a charming hairdresser
DELIMIT fix limits
DELIVER cede; consign; rescue; save
DELOUSE to remove lice
DELPHIC oracular
DELPHIN classical edition
DELTAIC delta-like
DELTOID a muscle   md
DELUDED misled; beguiled; gulled
DELUDER deceiver; trickster; hoaxer
DELUGED flooded; inundated; swamped
DELVING digging; excavating
DEMENTI official denial (Fr.)
DEMERIT a fault; defect
DEMERSE immerse; drown
DEMESNE lord's farming land (feudal)
DEMETON chemical insecticide
DEMIGOD almost worshipped person
DEMIREP a lady of doubtful virtue
DEMISED bequeathed; willed
DEMODED old fashioned
DEMONIC fiendish; satanic; diabolical
DEMONRY devilry
DEMONYM pseudonym using pop. style
DEMOTIC popular; common
DENDRAL living in trees
DENDRON dendrite of nerve-cell
DENIZEN alien inhabitant; resident
DENOTED indicated; signified
DENSELY closely; thickly
DENSEST thickest; closest
DENSITY compactness; stolidness
DENTARY (teeth)
DENTATE toothed
DENTELS toothed ornaments
DENTINE ivory tissue
DENTING dinting; notching
DENTIST tooth doctor   md
DENTIZE (dental work)
DENTOID tooth-like
DENTURE false teeth
DENUDED stripped; bared; divested
DENYING controverting; refuting
DEODAND a forfeit (obs.)   lw
DEODATE heavenly gift
DEPETER stone-imitating plasterwork   bd
DEPLANE cf. detrain
EPLETE to empty; exhaust; drain
EPLORE lament; grieve; bewail
EPLUME to pluck
EPONED testified   lw
EPOSAL dismissal; sacking
EPOSED bore witness; ousted
EPOSIT store; lodge; intrust

DEPRAVE corrupt; debase; vitiate
DEPRESS damp; dishearten; sadden
DEPRIVE strip; rob; divest
DEPUTED delegated; authorized
DERAIGN darrain; justify (obs.)
DERANGE disturb; upset; ruffle
DERATED freed from liability
DERBEND Turkish guard house
DERIDED jeer; scorned; lampooned
DERIDER a mocker; scoffer
DERIVED deduced; traced; obtained
DERMOID like skin
DERNFUL solitary; mournful
DERNIER final; last (Fr.)
DERRICK form of crane   nt
DERRING daring
DERVISH Moslem monk
DESCANT comment freely; dilate
DESCANT part song; a commentary
DESCEND dismount; alight; drop; sink
DESCENT slope; decline; origin; raid
DESERVE earn; win; merit; justify
DESIRED wanted; solicited; coveted
DESIRER craver; yearner; fancier
DESKILL simplify industrial work
DESMINE stilbite; zeolitic mineral   mn
DESMOID tufty
DESPAIR hopelessness; despondency
DESPISE disdain; contemn; scorn; scout
DESPITE in spite of; malice
DESPOIL rob; bereave; strip; rifle
DESPOND despair; dejectedness
DESSERT a fruit course; afters   ck
DESTINE to ordain; appoint
DESTINY fate; fortune; doom; Kismet
DESTROY devour; demolish; raze
DETENTE relaxing political strain
DETERGE cleanse; wipe
DETERMA a useful wood from Guyana   fr
DETINUE writ of distraint   lw
DETRACT defame; disparage; traduce
DETRAIN alight from train
DETRUDE force down
DETUNER jet-engine noise-reduction
   structure
DEUTZIA a white flower   bt
DEVALUE depreciate
DEVELOP grow; unfold; expand
DEVIATE swerve; turn; tack; digress
DEVILED stuffed; seasoned before frying
DEVILET small demon; imp
DEVILRY cruel mischief; diabolism
DEVIOUS wandering; erratic; tortuous
DEVISED contrived; willed; concocted
DEVISEE legatee
DEVISER inventor; schemer; planner
DEVISOR testator
DEVOLVE deliver; depute; impose
DEVOTED loving; ardent; attached
DEVOTEE an addict; a fan; zealot
DEWANNY office of dewan (India)

DEW-CLAW rudimentary claw   zo
DEW-DROP drop of earth condensation
DEW-FALL aqueous precipitation
DEWLAPT with a dewlap
DEW-POND pond fed by condensation
DEW-WORM earthworm   zo
DEXTRAL (not left)
DEXTRAN synthetic blood plasma
DEXTRIN starch gum
DHAGOBA Buddhist mound   rl
DHOOLIE covered litter
DHOOTIE Indian loin-cloth fabric   tx
DHURRIE Indian curtain
DIABASE variously defined rock type   mn
DIABOLO a game
DIACOPE tmesis
DIADROM a beat; a vibration
DIAGRAM graph; sketch; drawing
DIALECT idiom; parlance
DIALIST dial-maker
DIALIZE separate   ch
DIALLED rang up
DIAMINE 2-amino-group compound   ch
DIAMOND hard valuable stone   mn
DIANDER (two stamens)   bt
DIAPASM toilet powder
DIAPSID condition of skulls   zo
DIARAIN diarial; daily
DIARCHY dual monarchy
DIARIES daily records
DIARISE to record
DIARIST a chronicler
DIASTER stage in cell-division   cy
DIATOMS seaweed   bt
DIATONI face-dressed quoins   bd
DIAXONE bipolar nerve cell   zo
DIBASIC giving two salts   ch
DIBATAG N. African gazelle   zo
DIBBING dipping
DIBBLED made holes in the ground
DIBBLER planted
DICE-BOX dice holder
DICEING throwing dice
DICERAS clams   zo
DICHORD lyre   mu
DICKITE hydrated aluminium silicate   mn
DICLINY state of sex separation   bt
DICTATE enjoin; command; bid
DICTION style; speech; phraseology
DIDACHE apostolic teaching
DIDDLED out-witted; cajoled; cozened
DIDDLER a cheat; swindler; cajoler
DIDIDAE the dodo, etc.   zo
DIE-AWAY languishing
DIE-CAST (condenser construction)
DIEDRAL dihedral
DIE-HARD last ditcher
DIETARY course of diet
DIETING banting; slimming
DIETIST dietitian
DIE-WORK die-cutting

DIFFORM irregular
DIFFUSE spread; copious; prolix
DIGAMMA obsolete Greek letter
DIGGING delving; grubbing; thrusting
DIGHTLY finely apparelled (obs.)
DIGITAL integral
DIGLYPH grooved face
DIGNIFY ennoble; exalt; grace
DIGNITY majesty; decorum; rank
DIGRAPH (two letters)
DIGRESS deviate; wander; swerve
DIGYNIA curious plant; (two pistils)   bt
DIKETEN ketene dimer   ch
DILATED enlarged; expatiated
DILATER an expander; amplifier
DILATOR a muscle   md
DILEMMA quandary; plight; strait
DILLING darling; weakling
DILL-OIL a carminative   md
DILUENT a diluter; reducer
DILUTED watered; attenuated
DILUTEE unskilled worker (industrial)
DILUTER thinner
DIMEFOX chemical insecticide
DIMETER (poetry)
DIM-EYED with weak vision; weepy
DIMMING blurring; clouding; dulling
DIMMISH somewhat obscure
DIMNESS vagueness; dinginess
DIMPLED showing dimples
DINETTE a dining compartment
DINGING ringing; urging
DINGOES wild dogs of Australia   zo
DINMONT shorn wether   zo
DINNING advocating clamorously
DINOCAP crotonate fungicide   ch
DINOSAM } chem. insecticide/
DINOSEB } fungicide
DINTING denting; striking
DIOCESE a bishopric   rl
DIOCOEL diencephalon lumen   zo
DIODONE iodine x-ray preparation
DIOECIA genus of plants   bt
DIONAEA Venus's fly-trap   bt
DIOPSIS fly genus   zo
DIOPTER optical measurement   me
DIOPTER speculum; theodolite
DIOPTRE unit of lens power   ps
DIORAMA panorama
DIORISM definition
DIORITE igneous rock   mn
DIOXIDE oxygen-based oxide   ch
DIPHONE a shorthand sign
DIPLOID twin chromosomes   me
DIPLOMA a certificate
DIPLONT diploid-nuclei-bearing plant body
DIPOLAR with two poles
DIPPING dibbing; plunging; immersing
DIPTERA two-winged insect   zo
DIPTOTE noun with 2 cases only
DIP-TRAP bend in a pipe

DIPTYCH pictorial altar-piece   rl
DIREFUL calamitous; baleful; awful
DIRKING stabbing
DIRT-BED (quarrying)
DIRTIED soiled; sullied; begrimed
DIRTIER grubbier
DIRTILY filthily
DIRT-PIE mud-pie
DISABLE unfit; incapacitate; maim
DISAGIO money-exchange charge
DISALLY separate; sunder
DISAVOW repudiate; disown; deny
DISBAND disperse ; disembody
DISBARK disembark
DISBEND unbend (obs.)
DISCAGE release; unmew
DISCANT descant; discourse
DISCARD cast; reject; abandon
DISCASE strip; unpack
DISCEPT debate; dispute
DISCERN espy; perceive; discriminate
DISCERP tear off; separate
DISCOID flat like a disc
DISCORD strife; brawl; animosity
DISCOUS broad; flat
DISCUSS debate; argue; consume
DISDAIN spurn; contemn; ignore
DISEASE malady; complaint   md
DISEDGE to blunt
DISEUSE woman reciter (Fr.)
DISFAME disrepute; evil reputation
DISFORM alter; deform; disfigure
DISGOWN unfrock
DISGUST nausea; aversion; loathing
DISHELM remove helmet
DISHFUL filling a dish
DISHING thwarting; frustrating
DISHOME evict
DISHORN remove horns
DISJOIN part; detach; sunder; sever
DISJUNE dejeuner; lunch (Sc.)
DISLEAF deprive of leaves
DISLEAL disloyal; dishonourable
DISLIKE hate; detest; antipathy
DISLIMB dismember
DISLIMN obliterate; efface (obs.)
DISLINK unlink; disjoin
DISLOAD unburden; unload
DISMALS mournings
DISMASK unmask; uncover; reveal
DISMAST remove masts   nt
DISMISS cashier; discharge; sack
DISNEST eject
DISOBEY transgress; disregard; infringe
DISOMUS 2-bodied monster   md
DISPAIR separate; uncouple
DISPARK set at large
DISPART separate
DISPEND expend; disburse (obs.)
DISPLAY parade; flaunt; show; evince
DISPONE hand over   lw

DISPORT sport; gambol; frolic; wanton
DISPOSE sell; transfer; arrange
DISPOST displace
DISPUTE argue; wrangle; bicker
DISRANK degrade
DISRATE reduce to lower rating
DISROBE unrobe; strip; divest; bare
DISROOT uproot; eradicate
DISRUPT break up; disintegrate
DISSEAT unseat
DISSECT anatomize; analyse; cut
DISSENT disagree; differ
DISSERT discourse; dissertation (obs.)
DISTAFF staff for holding unspun flax
DISTAFF the opposite of spear-side
DISTAIN sully; stain
DISTANT remote; far; aloof; reserved
DISTEND dilate; swell; expand; bloat
DISTENT distended (Spens.)
DISTICH rhyming couplet
DISTOMA genus of worms   zo
DISTORT pervert; misrepresent
DISTRIX hair-end splitting   md
DISTUNE put out of tune
DISTURB molest; confuse; vex; annoy
DISTYLE portico
DISUSED obsolete; neglected; abandoned
DISWARN dissuade
DISWONT deprive of wonted usage
DISYOKE unyoke
DITCHED ⎰ fallen into the sea (RAF)
DITCHED ⎱ discarded; failed examination
DITCHER ditch clearer
DITHERY nervous; agitated; tremulous
DITTANY candle-plant   bt
DITTIED sung
DITTIES sonnets; shanties
DIURNAL daily; quotidian; journal
DIVERGE fork; radiate; part
DIVERSE unlike; different; varied
DIVIDED severed; sundered; separated
DIVIDER distributor; apportioner
DIVINER predictor; seer; magician
DIVISOR (arithmetic)
DIVORCE dissever; part; alienate
DIVULGE tell; reveal; disclose; impact
DIVULSE rend apart
DIVVY-UP divide
DIZENED bedecked
DIZZARD blockhead
DIZZIED dazed; bewildered; confused
DIZZIER giddier
DIZZILY confusedly
DJEREED ⎰ blunt Turkish javelin
DJERRID ⎱
DJIBBAH ⎰ Eastern garment
DJUBBAH ⎱
DOBHASH interpreter (Hindu)
DOCETAE an ungodly sect
DOCETIC heretical
DOCIBLE docile; tractable; amenable

DOCIOUS docile
DOCKAGE dock dues
DOCKING curtailing; clipping — nt
DOCKIZE to convert into docks
DOCQUET docket; summary; list
DODDART hockey (obs.)
DODDING lopping; polling
DODGERY trickery; prevarication
DODGING evading; quibbling
DOESKIN soft leather
DOFFING divesting; putting off
DOG-BANE plant with a bitter root — bt
DOG-BELT part of dog harness
DOG-BOLT arrow; dog-meal
DOG-CART two-wheeled vehicle
DOG-DAYS (occur in July and August)
DOGEATE office of doge
DOG-FISH tope; small shark — zo
DOGGING following closely; tailing
DOGGISH rather posh
DOGGREL doggerel; trashy verse
DOGHEAD gunlock hammer
DOG-HOLE not a luxurious abode
DOGHOOD cf. manhood
DOGLIKE having canine attributes
DOG-NAIL large nail
DOG-ROSE wild rose — bt
DOG'S-EAR a fold in a page in a book
DOGSHIP personality of a dog
DOG-SICK sick as a dog
DOGSKIN glove leather
DOG'S-RUE a plant; Scrophularia — bt
DOG-STAR Sirius
DOG-TICK a parasite — zo
DOGTROT jog
DOG-VANE wind-vane — nt
DOGWOOD flowering bush — bt
DOLABRA Roman hatchet
DOLEFUL woe-begone; dismal; rueful
DOLLIED hammered; laundered
DOLLIER an ore-crusher
DOLLMAN Turkish robe
DOLPHIN fish; a spar — zo
DOLTISH stupid; stolid; witless
DOMABLE tamable; tractable
DOMICAL dome-shaped
DOMINIE schoolmaster (Sc.)
DOMINUS Master; Lord
DONATOR donor; presenter; giver
DONNERD donnert; stunned (Sc.)
DONNING putting on; assuming
DONNISH like a don
DONNISM self-importance
DONSHIP estate of being a don
DOOMING condemning; judging
DOORING door-case
DOORMAT boot-scraping mat
DOORWAY portico
DOPPLER change of frequency — el
DORHAWK nightjar — zo
DORKING a fowl — zo

DORLACH bundle; valise (Sc.)
DORMANT quiescent; latent
DORMICE sleepy rodents — zo
DORNICK \
DORNOCK / figured linen — tx
DORTOUR dorter; dormitory — rl
DOSSIER file of papers; a brief (Fr.)
DOTTARD decayed tree
DOTTIER barmier; more foolish
DOTTING spotting; stippling
DOTTREL plover — zo
DOUBLED turned; ran; repeated
DOUBLER duplicator
DOUBLET jerkin; one of a pair
DOUBTED distrusted; suspected
DOUBTER an unbelieving Thomas
DOUCELY sweetly
DOUCETS \
DOWCETS / stones of deer — zo
DOUCEUR tip; vail; gratuity
DOUCHED sprayed
DOUCINE ornamental moulding
DOUGHTY valiant; intrepid; dauntless
DOUPION double cocoon — zo
DOUREST grimmest; staunchest
DOURINE breeding-horse infection — vt
DOUSING \ dipping; extinguishing;
DOWSING / water-divining
DOUTING extinguishing; quenching
DOVECOT dove-cote — zo
DOVEKIE little auk (Sc.) — zo
DOVELET young dove — zo
DOVERED slumbered
DOWABLE endowable
DOWAGER widow with a jointure
DOWDILY untidily; slovenly
DOWERED gifted
DOWN-BED feather bed
DOWNING felling; overcoming
DOWSING water-divining
DOYENNE senior lady
DOZENTH 12th
DRABBER more dingy
DRABBET smocking
DRABBLE befoul; draggle
DRABLER additional sail — nt
DRACHMA Greek silver coin — me
DRACINA dragon's blood palm — bt
DRACINE dracina; a dye — bt
DRACONE nylon/rubber liquids container
DRACULA Bram Stoker's batman
DRAFTED outlined; detached
DRAFT-OX draught-ox — zo
DRAG-BAR draw-bar
DRAGGED tugged; hauled; lingered
DRAGGLE bemire; drabble
DRAG-MAN a fisherman
DRAG-NET his net
DRAGOON compel; coerce; cavalryman
DRAINED filtered; exhausted; emptied
DRAINER a colander

DRAPERY haberdashery	**DROUTHY** thirsty; very dry
DRAPIER a Swift 'nom de plume'	**DROWNED** overflowed; submerged
DRAPING covering; dressing	**DROWSED** dozed; slumbered; dovered
DRAPPIE a wee drop (Sc.)	**DRUBBED** thrashed; thumped; mauled
DRASTIC severe; forcible; efficacious	**DRUBBER** a beater
DRATTED confounded	**DRUDGED** plodded; toiled; slaved
DRAUGHT dose; breeze; outline	**DRUDGER** toiler; menial; scullion
DRAWBAR connecting rod	**DRUGGED** stupefied; physicked **md**
DRAWBOY a weaving assistant	**DRUGGER** drogher; small ship **nt**
DRAWING pulling; sketch; plan	**DRUGGET** carpet covering
DRAWLED dawdled; droned	**DRUIDIC** (Druids)
DRAWLER monotonous speaker	**DRUMBLE** to drone
DRAW-NET bird net	**DRUMLIN** long glacially-formed hill **gl**
DRAWN-ON printing technique	**DRUMMED** expelled **mu**
DRAYAGE charge for a dray	**DRUMMER** commercial traveller **mu**
DRAYMAN dray-driver	**DRUNKEN** inebriated; crapulous; tipsy
DREADED apprehended; feared	**DRUSIAN** a Syrian
DREADER an alarmist	**DRYADES** wood nymphs; trees **bt**
DREAMED dreamt; imagined	**DRY-BEAT** (blows without blood)
DREAMER visionary; idealist	**DRY-BONE** silicate of zinc **mn**
DREDGED sprinkled	**DRY-CELL** type of battery **el**
DREDGER machine for dredging	**DRY-DOCK** ship repair stage **nt**
DREEING enduring; bearing (Sc.)	**DRY-EYED** tearless
DRESDEN Meissen porcelain	**DRYNESS** aridity; drought; thirst
DRESSED cooked; decked; arrayed in	**DRY-PILE** voltaic battery
DRESSER kitchen sideboard	**DRY-RENT** (no distress) **lw**
DREULED slavered; dribbled	**DRY-SALT** preserve; cure
DRIBBED inveigled; filched	**DRYSHOD** with shoes not wet
DRIBBLE (football); trickle; drip; ooze	**DUALINE** dualin; form of dynamite
DRIBLET driplet; a small quantity	**DUALISM** a doctrine; Manichaeism
DRIFTED floated; enlarged	**DUALIST** (twofoldness in the universe)
DRIFTER wanderer **nt**	**DUALITY** doubleness
DRILLED trained; perforated; pierced	**DUALIZE** split in twain
DRINKER reveller; carouser; toper	**DUARCHY** diarchy; dual control
DRIP-DRY non-iron fabric	**DUBBING** dubbin; grease; entitling
DRIPPED dropped; oozed; trickled	**DUBIATE** to doubt; to hesitate
DRIP-TIP a leaf-point **bt**	**DUBIETY** doubtfulness; uncertainty
DRIVE-IN service for motorists	**DUBIOUS** undecided; vacillating
DRIVING dragooning; urging; forcing	**DUCALLY** in ducal style
DRIZZLE fine rain	**DUCHESS** duke's wife
DRIZZLY with fine rain	**DUCK-ANT** Jamaican termite **zo**
DROGHER coasting vessel **nt**	**DUCKING** a soaking; diving **zo**
DROGMAN dragoman; interpreter	**DUCTILE** tractile; malleable
DROGUET ribbed fabric	**DUCTULE** narrow-lumen duct **zo**
DROICHY dwarfish (Gael.)	**DUDDERY** rags; old clo' shop
DROILED toiled tediously	**DUDGEON** dagger; sullenness
DROLLED jested; clowned	**DUE-BILL** accepted debt
DROLLER farceur; funnier; odder	**DUELIST** fighter
DROMOND fast sailing ship **nt**	**DUELLED** fought a duel
DRONING prosing; humming	**DUELLER** combatant in single fight
DRONISH lazy	**DUENESS** fitness; propriety; seemliness
DROOLED slavered; dribbled	**DUFFING** sham; furbishing up
DROOPED withered; declined	**DUKEDOM** duke's realm
DROPLET a drip; bead of moisture	**DULCIFY** sweeten
DROP-NET a fishing-net	**DULCINE** manna-sugar; mannite
DROP-OUT resign; computer error	**DULCITE** saccharine **ch**
DROPPED dripped; fell; quitted	**DULCOSE** dulcine
DROPPER end fly of a cast	**DULLARD** stupid fellow; blockhead
DROSERA sun-dew **bt**	**DULLEST** bluntest; most obtuse
DROSHKY Russian vehicle	**DULLING** allaying; benumbing
DROUGHT aridity; dryness	**DULLISH** rather dull; somewhat inert

DULNESS dullness; stupidity; apathy
DULOSIS ant slavery zo
DUMPING heaping (exporting)
DUMPISH in the dumps
DUN-BIRD pochard duck zo
DUNCERY dulness; stupidity
DUNCIAD Pope's epic poem
DUNCISH not clever
DUNEDIN Edinburgh
DUNFISH cured cod-fish ck
DUNGEON dark prison; cell
DUNKERS Tunkers; triple baptists
DUNNAGE packing; baggage; timber
DUNNING debt collecting; fish curing
DUNNISH dirty brown
DUNNOCK hedge-sparrow zo
DUODENA ancient jury lw
DUOTONE two-colour half-tone printing
DUO-TYPE 2 like plates for diff. colours pr
DUPABLE credulous; gullible
DUPPING opening as a door
DURABLE lasting; abiding; stable
DURABLY permanently; long lasting
DURAMEN heart-wood bt
DURANCE captivity; duress; restraint
DURANTE for life
DUREFUL long lasting
DURESSE severity; constraint (Fr.)
DURIRON acid-resistant iron alloy ml
DURMAST an oak bt
DURSLEY bloodless blows lw
DUSKIER more sable or swarthy
DUSKILY dimly; darkly
DUSKISH shadowy
DUSTBIN trash receptacle
DUSTIER more flocculent
DUSTING a beating
DUSTMAN garbage collector
DUSTPAN house cleaning implement
DUTEOUS obsequious; deferential
DUTIFUL obedient; respectful
DUUMVIR Roman magistrates
DVORNIK Russian concierge
DWARFED stunted; eclipsed
DWELLED sojourned; abode; inhabited
DWELLER resident; inmate; indigene
DWINDLE diminish; decrease; shrink
DYARCHY duarchy; dual control
DYELINE document-copying process pr
DYE-WOOD (various woods) bt
DYE-WORK dyeing establishment
DYINGLY deathly
DYNAMIC forceful
DYNASTY house; family; succession
DYPTICH codex book between wood
  covers
DYSLOGY disapproval; disapprobation
DYSNOMY bad laws
DYSOPSY poor sight md
DYTICUS water-beetles zo
DYVOURY bankruptcy lw

E

EAGERLY avidly; ardently; fervently
EANLING young lamb zo
EARACHE a pain in the ear md
EARDROP a pendant; earring
EAR-DRUM tympanum md
EAR-HOLE aural portal
EARLDOM the seignory of an earl
EARLESS reluctant to hear
EARLIER sooner
EARLOCK love-lock
EARMARK identity mark for sheep
EARNEST pledge; steady; persevering
EARNING winning; meriting; acquiring
EAR-PICK tool for cleaning ears
EARRING pendant; eardrop
EARSHOT hearing distance
EARTHED burrowed el, ro
EARTHEN of clay
EARTHLY carnal; mundane; terrestrial
EASEFUL restful; tranquil; contented
EASIEST least difficult; simplest
EAST-END east part of city
EASTERN oriental; auroral
EASTING east of any meridian nt
EATABLE edible; succulent; esculent
EBB-TIDE retrogression
EBONIST ebony worker
EBONITE vulcanite
EBONIZE ebonise
EBRIETY intoxication; intemperance
EBRIOSE fuddled; crapulous; tipsy
EBRIOUS fond of the bottle; temulent
ECBASIS } rhetorical treatment
ECBATIC }
ECCRINE cell-excretory glandular md
ECDEMIC foreign; not endemic
ECDYSIS moulting; sloughing
ECHAPPE (horse-breeding)
ECHELLE scale; ladder (Fr.)
ECHELON a ladder formation; cycling
ECHIDNA Australian ant-eater zo
ECHIMYD S. American dormouse zo
ECHINUS sea-urchin zo
ECHOING resounding; repeating
ECHOISM onomatopoeia
ECHOIST a yes-man
ECLIPSE shroud; veil; surpass
ECLOGUE pastoral poem
ECOLOGY biological geography
ECONOMY care; thrift; providence
ECOTONE plant-community boundary bt
ECOUTES listening posts (Fr.)
ECSTASY rapture; fervour; delight
ECTASIS mispronunciation
ECTHYMA a rash md
ECTOPIA dislocation md
ECTOPIC displaced
ECTOZOA parasites zo
ECTYPAL actual copy

EDACITY greed; voracity; rapacity
EDAPHON soil community of living organisms
EDDERED bound by an edder
EDDYING swirling; whirling; vortical
EDELITE a silicate   mn
EDENTAL toothless
EDICTAL laid down; ordered
EDIFICE a stylish building
EDIFIED benefited spiritually
EDIFIER an uplifter
EDITING revising; annotating
EDITION issue; number; impression
EDUCATE teach; tutor; school; train
EDUCING extracting; eliciting
EDUCTOR corkscrew
EELBUCK basket-net
EEL-FARE a young eel   zo
EEL-POUT blenny   zo
EFFABLE explicable; utterable
EFFACED erased; defaced
EFFECTS personal estate
EFFENDI Turkish title
EFFORCE ravish; rape
EFFULGE gleam; glisten; coruscate
EFFUSED emanated; diffused
EGALITY parity; equality
EGESTED cast out; ejected
EGG-BIRD tern   zo
EGG-CELL a zygote   zo
EGG-COSY oval muff
EGG-FLIP a bracer; drink
EGGHEAD intellectual
EGOTISM self-sufficiency; vanity
EGOTIST egoist
EGOTIZE (excess of 'I')
EGRETTE spray of gems; aigrette
EIDETIC one having vivid mental pictures   pc
EIDOLON apparition; phantom
EIRENIC irenic; peaceful
EJECTED threw out; dispossessed
EJECTOR chucker-out
ELAIDIC } oil products   ch
ELAIDIN }
ELANCED threw; darted
ELAPSED intervened; slid away; passed
ELASTIC resilient; springy
ELASTIN elastic
ELATERY elastic force; elasticity
ELATINE water-wort   bt
ELATING crowing; exalting
ELATION gratification; exhilaration
ELAULIC with oil in pipes   hy
ELBAITE tourmaline variety   mn
ELBOWED thrust aside; nudged
ELDERLY getting on in years
ELEATIC philosophic
ELECTED chosen; picked; preferred
ELECTOR voter; German title
ELECTRO plated metal

ELEGANT refined; graceful; tasteful
ELEGIAC a lament; dirge
ELEGIST plaintive writer
ELEGIZE lament in writing
ELEIDIN skin cells substance   zo
ELEMENT part; component; ingredient
ELEVATE elate; raise; hoist; promote
ELEVENS an interim
ELF-BOLT elf-arrow
ELF-LAND fairy-land
ELF-LOCK tangled hair
ELF-SHOT flint arrow-head
ELF-WORT elecampane   bt
ELIDING rebutting; shortening
ELIMATE to file; to polish
ELISION metric suppression
ELK-WOOD umbrella-tree   bt
ELLAGIC of gall-nuts   bt
ELLIPSE oval
ELL-WAND (a yard and a quarter)
ELOGIST orator at a funeral
ELOGIUM panegyric
ELOHIST Pentateuch author
ELOINED removed; separated; banished
ELOPING sloping; bolting; decamping
ELUDING dodging; evading; baffling
ELUSION evasion; avoidance
ELUSIVE illustory; deceptive; fugitive
ELUSORY hard to solve; intangible
ELUTION ablution
ELUVIUM detritus from rock weathering
ELYSIAN delightful; heavenly
ELYSIUM Greek paradise
ELYTRAL shield-like   zo
ELYTRON } wing-sheath of beetles   zo
ELYTRUM }
ELZEVIR edition of classics
EMANANT proceeding from
EMANATE originate; issue; flow
EMARCID wilted
EMBALED packed; bundled
EMBARGO a prohibition; veto
EMBASSY ambassadorial residence
EMBATHE to bathe
EMBAYED land-locked
EMBLAZE embellish; imblaze
EMBLEMA inlaid ornament
EMBLICA Indian tree   bt
EMBLOOM bloom
EMBOGUE debouch; discharge
EMBOLUS wedge; a clot   md
EMBOSOM to hug; embrace; enfold
EMBOWER imbower; to shelter
EMBOXED enclosed
EMBRACE clasp; welcome; include
EMBRAID to braid (obs.)
EMBRAIL brail; lash
EMBRAVE embellish; inspirit
EMBREAD embraid
EMBROIL implicate; start trouble
EMBROWN to brown

EMBRUED ensanguined heraldically   hd
EMBRUTE to deteriorate; brutalize
EMBRYON an embryo   bt, zo
EMENDED amended; corrected
EMERALD smaragdus; brilliant green
EMERGED resulted; emanated; arose
EMERITI honourably discharged
EMETINE ipecacuanha alkaloid
EMICANT sparkling; sparking
EMINENT exalted; prominent
EMIRATE the domain of emir
EMITRON early UK TV tube
EMITTED circulated; exhaled; gushed
EMITTER transistor electrode   el
EMMEWED } confined; cooped up
ENMEWED } also inmewed
EMOTION passion; agitation; feeling
EMOTIVE emotional; passionate
EMPALED impaled; transfixed; fenced
EMPANEL enrol
EMPATHY sympathetic reaction
EMPERIL endanger
EMPEROR head of an empire
EMPIGHT placed; fixed
EMPIRIC based on practical experience
EMPIRIC a quack; charlatan
EMPLANE cf. embark
EMPLEAD prosecute   lw
EMPLUME to feather
EMPOWER authorize; warrant; allow
EMPRESS female ruler of empire
EMPRISE a dangerous enterprise
EMPTIED drained; depleted; discharged
EMPTIER more inane and vacuous
EMPTION purchase
EMULATE to vie; compete; rival
EMULOUS striving to equal
EMULSIC emulsive   md
EMULSIN almond ferment   ch
EMU-WREN an Australian bird   zo
ENABLED authorized; allowed
ENACTED decreed; ordained
ENACTOR law-maker   lw
ENAMOUR charm; fascinate; enslave
ENARMED with weapon   hd
ENATION plant or leaf outgrowth   bt
ENCAGED incaged; cooped
ENCASED incased; enclosed
ENCAVED cached in a cave
ENOENIA commemorations, festivals
ENCHAFE to rub warm
ENCHAIN bind; fetter; shackle
ENCHANT enamour; bewitch; captivate
ENCHASE set with jewels; engrave
ENCHEER hearten; exhilarate
ENCHYMA injection; infusion   md
ENCLASP embrace; hug; enfold
ENCLAVE an inlier
ENCLOSE envelop; fence; wrap
ENCLOUD mystify
ENCOMIC of kinky, woolly hair

ENCORED repeated by request
ENCRATY abstinence; self-control
ENCRUST coat; plaster
ENDARCH xylem strand characteristic   bt
ENDEMIC local; indigenous
ENDERON true skin   md
ENDEWED endowed (obs.)
END-GAME chess
ENDIRON andiron; firedog
ENDLESS eternal; interminable
ENDLONG not sideways
ENDMOST uttermost
END-NOTE additional printed information
ENDOGEN botanical growth   bt
ENDORSE indorse; assign; ratify
ENDOWED supplied; bequeathed
ENDOWER benefactor; donor
END-SHIP a village (obs.)
ENDUING induing; investing
ENDURED tolerated; brooked; bore
ENDURER stayer; patient sufferer
ENDWAYS on end; upright
ENDWISE endways
ENDYSIS development of new hair/skin
ENERGIC active; energetic
ENFACED opposite to endorsed
ENFELON make fierce (obs.)
ENFEOFF assignment   lw
ENFILED heraldic sword thrust   hd
ENFLESH turn into flesh
ENFORCE compel; oblige; coerce
ENGAGED plighted; stipulated
ENGAGER employment agent
ENGINED powered; racked
ENGLISH of England
ENGLOBE inglobe; ensphere
ENGLOOM to depress
ENGORGE stuff with food; engulf
ENGRACE bring into favour
ENGRAFT insert; graft
ENGRAIL spot with dots   hd
ENGRAIN dye; permeate
ENGRASP clutch; seize
ENGRAVE cut; chisel; carve
ENGROSS monopolize; absorb; copy
ENGUARD defend
ENHANCE to intensify; heighten
ENISLED isolated
ENJOYED relished; liked; fancied
ENJOYER appreciator; gourmet
ENLACED entwined; inlaced
ENLARGE amplify; extend; expand
ENLIVEN wake; arouse; quicken
ENMURED immured; imprisoned
ENNICHE to enshrine
ENNOBLE exalt; raise; aggrandize
ENNUIED bored stiff
ENODING unknotting
ENOMOTY Spartan band
ENOUNCE proclaim; announce
ENPLANE to board an aeroplane

ENPRINT small enlargement · · · pg
ENQUIRE inquire; investigate; ask
ENQUIRY inquiry; question; search
ENRACED enrooted
ENRAGED exasperated; incensed
ENRIDGE to furrow
ENRIPEN to mellow; mature
ENROBED attired; invested
ENROUGH to roughen
ENSILED stored in a pit
ENSKIED raised to heaven
ENSLAVE enthral; captivate; subjugate
ENSNARE entrap; allure; inveigle
ENSNARL entangle; ravel
ENSOBER to calm down
ENSTAMP impress; imprint
ENSTEEP immerse; duck; souse
ENSTYLE to call; to name
ENSUING resulting; issuing; accruing
ENSURED insured; made certain
ENSWEEP pass over rapidly
ENSWEPT scoured
ENTAMED subdued; domesticated
ENTASIA spasm · · · md
ENTASIS architectural swell
ENTENTE understanding
ENTEQUE S. Amer. farm-stock
  septicaemia · · · vt
ENTERED began; recorded; penetrated
ENTERER entrant; competitor
ENTERIC typhoid fever · · · md
ENTERON collenterata body cavity · · · zo
ENTHEAL divinely inspired
ENTHRAL inthral; enslave
ENTHUSE to gush
ENTICED allured; attracted
ENTICER seducer; cajoler; wheedler
ENTITLE intitle; qualify; allow
ENTOMIC (insects) · · · zo
ENTONIC of high tension
ENTOTIC (interior of ear) · · · md
ENTOZOA internal parasites · · · zo
ENTRAIL interweave; plait
ENTRAIN to board a train
ENTRANT intrant; competitor
ENTREAT beg; implore; importune
ENTROPY dissipation of energy
ENTRUST intrust; confide
ENTUNED chanted; sang
ENTWINE weave; interlace; twist
ENTWIST intwist; wring; contort
ENURING inuring; hardening
ENVAULT entomb
ENVELOP enwrap; enfold; encase
ENVENOM to poison
ENVIOUS jealous; invidious; grudging
ENVIRON envelop; encompass; engird
ENVYING grudging; coveting
ENWHEEL encircle; surround
ENWOUND entwined; woven
ENWOVEN interwoven

ENZONED girdled; belted·
EOBIONT stage in biopoiesis · · · bl
EPACRID of heathlike shrubs · · · bt
EPAGOGE figure of speech
EPARCHY prefecture
EPAULET shoulder-piece
EPAXIAL above the axis · · · zo
EPERGNE ornamental stand
EPHEBIC adult; of optimum period · · · zo
EPHEBUS young Greek citizen
EPHELIS freckle · · · md
EPIBOLY overgrowth · · · zo
EPICARP the rind · · · bt
EPICEDE funeral ode
EPICENE common to both sexes
EPICHIL orchid labellum end · · · bt
EPICISM sagas; heroic poems; etc
EPICIST epic writer
EPICOLE harmless parasite animal · · · ec
EPICURE gourmet; voluptuary
EPICYTE ectoplasm cuticular layer · · · zo
EPIDEME wing articulation sclerite · · · zo
EPIDOTE a silicate · · · mn
EPIGEAL low growing
EPIGEAN found on ground · · · bt
EPIGEIC with stolons on soil surface · · · bt
EPIGENE mineral change
EPIGONE a descendant
EPIGONE spore-bag · · · bt
EPIGRAM barbed wisdom
EPIHYAL hyoid arch element · · · zo
EPILATE remove (hair)
EPILOIA development defect affliction · · · md
EPIMERE mesothelial-wall zone in vert.'s
EPIMYTH moral of story
EPIOTIC a bone in vertebrate skull · · · zo
EPISODE interesting incident
EPISOME genetically active bacteria
  particle
EPISTLE lengthy letter
EPITAPH monumental inscription
EPITAXY crystal growth or deposition
EPITHEM lotion; poultice
EPITHET an appellative; adjective
EPITOME brief summary; abstract
EPIZOIC carried by/inhabiting living
  animal · · · zo
EPIZOON epizoan; parasite · · · zo
EPOCHAL remarkable; outstanding
EPOXIDE plastic resin
EPULARY festive
EQUABLE fair; serene; uniform; calm
EQUABLY uniformly; justly
EQUALLY evenly
EQUATED made equal; balanced
EQUATOR a great circle
EQUERRY mounted officer
EQUINAL horsy
EQUINIA glanders · · · md
EQUINOX (fifty-fifty)
EQUINUS foot deformity · · · md

EQUITES noble Romans
ERASING expunging; deleting
ERASION erasure; deletion; obliteration
ERASURE effacement; cancellation
ERECTED raised; constructed; uplifted
ERECTER a builder; prefabricator
ERECTLY uprightly; upstanding
ERECTOR erecting lens
ERELONG before long
EREMITE hermit; a solitary
EREPSIN an enzyme
ERGOTED afflicted with fungus   bt
ERGUSIA vitamin A
ERICOID with heather-like leaves   bt
ERINEUM leafy excrescence   bt
ERINITE arseniate of copper   mn
ERINOID a plastic material (milk)
ERINYES the Furies
ERISTIC controversial
ERL-KING (Norse mythology)
ERMELIN ermine; the stoat   zo
ERMINED adorned with fur
ERMINES white spots   hd
ERODENT consuming; erosive
ERODING corroding; eating away
EROSION corrosion
EROSIVE gnawing; virulent; acid
EROTEME interrogation mark
EROTICA pornographic literature
ERRABLE fallible; aberrant
ERRATIC rambling; vagrant; capricious
ERRATUM an error; misprint; mistake
ERRHINE medical snuff   md
ERUDITE scholarly; learned
ERUGATE smoothed
ERUPTED exploded; ejected
ESCAPED eluded; avoided; leaked
ESCAPER danger dodger
ESCHARA net-like coral   zo
ESCHEAT forfeiture; confiscate   lw
ESCRIME fencing; swordsmanship (Fr.)
ESCROLL heraldic scroll   hd
ESCUAGE feudal tenure
ESCULIN alkaloid (horse chestnut)   ch
ESERINE alkaloid (Calabar bean)   ch
ESKIMOS inhabitants of Arctic America
ESOPIAN fabulous (Aesop)
ESOTERY mysticism; necromancy
ESPADON Spanish sword
ESPARTO grass (Spain & Algeria)   bt
ESPINEL kind of ruby   mn
ESPOUSE to marry; betroth
ESPYING observing; discovering
ESQUIRE originally a shield-bearer
ESSAYED assayed; tested; tried
ESSAYER essay writer
ESSENCE extract; quiddity
ESSENES Jewish fraternity
ESSOIGN essoin; excuse for absence
ESTIVAL (summer)
ESTOILE heraldic star   hd

ESTRADE a dais (Fr.)
ESTREAT true extract   lw
ESTUARY river mouth; firth; frith
ESURINE aperitif; a cocktail
ETAERIO berried fruit (strawberry)   b
ETAGERE set of shelves (Fr.)
ETATISM central control (government)
ETCHANT copper-removing chemical   cl
ETCHING engraving; an impression
ETERNAL endless; perennial; immortal
ETESIAN Levant wind
ETHERIA river-oyster   z
ETHICAL moral
ETHIOPS dark-coloured
ETHMOID sieve-like; like a temse
ETOILIN yellow chlorophyll   cl
ETONIAN of Eton (College)
EUCHRED outwitted (USA)
EUCLASE beryl   m
EUCRITE coarse-grained igneous rock   g
EUDOXID monogastric stage in siphonofora
EUGAMIC of maturity-period   z
EUGENIA a large genus of spices   b
EUGENIC (birth influence)
EUGENIN clove camphor
EUGENOL constituent of clove/cinnamon oil
EULALIA an ornamental grass
EULOGIA praises; panegyrics
EULOGIC commendatory; laudatory
EUPATHY contentment/moderation
EUPEPSY hearty digestion   m
EUPHONY melodious sound
EUPHROE ridge-pole
EUPNOEA free respiration   m
EURIPUS strait having violent tides
EURITIC like granite   m
EURYALE water-lilies   b
EUSTYLE columnar building style
EUTERPE muse of music
EUTONIA firmness of tone   m
EUTROPY variation in chem. compounds
EVACUEE a displaced person
EVADING eluding; dodging; foiling
EVANGEL the gospel; good news
EVANISH vanish; disappear
EVASION subterfuge; prevarication
EVASIVE elusive; elusory; slippery
EVENING eventide; night-fall; twilight
EVERTED turned inside out
EVICTED dispossessed; ejected   lw
EVICTOR chucker-out   lw
EVIDENT obvious; patent; manifest
EVIL-EYE a bewitching look
EVINCED manifested; proved
EVIRATE castrate; geld
EVITATE to avoid (Shak.)
EVOCATE to summon spirits
EVOKING rousing; exciting; eliciting
EVOLUTE geometric curve

EVOLVED unfolded; emitted; educed
WE-LAMB poor man's only possession
XACTED demanded; levied
XACTER extortioner
XACTLY just so; precisely; literally
XACTOR a tax collector
XALTED lofty; ennobled; elevated
XALTER magnifier; extoller
XAMINE inquire; scrutinize
XAMPLE model; pattern; sample
XANGIA blood-vessel   **md**
XARATE of pupae with free members   **zo**
XARCHY a vice-royalty
XCERPT an extract; cutting; citation
XCHEAT escheat; confiscate   **lw**
XCIPLE outer apothecium wall layer   **bt**
XCISED cut out; removed
XCITED provoked; irritated; inflamed
XCITER rouser; stimulant; agitator
XCITON electron pair in semiconductor   **el**
XCITOR stimulating to activity   **zo**
XCLAIM vociferate; ejaculate
XCLAVE opposite to enclave
XCLUDE prohibit; debar; preclude
XCRETA human or animal waste   **md**
XCURSE to digress; to wander
XCUSED released; pardoned; condoned
XECUTE accomplish; put to death   **lw**
XEDRAE halls; recesses
XEGETE theological exponent
XERGUE date space on coin
XERTED strove; applied; used
XHALED emitted; evaporated; breathed
XHAUST drain; empty; expend; tire
XHIBIT display; manifest; evince
XHUMED disinterred; unearthed
XHUMER a resurrectionist
XIGENT urgent; critical; importunate
XILIAN exiled Jew
XILING banishing; proscribing
XILITY tenuity; slenderness
XISTED was; lasted; endured; subsisted
XITIAL destructive to life
XOCONE of insect compound eyes   **zo**
XODERM outer cell layer in porifera   **zo**
XODIST an emigrant
XOGAMY mixed marriage
XOMION Greek sleeveless vest
XOTISM (not indigenous)
XOTYPE kind marked by non-heritability   **zo**
XPANSE stretch; extent; space
X-PARTE prejudiced; biased
XPENSE cost; outlay; charge; price
XPIATE atone
XPIRED exhaled; ended; stopped
XPLAIN elucidate; interpret; expound
XPLODE burst; detonate; discharge
XPLOIT feat; deed; achievement
XPLORE search; prospect; examine
XPOSAL exposure; revelation

EXPOSED unmasked; debunked
EXPOSER revealer; nark
EXPOUND explain; unfold; interpret
EXPRESS explicit; exude; speedy
EXPUNGE erase; abrogate; cancel
EXPURGE purify; expurgate
EXSCIND cut out; exsect
EXTATIC ecstatic; rapturous
EXTINCT defunct; obsolete; quenched
EXTRACT decoction; essence; juice
EXTRACT extort; derive; select
EXTREME utmost; ultimate; excessive
EXTRUDE expel; eject; force out
EXUDING sweating; oozing; dripping
EXULTED crowed; triumphed; boasted
EXUVIAE cast-off skins, etc.   **zo**
EXUVIAL (cast skins)   **zo**
EYE-BALL eye orb
EYE-BATH eye basin
EYE-BEAM a glance
EYE-BOLT (for hooks)   **nt**
EYE-BROW a hairy arch
EYE-DROP a tear
EYE-FLAP blinker
EYE-HOLE peep-hole
EYELASH cilliary hair
EYELESS blind; unobservant
EYELIAD wanton glance
EYESHOT range of vision; by eye
EYESORE a hideosity
EYESPOT (peacock's feather)
EYEWASH humbug; window dressing
EYE-WINK a wink (Shak.)

F

FABELLA small sesamoid bone in mammals   **zo**
FABLIAU 12th cent. topical verse (Fr.)
FABLING romancing
FABRILE (handicraft)
FABULAR legendary
FACETED having facets
FACETIA witty remarks, jokes, indecent writings
FACETTE listel; flat surface between flutes
FACONNE woven figurative design   **wv**
FACTICE veg. oil vulcanisation product **ch**
FACTION cabal; clique; dissension
FACTORY works; mill; workshop
FACTUAL real; actual; authentic
FACTURE manufacture; workmanship
FACULAE large bright areas of sun photosphere
FACULTY knack; skill; dexterity
FADAISE trivial remark (Fr.)
FADDING shellac lacquering
FADDISH rather crotchety
FADDIST with-it person
FADDLED trifled; played
FADEDLY insipidly

FADE-OUT an evanescence   cn
FADGING suiting; prospering
FAGGERY drudgery
FAGGING enforced service
FAGOTTO bassoon   mu
FAHLERZ copper crystal ore   mn
FAIENCE fayence; glazed pottery
FAILING a foible; declining; miscarry
FAILURE fiasco; ruin; collapse
FAINING wishing; desiring
FAINTED swooned; languished
FAINTER weaker; paler; dimmer
FAINTLY dimly; indistinctly
FAIREST clearest; purest
FAIRIES enchantresses; pixies
FAIRILY like a fairy; elf-like
FAIRING a present; streamlining
FAIRISH reasonably fair
FAIRWAY (golf); navigable channel
FAITOUR impostor; scoundrel
FALANGE Spanish fascist party
FALBALA furbelow; puckered flounce
FALCADE (equitation); curvetting
FALCATE hooked; like a crescent
FALCULA claw   zo
FALDAGE a farming privilege
FALDEE grazing fee
FALERNE sweet white wine
FALLACY a sophism; chimera; untruth
FALLALS showy trifles
FALLING erring; tumbling; dropping
FALLOUT radioactive contamination
FALSELY fallaciously; untruly
FALSEST most disloyal
FALSIES artificial bust
FALSIFY counterfeit; belie; fake
FALSISH somewhat erroneous
FALSISM obvious falsity
FALSITY fallacy; fabrication
FAMULUS magician's assistant
FANATIC bigot; zealot; visionary
FANCIED favoured; imagined; thought
FANCIER expert; breeder
FANFARE flourish of trumpets
FANGLED newly contrived
FAN-MAIL letters of adulation
FANNING extending; winnowing
FAN-PALM the talipot palm   bt
FANTAIL pigeon; a gas burner   zo
FANTASM spook; phantasm
FANTAST visionary; enthusiast
FANTASY caprice; mental conception
FARADAY unit of electrolysis
FARADIC inductive
FARAWAY distant; remote
FARCEUR satirical jester
FARCING edible stuffing; force-meat
FARCIFY to burlesque
FARDAGE dunnage; packing (Fr.)   nt
FARMERY homestead
FARMING leasing of taxes

FARMOST uttermost; furthest
FARNESS remoteness
FARRAGO a medley; hodge-podge
FARRIER shoeing-smith; a vet
FARTHEL farl; oatcake
FARTHER besides; further; beyond
FASCETS glass-making tools   tc
FASCIAE fillets; name boards
FASCIAL (fasces)
FASCINE bound brushwood
FASCISM anti-socialism
FASCIST political party (Italy)
FASHERY annoyance; vexation
FASHING worrying; bothering
FASHION mode; vogue; style; mould
FAST-DAY non-eating day   r
FASTEST swiftest; fleetest; closest
FASTING abstaining from food
FASTISH rather dissipated
FATALLY mortally; calamitously
FAT-BODY fatty tissue in amphibians,
   insects   zc
FATEFUL ominous; portentous
FAT-HEAD blockhead; moron; dunce
FATIDIC prophetic; oracular
FATIGUE tire; jade; lassitude
FATLING young fatted animal   zc
FATLUTE luting
FATNESS obesity; corpulence; fertility
FATTEST most obese
FATTING fattening
FATTISH rather plump; adipose
FATUITY self-complacency; folly
FATUOUS illusory; imbecile; witless
FAUCIAL pertaining to fauces
FAULTED displaced; (tennis)
FAULTER defaulter
FAUNIST naturalist
FAVOURS party badges
FAWNING sycophantic; cringing
FAYENCE faience; pottery
FEARFUL dismayed; dire
FEARING dreading; revering; timid
FEASTED caroused; gratified
FEASTER a Lucullus
FEATHER adorn; quill; (oar)   zc
FEATURE characteristic; aspect; trait
FEAZING unravelling
FEBRILE feverish
FECULUM starchy extract
FEDERAL confederated
FEEDING pasture; eating; subsisting
FEE-FARM tenure without fealty
FEELING sensibility; perception
FEERING first furrow (Sc.)
FEE-TAIL entailed estate
FEEZING twisting; unscrewing
FEIGNED simulated; shammed
FEINTED feigned
FELIDAE, FELINAE the cat genus   zc
FELLING hewing; cutting down

FELONRY the convict class
FELSITE igneous rock   mn
FELSPAR metamorphic rock   mn
FELTING felt cloth
FELUCCA Mediterranean vessel   nt
FELWORT mullein   bt
FEMINAL womanly
FEMORAL (thigh)   md
FENCING hedging; evading
FENDING warding off; averting
FEN-DUCK shoveller-duck   zo
FEN-FIRE will o' the wisp
FENGITE alabaster   mn
FENNISH marshy; boggy; swampy
FENURON chemical weedkiller
FEODARY feudal tenure
FEOFFEE receiver of a fief
FEOFFOR feoffer; fief-granter
FERDWIT a quittance; penalty
FERINGI European in India
FERMATA a pause   mu
FERMENT inflame; commotion; yeast
FERMION generalized particle in statist. theory
FERMIUM man-made element   ch
FERNERY fern garden   bt
FERN-OWL night-jar   zo
FERRARA a sword-blade (It.)
FERRATE an iron salt   ch
FERRIED transported
FERRIES ferry-boats
FERRITE ferro-magnetic (ceramics)   ch
FERROUS (iron)   ch
FERRUGO plant-rust; fungus   bt
FERRULE protecting cap
FERTILE inventive; prolific; fruitful
FERULED caned; punished
FERVENT zealous; ardent; glowing
FERVOUR eagerness; intensity; ardour
FESTIVE joyous; convivial; gay
FESTOON wreath; garland
FESTUCA grass genus   bt
FETCHED brought; conveyed; reached
FETCHER collector; heaver
FETLOCK a tuft of hair   zo
FEUDARY feodary   lw
FEUDING quarrelling (ice hockey)
FEUDIST writer on feudal law   lw
FEU-DUTY annual payment (Sc.)
FEVERED agitated; febrile
FEWNESS paucity; scarcity; sparsity
FIANCEE betrothed woman
FIBBERY mendacity
FIBBING prevaricating
FIBROID like fibre
FIBROIN cobweb material
FIBROIN tough elastic protein   bc
FIBROMA fibrous tumour   md
FIBROSE filamental
FIBROUS stringy
FIBSTER petty liar

FIBULAR (leg bone)   md
FICARIA celandine   bt
FICTILE plastic; mouldable
FICTION romance; fantasy; invention
FICTIVE imaginative; feigned
FIDALGO Portuguese hidalgo
FIDDLED trifled; meddled
FIDDLER a crab; violinist   zo
FIDDLEY hatchway railing   nt
FIDGETY restless; uneasy; impatient
FIELDED (cricket); (base-ball)
FIELDER not one of the batting side
FIERCER more violent
FIERILY vehemently; ardently
FIFTEEN a Rugby side
FIG-CAKE sweetmeat   ck
FIGGERY dressy ornament
FIGGING dressing up
FIGHTER combatant; warrior
FIG-LEAF early dress material   bt
FIGMENT a fabrication
FIG-TREE Mediterranean plant   bt
FIGURAL pictorial; figurate
FIGURED computed; depicted
FIGWORT a plant   bt
FILACER } Law officer dealing with writs
FILAZER }   and pleas   lw
FILARIA parasitic worms   zo
FILBERT hazel-nut   bt
FILCHED purloined; stole
FILCHER pickpocket; pilferer
FILEMOT dead-leaf colour
FILIATE affiliate; adopt
FILIBEG the kilt
FILICAL (ferns)   bt
FILICES the ferns   bt
FILINGS file fragments
FILLING satisfying; replenishing
FILM-FAN a devotee; star-worshipper
FILMING recording in celluloid
FIMBRIA fringe
FIMETIC foul in thought
FINABLE liable to a fine; amerceable
FINALLY ultimately; lastly; eventually
FINANCE money affairs; revenue
FINBACK rorqual whale   zo
FINCHED striped; spotted
FINDING verdict; discovering
FINECUT chopped into small pieces
FINESSE subtlety; craft; artifice
FIN-FISH fin-back whale   zo
FIN-FOOT tropical bird   zo
FINGENT moulding
FINICAL fastidious; dainty; faddy
FINICKY niggling; meticulous
FINIKIN finicking; finicky
FINLESS having no flipper
FINNACK } white sea-trout
FINNOCK }   zo
FINNISH of the Finns
FIN-TOED web-footed

FIORITE volcanic residue	mn	**FLANEUR** an idling gossip
FIRE-ARM weapon		**FLANGED** having a raised edge
FIRE-BAR furnace bar		**FLANKED** bordered by; side by side
FIRE-BOX boiler fuel chamber		**FLANKER** that which lies beside
FIRE-BUG an incendiary		**FLANNEL** woollen fabric; mullein genus
FIREDOG an andiron		**FLAPPER** bird; girl	zc
FIREFLY a luminous beetle	zo	**FLARING** funnel-shaped; glaring
FIREMAN fire fighter		**FLASHED** glistened; sparkled; gleamed
FIRE-NEW brand-new		**FLASHER** would-be-wit
FIRE-PAN brazier; priming pan		**FLASKET** basket; flask
FIRE-POT incendiary bomb		**FLATLET** a small flat
FIRMARY tenant's rights	lw	**FLATTED** flattened; depressed
FIRMING confirming; establishing		**FLATTEN** level; lay low
FIRRING wood strips for roof boarding basis		**FLATTER** coax; cajole; compliment
FISH-DAY fast day		**FLAUNTY** showy; gaudy
FISHERY fish-breeding station		**FLAVEDO** yellowness	bt
FISH-FAG fish-wife		**FLAVIAN** (Flavius Vespasian)
FISH-FLY a bait	zo	**FLAVINE** a yellow dye	bt
FISH-GIG fishing appliance		**FLAVONE** yellow plant pigment	ch
FISH-GOD Dagon		**FLAVOUR** zest; savour; taste; relish
FISHIFY to turn into a fish (Shak.)		**FLAWING** cracking; marring
FISHILY in a fishy manner		**FLAYING** skinning; excoriating
FISHING angling; piscatorial pursuit		**FLEABAG** sleeping bag
FISH-MAW swimming bladder		**FLEAPIT** shabby room; theatre
FISH-OIL nutrient-rich oil		**FLECKED** spotted
FISHWAY fish-ladder		**FLECKER** to dapple
FISKERY friskiness		**FLEDGED** ready for flight
FISSILE cleavable; laminate		**FLEECED** clipped; shorn
FISSION fissure; rent; rift; fracture		**FLEECER** white collar bandit
FISSIVE fissile		**FLEEING** absconding; retreating
FISSURE cleft; crevice; interstice		**FLEERED** mocked; scoffed
FISTING pommelling		**FLEERER** a derider; flouter
FIST-LAW might is right		**FLEETED** flitted; flew; sped
FISTUCA pile-driver		**FLEETLY** swiftly; nimbly; rapidly
FISTULA ulcer; reed	md	**FLEMING** a native of Flanders
FITCHED pointed	hd	**FLEMISH** language of Flemings
FITCHEE fitched		**FLENSED** cut blubber
FITCHET polecat; foumart	zo	**FLESHED** satiated; glutted
FITMENT a fitting		**FLESHER** butcher; red-backed shrike	zc
FITNESS aptness; decency; seemliness		**FLESHLY** carnal; sensual; fat; obese
FITTAGE brokerage		**FLETTON** pink/yellow indented brick	bt
FITTING a fixture; appropriate		**FLEURET** floral decoration; fencing-foil
FITWEED anti-hysteric plant	bt	**FLEURON** type flower in printing
FIXABLE securable		**FLEXILE** pliable; pliant; supple
FIXEDLY firmly; steadfastly		**FLEXING** bending; turning
FIXTURE appointment; engagement		**FLEXION** inclination; a bow
FIZZING spluttering; hissing		**FLEXURE** bending; curvature
FIZZLED failed; flopped		**FLICKED** flipped
FLACCID flabby; tabid; loose; limp		**FLICKER** twinkle; scintillate
FLACKER flutter like a bird		**FLIGHTY** volatile; mercurial; fickle
FLACKET flask; flasket		**FLINDER** splinter; fragment
FLACKIE straw packing		**FLINGER** hurler
FLAFFER to flutter (Sc.)		**FLIP-DOG** liquor heater	zc
FLAG-DAY day when flags sold for charity		**FLIPPED** filliped; flicked
FLAGGED signalled; drooped		**FLIPPER** fore-limb of a cetacean	zc
FLAG-MAN signaller		**FLIRTED** coquetted; flicked
FLAKING crumbling		**FLITTER** flutter; a tatter
FLAMING blazing; burning; glowing		**FLOATED** drifted; wafted
FLAMMED hoaxed		**FLOATER** not a sinker
FLAMMER splitting knife	to	**FLOCCUS** tuft of hair; down
		FLOCKED crowded; swarmed; thronged

FLOCKLY like sheep
FLOGGED scourged; lashed
FLOGGER graining brush   pt
FLOODED swamped; inundated; deluged
FLOOKAN slimy clay
FLOORED overthrown; baffled
FLOORER knockdown blow
FLOPPED failed; fizzled
FLOREAL 8th month (Fr. Revolution)
FLORIST a nurseryman
FLOROON flower border
FLORUIT a life-time
FLOTAGE buoyancy
FLOTSAM recovered wreckage
FLOUNCE a jerky movement
FLOURED powdered
FLOUTED jeered; insulted
FLOUTER mocker; derider
FLOWAGE flow; current; discharge
FLOWERY florid; ornate; figurative
FLOWING fluent; copious; smooth
FLUENCY also fluence; exuberance
FLUEWAY smoke and gas duct
FLUFFED bungled; foozled
FLUIDAL flowing; liquid
FLUIDIC fluid
FLUIDLY liquidly
FLUKILY by a fluke
FLUKING scoring by chance
FLUMMOX perplex; defeat
FLUMPED slumped
FLUNKEY footman; snob; toady
FLUORIC (fluorine)   ch
FLUSHED blushed; roused; disturbed
FLUSHER lesser butcher-bird   zo
FLUSTER agitation; disconcert; bustle
FLUSTRA sea-mat; polyzoa   zo
FLUTINA accordion   mu
FLUTING grooving
FLUTIST flautist
FLUTTER speculation; palpitate   el
FLUVIAL (rivers)
FLUXIDE fusible
FLUXING melting
FLUXION fusion; variation; change
FLYAWAY flighty
FLYBACK electronics term   el
FLY-BILL hand-bill
FLY-BLOW fly-larva   zo
FLY-BOAT canal boat
FLY-BOMB pilotless aerial torpedo
FLY-BOOK (fishing)
FLY-FLAP fly-whisk
FLY-HALF (football)
FLY-LEAF blank page
FLY-LINE fishing line
FLY-OVER road or rail crossing
FLY-PAST flight by aircraft
FLY-RAIL table leaf support
FLY-TRAP an insectivorous plant   bt
FOALING colt-birth

FOAMING raging; bubbling; creaming
FOBBING cheating; tricking
FOCUSED concentrated
FODIENT pertaining to digging
FOE-LIKE hostile; inimical; adverse
FOG-BANK accumulation of fog
FOG-BELL sea warning device
FOGGAGE coarse grass   bt
FOGGIER murkier; more opaque
FOGGILY mistily
FOGGING obscuring
FOGHORN sea warning device   nt
FOGLAMP penetrating headlight
FOGLESS clear
FOG-RING bank of fog
FOGYISH antiquated
FOGYISM dull notions
FOILING tracery; deer track
FOILIST fencer
FOINING thrusting; tilting
FOISTED falsified; thrust
FOISTER palmer; imposer; cheat
FOLDAGE sheep folding rights
FOLDING a fold; sheep penning
FOLIAGE leafage; boscage
FOLIATE a curve; laminate
FOLINIC acid constituent of folic acid
FOLIOED in folios or pages
FOLIOLE leaflet   bt
FOLIOSE leafy
FOLIOUS thin; unsubstantial
FOLLIES imbecilities; inanities
FOMITES porous substances   ch
FONDANT soft sweet
FONDEST most affectionate
FONDING doting
FONDLED caressed; dandled
FONDLER sugar daddy
FONDUTA cheese/truffle fondue (N. Italy)   ck
FONTEIN S. African spring
FONTLET small font   rl
FOODFUL nourishing; nutritious
FOOLERY clowning; buffoonery
FOOLING hoodwinking; beguiling
FOOLISH doltish; stupid; irrational
FOOT-BAR aeroplane rudder control   ae
FOOTBOY page; bell-hop
FOOTHOT hot-foot; immediately
FOOTING basis; entrance fee
FOOTLED pottered
FOOTMAN flunkey; lackey
FOOTPAD highwayman
FOOT-ROT disease of sheep   vt
FOOT-TON a measure of work   me
FOOTWAY footpath
FOOZLED footled; mishit
FOOZLED bungler
FOPLING young dandy
FOPPERY affectation; coxcombry
FOPPISH finical; dressy

FORAGED plundered; pillaged
FORAGER ravager; a cap
FORAMEN a pore   md
FORAYED invaded; raided
FORAYER marauder
FORBADE vetoed; banned; inhibited
FORBEAR ancestor; refrain; abstain
FORBORE desisted; withheld; shunned
FORCEPS pliers   to
FORCING plant culture; coercing
FORCITE dynamite
FORCQUE fork; mine sump   mn
FORDING crossing
FORDONE tired out
FOREARM lower part of arm   pl
FOREBAY pipeline head reservoir   hy
FORE-BOW front of saddle
FORE-CAR (motor-cycle)
FOREDAY forenoon
FOREDID overpowered; undid
FORE-END the front end
FORE-GUT part of animal alimentary canal
FOREIGN alien; exotic; strange
FORELAY ambush
FORELEG front leg
FOREMAN boss; overseer; ganger   lw
FORERAN preceded; ushered
FORERUN herald
FORESAW foretold; forecast
FORESAY predict; presage; augar
FORESEE anticipate; forecast
FORETOP part of rigging   nt
FOREVER everlasting; always
FORFANG an ancient felony   lw
FORFEIT alienate; penalty; fine
FORFEND to avert; ward off
FORGAVE pardoned; absolved
FORGERY counterfeiting
FORGING shaping; hammering
FORGIVE remit; excuse
FORGONE past; predetermined
FORKFUL fork-load
FORKING branching; dividing
FORLORN desolate; lost; hapless
FORMANT vowel pitch
FORMATE (formic acid)   ch
FORMFUL imaginative; creative
FORMING shaping; moulding
FORMOXY organic radical   ch
FORMULA set of symbols
FORNENT directly opposite (Sc.)
FORPINE waste away (obs.)
FORSAKE abandon; quit; desert
FORSOOK renounced; relinquished
FORTIFY strengthen; brace
FORTLET small redoubt
FORTUNE luck; Kismet; felicity
FORWARD bold; brazen; quicken
FORWENT foregone
FORWORN tired out (obs.)
FOSSICK prospect; rummage

FOSSWAY Roman road
FOUDRIE jurisdiction (Sc.)
FOUGADE fougasse; mine
FOULARD silk
FOULDER to flame; gleam (obs.)
FOULING (gun-barrels); soiling
FOUMART the polecat; fitchew   zo
FOUNDED started; established
FOUNDER collapsed; originator
FOUNDRY (metal-casting)
FOURGON baggage wagon
FOVEATE pitted   bt
FOVEOLA dent; depression   md
FOVILLA (pollen)   bt
FOWLING falconry
FOWLRUN poultry yard
FOX-CASE fox-skin
FOX-EVIL baldness   md
FOXHOLE defensive trench
FOXHUNT English diversion
FOXLIKE cunning
FOXSHIP craftiness
FOXTAIL a grass   bt
FOX-TRAP a snare
FOX-TROT a dance
FOYAITE nepheline-syenite variety   gl
FRABBIT peevish
FRACHES glass annealing trays
FRACTED broken   hd
FRAGILE delicate; infirm; brittle
FRAILLY weakly; feebly
FRAILTY foible; weakness; infirmity
FRAISED defended by pointed stakes
FRAKTUR German black-letter type
FRAME-UP a plot
FRAMING forming; devising
FRAMPEL quarrelsome; peevish
FRANCIC Frankish
FRANION boon companion; paramour
FRANKED exempt; post paid
FRANKLY candidly; openly; unreserved
FRANTIC frenzied; raving; distracted
FRAPPED bound   nt
FRATCHY quarrelsome
FRATERY refectory in monastery   rl
FRAUGHT laden; pregnant; surcharged
FRAYING peel of deer's horn
FRAZZLE tatters; shreds
FREAKED streaked; checkered
FRECKLE macula
FRECKLY spotted
FREEDOM liberty; informality; scope
FREEING loosing; liberating
FREEMAN privileged citizen
FREESIA bulbous plant   bt
FREEWAY by pass; motorway
FREEZER refrigerator
FREIGHT cargo; burden; burthen
FRENATE bristly   zo
FRESHEN refresh; invigorate; revive
FRESHER freshman; less faded

FRESHES a flood; a spate
FRESHET flooding of a river
FRESHLY recently; briskly; newly
FRESNEL unit of optical frequency
FRETFUL petulant; testy; fractious
FRET-SAW woodworking tool   **to**
FRETTED frayed; abraded; harassed
FRETTEN pock-pitted
FRETTER a worried woman
FRIABLE crumbly; powdery
FRIARLY unsophisticated
FRIBBLE frivolous; to trifle; totter
FRIEZED shaggy with nap; ornamented
FRIGATE a war-ship   **nt**
FRIJOLE Mexican bean   **bt**
FRILLED adorned like a ham
FRINGED bordered; edged
FRIPPER old clothes merchant
FRISEUR hairdresser
FRISIAN Frieslander; cattle   **zo**
FRISKED gambolled; searched
FRISKER a gad-about; a searcher
FRISKET a printing frame
FRISLET small ruffle
FRISURE a crisping of the hair
FRITTED fused; baked
FRITTER pancake; fragment; dissipate
FRIZING stripping grain surface   **le**
FRIZZED curled
FRIZZLE to fry; to crisp; to splutter
FRIZZLY curly
FROCKED wearing a frock
FROGBIT aquatic plant   **bt**
FROGERY a frog pool   **zo**
FROGGED braided
FROG-MAN special type of diver   **nt**
FRONDED leafy   **bt**
FRONTAL a pediment; head on
FRONTED faced; encountered
FRONTON a pelota ground (Sp.)
FROSTED roughened
FROTHED foamed
FROUNCE wrinkle; frown
FROWARD perverse; wayward
FROWNED scowled; glowered
FROWSTY foul and stuffy
FRUCTED bearing fruit
FRUGGIN oven stirring pole
FRUITED bore fruit
FRUITER fruit grower
FRUMPED jeered
FRUMPER scoffer; mocker
FRUSTUM a conic section
FRUTIFY fructify; team; produce
FUBBERY deception
FUCATED painted deceptively
FUCHSIA a flowering shrub   **bt**
FUCHSIN red fuchsia dye
FUDDLED bemused; fuzzled
FUDDLER drunkard; toper
FUDGING faking

FUEHRER German leader
FUELLER stoker
FUFFING puffing
FUGUIST fugue composer   **mu**
FULCRUM support for lever
FULGENT dazzling; radiant; brilliant
FULGORA lantern fly   **zo**
FULGOUR splendour
FULLAGE fuller's pay
FULLERY cloth works
FULLEST amplest; most exhaustive
FULL-HOT vehement; blazing
FULLING (cloth process)
FULL-PAY not docked
FULMINE fulminate
FULNESS repletion; plenty; plentitude
FULSOME obsequious; nauseous
FULVOUS tawny; fulvid
FUMARIA genus of plants   **bt**
FUMARIC a vegetable extract   **bt**
FUMARIN chemical rodenticide
FUMBLED bungled; groped
FUMBLER foozler
FUMETTE smell of high game
FUMITER the fumitory plant   **bt**
FUNARIA genus of mosses   **bt**
FUNDING forming a reserve
FUNERAL sepulture; obsequies
FUN FAIR amusement park
FUNGATE (fungic acid)   **ch**
FUNGITE fossil coral   **mn**
FUNGOID fungus   **bt**
FUNICLE ligature; a fibre   **bt**
FUNKING panicking; fearing
FUNNILY comically; humorously
FUNNING joking; diverting
FURBISH burnish; rub; polish
FURCATE forked
FURCULA the merrythought   **zo**
FURIOSO all out   **mu**
FURIOUS frantic; raging; frenzied
FURLANA forlana; Venetian dance
FURLING wrapping; rolling
FURLONG 220 yards (201 m)   **me**
FURMETY frumenty; porridge
FURNACE firebox
FURNISH equip; supply; produce
FURRIER a dealer in furs
FURRING (lathing); encrusting
FURROWY in furrows
FURTHER farther; promote; encourage
FURTIVE stealthy; sly; clandestine
FUSCINE an oil extract   **ch**
FUSCITE crystallized pyrargillite   **mn**
FUSCOUS swarthy
FUSIBLE able to be melted
FUSSIER more fidgety
FUSSILY restlessly
FUSSING making trouble
FUSS-POT anxious busy-body
FUSTIAN coarse cloth; bombastic

FUSTIER mouldier; mustier
FUTCHEL supporting bar
FUTHORC Runic alphabet
FUTTOCK ship's timber
FUZZIER curlier; more crinkled
FUZZLED fuddled; inebriated
FYRDUNG Saxon martial array

G

GABBARD gabbart; a barge   nt
GABBING gossiping
GABBLED gaggled; chattered
GABBLER a babbler
GABELER salt tax collector
GADELLE currant (Fr.)   bt
GADDING roving; wandering
GADDISH restless
GADLING gauntlet spike
GADROON ornamented edge
GADSMAN ploughman
GADWALL migratory duck   zo
GAEKWAR Gaikwar; (Baroda)
GAFFING (fishing); gambling
GAGGING interpolation; silencing
GAGGLED gabbled
GAHNITE spinel-group mineral   mn
GAINFUL lucrative; beneficial
GAINING profiting; winning; acquiring
GAINSAY dispute; contradict
GAIRISH garish; gaudy
GAITERS gambadoes
GALANTY (shadow pantomime)
GALATEA Pygmalion's statue
GALATEA cotton fabric
GALEATE crested   zo
GALEENY guinea-fowl   zo
GALENIC (lead)
GALETTE a gateau
GALILEE West porch   rl
GALILEO eminent astronomer
GALIPOT pine-resin   bt
GALLANT courtly; valiant; a beau
GALLA-OX Abyssinian ox   zo
GALLATE (gallic acid)   ch
GALLEON treasure ship   nt
GALLERY corridor; passage; balcony
GALL-FLY a pest   zo
GALLICE in French
GALLING irritating; exasperating
GALLIOT galiot; brigantine   nt
GALLIUM a metallic element   ch
GALLIZE (wine-making)
GALL-NUT a pestiferous growth   bt
GALLOON woven fabric; lace
GALLOWS (Tyburn)
GALOCHE galosh; rubber over-shoe
GALOPIN kitchen-boy (Sc.)
GALUMPH bound exultingly
GAMBADO mud-gaiter; caper

GAMBIAN native of Gambia (W. Africa)
GAMBIER catechu; a dye   bt
GAMBIST a viol player   mu
GAMBLED staked; ventured; hazarded
GAMBLER speculator; wagerer
GAMBOGE also camboge
GAMBREL butcher's crook; roof   ar
GAME-BAG hunter's bag
GAME-EGG a bad egg   zo
GAMEFUL sportive
GAME-LEG lameness   md
GAMETAL gametic; reproductive
GAMETID sporont-body bud cell   zo
GAMMOCK sky-larking; gammon
GAMPISH bulging; slatternly
GANCHED (Turkish execution)
GANGING going (Sc.); joining   el
GANGLIA nerve-centre   md
GANGREL vagrant; vagabond
GANG-SAW multiple saw   to
GANGWAY a passage   nt
GANOIDS fish of sturgeon type   zo
GANOSIS reducing shine on marble
GANTLET gauntler
GANTREE loom jacquard frame   wv
GAPPING opening; cleaving
GARBAGE refuse; offal
GARBLED (suppressio veri)
GARBLER (suggestio falsi)
GARBOIL uproar; turmoil (Shak.)
GARBURE Pyrenean ragout/soup   ck
GARDANT full-faced   hd
GARFISH sea-fish; belone   zo
GARGLED warbled
GARLAND wreath; chaplet; festoon
GARMENT vesture; raiment; apparel
GARNISH adorn; pewter ware
GAROTTE garrotte; throttle
GARPIKE the garfish   zo
GARVOCK a sprat; garvie (Sc.)   zo
GAS-BUOY marine device   nt
GAS-COAL anthracite
GAS-COKE coal residuum
GASEITY gaseousness
GASEOUS containing gas
GAS-FIRE heating unit
GASHFUL mutilated; hideous
GASHING slicing; slitting
GASKINS leggings
GAS-LAMP Victorian lighting
GAS-LIME (gas filtration)
GAS-MAIN chief gas conduit
GAS-MASK war protection device
GAS-OVEN kitchen furniture
GASPING spasmodic breathing
GAS-PIPE gas conduit
GAS-RING cooker
GASSING loquacity
GASSOUL mineral soap (Morocco)
GAS-TANK gas storage receptacle
GASTRIC gastral; (stomach)   md

GATEMAN gate-keeper
GATEWAY entrance
GATLING a gun
GAUDERY finery; gew-gaws
GAUDIED embellished
GAUDILY ostentatiously
GAUFFER to crimp
GAUFFRE a batter cake
GAUGING mensuration; estimating
GAULISH (Gaul)
GAULTER gault or clay digger
GAUMING daubing; smearing
GAUNTLY lankily; leanly
GAUNTRY gantry; travelling crane
GAVELET land forfeiture   lw
GAVILAN species of hawk   zo
GAVOTTE a country dance   mu
GAYNESS merriment; hilarity
GAYSOME blithe; vivacious; jolly
GAZEFUL regardant; contemplative
GAZELLE graceful animal   zo
GAZETTE journal; newspaper; record
GEAR-BOX motor-engine
GEARING train of wheels
GEDRITE orthorhombic amphibole   mn
GEGGERY trickery (Sc.)
GEHENNA place of abomination
GELABLE congealable
GELATIN gelatine
GELDING emasculated horse   zo
GELIDLY frigidity
GELLOCK crowbar; gavelock   to
GEMMATE budding
GEMMERY, GEMMARY jewellery
GEMMING budding
GEMMULE small bud   bt
GEMSBOK S. African antelope   zo
GENAPPE worsted yarn
GENERAL vague; inexact; usual
GENERIC collective; characteristic
GENESIS starting point
GENETIC originating
GENETTE genet; civit   zo
GENEVAN Calvanist   rl
GENIPAP orange-like fruit   bt
GENISTA broom plant; (Plantagenet)   bt
GENITAL generic
GENITOR creator
GENOESE of Genoa
GENTEEL elegant; polite; mincing
GENTIAN plant genus   bt
GENTILE not a Jew
GENTLER milder; more kindly
GENUINE sincere; authentic; veritable
GEOCOLE periodically soil-dwelling organism
GEODESY (earth measurements)
GEOGONY (earth formations)
GEOIDAL earth-shaped
GEOLOGY study of rocks
GEONOMY physical geography

GEORAMA globular map
GEORDIE mine-lamp; guinea   nm
GEORGIC rural poetry
GEOTOME soil-sample taker   bt
GEOXENE accidentally soil-dwelling organism
GERMANE relevant; apposite; pertinent
GERMULE a small germ   md
GERVAIS cream cheese (Fr.)   ck
GESTALT total perception; art as unity
GESTAPO German secret police
GESTATE carry in womb
GESTURE sign; signal; action
GETABLE obtainable; procurable
GET-AWAY escape
GETTING acquisition; gaining; reaching
GHASTLY fearsome; spectral; awful
GHERKIN small cucumber   bt
GHILGAI Australian dewpond
GHILLIE game-keeper (Sc.)
GHOSTLY weird; spiritual; spectral
GIANTLY gigantic; Cyclopean
GIANTRY giants collectively
GIBBOSE humped
GIBBOUS convex   as
GIBLETS kidneys and liver
GIDDILY vertiginously
GIFTING endowing; bestowing
GIG-MILL nap-raising device
GILBERT magnetic potential
GILDING painting gold
GILLIAN sweetheart
GILLION 10 to the 9th power
GILL-LID gill covering   zo
GILVOUS brownish   bt
GIMBALS compass suspender
GIMBLET gimlet   to
GIMMICK publicity trick
GIN-FIZZ a beverage
GINGALL swivel gun
GINGERY hot-flavoured
GINGHAM umbrella; gamp; (material)   tx
GINGILI sesame-oil   bt
GINGING mine-shaft lining   mn
GIN-MILL off-licence (Amer.)
GINNING cotton making
GINSENG a Chinese pick-me-up   bt
GIN-SHOP gin-palace
GIN-TRAP animal snare
GIPPING gutting
GIPSIES Zingari
GIRAFFE the camelopard   zo
GIRASOL fire-opal   mn
GIRDING a covering; reproaching
GIRDLED zoned; belted
GIRDLER girdle maker
GIRLISH very young; lady-like
GIRNING grumbling (Sc.)
GIRROCK garfish   zo
GIRTHED girdled; bound
GISARME battle-axe; bill; halberd

GITTERN cithern; guitar	mu
GIZZARD grinding organ of a bird	
GLACIAL icy	
GLACIER moving ice layer	
GLADDEN delight; gratify; rejoice	
GLADDER brighter; more cheerful	
GLAD-EYE an invitation	
GLADIUS swordfish	zo
GLADWYN purple iris	bt
GLAIDIN glutin; (wheat)	
GLAIKIT giddy; foolish (Sc.)	
GLAIRED varnished	
GLAMOUR fascination; witchery	
GLANCED glimpsed; ricocheted	
GLARING refulgent; bare-faced	
GLASSES specs	
GLAUCUS genus of molluscs	zo
GLAZIER pane-setter	
GLAZING (windows); (pottery)	
GLEAMED shone; flashed; glinted	
GLEANED gathered; culled; harvested	
GLEANER Ruth	
GLEBOUS gleby; turfy	
GLEDGED squinted	
GLEEFUL gay; lively; hilarious	
GLEEMAN minstrel	
GLENOID cupped	md
GLEYING squinting	
GLIADIN gliadine; glutin	ch
GLIDING flowing; skimming; sliding	
GLIMMER gleam; inkling	
GLIMPSE glance; view; look	
GLINTED gleamed; sparkled	
GLIRINE rodent-like	
GLISTEN shine; coruscate; scintillate	
GLISTER glitter; lustre; sparkle	
GLITTER glisten; brilliance; radiance	
GLOAMED grew dark	
GLOATED exulted; revelled	
GLOBARD a glow-worm	zo
GLOBATE spheroidal	
GLOBING encircling	
GLOBOID spherical	
GLOBOSE round	
GLOBOUS globular	
GLOBULE corpuscle	
GLONOIN trinitroglycerine alcohol solution	
GLOOMED obscured; dimmed; moped	
GLORIED exalted; took pride in	
GLORIFY honour; magnify; extol; bless	
GLOSSED explained; palliated	
GLOSSER polisher; commentator	
GLOSSIC phonetic alphabet	
GLOTTIC glottal	md
GLOTTIS (larynx)	md
GLOWING vehement, ardent; fervid	
GLOZING specious representation	
GLUCIDE saccharin, gluside	ch
GLUCINA an oxide	ch
GLUCOSE sugar	
GLUE-POT gum receptacle	

GLUMMER more dismal and dejected	
GLUMOUS husky	bt
GLUTEUS hind-limb muscle in vertebrates	
GLUTTED gorged; surfeited; crammed	
GLUTTON the wolverine	zo
GLYCINE amino-acetic acid	ch
GLYOXOL yellow dialdehyde liquid	ch
GLYPHIC word picture; plastic model	
GLYPTIC engraved; figured	
GMELINA (verbena)	bt
GNARING snarling; growling	
GNARLED knotty; gnarred	
GNARRED gnarled; knotty	
GNASHED ground	
GNATHIC (jaws); gnathal	md
GNATHOS ventral sclerite in m. lepidoptera	
GNAT-NET mosquito-net	
GNAWING champing; eroding	
GNOCCHI maize/potato dumplings (It.)	ck
GNOSTIC speculative believer	
GOADING inciting; annoying	
GO-AHEAD enterprising	
GOATISH lustful	
GOBBING coal refuse	
GOBBLER turkey-cock	zo
GOBBLER gourmandizer	
GOBELIN French tapestry	
GODDARD pewter cup	
GODDESS female deity	
GODETIA a garden annual	bt
GODHEAD divine nature	
GODHOOD state of being god	
GODILLE wavy ski-descent technique	
GODLESS atheistic; irreligious; profane	
GODLIER more righteous	
GODLIKE deific	
GODLILY devoutly	
GODLING an inferior deity	
GODROON gadroon; beading	
GODSEND windfall; a crowning mercy	
GODSHIP deification	
GODWARD heavenward	
GOGGLED lobster-eyed	
GOGGLES eye-protectors	
GOITRED afflicted with bronchocele	
GOLD-CUP buttercup	bt
GOLDING an apple; hops	bt
GOLDNEY a bream	zo
GOLFING mild sport	
GOLIARD wandering jester	
GOLIATH large beetle	zo
GOMBEEN money-lending; usury (Irish)	
GOMELIN cotton starch	
GOMERIL a lout; stupid fellow (Sc.)	
GONAGRA gout	md
GONDOLA car of an airship	nt
GONGING prelude to a fine	
GONIDA lichen-spores	bt
GONITIS stifle joint inflammation	vt
GONOPOD external insect-reproduction organ	zo

GOOD-BYE adieu	GRANGER farm bailiff	
GOOD-DAY conventional greeting	GRANITE igneous crystalline rock	mn
GOOD-DEN ⎫	GRANNOM grandam	
GOOD-E'EN ⎭ good evening	GRANTED ceded; allotted; vouchsafed	
GOOD-EGG! cordial approval	GRANTEE the receiver	lw
GOODISH not so bad	GRANTER the bestower	
GOODMAN a husband	GRANTOR conveyor	lw
GOOD-NOW exclamation of wonder	GRANULE small particle	
GOONDIE Australian native hut	GRAPERY vinery	bt
GOOSERY cf. swannery zo	GRAPHIC pictorial; striking; vivid	
GOPURAM Hindu gate tower ar	GRAPNEL grappling-iron	
GORCOCK red grouse zo	GRAPPLE grasp; clutch; grip	
GOR-CROW carrion crow zo	GRASPED clasped; gripped; understood	
GORDIAN intricate; (knot)	GRASPER clasper; grabber	
GORDIUS hair-worm zo	GRASSED brought down	
GORGING cramming; stuffing	GRASSER extra printing hand	
GORILLA largest anthropoid ape zo	GRASSUM a premium lw	
GORMAND gourmand; glutton	GRATIFY please; humour; gladden	
GORSEDD Welsh bardic assembly	GRATING harsh; offensive; jarring	
GOSHAWK short-winged hawk zo	GRAVEDO cold in the head md	
GOSLING a young goose zo	GRAVELY seriously; staidly; soberly	
GOSNICK small sea-fish; skipper zo	GRAVEST most serious; very cogent	
GOSSIPY chatty; loquacious	GRAVIED served with gravy	
GOSSOON a boy (Irish)	GRAVING engraving; scraping	
GOUACHE (water-colour painting)	GRAVITA gravely mu	
GOUGING scooping	GRAVITY enormity; importance	
GOULARD lead acetate ch	GRAVURE photogravure	
GOULASH a ragout; (cards) ck	GRAZIER a pastor; shepherd	
GOURAMI tropical fish zo	GRAZING glancing; touching; browsing	
GOURMET a dainty feeder; epicure	GREASED lubricated; oiled	
GOURNET gurnet zo	GREASER lubricator; a dago	
GOWN-MAN a divine, etc.	GREATEN enhance; enlarge; augment	
GRAB-BAG lucky-dip bag	GREATER bulkier; bigger; larger	
GRABBED clutched; snatched	GREATLY vastly; notably; immensely	
GRABBER gripper; pincher	GREAVES leg-armour	
GRABBLE sprawl; grope; paw	GREAVES tallow refuse; cracklings	
GRACILE slender	GRECIAN Greek (poetic)	
GRACING adorning; decking	GRECISM Greek idiom	
GRACKLE Indian thrush zo	GRECIZE to Hellenize	
GRADATE to blend colour	GRECQUE coffee-machine	
GRADELY orderly; really good	GREENED hoaxed; duped; gulled	
GRADINE sculptor's chisel to	GREENER more verdant	
GRADING a decoration; classifying	GREENFLY verdantly	
GRADUAL step by step	GREENTH verdure	
GRAFFER notary; scrivener lw	GREETED accosted; welcomed	
GRAFTED incorporated	GREMIAL Bishop's pinafore rl	
GRAFTER swindler	GREMLIN aerial imp	
GRAINED (painted wood)	GRENADE hand-bomb	
GRAINER grain-painter	GREY-HEN stone bottle	
GRALLAE wading birds zo	GREY-HEN female grouse zo	
GRALLIC stilted	GREY-FLY gray-fly zo	
GRAMARY magic; wizardry	GREY-LAG wild goose zo	
GRAMMAR a treatise	GREY-OWL tawny owl zo	
GRAMPUS dolphin; killer whale zo	GREYISH grayish	
GRANARY grain-store	GREYLAG gray-lag; grey goose zo	
GRANDAD grandpa	GRIDDED marked in squares	
GRANDAM a grannie	GRIDDLE sieve; a grid	
GRANDEE Spanish nobleman	GRIDING grating; jarring	
GRANDER finer; superior; sublime	GRIEVED lamented; mourned	
GRANDLY splendidly; superbly	GRIFFIN greenhorn; a duenna	
GRANDMA grandam	GRIFFIN heraldic monster hd	

GRIFFON griffin; a dog   zo
GRILLED broiled; cross-examined
GRIMACE a moué; facial distortion
GRIMING fouling; soiling
GRIMMER dourer; fiercer; more grisly
GRINDER a molar
GRINNED smiled broadly
GRIPING grasping; trenching
GRIPPED seized; held; clutched
GRIPPER a bailiff
GRIPPLE usurious; tenacious
GRIQUAS Dutch half-castes
GRISKIN lean bacon
GRISLED grizzled; grey
GRISTLE a cartilage
GRISTLY cartilaginous
GRITTED grated; ground
GRIZZLE whimper; gray
GRIZZLY grey; a bear   zo
GROANED moaned; bewailed
GROBIAN clumsy lout
GROCERY provision shop
GROGRAM fabric of silk and mohair   tx
GROINED arched
GROLIER (bookbinding)
GROMMET ring of rope
GROOMED soigné
GROOVED furrowed; scooped
GROPING seeking blindly; stumbling
GROSSER coarser; rougher
GROSSLY flagrantly; outrageously
GROTIAN (legal philosophy)
GROUNDS reasons; dregs; lees
GROUPED graded; classified
GROUPER an arranger
GROUSED complained; murmured
GROUSER grumbler
GROUTED filled with cement
GROWING raising; waxing
GROWLED snarled
GROWLER a four-wheeled cab
GROWN-UP an adult
GRUB-AXE a hoe   to
GRUBBED dug up
GRUBBER an investigator
GRUBBLE grope; grabble
GRUDGED envied; coveted
GRUFFER surlier; rougher
GRUFFLY churlishly; roughly; bluntly
GRUMBLE grouse; complain; repine
GRUMMET a grommet; a rope ring
GRUMOSE clustered
GRUMOUS clotted
GRUNDEL loach or rock-goby   zo
GRUNTER a pig; a gurnet   zo
GRUYERE a Swiss cheese
GRYLLID pertaining to crickets
GRYPHON griffin; heraldic monster   hd
GRYSBOK S. African antelope   zo
GUAJIRA peasant dance (Cuba)
GUANACO huanco; camel   zo

GUANINE purine base in living tissues   b
GUARANA Brazil cocoa   b
GUARANI (Paraguay)   nn
GUARDED wary; watchful; defended
GUDGEON an axle; a fish   ze
GUELDER rose; snowball tree   b
GUENONS a monkey genus   ze
GUERDON a reward; recompense
GUEREZA the Abyssinian monkey   ze
GUERITE watch-tower
GUESSED divined; solved; supposed
GUESSER a conjecturer
GUESTAN to be a guest (Sc.)
GUIACUM lignum vitae   b
GUICHET small window as for tickets (Fr.)
GUIDING leading; directing; piloting
GUILDER Dutch gold coin   nn
GUILDRY a guild
GUINEAN (W. African)
GUIPURE a heavy lace
GUISARD a Christmas mummer
GULLERY imposture
GULLIED water-worn
GULLIES ravines; knives
GULLING greening; duping
GUM-BOIL inflamed swelling   me
GUM-BOOT rubber shoe
GUMDROP a confection
GUMMING fruit-tree disease; cementing   b
GUMMOUS gummy; mucilaginous
GUM-RASH red gum; strophulus   me
GUM-THUS resin from Amer. pine   b
GUM-TREE (quandary)   b
GUMWOOD similar grain to rosewood   b
GUNBOAT small warship   n
GUN-DECK area of guns   n
GUN-FIRE time signal
GUNLOCK firing mechanism
GUNNAGE (number of guns)   n
GUNNERY the craft of the artillery
GUNNING shooting
GUN-PORT port-hole   n
GUN-ROOM a mess-room   n
GUNSHOT range
GUN-SITE location of gun
GUNWALE topmost plank   n
GURGLED purled; rippled
GURNARD gurnet fish   z
GUSHING spouting; flowing; effusive
GUSTILY in gusts; fitfully, breezily
GUTTATE spotted
GUTTING gipping; eviscerating
GUTTLED gulped; swallowed
GUTTULE small drop
GUTWORT a tord-boyau   b
GUZZLED swilled; gorged; caroused
GUZZLER gourmand
GWINIAD freshwater salmon   z
GWYNIAD small white fish   ze
GYMNAST athlete
GYPLURE moth sex attractant   z

GYRATED twirled; span; spun; rotated
GYRINID whirligig beetle   zo
GYRONNY heraldic triangulation   hd
GYROSYN flux-gate gyro compass   ae
GYTRASH a ghost

H

HABITAT home; abode; domicile
HABITED dressed; attired
HABITUE a frequenter
HACHURE engraved line
HACKBUT an arquebus
HACKERY Bengal ox-cart
HACKING cutting; notching; kicking
HACKLED combed
HACKLER flax-comber
HACKLET sea-bird; shearwater gull   zo
HACKLOG chopping block
HACKNEY horse; cab; trite   zo
HACK-SAW a saw for metal   to
HADDING a holding on lease (Sc.)
HADDJAR Persian dagger
HADDOCK a haddie (Sc.)   zo
HADROME xylem conducting tissues   bt
HAEMONY witch's bane plant   bt
HAFFETS the temples (Sc.)
HAFFLED prevaricated
HAFFLIN half-grown (Sc.)
HAFNIUM metallic element   ch
HAFTING fitting a handle
HAGANAH Jewish militia
HAGDOWN shearwater gull   zo
HAGFISH parasite fish   zo
HAGGADA Jewish commentary
HAGGARD stackyard; lean; hollow-eyed
HAGGING nagging; harassing
HAGGISH ugly; repulsive
HAGGLED mangled; bargained
HAGGLER higgler; bargainer
HAGSEED witch's offspring
HAGSHIP haggishness
HAGWEED broom   bt
HAILING raining; greeting
HAIRCUT barber service
HAIRNET coiffure cover
HAIR-OIL hair dressing
HAIRPIN aid to coiffure
HAITIAN native of Haiti
HALACHA ⎱ Jewish oral laws
HALAKAH ⎰ and traditions
HALBERD pike-like weapon
HALCYON kingfisher; calm   zo
HALF-ONE a golf handicap
HALF-PAY semi-retirement
HALFWAY intermediate position
HALF-WIT nitwit; moron
HALIBUT the largest flounder   zo
HALIDOM mascot; sanctuary
HALITUS exhaled air   md
HALLAGE market-hall dues
HALLIER bird net

HALLION hallyon; hallian; rascal
HALOGAN salt producer group   ch
HALOGEN one of 7th-group elements
HALTERE capitate thread in diptera
HALTING faltering; hesitating
HALVANS ore-mining refuse   mn
HALVING tieing; bisecting
HALYARD halliard; running rope   nt
HAMBLED mutilated the foot
HAMBURG domestic fowl   zo
HAMITIC (Ham)
HAMMOCK canvas hanging bed   nt
HAMSTER a rodent   zo
HAMULAR, HAMULUS small hook;
    hooked; hamate
HANAPER hamper; treasury
HANDBAG a reticule
HANDFUL gowpen (Sc.)
HANDIER more dexterous
HANDILY conveniently; adjacently
HANDING presenting; delivering
HANDJAR Persian dagger
HANDLED dealt with; manipulated
HANDLER dealer
HANDOUT prepared statement; sample
HANDSAW carpenter's tool   to
HANDSEL earnest money; a present
HANDSET telephone
HANGDOG sullen; morose
HANGING dangling; depending
HANGMAN topsman; public executioner
HANG-NET vertical net
HANKIES kerchiefs   tx
HANKING making into skeins
HANKLED entangled; involved
HANSARD Parliamentary records
HANSTER a freeman of a guild
HANUKAH Jewish feast day   rl
HANUMAN Hindu monkey-god
HAPLESS luckless
HAPLOID single chromosomes
HAPLONT special-nucleus-type plant
HAP'ORTH (halfpenny)
HAPPIER more expert; luckier
HAPPILY joyously; blissfully; gaily
HAPPING happening
HARBOUR shelter; haven; asylum
HARDEST densest; firmest; harshest
HARDIER pluckier; braver; tougher
HARDILY stoutly; intrepidly; resolutely
HARDISH somewhat hard
HARDOCK harlock; burdock   bt
HARD-PAN bed-rock
HARD-RUN greatly pressed
HARDSET beset by difficulty; hungry
HARDTOP fixed roof on a car
HARD-WON barely victorious
HAREING speeding
HARELIP fissured lip   md
HARICOT French bean   bt
HARKING listening; hurrying

HARLING process for protecting steel-clad houses
HARMALA wild rue   bt
HARMFUL noxious; baneful; baleful
HARMINE wild rue extract   ch
HARMING molesting; scathing
HARMONY unison; concord; amity
HARNESS gear; tackle; equipment
HARPING nagging; reiterating   mu
HARPIST a harper   mu
HARPOON barbed spear
HARRIED harassed; raided; ravaged
HARRIER hound; hawk   zo
HARSHEN stiffen; embitter
HARSHER rougher; severer; sterner
HARSHLY raucously; stridently
HARTALL orpiment   mn
HARTLEY unit of information; bits
HARVEST crop; yield; produce
HAS-BEEN diminished fame
HASHING muddling; mangling
HASHIRA narrow print (Jap.)
HASHISH bhang; the assassin's drug
HASLOCK wool on sheep's throat
HASSOCK cushion; tuft; pouffe
HASTATE spear-shaped
HASTIER quicker; rasher; brisker
HASTILY rapidly; hurriedly; abruptly
HASTING ripening early; expediting
HASTLER turn-spit
HATABLE odious; obnoxious
HATBAND ribbon in hat
HATCASE bonnet-box
HATCHED shaded; incubated
HATCHEL to heckle; to tease
HATCHER plotter; conspirator
HATCHES coverings   nt
HATCHET an axe   to
HATEFUL detestable; execrable; odious
HATLESS bareheaded
HAT-RACK place to hang hat
HAUBERK coat of mail
HAUGHTY arrogant; proud
HAULAGE a charge for conveyance
HAULIER carter
HAULING tugging; drawing; dragging
HAUNCHY with full hips
HAUNTED frequented; followed
HAUNTER frequent visitor
HAURLED dragged; rough-cast
HAUSTUS adult medicine dose
HAUTBOY strawberry; oboe   mu, bt
HAUTEUR disdain; arrogance; loftiness
HAUTPAS a dais
HAVENOT under-privileged
HAW-BUCK a clown
HAWKBIT a plant   bt
HAWKING falconry; peddlary; touting
HAWK-OWL snowy owl   zo
HAYBAND hay-rope
HAYCOCK gathered hay in stack

HAYFORK farm implement   t
HAYLOFT part of barn
HAYRICK regular hay pile
HAYSEED hick, bumpkin   b
HAY-TIER hay bundler
HAYWARD a warden
HAYWIRE in confusion
HAZELLY light brown
HAZIEST foggiest; vaguest
HEADILY impetuously; precipitately
HEADING adit; headline; intercepting
HEADMAN chief; boss
HEADWAY progress
HEAL-ALL valerian; a panacea   ▶
HEALING mollifying; remedying
HEALTHY hygienic; bracing; hale
HEAPING collecting; amassing
HEARING audition; trying   l
HEARKEN listen; attend; heed
HEARSAY rumour; report; gossip
HEARSED put in a hearse
HEARTED emboldened; cheered
HEARTEN encourage; rally; inspire
HEATHEN pagan; paynim; infidel
HEATHER ling; erica   ▶
HEATING warming; exciting
HEAVERS stevedores
HEAVE-TO storm tactics   ▶
HEAVIER weightier; denser
HEAVILY ponderously; onerously
HEAVING a rising; hoisting; throwing
HEBAMIC pert. to Socratic method
HEBENON hen-bane; poison   ▶
HEBETIC occurring at puberty
HEBRAIC Hebrew
HECKLED combed; questioned
HECKLER political enquirer
HECTARE 100 ares (Fr.)   n
HECTOID flushed; feverish; hectic
HEDEOMA penny-royal   ▶
HEDERAL of ivy
HEDGING guarding against loss
HEDONIC pleasure-seeking
HEEDFUL mindful; wary; cautious
HEEDING paying attention; regarding
HEELING (cockfighting); (football)
HEFTIER stronger; more vigorous
HEFTILY vigorously; powerfully
HEGUMEN Greek abbot
HEIGH-HO exclamation of complaisance
HEINOUS infamous; flagrant; atrocious
HEIRDOM succession
HEIRESS female inheritor
HELCOID ulcerous   n
HELIBUS, HELICAB helicopter bus/taxi
HELICAL spiral
HELICES circumvolutions; spirals
HELICON mount beloved by the Muses
HELIOID like the sun
HELIXIN an ivy extract   c
HELL-BOX receptacle for broken type   ▶

HELL-CAT malignant hag
HELLENE Greek
HELL-HAG author's invention
HELLISH diabolical; infernal; fiendish
HELMAGE guidance
HELOSIS condition of having corns   md
HELOTRY serfdom; bondage; (Sparta)
HELPFUL assistant; useful; beneficial
HELPING share; aiding; abetting
HELVING hafting; fitting a handle
HELVITE beryllium silicate   mn
HEMIONE half-ass; dziggetal   zo
HEMLOCK conine; poison   bt
HEMMING edging; besetting; sewing
HENBANE narcotic plant   bt
HENCOOP a fowl abode
HENNAED dyed with henna
HENNERY poultry farm
HENOTIC conciliatory
HENPECK nag; dominate
HENTING final furrow
HENWIFE chicken-girl
HEPARIN anticoagulant
HEPATIC liverish   md
HEPTADE seven
HEPTANE petrol constituent   ch
HEPTODE type of electric valve
HEPTOSE monosaccharide subgroup   ch
HERBAGE pasture
HERBARY herb garden
HERBIST herbalist; collector of simples
HERBLET small herb
HERBOUS herbaceous; herbose
HERDING tending; crowding
HERDMAN herdsman; ranchero
HEREOUT out of this
HERETIC unorthodox; schismatic
HERISSE bristled
HERITOR inheritor
HERLING young sea-trout   zo
HERNIAL (rupture)   md
HEROINE intrepid damsel
HEROISM valour; bravery; fortitude
HEROIZE lionize
HERONRY bird sanctuary   zo
HERRING tasty fish   zo
HERSELF reflexive pronoun
HERSHIP cattle-theft (Sc.)
HESSIAN jute fabric
HESSITE telluride of silver   mn
HETAIRA Greek dancing girl
HEXAGON a six-sided figure
HEXAPLA a Bible edition
HEXAPOD with six feet
HEXARCH with 6 protoxylem strands   bt
HEXERIS galley with 6 oar banks
HEXONIC chemical base
HEYDUCK Haiduk; Hungarian
HEY-PASS conjuror's command
HIBACHI charcoal brazier (Jap.)
HICATEE Central American tortoise   zo

HICKORY American nut-bearing tree   bt
HICKWAY small woodpecker   zo
HIDALGO Spanish Don; asteroid   as
HIDEOUS unshapely; monstrous; grisly
HIDE-OUT a cache
HIEMATE hibernate; to winter
HIGGLED negotiated; peddled; chaffered
HIGGLER haggler; bargainer; hawker
HIGHDAY holiday
HIGHEST tallest; loftiest
HIGHFED pampered
HIGH-HAT high-brow
HIGHLOW sort of shoe
HIGH-TOP a masthead (Shak.)
HIGHWAY public road
HILDING paltry; base; a deceiver
HILLIER steeper
HILLING earthing
HILLMAN a mountaineer
HILLOCK small hill
HILLTOP summit
HIMSELF reflexive pronoun
HINDBOW saddle cantle
HIND-GUT posterior of alimentary canal   zo
HINNIED whinnied
HINTING implying; suggesting
HIP-BATH portable sitting bath
HIP-BELT swordbelt
HIP-GOUT sciatica   md
HIP-KNOT gable ornament
HIP-LOCK wrestling trick
HIPPING grieving; glooming
HIPPOID like a horse
HIP-ROOF a type of roof
HIPSHOT dislocated hip
HIPSTER clothes held by a belt
HIRABLE for hire; leasable
HIRCINE goatish   zo
HIRSUTE hairy; rude
HIRUDIN anticoagulant chemical from leeches
HISKING breathing heavily
HISSING audible disapproval
HISTONE simple-protein group   ch
HISTORY chronicle; annals; account
HISTRIO histrion; an actor
HITCHED caught; fastened; attached
HITTING smiting; striking; succeeding
HITTITE ancient Near-Eastern people
HIVE-BEE honey-bee   zo
HOARDED garnered; amassed; secreted
HOARDER miser; husbandman
HOATZIN S. American bird   zo
HOAXING duping; gammoning
HOBBISH clownish
HOBBISM a moral philosophy
HOBBIST follower of Hobbes
HOBBLED hoppled; tethered
HOBBLER horse-soldier
HOBLIKE boorish; clownish

HOBNAIL boot-nail
HOBOISM vagrancy (USA)
HOCK-DAY old English festival
HOCKLED houghed; hamstrung
HOE-CAKE Indian meal cake
HOGBACK ridge; eskar
HOGCOTE pig-sty
HOGGERS miner's leg-wear
HOGGING bending
HOGGISH swinish; sordid; greedy
HOG-HERD swineherd
HOG-MANE clipped mane
HOG-PLUM tropical tree   bt
HOGSKIN pigskin
HOGWASH swill
HOGWEED cow parsnip   bt
HOISTED raised; heaved
HOISTER an elevator; lift
HOITING capering
HOLDALL a pack; luggage
HOLDING tenure; retaining; grasping
HOLIDAY festival; vacation
HOLIEST most sacred
HOLLAND coarse linen
HOLMIUM metallic element   ch
HOLM-OAK evergreen oak   bt
HOLSTER leather pistol case
HOLY-DAY feast day   rl
HOMAGER a vassal
HOMBURG gentleman's hat
HOMELOT home-plot
HOMELYN spotted ray   zo
HOMERIC of Homer; grandiose
HOMINID man (ancient and modern)
HOMONYM equivocation
HONESTY best political creed
HONEYED flattering; sweet
HONITON lace
HONKING (motoring); (geese)
HOODING covering; blinding
HOODLUM hooligan; rowdy; mobster
HOODOCK miserly (Sc.)
HOOFING walking
HOOKING ensnaring; bending
HOOKPIN floor nail
HOOP-ASH nettle-tree   bt
HOOPING binding; encircling
HOOTING decrying; booing
HOP-BACK brewer's vessel
HOPBIND, HOPBINE hop-vine   ht
HOPEFUL eager; expectant; confident
HOPEITE hydrated zinc phosphate   mn
HOP-FLEA a parasite   zo
HOPKILN an oast
HOPLITE Greek heavy-armed soldier
HOP-OAST hop-kiln
HOPPERS a hopping game
HOPPING skipping; leaping
HOPPLED hobbled; tethered
HOPPLES hobbles; rope shackles
HOP-POLE husbandry implement

HOP-TREE American shrub   bt
HOP-VINE hopbind   bt
HOP-YARD hop-garden
HORDEIN, HORDEUM barley starch/-
      genus   bt
HORDING crowding; herding; amassing
HORIZON where sea meets sky
HORMONE gland secretion   md
HORNBAR crossbar
HORN-BUG stag beetle   zo
HORNING debtor's summons   lw
HORNISH ungual
HORNITO volcanic smoke-hole
HORN-NUT a water-plant   bt
HORN-OWL tufted owl   zo
HORRENT bristling
HORRIFY appal; terrify; alarm; shock
HOSANNA beatific invocation   rl
HOSEMAN fireman
HOSIERY stock of stockings
HOSPICE guest-house   rl
HOSTAGE personal pledge
HOSTESS woman giving hospitality
HOSTILE inimical; adverse; opposed
HOSTLER ostler
HOTFLUE drying room
HOT-FOOT in haste
HOT-HEAD impetuous; rash
HOTNESS fieriness; ardency; fervency
HOT-SPOT internal combustion
HOTSPUR impetuous
HOTTEST most vehement
HOT-TROD Border pursuit
HOT-WALL (fruit culture)
HOUBARA ruffed bustard   zo
HOUGHED hockled; hamstrung
HOUNDED pursued; harassed; dogged
HOUSAGE storage fee
HOUSING saddle-cloth; sheltering
HOVERED vacillated; lingered
HOVERER waverer; flutterer
HOWADJI traveller; merchant (Arab)
HOWBEIT nevertheless
HOWDY-DO ado; fuss; commotion
HOWEVER notwithstanding
HOWLING dreary; lamenting; wailing
HUANACO guanaco; llama   zo
HUDDLED heaped; piled; mixed
HUDDLER bungler; confused cogitator
HUELESS colourless
HUFFILY petulantly; angrily; irritably
HUFFING puffing; swelling; (draughts)
HUFFISH hectoring; furious
HUFFKIN hot larded bread bun (Eng.) ck
HUGGING clasping; embracing; necking
HULKING big and clumsy
HULLING husking; shelling
HUMANLY ethically; rationally
HUMBLED abashed; humiliated
HUMBLER an abaser; mortifier
HUMBUZZ a bull-roarer

HUMDRUM commonplace; prosaic
HUMERAL Jewish veil
HUMERUS shoulder   md
HUMETTE heraldic fesse   hd
HUMIDLY damply; dankly
HUMMING bumming; droning
HUMMOCK hommock; hillock
HUMORAL vapourish
HUMULIN, HUMULUS hop extract/-
  genus   bt
HUNCHED bunched; crooked
HUNDRED cantred; county division
HUNGRED hungry; famished
HUNKERS the hams; haunches
HUNTING chasing; searching
HURDLED enclosed with a wattle fence
HURDLER racing jumper
HURKARU Hindu errand boy
HURLING casting; flinging; pitching
HURRIED scurried; accelerated; ran
HURRIED cursory; superficial
HURRIER hastener; quickener; urger
HURTFUL noxious; baleful; detrimental
HURTLED whizzed; crashed
HURTOIR a bumper
HUSBAND spouse
HUSHABY lullaby
HUSHING repressing; calming
HUSHION sort of sock (Sc.)
HUSKIES Eskimo dogs; toughs   zo
HUSKING removing husks
HUSSIES worthless women
HUSSITE (John Huss)
HUSTING an assembly; a council
HUSTLED bustled; elbowed
HUSTLER energiser; jostler
HUSWIFE hussif; housewife
HUTCHED cooped; boxed; confined
HUTMENT a hut
HUTTING temporary building
HYALINE glassy
HYALITE clear opal   mn
HYALOID vitreous
HYDRANT fire-plug
HYDRATE hydride; hydrous   ch
HYDRIAD water-nymph
HYDROID hydra-like
HYDROUS containing water
HYGEIAN hygienic
HYGIENE sanitary science
HYGROMA fluid-filled swelling   vt
HYLOIST materialist
HYMNARY hymn-book
HYMNING lauding
HYMNIST hymn-writer
HYMNODY hymn-singing
HYODONT pig-toothed
HYPERON cosmic-ray particle   nc
HYPNODY larval resting period   zo
HYPNOID resembling sleep
HYPOGEA cellars; basement

HYPOPUS development stage in cheese-
  mites
HYPPISH hippish; depressing
HYPURAL below the tail   zo
HYSTRIX the porcupine   zo

I

IAMBICS classic verse
IAMBISE satirize
IBERIAN Spanish and Portuguese
ICARIAN rash; headlong; adventurous
ICEBELT region of ice
ICEBERG floating ice mass
ICEBIRD little auk   zo
ICEBOAT for travel on ice
ICE-FALL a glacier
ICE-FERN frosty incrustations
ICE-FLOE mass of ice chunks in sea
ICE-FOOT belt of ice
ICE-HILL tobogganing slope
ICEPACK ice barrier at poles
ICEPAIL for chilling wine
ICE-RINK skating rink
ICE-SPAR ryacolite   mn
ICHABOD calamity (Heb.)
ICHNITE fossil footprint
ICHTHYS Christian emblem
ICINESS frigidity
ICTERIC jaundiced
ICTERUS jaundice   md
ICTINUS designer of the Parthenon
IDALIAN sacred to Venus
IDEALLY intellectually; mentally
IDENTIC identical
IDIOTCY imbecility; insanity
IDIOTIC fatuous; witless; inane
IDLESSE idleness
IDOLISM idolatry
IDOLIST idolater
IDOLIZE idolise; deify; adore; venerate
IDYLIST writer of idylls
IDYLLIC pastoral; poetic
IGNEOUS volcanic in origin
IGNITED lit; kindled; inflamed
IGNITER primer; detonator
IGNITOR electrode of ignition
IGNOBLE dishonourable; low; base
IGNOBLY infamously; unworthily
IGNORED disregarded; neglected
IGOROTE Filipino
IJOLITE coarse-grained igneous rock   gl
ILEITIS ileum inflammation   md
ILLAPSE glide; slip; a seizure
ILL-BRED poorly brought up
ILLEGAL unlawful; illegitimate; illicit
ILLEISM too much 'he'
ILL-FAME of bad repute
ILLICIT forbidden; banned; prohibited
ILLNESS malady; disease; ailment
ILLOCAL not local

ILL-TIME mistime
ILL-TURN unkindly act
ILLUDED deceived; deluded
ILLUMED elucidated; brightened
ILL-USED badly treated
ILL-WILL enmity; odium; spite; malice
ILVAITE hydrous iron silicate   mn
IMAGERY fanciful concept
IMAGINE dream; think; suppose
IMAGING imagining
IMAMATE the Caliphate
IMBATHE bathe
IMBIBED swallowed; absorbed
IMBIBER a toper; drunkard
IMBLAZE emblaze; illuminate
IMBOSOM embosom; caress
IMBOUND impound
IMBOWED embowed; arched
IMBOWER embower; shelter
IMBREED inbreed
IMBREKE houseleek   bt
IMBROWN embrown; tan
IMBRUED drenched; soaked; stained
IMBRUTE to brutalize
IMBUING pervading; drenching
IMBURSE to finance
IMITANT counterfeit
IMITATE ape; copy; mimic; parody
IMMENSE titanic; colossal; boundless
IMMERGE }   plunge into; souse;
IMMERSE }   to engross; duck
IMMIXED mixed; blended
IMMORAL depraved; vicious
IMMURED shut up; imprisoned
IMPAINT to colour
IMPALED fenced in; spiked; transfixed
IMPALSY strike with palsy
IMPANEL empanel; enrol
IMPASSE deadlock
IMPASTE knead
IMPASTO thick colour
IMPAVID fearless; undaunted
IMPEACH call to account
IMPEARL decorate with pearls
IMPEDED hindered; obstructed
IMPERIL endanger; hazard; jeopardize
IMPETUS momentum
IMPEYAN Indian pheasant   zo
IMPFING crystallisation technique
IMPIETY iniquity; profanity
IMPINGE to touch upon; infringe
IMPIOUS irreverent; ungodly
IMPLANT to graft; infuse; instil
IMPLATE to sheathe
IMPLEAD impeach; plead
IMPLIED understood; insinuated
IMPLORE entreat; crave; adjure
IMPONED wagered; inflicted
IMPOSED forced; misled
IMPOSER impostor; charlatan
IMPOUND confine; confiscate

IMPREGN impregnate
IMPRESS stamp; mark; imprint
IMPREST advanced cash
IMPRINT impress; fix on the mind
IMPROVE amend; ameliorate; raise
IMPULSE stimulus; urge to action
IMPUTED attributed; implied
IMPUTER ascriber
IN-AND-IN overly inbred
INANELY vapidly; stupidly
INANITY fatuity; emptiness
INAPTLY untimely; unsuitably
INBEING inherence
INBOARD within the ship
INBOUND inward bound
INBREAK inburst
INBREED mate with relative
INBURST irruption
INCAGED encaged; confined
INCENSE to inflame; madden; enrage
INCHASE enchase; engrave
INCHEST embox; encase
INCHING moving gradually
INCHPIN deer's sweetbread
INCIPIT here begins; originating (Lat.)
INCISED cut; engraved
INCISOR cutting tooth
INCITED roused; fomented; egged
INCITER agitator; agent provocateur
INCIVIL uncivil; impolite (obs.)
INCLASP embrace; enclasp
INCLAVE heraldic dovetail   hd
INCLINE slope; tend; predispose
INCLOSE enclose; envelop; wrap
INCLUDE embody; comprise; contain
INCOMER new arrival
INCRUST encrust
INCUBUS incumbrance; dead weight
INCURVE bend
INCUSED hammered; stamped
INDICAN a glucoside or acid   ch
INDICES mathematical exponents
INDICIA indications
INDITED scribbled; wrote; dictated
INDITER a writer; composer; penman
INDOLES inherent disposition
INDOORS within house
INDORSE endorse; countersign; ratify
INDOXYL isomer of oxindole   ch
INDRAFT inflow; indraught
INDRAWN retracted
INDUCED impelled; prompted
INDUCER persuader; instigator
INDUING enduing; investing; endowing
INDULGE pamper; humour; gratify
INDWELL inhabit; occupy
INEARTH inter; bury; inhume
INEPTLY not aptly; pointlessly
INERTIA inertness; indolence
INERTLY sluggishly; torpidly
INEXACT unexact; incorrect; faulty

INEYING inoculating; grafting
INFAMED defamed; libelled; aspersed
INFANCY under 18
INFANTA Spanish princess
INFANTE Spanish prince
INFARCT blood-deprived necrotic tissue md
INFAUST unlucky; unfortunate
INFERNO hell
INFIDEL disbeliever; paynim; heathen
INFIELD cultivated ground
INFIELD cf. outfield (cricket)
INFIXED fastened; clamped
INFLAME excite; fan; kindle; incense
INFLATE elate; expand; distend; bloat
INFLECT deflect; curve; bend
INFLICT impose; lay; punish
INFULAE priestly badges rl
INFUSED inspired; instilled; inculcated
INFUSER a coffee machine
INGENER a designer (Shak.)
INGENUE naïve girl
INGESTA food md
INGLOBE englobe; encircle; ensphere
INGOING entrance; entry
INGRAFT engraft; instil; introduce
INGRAIN engrain; permeate
INGRATE ungrateful person (obs.)
INGRESS entrance; portal
INGROSS engross (obs.)
INHABIT dwell; occupy
INHALED breathed
INHALER a respirator
INHAUST to drink in (obs.)
INHERED adhered; stuck
INHERIT acquire by bequest
INHERSE to bury (Shak.)
INHIBIT ban; prohibit; restrain
INHUMAN merciless; fell; ruthless
INHUMED interred; buried
INITIAL incipient; primary letter
INJELLY gelatinise
INJOINT to join (obs.)
INJURED offended; marred; maltreated
INJURER abuser; impairer
INKHORN portable inkpot
INKLING hint; suggestion; innuendo
INKNEED knock-kneed
INKWELL ink-cup
INLACED enlaced; entwined
INLAWED cf. outlawed
INLAYER inlay worker
INMEATS the entrails
INNERVE invigorate; insinew
INNINGS reclaimed land; (cricket)
INNUENT significant
IN-PHASE (electrical)
INQUEST judicial inquiry lw
INQUIRE enquire; ask; interrogate
INQUIRY enquiry; examination
INSCULP engrave; carve (obs.)

INSHELL to hide as in a shell (obs.)
INSHORE close to the beach
INSIDER in the know
INSIGHT vision; perception
INSINEW innerve; invigorate
INSIPID tasteless; vapid; flat; tedious
INSNARE ensnare; entrap; inveigle
INSOOTH in truth
INSPECT supervise; investigate
INSPIRE animate; inflame; imbue
INSTALL instal; instate; induct; invest
INSTANT current; urgent; prompt
INSTATE install; inaugurate; introduce
INSTEAD in place of; in lieu
INSTEEP immerse; souse; duck
INSTILL instil; implant; inculcate
INSTYLE entitle; to name
INSULAR isolated; narrow-minded
INSULIN (diabetes treatment) md
INSURED ensured; guaranteed
INSURER underwriter
INSWEPT narrowed
INTEGER whole; a whole number
INTENSE acute; vehement; extreme
INTERIM a pause; in the meantime
INTERNE inmate; boarder
INTHRAL enthral; enslave; captivate
INTITLE entitle; intitule (obs.)
INTONED chanted
INTRANT entrant; entering; penetrating
INTREAT entreat; crave; importune
INTROIT opening anthem rl
INTRUDE obtrude; trespass; butt in
INTRUST entrust; commit; confide
INTWINE entwine; reticulate; weave
INTWIST entwist; ravel; interlace
INULASE an enzyme md
INURING enuring; habituating
INUTILE useless (Fr.)
INVADED violated; entered; occupied
INVADER aggressor; raider; attacker
INVALID null and void; infirm; weak
INVEIGH revile; reproach; upbraid
INVERSE reciprocal; inverted
INVEXED arched hd
INVIOUS impassable; untrodden
INVITED bid; bequested; asked
INVITER allurer; solicitor; enticer
INVOICE bill; schedule; inventory
INVOKED adjured; implored; besought
INVOKER summoner; conjuror
INVOLVE implicate; entangle; embrace
INWARDS internally
INWEAVE complicate; intwine
INWHEEL encircle; surround
INWOVEN intertwined
IODIZED treated with iodine
IONIZED electrified
IPAZINE chemical weedkiller
IPOMAEA convolvulus bt
IPSEITY selfhood

IRACUND irascible; choleric; petulant
IRANIAN Persian
IRENICS pacific theology
IRICISM Irish bull
IRIDEAE iris plants   bt
IRIDISE make iridescent
IRIDIUM metallic element   ch
IRISHRY Irish people
IRKSOME wearisome; tiresome; tedious
IRONIES sarcastic censures
IRONING flattening
IRONIST ironical talker
ISAGOGE a treatise
ISATINE isatin; indigo; woad   ch
ISCHIUM pelvic bone in tetrapods   zo
ISERINE titanic steel
ISHMAEL an outcast
ISIDIUM excrescence on lichen   bt
ISLAMIC Mohammedan; Moslem
ISLEMAN islander
ISMATIC faddish; fond of isms
ISOBASE land-depression line   gl
ISOBATH under-sea contour
ISODOMA form of masonry
ISODONT uniform teeth
ISODRIN chemical insecticide
ISOETES quill-worts   bt
ISOGAMY union of equal gametes   bt, zo
ISOGENY similar origin
ISOGRAM map line linking like places
ISOHYET (seasonal) rainfall map
ISOLATE insulate; segregate; dissociate
ISONEPH equal-cloudiness line   mt
ISONETH cloud map   mt
ISONOMY equal rights
ISONYMY paronymy; equal   lw
ISOPODA crustaceans   zo
ISOPYRE impure opal   mn
ISOTACH equal wind-speed line   mt
ISOTAXY polymerization characteristic
ISOTONE stable nucleus (atom)
ISOTOPE allied element   ch
ISOTRON isotope-separating device   nc
ISOTYPE picture writing
ISOZYME like/unlike enzyme form   bc
ISRAELI Jew (Israel)
ISSUANT issuing   hd
ISSUING emanating; proceeding
ISTHMUS land joining larger masses
ITACISM Greek egotism
ITALIAN of Italy
ITALICS sloping letters
ITCHING desirous
ITEMIZE particularize
ITERACY repetition
ITERANT repeating
ITERATE recapitulate
IVORIED provided with teeth
IVY-BUSH Bacchus's bush   bt
IXIODIC infested with ticks   md, vt
IXOLITE fossil resin   mn

J

JABBING prodding; stabbing
JACAMAR tropical kingfisher   zo
JACCHUS marmoset   zo
JACINTH hyacinth; a gem   bt
JACKASS male moke   zo
JACKBIT blast-hole drill end   mn
JACKDAW a daw   zo
JACKING lifting; abandoning
JACKPOT (poker)
JACKSAW goosander   zo
JACK-TAR a sailor   nt
JACOBIN revolutionary
JACOBUS James I sovereign   nm
JACONET muslin
JADEDLY wearily
JADEITE a silicate   mn
JAGGERY palm sap sugar
JAGGING notching; carousing
JAGHIRE land revenues (Hindu)
JAHVIST scriptural writer
JAILING gaoling; imprisoning
JAINISM an Indian religion
JALAPIN a purge   md
JALOUSE to suspect (Sc.)
JAMADAR jemidar; Indian lieutenant
JAMBONE (cards on table at euchre)
JAMDANI flowery muslin   tx
JAMDARI figured muslin   tx
JAMEWAR goat hair cloth
JAMMING squeezing; pressing
JAMRACH animal mart
JAMSHID King of the genii
JANEITE (Jane Austen)
JANGADA timber raft
JANGLED jingled; discordant
JANGLER wrangler
JANITOR doorkeeper
JANIZAR Janissary; Turkish soldier
JANNOCK bannock; a cake
JANNOCK straightforward
JANTILY jauntily; airily; finically
JANTING jaunting; rambling
JANUARY 1st month
JAP-SILK a thin kind of silk
JARGOON a gem; zircon   mn
JARKMAN begging letter writer
JARRING discordant; grating; clashing
JASHAWK young hawk   zo
JASMINE fragrant flower   bt
JASPERY like jasper   mn
JASPOID jaspery
JAUNDER gossip (Sc.)
JAUNTED rambled; strolled
JAUPING spattering (Sc.)
JAVELIN a throwing spear
JAWBONE Samson's lethal weapon   md
JAW-FALL depression
JAW-FOOT maxilliped   zo
JAW-HOLE a sink

JAW-ROPE sailing tackle   **nt**
JAYWALK walk irresponsibly on roadways
JAZZING dancing   **mu**
JEALOUS envious; covetous; resentful
JECORAL pertaining to the liver
JEDCOCK jack snipe   **zo**
JEDDART rough justice (Sc.)
JEERING derision; taunting; scoffing
JEJUNUM digestive organ   **md**
JELLIED congealed
JELLIFY to become gelatinous
JELLYBY (a philanthropist)
JEMIDAR jamadar; Indian officer
JEMIMAS elastic-sided boots
JENKINS society reporter; toady
JEOFAIL an oversight   **lw**
JEOPARD to hazard; to endanger
JERKING twitching; jolting
JERVINE white hellebore alkaloid   **ch**
JESSAMY jasmine; a dandy   **bt**
JESSANT heraldic uprising   **hd**
JESTFUL humorous; witty; sportive
JESTING joking; quipping
JETTIED projected; jutted
JETTING spouting; emitting
JEWELRY gems; trinkets
JEW'S-EAR edible fungus   **bt**
JEZEBEL a courtesan
JEZHAIL jezail; Afghan rifle
JIBBING balking; shying
JIB-BOOM part of rigging   **nt**
JIB-DOOR flush door
JIGAJOG jig-jog; also jickajog
JIGGERS tropical foot complaint   **md**
JIGGING sieving; dancing
JIGGISH frivolous; frolicsome
JIGGLED joggled; wriggled
JILTING discarding; rejecting
JIMCROW of black segregation (Amer.)
JIM-JAMS nervous apprehension
JINGLED jangled; tingled
JINGLET sleigh-bell clapper
JINKING dodging; twisting
JITTERS fear; distortion   **el**
JITTERY nervy; agitated; dithery
JOBBERY intrigue
JOBBING doing small jobs
JOBLESS unemployed
JOCULAR jocose; facetious; droll
JOGGING stimulating; nudging
JOGGLED jostled; shook
JOGGLES stone jointing
JOG-TROT easy running pace
JOHNIAN (St. John's Col. Cam.)
JOINDER united action   **lw**
JOINERY carpentry
JOINING uniting; linking; connecting
JOINTED articulated
JOINTER smoothing plane   **to**
JOINTLY in concert; unitedly
JOISTED (floor-laying)

JOLLIER merrier; more genial
JOLLIFY celebrate; carouse
JOLLILY heartily; mirthfully
JOLLITY joviality; hilarity; frolic
JOLTING jerking; shaking
JONGLER a wandering minstrel
JONQUIL narcissus   **bt**
JOOKERY jokery; trickery
JOTTING a memorandum
JOUNCED shook; jolted
JOURNAL diary; newspaper; log
JOURNAL spindle bearing; gazette
JOURNEY jaunt; excursion; travel
JOUSTED tilted
JOYANCE gaiety; festivity
JOY-RIDE riding vehicle for pleasure
JUBILEE fiftieth anniversary
JUDAISE practice Judaism
JUDAISM Jewish rites
JUDAIST follower of Jew. rites
JUDAIZE to enforce Judaism
JUDCOCK jack snipe   **zo**
JUDGING trying; deeming; estimating
JUFFERS square timber
JUGATED coupled; yoked
JUGGING imprisoning; stewing
JUGGINS a simpleton
JUGGLED conjured; swindled
JUGGLER conjuror; wizard; marabout
JUGLANS walnut-genus   **bt**
JUGULAR (vein)   **md**
JUGULUM breast/neck region in birds   **zo**
JUJITSU ⎫
JUJUTSA ⎬ Japanese wrestling
JUKE-BOX electric gramophone (USA)
JUMBLED disordered; confused
JUMBLER a muddler
JUMELLÉ paired
JUMPING bounding; (claims)
JUNCATE junket; picnic; spree
JUNCOUS rush-like
JUNIPER coniferous tree; gin-berry   **bt**
JUNKING coal-cutting process   **mn**
JUNKMAN junk-dealer
JUPETTE short petticoat
JUPITER a planet
JURALLY lawfully; legally   **lw**
JURY-BOX where jury sits
JURY-MAN juror   **lw**
JUSSIVE imperative
JUSTICE equity; fairness; impartiality
JUSTIFY vindicate; exonerate; excuse
JUTTING projecting; beetling
JUVENAL a youth
JUWANZA camel-thorn   **bt**
JYNGINE of wryneck bird family   **zo**

K

KABBALA cabbala; shrine
KABBALA Jewish oral tradition

KACHINA doll (Amer. Indian)			**KHAMSIN** hot wind of the Sahara	
KADAYIF Baklava-type pastry (Turk.)	ck		**KHANATE** khan's jurisdiction	
KADDISH Jewish funeral prayer			**KHEDDAH** enclosure; (eleph. hunting)	
KAINITE chemical fertilizer	ch		**KHEDIVA** } wife of the	
KAKAVIA fish soup; cooking pot (Gr.)	ck		**KHEDIVE** } Egyptian viceroy	
KAKODYL cacodyl; noisome liquid			**KHOTBAH** } Mahommedan prayer	
KALENDS 1st day of Roman month			**KHUTBAH** } and service	r
KALMUCK Calmuck; Mongolian			**KIBBLED** fine-ground in a hand mill	
KAMERAD (surrender)			**KIBBUTZ** communal farm (Israel)	
KAMICHI Brazilian tropical bird	zo		**KIBITKA** Russian vehicle	
KAMPONG (Malay) court-yard			**KICKING** spurning; punting	
KANAGAI lacquer work (Japan)			**KICK-OFF** start of play	
KANDITE kaolin minerals group	mn		**KIDDIES** youngsters	
KANTHAL high-resistivity alloy	ml		**KIDDING** bluffing	
KANTIAN (Kant); Kantist			**KIDLING** a young kid	zo
KANTISM a philosophy			**KIDSKIN** goat leather	
KAPITIA lacquer (Sri Lanka)			**KIKUMON** imperial crest of Japan	
KARAGAN Russian fox	zo		**KILLDEE** N. Amer. ring plover	zo
KARAITE strict Jewish sect	rl		**KILLICK** a small anchor	n
KARATAS W. Indian pineapple	bt		**KILLING** slaying; butchering; tiring	
KASHGAR white silky Asian wool	tx		**KILL-JOY** a sourpuss	
KATHODE negative electrode			**KILLOCK** killick; small anchor	n
KATYDID N. Amer. grasshopper	zo		**KILN-DRY** dessicate	
KEATITE synthetic silica form	mn		**KILOVAR** volt-ampères unit	e
KEBBOCK kebbuck; a cheese (Sc.)			**KILTING** trussing up (Sc.)	
KECKLED cackled			**KINDEST** most benevolent	
KEDGING warping	nt		**KINDLED** ignited; fired; incited	
KEDLACK wild mustard	bt		**KINDLER** an igniter	
KEEKING peeping; prying			**KINDRED** relations; related; kin	
KEELAGE harbour duty			**KINETIC** force in motion	
KEELING a codling	zo		**KINETIN** plant growth substance	b
KEELMAN bargee			**KINGCUP** marsh marigold	b
KEELSON keel-plate	nt		**KINGDOM** monarchy; realm; dominion	
KEENING wailing; mourning			**KINGLET** golden-crested wren	zo
KEEPING lasting; retaining; observing			**KING-PIN** head of organisation	
KEEVING (fermentation)			**KINKING** twisting; looping	
KEITLOA S. African rhinoceros	zo		**KINLESS** without kindred	
KELKING beating; thrashing			**KINSHIP** relationship	
KENNICK tinker jargon			**KINSMAN** a connection	
KENNING range of vision; knowing			**KIP-SHOP** house of ill-fame	
KENOSIS } divine abnegation			**KIPSKIN** kip-leather	
KENOTIC }			**KIRGHIZ** Central Asian	
KENTISH of Kent			**KIRIMON** kikumon; a chrysanthemum	
KERASIN brain-substance cerebroside	ch		**KIRKTON** a village (Sc.)	
KERATIN (horn and hair)	md		**KIRTLED** with petticoat	
KERMESS Dutch fair			**KIRUNDI** language of Burundi (Africa)	
KERNING granulating			**KISSING** bussing	
KERNISH clownish			**KITCHEN** cook-house; galley	
KERNITE sodium borate	mn		**KLICKED** clicked	
KESTREL a falcon	zo		**KLIPDAS** S. African rock-badger	zo
KETCHUP a sauce			**KLIPPEN** hill-top outliers	g
KETOSIS fat-metabolism toxaemia	md		**KLODNIK** iced beetroot soup (Pol.)	ck
KEYBOLT part of lock			**KNABBED** gnawed; bitten	
KEYCOLD cold as a key			**KNACKER** cat's meat purveyor	
KEYED-UP tense with suspense			**KNAPPED** snapped; nibbled	
KEYHOLE orifice for key			**KNAPPER** flint worker	
KEYNOTE which sets tone	mu		**KNAPPLE** snap; nibble	
KEY-RING key holder			**KNARRED** knotted	
KEY-SEAT a groove			**KNAVERY** roguery; trickery; fraud	
KEYWORD word showing topic discussed			**KNAVISH** rascally; fraudulent	
KHALIFA khalif; calif			**KNEADED** massaged; mixed	

KNEADER dough-mixer	**LACQUEY** lackey; footman; flunkey	
KNEECAP knee-pan md	**LACTASE** lactose-dissolving enzyme	
KNELLED knolled; tolled	**LACTATE** (lactine)	ch
KNESSET Israeli Parliament	**LACTEAL** lactean; milky	
KNIFING stabbing	**LACTONE** hydroxy acid anhydride	
KNITTED contracted	**LACTOSE, LACTINE** sugar of milk	
KNITTLE a draw-thread	**LACTUCA** lettuce genus	bt
KNOBBED knobby	**LACUNAE** gaps; blanks; chasms	
KNOBBLE small boss	**LACUNAL** discontinuously	
KNOBBLY knobby; knotty	**LACUNAR** (panelled ceiling)	
KNOCKED buffeted; rapped; hit	**LADANUM** resinous extract	md
KNOCKER a rapper	**LADINOS** mixed race (El Salvador)	
KNOCK-ON (Rugby)	**LADLING** spooning	
KNOCK-UP practice game (tennis)	**LADY-BUG** lady-fly	zo
KNOLLED knelled; tolled	**LADY-COW** the ladybird	zo
KNOLLER bell-toller	**LADY-DAY** March 25th	
KNOPPER gall-nut bt	**LADYISH** genteel; affected	
KNOTTED tied; kinked; entangled	**LADYISM** gentility	
KNOW-ALL a wiseacre	**LAETARE** 4th Sunday in Lent	
KNOW-HOW technical expertise	**LAGGARD** lagging; sluggard	
KNOWING pawky; shrewd; astute	**LAGGING** hysteresis; dawdling	
KNUCKLE submit md	**LAGOMYS** (tailless hares)	zo
KOFTGAR metal inlayer (Hindu)	**LAGOPUS** grouse genus	zo
KOLA-NUT cola-nut bt	**LAGOTIC** rabbit-eared	
KOLKHOZ Soviet collective farm	**LAICISE, LAICIZE** commit to laymen	
KOMATIC long Eskimo sledge	**LAIRAGE** cattle depot; lair	
KORANIC (Koran)	**LAKELET** pool; mere; pond	
KO-TOWED made obeisance	**LAKSHMI** wife of Vishnu	rl
KOUMISS fermented mare's milk	**LALIQUE** artistic glassware	
KREATIN creatin; muscle constituent	**LALLANS** Lowland Scots (dial)	
KREMLIN citadel (Moscow)	**LALLING** repetition of a sound	
KRIMMER grey lambskin fur	**LAMAISM** Tibetan Buddhism	rl
KRISHNA an incarnation of Vishnu	**LAMAIST** spirit-worshipper	rl
KRUPSIS a theological doctrine	**LAMB-ALE** shearing feast	
KRYPTOL electrical resistant	**LAMBENT** softly radiant	
KRYPTON gaseous element ch	**LAMBERT** unit of brightness	me
KUH-HORN Alpine horn mu	**LAMBING** yeaning	
KUMQUAT Chinese citron bt	**LAMBKIN** baby lamb	zo
KURBASH Arab hippo-hide whip	**LAMBOYS** armoured kilts	
KURDISH (Kurd)	**LAMELLA** thin plate or scale	zo
KURHAUS spa pavilion (Ger.)	**LAMETER** ⎫ lamiter; a cripple	
KURSAAL the pump-room of a spa	**LAMIGER** ⎭	
KUWAITI native of Kuwait	**LAMETTA** metal foil	
KYANISE rot-proofing of timber	**LAMINAR** laminal; in plates	
KYANITE aluminium silicate mn	**LAMMING** thrashing	
	LAMPATE a salt	ch
	LAMPERN lamprey	zo
L	**LAMP-FLY** fire-fly	zo
	LAMPING ultraviolet detection	
LABARUM symbolical banner	**LAMPION** fairy lamp	
LABIATE lip-like	**LAMP-LIT** artificially illuminated	
LABROSE thick-lipped	**LAMPOON** a satirical article	
LACCATE as if varnished bt	**LAMPREY** eel-like fish	zo
LACCINE (shellac)	**LANATED** woolly	
LACEMAN lace-dealer	**LANCERS** (cavalry); a dance	
LACERTA lizard genus zo	**LANCING** piercing; cutting	
LACINIA leaf incision; maxilla lobe bt, zo	**LANDING** disembarking; floor; (fish)	
LACK-ALL destitute	**LANDLER** Tyrolean waltz	
LACKING needing; wanting	**LANDMAN** landsman	
LAC-LAKE lac dye	**LANDTAG** governing body	
LACONIC concise; pithy; curt; terse	**LAND-TAX** type of impost	
LACQUER varnish		

LANGAHA snake (Madagascar)	zo	
LANGITE copper sulphate	mn	
LANGLEY unit of radiation	me	
LANGREL chain-shot		
LANGUED heraldic tongue	hd	
LANGUET tongue-shaped		
LANGUID feeble; listless; enervated		
LANGUOR langure; lassitude		
LANIARY slaughter house		
LANIARY canine tooth		
LANIATE tear in pieces		
LANKIER taller and thinner		
LANOLIN an ointment	md	
LANTANA verbena	bt	
LANTERN lanthorn		
LANYARD laniard; short rope		
LAOCOON (sculptured group)		
LAOTIAN native of Laos		
LAO-THAI language of Laos		
LAPILLI volcanic stones		
LAPPING polishing; wrapping; drinking		
LAPPISH Laplandish; Lapp		
LAPSING slipping; failing		
LAPUTAN visionary		
LAPWING peewit	zo	
LAPWORK overlapping work		
LARCENY theft; pilfering	lw	
LARCHES conifers	bt	
LARDING smearing with lard		
LARD-OIL a lubricant		
LARDOON strip of bacon		
LARGELY greatly; abundantly		
LARGESS bounty; alms; gift		
LARGEST most capacious; biggest		
LARGISH somewhat extensive		
LARIGOT 6-f organ pitch	mu	
LARIKIN larrikin; hooligan (Aust.)		
LARKING sporting; on the spree		
LARMIER drip-stone; corona		
LARNITE orthosilicate of calcium	mn	
LARVATE larval; masked	zo	
LASAGNA flat pasta strip (It.)		
LASHING scourging; upbraiding		
LASHKAR N. Indian tribal force		
LASKETS gaskets	nt	
LASSOED noosed		
LASSOES lariats		
LASTAGE ballast; fishing dues		
LASTING abiding; enduring; durable		
LASTING strong twill cloth	tx	
LATAKIA Syrian tobacco	bt	
LATCHED fastened; grasped		
LATCHES laskets	nt	
LATCHET shoe-fastening		
LATCHET sapphirine gurnet	zo	
LATEBRA an egg cavity	zo	
LATENCE suspended activity		
LATENCY force in suspense		
LATERAL side by side		
LATERAN Roman cathedral	rl	
LATHING lath work		

LATRANT barking		
LATRINE camp privy; toilet		
LATROBE a form of stove		
LATTICE a network		
LATVIAN Lettish		
LAUDING extolling; praising		
LAUGHED derided		
LAUNDER wash; ore trough		
LAUNDRY the wash		
LAURELS bays of victory	bt
LAURITE a sulphide	mn
LAUWINE avalanche		
LAVOLTA an old dance		
LAVROCK lark	zo
LAW-BOOK case book	lw
LAW-CALF (bound in calf)		
LAWLESS wild; rebellious; disorderly		
LAW-LORD Lords' legal man	lw
LAW-LORE Blackstone's		
LAW-SUIT case in court	lw
LAXATOR a muscle	md
LAXNESS slackness; negligence		
LAY-DAYS (cargo lading)		
LAYERED stratified		
LAYETTE infant's outfit		
LAYLAND pasture land		
LAYLOCK lilac	bt
LAY-LORD civil lord	nt
LAZARET hospital		
LAZARLY leprous		
LAZARUS a poor man		
LAZIEST most sluggish; idlest		
LAZY-BED potato-bed		
L-DRIVER learner driver		
LEACHED strained through wood-ash		
LEADING chief; principal; main		
LEAD-OFF beginning		
LEAFAGE foliage; boscage		
LEAF-BED gemma	b
LEAF-FAT fat in layers		
LEAFING leaf-growth		
LEAFLET handbill; small pamphlet		
LEAGUED united; coalesced		
LEAGUER camp; ally		
LEAKAGE divulgence; percolation		
LEAKING oozing; escaping		
LEANDER channel swimmer		
LEANEST thinnest; lankiest		
LEANING penchant; bias; relying		
LEAPING jumping; springing		
LEARNED erudite; scholarly		
LEARNER pupil; tyro; student		
LEASHED bound; under control		
LEASING falsehood; letting		
LEASOWE a pasture		
LEATHER to thrash; to tan		
LEAVING desisting; bequeathing		
LECTERN lectern; reading desk	
LECTION a reading		
LECTUAL necessitating bed-rest		
LECTURE reproof; rebuke; discourse		

LEECHED healed	**md**	
LEECHEE Chinese fruit	**bt**	
LEEFANG jib sheet	**nt**	
LEEMOST most leeward		
LEERILY wideawake; sly; fly		
LEERING ogling		
LEE-SIDE, LEEGAGE sheltered side	**nt**	
LEE-TIDE tide with the wind		
LEEWARD down wind		
LEFT-ARM cricket		
LEGALLY legitimately; licitly		
LEGATEE inheritor	**lw**	
LEG-BAIL (absconding)		
LEGGERS barge-pushers		
LEGGING a gaiter		
LEGGISM black-leggism		
LEGHORN straw hat; fowl	**zo**	
LEGIBLE readable		
LEGIBLY clearly written		
LEG-IRON a fetter		
LEGITIM Bairn's Part	**lw**	
LEGLESS apodal		
LEG-PULL a draw		
LEGTRAP (cricket)		
LEGUMEN vegetable casein	**bt**	
LEISTER fishing spear (Ice.)		
LEISURE restful ease		
LEMMATA logical premises		
LEMMING Arctic rodent	**zo**	
LEMNIAN (Lemnos)		
LEMPIRA Honduras	**nm**	
LEMURES ghosts of evil doers		
LENDING loaning; advancing		
LENGTHY extended; protracted		
LENIENT mild; clement; merciful		
LENTIGO a rash; freckle	**md**	
LENTISK mastic tree	**bt**	
LENTOID lens-shaped		
LENTOUS viscous; tenacious		
LEONERO puma hunting dogs	**zo**	
LEONIDS meteor shower		
LEONINE like a lion		
LEOPARD also libbard	**zo**	
LEPROMA leprous swelling	**md**	
LEPROSE scurfy	**md**	
LEPROSY } dread disease	**md**	
LEPROUS }		
LEPTOME phloem elements	**bt**	
LESBIAN female homosexual		
LESOTHO Basuto (S. Africa)		
LETCHED percolated; filtered		
LET-DOWN an avoidable failure		
LETHEAN oblivious		
LETTERN lectern; reading desk		
LETTING preventing; hindering		
LETTISH Latvian; Lettic		
LETTUCE salad plant	**bt**	
LEUCINE (decomposition)	**md**	
LEUCITE volcanic rock	**mn**	
LEUCOMA wall-eye	**md**	
LEUCOUS albino		
LEVATOR a muscle	**md**	
LEVECHE dry S.W. wind in Spain	**mt**	
LEVELER leveller		
LEVELLY evenly; horizontally		
LEVERED raised; lifted		
LEVERET young hare	**zo**	
LEVITIC (Levi)		
LEVYING collecting; exacting		
LEXICAL alphabetically arranged		
LEXICON dictionary		
LIAISON co-ordination; intrigue		
LIASSIC geological formation		
LIBERAL bounteous; generous		
LIBERTY freedom; emancipation		
LIBRARY a voluminous apartment		
LIBRATE to balance; poise; oscillate		
LICENCE permission; excess; warrant		
LICENSE to permit; allow; authorize		
LICH-OWL screech-owl	**zo**	
LICH-WAY lych-way		
LICITLY lawfully; legally; legitimately		
LICKING a flogging; a thrashing		
LIE-ABED a sluggard		
LIFT-BOY, LIFTMAN elevator operator		
LIFTING elating; stealing; raising		
LIGATED bandaged	**md**	
LIGHTED lit; ignited; illumined		
LIGHTEN enlighten; alleviate; ease		
LIGHTER barge; brighter; igniter		
LIGHTLY buoyantly; airily; joyfully		
LIGNIFY become woody		
LIGNINE woody fibre	**bt**	
LIGNITE brown coal	**mn**	
LIGNOSE cellulose		
LIGROIN paraffin		
LIGULAR strap-shaped	**bt**	
LIKABLE attractive; lovable; amiable		
LIKENED resembled; compared		
LILY-PAD water-lily leaf	**bt**	
LIMAÇON heart-shaped curve	**ma**	
LIMBATE bordered; edged		
LIMBING dismembering		
LIMBOUS overlapping	**zo**	
LIMBRIC plain-weave cotton cloth	**tx**	
LIME-LIT illuminated		
LIME-PIT limestone quarry		
LIMINAL almost conscious		
LIMITED restricted; circumscribed		
LIMITER restrainer		
LIMNING water-colour painting		
LIMNITE iron ore	**mn**	
LIMOSIS abnormal hunger	**md**	
LIMPING halting; walking lamely		
LIMPKIN tropical crane	**zo**	
LINCTUS soothing syrup	**md**	
LINEAGE ancestry; extraction; race		
LINEATE lined		
LINEMAN railwayman, P.O. man	**el**	
LINE-OUT rugby football		
LINGISM Swedish drill		
LINGUAL (tongue)		

LINKAGE (mechanics)		
LINKBOY torch bearer		
LINKING connecting; joining		
LINKMAN linkboy		
LINNEAN (Linnaeus, botanist)		
LINOXYN dried film of linseed oil	pt	
LINSANG Indian civet	zo	
LINSEED flax-seed	bt	
LIONCEL small lion	hd	
LION-CUB baby lion	zo	
LIONESS lady lion	zo	
LIONISM tuft hunting		
LIONIZE heroize		
LIP-BORN hearsay; not genuine		
LIP-GOOD good promiser		
LIPPING uttering; (golf)		
LIQUATE liquefy		
LIQUEFY dissolve; melt; fuse		
LIQUEUR a cordial		
LIRELLA ridged apothecium	bt	
LISPING expressing childishly		
LISSOME svelte; lissom; agile		
LISTFUL attentive; heedful		
LISTING tabulation; choosing		
LITERAL au pied de la lettre		
LITHATE (lithium)	ch	
LITHELY actively; pliantly		
LITHIUM metallic element	ch	
LITHOID stone-like		
LITOTES (figure of speech)		
LITTERY covered with litter		
LITUATE forked		
LITURGE leader in public worship	rl	
LITURGY ritual	rl	
LIVABLE habitable		
LIVENED cheered up; enlivened		
LIVE-OAK American oak	bt	
LIVERED (lily-livered)		
LLANERO S. American plain dweller		
LOADING cargo; lading; charging		
LOAFING loitering; idling		
LOAMING earthing		
LOANING lending; advancing		
LOATHED hated; detested		
LOATHER an abhorrer		
LOATHLY reluctant; unwilling; hateful		
LOBBIED sought votes		
LOBBIES vestibules		
LOBBING pitching		
LOBCOCK a lubber; a lubbard		
LOBELET small lobe		
LOBELIA a flower genus	bt	
LOBIPED having lobate feet	zo	
LOBSTER a decapod	zo	
LOBULAR lobed		
LOBULUS small lobe		
LOBWORM lug-worm	zo	
LOCALLY in the vicinity		
LOCATED placed; fixed; found		
LOCATOR finder		
LOCKAGE canal dues		

LOCKIAN (Locke's philosophy)		
LOCKING grappling; securing		
LOCKIST philosopher		
LOCK-JAW tetanus	md	
LOCK-MAN under-sheriff (I. of M.)		
LOCK-OUT (industrial)	cp, el	
LOCKRAM coarse linen	tx	
LOCULAR cell-like		
LOCULUS small cell		
LOCUSTA carob-tree	bt	
LODGING quarters; abode; harbour		
LOFTIER of greater eminence		
LOFTILY arrogantly		
LOFTING raising; lifting		
LOGATOM artificial testing word	ac	
LOGBOOK official record	nt	
LOG-CHIP log-line board	nt	
LOGGATS (ninepins)		
LOGGING recording	nt	
LOG-HEAD a blockhead		
LOG-HEAP log-pile; wood-pile		
LOGICAL reasonable; deductive		
LOGLINE rope to log float	nt	
LOG-REEL for puzzling sailors	nt	
LOG-ROLL pull strings		
LOG-SHIP log-chip	nt	
LOGWOOD (red dye)	bt	
LOLLARD religious sect		
LOLLING lounging; (tongue)		
LOMARIA ferns	bt	
LOMBARD a banker; a money lender		
LONG-AGO remote in time		
LONGBOW medieval weapon		
LONGEST most protracted		
LONG-HOP (cricket)		
LONGING eager desire; yearning		
LONGISH somewhat long		
LONG-LEG (cricket)		
LONG-OIL high-oil-content varnish	pt	
LONG-RUN final issue		
LOOBILY like a looby; clumsily		
LOOKING search; watching; scanning		
LOOKOUT sentinel; gazebo; view		
LOOK-SEE glance; hasty visit		
LOOMING a mirage; threatening		
LOONING cry of the loon		
LOOPERS (moth caterpillars)	zo	
LOOPING circling		
LOOSELY vaguely; diffusely; slackly		
LOOSING relaxing; releasing		
LOOTING pillaging; rifling		
LOPPING amputating; curtailing		
LORDING lordling		
LORELEI a siren; rock on the Rhine		
LORETTE a Delilah		
LORGNON an eye-glass		
LORIMER loriner		
LORINER bridle-maker		
LOSABLE easily mislaid		
LOTTERY game of chance		
LOTTING cataloguing		

LOUDEST showiest; noisiest
LOUKOUM lokum; Turkish delight
LOUNDER to beat; a blow (Sc.)
LOUNGED reclined; lolled
LOUNGER flaneur; loafer; idler
LOURING threatening; menacing
LOUSILY inferior word
LOUTISH clumsy
LOVABLE amiable; charming; winsome
LOVE-ALL no score tennis
LOVE-DAY settling day (Shak.)
LOVEMAN a plant   bt
LOVERED having a lover
LOVERLY passionate; devoted
LOW-BELL (night-fowling)
LOW-BORN of humble birth
LOW-BRED poorly reared
LOWBROW unintellectual
LOWDOWN rascally
LOWERED threatened; frowned
LOW-GEAR low speed machine   au
LOWLAND netherland
LOW-LIFE humble life
LOWLILY humbly; meekly
LOWNESS dejection; depression
LOW-TIDE when tide is out
LOXOTIC oblique; distorted
LOYALLY faithfully; devotedly
LOYALTY fealty; fidelity
LOZENGE a rhomb; cachou   to, md
LOZENGY lozenged   hd
LUBBARD a lubber
LUCANUS stag beetle   zo
LUCARNE luthern; dormer window
LUCENCE | brightness; sheen;
LUCENCY | radiance; effulgence
LUCERNE plant for fodder   bt
LUCIDLY clearly; limpidly; radiantly
LUCIFER Satan; a match
LUCIGEN powerful oil lamp
LUCKIER more fortunate
LUCKILY happily; fortunately
LUFFING turning toward wind   nt
LUGGAGE baggage; impedimenta
LUGGING tugging; dragging; hauling
LUGMARK earmark
LUGSAIL 4-cornered sail   nt
LUGWORM lob-worm   zo
LUK-CHIN hybrid Chinese
LULLABY soporific song
LULLING soothing; waning; subsiding
LUMBAGO muscular rheumatism   md
LUMINAL narcotic drug   md
LUMPIER bumpier; more awkward
LUMPING bulky
LUMPISH dull; heavy
LUMP-SUM cash down payment
LUNATIC maniac; crazy; insane
LUNETTE bastion; watch glass
LUNULAR crescent shaped
LUNULET lunular spot

LUPULIN hop extract
LUPULUS hop plant   bt
LURCHED pitched; lurked; shifted
LURCHER a lurker; dog   zo
LURKING skulking; awaiting
LUSHING swilling; toping
LUSTFUL lascivious
LUSTIER stronger; sturdier
LUSTILY vigorously
LUSTING desirous
LUSTRAL (purification)
LUSTRUM period of 5 years
LUTEOUS fulvous; tawny
LUTETIA old name for Paris
LUTHERN lucarne; dormer-window
LUTRINE (otter)   zo
LUXATED dislocated
LYCHNIC (vespers, Greek church)
LYCHNIS campion plants   bt
LYCOPOD a moss   bt
LYCOSID wolf spider   zo
LYDDITE a high explosive
LYING-IN awaiting birth
LYINGLY falsely; mendaciously
LYMNATO decorating by spray-gun
    technique
LYMPHAD sailing vessel (Sc.)   nt
LYNCEAN lynx-eyed   zo
LYNCHED summarily dealt with
LYNCHET unploughed strip
LYRATED lyre-shaped
LYRICAL musically poetic

M

MACABRE gruesome; grisly
MACACUS baboon   zo
MACADAM road material
MACAQUE monkey   zo
MACCHIA first undersketch of painting
MACE-ALE spiced ale
MACERAL elementary coal constituent   mn
MACHAIR low-lying ground (Gael.)
MACHETE West Indian knife
MACHINE complicated device
MACKITE asbestos plaster
MACRAME fringe; corded edging
MACRONT post-schizogony stage:
    neosporidia
MACULAE dark sun-spots
MACULAR of body tissue spots
MAD-BRED passionately conceived
MADDEST craziest
MADDING raging; distracted
MADEIRA a wine; a cake
MADLING a lunatic
MADNESS mania; delirium; frenzy
MADONNA Our Lady
MADOQUA Abyssinian antelope   zo
MADRIER mine-plank   mn

MADRONA ⎫ evergreen tree of		
MADRONO ⎰ California	bt	
MADWEED black horehound	bt	
MADWORT mugwort; cure for rabies	bt	
MAESTRO eminent conductor	mu	
MAFFICK rejoice riotously		
MAFFLED muddle-headed		
MAGENTA red aniline dy		
MAGGOTY whimsical		
MAGICAL talismanic; supernatural		
MAGINOT French defensive line		
MAGNATE one of the great		
MAGNETO a generator		
MAGNIFY praise; enlarge; augment		
MAHALEB cherry (Arab.)	bt	
MAHATMA adept in esoteric Buddhism		
MAHDISM (Mahdi)	rl	
MAHDIST Moslem dervish		
MAHJONG Chinese game		
MAHOUND Moslem evil spirit		
MAHSEER Indian river fish	zo	
MAIL-BAG post sack		
MAIL-CAR postal van		
MAILING posting		
MAIL-VAN post vehicle		
MAIMING mutilating; crippling		
MAINOUR stolen property	lw	
MAINTOP part of rigging	nt	
MAISTER maestro; master		
MAIZENA maize-meal	bt	
MAJESTY grandeur; magnificence		
MAJORAT primogeniture (Fr.)		
MALACCA cane	bt	
MALACIA pathological tissue softening	md	
MALACON variety of zircon	mn	
MALAISE unease; disquiet		
MALARIA fever	md	
MALAYAN (Malay)		
MALEFIC maleficent; baneful; noxious		
MALICHO villainy		
MALISON a curse; malediction		
MALLARD wild duck	zo	
MALLEIN glanders inoculum	vt	
MALLEUS ear bone	md	
MALLING beating; mauling		
MALMSEY canary wine		
MALTASE an enzyme	zo	
MALTESE native or language of Malta		
MALTING brewing		
MALTMAN maltster		
MALTOSE starch sugar	ch	
MAMELON rounded mound		
MAMMARY (breasts)		
MAMMATE (mammals)	zo	
MAMMOCK shapeless mass; to mangle		
MAMMOSE like a bosom		
MAMMOTH elephantine; colossal	zo	
MAMMULA small protuberance		
MANACLE handcuff; shackle; fetter		
MANAGED contrived; administered		
MANAGER controller; director		

MANAKIN small bird; manikin	zo	
MANATEE sea-cow; dugong	zo	
MANCHET small French loaf		
MANCHOO Chinese ruler		
MANDATE command; charge; edict		
MANDIOC cassava shrub	bt	
MANDOLA mandora; guitar	mu	
MANDREL lathe-head		
MANDRIL mandrel; spindle		
MANETON heavy gripping pinch-bolt	ae	
MANGABY monkey (Madagascar)	zo	
MANGLED calendered		
MANGLER indifferent carver		
MANGOLD mangel-wurzel	bt	
MANHOLE underground-channel exit		
MANHOOD man's ideal		
MAN-HOUR unit of work	me	
MAN-HUNT search for fugitive		
MANIHOC ⎫ mandioc; tapioca;		
MANIHOT ⎰ cassava	bt	
MANIKIN manakin; dwarf; a bird	zo	
MANILIO arm-ring; copper coin	nm	
MANILLA cheroot; cigar		
MANILLE a card value		
MANIPLE handful; scarf	lw	
MANITOU Great Spirit		
MANKIND blot on creation		
MANLIKE as a man		
MAN-MADE hand-made		
MANNING providing a crew		
MANNISH masculine		
MANNITE manna-sugar	bt	
MANNOSE a hexose	ch	
MAN-ROPE handrail	nt	
MANSARD (roof)	ar	
MANSION residence; house		
MANTLED cloaked; disguised		
MANTLET cloak; testudo		
MAN-TRAP snare for trespassers		
MANUALE case for papyrus rolled text		
MANUMIT free from slavery		
MANURED fertilized		
MANURER cultivator		
MANX-CAT tailless cat	zo	
MAORMOR royal steward (Sc.)		
MAPPERY map-work		
MAPPING surveying; delineating		
MAPPIST cartographer		
MARABOU adjutant stork	zo	
MARACAN parrot	zo	
MARACAS Cuban instrument	mu	
MARATHI Mahratta language		
MARBLED veined		
MARBLER (decorator)		
MARCATO precisely	mu	
MARCHED bordered; advanced		
MARCHEN folk-stories		
MARCHER border-defender		
MARCHES boundaries		
MAREMMA marsh; malaria	md	
MARGODE bluish stone	mn	

MARGOSA Indian tree	bt	**MATELOT** a sailor (Fr.)	
MARIKIN marmoset	zo	**MATERIA** matter	md
MARIMBA kind of xylophone	mu	**MATINAL** a.m.	
MARINER sailor; seafarer	nt	**MATINEE** afternoon performance	
MARIPUT civet	zo	**MATRASS** chemical retort	
MARITAL (husband)		**MAT-REED** reed-mace	bt
MARKHOR wild goat	zo	**MATRICE** matrix; die	
MARKING branding; labelling		**MATROSS** assistant gunner	
MARLINE rope		**MATTERY** purulent	md
MARLING binding	nt	**MATTING** mat-work	
MARLITE variety of marl	mn	**MATTINS** daily service	rl
MARLPIT clay-pit		**MATTOCK** pick-adze	to
MARMITE cooking vessel		**MATTOID** congenital idiot	
MARMOSE opossum	zo	**MATURED** mellow; ripened; payable	
MARPLOT spoil-sport		**MAUDLIN** drunk and whining	
MARQUEE large tent		**MAULING** malling; hammering	
MARQUIS French nobleman		**MAUNDER** mutter; to drivel	
MARRANO Jew converted to Christianity		**MAURIST** a Benedictine	rl
MARRIED spliced; wedded		**MAUTHER** mother (dialect)	
MARRING spoiling; interrupting		**MAWKISH** squeamish	
MARROWY full of marrow		**MAW-SEED** poppy-seed	bt
MARSALA a light wine		**MAW-WORM** tape-worm	zo
MARSHAL arrange; harbinger		**MAXILLA** upper jaw-bone	pl
MARTEXT careless preacher		**MAXIMAL** aphoristic	
MARTIAL warlike; military		**MAXIMED** proverbial	
MARTINI rifle; cocktail		**MAXIMUM** highest value	
MARTITE variety of haematite	mn	**MAXWELL** unit of magnetic flux	el
MARTLET house martin	hd, zo	**MAY-BIRD** wood-thrush	zo
MARXIAN a socialist		**MAY-DUKE** cherry	bt
MARXISM communism		**MAYFAIR** fashionable locality	
MARXIST communist		**MAY-GAME** May-day sport	
MARYBUD marigold	bt	**MAY-LADY** May-queen	
MASCARA eye shading (cosmetics)		**MAY-LILY** spring flower	bt
MASCLED net-like		**MAY-MORN** freshness	
MASCULE } lozenge-shaped	hd	**MAYORAL** (mayor)	
MASCULY }		**MAY-POLE** flower-decked pole	
MASHING mixing		**MAY-TIME** season of May	
MASHLIN } mashlum; mashlim		**MAY-WEED** camomile	bt
MASHLIM } mixed grain		**MAZAGAN** bean	bt
MASH-TUB where malt processed		**MAZARIN** deep blue	
MASKING revelling; disguising		**MAZDEAN** godlike	
MASONIC (freemasonry)		**MAZEFUL** intricate; daedalian	
MASONRY stonework		**MAZURKA** dance	mu
MASSAGE friction	md	**MAZZARD** skull; cherry	
MASSEUR rubdown giver		**MEADOWY** pasturable	
MASSING accumulating; heaping		**MEAL-ARK** meal-chest	
MASSIVE bulky; weighty; ponderous		**MEALMAN** grain merchant	
MASSORA Biblical references		**MEANDER** wander; twist and turn	
MASTABA Egyptian tomb		**MEANING** purport; import; signifying	
MASTERY skill; supremacy		**MEASLED** spotted	md
MASTFUL full of beech-nuts		**MEASLES** children's disease	md
MASTICH gum; mastic	bt	**MEASURE** mete; gauge; value; degree	
MASTIFF large strong dog	zo	**MEAT-FLY** blow-fly	zo
MASTING system of masts	nt	**MEAT-TEA** high tea	
MASTOID nipple-shaped	md	**MEAT-TUB** pickling tub	
MASTOID bone behind ear	md	**MECCANO** constructional devices	
MATADOR bull-fighter		**MECHLIN** lace	
MATADOR a domino game		**MECONIC** (opium)	md
MATCHED tallied; harmonized		**MEDALET** small medal	rl
MATCHES contests; lucifers		**MEDDLED** interfered; muddled	
MATCHET machete; cutlass		**MEDDLER** busybody	

MEDIACY interposition
MEDIANT a tone   mu
MEDIATE intermediate
MEDICAL curative; sanatory   md
MEDINAL soporific drug   md
MEDULLA marrow; pith   md
MEDUSAE Gorgons; hydrozoans   zo
MEDUSAN (petrifying)
MEERKAT mongoose (S. Africa)   zo
MEETING encounter; concourse; duel
MEGABIT million-bits unit   cp
MEGAERA one of the Furies
MEGA-ERG a million ergs   me
MEGAFOG multiple foghorn
MEGAPOD having large feet   zo
MEGARON ancient Gk. house
MEGATON measure of explosive force   me
MEGRIMS giddiness; staggers   vt
MEIOSIS hyperbole
MEISSEN (Dresden china)
MELANGE medley; farrago; jumble
MELANIC black
MELANIN black skin pigment   md
MELASMA black spots   md
MELILOT sweet-scented clover   bt
MELISMA melodic ornamentation   mu
MELISSA herb; balm   bt
MELLITE honey-stone   mn
MELLOWY mellow; soft; unctuous
MELODIC melodious; harmonious
MELROSE honey of roses
MELTING fusing; softening; melting
MEMBRAL (limbs)   md
MEMENTO keepsake; souvenir
MENACED alarmed; frightened
MENACER threatener; intimidator
MENDING repairing; amending
MEN-FOLK group of men
MENGITE anybody's guess   mn
MENINGE brain tissue-envelope   zo
MENIVER miniver; ermine & lambskin
MENTHOL peppermint camphor   ch
MENTION remark; state; cite; declare
MERANTI Malayan hardwood   fr
MERCERY haberdashery
MERCIES usually small
MERCURY planet; quicksilver   ch
MERCURY Hermes; messenger
MERGING absorbing; involving
MERISIS cell-division size increase   cy
MERITED deserved; earned; incurred
MERLING the whiting   zo
MERMAID famous Inn at Rye
MERRIER more cheerful
MERRILY joyously; blithely; happily
MERSION immersion
MESALLY centrally
MESARCH metal/protoxylem relationship   bt
MESEEMS it seems to me
MESHING ensnaring; netting

MESOBAR region of normal atmosph. pressure   mt
MESODIC (intermediate system)
MESOPOD central-stipe fungus fruit   bt
MESOTIC paired cartilage in birds   zo
MESSAGE despatch; missive; errand
MESSIAH also Messias
MESSING muddling; communal feeding
MESS-TIN a soldier's canteen
MESTINO } half-caste Spanish-Indian
MESTIZO }
METAGON cytoplasmic particle: paramecium
METAZOA multicellular animalculae   zo
METHANE marsh-gas   ch
METHION anticonvulsant chemical   pm
METOCHE an architectural interval
METONIC lunar cycle of 19 years
METONYM attribute representing a thing
METOPIC superficial
METOPON opium-based drug   md
METOTIC behind auditory vesicle   zo
METOVUM nutrition-surrounded ovum   zo
METRICS versification; mensuration
METRIFY versify; poetise
METRIST a ballad-monger
METTLED high-spirited
MEWLING squalling
MEXICAN of Mexico
MEZQUIT mesquit; a Mexican tree   bt
MIASMAL airborne infection   md
MIAUING mewing
MIAULED caterwauled
MICELLA foundation structure of cell walls
MICELLE aggregate of molecules   ch
MICHING pilfering
MICROBE germ; bacillus   md
MICROHM electrical resistance   me
MIDDEST middlemost
MIDGARD cf. Asgard (Scand.)
MID-HOUR crossword combination
MID-IRON golf-club
MIDLAND some way from the coast
MID-LIFE halfway to death
MIDMOST middlemost; central
MID-NOON midday
MIDRASH Jewish commentary
MIDRIFF diaphragm; garment   md
MIDSHIP middle of ship   nt
MIDWIFE birth assistant
MIEMITE limestone   mn
MIGRANT nomad; wandering; roving
MIGRATE emigrate
MILDEST calmest; blandest
MILDEWY mouldy; musty; rusty
MILEAGE distance travelled
MILFOIL the yarrow   bt
MILIARY a fever   md
MILIOLA (fossil millet)   mn
MILITIA citizen army
MILK-BAR snack bar

MILKMAN milk distributor
MILK-RUN routine round
MILKSOP effeminate fellow
MILL-COG water-wheel tooth
MILL-DAM mill reservoir
MILLIAD 1000 years
MILLIER a thousand kilos (2204 lb)　　**me**
MILLING struggling; grinding
MILLION 1,000,000
MILLREA ⎱ Portuguese and Brazilian
MILREIS ⎰　　coins　　**nm**
MILTING spawning
MILVINE (kite family)
MIMESIS mimicry
MIMETIC imitative
MIMICAL mocking
MIMICRY impersonation; miming
MIMULUS musk plant　　**bt**
MINARET slender tower
MINCING affected; chopping; cutting
MINDFUL heedful; wary; attentive
MINDING marking; disliking; objecting
MINERAL earth substance
MINERVA Pallas Athene
MINETTE biotite-orthoclase lamprophyre
MINEVER ⎱ miniver; ermine & lambskin
MINIVER ⎰
MINGLED joined; associated; jumbled
MINGLER a mixer; blender; compound
MINIATE to paint red
MINICAB hired car
MINIBUS four-wheeled vehicle
MINIKIN small pin; pet; favourite
MINIMAL smallest
MINIMUM least quantity
MINIMUS smallest; youngest
MINIOUS vermilion
MINIVER unspotted ermine fur
MINORCA a fowl　　**zo**
MINSTER cathedral　　**rl**
MINTAGE coinage; mint dues
MINTING coining; inventing
MINTMAN coiner
MINUEND (subtraction)
MINUTED briefly recorded
MIOCENE geological period
MIOLNIR Thor's hammer
MIPAFOX chemical insecticide
MIRACLE prodigy; supernatural event
MIRADOR balcony or gallery (Sp.)
MIRATON beef/onion stew (Fr.)　　**ck**
MIRBANE (bitter almonds)
MIRIFIC marvellous; wondrous
MISBORN born to misfortune
MISCALL revile; abuse
MISCAST wrong addition; in wrong role
MISCITE quote erroneously
MISCOPY copy amiss
MISCUED (billiards)
MISDATE put wrong date on
MISDEAL faulty card distribution

MISDEED fault; crime; trespass
MISDEEM judge wrongly
MISDOER delinquent; malefactor
MISDONE ill-done
MISDRAW draft badly
MISERLY parsimonious; niggardly
MISFALL mishap; misadventure
MISFIRE fail to go off
MISGAVE filled with doubt
MISGIVE mistrust; doubt
MISHNAH ⎱ Jewish Oral Law
MISHNIC ⎰
MISKICK football
MISLAID temporarily lost
MISLEAD dupe; delude; hoodwink
MISLIKE dislike; aversion
MISLIVE live a bad life
MISLUCK ill fortune; misfortune
MISNAME misterm; miscall
MISPLAY foozle
MISRATE rate erroneously
MISREAD read incorrectly
MISRULE anarchy; chaos; riot
MISSAID incorrectly stated
MISSEEM appear falsely
MISSEND ⎱ wrongly addressed
MISSENT ⎰
MISS-HIT cricket
MISSILE bullet; projectile
MISSING lost; lacking; absent
MISSION trust; errand; embassy
MISSISH girlish; affected
MISSIVE missile; letter; message
MISSTEP a false step
MISSUIT not harmonize
MISTAKE err; error; fault; oversight
MISTELL misstate; misrepresent
MISTERM mischance; miscall
MISTERY a craft or trade
MISTFUL clouded; foggy
MISTICO coasting vessel　　**nt**
MISTILY hazily; obscurely
MISTIME judge occasion poorly
MISTRAL a northerly wind (Fr.)
MISUSED abused; squandered
MISWEEN judge wrongly
MISWEND wander; stray
MISYOKE yoke improperly
MITHRAS a Persian divinity
MITOSIS complex cell division
MITRATE mitre-shaped
MITRING joining wood pieces at 90°　　**cr**
MIXABLE made-up word
MIXEDLY confoundedly
MIXTION gold-leaf fixative
MIXTURE medley; hotch-potch
MIZMAZE a labyrinth; a maze; amazed
MIZZLED decamped
MJOLNIR, MIOLNIR Thor's hammer
MOABITE a tribe
MOANFUL mournful; grievous

MOANING deploring; repining
MOBBING crowding around
MOBBISH tumultuous; disorderly
MOBILES free-hanging ornaments
MOB-RULE a form of democracy
MOBSMAN well-dressed swindler
MOBSTER gangster; hoodlam; ruffian
MOCKADO ancient woollen fabric; tawdry
MOCKERY scorn; derision; ridicule
MOCKING taunting; jeering
MOCK-ORE a zinc ore   mn
MOCK-SUN a parhelion
MODALLY conditionally
MODESTY chastity; propriety
MODICUM small quantity
MODISTE dressmaker
MODULAR proportional
MODULUS factor of a function
MODWALL bee-eater   zo
MOELLON masonry-filling
MOFETTE (earth-fissures)
MOHICAN Algonquin Indian
MOHSITE titanite of iron   mn
MOIDERT bewildered (Sc.)
MOIDORE Portuguese gold coin   nm
MOILING toiling; drudging
MOINEAU bastion (Fr.)
MOISTEN damp; add water
MOLASSE sandstone   mn
MOLE-RAT a rodent   zo
MOLIMEN strenuous effort
MOLLIFY pacify; alleviate; soothe
MOLLINE emollient base
MOLLUSC ⎫ snails; gasteropods;
MOLLUSK ⎭ cuttlefish; cephalopods   zo
MOLOSSI (3 long syllables)
MOMENTA masses having velocity
MONACID with one hydroxyl group   ch
MONADIC of monads   ch
MONARCH despot; king; ruler
MONAXON of one axis only   zo
MONEPIC comprising one word
MONERAL ⎫
MONERAN ⎬ protozoans
MONERON ⎭
MONEYED rich; wealthy; opulent
MONEYER coiner
MONGREL mixed breed
MONIKER nickname
MONITOR mentor; advisor; lizard   zo
MONKERY monk-life
MONKEYS primates   zo
MONKISH monastic
MONOCLE eye-glass
MONODIC monotonous and mournful
MONODON narwhal   zo
MONOGYN type of plant   bt
MONOMER single-molecule substance   ch
MONONYM monomial name, term
MONOTIC affecting 1 ear only
MONSOON Indian rainy season

MONSTER ogre; marvel; prodigy
MONTAGE film editing   cr
MONTANT fencing term
MONTERO horseman-cap (Sp.)
MONTHLY menses
MONTOIR mounting-stone (Fr.)
MONTURE saddle-horse (Fr.)
MONURON chemical weedkiller
MOOCHED loitered; mouched
MOODILY morosely; capriciously
MOOKTAR Indian lawyer   lw
MOOLVEE doctor of Moslem law
MOONEYE lake fish   zo
MOONING day-dreaming
MOONISH fickle; variable
MOONLIT visible in moonlight
MOON-MAD moonstruck
MOON-SET the setting of the moon
MOORAGE anchorage
MOORHEN water-hen   ze
MOOR-ILL cattle disease (Sc.)
MOORING boat tie-up   nt
MOORISH Moresque; arabesque
MOOTING suggesting; debating
MOOTMEN debating law students   lw
MOPPING dabbing; wiping
MORAINE glacial debris
MORALER moraliser (Shak.)
MORALLY ethically; virtuously
MORASSY marshy; swampy; boggy
MORBLEU a French oath
MORCEAU morsel (Fr.)
MORDANT biting; caustic
MORDENT a trill   m
MORELLA ⎫
MORELLO ⎭ dark-red cherry   b
MORESCO arabesque; morisco
MORGANA (Fata)
MORGLAY claymore
MORICHE American palm   b
MORINGA Malay tree   b
MORISCO Moorish; moresco
MORLING dead sheep or its wool
MORMOPS repulsive looking bats   z
MORNING dayspring; daybreak
MOROCCO goatskin leather
MOROSIS feeble-mindedness
MORPHEW scurf
MORPHIA opium extract   m
MORPHIC morphological
MURRHUA (cod)   z
MORRICE Morris; Moorish
MORRION open helmet
MORSURE the act of biting
MORTISE, MORTICE a joint in carpentry   c
MORTIER cap of state (Fr.)
MORTIFY putrefy; fester; corrupt
MORTIFY bodily self-denial; humiliate
MOSAISM (Moses)
MOSCHUS musk deer   z

MOSELLE light wine
MOSS-HAG a slough in a bog
MOTACIL wag-tail zo
MOTHERY concreted; maternal
MOTTLED variegated; spotted
MOTTOES pithy maxims
MOUCHER skulker
MOUFLON wild sheep zo
MOUILLE liquid tone
MOULAGE casting footprints
MOULDED kneaded; shaped
MOULDER metal-caster; crumble
MOULDIE a torpedo nt
MOULTED shed
MOULVIE ⎫ Mahommedan priest;
MOULWEE ⎭ a learned man rl
MOUNDED banked; fortified
MOUNTED on horseback; ascended
MOUNTER climber
MOURNED grieved; keened; wailed
MOURNER bewailer
MOUSING cat-work; lashing
MOUSMEE geisha
MOUTHED orated; chewed
MOUTHER stump-orator; ranter
MOVABLE portable; mobile
MOW-BURN (hay)
MOZARAB (Christian Spaniard)
MOZETTA cardinal's cape rl
MUCIGEN chalice-cells substance zo
MUCKING muffing; muddling
MUD-BATH health measure
MUD-BOAT dredger nt
MUD-CART night-soil pick-up service
MUD-CONE mud volcano
MUDDIED fouled; dirtied; soiled
MUDDING smearing with mud
MUDDLED misused; confused; fuddled
MUDDLER mixer
MUD-FISH the bow-fin zo
MUD-FLAT low-tide bank
MUD-HOLE waterside residence
MUD-LARK a gamin
MUDLINE water/slurry division line mn
MUD-SCOW (dredging)
MUD-SILL tide mud level
MUD-WALL soil embankment
MUD-WORT aquatic plant bt
MUEDDIN ⎫ Moslem priest
MUEZZIN ⎭ rl
MUFFING botching; fluffing
MUFFLED deadened; dulled
MUFFLER scarf
MUFFLON wild sheep
MUGGARD sullen; displeased
MUGGENT wild freshwater duck zo
MUGGING swotting; ruffianly attack
MUGGINS simpleton; a juggins
MUGGISH damp and warm
MUGIENT bellowing like cattle
MUGWORT wormwood plant bt

MUGWUMP independent politician
MULATTO half-breed
MULCHED ⎫ applied top dressing
MULSHED ⎭
MULCTED fined; penalized; amerced
MULETTE Portuguese sailing vessel
MULLEIN yellow plant bt
MULLING warming and spicing
MULLION munnion; uprt. window bar
MULLITE aluminium silicate mn
MULLOCK rubbish; dirt
MULTOCA Turkish law lw
MULTURE grain grinding
MUMBLED muttered
MUMBLER indistinct articulator
MU-MESON elementary particle nc
MUMMERY masquerading; buffoonery
MUMMIED mummified
MUMMIFY embalm
MUMMING mummery; burlesquing
MUMMOCK ragged coat
MUMPING mockery; begging tricks
MUMPISH dull; sullen
MUNCHED crunched; chewed
MUNCHER a masticator
MUNDANE worldly; secular; temporal
MUNDIFY cleanse; purify
MUNJEET Siberian madder bt
MUNNION a mullion
MUNTING a door upright
MUNTJAK barking deer zo
MURAENA eel genus zo
MUREXAN purple dye
MUREXES ⎫ shellfish zo
MURICES ⎭ Tyrian dye
MURGEON a wry face; grimace (Sc.)
MURIATE hydrochloric ch
MURKIER more overcast
MURKILY duskily; luridly; darkly
MURRAIN cattle disease vt
MURRINE fluorspar mn
MURRION morion; helmet
MURTHER murder
MUSCARI grape hyacinth bt
MUSCITE fossil moss mn
MUSCLED muscular
MUSCOID moss-like bt
MUSEFUL pensive; meditative
MUSETTE small bagpipe mu
MUSHING dog-sleighing
MUSICAL tuneful; harmonious
MUSIMON moufflon zo
MUSK-BAG perfume sachet
MUSK-CAT civet cat zo
MUSKILY like musk
MUSK-RAT the musquash zo
MUSROLE nose-band of a bridle
MUSTANG wild horse zo
MUSTARD sinapis bt
MUSTELA weasel zo
MUSTILY sourly; acridly; frowsily

MUSTING growing mouldy and rank
MUTABLE changeful; fickle; unstable
MUTABLY variably; inconstantly
MUTAGEN mutation producer md
MUTANDA things to be altered
MUTTONY resembling mutton
MUZZILY confusedly; dizzily
MUZZLED forcibly restrained
MYALGIA cramp md
MYALGIC tense; stiff md
MYALISM W. Ind. magic cult
MYARIAN (mussels) zo
MYCELIA mushroom spawn bt
MYCETES ⎫
MYCETIS ⎬ howling monkeys zo
MYCOSIS fungoid growth md
MYCOTIC fungoid bt
MYELOID marrow-like
MYELOMA bone-marrow malignancy md
MYIASIS parasitism by fly larvae vt
MYLODON extinct sloth zo
MYNHEER Dutchman
MYOCELE muscle hernia md
MYOCOEL coelomic space in myotome zo
MYOCYTE ectoplasm layer of protozoa zo
MYODOME eye-muscle chamber zo
MYOGRAM (muscular movement)
MYOLOGY (muscles) md
MYOMERE somite muscles zo
MYONEME ectoplasm fibril in protozoa zo
MYOTOME muscle merome zo
MYOTOMY dissection md
MYOXINE pertaining to dormice
MYRINGA ear-drum
MYRRHIC (myrrh) bt
MYRRHIN extract of myrrh bt
MYRRHOL myrrh-oil bt
MYSTERY mistery; a craft; enigma
MYSTICS a sect
MYSTIFY nonplus; perplex; bewilder
MYTHIST a recorder of legends
MYTILUS mollusc genus; mussels zo
MYXOPOD a protozoan zo

N

NABBING grabbing; seizing
NACARAT bright orange-red colour
NACELLE body of aeroplane
NACODAH Arab sea-captain
NACRITE pearl-like mn
NACRITE clay mineral mn
NACROUS pearly
NAEVOID (birthmark) md
NAEVOUS freckled
NAGGING incessant scolding
NAIADES water nymphs
NAILERY nail factory
NAILING spiking; fastening
NAIL-ROD nail material
NAIVELY artlessly; candidly

NAIVETE ingenuousness
NAIVETY unaffected simplicity
NAKEDLY starkly
NAMABLE nameable; nomenclatory
NAMAQUA African dove zo
NANDINE civet cat (W. Africa) zo
NANKEEN buff-coloured cloth (Nankin)
NAOLOGY study of church buildings
NAPHTHA rock-oil mn
NAPLESS threadbare
NAPPING dozing; snoozing; unalert
NARCOMA narcotics coma md
NARCOUS, NARCOSE stupor-inducing
NARDINE spikenard bt
NARGILE Eastern pipe; hubble-bubble
NARRATE chronicle; describe; report
NARTHEX porch with lean-to roof r
NARWHAL sea-unicorn zo
NASALIS proboscis monkey ze
NASALLY through the nose
NASARDE organ stop mu
NASCENT natal; originating; incipient
NASITIS nasal inflammation md
NASMYTH inventor of steam hammer
NASTIER more disagreeable
NASTILY offensively; nauseously
NATTERY peevish; captious
NATTIER French blue; smarter
NATTILY neatly; sprucely
NATURAL an idiot; normal; inherent
NATURED temperamentally disposed
NATUREL unadulterated
NAUGHTY froward; perverse
NAUPLII crustaceans ze
NAUTICS art of navigation n
NAUTILI cuttlefish ze
NAVARCH an admiral (Greek)
NAVARHO aircraft navigation system
NAVARIN mutton/vegetable stew ck
NAVETTE rape plant b
NAVY-CUT rope-bound tobacco sliced
NAVVIES labourers; canal diggers
NAYWORD by-word; watch-word
NAZI-ISM German national socialism
NEAD-END show end
NEALOGY embryology mc
NEAREST closest; stingiest
NEARING approaching, drawing nigh
NEATEST sprucest; tidiest; trimmest
NEBULAE gaseous matter
NEBULAR cloudy; vague; hazy
NECKING embracing; an annulet a
NECKLET small necklace
NECKTIE cravat
NECTARY honey-gland b
NEEDFUL essential; vital; requisite
NEEDIER rather worse off
NEEDILY necessitously
NEEDING wanting; lacking
NEEDLED pierced; embroidered
NEEZING, NEESING sneezing

NEGATED denied; mollified
NEGATER computer inverter
NEGATUR it is denied   lw
NEGLECT disregard; omission
NEGLIGE loose attire; negligee
NEGRESS coloured woman
NEGRITO pygmy (Polynesia)
NEGROID negro-type
NEGUNDO box-elder   bt
NEIGHED whinnied
NEITHER not either; not the one
NELUMBO water-lily; lotus
NEMATIC of substance with parallel orientation   ps
NEMESIC retributive
NEMESIS goddess of vengeance
NEMORAL arboreal
NEOCENE geological formation
NEOLITE silicate of aluminium   mn
NEOLOGY (new terms); rationalism
NEORAMA view of building interior
NEOTENY larval-character retention   zo
NEOZOIC geological system
NEPHRIA Bright's disease   md
NEPHRIC of the kidney   zo
NEPOTIC favouring the family
NEPTUNE sea-god; planet
NEREITE fossil centipede   mn
NERITIC of shallow coastal waters
NERVATE veined   bt
NERVINE nerve tonic   md
NERVING summoning resolution
NERVOUS sensitive; timid; fearful
NERVOSE having nerves
NERVULE } vein in leaf   bt
NERVURE } or insect's wing   zo
NESIOTE living on an island
NEST-EGG cash savings
NESTING nidification
NESTLED cherished; lay close
NESTLER a snuggler; cuddler
NET-BALL a girl's game
NET-CORD (tennis)
NET-FISH caught trout   zo
NETSUKE Japanese fastening
NETTING snaring
NETTLED stung; fretted; irritated
NETTLER a provoker
NETWORK reticulation; mesh
NEURINE nerve-matter   md
NEUROID nerve-like
NEUROMA tumour   md
NEURONE nerve cell
NEUROSE veined
NEURULA stage of embryo development   zo
NEUSTON water-surface animals   ec
NEUTRAL unbiased; indifferent
NEUTRON uncharged particle   nc
NEVADOS Andean winds (Ecuador)
NEW-BORN just hatched

NEWCOME recently arrived
NEW-LAID fresh eggs
NEW-MADE novel; fresh; neoteric
NEWNESS novelty
NEWSBOY paper seller
NEWSMAN reporter
NIAGARA cataract; deluge; torrent
NIBBLED bit; pilfered; carped
NIBBLER dainty feeder
NIBLICK a golf club
NICKING stealing; notching
NICTATE wink
NIDGING stone dressing
NIGELLA love-in-a-mist   bt
NIGGARD a miser; covetous; sparing
NIGGERY negroid
NIGGLED trifled
NIGGLER fuss-pot
NIGHTED benighted
NIGHTIE nightdress; robe de nuit
NIGHTLY every evening
NIGRINE an ore of titanium   mn
NIGRITE insulating material
NILLING unwilling
NILOTIC (Nile)
NIMBLER more agile; quicker; swifter
NIMIETY excessiveness
NIMONIC high-temperature-work alloy   ml
NINE-PIN skittle
NIOBEAN (Niobe); lachrymose; tearful
NIOBIUM metallic element   ch
NIPBONE herb comfrey   bt
NIPPERS small pincers   to
NIPPIER quicker; more agile
NIPPIES waitresses
NIPPING biting; pinching
NIRVANA tranquility; earthly paradise
NITENCY effort; brightness
NITHING poltroon
NITRATE nitrite   ch
NITRIDE metal/nitrogen compound   ch
NITRIFY convert to nitre   ch
NITRILE alkyl cyanide   ch
NITROUS nitrose   ch
NIVEOUS snowy
NJORTHR a Vanir (Norse)
NOACHIC of Noah's time
NOBBLED stole; tampered with a horse
NOBBLER confederate; doper
NOBLESS noblesse; nobility
NOBLEST most illustrious
NO-CLAIM (insurance)
NOCTUID nocturnal moth   zo
NOCTULE bat   zo
NOCTURN a service of psalms   rl
NOCUOUS harmful; noxious; baleful
NODATED knotted
NODDING (auction); unwary; nutation
NODICAL (ecliptic point)   as
NODULAR (intersections)
NODULED knotted

NODULUS small knop
NOEMICS intellectual science
NOETIAN a dogmatic theologian
NOGGING brick and wood-work
NOISILY rowdily; loudly; uproariously
NOISING bruiting; rumouring
NOISOME noysome; disgusting
NOMADIC wandering; migratory
NOMANCY divination
NOMARCH Greek provincial governor
NOMBLES entrails of deer
NOMBRIL escutcheon centre
NOMINAL titular; ostensible
NOMINEE prospective candidate
NON-ACID alkali
NON-AGED under 18
NONAGON nine-sided figure
NONPLUS perplex; astound; bewilder
NON-SKID steady grip tyres
NONSTOP perpetual motion
NONSUCH fodder plant   bt
NON-SUIT no case   lw
NON-TERM vacation   lw
NONUPLE 9-fold
NOOLOGY psychology
NOONDAY 12 o'clock midday
NOONING siesta
NOOSING lassoing; snaring
NORFOLK loose jacket
NORIMON Japanese palanquin
NOR-LAND north country
NORTHER north wind
NORWICH school of painting
NOSE-BAG horse's lunchbox
NOSEGAY bouquet
NOSE-LED befooled
NOSTRIL nose passage
NOSTRUM panacea; quack; medicine
NOTABLE signal; famous; memorable
NOTABLY conspicuously; notoriously
NOTAEUM bird's back   zo
NOTANDA memoranda
NOTCHED scored; nicked
NOTCHEL to repudiate
NOTEDLY markedly; particularly
NOTELET small note
NOTHING nihil; zero; naught
NOTHOUS spurious; bastard
NO-THROW barely twisted silk thread   tx
NOTICED observed; heeded; marked
NOTITIA a catalogue
NOUMENA opp. to phenomena
NOURISH cherish; foster; encourage
NOURSLE to bring up; to nurse
NOVALIA reclaimed land
NOVELLA supplemental decrees
NOVELTY newness
NOVOLAK phenol condensation product ch
NOWHERE address unknown
NOXIOUS hurtful; nocuous; baneful
NOYADES organised drownings (Fr.)

NOYSOME noisome; nauseating
NUCLEAL nuclear; (nucleus)
NUCLEAR central, like a kernel
NUCLEUS kernel; centre; head of comet
NUCLEIC nucleoprotein non-protein part bc
NUCLEIN cell matter
NUCLEOR nucleon core   nc
NUCLIDE atom-nucleus-distinguished isotope
NUDGING elbowing; jostling
NULLIFY annul; rescind; revoke; repeal
NULLITY invalidity; noughtiness
NUMBERS a biblical book   rl
NUMBING deadening; paralyzing
NUMBLES entrails of deer
NUMERAL digit; figure
NUMERIC numerical
NUMMARY numismatics   nm
NUNATAK projecting rock (Eskimo)
NUN-BUOY conical buoy
NUNDINE market day (Roman)
NUNHOOD nunation
NUNNERY convent   rl
NUNNISH sisterly; conventual
NUPTIAL conjugal; bridal; hymeneal
NURAGHE Sardinian fort
NURLING milling an edge
NURSERY (canons); training centre
NURSING fostering; developing
NURTURE upbringing; sustenance
NUT-BUSH hazel   bt
NUT-GALL dyestuff source   bt
NUT-HOOK crooked stick
NUT-LOAF, NUT-MEAT vegetarian
NUT-MEAL nut-flour rissole   ck
NUT-PINE food-producing tree   bt
NUTTING gathering nuts
NUT-TREE hazel   bt
NUT-WOOD panel wood   bt
NUZZLED nestled; cuddled
NYCTALA genus of owls   zo
NYLGHAU antelope (Ind.)   zo
NYMPHAL young and beautiful
NYMPHLY, NYMPHIC girlish

O

OAFLIKE doltish; stupid; idiotic
OAK-BARK could be cork   bt
OAK-FERN 3-branched polypody   bt
OAK-GALL tree excrescence   bt
OAK-LEAF colonel's decoration   bt
OAKLING young oak   bt
OARFISH ribbon-fish
OARLOCK rowlock
OARSMAN sculler
OAT-CAKE Gaelic delicacy   ck
OAT-MALT malt from oats
OATMEAL rolled oats
OBCONIC funnel-shaped
OBDUCED drawn over; covered

OBDURED hardened; inured
OBELION part of skull
OBELISK printer's dagger (†)
OBELIZE mark as spurious
OBESITY corpulence; fatness
OBEYING submitting; complying
OBITUAL funereal
OBLIGED gratified; forced; bound
OBLIGEE under bond
OBLIGER favourer
OBLIGOR bond giver — lw
OBLIQUE askew; crooked; aslant
OBLOQUY calumny; censure; odium
OBOLARY poverty-stricken
OBOVATE, OBOVOID egg-shaped
OBSCENE repulsive; lewd
OBSCURE recondite; indistinct
OBSEQUY funeral rite
OBSERVE mark; notice; espy; remark
OBTRUDE intrude; thrust; interfere
OBVERSE head of coin
OBVIATE get round; preclude
OBVIOUS evident; patent; palpable
OCARINA instrument (Sicily) — mu
OCCIPUT back of head — md
OCCLUDE absorb; include
OCEANIC of oceans
OCEANID ocean nymph
OCEANUS ocean god
OCELLAR ocellate; with 'eyes' — zo
OCELLUS single eye; a spot
OCELOID of the leopard type — zo
OCHROID pale yellow
OCREATE wearing boots/leggings
OCTAGON 8-sided figure
OCTAPLA eight-fold text
OCTAVUS eighth (Latin)
OCTETTE group of eight
OCTOBER 10th month
OCTOFID eight segments — bt
OCTOPOD eight-footed — zo
OCTOPUS cuttlefish; squid — zo
OCTUPLE eightfold
OCTYLIC (organic radicle) — ch
OCULATE eyed
OCULIST eye doctor — md
OCYPETE one of the Harpies
ODALISK woman slave (Turk.)
ODDMENT remnant
ODDNESS oddity; eccentricity
ODFORCE mesmeric force
ODONTIC pertaining to teeth — at
ODORANT odorous; fragrant
ODORINE a bone distillate
ODOROUS fragrant; redolent
ODYSSEY perilous journey
OEDEMIA surf-ducks — zo
OEDIPUS a solver; King of Thebes
OENOMEL wine and honey
OERSTED magnetic field intensity — me
OESTRUM frenzy; orgasm

OESTRUS gadfly — zo
OFF-BEAT unusual, advanced — mu
OFFCOME apology; pretext (Sc.)
OFFENCE crime; injury; assault
OFFERED proffered; tendered; essayed
OFFERER a bookie; volunteer
OFFHAND casual; impolite
OFFICER person holding office
OFF-LINE aside from — cp
OFFSCUM offscouring
OFFSIDE right-hand side; football fault
OFFWARD leaning off
OGHAMIC (Irish script)
OGREISH like an ogre
OGYGIAN prehistoric; primeval
OIL-BATH bicycle accessory
OIL-BIRD the guacharo — zo
OIL-CAKE cattle food
OIL-GOLD (gold leaf)
OIL-MEAL ground linseed cake
OIL-MILL oil factory
OIL-PALM oil source — bt
OIL-SHOP lubricatorium
OILSILK oil-impregnated fabric — tx
OILSKIN waterproof garment
OIL-SUMP drainage cavity in motor
OIL-WELL petroleum well
OJIBWAY Algonquin Indian
OLDNESS senility
OLDSTER middle-aged
OLD-TIME old fashioned; quondam
OLEFINE hydro-carbons — ch
OLIFANT elephant — zo
OLIGIST haematite — mn
OLITORY (kitchen-garden)
OLIVARY olive shaped; oval
OLIVINE chrysolite — mn
OLYMPIC of Olympus
OLYMPUS abode of the gods
OMENING auguring; presaging
OMENTAL } peritoneum — md
OMENTUM }
OMICRON Greek letter 'o'
OMINOUS portentous; inauspicious
OMITTED left out; neglected; dropped
OMNEITY state of including all things
OMNIBUS bus; compendium
OMNIFIC all-creating
ONANISM self-satisfaction
ONCOSTS overhead costs (Sc.)
ONCOTIC osmotic pressure of colloids
ONDATRA musk-rat
ONE-EYED limited in vision
ONEFOLD single
ONEIRIC pertaining to dream — pc
ONENESS unity; concord
ONERARY operose; oppressive
ONEROUS burdensome; weighty
ONESELF me, you or anybody
ONE-STEP a dance
ONE-TIME former; previous

ONGOING proceeding; event	
ONICOLO cameo-onyx	mn
ONOCLEA fern genus	bt
ONOLOGY prattle	
ONSHORE towards the land	
ONSTEAD farmstead (Sc.)	
ONWARDS forward; advancing	
ONYCHIA a whitlow	md
ONYMISE categorise	
ONYMOUS not anonymous	
OOCYTIN substance in spermatazoa	bl
OOECIUM brood pouch	zo
OOGRAPH egg drawing device	
OOLITIC granular	
OOLOGIC (birds' eggs)	zo
OOLYSIS conversion to leaf	bt
OOMETRY egg measurement	
OOPHYTE gametophyte	bt
OOPLASM central cytoplasm in oomycetes	
OOSPORE fertilized ovum	zo
OOTHECA egg-carrying structure	zo
OOZOOID zooid arising from ovum	zo
OPACITY opaqueness; obscurity	
OPACOUS opaque; untransparent	
OPALINE opalescent	
OPALIZE opalise	
OPEN-AIR out-door	
OPEN-END radio; contract	
OPENING aperture; breach; orifice	
OPEN-JAW air ticket (two way)	
OPERAND quantity to be worked on	
	cp, ma
OPERANT a worker; artisan; employee	
OPERATE function; manipulate	md
OPEROSE tedious	
OPEROUS laborious; toilsome	
OPETIDE spring-tide	
OPHIDIA snakes	zo
OPHIURA starfish	zo
OPIATED drugged	
OPINANT of opinion	
OPINING opinion; a notion; supposing	
OPINION conception; idea; conjecture	
OPORICE preserved fruit	
OPOSSUM a marsupial	zo
OPPIDAN town boy (Eton)	
OPPOSED combatted; competed	
OPPOSER rival; resister	
OPPRESS persecute; crush; maltreat	
OPSONIC } germ-resisting corpuscles	md
OPSONIN }	
OPTICAL of vision	
OPTICON brain zone in insects	zo
OPTIMUM best value	
OPULENT wealthy; affluent	
OPUNTIA cactus family	bt
OPUSCLE opusculum; a small work	
ORAISON orison; a prayer	rl
ORARIAN coastal	
ORARION, ORARIUM stole	rl
ORATING spouting; declaiming	
ORATION speech; harangue; address	

ORATORY eloquence; chapel	r
ORATRIX lady speaker	
ORBIFIC world-creating	
ORBITAL revolutionary; elliptic	
ORBLESS without knobs	
ORBLIKE globular	
ORCHARD garden of fruit-trees	
ORCINOL dihydric phenol	ch
ORDERED regulated; commanded	
ORDERER controller; manager	
ORDERLY methodical; (military)	
ORDINAL a number	
ORDINEE young deacon	r
OREADES mountain nymphs	
ORECTIC pert. to desires/satisfaction	
ORGANIC vital; radical; fundamental	
ORGANON } organised enquiry	
ORGANUM }	
ORGANRY organ music	mu
ORGIAST a Bacchanalian	
ORIENCY brightness of colour	
ORIFICE aperture; vent; pore	
ORIFORM mouth-shaped	
ORIGAMI paper cut-out, fold designs (Jap.)	
ORLEANS cloth; plum	b
OROGENY (mountain formation)	
OROLOGY mountain lore	
OROTUND full voiced	
ORPHEAN enchanting	
ORPHEUS a maker of melodies	
ORPHISM cult of Bacchus	
ORPHREY embroidered border	
ORTHITE allanite	mn
ORTHROS morning service (Greek)	
ORTOLAN garden bunting	z
ORVIETO a white wine	
OSAZONE fraction of monosaccharide	ch
OSBORNE convalescent home, I.O.W.	
OSCHEAL scrotal	
OSCINES singing birds	z
OSCULAR (kissing)	
OSCULUM exhalant aperture in porifera	
OSIERED with withes	
OSMANLI a Turk; Ottoman dynasty	
OSMATIC having olfactory organs	
OSMIOUS containing osmium	ch
OSMOSIS diffusion	ch
OSMOTIC diffusible	
OSMUNDA royal fern	b
OSSELET morbid growth	
OSSEOUS bony	
OSSICLE small bone	
OSSIFIC bony	mo
OSSUARY charnel-house	
OSTEOID like bone	
OSTERIA hostelry (It.)	
OSTIARY church janitor	r
OSTIOLE spore-door	b
OSTIOMA bone tumour	mo
OSTITIS inflammation	mo
OSTRICH also estrich	zo
OTALGIA ear-ache	me

OTARINE referring to seals   **zo**
OTIDINE pertaining to bustards   **zo**
OTOCYST auditory vesicle   **md**
OTOLITH ear-stone   **md**
OTOLOGY ear science   **md**
OTTOMAN Turk; sofa; divan
OURSELF our kingly self
OUSTING ejecting; evicting; dislodging
OUT-BACK one from the back country
OUTBRAG out-boast
OUTBURN burn away
OUTCAST pariah; exile
OUTCOME issue; sequel; upshot
OUTCROP geological fault
OUTDARE outventure
OUTDONE surpassed; eclipsed
OUTDOOR open air
OUTEDGE farthest extremity
OUTFACE to brave
OUTFALL the place of discharge
OUTFLEW L. Carroll-type word
OUTFLOW outlet
OUTFOOT out-pace; outsail
OUTGATE exit
OUTGAZE look longer than
OUTGIVE surpass in liberality
OUTGOER opposite of incomer
OUTGONE over-reached; went beyond
OUTGROW get too old for
OUTGUSH outpour; outwell
OUTHAUL a rope   **nt**
OUTHIRE to let out
OUTJEST write dictionary definitions
OUTLAND foreign
OUTLASH sudden outburst
OUTLAST survive; outlive; outwear
OUTLEAP a sally
OUTLIER outcrop
OUTLINE draft; sketch; profile
OUTLIVE survive
OUTLOOK prospect; future; view
OUTMATE overmatch; checkmate
OUTMOST furthest outward
OUTMOVE out-manoeuvre
OUTNAME surpass in reputation
OUTNESS externality; objectiveness
OUTPACE outrun
OUTPART remote part
OUTPEER excel
OUTPLAY out-manoeuvre
OUTPORT branch port
OUTPOST detached fort
OUTPOUR stream; spout
OUTPRAY surpass in prayer
OUTRAGE wanton mischief; abuse
OUTRANK precede
OUTRAZE exterminate
OUTRIDE win horse race
OUTROAD a foray (Sc.)
OUTROAR an uproar
OUTROOT uproot; eradicate
OUTRUSH a raid; a foray

OUTSAIL win yacht race
OUTSELL succeed in America
OUTSERT extra outside binding leaf   **pr**
OUTSHOT a projection
OUTSIDE external; exterior; superficial
OUTSIZE extra big
OUTSOAR word invented to fill space
OUTSOLD outvend
OUTSOLE outer sole
OUTSPAN to unyoke
OUTSTAY stay longer than
OUTSTEP overstep
OUTTALK over jabber
OUTTURN output; production
OUTVIED surpassed; exceeded
OUTVOTE get majority
OUTWALK outpace
OUTWALL outer wall
OUTWARD ostensible; apparent
OUTWEAR last longer; outlast
OUTWELL outgush
OUTWENT outstripped
OUTWIND extricate
OUTWING out-flank
OUTWITH beyond the scope of (Sc.)
OUTWORE lasted longer than
OUTWORK redoubt; ravelin
OUTWORN worn out; exhausted
OUVRAGE work (Fr.)
OVARIAN (ovary)
OVATION enthusiastic applause
OVEN-TIT willow-warbler   **zo**
OVERACT act too much
OVERALL protective garment
OVERARM bowling (cricket)
OVER-ATE surfeited
OVERAWE intimidate; daunt; cow
OVERBID succeed at auction
OVERBUY buy too much
OVERDUE in arrears; outstanding
OVERDYE dye too deeply
OVEREAT gourmandize
OVEREYE overlook
OVERFAR a bit much
OVERFLY soar beyond; fly over
OVERLAP lie partly over another
OVERLAY overwhelm
OVERLIE to smother
OVERMAN foreman
OVERMAN mining manager; umpire
OVERPAY pay too much
OVERPLY over-exert
OVERRAN outran; invaded
OVERRUN swarm; infest; printing   **pr**
OVERSAW superintended
OVERSEA foreign
OVERSEE superintend
OVERSET upset
OVERSEW stitch fit to burst
OVERTAX aim of Labour party
OVERTLY openly; publicly; patently
OVERTOP surpass

OVICELL brood-pouch in ectoprocta	zo	
OVICIDE killing of eggs/sheep		
OVIDIAN (Ovid)		
OVIDUCT ovary passage	md	
OVIFORM oval		
OVOIDAL ovoid; egg-shaped		
OVOLOGY egg-lore		
OVULARY (seed)	bt	
OVULITE fossil egg	mn	
OWENITE (Robert Owen)		
OWL-EYED with big orbs		
OWL-LIKE fairly wise		
OXALATE of oxalic acid	ch	
OXALITE oxalate of iron	mn	
OXAMIDE oxalic acid amide	ch	
OXHEART kind of large sweet cherry		
OXIDANT combustive agent	ch	
OXIDASE enzyme	ch	
OXIDATE oxidize	ch	
OXIDIZE to rust	ch	
OXIMIDE oxamic acid compound	ch	
OXONIAN of Oxford		
OX-STALL home for non-bulls		
OXYACID proton-giving hydroxide	ch	
OXYDANT oxygen component in rocket	ae	
OXYNTIC secreting acid (of stom. glands)		
OXYOPIA acute vision	md	
OXYSALT containing oxygen	ch	
OXYTONE accented syllable		
OZONIDE explosive organic compound	ch	
OZONIZE charge with ozone		
OZONOUS ozonic		

P

PABULAR yielding food		
PABULUM aliment; fodder; nutriment		
PACABLE appeasable		
PACATED calmed; quieted; pacified		
PACHISI pachesi; Indian backgammon		
PACHYMA fungus genus	bt	
PACIFIC peaceful; tranquil; irenic		
PACKAGE bale; bundle; parcel		
PACK-ICE icy-sea barrier		
PACKING crowding; stowing		
PACKMAN peddler; hawker; tallyman		
PACKWAX tendon in animals' necks	zo	
PACKWAY bridle path		
PACTION a pact; covenant; bond		
PADDING stuffing		
PADDLED dabbled; propelled		
PADDLER canoeist		
PADDOCK frog or toad	zo	
PADDOCK puddock; field		
PADELLA small lamp		
PADISHA Persian title		
PADLOCK heavy durable lock		
PADRONE Italian employer		
PAD-TREE harness frame		
PAENULA chasuble	rl	
PAEONIN red colouring matter		

PAGEANT spectacle; display; pompous		
PAGINAL (pages)		
PAHLEVI pehlevi, early Persian dialect		
PAILFUL the contents of a bucket		
PAILLON metal backing		
PAINFUL grievous; vexatious; sore		
PAINING afflicting; tormenting; aching		
PAINTED limned; bedizened; daubed		
PAINTER artist in colour; depictor		
PAINTER R.A.; mooring rope	nt	
PAIRING mating; (voting)		
PAJAMAS pyjamas; slumber wear		
PAKFONG } German silver		
PAKTONG }		
PALABRA palaver (Sp.)		
PALADIN knight errant		
PALAMAE toe-webbings	zo	
PALATAL (palate)	md	
PALAVER conference; pow-wow		
PALE-ALE type of brew		
PALEOUS like chaff		
PALETOT loose overcoat		
PALETTE artist's board		
PALFREY saddle-horse	zo	
PALINAL retrogressive	md	
PALLIAL (mantle of mollusc)	zo	
PALLING covering; surfeiting		
PALLIUM archbishop's pall	rl	
PALLIUM mantle-like brain/shell tissue	pl	
PALLONE Italian ball-game		
PALMARY worthy; capital		
PALMATE web-footed	zo	
PALMERY palm-house	bt	
PALMING concealing; handling		
PALMIST fortune teller		
PALM-OIL bribery		
PALMYRA East Indian palm	bt	
PALOOKA guy; nitwit; simpleton		
PALPATE to handle		
PALSHIP comradeship		
PALSIED paralyzed		
PALUDAL marshy; malarial; fenny		
PAMPERO westerly wind (S. America)		
PANACEA universal remedy		
PANACHE plume; self-esteem		
PANAGIA all holy; an ornament	rl	
PANCAKE aeroplane descent; thin cake fried in pan	ae, ck	
PANDEAN of Pan		
PANDECT digest of Roman Law		
PANDION osprey genus	zo	
PANDORA (her fateful box); sea-bream	zo	
PANDORE a lute	mu	
PANDOUR } Hungarian soldier;		
PANDOOR } a robber		
PANDURA Neapolitan guitar	mu	
PANEITY state of being bread	rl	
PANFISH small non-commercial food fish		
PANGANI East African ivory		
PANGING paining; causing anguish		
PANICKY jumpy; nervous; fearful		
PANICLE a small web	bt	

PANICUM millet   bt
PANIKIN tin mug
PANNADE curvetting
PANNAGE swine food
PANNIER (dress); basket; corbel
PANNING washing; yielding
PANNOSE like felt
PANOCHA coarse sugar (Mexico)
PANOPLY complete armour
PAN-PIPE mouth-organ   mu
PANSIED with pansies
PANTHER leopard   zo
PANTHOS Divinity made manifest
PANTIES undies
PANTILE pentile; curved tile
PANTING palpitating; desirous
PANTLER butler
PANURGE a Rabelaisian rascal
PANURGY skill in work
PAPALLY popishly
PAPERED sand-papered
PAPERER paperhanger
PAPHIAN (worship of Venus)
PAPILIO butterfly   zo
PAPILLA nerve extremity   md
PAPMEAT soft food
PAPOOSE North American Indian infant
PAPPING feeding with pap
PAPPOSE pappous; downy
PAPRIKA red pepper (Turkish)   bt
PAPULAE dermal gills in echinodermata
PAPULAR pimply   md
PAPYRUS sedge; scroll   bt
PARABLE allegorical similitude
PARACME decline; decadence
PARADED displayed; vaunted
PARADOS rampart
PARADOX surprising statement
PARAGON model of perfection
PARAMOS semi-tundra (Andes)
PARAPET rampart
PARASOL sunshade
PARBAKE bake partially   ck
PARBOIL boil partially   ck
PARCHED scorched; dried; shrivelled
PARDIEU in truth
PARDINE like a leopard, spotted
PAREIRA drug (Brazilian plant)   bt
PARELLA litmus lichen   bt
PARELLE perelle
PARERGY subsidiary work
PARESIS paralysis   md
PARETIC partially paralyzed   md
PARFAIT cold egg/creme dessert   ck
PARGING pargeting; external plaster work
PARISON intermediate glass shape   gs
PARITOR beadle; apparitor
PARKING lodging; collecting
PARLOUR the Mayor's sanctum
PARLOUS perilous; difficult; precarious
PARODIC (parody); farcical
PAROTIC auricular   md

PAROTID ⎫
PAROTIS ⎬ (salivary gland)   md
PARQUET flooring; pit of theatre
PARRIED avoided; warded off; fended
PARSING grammatical exercise
PARSLEY a culinary herb   bt
PARSNIP parsnep; a vegetable   bt
PARTAKE to share; participate
PARTIAL biased; restricted; fond
PARTIES sides; jamborees
PARTING division; separating; breaking
PARTITE partially parted   bt
PARTLET a ruff; a collar; a hen   zo
PARTNER colleague; associate; buddy
PARULIS gumboil   md
PARVENU upstart
PARVISE porch; church garden   rl
PARVULE tiny pill
PASCHAL (Easter)
PASCUAL grazing; pasturing
PASQUIL ⎫
PASQUIN ⎬ lampoon; satire
PASSADE ⎫ sword thrust;
PASSADO ⎬ equestrian exercise
PASSAGE alley; clause; contest
PASSANT walking   hd
PASSING brief; transient; exceeding
PASSION ardour; fervour; wrath
PASSIVE patient; resigned; inert
PASS-KEY a master-key
PASSMAN (honours)
PASTE-IN late correction, insert   pr
PASTERN (fetlock)
PASTE-UP extended arrangement of proof
sheets   pr
PASTIES patties; pies
PASTIME recreation; sport; diversion
PASTING cementing; gumming
PASTOSE painted thickly
PASTURE herbage; meadowland
PATAMAR coasting vessel (Indian)
PATBALL tennis of sorts
PATCHED repaired clumsily
PATCHER repairer; botcher
PATELLA limpet   zo
PATELLA knee-cap; saucer   md
PATERAE shallow dishes
PATHWAY footway; track; trail
PATIENT long-suffering   md
PATNESS celerity in the uptake
PATONCE heraldic curved cross   hd
PATRIAL racial; national
PATRICO gipsy priest; patercove
PATRIOT staunch non-cosmopolitan
PATRIST a theologian
PATROON American proprietor
PATTERN model; exempler; paragon
PATTIES pasties; pies
PATTING tapping
PATTRAS wooden wall-plug
PATULIN penicillium antibiotic   pm
PATURON chelicerae segment in spiders

PAUCITY fewness; exiguity; lack
PAULINE (St Paul)
PAUNCHY obese; stout
PAUSING halting; wavering; tarrying
PAVIAGE road tax (Fr.)
PAVIOUR pavement layer
PAWNING pledging; hypothecating
PAXILLA spine in asteroidea   **zo**
PAXIUBA South American palm   **bt**
PAYABLE due; profitable
PAY-BILL order to pay
PAY-BOOK record of payments
PAY-DIRT alluvial deposit
PAY-LIST pay-roll
PAYLOAD plane's cargo
PAYMENT recompense; reward
PAYNISE to preserve wood
PAY-ROLL pay-list
PAYSAGE landscape (Fr.)
PEACHED divulged
PEACHER an informant
PEA-COAT pea-jacket
PEACOCK pavonine   **zo**
PEA-CRAB small crustacean   **zo**
PEA-FOWL a species of Pavo genus   **zo**
PEAKING raising a yard obliquely   **nt**
PEAKISH off colour; sickly
PEALING ringing; resounding
PEANISM song of praise or triumph
PEARLED made success as oyster
PEARLIN lace made of silk thread
PEASANT a rustic; swain; hind
PEASCOD pea-pod   **bt**
PEA-SOUP London fog
PEAT-BED damp doss
PEAT-BOG Irish fuel source
PEAT-HAG peat-hole
PEAVIES lumbermen's levers
PEBBLED shingled
PEBRINE silk-worm disease
PECCANT sinning; guilty; criminal
PECCARY S. American pig   **zo**
PECCAVI confession of error
PECKING picking up; striking
PECKISH hungry
PECTASE gel-forming plant enzyme   **bt**
PECTATE pectose; gelatinous
PECTINE jelly
PECTOSE carbohydrate plant constituent
PEDDLED retailed; trifled
PEDDLER hawker; huckster
PEDESIS molecular vibration
PEDICEL ⎱ small stalk
PEDICLE ⎰   **bt**
PEDLARY hawking
PEDRAIL tracked vehicle
PEELING excoriating; skinning
PEELITE follower of Sir R. Peel
PEENING hammer-blow metal-working
PEEPING snooping; peering
PEERAGE Debrett

PEERESS consort of a peer
PEERING prying; gazing; appearing
PEEVERS hop-scotch (Sc.)
PEEVISH querulous; snappish
PEEWEEP peewit; pewit   **zo**
PEGASUS winged horse of the Muses
PEGASUS (fish); constellation   **zo**
PEGGING fastening; (croquet)
PEGWOOD clock-hole cleaning sticks
PEHLEVI pahlavi, early Persian dialect
PEISHWA Mahratta prime minister
PELAGIC (deep sea)
PELAMID bonito; mackerel type   **zo**
PELASGI Greek tribe
PELICAN genus of birds   **zo**
PELIOMA livid spot   **md**
PELISSE fur-coat
PELLAGE duty on skins
PELOPID a son of Pelops
PELORIA ⎱ abnormalism   **md**
PELORIC ⎰
PELORUS pivoted dial   **nv**
PELOTON coiled hypha in fungi   **bt**
PELTAST soldier with buckler
PELTATE shield-like
PELTING pouring; throwing
PENALLY by way of punishment
PENALTY handicap; retribution
PENANCE punishment; humiliation
PENATES Roman household gods
PEN-CASE pen-holder
PENDANT an ornament; pennant
PENDENT hanging; dangling
PENDING awaiting decision
PENEIAN (river Peneus in Vale of Tempe)
PEN-FISH sparoid fish   **zo**
PENFOLD pinfold; enclosure for cattle
PENGUIN Antarctic sea-bird   **zo**
PENICIL paint-brush
PEN-NAME pseudonym; nom de plume
PENNANT a long streamer   **nt**
PENNATE winged; pinnate   **zo**
PENNIED having a cash asset
PENNIES pence   **nm**
PENNILL stanza (Eisteddfod)
PENNINE magnesium/aluminium silicate
PENNING inditing; cooping
PENSILE pendulous; suspended
PENSION (boarding house); annuity
PENSIVE meditative; thoughtful
PENTACT five rayed
PENTANE (paraffin)   **ch**
PENTICE pent-house; a sloping roof
PENTODE pentone; wireless adjunct
PENTOSE a form of sugar   **ch**
PENTZIA S. African shrub   **bt**
PENUCHE type of fudge   **ck**
PEONAGE ⎱ agricultural servitude
PEONISM ⎰
PEONIES paeonies   **bt**
PEOPLED inhabited

EPERIN volcanic tufa	mn	
EPPERY irascible; choleric		
EP-PILL stimulant		
EPSINE an enzyme	md	
EP-TALK encouragement		
EPTICS digestion	md	
EPTIDE protein-breakdown substance	ch	
EPTONE digestive product	md	
ER-ACID hydrogen-peroxide/acid product		
ERBEND bonding stone		
ERCALE woven cambric		
ERCASE perhaps		
ER-CENT out of 100		
ERCEPT that which is perceived		
ERCHED roosted; settled		
ERCHER candle; rooster	zo	
ERCINE like a perch; percoid	zo	
ERCOCT well cooked		
ERCOID perch-like	zo	
ERCUSS strike; tap		
ERDURE endure; persist		
EREGAL fully equal		
EREION thorax of crustacea	zo	
ERELLE parella; lichen	bt	
ARELLE		
ERFECT to complete; faultless		
ERFIDY betrayal; treachery		
ERFORM fulfil; act; execute; effect		
ERFUME scent; aroma; fragrance		
ERFUSE sprinkle; bedew; permeate		
ERGOLA pergula; arbour		
ERHAPS aiblins; peradventure		
ERIAPT amulet; charm; talisman		
ERIDOT green jewel; olivine	mn	
ERIGEE lowest point of an earth orbit		
ERIKON detector	ro	
ERIQUE Louisiana tobacco		
ERIWIG peruke		
ERJURE forswear		
ERJURY false testimony	lw	
ERKIER more irrepressible		
ERKILY saucily; jauntily; airily		
ERKING peering; smartening up		
ERLITE vitreous rock	mn	
ERMAGY small Turkish boat		
ERMIAN geological formation		
ERMUTE commute; change		
EROPOD rudimentary leg	zo	
ERORAL surrounding the mouth	zo	
EROSIS slipped tendon	vt	
ERPEND ratiocinate; cogitate		
ERPEND bonding stone		
ERPLEX puzzle; nonplus; embarrass		
ERRIER catapult; a table water		
ER-SALT salt corresponding to per-acid		
ERSEID a meteor from Perseus		
ERSEUS slew Medusa; a constellation		
ERSIAN Iranian		
ERSIST persevere; continue; last		
ERSONA (grata); actor's mask		
ERSPEX a glazing material		

PERTAIN to relate to; concern		
PERTURB disturb; agitate; disquiet		
PERTUSE riddled; bored		
PERUSAL careful reading		
PERUSED read; studied; examined		
PERUSER a scrutineer of pages	pr	
PERVADE perfuse; impregnate; imbue		
PERVERT deviate; lead astray		
PESHITO Syriac Testament	rl	
PESKILY annoyingly		
PESTLED pounded in a mortar		
PETASMA curtainlike structure in prawns	zo	
PETASUS Mercury's winged cap		
PETERED pottered; exhausted; (cards)		
PETEREL petrel; Mother Carey's chick	zo	
PETIOLE leaf-stalk; pedicle	bt	
PETRAIL heavy framing beam	cr	
PETRARY catapult for stones		
PETREAN stony		
PETRIFY stupefy; dumbfound; stun		
PETRINE according to St Peter	rl	
PETROUS rocklike		
PETTILY meanly; trivially		
PETTING fondling; canoodling		
PETTISH peevish; fretful; querulous		
PETUNIA a flower	bt	
PETZITE silver/gold telluride	mn	
PEW-RENT rent paid for use of pew	rl	
PEWTERY (pewter)		
PFENNIG German copper coin	nm	
PHACOID lenticular	md	
PHAETON sky-hog; four-wheel carriage		
PHAETON boatswain-bird	zo	
PHALANX compact body		
PHALLIC Bacchanalian		
PHALLUS symbol of procreation		
PHANTOM spectral; illusive; ghost		
PHARAOH Egyptian title		
PHARATE of development phase in insects		
PHARYNX upper part of gullet	md	
PHASING adjustment picture	tv	
PHELLEM tissue external to phellogen	bt	
PHENATE (phenol)	ch	
PHENOIC carbolic	ch	
PHIDIAS Greek sculptor		
PHILTRE philter; love potion		
PHINEAS mascot of Univ. Coll. Hosp.		
PHLOEUM phloem; bark-fibre	bt	
PHOCINE (seals)	zo	
PHOEBUS Apollo; the sun		
PHOENIX date palm; fabulous bird	zo	
PHONATE to utter inarticulately		
PHONEME relevant sound (linguistics)		
PHONICS harmony; phonetics		
PHONING telephoning		
PHORESY transport by clinging to animal	zo	
PHORONE acetone condensation product	ch	
PHOTICS science of light		
PHOTISM colour sensation		

PHRAGMA septum or partition	zo	**PIG-WASH** hog-wash	
PHRASED expressed; styled		**PIKELET** ⎱ a crumpet;	
PHRASER phrase-monger		**PIKELIN** ⎰ a tea-cake	
PHRATRY tribal subdivision		**PIKEMAN** turnpike gatekeeper	
PHRENIC diaphragmatic	md	**PIKRITE** igneous rock	m
PHRENSY frenzy; madness; delirium		**PILCHER** a scabbard	
PHYSICS a science		**PILEATE** cap-shaped	
PHYTOID plant-like	bt	**PILFERY** petty theft; larceny	lw
PIACERE at pleasure	mu	**PILGRIM** palmer; devotee; wayfarer	
PIAFFER a horse gait		**PILKINS** pill-corn; oats	b
PIANINA small piano	mu	**PILLAGE** rifle; sack; ravage; loot	
PIANISM musical technique	mu	**PILLBOX** concrete emplacement	
PIANIST an expert on the ivories	mu	**PILLING** blackballing	
PIANOLA self-playing piano	mu	**PILLION** padded saddle	
PIARIST philanthropist, A.D. 1617		**PILLORY** expose to ridicule	
PIASTRE (Egypt)	mn	**PILLOWY** yielding; soft	
PIBROCH a tune; bagpipe (Sc.)	mu	**PILOTED** steered; conducted; guided	
PICADOR mounted bull-fighter		**PILOTIS** building on columns	a
PICAMAR tar extract		**PILTOCK** coalfish	z
PICCAGE pitch-money	lw	**PILULAR** (pills)	
PICCOLO small flute	mu	**PIMELIC** a fat product	c
PICEOUS pitch-black		**PIMENTA** ⎱ allspice;	b
PICKAXE pointed chopper	to	**PIMENTO** ⎰ Jamaica pepper	
PICKING petty larceny; choosing		**PIMPLED** blotched	
PICKLED preserved		**PINACOL** tetra alkyl glycol	c
PICK-OFF automation device		**PINBONE** hipbone of quadruped	z
PICOTEE carnation	bt	**PIN-CASE** pin etui	
PICOTTE little lace loop		**PINCERS** pliers	t
PICQUET piquet; card game		**PINCHED** gripped; purloined	
PICRATE an explosive; lyddite	ch	**PINCHER** sea fish	z
PICRINE foxglove extract	bt	**PINCHES** nips	
PICRITE olivine; peridot	mn	**PINDARI** Indian freebooter	
PICTISH Celtic		**PINE-OIL** oil from resin	
PICTURE portrait; drawing; imagine		**PINETUM** plantation of pine-trees	b
PIDDOCK mollusc	zo	**PIN-FIRE** (cartridge)	
PIEBALD pyebald		**PIN-FISH** a scaly fish; sailor's choice	z
PIECING patching; uniting		**PINFOLD** cattle pound	
PIERAGE pier tolls		**PINGING** like a bullet	
PIERCED transfixed; impaled		**PINGUID** fat; greasy; unctuous	p
PIERCER borer; gimlet; drill		**PINHEAD** top of a pin; minute	
PIERIAN (Muses); (Mount Pierus)		**PIN-HOLD** pin-housing	
PIERROT an entertainer		**PINHOLE** tiny aperture	
PIETISM sanctimoniousness		**PINK-EYE** a horse disease	
PIETIST religious sect		**PINKING** scalloping; knocking	
PIEWIFE lapwing	zo	**PINKISH** somewhat pink	
PIEZOID piezo crystal blank	el	**PINNACE** a man-of-war's boat	r
PIFFERO oboe; organ-stop	mu	**PINNATE** pennate; feathered	b
PIFFLED chattered; drivelled		**PINNING** making fast	
PIG-DEER invented animal	zo	**PINNOCK** tom-tit	z
PIGEYED with small eyes		**PINNULA** ⎱ branchlet;	b
PIGGERY pig-sty		**PINNULE** ⎰ small feather	z
PIGGING living higgledy-piggledy		**PINTADO** guinea-fowl; chintz	ze
PIGGISH hoggish; swinish; messy		**PINTAIL** a duck	z
PIGHTLE small enclosure		**PINT-POT** vessel holding pint	m
PIG-IRON iron ingots		**PIN-WORK** (flexing flax)	
PIG-LEAD cast lead		**PIONEER** forerunner; initiator	
PIGMEAN pygmean; Lilliputian		**PIONING** pioneering (Spens.)	
PIGMENT paint; colour; tincture	pt	**PIOUSLY** devoutly; religiously	
PIGMIES pygmies		**PIP-EMMA** p.m., (signalling)	
PIGNONS fir-cone seeds	bt	**PIPERIC** peppery	
PIGSKIN (leather); (saddle)		**PIPETTE** graduated tube	
PIGTAIL plait of hair		**PIPLESS** seedless	b

PIPPING pilling; defeating
IQUANT stimulating; caustic; tart
IQUING irritating; nettling
IRAGUA a dug-out canoe   nt
IRATED plundered; marauded
IRATIC infringing; piratical
IROGUE flat-bottomed boat (Sp.)
ISCARY fishing rights
ISCINA basin; fish-pond   rl
ISCINE fishy; swimming pool (Fr.)
ISMIRE an ant; emmet   zo
ISTOLE Spanish golden coin   nm
ITAPAT in a flutter
ITCHED flung; tossed; planted; cast
ITCHER eared jug; (base-ball)
ITCOAL coal from underground   mn
ITEOUS woeful; sorry; compassionate
ITFALL a trap; snare; danger
IT-HEAD top of coal mine
ITHILY tersely; concisely; briefly
ITHING extracting the marrow
ITH-RAY root or stem cell sheet   bt
ITIFUL humane; lenient; wretched
IT-MIRK dark as pitch (Sc.)
ITTING corrosion; striving
ITTITE playgoer
ITUITA }
ITUITE } phlegm   md
ITYING commiserating; condoling
IVOTAL axial
IVOTED hinged; centred on
IXY-LED bewildered
LACARD bill; poster; notice
LACATE pacify; conciliate; appease
LACEBO R.C. mass   rl
LACING identifying; assigning
LACKET slit; pocket
LACODE platelike structure   zo
LACOID scaly
LACULA small plate; plaque
LAFOND ceiling; a soffit
LAGIUM kidnapping   lw
LAGUED distracted
LAGUER a vexatious person
LAGULA chitinous plate in solifugae   zo
LAIDED wearing a tartan
LAINER clearer; more obvious
LAINLY simply; clearly; candidly
LAITED folded; woven
LAITER an interlacer
LANARY flat; level
LANÇON octagonally hewn log   fr
LANING smoothing; aeroplaning
LANISH to hammer smooth
LANKED laid down; floored
LANNED sketched; schemed
LANNER a projector; designer
LANTAR (sole of foot)
LANTED instilled; inculcated; sown
LANTER settler; grower
LANULA embryo protoplasm   zo
LANXTY Welsh lament

PLASHED splashed; dabbled
PLASMIC proto-plasmic
PLASMID changeable cytoplasm structure   bl
PLASMIN fibrin-destroying blood substance
PLASMON flour-like food
PLASTER sinapism; daub; stucco
PLASTIC elastic; pliable; yielding
PLASTID living cell   zo
PLATANE plane-tree   bt
PLATEAU tableland; highland
PLATINA platinum   ch
PLATING sheathing
PLATOON a squad
PLATTED plaited; weaved
PLATTER wooden plate
PLAUDIT applause; approbation
PLAY-BOX theatre seat
PLAYBOY Lothario
PLAY-DAY holiday
PLAYFUL sportive; frolicsome
PLAYING acting; competing; romping
PLEADED entreated; argued   lw
PLEADER barrister; advocate   lw
PLEASED delighted; contented; obliged
PLEASER charmer; gratifier
PLEATED platted; interlaced
PLECTRE plectrum; plectron   mu
PLEDGED pawned; engaged
PLEDGEE pawnbroker
PLEDGER pawnbroker's customer
PLEDGET lint compress   md
PLEIADS the Pleiades; 7 stars in Taurus
PLENARY in full; complete; entire
PLENISH provide; equip
PLENIST spacious materialist
PLEOPOD abdominal swimming appendage   zo
PLEROMA abundance; fullness
PLEROME centre of apical meristem   bt
PLEURAL (lungs)   md
PLEURON shell extension   zo
PLEXURE weaving; texture
PLIABLE limber; tractable; supple
PLIABLY flexibly; lithely
PLIANCY flexibility
PLICATE folded; plaited
PLIFORM in the form of a fold
PLIMMED swollen
PLISKIE plight (Sc.)
PLODDED toiled; drudged
PLODDER steady worker
PLOPPED plumped
PLOSIVE explosive (sound)
PLOTFUL full of schemes
PLOTTED planned; schemed; concocted
PLOTTER intriguer; conspirator
PLOTTIE mulled wine (Sc.)
PLOUTER to paddle or dabble
PLOW-BOY ploughboy

PLOWING ploughing	
PLOWMAN ploughman, (lunch)	
PLUCKED failed to pass; pulled	
PLUCKER feather remover	
PLUGGED plodded; shot; sealed	
PLUGGER stopper	
PLUMAGE plumery; feathers	
PLUMBED measured; made vertical	
PLUMBER lead-worker	
PLUMBUM, PLUMBIC lead	ch
PLUMCOT plum-apricot	bt
PLUMERY display of plumes	
PLUMING self-congratulation	
PLUMIST feather-dresser	
PLUMMET lead bob	
PLUMOSE plumous; feathery	
PLUMPED fell suddenly	
PLUMPER chubbier; fatter; stouter	
PLUMPLY roundly; fully	
PLUMULE plumula; bud	bt
PLUNDER loot; spoil; pillage; booty	
PLUNGED dived; gambled heavily	
PLUNGER part of a pump	
PLUNKET blue colour	
PLUTEUS pelagic larval form	zo
PLUVIAL rainy; humid	
PLUVIUS Jupiter pluvius	
PLY-WOOD laminated wood	
POACEAE the grasses	bt
POACHED trespassed; stabbed; (eggs)	
POACHER a toiler; setter of snares	
POCHARD a duck	zo
POCHOIR stencil colour process	pr
POCK-PIT pock-mark	md
PODAGRA gout	md
PODALIC pertaining to feet	
PODDING producing pods	
PODESTA Italian magistrate	
PODITIC (crab's leg)	zo
PODRIDA Spanish stew	
POE-BIRD tui; parson bird; (NZ)	zo
POEISIS creation	
POETESS lyrical lady	
POETICS criticism of poetry	
POETIZE poetise; versify	
POINDED pounded; distrained	lw
POINTED acute; sharp; keen; significant	
POINTEL pencil; spike; style	
POINTER fescue; indicator	zo
POISING balancing; loading	
POITREL horse-armour	
POLACCA Mediterranean sailing vessel	
POLAIRE ancient leather satchel for books	
POLARON trapped electron	el
POLARIS guided missile	
POLDERS reclaimed land	
POLE-AXE poll-axe	to
POLE-CAT civet	zo
POLEMIC controversial; contentious	
POLENTA Italian porridge	
POLICED regulated	

POLIGAR S. Ind. village chieftain	
POLITER more courteous or civil	
POLITIC statesmanlike; discreet	
POLLACK sea-fish, pollock, chub	z
POLLARD stag after casting his antlers	
POLLARD lopped; bran; the chub	z
POLL-AXE pole-axe	t
POLLENT strong; mighty; puissant	
POLLING voting; lopping	
POLL-MAN pass-man (Cam.)	
POLL-TAX capitation tax	
POLLUTE defile; profane; corrupt	
POLOIST polo player	
POLONYM joint-authorship name, work	
POLYACT rayed	
POLYGON angular figure	
POLYGYN plant genus	
POLYMER complex compound	c
POLYOPY multiple vision	
POLYOSE polysaccharide	c
POLYPOD having all appendages	z
POLYPUS sea-anemone; coral	z
POLYZOA barnacles	z
POMATUM an unguent	
POMELOE citron of shaddock kind	
POMEROY the king-apple	
POMFRET a fish	z
POMMAGE crushed apples	
POMMARD a Burgundy wine	
POMPANO edible fish (N. Amer.)	z
POMPION pumpkin	
POMPIRE an apple	
POMPOSO with due pomp	m
POMPOUS self-important; grandiose	
PONCEAU poppy; poppy-coloured	
PONDAGE water in a pond	
PONDING collecting into a pond	
PONIARD dagger	
PONTAGE bridge toll	
PONTIFF high priest; pope	
PONTINE Roman marsh	
PONTOON bridge of boats; card game	
POOH-BAH a pluralist	
POOLING merging; combining	
POOPING (following sea)	
POOR-BOX alms for the poor	
POOREST most necessitous; neediest	
POOR-LAW charity provisions	
POPCORN parched maize	
POPEDOM papality	
POP-EYED with protruding eyes	
POPOVER Amer. 'Yorkshire pudding'	c
POPPIED drowsy; slumbrous; narcotic	
POPPING exploding; pawning; darting	
POPPLED rippled; bubbled	
POP-SHOP pawn-shop	
POPULAR familiar; prevailing; current	
POP-WEED bladder-wort	
PORCATE ridged	
PORCINE piggy; swinish; suiform	z
PORIFER a sponge	

PORK-PIE type of hat
POROSIS bone formation   **md**
POROTIC (porosis); callous   **md**
PORPHIN pyrrole/methene nucleus group   **ch**
PORRECT extended
PORRIGO dandruff   **md**
PORTAGE porterage
PORT-BAR harbour bar
PORTEND foretell; augur; bode
PORTENT an evil omen; presage
PORTICO porch; stoa; colonnade
PORTIFY aggrandise
PORTING carrying; conveying   **nt**
PORTION bit; part; share; division
PORTRAY paint; describe
PORZANA water-rail; crake   **zo**
POSAUNE German trombone   **mu**
POSITED postulated
POSSESS own; hold; keep; control
POSTAGE mail carriage fee
POST-BAG sack for letters
POST-BOY mail collector
POST-BOX letter-box
POST-DAY day for sending/getting mail
POSTEEN Kashmir sheepskin coat
POSTERN back-door; small gate
POSTFIX affix; suffix; append
POSTING mailing; recording
POSTMAN letter carrier
POSTURE pose; attitude; position
POST-WAR since hostilities
POTABLE drinkable; liquid
POTAGER porringer
POTAMIC pertaining to rivers
POTANCE part of a watch
POTARGO a pickle
POTASSA potash   **ch**
POTATOR an imbiber; toper
POTCHER paper-pulp machine   **pp**
POTENCE heraldic gibbet   **hd**
POTENCE inverted cock   **hr**
POTENCY ability; power; influence
POT-HEAD dunderhead
POTHEEN Irish whiskey
POT-HERB cookery flavouring
POT-HOLE earth cavity
POT-HOOK fireplace hook
POTICHE porcelain vase
POT-LIFE period in pot before paint jells
POT-LUCK makeshift meal
POTOROO rat kangaroo   **zo**
POT-SHOP small inn
POT-SHOT random round
POTTAGE a mess; a stew
POTTERY earthenware
POTTING preserving; shooting
POUCHED bagged; marsupial   **zo**
POULARD plump pullet   **zo**
POULTER poulterer (Shak.)
POULTRY fattened fowls   **zo**

POUNCED with claws; sprang; swooped
POUNDAL unit of force   **me**
POUNDED confined; bruised
POUNDER pestle
POURING streaming; gushing
POUTING registering displeasure
POVERTY want; penury; indigence
POWDERY pulverous; floury; dusty
POWERED engined
PRACTIC deceitful; skilful (Shak.)
PRAESES academical disputers
PRAETOR Roman magistrate
PRAIRIE treeless grassy lands
PRAISED lauded; glorified
PRAISER laudator; extoller; eulogizer
PRAKARA temple passage (India)
PRAKRIT Sanskrit and allied languages
PRALINE sweetmeat; nuts in sugar
PRANCED strutted; bounded
PRANGED bombed heavily; struck
PRANKED all dressed up; prinked
PRANKER practical joker; a dude
PRATIES potatoes (Irish)   **bt**
PRATING babbling; boasting
PRATTLE idle chatter
PRAYING imploring; craving; begging
PREACHY tediously didactic
PREBEND canon's stipend   **rl**
PRECEDE herald; usher; introduce
PRECEPT behest; maxim; rule; canon
PRECIPE writ   **lw**
PRECISE exact; accurate; finical
PREDATE ante-date
PREDIAL (farm estate)
PREDICT presage; portend; foretell
PREDONE worn-out; exhausted
PREDOOM prejudge
PRE-ECHO prior sound from record defect
PREEMPT bespeak at a high price
PREENED tidied up
PREFACE preamble; proem; prologue
PREFECT French magistrate; monitor
PREFINE limit; delimit
PREFORM form beforehand
PREFORM larger moulding composition
PREHEAT heat (oven) up for use   **ck**
PRELACY episcopacy   **rl**
PRELATE church dignitary   **rl**
PRELECT discourse; lecture; address
PRELIMS introductory features of book
PRELIMS examinations
PRELUDE preface; exordium   **mu**
PREMIAL at a premium
PREMIER first; principal; P.M.
PREMISE antecedent proposition
PREMISS logical premise
PREMIUM bounty; fee; reward; bonus
PRENDER right of seizure   **lw**
PREORAL in front of the jaw
PREPAID paid in advance
PREPARE make ready; manufacture

PREPUCE foreskin, penile cover **md**
PREPUPA insect stage before larval ecdysis
PRERUPT abrupt; steep
PRESAGE foretell; predict; prophesy
PRESEEN foreseen
PRESELL promote products in advance
PRESENT here; now; existing; current
PRESENT exhibit; proffer; gift
PRESIDE officiate; direct; control
PRESSED urged; crushed; encroached
PRESSER squeezer
PRESSOR causing arterial pressure rise **zo**
PRESTER mythical medieval priest
PRESUME assume; reckon; venture
PRETEND feign; simulate; claim
PRETEXT excuse; plea; cloak
PRETONE (accented syllable)
PRETZEL crisp biscuit
PREVAIL dominate; win; succeed
PREVENE precede
PREVENT hinder; hamper; thwart
PREVIEW foresee
PREVISE forewarn; foresee
PREWARN give notice of
PREYFUL predatory
PREYING plundering; wasting; robbing
PRIAPUS god of procreation
PRICING costing; valuing; rating
PRICKED spurred; punctured; bored
PRICKER prickle; light horseman
PRICKET early candlestick
PRICKET a young buck **zo**
PRICKET stone-crop **bt**
PRICKLE to prick; a thorn **bt**
PRICKLY spinate; spicate
PRIDIAN of yesterday
PRIDING valuing; esteeming highly
PRIDWIN King Arthur's shield
PRIGGED filched; purloined; nabbed
PRIGGER thief; pincher
PRIMACY archbishopric **rl**
PRIMAGE a lading charge
PRIMARY main; first; pristine; initial
PRIMATE archbishop **rl**
PRIMELY originally; excellently
PRIMERO card game
PRIMEUR early crop
PRIMINE outer husk **bt**
PRIMING (powder); first coat **pt**
PRIMMED formed precisely
PRIMSIE demure; prim (Sc.)
PRIMULA primrose genus **bt**
PRINKED pranked; all dressed up
PRINKER (dressed showily)
PRINTED published; pressed; issued
PRINTER typographer
PRISAGE a levy on wines
PRISERE primary succession **bt**
PRISING forcing open; levering
PRISTIS saw-fish **zo**
PRITHEE I pray thee

PRIVACY seclusion; solitude; retreat
PRIVATE soldier; personal; unofficial
PRIVILY privately; confidentially
PRIVITY secrecy; cognizance
PRIZAGE prisage; crown levy
PRIZING appreciating; valuing
PROBANG whalebone swab **mc**
PROBATE proof of a will **lw**
PROBING scrutinizing; testing; sifting
PROBITY proved integrity; sincerity
PROBLEM enigma; query; conundrum
PROCARP female organ in rhodophyta **b**
PROCEED advance; continue; act
PROCESS operation; course; progress
PROCTOR university official **lw**
PROCURE get; obtain; induce
PROCYON lesser Dog-star
PRODDED goaded; shoved; poked
PRODDER inciter; stimulator
PRODIGY marvel; wonder; portent
PRODUCE engender; showed; bear
PRODUCT proceeds; yield; result
PROFACE May it profit you!
PROFANE desecrate; secular
PROFESS own; aver; proclaim
PROFFER offer; tender; volunteer
PROFILE outline; side view
PROFUSE lavish; prodigal; copious
PROGENY offspring; issue; young
PROGGED begged; prodded; (proctored)
PROGRAM programme; syllabus
PROJECT propel; contrive; jut
PROLATE extended
PROLEGS legs of caterpillars **z**
PROLINE protein cleavage product **c**
PROLONG protract; lengthen; sustain
PROMINE cancer-cell growth stimulant **m**
PROMISE pledge; engage; stipulate
PROMOTE further; aid; elevate
PRONAOS temple porch
PRONATE face or palms downwards
PRONELY lying down
PRONGED fork-like; bifurcated
PRONOTA beetles' backs **z**
PRONOUN word replacing noun
PROOFED tried; tested
PROOTIC an ear-bone **m**
PROPALE to disclose
PROPANE paraffin gas
PROPEND to favour; lean forward
PROPENE propyl alcohol **c**
PROPHAM chemical herbicide
PROPHET seer; augur; preacher
PROPINE pledge; guarantee
PROPINE methyl acetylene **c**
PROPOSE suggest; intend; purpose
PROPPED shored; strutted; supported
PROPUGN vindicate; defend
PRORATE assess pro rata
PRORSAD prorsal; anterior **m**
PROSAIC unexciting; dull; humdrum

PROSIFY turn into prose		
PROSILY unimaginatively		
PROSING talking tediously		
PROSODY (harmonious writing)		
PROSPER thrive; flourish; succeed		
PROTEAN in many guises		
PROTECT shield; defend; ward		
PROTEGE trusted nominee		
PROTEID \ complex substances in food,		
PROTEIN / necessary for diet	ch	
PROTEND hold out; extend		
PROTEST expostulate; exclaim; object		
PROTEUS sea-god of Carpathian Sea		
PROTIUM hydrogen isotope	ch	
PROTYLE hypothetical nucleus		
PROUDER more arrogant and haughty		
PROUDLY majestically; imperiously		
PROVAND provision; provend (Shak.)		
PROVANT of inferior quality		
PROVERB saw; adage; aphorism		
PROVIDE supply; produce; survey		
PROVINE (vine culture)		
PROVING establishing; testing		
PROVISO a condition		
PROVOKE infuriate; enrage; rouse		
PROVOST magistrate	rl	
PROWESS valour; skill; dexterity		
PROWEST most valiant, (obs.)		
PROWLED slunk; roved; roamed		
PROWLER stealthy stalker		
PROXIME nearest		
PROXIMO next month		
PRUDENT wise; cautious; frugal		
PRUDERY mock modesty		
PRUDISH very formal; puritanical		
PRUNING lopping; clipping; trimming		
PRURIGO an itch	md	
PRUSSIC acid; a cyanide	ch	
PRYTANY Athenian Council division		
PRYTHEE I pray thee!		
PSALTER psalm book; rosary		
PSCHENT royal crown of ancient Egypt		
PSOATIC (tenderloin)	md	
PSYCHAL spiritualistic		
PSYCHIC not based on materialism		
PTARMIC sneezing mixture	md	
PTERION (craniology)	md	
PTEROMA Greek peridrome; side-wall		
PTEROPE flying fox; fruit-bat	zo	
PTOMAIN ptomaine; toxic matter	md	
PTYALIN (saliva)	md	
PUBERAL of age		
PUBERTY the generative age		
PUBLISH announce; disclose; blazon		
PUCELLA wine-glass top opener	gs	
PUCELLE Joan of Arc		
PUCERON plant louse	zo	
PUCKERY wrinkled		
PUCKISH impish; mischievous		
PUDDING fruity farinaceous food		
PUDDLED stirred up the mud		

PUDDLER iron-worker		
PUDENCY modesty; bashfulness		
PUEBLAN Mexican aborigine		
PUERILE childish		
PUERING skin-steeping/softening	le	
PUFF-BOX compact		
PUFFERY \ extravagant;		
PUFFING / advertisement		
PUFFIER more swollen		
PUFFILY bombastically		
PUGAREE puggree; puggery; Ind. scarf		
PUGGING (sound prevention); ceramics		
PUGGREE Indian scarf for topee		
PUGMILL clay mill		
PUG-NOSE retroussé		
PULIALL herb pennyroyal	bt	
PULLIES pulley-wheels		
PULLING extracting; wresting; towing		
PULLMAN (railway carriage)		
PULL-OUT extensible		
PULPIFY mash		
PULPING reducing to pulp		
PULPOUS pulpy		
PULSATE throb; palpitate; quiver		
PULSING beating; vibrating; throbbing		
PULSION propulsion		
PUMMAGE crushed apples		
PUMPAGE the amount pumped		
PUMPING extracting information		
PUMPKIN pumpion; quashey; a gourd	bt	
PUMP-ROD part of engine	au	
PUNCHED perforated; struck		
PUNCHER a bruiser; a drover		
PUNCH-UP fist-fight (boxing)		
PUNCTUM marking dot; tiny aperture	zo	
PUNGENT acrid; caustic; tart		
PUNJABI an Indo-Aryan language		
PUNNAGE punning		
PUNNING quipping		
PUNSTER a pun maker		
PUNT-GUN for hijacking scull		
PUNTING gaming; (football)		
PUPATED formed a chrysalis	zo	
PURANIC (Brahmin scriptures)	rl	
PURBECK Dorset stone	mn	
PURFLED decorated	ar	
PURFLEW wrought border		
PURGING cleaning up; pruning		
PURITAN religious bigot		
PURLIEU slum; environs		
PURLINE timber-work		
PURLING rippling		
PURLOIN steal; pilfer; filch		
PURPLED dyed purple		
PURPLES livid spots	md	
PURPORT signification; import		
PURPOSE aim; intent; object		
PURPURA Tyrian purple	zo	
PURPURE heraldic purple	hd	
PURRING curring; (feline felicitude)		
PURROCK paddock		

PURSING wrinkling
PURSUED continued; hunted; practised
PURSUER plaintiff (Sc.)   lw
PURSUIT chase; search; calling
PURVIEW extent; scope; range
PUSHFUL enterprising; self-assertive
PUSHING vigorous; jostling; thrusting
PUSHPIN a game
PUSH-ROD auto engine part   au
PUSTAKA magic/divine book of bark
    strips (Indon.)
PUSTULE pimple   md
PUTAMEN fruit-stone; husk   bt
PUTAMEN lenticular nucleus   md
PUTRIFY rot; decay; decompose
PUTTIED fixed with putty
PUTTIER glazier
PUTTIES leg-wear; puttees
PUTTING (golf); (the weight)
PUTTOCK kite; buzzard   zo
PUTWITH acknowledgement, addenda for
    book
PUZZLED perplexed; mystified
PUZZLER poser; riddler
PYAEMIA blood-poisoning   md
PYAEMIC suffering from pyaemia   md
PYCNITE topaz   mn
PYCNIUM spermogonium in uredinales   bt
PYEBALD piebald
PYE-BOOK rules to determine Easter date
PYGMEAN pigmean; dwarfish
PYJAMAS also pajamas; nightwear
PYLORIC of stomach-intestine entry   zo
PYLORUS an outlet   md
PYRAMID triangular solid
PYRENIN paranuclein   cy
PYRETIC fever-reducer   md
PYREXIA fever   md
PYREXIC feverish   md
PYRITES an iron ore
PYRITIC (pyrites)
PYROGEN fever inducer   md
PYROSIS indigestion   md
PYROTIC caustic; burning   md
PYRRHIC war dance; costly
PYRROLE coal-tar constituent   ch
PYRUVIC of an α-keto acid   bc
PYTHIAD a period
PYTHIAN oracular
PYXIDIA capsules   bt

Q

QUABIRD night heron   zo
QUACKED boasted; practised quackery
QUACKLE croak; quack
QUADRAT filling piece in printing   pr
QUADREL square tile
QUADRIC quadratic
QUAFFED tippled; swilled; caroused

QUAFFER deep drinker; soaker; toper
QUAHAUG American clam   zo
QUAILED flinched; cowered; blenched
QUAKERS a sect
QUAKERY Quakerism
QUAKING shaking; quivering
QUALIFY entitle; regulate; dilute
QUALITY trait; attribute; grade
QUAMASH camass lily   b
QUANACO S. American llama   zo
QUANNET flat file   t
QUANTIC algebraic function
QUANTUM a sufficiency
QUARREL wrangle; brawl; bicker
QUARREL cross-bow bolt; diam. pane
QUARTAN every fourth day
QUARTER district; region; clemency
QUARTET quartette   m
QUARTIC of the fourth degree
QUARTZY (quartz)
QUASARS quasi-stellar radio sources
QUASHED rendered void; nullified
QUASHEY pumpkin; a gourd   b
QUASSIA bitter tonic   b
QUASSIN bitter extract   b
QUATERN a quarter; 4 pound loaf
QUAVERY tremulous; quivery; tottery
QUAYAGE quay dues
QUEACHY bog-like; unsteady; yielding
QUEENED played the queen
QUEENLY regal
QUEERED put at a disadvantage
QUEERER odder; rummier; stranger
QUEERLY quaintly; whimsically
QUELLED crushed; allayed; quenched
QUELLER subduer; represser
QUERCUS oak   b
QUERELA complaint
QUERENT inquirer; plaintiff   lv
QUERIED doubted; challenged
QUERIST questioner; interrogator
QUERLED twirled
QUERNAL oaken
QUESTED sought; requested
QUESTER a seeker; searcher; candidate
QUESTOR Roman treasury official
QUETZAL resplendent trogon   nm, z
QUIBBED quipped; sneered
QUIBBLE prevaricate; cavil; trifle
QUICKEN revive; rouse; expedite
QUICKER faster; more swiftly
QUICKIE a fatuous film
QUICKLY rapidly; speedily; pronto
QUIDDIT a quibble
QUIDDLE to potter
QUISCHE be still; calm; be silent
QUIETED calmed; assuaged; mollified
QUIETEN lull; allay; pacify; soothe
QUIETER more placid or secluded
QUIETLY peacefully; serenely
QUIETUS discharge; death

QUILLED pleated; crimped
QUILLET a quibble; a furrow
QUILLON part of a sword-guard
QUILTED padded; tufted
QUILTER coverlet maker
QUINARY in fives
QUINATE five-leafed   bt
QUININE (cinchona)   md, bt
QUINNAT king salmon   zo
QUINONE (benzene)   ch
QUINTAD pentad
QUINTAL a hundredweight   me
QUINTAL 100 lb or 100 kg   me
QUINTAN recurring ague   md
QUINTAR (Albania)   nm
QUINTET 5-part music   mu
QUINTIC fifth degree
QUINTUS the fifth (Latin)
QUIPPED quibbled; taunted
QUIRING singing in unison
QUITTAL repayment; requital
QUITTED abandoned; forsook; left
QUITTER shirker; horse ulcer; deserter   vt
QUITTOR chronic foot cartilage suppura-
tion   vt
QUI-VIVE alert
QUIXOTE a chivalrous Don
QUIZZED bantered; chaffed
QUIZZER a joker
QUODLIN codlin; an apple   bt
QUONDAM former
QUOTING citing; pricing
QUOTITY quantity

R

RABATED beaten down; abated
RABBANA raffia matting (Madagascar)
RABBITY petty; rabbit-like
RABBLER puddler; iron-worker
RABBONI Jewish title
RABIDLY frantically; maniacally
RABIFIC causing hydrophobia   md
RABINET ancient gun
RABIOUS raging mad
RACCOON N. American racoon   zo
RACE-CUP a trophy
RACEMED clustered   bt
RACEMIC acid from grapes   ch
RACEWAY sluice
RACKETY bobbery; clamorous
RACKING decanting; straining
RACQUET racket
RADDLED interwoven; painted
RADDOCK ruddock; robin   zo
RADIALE radiocarpal bone   md
RADIANT beaming; effulgent; shining
RADIATE sparkle; glitter; emit
RADICAL innate; extreme; inborn
RADICEL small root   bt

RADICLE root; corm; rootlet   bt
RADIOED transmitted by wireless
RADULAR rasping; rough
RAFFING sweeping; snatching
RAFFISH rakish; dissipated
RAFFLED notched; (lottery)
RAFFLER lottery organizer
RAFT-DOG iron clamp
RAFTING raft-work
RAG-BOLT iron holdfast
RAG-BUSH heathen shrine   bt
RAG-DUST rag refuse
RAGEFUL angered; wroth; ireful
RAG-FAIR old clothes sale
RAGGERY rags collectively
RAGGING plaguing; rampaging
RAG-SHOP ragpicker's emporium
RAGTIME syncopation   mu
RAGULED jagged   hd
RAG-WEED ragwort   bt
RAG-WOOL shoddy
RAGWORK mason's work using stones
RAGWORT rag-weed   bt
RAIDING foraying; pillaging
RAILBUS bus-engine railway coach   rw
RAILCAR self-propelled rail coach   rw
RAILING fencing; nagging; rating
RAILSAW portable saw   to
RAILWAY railroad
RAIMENT garb; vesture; apparel
RAINBOW water-refracted sunlight
RAINING pouring; showering
RAINMAP weather chart
RAISING erecting; levying; growing
RAKE-OFF rebate
RAKSHAS ghouls (Hindu mythology)
RALLIED recovered; reformed
RALLIES bouts; jamborees
RALLINE (water-rails, etc.)   zo
RAMADAN Mohammedan fast   rl
RAMAZAN Ramadan   rl
RAMBADE boarding platform   nt
RAMBLED sauntered; maundered
RAMBLER Dr Johnson's magazine
RAMBLER a climbing rose   bt
RAMEKIN a cheese savoury
RAMENTA scales on ferns   bt
RAMEOUS branching; ramulous
RAM-HEAD iron lever; a cuckold
RAMLINE guide line in ship-building
RAMMING thrusting; forcing
RAMMISH rank; strong-scented
RAMPAGE frolic
RAMPANT exuberant
RAMPART rampire; fortified mound
RAMPICK } dead-tree;
RAMPIKE } tree-stump
RAMPING creeping; climbing; bounding
RAMPION campanula   bt
RAMPLER a rover (Sc.)
RAMSKIN cheese cake; ramekin   bt

RAMSONS garlic, broad-leaved	bt
RAMSTAM reckless; headlong (Sc.)	
RAMULUS small branch	bt
RANCHED (stock farming)	
RANCHER stock-breeder	
RANCOUR deep-seated enmity	
RANGERS riflemen	
RANGIER scythe (heraldic)	hd
RANGING ranking; roving; extending	
RANIDAE the frogs	zo
RANKEST coarsest; most rancid	
RANKING grading; ranging	
RANKLED festered; smouldered	
RANSACK rummage; pillage; plunder	
RANTING orating; declaiming; raving	
RANTOCK goosander	zo
RAPE-OIL cole-seed oil	bt
RAPFULL full of wind	nt
RAPHAEL an archangel; a painter	
RAPHIDE plant-cell crystal	bt
RAPIDLY speedily; swiftly; despatch	
RAPLOCH homespun (Sc.)	
RAPPING knocking; hitting; beating	
RAPPING mould pattern loosening	fd
RAPPORT harmony; consonance	
RAPTURE ecstasy; beatitude; bliss	
RAREBIT dainty morsel	
RASHING thin layer of shale/poor coal	mn
RASORES gallinaceous birds	zo
RASPING grating; abrading	
RASTRUM a music-pen	mu
RATABLE taxable; assessable	
RATABLY by rate	
RATAFIA almond-flavoured biscuit	
RATATAT drumming	mu
RATCHED stretched; racked	
RATCHEL ratchil; loose stones	
RATCHET pawl; toothed bar	
RAT-HOLE retreat for rat	
RATITAE (ostriches, emus, kiwis)	zo
RATLINE ⎫ step of rigging ladder	
RATLING ⎭	nt
RAT-RACE career competition	
RAT-TAIL tapering	
RATTEEN twilled wool	
RATTERY apostacy	
RATTING quitting; abandoning	
RATTLED clattered; shaken	
RATTLER snake	zo
RATTOON young sugar-cane	bt
RAT-TRAP bicycle pedal	
RAUCITY hoarseness	
RAUCOUS harsh; roopy	
RAVAGED laid waste; devastated	
RAVAGER despoiler; plunderer	
RAVELIN part of a fort	
RAVENED preyed; plundered	
RAVENER ravager; devourer	
RAVINED gullied	
RAVIOLI meat-filled pasta cases (It.)	
RAWBONE gaunt, lean person	

RAWCOLD damp and cold (Shak.)	
RAWHEAD bugaboo	
RAWHIDE untanned skin	
RAWNESS immaturity; callowness	
RAWPORT porthole for an oar	nt
RAYLESS dark	
REACHED attained; arrived; stretched	
REACHER stretcher	
REACTED took violent action	
REACTOR atomic power generator	
READIED prepared	
READIER prompter; more glib	
READILY willingly; cheerfully	
READING recital; version; studying	
READMIT glove used when reading	
REAGENT active agent	ch
REAGREE reconcile	
REALGAR red arsenic	mn
REALIEN objects for study; teaching aids	
REALISM naturalism	
REALIST a facer of facts	
REALITY actuality; truth; verity	
REALIZE realise; convert into cash	
REALLOT re-assign	
REALTOR estate agent USA	
REAMING enlarging	
REANNEX reunite	
REAPING harvesting; gathering	
REAPPLY try it again	
REARGUE rehash	
REARING breeding; lifting, raising	
REARISE reascend	
REARMED re-equipped	
RE-AROSE got up again	
REAUMUR (thermometer)	
REAVING bereaving; ravaging	
REAWAKE rouse again	
REBATED blunted; diminished	
REBIRTH renascence	
REBLOOM impossible action	
REBOANT resounding; reverberating	
REBORED ennui resumed	
REBOUND bounce; recoil	
REBRACE race by rebels	
REBUILD re-edify	
REBUILT re-erected	
REBUKED chidden; upbraided	
REBUKER reproacher	
REBURSE repay	
RECARRY carry anew	
RECEDED retreated; withdrew	
RECEIPT a recipe; formula; quittance	
RECEIVE welcome; acquire; get	
RECENCY newness	
RECHEAT recall hounds	
RECITAL concert; narration	
RECITED narrated; rehearsed	
RECITER relater	
RECKING caring; heeding	
RECLAIM rescue; salve; regain	
RECLAME notoriety	

RECLASP refasten		
RECLINE lean; lie; rest; repose		
RECLOSE fail to keep open		
RECLUSE sequestered; a hermit		
RECOAST coast back		
RECOUNT tell; relate; enumerate		
RECOUPE heraldic division	hd	
RECOURE recover (Spens.)		
RE-COVER cover anew		
RECOVER rally; revive; retrieve		
RECROSS go back over		
RECRUIT enlist; recuperate; novice		
RECTIFY amend; correct; redress		
RECTION grammatical influence		
RECTORY rector's benefice	rl	
RECTRIX steering feather	zo	
RECURVE reflex		
RED-BIRD bull-finch	zo	
RED-BOOK a register		
RED-CENT copper cent	nm	
RED-CLAY raddle; reddle		
RED-COAT a soldier		
RED-COCK incendiary fire		
RED-CRAG Pliocene rock	mn	
RED-DEER the common stag	zo	
REDDEST ultra-radical		
REDDING arranging (Sc.)		
REDDISH rubicund; Titian		
RED-DRUM red-bass	zo	
RED-EYED needing sleep		
RED-FISH Pacific salmon	zo	
RED-HAND (Ulster)		
RED-HEAD a duck	zo	
RED-LEAD minium		
RED-LEGS purple sandpiper	zo	
REDNESS ruddiness		
REDORSE reverse of dorsal		
REDOUBT fort		
REDOUND conduce; lead; tend		
REDPOLL linnet	zo	
REDRAFT revised copy		
REDRAWN drawn again		
REDRESS remedy; reparation		
REDRIVE drive back		
RED-ROOT buckthorn	bt	
RED-SEAR to break when too hot		
RED-SEED small crustaceans	zo	
REDSKIN N. American Indian		
RED-TAIL North American buzzard	zo	
RED-TAPE routine		
REDUCED curtailed; abridged		
REDUCER contractor		
RED-WEED the poppy		
REDWING fieldfare	zo	
REDWOOD sequoia	bt	
RE-EDIFY rebuild		
REEDING moulding	ar	
REEFING shortening sail	ht	
REEKING fuming; smoking		
REELING staggering; vacillating		
REEMING caulking	nt	

RE-ENTRY regress; return		
RE-EQUIP rearm		
RE-ERECT rebuild		
REEVING (passing a rope)	nt	
REFEOFF reinvest in a fief		
REFEREE umpire; arbitrator; judge		
REFINED highly cultivated		
REFINER purifier; clarifier		
REFLAME flare up again		
REFLECT mirror; muse; mediate		
REFORGE fashion anew		
REFRACT to bend at an angle		
REFRAIN chorus; forgo; abstain		
REFRESH invigorate; revive; brace		
REFUGED took sanctuary		
REFUGEE a displaced person		
REFUSAL declination; denial		
REFUSED declined; denied; vetoed		
REFUSER repudiator		
REFUTED disproved; confuted		
REFUTER rebutter		
REGALED entertained sumptuously		
REGALIA insignia of sovereignty		
REGALLY royally		
REGATTA gondola race	nt	
REGENCY also regence		
REGIBLE governable		
REGIMEN regulation; diet		
REGNANT ruling		
REGORGE vomit		
REGRADE re-assess		
REGRANT grant again		
REGRATE retail		
REGREDE regrade (obs.)		
REGREET welcome again		
REGRESS return; re-entry		
REGULAR steady; systematic; normal		
REGULON enzyme-production gene group		
		gn
REGULUS star in Leo		
REGULUS line set in ruled surface	ma	
REIGNED ruled; administered		
REINING curbing; restraining		
REINTER to bury again		
REIT-BOK S. African buck	zo	
REJOICE revel; exult; gladden		
REJOINT make a new joint		
REJOURN adjourn; defer		
RELAPSE delapse; backsliding; revert		
RELATED akin; connected; recited		
RELATER relator; delator		
RELATOR informant	lw	
RELAXED loosened; slackened; abated		
RELAYED transmitted	ro	
RELEASE set free; emancipate; liberate		
RE-LEASE lease again		
RELIANT confident; self-assured		
RELIEVE release; allay; assuage		
RELIEVO rilievo; in relief		
RELIGHT rekindle; reignite		
RELIQUE a relic (Fr.)		

RELIVED lived again	**REPTILE** snake; serpent	zo
RELUMED rekindled	**REPULSE** rebuff; deter; reject	
RELYING depending; trusting	**REPUTED** alleged; deemed; reckoned	
REMAINS (literary productions)	**REQUERE** request (Spens.)	
REMANET delayed lawsuit — lw	**REQUEST** demand; entreat; solicit	
REMEANT coming back (obs.)	**REQUIEM** a mass	rl
REMEGIA a moth genus — zo	**REQUIRE** want; lack; desire; need	
REMERCY to thank (Spens.)	**REQUITE** repay; reward; avenge	
REMERGE merge again	**REREDOS** altar screen	rl
REMIGES flight feathers — zo	**RESCIND** revoke; quash; cancel	
REMIPED oar-shaped feet — zo	**RE-SCORE** try again	mu
REMISED released; surrendered — lw	**RESCUED** freed; liberated	
REMNANT residue; odd lot; fragment	**RESCUER** deliverer; saviour	
REMODEL refashion; remake; redesign	**RESEIZE** (legal confiscation)	lw
REMORSE anguish; compunction	**RESERVE** withhold; restraint	
REMOTER farther off	**RESHAPE** remould; remodel	
REMOULD shape anew	**RESIANT** resident	lw
REMOUNT a fresh horse — zo	**RESIDED** abode; inhered	
REMOVAL euphemism for murder	**RESIDER** sojourner; dweller	
REMOVED dislodged; abstracted	**RESIDUE** remainder; dregs	
REMOVER shifter	**RESILED** started back; receded	
REMPHAN Israelitish idol	**RESOLVE** determine; resolution	
REMPLOY for disabled workers	**RESOUND** reverberate; extol	
RENAMED rechristened	**RE-SOUND** sound again; echo	
RENDING ripping; tearing; severing	**RESPEAK** repeat; reply	
RENEGED denied; revoked	**RESPECT** revere; honour; esteem	
RENEWAL refreshment	**RESPIRE** breathe; inhale	
RENEWED repeated; rejuvenated	**RESPITE** reprieve; pause; rest	
RENEWER renovator	**RE-SPOKE** reiterated	
RENT-DAY time to pay or flit	**RESPOND** answer; accord; tally	
RENTIER estate or fund holder	**RESSAUT** a projection	a
RENTING letting; leasing	**RESTANT** persistent; remaining	
RENUENT nodding	**RESTATE** re-assert; recite	
REORDER bid again	**RESTAUR** claim for indemnity	lw
REPAINT (a golf ball)	**REST-DAY** the Sabbath	
REPAPER (a palindrome)	**RESTFUL** tranquil; quiescent; irenic	
REPINED fretted; murmured; envied	**RESTIFF** restive (obs.)	
REPINER plaintive person	**RESTILY** stubbornly; recalcitrantly	
REPIQUE (piquet)	**RESTING** reposing; relaxing; leaning	
REPLACE reinstate; refund	**RESTIVE** refractory; obstinate	
REPLAIT refold	**RESTOCK** replenish	
REPLETE crammed; fraught	**RESTORE** reinstate; repair; heal	
REPLEVY to bail — lw	**RE-STORE** return to store	
REPLICA a copy; duplicate	**RESUING** pre-mining technique	m
REPLIED answered; folded back	**RESUMED** renewed; continued	
REPLIER respondent	**RESURGE** rise again	
REPLUME to preen	**RETABLE** altar shelf for candles	
REPOINT sharpen; accentuate	**RETAKEN** recaptured	
REPONED replaced; relied	**RETAKER** recaptor	
REPOSAL rest; sleep; ease	**RETENUE** self-control	
REPOSED settled; reclined	**RETIARY** net-like, (gladiator)	
REPOSER slumberer	**RETICLE** small net; reticule	
REPOSIT deposit	**RETINAL** (retina)	m
REPRESS crush; check; restrain	**RETINOL** resin oil	
REPRIEF reproof (obs.)	**RETINUE** suite; escort; bodyguard	
REPRINT a subsequent edition	**RETIPED** having veined feet	a
REPRISE a deduction — lw	**RETIRAL** withdrawal; departure	
REPRIVE deprive (obs.)	**RETIRED** left; retreated; secluded	
REPROOF reprief; censure	**RETOUCH** re-engrave; revise	
REPROVE chide; upbraid	**RETOURN** to turn back (obs.)	
REPTANT creeping; reptilian — zo	**RETRACE** return by the same road	

RETRACT adjure; recant; revoke
RETRAIT portrait; retired (Spens.)
RETRATE retreat (Spens.)
RETREAD repair of a tyre
RETREAT recede; asylum; refuse
RETRIAL repeating court case   lw
RETRUDE to thrust back
RETRUSE abstruse; hidden; occult
RETTERY flax mill
RETTING prepared flax
RETYRED (motoring)
REUNIFY rejoin
REUNION social gathering
REUNITE reconcile; recombine
REURGED entreated again
REUTTER repeat; reiterate
REVALUE re-assess
REVELRY carousal; debauch; orgy
REVENGE requite; retaliate; vindicate
REVENUE income; return; reward
REVERED honoured; worshipped
REVERER venerator
REVERIE dreaminess; trance; vision
REVERSE misfortune; opposite
REVERSI a counter-game
REVERSO left-hand page of a book
REVESTU heraldic squaring   hd
REVILED aspersed; villified; abused
REVILER traducer; upbraider
REVINCE refute; disprove (obs.)
REVISAL revision; reviewal
REVISED amended; altered
REVISER also revisor; editor
REVISIT return to the same place
REVIVAL a religious awakening
REVIVED quickened; resuscitated
REVIVER invigorator; rouser
REVIVOR renewed action   lw
REVOKED reneged; repealed; quashed
REVOLVE rotate; spin; whirl; circle
REVOMIT regorge
REVVING spinning at speed
REWAKEN re-arouse
REWRITE transcribe
REYNARD the fox
RHABDOM rodlike body in arthropoda eye   zo
    zo
RHABDOS a straight spicule   bt
RHAETIC Rhaetian
RHAGADE wet-skin crack
RHAGOSE spongy
RHAMNUS buckthorn, etc.   bt
RHATANY Peruvian shrub   bt
RHEMISH (Rheims)
RHENISH (Rhine)
RHENIUM metallic element   ch
RHESIAN (Indian sacred monkey)   zo
RHIZINE ⎫ rhizina; root-like
RHIZOID ⎬   bt
RHIZOMA ⎫ sucker-root
RHIZOME ⎭   bt

RHIZOTA small aquatic animals   zo
RHIZOTE rooted   bt
RHODIAN Rhodesian; (Rhodes)
RHODIUM hard white metal   ch
RHODORA rhododendron   bt
RHOMBIS ⎫ oblique angled
RHOMBUS ⎭ parallelogram
RHONCUS harsh bronchial-tube sound   md
RHOPODE a marine invertebrate   zo
RHUBARB pudding plant   bt
RHYMING versifying
RHYMIST ballad-monger
RHYNCHO snouted
RHYPHUS genus of gnats   zo
RHYTINA dugong; manatee, etc.   zo
RIB-BAND (shipbuilding)   nt
RIBBING lampooning, ridiculing
RIBBONS driving reins
RIBLIKE lying like slats
RIBSTON pippin; an apple   bt
RICASSO part of rapier-blade
RICE-HEN American fowl   zo
RICINUS castor-oil plant   bt
RICKERS tree stems for spars
RICKETS softness of the bones   md
RICKETY shaky; unstable; feeble
RICKING wrenching; spraining
RICKSHA jinricksha; carriage
RICOTTA bland creamy Ital. cheese   ck
RIDABLE rideable
RIDDING freeing; banishing; clearing
RIDDLED full of holes
RIDDLER propounder of riddles
RIDERED stakes laid across bars
RIDOTTO musical entertainment (It.)
RIETBOK rietboc; reedbuck (S. Africa)   zo
RIFFLER curved file   to
RIFLING spiral grooving; ransacking
RIFTING riving; cleaving; splitting   nt
RIGAREE broken design band; collar   gs
RIGGING manipulating; tackle   nt
RIGGISH wanton
RIGGITE jester; trickster (obs.)
RIGHTED redressed; rectified; adjusted
RIGHTEN set right; settle
RIGHTER redresser of wrongs
RIGHTLY properly; correctly
RIGIDLY inflexibly; staunchly
RIGSDAG Danish Parliament
RIG-VEDA Vedic doctrine   rl
RIKSDAG Swedish Parliament
RILIEVO relievo; in relief
RILLING flowing; purling; rippling
RIMFIRE a cartridge
RIMLESS unframed
RIMMING making a border or edge
RIMPLED wrinkled; rumpled
RINDING peeling; excoriating
RING-DOG used for hauling timber   fr
RINGENT irregular and gaping
RINGHAL spitting cobra   zo

RINGING resounding	
RINGLET circlet	
RINGMAN third finger, Zulu chief	
RING-NET butterfly-net	
RING-SAW scroll-saw	to
RINKING roller-skating	
RINSING cleansing	
RIOLITE silver selenide	mn
RIOTING disorder; lawlessness	
RIOTISE riot; extravagance (Spens.)	
RIOTOUS turbulent; tumultuous	
RIPCORD parachute release cord	
RIPIENO supplementary	mu
RIPOSTE lightning repartee	
RIPPING splendid; tearing	
RIPPLED purled; rilled	
RIPPLER comb for flax	to
RIPPLET tiny ripple	
RIPSACK Californian whale	zo
RIPTIDE fast flowing current	
RISBERM glacis below jetties	
RISIBLE laughable; droll; absurd	
RISIBLY amusingly; farcically	
RISKIER more hazardous	
RISKING venturing; chancing; hazarding	
RISOTTO rice and onions	
RISSOLE an entrée	
RISTORI woman's jacket	
RITTOCK tern	zo
RIVALRY emulation; competition	
RIVERET small river; stream; rivulet	
RIVETED fastened	
RIVETER clincher	
RIVIERA fashionable resort	
RIVIERE a necklace of jewels	
RIVULET stream; brook; riveret	
RIZOMED heraldic grains	hd
ROADBED road foundation	
ROADCAR rural streetcar	
ROAD-HOG a motor pest	
ROADING team racing	
ROADMAN road repairer	
ROAD-MAP plan of road network	
ROADWAY highway; turnpike; autobahn	
ROAMING roving; wandering	
ROARING bellowing; shouting; bawling	
ROASTED parched; bantered	
ROASTER gridiron	
ROBBERY piracy; spoliation; pillage	
ROBBING stealing; depriving; theft	
ROBINET chaffinch	zo
ROBINIA acacia	bt
ROCK-CAM cam on rocking shaft	
ROCK-DOE chamois	zo
ROCK-EEL slippery customer	zo
ROCKERY rock garden	
ROCKIER more unstable	
ROCKILY reeling; tottery	
ROCKING lulling; staggering	
ROCK-OIL petroleum; naphtha	mn
ROCKOON balloon/rocket technique	sp
ROCK-TAR petroleum	mn
RODLIKE cylindrical	
ROD-LINE fishing line	
RODOMEL roses and honey	
ROD-RING (fishing-rod)	
RODSTER an angler	
ROE-BUCK male roe-deer	zo
ROE-DEER small deer species	zo
ROGUERY knavery; fraudulence	
ROGUISH arch; wanton; puckish	
ROILING riling; angering	
ROINISH roinous; mangy	
ROISTER to bluster; swagger; bully	
ROKEAGE parched Indian corn	
ROKELAY short cloak; roguelaure	
ROLLICK frolic	
ROLLING trundling; wallowing; lurching	
ROLLMOP cured spiced herring	ck
ROLLOCK rowlock; also rullock	nt
ROLLWAY an incline; a shoot	
ROMAIKA modern Greek dance	
ROMAINE cos; firm-leafed lettuce	
ROMALEA a locust genus	zo
ROMANCE historical fiction	
ROMANIC derived from Latin	
ROMAUNT a romance; exaggeration	
ROMEINE (antimony and lime)	mn
ROMEITE antimonite of calcium	mn
ROMMANY gipsy language	
ROMPERS children's overalls	
ROMPING frolicking; capering	
ROMPISH frisky; sportive; frolicsome	
RONCHIL ronquil, a N. Pacific fish	zo
RONDEAU verse with a refrain	mu
RONDENA Andalusian serenade	mu
RONDEUR rounded contour, shape	
RONGEUR surgical forceps	md
RONQUIL ronchil, sea-fish	zo
RONTGEN (X-rays)	
ROOFING materials for roof	
ROOFLET small roof	
ROOINEK an Englishman (S. Africa)	
ROOKERY (rooks); (seals); (penguins)	zo
ROOKING defrauding; fleecing	
ROOK-PIE unsavoury dish	
ROOMAGE stowage	
ROOMFUL quantity of roses	
ROOMIER more extensive	
ROOMILY spaciously	
ROOMING lodging	
ROOSTED perched; slept	
ROOSTER chanticleer	zo
ROOTAGE manner of rooting	
ROOTCAP tip at end of root	bt
ROOTERY pile of stumps	
ROOTING eradicating; implanting	
ROOTLED rummaged; dug	
ROOTLET radicle; a root fibre	b
ROPALIC club-shaped	
ROPEWAY aerial transport	
RORQUAL a whale	zo

ROSALIA progressive melody   mu
ROSATED crowned with roses
ROSEATE rosy; blushing
ROSEBAY willow-herb   bt
ROSE-BIT (for countersinking)   to
ROSE-BOX a plant   bt
ROSE-BUD what Citizen Kane said   bt
ROSE-BUG rose-chafer   zo
ROSE-CUT (diamond-cutting)
ROSE-HAW } the fruit of the wild rose   bt
ROSE-HIP }
ROSELET ermine's summer fur
ROSELLA a parakeet   zo
ROSELLE rose-mallow   bt
ROSEOLA a rash   md
ROSE-RED pretty pink
ROSETTA inscribed stone (Ptolemy V)
ROSETTE a favour
ROSIEST most blushing
ROSINED resined; gingered up
ROSLAND moorland
ROSOLIO raisin brandy
ROSSING removing bark
ROSTRAL beak-like
ROSTRUM platform; pulpit; a beak
ROSULAR (leaves in clusters)
ROTALIA foraminifers   zo
ROTATED revolved; spun; twirled
ROTATOR a rotor
ROTCHET red gurnard   zo
ROTCHIE little auk; sea-dove   zo
ROTELLA round shield
ROTIFER an animalcule   zo
ROTODIP car-painting technique
ROTONDE ruff; cope (Fr.)
ROTTING decaying; fooling
ROTTOLO Levantine weight   me
ROTULAR (patella)   md
ROTUNDA circular building
ROUCHED puckered
ROUELLE wheel-like amulet
ROUERIE debauchery
ROUGHED rasped; (horse-shoes)
ROUGHEN scarify; coarsen
ROUGHER ruder; harsher; coarser
ROUGHIE dried heath (Sc.)
ROUGHLY boisterously; crudely
ROUGH-UP violent fight
ROUGING painting with rouge
ROULADE melodious passage   mu
ROULEAU packet of coins
ROUNDED curved; turned
ROUNDEL a Norman shield; a ballad
ROUNDER more like a circle
ROUNDLY boldly; openly; plainly
ROUND-UP a rodeo
ROUPING selling by auction (Sc.)
ROUSANT starting up   hd
ROUSING stimulating; brisk; lively
ROUSTER vagrant; vagabond
ROUTHIE plentiful; abundant (Sc.)

ROUTIER armed brigand (Fr.)
ROUTINE regularity; system
ROUTING rooting; defeating
ROUTISH clamorous; disorderly
ROWABLE a truly oarful state
ROWBOAT pleasure vessel   nt
ROWDIER more uproarious or rampant
ROWDILY turbulently; noisily
ROWLOCK rollock; rullock   nt
ROWPORT oar-hole
ROYALET petty king; princelet
ROYALLY regally; imperially
ROYALTY author's perquisite
ROYNISH roinish; mangy
ROYSTON hooded crow   zo
ROYTISH rowdy; wild (obs.)
ROZELLE hibiscus   bt
RUB-A-DUB beat of drum
RUBASSE Ancona ruby   mn
RUBBING chafing; tracing; scouring
RUBBISH trash; litter; lumber
RUB-DOWN aphrodisiac
RUBELLA German measles   md
RUBIATE madder
RUBICAN roan
RUBICEL variety of ruby   mn
RUBICON boundary; fateful river
RUBIFIC making red
RUBIOUS ruby-red
RUBYING reddening
RUCHING a plaited frilling
RUCKING creasing; ruffling
RUCKLED wrinkled; rucked
RUCTION uproar; turmoil; disturbance
RUDDIED reddened
RUDDIER rosier; more rubicund
RUDDILY glowingly
RUDDLED interwoven; ochred
RUDDOCK robin; apple   bt, zo
RUDERAL waste growth   bt
RUDESBY uncivil fellow (Shak.)
RUELLIA a plant genus   bt
RUE-WORT herb of grace   bt
RUFFIAN desperado; apache; rascal
RUFFING trumping; ruffling
RUFFLED disordered; agitated
RUFFLER a bully
RUGGING heavy napped cloth
RUINATE demolish; destroy (Shak.)
RUINING wrecking; demolishing
RUINOUS pernicious; calamitous
RULABLE allowable; governable
RULLION veldt-shoe; virago
RUMBLED reverberated
RUMBLER tum
RUMINAL ruminant   zo
RUMMAGE search; ransack
RUMMIER stranger; droller; quainter
RUMMILY oddly; whimsically
RUMNESS queerness; oddity
RUMPLED rimpled; crushed

RUM-SHOP a tavern
RUNAWAY fugitive; deserter; renegade
RUNDALE land tenure
RUNDLED rounded like a rung
RUNDLET small barrel; runlet
RUN-DOWN exhausted; weak; anaemic
RUN-LINE long straight rapidly painted line
RUNNING in succession, careering
RUN-OVER continuation over page/body
RUPTION eruption
RUPTIVE ruptile; liable to snap
RUPTURE fracture; breach; rift
RURALLY rustically
RUSALKA water-nymph (Rus.)
RUSHING dashing; careering; flying
RUSH-MAT reed pad
RUSH-NUT edible tuber   bt
RUSSETY reddish-brown
RUSSIAN of Russia
RUSSIFY to muscovate
RUSSULA red fungus   bt
RUSTFUL rusty
RUSTICA ancient Rom. manuscript style
RUSTIER less practised
RUSTILY fustily; mustily
RUSTING oxidizing
RUSTLED stirred
RUSTLER cattle-thief
RUSTRED lozenge-shaped   hd
RUTHFUL compassionate
RUTTIER routier, bearings chart   nv
RUTTING grooving; furrowing; pairing
RUTTISH lustful
RYE-MOTH a havest pest   zo
RYE-WOLF (German folk lore)   zo
RYE-WORM larva of rye-moth   zo

S

SABAISM } star worship, ancient religion
SABEISM } of Persia and Chaldea
SABAOTH armies (Hebrew)
SABBATH day of rest
SABELLA sea-worms   zo
SABRING cutting with a sabre
SABURRA grittiness of the tongue
SACCADE sudden check   mu
SACCATA molluscs   zo
SACCATE sack-like
SACCULE small pouch
SACELLA altars; sanctuaries
SACKAGE pillage
SACKBUT sacbut; dulcimer   mu
SACKFUL bagful
SACKING looting; plundering
SACODES beetle genus   zo
SACRARY a holy place (obs.)
SACRING consecration   rl
SACRIST sacristan; a sexton   rl
SADDEST most dismal and depressing

SADDLED loaded; hampered
SADDLER owner of wells
SAD-EYED mournful
SADIRON box-iron; flat-iron
SADNESS sorrowfulness; melancholy
SADTREE night jasmine   bt
SAFFIAN (tanned skins)
SAFFRON plant; a colour; flavour   bt, ck
SAGAMAN a bard; narrator of sagas
SAGATHY woollen stuff
SAGESSE wisdom (Fr.)
SAGGARD box for baking porcelain
SAGGING bending; including
SAGITTA a Northern constellation; an arrow (Lat.)
SAGOUIN capuchin monkey   zo
SAGUARO giant cactus   bt
SAHLITE augite   mn
SAIL-ARM (windmill)
SAILING cruising   nt
SAIMIRI squirrel monkey   zo
SAINTED canonized
SAINTLY holy; devout; religious
SAIRING enough (Sc.)
SAIVISM worship of Siva   rl
SALABLE saleable; vendible
SALADIN a Soldan; a Sultan
SALAMBA fishing device (Manila)
SALAMIS insect genus   zo
SALIANT salient; leaping; projecting
SALICIN willow extract   ch
SALIENT Ypres; prominent
SALIERE salt-cellar (Fr.)
SALIGOT water caltrops   bt
SALIQUE salic (male succession)
SALIVAL salivary
SALLIED dashed out
SALLOWY yellowish; jaundiced
SALMIAC sal-ammoniac   ch
SALMINE fish-testicle protamine   ch
SALPIAN ascidian   zo
SALPINX Eustachian tube   md
SALSAFY } oyster plant;   bt
SALSIFY } purple goat's beard
SALSOLA glass-wort   bt
SALTANT dancing; leaping
SALTANT suddenly developed variant   bl
SALTATE to dance; leap; jump; skip
SALT-BOX salt cellar
SALT-CAT pigeon medicine
SALTERN salt factory
SALTIER saltire
SALTING sea-marsh; pickling; curing
SALTIRE St Andrew's cross
SALTISH brackish; briny
SALT-PAN evaporating pan
SALT-PIT Russian place of work
SALUTED honoured; kissed; greeted
SALUTER that which salutes
SALVAGE rescue; compensation
SALVETE greetings to new members

288

SALVING healing; restoration		
SAMADHI broken; mind/body link in yoga		
SAMBHUR Indian stag	zo
SAMBUCA ancient harp	mu
SAMBUKE sambuca	mu
SAMIOTE native of Samos	
SAMISEN Japanese guitar	
SAMNITE Sabine tribe	
SAMOGON illicitly distilled vodka (Rus.)	
SAMOLUS primrose genus	bt
SAMOVAR Russian tea-urn	
SAMOYED sledge-dog; Mongolian	zo
SAMPLED tried; tasted	
SAMPLER needlework; pattern	
SAMSHOO rice spirit (China)	
SAMURAI Japanese military class	
SANCTUM a refuge; a shrine	rl
SANCTUS a hymn	rl
SANDBAG a convenient weapon	
SAND-BAR estuarine barrier	
SANDBED a mould	
SANDBOX also a W. Indian tree	bt
SAND-BOY proverbially a happy lad	
SANDBUG digger-wasp	zo
SANDBUR a weed	bt
SAND-DAB plaice	zo
SAND-EEL small fish	zo
SANDERS red sandal-wood	bt
SAND-FLY a biting midge	zo
SANDING burying oysters	
SANDISH gritty; friable	
SANDJET sand-blast	
SAND-LOB lug-worm	zo
SANDMAN children's sleep-giver	
SAND-PIT source of sand	
SAND-RAT the camass rat	zo
SANHITA Vedic hymns	
SANICLE healing plant	bt
SANKHYA Hindu philosophy	
SAPAJOU S. Amer. spider-monkey	zo
SAPERDA boring beetles	zo
SAP-HEAD (fortification)	
SAPHENA prominent vein	md
SAPIENT wise; sage; clever; astute	
SAPLESS dry; not juicy	
SAPLING young tree	bt
SAPLING young grey-hound	zo
SAPONIN soapwort extract	
SAPPHIC (Sappho)	
SAPPING undermining	
SAPPLES soap-suds (Sc.)	
SAPROBE plant growing in foul water	
SAPSAGO a green Swiss cheese	
SAPWOOD the alburnum	bt
SARACEN Arab	
SARAFAN Russian gala-dress	
SARAWAK glossy yellow cane	
SARCASM irony; satire; ridicule	
SARCELE partly cut through	
SARCINA fungoid plant	bt
SARCINE (muscular tissue)	md
SARCODE protoplasm	
SARCODY conversion to fleshlike state	
SARCOID flesh-like	
SARCOMA tumour	md
SARCOUS fleshy	
SARDANA folk dance (Catalan)	
SARDINE the young of the pilchard	zo
SARDIUS sard; a quartz	mn
SARGINA mullet genus	zo
SARIGUE opossum (Brazil)	zo
SARKING roof sheathing	
SARMENT a runner; filiform stem	bt
SARPLAR sarpler; packing cloth	
SARSNET fine woven silk	
SARTAGE forest clearing	
SASHERY sashes	
SASHING window framing	
SASSABY tsessebe; hartebeest	zo
SASSING cheeking; saucing	
SATANIC infernal; diabolical; devilish	
SATCHEL small sack or container	
SATIATE glutted; to cloy; to gorge	
SATIETY a surfeit	
SATINET thin satin	
SATIRIC sarcastic; ironical; mordant	
SATISFY gratify; requite; settle	
SATRAPY Persian province	
SATSUMA Japanese pottery; citrus fruit	bt
SATTARA ribbed woollen material	
SATTEEN ratteen; thick woollen fabric	
SATYRAL Satyr-like	
SATYRIC lustful	
SATYRUS orang-utan genus	zo
SAUCIER ruder; more impudent	
SAUCILY pertly; flippantly; pungently	
SAUCING sassing; seasoning	
SAUNTER dawdle; stroll; dally	
SAURIAN lizard; reptile	zo
SAUROID reptilian	
SAUSAGE minced meat packed into skin	ck
SAUTOIR diagonal ribbon	hd
SAVABLE salvable	
SAVAGED attacked brutally	
SAVANNA treeless plain	
SAVARIN syrup-soaked yeast cake	ck
SAVE-ALL an economizer	
SAVELOY red smoked pork sausage	ck
SAVIGNY red Burgundy wine	
SAVINGS a nest-egg	
SAVIOUR Messiah	rl
SAVOURY of grateful savour	
SAW-BACK a caterpillar	zo
SAWBILL goosander; merganser	zo
SAWBUCK sawhorse	
SAWDUST carpentry by-product	
SAWFILE triangular file	to
SAWFISH serrated-proboscis fish	zo
SAWHORN an insect	zo
SAWMILL lumber factory	
SAWWHET Acadian owl	zo
SAWWORT a plant	bt

SAXHORN brass wind-instrument   **mu**
SAXONIC Saxon
SAY-CAST coarse part of wool, from tail   **tx**
SAYETTE serge; woollen yarn
SCABBED mean; worthless
SCABBLE scapple; (stone-dressing)
SCABIES the itch   **md**
SCABRID scabrous; rough; rugged
SCADDLE skaddle; hurtful; impish
SCAGLIA Italian calcareous rock   **mn**
SCALADE ⎱ assault by escalade
SCALADO ⎰
SCALARY stepped like a ladder
SCALDED immersed in boiling water
SCALDER Norse minstrel or bard
SCALDIC (Norse ballads)
SCALENE irregular triangle
SCALING removal of loosened rock   **mn**
SCALING fish scales; boiler cleaning
SCALLED scurfy; scabby
SCALLOP scollop; shellfish   **zo**
SCALLOP pilgrim badge; (border)
SCALOPS American shrew-moles   **zo**
SCALPED laid bare
SCALPEL dissecting knife   **md**
SCALPER hair-raising savage
SCAMBLE shamble; scramble; mangle
SCAMMEL bar-tailed godwit   **zo**
SCAMMUM geometrical figure
SCAMPED skimped
SCAMPER scurry; run; hasten
SCANDAL disgrace; infamy; discredit
SCANDIX Venus' comb   **bt**
SCANNED scrutinized; perused
SCANNER television or radar beam
SCANTED limited; stinted
SCANTLE cut into small pieces
SCANTLY scantily; niggardly
SCAPNET minnow-net
SCAPPLE stone-dressing
SCAPULA shoulder blade   **md**
SCARCER rarer; less plentiful
SCARFED (timber joint)
SCARIFY to scratch; to harrow
SCARING affrighting; daunting
SCARLET bright orangish red
SCAROID like parrot fish
SCARPED made precipitous
SCARRED disfigured
SCARVES kerchiefs; cravats
SCATHED injured; damaged; hurt
SCATTER disperse; strew; dispel
SCAUPER engraver's tool   **to**
SCAURIE young gull (Sc.)
SCENERY prospect; view; landscape
SCENTED perfumed; smelt; suspected
SCEPSIS philosophic doubt
SCEPTIC skeptic, a doubter
SCEPTRE royal mace
SCEPTRY rather royal

SCHAPPE spun silk
SCHELLY white fish   **zo**
SCHEMED plotted; planned; contrived
SCHEMER intriguer; plotter
SCHEPEN magistrate (Dutch)
SCHERZO playfully   **mu**
SCHESIS habitude; wont
SCHETIC constitutional; habitual
SCHINUS mastic-tree   **bt**
S-CHISEL well-boring cutter   **to**
SCHISMA tonal difference   **mu**
SCHLICH ore slime
SCHLOSS castle; ancient seat (Ger.)
SCHMUCK unsophisticated person; idiot (Jew.)
SCHNAPS schnapps; akvavit; eau de vie
SCHOLAR student; pupil; disciple
SCHOLIA marginal notes
SCHORLY tourmaline   **mn**
SCIATIC affecting the hip   **md**
SCIBILE knowable
SCIENCE knowledge; reduced to system
SCINCUS lizard; skink; a saurian   **zo**
SCIOLTO with abandon   **mu**
SCIRPUS bulrush genus   **bt**
SCISSEL ⎱ metal clippings
SCISSIL ⎰
SCISSOR to cut
SCIURUS squirrel genus   **zo**
SCLERAL hard; ossified   **md**
SCLERIA sedges   **bt**
SCOBINA ends of grass   **bt**
SCOFFED mocked; jeered; derided
SCOFFER a taunter; ridiculer
SCOLDER chided; nagged; rebuked
SCOLDER railer; upbraider
SCOLITE fossil worm   **mn**
SCOLLOP scallop   **zo**
SCOMBER mackerel genus   **zo**
SCOONED skimmed; glided
SCOONER a schooner   **nt**
SCOOPED hollowed out; dredged
SCOOPER a water-fowl; the avocet   **zo**
SCOOTED bolted; squirted
SCOOTER ice-boat; toy; light motorcycle
SCOPATE brush-like
SCOPTIC bantering; jesting
SCOPULA small tuft of hairs   **zo**
SCORIAC ashy
SCORIAE volcanic ashes   **mn**
SCORIFY reduce to ashes
SCORING recording; scratching
SCORNED disdained; spurned
SCORNER contemner; flouter
SCORPER a gouge   **to**
SCORPIO (Zodiac); scorpion   **zo**
SCOTICE in Scottish   **rl**
SCOTISM doctrine of Duns Scotus
SCOTIST a theologian   **rl**
SCOTOMA blind spot   **md**
SCOTOMY scotoma; dizziness   **md**

SCOURED scurried; purged; rinsed
SCOURER scrubber; polisher; scraper
SCOURGE lash; chastise; plague
SCOUTED scorned; ridiculed
SCOUTER stone-flaker
SCOWLED registered displeasure
SCRAGGY lean and bony
SCRANCH scrunch; grind
SCRANKY scraggy; lank (Sc.)
SCRANNY lean; spare
SCRAPED erased; rubbed; rasped
SCRAPER miser; indifferent fiddler
SCRAPIE chronic nervous sheep disease   vt
SCRAPPY fragmentary
SCRATCH lacerate; zero handicap
SCRATCH withdraw from contest
SCRAWLY scribbled; ill-formed
SCRAWNY raw-boned
SCREECH scraich; scraigh
SCREEVE to write begging letters
SCREWED twisted; tipsy
SCREWER screw-driver; extortioner
SCRIBAL clerical
SCRIBED wrote; recorded; marked
SCRIBER engraving tool   to
SCRIEVE glide swiftly (Sc.)
SCRIMER fencer (Shak.)
SCRINGE cringe; flinch; grate
SCRITCH screech; a thrush   zo
SCROGGY having thick undergrowth
SCROOGE scrudge; squeeze
SCROUGE squeeze; to crowd
SCROTAL of the scrotum
SCROTUM testicle sac in mammals   zo
SCRUBBY stunted; squabby
SCRUFFY scurfy; scaly
SCRUNCH crunch; crush
SCRUPLE 20 grains, troy weight   me
SCRYING crystal gazing
SCUDDED ran before the wind   nt
SCUDDLE scuttle; skuttle
SCUDLER a scullion
SCUFFLE struggle; a hoe   to
SCULLED rowed   nt
SCULLER an oarsman
SCULPIN sea-fish; dragonet; bull-head
SCUMBER fox-dung   zo
SCUMBLE overlay painting
SCUMMER a skimmer of scum
SCUNNER loathing; prejudice (Sc.)
SCUPPER vent; annihilate
SCUPPET scoppet; shovel
SCURRIL scurrilous; foul-mouthed
SCURRIT lesser tern   zo
SCURVEY vitamin-deficiency disease   md
SCUTAGE feudal tax
SCUTATE like a shield
SCUTTER scurry
SCUTTLE (coal); hatchway; sink   nt
SCYMNUS ladybirds; sharks   zo
SCYPHUS a large drinking-cup (Greek)

SCYPHUS podetium end widening   bt
SCYTALE secret message (Greek)
SCYTALE coral snake   zo
SCYTHED mowed; cut
SCYTHIC scythian
SEA-BANK protective bank
SEA-BASS marine fish   zo
SEA-BEAN small univalve shell   bt, zo
SEA-BEAR seal; polar bear   zo
SEA-BEAT lashed by the waves
SEA-BEET rare vegetable   bt
SEA-BELT fucus plant   bt
SEA-BIRD aquatic bird   zo
SEA-BOAT (sea-worthy)
SEA-BORN produced by the sea
SEA-CALF common seal   zo
SEA-CARD compass card   nt
SEA-CLAM a bivalve   zo
SEA-COAL cash   mn
SEA-COCK gurnard; a valve   zo
SEA-COOK marine father   nt
SEA-COOT exotic ocean bird   zo
SEA-CORN spawn   zo
SEA-CRAB ocean crustacean   zo
SEA-CROW cormorant   zo
SEA-DACE bass   zo
SEA-DOVE little auk   zo
SEA-DUCK eider-duck   zo
SEA-FIRE phosphorescence
SEA-FISH cod and others   zo
SEA-FOAM meerschaum   mn
SEA-FOLK sailors
SEA-FOOD fish as food   zo
SEA-GAGE depth gauge
SEA-GATE harbour bar
SEA-GIRT insular
SEA-GOWN dress worn at sea
SEAGULL marine bird   zo
SEA-HAAR sea-mist
SEA-HALL hall below the sea
SEA-HARE mollusc   zo
SEA-HAWK a skua   zo
SEAHOLM sea-holly   bt
SEAKALE a cruciferous plant   bt
SEA-KING a viking
SEA-LACE (seaweed)   bt
SEA-LARK the dunlin   zo
SEA-LEGS acclimatization to sailing
SEALERY seal-fishing station
SEALIKE unrivery
SEA-LILY sea-urchin   zo
SEA-LINE horizon; sky-line
SEALING confirming; seal-hunting
SEA-LION large seal   zo
SEAL-OFF closure
SEA-LUCE hake   zo
SEA-MAID mermaid
SEA-MALL sea-gull   zo
SEA-MARK land or sea-mark
SEA-MILE geographical mile; 6080 feet (1853 m)

SEAMING sewing together; scarring	
SEA-MINK whiting	zo
SEA-MONK monk-seal	zo
SEA-MOSS seaweed	bt
SEAM-SET tinman's punch	to
SEA-OOZE soft mud	
SEA-PASS passport	
SEA-PEAR sea-squirt	zo
SEA-PECK the dunlin	zo
SEA-PERT the opah fish	zo
SEA-PIKE pike	zo
SEA-PINK the thrift	bt
SEA-PORK an ascidian	zo
SEAPORT harbour for large ships	
SEA-REED mat grass	bt
SEARING cauterizing	
SEA-RISK marine hazard	
SEA-ROLL sea-cucumber	zo
SEA-ROOM manoeuvre space	
SEA-ROSE sea-anemone	zo
SEA-RUFF sea-bream	zo
SEA-SALT cookery condiment	mn
SEASICK mal-de-mer	
SEASIDE beach	
SEA-SLUG a nudibranch	zo
SEA-TANG sea-tangle-weed	
SEATING installing; settling	
SEA-TOAD the angler	zo
SEA-TOST common or garden tost	
SEA-TURN a gale from the sea	
SEAVIEW glimpse of the briny	
SEA-WALL retaining wall	
SEA-WANE wampum	
SEAWARD toward the sea	
SEA-WARE seaweed; sea-wrack	bt
SEAWEED tangle; algae	bt
SEA-WHIP a zoophyte	zo
SEA-WIFE wrasse	zo
SEA-WING a sail	
SEA-WOLD imaginary tract	
SEA-WOLF wolf fish; pirate	zo
SEA-WORM marine annelid	zo
SEBACIC fatty acid	ch
SEBILLA wooden bowl	
SEBUNDY a sepoy	
SECANCY intersection	
SECEDED withdrew; separated	
SECEDER separationist	
SECHIUM genus of gourds	bt
SECLUDE segregate; shut up	
SECONDO bass of duet	mu
SECRECY privacy; stealth; reticence	
SECRETE hide; conceal; cache; yield	
SECTANT geometric figure	
SECTARY sectarian	
SECTILE sliceable	
SECTION portion; division; segment	
SECTIST dissenter	
SECTIVE divisible	
SECULAR of the world; lay; temporal	
SECURED obtained; ensured; fastened	

SECURER protector; guardian; safer	
SEDILIA altar seats	rl
SEDUCED enticed; led astray	
SEDUCER a libertine	
SEEABLE visible	
SEE-CAWK the American skunk	zo
SEED-BAG germ-pouch	
SEED-BED plantation	
SEED-BUD germ of the fruit	bt
SEED-COD seed-basket; husk	
SEEDFUL promising; hopeful	
SEEDILY shabbily	
SEEDING (tournaments); sowing	
SEED-LAC dried resin	
SEED-LOP seed container	bt
SEED-OIL linseed oil	
SEEKING inquiring; questing	
SEELING closing the eyelids	
SEEMING specious; guise; apparent	
SEEPAGE leakage; oozings	
SEETHED boiled; soaked	
SEETHER boiling pot	
SEGGROM ragwort	bt
SEGMENT a portion; section	
SEINING netting fish	
SEISING taking possession	lw
SEISMAL seismic; (earthquake)	
SEISTAN Persian summer north wind	mt
SEISURA Australian fly-catchers	zo
SEIURUS wagtail genus	zo
SEIZING (ropes); grappling; binding	
SEIZURE grasp; possession	lw
SEJEANT sitting	hd
SELACHE shark genus	zo
SELENIC (selenium)	ch
SELF-FED automatic	
SELFISH egotistical; mean; ungenerous	
SELFISM selfishness	
SELFIST egoist	
SELINUM milk-parsley	bt
SELLING vending; hawking; betraying	
SELTZER mineral water	
SELVAGE selvedge; border	
SEMATIC significant	
SEMEION metrical mark	
SEMI-APE a lemur	zo
SEMI-GOD demi-god	
SEMILOR imitation gold	
SEMINAL rudimentary; original	
SEMINAR teacher in a seminary, special study group	
SEMIPED (prosody); a half-foot	
SEMI-RAG paper with some rag content	
SEMITIC Jewish; Hebrew	
SENATOR a counsellor	
SENATUS governing body	
SENCION } groundsel; ragwort	bt
SENECIO }	
SENDING despatching; forwarding	
SEND-OFF farewell party	
SENEGAL African fire-bird	zo

SENIORY council of elders
SENSATE sensible
SENSILE sensitive
SENSING understanding; feeling
SENSION perception
SENSISM sensualism
SENSIST sensationalist
SENSORY nerve system   md
SENSUAL voluptuous
SEPIARY ⎫
SEPIOID ⎭ referring to cuttlefish   zo
SEPIOST cuttle-bone   zo
SEPPUKU hara-kiri (Jap.)
SEPTATE partitioned
SEPTIME fencing posture
SEQUELA a consequence   md
SEQUENT following; succeeding
SEQUOIA Californian red-wood   bt
SERAPIS Apis; Goddess of fertility
SERBIAN Servian
SERENED tranquilized
SERENER calmer; more placid
SERENOA dwarf-palms (Florida)   bt
SERFAGE serfdom; slavery
SERFDOM villenage; thraldom
SERIATE in series; serial
SERICIN silk
SERICON alchemic red
SERIEMA cariama; (heron)   zo
SERIFIC silk-producing
SERINGA flowering shrub   bt
SERINUS canary genus   zo
SERIOLA amber fish   zo
SERIOUS grave; sedate; staid
SERMENT oath
SERPENT snake; reptile   zo
SERPIGO ring-worm   md
SERPULA sea-worms   zo
SERRATE serrous; notched
SERRIED at close interval
SERRULA comblike ridge on chelicerae
  zo
SERTOLI of seminiferous tubule cells   zo
SERTULE collection of plants   bt
SERVAGE servitude; enthralment
SERVANT retainer; henchman; menial
SERVIAN Serbian; Serb
SERVICE duty; performance; utility
SERVILE fawning; sycophantic
SERVING ministering; (tennis)   rl
SERVITE mendicant monk, 13th Cent.
SESAMUM sesame genus   bt
SESOTHO Basuto language (S. Africa)
SESSILE (no stalk)   bt
SESSION meeting; assize; sitting
SESTINA sestine; verse (Fr.)
SESTOLE sextuplet
SETARIA spiky grasses   bt
SET-BACK check; reverse; recess   ar
SET-DOWN a rebuff
SETLESS no score; tennis   mu

SETTIMA ⎫
SETTIMO ⎭ the interval of a seventh
SETTING appointing; congealing
SETTLED fixed; paid; sank; serene
SETTLER coloniser; arbitrator
SETWALL valerian   bt
SETWORK (boat-building); (plaster)
SEVENTH ordinal number
SEVENTY cardinal number
SEVERAL sundry; diverse; various
SEVERED cut; rent; divided
SEVERER stricter; simple
SEVRUGA caviare-fish   zo
SEWED-UP stranded   nt
SEXFOIL six-leafed plant   bt
SEXLESS of indeterminate gender
SEXTAIN (six lines)
SEXTANS Roman bronze coin   nm
SEXTANT optical instrument   nt
SEXTERN quire of 6 sheets   pp
SEXTILE planet aspect
SEXUALE sexually-reproducing individual
  zo

SHABASH bravo! (Pers.)
SHACKED tramped; hibernated
SHACKLE manacle; gyve; bond; fetter
SHADFLY May-fly   zo
SHADIER more dubious
SHADILY umbrageously
SHADINE American sardine   zo
SHADING screening; tinting
SHADOOF water-raising device (Nile)
SHADOWY obscure; dim; gloomy
SHAFTED handled; hafted
SHAGGED shaggy; rough; rugged
SHAHEEN peregrine falcon   zo
SHAITAN Satan (Arabic)
SHAKE-UP upheaval reorganisation
SHAKILY insecure; precariously
SHAKING quaking; jarring; jolting
SHALLON an edible fruit   bt
SHALLOP rowing boat; skiff   nt
SHALLOT small type of onion   bt
SHALLOW superficial; rudd-fish   zo
SHAMBLE shuffle along
SHAMING humiliating; abasing
SHAMMED simulated; feigned
SHAMMER impostor; malingerer
SHAMPOO hair-washing
SHANDRY rickety conveyance (Irish)
SHANGIE shackle (Sc.)
SHANGTI Chinese for God   rl
SHANKED (golf)
SHAPELY finely formed
SHAPING moulding; fashioning
SHARDED beetle-winged   zo
SHARING apportioning; dividing
SHARKED cheated; duped; gulled
SHARKER shark-hunter
SHARPED tricked; defrauded; duped
SHARPEN strop; point; whet

SHARPER a trickster; cheat; rogue
SHARPIE oysterman's boat   nt
SHARPLY keenly; acutely; tartly
SHASTER Hindu Bible   rl
SHASTRA sacred Hindu book   rl
SHATTER splinter; disrupt; smash
SHAVIAN (Bernard Shaw)
SHAVING slicing; paring; grazing
SHEAFED bundled in sheaves
SHEARED reaped; cut through
SHEARER clipper; reaper; cutter
SHEATHE encase; cover
SHEATHY like a scabbard
SHEAVED collected in sheaves
SHEBANG store; saloon
SHEBEEN Irish whiskey shop
SHEDDER emitter; diffuser
SHEERED moved away
SHEETED covered with sheets
SHELLAC resin lac   bt
SHELLED bombarded; husked
SHELLER huller; shucker
SHELTER screen; asylum; refuge
SHELTIE Shetland pony   zo
SHELVED put aside; pigeonholed
SHELVES ledges
SHEPPEY sheep-cote
SHERBET a cooling drink
SHEREEF an amir; emir
SHERIAT Islamic law   lw
SHERIFF county officer   lw
SHEWING showing; demonstration
SHIFTED changed; altered; quitted
SHIFTER remover; contriver
SHIITES Persian sectarians
SHIKARI hunter (India)
SHILPIT washy; feeble (Sc.)
SHIMMED wedged
SHIMMER gleam; glisten; glimmer
SHINGLE tile; style of hair-cutting
SHINGLY pebbly
SHINING resplendent; coruscating
SHINNED climbed
SHIP-BOY sailor's solace   nt
SHIPFUL boat-load
SHIPLAP rebate-cut sheathing boards   cr
SHIP-MAN a sailor   nt
SHIPPED embarked; (oars)
SHIPPEN sheep-pen; stable
SHIPPER exporter
SHIPTON a prophetess
SHIP-WAY (dry dock)
SHIRKED evaded; avoided; scamped
SHIRKER malingerer; dodger
SHIRLEY bull-finch   zo
SHIRLEY poppy   bt
SHIRRED puckered
SHIRTED wearing a shirt
SHITTAH } acacia;   bt
SHITTIM } (Tabernacle wood)
SHIVERY brittle; chilly

SHIZOKU Japanese gentry
SHOALED became shallow
SHOALER coasting-vessel   nt
SHOCKED offended; surprised
SHOCKER sensational novel
SHOE-BOY a shiner
SHOEING farrier's work
SHOE-PEG a nail
SHOE-TIE shoe-lace
SHOGGED jolted; jogged
SHOOING scaring away
SHOOKED packed
SHOOTER marksman; sniper
SHOPBOY assistant, errand boy
SHOPMAN shop/factory foreman
SHOPPED imprisoned; framed
SHOPPER peripatetic buyer
SHORAGE landing charge
SHORING props; buttressing
SHORTED circuit fault   e
SHORTEN abbreviate; abridge; curtail
SHORTER briefer; terser; curter
SHOTGUN light sporting gun
SHOT-PUT putting the weight (sport)
SHOTTED loaded
SHOTTEN dislocated; curdled
SHOUTED yelled; bawled; roared
SHOUTER crier; vociferator
SHOVING propelling; pushing; jostling
SHOW-BOX presentation carton
SHOW-END (roll of cloth)
SHOWERY pluvial
SHOWILY ostentatiously; flashily
SHOWING representation; displaying
SHOWMAN exhibitor
SHOW-OFF play for admiration; swank
SHREDDY ragged; fragmentary
SHRILLY piercingly; sharply
SHRINAL sacred; hallowed
SHRINED enshrined
SHRIVEL to dry up; parch
SHRIVEN given absolution
SHRIVER a confessor; absolver
SHROUDS winding sheets
SHROUDY giving shelter
SHRUBBY full of shrubs   b
SHUCKER husker; huller; sheller
SHUDDER shake; quiver; shiver
SHUFFLE mix; cavil; quibble; (cards)
SHUNNED avoided; eluded
SHUNNER eschewer; evader
SHUNTED turned aside
SHUNTER a railway-man
SHUT-EYE sleep; a nap
SHUTTER window   p
SHUTTLE sliding thread-holder
SHYLOCK rapacious usurer
SHYNESS bashfulness; coyness
SHYSTER rascally lawyer
SIAMANG Malay gibbon   z
SIAMESE (inseparables)

IBILUS sibilant rhoncus
IBLING one's brother or sister
ICCATE dessicate; dry; parch
ICCITY aridity; dryness
ICK BAY hospital ward — nt
ICKBED clinic
ICKEST very poorly
ICKISH unwell; out of sorts
ICKLED with sickle
ICK-PAY wages during illness
IC-LIKE such like
IDEARM sword or bayonet
IDEBOX (theatre)
IDECAR cocktail (motorcycle)
IDECUT branch canal
IDE-ROD coupling rod
IDLING edging away
IENESE of Sienna
IENITE syenite; hornblende — mn
IFFLED whistled
IFFLET small whistle
IFTING scrutinizing; sorting; sieving
IGHFUL grievous
IGHING lamenting; repining
IGHTED seen; viewed; glimpsed
IGHTER a trial shot
IGHTLY handsome
IGMATE (sigma)
IGMOID curve of beauty
IGNATE designate
IGNIFY indicate; betoken; portend
IGNING subscribing; gesturing
IGNIOR signor (It.)
IGNORA an Italian lady
IGNORY seigniory; overlordship
IKHISM monotheistic sect
ILENCE quiescence; dumbness
ILENUS foster-father of Bacchus
ILESIA cotton fabric
ILICIC (silica) — ch
ILICLE broad pod — bt
ILICON an element — ch
ILIQUA) seed vessel; — bt
ILIQUE) carat — me
ILKIER more lustrous
ILKING silk chiffon application to books
ILKMAN silk-mercer
ILLAGO a fish genus — zo
ILLERY a white wine
ILLIER more witless
ILLILY inanely; foolishly; ineptly
ILOXEN polymerized silicon analogue — ch
ILTING depositing mud
ILURUS cat-fish — zo
ILVERN of silver
ILVERY bright; clear; sweet
IMARRE a cymar; a costume
IMILAR alike; analogous; twin
IMILIA similes; metaphors
IMILOR semilor; imitation gold
IMIOUS ape-like; simian — zo

SIMITAR scimitar
SIMPKIN champagne
SIMPLER herbalist; plainer; easier
SIMPSON groundsel — bt
SIMULAR counterfeit; feigned
SIMURGH fabulous bird (Pers.)
SINAPIS sinapin; mustard — bt
SINBORN illegitimate
SINBRED raised to vice
SINCERE true; genuine; honest
SINEWED powerful; vigorous
SINGING the vocal art
SINGLED selected; separated
SINGLES tennis; reeled silk
SINGLET undervest
SINGULT a sob; a sigh
SINICAL (sine)
SINKAGE excess space for margins, headings
SINKING foundering; declining
SINLESS innocent; blameless
SINNING transgressing
SINOPIA) red pigment;
SINOPIS) sinople; sinoper
SINSICK repentant
SINSYNE since (Sc.)
SINUATE insinuate; curved
SINUOUS sinuose; winding
SINWORN fabulous monster
SIPPING supping
SIREDON larval salamander — zo
SIRENIA sea-cows — zo
SIRGANG green jackdaw — zo
SIRLOIN surloin
SIROCCO hot desert wind
SISTINE, SIXTINE (Pope Sixtus) — rl
SISTING summoning (Sc.) — lw
SISTRUM holy rattle (Egypt) — mu
SITFAST ulcer — md
SITHENS since; after that
SITTINE (nut-hatches) — zo
SITTING session; incubating
SITUATE permanently fixed
SIVAITE follower of Sivia — rl
SIXFOLD 6 times as much
SIXTEEN age of sweetness
SIZABLE of a size; bulky
SIZZLED frizzled
SJAMBOK S. Afr. raw hide whip
SKEETER mosquito — zo
SKELDER swindle
SKELLUM a rascal; scamp; scoundrel
SKELTER skedaddle
SKEPFUL basketful
SKEPTIC sceptic; doubting
SKETCHY vague; incomplete
SKEWGEE crooked; skewed
SKIDDED scotched; slipped
SKIDLID crash helmet
SKID-PAN motorists' training ground
SKIFFLE folk-song and jazz — mu

SKI-JUMP skiing slide
SKILFUL dexterous; adept; expert
SKI-LIFT cable or funicular lift
SKILLED expert; artful; adroit
SKILLET iron cooking pot
SKIMMED glided; grazed
SKIMMER scoop; bird   zo
SKIMPED stinted
SKINFUL amount of drunkenness
SKINKER tapster; barman
SKINNED peeled; fleeced
SKINNER a furrier
SKIPPED omitted; jumped
SKIPPER a fish; a captain   zo
SKIPPET seal-box; boat   nt
SKIRLED shrieked shrilly
SKIRRET water-parsnip   bt
SKIRTED bordered
SKIRTER a dodger
SKI-SUIT winter costume
SKITTER glide; skim
SKITTLE bowl out; knock down
SKIVING leather splitting; work dodging
SKULKED lurked
SKULKER a shirker; malingerer
SKULPIN sea-fish   zo
SKYBLUE azure
SKYBORN heaven-born
SKYHIGH excessively elevated
SKYLARK the laverock   zo
SKYLINE horizon; sea-line
SKYSAIL sail above royal   nt
SKYTEEN satin weave shirting   tx
SKYWARD heading upward
SLABBED cut into thick slices
SLABBER slobber; dribble; slaver
SLACKED eased off
SLACKEN relax; mitigate; abate
SLACKER skulker; sluggard; idler
SLACKLY negligently; laxly
SLAINTE! Good health! (Irish)
SLAKING quenching; allaying
SLAMKIN a slut; loose gown
SLAMMED banged
SLANDER malign; traduce; obloquy
SLANGED abused; vituperated
SLANKET strip of land; slang
SLANTED sloped; tilted
SLANTLY slantwise; atilt; obliquely
SLAPPED smacked; spanked
SLAPPER slap-up affair
SLASHED gashed; cut
SLASHER cutting tool   to
SLATHER lots of
SLATING roofing; reprimand; abusing
SLATTER to be wasteful; slovenly
SLAVDOM Slavs collectively
SLAVERY serfdom; thraldom; bondage
SLAVING drudging; moiling
SLAVISH servile; obsequious
SLAYING destroying; despatching

SLEAVED not spun; raw
SLEAVED separated; divided
SLEDDED on a sled
SLEDGED sledded; mushed
SLEEKED glided; smoothed
SLEEKEN to smooth
SLEEKER slicker
SLEEKIT smooth-tongued (Sc.)
SLEEKLY fair spoken; glossily; silky
SLEEPER (various meanings)
SLEETED hailed and snowed
SLEIDED unwoven; sleaved
SLEIGHT dexterity; skill; adroitness
SLENDER frail; slim; slight
SLEYING swinging askew
SLICING severing; (golf)
SLICKER smarter; more deft
SLIDDER to slither; slip; slide
SLIDING a lapse; varying
SLIGHTLY superficial
SLIMILY viscously; muddily
SLIMMER more slender; lankier
SLINGER of slongs
SLIPPED conveyed secretly
SLIPPER steel cradle; mule
SLIPWAY (shipbuilding)
SLITHER slide about
SLITTED slashed; split
SLITTER a cutter
SLOBBER slabber; dribble; slaver
SLOCKEN slake; quench
SLOE-GIN pleasant drink
SLOGGED hit hard
SLOGGER mighty smiter
SLOPING inclined; declinous; oblique
SLOPPED spilt
SLOTTED grooved
SLOTTER to foul; filth
SLOUCHY slackly
SLOUGHY swampy; miry; queachy
SLOVENE language and people (Yugoslavia)
SLOWEST dullest; tardiest
SLOWING delaying; retarding
SLUBBER to scamp; slabber
SLUDGER sewage dumping vessel
SLUGGED bashed; coshed
SLUICED drenched; flushed
SLUMBER sleep; repose; doze
SLUMMER slum visitor
SLUMPED fell heavily
SLUNKEN shrivelled
SLURRED sullied; disparaged   m
SLUTCHY residual; mucky
SLYNESS sliness; craft; cunning
SMACKED slapped; spanked
SMACKER a resounding kiss
SMARAGD the emerald   m
SMARTED endured sharp pain
SMARTEN brighten; quicken
SMARTER brisker; sprucer

SMARTLY promptly; readily; alertly
SMASHED disrupted; broken
SMASHER snide coin passer
SMASH-UP a crash
SMATTER slight superficial knowledge
SMEARED daubed; contaminated
SMEARER overshoot-cancelling circuit   **tc**
SMECTIC with parallel-oriented atoms   **ps**
SMEDDUM energy; powder
SMELLED had an odour; smelt
SMELLER the proboscis
SMELTER ore-worker
SMERLIN loach fish   **zo**
SMICKER to smirk; ogle; leer
SMICKET a smock
SMICKLY amorously
SMIDGEN a bittock; a trifle
SMILING smirking
SMIRKED simpered
SMITING striking; buffeting; hitting
SMITTEN afflicted; chastened
SMITTLE to infect
SMOKIER reekier
SMOKILY fumily
SMOKING bloating; quizzing
SMOLDER smoulder
SMOOTHE palliate; flatter; flatten
SMOTHER stifle; suppress (cricket)
SMOUSER pedlar (S. Africa)
SMUDGED blurred; blotted
SMUDGER plumber
SMUGGLE convey secretly; snuggle
SMYTRIE a crowd of children (Sc.)
SNABBLE snaffle; plunder; eat
SNAFFLE a bit; appropriate; filch
SNAGGED snaggy
SNAGGER a cutter   **to**
SNAKING rope-winding   **nt**
SNAKISH reptilian; serpentine
SNAPING bevelling
SNAPPED caught; broke; photographed
SNAPPER a turtle   **zo**
SNARING entrapping; catching
SNARLED entangled; complicated
SNARLER growler; grumbler
SNATCHY irregular
SNEAKER soft soled shoe
SNEAKER short drink
SNECKED latched; fastened (Sc.)
SNECK-UP go hang!
SNEDDEN sand-eel   **zo**
SNEERER derider; taunter
SNEEZED snoze
SNICKER snigger; giggle
SNIFFED snuffed; inhaled
SNIFFLE snuffle
SNIFTER dram; radio-detector
SNIGGER snicker; giggle
SNIGGLE ensnare
SNIPING shooting from ambush
SNIPPER a tailor

SNIPPET a cutting
SNIRTLE snigger
SNOODED wearing a fillet
SNOOKER (pool)
SNOOPER a nosy Parker
SNOOZER a daydreamer
SNORKEL breathing pipe (U-boat)   **nt**
SNORTER a fast one (cricket)
SNOTTER bowsprit housing   **nt**
SNOUTED with snout
SNOW-BOX (stage snowstorm)
SNOW-FED (streams)
SNOW-FLY a stone-fly   **zo**
SNOW-ICE frozen slush
SNOW-MAN snowball in human form
SNOW-OWL the great white owl   **zo**
SNUBBED deliberately slighted
SNUBBER shock absorber
SNUFFED sniffed
SNUFFER a snuff taker
SNUFFLE nasal catarrh   **md**
SNUGGLE smuggle; cuddle; fondle
SNUGIFY to make cosy
SNUZZLE nuzzle
SOAKAGE absorption
SOAKING drenching; steeping; imbruing
SO-AND-SO a vague definition
SOAP-BOX orator's platform
SOAP-PAN soap boiler
SOAPING flattering; lathering
SOARANT heraldic flying   **hd**
SOARING mental uplift; aspiring
SOBBING lamentation; ululation
SOBERED enjoyed morning after
SOBERLY staidly
SOBOLES botanical suckers   **bt**
SOCAGER socage tenant
SOCCAGE land tenure   **lw**
SOCIETY company; sodality; élite
SOCKEYE Pacific salmon   **zo**
SOCKING beating; throwing
SODA-ASH impure sodium carbonate   **mn**
SODDING turfing
SOFA-BED day-bed; divan; ottoman
SOFTEST gentlest; easiest
SOFTISH yielding; compliant
SOGGING saturating
SOIGNEE admirably turned out (Fr.)
SOILING staining; tarnishing
SOILURE pollution
SOJOURN visit; tarry; remain; abide
SOKEMAN tenant by socage   **lw**
SOLACED consoled; comforted
SOLANUM night-shade genus   **bt**
SOLDIER warrior; man-at-arms
SOLENIA enteron diverticula in hydroids   **zo**
SOLICIT importune; canvass; crave
SOLIDLY compactly; firmly; densely
SOLIDUM complete sum
SOLIDUS 's' for shilling   **nm**

SOLIPED not cloven-hoofed	zo	**SOUFFLE** blowing sound over heart	md
SOLOIST lone musician	mu	**SOULFUL** spiritually emotional	
SOLOMON wisdom personified		**SOUNDLY** thoroughly; validly	
SOLONIC wise like Solon		**SOUNDED** vibrated; tested	nt
SOLPUGA a spider genus	zo	**SOUNDER** (Morse)	
SOLUBLE capable of solution		**SOUNDER** boar; herd of swine	zo
SOLVEND a substance to be dissolved		**SOUNDEX** consonant-based coding system	
SOLVENT able to pay all debts		**SOUPCON** a suspicion; a taste (Fr.)	
SOLVING elucidating; unravelling		**SOUREST** most acid; rankest	
SOMATIC corporeal; bodily		**SOURING** acidulating	
SOMEHOW in one way or another		**SOURISH** tart; acetous; acrid	
SOMEONE unspecified person		**SOUROCK** sorrel	bt
SOMNIAL dreamy		**SOURSOP** American custard apple	bt
SONANCE sonancy; a call (Shak.)		**SOUSING** pickling; drenching	
SONCHUS sow-thistle genus	bt	**SOUTANE** cassock	rl
SONDELI Indian musk-rat	zo	**SOUTHER** south wind	
SONGFUL full of glee		**SOUTHLY** southerly	
SONGMAN balladmonger		**SOU'WEST** S.W.	
SONLESS defiliated		**SOVKHOZ** state-owned farm (Rus.)	
SONNITE Sunnite; orthodox Moslem	rl	**SOWBACK** gravel ridge	
SONSHIP cf. daughterdom		**SOYBEAN** oil-rich Asiatic legume	bt, ck
SOOTHED assuaged; pacified; cajoled		**SOZZLED** sossled; tipsy; fuddled	
SOOTHER diplomatist; mollifier		**SPACIAL** extensive; commodious	
SOOTHLY truly		**SPACING** arranging intervals	
SOOTING (sparking plugs)		**SPADDLE** spittle; small spade	to
SOOTISH like soot		**SPADING** digging	
SOPHISM a fallacy; specious argument		**SPADONE** double-handed sword	
SOPHIST captious reasoner		**SPAEMAN** diviner (Sc.)	
SOPHORA pagoda tree	bt	**SPAIRGE** sparge; sprinkle	
SOPIENT a soporific		**SPALING** a bracing; cross-band	
SOPPING soaking; steeping		**SPALLED** chipped; splintered	
SOPRANI several sopranos	mu	**SPANCEL** cow-hobble	
SOPRANO female treble	mu	**SPANDAU** German light machine gun	
SORBENT an absorbent		**SPANGLE** glittering disc	
SORBIAN ⎫ Slavonic race in Saxony		**SPANGLY** sparkling	
SORBISH ⎭		**SPANIEL** fawning; mean	zo
SORBILE that can be sipped/drunk		**SPANISH** Iberian	
SORBINE ⎫ sorbate; sweet berry		**SPANKED** slapped; speeded	
SORBITE ⎭ extract	bt	**SPANKER** a sail	nt
SORBOSE keto hexose	ch	**SPANNED** measured; embraced	
SORCERY witchcraft; enchantment		**SPANNER** monkey-wrench	
SORDINE a mute	mu	**SPAN-NEW** brand-new	
SORDONO (oboe)	mu	**SPARELY** sparingly; charily	
SOREHON Irish tenure		**SPARGED** sprinkled; sprayed	
SORGHUM sugar-cane	bt	**SPARGER** sprinkler; diffuser	
SORICID like a shrew		**SPARING** frugal; parsimonious	
SORITES syllogistic argument		**SPARKED** played the gallant	
SORNING obtruding; sponging on		**SPARKLE** coruscate; twinkle	
SORORAL sisterly		**SPAROID** like sea bream	
SOROSIS mulberry type of fruit	bt	**SPARRED** disputed; wrangled, boxed	
SOROSIS woman's club		**SPARRER** boxing partner	
SORRILY meanly; pitiably		**SPARROW** a small finch	zo
SORTING disposing; classifying		**SPARSIM** here and there (Lat.)	
SOSPIRO a breathing rest	mu	**SPARTAN** austere; hardy; undaunted	
SOSTRUM life-saving reward (Greek)		**SPASTIC** spasmodic	
SOTTING tippling; toping; boozing		**SPATHED** ensheathed	
SOTTISE blundering act (Fr.)		**SPATHIC** laminated; foliated	
SOTTISH besotted; foolish		**SPATIAL** spacial, wide; spacious	
SOUBISE onion sauce	ck	**SPATTER** asperse; besprinkle; splash	
SOUCHET boiled fish	ck	**SPATTLE** ⎫ spaddle; spittle;	
SOUFFLE frothy egg-dish	ck	**SPATULA** ⎭ a blade; a small spade	me

298

SPATULE (tail feather) zo
SPAWLED slavered
SPAWNED deposited eggs
SPAWNER female fish zo
SPAYING gelding
SPEAKER (House of Commons)
SPEARED lanced; pierced; impaled
SPEARER spearman
SPECIAL distinctive; particular
SPECIES group; genus; class; kind
SPECIFY definite; indicate; detail
SPECKED spotted; speckled
SPECKLE small speck or stain
SPECTRA (spectrum); images
SPECTRE apparition; spook; hobgoblin
SPECULA mirrors; reflectors
SPEEDED ran; hastened; executed
SPEEDER pace-maker
SPEED-UP accelerate
SPELDER a splinter; chip
SPELEAN troglodytic
SPELLED charmed; entranced; spelt
SPELLER spelling book
SPELTER soldering alloy
SPENCER butler; jacket
SPENCER gaff-sail nt
SPENDER prodigal; wastrel; waster
SPERKET spirket; harness hook
SPEWING vomiting
SPHACEL gangrene md
SPHENIC wedge-like
SPHERAL ball-like; globular
SPHERED englobed
SPHERIC spherical
SPHYRNA hammer-headed sharks
SPICATE } spicous; prickly;
SPICOSE } spinous; thorny; spinate
SPICERY (spices)
SPICILY pungently; piquantly
SPICING seasoning; varying
SPICULE } small pine; bt
SPICULA } spike or ear
SPIDERY very thin
SPIEGEL steel alloy
SPIGNEL baldmoney; a plant bt
SPIKING impaling; transfixing
SPILING building-piles
SPILITE fine-grained igneous rock gl
SPILLED spilt; wasted; slopped
SPILLER reefing rope nt
SPILOMA birthmark; a naevus md
SPINACH spinage bt
SPINATE spiky; spicate bt
SPINDLE axis; arbor
SPINDLY fusiform; slender
SPINNER a bait; textile operator
SPINNEY spinny; copse
SPINODE cusp in a curve
SPIN-OFF incidental by-product; side effect
SPINOSE spinous; thorny bt
SPINULA spicule bt

SPINULE small spine bt
SPIRAEA a plant genus bt
SPIRANT fricative consonant; a sibilant
SPIRING tapering; sprouting
SPIRITY mettlesome; alcoholic
SPIRKET sperket; harness hook
SPIRTED spurted; spouted; gushed
SPIRTLE to spirt; to spurt
SPIRULA cephalopods; cuttle-fish zo
SPITBOX a cuspidor
SPITING grudging; thwarting
SPITTED transfixed ck
SPITTER young deer zo
SPITTLE small spade; saliva
SPIZINE (buntings; finches) zo
SPLASHY wet and muddy
SPLAYED sloped; slanted
SPLEENY ill-humoured; fretful
SPLEGET a swab md
SPLENIC spleeny; fretful; melancholy
SPLICED interwoven; married
SPLINTS surgical appliances md
SPLODGE daub; patch
SPLODGY stained; blotched
SPLOTCH smear; stain
SPLURGE rowdiness
SPLURGY boisterous; spend freely
SPODIUM ivory-black
SPOFFLE to bustle; to fuss
SPOILED pillaged; ruined; marred
SPOILER plunderer; bungler
SPOLIUM church property rl
SPONDEE poetic foot (2 long syllables)
SPONDYL a vertebra; a joint md
SPONGED deleted; purged; sorned
SPONGER a parasite; sorner
SPONGIN horny skeletal substance in porifera zo
SPONSAL (marriage)
SPONSON protecting bracket nt
SPONSOR guarantor; a surety
SPOOFED hoodwinked; hoaxed
SPOOLED wound on spools
SPOOMED scudded before the wind
SPOONED hit into the air; courted
SPOONEY love-sick
SPOORER tracker
SPOROID sporous; sporelike bt
SPORONT stage in protozoa life history
SPORRAN kilt-pouch
SPORTED wore; trifled; romped
SPORTER jester; player
SPORULE small spore bt
SPOTTED spied; detected; pied
SPOTTER sharp-sighted look-out
SPOUSAL nuptial; matrimonial
SPOUTED orated; spirted; pawned
SPOUTER declaimer; whale zo
SPRAICH shriek; cry (Sc.)
SPRAYED sprinkled; spumed; affused
SPRAYEY branching

SPREAGH plunder (Sc.)
SPRIGGY full of sprigs
SPRIGHT sprite; a spirit; a ghost
SPRINGE spring trap; a gin
SPRINTS bicycle wheels
SPRINGY vernal; elastic
SPRUCED smartened up; prinked
SPRUNNY spruce; a sweetheart
SPRYEST spriest; gayest; pertest
SPUMING spumous; frothy; foamy
SPUMONE ice-cream in varied layers (It.)
SPUN-HAY twisted hay
SPUN-OUT long drawn
SPUR-DOG a shark   zo
SPURIAE bastard quills   zo
SPURNED rejected; scouted; contemned
SPURNER a disdainer
SPURRED goaded; impelled; galloped
SPURRER inciter; instigator
SPURREY a plant   bt
SPURTED spirted; gushed; sprinted
SPURTLE spurt; spirtle
SPURWAY bridle-path
SPUTNIK earth satellite (Russian)
SPUTTER splutter
SPY-BOAT vessel for secret agents   nt
SPY-HOLE peep-hole; Judas' hole
SPYNDLE unit of length of jute/flax yarn
SQUABBY squaddy; squat; tubby
SQUACCO crested heron   zo
SQUALID sordid; unclean; filthy
SQUALLY gusty; blustering
SQUALOR dirtiness; foulness
SQUALUS shark   zo
SQUARED adjusted; tallied; bribed
SQUASHY pulpy; soft
SQUATTY squabby; clumsy
SQUEASY scrupulous; squeamish
SQUEEZE compress; crush; pinch; nip
SQUEEZY congested; squashy
SQUELCH crush; suppress; quash
SQUIFFY tipsy; inebriated; sozzled
SQUINCH small stone arch; tight squeeze
SQUINNY to look asquint; meagre
SQUIRED escorted
SQUITCH quitch-grass   bt
SRADDHA Hindu devotional offerings   rl
STABBED wounded; pierced
STABBER awl; marlinspike   to
STABLED stalled
STABLER stable-keeper
STABLES a trumpet call   mu
STACHYS hedge-nettle genus   bt
STACKED piled; (cards)
STACKER haymaker
STADDLE crutch; support
STADIUM arena; running track
STAFFED manned by
STAGERY scenic exhibition
STAGGER astound; lurch; reel; sway
STAGING a structure; producing

STAIDLY steadily; sedately; soberly
STAINED foxed; tarnished; sullied
STAINER a dyer
STAITHE coaling stage
STAKING hazarding; wagering
STALDER cask rack
STALELY mustily; effetely; insipidly
STALEST most trite
STALKED with peduncle   bt
STALKER stealthy sportsman
STALLED fatted; lost speed
STALLOY silicon-content steel   ml
STAMINA endurance; vitality; vigour
STAMMEL rough red cloth
STAMMER stutter
STAMNOS Greek urn
STAMPED impressed; crushed; branded
STAMPER ore crusher
STAND-BY a reserve
STANDER provider; candidate
STAND-IN deputy; substitute
STAND-TO military readiness
STAND-UP well fought
STANIEL ⎫ stanyel; kestrel;
STANNEL ⎬ windhover   zo
STANNIC (of tin)
STANNUM tin, metallic element   ch
STAPLED connected together
STAPLER a dealer; clipping machine
STARCHY stiff; formal; precise
STARDOM film eminence
STARING glaring; gaping; prominent
STARKEN stiffen; make obstinate
STARKLY completely; absolutely
STARLET junior actress
STAR-LIT almost invisible
STARRED shone; bespangled
STARTED winced; roused; began
STARTER also ran
STARTLE alarm; frighten; surprise
STARVED famished; emaciated
STASIMA choral odes (Greek)
STATANT standing   hd
STATELY lofty; magnificent; imposing
STATICE sea-lavender   bt
STATICS conditions for equilibrium
STATING narrating; affirming
STATION Australian stock-farm; place
STATISM policy; art of government
STATIST statistical expert
STATIVE fixed; standing still
STATOHM obsolete electrostatic unit el, me
STATUED with statues
STATURE natural height
STATUTE an enactment; decree   lw
STAUNCH stanch; trusty; steadfast
STAVING delaying; broaching
STAYING enduring; detaining; abiding
STAY-PUT semi-permanent
STEALER purloiner; peculator
STEALTH furtiveness; secrecy

STEAMED vaporized
STEAMER cooking vessel; ship   nt
STEARIC of candle grease   ch
STEARIN fat; wax; stearic acid
STEELED hardened; nerved
STEEPED soaked; drenched; imbrued
STEEPEN to make steep
STEEPER soaking vat
STEEPLE a spire   rl
STEEPLY almost sheer; abruptly
STEERED conned; controlled; directed
STEERER pilot; guide; director
STEEVED packed closely
STELENE pillar-like; columnar
STELLAR astral; starry
STEMLET small stalk
STEMMED compressed
STEMPLE, STEMPEL cross-beam
STEMSON jointing timber   nt
STENCHY odoriferous
STENCIL pattern plate
STENGAH whisky and soda (Malay)
STENODE supersonic heterodyne receiver
STENTER fabric-stretching machine   tx
STENTOR a loud speaker
STEP-INS elastic-held shoes; underwear
STEPNEY spare-wheel; (born at sea)
STEPPED paced; walked; fixed
STEPPER horse with high action
STEPSON spouse's earlier product
STERILE barren; germ-free; acarpous
STERLET sturgeon   zo
STERNAL (breast-bone)   me
STERNER harsher; more austere
STERNLY severely; strictly; dourly
STERNUM breast-bone   me
STEROID sterol compound   ch
STERTOR noisy breathing   md
STETSON a hat (USA)
STEVING stowing   nt
STEWARD seneschal; bailiff   nt
STEWING simmering; worrying
STEW-CAN   \ vessels used
STEW-PAN, STEW-POT ∫ for stews
STHENIA strength   md
STIBIAL (antimony)
STIBINE antimony hydride   ch
STIBIUM antimony   ch
STICHIC rhythmic
STICHOS a line of verse
STICKER last ditcher; adherent
STICKLE a rapid in a stream
STIFFEN harden
STIFFER more rigid; harder; primmer
STIFFLY rigidly; firmly; starchy
STIFLED suffocated; smothered
STILLED hushed; calmed; distilled
STILLER pacifier; composer
STILTED pompous; bombastic
STILTON a cheese
STIMIED obstructed; (golf)

STIMULI incentives; spurs
STINGER insect's proboscis
STINKER despicable person
STINTED restricted; rationed
STINTER pincher; restrainer
STIPATE crowded   bt
STIPEND salary; emolument
STIPPLE to make dots
STIPTIC astringent   md
STIPULA \ leaf appendage   bt
STIPULE ∫
STIRPES forefathers; races
STIRRED roused; incited; bustled
STIRRER thriller; agitator; disturber
STIRRUP foot-holder for rider
STIVING stewing
STOAKED choked; stopped   nt
STOCKED stored; saved; hoarded
STOICAL passionless; unfeeling
STOKING adding fuel
STOLLEN sweet German yeast bread   ck
STOMACH to brook; to resent   md
STOMATA breathing pore   md
STOMIUM fern-sporangium-wall part   bt
STONIED astonished; amazed
STONILY obdurately; unrelentingly
STONING pelting; (fruit)
STOOGED loitered; filled in time
STOOKED set up in sheaves
STOOKER harvest worker
STOOMED fermented
STOOPED condescended; swooped
STOOPER bender
STOOTER Dutch silver coin   nm
STOPGAP locum tenens
STOPING series of ledges
STOPPED restrained; repressed; closed
STOPPER \ plug; cork; tampion
STOPPLE ∫
STORAGE safe custody
STORIED legendary; fabled
STORIES floors; tales
STORING garnering; hoarding
STORMED assaulted; raved; raged
STORMER blusterer
STOTTER rebound; a bounce (Sc.)
STOUTEN hearten; encheer
STOUTER more corpulent; braver
STOUTLY sturdily; stalwartly; robust
STOVING a heat treatment
STOWAGE packing; loading
STOWING arranging; packing
STRAIKS wheel-plates; strakes
STRANGE unfamiliar; abnormal; exotic
STRAPPY strong; fit; many straps
STRATUM rock formation
STRATUS cloud formation
STRAWED strewed
STRAYED erred; roved; deviated
STRAYER wandered; vagrant
STRAYNE strain; stress (Spens.)

STREAKY striped
STREAMY well watered
STRETCH reach; strain; expand
STRETTO quick and sharp   mu
STREWED strewn; scattered
STRIATE streaky; scratched
STRIDOR harsh noise; a jar
STRIGES the owl genus   zo
STRIGIL skin-scraper
STRIKER bashful worker; firing pin
STRINGY filamentous
STRIOLA small/weak stria; scratch
STRIPED streaked
STRIPES a tiger   zo
STRIP-IN recombining photo material
STRIVEN strove; struggled; tussled
STRIVER emulator; trier; competitor
STROBIC rate of turning; spinning
STROCAL glass-maker's shovel
STROKED rubbed gently; (rowing)
STROKEN struck (Spens.)
STROKER rubber; soother
STROPHE a stanza (Greek)
STRUDEL Austrian thin-dough pastry   ck
STUBBED blunted; obtuse; extirpated
STUBBLE corn stumps   bt
STUBBLY like stubble; unshaven
STUCKLE clump of sheaves
STUCK-UP arrogant; pompous
STUDDED (shirts); (nails)
STUDDLE a trestle
STUDENT pupil; scholar; philomath
STUDIED conned; pondered; worked
STUDIER student; scrutinizer
STUFFED padded; crowded; rammed
STUFFER packer; crammer
STUMBLE trip; slip; blunder; lurch
STUMBLY apt to stumble
STUMMED fortified; doctored
STUMMEL tobacco pipe (German)
STUMPED at a loss; (cricket)
STUMPER wicket-keeper
STUNNED dumbfounded; amazed
STUNNED an astonisher; stupefier
STUNTED dwarfed; pygmean; runty
STUPEFY bemuse; dope; benumb
STUPENT struck with stupor
STUPOSE tufted; scaly; matted
STURNUS starling genus   zo
STUTTER stammer; hesitant utterance
STYGIAN infernal; black; murky
STYLATE styloid; like a style or pen
STYLING naming; designating
STYLISH modish; chic; elegant
STYLIST fine writer
STYLITE pillar-dweller
STYLIZE to make conventional
STYLOID pen-like
STYMIED stimied; obstructed; (golf)
STYPSIS use of styptics   md
STYPTIC stiptic; astringent   md

SUASIVE urbane; agreeable
SUASORY convincing
SUAVELY pleasantly; blandly
SUAVITY affability; sweetness
SUBACID rather acid
SUBADAR Mogul governor
SUBARID slightly arid
SUBBASS low organ note   mu
SUBEDAR native captain
SUBBING acting as substitute; subediting
SUBCOXA segment of primitive leg in
   insects   zo
SUBDEAN under-dean   rl
SUBDUAL conquest; subjugation
SUBDUCE withdraw
SUBDUCT subtract
SUBDUED piano; routed; worsted
SUBDUER queller; vanquisher
SUBEDIT (edit)
SUBERIC of cork
SUBERIN cork-cell fatty mixture   bt
SUBFUSC subfusk; dusky
SUBGENS sub-clan
SUB-HEAD sub-title
SUBJECT thesis; topic; subservient
SUBJOIN append; affix; postfix
SUBLATE carry off; take away
SUBLIME exalted; lofty; superb
SUBNUDE almost leafless   bt
SUBOVAL almost ovate
SUBPENA subpoena; writ   lw
SUBRENT sublet
SUBSALT below the salt   ch
SUBSIDE sink; ebb; wane; abate
SUBSIDY a grant; dole; monetary aid
SUBSIGN undersign
SUBSIST live; exist; endure
SUBSOIL the under-soil
SUBSUME include as comprehended
SUBTACK an under-lease (Sc.)
SUBTEND embrace; enfold
SUBTILE subtle; cunningly devised
SUBTLER wilier; craftier
SUBTYPE subdivision
SUBURBS outlying districts
SUBVENE aid; support
SUBVERT overthrow; ruin; corrupt
SUCCADE candied fruit
SUCCEED follow; prosper; win
SUCCESS prosperity; victory; triumph
SUCCISE ending below abruptly   bt
SUCCORY chicory   bt
SUCCOSE sappy
SUCCOUR aid; help; support; foster
SUCCUBA battering demons; spirits
SUCCULA capstan; winch
SUCCUMB yield; submit; die; capitulate
SUCCUSS to shake suddenly
SUCKING absorbing; imbibing
SUCKLED nursed
SUCKLER an infant; a suckling

SUCROSE cane sugar
SUCTION vacuum-filling
SUDANIC group of languages (Sudan)
SUDORAL sweaty; perspiring
SUFFETE Punic official
SUFFICE to content; be enough; avail
SUFFUSE diffuse; blush; overspread
SUGARED candied; sweetened
SUGGEST hint; insinuate; propose
SUGGING sea-rocked when stranded   nt
SUICIDE felo-de-se
SUIFORM pig-like; swinish
SUITING pleasing; according   tx
SULCATE grooved; furrowed
SULKIER more sullen
SULKILY morosely; sullenly; surlily
SULKING glowering
SULLAGE dross; scum
SULLENS morose; temper; the sulks
SULLIED tainted; tarnished; defamed
SULPHUR brimstone   ch
SULTANA raisin; marsh bird   bt, zo
SUMATRA Malaccan summer squall   mt
SUMLESS beyond count
SUMMARY epitome; abstract; digest
SUMMERY summerlike
SUMMING summary; adding; counting
SUMMIST writer of a compendium
SUMMONS writ; citation   lw
SUMPTER pack-horse   zo
SUN-BATH outdoor near-nudity
SUNBEAM ray from the sun
SUNBEAT struck by the sun's rays
SUNBIRD humming bird   zo
SUNBURN tan
SUNCLAD radiant
SUNDARI hardwood tree (Borneo)   bt
SUNDAWN dawn-light
SUNDIAL stylish timepiece
SUNDOWN sunset
SUNDROP primrose (Amer.)
SUNFISH shark   zo
SUN-KIST kissed by the sun
SUN-LAMP ultra-violet ray
SUNLESS cloudy; overcast
SUNLIKE solar
SUNMYTH a solar myth
SUNNING sun-bathing
SUNNITE Sonnite; orthodox Muslim
SUNRISE dawn; cock-crow
SUNROSE sunflower   bt
SUNSPOT solar phenomenon   as
SUNWARD towards the sun
SUNWISE clock-wise
SUPPING eat evening meal
SUPPLED made pliant
SUPPORT prop; uphold; assist
SUPPOSE surmise; fancy; deem
SUPREME dominant; paramount
SURANAL above the anus   zo
SURBASE cornice; base moulding

SURCOAT coat worn over chain mail
SURDITY lack of resonance
SURFACE exterior; superficies
SURFEIT excess; plethora; cloy; gorge
SURFMAN skilled boatman
SURGENT swelling; heaving
SURGEON who treats people by operation
SURGERY cutting into bodies   md
SURGING swirling; billowing
SURLIER more churlish and crusty
SURLILY gruffly; sullenly; morosely
SURLOIN sirloin beef
SURMISE conjecture; suppose; imagine
SURNAME sirname; cognomen
SURPASS excel; exceed; outdo
SURPLUS residuum; balance; excess
SURSIZE feudal penalty   lw
SURTOUT overcoat
SURVIVE outlive; endure; outlast
SUSCEPT parasite's host
SUSPECT doubtful; mistrust; distrust
SUSPEND hang; postpone; relieve
SUSPIRE sign; yearn; breathe
SUSTAIN uphold; bear; endure
SUTLERY ⎫ sutler's occupation
SUTLING ⎭ commissariat
SUTURAL sewn; seamy; stitched
SUTURED sewn together
SWABBED washed; mopped
SWABBER scrubber; mopper-up
SWABIAN (South German)
SWADDLE swathe; wrap; bind
SWAGGED sagged; leant
SWAGGER strut; ruffle; boast
SWAGING assuaging; mitigating
SWAGING metal-rod tapering   mt
SWAGMAN burglar
SWAHILI East African language
SWALING wasting; consuming; burning
SWALLET underground stream
SWALLOW voracity; engulf; absorb   zo
SWAMPED overwhelmed; inundated
SWANKED boasted; bragged
SWANKIE swipes; thin beer
SWANPAN Chinese abacus
SWAPPED bartered; exchanged
SWARAJI home rule (India)
SWARDED grassy; turfy
SWARFED fainted; swooned; dwalmed
SWARMED thronged; teemed; clustered
SWARTHY tawny; swart; dark
SWASHED blustered; swanked
SWASHER swash-buckler
SWATTED hit with a fly swat
SWATTER fly-killer
SWAYING governing; oscillating
SWEALED guttered like a candle
SWEARER blasphemer
SWEATED drudged; oozed; reeked
SWEATER a pullover; jersey
SWEDISH (Sweden)

SWEEPER an artist of the brush
SWEETEN to palliate; dulcify
SWEETER more fragrant
SWEETIE sweetmeat; confectionery
SWEETLY dulcetly; fragrantly
SWELLED inflated; heaved; bulged
SWELLEL American squirrel   zo
SWELLET rush of water in a mine
SWELTER perspire; sweat
SWELTRY sultry; oppressive
SWERVED deviated; turned aside
SWERVER curve-swinger
SWIFTER faster; nimbler; quicker
SWIFTLY rapidly; promptly; suddenly
SWIGGED drank deep; quaffed
SWILLED rinsed; washed; boozed
SWILLER copious absorber
SWIMMER water-spider   zo
SWINDLE fraud; dupe; cheat
SWINERY piggery
SWINGED beaten up; punished
SWINGEL } loose end of flail
SWINGLE } swipple
SWINGER skew-bored gramophone record
       ac
SWINISH hoggish; suiform
SWINKED drudged; moiled; toiled
SWIPING slogging; lashing out
SWIRLED whirled; eddied
SWISHED flogged
SWISHER a wielder of the birch
SWITHER hesitate; doubt; fright
SWITZER Swiss bodyguard; a Swiss
SWIZZLE a mixed drink
SWOLLEN distended; enlarged; bloated
SWOONED fainted; swarfed; dwalmed
SWOOPED caught on the wing
SWOPPED swapped; bartered
SWOTTED studied hard
SYBOTIC pertaining to swineherd
SYCOSIS barber's itch   md
SYENITE Egyptian granite   mn
SYLPHID small sylph; fairy
SYLVINE potassium chloride   ch
SYLVITE potassium chloride   ch
SYMBION symbiotic organism   zo
SYMPTOM token; indication; sign
SYNACMY floral maturity   bt
SYNAPSE nerve junction   md
SYNAPTE Greek litany   rl
SYNAXIS an assembly for worship
SYNCARP multiple fleshy fruit   bt
SYNCOPE contraction; collapse
SYNCHRO transformer for transmitting
    angular data
SYNERGY co-operation
SYNESIS harmonious construction
SYNNEMA erect bunch of hyphae   bt
SYNOCHA fever   md
SYNOCIL a growth on sponges
SYNODAL bishop's benefit   rl

SYNODIC (synod); conventional
SYNONYM a word of similar significance
SYNOTUS long-eared bat   zo
SYNOVIA lubrication   md
SYNTONY wireless tuning
SYRINGA mock-orange   bt
SYRINGE a squirt; to spray
SYSTOLE contraction of the heart   mc
SYSTYLE a stylish portico
SYSTYLE type of colonnade   ar

T

TABANAC French white wine
TABANUS horse-fly or gad-fly   zo
TABARET satin striped silk
TABELLA lozenge   md
TABETIC consumptive   md
TABIDLY tabific; tabetic
TABINET curtain material
TABLEAU vivid picture (Fr.)
TABLIER apron; chess-board
TABLING setting down in order
TABLOID multum in parvo   md
TABOOED banned; barred; accursed
TABORER drummer   mu
TABORET small drum   mu
TABULAR listed; tabulated
TACHYON fast-moving particle   nc
TACITLY noiselessly implied
TACKILY stickily; adhesively
TACKING stitching; fastening   nt
TACKLED seized; grappled with
TACK-RAG dust/grit remover   pt
TACTFUL diplomatic and sensitive
TACTICS cunning moves
TACTILE tangible; perceptible
TACTION sense of touch; contact
TACTOID double-reflecting droplet   ch, ps
TACTUAL tactile; palpable
TADORNA duck genus   zo
TADPOLE embryonic frog; polliwog   zo
TADZHIK Central Asian people
TAENITE iron-nickel solution   mn
TAFFETA wavy fabric
TAFFETY taffeta; lustrous silk
TAGALOG language (Philippines)
TAGETES French marigolds   bt
TAGGERS thin sheet iron
TAGGING following; tailing; tacking
TAGMEME smallest meaningful speech unit
TAGSORE sheep disease   vt
TAGTAIL worm; parasite   vt
TAILAGE entail
TAILCAP leather fold on book spine
TAILEND fag-end
TAILING following; a winter sport
TAILZIE deed of entail   lw
TAINTED infected; stained; sullied
TAIPING Chinese rebel
TAKE-OFF a burlesque; a start

TAKINGS cash receipts		**TAPIOCA** cassava	bt
TAKSPAN pine-roof shingles	ar	**TAPLASH** stale swipes	
TALARIA Mercury's winged sandals		**TAPPING** broaching; screwcutting	
TALCITE nacrite	mn	**TAPROOM** bar	
TALCOSE talcous; a talc		**TAPROOT** main sustenance root	bt
TALEFUL newsy		**TAPSTER, TAPSMAN** bartender	
TALIPED club footed		**TARBUSH** tarboosh; fez	
TALIPES slub-foot	md	**TARDIER** slower; later; slacker	
TALIPOT ⎫ talipat; fan-palm		**TARDILY** slowly; reluctantly	
TALIPUT ⎭	bt	**TARNISH** sully; soil; stain	
TALKIES talking films		**TARRACE** volcanic earth	
TALKING prating; discoursing		**TARRIED** loitered; lingered; sojourned	
TALLAGE ancient tax		**TARRIER** dawdler; estate register	lw
TALLBOY chest of drawers		**TARRING** covering with bitumen	
TALLEST loftiest; highest		**TARROCK** arctic tern	zo
TALLIED agreed; correspond; fitted		**TARSIER** lemur; the malmag	zo
TALLIER tally-keeper		**TARTARY** Tartarus; nethermost hell	
TALLISH rather tall		**TARTISH** somewhat sharp	
TALLITH praying mantle (Heb.)		**TARTLET** small tart	
TALLOWY fatty		**TASHRIF** respect; compliment (Ind.)	
TALLY-HO hunting call		**TASKING** taskwork; drudgery; toiling	
TALONED with claws		**TASTIER** choicer; more succulent	
TAMABLE docile; tractable		**TASTILY** artistically	
TAMANOA ant-eater	zo	**TASTING** relishing; enjoying; gustation	
TAMARIN S. American monkey	zo	**TATARIC** Mongolian, Turkish, etc.	
TAMASHA entertainment (India)		**TATOUAY** armadillo; peba; tatou	zo
TAMBOUR drum; embroidery	mu	**TATTERY** in rags	
TAMILIC ⎫ Tamil; a dialect of Sri Lanka		**TATTING** lace work	
TAMULIC ⎭		**TATTLED** gossiped; chatted; prated	
TAMMANY political organisation, US		**TATTLER** tale-bearer	
TAMPING (blasting)		**TAUNTED** derided; flouted; scorned	
TAMPION also tompion; a stopper		**TAUNTER** mocker; upbraider; reviler	
TANADAR Hindu police officer		**TAURIAN** (bulls)	
TANAGER American finch	zo	**TAURIDS** meteoric shower	
TANAGRA finches	zo	**TAURINE** ox extract	md
TANAGRA terracotta ware		**TAUTEST** tightest; tensest	
TANGENT meeting but not intersecting		**TAXABLE** rateable	
TANGHIN poison tree (Madagascar)	bt	**TAXCART** small farm cart	
TANGING twanging; flavouring		**TAXFREE** scot-free	
TANGLED jumbled; matted; twisted		**TAXICAB** hire car	
TANGRAM Chinese jigsaw		**TAXI-ING** runway movements	ae
TANKAGE storage		**TAXI-MAN** cab driver	
TANKARD drinking vessel		**TEA-CAKE** scone or bun for tea	
TANKCAR tanker; oil-tank		**TEACH-IN** active seminar discussion	
TANKING waterproofing a basement		**TEACHTA** member of parliament (Irish)	
TANLING sun-bather		**TEA-COSY** pot warmer	
TANNAGE tanning materials		**TEA-GOWN** long afternoon dress	
TANNATE a salt of tannic acid	ch	**TEA-LEAD** (tea-chest linings)	
TANNERY leather factory		**TEA-LEAF** blade of tea	bt
TANNING leathering		**TEA-ROSE** tea-scented rose	bt
TANRIDE riding school		**TEA-SHOP** shop serving tea	
TANSPUD bark-peeling tool	to	**TEA-TIME** 4/5 o'clock	
TANTARA fanfare	mu	**TEA-TRAY** on which tea carried	
TANTITY tantamount		**TEA-TREE** Asian camellia; shrub	bt
TANTIVY at speed		**TEACHER** master; tutor; pedagogue	
TANTONY smallest pig in litter	zo	**TEAMING** grouping; selecting	
TANTRUM temper; petulance		**TEARBAG** lachrymal gland	md
TANYARD tanning place		**TEARFUL** maudlin; weeping; Niobean	
TAPBOLT screw bolt		**TEAR-GAS** riot repellant; eye irritant	ch
TAPERED conical; pointed		**TEARING** rending; raving; raging	
TAPETUM (retina)	md	**TEARPIT** a lachrymal depression	

TEASING tantalizing; plaguing	
TEATHED manured by live stock	
TECHILY fretfully; peevishly	
TECHNIC technique; technical	
TECTRIX a wing or tail feather	zo
TEDDING spreading	
TEDIOUS wearisome; hum-drum	
TEEMFUL prolific; swarming	
TEEMING fruitful; abundant	
TEENAGE thirteen to nineteen	
TEENING troubling; provoking	
TEGULAR (tiles)	
TEGUMEN abdomen segment in lepidoptera	
TEKTITE non-volcanic natural glass	mn
TELAMON statue supporting masonry	
TELECAR mobile telegraph office	
TELEOST osseous	
TELERGY telepathy	
TELESIA sapphire	mn
TELLING effective; informing	
TELPHER system of electric traction	
TEL-QUEL exchange rate	
TELSTAR television satellite	
TEMENOS temple precinct (Greek)	
TEMPEAN delightful; (Vale of Tempe)	
TEMPERA oilless paint; distemper	
TEMPEST hurricane; typhoon; gale	
TEMPLAR student of law	lw
TEMPLED in a temple	
TEMPLET template; jig	to
TEMPTED allured; tried; solicited	
TEMPTER a decoy; an enticer	
TENABLE maintainable; rational	
TENANCY tenure	
TENDING tendentious; trending	
TENDRIL twining shoot	bt
TENERAL immature	zo
TENFOLD decuple	
TENIOID like tapeworms	zo
TENONED mortised	
TENONER tenon cutter	to
TEN-PINS cf. Nine-pins	
TENSELY tauty; tightly	
TENSEST stiffest; most emotional	
TENSILE ductile	
TENSION strain; stress; exigency	
TENSITY tenseness; urgency	
TENSIVE intensive	
TENTBED canopied bed	
TENT-FLY part of tent	
TENTFUL tent fully occupied	
TENTGUY tent-rope, not its occupant	
TENTING probing; searching; camping	
TENTORY the awning of a tent	
TENTPEG, TENTPIN used anent a tent	
TENTURE wall hangings	
TENUATE thin; attenuate	
TENUITY rarity; thinness	
TENUOUS diffused; slender	
TEQUILA fermented sap drink (Mex.)	
TERBIUM a metallic element	ch
TERCINE seed-coat	bt
TEREBIC (turpentine)	bt
TEREBRA Roman ram; ovipositor	zo
TEREKIA sandpiper genus	zo
TERGANT recursant	hd
TERGITE back of an anthropod	zo
TERM-FEE periodic payment	lw
TERMING naming; denominating	
TERMINI boundaries; extremities	
TERMITE white ant	zo
TERNARY in threes	
TERNATE three-leafed	bt
TERNERY tern breeding ground	
TERNION (twelve pages)	
TERPENE terebene	ch
TERRACE raised beach	
TERRAIN geological features	
TERRANE area covered by certain rock	gl
TERRAZO Venetian mosaic	
TERRENE terrestrial; earthy	
TERRIER fine fighter	zo
TERRIER tarrier; register	lw
TERRIFY alarm; appal; dismay	
TERRINE earthenware cooking dish	
TERSELY concisely; briefly; laconically	
TERSION wiping	
TERTIAL wing feather	zo
TERTIAN on alternate days	
TESSERA mosaic block	
TESTACY testate	lw
TESTATE leaving a will	lw
TEST-BAN nuclear weapons agreement	
TESTERN testril; a sixpence	nm
TESTIER more irritable or irascible	
TESTIFY affirm; avow; depose; depone	
TESTILY peevishly; petulantly	
TESTING proving; trying	
TESTOON Henry VIII shilling	nm
TESTRIL a tester; a sixpence	nm
TESTUDO tortoise; early tank	zo
TETANIC as in tetanus	me
TETANUS lock-jaw	me
TETRACT having four rays	
TETRODE a thermionic valve	
TETROSE monosaccharide	ch
TEXTILE woven fabric	
TEXT-MAN a quoter	
TEXTUAL authoritative	
TEXTURA medieval handwriting, Goth. dark type	pr
TEXTURE a web; structure; fabric	
THALIAN comic	
THALLUS a stem formation	
THALWEG longitudinal river profile	g
THAMMUZ Osiris; Adonis	
THANAGE thanedom	
THANKED gratefully acknowledged	
THAPSIA plant genus	b
THAWING melting; dissolving	
THEATRE operations; drama	me
THEBAIA thebain; opium	me

THEBAIC Theban
THECATE sheathed; encased   bt
THECIUM spore-case   bt
THEORBO lute with 11 strings   mu
THEOREM logical proposition
THERAPY the curative art   md
THEREAT on that account
THEREBY in consequence
THEREIN inside that
THEREOF about that
THEREON upon that
THERETO in addition
THERIAC alleged antidote   md
THERMAL thermic; warm
THERMIE heat-calory unit (Fr.)
THERMIT incendiary mixture
THERMOS flask
THEROID animal-like   zo
THESEUS slew Minotaur in Labyrinth
THESPIS founder of Greek drama
THEURGY miracle making
THIAMIN B vitamin   ch
THICKEN condense; coagulate; curdle
THICKER closer; duller; muddier
THICKET underwood
THICKLY solidly; densely; closely
THICKUN £1; a sovereign   nm
THIEVED stole; peculated; purloined
THIGGED cadged; begged
THIGGER threatening beggar; sorner
THILLER wheel-horse; shaft-horse   zo
THIMBLE iron rope ring   nt
THINKER cogitator; (Rodin)
THINNED attenuated; reduced
THINNER slimmer; slighter
THIRSTY dry; parched; craving
THISTLE emblem of Scotland; weed   bt
THISTLY overgrown with thistles
THITHER to there; yonder
THOLING enduring; yielding
THOMISM } doctrines of Thomas
THOMIST } Aquinas   rl
THORIDE radioactive isotope   nc
THORITE thorium silicate   mn
THORIUM a metallic element   ch
THOUGHT solicitude; concern; care
THOUING treating with familiarity
THRATCH gasp for breath (Sc.)
THREADY filamentous
THREAVE 24 sheaves
THRIFTY frugal; economical; thriving
THRIVED waxed; luxuriated
THRIVEN flourished; grown
THRIVER prosperer
THROATY guttural
THRONAL like a throne
THRONED exalted
THROUGH clear; unobstructed
THROWER caster; hurler; heaver
THROW-IN football
THRUMMY shaggy cloth; fringed

THUGGEE thug; assassin
THULITE Norwegian rock   mn
THULIUM a metallic element   ch
THUMBED beckoned for a lift
THUMMIM a perfect mystery
THUMPED struck heavily; drubbed
THUMPER whacker
THUNDER denounce; rumble
THURIFY to cense frankincense
THWAITE reclaimed land
THYMINE animal nucleoprotein constituent   bc
THYMOMA tumour in thymus   md
THYRITE voltage-rise limiting device   el
THYROID shield-like gland   md
THYRSUS ivy staff (Bacchus)
THYRSUS densely branched inflorescence   bt
THYSELF reflexive pronoun
TIARAED wearing a tiara
TIBETAN of Tibet
TIBICEN flute player   mu
TICKING bedding material; marking
TICKLED titillated; amused
TICKLER enlivener
TIDDLER small fry   zo
TIDERIP rough water
TIDEWAY a channel
TIDIEST neatest; sprucest
TIDINGS news; intelligence; message
TIE-BACK window drape fastener
TIE-BEAM rafter retainer
TIERCEL male hawk   zo
TIERCET triple rhyme
TIFFANY gauze; thin silk
TIGELLA short stem   bt
TIGHTEN increase the strain
TIGHTER more compact; closer
TIGHTLY tautly; tensely
TIGLINE croton oil   bt
TIGRESS fierce female tiger   zo
TIGRINE marked like a tiger
TIGRISH fierce
TIGROID of nerve-cell granules   cy
TILBURY dog-cart
TILE-ORE copper ore   mn
TILE-RED brownish-red
TILLAGE cultivation
TILLING husbandry
TILLITE till; boulder clay
TILSEED seed of sesamum indicum   bt
TILTING slanting; forging
TIMBALE a fowl dish
TIMBREL tambourine   mu
TIMEFUL seasonable; timely
TIME-GUN parting shot
TIME-LAG an interim; delay
TIME-OFF leisure; break
TIMIDLY fearfully; diffidently
TIMOTHY cat's tail grass   bt
TIMPANI tympani   mu

TIMPANO kettle-drum	mu	
TINAMOU S. American quail	zo	
TINCHEL ⎫ deer battue		
TINCHIL ⎭		
TINDERY inflammable		
TIN-FISH torpedo	nt	
TINFOIL leaf aluminium		
TINGING ringing; tinking		
TINGLED thrilled; smarted		
TINIEST smallest; puniest; microscopic		
TINKING tinkling; ringing		
TINKLED rang; clinked		
TINKLER small bell		
TIN-MINE Cornish hole		
TINNING covering with tin		
TINNOCK blue tit	zo	
TIN-TACK tack of/for tin		
TINTAGE colouring; shading		
TINTIES coloured films		
TINTING tingeing		
TINTYPE ferro-type		
TINWARE tin pots		
TIN-ZINC metal finish	ml	
TIPCART rubbish barrow		
TIPPING (flute playing); hinting	mu	
TIPPLED drank deep		
TIPPLER steady absorber		
TIPSIFY inebriate		
TIPSILY drunkenly		
TIPSTER racing tout		
TIPTOED walked warily		
TIQUEUR person suffering from tic	md	
TIRASSE pedal coupling	mu	
TIRLING quivering; vibrating; twisting		
TISSUED woven; variegated		
TITANIA fairy queen		
TITANIC gigantic; colossal		
TITHING township		
TITLARK meadow pipit	zo	
TITLING title pages		
TITLING hedge sparrow	zo	
TITMICE tits	zo	
TITOISM political practice		
TITRATE (volumetric analysis)	ch	
TITTUPY frisky		
TITULAR nominal		
TIVERED marked with ochre		
TOADIED cringed; truckled; fawned		
TOADIES sycophants		
TOASTED dried; warmed		
TOASTER bread burner		
TOBACCO insidious narcotic		
TOBASCO red pepper		
TOBOGAN toboggan		
TOBYMAN highwayman		
TOCCATA a touchy composition	mu	
TODDLED strolled; meandered		
TODDLER a tiny tot		
TOE-HOLD foot grip for climber		
TOENAIL horn on foot digits		
TOFTMAN a cottager		

TOGGERY raiment		
TOILFUL wearisome		
TOILING moiling; labouring; snaring		
TOKENED spotted; marked		
TOLLAGE dues		
TOLLBAR toll-gate		
TOLLING knelling; annulling	lv
TOLLMAN toll-gatherer		
TOLUENE methyl benzene	ch
TOMALLY lobster liver	ze
TOMATIN tomato anti-biotic	ch
TOMBOLA a form of lottery		
TOMFOOL buffoon		
TOMOSIS disease of cotton plant	b
TOMPION inking pad; clockmaker		
TONGUED possessing a tongue		
TO-NIGHT night of this day		
TONNAGE amount of tons		
TONNEAU back-seat part of motor-car	a
TONSILE clippable		
TONSURE shaving; (shorn)		
TONTINE co-operative loan		
TOOL-BOX container for implements		
TOOLING (bookbinding); driving		
TOOTHED dentate		
TOOTING prying; hornblowing		
TOOTLED played the flute	m
TOPARCH a Greek governor		
TOPBOOT high-rising shoe		
TOPCOAT light overcoat		
TOP-EDGE smooth gilded upper book edg	
TOPFULL brimming (Shak.)		
TOPHOLE first-rate		
TOP-HUNG of top-hinged window-sash	b
TOPIARY ornamental clipping		
TOPICAL local; particular; allusive		
TOPKNOT plume or crest of feathers	a
TOPLESS without a lid; bare-bosomed		
TOPMAST elevated mast	
TOPMOST highest		
TOPONYM topographical name		
TOPPING of a high order		
TOPPLED tumbled down		
TOPSAIL part of rigging	
TOPSIDE the upper part		
TOPSMAN bailiff; public hangman		
TOPSOIL planting earth		
TORBITE peat fuel		
TORCHER torch-bearer; linkman		
TORCHON geometric lace		
TORGOCH a species of char	a
TORMENT rag; rack; plague; harry		
TORMINA griping pains	n
TORNADO cyclone; hurricane; typhoon		
TORNOTE with blunt extremities		
TORPEDO ray fish; the tin fish		
TORPENT torpid; inert		
TORPIFY benumb		
TORQUED wreathed	
TORREFY parch; roast; scorch		
TORRENT stream; flood; current		

TORSADE twisted scroll	**TRAINED** proficient; skilled
TORSION twisting force	**TRAINEE** man under instruction
TORSIVE spiral	**TRAINER** a coach
TORSTEN an iron ore mn	**TRAIPSE** to tramp
TORTEAU red circlet hd	**TRAITOR** quisling; betrayer
TORTILE coiled; wreathed	**TRAJECT** ferry; project
TORTIVE twisted; tortile; tortuous	**TRAMCAR** passenger carriage on lines
TORTRIX a moth genus zo	**TRAMMEL** bird-net; compass; hamper
TORTURE torment; agony; pang	**TRAMPED** toured; walked; trudged
TORULUS antenna socket zo	**TRAMPER** vagrant; stroller; hiker
TORVOUS grim; stern in aspect	**TRAMPLE** crush; spurn; squelch
TORYISM Conservatism	**TRAMPOT** socket for a spindle
TOSSILY perty	**TRAMWAY** street railway
TOSSING (deciding); agitating; shaking	**TRANCED** in a dream; enraptured
TOSS-POT toper	**TRANCHE** slice; book edge; portrayal of
TOTALLY wholly; entirely; completely	life
TOTEMIC (totems); emblematic	**TRANECT** ferry; traject
TOTTERY shaky; unsteady	**TRANGLE** small band hd
TOTTING adding up	**TRANKUM** a gew-gaw
TOUCHED sympathetic; impinged	**TRANNEL** wooden nail
TOUCHER a close call	**TRANSIT** conveyance; passage
TOUGHEN indurate; harden	**TRANSOM** cross-beam nt
TOUGHLY stubbornly; tenaciously	**TRANTER** pedlar
TOURACO African bird zo	**TRAPEZE** swinging cross-bar
TOURING journeying	**TRAPPED** adorned; caught
TOURISM co-ordinated travel	**TRAPPER** setter of snares
TOURIST tripper; excursionist	**TRASHED** lopped; crushed; hindered
TOURNEY tournament	**TRAVAIL** toil; labour; affliction
TOUSING teasing; worrying	**TRAWLED** fished nt
TOUSLED unkempt; in disarray	**TRAWLER** fishing boat nt
TOUTING seeking custom	**TRAYLED** interwoven (Spens.)
TOWARDS in direction of	**TREACLE** molasses; dark syrup
TOWBOAT tug nt	**TREACLY** viscous and sweet
TOWERED with towers	**TREADER** trampler
TOWIRON whaling toggle-iron	**TREADLE** pedal
TOWLINE tow rope	**TREASON** treachery; disloyalty
TOWNISH urban	**TREATED** entertained; doctored
TOWPATH boat-haulage path	**TREATER** negotiator
TOW|ROPE boat-haulage rope	**TREBLED** tripled; threefold
TOXEMIA blood poisoning md	**TREDDLE** a treadle (obs.)
TOXEMIC septicaemic md	**TREEING** cornering
TOXICAL poisonous	**TREFOIL** (clover) ar
TOXODON extinct rhinoceros zo	**TREGOHM** million megohms el
TOYSHOP plaything emporium	**TREHALA** Turkish manna bt
TOYSOME playful	**TREKKED** migrated
TOYWORT shepherd's purse bt	**TREKKER** (ox-wagons, S. Africa)
TRACERY ornamental stonework	**TRELLIS** lattice work
TRACHEA wind-pipe md	**TREMBLE** quiver; shake; oscillate
TRACHLE to draggle (Sc.)	**TREMBLY** tottery; unsteady
TRACING a copy; traversing	**TREMOLO** vibrato mu
TRACKED trailed; traversed	**TRENAIL** wooden nail
TRACKER a sleuth	**TRENDED** tended; inclined; gravitated
TRACTOR mechanical plough	**TRENDLE** a roller
TRADE-IN part-exchange	**TRENTAL** 30 masses rl
TRADING commerce; barter	**TREPANG** sea-slug zo
TRADUCE misrepresent; libel; slander	**TRESSED** curled
TRAFFIC intercourse; transport; deal	**TRESSEL** trestle; a movable framework
TRAGEDY drama; calamity	**TRESTLE** a support
TRAIKET worn out (Sc.)	**TREVISS** cross-beam
TRAILED followed; dragged; dogged	**TRIABLE** (jurisdiction) lw
TRAILER tracker; towed vehicle	**TRIADIC** trivalent ch

TRIAENE spicule in porifera	zo
TRIARCH with 3 xylem strands in stele	bt
TRIATIC jumper stay	nt
TRIAXON with three axes	
TRIBBLE paper drying frame	
TRIBLET a goldsmith's mandril	to
TRIBUNE Roman magistrate; platform	
TRIBUTE tax; impost; toil; offering	
TRICEPS extensor muscle	md
TRICHAS American warblers	zo
TRICING hauling; clewing	nt
TRICKED defrauded; hoaxed	
TRICKER trickster	
TRICKLE drip; ooze; percolate	
TRICKLY trickling	
TRICKSY artful; deft	
TRICORN three-cornered	
TRIDARN having three tiers	
TRIDENT Neptune's sceptre	
TRIDUAN every third day	
TRIDUUM period of three days	
TRIFLED dallied; toyed; played	
TRIFLER philanderer; idler; fribbler	
TRIFOLY trefoil	bt
TRIFORM triple form	
TRIGAMY cf. bigamy	
TRIGGED skidded; obstructed	
TRIGGER a detent	
TRIGLOT in three languages	
TRIGONE triangular area	
TRIGRAM a triphthong; a trigraph	
TRILABE surgical fork	md
TRILITH stone doorway	ar
TRILLED warbled; quavered	
TRILOGY a series of three books in literature	
TRIMERA type of beetle	zo
TRIMMED clipped; balanced; rebuked	
TRIMMER fishing float; time-server	
TRINARY ternary; threefold	
TRINDLE trundle; trickle	
TRINGLE curtain rod (Fr.)	
TRINITY unit of 3	rl
TRINKET small ornament	
TRINKLE trickle or tinkle	
TRIOLET poetic stanza	
TRIONAL hypnotic drug	md
TRIONES 7 stars in Ursa Major	
TRIPACK 3-emulsion-base process	pg
TRIPARA woman giving birth 3 times	
TRIPERY tripe-booth	
TRIPLED trebled	
TRIPLET three of a kind	mu
TRIPODY verse measure of 3 feet	
TRIPOLI polishing powder; diatomite	
TRIPOLY Michaelmas daisy	bt
TRIPPED erred; slipped; stumbled	
TRIPPER excursionist; dancer	
TRIPSIS shampooing; pulverizing	
TRIREME a galley	nt
TRISECT cut into three	

TRISEME (tribrach)	
TRISMUS lock-jaw; tetanus	md
TRISULA Siva's trident	
TRITELY jejunely; hackneyed	
TRITIUM very rare isotope of hydrogen	
TRITOMA red-hot poker	bt
TRITONE dissonant interval	mu
TRIUMPH exultation; success; ovation	
TRIVIAL trifling; slight; paltry	
TRIVIUM grammar; logic and rhetoric	
TROCHAL wheel-shaped	zo
TROCHEE long and short foot metre	
TROCHUS gastropod genus	zo
TRODDEN trampled	
TROGGIN pedlary	
TROLAND unit of illuminance (optics)	
TROLLED sang; fished; rambled	
TROLLER trolley; trolly	
TROLLEY truck; metal pulley	
TROLLOL sing; troll; trill	
TROLLOP a slattern; a slut	
TROMMEL mining sieve	
TROMPIL blast regulating device	
TRONAGE wool-tax	
TROOPED thronged; (the colours)	
TROOPER mounted man; ship	nt
TROPHIC (nutrition)	
TROPICS (Cancer and Capricorn)	
TROPINE constituent of atropine	md
TROPISM enforced turning movement	
TROPIST figurative speaker	
TROTTER pig's foot	
TROUBLE disturb; worry; trial; dolour	
TROUNCE to larrup; castigate	
TROUPER strolling player	
TROUSSE set of instruments	md
TROWING trusting; believing	
TRUANCY vagrancy	
TRUCAGE counterfeiting a picture	
TRUCKED bartered; trafficked	
TRUCKER exchange agent	
TRUCKLE roller; yield; submit	
TRUDGED walked wearily; tramped	
TRUDGEN a swimming stroke	
TRUFFLE an edible fungus	bt
TRUMEAU part of a wall	
TRUMPED deceived; ruffed	
TRUMPET proclaim; blazon	mu
TRUNCAL main; principal	
TRUNCUS main blood vessel	zo
TRUNDLE wheel; truck; to roll	
TRUNDLE spool of golden thread	
TRUSSED bound; tied up	
TRUSTED credited; confided	
TRUSTEE guardian; fiduciary	
TRUSTER an optimist; creditor	
TRYABLE triable	lw
TRYPETA boring flies	zo
TRYPSIN pepsin	md
TRYPTIC peptic; digestive	md
TRY-SAIL part of rigging	nt

TRYSTED rendezvoused; appointed
TRYSTER tryst convener
TSABIAN star-worshipper; sabian
TSANTSA head-shrinking technique
TSARINA Empress of Russia
TSARIST Russian royalist
T-SQUARE draughtsman's tool
TUATERA tuatara; NZ lizard   zo
TUBBING mine shaft lining; bathing   mn
TUBBISH rotund   zo
TUB-FISH sapphirine gurnard   zo
TUBICEN trumpeter   mu
TUB-SIZE strengthening dip for handmade paper
TUBULAR hollow; fistular; capillary
TUCK-BOX treats for schoolboys
TUCKING cramming; folding; gathering
TUCK-OUT tuck-in; blow-out
TUEFALL a pent-house
TUESDAY a weekday
TUESITE slate pencil material   mn
TUFTING adorning with tufts
TUGBOAT small powerful boat   nt
TUGGING lugging; pulling; hauling
TUGHRIK (Mongolia)   nm
TUITION instruction; education
TULCHAN spoof calf
TULLIAN (Tullius Cicero)
TUMBLED rumpled; fallen; twigged
TUMBLER pigeon; glass; acrobat   zo
TUMBREL tumbril; two-wheeled cart
TUMIDLY pompously; turgidly; puffily
TUMPING humping; carrying
TUMULAR heaped
TUMULUS burial mound
TUNABLE melodious; musical
TUNABLY harmoniously
TUNDISH wine funnel
TUNEFUL musical; dulcet
TUNG-OIL wood-oil   bt
TUNICIN animal cellulose   zo
TUNICLE small tunic
TUNMOOT village council
TUNNAGE (and poundage) wine tax
TUNNERY tunny-netting area
TUPPING hammering; butting
TURACIN carmine
TURAKOO gaudy bird; plantain-eater   zo
TURBARY turf digging rights
TURBINE rotary engine
TURDINE thrush-like
TURFING laying turf; swarding
TURFITE racing fan
TURGENT swelling; distended; tumid
TURGITE a form of haematite   mn
TURKISH, TURKMEN (Turkestan)
TURKOIS turquoise   mn
TURMOIL tumult; ado; hubbub
TURNCAP chimney cowl
TURNERY lathe work
TURNING flexure; spinning; fermenting

TURNKEY prison warder
TURN-OUT an equipage
TURN-UPS trouser leg folds
TURPETH purgative plant   bt
TURTLER turtle-hunter
TUSSIVE afflicted with a cough
TUSSLED struggled; fought; battled
TUSSOCK tuffet; tuft
TUSSORE coarse silk   tx
TUTAMEN a protection; a defence
TUTANIA Britannia metal
TUTELAR protective
TUTENAG a Chinese alloy; zinc
TUTORED taught; educated; instructed
TUTULUS Etruscan head-dress
TUT-WORK excavation piece-work   mn
TWADDLE verbiage; balderdash; prattle
TWANGED played the banjo   mu
TWANGLE to twang
TWANKAY green tea
TWANKED twanged; twangled
TWATTLE gabble
TWEAKED twitched; pinched
TWEEDLE (fiddle); wheedle
TWEELED twiller (Sc.)
TWEENIE a maid
TWEETER loudspeaker   ac
TWELFTH ordinal number
TWIBILL mattock; axe   to
TWIDDLE twist; tweedle
TWIGGED understood; observed
TWIGGEN of wicker
TWINGED twitched; pained
TWINING twisting; meandering; coiling
TWINKLE wink; glimmer; scintillate
TWINNED two at a time
TWINSET matching sweater and cardigan
TWINTER beast, two winters old
TWIN-TOP (motoring)   au
TWIRLED span; rotated; whirled
TWIRLER spinner; twister
TWISTED spun; contorted; tangled
TWISTER a puzzle; perverter; tornado
TWISTLE twist; a wrench (Sc.)
TWISTOR computer memory device
TWITTED reproached; rallied; taunted
TWITTEN by-lane
TWITTER an upbraider; chirp; palpitate
TWIZZLE turn and twist
TWO-FOLD twi-fold; double
TWO-LINE size of printing type; whip   pr
TWONESS doubleness
TWOSOME a couple
TWOSTEP a dance   mu
TWO-TIME double-cross   mu
TYCHISM theory based on chance
TYING-IN tubular scaffolding, interior grip   pt
TYING-UP mooring a vessel; setting book-bands; binding; securing   nt, pr
TYLARUS padded hoof   zo

TYLOPOD camel-footed
TYLOSIS eye-trouble   md
TYLOTIC eye-inflammation   md
TYMPANA ear-drums   md
TYMPANO timpano; a drum   mu
TYMPANY turgidity; flatulence   md
TYNWALD parliament (Isle of Man)
TYPE-BAR a line of type   pr
TYPHOID a fever   md
TYPHOON cyclone; hurricane
TYPHOUS enteric   md
TYPICAL emblematic; characteristic
TYPONYM type-name
TYRANNY despotism; iron rule
TZARINA Tsarina (Russia)
TZIGANE gipsy (Hungary)

U

UBEROUS fruitful
UDALLER odaller; freeholder
UDARNIK 'shock' worker (Rus.)
UKULELE Hawaian guitar   mu
ULEXITE hydrated sodium/calcium borate
   mn
ULLALOO Irish lament
ULNARIA arm-bones   pl
ULONCUS swollen gums   md
ULULANT wailing; sobbing
ULULATE howl; hoot
ULYSSES Odysseus; a wanderer
UMBERED tinged with umber
UMBONAL protuberant
UMBONES bosses on shields
UMBONIC humpy
UMBRAGE shade; resentment
UMBRERE helmet visor
UMBRIAN (Raphael)
UMBRINE dull darkish brown   bt
UMBRINE a fish   zo
UMBROSE shady; umbrageous
UMPIRED arbitrated; judged
UMPTEEN more than ten
UNACTED never staged
UNAGING immortal
UNAIDED single-handed
UNAIRED possibly damp; stuffy
UNALIST holding one benefice   rl
UNAPTLY not à propos
UNARMED defenceless
UNASKED gratuitously
UNAWARE ignorant; uninformed
UNBATED unblunted; non-stop
UNBAYED opened up
UNBEGUN not started
UNBLIND restore vision
UNBLOCK to clear; (cards)
UNBLOWN not sounded; in the bud
UNBORNE not carried
UNBOSOM freely disclose

UNBOUND loose
UNBOWED unsubdued
UNBRACE relax; free from tension
UNBRAID disentangle
UNBRUTE domesticate; tame
UNBUILT not yet constructed
UNBURNT unconsumed
UNCAGED released; freed
UNCANNY eerie; weird; mysterious
UNCARED untended; unheeded
UNCASED taken out; displayed
UNCEDED not transferred or granted
UNCHAIN free; let loose; unfetter
UNCHARM unspell; exorcise
UNCHARY heedless; not frugal
UNCINAL hook-shaped
UNCINUS small hook   me
UNCIVIL incivil; impolite
UNCLASP unfasten; disconnect
UNCLEAN foul; dirty; leprous
UNCLEAR confused; unintelligible
UNCLING unclasp; disengage
UNCLOAK disrobe; unveil; unmask
UNCLOSE open; babbling
UNCLOUD free from obscurity
UNCOUTH boorish; rustic; rough
UNCOVER lay open; disclose
UNCROSS (the legs)
UNCROWN dethrone
UNCTION an anointing
UNCULAR avuncular
UNDATED waved
UNDEIFY remove a god
UNDERDO cook insufficiently
UNDERGO experience; bear; suffer
UNDIGHT to undress
UNDOING opening; unravelling; ruining
UNDRAPE strip; uncover
UNDRAWN not delineated
UNDRESS not full parade uniform
UNDRIED wet; green
UNEARED untilled (Shak.)
UNEARTH disclose; reveal; discover
UNEATEN not consumed
UNEQUAL varying; not uniform
UNEXACT inexact; inaccurate
UNFADED unwithered
UNFAITH infidelity
UNFENCE remove a hedge
UNFILED unrasped; (papers)
UNFITLY unsuitably; improperly
UNFIXED unsettled
UNFLESH reduce to a skeleton
UNFLUSH lose colour
UNFOUND still lost; not met with
UNFROCK deprive of office
UNFUMED not fumigated
UNFUSED not melted
UNFUZED (shells)   m
UNGIVEN not conceded
UNGLAZE remove the glass

UNGLOVE bare the hand		
UNGLUED unstuck		
UNGODLY sinful; impious; profane		
UNGRATE ungrateful person		
UNGUARD leave defenceless		
UNGUENT an ointment	md	
UNGULAR (hoof; nails; etc.)	zo	
UNGYVED unfettered		
UNHABLE incapable (Spens.)		
UNHANDY awkward; clumsy		
UNHAPPY sad; grievous; sorrowful		
UNHARDY irresolute; delicate		
UNHASTY slow; deliberate		
UNHEARD inaudible; obscure		
UNHEART to discourage (Shak.)		
UNHEEDY careless; rash		
UNHINGE to unsettle; derange		
UNHIRED not engaged		
UNHITCH loosen; unfasten		
UNHIVED driven from shelter		
UNHOARD dissipate; spend		
UNHOPED unexpected		
UNHORSE force to dismount		
UNHOUSE evict		
UNIAXAL uniaxial		
UNICITY oneness; sameness		
UNICORN a fabulous animal; oryx	zo	
UNIDEAL realistic; prosaic		
UNIFIED united; merged		
UNIFIER amalgamator; merger		
UNIFOIL bearing only one leaf	bt	
UNIFORM consistent; steady		
UNITAGE measurement		
UNITARY monistic; integral		
UNITATE remainder after division		
UNITERM key-word graphic index system		
UNITING combining; concerting		
UNITION conjunction		
UNITIVE harmonising		
UNITIZE to treat as one unit		
UNJOINT disconnect		
UNKEMPT uncombed; rough		
UNKNOWN nameless; anonymous		
UNLACED not done up; untied		
UNLADEN unladed; unloaded		
UNLATCH to open		
UNLEARN to forget		
UNLEASH remove all constraint		
UNLEAVE strip of leaves		
UNLEVEL uneven; rough		
UNLIMED freed from lime		
UNLINED (paper); unruled		
UNLIVED bereft of life (Shak.)		
UNLOOSE unleash; unfasten		
UNLOVED disliked		
UNLUCKY ill-starred; hapless		
UNLUSTY weak; infirm; sickly		
UNLUTED unglued; uncemented		
UNMANLY effeminate; cowardly		
UNMARRY divorce		
UNMEANT not intended		

UNMETED not measured		
UNMEWED set free; released		
UNMIXED pure; unadulterated		
UNMOIST dehydrated; dry; arid		
UNMORAL immoral; licentious		
UNMOULD change the form of		
UNMOVED impassive; serene; quiet		
UNNAMED anonymous		
UNNERVE frighten; intimidate		
UNNOBLE ignoble (Spens.)		
UNNOTED undistinguished		
UNOFTEN infrequently		
UNOILED free from lubrication		
UNORDER countermand		
UNOWNED unacknowledged		
UNPAGED unnumbered (of prelim. pages)		
UNPAINT efface		
UNPANEL to unsaddle		
UNPAVED uncobbled		
UNPENAL without penalty		
UNPERCH dislodge; unroost		
UNPLACE displace		
UNPLAIT unbraid; unravel		
UNPLUMB not vertical		
UNPLUME pluck		
UNQUEEN dethrone		
UNQUIET unease; restless		
UNQUOTE end quotation		
UNRAKED untilled		
UNRAVEL disentangle; solve		
UNREADY irresolute; slow		
UNREEVE withdraw a rope	nt
UNRIVET undo; loosen; detach		
UNROBED undressed		
UNROUGH moderately smooth		
UNROYAL unkingly		
UNRULED uncontrolled; unlined		
UNSATED rapacious; not satisfied		
UNSCALY having no scales	zo
UNSCREW untwist; unfasten		
UNSENSE to stun		
UNSEXED lacking femininity		
UNSHELL unhusk; release		
UNSHORN unshaven; unclipped		
UNSHOWN not exhibited		
UNSIGHT cricket		
UNSIZED not stiffened		
UNSLING release from slings		
UNSLUNG not projected		
UNSMOTE unsmitten		
UNSNARL disentangle; unravel		
UNSOLID fluid; unsubstantial		
UNSOUND erroneous; defective		
UNSPELL uncharm; exorcise		
UNSPENT unexhausted; still moving		
UNSPIED unobserved; undetected		
UNSPIKE pull out prickles		
UNSPILT not shed; not slopped		
UNSPLIT undivided		
UNSPOIL restore		
UNSTACK disperse; dishevel		

UNSTAID unsteady; unstable
UNSTATE deprive of dignity
UNSTEEL soften; disarm
UNSTICK ungum; tear free
UNSTRAP loosen
UNSTUCK loosened; dished
UNSTUNG depierced
UNSUNNY dull; shady
UNSWEAR recall an oath
UNSWEET inharmonious; acid
UNSWEPT unbrushed
UNSWORN not on oath
UNTAKEN left; relinquished
UNTAMED savage; barbaric
UNTAXED not charged
UNTHINK dismiss from the mind
UNTILED detesselated
UNTIRED unwearied
UNTOOTH extract
UNTRIED inexperienced; new
UNTRULY falsely; erroneously
UNTRUSS take apart; dissect
UNTRUTH lie; imposture; error
UNTUNED not set to play   ro, mu
UNTWINE untwist; unravel
UNTWIST disentangle
UNTYING unknotting
UNURGED unsolicited
UNUSUAL bizarre; queer; odd; rum
UNVEXED unharassed; untroubled
UNVOWED not bound by oath
UNWAGED unsalaried
UNWAYED trackless
UNWEARY unspent; unflagging
UNWEAVE unplait
UNWHIPT unbirched
UNWIRED unstrung
UNWITCH uncharm; unspell
UNWITTY lacking humour; prosaic
UNWOOED uncourted; unsolicited
UNWOUND untwined; uncoiled
UNWOVEN not made into cloth
UNWRUNG not galled
UNYOKED unrestrained (Shak.)
UNZONED unbelted
UPBLAZE to flare up
UPBORNE carried aloft
UPBOUND tied; restricted
UPBRAID rebuke; chide; taunt
UPBREAK shoot up
UPBURST outburst
UPCHEER encourage
UPCLIMB ascend
UPENDED stood on end
UPFIELD cricket
UPGAZED looked upwards
UPGRADE on the rise
UPHEAVE lift up; raise
UPHOARD secrete; amass; garner
UPLYING elevated
UPPLUCK gather up; uproot

UPRAISE to nurture; uplift
UPRIGHT vertical; honest; just
UPRISEN ascended
UPROUSE awaken
UPSHIFT change gear
UPSHOOT a sprout   bt
UPSPEAR shoot up straight
UPSTAGE (theatrical)
UPSTAND to stand up; to rise
UPSTARE upgaze
UPSTART parvenu; meadow saffron   bt
UPSURGE upswell
UPSWARM opposite of downscool
UPSWEEP woman's coiffure
UPSWELL upsurge
UPTHROW an upheaval
UPTIGHT unduly inhibited
UPTRACE to trace
UP-TRAIN train to London
UPTRILL sing high
UPWARDS upward; upwardly
URAEMIA kidney disease   md
URALITE fireproof material   mn
URANIAN astronomical
URANIDE element beyond protactinium
    ch
URANITE a green uranium ore   mn
URANIUM metallic element   ch
URANOUS containing uranium   ch
URETHRA urinary duct   zo
URGENCY importunity; stress
URICASE uric acid salt
URIDINE crystalline nucleoside   ch
URINANT bent fish   hd
URINARY of the bladder/urine   md
URINATE to pass body water   md
UROCYON American grey fox   zo
UROCYST the bladder   pl
UROLOGY study of urinary tract   md
UROSOME caudal segment   md
URSINAL ursine; bearish   zo
URTICAL (nettles)   bt
USELESS vain; bootless; abortive
USHERED introduced; foreran; heralded
USITATE usually; customary
USUALLY normally; generally
USURPED arrogated; seized; assumed
USURPER a dictator
UTENSIL implement; vessel
UTERINE of the uterus   md
UTILISE utilize; employ; apply
UTILITY usefulness
UTOPIAN imaginary; chimerical; ideal
UTOPISM unpractical hopefulness
UTOPIST optimist; visionary
UTRICLE small cell or bladder   md
UTTERED issued; pronounced; said
UTTERER promulgator; (counterfeit)
UTTERLY absolutely; completely
UVEITIS eye congestion   md
UXORIAL dotingly fond of a wife

V

VACANCY void; emptiness; listlessness
VACATED left; abandoned
VACATOR a quitter
VACATUR annulment — lw
VACCINE lymph — md
VACHERY cow-house; dairy
VACUATE make a vacuum
VACUIST vacant believer
VACUITY emptiness; a void
VACUOLE minute cavity
VACUOUS void; unfilled
VAGITUS cry of a new-born child
VAGRANT vagabond; nomad; tramp
VAGUELY dimly; indefinitely
VAGUEST most uncertain
VAILING veiling; tipping
VAINEST most conceited
VALANCE draped border
VALENCE } combining power — ch
VALENCY }
VALERIC derived from valerian — bt
VALIANT intrepid; gallant; doughty
VALIDLY with legal force
VALINCH cask tap
VALLARY (rampart)
VALLATE cup-shaped
VALONIA acorn-cup (Levant) — bt
VALSOID with perithecia in circle — bt
VALUING esteeming; appraising
VALVATE valvular
VALVLET valvula; small valve
VALVULA cerebellum process in fish — zo
VALVULE valvula; small valve
VAMOOSE to retire
VAMOSED decamped
VAMPING patching; bewitching — mu
VAMPIRE blood-sucker; a bat — zo
VAMPLET spear buckler
VANADIC of vanadium — ch
VANADYL electrolyte cation — ch
VANDYKE lace collar
VANESSA butterfly genus (Swift) — zo
VAN-FOSS a moat
VANILLA orchid; a flavour — bt
VANNING mining operation
VANSIRE mongoose (Madagascar) — zo
VANTAGE (tennis); advantage
VANWARD vanguard
VAPIDLY inertly; insipidly; languidly
VAPOURS nervous malady — md
VAPOURY hypochondriac
VAQUERO S. American cow-puncher
VARANUS monitor lizard — zo
VAREUSE seaman's jersey, jacket
VARIANT different; diverse
VARIATE to vary; alter
VARICES knotted veins — md
VARIETY diversity; assortment
VARIOLA smallpox — md

VARIOLE pitted
VARIOUS sundry; several; numerous
VARMINT vermin — zo
VARNISH to gloss over; palliate
VARSITY university
VARVELS vervels; rings on a hawk
VARYING differing; deviating; altering
VASTATE make immune
VASTEST bulkiest; greatest
VATICAN papal power
VATTING mixing wines; customs
VAUDOIS Waldensian
VAULTED arched; sprang
VAULTER bounder
VAUNTED boosted; bragged
VAUNTER braggart; boaster
VAVASOR titled landowner
VECTION porterage; convection
VEDANGA Veda commentary
VEDANTA Veda philosophy
VEDETTE vidette; mounted scout
VEERING shifting; changing; varying
VEGETAL vegetable; plant — bt
VEHICLE (painting); car; conveyance
VEILING veil material
VEINAGE vein system — bt, md
VEINING ramification
VEINLET small vein
VEINOUS (veins)
VEINULE veinlet
VELAMEN a membrane — md
VELARIA Roman amphitheatre awning
VELIGER larval stage of mollusca — zo
VELLING cutting turf
VELLUMY like vellum
VELOURS plush fabric
VELOUTE creamy meat sauce — ck
VELVETY smooth
VENALLY mercenary
VENATIC sporting
VENDACE a lake fish — zo
VENDING selling; bartering
VENERER gamekeeper
VENISON deer meat
VENOMED poisoned
VENTAGE escape hole
VENTAIL helmet visor
VENTING releasing; uttering; emitting
VENTOSE windy; breezy
VENTOSE Republican month (Fr.)
VENT-PEG a spile; spigot
VENTRAD ventrally — zo
VENTRAL abdominal — md
VENTRIC ventral
VENTURE hazard; chance; dare
VENTURI convergent/divergent duct — ae
VERANDA verandah; open portico
VERBENA vervain — bt
VERBIFY verbalise
VERBILE person stimulated by words — pc
VERBOSE wordy; prolix; loquacious

VERDANT unsophisticated; green
VERDICT decision; finding; judgment
VERDITE green S. Afr. rock   mn
VERDURE green growth
VERGENT bordering; tending
VERGING inclining; adjacent to
VERGLAS thin ice or frost layer
VERIEST absolute; truest
VERISMO expressionist objectivity (art)
VERITAS French shipping bureau
VERMEIL a glaze; ormolu
VERMIAN wormlike   zo
VERMILY vermilion
VERMUTH vermouth; absinth
VERNANT spring-like; vernal
VERNATE to flourish
VERNIER measuring device
VERONAL an opiate   md
VERRUCA a wart   bt, md
VERSANT conversant; familiar
VERSENE sodium versenate   ch
VERSIFY relate in verse
VERSINE function of an angle   ma
VERSING relating in rhyme
VERSION an account; interpretation
VERSUAL paragraphic
VERSUTE crafty; wily
VERTIGO dizziness; giddiness   md
VERULED ringed   hd
VERULES concentric rings   hd
VERVAIN verbena   bt
VERVELS varvels; rings on a hawk
VESANIA insanity   md
VESICAL } bladder-like   md
VESICLE }   cavity or cell
VESPINE wasplike
VESPOID wasplike   zo
VESTIGE footprint; trace; mark
VESTING fabric for vests; investing
VESTLET a sea-anemone   zo
VESTRAL (vestry)
VESTURE clothing; garment; dress
VETERAN experienced; seasoned
VETIVER a fragrant grass   bt
VETOING prohibiting; barring; banning
VETTING examining
VETTURA Italian cab
VEXILLA processional banners
VIADUCT raised road
VIALFUL a bottleful
VIARIAN wayfarer
VIBICES feverish spots   md
VIBRANT resonant; undulous
VIBRATE oscillate; quiver; sway
VIBRATO tremolo   mu
VIBRION mobile bacterium   md
VICEROY king's deputy
VICINAL adjoining; near; neighbouring
VICIOUS depraved; sinful; defective
VICTORY success; mastery; triumph
VICTRIX a lady winner

VICTUAL provide provisions
VIDENDA things to be seen
VIDETTE vedette; mounted scout
VIDIMUS an inspection; summary
VIDUAGE } viduity; widowhood
VIDUATE }
VIDUOUS widowed
VIEWING surveying; scanning; eyeing
VIGONIA llama wool fabric
VILAYET Turkish province
VILLAGE hamlet; thorpe
VILLAIN miscreant; rascal; rogue
VILLEIN serf; villager
VILLINO small villa in a park
VILLOSE shaggy
VILLOUS hairy
VIMINAL of twigs
VINALIA Roman wine festival
VINASSE wine dregs
VINCULA brackets; several similarly
    treated terms   ma
VINEGAR acetic acid; sour wine
VINGT-UN card game
VINTAGE gathering of grapes
VINTNER wine-seller
VIOLANE violet-blue diopside   mr
VIOLATE outrage; break; profane
VIOLENT fierce; vehement; furious
VIOLINE poisonous extract   b
VIOLIST viola player   mu
VIOLONE double-bass   mu
VIRELAY roundelay (Fr.)
VIRGATE wand-like; slender and straight
VIRGATE a quarter of a hide   me
VIRGULE small rod; a comma
VIROSIS viral infection   md
VIRTUAL potential; implicit
VISAGED envisaged
VIS-A-VIS face to face
VISCERA internal organs   md
VISCOUS sticky; glutinous; tenacious
VISEITE zeolite   mr
VISIBLE patent; evident; apparent
VISIBLY obviously; manifestly
VISITED stayed; chastised; afflicted
VISITOR visiter; a caller
VISNOMY physiognomy (Spens.)
VISORED masked
VIS-VIVA striking energy
VITALLY essentially
VITAMIN a food element
VITIATE to spoil; impair; debase
VITRAIL stained-glass window
VITRAIN a type of coal   mr
VITREUM eye-fluid   md
VITRICS glass-making
VITRIFY to glaze
VITRINA glass snails   zo
VITRINE glass show case
VITRIOL sulphuric acid   ch
VITRITE black glass

VITTATE with longitudinal stripes bt
VITULAR (calf); (veal)
VIVENCY existence
VIVERRA civet genus zo
VIVIDLY animatedly; brilliantly
VIVIFIC enlivening
VIXENLY snappish
VOCABLE a word; a name
VOCALIC containing vowels
VOCALLY by voice
VOCODER synthetic speech device
VOCULAR vocal
VOETSAK begone! (S. Africa)
VOGLITE uranium ore mn
VOICING expressing
VOIDAGE fractional quantity of voids
VOIDING ejecting; emptying
VOIVODE, VAIVODE Balkan governor
VOLABLE nimble-witted; volatile
VOLANTE Spanish vehicle
VOLAPUK universal language
VOLCANO eruptive mountain
VOLSUNG Odin's grandson
VOLTAGE amount of volts el, me
VOLTAIC galvanic
VOLUBLE having the gift of the gab
VOLUBLY glibly; fluently
VOLUMED bulky
VOLUMEN rolled papyrus text
VOLUSPA song of the sybil (Scand.)
VOLUTED with spiral scroll
VOMITUS vomited matter md
VOTABLE enfranchised
VOUCHED warranted; attested
VOUCHEE warrantee lw
VOUCHER a witness; a pass
VOWELLY full of vowels
VOYAGED cruised; traversed
VOYAGER ocean traveller
VULGATE authentic Latin Bible rl
VULPINE foxy; cunning
VULTURE carrion-eating bird zo
VULTURN Australian turkey zo

W

WABBLER a wobbler
WABSTER webster; weaver
WADABLE fordable
WADDING stuffing
WADDLED walked like a duck
WADDLER wobbly walker
WAD-HOOK an extractor to
WADMOLL woollen cloth
WADSETT a mortgage lw
WAENESS sadness (Sc.)
WAESOME woesome; woeful; pitiful
WAFERED sealed; secured
WAFTAGE transportation
WAFTING floating; airing; beckoning

WAFTURE waftage; wavure
WAGERED hazarded; risked; staked
WAGERER a better
WAGGERY sportive merriment
WAGGING vibrating; stirring
WAGGISH droll; facetious; jocular
WAGGLED wiggled; swayed
WAGONED carted; transported
WAGONER cart-driver
WAGSOME whimsical; witty
WAGTAIL bird; joinery zo
WAGWANT totter-grass bt
WAHABEE primitive Moslem rl
WAILFUL mournful; sorrowful; grievous
WAILING bemoaning; lamenting
WAINAGE transport
WAISTED narrowed
WAISTER whaling greenhorn
WAITING attendance; biding; tarrying
WAIVING relinquishing; remitting
WAIVODE Polish governor
WAKEFUL alert; wary; vigilant
WAKEMAN watchman
WAKENED stimulated; excited
WAKENER a rouser; knocker-up
WALKING pedestrianism; hiking
WALK-OUT industrial strike; protest
WALLABA timber tree (Guyana) bt
WALLABY kangaroo-like animal zo
WALLACH Wallack; a Wallachian
WALL-EYE eye condition md
WALLING wall material
WALLOON Belgian dialect
WALL-RUE a fern bt
WALTZED cut a figure
WALTZER ballroom athlete
WAMBLED rumbled
WAME-TOW belly-band
WAMPISH to flourish; to brandish (Sc.)
WAN-EYED languid; sad
WANGHEE a cane; a stick
WANGLED acquired by craft
WANHOPE despair
WANHORN a plant bt
WANNESS pallor; paleness
WANNISH sickly
WANTAGE deficiency; lack
WANTING absent; desiring; needing
WANTWIT a numskull; nitwit
WAPACUT American snowy owl zo
WARATAH Australian plant bt
WARBLED quavered; trilled; carolled
WARBLER a songster zo
WARBLES saddle-sores; tumours
WARDAGE watch-tax
WARDIAN botanist's case
WARDING repelling; fending; guarding
WARD-WIT warder's quittance
WAREFUL wary; cautious; vigilant
WARFARE strife; hostilities
WARHEAD explosive part of missile

WARHOOP war-cry; slogan
WARIEST most circumspect
WARISON a reward; a gift
WARLIKE belligerent; martial
WARLOCK wizard; a spell
WARLORD Junker militarist
WARMEST keenest; most ardent
WARMING heating
WARNING caution; notification; omen
WARPATH hostile expedition
WARPING twisting; distorting
WARPING non-flatness in gramophone records
WARRANT authority; right; justify
WARRING contending; striving
WARRIOR veteran fighter
WAR-RISK (insurance)
WAR-SCOT war-tax; a levy
WARSHIP battleship, etc.   nt
WARSONG song on martial theme
WART-HOG an African ungulate   zo
WARWOLF military engine
WARWORN battle-weary
WASH-DAY laundry day
WASHING ablution; rinsing
WASH-OUT a failure
WASHPOT (Moab)
WASHTUB scrubbing vessel
WASP-FLY fly resembling wasp   zo
WASPISH resentful; irritable
WASSAIL an occasion; punch
WASTAGE dissipation
WASTING emaciation
WASTREL waif; a dud
WATCHED guarded; tended; noted
WATCHER watchman
WATCHET light blue
WATERED wavy; moistened; sprinkled
WATERER irrigator
WATTLED (hurdles); (cocks-comb)
WAULING howling; caterwauling
WAVELET a ripple
WAVERED faltered; swayed
WAVERER hesitator
WAVESON flotsam
WAVICLE quantum mechanical entity   ps
WAX-BEAN butter-bean   bt
WAXBILL (weaver-bird)   zo
WAX-DOLL poupée (Fr.)
WAX-MOTH (a bee scourge)   zo
WAX-PALM wax-producing tree   bt
WAX-TREE American gamboge tree   bt
WAXWING a crested bird   zo
WAXWORK wax statue counterfeiting life
WAYBILL a list (transport)
WAYFARE to walk
WAYGONE exhausted; wayworn
WAYLAND a legendary smith
WAYLESS pathless; trackless
WAY-MARK sign-post
WAY-POST guide-post

WAYSIDE of the roadside
WAYWARD froward; wilful; unruly
WAYWISE directional capacity
WAYWODE waivode; Polish governor
WAYWORN exhausted; spent
WEAKEST puniest
WEALDEN (weald of Kent)
WEALTHY opulent; affluent; rich
WEANING alienating; detaching
WEARIED fatigued; jaded; careworn
WEARIER more jaded and tired
WEARILY tediously
WEARING exhausting
WEARISH withered; washy
WEASAND ⎫
WEAZAND ⎬ windpipe; throat   mc
WEATHER climate; endure; overcome
WEAVING cloth-making
WEBBING hempen fabric
WEB-EYED filmy-eyed   me
WEB-FOOT characteristic of aquatic birds
WEBSTER wabster; a weaver
WEB-TOED with webs between toes
WEDDING nuptials; espousal; marriage
WEDGING a timber joint; compressing
WEDLOCK matrimony
WEEDERY cf. fernery
WEEDING eliminating; purging
WEE-FREE Independent Liberal
WEEKDAY daily except Sunday; work day
WEEKEND Saturday and Sunday
WEENING thinking; imagining
WEEPING sobbing; crying; bewailing
WEEVILY full of weevils   zo
WEFTAGE texture
WEIGHED pondered; pressed; (anchor)
WEIGHER weighing machine
WEIGH-IN pre-contest weight check
WEIGHTY ponderous; onerous; grave
WEIRDER more fantastic
WEIRDLY errily; uncannily
WELAWAY alas!
WELCHER welsher; absconding bookie
WELCOME salutation; greeting
WELDING welded joint
WELFARE comfort; prosperity; weal
WELLING springing; gushing
WELL-MET all hail! welcome!
WELL-OFF well-to-do; prosperous
WELL-SET firmly set
WELL-WON honestly gained
WELSHED decamped; absconded
WELSHER absconding bookie
WELTING shoe-edging
WENDING wandering; strolling
WENDISH the Wend dialect
WENLOCK limestone   mn
WENNISH cyst-like
WERGILD ⎫ fine for murder;
WERGOLD ⎬ blood money
WERWOLF werewolf; wolf-man

WEST-END fashionable; stylish
WESTERN occidental
WESTING westerly
WET-DOCK dock where ship can float
WETNESS dampness; humidity
WET-SHOD with wet feet
WETTEST supersaturated
WET-TIME wages for rainy days
WETTING moistening; drenching
WETTISH rather rainy
WETWOOD high-water-content wood   fr
WHACKED beaten; defeated; smitten
WHACKER of large size; formidable
WHAISLE wheeze (Sc.)
WHALERY whale-fishing industry
WHALING thrashing
WHANGEE bamboo cane   bt
WHAPPED struck; fluttered
WHARFED brought to shore   nt
WHARVES quays; docks
WHATNOT a piece of furniture
WHATTEN what kind of (Sc.)
WHEATEN of wheat   bt
WHEEDLE to coax; to cajole
WHEELED with wheels
WHEELER shaft-horse; cyclist   zo
WHEELER wheelwright
WHEEZED breathed asthmatically
WHEEZLE whaizle; whaisle; obtain
WHELKED ridged
WHELPED littered
WHEMMLE an upset (Sc.)
WHEREAS in view of fact that
WHEREAT thereupon
WHEREBY through which
WHEREIN within which
WHEREOF whence
WHEREON upon which
WHERESO not actually a word
WHERETO to which
WHERRET to worrit; a blow
WHETHER if; in the case of
WHETILE woodpecker   zo
WHETTED stimulated; urged
WHETTER a sharpener
WHEWING whistling with surprise
WHEYISH like whey
WHEY-TUB cream-tub
WHIFFED puffed
WHIFFER a puffer
WHIFFET whipper-snapper
WHIFFLE a flute; prevaricate   mu
WHILERE recently
WHILING loitering; passing the time
WHIMPER whine; cry; moan
WHIMPLE wimple; head-dress
WHIMSEY whimsy; a caprice; crotchet
WHINGER dirk; hangar (Sc.)
WHINING complaining; snivelling
WHIPCAT a tailor
WHIPPED lashed; beaten; thrashed

WHIPPER a flagellant
WHIPPET greyhound; small tank   zo
WHIP-RAY a sea-fish   zo
WHIPSAW frame-held narrow saw   to
WHIP-TOP whipping top
WHIRLED span; spun; revved
WHIRRED whurred; rotated
WHIRLER a whirligig
WHIRRET wherrit; vex; a blow
WHISHED whizzed
WHISKER hair of man's cheek
WHISKET a basket
WHISKEY whisky; a light dog-cart
WHISPER murmur; disclose
WHISTLE bosun's pipe   nt
WHISTLY silently
WHITELY palely; pallidly
WHITEST purest; lightest
WHITHER to which place
WHITING whitewash; a fish   zo
WHITISH near white
WHITLOW an abscess   md
WHITSUL curds and whey
WHITSUN Whitsuntide
WHITTAW a saddler
WHITTLE shawl; to cut; pare
WHIZZED tore through the air
WHIZZER a fast one
WHOEVER anyone at all
WHOMMLE confusion; overwhelm
WHOOBUB hubbub
WHOOPEE a joyous cry; a revel
WHOOPED hooted; yelled; shouted
WHOOPER the hooper swan   zo
WHOPPED beat; defeated
WHOPPER whacker
WHORLED spiral; convoluted
WICKING cannoning when curling
WICKIUP shelter (Amer. Indian)
WIDENED extended; broadened
WIDENER an enlarger; a reamer
WIDGEON migratory duck   zo
WIDOWED bereaved; viduous
WIDOWER bereaved husband
WIELDED handled; plied; governed
WIELDER a controller; user
WIGGERS dandelion   bt
WIGGERY false hair
WIGGING a scolding; reprimand
WIGGLED waggled
WIGGLER a wriggler
WIGHTLY courageously; nimbly
WIGLESS deperuked
WILD-ASS the onager   zo
WILDCAT speculative; strike (indust.)   zo
WILDEST most turbulent and rash
WILDING growing wild; crab-apple   bt
WILDISH rather wild
WILD-OAT youthful crop   bt
WILIEST craftiest; pawkiest
WILLING inclined; devising

WILLOCK young guillemot	zo
WILLOWY slender; pliant	
WILSOME wilful; stubborn; wayward	
WILTING drooping; fading	
WIMBERY whortleberry	bt
WIMBLED drilled; bored	
WIMBREL whimbrel; small curlew	zo
WIMPLED puckered; wrinkled	
WINCHED hoisted; hauled up	
WINDAGE clearance	
WINDBAG a would-be orator	
WIND-EGG an addled egg	zo
WIND-GUN air-gun	
WINDIER breezier; more alarmed	
WINDILY breezily; panic-struck	
WINDING tortuous; changing; scenting	
WINDROW hay or peat in rows	
WINDSOR Royal House	
WINEBAG wine-skin; a tippler	
WINEFAT a vat	
WINESAP American winter apple	bt
WING-ICE (ice on aircraft)	
WINGING flying; wounding	
WINGLET bastard wing	zo
WINKERS flashing lights	au
WINKING nictitating; conniving at	
WINNING charming; acquiring; getting	
WINNOCK windock; a window (Sc.)	
WINSOME engaging; taking; seductive	
WINTERY wintry; hyemal	
WIPE-OUT intense interference	tc
WIREBAR copper in tapered ingots	ml
WIREMAN linesman	
WIREWAY telpherage; aerial transport	
WIRIEST leanest; toughest	
WISE-GUY clever trickster; smart Alec	
WISHFUL desirous; eager and anxious	
WISTFUL pensive; meditative; yearning	
WISTITI marmoset	zo
WITCHED bewitched; charmed	
WITCHEN mountain ash; rowan	bt
WITHERS (horse's neck)	
WITHIES willow twigs	bt
WITHOUT outside; except; lacking	
WITLESS indiscreet; thoughtless	
WITLOOF chicory	bt
WITNESS attest; testimony; see	
WITTIER droller; more facetious	
WITTILY jocularly; humorously	
WITTING wotting; knowing	
WITWALL golden oriole	zo
WIZENED shrivelled; wimpled	
WOBBLED deviated	
WOBBLER wabbler; vacillator	
WOESOME woeful; waesome	
WOLF-DOG sheep-dog	zo
WOLFISH wolvish; rapacious; ravenous	
WOLFKIN young wolf	
WOLF-NET large fishing net	
WOLFRAM tungsten	ch
WOLSUNG grandson of Odin	

WOMANED chaperoned	
WOMANLY feminine	
WOMMERA } spear; throwing	
WOOMERA } stick (Australian)	
WONGSHY yellow dye (Chinese)	
WOOD-ANT the red ant	zo
WOODCUT a print from a wooden block	
WOOD-GOD sylvan deity	
WOODMAN a forester	
WOODNUT hazel-nut	bt
WOOD-OIL balsam	bt
WOOD-OWL brown owl	zo
WOOD-TAR a distillate	ch
WOOD-TIN tin-stone	mn
WOOLDED roped; lashed	
WOOLDER lashing stick	
WOOLFAT lanolin	zo
WOOLLEN of wool	
WOOLMAN wool dealer	
WOOLSAW evil spirit (C. American)	
WOOLSEY a dress material	
WOORALI } wourali; curari;	
WORRARA } arrow poison	
WORDILY verbose; prolix; garrulously	
WORDING phrasing; expressing	
WORDISH wordy; loquacious	
WORKBAG lady's sewing bag	
WORKBOX box of work materials	
WORKDAY M., T., W., Th., F.	
WORKING fermenting; drudging	
WORKMAN a toiler; operative	
WORK-OUT gymnastic exercise	
WORKSHY allergic to labour	
WORLDLY earthy; secular; mundane	
WORMING (rope); squirming	
WORN-OUT exhausted	
WORRIED harassed; bothered; troubled	
WORRIER a worrit; a hector	
WORSHIP adoration; idolize; venerate	
WORSTED wool yarn	
WOULD-BE aspiring	
WOULDST (thou) would	
WOUNDED injured; hurt; damaged	
WOUNDER a pain-giver	
WRANGLE brangle; bicker; brawl	
WRAPPED covered; swathed; wound	
WRAPPER envelope; scarf	
WRAULED } caterwauled;	
WRAWLED } howled	
WREAKED inflicted	
WREAKER an avenger	
WREATHE entwine; to garland	
WREATHY twisty; interlaced	
WRECKED shattered; ruined; destroyed	
WRECKER saboteur; blighter	
WREN-TIT Californian bird	zo
WRESTED wrenched; forced; pulled	
WRESTER a twister	
WRESTLE grapple; strive; contend	
WRICKED ricked; sprained	
WRIGGLE worm; squirm; writhe	

WRIGGLY tortuous; sinuous
WRINGER a mangle
WRINKLE crinkle; pucker
WRINKLY creased; rumpled
WRITE-UP flattering notice
WRITHED squirmed; wriggled
WRITHEN contorted; coiled
WRITHLE to wrinkle; to shrivel
WRITING calligraphy; penmanship
WRITTEN inscribed; indited
WRONGED maltreated; oppressed
WRONGER a wrong-un; evil-doer
WRONGLY falsely; unjustly
WROUGHT worked; effected
WRYBILL a New Zealand plover   zo
WRYNECK (woodpecker)   zo
WRYNESS crookedness
WUSTITE cubic iron oxide   mn
WUZZENT wizened (Sc.)
WYANDOT Iraquoian Indian; fowl   zo
WYCH-ELM witch-elm   bt

X

XANTHIC an acid; yellow   ch
XANTHIN yellow extract   bt
XENURUS genus of armadillos   zo
XERASIA } hair disease; dryness of the
XEROSIS } scalp   md
XERODES dry tumour   md
XEROTES }
XEROTIC } dryness of the body   md
XIPHIAS sword-fish genus   zo
XIPHIAS a Southern constellation
XIPHOID ensiform
XYLENOL monohydric phenol   ch
XYLOPIA bitter plants   bt
XYLOLIN wood pulp fabric

Y

YACHTED cruised
YACHTER yachtsman
YAHWISM worship of Jehovah   rl
YAHWIST Jehovist   rl
YAMADOU nutmeg oil   bt
YANKING jerking; heaving; hauling
YAPPING yelping; yauping
YAPSTER a yelper
YARDAGE yard dues
YARDAGE yard-volume of excavation   ce
YARD-ARM place for hanging   nt
YARDING enclosing
YARD-MAN (farm); (railway)
YARNING narrating
YARRING snarling
YARRISH rough dry taste
YASHMAK Moslem woman's double veil
YATAGAN Turkish knife
YAUPING yelping
YAWLING howling; screaming
YAWNING gaping

YEANING } bringing forth young;
YEENING } lambing
YEARNED desirous; grieved
YEGGMAN criminal tramp (USA)
YELDRIN yellow bunting   zo
YELLING howling
YELLOCH to yell; a yell (Sc.)
YELLOWS an animal disease
YELLOWY yellowish; sallowy
YELPING yauping; yapping
YERKING chucking; jerking
YESTERN (yesterday)
YEW-TREE (bow-wood)   bt
YEZIDIS devil worshippers
YIDDISH Jewish dialect
YIELDED rendered; resigned; conceded
YIELDER capitulator; abdicator
YODELER Tyrolese singer
YOGHURT fermented milk
YOICKED shouted Yoicks
YOLDING }
YOLDRIN } yorling; yellow-hammer   zo
YORKIST (War of Roses)
YOUGHAL needle-point lace
YOUNGER not so old
YOUNGLY inexperienced; juvenile
YOUNKER a stripling; youngster
YOUTHLY youthful; immature
YOWLING howling; bawling
YPERITE poison gas   ch
YTTRIUM a metallic element   ch
YULE-LOG Christmas fire
YU-STONE high-quality jade   mn

Z

ZABAISM star worship
ZABTIEH Zaptieh; Turkish policeman
ZADKIEL (almanac)
ZALACCA dragon's blood palm   bt
ZAMARRA sheepskin jacket (Sp.)
ZAMOUSE W. African ox   zo
ZANELLA umbrella fabric
ZANJERO irrigation officer
ZANONIA cucumber   bt
ZANYING fooling
ZANYISM buffoonery
ZAPATEO shoe dance (S. Amer.)
ZAPHARA sky blue dye used in pottery
ZAREEBA zareba; stockade
ZARNICH realgar; orpiment   mn
ZEALANT a zealot; enthusiast; bigot
ZEALFUL zealous; enthusiastic; eager
ZEALOUS fervent; ardent; fervid
ZEBRASS a cross-breed; zebra and ass   zo
ZEBRINE zebra type   zo
ZEBRULA (zebra and horse)   zo
ZEDOARY aromatic root   bt
ZEITNOT clockbound administration: chess term
ZEMSTVO Russian local assembly

ZEOLITE aluminium silicate	mn
ZEROING concentrating firepower	
ZESTFUL piquant; eager; keen	
ZESTING flavouring; relishing	
ZETETIC a seeker; a Pyrrhonist	
ZEUGITE nuclear-fission cell	nc
ZEUXITE a silicate of aluminium	mn
ZIMOCCA bath-sponge	
ZINCALI Spanish gipsies	
ZINCATE zinc oxide	ch
ZINCIFY coat with zinc	
ZINCITE red zinc ore	mn
ZINCODE⎫ positive pole electrode;	
ZINCOID ⎭ anode	
ZINCOUS (zinc)	
ZINGARI (cricket); gipsies (It.)	
ZINGARO zingane; zingano (It.)	
ZIONISM Jewish Nationalism	
ZIONIST who supports free Israel	
ZIPCORD parachute release cord	
ZIPHIUS swordfish genus	zo
ZIPPING pinging; whizzing; fastening	
ZITHERN cithara	mu
ZITHERN or zither	mu
ZIZANIA aquatic grasses; (rice)	bt
ZOARIUM polyzoan	zo
ZOCCOLO square base	ar
ZOILEAN supercritical	
ZOILISM carping criticism	
ZOILIST a caviller	
ZOISITE a silicate; an epidote	mn
ZOLAISM excessive naturalism	
ZONALLY girdling	

ZONULAR belted	
ZONULET small girdle	
ZONURUS saurian genus	zo
ZOOECIA polyp cells	zo
ZOOGAMY reproduction	
ZOOGENY ⎫ zoological origins	zo
ZOOGONY ⎭	zo
ZOOIDAL animal-like	zo
ZOOLITE ⎫ a fossil animal	mn
ZOOLITH ⎭	zo
ZOOLOGY study of animals	zo
ZOOMING flying low	
ZOONITE articulated segment	
ZOONOMY natural laws	
ZOOPERY experimenting on lower animals	
ZOOTAXY systematic zoology	
ZOOTOMY animal anatomy	
ZOPISSA pitch used medicinally	md
ZORGITE a metallic ore	mn
ZORILLA ⎫	
ZORILLE ⎬ American skunk	zo
ZORRINO ⎭	
ZOTHECA alcove (Greek)	
ZUFFOLO Italian flute	mu
ZUNYITE orthosilicate of aluminium	mn
ZURLITE a Vesuvian mineral	mn
ZYGAENA a shark genus	zo
ZYGOSIS conjugation	zo
ZYGOTIC of a zygote	bt, zo
ZYMOGEN a fermentor	ch
ZYMOSIS inflammation	md
ZYMOTIC bacteriological	md
ZYMURGY fermentation	ch

A

AARDVARK ant-bear (S. Afr.) **zo**
AARD-WOLF African wolf **zo**
AARONITE Hebrew priest **rl**
AASVOGEL vulture (S. Afr.)
ABACTION cattle-theft; rustling
ABACULUS counting-frame; tablet
ABAMPERE absolute electromagnetic unit
ABAMURUS buttress
ABAPICAL distant from apex, apposite pole
ABASHING humiliating; shaming
ABATABLE reducible; alleviable
ABAT-JOUR skylight; reflector
ABATTOIR slaughter-house
ABAT-VOIX canopy over pulpit **rl**
ABBATESS abbess; Lady Superior **rl**
ABBATIAL under abbey control **rl**
ABDALAVI Egyptian musk melon **bt**
ABDERIAN given to laughter
ABDERITE a Thracian; Democrites
ABDICANT renouncing; an abdicator
ABDICATE resign; cede; renounce
ABDITORY secret repository **rl**
ABDUCENT retracting; separating
ABDUCING abducting; kidnapping **lw**
ABDUCTED removed; took by fraud
ABDUCTOR kidnapper; a muscle **md**
ABELIANS ⎱ a sect practising marriage
ABELITES ⎰ chastity (Abel) **rl**
ABELMOSK Syrian mallow **bt**
ABERDEEN a terrier **zo**
ABERRANT abnormal; rambling
ABERRATE deviate; diverge; wander
ABERRING straying; digressing
ABETMENT aiding and abetting **lw**
ABETTING conniving; encouraging
ABEYANCE suspension; dormancy
ABEYANCE cessation; contemplation
ABHORRED hated; loathed; detested
ABHORRER Tory nickname, A.D. 1680
ABIDANCE abode; dwelling; habitation
ABIETENE abietine; balsam **bt**
ABIOGENY spontaneous generation
ABJECTLY servilely; despicably
ABJURING apostasy; forswearing
ABLATION removal; attrition
ABLATIVE the sixth case in Latin
ABLEGATE despatch; depute; delegate
ABLEGATE a Papal envoy **rl**
ABLENESS ability; skill, vigour
ABLEPSIA ablepsy; blindness **md**
ABLOCATE hire; lease; let
ABLUTION purification; baptism **rl**
ABLUVION water-deposited detritus
ABNEGATE deny; adjure; renounce
ABNODATE untie; remove the knots
ABNORMAL odd; irregular; monstrous
ABOCOCKE peaked cap of 15th century
ABOMASUS abomasum; cow's stomach
ABORTING miscarrying; frustrating

ABORTION a hideosity; vain effort
ABORTIVE premature: broken off
ABRADANT disintegrator; scraper
ABRADING grinding; abrasing; fraying
ABRASION surface wound: attrition
ABRASIVE scratchy: gritty: rough
ABRASTOL a preservative **ch**
ABRIDGED epitomized; curtailed
ABROGATE cancel; repeal; quash
ABRUPTED rent; torn asunder
ABSCISSA an axial line in geometry
ABSENTED played truant
ABSENTEE deliberate duty dodger
ABSENTLY dreamily; inattentively
ABSINTHE wormwood; French liqueur **bt**
ABSOLUTE pure; despotic; supreme
ABSOLVED acquitted; excused
ABSOLVER a pardoner; forgiver
ABSONANT irrational; discordant
ABSONOUS incongruous; out of tune
ABSORBED imbibed; preoccupied
ABSTERGE purge; wipe away
ABSTRACT detach; purloin; abstruse
ABSTRACT gist; summary; epitomize
ABSTRUSE recondite; occult; obscure
ABSURDLY irrationally; foolishly
ABUNDANT profuse; plentiful; copious
ABUSABLE violable; misapplicable
ABUTILON plant genus; the jute **bt**
ABUTMENT an arch support; adjacency
ABUTTALS estate boundaries **lw**
ABUTTING bordering; alongside
ACADEMIC scholastic; literary
ACALEPHA hydrozoa (jellyfish) **zo**
ACANTHUS a 'capital' plant **bt**
ACARDIAC heartless
ACARIDAE mites; ticks, etc **zo**
ACARPOUS sterile; barren **bt**
ACAUDATE tailless; acaudal **zo**
ACAULOUS acauline; stalkless **bt**
ACCEDING complying; consenting
ACCENSOR R.C. candle-trimmer **rl**
ACCENTED stressed; emphasized
ACCENTOR the hedge-sparrow **zo**
ACCENTOR leading singer **mu**
ACCEPTED admitted; acknowledged
ACCEPTER ⎱ the recipient of a Bill of
ACCEPTOR ⎰ Exchange
ACCIDENT mischance; fortuity; hap
ACCLINAL sloping; atilt
ACCOLADE (knighthood), an embrace
ACCOLENT neighbour; borderer
ACCOLLED collared **hd**
ACCORDED harmonized; granted
ACCOSTED hailed; greeted; addressed
ACCOUNTS recorded transactions
ACCOUPLE to link together
ACCOUTRE dress in military array
ACCREDIT authorize; empower; entrust
ACCRETED grew; increased
ACCROACH usurp; encroach

ACCRUING accumulating; resulting	
ACCURACY precision; exactness; truth	
ACCURATE correct; unerring	
ACCURSED execrable; doomed	
ACCUSANT informer; accuser	lw
ACCUSING charging; impeaching	
ACCUSTOM habituate; familiarize	
ACELDEMA the field of blood (Hebrew)	
ACENTRIC out of centre	
ACEPHALA oyster genus	zo
ACERBATE exasperate; embitter	
ACERBENT caustic; astringent	
ACERBITY bitterness; sour taste	
ACERVATE clustered	
ACESCENT turning sour	
ACETATED (acetic acid)	ch
ACHENIUM single-seeded fruit	bt
ACHERSET 8 bushel measure	me
ACHEWEED gout-weed	bt
ACHIEVED won; attained; perfected	
ACHIEVER a performer; an executant	
ACHILOUS lipless	bt
ACHIRITE dioptase	mn
ACHROITE tourmaline	mn
ACICULAE spikes and prickles	bt, zo
ACICULAR needle-shaped	
ACIDIFIC producing acid	ch
ACIDNESS bitterness; tartness	
ACIDOSIS acidity	md
ACIERAGE steel electro-plating	
ACIERATE turn into steel	
ACNESTIS part of spine	zo
ACOEMETI religious community	
ACONITIC (wolf's-bane, monk's-hood)	bt
ACORN-CUP acorn top, case	bt
ACOUSTIC relating to sound	
ACQUAINT notify; apprize; teach	to
ACQUIRED scrounged; won; procured	
ACRIDIAN locust	zo
ACRIDITY pungency; harshness	
ACRIMONY sharpness of temper	
ACRITUDE corrosive quality	
ACROATIC esoteric; (oral instruction)	
ACROLEIN acryl aldehyde, propenal	ch
ACROLITH statue with wooden body	
ACROMIUM ventral process	
ACROSOME head of sperm	zo
ACROSTIC word puzzle in verse	
ACROTISM lack of pulsation	md
ACTINISM effect of light rays	
ACTINIUM radio-active element	ch
ACTINOID star-shaped	zo
ACTIVATE to move to activity	
ACTIVELY energetically; sedulously	
ACTIVISM practical idealism	
ACTIVIST production promoter (indust.)	
ACTIVITY agility; alertness	
ACTUALLY really; as a fact	
ACTUATED influenced; set in motion	
ACUITION accentuation	
ACULEATE spiky; pointed	bt

ACUTANCE clarity of enlargement	pt
ADAMITIC Adamic; nudistic	
ADAPTING adjusting; suiting	
ADAPTIVE adaptable; conformable	
ADDEEMED adjudged; considered	
ADDENDUM adjunct; appendix	
ADDER-FLY dragonfly	zo
ADDICTED wont; prone; inclined	
ADDITION accession; summation	
ADDITIVE additional; further	ch
ADDORSED back to back	hd
ADDUCENT retracting (muscles)	md
ADDUCING citing; alleging	
ADDUCTOR a muscle	pl
ADENITIS } inflammation of the	
ADENOIDS } nasal glands	md
ADEPTION attainment; perfection	
ADEQUACY sufficiency; fitness	
ADEQUATE suitable; condign	
ADFECTED compounded	
ADHERENT partisan; adhesive	
ADHERING cohering; cleaving	
ADHESION coalescence; attachment	
ADHESIVE tenacious; gummy	
ADIANTUM maiden-hair fern	bt
ADIPOSIS fat-deposit illness	md
ADJACENT contiguous; close by	
ADJECTED added to; joined	
ADJOINED connected; neighbouring	
ADJUDGED awarded; deemed	
ADJURING charging on oath	lw
ADJUSTER arranger; fitter	
ADJUTAGE tubular connection	
ADJUTANT assistant; regimental officer	
ADJUTANT Indian scavenging stork	zo
ADJUTRIX lady help	
ADJUVANT helping; intensifier	md
ADMIRING respecting; marvelling	
ADMITTED included; conceded	
ADMIXING mingling with	
ADMONISH warn; reprove; exhort	
ADNATION length attachment of organs	bt
ADOPTING choosing; embracing	
ADOPTION formal acceptance	
ADOPTIVE selective	
ADORABLE reverential; venerable	
ADORABLY worshipfully; devotedly	
ADORNING embellishing; decking	
ADRECTAL adjacent to the rectum	md
ADROITLY dexterously; adeptly	
ADSCRIPT conscript; postscript	
ADSORBED condensed	
ADULARIA moonstone	mn
ADULATED lauded; flattered	
ADULATOR sycophant; yes-man	
ADULTERY ex-marital cohabitation	
ADUNCATE hooked	bt
ADUSTION cauterization	md
ADVANCED in the van; lent; marched	
ADVANCER promoter	
ADVENING acceding	

ADVERTED drew attention to
ADVISING counselling; notifying
ADVISORY hortative
ADVOCAAT brandy-eggyolk liqueur (Dutch)
ADVOCACY defence; support
ADVOCATE barrister; recommend   lw
ADVOWSON patronage of benefice   rl
ADYNAMIA loss of vitality   md
ADYNAMIC slack; lifeless; listless
AEGROTAT academic certificate   md
AERARIAN voteless Roman freeman
AERATING charging with gas
AERATION gasification
AERIALLY ethereally
AERIFIED inflated
AERIFORM unsubstantial
AEROBOMB a bomb
AEROCYST seaweed air cell   bt
AERODART dart dropped by airman
AERODYNE aircraft   ae
AEROFOIL lifting surface
AEROGRAM wireless message; letter
AEROLITE \ meteoric stone;
AEROLITH / meteorite   mn
AEROLOGY meteorology
AERONAUT airman; balloonist
AEROSTAT barrage balloon
AESCULIN horse-chestnut extract   bt
AESTHETE professed beauty lover
AESTIVAL estival (summer)
AFEBRILE unaccompanied by fever   md
AFFECTED moved; unnatural; insincere
AFFEERED fixed; confirmed
AFFERENT conducting inwards   md
AFFIANCE confidence; betroth
AFFINAGE metal refining
AFFINING refining; purifying
AFFINITY relationship; attraction
AFFIRMED confirmed; ratified
AFFIRMER testifier; a Quaker   rl
AFFIXING attaching; connecting
AFFLATUS inspiration; ecstasy
AFFLUENT a tributary; wealthy
AFFORCED ravished
AFFORDED yielded; bore the cost
AFFOREST convert into forest
AFFRIGHT sudden terror; frighten
AFFRONTE confronting   hd
AFFUSING spraying; bedewing   rl
AFFUSION baptismal sprinkling   rl
AFTER-ALL in conclusion
AFTER-WIT wisdom after the event
AGAL-WOOD aloes-wood   bt
AGAR-AGAR seaweed   bt
AGASTRIC stomachless   zo
AGATIZED turned into agate
AGEDNESS antiquity; senility
AGENESIS imperfect development
AGENTIAL acting through an agent
AGGRIEVE give sorrow; injure

AGIOTAGE (stock-jobbing)
AGISTAGE tax on pasturage   lw
AGITABLE excitable; tremulous
AGITATED roused; instigated
AGITATOR agent provocateur
AGLIMMER shimmering
AGLOSSAL tongueless   zo
AGNATION male descent   lw
AGNOSTIC humanist; positivist
AGONISED tormented
AGRAPHIA inability to write   md
AGRARIAN relating to land
AGREEING matching; tallying
AGRESTAL weedlike   bt
AGRESTIC rustic; unpolished
AGRIMONY liverwort   bt
AGRONOMY scientific farming
AGUE-CAKE a tumour   md
AGUE-TREE sassafras tree   bt
AIGRETTE egret's plume   zo
AIGUILLE spire; peak; rock-drill
AILLETTE ailette; epaulet
AIR-BORNE no earthly connection
AIR-BRAKE brake operated by air
AIR-BRICK ventilating brick
AIRBRUSH fixative spray
AIR-BUILT chimerical; baseless
AIRCRAFT flying machines
AIR-DRAIN an airspace   ar
AIR-DRAWN imaginary; visionary
AIREDALE terrier   zo
AIRFIELD landing ground
AIR-FLEET unified collection of aeroplanes
AIR-FLOAT sand-shaking process   mn
AIRFRAME fuselage   ae
AIRGRAPH air mail letter; microfilm
AIRINESS lightness; gaiety
AIR-LINER commercial passenger plane
AIR-PILOT a flyer; a navigator
AIRPLANE aeroplane
AIRPOISE aneroid barometer
AIR-POWER air war potential
AIRSCREW propeller
AIRSHAFT ventilation shaft
AIRSPACE cubic content
AIR-STOVE heating apparatus
AIR-STRIP landing strip
AIR-SWEPT dry grinding process   mn
AIRTIGHT impermeable to air
AIRTRUNK ventilating shaft
AKINESIA muscular weakness/paralysis   md
ALACRITY briskness; agility; readiness
ALARM-GUN signal of distress
ALARMING calling to arms; ominous
ALARMIST Jeremiah; panic-monger
ALBACORE \ tunny-fish;   zo
ALBICORE / species of thynnus
ALBANIAN (Albania)
ALBINESS female albino
ALBINISM deficiency of pigment

ALBORADA folk music (Sp.)	mu		**ALLOSOME** non-typical chromosome	c⸱
ALBUMESS Lamb's album-keeper			**ALLOTTED** meted; assigned; dispensed	
ALBURNUM sap-wood	bt		**ALLOTTEE** a sharer	
ALCAHEST) universal solvent of the			**ALLOTYPE** varying type specimen	
ALKAHEST) alchemists			**ALL-OUTER** extremist; zealot	
ALCATRAS ocean birds; pelican	zo		**ALLOWING** conceding; admitting	
ALCHEMIC relating to alchemy			**ALLOYAGE** the alloying of metals	m
ALDEHYDE a volatile liquid	ch		**ALLOYING** blending; debasing	
ALDERMAN a civic dignitary			**ALLSPICE** Jamaica pepper	b
ALDOLASE an enzyme	ch		**ALLUDING** hinting; insinuating	
ALEATORY depending on dice			**ALLURING** enticing; tempting	
ALEBENCH alehouse bench			**ALLUSION** hint; reference	
ALEBERRY hot ale with sops			**ALLUSIVE** relative; innuent	
ALEHOUSE (no spirit licence)			**ALLUSORY** symbolical; figurative	
ALEMBDAR Sultan's standard-bearer			**ALLUVIAL** sedimentary	
ALE-STAKE an alehouse sign			**ALLUVION** alluvial land	
ALEURONE a protein in seeds	bt		**ALLUVIUM** water-borne silt	
ALFRESCO in the open air			**ALMAGEST** astronomical problems	as
ALGERINE Algerian; pirate			**ALMIGHTY** all-powerful; omnipotent	
ALGIDITY chilliness			**ALMSDEED** act of charity	
ALGOLOGY the study of seaweeds	bt		**ALMSGATE** (where alms were given)	
ALGONKIN Canadian Indian			**ALOMANCY** divination by salt	
ALGORISM the decimal system			**ALOPECIA** baldness; fox-evil	me
ALGRAPHY aluminium printing			**ALPHABET** order or list of letters	
ALHAMBRA Moorish palace			**ALPHA-RAY** a radio-active ray	
ALICANTE Spanish red wine			**ALPHENIC** white barley-sugar	cl
ALIENAGE estrangement			**ALPINIST** mountaineer	
ALIENATE transfer; misapply			**ALQUIFOU** Cornish lead ore	m⸱
ALIENISM study of insanity	md		**ALSATIAN** sheep-dog; debauchee	z⸱
ALIENIST mental specialist	md		**ALTARAGE** altar offerings	⸱
ALIGHTED stepped off; descended			**ALTERANT** production of change	
ALIGNING adjusting; dressing			**ALTER-EGO** second self	
ALIQUANT a remainder			**ALTERING** varying; changing	
ALITRUNK winged segment	zo		**ALTERITY** being otherwise	
ALIZARIN madder; synthetic dye			**ALTERNAT** precedence by rotation	
ALKALIES caustic bases			**ALTHEINE** asparagine	b
ALKALIFY) neutralize an acid;			**ALTHOUGH** notwithstanding	
ALKALIZE) alkalise	ch		**ALTINCAR** unrefined borax	c⸱
ALKALINE salty	ch		**ALTITUDE** height; eminence	
ALKALOID active part of a drug	md		**ALTO-CLEFF** C on 3rd line of staff	m⸱
ALKERMES a crimson cordial			**ALTRUISM** self-sacrifice	
ALLANITE cerium silicate	ch		**ALTRUIST** philanthropist	
ALLAYING stilling; mitigating			**ALUMINIC** containing aluminium	m⸱
ALL-BURNT rocket-fuel exhaustion			**ALUMINUM** aluminium	c⸱
moment			**ALUNOGEN** aluminium sulphite	c⸱
ALL-CLEAR end of danger			**ALVEATED** hollowed out; saucer-shape	
ALLEGING asserting as a fact			**ALVEOLAR** like a honey-comb	
ALLEGORY parable; metaphor			**ALVEOLUS** alveole; tooth socket	
ALLELUIA alleluyah; halleluiah			**AMADAVAT** a weaver-bird	z⸱
ALLERGIC antipathetic			**AMANDINE** sweet almond ointment	
ALLERION heraldic beakless eagle	hd		**AMANDOLA** green marble	m
ALLEY-WAY narrow passage			**AMANITIN** poison in fungi	c⸱
ALL-FIRED infernal; hell-fired			**AMARACUS** marjoram	b
ALL-FOURS (cards); mode of progress			**AMARANTH** love-lies-bleeding	b
ALLIANCE union by treaty; coalition			**AMASSING** piling up; accumulating	
ALLIGATE to bind together			**AMAZEDLY** confusedly; dazedly	
ALLOCATE allot; assign; share			**AMBERITE** smokeless explosive	c⸱
ALLODIAL freehold; not feudal			**AMBITION** desire; aspiration	
ALLODIUM freehold estate	lw		**AMBIVERT** one turned both ways	p⸱
ALLOGAMY cross-fertilization	bt		**AMBLYGON** obtuse-angled	
ALLOPATH user of healing drugs	md		**AMBREADA** spurious amber	

AMBREATE salt of ambreic acid	ch	
AMBROSIA food of the gods; bee-bread		
AMBROSIN Milanese coin	nm	
AMBULANT peripatetic; hiking		
AMBULATE saunter; walk; stroll; hike		
AMBUSHED caught unaware		
AMENABLE liable; pliant; subject		
AMENABLY docilely; responsively		
AMENANCE conduct; behaviour		
AMENDING rectifying; correcting		
AMERCING fining; mulcting		
AMERICAN Yankee		
AMETHYST anti-inebriation jewel	mn	
AMIANTUS fibrous asbestos	mn	
AMICABLE friendly; neighbourly		
AMICABLY benignly; peacefully		
AMIDMOST in the very centre		
AMISSING lost; wanting		
AMITOSIS constriction-division of nucleus		
AMITOTIC characterized by amitosis	cy	
AMMODYTE sand-eel	zo	
AMMONIAC of nature of ammonia	ch	
AMMONITE explosive		
AMMONITE spiral fossil	zo	
AMMONIUM base of ammonia	ch	
AMNIOTIC a membrane	md	
AMOEBEAN alternately answering		
AMOEBEUM poetic dialogue		
AMOEBOID) of simple structure	zo	
AMOEBOUS) like a protozoon	zo	
AMORETTO cupid; a lover		
AMORTIZE transfer property	lw	
AMOUNTED reached; rose; resulted		
AMPELITE anti-pest earth	mn	
AMPHIBIA amphibians	zo	
AMPHIGEN a lichen-like plant	bt	
AMPHIONT a zygote; an egg-shell	zo	
AMPHORAL like a two-handled vase		
AMPHORIC hollow sounding	md	
AMPULLAR like a two-handled flask		
AMPUTATE lop; prune; sever		
AMULETIC like an amulet; charming		
AMURCOUS foul with dregs		
AMUSABLE capable of enjoyment		
AMUSETTE light field gun		
ANABASIS a military advance		
ANABATIC of hot-air convection winds	mt	
ANABLEPS a genus of fish	zo	
ANABOLIC body-building	md	
ANACONDA python (S. America)	zo	
ANAFRONT frontal-zone warm-air rise	mt	
ANAGLYPH a cameo; stereoscopic		
ANAGOGIC mystical; allegorical		
ANAGRAPH catalogue; inventory		
ANALECTS collection of lit'y fragments		
ANALEMMA pedestal of sundial		
ANALEPSY recurring epilepsy	md	
ANALOGIC analogous; alike; akin		
ANALOGON) similarity; synonym;		
ANALOGUE) a corresponding part		
ANALYSED examined		

ANALYSER scrutator; analyst		
ANALYSIS opposite of synthesis		
ANALYTIC inductive		
ANANGIAN lacking vascular system	pl	
ANAPAEST a reversed dactyl		
ANAPHASE nuclear division stage		
ANAPHORA rhetorical repetition	rl	
ANARCHIC lawless and turbulent		
ANASARCA dropsy	md	
ANATHEMA excommunication	rl	
ANATOMIC internal	md	
ANCESTOR forefather; forebear		
ANCESTRY lineage; descent		
ANCHORED fixed securely		
ANCHORET anchorite; hermit	rl	
ANCONEAL relating to the elbow	md	
ANDERSON a steel shelter		
ANDESINE felspar; andes	mn	
ANDESITE igneous rock, Andes	mn	
ANDORRAN (Andorra)		
ANDIRONS fire-dogs		
ANDROGEN male hormone	bc	
ANECDOTE a chatty relation		
ANECHOIC echoless	ac	
ANEURISM) dilated artery;	md	
ANEURYSM) abnormal enlargement		
ANGEL-BED open bed without posts		
ANGELICA plant; Californian wine	bt	
ANGERING inflaming; infuriating		
ANGLICAN Church of England	rl	
ANGLOMAN anglo-maniac		
ANGRIEST exceedingly irate		
ANGSTROM light wave-length unit	lt, me	
ANGULATE angular		
ANHEDRAL allotriomorphic	gl	
ANIENTED annulled		
ANIMALLY beastly		
ANIMATED enlivened		
ANIMATOR a rouser		
ANIMETTA cloth for chalice	rl	
ANIRIDIA absence of iris	md	
ANISETTE liqueur from aniseed		
ANNALISE record historical events		
ANNALIST writer of annals		
ANNAMITE native of Annam, Vietnam		
ANNEALED tempered		
ANNELIDA worms	zo	
ANNEXING attaching; taking over		
ANNOTATE add notes to; commentate		
ANNOUNCE pronounce; proclaim		
ANNOYING irritating; vexatious		
ANNUALLY yearly; every year		
ANNULARY ring bearing (fourth finger)		
ANNULATE dividing into rings		
ANNULLED rendered void; abolished		
ANNULLER a voider		
ANNULOSE annular; ringed	zo	
ANODISED treated electrically		
ANOINTED consecrated; Messiah	rl	
ANOREXIA loss of appetite	md	
ANORTHIC oblique angled (crystal)		

ANOVULAR eggless   pl
ANSERINE gooselike; stupid; silly
ANSWERED solved; responded; refuted
ANTALGIC anodyne; pain-killer   md
ANT-EATER ant-bear, etc.   zo
ANTECEDE precede
ANTEDATE anticipate
ANTEFIXA ornamental tiling
ANTELOPE antilope   zo
ANTENATI born before a given date
ANTENNAE feelers; aerials   zo
ANTENNAL relating to the above
ANTENODE (maximum displacement)   el
ANTEPAST antipasta; pre-meal appetizer
ANTEPORT outer gate or harbour
ANTERIOR prior; before
ANTEROOM antechamber
ANTHELIA luminous rings around sun
ANTHELIX antihelix; part of the ear   pl
ANTHEMIS plant genus; camomile   bt
ANTHERAL (pollen bearing anthers)   bt
ANTHESIS full bloom   bt
ANTHOZOA sea-anemones; corals   zo
ANTIACID antacid medicine   md
ANTI-ARMY pacifist
ANTIBODY a counteractive   md
ANTICIZE to play antics
ANTICOUS centripetal   bt
ANTIDOTE counter-measure
ANTI-ICER anti-freeze
ANTIGENY sexual dimorphism   zo
ANTILOGY contradiction; antinomy
ANTILOPE antelope   zo
ANTIMASK grotesque interlude
ANTIMIST preventing misting up   ch
ANTIMONY stibium; a white metal   mn
ANTI-NAZI anti-Hitlerite   ch
ANTINODE radio term   ro
ANTINOMY legal contradiction   lw
ANTINOUS ideal of youthful beauty
ANTIPHON anthem; alternate chanting
ANTIPODE } directly opposite;
ANTIPOLE } the opposite
ANTIPOPE opposition pope; (Avignon)
ANTISERA antibiotics   md
ANTISPIN assisting recovery from spin
ANTISTES chief priest or prelate   rl
ANTI-TANK (guns, mines, etc.)
ANTITYPE typical example
ANTLERED furnished with antlers
ANTRORSE up-turning
ANYTHING an unspecified object
ANYWHERE an undefined locality
AORISTIC indefinite as to time
AORTITIS inflammation of artery   md
APAGOGIC reducing to an absurdity
APELLOUS without a skin   md
APERIENT a laxative; an opening   md
APERITIF a cocktail
APERTURE gap; hole; lens   pg
APEX-BEAT heartbeat visibility point   md, pl

APHANITE horn-blende, quartz, etc.
APHELION an astronomical distance
APHIDIAN (green-fly)   z
APHLEBIA lateral fern outgrowth   b
APHONOUS voiceless; dumb   m
APHORISM a maxim; a saw
APHORIST a writer of adages
APHORIZE aphorise; define briefly
APHTHOUS ulcerous   m
APIARIAN concerning bees   z
APIARIST a bee expert
APICALLY topmost; at the apex
APLASTIC not easily moulded
APLUSTRE ornament on stern
APNEUSIS state of maintained inspiratic
APOCONYM name made by shortenir word
APOCRINE of gland-cell breakdown   m
APODOSIS consequent clause
APOGAEIC (apogees and aphelions)
APOGRAPH a copy; transcript
APOLLYON the destroying angel
APOLOGIA vindication; formal defence
APOLOGIA excuses
APOLOGUE moral fable; allegory
APOPHYGE base of column
APOPLEXY loss of mental control   m
APOSITIA aversion to food   m
APOSTACY } abandonment of principl
APOSTASY } recantation
APOSTATE a renegade
APOSTEME apostume; an abscess   m
APOTHEGM sententious maxim
APPALLED terrified; dismayed
APPANAGE territorial dependency
APPARENT obvious; evident; palpable
APPEALED implored; entreated
APPEALER a suppliant; invoker
APPEARED emerged; dawned; arrived
APPEASED soothed; allayed; mollified
APPEASER pacifier; tranquillizer
APPELLEE defendant in an appeal   l
APPELLOR prosecutor
APPENDED subjoined; attached
APPENDIX supplement; addendum   m
APPETENT desirous; solicitous
APPETITE craving; longing; hunger
APPETIZE to create a desire
APPLAUSE praise; laudation
APPLE-PIE neat; orderly; bed
APPLE-PIP apple-seed
APPLIQUE applied work
APPLYING employing; requesting
APPOSITE fit; suitable; pertinent
APPRAISE set a value to; rate; survey
APPRISED informed; notified; told
APPRIZED appreciated; valued
APPROACH advance; resemble; avenue
APPROVAL approbation; sanction
APPROVED commended; ratified
APPROVER ratifier; king's evidence

APPULSED driven; struck; attacked
APRES-SKI clothes: party after snow sports
APRON-MAN a mechanic
APTEROUS wingless   zo
APTITUDE readiness; knack; faculty
APYRETIC feverless   md
APYREXIA intermittent fever   md
AQUACADE musical water show
AQUALUNG diver's oxygen pack
AQUARIUM tanks of aquatic animals
AQUARIUS water-carrier (zodiac)
AQUASTAT boiler temperature regulator
AQUATINT a print; (engrav. on copper)
AQUATONE photo printing process   pg
AQUEDUCT artificial water channel
AQUIFORM liquid
AQUILINE like an eagle; hooked
AQUOSITY sloppiness
ARACHNID spider; mite or scorpion   zo
ARAINGEE gallery of a mine
ARAMAISM an Aramaic idiom
ARANEOUS araneose; cobwebby   zo
ARAPUNGA the bell-bird; campanero   zo
ARBALIST arbalest; cross-bow
ARBITRAL arbitrational
ARBOREAL tree-like   bt
ARBORETA shrubberies
ARBORIST tree expert; herbalist
ARBOROUS woody; arboreal
ARBOURED with shady bowers
ARBUSCLE dwarf tree   bt
ARBUSTUM copse; shrubbery   bt
ARBUTEAN (strawberry tree)   bt
ARCADIAN pastoral; rustic
ARCATURE a small arcade
ARCHAEAN geologically remote
ARCHAISM an archaic expression
ARCHAIZE archaise; use archaisms
ARCHDUKE a princely title
ARCHICAL chief; primary
ARCHIVAL documentary
ARCHIVES record office; records
ARCHLIKE arcuate; iridian
ARCHLUTE double-stringed lute   mu
ARCH-MOCK the height of mockery
ARCHNESS roguishness
ARCH-POET Poet Laureate
ARCHWISE bowed
ARCTURUS Bear-guard; star in Boötes
ARDENTLY fiercely, zealously
AREFYING withering; desiccating
ARENARIA sandwort; chickweed   bt
AREOLATE divided into small areas
ARESCENT drying   bt
ARGEMONE silver-weed   bt
ARGENTAN German silver
ARGENTIC argental; silvery
ARGENTUM silver; Ag.   ch
ARGINASE enzyme   pl
ARGONAUT (golden fleece); cuttlefish

ARGOSIES richly laden vessels
ARGUABLE debatable
ARGUFIED wrangled
ARGUMENT discussion; an abstract
ARGUTELY keenly; shrewdly; piercing
ARIANISE convert to Arianism   rl
ARIANISM doctrine of Arius
ARIDNESS dryness; sterility
ARILLARY (exterior coating of a seed)   bt
ARISINGS replaced materials after refit   nv
ARISTATE awned; bearded   bt
ARMAMENT munitions; arms; guns
ARMARIAN monastic librarian
ARMARIUM scroll; book cupboard
ARMATURE armour; rotor of dynamo
ARM-CHAIR an elbow-chair
ARMENIAN a native; a sect   rl
ARMIGERO esquire; armour-bearer
ARMILLET small bracelet; armlet
ARMINIAN (opposed to Calvinism)   rl
ARMORIAL relating to coats-of-arms
ARMORIST expert in heraldry
ARMOURED plated
ARMOURER artificer; manufacturer
ARMOZEEN } taffeta or silk, used for
ARMOZINE } clerical gowns
AROMATIC fragrant; pungent
AROUSING stirring
ARPEGGIO harplike chord   mu
ARQUEBUS heavy musket
ARRANGED settled; grouped
ARRANGER planner; orchestrator
ARRANTLY infamously; notoriously
ARRASENE Arras embroidery
ARRAUGHT taken by force
ARRAYING disposing; adorning
ARRECTED erect; upright
ARRESTED halted; seized; captured
ARRESTER an apprehender   lw
ARRETTED accused
ARRIDING gratifying; pleasing
ARRIVING reaching; attaining; landing
ARROGANT haughty; overbearing
ARROGATE usurp; assume
ARRONDEE segmented heraldic cross   hd
ARROSION corrosion; gnawing
ARSENATE }
ARSENITE } arsenical salts   ch
ARSONIST } felon who deliberately sets
ARSONITE } fire to property
ARTERIAL (arteries); (roads)   md
ARTESIAN (deep wells)
ARTFULLY craftily
ARTICLED bound by agreement   lw
ARTIFACT product of primitive art
ARTIFICE stratagem; trick; device
ARTISTIC tasteful; aesthetic
ARTISTRY vocation; workmanship
ARUSPICE haruspex; soothsayer
ARUSPICY divination by augury
ARVICOLA vole genus   zo

ASBESTIC made of asbestos   mn
ASBESTOS incombustible material
ASCENDED rose; mounted
ASCENDER part of letters in printing   pr
ASCIDIUM bottle-like appendage   bt
ASCORBIC acid; vitamin 'C'   ch
ASCRIBED attributed; assigned
ASH-LEACH tub for washing wood-ash
ASH-PLANT ash sapling; walking stick
ASH-STAND ash-tray
ASHY-GRAY ashy in colour
ASPARTIC obtained from asparagus   bt
ASPERATE to roughen
ASPERGES ceremonial sprinkling   rl
ASPERITY harshness; sourness; acerbity
ASPERSED sprinkled; slandered; abused
ASPHODEL a lily; a daffodil   bt
ASPHYXIA suffocation   md
ASPIRANT suitor; candidate
ASPIRATE to emphasize the 'h' sound
ASPIRING longing; hoping; soaring
ASPOROUS without spores   bt
ASPORTED stolen away
ASSAILED assaulted; attacked; vilified
ASSAILER aggressor; invader; traducer
ASSAMESE native of Assam (language)
ASSARTED grubbed up trees and bushes
ASSASSIN a thug primed with hashish
ASSAYING testing; analysing
ASSEMBLE convene; muster; congregate
ASSEMBLY meeting; company
ASSENTED concurred; agreed; acquiesced
ASSENTER assentor; approver
ASSERTED maintained; averred
ASSESSED taxed; rated; appraised
ASSESSOR tax-master; valuer   lw
ASSIDENT alongside; accompanying
ASSIETTE oblong dish; plate (Fr.)
ASSIGNAT paper currency, Fr. Rev.   nm
ASSIGNED allotted; specified
ASSIGNEE a recipient
ASSIGNOR transferrer of an interest
ASSINEGO small donkey; fool; dolt   zo
ASSISTED aided; abetted; sustained
ASSIZING assessing; regulating
ASSONANT harmonious; rhythmical
ASSONATE correspond in sound   mu
ASSORTED mixed; varied; classified
ASSUAGED allayed; abated; appeased
ASSUAGER mitigator; alleviator
ASSUMING arrogant; presumptuous
ASSURANT holder of insurance policy
ASSURING affirming; pledging
ASSYRIAN a descendant of Shem
ASTACIAN shellfish, lobster type   zo
ASTERIAS starfish genus   zo
ASTERISK the mark (*)
ASTERISM small cluster of stars   as
ASTERNAL not joined to breastbone
ASTEROID minor planet; star-shaped
ASTHENIA lack of vitality; debility

ASTHENIC feeble; weak   md
ASTOMATA an order of infusoria   zo
ASTOMOUS astomatous; mouthless
ASTONIED astounded; stunned; dazed
ASTONISH amaze; startle; surprise
ASTRAGAL a rounded moulding
ASTRINGE constrict; constrain
ASTUNNED astonished; mazed; dazed
ASTUTELY cunningly; craftily
ASYSTOLE heart failure   md
ATABRINE quinine type   md
ATARAXIA stoical indifference
ATHEIZED converted to disbelief
ATHELING Anglo-Saxon noble
ATHENIAN a Greek capitalist
ATHERINE fish genus; mullets; smelts   zo
ATHEROMA disease of arteries   md
ATHLETIC strong; vigorous; sinewy
ATLANTES male supporting figures
ATLANTIC the herring pond
ATLANTIS legendary island
ATMOLOGY science of vaporization
ATOMICAL atomic; minute
ATOMIZED vaporized
ATOMIZER a spray
ATONABLE expiable; amendable
ATREMBLE dithering
ATROCITY a Hunnish act
ATROPHIC emaciated; withered
ATROPINE bella-donna   md
ATROPISM illness due to atropine   md
ATROPOUS upturned; erect   bt
ATTACHED fond; bound; arrested   lw
ATTACKED assaulted; set about
ATTACKER assailant; invader; violator
ATTAINED achieved; secured; won
ATTENDED served; escorted; hearkened
ATTENDER attendant; close listener
ATTENTAT attempted assassination
ATTESTED invoked; endorsed
ATTESTOR attester; a witness
ATTICISM witty remark; Attic salt
ATTICIZE to use Athenian idioms
ATTINGED touched lightly; affected
ATTIRING arraying; adorning; robing
ATTITUDE pose; posture; bearing
ATTORNED transferred homage
ATTORNEY lawyer; solicitor   lw
ATTRITED worn away; abraded; erased
ATTRITUS a grade of coal   mn
ATTUNING harmonizing   mu
AUBUSSON style of carpet
AUCUPATE to go bird-catching
AUDACITY boldness; effrontery; daring
AUDIENCE formal interview; listeners
AUDITING examining accounts
AUDITION a test of competency
AUDITIVE audible
AUDITORY an audience; auditorium
AUGURATE foretell by divination
AUGURIAL ominous

AUGURIES prognostications; portents
AUGURING presaging; prophesying
AUGUSTAN (Emperor Augustus)
AUGUSTLY majestically; imposingly
AULARIAN member of an Oxford Hall
AURELIAN (Emperor Aurelius)
AUREOLED in a halo   rl
AURICLED eared   bt
AURICULA the primula   bt
AURIFORM ear-shaped
AURILAVE an ear-washing instrument   md
AUROREAN rosy; dawning
AURULENT golden
AUSONIAN Italian
AUSTRIAN of Austria
AUTACOID a hormone; a chalone   md
AUTARCHY autocracy; absolutism
AUTARKIC self-sufficient
AUTISTIC withdrawn   pc
AUTOBAHN fast motorway
AUTOCADE motor cavalcade
AUTOCARP self-fertilised fruit   bt
AUTOCODE computer operation procedure
AUTOCRAT absolute ruler   rl
AUTOCYST parasite-formed membrane   zo
AUTO-DA-FE Inquisitional judgment
AUTO-DYNE frequency stabilizer
AUTO-GAMY self-fertilization   bt
AUTO-GENY spontaneous generation
AUTOGYRO a type of aircraft   ae
AUTOLOGY the study of self
AUTOMATA automatons; robots
AUTOMATH a self-taught man
AUTONOMY self-government
AUTOPSIA autopsy; post-mortem   md
AUTOPTIC seen with one's own eyes
AUTOSLED snow vehicle
AUTOSOME non-sexual chromosome   cy
AUTOTOMY amputation; cell division
AUTOTYPE ⎫
AUTOTYPY ⎬ carbon copy process
AUTUMNAL peculiar to the autumn
AUTUNITE phosphate of uranium   ch
AUXILIAR subsidiary; assisting
AUXOCYTE cell with meiosis   cy
AVAILING profiting; sufficing; using
AVELLANE heraldic cross of filberts   hd
AVENGING vindicating; retaliating
AVENTAIL visor; opening in a helmet
AVENTURE fatal accident   lw
AVERAGED equated; proportional
AVERCAKE oatcake   ck
AVERMENT affirmation
AVERNIAN Plutonic; infernal
AVERRING declaring; alleging
AVERSANT heraldic reversal   hd
AVERSELY unwillingly; reluctantly
AVERSION dislike; hatred; allergy
AVIARIST keeper of caged birds
AVIATING flying
AVIATION travel by air

AVIFAUNA local birds   zo
AVISEFUL wary; watchful; circumspect
AVOIDING eschewing; shunning
AVOIDISM trouble evasion
AVOUCHED guaranteed
AVOWABLE affirmable; declarable
AVOWABLY deposably; admittedly
AVOWANCE avowal; confession
AVOWEDLY openly; frankly
AVULSION forcible separation
AWAITING abiding; expecting
AWAKABLE not dead-asleep
AWAKENED spurred; stimulated
AWAKENER a rouser
AWANTING wanting; lacking; absent
AWARDING decreeing; bestowing
AWEARIED jaded; spent; worn
AWEATHER the weather-side   nt
AXE-HELVE handle of an axe
AXE-STONE jade   mn
AXILLARY (armpit); branch angle   bt
AXIOLOGY theory of value
AXIOTRON value with controlled stream
AXLETREE spindle
AXOIDEAN axial
AXOPLASM material around axon
AYENBITE remorse
AZOTIZED nitrogenized

B

BABAKOTO a large lemur   zo
BABBLING prattling; gossiping
BABELDOM state of confusion
BABIRUSA pig-deer of Sri Lanka   zo
BABISHLY childishly
BABOODOM realm of red tape
BABOOISM plethora of verbiage
BABOUCHE oriental slipper
BABY-FACE term of endearment
BABY-FARM baby-boarding house
BABY-HOOD state of infancy
BACCARAT a card game
BACCHANT bacchanalian
BACILLAR like baccili   md
BACILLUS rod-like organism   md
BACHELOR a degree-man; unmarried man
BACK-BAND cart-saddle band
BACK-BITE to speak evil; asperse
BACK-BOND conditional deed
BACKBONE reliability; spine   md
BACK-CHAT impertinent rejoinder
BACK-COCK pendulum bracket   hr
BACK-DOOR clandestine; furtive
BACK-DROP drop scene
BACK-DUTY unpaid tax   lw
BACK-FALL a wrestling throw
BACKFIRE a blow back
BACK-FLAP folding shutter
BACK-FLOW reverse liquid flow   hy
BACK-FOLD foldable part of shutter   jn

BACK-GEAR lathe speed-reducer   eg
BACKHAND (writing); (stroke)
BACK-HEEL rugby football
BACK-IRON plane stiffening plate   ci
BACK-KICK violent engine reversal   eg
BACKLASH gear wear
BACKMOST hindermost
BACK-RAKE surface/base relation   eg
BACK-RENT dues
BACK-REST loom bar   tx
BACK-ROOM behind the scenes
BACKSIDE posterior
BACKSPIN backwards rotary motion of
    ball
BACK-STEP cycle mounting step
BACKSTOP armature-travel-limiting relay
BACK-VELD back blocks (S. Africa)
BACK-WALL semi-conductor photovoltaic
                                      eg
BACKWARD hesitating; reluctant
BACKWASH backward current; wake
BACK-WAVE spacing wave   tc
BACKWORK non-mining colliery activity
BACKWORM filanders; hawk-disease   zo
BACONIAN (Bacon); inductive
BACTERIA fungoid growths   md
BACTRIAN two-humped camel   zo
BACULINE rod-like
BACULITE fossil cuttlefish   mn
BADGERED pestered; worried
BADGERLY grey like a badger
BADIGEON sculptor's cement
BADINAGE persiflage; chaff
BAFFETAS Indian muslin
BAFFLING defeating; hoodwinking
BAGHEERA the black panther (India)   zo
BAGPIPER a piper   mu
BAGUETTE round moulding   ar
BAILABLE able to be bailed   lw
BAIL-BALL cricket ball bail high
BAIL-BOND security for appearance
BAIL-DOCK room at Old Bailey   lw
BAILMENT delivery of goods in trust   lw
BAILSMAN guarantor of bond   lw
BAKELITE a plastic material
BAKEMEAT pastry; pies
BAKSHISH discount; commission; tip
BALANCED in equilibrium
BALANCER acrobat; tumbler
BALANITE fossil barnacle   mn
BALCONET miniature balcony
BALDCOOT baldicoot; coot; monk   zo
BALDHEAD no hair apparent
BALDMONY gentian   bt
BALDNESS alopecia   md
BALD-PATE species of wild duck   zo
BALDRICK shoulder belt
BALE-FIRE signal-fire; funeral pyre
BALK-BACK fibrous-back cloth   tx
BALK-LINE baulk-line (billiards)
BALLADER ballad-monger

BALLADRY patriotic or epic verse
BALL-CLAY fine-textured detrital clay   gl
BALL-COCK stopcock in a cistern
BALLIAGE an export duty
BALLISTA ancient catapult
BALLONET small balloon; gas bag
BALLOTED drew lots for; voted
BALL-PANE part flat, part globular   to
BALLROOM location for stately measures
BALLYHOO bunkum; false fame
BALLYRAG bullyrag; torment
BALMORAL bonnet; boot; petticoat
BALNEARY a bathroom
BALOTADE an equine feat
BALSAMIC soothing; demulcent
BALUSTER supporting column   ar
BANALITY triviality; triteness
BANDAGED surgically bound
BANDANNA Indian silk kerchief
BANDEAUX hair-bands or fillets
BAND-EDGE between 2 defined limits   el
BANDELET bandlet   ar
BANDEROL bannerol; small banner
BANDFISH long lean fish   zo
BANDITTI bandits; robbers; outlaws
BAND-PASS freely passing specific
    currents
BANDSMAN a player
BANDSTER sheaf-binder
BAND-STOP attenuating specific currents
BANDYING tossing about
BANEWORT deadly nightshade   bt
BANG-BANG servo control mechanism   am
BANGSTER bragart; victor
BANGTAIL square-cut tail
BANISHED expelled; outlawed
BANISTER baluster; stair railings
BANJOIST fretful player   mu
BANKABLE receivable at a bank
BANK-BILL note of exchange
BANK-BOOK pass-book
BANK-NOTE promissory note
BANK-RATE Bank of England rate
BANKRUPT insolvent; broke
BANKSMAN overseer at pit-mouth
BANLIEUE environs of a town (Fr.)
BANNERED beflagged
BANNERET knighthood
BANNEROL banderol; small banner
BANTERED railed; chaffed
BANTERER joker; jester
BANTLING young child; bratling
BANXRING insect-eating-squirrel   zo
BAPHOMET Templar's idol
BAPTIZED baptised; immersed   rl
BARATHEA woven fabric   tx
BARBACAN barbicon; outer defence
BARBARED shaved; shorn
BARBARIC foreign; savage; Hunnish
BARBATED bearded; awned   bt
BARBECUE out-door cookery

BARBERRY thorny shrub; berberry   bt
BARBETTE armoured defence
BARBICAN barbacan; gun-port
BARBITON antique form of lyre   mu
BAR-CRAMP plank-gluing bar   to
BARDLING bardlet; poetaster; rhymster
BAREBACK unsaddled
BAREBOAT chartering contract   lw
BAREBONE (Parliament); lean; thin
BAREFOOT bootless
BARESARK without shirt of mail
BARGEMAN barge owner; bargee
BARGHEST a dog-like goblin
BARILLET watch-spring case
BARITONE (between tenor and bass)   mu
BARKMILL bark-crusher
BARNABAS cornflour   bt
BARNACLE a twitch; cirriped; goose   zo
BARN-DOOR a farm portal
BARNEKIN outermost castle ward
BARNYARD the rooster's realm
BAROLOGY the science of weight
BAROMETZ a fern   bt
BARONAGE cf. peerage
BARONESS wife or widow of baron
BARONIAL noble and spacious
BAROUCHE four-wheeled carriage
BAR-POSTS supports of field-gate
BARRACAN material of camel-hair
BARRACKS the soldier's home
BARRANCO barranca; deep gorge
BARRATOR encourager of litigation   lw
BARRATRY traffic in church offices   rl
BARRENLY sterilely; unfruitfully
BARRULET horizontal heraldic bar   hd
BAR-SHEAR bar-cutter   to
BARTERED exchanged commodities
BARTERER a dealer
BARTIZAN small overhanging turret
BASALTIC allied to basalt   mn
BASANITE touchstone; flinty slate   mn
BASCINET helmet of XVth century
BASEBALL national game (USA)
BASEBAND frequency modulation
BASE-BORN of low parentage
BASE-BRED of low breeding
BASELESS lacking any foundation
BASE-LINE a surveyor's base   me
BASEMENT floor below ground level
BASENESS vileness; meanness
BASE-PAIR complementary acid bases   bc
BASE-RICH iron-rich soil
BASE-VIOL bass-viol; violoncello   mu
BASHLESS unashamed; undaunted
BASICITY ratio of acid to base   ch
BASIFIER an alkali   ch
BASILIAN monk of St. Basil   rl
BASILICA church   rl
BASILICA public hall (Roman)
BASILING grinding to an angle
BASILISK dragon; lizard; cannon   zo

BASINFUL bowlful
BASIPHIL attracted to basic dyes   zo
BASKETED hampered
BASKETRY wickerwork
BASOPHIL attracted to basic dyes
BASQUINE Basque outer petticoat
BASS-DRUM deep-noted drum   mu
BASSETTE tenor or small bass viol   mu
BASS-HORN deep-toned bassoon   mu
BASSINET wickerwork perambulator
BASS-TUBA euphonium   mu
BASS-VIOL base-viol; violoncello   mu
BASSWOOD (N. Amer.)   bt
BASTAARD Dutch half-breed (S. Afr.)
BASTARDY illegitimacy
BASTERNA mule-borne litter
BASTILLE old castle; state prison
BATAVIAN native of Batavia
BATELESS irrepressible
BATHABLE washable
BATHETIC anticlimatic; bombastic
BATHMISM inherent divergence
BATHORSE pack-horse   zo
BATH-RAIL side-grip
BATHROOM balneary
BATSWING flat gas flame
BATTELED (Oxford University)
BATTENED grew fat; secured
BATTERED pounded; shattered
BATTLING striving; warring
BATUCADA batuque; dance (Brazil)   mu
BAUDEKIN silk brocade; canopy   rl
BAUDRONS Scottish name for the cat
BAULKING balking; checking
BAVARIAN of Bavaria
BAWDRICK baldrick; shoulder belt
BAYADERE Indian nautch girl
BAYARDLY blindly
BAYBERRY war-myrtle   bt
BDELLIUM aromatic gum-resin   bt
BEACHING running ashore
BEACONED lit up
BEADLERY beadle's jurisdiction
BEAD-ROLL names for masses   rl
BEADSMAN almsman
BEAD-TREE the azedarac   bt
BEAD-WORK ornamental work
BEAK-HEAD Romanesque ornament
BEAKIRON bickern; anvil point
BEAM-BIRD spotted flycatcher   zo
BEAM-EDGE searchlight angle   lt
BEAM-FLUX total light flux   lt
BEAM-TRAP electron beam-catching
electrode
BEAM-TREE a hardwood tree   bt
BEAN-KING king of the revels
BEARABLE tolerable; supportable
BEARABLY endurably; moderately
BEARBIND bearbine; bindweed   bt
BEARDING meeting face to face
BEAR-HERD bear-keeper

BEARINGS sense of direction
BEARLIKE rude and rough; ursine
BEAR'S-EAR primula auricula — bt
BEARSKIN headdress of the guards
BEARWARD bear-leader; Arcturus
BEASTIES small animals — zo
BEASTISH brutal; animal
BEATIFIC ecstatic; rapturous
BEAT-NOTE rhythmic accentuation
BEAUFREY beam or joist
BEAUPERE father-in-law (Fr.)
BEAUTIES lovelies
BEAUTIFY adorn; array; garnish
BEAVERED covered with beaver fur
BECALMED motionless; tranquillized
BECHAMEL savoury sauce
BECHANCE befall; accidentally
BECKONED nodded; called; invited
BECOMING befitting; graceful
BECUEING scowing of an anchor on rocks — nt
BECURLED with ringlets
BEDABBLE dabble; sprinkle
BEDAGGLE drag through the mire
BEDARKEN obscure; eclipse
BEDASHED bespattered
BEDAUBED smeared; plastered
BED-CHAIR bed back-rest
BEDECKED robed; embellished
BEDEGUAR a rose scourge — bt, zo
BEDESMAN see beadsman — rl
BEDEWEEN the birch tree — bt
BEDEWING sprinkling
BED-GOING retiring
BEDIMMED blurred; tarnished; dulled
BED-LINEN sheets, etc.
BEDMAKER college servant
BEDPLATE foundation plate
BEDPLATE engine-frame base — eg
BED-QUILT an overlay
BEDRENCH saturate; immerse; soak
BEDSTAFF cudgel, truncheon
BEDSTEAD a framework
BEDSTRAW a plant — bt
BED-TABLE table for use in bed
BEDUCKED soused
BEDUSTED smothered with dust
BEDWARDS on the way to bed
BEE-BREAD pollen collected by bees — bt
BEECH-OIL beech nut oil
BEE-EATER a bird — zo
BEEFIEST heftiest; lustiest
BEEFWOOD an Australian wood — bt
BEER-PUMP beer-pull, spout
BEERSHOP inn; alehouse; tavern
BEESWING dregs of port
BEETLING overhanging; projecting
BEETRAVE beetroot — bt
BEETROOT beetrave — bt
BEFITTED suitable; becoming; worthy
BEFLOWER cover with flowers

BEFOGGED dimmed; confused
BEFOOLED deluded; hoaxed; gulled
BEFOULED polluted; begrimed
BEFRIEND favour; patronize; aid
BEFRINGE adorn with fringes
BEFURRED covered with fur
BEGETTER a sire
BEGGABLE borrowable
BEGGARED rendered penniless
BEGGARLY paltry; mean; abject
BEGINNER tyro; novice; neophyte
BEGIRDED belted
BEGIRDLE encompass; encircle
BEGOTTEN born; produced
BEGREASE lubricate
BEGRIMED soiled; grubby
BEGRUDGE envy
BEGUILED deluded; diverted
BEGUILER cheat; deceiver
BEHAVING comme il faut
BEHEADAL an execution
BEHEADED decapitated
BEHEMOTH Job's hippopotamus — zo
BEHOLDEN grateful; indebted
BEHOLDER observer; surveyor
BEHOVING being necessary
BEINNESS comfort; well-being
BEJESUIT initiate in Jesuitism — rl
BEKISSED smothered in kisses
BELABOUR to thrash; whack
BELACING adorning with lace
BELAMOUR a gallant; a fair lady
BELATING being late
BELAUDED eulogized
BELAYING fastening — nt
BELCHING eructating
BELFRIED having belfries
BELFRIES steeples; watch-towers — rl
BELIEVED credited; fancied
BELIEVER theist; devotee; pietist
BELITTLE disparage; deprecate
BELLBIND, BELL-BINE bindweed — bt
BELL-BIRD New Zealand bird — zo
BELL-BUOY the sailor's warning — nt
BELLCOTE small belfry
BELLOWED roared; bawled
BELL-PULL bell-rope
BELL-PUSH push-button bell switch — el
BELL-ROPE a ringer
BELL-TENT conical canvas tent
BELLWORT a campanula — bt
BELLYFUL replete
BELLY-GOD greedy; epicure
BELLYING swelling; billowing
BELONGED owned by; pertained
BELOVING loving; fond; doting
BELT-FORK belt-transfer prongs — eg
BELT-SLIP pulley-face belt slippage — eg
BELZEBUB Beelzebub
BEMASKED wearing a mask
BEMIRING soiling

BEMOANED bewailed; lamented	**BESPREAD** broadcast; disseminate
BEMUDDLE mess up	**BESSEMER** a steel process
BEMUFFLE wrap up	**BESTIARY** book about beasts
BENCHING sitting on a bench	**BESTOWAL** gift; grant; distribution
BENDABLE not rigid	**BESTOWED** gave; presented; awarded
BENEAPED aground at low tide nt	**BESTOWER** donor; feoffer
BENEDICK } newly married man;	**BESTREAK** mark with streaks
BENEDICT } learned saint rl	**BESTREWN** scattered; dispersed
BENEFICE church living	**BESTRIDE** astride
BENIGNLY kindly; benevolently	**BESTRODE** traversed; mounted
BENITIER holy water vessel	**BETAFITE** hydrous uranium compound
BENJAMIN gum; overcoat	mn
BENOTING noting fully	**BETAKING** removing to; applying to
BENT-TAIL having a bent shank eg	**BETA-RAYS** radium-rays
BENUMBED torpid	**BETATRON** electron speeding machine
BENZOATE a salt ch	**BETEARED** tearful; bedimmed
BEPEPPER shoot repeatedly	**BETEL-NUT** areca nut palm bt
BEPESTER annoy persistently	**BETIDING** happening; befalling
BEPITIED commiserated	**BETONGUE** scold; rail; nag
BEPLUMED with plumes	**BETOSSED** thrown about
BEPOMMEL belabour	**BETRAYAL** breach of trust
BEPOWDER pulverize	**BETRAYED** ensnared; beguiled
BEPRAISE laud	**BETRAYER** seducer; a Judas; traitor
BEPUFFED flattered	**BETTERED** ameliorated; improved
BEQUEATH entrust	**BETULINE** birch camphor bt
BERATING scolding	**BEVELING** rounded edge
BERBERIN barberry extract ch	**BEVELLED** basiled; on the slant
BERBERRY the barberry bt	**BEVERAGE** drink; potion; potation
BEREAVED bereft bt	**BEVILLED** sloping lines hd
BERGAMOT citron; perfume; pear bt	**BEWAILED** lamented
BERGMEHL crystalline earth mn	**BEWARING** minding; avoiding
BERGMOTE a miner's court	**BEWIGGED** with wig; scolded
BERHYMED celebrated in verse	**BEWILDER** perplex; confuse
BERI-BERI a tropical disease md	**BEWINTER** to chill
BERNOUSE burnouse; Arab mantle	**BEWRAYED** disclosed
BERRYING producing berries	**BEWRAYER** betrayer
BERTHAGE dock fees	**BEZONIAN** beggar; rascal
BERTHING docking nt	**BHEESTIE** Hindu water-carrier
BESCRAWL scribble	**BIANCONI** Irish car
BESCREAM yell the house down	**BIBATION** tippling
BESCREEN shelter	**BIBLICAL** scriptured
BESEEMED befitted	**BIBULOUS** absorbing
BESEEMLY becoming; fit; suitable	**BIB-VALVE** disc-closed draw-off tap eg
BESETTER an assailant	**BICAUDAL** with two tails
BESHADOW overshadow	**BICKERED** squabbled
BESIDERY variety of pear bt	**BICOLOUR** of two colours
BESIEGED beleaguered; encircled	**BICONVEX** lens pt
BESIEGER an investor	**BICRURAL** two-legged
BESILVER electro-plate	**BICUSPID** having two cusps bt
BESLAVED enslaved	**BICYCLED** cycled
BESLAVER slobber	**BIDDABLE** worthy of being bid
BESLIMED bemired	**BIDENTAL** with two teeth
BESMIRCH besmutch; beslime	**BIENNIAL** once in two years
BESNOWED snowed up	**BIER-BALK** right of way for funerals
BESOILED defiled	**BIFACIAL** doublefaced
BESORTED suited; fitted	**BIFEROUS** two crops each year bt
BESOTTED drunk; crapulous; inebriated	**BIFIDATE** cleft in twain bt
BESOUGHT entreated; implored	**BIFORATE** having two pores
BESOULED endowed with a soul	**BIGAMIST** one living in bigamy lw
BESPICED highly seasoned	**BIGAMOUS** involving bigamy
BESPOKEN made to order	**BIGAROON** white-heart cherry bt

BIG-BONED bony; osseous
BIGGONET cap; deerstalker
BIGNONIA plant genus   bt
BIG-SWOLN ready to burst
BIJOUTRY bijouterie; trinkets
BIJUGATE twin   bt
BIJUGOUS paired
BIJWONER squatter (S. Africa)
BILANDER Dutch barge   nt
BILBERRY whortleberry   bt
BILEDUCT a canal   md
BILL-BOOK account book
BILLETED quartered
BILLETEE person billeted
BILLFISH lake fish (N. Amer.)   zo
BILLHEAD letterhead, printing
BILLHOOK hedge cutting tool   to
BILLIARD (used for billiards)
BILLOWED surged; swelled
BILLY-BOY bluff-bowed ketch   nt
BILLY-CAN bush teapot
BILOBATE with two lobes
BIMANOUS two-headed
BIMANUAL done with both hands   md
BIMARINE between two seas
BISMATIC with 2 nipples   zo
BIMENSAL six times in one year
BIMESTER two-monthly
BIMIRROR slightly inclined mirror pair
BINAURAL adapted for two ears
BINBASHI Turkish army officer
BINDWEED bearbine; convolvulus   bt
BINNACLE bittacle; compass box   nt
BINOMIAL consisting of two terms
BINOXIDE a peroxide   ch
BIO-ASSAY drug-power test on animals
   pm
BIOBLAST parturient protoplasm
BIOCYTIN vitamin in yeast
BIOGENIC produced by living organisms
BIOGRAPH bioscope; zoetrope
BIOLYTIC destructive to life
BIOMETER life-measuring instrument   bl
BIOMETRY life mensuration
BIONOMIC ecological   bl
BIOPHORE minute growth-capable particle
BIOPLASM protoplasm   zo
BIOSCOPE early cinematograph
BIOSOPHY made of life
BIPAROUS twin-producing
BIPENNIS two edged battle-axe
BIQUARTZ saccharimeter analyser   lt
BIRADIAL part radial, part bilateral   zo
BIRAMOUS double-branched
BIRCHING corporal punishment
BIRD-BATH garden ornament
BIRD-BOLT blunt arrow
BIRD-CAGE London walk
BIRD-CALL bird whistle
BIRD-EYED quick-sighted; eagle-eyed
BIRD-LICE avian irritants   zo

BIRDLIKE aviform
BIRD-LIME sticky stuff
BIRD-SEED not sown but cropped
BIRD'S-EYE seen from above; tobacco
BIRD-SONG warbling of birds
BIRRETUM judge's black cap   lw
BIRTHDAY an anniversary
BIRTHDOM privilege of birth
BISCAYAN Basque
BISCOTIN sweet biscuit
BISECTED halved; split in twain
BISECTOR an equal divisor
BISERIAL in two series
BISETOSE double-bristled   bt, zo
BISEXUAL hetero- and homosexual
BISHOPED horse coping   vt, zo
BISTABLE with 2 stable states   tc
BISTATIC transmitter/receiver apart   rd
BISTOURY surgical knife   md
BITING-IN (etching)
BITINGLY acidly; mordantly
BITMAKER lorimer; loriner
BITMOUTH bit of a bridle
BITTACLE compass housing   nt
BITTERED soured
BITTERLY acrimoniously
BIVALENT diatomic valency   ch
BI-WEEKLY periodically
BIZCACHA chinchilla, rodent   zo
BLABBING telling; tatling
BLACK-ART necromancy
BLACK-BOX computer control unit; flight
   recorder   ae
BLACKCAP a warbler   zo
BLACK-FLY turnip-flea   zo
BLACK-GUM N. American tree   bt
BLACKING a polish
BLACKISH somewhat dark
BLACKLEG strike-breaker
BLACK-NEB crow; crane, etc.   zo
BLACK-OUT airman's blindness
BLACKPOT coarse ceramic
BLACK-ROD Usher to House of Lords
BLACK-WAD ore of manganese   mn
BLADDERY vesicular   md
BLAMABLE censurable
BLAMABLY reprehensibly
BLAMEFUL culpable
BLANCARD bleached woven cloth
BLANCHED deprived of colour
BLANCHER white-washer
BLANDEST smoothest; mildest
BLANDISH flatter; coax; cajole
BLANKEST most vacant
BLANKING frustrating
BLASTEMA an off-shoot   bt
BLASTING detonating; cursing
BLAST-OFF launching of rocket
BLASTULAR embryonic cell   bl
BLATANCY obtrusive vulgarity
BLAUWBOK antelope, (S. Africa)   zo

BLAZONED embellished	
BLAZONER a broadcaster	
BLAZONRY heraldic painting	
BLEACHED blanched	
BLEACHER colour extractor	
BLEAKEST coldest; barest; chilliest	
BLEAKISH cold and cheerless	
BLEATING blethering	
BLEEDING blood-letting	
BLENCHED flinched; paled	
BLENDING intermingling; harmonizing	
BLENHEIM spaniel; apple; plane	zo, bt
BLESSING divine favour; boon; gain	
BLETTING decaying	.rl
BLIGHTED mildewed	
BLIGHTER pestilent fellow	
BLIMBING a fruit	
BLIMPERY blatant inefficiency	
BLINDAGE camouflage	
BLINDEST most ignorant and heedless	
BLINDING hoodwinking	
BLINKARD a blinker or winker	
BLINKERS eye-shades	
BLINKING ignoring; winking; gleaming	
BLISSFUL rapturous; ecstatic	
BLISTERY vesicated	
BLITHELY joyously	
BLITHEST merriest	
BLITZING bombing	
BLIZZARD violent snowstorm	
BLOATING smoking; inflating; swelling	
BLOCKADE encirclement	
BLOCKING obstructing; shaping	
BLOCKISH like a blockhead	
BLOCK-TIN pure tin	pb
BLODWYTE fine for bloodshedding	
BLONCKET gray	
BLOOD-HOT 98.6°F (37°C)	md
BLOODIED stained with gore	
BLOODILY sanguinely	
BLOODING fox-hunting rite	
BLOOD-RED a gory hue	
BLOOD-TAX conscription	
BLOOD-WON dearly bought	
BLOOMERS garments; blunders	
BLOOMERY forge for smelted iron	
BLOOMING flourishing	
BLOSSOMY full of blossom	
BLOTCHED pimpled; maculose	
BLOTTING obliterating	
BLOW-BALL dandelion head	bt
BLOW-HOLE a whale's nostril	zo
BLOW-LAMP intense local-heat apparatus	
BLOW-MILK skim-milk	
BLOWPIPE a tube; blow-gun	
BLUDGEON truncheon; heavy stick	
BLUE-BACK the field-fare	
BLUEBIRD American warbler	zo
BLUE-BOOK Parliamentary report	
BLUECOAT Christ's Hospital schoolboy	
BLUE-EYED innocent; promising	

BLUE-FISH mackerel	zo
BLUE-FUNK alarm and despondency	
BLUEGILL common Amer. sunfish	
BLUEGOWN King's bedesman	
BLUENESS azureness	
BLUENOSE a Nova Scotian	
BLUE-PILL mercurial pill	md
BLUE-POLL salmon type	zo
BLUE-WING a duck	zo
BLUFFEST most outspoken	
BLUFFING acting deceptively	
BLUISHLY rather blue	
BLUNGING puddling clay	
BLUNTING dulling; benumbing	
BLUNTISH not sharp	
BLURRING dimming; obscuring	
BLURTING uttering hastily	
BLUSHFUL modest	
BLUSHING showing shame; flushing	
BLUSTERY stormy	
BOARDING embarking; lodging	nt
BOARFISH red and silver fish	zo
BOASTFUL vaunting	
BOASTING bragging; bucking; crowing	
BOATABLE navigable	
BOATBILL a heron	zo
BOAT-HOOK aduncous adjunct	
BOAT-RACE aquatic contest	
BOAT-ROPE a painter	
BOBBINET netted lace	
BOBOLINK the rice-bird	zo
BOB-WHITE American partridge	zo
BOCK-BEER lager beer	
BOCKELET a hawk	zo
BOCKLAND freehold land	lw
BODEMENT a presentiment	
BODILESS incorporeal	
BODLEIAN (Oxford Library)	
BODY-LINE (bowling at cricket)	
BODY-WALL perivisceral cavity wall	zo
BOG-BERRY cranberry	bt
BOG-EARTH peat	mn
BOGEYISM frightfulness	
BOGEYMAN hobgoblin	
BOGGLING wavering; havering	
BOG-WHORT whortleberry	bt
BOHEMIAN unconventional	
BOLD-FACE brazen	
BOLDNESS courage; audacity	
BOLIVIAN (Bolivia)	
BOLL-WORM cotton-worm; weevil	zo
BOLOMETER head radiation meter	
BOLT-BOAT cobble	nt
BOLT-HEAD a matrass	
BOLT-HOLE escape hole	
BOLT-ROPE rope round sail	nt
BOMB-FREE no raiders	
BOMBIATE a bombic salt	ch
BOM-PROOF book-club advance copy	pr
BONA-FIDE in good faith	
BONDAGER helpful tenant	

BOND-DEBT bond-held debt	lw
BONDMAID slave	
BONDSMAN surety; bondman	lw
BONE-ACHE a pain	md
BONE-CAVE (prehistoric bones)	
BONE-DUST manure	
BONE-IDLE inert	
BONELACE bobbin-lace	
BONELESS spineless	
BONHOMIE geniality	
BONIFACE an innkeeper	
BONING-IN peg-lining	sv
BONNETED with hat or hood	
BONSENSE opposite of nonsense	
BONSPIEL curling match	
BONTEBOK S. African antelope	zo
BOOBY-HUT covered sleigh	
BOOBYISH dullish	
BOOBYISM stupidity	
BOOHOOED lamented loudly	
BOOKCASE shelved case	
BOOK-CLUB literary association	
BOOK-DEBT outstanding account	
BOOKLESS unlearned	
BOOKMARK book-marker	
BOOK-MATE schoolfellow	
BOOK-NAME nonce name	
BOOK-OATH Bible oath	
BOOK-POST a postal facility (obs.)	
BOOKSHOP voluminous emporium	
BOOKWORM avid reader	
BOOSTING advertising; pushing	
BOOT HOOK helpful appliance	
BOOTHOSE spats	
BOOTIKIN leggings	
BOOTJACK a boot remover	
BOOTLACE a latchet	
BOOTLAST last for boot-making	
BOOTLESS unavailing	
BOOTLICK a lickspittle	
BOOT-TREE (for a shapely boot)	
BORACHIO leather wine bag	
BORACITE magnesium borate	ch
BORDEAUX claret	
BORDERED edged	
BORDERER border dweller	
BORDLAND reserved domain land	lw
BORD-LODE timber carrying	
BORECOLE winter cabbage	bt
BOREWORM teredo	zo
BORROWED assumed; hypothecated	
BORROWER cadger	
BORSTALL hill road	
BOSTANGI Turkish seraglio guards	
BOTANIST plant studier	bt
BOTANIZE pick flowers	
BOTCHERY patchwork	
BOTCHING clumsy repair work	
BOTHERED plagued	
BOTRYOID like a bunch of grapes	
BOTSWANA (Bechuanaland)	

BOTTLING preserving	
BOTTOMED fathomed	
BOTTOMRY loan secured by ship	
BOTULISM form of poisoning	md
BOUDERIE pouting; petulance	
BOUFFANT puffed out	
BOUGHTEN bought (archaic)	
BOUILLON broth; soup	
BOUNCING resilient	
BOUNDARY limit; (cricket)	
BOUNDING leaping; bordering	
BOUNTREE see bourtree	bt
BOURETTE tufted waste-silk yarn	tx
BOURGEON bud; sprout	
BOURTREE the elder	bt
BOVIFORM ox-like	
BOW-BRACE archer's string-guard	
BOW-DRILL rotary drill	
BOW-GRACE a fender	nt
BOWINGLY subserviently; courteously	
BOW-PIECE bow-chaser, (gun)	nt
BOWSPRIT a spar	nt
BOX-DRAIN enclosed drain	
BOX-ELDER ash-leaved maple	bt
BOX-FRAME 1-piece traction-motor frame	
	el
BOX-LOBBY passage in theatre	
BOX-PLATE web-plate steel	bd
BOX-PLEAT a double fold	
BOX-THORN a shrub	bt
BOYISHLY puerilely	
BOY'S-PLAY a prank; trifling	
BRACCATE with feathered feet	zo
BRACELET a handcuff; ornament	
BRACHIAL belonging to the arm	
BRACKISH somewhat salt	
BRACTEAL leaf formation	bt
BRADBURY £1 note (obs.)	
BRADSHAW railway guide	
BRADYPOD a sloth	zo
BRAGGART boaster	
BRAGGING vaunting	
BRAIDING plaiting; upbraiding	
BRAILING hauling in; trussing	nt
BRAIN-FAG nervous exhaustion	
BRAINING dashing out the brains	
BRAINISH brain-sick; furious	
BRAINPAN part of the skull	md
BRAISING a form of cookery	
BRAKE-MAN a controller	
BRAKE-VAN the guard's domain	
BRAMBLED overgrown	
BRANCARD horse-borne litter	
BRANCHED forked; ramified	
BRANCHER young bird	zo
BRANDIED laced with brandy	
BRANDING stigmatizing; marking	
BRANDISE a trivet	
BRANDISH flourish; wave; shake	
BRAND-NEW bran-new	
BRANGLED wrangled	

BRANTAIL the redstart; a warbler	**zo**	
BRANT-FOX a kind of small fox	**zo**	
BRASSAGÉ cost of mintage		
BRASSARD an armlet		
BRASSART arm armour		
BRASS-HAT big-wig		
BRASSICA the cabbage genus	**bt**	
BRASSOCK field mustard	**bt**	
BRATLING small brat		
BRATTICE brettice; partition		
BRAUNITE manganese oxide	**ch**	
BRAWLING wrangling		
BRAZENED shameless		
BRAZENLY impudently; boldly		
BRAZENRY effrontery		
BRAZILIN a red dye	**bt**	
BREACHED violated; tore open		
BREACHES gaps; violations		
BREAD-NUT a fruit	**bt**	
BREAKAGE rupture; fracture		
BREAKING smashing; infringing		
BREAKMAN brake's-man		
BREAK-OUT molten-metal escape	**fd**	
BREAKVOW a perjurer		
BREAMING cleaning ship's bottom		
BREASTED confronted		
BREATHED exhaled; respired		
BREATHER a respite		
BREECHED put into trousers		
BREECHES pantaloons		
BREEDING lineage; begetting		
BREEZING of unclear photo image	**cn**	
BRELOGUE watch-chain ornament		
BRENNAGE an ancient tribute		
BREPHNIC neanic, of adolescent period	**zo**	
BRETHREN brothers; kindred		
BRETTICE brattice; partition		
BREVETCY brevet rank		
BREVIARY prayer-book, R.C.	**rl**	
BREVIATE epitome; a brief	**lw**	
BREVIPED short-legged	**zo**	
BREVIPEN short-winged	**zo**	
BREWSTER brewer; maltster		
BRIAREAN many handed		
BRIBABLE venal; corrupt		
BRICK-AXE 2-bladed brick-dressing axe		
BRICKBAT half-a-brick		
BRICKING building; wrecking		
BRICK-RED dark orange-red		
BRICK-TEA tea in blocks		
BRIDE-ALE ale at a marriage		
BRIDE-BED marriage-bed		
BRIDGING joining up		
BRIDLING controlling; scorning; ruffling		
BRIEFING giving final instructions		
BRIEFMAN brief compiler		
BRIGADED combined		
BRIGHTEN clarify		
BRIGHTLY brilliantly		
BRIGUING canvassing		
BRIMLESS rimless		

BRIMMING full; verging		
BRINDLED streaky brown		
BRINEPAN } salt extraction		
BRINEPIT } by evaporation		
BRINGING conveying; fetching		
BRISANCE shattering effect		
BRISKING quickening		
BRISKISH rather spry		
BRISLING small sardine or sprat	**zo**	
BRISTLED ruffled		
BRITTLED (cooking venison)		
BRITZSKA Polish carriage		
BROACHED pierced		
BROACHER first proposer		
BROAD-AXE heavy axe	**to**	
BROADEST vastest; amplest		
BROADISH rather broad		
BROCADED embroidered		
BROCATEL coarse brocade		
BROCCOLI cultivated cabbage	**bt**	
BROCHURE pamphlet; leaflet		
BRODEKIN buskin; half-boot		
BROIDERY embroidery		
BROILING grilling		
BROKENLY disconnectedly		
BROKERLY mean; low; servile		
BROMELIA the pineapple	**bt**	
BROMELIN proteolytic enzyme	**ch**	
BROMIDIC dull; addict	**md**	
BROMIZED made to smell	**ch**	
BRONCHIC (windpipe)		
BRONZIFY make into bronze		
BRONZING metallic-lustre-giving	**pt**	
BRONZITE lustrous diallage	**mn**	
BROODING pondering; incubating		
BROOD-SAC cockroach egg chamber	**zo**	
BROOKING bearing; enduring		
BROOKITE crystalline titanium oxide	**mn**	
BROOKLET streamlet		
BROOMING sweeping; breaming		
BROUGHAM one-horsed carriage		
BROUHAHA fuss and bother		
BROWBEAT bully; overbear; haze		
BROWLESS shameless		
BROWNING a process; a rifle		
BROWNISH somewhat sunburnt		
BROWNIST congregationalist (now URC)	**rl**	
BROW-POST a main beam		
BROWSICK dejected; melancholy		
BROWSING pasturing		
BRUISING contusing		
BRUMAIRE November (Fr. Rev. cal.)		
BRUNETTE dark hair and eyes		
BRUSH-BOX brush-holder container	**el**	
BRUSHING sweeping; brisk		
BRUSSELS (carpets); (sprouts)		
BRUSTLED crackled; bullied		
BRUTALLY ferociously; ruthlessly		
BRYOLOGY study of mosses		
BRYONINE extract of bryony	**ch**	

BUBBLING gurgling; cheating	
BUCCANED (smoked meat)	
BUCCINAL like a trumpet	
BUCCINUM a whelk	zo
BUCHERON Canadian forest worker	fr
BUCKBEAN a water-plant	bt
BUCKETED rode furiously	
BUCKHORN buck's horn	zo
BUCK-JUMP quick plunging leap	
BUCKLING curling; fastening	
BUCKMAST beech-mast	bt
BUCKRAKE tractor transport attachment	
	ag
BUCKSHEE gratuity; commission; free	
BUCKSHOT large shot	
BUCKSKIN soft yellow leather	
BUCRANIA ornamental ox-skulls	
BUDDHISM } religion founded	
BUDDHIST } by Sakyamuni	rl
BUDDLING ore washing	
BUDGEREE good (Australian)	
BUDGETED made provision	
BUFFCOAT a soldier; a jacket	
BUFFETED struck; clouted	
BUFONITE toadstone	mn
BUHL-WORK inlaid tortoiseshell	
BUILDING erecting; pile; structure	
BULGARIC Bulgarian	
BULKHEAD (ship construction)	
BULK-TEST radiation test sample	nc
BULL-BEEF coarse beef	
BULL-CALF male calf	zo
BULLDOSE to haze; intimidate; coerce	
BULLDOZE rase or level	
BULLETIN official report	
BULL-FROG North American frog	zo
BULLHEAD miller's thumb (fish)	zo
BULLIRAG to badger; ballyrag	
BULLNOSE rounded edge	ar
BULLRING Spanish arena	
BULL'S-EYE glass window; sweet	
BULLWEED knap-weed	bt
BULLWORT bishop's-weed	bt
BULLYING browbeating; threatening	
BULLYISM hectoring; blustering	
BULLYRAG abuse vehemently	
BULRUSHY full of rushes	bt
BUMMALOE Bombay duck (fish)	zo
BUMMAREE fish-factor; money-lender	
BUMP-BALL cricket	
BUNCHING clustering; grouping	
BUNDLING faggoting	
BUN-FIGHT tea party	
BUNGALOW one-storied house	
BUNGHOLE hole in a cask	
BUNGLING awkward; clumsy	
BUNGVENT spile-hole in bung	
BUNKERED coaled; in difficulties	
BUNODONT a dental malady	md
BUNTLINE a sheet	nt
BUOYANCY specific lightness	

BURBERRY a waterproof	
BURDENED laden; overloaded	
BURGAMOT bergamot; citron	b
BURGANET } Burgundian helmet;	
BURGONET } helmet with visor	
BURGLARY felony at night	
BURGLING stealing; robbing	
BURGRAVE German governor	
BURGUNDY French wine	
BURINIST engraver	
BURLETTA burlesque; comic opera	m
BURNOOSE Arab cloak	
BURNT-EAR corn-disease	b
BURROWED excavated; tunnelled	
BURROWER a rabbit	
BURR-PUMP large pump	n
BURSALIS a muscle	m
BURSCHEN German students	
BURSITIS bursa inflammation	m
BURSTING exploding; rending	
BUSH-BABY night-ape (S. Africa)	z
BUSH-BRED reared in back country	
BUSHBUCK antelope (S. Africa)	z
BUSHELER a clothes-repairer (USA)	
BUSH-ROPE a liana; a creeper	b
BUSH-VELD bush country (S. Africa)	
BUSINESS stage-craft; occupation	
BUSKINED booted	
BUSYBODY officious person	
BUSYLESS being idle	
BUSYNESS state of being busy	
BUTCHERY slaughter; massacre	
BUTCHING butchery (dialect)	
BUTTERED missed	
BUTTERIS farrier's knife	t
BUTTONED fastened	
BUTTRESS support; prop	
BUTTRICE farrier's knife	t
BUTYRATE salt of butyric acid	c
BUTYROUS buttery; oleaginous	
BY-BIDDER auction-bid encourager	
BYCOCKET peaked cap (XVth Cent.)	
BY-CORNER odd corner	
BY-DESIGN subsidiary purpose	
BY-LANDER bilander; hoy	n
BY-MATTER something incidental	
BY-MOTIVE unavowed motive	
BY-PASSED avoided	
BYRONISM Lord Byron's phrase	
BY-SPEECH casual speech	
BY-STREET side street	
BY-STROKE sly stroke	
BY-THE-BYE by the way	

C

CABACHON jewel without facets	
CABALISM occultism; mystic science	
CABALIST an adept	
CABALLED plotted; conspired	
CABALLER schemer; intriguer	

CABBAGED filched; purloined; stole		
CABBLING smashing into small pieces		
CABIN-BOY waits on ship's passengers		
CABINING confining; cooping up		
CABIRIAN fire-worshipper (Lemnos)		
CABLE-WAY blondin; tower-supported		
cables		ce
CABOCHED } heraldic head without		
CABOSHED } a neck		hd
CABOODLE the whole lot		
CABOTAGE coasting trade		
CABRIOLE capriole; to leap; to caper		
CAB-STAND a rank		
CACHALOT } the sperm whale		zo
CACHOLOT }		
CACHEMIC unhealthy		md
CACHEPOT ornamental flower-pot		
CACHEXIA severe emaciation		md
CACHUCHA Spanish dance		mu
CACHUNDE aromatic medicine		md
CACKEREL a species of fish		zo
CACKLING gossiping; chattering		
CACODOXY erroneous opinion		
CACOLOGY bad pronunciation		
CADASTRE a survey of land		
CADENCED modulated; rhythmical		
CADILLAC a pear; motor car		bt
CADUCEUS Mercury's wand		
CADUCITY frailty; transitoriness		
CADUCOUS early falling (leaves)		bt
CAERLEON King Arthur's residence		
CAESIOUS blue-grey		
CAESURAL (metric pause)		
CAFFEINE coffee alkaloid		ch
CAGELING a bird in a cage		
CAILLACH an old woman (Gael.)		
CAIMACAM Turkish governor		
CAISSOON caisson; watertight chest		
CAJOLERY flattery; blandishment		
CAJOLING wheedling; coaxing		
CAKESHOP (confectionery)		
CAKE-WALK a caper		
CALABASH gourd		bt
CALADIUM plant genus		bt
CALAMARY cuttlefish		zo
CALAMBAC aloes-wood		bt
CALAMINE zinc ore		mn
CALAMINT aromatic plant		bt
CALAMITE tremolite		mn
CALAMITY disaster; affliction		
CALANDER a lark		zo
CALANDRA grain-weevil		zo
CALANGAY white cockatoo		zo
CALATHUS work-basket		
CALCEATE shod; to shoe		
CALCEDON opaline quartz		mn
CALCINED reduced to quick-lime		
CALCINER high-temperature heat device		
CALC-SPAR calcite		mn
CALC-TUFF a limestone		mn
CALCULUS stone; (calculation)		md

CALENDAR almanac; register; list		
CALENDER hot-rolling machine		
CALFLESS spindle-shanked		
CALF-LOVE an early attachment		
CALF-SKIN binding leather		
CALIBRED bored; gauged		
CALIDITY warmth; fervency; ardency		
CALIDUCT a heating pipe		
CALIFATE rank of calif		
CALIPASH green turtle fat		
CALIPERS a measuring device		to
CALIPPIC (Metonic cycles)		me
CALISAYA Peruvian bark		bt
CALIXTIN Hussite		rl
CALLAITE turquoise		mn
CALL-BIRD a decoy		zo
CALL-GIRL prostitute		
CALLIOPE muse of epic poetry		
CALL-LOAN cash on demand		
CALL-NOTE bird-call		
CALL-OVER a roll-call		
CALMNESS placidity; tranquillity		
CALORIST a heat theorist		
CALORIZE aluminium-spray steel surfaces		
		ml
CALOTYPE talbot-type		pg
CALTROPS a plant		bt
CALVERED crimped; pickled		
CALVILLE an apple		bt
CALYCINE cuplike		bt
CALYCOID like a calyx		
CALYMENE trilobite genus		zo
CALYPTRA a covering		bt
CAMASSIA kind of hyacinth		bt
CAMATINA acorns for tanning		
CAMBERED slightly arched		
CAMBOGIA gamboge gum		ch
CAMBRIAN Welsh		
CAMELEER camel driver		
CAMELEON chameleon		zo
CAMELINE camlet; camel hair		
CAMELISH obstinate		
CAMELLIA an evergreen		bt
CAMERATE to build arch shape		ar
CAMISADE } night attack with white		
CAMISADO } shirts over armour		
CAMISOLE a straight-jacket		
CAMISTER a clergyman		rl
CAMOMILE a bitter plant		bt
CAMPAIGN open country; crusade		
CAMP-FIRE outdoor heating element		
CAMPHENE camphine; camphor		ch
CAMP-SHOT a pile revetment		
CAM-SHAFT part of machinery		au
CAMSTONE whitening for doorsteps		
CAM-WHEEL an eccentric		
CANADIAN Canuck		
CANAIGRE Texan dock		bt
CANALIZE make into a canal		
CANARESE natives of Canara		
CANASTER a kind of tobacco		bt

CANCELLI bars of lattice-work	rl	
CANCRINE crab-like	zo	
CANCROID like cancer	md	
CANDIDLY frankly; sincerely; naively		
CANDYING preserving in sugar		
CANE-HOLE trench for sugar canes		
CANE-MILL sugar crushing mill		
CANEPHOR basket-bearing figure		
CANEWARE yellowish stoneware dishes		
CANICULA the dog-star; Sirius		
CANISTER a tin; tea chest; case-shot		
CANITIES whiteness of the hair	md	
CANKERED corroded; infected		
CANNABIN cannabic extract	ch	
CANNABIS hemp; bhang	bt	
CANNELON mince-pie		
CANNIBAL anthropophagite		
CANNIKIN pannikin; a billy		
CANNONED (billiards); collided		
CANNULAR tubular		
CANOEIST a paddler		
CANON-BIT cannon-bit; (horse-bit)		
CANONESS a beneficiary	rl	
CANONIST ecclesiastical expert	rl	
CANONIZE besaint	rl	
CANON-LAW diocesan digest	rl	
CANOODLE caress; fondle		
CANOPIED with an awning		
CANOROUS tuneful; musical; melodious		
CANSTICK candlestick (Shak.)		
CANTERED galloped easily		
CANTHOOK lumberman's lever	to	
CANTICLE song or chant		
CANTICUM a canticle	rl	
CANTLING brick-firing course	bd	
CANTONAL referring to a district		
CANTONED divided into cantons		
CANTORIS of the precentor	rl	
CANZONET air or song		
CAPACITY volume; capability; faculty		
CAPE-CART two-wheeled vehicle (SA)		
CAPELINE bandage; lady's wrap	md	
CAPELLET enlarged hock		
CAPERING frolicsome frisking		
CAPER-TEA black tea	bt	
CAPIBARA Brazilian rodent	zo	
CAPYBARA allied to the guinea-pig		
CAPITANO a head-man		
CAPITATE growing to a head	bt	
CAPONIER gallery in a fort		
CAPONISE castrate; geld; emasculate		
CAPOTING winning all tricks at piquet		
CAP-PAPER wrapping or writing paper		
CAPRIFIG pollinating inedible fig	bt	
CAPRIPED goat-footed		
CAPROATE a butric salt	ch	
CAPRYLIC normal; acidic	ch	
CAP-SCREW nutless screw-bolt	eg	
CAPSICUM red pepper; chilli	bt	
CAPSTONE fossil sea-urchin	mn	
CAPSULAR in capsule form		

CAPTIOUS hypercritical; censorious		
CAPTURED caught; arrested		
CAPUCCIO a hood or cowl		
CAPUCHIN monk; hooded cloak	rl	
CAPUCINE hooded monkey; pigeon	zo	
CARABINE carbine; short rifle		
CARACARA Brazilian carrion-hawk	zo	
CARACOLE spiral staircase	ar	
CARACOLE equestrian turn; shell	zo	
CARACOLY alloy of gold and silver		
CARAPACE tortoise shell; etc.	zo	
CARAP-OIL crab-wood oil	bt	
CARBOLIC phenol	ch	
CARBOLOY carbide alloy for cutting tools		
CARBONIC of carbon	ch	
CARBONYL metal/carbon-monoxide product	ch	
CARBURET impregnant with carbon		
CARCAJOU wolverine or glutton		
CARCANET collar of jewels		
CARDAMOM aromatic spice	md	
CARD-CASE a receptacle		
CARDIACE heart-shaped jewel		
CARDIGAN knitted woollen jacket		
CARDINAL short cloak; principal	rl	
CARDIOID heart-shaped curve		
CARDITIS inflammation of heart	md	
CAREENED laid on one side	nt	
CAREERED raced; rushed; dashed		
CAREFREE joyous		
CARELESS heedless; remiss; incautious		
CARESSED fondled; embraced; petted		
CAREWORN grief-stricken		
CARGOOSE crested grebe	zo	
CARIACOU Virginian deer	zo	
CARIBBEE a Caribbean		
CARICOUS like a fig	bt	
CARILLON a ring of bells		
CARINATE keel-shaped	bt	
CARL-HEMP female hemp plant		
CARNAGED slaughtered; butchered		
CARNALLY sensuously		
CARNAUBA Brazilian palm	bt	
CARNEOUS fleshly		
CARNIFEX public executioner		
CARNIVAL revelry; masquerade		
CAROLINE time of King Charles		
CAROLLED warbled; sang	mu	
CAROTEEL East Indian weight	me	
CAROTENE vitamin A		
CAROUSAL a jollification; orgies		
CAROUSED held carnival; feasted		
CAROUSEL tournament; tourney		
CAROUSER a noisy reveller		
CARPETED told off; rebuked		
CARRIAGE cab; burden; behaviour		
CARRIOLE open carriage; sledge		
CARRITCH catechism (Sc.)		
CARRYING transporting; conveying		
CART-LOAD a measure of capacity		
CARTOUCH cartouche; hieroglyph		

CARUCAGE tax on ploughs
CARUCATE (plough-land)
CARUNCEL fleshy excrescence   md
CARYATIC (Caryatides)
CARYATID a lady supporter   ar
CARYOKAR butter-nut tree   bt
CASANOVA type of salad   ck
CASCABEL swell on cannon's mouth
CASCADED fell in torrents
CASCALHO diamond-bearing earth
CASEMATE armoured chamber
CASEMENT hinged window
CASE-SHOT short range ammunition
CASE-WORM caddis-worm   zo
CASHMERE silky goat's hair
CASKETED enshrined; coffined
CASSETTE container
CASS-WEED shepherd's purse   bt
CASTANEA chestnut-tree   bt
CASTANET a clapper   mu
CASTAWAY wrecked; rejected
CAST-IRON rigid; inflexible
CASTLERY feudal castle control
CASTLING (chess)
CASTRATE geld; emasculate
CASTRATO high voiced singer   mu
CASUALLY accidentally; fortuitously
CASUALTY killed or wounded
CATACOMB cave sepulchre
CATALASE hydrogen-peroxide-
decomposing enzyme   ch
CATALYST ⎫ (unchanged substance
CATALYSE ⎬ assisting chemical action)
CATAPULT a pellet projector
CATARACT waterfall; eye trouble   md
CAT-BLOCK anchor-tackle   nt
CATCH-ALL general jumble container
CATCHFLY certain plants   bt
CATCHING infectious; charming
CATCH-PIT sump; matter-retaining
catchment
CATEGORY order; class; division
CATENARY like a chain
CATENATE chain-like   bt
CATENOID catenary revolution surface   ma
CATERESS lady provider
CATERING food and entertainment
CATHEDRA bishop's throne   rl
CATHETUS perpendicular line
CATHEXIS concentration of psychic
energy
CATHISMA part of the psalter
CATHODAL negative electrode   el
CATHODIC produced by cathode reaction
  el
CATHOLIC universal; liberal; tolerant
CATILINE daring conspirator
CATODONT teeth on lower jaw only
CATOLYTE electrolyte next to cathode   el
CATONIAN resembling Cato; severe
CATOPSIS morbid keen-sightedness

CAT'S-FOOT ground ivy   bt
CAT'S-TAIL the reed mace   bt
CAT-STICK tip-cat's stick
CAUDATED having a tail; tailed
CAUDICES stems of trees   bt
CAUDICLE an orchid stalk   bt
CAULDRON bowl-shaped boiler
CAULICLE caudicle; small stalk   bt
CAULKING filling in cracks   nt
CAUSALLY resultantly; productively
CAUSERIE gossip; small talk
CAUSEUSE settee for two
CAUSEWAY roadway over wet ground
CAUTIOUS wary; discreet; watchful
CAVALIER haughty; disdainful; beau
CAVATINA short simple air   mu
CAVATION excavation
CAVEATED warned   lw
CAVEATOR caveat lodger   lw
CAVE-BEAR extinct animal   zo
CAVERNED hollowed out
CAVESSON horse-breaking appliance
CAVICORN hollow-horned   zo
CAVILLED objected; carped; criticized
CAVILLER captious critic
CAVORTED pranced
CELERIAC turnip-rooted celery   bt
CELERITY rapidity; swiftness; speed
CELIBACY the unmarried state
CELIBATE unwed
CELLARER wine steward; Simon
CELLARET small wine container
CELLULAR honeycombed; alveolated
CEMENTED glued; united; stuck
CEMETERY burial ground; necropolis
CENATION supping
CENOBITE religious order   rl
CENOTAPH a monument; memorial
CENOZIAC tertiary geological period
CENSORED blue-pencilled
CENSURED reprimanded; rebuked
CENTAURY rose-pink flower   bt
CENTERED centred; localized
CENTIARE a square metre   me
CENTIBAR a meteor measurement   me
CENTOISM literary patchwork
CENTOIST platitudinarian
CENTRING football kick; centering
CENTROID centre of gravity
CENTUPLE a hundredfold
CEPHALGY headache   md
CEPHALIC remedy for head-pains   md
CEPHALIN phosphatide substance in brain
CERAMICS pottery
CERASINE plum gum   bt
CERASTES a horned snake   zo
CERATITE species of ammonite   mn
CERATODE horny structure
CERATOID ceratose; horny
CERBERUS hell's watch-dog   zo
CEREALIA corn and grass   bt

CEREALIN a bran extract   ch
CEREBRAL brainy
CEREBRIC cerebral   md
CEREBRIN something in the brain
CEREBRUM part of the brain   md
CEREMENT shroud dipped in wax
CEREMONY prescribed formality
CERESINE refined ozocerite   el
CERNUOUS drooping   bt
CERTINAL a phenol developer   pg
CERULEAN sky-blue
CERULEIN olive-green
CERUSITE white lead   mn
CERVELAT saveloy; pork-brain sausage
CERVICAL relating to the neck
CESAREAN (Julius Caesar)   md
CESSPOOL drainage pit; midden
CESTODES tapeworm   md
CETACEAN whale or dolphin;   zo
CETOLOGY their natural history   zo
CETRARIA lichen; Iceland moss   bt
CHACONNE slow dance and music
CHADBAND a canting hypocrite
CHAFEWAX sealing-wax officer
CHAFFERY haggling; bargaining
CHAFFING bantering; scoffing
CHAFFRON horse armour
CHAINING restraining; fettering
CHAINLET small chain
CHAIR-BED convertible contraption
CHAIRING carrying in triumph
CHAIRMAN president or carrier
CHALDAIC Babylonian
CHALDRON 25 cwt (1270 kg) of coal   me
CHALICED cup-like
CHALKING recording in chalk
CHALKPIT a quarry
CHALONIC inhibitory, depressive   zo
CHAMBREL horse's hind leg joint
CHAMFRON horse's head armour
CHAMORRO native; language (Guam, Marianas)
CHAMPING chewing; gnawing; biting
CHAMPION defender; hero; victor
CHANCERY court of justice   lw
CHANCING risking; happening
CHANDLER candle-maker; dealer
CHANFRIN fore-part of horse's head
CHANGING altering; varying
CHANTING intoning; reciting
CHAPATTY flat unleavened bread (India)
CHAPBOOK book hawked by chapmen
CHAPELET stirrups and leathers
CHAPELRY chapel district   rl
CHAPERON an escort; a cap
CHAPITER capital of a column
CHAPLAIN a sky-pilot   rl
CHAPLASH yellow-brown durable wood   fr
CHAPLESS without a lower jaw
CHAPPING cleaving
CHAPTREL arch-supporting capital

CHARCOAL charred wood
CHARGING rushing; costing; enjoining
CHARISMA magnetic personality; grace
CHARLIES night watchmen
CHARLOCK wild mustard   b
CHARMING fascinating; captivating
CHARRING scorching; toasting
CHARTING mapping; recording
CHARTISM (universal suffrage;
CHARTIST payment of M.P.s, etc.)
CHASSEUR light-armed soldier
CHASTELY virtuously; modestly
CHASTISE flog; castigate; discipline
CHASTITY sexual abstinence
CHASUBLE vestment over alb
CHATELET small castle
CHATTELS miscellaneous property
CHATTING friendly converse
CHATWOOD fuel; ducal mansion
CHAUFFER portable furnace
CHAUNTER chanter of bagpipes   m
CHAUSSES trunk-hose; leg-armour
CHAY-ROOT Indian red dye   b
CHEATERY fraud; deception
CHEATING knavery; duping
CHECHAKO tenderfoot (Alaska)
CHECKERS a draughts game
CHECKING reproving; impeding
CHEEKING saucy behaviour
CHEEPING piping; chirping
CHEERFUL merry and bright
CHEERILY joyfully; gaily; blithely
CHEERING applause; comforting
CHELIFER book-scorpion   z
CHELLEAN early Palaeolithic
CHELONIA tortoises and turtles   z
CHEMICAL chymical
CHEMOSIS eye-disease symptom   m
CHEMURGY applied organic chemistry
CHENILLE fluffy silk or cotton
CHERUBIC angelic
CHERUBIM a celestial spirit
CHESHIRE cheese; fading cat   z
CHESIBLE see chasuble
CHESSMAN a piece
CHESTING encasing; boxing
CHESTNUT old joke; conker   b
CHEVEREL kid-skin;   z
CHEVERIL flexible leather
CHEVILLE bridge of a violin   m
CHEVYING chasing; pursuing
CHIASMUS inverse parallelism
CHIASTIC crossed
CHICANED cheated; tricked
CHICANER a swindler; artful dodger
CHICCORY chicory   b
CHICKING sprouting
CHICK-PEA small pea   b
CHIEFAGE capitation; poll tax
CHIEFRIE small feudal rent   lw
CHILD-BED lying in

CHILDING bearing children
CHILDISH puerile; infantile
CHILDREN kids
CHILIASM doctrine of millennium
CHILIAST believer in that doctrine
CHILLIER cooler; colder
CHILLING discouraging; depressful
CHILTERN (stewardship)
CHIMAERA fabulous monster   zo
CHIMERIC fanciful; delusive
CHINAMAN Chinese
CHINAMPA floating garden
CHIN-CHIN a toast
CHINKING jingling
CHINOITE green mineral
CHINREST violin
CHINSCAB a sheep-disease   vt
CHINSING caulking
CHIPMUCK ⎫ the ground-squirrel
CHIPMUNK ⎭ of North America   zo
CHIPPING chaffing; chopping; fracturing
CHIPSHOT golf
CHIRAGRA gout in the hands   md
CHIRPING cheeping
CHIRRING cooing; curring; purring
CHIT-CHAT small talk
CHIVALRY gallantry
CHLOASMA a skin disease   md
CHLORATE salt of chloric acid   ch
CHLORIDE compound of chlorine   ch
CHLORINE a yellow gas   ch
CHLORITE olive-green mineral   mn
CHLOROID ⎫
CHLOROUS ⎭ pertaining to chlorine   ch
CHOANITE fossil sponge   mn
CHOICELY discriminately; exquisitely
CHOIR-BOY a sweet singer   rl
CHOIRING singing in unison
CHOLERIC irascible; testy; petulant
CHOLIAMB iambic metre
CHONDRAL cartilaginous   md
CHONDRIN gelatinous liquid   md
CHOOSING selecting; picking
CHOP-CHOP hurry!
CHOPNESS kind of spade
CHOPPING and changing; veering
CHOP-SUEY a succulent Chinese dish   ck
CHORAGIC (musical production)
CHORALLY (choir or chorus)
CHORDATA vertebrates, etc.   zo
CHORDING stringing
CHOREGUS choragus   mu
CHORIAMB iambic metre
CHORISIS separation   bt
CHORTLED chuckled loudly
CHORUSED concerted
CHOULTRY caravanserai; inn
CHOUSING swindling
CHOW-CHOW ginger chutney
CHOW-MEIN Chinese dish   ck
CHRESARD plant water supply in earth

CHRISMAL (consecrated oil)   rl
CHRISTEN baptize   rl
CHROMATE salt of chromic acid   ch
CHROMIUM a metallic element   ch
CHROMULE colouring matter   bt
CHRYSENE coal-tar component   ch
CHTHONIC subterranean
CHUCKIES a game with pebbles
CHUCKING throwing; jerking; gripping
CHUCKLED exulted
CHUFFILY clownishly; churlishly
CHUMMAGE chamber-fellowship
CHUMMERY friendship; intimacy
CHUMMING messing together
CHUMP-END thick end
CHUMSHIP comradeship (Sc.)
CHUPATTY unleavened bread (Ind.)   ck
CHURINGA Australian amulet
CHURLISH surly and sullen
CHURNING agitating; rotating; foaming
CHYLIFIC producing chyle   md
CHYMICAL chemical
CHYMOSIN gastric enzyme, rennin   ch
CIBATION feeding
CIBORIUM eucharistic vessel   rl
CICATRIX a scar   md
CICERONE guide
CICISBEI sword-knots
CICISBEO philanderer
CICURATE to tame
CIDER-CUP a beverage
CIDERIST cider-maker
CIDERKIN inferior cider
CILIATED with eyelashes
CILIFORM (fine filaments)   bt
CIMBRIAN a German tribe
CIMOLITE fuller's earth   mn
CINCHING tightening roll of film   cn
CINCHONA Peruvian bark   md
CINCTURE girdle; belt
CINDROUS ashy
CINEFILM moving-picture film   cn
CINERAMA wide screen film   cn
CINERARY cindery
CINEREAL like ashes
CINGULUM band; zone; belt
CINNABAR dragon's blood   mn
CINNAMIC cinnamon type   bt
CINNAMON a spicy bark   bt
CIPHERED written in code
CIRCAEAN infatuating (Circe)
CIRCINUS the compasses (Astronomical)
CIRCLING flying around
CIRCUITY indirect approach
CIRCULAR round; printed leaflet
CIRRHOSE ⎫ terminating in a
CIRRHOUS ⎭ tendril or curl   bt
CIRRIPED a barnacle   zo
CISELEUR engraver; chaser
CISELURE chased metal-work
CISTELLA capsular shield   bt

CISTVAEN stone tomb
CITATION mention in despatches
CITATORY citing; summoning
CITREOUS citric; lemon flavoured
CITRININ bacteriostat
CITY-BRED raised in town
CIVET-CAT polecat   zo
CIVETING scenting with civet
CIVILIAN non-military
CIVILIST civil law expert
CIVILITY politeness; courtesy
CIVILIZE reclaim from barbarism
CLACK-BOX valve container
CLACKING clicking; jabbering
CLADDING metal-surfacing coins   ar
CLADONIA reindeer moss   bt
CLAGGING adhesion of blacking   ml
CLAIMANT assertor of claims
CLAIMING demanding; arrogating
CLAMANCY urgency; exigency
CLAM-BAKE seaside picnic (USA)
CLAMMING daubing; clogging
CLAMPING fastening; clumping
CLANGING resounding; clanking
CLANGOUR din; clamour
CLANGOUS resonant
CLANKING clanging; clashing
CLANNISH cliquish
CLANSHIP loyalty; sodality
CLANSMAN one of a clan
CLAP-DISH wooden platter
CLAPPING applauding; putting away
CLAP-SILL frame of lock-gates
CLAP-TRAP speciosity; theatrical
CLAQUEUR hired applauder
CLARENCE four-wheeled cab
CLARINET reed instrument   mu
CLASHING colliding; jarring; differing
CLASPING fastening; grasping; hugging
CLASP-NUT split/lathe nut   eg
CLASSIER superior; loftier; finer
CLASSIFY arrange; tabulate
CLASSING grading; grouping; ranging
CLASSMAN a graduate
CLASS-WAR engineered strife
CLAUDIAN (Roman Emperors)
CLAUSURE closure; stoppage
CLAVATED with knobs on
CLAVECIN harpsichord   mu
CLAVIARY index of keys
CLAVICLE collar-bone   md
CLAVIGER clubman; key-man
CLAWBACK a sycophant
CLAW-FOOT foot deformity   md
CLAW-HAND hand deformity   md
CLAWLESS no claws
CLAWSICK foot-rot   vt
CLAY-COLD lifeless
CLAY-MARL chalky clay   mn
CLAY-MILL clay mixing mill
CLAYMORE Scottish broad-sword

CLAYWEED coltsfoot   bt
CLEADING coffer dam; lock-gate boarding   eg
CLEANING washing; purifying; clearing
CLEANISH rather clean
CLEANSED purged; purified
CLEANSER a detergent; purifier
CLEARAGE removal
CLEAR-CUT sharply outlined
CLEAREST plainest; purest
CLEARING (banking; woodcutting)
CLEAVAGE fracture; fissure; separation
CLEAVERS goose-grass   bt
CLEAVING splitting; riving
CLEAVING clinging; uniting; adhering
CLECKING a brood; a clutch   ze
CLEMATIS traveller's joy, etc.   bt
CLEMENCY clemence; leniency; mercy
CLENCHED clinched; gripped
CLERICAL priestly
CLERKAGE clerical work
CLERKDOM babooism
CLERKERY accountancy
CLERKISH somewhat learned
CLEVEITE Norwegian pitchblende   mu
CLEVERER more astute; abler
CLEVERLY dexterously; adroitly
CLICKING progressing satisfactorily
CLIENTAL dependent
CLIENTED supplied with clients
CLIMATIC due to climate
CLIMBING scrambling; scaling
CLINCHED clenched; held fast
CLINCHER decisive reply
CLINGING embracing; tenacious
CLINICAL bedside   me
CLINIQUE nursing-home   me
CLINKANT glittering
CLINKING jingling
CLIPPERS cutting tools   te
CLIPPING shearing; trimming
CLIQUISH clannish
CLIQUISM exclusiveness
CLITELLA bands of worms   ze
CLITHERS burweed   b
CLITHRAL completely roofed
CLOAKAGE disguise; pretext
CLOAK-BAG portmanteau
CLOAKING hiding; veiling; screening
CLOCHARD tramp (Fr.)
CLOCKING checking in; timing
CLODDING clotting
CLODDISH boorish; rustic
CLODPATE dolt; blockhead
CLODPOOL dullard; clotpoll
CLOGGING coalescing; impeding
CLOISTER an ambulatory
CLOSE-CUT close-bodied; cropped
CLOSETED secluded
CLOTHIER cloth merchant; tailor
CLOTHING garments; dress; draping

CLOTPOLL clodpate
CLOTTING coagulating; curdling
CLOUDAGE cloudiness
CLOUDERY cloudage
CLOUDILY mistily
CLOUDING obscuring; dimming
CLOUDLET a little cloud
CLOURING chisel indentations on walls **ar**
CLOUTING patching; buffeting
CLOVERED in clover
CLOWNERY buffoonery; burlesque
CLOWNING playing the fool; jesting
CLOWNISH ungainly; rude; boorish
CLOYLESS insatiable
CLOYMENT a surfeit; a glut
CLOYSOME palling
CLUBBING combining; bludgeoning
CLUBBISH rustic; congenial
CLUBBISM the club system
CLUBBIST frequenter of clubs
CLUB-FIST large heavy fist
CLUBFOOT taliped **md**
CLUBHAUL tacking **nt**
CLUB-LAND (Pall Mall, etc.)
CLUB-MOSS lycopodium **bt**
CLUB-ROOM a meeting room
CLUB-ROOT a plant disease **bt**
CLUB-RUSH bulrush **bt**
CLUCKING hen-talk
CLUELESS without a trace
CLUMPING (bootmaking); bunching
CLUMSIER more awkward
CLUMSILY maladroitly
CLUPEOID like a herring **zo**
CLUSTERY in clusters or bunches **bt**
CLUTCHED caught; gripped; clasped
CLYFAKER a pickpocket
CLYPEATE like a shield; oscutate
COACHBOX driver's seat
COACH-DOG Dalmatian **zo**
COACHFUL full inside
COACHING tutoring; driving; training
COACHMAN a coachee
COACTING alliance; working together
COACTION compulsion; coercion
COACTIVE working in unison
COAGENCY joint action
COAGULUM a blood clot **md**
COALESCE mix; unite; amalgamate
COALFISH black-backed cod **zo**
COAL-HOLE small coal-cellar
COAL-MINE coal-pit
COAL-SHIP a collier **nt**
COALWORK a colliery
COAMINGS raised work **nt**
COARSELY crudely; churlishly
COARSEST roughest; grossest
COARSISH rather coarse
CO-ASSUME agree
COASTING (shipping, cycling) **nt**
COAT-CARD court-card

COAT-LINK two buttons and a link
COBALTIC rather blue
COBBLING shoe-repairing
COBCOALS cobbles **mn**
CO-BISHOP joint bishop **rl**
COBSTONE large rounded stone **mn**
COBWEBBY araneous
COCCAGEE cider apple **bt**
COCCIDIA parasites **md**
COCCULUS narcotic plant **bt**
COCHLEAN spiral
COCHLEAR twisted; spiral
COCKADED bearing a badge
COCKATOO crested parrot **zo**
COCKAYNE cocaigne; land of plenty
COCK-BILL (anchor-dropping) **nt**
COCK-BEAD hanging decorative bead
COCK-BOAT cog; small boat **nt**
COCK-CROW dawn
COCKERED pampered
COCKEREL young cock **zo**
COCK-EYED asquint; crooked **md**
COCKLING puckering; wrinkling
COCKLOFT top loft
COCK-SHOT cock-shy; random round
COCSHUT eventide; twilight
COCKSPUR Virginian hawthorn **bt**
COCKSURE absolutely certain
COCKTAIL alcoholic drink; beetle **zo**
COCOA-NUT cokernut **bt**
COCOBOLO hard wood used for knife handles
COCTIBLE able to be cooked
CODDCELL single electric cell
CODDLING pampering; indulging
CODIFIED systematized
CODIFIER a compiler; collator
CODSHEAD type of yacht **nv**
CO-EDITOR joint editor
COENZYME a fellow enzyme
COERCING compelling; curbing
COERCION force; constraint
COERCIVE repressive; compulsive
COESTATE union of estates
COEXPAND dilate simultaneously
COEXTEND march together
COFFERED in a box
COFFERER a treasurer
COFFINED enclosed
COGENTLY forcibly; potently
COGITATE ponder; meditate; ruminate
COGNIZEE fine receiver **lw**
COGNIZOR exacter of a fine **lw**
COGNOMEN the surname
COGNOSCE give judgment **lw**
COGNOVIT acceptance of claim **lw**
COGWHEEL spur-wheel
COHERENT connected; consistent
COHERING adhering; uniting
COHESION congruity; adhesion
COHESIVE sticky; gummy

COHOBATE distil	ch
COIFFEUR hairdresser	
COIFFURE a headdress	
COIGNING extorting	
COINCIDE happen simultaneously	
CO-INHERE exist together	
COINLESS impecunious; broke	
COISTRIL a groom; see coystril	
COKE-OVEN coal carbonization process	
COKERNUT coconut	
COLANDER perforated bowl	
COLATION filtration	
COLATURE straining	
COLDNESS frigidity	
COLD-SETT Smith's chisel	
COLDSHUT casting imperfection	
COLD-TYPE printing	
COLE-RAPE the turnip	bt
COLESEED cabbage seed	bt
COLESLAW cabbage salad	
COLEWORT young cabbage	bt
COLISEUM Roman ruin	
COLLAGEN gelatine	ch
COLLAPSE breakdown; subside; faint	
COLLARED pressed; caught	
COLLARET small collar	
COLLATED collected; assembled	
COLLATOR codifier; donor	
COLLEGER Eton scholar	
COLLETIC sticky; mucilaginous	
COLLIDED crashed; encountered	
COLLIERY coal-mine	
COLLOGUE plot; confer	
COLLOQUY dialogue; conversation	
COLLUDED acted in collusion	
COLLUDER conspirator; plotter	
COLLYING fouling	
COLONIAL colonist	
COLONIST a settler in the colonies	
COLONIZE establish a colony	
COLOPEXY abdominal operation	md
COLOPHON publisher's tallymark	
COLORATE coloured; dyed	
COLORINE madder extract	bt
COLOSSAL gigantic; herculean; titanic	
COLOSSUS Apollo's statue	
COLOTOMY colonic incision	md
COLOURED specious; painted; tinged	
COLSTAFF carrying pole	
COLUMBIC containing niobium	mn
COLUMNAR in columns	
COLUMNED having pillars	
COMATOSE lethargic; drowsy	
COMATOUS sleepy; torpid	
COMBINED united; coalesced	
COMBINER a merger; blender	
COMBLESS lacking comb or crest	
COME-BACK repartee; return	
COMEDIAN actor; player; performer	
COMEDIST writer of comedy	
COME-DOWN humiliation; anti-climax	

COMELILY attractively; gracefully	
COMETARY planetarium; orrery	
COMING-IN entrance; income	
COMITIAL relating to assemblies	
COMMANDO a fighting force	
COMMATIC staccato; concise	
COMMENCE initiate; begin; originate	
COMMERCE barter; trade; traffic	
COMMIXED blended; combined	
COMMONED held in common	
COMMONER an M.P., not a nobleman	
COMMONEY a playing-marble	
COMMONLY usually; frequently	
COMMONTY common land	
COMMOVED agitated; disturbed	
COMMUNAL public	
COMMUNED held private converse	
COMMUTED exchanged; altered	
COMMUTER season ticket holder	
COMPAGES a complex structure	
COMPARED likened	
COMPESCE to curb	
COMPETED strove; emulated	
COMPILED amassed; composed	
COMPILER literary hack	
COMPLAIN grumble; grouse; repine	
COMPLECT embrace	
COMPLETE ended; perfect; fulfil	
COMPLICE an accomplice	
COMPLIED met; yielded; fulfilled	
COMPLIER an active agent	
COMPLINE evening service, R. C.	r▶
COMPONED heraldic squares	hd
COMPOSED calm; invented; produced	
COMPOSER a creator; writer	mu
COMPOSTO compounded; medley	mu
COMPOUND combine; agree; mingle	
COMPRESS abridge; condense; bandage	
COMPRINT pirate	lw
COMPRISE include; embrace; contain	
COMPTOIR cash-desk	
COMPUTED calculated; rated	
COMPUTER actuary; reckoner	
CONACRED sub-let	
CONARIAL } relating to the	
CONARIUM } pineal gland	md
CONATION volition	
CONATIVE endeavouring	
CONCAUSE secondary cause	
CONCAVED hollowed	
CONCEDED granted; allowed; yielded	
CONCEDER a donor; relinquisher	
CONCEIVE imagine; think; fancy; plan	
CONCERTO full accompaniment	mu▶
CONCETTO a right merry conceit	
CONCHITE fossil shell	mu▶
CONCHOID shell-like curve	
CONCLAVE synod; assembly; council	
CONCLUDE close; terminate; infer	
CONCOURS a gathering (Fr.)	
CONCRETE not abstract; solid; cement	

CONDENSE compress; solidify; shorten
CONDITED pickled; preserved
CONDOLED sympathized; commiserated
CONDONED pardoned; forgave
CONDUCED aided; led; promoted
CONE-GEAR variable-speed belt drive
CONFALON gonfalon; banneret
CONFERVA a seaweed   bt
CONFETTI scraps of paper
CONFETTI (substitute for rice)
CONFIDED entrusted; hoped; relied
CONFIDER teller of secrets
CONFINED limited; shut-up; restrained
CONFINER borderer; neighbour
CONFIXED fastened
CONFLATE collect; assemble;
CONFLICT combat; clash; discord
CONFOUND amaze; mystify
CONFRERE colleague; companion
CONFRONT face; beard; oppose
CONFUSED in disarray; flurried
CONFUTED disproved; overcame
CONGENER an affinity
CONGIARY Roman gift of wine
CONGLOBE to ball; ensphere
CONGREET salute mutually
CONGRESS representative assembly
CONGREVE lucifer; rocket
CONICINE hemlock   md
CONICITY conicalness
CONIFORM conical
CONJOINT associated; connected
CONJUGAL matrimonial
CONJUNCT concurrent; united
CONJURED bound by oath
CONJURER ⎫ magician; juggler;
CONJUROR ⎭ wizard; marabout
CONJUSTO with gusto   mu
CONNIVED overlooked; permitted
CONNIVER confidence man; accessory
CONNOTED included; implied
CONOICAL almost conical
CONOIDIC conoidal
CONQUEST victory; subjugation
CONSERVE preserve; maintain
CONSIDER contemplate; regard; ponder
CONSOLED solaced; assuaged; cheered
CONSOLER a comforter; soother
CONSOMME clear soup
CONSOUND herb comfrey   bt
CONSPIRE plot; intrigue; machinate
CONSPUED defamed; execrated
CONSTANT unchangeable; perpetual
CONSTRUE translate; interpret
CONSULAR a service
CONSULTA council
CONSUMED dissipated; squandered
CONSUMER devourer; waster; eater
CONSUMPT quantity consumed
CONTANGO premium; discount
CONTEMPT disdain; scorn; derision

CONTENTS the inside
CONTERNO contour; outline (It.)
CONTINUE endure; extend; persist
CONTLINE intervening space
CONTOURA copying device
CONTRACT agreement; abridge
CONTRAIL condensation trail   mt
CONTRARY otherwise; opposite
CONTRAST difference; compare
CONTRATE opposed; mitred
CONTRITE penitent; repentant; humble
CONTRIVE bring about; scheme
CONTUSED bruised; crushed; knocked
CONUSANT knowing; cognizable
CONVENED called together; gathered
CONVENER summoner
CONVERGE approach; incline
CONVERSE talk; parley; reciprocal
CONVEXED vaulted
CONVEXLY in convex form
CONVEYED stolen; imparted
CONVEYER imposter; conveyancer
CONVEYOR transporter; carrier
CONVINCE persuade; satisfy; prove
CONVOKED convened; mustered
CONVOLVE roll together
CONVOYED escorted; guarded
CONVULSE writhe; agitate; perturb
CONY-SKIN rabbit-skin
CONY-WOOL rabbit's fur
COOEEING hailing in Australia
COOK-ROOM cook-house; caboose
COOK-SHOP eating-house
COOLNESS indifference; frigidity
COOPERED repaired; doctored
CO-OPTING electing
CO-OPTION adoption; election
COPATAIN high-crowned; pointed
COPEPODA water-boatmen   zo
COPHOSIS deafness   md
COPHOUSE tool-house
COPOPSIA eye-strain   md
COPPERAS sulphate of iron   ch
COPPERED covered with copper
COPULATE unite; couple
COPYBOOK exercise book; example
COPYHOLD not freehold   lw
COQUETRY flirtation; philandering
COQUETTE a flirt; a jilt
CORACITE uraninite   mn
CORACOID like a crow's beak
CORANACH coronach; a dirge
CORDATED heart-shaped   bt
CORDINER cordwainer; shoemaker
CORDOVAN goatskin leather
CORDUROY ribbed cloth
CORDWAIN Spanish leather
CORD-WOOD firewood
CO-REGENT joint ruler
CORE-SAND linseed moulding mixture
CORK-SOLE inner shoe-sole

CORK-TREE quercus suber	bt
CORKWING a sea-fish	zo
CORKWOOD an American tree	bt
CORN-BALL pop-corn	
CORN-BEEF corned beef	
CORN-BIND convulvulus	bt
CORNCAKE Indian meal cake	ck
CORNEOUS horny	
CORNERED brought to bay; controlled	
CORNETCY rank of a cornet	
CORNFLAG gladiolus	bt
CORNICLE a little horn	
CORNICLE honeydew tube in aphids	zo
CORNIFIC horn-producing	
CORNLAND grain-land	
CORNLOFT granary	
CORNMEAL coarse maize flour	ck
CORN-MILL a grinder; quern	
CORN-MINT calamint	bt
CORN-MOTH a pest	zo
CORN-PIPE straw-pipe	
CORN-PONE bread (Indian corn)	
CORN-RENT rent paid in corn	
CORNUTED with horns	
CORN-WAIN farm-cart	
COROCORE Malay boat	nt
COROLLET a floret	bt
CORONACH coranach; a lament	
CORONARY crown-shaped, heart artery	
	md
CORONATE crowned	
CORONIUM gaseous element	ch
CORONOID coracoid	
CORONULE downy tuft on seeds	bt
CORPORAL bodily; material; an N.C.O.	
CORPORAS fine linen	rl
CORRIDOR passage-way; gallery	
CORRIVAL co-rival	
CORRODED eaten away; rusted; eroded	
CORSELET corslet; leather cuirass	
CORSICAN (Napoleon)	
CORTICAL external; made of bark	bt
CORUNDUM emerald; ruby; sapphire	
CORVETTE a warship	nt
CORYBANT priest of Cybele	
CORYMBUS top-knot	
CORYPHEE ballet-dancer	mu
CORYSTES masked crab	zo
COSECANT an inverse sine	
COSENAGE ⎱ cousinhood;	
COSINAGE ⎰ a writ	lw
COSHERED pampered; coddled	
COSHERER (free board and lodgings)	
COSINESS snugness	
COSMETIC a beautifier	
COSMICAL relating to the universe	
COSSETED petted; fondled; caressed	
COSTATED ribbed	
COST-BOOK account book	
COST-FREE free of charge	
COSTLESS without price; free	
COSTLIER more expensive; dearer	
COSTMARY aromatic plant	bt
COST-PLUS war contract price	
COSTUMED garbed; dressed; robed	
COSTUMER costumier; dressmaker	
CO-SURETY joint security	
COTCHELL privately-sold timber	
COTELINE ribbed muslin	
CO-TENANT joint tenant	
COTHOUSE a cottar's house	
COTILLON cotillion; round dance	mu
COTQUEAN a womanly man	
COTSWOLD sheep	zo
COTTABUS wine throwing contest	
COTTAGED covered with cottages	
COTTAGER small holder	
COTTONED attracted to; understood	
COTYLOID cup-shaped	
COUCHANT reclining	hd
COUCHING removing cataract	md
COUGHING a raucous noise	
COULISSE theatrical side-scene	
COUMARIC from Tonka beans	bt
COUMARIN a scent	bt
COUNTESS wife of earl or count	
COUNTING reckoning; enumerating	
COUNT-OUT adjournment; boxing	
COUPELET cabriolet	
COUPLING linking; a link	mu
COURANTE French dance; a paper	
COURANTO musical piece	mu
COURSING racing; chasing; pursuing	
COURT-DAY sessions-day	lw
COURTESY polished manners	
COURTIER courtesy personified	
COURTING wooing; soliciting; inviting	
COUSCOUS semolina/meat dish (N. Afr.)	
	ck
COUSINLY friendly	
COUSINRY kin; relations	
COUTILLE material for corsets	
COVALENT bond: 1 electron to 2 atoms	
COVENANT contract; bond; pact	
COVENTRY ostracism	
COVERAGE protection; insurance	
COVER-ALL an overlay	
COVERCLE a lid	
COVERING protecting; including	
COVERLET bed cover; counterpane	
COVERLID coverlet	
COVERTLY surreptitiously; insidiously	
COVETING acquisitiveness	
COVETOUS avaricious; rapacious	
COVINOUS collusive; fraudulent	
COWARDLY timidly; cravenly	
COWBERRY whortleberry	bt
COWERING crouching; cringing	
COWGRASS meadow trefoil	bt
COWHIDED whipped	
COWHOUSE a byre	
COW-LEECH cow doctor	

CO-WORKER fellow toiler
COWPILOT West Indian fish zo
COWPLANT plant (Sri Lanka) bt
COW-THIEF a rustler
COW-WHEAT annual plant bt
COXALGIA hip disease md
COXINESS conceit; bumptiousness
COXSWAIN steersman; cox nt
COYSTREL ⎰ coistral; a groom;
COYSTRIL ⎱ custrel; a knave
COZENAGE deception; deceit; fraud
COZENING cheating; swindling
CRABBING peevish criticism; grousing
CRABTREE crab-apple bt
CRABWOOD S. American tree bt
CRAB-YAWS foot disease md
CRACKING distilling; splitting
CRACK-JAW difficult to pronounce
CRACKLED crepitated
CRACKLING china-ware
CRACKNEL a biscuit
CRACK-POT a maniac; crazy
CRACOWES pointed shoes
CRADLING timber framework
CRAFTIER slyer; more cunning
CRAFTILY shrewdly; pawkily
CRAGSMAN rock-climber
CRAM-FULL no more room
CRAMMING stuffing; tutoring
CRAMOISY crimson; cremosin
CRAMPING restraining; impeding
CRAMPONS grappling-irons
CRANE-FLY daddy-longlegs zo
CRANKING winding; turning; twisting
CRANK-PIN link; crank/connecting rod eg
CRANNIED full of chinks
CRANNIES nooks; fissures
CRASHING blundering; clashing
CRATCHES mangers; swollen pastern
CRAVENLY cowardly
CRAW-CRAW tropical skin disease md
CRAWFISH crayfish; langouste zo
CRAWLING on all fours; creeping
CRAYFISH crawfish zo
CRAYONED drawn with chalk
CRAZIEST maddest; most idiotic
CREAKING grating
CREAMERY milk-bar; dairy
CREAMING foaming; mantling
CREAM-NUT Brazil nut bt
CREAM-POT cosmetic container
CREASING folding
CREASOTE creosote ch
CREATINE kreatine; gristle md
CREATING begetting; fashioning
CREATION the universe; cosmos
CREATIVE inventive; productive
CREATRIX a designing lady
CREATURE term of contempt
CREDENCE belief; credit; reliance rl

CREDENDA articles of faith rl
CREDENZA low cupboard on floor
CREDIBLE trustworthy; believable
CREDIBLY conceivably
CREDITED trusted; accepted
CREDITOR a lender; mortgagee
CREEPING crawling; cringing; stealing
CREMATED reduced to ashes
CREMATOR incinerator
CREMORNE French-window bolt
CREMOSIN crimson; cramoisy
CRENATED notched
CRENELET small loophole
CRENELLE loophole
CREOLIAN Creole
CREOSOTE coal-tar derivative ch
CREPANCE brushing (horse)
CREPITUS lung-rattle md
CRESCENT Turkish emblem
CRESCIVE growing; increasing
CRESTING topping
CRETATED chalked
CRETONNE patterned cloth
CREUTZER Austrian copper coin nm
CREVASSE fissure in glacier
CREVICED rent; cracked; flawed
CRIBBAGE card game
CRIBBING shift lining; copying
CRIBBLED sifted; riddled
CRIBRATE perforated
CRIBROSE full of holes
CRIB-WORK a form of structure
CRICETUS genus of rodents zo
CRIMEFUL criminal; wicked; culpable
CRIMINAL felon; convict; illegal lw
CRIMPAGE press-gang work
CRIMPING plaiting; crisping
CRIMPLED curled
CRINATED hairy
CRINGING fawning; crouching; servile
CRINKLED wrinkled; corrugated
CRIPPLED disabled; impaired; maimed
CRISPATE curly
CRISPING crimping; twisting; waving
CRISTATE crested; tufted
CRITERIA standards of judgment
CRITHMUM the samphire bt
CRITICAL crucial; fault-finding
CRITIQUE literary notice
CROAKING woeful; calamitous
CROCEOUS yellow; like saffron
CROCKERY earthenware
CROCKING blackening with soot
CROCOITE chromate of lead mn
CROFTING farming
CROMLECH ancient stone circle
CROMORNA organ-stop mu
CROODLED cowered
CROOKING bending; inflecting
CROONING moaning; lamenting
CROPPING harvesting; lopping; cutting

CROP-SICK sick of a surfeit		
CROSS-BAR transverse bar		
CROSSBIT cheated		
CROSS-BOW a weapon		
CROSS-BUN hot cross-bun		
CROSS-CUT short cut; large saw	to	
CROSSING a ford; traversing		
CROSSLET small heraldic cross	hd	
CROSS-PLY standard flexible-tread	au	
CROSS-ROW the alphabet		
CROSS-SEA choppy sea		
CROSS-TIE railway sleeper		
CROSSWAY by-way		
CROTALUM castanet; small bell	mu	
CROTCHED forked	mu	
CROTCHET whimsey; fancy; conceit		
CROTONIC (croton-oil)	bt	
CROTTLES lichens used for dyeing	bt	
CROUCHED cringed; fawned; truckled		
CROUPADE equestrian feat		
CROUPIER a raker of shekels		
CROUPOUS croupy	md	
CROW-BILL forceps	md	
CROWDING urging; pressing; swarming		
CROWFOOT ranunculus	bt	
CROWMILL crow-trap		
CROWNING a coronation		
CROWNING (mercy) completing		
CROWNLET small crown		
CROWN-SAW circular saw	to	
CROW-SILK aquatic plant	bt	
CRUCIATE cruciform		
CRUCIBLE melting pot		
CRUCIFER cross-bearer		
CRUCIFIX religious emblem	rl	
CRUDITES raw-vegetable salad	ck	
CRUELEST most ruthless; harshest		
CRUISING voyaging; sailing		
CRUMBING covering with crumbs		
CRUMBLED disintegrated; crushed		
CRUMENAL a purse		
CRUMPLED ruffled; rumpled; wrinkled		
CRUNCHED munched		
CRUSADED followed the cross		
CRUSADER valiant enthusiast		
CRUSHING subduing; overpowering		
CRUSTILY morosely; sullenly		
CRUSTOSE uninterrupted crust	bt	
CRUTCHED on crutches		
CRUTCHET the perch, fish	zo	
CRUZEIRO Brazil currency unit	nm	
CRYOLITE a transparent stone	mn	
CRYOSTAT low-temperature thermostat	ps	
CRYOTRON small electronic switch	el	
CUBATION ⎱ determination of cubic		
CUBATURE ⎰ contents		
CUBEBINE a carminative	md	
CUBIFORM cubical		
CUBOIDAL cube-like		
CUCHILLA uplands (S. Amer.)		
CUCUMBER a creeping plant	bt	

CUCURBIT distilling vessel	ch	
CUDDLING fondling; petting; hugging		
CUFFLINK wrist adornment		
CUL-DE-SAC dead-end		
CULINARY au cordon bleu		
CULLYING imposing on		
CULLYISM being a simpleton		
CULPABLE censurable; blameworthy		
CULPABLY guiltily; sinfully		
CULTRATE knife-like		
CULTURED intellectual; refined		
CULVERIN a cannon		
CUMBERED hampered; clogged		
CUMBRIAN (Cumberland)		
CUMBROUS unhandy; clumsy		
CUMULATE amass; collect		
CUMULOSE heaped		
CUNABULA a cradle; incunabula		
CUNABULA books prior to A.D. 1500		
CUNARDER a Cunard steamship		
CUNEATED wedge-shaped; cuneiform		
CUNIFORM Assyrian writing, etc.		
CUPBOARD a repository		
CUP-CHUCK bell-chuck on lathe	eg	
CUPIDITY covetousness; avarice; desire		
CUP-JOINT male/female pipe joint		
CUPREOUS like copper		
CURARINE curari extract	ch	
CURARISE to poison with curari		
CURASSOW S. American turkey	zo	
CURATIVE healing; restorative		
CURATORY remedial; antidotal		
CURBLESS without restraint		
CURB-ROOF bent roof		
CURCULIO corn-worm; weevil	zo	
CURDLING congealing; thickening		
CURLICUE a fantastic curl; pig's tail		
CURLIWIG a curved piece		
CURRENCY coin; flow; circulation		
CURRICLE two-wheeled chaise		
CURRYING (food; leather; horse)		
CURSEDLY execrably		
CURSITOR Chancery writ writer	lw	
CURSORES running birds	zo	
CURTLEAX cutlass; curtal-ax		
CURTNESS abruptness; terseness		
CURTSIED made obeisance		
CURVATED curved; bent		
CURVITAL not straight		
CUSPIDAL pointed		
CUSPIDOR a spittoon		
CUSTOMED wont; habituated		
CUSTOMER purchaser; client; patron		
CUT-AWAY a style of coat or dress		
CUTCHERY Indian court	lw	
CUT-GLASS art glassware		
CUTHBERT Northumbrian apostle	rl	
CUTIKINS spats (Sc.)		
CUT-PRICE cheap		
CUTPURSE pickpocket		
CUTWATER prow	nt	

CYANOGEN poisonous gas   ch
CYANOSIS skin disease   md
CYANOTIC (blue jaundice)   md
CYCLAMEN primrose family   bt
CYCLE-CAR a combination
CYCLICAL circular; epic
CYCLONIC like a hurricane
CYCLOPIC gigantic; monstrous
CYCLOSIS circulation; cell movement
CYLINDER solid roller
CYMATIUM cyme; a moulding   ar
CYNANCHE sore throat   md
CYNICISM misanthropy
CYNOSURE centre of attraction
CYRENAIC of Cyrene
CYRILLIC (Slavic alphabet)
CYSTICLE small cyst   md
CYSTITIS inflammation of bladder   md
CYTISINE laburnum alkaloid
CYTOLOGY study of cells
CYTOSINE nucleic acid hydrolysis   ch
CYTOSOME cell cytoplasm   zo
CYTOZOIC intra-cellular; living in a cell
CZECHISH Czech language

D

DABBLING meddling; trifling
DAB-CHICK also dob-chick   zo
DACRYOMA defective tear duct   md
DACRYOPS eyelid cyst   md
DACTYLAR (finger); (toe)
DACTYLIC (verse)
DADDLING tottering locomotion
DAEDALUS human glider
DAEMONIC diabolical; satanic
DAFFODIL Lent lily   bt, rl
DAFTNESS lunacy, stupidity
DAGGERED stabbed
DAGGLING trapesing
DAG-SWAIN coarse woollen fabric   tx
DAHABIEH Nile boat   nt
DAINTILY delicately; elegantly
DAIQUIRI rum drink
DAIRYING farming
DAIRYMAN dairy keeper; milkman
DALESMAN Lake District man
DALLYING trifling; delaying; fondling
DALMAHOY bushy bob-wig
DALMATIC long white vestment   rl
DAMAGING injuring; impairing
DAMASKED variegated
DAMASKIN Damascus sword
DAMASSIN damask cloth
DAMBOARD draughtboard
DAME-WORT dame's violet   bt
DAMNABLE pernicious; execrable
DAMOCLES his sword was a hanger

DAMPENED moistened; discouraged
DAMPNESS humidity
DANALITE iron/beryllium silicate   mn
DANCETTE Norman zigzag moulding   ar
DANDERED sauntered (Sc.)
DANDIEST neatest
DANDLING fondling; caressing
DANDRUFF dandruff; scurf   md
DANDYISE dress ostentatiously
DANDYISH foppish
DANDYISM elegance in attire
DANE-GELD tribute paid to Danes
DANELAGH Danish England (A.D. 878)
DANE-WEED a plant   bt
DANE-WORT dwarf elder   bt
DANGLING hanging by a thread
DANSEUSE ballerina
DANUBIAN (Danube)
DAPEDIUS ganoid fish   zo
DAPHNITE iron-rich chlorite   mn
DAPPERLY variegated
DAPPLING shading; spotting
DARING-DO derring-do
DARINGLY intrepidly; bravely
DARKENED obscured; clouded
DARKLING gloomy; sombre
DARKNESS ignorance; blindness
DARK-ROOM a developing locality
DARKSOME mysterious; dismal
DASTARDY cowardice; base timidity
DASYURES Australian marsupials   zo
DATELESS immemorial; timeless
DATE-LINE where East meets West
DATE-PALM Biblical palm   bt, rl
DATE-PLUM persimmon   bt
DATE-TREE (many varieties)   bt
DATOLITE a silicate   mn
DATURINE thorn-apple alkaloid   ch
DAUBSTER poor painter
DAUGHTER person's female child
DAUNTING intimidating; dismaying
DAUPHINE French princess
DAVY-LAMP miner's lamp   mn
DAWDLING dallying; lagging; trifling
DAYBREAK dawn; dawning; day-spring
DAY-DREAM reverie; visionary scheme
DAYLIGHT illumination
DAYSHIFT working period (industrial)
DAY-SIGHT night-blindness
DAY-TO-DAY ephemeral
DAY-WOMAN daily woman
DAZZLING bewildering; confusing
DEAD-BEAT exhausted
DEAD-BORN still-born
DEADENED retarded; benumbed
DEAD-FALL animal trap
DEAD-FIRE death omen
DEAD-HEAD (on the free list)
DEAD-HEAT bracketed
DEADLIER more malignant
DEAD-LIFT (no leverage or help)

DEADLINE a boundary; time-limit
DEADLOCK no compromise; impasse
DEAD LOSS complete loss
DEAD-MEAT meat for market
DEADNESS inertness; inertia
DEAD-PULL dead-lift
DEADRISE design of rise from ship's
bottom   nt
DEAD-ROPE fixed rope in dead-eye
DEAD-SHOT unerring marksman
DEAD-WALL windowless wall
DEAD-WIND calm
DEAD-WOOD decayed or useless wood
DEAD-WORK unprofitable work
DEAD-WORT species of elder   bt
DEAFENED stunned
DEAF-MUTE deaf and dumb
DEAFNESS hard of hearing   md
DEAL-FISH a thin fish   zo
DEANSHIP office of dean   rl
DEARNESS costliness; tenderness
DEARNFUL solitary; mournful
DEATH-BED the passing place
DEATHFUL fateful; moribund
DE-BANNED freed; de-restricted
DEBARKED landed
DEBARRED excluded; prohibited
DEBASING degrading; vitiating
DEBATING discussing; disputing
DEBILITY functional weakness
DEBITING charging
DEBONAIR genial; cheerful; merry
DEBOUCHE an opening; a market
DEBOUTED expelled; ejected
DEBTLESS owing naught
DEBUNKED shown up
DEBUTANT a starter
DECADENT degenerate
DECAGRAM 10 grams   me
DECALAGE wing chords angle   ae
DECAMPED sloped off; fled; bolted
DECANTED poured out
DECANTER glass wine bottle
DECAYING rotting; declining; ebbing
DECEASED dead; departed; defunct
DECEIVED beguiled; duped; gulled
DECEIVER impostor; trickster
DECEMBER 10th Roman month
DECEMFID ten-cleft   bt
DECEMVIR Roman magistrate
DECENTLY comme il faut
DECERNED judged; decreed
DECICAIN local anaesthetic   pm
DECIDING settling; resolving
DECIDUAL able to be cast off
DECIGRAM one-tenth of gram   me
DECIMATE kill one in ten
DECIPHER decode
DECISION verdict; firmness
DECISIVE final; conclusive
DECISORY determining

DECK-GAME (bull-board, etc.)
DECK-HAND an A.B.   nt
DECK-LOAD deck-cargo
DECLARED said; announced; averred
DECLINAL sloping downward
DECLINED pined; sank; shunned
DECLINER a refuser
DECLUTCH gear-changing (motoring)
DECOCTED cooked; digested
DECODING deciphering
DECOLOUR bleach
DECORATE deck; embellish; garnish
DECOROUS proper; befitting; seemly
DECOYING luring; enticing; inveigling
DECREASE minimize; reduce; curtail
DECREPIT broken down
DECRETAL a Papal decree   rl
DECRYING disparaging; vilifying
DECUPLED tenfold
DECURION controller of ten
DECURVED bent down   bt
DEDENDUM wheel/cylinder radial distance
DEDICANT dedicator
DEDICATE devote; consecrate; assign
DEDITION surrender
DEDUCING inferring; drawing; deriving
DEDUCTED subtracted; withdrawn
DEEDLESS inactive
DEED-POLL a legal instrument   lw
DEEMSTER Manx judge   lw
DEEP-DYED extreme; rascally
DEEPENED became more mysterious
DEEP-LAID cunning; intricate
DEEP-MOST uttermost
DEEPNESS profundity
DEEP-READ scholarly
DEERFOOT leathercraft   to
DEER-HAIR heath club-rush   bt
DEER-HERD a herd of deer
DEER-LICK salt lick
DEER-NECK scraggy
DEER-PARK paddock enclosure, zoo
DEERSKIN leather
DEFACING disfiguring; marring; spoiling
DEFAMING slandering; traducing
DEFEATED frustrated; overthrown
DEFECATE purify; purge; empty bowels
DEFENCED fortified; covered
DEFENDED warded off; shielded
DEFENDER protector; advocate
DEFERENT a conveyor; deferential
DEFERRED postponed; adjourned
DEFERRER a procrastinator
DEFIANCE a challenge; provocation
DEFILADE cf. enfilade
DEFILING polluting; corrupting
DEFINING explaining; specifying
DEFINITE precise; exact; certain
DEFLATED punctured
DEFLEXED bent
DEFLOWER sully; seduce; ravish

DEFLUENT flowing
DEFORCED resisted   lw
DEFOREST clear of trees
DEFORMED disfigured; misshapen
DEFORMER destroyer of symmetry
DEFRAYAL payment
DEFRAYED met the cost; paid
DEFRAYER liquidator; settler
DEFTNESS adroitness; dexterity
DEGAUSSE neutralize magnetic mine
DEGRADED reduced in rank
DEGREASE remove the grease
DEHORNED dodded (cattle)
DEIFICAL making divine
DEIFYING idolizing; exalting
DEIGNING condescending; vouchsafing
DEISHEAL clockwise
DEJECTED downcast; chapfallen
DEJECTLY gloomily; dolefully
DEJEUNER breakfast; lunch (Fr.)
DELATING informing
DELATION informer's accusation
DELAYING retarding; hindering
DELECTUS classical anthology
DELEGACY representation
DELEGATE deputy; commissioner
DELETING obliterating; effacing
DELETION erasure; expunction
DELETIVE delible
DELETORY erasive; blotting
DELIBATE taste; sip
DELICACY consideration; tact; relish
DELICATE dainty; frail; slight
DELIMING hide lime-salt removal
DELIRIUM mental aberration; mania
DELIVERY rescue; distribution
DELOUSED cleared of vermin
DELPHIAN oracular
DELPHINE dauphin; dolphin   zo
DELUBRUM shrine; sanctuary
DELUDING duping; gulling; misleading
DELUGING pouring; inundating
DELUSION fallacy; imposture
DELUSIVE deceptive; fallacious
DELUSORY illusory; deceitful
DEMAGOGY popular oration technique
DEMANDED queried; exacted; claimed
DEMARCHE ultimatum; counter-stroke
DEMEANED degraded; behaved
DEMENTED daft; crazy; deranged
DEMENTIA insanity; lunacy   md
DEMERARA brown sugar   bt
DEMERSAL near sea bottom
DEMERSED sub-aqueous
DEMIBAIN small bath
DEMIJOHN bottle enclosed in wicker
DEMILUNE ravelin (fort.)
DEMISING bequeathing; devising
DEMISSLY humbly
DEMISTER windscreen condensation
preventive   au

DEMI-TINT a shade
DEMI-TONE a semitone
DEMITTED dismissed; resigned
DEMIURGE Plato's world-maker
DEMI-VOLT an equestrian trick
DEMI-WOLF progeny of dog and wolf   zo
DEMOBBED demobilized; discharged
DEMOCRAT upholder of democracy
DEMOLISH destroy; raze; dismantle
DEMOLOGY social statistics
DEMONESS a diabolical lady
DEMONIAC possessed; infernal
DEMONISM Satanic cult
DEMONIST devil worshipper
DEMONIZE turn into a devil
DEMONOMY dominion of devils
DEMPSTER see deemster
DEMURELY gravely; sedately; modestly
DEMURRED hesitated; wavered; paused
DEMURRER a plea; objector   lw
DEMYSHIP an Oxford scholarship
DENARIUS former English penny; d   nm
DENATURE denaturalize
DENDRITE dendroit   mn
DENDROID tree-like
DENDROIT tree-like fossil   mn
DENEGATE deny; contradict; refute
DENEHOLE shaft cut in chalk
DENIABLE controvertible; refutable
DENOTATE denote; signify
DENOTING indicating; designating
DENOUNCE impeach; censure; threaten
DENTAGRA toothache   md
DENTATED with teeth; notched
DENTELLE tooth-like decoration or edging
DENTICLE small projection
DENTIZED toothed
DENUDATE strip bare; divest
DENUDING strip teasing
DEPARTED left; gone away; withdrew
DEPARTER metal refiner
DEPENDED relief; trusted; hung
DEPICTED described; limned; portrayed
DEPICTOR painter; artist
DEPILATE remove hair
DEPLETED emptied; drained
DEPLORED lamented; bewailed; grieved
DEPLOYED extended; unfolded
DEPLUMED plucked
DEPONENT a witness   lw
DEPONING testifying under oath   lw
DEPORTED expelled; banished
DEPORTEE reported; forcibly removed
DEPOSING ousting; removing
DEPRAVED corrupt; vicious; profligate
DEPRAVER vilifier; reprobate
DEPRIVED robbed; dispossessed
DEPRIVER a despoiler; brigand
DEPURATE cleanse; purify
DEPUTING authorizing; charging
DEPUTIZE delegate; act for another

DERAILED off the lines
DERAILER train-wrecker
DERANGED disordered; insane; mad
DERATING reducing liability
DERATION free from restriction
DERBY-DAY a Wednesday
DERBY-DOG also ran
DERBYITE volunteer of 1915
DERELICT abandoned; deserted; left
DERIDING mocking; lampooning
DERISION laughing stock; mockery
DERISIVE scoffing; ridiculous
DERISORY scornful; contemptuous
DERIVATE a derivative
DERIVING deducing; tracing; obtaining
DERMATIC relating to the skin   md
DEROGATE disparage; detract
DESCRIBE portray; narrate; tell
DESCRIED observed; espied; discerned
DESERTED forlorn; left; abandoned
DESERTER quitter; renegade; turncoat
DESERVED justified; merited; earned
DESERVER meritorious person
DESIGNED projected; invented; drew
DESIGNER schemer; contriver
DESILVER extract silver from
DESIRING craving; wanting
DESIROUS covetous; eager; longing
DESISTED stopped; ceased; forbore
DESK-WORK clerical work
DESOLATE solitary; deserted
DESPATCH dispatch; hasten; kill
DESPISAL contempt; scorn
DESPISED disdained; ignored; scouted
DESPISER scorner; contemner
DESPITED vexed; offended; teased
DESPOTAT territory under despot
DESPOTIC tyrannical; arbitrary
DESTINED ordained; fated
DESTRIER second charger   zo
DETACHED isolated; disengaged
DETAILED particularized; recounted
DETAILER enumerator; narrator
DETAINED delayed; restrained; held
DETAINER withholder of goods   lw
DETECTED found out; unmasked
DETECTOR detecter; discoverer
DETERGED cleansed; wiped
DETERRED prevented; hindered
DETESTED odious; abominated; loathed
DETESTER abhorrer
DETHRONE depose; discrown
DETONATE explode violently
DETONIZE fulminate
DETRITAL (detritus); residual
DETRITED worn down; eroded
DETRITUS disintegrated material
DETRUDED extruded; thrust
DEUCE-ACE a throw at dice
DEUCEDLY confoundedly
DEUTERON charged particle   ch

DEUTOVUM development stage in acarina
  zo
DEVALUED depreciated
DEVELOPE evolve; unfold; amplify
DEVESTED divested; alienated
DEVIATED swerved; strayed; veered
DEVIATOR a wanderer
DEVILDOM kingdom of hell
DEVILESS demoness
DEVILISH fiendish; malignant; diabolic
DEVILISM devil worship
DEVILKIN imp
DEVILLED highly seasoned; curried
DEVILTRY devilry; devilship
DEVISING scheming; bequeathing
DEVOLUTE transfer; depute
DEVOLVED handed over
DEVONIAN geological formation   mn
DEVOTING dedicating; consecrating
DEVOTION zeal; piety; attachment
DEVOURED bolted; consumed; gobbled
DEVOURER absorber; destroyer
DEVOUTLY earnestly; piously; holily
DEWBERRY the bramble   bt
DEWINESS precipitation
DEW-POINT a critical temperature
DEWSTONE a limestone   mn
DEXTRINE starch gum   ch
DEXTRONE synthetic blood
DEXTROSE glucose sugar   ch
DEXTROUS dexterous; skilful
DEZINKED freed from zinc
DIABASIC greenstone type   mn
DIABETES sugar sickness   md
DIABETIC of diabetes   md
DIABLERY diablerie; impishness
DIABOLIC satanic; demoniac; fiendish
DIACETYL colour/flavour constituent in butter
DIACHYMA cellular tissue   bt
DIACOELE 3rd brain ventricle in craniata
  zo
DIACONAL (deacon)   rl
DIACTINE having two rays   bt
DIADELPH twin   bt
DIADEMED crowned
DIADEXIS disease mutation   md
DIADOCHI ancient governors (Gr.)
DIAGLYTH an intaglio; carved gem
DIAGNOSE identify   md
DIAGONAL cross-tie
DIAGRAPH drawing instrument
DIALLAGE monoclinic pyroxene   mn
DIALLAGE rhetorical argument
DIALLING (telephoning)
DIALOGIC in dialogue form
DIALOGUE two talking
DIALYSIS debility   ch, md
DIALYTIC unbracing
DIALYZED ⎱ (analysis of soluble sub-
DIALYZER ⎰ stances)   ch

DIAMETER an exact bisector
DIANDRIA two-stemmed plants bt
DIANODAL traversing a node
DIANTHUS carnations, pinks, etc. bt
DIAPASON concord of sounds mu
DIAPAUSE life-cycle stage in insects zo
DIAPENTE interval of a fifth mu
DIAPERED figured
DIAPHANE transparent woven silk tx
DIAPHONE electrical fog-signal
DIARIZED recorded in a diary
DIASPORA Jew dispersion
DIASPORE aluminium hydrate mn
DIASTASE malt sugar
DIASTEMA tooth-gap in jaw; stage of protoplasm
DIASTOLE heart dilatation md
DIASTYLE proportion in colonnades ar
DIATOMIC (two atoms) ch
DIATONIC natural scale mu
DIATRIBE stream of invective; tirade
DIBBLING planting
DIBSTONE stone used in a game
DICARYON simultaneously dividing nuclei cy
DICE-COAL small coal mn
DICENTRA bleeding-heart bt
DICE-PLAY dicing
DICHLONE chemical fungicide ch
DICHROIC double refraction
DICKERED bargained
DICLINIC crystalline shape
DICLORAN chemical fungicide ch
DICROTIC double pulsation md
DICTATED bid; prescribed; ordained
DICTATOR autocrat; despot; tyrant
DICYCLIC with 2-whorled perianth bt
DIDACTIC instructive; moral; directive
DIDACTYL with all hind-foot toes separate
DIDAPPER dabchick zo
DIDDERED shivered
DIDDLING cheating; trifling; dawdling
DIDYMATE in pairs; twins bt, zo
DIDYMIUM a rare metal ch
DIDYMOUS growing in pairs bt
DIEGESIS explanation; narrative
DIELYTRA the bleeding-heart bt
DIE-STOCK die-holder
DIETETIC (food regime)
DIFFERED disagreed; diverged; varied
DIFFRACT break; refract
DIFFUSED disseminated; spread
DIFFUSER a spray
DIGAMIST married twice
DIGENITE cubic copper sulphide mn
DIGESTED classified; codified; arranged
DIGESTER a stock-pot
DIGGABLE suitable for spade work
DIGGINGS (gold); lodgings
DIGITATE having five leaflets bt
DIGITRON numerical read-out glow tube el

DIGITULE fingerlike process zo
DIGONOUS with two angles bt
DIGYNIAN } flowers having
DIGYNOUS } cleft styles bt
DIHEDRAL angle between planes
DIHEDRON geometric figures
DIHEPTAL of 14 in number el
DIHYBRID from parents different in 2 aspects gn
DIKETONE CO-group-containing compound ch
DILATANT swelling; elastic
DILATING expanding; stretching
DILATION distention; amplification
DILATIVE expansive
DILATORY tardy; dallying; lagging
DILIGENT busy; industrious; assiduous
DILLY-BAG Australian rush-bag
DILUTING attenuating; weakening
DILUTION watering; reducing
DILUVIAL alluvial
DILUVIUM glacial or flood deposit
DIMEDONE alcohol-detecting reagent ch
DIMEGALY with different-sized spermatozoa zo
DIMERISM duplex arrangement
DIMEROUS in two parts
DIMETRIC tetragonal
DIMINISH cut; abate; lessen; curtail
DIMPLING smiling
DIMYARIA molluscs zo
DINAMODE unit of work, metre-ton
DINARCHY dual control
DINER-OUT a table companion
DING-DONG hammer and tongs
DINGHIES small boats nt
DINGIEST dullest; dirtiest
DINORNIS moa-bird, N. Zealand zo
DINOSAUR extinct lizard zo
DIOCESAN a bishop rl
DIOGENIC (Diogenes); cynical
DIOPSIDE augite mn
DIOPTASE copper silicate
DIOPTRIC (refraction of light)
DIORAMIC (peep-show)
DIORITIC (igneous rock, diorite) mn
DIOSCURI Castor and Pollux
DIPCHICK dabchick zo
DIPHASIC in two phases
DIPHENYL coal-tar chemical
DIPLEGIA paralysis md
DIPLEXER two-way transmitter el
DIPLOGEN deuterium; heavy hydrogen
DIPLOMAT ambassador; envoy
DIPLOPIA double vision md
DIPLOSIS chromosome doubling cy
DIPNOOUS having lungs and gills zo
DIPROTON two-proton system
DIPSACUS the teasel bt
DIPSOSIS morbid thirst md
DIPTERAL with two wings zo

DIPTERAN a fly zo
DIPTEROS (double peristyle) ar
DIPTYCHA writing tablets
DIRECTED addressed; enjoined
DIRECTLY expressly; soon; forthwith
DIRECTOR manager; controller
DIRENESS horror; calamity
DIRIGENT directing
DIRTIEST filthiest; most sordid
DIRTYING fouling; soiling
DISABLED incapacitated; crippled
DISABUSE enlighten; undeceive
DISACRYL acrolin polymer ch
DISADORN deprive of ornament
DISAGREE differ; vary; deviate
DISALLOW reject; forbid; disclaim
DISANNEX disunite; disjoin
DISARMED subdued; stripped
DISARRAY disorder; undress
DISASTER calamity; catastrophe
DISBENCH unseat
DISBLOOM disbud
DISBOSOM reveal
DISBOWEL disembowel
DISBURSE expend; spend
DISCANDY melt; dissolve
DISCASED undressed
DISCHARM disenchant
DISCINCT ungirded
DISCIPLE learner; follower; pupil
DISCLAIM disown; reject; renounce
DISCLOSE reveal; tell; betray
DISCOUNT allowance; forestall; deduct
DISCOVER detect; espy; divulge
DISCRASE a silver salt ch
DISCREET circumspect; prudent
DISCRETE separate; distinct
DISCROWN depose; dethrone
DISCSEAL form of valve
DISEASED indisposed; unhealthy; sickly
DISEDGED blunted
DISEDIFY scandalize
DISENACT repeal; annul
DISENDOW deprive of endowments
DISENROL cashier
DISFLESH disembody
DISFROCK expel from clergy rl
DISGAVEL a change in tenure lw
DISGORGE surrender; eject; vent
DISGRACE ignominy; dishonour
DISGRADE reduce in rank; disrate
DISGUISE conceal; mask; cloak
DISHABIT dislodge
DISHERIT disinherit
DISHEVEL disarray
DISHORSE unhorse
DISINTER exhume; unbury
DISINURE render unfamiliar
DISIPPUS an American butterfly zo
DISJOINT dislocate
DISJUNCT discontinuous

DISLEAVE deprive of leaves
DISLIKED detested; hated; loathed
DISLIKEN made unlike
DISLODGE evict; eject; oust
DISLOYAL false; perfidious
DISMALLY drearily; dolefully
DISMAYED terror-struck; appalled
DISMOUNT alight; descend; unhorse
DISORBED thrown from its orbit
DISORDER confusion; turbulence
DISOWNED repudiated; denied
DISPATCH despatch; expedite; send
DISPATHY antipathy; allergy
DISPEACE unrest; unease
DISPENSE administer; dispence
DISPERSE scatter; diffuse; dispel
DISPIRIT discourage; dishearten
DISPLACE remove; discharge; oust
DISPLAIT untwist; unravel
DISPLANT uproot; eradicate
DISPLUME pluck
DISPONED disposed
DISPONEE } (conveyance of property in
DISPONER }   legal form) lw
DISPONGE dispunge; expunge
DISPOPED deprived of popedom rl
DISPOSAL right of bestowing
DISPOSED inclined; arranged; biased
DISPOSER administrator
DISPREAD extend; expand
DISPRIZE undervalue; belittle
DISPROOF refutation; rebuttal
DISPROVE confute; refute
DISPUNGE disponge; expunge
DISPUTED contested; wrangled
DISPUTER arguer; debater
DISQUIET to vex; unease; anxiety
DISRATED reduced in rank; degraded
DISROBED divested; denuded
DISROBER raiment remover
DISSEIZE dispossess lw
DISSERVE to perform an ill turn
DISSEVER cut in two; rend
DISSIGHT an eyesore
DISSOLVE loosen; liquefy; end
DISSUADE deter; disincline
DISTALIA 5 bones in tetrapod limb zo
DISTALLY remote
DISTANCE interval; space; outstrip
DISTASTE aversion; antipathy
DISTHENE cyanite; kyanite mn
DISTINCT definite; clear
DISTITLE deprive of right
DISTOMUM liver-fluke parasite zo
DISTRACT divert; harass; bewilder
DISTRAIN seize for debt lw
DISTRAIT absent-minded
DISTREAM overflow
DISTRESS anguish; suffering; worry
DISTRICT territory; region; quarter
DISTRUST discredit; doubt; suspect

DISTUNED put out of tune	
DISUNION breach of concord	
DISUNITE separate; disrupt	
DISUNITY isolation; dissension	
DISUSAGE disuse; desuetude	
DISUSING abandoning	
DISVALUE underrate; disprize	
DISYOKED untrammelled	
DITCH-DOG dead dog	zo
DITCHING excavating; clearing	
DITHECAL with two spore-cases	bt
DITHEISM } co-existence of a good	
DITHEIST } and an evil god	
DITHERED shivered; hesitated	
DITOKOUS having twins	
DITROITE coarse-grained alkali/syenite rock	mn
DITTY-BAG sailor's kit-bag	
DITTY-BOX sailor's treasure-box	
DIVAGATE digress; wander	
DIVALENT bivalent	ch
DIVE-BOMB aerial attack	
DIVERGED deviated; digressed; veered	
DIVERTED distracted; amused	
DIVERTER an entertainer	
DIVESTED stripped; deprived; bared	
DIVIDEND interest; share; profit	
DIVIDING cleaving; parting	
DIVI-DIVI pods used in tanning	bt
DIVIDUAL shared in common	
DIVINELY heavenly; exquisitely	
DIVINIFY treat as divine	
DIVINITY deity; theology	rl
DIVINIZE divinise; deify	
DIVISION category; army unit	
DIVISIVE dissentient; discordant	
DIVORCED forced assunder	
DIVORCEE person divorced	
DIVORCER divorcing person	
DIVULGED communicated; revealed	
DIVULGER betrayer of secrets	
DIZENING dressing gaudily	
DIZZYING confusing	
DOCETISM doctrine of a sect	rl
DOCETIST a 2nd-century heretic	rl
DOCHMIAC Greek metrical foot	
DOCILITY pliance; tameness	
DOCIMACY metallurgy	
DOCKIZED erected docks	
DOCKYARD naval establishment	nt
DOCTORAL (doctor)	
DOCTORED treated; doped	md
DOCTORLY scholarly	
DOCTRINE dogma; creed; tenet	
DOCUMENT writing; record; writ	
DODDERED quaked; tottered	
DODDERER senile senior	
DODECANE paraffin	ch
DODIPOLL dolt; numbskull	
DODONIAN oracular	
DOGBERRY ignorant parish official	

DOG-BRIER dog-rose	bt
DOG-CHEAP bargain price	
DOG-EARED crinkled corner	
DOGESHIP Venetian office	
DOG-FACED unprepossessing	
DOGGEDLY obstinately; stolidly	
DOGGEREL bad verse	
DOGGONED confounded	
DOG-GRASS couch grass	bt
DOG-HOUSE kennel	
DOG-LATIN barbarous Latin	
DOG-LEECH a vet.	
DOGMATIC dictatorial; arbitrary	
DOG'S-BANE a poisonous plant	bt
DOG'S-BODY utility man	
DOG-SLEEP cat-nap	
DOG'S-MEAT offal	
DOG'S-NOSE beer and gin	
DOG-TIRED spent	
DOG-TOOTH a Norman moulding	ar
DOG-TRICK a currish wile	
DOG-WATCH short $\frac{1}{2}$-watch	nt
DOG-WEARY exhausted	
DOG-WHEAT dog-grass	bt
DOG-WHELK kind of mollusc	zo
DOLDRUMS calm zone; depression	
DOLERITE medium-grain-size igneous rock	gl
DOLESOME dismal; rueful	
DOLICHOS hyacinth bean	bt
DO-LITTLE a lazy-bones	
DOLLARED flush; wealthy	
DOLLED-UP dressed showily	
DOLLHOOD dollship	
DOLLY-MOP handled mop	
DOLLY-TUB washing tub	
DOLOMITE magnesian limestone	mn
DOLOROSO pathetically	mu
DOLOROUS sorrowful; dolesome	
DOMAINAL } (landed estate)	
DOMANIAL } (scope)	
DOMELIKE dome shaped	
DOMESMAN judge; umpire	
DOMESTIC household; maid	
DOMICILE habitation; residence	
DOMIFIED (horoscope)	
DOMINANT prevailing; ruling	
DOMINATE control; override	
DOMINEER to hector; to sway	
DOMINION sovereignty	
DOMINIUM ownership	
DOMINOES hooded capes; a game	
DONATING giving; bestowing	
DONATION presentation; offering; alms	
DONATISM a Christian cult	rl
DONATIVE gratuity; benefice; largesse	
DONATORY recipient of land	lw
DONNERED stunned (Sc.)	
DOOLTREE duletree; the gallows	
DOOM-PALM Egyptian palm	bt
DOOMSDAY domesday (Book)	

DOOMSMAN domesman; judge	**DOZINESS** drowsiness	
DOOR-BELL a ringer	**DRABBETT** } twilled linen used for	
DOOR-CASE door framework	**DRABETTE** } smocks	
DOOR-KNOB a handle	**DRABBISH** slatternly; dowdy	
DOORLESS without portal	**DRABBLED** fouled with mire	
DOORNAIL considered as dead	**DRABBLER** a sail extension	nt
DOOR-POST regarded as deaf	**DRACANTH** gum; tragacanth	bt
DOOR-SILL lower framework	**DRACONIN** dragon's blood	
DOOR-STEP slice of bread (slang)	**DRACONIC** (Draco); severe	
DOOR-YARD an enclosure	**DRAFFISH** dreggy; worthless	
DORICISM Doric in expression	**DRAFT-BAR** swingle-tree	
DORMANCY abeyance; latency	**DRAFTING** sketching; drawing	
DORMOUSE somnolent rodent	zo **DRAG-BOLT** draw-bar	
DORR-HAWK nightjar	zo **DRAGGING** tugging; tedious	
DORSALIS dorsal organ artery	zo **DRAGGLED** wet and dirty	
DOSOLOGY science of doses	md **DRAG-HOOK** a connection	
DOTATION donation; dowry	**DRAG-HUNT** foxing the hounds	
DOTINGLY stupidly; fondly	**DRAGOMAN** guide; interpreter	
DOTTEREL a plover	zo **DRAGONET** small dragon; a fish	zo
DOUANIER custom-house officer (Fr.)	**DRAGONNE** heraldic lion-dragon	ho
DOUBLETS (dice)	**DRAG-SHOE** a brake	
DOUBLING folding; running	**DRAGSMAN** coach-driver (horse-drawn)	
DOUBLOON Spanish guinea	nm **DRAILING** trailing; draggling	
DOUBLURE book-binding	**DRAINAGE** sewage system	
DOUBTFUL uncertain; ambiguous	**DRAINING** emptying; exhausting	
DOUBTING distrusting; querying	**DRAMATIC** theatrical	
DOUBTIVE questionable; dubious	**DRAMBUIE** whisky liqueur	
DOUCHING spraying	**DRAMMOCK** drummock; skilly; gruel	
DOUGHBOY American soldier	**DRAM-SHOP** shebeen; illicit bar	
DOUGHNUT a confection	**DRAUGHTS** a game	
DOUM-PALM doom palm	bt **DRAUGHTY** inconveniently airy	
DOURNESS obstinacy; grimness	**DRAWABLE** representable	
DOVECOTE pigeon house	**DRAWBACK** detriment; defect	
DOVE-EYED meek-eyed	**DRAWBOLT** coupling pin	
DOVELIKE gentle; innocent	**DRAWBORE** carpentry	
DOVERING snoozing	**DRAWGATE** sluice gate	
DOVESHIP qualities of a dove	**DRAW-GEAR** harness; railway coupling	
DOVETAIL a joint; synchronise	**DRAWLING** droning	
DOWDYISH rather slovenly	**DRAW-LINK** a couple	
DOWDYISM shabbiness	**DRAW-WELL** deep well	
DOWELLED pinned together	**DREADFUL** frightful; dire; horrific	
DOWEL-PIN a fastening	**DREADING** fearing; awing	
DOWERING endowing; bequeathing	**DREAMERY** reverie	
DOWFNESS lethargy; dullness	**DREAMFUL** fanciful; dreamy	
DOWNBEAR depress	**DREAMILY** vaguely	
DOWNBORE discouraged	**DREAMING** imagining	
DOWNCAST dejected	**DREARILY** gloomily; dismally	
DOWNCOME sudden fall	**DREDGING** deepening; sprinkling	
DOWNFALL debacle; ruin	**DREGGISH** foul with lees	
DOWNHAUL a sheet	nt **DRENCHED** saturated; inundated	
DOWNHILL a declivity	**DRENCHER** a soaker	
DOWNLAND hilly pasture land	**DRESSING** alignment; draping	mo
DOWN-LINE (railways)	**DRIBBLED** slavered	
DOWNPIPE rainwater runaway	**DRIBBLER** (footballer)	
DOWNPOUR continuous heavy rain	**DRIBBLET** a small drop	
DOWNRUSH downward draught	**DRIFTAGE** leeway	nt
DOWNTROD trampled; tyrannised	**DRIFT-ICE** bits of iceberg	
DOWNTOWN business centre	**DRIFTING** passively awaiting events	
DOWNWARD descending	**DRIFT-NET** drifting herring net	
DOWNWEED cottonweed	bt **DRIFT-WAY** cattle-road; leeway	
DOXOLOGY hymn of praise	rl **DRILL-BOW** a boring device	tc

DRILL-BOX seed-box	**DUCKLING** young duck	zo
DRILLING training; perforating	**DUCK-MOLE** duckbill	zo
DRINKING imbibing; carousing	**DUCK'S-EGG** a zero (cricket)	
DRIP-FLAP part of balloon	ae	**DUCK-SHOT** pellets for wild fowl	
DRIPPING (fat); (tap)	**DUCK-WEED** a water weed	bt
DRIVABLE conducible	**DUCTLESS** endocrine gland	md
DRIZZLED rained	**DUELLING** ⎫ fighting in single combat	
DROGHING coastal trade, W. Indies	**DUELLIST** ⎭	
DROILING drudging; loitering	**DUELSOME** prone to duelling	
DROLLERY buffoonery; waggery	**DUETTINO** short duet	mu
DROLLING jesting; clowning	**DUETTIST** a performer	mu
DROLLISH fairly facetious	**DUKELING** a petty duke	
DROMICAL (race-course)	**DUKERIES** ducal country seats	
DRONE-FLY drone-bee	zo	**DUKESHIP** ducal rank	
DROOLING slavering; slobbering	**DULCIMER** stringed instrument	mu
DROOPING withering; languishing	**DULCITOR** saccharine	
DROP-DOWN short first title in book	**DULE-TREE** dool-tree; the gallows	
DROP-GOAL four points	**DULL-EYED** lacking expression	
DROPHEAD convertible automobile	au	**DULL-HEAD** a dolt	
DROPKICK football	**DULLNESS** dulness; apathy	
DROPPING flock of sheldrakes	zo	**DUMB-BELL** no ringing tone	
DROP-RIPE ready to fall	**DUMB-CAKE** (baked on St. Mark's Eve)	
DROPSHOT tennis	**DUMB-CANE** (causing dumbness)	bt
DROP-SLIP book stockist's order	**DUMBNESS** muteness	
DROPWISE in drops	**DUMB-SHOW** pantomine	
DROPWORT meadow-sweet	bt	**DUMMERER** bogus mute	
DROTCHEL idle wench; slut	**DUMOSITY** prickliness	
DROUGHTY thirsty; arid	**DUMPLING** pudding	
DROWNING submerging; overwhelming	**DUNCEDOM** the class of dunces	
DROWSILY sleepily	**DUN-DIVER** goosander	zo
DROWSING dozing	**DUNGAREE** Indian cloth; overalls	
DRUBBING beating; mauling	**DUNG-FORK** a gardening implement	
DRUDGERY slavery; ignoble toil	**DUNG-HILL** cock's castle	
DRUDGING moiling; plodding	**DUNG-MERE** ⎫ manure pit	
DRUDGISM menial occupation	**DUNG-YARD** ⎭	
DRUGFAST drugproof; immune	md	**DUODENAL** ⎫ the first of the small	
DRUGGING inducing stupor	**DUODENUM** ⎭ intestines	md
DRUGGIST chemist; chymist	**DUOLOGUE** conversation	
DRUIDESS lady soothsayer	**DUOPHASE** choke-use in valve circuit	el
DRUIDISM Celtic cult	**DURATION** indefinite length of time	
DRUMFIRE continuous fire	**DUSKNESS** twilight	
DRUMFISH North American fish	zo	**DUST-BALL** horse disease	
DRUMHEAD (service; court-martial)	**DUST-CART** rubbish conveyor	
DRUMMING vibrating	**DUST-COAT** light overcoat	
DRUNKARD toper; dipsomaniac	**DUST-HOLE** ash-bin	
DRY-BIBLE cattle-disease	zo	**DUTCHMAN** Hollander	
DRY-CLEAN without using water	**DUTIABLE** subject to customs	
DRY-GOODS drapery	**DUTY-FREE** not customary	
DRY-PLATE photographic plate	**DWARFING** stunting; overshadowing	
DRY-POINT engraving needle	**DWARFISH** pygmy; undersized; tiny	
DRY-STEAM (no unevaporated water)	**DWARFISM** growth-hindering condition	
DRY-STONE (no mortar used)		md
DRY-STOVE hot-house	**DWELLING** domicile; habitat	
DUALIZED halved; split in twain	**DWINDLED** declined; shrank	
DUBITATE to doubt; to vacillate	**DYE-HOUSE** where dyeing is done	
DUCATOON scudo; silver coin	nm	**DYE-STUFF** dye material	
DUCHESSE a table-cover	**DYEWORKS** coloration factory	
DUCKBILL platypus	zo	**DYNAMICS** masses in motion	
DUCK-DIVE swimming-dive	**DYNAMISM** ⎫ the theory of	
DUCK-FOOT lowered inverted commas	**DYNAMIST** ⎭ imminent energy	
DUCK-HAWK marsh-harrier	zo	**DYNAMITE** powerful explosive	

DYNASTIC in succession
DYNATRON electrical oscillation
DYSBASIA walking difficulty   md
DYSCHROA skin disease   md
DYSGENIC detrimental to the race
DYSLALIA over-age baby talk
DYSLEXIA reading learning difficulty
DYSLUITE manganese ore   mn
DYSODILE lignite   mn
DYSOPSIA dimness of sight   md
DYSOREXY depraved appetite   md
DYSPATHY antipathy
DYSPEPSY indigestion   md
DYSPHONY difficulty of speaking
DYSPNOEA difficulty in breathing   md
DYSTOCIA difficult birth-labour   md
DYSTOMIC (imperfect fracture)   mn

E

EAGLE-OWL great horned owl   zo
EAGLE-RAY devil-fish   zo
EAR-BORED (for ear-rings)
EARPHONE a receiver
EAR-SHELL a sea-shell   zo
EARTH-BAG sandbag
EARTH-FED earthly contented
EARTH-HOG aardvark   zo
EARTHING burrowing; burying
EARTH-NUT pig-nut; peanut   bt
EARTH-PEA hog peanut   bt
EAR-TO-EAR a definite distance
EASELESS non-stop; uneasy
EASEMENT relief; privilege
EASINESS facility; comfort; quiet
EASTERLY oriental
EASTLAND the Orient
EASTMOST farthest east
EASTWARD toward the rising sun
EASY-CARE minimal-creasing fabrics   tx
EAU-DE-NIL dull green colour (Nile)
EAU-DE-VIE brandy; akvavit
EBENEZER memorial stone; chapel
EBIONISE ⎫ (Jewish Christian sect
EBIONISM ⎬ that upheld the
EBIONITE ⎭ Mosaic laws)   rl
EBLANINE volatile crystal   ch
EBONIZED blackened
EBRIATED intoxicated
EBURNEAN ⎱ like ivory
EBURNINE ⎰
ECAUDATE tailless; Manx   zo
ECCLESIA an assembly; a church   rl
ECCYESIS external foetus development
ECGONINE coca-base alkaloid   ch
ECHINATE prickly; bristled
ECHINITE fossil sea-urchin   mn
ECHINOID like a sea-urchin   zo
ECHINOPS globe thistle, etc.   bt

ECHIODON sand-eel type   zo
ECHOLESS no repetition
ECLAMPSY epilepsy   md
ECLECTIC selected; picked
ECLIPSED obscured; disgraced
ECLIPTIC a great circle
ECLOGITE crystalline rock   mn
ECLOSION emergence from egg case   zo
ECOCLINE trans-habitat cline   ec
ECONOMIC frugal; thrifty; careful
ECOPHENE physiologically habitat-affec-
     ted type
ECOSTATE ribless   bt
ECPHASIS explicit declaration
ECRASEUR surgical instrument   md
ECSTATIC rapturous; beatific
ECTOCYST outer cyst layer; exoskeleton   zo
ECTODERM outer skin   md
ECTOGENY pollen effect on female plant
     organs   bt
ECTOLOPH mammalian tooth edge   zo
ECTOZOAN an external parasite   zo
ECUMENIC universal; catholic; general
EDACIOUS greedy; voracious
EDDERING making up fences
EDDY-WIND back draught
EDENTATA ⎱ animal lacking
EDENTATE ⎰ front teeth   zo
EDGE-BONE aitch bone; rump bone
EDGELESS blunt
EDGE-RAIL an iron rail
EDGE-TOOL cutting tool   to
EDGEWAYS ⎱ sideways
EDGEWISE ⎰
EDGINESS angularity
EDIFYING enlightening; instructive
EDITRESS woman editor
EDUCABLE teachable
EDUCATED instructed; taught; literate
EDUCATOR tutor
EDUCIBLE deducible; extractible
EDUCTION extraction; deduction
EEL-GRASS grass-wrack   bt
EEL-SPEAR fisherman's fork
EERINESS weirdness; creepiness
EFFACING expunging; deleting; erasing
EFFECTED accomplished; executed
EFFECTOR effecter; creator
EFFERENT conveying outward
EFFICACY production power
EFFIGIAL relating to images
EFFIGIES images; likenesses; guys
EFFLUENT a stream; outflow
EFFLUVIA noxious exhalations
EFFORCED ravished; compelled
EFFULGED shone; beamed
EFFUSING shedding; pouring
EFFUSION emanation
EFFUSIVE demonstrative
EFTSOONS soon after; again
EGESTING discharging

EGESTION excretion
EGG-APPLE brinjal; aubergine — bt
EGG-DANCE ancient blindfold hop
EGG-GLAIR pre-gilding eggwhite surface — pt
EGG-GLASS sand-glass
EGG-PLANT brinjal; aubergine — bt
EGG-SHELL thin porcelain; paint
EGG-SLICE frying spatula — ck
EGG-SPOON small pointed spoon
EGG-TOOTH knob on chick's beak
EGG-WHISK wire brush
EGLATERE eglantine; sweetbriar — bt
EGOISTIC self-assertive
EGOPHONY a pleurisy symptom — md
EGOTIZED self-conceited
EGRESSED departed; left
EGYPTIAN a gipsy; a tiny peg (anag.)
EIGHTEEN 1½ dozen
EIGHTHLY an ordinal number
EJECTING rejecting; cashiering
EJECTION discharge; dismissal
EJECTIVE expulsive; emissive
ELAIDATE ⎫
ELAIODIC ⎬ castor-oil derivative — ch
ELANCING darting; casting; launching
ELAPHINE like a stag — zo
ELAPSING slipping away
ELAPSION lapse; interval
ELATEDLY in high spirits
ELATERIN cucumber extract — ch
ELBOWING jostling; nudging
ELDER-GUN pop-gun
ELDORADO land of fabulous wealth
ELDRITCH weird (Sc.)
ELECTING choosing; preferring
ELECTION freewill; choice; acceptance
ELECTIVE selective; preferential
ELECTRET permanently polarized material — el
ELECTRIC stimulating
ELECTRON (negative electricity)
ELECTRUM silver and gold alloy
ELEGANCE refinement; taste; grace
ELEGANCY beauty of propriety
ELEGANTE lady of fashion
ELEGIAST sorrowful bard
ELEGIZED lamented in verse
ELENCHIC elenctic; refutatory
ELENCHUS a sophism
ELEPHANT size of paper; mammoth — zo
ELEUSINE tropical grass — bt
ELEVATED high; exalted; dignified
ELEVATOR a lift; animator
ELEVENTH (hour)
ELF-ARROW flint arrow-head
ELF-CHILD a changeling
ELICITED deduced; extracted; evoked
ELIDABLE suppressible
ELIGIBLE fit; fully qualified
ELIGIBLY desirably; worthily

ELIMATED polished; smoothed
ELINGUID tongue-tied
ELLIPSIS gap; omission; hiatus
ELLIPTIC oval
ELOCULAR without partitions
ELOINING banishing
ELONGATE stretch; extend; lengthen
ELOQUENT fluent and impressive
ELSEWISE otherwise; differently
ELUDIBLE avoidable; escapable
ELVANITE crystalline rock — mn
ELVE-LOCK elf-lock
ELVISHLY mischievously; impishly
ELYDORIC oil and water-colour
ELYTRINE (beetle wing material) — zo
EMACIATE waste away; decline; pine
EMANATED derived from; originated
EMBALING bundling; packing
EMBALMED filled with sweet scent
EMBALMER preserver; mortician
EMBANKED mounded
EMBARKED ventured; undertook
EMBARRED encaged; shut in
EMBATTLE draw up for battle
EMBAYING enclosing in a bay
EMBEDDED firmly established
EMBEZZLE appropriate; peculate
EMBITTER exacerbate; exasperate
EMBLAZED displayed; bedecked
EMBLAZON blaze; adorn; embellish
EMBODIED incorporated; integrated
EMBODIER codifier; merger
EMBOGGED mired; bogged
EMBOGUED emptied; discharged; fell
EMBOLDEN encourage; reassure; impel
EMBOLISM intercalation
EMBOLITE a silver ore — mn
EMBOLIUM narrow corium strip in hemiptera
EMBORDER adorn with a border
EMBOSSED ornamented in relief
EMBOSSER a craftsman
EMBOTTLE to bottle
EMBOWING arching; vaulting
EMBRACED embodied; clasped; hugged
EMBRACER corrupter of a jury — lw
EMBRAVED inspired (obs.)
EMBRONZE fashion in bronze
EMBRUTED brutalized
EMBRYOUS inaugural
EMBUSQUE shirker in a cushy job (Fr.)
EMBUSSED loaded on a bus
EMENDALS repair-work
EMENDATE to correct; to rectify
EMENDING amending; reforming
EMERGENT pressing; urgent
EMERGING issuing; arising
EMERITED put on retired list
EMERITUS retired with honour
EMERSION reappearance; emergence
EMETICAL ejective — md

EMIGRANT distant home seeker	**ENCASTRE** end-fixed, of a beam	**bd**
EMIGRATE migrate; remove	**ENCAVING** hiding in a cave	
EMINENCE distinction; celebrity	**ENCEINTE** pregnant	
EMINENCY a title	**ENCHAFER** warmed up (obs.)	
EMISSARY envoy; spy; agent	**ENCHARGE** to trust	
EMISSILE capable of being emitted	**ENCHASED** decorated	
EMISSION discharge; ejection	**ENCHISEL** to chisel	
EMISSIVE emanative; expulsive	**ENCHORIC** demotic	
EMISSORY a duct; channel **md**	**ENCIRCLE** encompass; hem; environ	
EMITTING issuing; delivering	**ENCLISIS**) (grammatical	
EMMANUEL Immanuel; Messiah **rl**	**ENCLITIC**) accentuation)	
EMMARBLE enmarble; petrify	**ENCLOSED** wrapped; enveloped	
EMMEWING confining; penning	**ENCLOSER** incloser	
EMPACKET to pack up	**ENCLOTHE** to clothe	
EMPALING transfixing	**ENCOFFIN** prepare for burial	
EMPARKED enclosed	**ENCOLLAR** encircle	
EMPATRON patronise	**ENCOLOUR** tinge	
EMPAWNED pledged	**ENCOLURE** horse's mane	
EMPEOPLE populate (obs.)	**ENCOMIUM** panegyric; eulogy	
EMPERISH impair (obs.)	**ENCORING** calling for a repeat	
EMPHASIS stress; force; accent	**ENCRADLE** lay in a cradle	
EMPHATIC definite; positive; earnest	**ENCRINAL**)	
EMPIERCE pierce (obs.)	**ENCRINIC**) (fossilized sea-lilies) **mn**	
EMPLANED boarded an aeroplane	**ENCROACH** trench; intrude; infringe	
EMPLOYED at work; occupied	**ENCUMBER** burden; clog; obstruct	
EMPLOYEE a wage earner; hand	**ENCURLED** interlaced	
EMPLOYER the boss	**ENCYCLIC** circular	
EMPLUMED plumed	**ENCYSTED** enclosed	
EMPLUNGE plunge (obs.)	**ENDAMAGE** cause loss; spoil	
EMPOISON embitter; envenom	**ENDANGER** hazard; imperil; jeopardize	
EMPORIUM large store; mart	**ENDEARED** beloved; made fond	
EMPTYING exhausting; discharging	**ENDEMIAL** locally prevalent	
EMPTYSIS haemorrhage **md**	**ENDENIZE** naturalize	
EMPURPLE to dye	**ENDERMIC** (through the skin) **md**	
EMPUZZLE mystify; bewilder; nonplus	**ENDOCARP** inner coat of fruit **bt**	
EMPYREAL ethereal aerial; sublime	**ENDOCYST** inner membrane **zo**	
EMPYREAN highest; heaven	**ENDODERM** inner skin **zo**	
EMULATED vied; strcve; competed	**ENDOGAMY** tribal intermarriage	
EMULATOR rival; copyist	**ENDORSED** ratified; approved	
EMULGENT flowing; oozing	**ENDORSEE** the assignee	
EMULSIFY liquate; blend	**ENDOSARC** endoplasm **bt**	
EMULSINE a fermented mixture	**ENDOSOME** protozoa nuclei central mass	
EMULSION milky liquid	**zo**	
EMULSIVE milk-like	**ENDOWING** presenting; bequeathing	
ENABLING empowering; allowing	**ENDOZOIC** living inside animal **bt**	
ENACTING decreeing; ordaining	**ENDPAPER** link between cover & book	
ENACTIVE authoritative	**END-PLATE** muscle motor-nerve ending **zo**	
ENACTURE purpose; action (Shak.)	**END-PLATE** type of electrode **el**	
ENALLAGE change of tense, etc.	**ENDRUDGE** enslave	
ENALURON heraldic bordure **hd**	**ENDURING** lasting; persisting	
ENARCHED like a rainbow	**ENERGICO** with vitality **mu**	
ENASCENT being born	**ENERGIZE** animate; excite; force	
ENAUNTER lest by chance (obs.)	**ENERVATE** weaken; sap; relax	
ENCAENIA festival; commemoration	**ENFACING** (cf. endorsing)	
ENCAGING confining; mewing	**ENFAMISH** to famish	
ENCALLOW brick claypit surface mould	**ENFEEBLE** debilitate; paralyse	
bd	**ENFETTER** manacle; shackle	
ENCAMPED pitched; settled	**ENFILADE** to rake	
ENCARPUS festoon of fruit **ar**	**ENFOLDED** clasped; enclosed	
ENCASHED realized; cashed	**ENFORCED** compelled; obliged	
ENCASING boxing; packing	**ENFORCER** active agent	

ENFOREST afforest
ENFORMED fashioned
ENFRAMED placed in a frame
ENGAGING winning; charming
ENGENDER produce; beget
ENGILDED gilt
ENGINEER scheme; a sapper
ENGINERY implement of war
ENGINING contriving; racking
ENGIRDED encircled
ENGIRDLE encompass; encircle
ENGLANTE heraldic acorns, etc.   **hd**
ENGORGED glutted
ENGOULED heraldic absorption   **hd**
ENGRAVED scribed; chiselled; cut
ENGRAVER carver; sculptor
ENGROOVE cut a furrow
ENGULFED devoured; overwhelmed
ENHANCED heightened; raised
ENHANCER augmenter
ENHARDEN encourage; harden
ENHUNGER affamish
ENHYDRIC containing moisture
ENJAILED put in prison; jugged
ENJOINED commanded; directed
ENJOINER prohibiter
ENJOYING appreciating; delighting in
ENKERNEL put in a nutshell
ENKINDLE rouse; inflame; ignite
ENLACING encircling; entwining
ENLARDED basted
ENLARGED dilated; expanded
ENLARGER an amplifier
ENLINKED coupled; connected
ENLISTED enrolled; engaged
ENLOCKED enclosed; shut up
ENMARBLE emmarble; harden
ENMESHED entrapped; caught
ENMOSSED mossy
ENMURING immuring; imprisoning
ENNEADIC nine of
ENNEAGON nine-sided polygon
ENNEATIC ninth
ENNOBLED made illustrious
ENORMITY atrocity; depravity
ENORMOUS vast; monstrous; gigantic
ENOUNCED proclaimed; enunciated
ENPLANED (cf. entrained)
ENQUIRED inquired; investigated
ENQUIRER a snooper; questioner
ENRAGING maddening; exasperating
ENRAVISH enrapture; entrance
ENRICHED endowed; adorned
ENRICHER a fertilizer
ENRIDGED furrowed; corrugated
ENRINGED encircled
ENROBING dressing
ENROLLED registered; recorded
ENROLLER inscriber
ENROOTED firmly fixed; established
ENSAMPLE a pattern; a model

ENSCONCE protect; hide; harbour
ENSALADA onion/tomato salad (Sp.)   **ck**
ENSEALED sealed up
ENSEAMED seamed
ENSEARED dried up
ENSEMBLE all together   **mu**
ENSHIELD guard; screen
ENSHRINE treasure; cherish
ENSHROUD veil; mask; conceal
ENSIFORM like a sword
ENSIGNCY rank of ensign
ENSIGNED distinctively marked
ENSILAGE preservation of fodder
ENSILING storing in a pit
ENSLAVED in bondage; enthralled
ENSLAVER captor; subjugator
ENSNARED trapped; inveigled
ENSOULED animated
ENSPHERE englobe
ENSTYLED by name of
ENSURING assuring; safe-guarding
ENSWATHE bandage; wrap
ENTACKLE supply with gear
ENTAILED settled on heirs
ENTAILER a deviser
ENTANGLE mat; ravel; implicate
ENTELLUS sacred monkey   **zo**
ENTENDER treat kindly
ENTERING penetrating; noting
ENTHALPY thermodynamic property
ENTHRILL to pierce (obs.)
ENTHRONE install; exalt; elevate
ENTHUSED became ardent
ENTICING alluring; coaxing
ENTIRELY fully; perfectly
ENTIRETY aggregate; completeness
ENTITLED styled; dubbed; empowered
ENTOILED snared; trapped
ENTOMBED buried; interred
ENTOMOID like an insect   **zo**
ENTOPTIC inner vision
ENTOZOIC } referring to   **zo**
ENTOZOON } internal parasites
ENTR'ACTE an interval   **mu**
ENTRAILS internal parts; offal   **md**
ENTRANCE entry; to ravish
ENTREATY urgent request; petition
ENTREMET sweet dish   **ck**
ENTRENCH fortify; encroach
ENTREPAS an amble (Fr.)
ENTREPOT emporium; transit depot
ENTRESOL mezzanine storey
ENTWINED woven; plaited; twisted
ENVAPOUR surround with vapour
ENVASSAL enslave; enthral
ENVEIGLE inveigle; lure; seduce
ENVELOPE a cover; surround
ENVIABLE most desirable
ENVIABLY covetously; grudgingly
ENVIRONS suburbs; vicinity
ENVISAGE to face; to consider

ENVOLUME include
ENZOOTIC (localized disease) zo
EOLIENNE dress material; silk and wool
EOLIPILE experimental flask
EOLITHIC pre-palaeolithic
EPAGOGIC inductive
EPALPATE no feelers zo
EPANODOS rhetorical recapitulation
EPENDYMA spinal cord epithelium in vertebrates
EPENETIC laudatory
EPHEMERA may-flies; etc. zo
EPHESIAN debauchee; (Ephesus)
EPIBLAST outer skin md
EPICALEX outer calyx bt
EPICERIE grocery; spices (Fr.)
EPICOELE cerebellum ventricle in craniata zo
EPICOLIC (abdomen over colon) md
EPICOTYL axis of feather or seedling bt, zo
EPICRINE type of secretion gland cy
EPICYCLE circulating circle
EPIDEMIC locally prevalent md
EPIDOTIC (vitreous ore) mn
EPIGAMIC appealing to opposite sex zo
EPIGEOUS low growing bt
EPIGRAPH motto; inscription
EPILEPSY fits md
EPILOGIC concluding
EPILOGUE farewell speech
EPIMACUS heraldic griffin hd
EPIMERAL (segment above joint) zo
EPIMERON posterior of sclerites in insects
EPIMORPH crystal natural cast mn
EPINASTY curvature bt
EPIORNIS extinct bird (Madagascar) zo
EPIPHANY January 6th rl
EPIPHORA streams of tears md
EPIPHYTE (mistletoe, orchids) bt
EPIPLASM residual cytoplasm in ascus bt
EPIPLOCE rhetorical climax
EPIPODIA lateral foot lobes in gastropoda zo
EPIPROCT plate over insect anus zo
EPIPUBIC before or above pubis zo
EPIPOLIC fluorescent
EPISCOPE projection lantern lt
EPISCOPY superintendence; search rl
EPISPORE outside spore-wall layer bt
EPISEMON city badge (Gr.)
EPISODAL digressive; accidental
EPISODIC incidental; subordinate
EPISPERM outer seed cover bt
EPISTLER letter-writer; scribe
EPISTOME face/mouth region in various creatures
EPISTYLE the architrave ar
EPITASIS climax; culmination
EPITAXY unified crystal growth
EPITHECA diatom cell valve bt
EPITONIC overstrained

EPITRITE metrical foot
EPITROPE rhetorical concession
EPIZOOTY animal epidemic zo
EPLICATE unplaited
EPONYMIC yclept
EPOPOEIA epic poetry
EPSOMITE Epsom salts mn
EPULOTIC cicatrizing md
EQUALISE equalize; even
EQUALITY uniformity; sameness
EQUALLED rivalled
EQUATING balancing
EQUATION allowance for inaccuracy
EQUIFORM of equal shape; similar
EQUIPAGE outfit; effects; train
EQUIPPED accoutred; armed
EQUITANT riding astraddle
EQUIVOKE an equivocation
ERADIATE emit; sparkle
ERASABLE effaceable
ERASTIAN follower of Erastus
ERECTILE capable of elevation
ERECTING raising; building
ERECTION structure; edifice
ERECTIVE setting upright
EREMETIC secluded; solitary; hermetic
EREPTION snatching; wresting
ERETHISM acute irritation md
EREWHILE formerly
ERGATOID like a worker insect zo
ERGONOMY physiological distinction of functions
ERGOSOME unit of cell-protein synthesis bl
ERGOTINE ⎫ parasitical fungus
ERGOTISE ⎬ found in rye, etc. bt
ERGOTISM ⎭ of poisonous nature
ERIGERON flea-bane genus bt
ERIONITE uncommon zeolite mn
ERMINOIS heraldic fur hd
EROTESIS rhetorical question
EROTETIC interrogatory
EROTICAL amatory; amorous
EROTICAL (Eros)
ERRANTLY like knights of old
ERRANTRY rambling; roving
ERRORIST fallacious fellow
ERUCTATE belch
ERUGATED wrinkled; corrugated
ERUMPENT breaking out bt
ERUPTING casting out
ERUPTION outburst
ERUPTIVE explosive
ERYCINIA insect genus zo
ERYSIMUM hare's ear, etc. bt
ERYTHEMA a skin disease md
ERYTHRON red blood cell
ESCALADE ⎫ attack by means of
ESCALADO ⎭ scaling ladders
ESCALATE increase in scope
ESCALLOP scallop; a bi-valve zo

ESCAMBIO (transfer of bills, Sp.)
ESCAPADE prank; adventure; frolic
ESCAPADO desperado
ESCAPING evading; eluding
ESCAPISM ⎫ the quest of a
ESCAPIST ⎭ mental anodyne
ESCARGOT edible snail　　　　　ck
ESCAROLE dark green salad plant　ck
ESCARPED steeply sloped
ESCHALOT small onion　　　　　bt
ESCHEWED shunned; avoided
ESCHEWER escapist
ESCORIAL Spanish royal palace
ESCORTED attended; conducted
ESCOTTED taxed; maintained　　　lw
ESCOUADE a squad (Fr.)
ESCULENT edible
ESOTERIC secret; mysterious
ESPALIER trellised trees
ESPARCET sainfoin　　　　　　bt
ESPECIAL particular; special
ESPIBAWN ox-eye daisy　　　　bt
ESPIOTTE species of rye　　　　bt
ESPOUSAL betrothal
ESPOUSED married
ESPOUSER wooer
ESPUNDIA S. Amer. skin infection　md
ESQUIRED escorted; protected
ESSAYING attempting; endeavouring
ESSAYISH experimental
ESSAYIST a scribe; writer
ESSAYKIN short essay
ESSENCED perfumed
ESSENISM Essene doctrine
ESSEXITE alkali-gabbro igneous rock　gl
ESSOINED excused for absence
ESSOINER attendance excuser　　lw
ESSONITE yellow garnet　　　　mn
ESSORANT heraldic wings　　　　hd
ESTANCIA cattle ranch, S. America
ESTEEMED held in high regard
ESTEEMER valuer; admirer
ESTERASE ester-hydrolising enzyme　ch
ESTHETIC aesthetic; perceptive
ESTIMATE appraise; calculate
ESTIVAGE method of ship loading
ESTIVATE pass the summer
ESTONIAN (former Baltic republic)
ESTOPPED impeded; barred　　　lw
ESTOPPEL a plea　　　　　　lw
ESTOVERS timber supplies　　　lw
ESTRANGE alienate; disaffect
ESTRAYED strayed
ESTRIDGE ostrich down　　　　zo
ESURIENT greedy; hungry
ETA-PATCH balloon patch
ETCETERA etc; etc.
ETEOSTIC a chronogram
ETERNITY perpetuity
ETERNIZE eternise; immortalise
ETHEREAL airy; heavenly; celestial

ETHERENE etherine; a gas　　　ch
ETHERISM effects of ether
ETHERIZE etherise; to gas　　　md
ETHEROLE a light oil　　　　　ch
ETHICIST moralist
ETHIOPIC Abyssinian; Ethiopian
ETHNARCH Greek governor
ETHNICAL racial; heathen; pagan
ETHOLOGY moral philosophy
ETHYLENE carburetted hydrogen　ch
ETIOLATE to blanch
ETIOLOGY study of causes
ETRURIAN ⎫ native to Etruria
ETRUSCAN ⎭
ETYPICAL exceptional; aberrant
EUCALYPT eucalyptus　　　　　bt
EUCARPIC with vegetative & reproductive
　　organs
EUCHARIS Amazon lilies, etc.　　bt
EUCTICAL supplicatory
EUCYCLIC made up of matching successive
　　whorls
EUGENICS eugenism
EUGENIST (race culture)
EUGUBINE (bronze tablets)
EUKARYON higher-organism nucleus　bl
EULACHAN candle-fish oil
EULOGIST panegyrist
EULOGIUM laudatory speech; encomium
EULOGIZE extol; applaud; flatter
EUMERISM aggregation of like parts　zo
EUMYDRIN atropine-like medicament　md
EUNICEAE a worm genus　　　　zo
EUONYMIN ⎫ an extract from the
EUONYMUS ⎭ spindle tree　　bt
EUPATORY hemp agrimony　　　bt
EUPATRID Athenian aristocrat
EUPEPSIA good digestion　　　md
EUPEPTIC highly digestible
EUPHONIA smooth enunciation
EUPHONIC harmonious; felicitous
EUPHONON harmonium　　　　mu
EUPHORIA satisfaction of the artist
EUPHRASY the eye-bright plant　md
EUPHUISM bombastic diction
EUPHUIST affected speaker; pedant
EUPHUIZE over-emphasize
EUPLOIDY polyploidy involving exact
　　haploid multiples　　　　　cy
EUPYRENE typical, of spermatozoa
EUPYRION a quick-match, etc.
EURASIAN European-Asiatic
EUROPIUM metallic element　　　ch
EURYTHMY symmetry; regularity
EUSEBIAN (Eusebius)　　　　　rl
EUTECTIC easily melted
EUTHERIA genus of mammals　　zo
EUTHROPY good digestion
EUXENITE uncommon rare-element
　　mineral　　　　　　　　mn
EVACUANT purgative　　　　　md

EVACUATE quit; abandon; forsake
EVADIBLE escapable; evasible
EVANESCE disappear; vanish
EVASIBLE avoidable; elusory
EVECTION convection
EVEN-DOWN downright
EVENFALL twilight
EVENNESS levelness; regularity
EVENSONG a service   rl
EVENTFUL full of incident; stirring
EVENTIDE evenfall; evening
EVENTUAL last; ultimate; final
EVERMORE always; eternally
EVERSION turning inside-out
EVERTING overturning; upsetting
EVERYDAY usual; common; routine
EVERYONE everybody
EVERYWAY in all ways
EVICTING expelling; ousting
EVICTION dispossession
EVIDENCE testimony; witness
EVILDOER malefactor; criminal
EVILNESS malignity; depravity
EVINCING demonstrating; exhibiting
EVINCIVE indicative
EVITABLE avoidable; escapable
EVOCATOR a summoner   lw
EVOLATIC volatile
EVOLVENT involute
EVOLVING unfolding
EVULGATE publish; divulge
EVULSION extraction
EWIGKEIT eternity (Ger.)
EXACTING enforcing; critical; rigid
EXACTION extortion; tribute
EXALTING extolling; honouring
EXAMINED inquired; studied
EXAMINEE candidate
EXAMINER scrutinizer; inspector
EXAMPLAR model; exemplar; pattern
EXANTHEM surface rash   md
EXCAVATE delve; dig; scoop
EXCEEDED surpassed; capped; excelled
EXCEEDER outdoer; surpasser
EXCEPTED excluded; omitted
EXCEPTOR objector
EXCERNED excreted; exuded
EXCESSED exceeded
EXCESSES debaucheries
EXCHANGE barter; commute
EXCISING cutting out
EXCISION extirpation; amputation
EXCITANT a stimulant
EXCITING rousing; inciting; inflaming
EXCITIVE provocative
EXCITRON mercury-arc rectifier   el
EXCLUDED banned; barred; vetoed
EXCURSED digressed; wandered
EXCURSUS supplemented treatise
EXCUSING remitting; condoning

EXCUSSED deciphered
EXECRATE curse; detest; abhor
EXECUTED beheaded; achieved
EXECUTER ⎫ executioner; agent   lw
EXECUTOR ⎭
EXEGESIS explanatory discourse
EXEGETIC elucidative
EXEMPLAR pattern; examplar; model
EXEMPTED excused; released
EXEQUIAL funereal
EXEQUIES burial rites
EXERCISE use; task; drill; exert
EXERGUAL date space on coin
EXERTING striving; wielding
EXERTION effort; strain; attempt
EXERTIVE labouring; toilsome
EXHALANT exhalent; evaporative
EXHALING breathing; emitting
EXHORTED encouraged; warned
EXHORTER incitor; adviser
EXHUMATE disinter; exhume
EXHUMING digging up
EXIGEANT exacting; importunate
EXIGENCY exigence; urgency
EXIGIBLE able to be levied
EXIGUITY scantiness; fineness
EXIGUOUS tiny; diminutive; minute
EXIMIOUS eminent; famous
EXINTINE floral membrane   bt
EXISTENT extant; living
EXISTING being; continuing
EXITIOUS deadly; malignant; noxious
EX-LIBRIS (book-plate)
EXOCHITE outer layer of fucales macrosporangium
EXOCOELE portion of coelenteron   zo
EXOCRINE of gland secretion; duct-carried   zo
EXOPHAGY selective cannibalism
EXORABLE not relentless; lenient
EXORCISM ⎫ deliverance from evil
EXORCIST ⎭   spirits
EXORCIZE exorcise
EXORDIAL introductory
EXORDIUM the beginning; preamble
EXOSMOSE diffusion
EXOSPORE outer layer of spore wall   bt
EXOSTOME part of ovule   bt
EXOTERIC openly professed; superficial
EXOTHERM heat liberator
EXOTOXIN bacterium released toxin   ba
EXPANDED stretched; dilated
EXPECTED awaited; forecast
EXPEDITE hasten; accelerate
EXPELLEE who got the boot
EXPENDED consumed; dissipated
EXPERTLY dexterously; adroitly
EXPIABLE atonable
EXPIATED made reparation
EXPIATOR indemnifier

EXPIRANT a dying person	**FADDLING** trifling; playing
EX-PIRATE retired free-booter	**FADELESS** imperishable; enduring
EXPIRING at death's door	**FADINGLY** decreasingly; vapidly
EXPLICIT clearly stated; categorical	**FAE-BERRY** fea-berry; gooseberry **bt**
EXPLODED burst; repudiated	**FAGGOTED** bundled
EXPLODER a machine	**FAGOTING** a kind of embroidery
EXPLORED scrutinized; plumbed	**FAILDYKE** turf-wall (Sc.)
EXPLORER investigator	**FAIL-SAFE** automatic protection-device
EXPONENT an executant	design
EXPORTED shipped; sent abroad	**FAINEANT** idler; do-nothing; sluggard
EXPORTER foreign trader	**FAINTEST** barely perceptible; dimmest
EXPOSING exhibiting; revealing	**FAINTING** swooning
EXPOSURE disclosure; revelation	**FAINTISH** giddy; languid
EXPUGNED overcome; conquered	**FAIR-COPY** correct copy
EXPUNGED erased; deleted	**FAIR-HAND** freehand
EXSECTED cut off	**FAIR-LEAD** a rope-guide **nt**
EXSERTED projecting; protruding	**FAIRNESS** honest dealing; equity
EXTENDED stretched; protracted	**FAIR-PLAY** justice; impartiality
EXTENDER dilator; expander	**FAIRYDOM** fairyland
EXTENSOR a muscle **pl**	**FAIRYISM** enchantment
EXTERIOR outer; outward	**FAITHFUL** leal; loyal; steadfast
EXTERNAL outer; foreign; exotic	**FAKEMENT** makeshift; swindle
EXTERNAT day school	**FAKIRISM** mysticism; poverty
EXTOLLER eulogizer	**FALCATED** like a sickle
EXTORTED wrested; extracted	**FALCHION** short curved sword
EXTRADOS convex surface of vault	**FALCONER** a hawker
EXTRORSE turned outward	**FALCONET** small hawk; cannon **zo**
EXTRUDED expelled; ejected	**FALCONRY** hawking
EXULTANT triumphant; jubilant	**FALDERAL** meaningless refrain
EXULTING crowing; rejoicing	**FALDETTA** hood and cape (Malta)
EXUVIATE moult; shed a skin	**FALLABLE** unstable; depreciable
EYEGLASS monocle	**FALLIBLE** liable to error; deceptive
EYEPIECE telescope lens	**FALLIBLY** erroneously
EYESALVE eyewash; ointment	**FALLOWED** ploughed but not sown
EYESIGHT vision	**FALL-TRAP** a snare
EYE-STALK eye-bearing stalk in crustacea	**FALSETTE** ⎱ shrill and unnatural
zo	**FALSETTO** ⎰ tone of voice **mu**
EYESTONE optical adjunct **md**	**FALSTAFF** fat face **pr**
EYE-TO-EYE vis-à-vis; face to face	**FALTERED** wavered; hesitated
EYETOOTH a canine tooth	**FAMELESS** undistinguished
EYEWATER tear; lotion	**FAMILIAR** unceremonious; intimate
	FAMILIST (16th century sect) **rl**
F	**FAMISHED** anhungered; starved
	FAMOUSLY remarkably; eminently
FABLIAUX French metric poetry	**FAMULIST** magician's attendant
FABULIST an Aesop	**FAN-BLAST** forced draught
FABULIZE fabulise; romance	**FANCIFUL** whimsical; capricious
FABULOUS feigned; fictitious; unreal	**FANCYING** preferring; imagining **mu**
FACE-ACHE neuralgia **md**	**FANDANGO** Spanish national dance
FACE-CARD court card	**FANFARON** swaggering bully; braggart
FACELESS lacking a physiognomy	**FANGLESS** toothless
FACE-PACK cosmetic	**FANLIGHT** window over front-door
FACETIAE witticisms; pleasantries	**FANTASIA** musical medley **mu**
FACETING cutting facets	**FAN-WHEEL** ventilating device
FACIALLY superficially; externally	**FARADAIC** ⎱ relating to a farad,
FACILITY dexterity; readiness; address	**FARADISE** the practical unit **me**
FACINGLY oppositely	**FARADISM** ⎰ of electrical capacity
FACTIOUS turbulent; riotous	**FARCICAL** ludicrous; absurd; droll
FACTOTUM general agent	**FARCY-BUD** glanders **vt**
FACULOUS spotted	**FARDELED** in bundles

FAREWELL adieu; good-bye; parting
FAR-FLUNG widely disseminated
FARINOSE mealy; floury
FARMABLE cultivatable
FARMYARD rooster's realm
FARRIERY veterinary work
FARROWED littered
FAR-SPENT well advanced
FARTHEST ultimate; yondmost
FARTHING four a penny (d)   **nm**
FASCHING German free-for-all carnival
FASCICLE a cluster
FASCIOLA narrow band of colour   **zo**
FASCIOLE ciliated spines in spatangoidea
FASCISTI Italian fascists
FASCISTS opponents of socialism
FASHIOUS vexatious; provocative
FASSAITE monoclinic pyroxene   **mn**
FASTENED secured; bound; tied
FASTNESS a stronghold; security
FATALISM   (belief in the inevitable)
FATALIST
FATALITY a calamity; disaster
FATHERED adopted; begat; sired
FATHERLY paternal; benign
FATHOMED comprehended; plumbed
FATIGUED weary; jaded; tired
FATTENED overfed
FATTENER a fat producer
FATTRELS ends of ribbon (Sc.)
FAULTFUL defective
FAULTILY imperfectly
FAULTING accusing
FAUTEUIL arm-chair; stall
FAUVETTE garden warbler   **zo**
FAVONIAN (west wind)
FAVOURED encouraged; approved
FAVOURER patron; supporter
FAYALITE an iron ore   **mn**
FEABERRY faeberry; gooseberry   **bt**
FEARLESS intrepid; undaunted; heroic
FEARSOME dread; awe inspiring
FEASIBLE workable; achievable
FEASIBLY practicable; possibly
FEAST-DAY a festival
FEASTFUL sumptuous; luxurious
FEASTING banqueting; carousing
FEAST-WON bribed by feasting
FEATEOUS dexterous; deft
FEATHERY with plumes
FEATNESS adroitness; neatness
FEATURED impersonated
FEBLESSE feebleness; irresoluteness
FEBRIFIC causing fever
FEBRUARY month of expiation
FECKLESS inefficient; spiritless
FECULENT muddy; turbid; fetid
FEDELINI macaroni
FEDERACY confederacy; alliance
FEDERARY a confederate
FEDERATE league together

FEEBLISH weakish
FEEDBACK sound; energy phenomenon   **el**
FEED-HEAD cistern of a boiler
FEED-PIPE water-pipe
FEED-PUMP a force-pump
FEE-GRIEF a private grief
FEER-TYPE positive process   **pg**
FEETLESS footless; apodal
FEIGNING counterfeiting; shamming
FEINTING pretending; misleading
FELDSPAR felspar   **mn**
FELICIDE cat-killing
FELICITY happiness; bliss; blessedness
FELINITY cattishness
FELLABLE capable of being felled
FELLAHIN Egyptian peasants
FELLNESS ruthlessness; ferocity
FELLOWED matched
FELLOWLY companionable
FELLSIDE mountain side
FELO-DE-SE suicide   **lw**
FELSITIC like porphyry   **mn**
FELSTONE (quartz and felspar)   **mn**
FELTERED matted together
FELTMARK imprint left in papermaking
FELTSIDE smooth side of roll of paper
FELTWORT the mullein   **bt**
FEMALITY feminality
FEMERELL louvre or ventilator
FEMICIDE lady-killing
FEMININE female; effeminate; tender
FEMINISM (women's rights)
FEMINIST advocate of feminism
FEMINIZE to make effeminate
FENBERRY cranberry   **bt**
FENCEFUL affording defence
FENCHONE dicyclic ketone   **ch**
FENCIBLE a home guard
FENESTER   a window
FENESTRA
FEN-GOOSE greylag goose   **zo**
FENOPROP chemical weedkiller
FENTHION chemical insecticide
FENUGREC sort of clover   **bt**
FEOFFING granting a fief
FERACITY fecundity; fruitfulness
FERETORY shrine for relics   **rl**
FERINELY wildly; savagely
FERN-SEED spores   **bt**
FERNSHAW a thicket of ferns   **bt**
FEROCITY cruelty; savagery
FERREOUS of iron
FERRETED unearthed
FERRETER investigator
FERRIAGE ferry charge
FERRITES ferro magnetic materials
    (ceramics)
FERRITIN liver protein
FERRULED tipped
FERRYING transporting
FERRY-MAN Charon (river Styx)

FERULING caning
FERVENCY ardour; devotion; eagerness
FERVIDLY hotly; zealously; with heat
FESTALLY joyously; jovially; merrily
FESTERED rankled
FESTIVAL mirthful; an occasion
FETCHING attractive; bringing
FETERITA dwarf sorghum   bt
FETISHES charms; talismans; amulets
FETTERED shackled; manacled
FETTLING conditioning
FEVERFEW a febrifuge   bt
FEVERING agitating; heating
FEVERISH inconstant; sultry
FEVEROUS restless; excited
FEWTRILS trifles (dial.)
FIBROGEN protein
FIBRILLA a filament   bt
FIBROSIS fibrous growth
FIBROTIC of fibrosis   md
FIBULATE ⎫
FIBULOUS ⎬ (leg bones)   md
FIDDLING trifling; fidgeting; cheating   mu
FIDELITY trust; staunchness
FIDGETED worried; fretted; chafed
FIDICULA small lute   mu
FIDUCIAL confident; precise; exact
FIELD-BED camp-bed
FIELD-DAY tactical exercise
FIELD-GUN mobile gun
FIELDING cricket
FIENDISH malicious; devilish
FIERCELY zealously; vehemently
FIERCEST most ferocious
FIERY-HOT blazing; impetuous
FIERY-NEW brand-new
FIFE-RAIL belaying pin rack   nt
FIFTIETH ordinal of fifty
FIG-APPLE a coreless apple   bt
FIG-EATER garden warbler   zo
FIGHTING contention; strife; faction
FIG-SHELL a univalve shell   zo
FIGULATE moulded
FIGULINE potter's clay   mn
FIGURANT male ballet dancer
FIGURATE of determinate form
FIGURIAL represented by a figure
FIGURINE small statuette (Fr.)
FIGURING calculating; symbolizing
FIGURIST one skilled in figures
FILAGREE filigree; metal lacework
FILAMENT slender thread
FILATORY spinning machine
FILATURE the reeling of silk
FILCHING pilfering; purloining
FILE-FISH a sea-fish   zo
FILIALLY like a son or daughter
FILIATED adopted; amalgamated
FILICORD fern-like plant   bt
FILIFORM thread-like
FILIGREE filagree; metallic lacework

FILIOQUE (clause in Nicene creed)   rl
FILIPINO (Philippines)
FILLETED strung together
FILLIBEG a kilt (Sc.)
FILLIPED flipped
FILMGOER a frequenter of cinemas
FILM-STAR popular actor/actress
FILOPINA ⎫
FILOPINO ⎬ philopina, a nut-game
FILTERED percolated; strained
FILTHIER grubbier
FILTHILY dirtily
FILTRATE filtered solution
FINALISM conclusiveness
FINALIST in the last round
FINALITY kismet; eventuality
FINANCED capitalized
FINDABLE discoverable
FINE-DRAW invisible mending
FINELESS endless; unlimited
FINENESS purity
FINE-SPUN elaborated
FINESSED acted artfully
FINESSER crafty person
FINGERED handled
FINGROMS woollen cloth
FINISHED ended
FINISHER final blow
FINITELY within limits
FINITUDE limitation
FINNIKIN crested pigeon   zo
FINOCHIO sweet fennel   bt
FINSCALE rudd, fish   zo
FIN-WHALE rorqual   zo
FIREARMS offensive weapons
FIREBACK ornamental plate
FIRE-BALL incendiary weapon
FIRE-BARS furnace bars
FIRE-BOAT fire-fighting steamboat
FIRECLAY used for fire-bricks   mn
FIRECOCK hydrant connexion
FIREDAMP explosive gas in mines
FIRE-EYED with fiery eyes
FIREFLAG flash of lightning
FIRE-GIRL woman fire fighter
FIRE-HOOK demolition hook
FIRE-HOSE portable piping
FIRE-KILN an oven
FIRELESS showing no flames
FIRELOCK antique musket
FIRE-PLUG valve in a water-main
FIRESHIP incendiary ship   nt
FIRESIDE the hearth
FIRE-STEP firing step in trench
FIRETAIL the redstart   zo
FIRETRAP (no means of escape)
FIRE-WARD fire-warden
FIREWEED a plant   bt
FIREWOOD chopped sticks
FIRMLESS wavering; unstable
FIRMNESS solidity; resolution

FIRST-AID emergency help	**FLAT-WORM** tape worm	zo
FIRST-DAY Sunday	**FLAUNTED** vaunted; paraded	
FISHABLE capable of being fished	**FLAUNTER** ostentatious person	
FISH-BALL fish-cake	**FLAUTIST** flute-player	mu
FISHBEAM beam of special form	**FLAWLESS** perfect; without blemish	
FISH-CAKE fish-ball	**FLAX-COMB** a heckle	
FISH-COOP box used for ice-fishing	**FLAX-LILY** New Zealand flax	b
FISH-GLUE an adhesive; isinglass	**FLAX-MILL** a factory	
FISH-HAWK the osprey	zo	**FLAX-SEED** linseed	b
FISH-HOOK barbed hook	**FLAX-TAIL** the reed-mace	b
FISH-MEAL fodder; fertilizer	**FLAX-WEED**) plants of doubtful	
FISH-POND fish storage tank	**FLAX-WORT**) provenance	b
FISH-ROOM part of ship	nt	**FLEA-BANE** flea-discouraging plant	b
FISH-SKIN fish epidermis	**FLEA-BITE** an inconvenient trifle	
FISHTAIL a gas jet; jewelry	**FLEAKING** reed covering under thatch	
FISH-WEIR a fishgarth	**FLEA-WORT** a plant	b
FISH-WIFE fish vendor	**FLECKING** dappling	
FISSIPED cloven hoof	**FLECTION** flexion; bending	
FISSURED cleft; cracked	**FLEECING** shearing; swindling	
FISTIANA boxing annals	**FLEERING** mocking; taunting	
FISTINUT pistachio nut	bt	**FLEETEST** fastest; swiftest	
FISTULAR tubular	**FLEETING** transient; passing; brief	
FITFULLY spasmodically; inconstantly	**FLENCHED** flensed	
FIVEFOLD 500%	**FLENSING** a whaling operation	
FIVELEAF cinquefoil	**FLESH-FLY** blow-fly; bluebottle	zo
FIXATION stability; firmness	**FLESHING** tights; scraping leather	
FIXATIVE a stabilizer	pg	**FLESHPOT** stock-pot; luxury	
FIXATURE hair cream	**FLETCHED** feathered (arrows)	
FIXIDITY permanence; constancy	**FLETCHER** arrow maker	
FIZZLING sizzling	**FLEXIBLE** pliant; tractable; lissom	
FLABBILY limply	**FLEXIBLY** sinuously; not rigidly	
FLAG-DAY charity or national day	**FLEXUOSE**) winding; wavering;	
FLAGGING signalling; wilting	**FLEXUOUS**) curving; elastic	
FLAGRANT notorious; glaring	**FLICHTER** flutter; quiver (Sc.)	
FLAG-SHIP leading ship	nt	**FLICKING** flipping	
FLAG-WORM green gentle	zo	**FLIGHTED** took wing	
FLAMBEAU a lighted torch	**FLIMFLAM** humbug; nonsense	
FLAMELET small flame	**FLIMSIES** carbon copies	
FLAMENCO folk dance, music (Sp.)	**FLIMSILY** unsubstantially	
FLAMINGO Amer. water bird	zo	**FLINCHED** winced; shrank back	
FLAMMING deluding	**FLINCHER** shrinker; coward	
FLAMMULE pictorial Japanese flame	**FLINDERS** fragments; flitters	
FLANCHED heraldic term; flanged	hd	**FLINGING** hurling; casting; pitching	
FLANERIE lounging (Fr.)	**FLINTIFY** turn into flint	
FLANKING bordering; touching	**FLIPFLAP** an entertaining device	
FLAP-JACK a confection; a compact	**FLIPFLOP** noise of walking	e
FLAPPING flopping; waving; shaking	**FLIPPANT** pert; saucy; glib	
FLASHILY transiently; gaudily	**FLIPPING** flicking	
FLASHING sparkling; gleaming	**FLIRTING** philandering; (fan)	
FLAT-BOAT a small craft	nt	**FLIRTISH** somewhat coquettish	
FLAT-FISH flounder, etc.	zo	**FLITTERN** a young oak (dial.)	
FLAT-FOOT flattie; policeman (slang)	**FLITTERS** flinders; fragments; glitter	
FLAT-HEAD a N. Amer. Indian	**FLITTING** migrating; hastening	
FLAT-IRON smoothing iron	**FLIXWEED** a hedge plant	b
FLATNESS monotony; depression	**FLOATAGE**) flotsam;	
FLAT-RACE not a steeplechase	**FLOATSAM**) shipwrecked goods	lw
FLATTERY insincere compliment	**FLOATING** circulating; wafting	
FLATTEST dullest; lowest; very level	**FLOCCOSE** tufted	
FLATTING a process	**FLOCCULE** small flock of wool	
FLATTISH comparatively level	**FLOCK-BED** bed stuffed with flock	
FLATWISE not edgewise	**FLOCK-GUN** dry spray for textile finishes	

FLOCKING congregating; crowding
FLOGGING a chastisement
FLOODING inundating; swamping
FLOOD-LIT illuminated
FLOOKING cross vein or fissure
FLOORAGE floor space
FLOORING material for floors
FLOPGATE diverting materials-moving gate   mn
FLOPPILY liply; flaccidly
FLOPPING breaking down
FLORALLY with flowers
FLORENCE wine; cloth   tx
FLORIAGE blossom
FLORICAN Indian bustard   zo
FLORIDLY ornately; exuberantly
FLOSCULE a floret; a bloom   bt
FLOTILLA small fleet   nt
FLOUNCED threw oneself about
FLOUNDER struggle; a fish   zo
FLOURING reducing to powder
FLOURISH prosper; wave; fanfare   mu
FLOUTING mocking; jeering
FLOWERED blossomed
FLOWERER plant flowering periodically
FLOW-LINE transport diagram showing movement
FLUENTLY volubly; easily
FLUFFING muffing
FLUIDICS science of liquid tube flow   ps
FLUIDIFY fluidise
FLUIDITY fluidism; liquidity
FLUMMERY a drink; humbug
FLUORENE coal tar product   mn
FLUORIDE tooth protector   ch
FLUORINE a gas   ch
FLUORITE fluorspar   mn
FLUOROUS derived from fluor
FLURRIED agitated; disconcerted
FLUSHING blushing; colouring
FLUSTERY confused; agitated
FLUXIBLE fusible
FLY-BLOWN shopworn, stale, dated
FLY-MAKER (fishing)
FLYPAPER a fly-trap
FLY-SHEET handbill; broadside
FLY-WATER an arsenical solution
FLY-WHEEL a conserver of momentum
FOAL-FOOT colt's foot   bt
FOCALIZE focalise; converge
FOCUSING correcting perspectives   pg
FODDERER cattle-feeder
FOG-BOUND wrapped in mist
FOGEYDOM senility
FOGGIEST most obscure; murkiest
FOG-SMOKE thick fog
FOILABLE able to be frustrated
FOILPLAY fencing
FOILSMAN fencer
FOLDEROL refrain of old song
FOLDLESS uncreased

FOLD-YARD cattle enclosure
FOLIAGED leafy
FOLIATED laminated
FOLICOLE living on leaves   bt
FOLKLAND common land   lw
FOLK-LORE legendary traditions
FOLKMOTE assembly of freemen
FOLK-SONG traditional song
FOLK-TALE fairy story
FOLKWAYS group tradition
FOLLICLE a pod   bt
FOLLOWED imitated; pursued
FOLLOWER partisan; adherent; copier
FOLLOW-ON cricket
FOLLOW-UP second stage support
FOMENTED excited; fanned
FOMENTER agent provocateur
FONDLING a beloved one
FONDNESS affection; predilection
FONTANEL a cavity   md
FONTANGE wire cap-frame
FOOD-CARD a rational requirement
FOODLESS lacking sustenance
FOOLSCAP paper, $17 \times 13\frac{1}{2}$ inches
FOOL-TRAP snare for simpletons
FOOTBALL national sport
FOOT-BATH bath to ease feet
FOOT-FALL footstep; tread
FOOTGEAR shoes and stockings
FOOT-HALT a sheep disease
FOOT-HILL an underfeature
FOOTHOLD support niche
FOOT-IRON carriage step; fetter
FOOTLESS with nothing to stand on
FOOTLING trifling; trivial; trumpery
FOOT-MARK foot-print
FOOT-MUFF foot-warmer
FOOT-NOTE an addendum
FOOT-PACE slow rate of progression
FOOTPATH pedestrian way
FOOT-POST pedestrian messenger
FOOT-RACE running match
FOOT-ROPE rope along a yard   nt
FOOT-RULE a 12-inch measure   me
FOOT-SLOG march; walk; tramp; hike
FOOTSORE with aching feet
FOOTSTEP footfall
FOOTWEAR foot-gear
FOOTWORK movement (sport)
FOOTWORN worn by many feet
FOOZLING bungling
FORAGING ravaging; searching
FORAMINA openings; orifices
FORAYING plundering; raiding
FORBORNE refrained; spared
FORCEDLY compulsorily; unnaturally
FORCEFUL coercive
FORCIBLE cogent
FORCIBLY violently
FORDABLE crossable wetshod
FORDOING ruining; exhausting

FOREBEAR forbear; ancestor	**FORGEMAN** coach-smith	
FOREBODE prognosticate; portended	**FORGIVEN** condoned; absolved	
FORE-BODY foreward part of ship	nt	**FORGIVER** pardoner; remitter
FORECAST prediction; prognosis	**FORGOING** preceding	
FOREDATE antedate	**FORKEDLY** furcated	
FOREDECK in the bows	nt	**FORKHEAD** (knuckle-joint)
FOREDONE overpowered	**FORKLESS** not branching	
FOREDOOM predestinate	**FORKTAIL** salmon; kite; crow	zo
FOREDOOR front door	**FORMALIN** an antiseptic	ch
FORE-EDGE front edge of book	**FORMALLY** precisely; ceremoniously	
FOREFEEL sense in anticipation	**FORMERLY** ci-devant; whilom	
FOREFELT anticipated	**FORMLESS** shapeless; chaotic	
FOREFOOT foremost end of keel	nt	**FORMULAE** sets of symbols
FOREGIFT lease premium	**FORMULAR** prescribed; formal	
FOREGOER vor-trekker	**FORRADER** further forward (slang)	
FOREGONE already decided	**FORSAKEN** left; abandoned; renounced	
FOREHAND cf. backhand	**FORSLACK** to relax (obs.)	
FOREHEAD brow; audacity; metope	**FORSOOTH** in truth; indeed	
FORE-HOOK strengthening piece	nt	**FORSPEAK** forbid; bewitch
FOREKNEW foresaw	**FORSPEND** exhaust; squander	
FOREKNOW know already	**FORSTALL** forestall (obs.)	
FORELAID previously arranged	**FORSWEAR** deny upon oath; abjure	
FORELAND headland; bluff; cape	**FORSWINK** exhaust; wear out	
FORELEND lend in anticipation	**FORSWORE** ⎫ pledged falsely;	
FORELENT previously loaned	**FORSWORN** ⎭ recanted	
FORELOCK sometimes a quiff	**FORSWUNK** over-laboured	
FOREMAST forward lower mast	nt	**FORTHINK** regret (obs.)
FOREMEAN intend	**FORTRESS** fortalice; citadel	
FOREMOST in the van; leading	**FORTUIST** believer in chance	
FORENAME Christian name	**FORTUITY** luck; accident	
FORENOON from sunrise to noon	**FORTUNED** presaged	
FORENSAL ⎫ concerning law-court	**FORWARDS** onward	
FORENSIC ⎭ procedure	**FORZANDO** emphatically	mu
FOREPART the beginning	**FOSSDYKE** Roman earthwork (Lincs.)	
FOREPEAK (in the bows)	nt	**FOSSETTE** dimple
FOREPLAN to scheme	**FOSSORES** burrowers	zo
FORE-RANK front rank	**FOSTERED** brought up; cherished	
FORE-READ prognosticate	**FOSTERER** a nurse	
FORE-RENT rent due before reaping	**FOSTRESS** foster-mother	
FORESAID previously mentioned	**FOTHERED** stopped a leak	nt
FORESAIL one of various sails	nt	**FOUGASSE** land-mine
FORESEEN expected; anticipated	**FOUL-FISH** fish when spawning	zo
FORESEER prophet	**FOUL-HOOK** not hooked in gills	
FORESHIP fore-part of ship	nt	**FOULNESS** dirt; grossness; scurrility
FORESHOW rehearse; predict	**FOUL-PLAY** unfair action	
FORESIDE front side	**FOUNDERY** foundry	ml
FORESTAL concerning forests	**FOUNDING** establishing; endowing	
FORESTAY part of rigging	nt	**FOUNTAIN** jet of water
FORESTER woodsman	**FOUNTFUL** full of springs	
FORESTRY arboriculture	**FOURCHEE** cross	hd
FORETELL predict; augur	**FOURFOLD** quadruple	
FORETIME the past; days of yore	**FOURLING** one of a quadruplet	
FORETOLD presaged; warned	**FOURNEAU** explosion chamber (Fr.)	
FOREWARD the van; the front	**FOURSOME** (dance; game; golf)	
FOREWARN caution; admonish; advise	**FOURTEEN** twice seven	
FOREWENT foregone; by-gone	**FOX-BRUSH** a trophy of the chase	
FOREWIND favouring breeze	**FOX-CHASE** hunting	
FOREWISH look forward to	**FOX-EARTH** reynard's home	
FOREWORD preface; prologue	**FOXGLOVE** digitalis	bt
FOREYARD (yard on foremast)	nt	**FOXGRAPE** variety of grape	bt
FORFAIRN down and out (Sc.)	**FOXHOUND** hunt dog	zo

FOXINESS craftiness; slyness		
FOX-SHARK thresher shark	zo	
FOX-SLEEP pretended sleep		
FOZINESS lack of spirit (Sc.)		
FRACTION part; particle; fragment		
FRACTURE break; rift; fissure		
FRAGARIA the strawberry	bt	
FRAGMENT shard; scrap; remnant		
FRAGRANT odoriferous; redolent		
FRAILISH somewhat weak; delicate		
FRAMABLE can be framed		
FRAME-SAW Italian saw	to	
FRANCATU russetin apple	bt	
FRANCIUM heaviest alkali metal	ch	
FRANK-FEE tenure in fee-simple	lw	
FRANKING remitting postage		
FRANKISH (Frank)		
FRANKLIN old English freeholder		
FRAPPAGE sharp slapping		
FRAPPING binding; lashing	nt	
FRASLING the perch	zo	
FRAUDFUL dishonest; knavish		
FRAULEIN German spinster		
FRAXININ extract from ash bark	ch	
FRAXINUS ash-tree genus	bt	
FREAKFUL } capricious; whimsical;		
FREAKISH } abnormal; erratic		
FRECKLED maculate		
FREEBORN not in vassalage		
FREE-CITY independent town		
FREE-COST cost free		
FREED-MAN emancipated slave		
FREEHAND without instrumental aid		
FREEHOLD held in fee-simple	lw	
FREE-LOVE promiscuity		
FREENESS freedom; liberty		
FREE-PORT (duties not levied)		
FREE-REED vibrating reed	mu	
FREE-SHOT legendary hunter		
FREE-SOIL (no slavery)		
FREE-TRIP tripping/closing mechanisms independent		
FREE-WILL voluntary; spontaneous		
FREEZE-UP immobility; infrozen		
FREEZING congealing; chilling		
FREMITUS palpable vibration	md	
FRENETIC frenzied; distracted		
FRENULUM a butterfly's bristle	zo	
FRENZIED maddened; furious		
FREQUENT oft repeated; recurrent		
FRESCADE a cool walk		
FRESCOED painted on plaster		
FRESCOER a washy painter		
FRESHISH almost fresh		
FRESHMAN first year student		
FRESH-NEW unpractised		
FRETTING worrying; fuming; abrading		
FRETWORK interlaced ornament		
FREUDIAN psycho-analytic		
FRIATION crumbling		
FRIBBLED frivolled; tottered		

FRIBBLER trifler		
FRICTION attrition; abrasion		
FRIENDED befriended; well-disposed		
FRIENDLY kind; favourable; amicable		
FRIESIAN Frisian; (Friesland)		
FRIGHTED affrighted; dismayed		
FRIGHTEN alarm; scare; intimidate		
FRIGIDLY coldly; icily		
FRILLING edging material		
FRINGENT } encircling; bordering		
FRINGING }		
FRIPPERY fallals; old clothes		
FRISETTE artificial curl		
FRISKFUL lively; sportive		
FRISKILY briskly; wantonly		
FRISKING capering; skipping; romping		
FRITTING pasty condition of powdered ore	gs, ml	
FRIZETTE see frisette		
FRIZZLED curled; fried		
FRIZZLER hairdresser; cloth-worker	tx	
FROCKING coarse jean		
FROG-FISH angler-fish	zo	
FROGGERY an abode of frogs		
FROGLING small frog	zo	
FROG-SPIT froth-fly	zo	
FROMWARD away from		
FRONDAGE leafage		
FRONDENT }		
FRONDOSE } leafy	bt	
FRONDOUS }		
FRONTAGE building line		
FRONTATE widening like a leaf		
FRONTIER boundary; border; march		
FRONTING facing; opposing		
FRONTLET fillet or browband		
FRONTOON a pediment	ar	
FROSTILY frigidly; icily; freezingly		
FROSTING icing		
FROTHERY mere froth; foam		
FROTH-FLY numerous parasites	zo	
FROTHILY verbosely		
FROTHING bubbling		
FROTTAGE coin-rubbing		
FROU-FROU flounced petticoat		
FROUNCED plaited; frowned		
FROWNING glowering; scowling		
FRUCTIFY to make fruitful; teem		
FRUCTOSE fruit sugar		
FRUGALLY economically; thriftily		
FRUITAGE crop; harvest; produce		
FRUIT-BUD flower to be fruit	bt	
FRUITERY fruit-loft		
FRUIT-FLY a pest	zo	
FRUITFUL productive; fecund; prolific		
FRUITING bearing fruit		
FRUITION fulfilment; realization		
FRUITIVE enjoying; gratifying		
FRUITLET a small fruit	bt	
FRUMENTY porridge of sorts		
FRUMPING insulting; flouting		

FRUMPISH old-fashioned; ill-natured
FRUSTULE shell of a diatom   bt
FUCHSINE magenta; rosaniline
   hydrochloride   ch
FUCHSITE green muscovite   mn
FUDDLING getting drunk
FUELLING stoking
FUGACITY instability; uncertainty
FUGITIVE volatile; vagabond; refugee
FUGLEMAN exemplary soldier
FULCRATE with supports   bt
FULGENCY effulgence; brilliance
FULGURAL (lightning); flashy
FULL-AGED of mature age
FULL-BACK (football)
FULL-BUTT head-on crash
FULL-EYED with prominent eyes
FULL-FACE cf. profile
FULLNESS fulness; repletion; profusion
FULL-STOP end of a period
FULL-TIME normal working hours
FULL-WAGE wireless rectifier
FULMINED fulminated; thundered
FULMINIC explosive; detonative
FUMARASE catalysing enzyme
FUMAROLE volcanic smoke hole
FUMATORY fumigating chamber
FUMBLING clumsy; groping
FUMELESS smokeless
FUMEWORT the fumitory plant   bt
FUMIGANT fume-producing
FUMIGATE disinfect
FUMITORY fumewort   bt
FUMOSITY smokiness; flatulence
FUNCTION duty; power; office
FUNDABLE able to be financed
FUNDLESS broke
FUNEBRAL, FUNEREAL sombre;
   woeful
FUNERARY mournful; dismal
FUNGIBLE interchangeable
FUNK-HOLE coward's corner
FURBELOW puckered flounce
FURCATED forked; branching
FURCULAR fork-shaped
FURFURAL fural solvent   ch
FURFUROL organic liquid   ch
FURIBUND raging; furious; frenzied
FURLOUGH leave of absence
FURMENTY see frumenty
FURRIERY the fur trade
FURROWED corrugated; ploughed
FURTHEST most distant; remotest
FURUNCLE a boil   md
FURY-LIKE furious; violent; frantic
FUSAROLE a classic moulding   ar
FUSELAGE body of aircraft
FUSEL-OIL malodorous spirit
FUSIFORM spindle-shaped
FUSILEER ⎱ armed with light
FUSILIER ⎰ flint-lock muskets
FUSTERIC a yellow dye   bt

FUSTILUG fat unwieldy person
FUTILELY unavailingly; ineffectually
FUTILITY uselessness; vanity
FUTURELY in time to come
FUTURISE anticipate; antedate
FUTURISM art movement
FUTURIST (Biblical prophesies)
FUTURITY future time; the hereafter
FUZZ-BALL puff-ball fungus   b
FUZZLING confusing; intoxicating

G

GABARAGE packing cloth
GABBATHA Pilate's judgment seat
GABBLING chattering; jabbering
GABIONED with gabions
GABLE-END part of house silhouette   a
GADABOUT roving busybody
GADHELIC Gaelic Celt language
GADLINGS steel spikes
GADZOOKS a mild expletive
GAGGLING noise of geese; cackling
GAG-TOOTH projecting tooth
GAIEMENT in lively style   mu
GAIETIES vivacities; jollities
GAINABLE procurable; attainable
GAINLESS unprofitable; bootless
GAINSAID contradicted; denied
GAIR-FOWL gare-fowl; great auk   ze
GALACTAN anhydride of galactose   ch
GALACTIA excess of milk   me
GALACTIC (the Milky Way)   a
GALACTIN sap of cow tree   b
GALALITH material made from milk
GALANGAL spicy tropical plant   b
GALATIAN inhabitant of Galatia
GALAXITE rare form of spinel   m
GALBANUM a gum   b
GALBULUS fleshy-scaled strobilus   b
GALEATED floral helmet
GALENISM Dr Galen's principles
GALENIST one of his followers
GALENITE sulphide of lead   m
GALENOID (galenite)
GALERITE fossil sea-urchin   m
GALILEAN (Galileo; Galilee)
GALL-DUCT body channel   m
GALLEASS ⎱ heavy type of
GALLIASS ⎰ galley   i
GALLIARD gay fellow; brisk; a dance
GALLICAN (Gaul or France)
GALLIPOT a glazed pot; artist's pot
GALLIVAT Malay pirate ship   n
GALLIZED (wine production)
GALLOPED rode at a gallop
GALLOPER mounted orderly
GALLOWAY a hardy horse   z
GALVANIC electric; (Galvani)
GAMBESON ⎱ doublet worn
GAMBISON ⎰ under armour

GAMBLING playing recklessly
GAMBOGIC (gamboge)
GAMBROON twilled linen cloth   tx
GAMEBIRD bird to be shot at
GAMECOCK fighting cock   zo
GAME-LAWS hunting regulations   lw
GAMENESS courage; endurance
GAMESOME sportive; gay; playful
GAMESTER a gambler
GAMMARUS genus of crustaceans   zo
GAMMONED pickled; bamboozled
GAMMONER practical joker
GAMOBIUM sexual generation in
   metagenesis   zo
GAMOGONY sporogony; gamete
   formation   zo
GANG-DAYS (Rogation week)   rl
GANGETIC (River Ganges)
GANGLAND criminal resort
GANGLIAC ganglial; (ganglion)
GANGLING slender
GANGLION nerve centre   md
GANGRENE mortification   md
GANGSMAN foreman
GANGSTER desperado; ruffian
GANGWEEK (Rogation week)   rl
GANISTER sandstone; fire-brick   mn
GANNETRY haunt of solan geese   zo
GANTLINE rope for sails/clothes   nt
GANYMEDE cupbearer to Zeus
GAOLBIRD an old lag
GAPINGLY widely open
GARBAGED eviscerated
GARBLING distorted; perverting
GARBOARD plank next to keel   nt
GARCINIA plant genus; mangosteen   bt
GARDENER a cultivator
GARDENIA sub-tropical shrub; flower   bt
GARE-FOWL gair-fowl; great auk   zo
GARGANEY sea-duck   zo
GARGLING warbling
GARGOYLE grotesque gutter-spout
GARISHLY gaudily; showily; tawdrily
GARLICKY like garlic   bt
GARNERED harvested; stored
GARRETED with watch-towers
GARRISON an armed force
GARROTTE strangle; throttle
GARRULUS crow genus; jay   zo
GARTERED with socks well up
GASALIER hanging pendant for gas
GAS-BLACK carbon-black pigment   pt
GASELIER hanging pendant for gas
GAS-GAUGE (for testing pressure)
GASIFORM gaseous
GAS-LIGHT 19th-cent. lighting
GAS-METER (for measuring volume)
GAS-MOTOR a gas engine
GASOGENE ⎫
GAZOGENE ⎬ aerating; apparatus
GASOLENE ⎫
GASOLINE ⎬ rectified petroleum; petrol

GAS-STOVE cooking stove
GASTIGHT air-tight
GASTRAEA primordial organism   zo
GASTRULA embryonic cup   zo
GAS-WATER (coal-gas purification)
GAS-WORKS a source of illumination
GATE-BILL record of fines
GATE-FINE fine when gated
GATEFOLD folded insert in a book
GATELESS without a gate
GATE-POST gate supporter
GATE-VEIN portal vein   md
GATHERED collected; acquired
GATHERER gleaner; collector
GAUDY-DAY festival
GAUDYING making merry
GAUNTLET iron glove
GAVELMAN tenant in gavelkind   lw
GAVELOCK crowbar; javelin
GAWNTREE barrel stand; gantry
GAZETTED published; recorded
GAZOGENE a gasogene
GAZPACHO Andalusian chilled soup   ck
GEAR-CASE part of auto works   au
GEGENION simple ion   ch
GELASTIC risible
GELATINE an animal jelly
GELATION solidification by cold
GELIDITY extreme cold
GEMATRIA a cabbalistic method
GEMINATE in pairs   bt
GEMINIDS meteoric shower   as
GEMINOUS double
GEMMATED budded   bt
GEMMEOUS gemlike
GEMSHORN an organ stop   mu
GENDARME armed policeman (Fr.)
GENDERED begat; sired; bred
GENERALE general principle
GENERANT a cause of production
GENERATE originate; beget; produce
GENEROUS munificent; liberal
GENESIAC (Genesis)
GENETICS study of heredity
GENETRIX ⎫ a mother,
GENITRIX ⎬ female parent
GENEVESE Genevan
GENIALLY heartily; cordially; jovially
GENITALS reproductive organs   zo
GENITIVE possessive case
GENITURE birth; procreation
GENOCIDE racial extermination
GENOMERE hypothetical gene constituent
   gn
GENOSOME chomosome part   cy
GENOTYPE individual's genetic constitu-
   tion
GENTILIC tribal; non-Jewish
GEOBIONT soil organism   ec
GEOCARPY underground fruit ripening   bt
GEOCLINE cline across organism's range
   features

GEODESIC } relating to measurements
GEODETIC } of the earth
GEOGNOST student of geognosy
GEOGNOSY petrography   b
GEOGONIC (formation of the earth)
GEOLATRY earth-worship
GEOMANCY a form of divination
GEOMETER a mathematician
GEOMETRY mensuration
GEONASTY groundward curvature   bt
GEONOMIC (physical laws)
GEOPHAGY earth-eating
GEOPHONE portable shock-wave recorder   gp
GEOPHYTE subterranean-budding plant bt
GEOPONIC agricultural; husbandry
GEOTAXIS gravity-stimulated movement response
GEORDIES Tynesiders
GEORGIAN a period; caucasian
GEOSCOPY observational knowledge
GERANIOL perfumery ester constituent ch
GERANIUM showy pink flower   bt
GERMANIC Teutonic
GERMCELL gamete
GERMINAL sprouting; French month
GEROCOMY regime for the aged   md
GERONTIC of individual's senescent period
GESTURAL gesticulating
GESTURED acted; posed; signalled
GHANAIAN native of Ghana
GHETTOES Jewish quarters
GHORKHAR Asiatic wild ass; onager
GHOSTING pattern staining; stand-in authorship
GHOULISH gruesome; fiendish
GIANTESS colossal lady
GIANTISM hugeness
GIANTIZE play the giant
GIBBSITE aluminium-hydroxide constituent of bauxite   mn
GIBINGLY scornfully; mockingly
GIB-STAFF water-gauge; pole
GIDDIEST most thoughtless
GIDDYING making dizzy
GIFTLING a small present
GIGANTIC enormous; elephantine
GIGGLING tittering; sniggering
GIG-LAMPS spectacles
GILLAROO species of trout   zo
GILLENIA rose genus   bt
GILL-FLAP a membrane   zo
GILT-EDGE aureate
GILT-HEAD sea-bream   zo
GILT-TAIL species of worm   zo
GIMCRACK a gewgaw; jimcrack
GIMLETED holed; bored
GINGERLY cautiously; warily
GINGIVAL relating to the gums   md
GIN-HORSE mill-horse   zo
GIN-HOUSE cotton factory

GIN-SLING a short drink
GIPSYDOM gipsy life
GIPSYISM cheating; flattery
GIRASOLE sunflower   b
GIRDLING encompassing; surrounding
GIRLHOOD juvenile femininity
GIRONDIN moderate republican
GIRTHING saddling; girdling
GIRT-LINE rigging line   n
GIVEABLE bestowable; presentable
GIVE-AWAY unintended disclosure
GLABRATE } smooth; without
GLABROUS } hair or down   b
GLACIATE freeze; polish by ice
GLADDEST very cheerful; merriest
GLADDING rejoicing; delighting; elating
GLADIATE sword-shaped
GLADIOLE sword-lily   b
GLADIOLI plural of gladiolus   b
GLADNESS joy; joyfulness; cheer
GLAD-RAGS party frocks
GLADSOME pleasurable; pleasant
GLAIRING varnishing
GLAIROUS viscous
GLANCING glimpsing; ricocheting
GLANDAGE feeding on acorns
GLANDERS a horse disease   v
GLANDULE small gland   m
GLAREOUS glairous; viscous
GLASSEYE a horse disease
GLASSFUL a measure of content
GLASSILY in a vitreous manner
GLASSING glazing
GLASSITE one of a Scottish sect
GLASS-POT (used for melting glass)   g
GLAUCIUM the yellow poppy   b
GLAUCOMA an eye-disease   m
GLAUCOUS a sea-green colour
GLEAMING resplendent; radiating
GLEANING harvesting; culling; picking
GLEDGING squinting
GLEESOME frolicsome; hilarious; lively
GLEISOIL poor-drainage-influenced soil type   s
GLIADINE yellow extract   b
GLIBNESS gift of the gab
GLIDDERY slippery
GLIMPSED viewed hurriedly; glanced
GLINTING gleaming
GLIOSOME cytoplasmic granule   c
GLISSADE a glide on a glacier
GLISSAUN the coal-fish   z
GLOAMING dusk; twilight
GLOATING revelling; crowing; exulting
GLOBATED spherical
GLOBULAR spheric; round
GLOBULET round particle
GLOBULIN (a blood constituent)   m
GLOOMILY despondently
GLOOMING obscuring; depressing
GLORIANA Queen Elizabeth

GLORIOLE a halo rl
GLORIOSA a lily bt
GLORIOUS illustrious; noble; eminent
GLORYING exulting; boasting
GLORY-PEA an Australian pea bt
GLOSSARY explanatory vocabulary
GLOSSILY smoothly; sleekly
GLOSSINA the tsetse fly zo
GLOSSING commenting; polishing
GLOSSIST annotator; glossarist
GLOWERED scowled; frowned
GLOW-LAMP incandescent lamp
GLOW-WORM a beetle zo
GLOXINIA flowering plant bt
GLUCAGON hormone increasing blood
  sugar md
GLUCINUM white metal; beryllium
GLUCONIC acid derived from glucose ch
GLUCOSID sugar compound ch
GLUE-LINE dielectric heating
GLUMMEST gloomiest; very morose
GLUMNESS sulkiness; depression
GLUMPISH sullen; splenetic; moody
GLUTAEUS posterior muscle md
GLUTELIN water-insoluble protein ch
GLUTENIN wheat glutelin protein ch
GLUTTING sating; saturating; cloying
GLUTTONY voracity; greed
GLYCEROL glycerine ch
GLYCOGEN animal starch ch
GLYCONIC kind of verse
GLYPTICS gem engraving
GNARLING gnawing
GNARRING snarling; growling
GNASHING grinding the teeth
GNATHISM (jaw measurement)
GNATHITE insect mouth-part zo
GNATLING small gnat zo
GNAT-WORM larva of gnat zo
GNOMICAL ⎫ relating to the art of
GNOMONIC ⎬ dialling
GOA-CEDAR a cypress bt
GOAL-LINE back-line (football)
GOAL-POST (football)
GOATHERD goat-minder
GOATLING small goat zo
GOAT-MOTH fabulous insect zo
GOATSKIN skin of goat
GOAT'S-RUE a plant bt
GOBBLING guzzling; turkey-noise
GODCHILD protegé
GOD'S-ACRE a graveyard
GODSMITH idol maker
GOD-SPEED a benediction
GOETHITE a hydrated iron oxide mn
GOFFERED crimped
GO-GETTER pushing person
GOGGLING rolling the eyes
GOINGS-ON queer happenings
GOITERED ⎫ afflicted with the
GOITROUS ⎬ goitre md

GOLCONDA diamond mine, Hyderabad
GOLD-DUST a plant bt
GOLDENLY splendidly; aureately
GOLDFISH a carp zo
GOLD-FOIL, GOLDLEAF thin gold
GOLD-LACE sumptuary decoration
GOLDLESS destitute of gold
GOLD-LILY the yellow lily bt
GOLD-MINE source of wealth
GOLD-RUSH prospector's scramble
GOLD-SIZE a varnish
GOLD-WIRE thread gold
GOLD-WORK mouth adornments
GOLF-CLUB tool for striking golf-ball
GOLGOTHA a charnel-house
GOLLYWOG grotesque doll
GOLOSHES overshoes
GOMARIST opponent of Arminians
GOMBROON Persian pottery
GONALGIA pain in the knee md
GONENESS that sinking feeling
GONFALON a banner
GONGYLUS (seaweed) bt
GONIMIUM lichen thallus cell bt
GONOCOEL gonad cavity zo
GONOCYTE sexual cell in porifera zo
GONODUCT genital products duct zo
GONOPORE reproductive elements opening
GONOSOME repro. individuals in animal
  colony zo
GONOTOME embryo somite zo
GOOD-DOER benefactor; patron
GOOD-FOLK the fairies
GOOD-LACK expression of pity
GOODLIER more excellent; fairer
GOODNESS kindness; beneficence
GOODWIFE a term of respect
GOODWILL benevolence; an asset
GOOGLIES deceptive spheres
GOOSE-CAP a silly person
GOOSE-EGG a zero; a duck zo
GORGEOUS splendid and showy
GORGONIA corals zo
GOSSAMER filmy cobweb
GOSSIPED chatted; tattled
GOSSIPRY small talk; intimacy
GOURMAND glutton; epicurean
GOUTWEED goutwort bt
GOVERNED controlled; ruled; swayed
GOVERNOR regulator; guardian
GOWNSMAN cf. townsman (university)
GRABBING snatching; clutching
GRABLINE life-line on a lifeboat nt
GRACE-CUP loving cup
GRACEFUL elegant and easy
GRACILIS land-vertebrate thigh muscle zo
GRACIOSO Spanish clown
GRACIOUS affable; polite; benign
GRADATED graded; blended
GRADATIM step by step
GRADIENT slope; incline

GRADUAND about to be a graduate		
GRADUATE pass; proportion; divide		
GRAECISM a Greek idiom		
GRAECIZE to turn into Greek		
GRAFFITI ancient wall scribblings		
GRAFFITO two colour plaster layers		
GRAFTING bribing; (gardening)		
GRAINAGE duties on grain		
GRAINING a process; a fish	zo	
GRAIN-TIN melted tin		
GRALLINE (wading birds)	zo	
GRALLOCK entrails of deer	zo	
GRAMARYE necromancy; magic		
GRANDDAD grandfather		
GRANDEST most magnificent; noblest		
GRANDEUR pomp; splendour; majesty		
GRANDSON son's son		
GRANITIC of granite	mn	
GRANTING conceding; conferring		
GRANULAR in grains		
GRAPHICS art of drawing		
GRAPHITE blacklead	mn	
GRAPHIUM a style (for writing)		
GRAPPLED seized; grasped; clutched		
GRASPING gripping; avaricious		
GRASSING turfing; laying low		
GRASS-OIL an essential oil	bt	
GRATEFUL thankful; beholden		
GRATIOLA hedge hyssop	bt	
GRATUITY tip; bonus; pourboire		
GRAVAMEN principal charge	lw	
GRAVELLY full of gravel		
GRAVITAS weight of dignity		
GRAY-EYED grey-eyed		
GRAYLING freshwater fish	zo	
GRAZIOSO gracefully	mu	
GREASILY unctuously		
GREASING lubricating; corrupting		
GREATEST largest; biggest; bulkiest		
GRECIZED Hellenized		
GREEDILY voraciously; eagerly		
GREENERY verdure; foliage		
GREEN-FLY a pest	zo	
GREENING hoaxing		
GREENISH somewhat green		
GREEN-TEA tea picked immature	bt	
GREETING welcoming; weeping (Sc.)		
GREFFIER notary (Channel Isles)	lw	
GREMLINS malignant aerial imps		
GREYCING greyhound racing		
GREYNESS grayness		
GRID-BIAS adjustment	ro	
GRIDELIN violet grey colour		
GRIDIRON a grill		
GRIEVOUS burdensome; heinous		
GRILLADE grilled meat (Fr.)		
GRILLAGE a cross-beam construction		
GRILLING broiling; interrogating		
GRIMACED smirked		
GRIMALDI an old clown		
GRIMMEST sternest; dourest		

GRIMNESS fierceness; dourness		
GRIMOIRE ancient handbook of black magic		
GRINDERY shoemakers' materials		
GRINDING pulverizing; crushing		
GRINNING smiling broadly		
GRIPEFUL distressing; colicky		
GRIPPING holding tight; clutching		
GRISELDA a very patient lady		
GRISEOUS grey; grizzled		
GRITTING grating; grinding; abrading		
GRIZZLED grey; grumbled		
GROANFUL mournful; lugubrious		
GROANING moaning; complaining		
GROGGERY a dram-shop		
GROGGING (extracting spirit)		
GROG-SHOP a pub		
GROINING angular curves	ar
GROMWELL a plant	bt
GROOMING making neat and tidy		
GROOVING furrowing; scoring		
GROSBEAK a finch	zo
GROSCHEN Austrian coin	nm
GROTTOES caves		
GROUNDED on the ground		
GROUNDER low ball at baseball		
GROUPING arranging; disposing		
GROUSING grumbling		
GROUTING filling in with concrete		
GROWABLE cultivatable		
GROWLERY a private den		
GROWLING grumbling; snarling		
GRUBBIER dirtier		
GRUBBING digging up		
GRUBBLED groped		
GRUDGING envying; coveting		
GRUESOME horrible; grisly; grim		
GRUMBLED complained; repined		
GRUMBLER grouser		
GRUMNESS surliness; dourness		
GRUMPHIE a sow	zo
GRUNDSEL groundsel	bt
GRYSBOCK steinbock, (S. Africa)	zo
GUACHERO oil-bird, (S. Amer.)	zo
GUAIACOL an odorous liquid	ch
GUAIACUM resinous lignum vitae	bt
GUANCHOS natives of Canary Islands		
GUARACHA a Cuban dance	mu
GUARANTY basis of security		
GUARDANT facing	he
GUARDFUL wary; cautious		
GUARDIAN warden; protector		
GUARDING watching; defending		
GUBBINGS wild Devonians		
GUELPHIC a royal family		
GUERILLA an irregular		
GUERNSEY a garment; a cow	z
GUESSING imagining		
GUGGLING gurgling		
GUICOWAR Galkwar		
GUIDABLE steerable		

GUIDANCE direction; government	
GUILEFUL crafty; insiduous	
GUILTILY criminally; culpably	
GUIMAUVE marsh-mallow	bt
GUJARATI language (Bombay)	
GULCHING pre-rock-fall sound	mn
GULF-WEED tropical seaweed	bt
GULLIBLE easily deceived	
GULLIVER swift traveller	
GULLYING making a channel	
GULOSITY voracity	
GUMPTION shrewd sense; nous	
GUM-RESIN gamboge	bt
GUN-LAYER who prepares guns for firing	
GUNMETAL alloy; copper and tin	
GUN-REACH gunshot; range	
GUNSMITH gun-maker	
GUNSTICK ramrod	
GUNSTOCK part of gun	
GUNSTONE stone projectile	
GURGLING purling; rippling	
GURKHALI language (Nepal)	
GUSTABLE tasty; savoury	
GUTTATED sprinkled; bedewed	
GUTTERED ran in drops	
GUTTLING gorging; swallowing	
GUTTURAL throaty	
GUYANESE (Guyana, S. Amer.)	
GUZZLING swilling; tippling; quaffing	
GYMKHANA sports meeting	
GYMNASIC gymnastic	
GYMNICAL athletic	
GYMNOTUS electric eel	zo
GYNANDER a plant	bt
GYNARCHY female government	
GYNECIUM women's quarters	
GYNERIUM pampas grass	bt
GYPSEOUS (gypsum)	mn
GYPSYISM gipsyism	
GYRATING spinning; rotating; whirling	
GYRATION rotation; revolution	
GYRATORY circling; revolutionary	
GYRODYNE speedy helicopter	ae
GYROIDAL spiral; winding	
GYROLITE hydrated calcium silicate	mn
GYROPTER helicopter	ae
GYROSTAT gyroscope	

H

HABENDUM descriptive clause	lw
HABITANT inhabitant; native	
HABITING dressing; arraying	
HABITUAL customary; usual; wonted	
HABITUDE customary manner	
HACIENDA estate or ranch (S. Amer.)	
HACKBOLT great shearwater gull	zo
HACKLING heckling; separating flax	
HAEMATIC acting on the blood	
HAEMATIN (haemoglobin)	md

HAGBERRY bird-cherry	bt
HAGGADAH ⎫ Rabinical commentary	
HAGGADIC ⎭ on Old Testament	rl
HAGGLING chaffering; bargaining	
HAGTAPER the mullein	bt
HAILSHOT small shot	
HAIRCORD kind of carpet	tx
HAIR-LACE hair ribbon	
HAIRLESS bald	
HAIRLINE a fine line	
HAIR-SALT epsomite	mn
HAIRWORK work done with hair	
HAIRWORM freshwater worm	zo
HALATION photographic defect	pg
HALENESS robustness; health	
HALF-BACK (football)	
HALF-BOOT (halfway to the knee)	
HALF-BRED mongrel	
HALF-COCK a safety position	
HALF-DEAD almost dead	
HALF-DECK half length deck	nt
HALF-DONE incomplete; under-done	
HALF-FACE the profile	
HALF-INCH map scale	
HALF-LIFE radio-activity period	ps
HALF-LINE light-shading technique	pr
HALFLING a youth	
HALF-MARK old coin, value 6s. 8d.	nm
HALFMAST a sign of mourning	
HALF-MILE athletics	
HALF-MOON a semicircle; demilune	
HALF-NOTE a semitone	
HALF-PAST, HALF-HOUR clock time	
HALF-PIKE short pike	
HALF-SEAS halfway	nt
HALF-SPAN lean-to	ar
HALF-SUIT body armour	
HALF-TIDE neither in nor out	
HALF-TIME an interval	
HALF-TINT intermediate tint	
HALF-TONE a printing process	pr
HALICORE dugong; sea-cow	zo
HALIOTIS mother-of-pearl shell	zo
HALL-DOOR front door	
HALLIARD running rope	nt
HALL-MARK a guarantee	
HALLOOED shouted	
HALLOWED reverenced; sanctified	
HALTERED roped; tethered	
HALTERES balancing wings	zo
HAMBLING mutilating the foot	
HAMIFORM hook-shaped	
HAMINDAS egg/peppers/onion casserole (Jew.)	ck
HAMMERED (Stock Exchange)	
HAMMERER hammer-man; smith	
HAMPERED impeded; packed; clogged	
HANDBALL an old pastime	
HANDBELL one rung by hand	mu
HANDBILL anouncement; broadcast	
HANDBOOK a manual	

HANDCART transport to hell
HANDCUFF manacle; fetter
HANDFAST hold; custody; betroth
HANDGEAR (manual control)
HANDGRIP, HANDHOLD climbing
HANDICAP penalty; allowance
HANDLESS awkward
HANDLINE line without a rod
HANDLING manipulation
HANDLIST convenient list
HANDLOOM for home weaving   **wv**
HAND-MADE product of home industry
HANDMAID an Abigail
HANDMILL a quern
HANDPICK select carefully
HANDPOST finger-post; guide
HANDRAIL support
HAND-SALE handshake deal
HANDSOME generous; good-looking
HAND-WORK sloid; sloyd
HANDYMAN jack-of-all-trades
HANGABLE dependable; suspensible
HANGER-ON parasite; retainer
HANGFIRE explosive-detonation delay   **mn**
HANGNAIL agnail   **md**
HANGNEST a bird   **zo**
HANG-OVER after-party reaction
HANKERED coveted; longed; yearned
HAPLODON mountain beaver   **zo**
HAPLOSIS chromosome halving   **cy**
HAPPENED chanced; occurred; befell
HAPTERON of plant attachment organs **bt**
HAQUETON padded jacket
HARA-KIRI happy despatch (Jap.)
HARANGUE tirade; declaim
HARASSED wearied; persecuted
HARASSER a guerilla
HARDBACK book published in stiff covers
HARDBAKE toffee almond cake   **ck**
HARDBEAM horn beam   **bt**
HARD-CASH ready money
HARD-CORE unwavering resistance
HARDENED inured; obdurate
HARDENER toughener   **ch**
HARD-FERN the northern fern   **bt**
HARD-HACK steeple-bush   **bt**
HARDIEST most robust; boldest
HARDNESS compactness; firmness
HARDSHIP injustice; tribulation
HARDTACK ship's biscuit   **nt**
HARDWARE ironmongery
HARDWOOD close-grained timber   **bt**
HAREBELL hairbell; campanula   **bt**
HAREFOOT swift of foot
HAREHUNE horehound   **bt**
HAREPIPE a snare
HARE'S-EAR a yellow flower   **bt**
HARI-KARI hara-kiri (Jap.)
HARLEIAN a literary society
HARLOTRY wantonness
HARMLESS innocuous; inoffensive

HARMONIC concordant; consonant
HARPINGS battens   **nt**
HARROWED lacerated; tortured; torn
HARROWER sensationalist
HARRYING harassing; raiding; vexing
HARTWORT plant; seseli type   **bt**
HASTATED spear-shaped   **bt**
HASTENED expedited; urged
HASTENER urgent reminder
HASTINGS early peas   **bt**
HATBRUSH brush for hats
HATCHERY incubator
HATCHETY sharp featured
HATCHING plotting; shading; breeding
HATCHWAY deck opening   **nt**
HATEABLE odious; detestable
HATSTAND like a hatrack, but different
HATTERIA tuatara; lizard, (NZ)   **zo**
HAT-TRICK 3 times successful
HAUNCHED having haunches
HAUNTING frequenting; obsessing
HAURIANT (fish on end)   **hd**
HAURLING dragging; trailing
HAUSFRAU housewife (Ger.)
HAVANNAH a cigar
HAVELOCK white cover for cap
HAVILDAR Warrant Officer (Ind.)
HAVOCKED devastated; wasted
HAWAIIAN (Hawai)
HAWFINCH grosbeak   **zo**
HAWK-BELL small bell on hawk's foot
HAWK-EYED lynx-eyed
HAWK-MOTH genus of moth   **zo**
HAWK-WEED genus of weed   **bt**
HAWTHORN the may   **bt**
HAY-FEVER pollen allergy   **md**
HAY-FIELD meadow
HAY-KNIFE stack-cutter
HAY-MAKER a swipe
HAY-STACK a hay-rick
HAZARDED imperilled; ventured
HAZARDER a gambler; speculator
HAZEL-HEN ruffled grouse   **zo**
HAZEL-NUT filbert   **bt**
HAZINESS uncertainty; vagueness
HEADACHE occipital disorder   **md**
HEADACHY off colour
HEAD-BAND book top; fillet
HEAD-BOOM jib-boom   **nt**
HEADFAST mooring rope   **nt**
HEADGEAR head-dress
HEADIEST most exhilarating
HEADLAMP (motor-car)
HEADLAND cape; promontory; ness
HEADLESS decapitated
HEADLINE newspaper superscripture
HEADLONG precipitately; steep; hasty
HEAD-MAIN main water supply
HEAD-MARK outstanding feature
HEAD-MOLD skull; a moulding   **md**
HEADMOST most advanced

HEAD-NOTE introductory note	**HELIOSIS** sunstroke	md
HEAD-PUMP sea-water pump	nt	**HELIOZIA** protozoa	zo
HEAD-RACE lead to water-wheel	**HELIPORT** helicopter airfield	ae
HEAD-RENT payment for use of a head	**HELLBENT** reckless	
HEAD-REST a support	**HELLBORN** } of satanic origin	
HEAD-RING Kaffir coiffure	**HELLBRED** }	
HEADSHIP supreme authority	**HELLENIC** Grecian	
HEAD-TIRE head-dress	**HELL-FIRE** Satan's illumination	
HEAD-WIND a contrary wind	**HELL-GATE** approach to inferno	
HEAD-WORD title word	**HELL-KITE** bird of ill-omen	zo
HEAD-WORK intellectual labour; sport	**HELLWARD** devilish progress	
HEALABLE remediable; curable	**HELMETED** double-domed	
HEARABLE audible	**HELMINTH** a worm	zo
HEARTILY cordially; sincerely; warmly	**HELMLESS** rudderless	
HEARTLET small heart	**HELMSMAN** steersman	
HEART-ROT central decay	bt	**HELOTAGE** } slavery; bondage;	
HEATHERY heathy; heath-clad	bt	**HELOTISM** } servitude; serfdom	
HEATH-HEN black grouse	zo	**HELPLESS** impotent; weak; powerless	
HEATH-PEA legendary plant	bt	**HELPMATE** wife; partner	
HEAT-SPOT a freckle	**HELPMEET** helpmate; helper	
HEAT-UNIT lot of hot air	me	**HELVETIA** Switzerland	
HEAT-WAVE calorific undulation	**HELVETIC** Swiss	
HEAVENLY celestial; seraphic	**HEMATITE** haematite	mn
HEAVIEST most ponderous	**HEMIGALE** Malayan civet	zo
HEBDOMAD a group of seven	**HEMIOLIC** 3 to 2 ratio	
HEBETANT making blunt; dulling	**HEMIONUS** dziggetai	zo
HEBETATE to dull; stupefy	**HEMIOPIA** faulty vision	md
HEBETUDE dullness; stupidity	**HEMIPODE** sort of quail	zo
HEBRAIST } concerned with	**HEMIPTER** cicada or bug	zo
HEBRAISM } Hebrew customs	**HEMISOME** symmetrical half of animal	zo
HEBRAIZE } and literature	**HEMP-PALM** a pretend plant	bt
HECATOMB sacrifice of 100	**HEMP-SEED** gallow's bird (Shak.)	
HECKLING hackling; combing	**HENCHMAN** servant; page; varlet	
HECKYMAL blue tit	zo	**HENEQUEN, HENEQUIN** sisal hemp	bt
HECTORED boasted; swaggered	**HEN-HOUSE** coop	
HECTORER brawler; bully; braggart	**HEN-HUSSY** a cotquean	
HECTORLY insolent; domineering	**HEN-MOULD** black spongy soil	
HEDGEHOG endangered species	zo	**HEN-PARTY** ladies' gossip group	
HEDGEHOP a low flight	**HEN-ROOST** poultry park	
HEDGEPIG young hedgehog	zo	**HEN-WOMAN** hen-wife	
HEDGEROW bushy boundary	bt	**HEPATITE** barium sulphate	mn
HEDONICS } doctrine that	**HEPATIZE** hepatise; livery-work	
HEDONISM } pleasure is the	**HEPATOMA** liver tumour	md
HEDONIST } highest good	**HEPTAGON** 7 sided figure	
HEEDLESS regardless; rash	**HEPTARCH** ruler of a heptarchy	
HEELBALL black wax	**HERALDED** proclaimed; blazoned	
HEEL-NICK cut-out portion of movable	**HERALDIC** } armorial bearings and	
type	pr	**HERALDRY** } ceremonial orders	hd
HEFTIEST sturdiest; beefiest	**HERBAGED** grass covered	
HEGELIAN (process of the spirit)	**HERBARIA** hortus siccus	bt
HEGEMONY leadership	**HERBELET** small herb	bt
HEGUMENE prior	rl	**HERBLESS** lacking vegetation	
HEIGHTEN enhance	**HERCULES** labour member of Tiryns	
HEIRLESS no heir	**HERD-BOOK** cattle stud-book	
HEIRLOOM family jewel	lw	**HERDSMAN** cow-puncher	
HEIRSHIP inherent right	**HEREAWAY** hereabouts	
HELCOSIS ulceration	md	**HEREDITY** inherent propensity	
HELCOTIC ulcerous	md	**HEREINTO** into this	
HELIACAL (sunlight)	**HERESIES** schisms	
HELICOID spiral	**HEREUNTO** unto this	
HELIODOR S. Afr. yellow beryl	mn	**HEREUPON** upon this; then	

HEREWITH by saying this	**HIP-JOINT** with-it nightclub
HERISSON spiked obstruction	**HIREABLE** on hire
HERITAGE patrimony; legacy	**HIRELESS** wageless
HERMETIC air-tight; mystic; occult	**HIRELING** mercenary
HERNIOID ruptured; hernial md	**HIRPLING** running lamely
HERNSHAW heronshaw; handsaw zo	**HIRRIENT** trilling sound
HEROICAL intrepid; valiant; epic	**HIRUDINE** like a leech
HEROICLY dauntlessly; daringly	**HISPANIC** Spanish
HEROIZED lionized; idealized	**HISTIOID** resembling tissue md
HEROSHIP heroism	**HISTORIC** authentic; genuine; famous
HERPETIC shingly md	**HISTRION** play-actor
HERTZIAN (low frequency waves)	**HITCHING** fastening; attaching
HERTZITE galena mn	**HITHERTO** till now
HESITANT vacillating; doubtful	**HIVELESS** not a single skep
HESITATE pause; waver; demur	**HIVE-NEST** multiple bird's nest zo
HESPERUS a wreck	**HOACTZIN** hoatzin; S. Amer. bird zo
HEXAGRAM Solomon's seal	**HOARDING** storing; treasuring; fence
HEXAPLAR sextuple	**HOARSELY** discordantly; raucously
HEY-GO-MAD joyous interjection	**HOASTMAN** member of a guild
HIBERNAL wintry	**HOBBLING** walking lamely; limping
HIBISCUS tropical mallow bt	**HOBBYISM** } cult of a favourite
HICCATEE Cen. Amer. tortoise zo	**HOBBYIST** } pursuit
HICCOUGH hiccup	**HOCKCART** (last harvest load)
HICCUPED belched politely	**HOCKHERB** a mallow bt
HICKWALL small woodpecker zo	**HOCKLING** mowing
HIDDENLY privily; furtively; covertly	**HOCK-TIDE** a festival
HIDE-ROPE a reim (S. Afr.)	**HOCUSSED** drugged; doped
HIDROSIS sweat md	**HOG-FRAME** (shipbuilding) nt
HIELAMAN native shield (Aust.)	**HOGGEREL** sheep of second year zo
HIERARCH chief priest rl	**HOGMANAY** Dec. 31st (Sc.)
HIERATIC priestly rl	**HOG-REEVE** medieval parish officer
HIERONYM sacred name used as surname	**HOG'S BEAN** henbane bt
HIGGLING haggling; chaffering	**HOG-SCORE** line on a curling rink
HIGH-BALL whisky and soda	**HOGSHEAD** large cask
HIGHBORN of noble birth	**HOGSTEER** wild boar zo
HIGHBRED not a hybrid	**HOHLRAUM** black-body radiator cavity
HIGHBROW so-called intellectual	ac
HIGH-HUNG elevated	**HOISTING** raising; lifting; elevating
HIGH-JUMP athletics; dismissal	**HOISTWAY** trap-door
HIGHLAND where the heart is	**HOLDBACK** check; retainer
HIGH-LIFE the jet set	**HOLDFAST** catch; grip
HIGH-MASS special service rl	**HOLDINGS** stock possessed by library
HIGHMOST topmost	**HOLEWORT** moschatel bt
HIGHNESS a rank; altitude	**HOLINESS** sanctity; devoutness rl
HIGHROAD thoroughfare	**HOLLANDS** geneva; schnapps
HIGH-SPOT climax	**HOLLOAED** shouted
HIGH-TIDE floodtide	**HOLLOWED** excavated; scooped
HIGH-TIME almost overdue	**HOLLOWLY** insincerely; vacantly
HIGTAPER the mullein bt	**HOLOGAMY** mature-cell fusion bt
HI-JACKED plundered a gang	**HOLOGRAM** laser optical imaging ps
HI-JACKER super-pirate	**HOLOPTIC** side eyes meeting zo
HILARITY gaiety; jollity; merriment	**HOLOZOIC** eating other organisms zo
HILL-FOLK hillmen; Covenanters	**HOLYROOD** holy cross rl
HILL-FORT stronghold; fastness	**HOLY-WEEK** the week before Easter
HILLOCKY hummocky	**HOLY-WRIT** the Scriptures rl
HILLSIDE a declivity	**HOMAGING** paying respects
HINDERED delayed; thwarted; impeded	**HOME-BIRD** stay-at-home
HINDERER obstructionist; opposer	**HOMEBORN** native; domestic
HINDMOST last; posterior	**HOMEBRED** natural; unpolished
HINDUISM doctrine and rites	**HOME-FARM** nearest fields to farmhouse
HINGEING depending on	**HOMEFELT** inward; private

HOME-GOER word rarely or never used	
HOMELAND native land	
HOMELESS on the streets	
HOMELIKE not ornate	
HOMELILY familiarly	
HOME-MADE better-tasting	
HOME-RULE autonomy	
HOMESICK nostalgia	
HOMESPUN rough worsted	
HOMEWARD return journey	
HOMEWORK out of school task	
HOMICIDE man-slaughter	lw
HOMILIST sermonizer	
HOMOBIUM alga/fungus association	bt
HOMODONT teeth all alike	zo
HOMODYNE (wireless telephony)	tc
HOMOGAMY hermaphroditism	bt
HOMOGENY similarity of nature	
HOMOLOGY affinity of structure	
HOMONYMY (similar sounding words)	
HOMOSOTE material for walls of huts	
HOMOTYPE ⎫ structural affinity	
HOMOTYPY ⎭	
HONDURAN (Honduras)	
HONESTLY uprightly; sincerely	
HONE-WORT herb parsley-piert	bt
HONEY-BAG nectar sac of bee	zo
HONEY-BEE nectar-sucker	zo
HONEYDEW tobacco; melon	bt
HONEY-POT a grape (S. Afr.)	bt
HONORARY gratuitous; unpaid	
HONOURED respected; revered	
HONOURER venerator	
HOODWINK befool; cheat; delude	
HOOFMARK imprint; slot	
HOOK-WORM a parasite	zo
HOOLIGAN ruffian; rascal; bully	
HOOP-IRON iron band	
HOOT-TOOT toot-toot!	
HOPELESS despairing; despondent	
HOPINGLY thinking wishfully	
HOPPLING hobbling	
HORATIAN (Horace)	
HORMESIS non-toxic organism stimulus	
	bt
HORNBEAK garfish	zo
HORNBEAM a tree	bt
HORNBILL picarian bird	zo
HORNFISH garfish	zo
HORNFOOT hoofed	
HORNGATE gate of dreams	
HORN-LEAD chloride of lead	mn
HORNLESS dodded	
HORNPIPE air; dance	mu
HORNWORT water-plant	bt
HOROLOGY works on clocks	
HORRIBLE revolting; fearful; dire	
HORRIBLY hideously; appallingly	
HORRIDLY foully; alarmingly	
HORRIFIC terrific; awful; frightful	
HORSE-BOX van	

HORSE-BOY stable-boy	
HORSE-CAR a carriage	
HORSE-FLY large sucking fly	zo
HORSE-HOE a harrow	
HORSEMAN rider; equestrian	
HORSE-WAY road or track	
HOSE-PIPE a duct	
HOSE-REEL firefighting equipment	
HOSPITAL an almshouse	
HOSPODOR Slav governor	
HOSTELRY inn; tavern; local	
HOT-BLAST pre-heated air	
HOTCHPOT farrago; mixture; medley	
HOTELIER hotel-keeper	
HOTHOUSE greenhouse	
HOT-PLATE a heating appliance	
HOT-PRESS a machine	
HOT-SHORT brittle	
HOTTONIA water-violet	bt
HOT-WATER trouble	
HOUGHING ham stringing	
HOUNDING pursuing; tracking; trailing	
HOUR-HAND time indicator	
HOUSE-BOY serving lad	
HOUSE-DOG watch dog	zo
HOUSE-FLY musca domestica	zo
HOUSE-TAX a levy	lw
HOVELLED meanly housed	
HOVELLER longshoreman	
HOVERING in suspense	
HOWIEITE triclinic hydrous silicate	ma
HOWITZER short cannon	
HUCKSTER an advertiser	
HUDDLING cowering in mass	
HUDIBRAS political satire by S. Butler	
HUGENESS bulk; immensity; vastness	
HUGUENOT French Protestant	rl
HUIA-BIRD New Zealand bird	zo
HUMANELY mercifully; benignly	
HUMANISM ⎫ pragmatism;	
HUMANIST ⎬ human interests,	
HUMANITY ⎭ grammar, rhetoric, etc.	
HUMANIZE enlighten; civilize	
HUMATION burial	
HUMBLING abasing; shaming	
HUMEFIED moistened	
HUMIDIFY to dampen	
HUMIDITY moisture	
HUMILITY humbleness; meekness	
HUMMOCKY hillocky	
HUMORISM facetiousness; jocularity	
HUMORIST jester; merryman	
HUMOROUS witty; droll; comical	
HUMOURED indulged; pampered	
HUMPBACK a whale; road-bridge	zo
HUMPLESS no depression here	
HUMSTRUM humdrum; monotonous	
HUNG-BEEF dried beef	
HUNGERED famished; hankered	
HUNGRILY cravingly	
HUNKERED squatted	

HUNTRESS a Diana
HUNTSMAN chasseur
HURDLING (athletics)
HURLBONE a horse bone   zo
HURLWIND whirlwind
HURRYING urging; speeding
HURTLESS uninjured; innoxious
HURTLING whizzing
HUSHED-UP undisclosed
HUSH-HUSH very secret
HUSH-MUSH highly confidential
HUSKIEST very hoarse
HUSTINGS electioneering platform
HUSTLING bustling; jostling; elbowing
HUTCHING cooping
HUZZAING shouting with joy
HYACINTH a gem; flower   mn, bt
HYALITIS optic inflammation   md
HYBODONT irregular teeth   md
HYDATISM a watery sound   md
HYDATOID aqueous
HYDRANTH nutrition polyp   zo
HYDRATED combined with water
HYDROFIN high speed motor-boat
HYDROGEL water soluble colloid   ch
HYDROGEN gaseous element   ch
HYDROMEL watered honey
HYDROMYS water-rats, etc.   zo
HYDROPIC thirsty
HYDROPSY dropsy   md
HYDROSOL colloidal solution
HYDROZOA jelly fish; etc.   zo
HYDRURET hybrid   ch
HYGIENIC salubrious; healthy
HYLICISM materialism
HYLICIST a philosopher
HYLOBATE a gibbon   zo
HYLOZOIC materialistic
HYMENEAL conjugal; matrimonial
HYMENEAN nuptial; bridal
HYMENIUM part of fungus   bt
HYMN-BOOK often A. & M.   rl
HYOIDEUS nerve branch in vertebrates zo
HYOSCINE poisonous alkaloid   md
HYPALGIA insusceptibility
HYPAXIAL below the axis   zo
HYPERGOL rocket fuel   sp
HYPERION a Titan
HYPHAEMA interior eye bleeding   md
HYPHENED linked
HYPHENIC jointed
HYPNOSIS hypnotism   md
HYPNOTIC mesmeric
HYPOARIA brain lobe in fish   zo
HYPOBOLE form of argument
HYPOCONE molar cusp   zo
HYPODERM cell layer under epidermis bt
HYPOGEAL underground
HYPOGEAN subterranean
HYPOGENE rock formation   mn
HYPOGEUM foundation

HYPOHYAL hyoid arch element   zo
HYPOMERE mesothelial wall zone   zo
HYPONOME water escape funnel   zo
HYPOTHEC debt security   lw
HYPOZOAN } below the limit of life   gl
HYPOZOIC }
HYSTERIA nervous disorder   md
HYSTERIC hysterical

I

IANTHINA purple sea-snails   zo
IATRICAL medical   md
IBSENISM (Henrik Ibsen)
ICE-BLINK a reflection; mirage
ICE-BOUND immobilized by ice
ICE-BROOK frozen brook
ICE-CREAM the content of a cornet
ICE-FIELD ice-floe
ICE-FLOAT ice-field
ICE-HOUSE building with ice in it
ICE-LEDGE much like any other ledge
ICE-PLANT frost flower   bt
ICE-SHEET glacial ice
ICE-WATER Amer. national drink
ICE-YACHT boat for transport on ice
ICHOROUS like ichor   md
ICHTHINE (fishes' eggs)   zo
ICHTHYIC fishlike
ICTERINE yellow
IDEALISM transcendency
IDEALIST visionary
IDEALITY perfection
IDEALIZE idealise
IDEATING fancying
IDEATION conception
IDEATIVE imaginative
IDENTIFY recognize; integrate
IDENTITY individuality; sameness
IDEOGRAM ideograph
IDEOLOGY metaphysics
IDIOTISH doltish; fatuous; inane
IDIOTISM imbecility; inanity
IDIOTIZE ridicule; befool
IDLEHOOD idleness
IDLENESS dolce far niente
IDOCRASE silicate of lime   mn
IDOLATER a heretic
IDOLATRY image worship
IDOLIZED idolised
IDOLIZER a fan
IGNATIAN (St Ignatius)   rl
IGNITING kindling; inflaming
IGNITION firing; lighting
IGNITRON mercury arc rectifier   el
IGNOMINY public disgrace; obloquy
IGNORANT uninstructed; unaware
IGNORING disregarding; overlooking
ILLAPSED glided
ILLATION inference
ILLATIVE deducive

ILL-BLOOD enmity; discord; rancour
ILL-FATED calamitous; unlucky
ILL-FAURD ill-favoured (Sc.)
ILLINIUM metallic element   ch
ILLIQUID financial
ILL-TIMED ill-judged
ILL-TREAT maltreat
ILLUDING deceiving
ILLUMINE enlighten; irradiate
ILLUMING elucidating
ILL-USAGE harsh treatment
ILLUSION delusion dream; fantasy
ILLUSIVE } deceptive; fugitive;
ILLUSORY } hallucinatory
ILLYRIAN a Yugoslav
ILMENITE titanate of iron   mn
IMAGINAL relating to an image   zo
IMAGINED fancied; thought
IMAGINER dreamer
IMBANDED banded together
IMBANKED embanked
IMBATHED immersed
IMBECILE idiot; moron; Bedlamite
IMBEDDED firmly fixed
IMBELLIC pacific
IMBIBING absorbing; swallowing
IMBITION dye transfer   pg
IMBOWING arching
IMBRUING drenching
IMBRUTED degenerated
IMBUMENT deep tincture
IMBURSED supplied with cash
IMITABLE easy to forge
IMITANCY mimicry
IMITATED parodied; aped
IMITATOR copy-cat; impersonator
IMMANELY savagely; brutally
IMMANENT inherent; innate
IMMANITY cruelty; inhumanity
IMMANTLE to cloak
IMMANUEL Emmanuel
IMMASKED disguised
IMMATURE unripe; crude; untimely
IMMERGED } submerged; soused;
IMMERSED } plunged; inundated
IMMESHED entangled; ensnared
IMMINENT impending; perilous
IMMINGLE mix; blend; amalgamate
IMMITTED injected; introduced
IMMIXING mingling; combining
IMMOBILE still; motionless; static
IMMODEST bold; indelicate; coarse
IMMOLATE sacrifice; surrender
IMMORTAL imperishable; deathless
IMMUNITY privilege; freedom
IMMUNIZE immunise; exempt
IMPACTED collided; struck
IMPAIRED enfeebled; blemished
IMPAIRER saboteur; marrer
IMPALING transfixing
IMPALMED grasped; handled

IMPANATE to sandwich
IMPARITY inequality; disproportion
IMPARKED enclosed
IMPARLED conversed; discussed
IMPARTED communicated; divulged
IMPARTER bestower; donator
IMPASTED kneaded
IMPAWNED pledged; mortgaged
IMPEDING obstructing; thwarting
IMPELLED urged; induced; drove
IMPELLER instigator; inciter
IMPENDED threatened; hovered
IMPENNED enclosed; encompassed
IMPERIAL short beard; a goatee
IMPERIUM sovereignty
IMPETIGO an eruption   md
IMPIERCE bore; drill
IMPINGER dust-measuring device   mn
IMPISHLY mischievously; wantonly
IMPLATED sheathed
IMPLEACH interweave
IMPLEDGE pawn; hypothecate
IMPLICIT tacit; implied; inferred
IMPLORED entreated; craved
IMPLORER supplicant; petitioner
IMPLUMED plucked
IMPLUNGE immerse; dive
IMPLYING indicating; connoting
IMPOCKET filch; steal
IMPOISON envenom; infect
IMPOLICY inexpedience
IMPOLITE positively rude; insolent
IMPONENT a backer; imposer; con-man
IMPONING wagering; betting
IMPOROUS gas-tight; impermeable
IMPORTED conveyed; denoted
IMPORTER foreign dealer
IMPOSING impressive; stately
IMPOSTOR trickster; charlatan
IMPOTENT helpless; incapable
IMPRIMIS in the first place
IMPRISON incarcerate; immure
IMPROPER unseemly; indelicate
IMPROVED bettered; amended
IMPROVER developer; rectifier
IMPUDENT saucy; shameless
IMPUGNED gainsaid; contradicted
IMPUGNER attacker; assailant
IMPUNITY exemption; immunity
IMPURELY unchastely; licentiously
IMPURITY an adulterant
IMPURPLE empurple
IMPUTING charging; insinuating
INACTION inertia; sloth; indolence
INACTIVE idle; torpid; supine
INAQUATE turn into water
INARABLE unfit for tillage
INASMUCH because
INAURATE gild
INBONDED brick-laying technique
INCAGING confining; mewing

INCANTON merge into a canton
INCARNED incarnated
INCASING encasing; enclosing
INCASKED barrelled
INCAVATE hollow out
INCENSED inflamed; enraged   hd
INCENSOR incense burner
INCEPTOR beginner; inaugurator
INCERTUM early rubble-filled masonry **bd**
INCHMEAL gradually
INCHOATE begun; immature; incipient
INCIDENT episode; event; casual
INCIRCLE encircle; encompass
INCISELY clear cut; acutely
INCISING scribing; engraving
INCISION cut; gash; slit
INCISIVE trenchant; sarcastic
INCISORY sharpness
INCISURA body notch; scar
INCISURE a cut; wound   pl
INCITANT stimulant; provocative
INCITING goading; arousing; spurring
INCIVISM lack of communal spirit
INCLINED disposed; biased; tilted
INCLINER sloping dial
INCLOSED enclosed; penned; enfolded
INCLOSER a fencer of common land
INCLUDED contained; embodied
INCOMING entrance; arrival
INCOMITY incivility; rudeness
INCORPSE incorporate (obs.)
INCREASE aggravate; augment
INCREATE create within
INCUBATE hatch
INCUBOUS (leaf formation)   bt
INCUDATE characteristic of rotifera   zo
INCUMBER encumber; hinder
INCURRED contracted; ran into
INCURVED bent
INCUSING stamping
INCUSSED forged; struck
INDAGATE investigate
INDAMINE used in dye-making   ch
INDEBTED under obligation
INDECENT unbecoming; coarse
INDENTED notched; toothed
INDEVOTE disloyal; unloving
INDEVOUT irreverent; impious
INDEXING compiling an index
INDIAMAN trading ship   nt
INDICANT symptomatic
INDICATE show; suggest; denote
INDICTED impeached; charged
INDICTEE a defendant
INDICTER an accuser
INDIGENE a native; aboriginal
INDIGENT poor; needy; necessitous
INDIRECT devious; tortuous; oblique
INDITING dictating; writing; penning
INDOCILE intractible; stubborn
INDOLENT lazy; sluggish; inert

INDORSED sanctioned; ratified
INDORSEE endorsee
INDORSER ratifier; confirmer
INDRENCH soak; saturate; steep
INDUCING actuating; urging
INDUCTED invested; installed   rl
INDUCTOR officiating minister
INDULGED gratified; humoured
INDULGER favourer
INDULINE a dye   ch
INDURATE harden; inure
INDUSIAL (caterpillar skins)   zo
INDUSIUM skin or cover   bt
INDUSTRY trade; assiduity; diligence
INDUVIAE withered leaves   bt
INEDIBLE uneatable
INEDITED unpublished
INEQUITY injustice; unfairness
INERMOUS no prickles   bt
INERTION sluggishness; indolence
INEXPERT unskilled; unversed
INFAMING defaming; discrediting
INFAMISE) publicly brand
INFAMIZE)   with infamy
INFAMOUS vile; notorious; heinous
INFANTLY childishly; infantile
INFANTRY foot-soldiers
INFECTED tainted; corrupted
INFECTER carrier of disease
INFECUND sterile; barren; unprolific
INFERIAE Roman sacrifices
INFERIOR poor; subordinate; mediocre
INFERNAL diabolical; fiendish; satanic
INFERRED deduced; argued; surmised
INFESTED overrun; thronged; beset
INFILTER permeate; seep
INFINITE boundless; unlimited
INFINITO perpetual   mu
INFINITY immensity
INFIRMLY irresolutely; feebly
INFLAMED exasperated; infuriated
INFLAMER agent provocateur
INFLATED distended; bloated; swollen
INFLATOR air-pump
INFLATUS inspiration
INFLEXED bent inwards
INFLOWED ran in
INFLUENT a tributary
INFOLDED embraced
INFORMAL unconventional; simple
INFORMED told; apprised; notified
INFORMER a sneak
INFRA-DIG beneath one's social standing
INFRA-RED beyond red in spectrum
INFRINGE violate; transgress
INFRUGAL prodigal; extravagant
INFUMATE to smoke
INFUSING inculcating; inspiring
INFUSION instillation; introduction
INFUSIVE penetrative
INFUSORY protozoic   zo

INGENIUM bent of mind		
INGROOVE engroove; furrow		
INGROWTH opposite of outgrowth		
INGUINAL (groin)	md	
INGULFED swallowed up		
INHALANT a vapourizer	md	
INHALING breathing		
INHERENT innate; congenital		
INHERING sticking fast		
INHERSED coffined		
INHESION inherence		
INHOOPED encaged; cooped		
INHUMING burying; interring		
INIMICAL allergic; hostile; contrary		
INIQUITY vice; sinfulness; offence		
INITIATE a novice; start; inaugurate		
INJECTED forced in; introduced		
INJECTOR kind of pump		
INJURING damaging; maltreating		
INKINESS state of being inky		
INKMAKER squid		
INKSTAND ink-holder		
INK-STONE sulphate of iron	mn	
INLACING enlacing		
INLANDER not an islander		
INLAWING clearing of attainder		
INLAYING ornamenting		
INLOCKED locked up		
INNATELY instinctively; naturally		
INNERVED invigorated		
INNOCENT guileless; blameless; sinless		
INNOVATE make changes; alter		
INNUENDO an insinuation		
INORNATE plain		
INOSITOL yeast growth agent	ch	
INQUIRED asked; investigated		
INQUIRER questioner; scrutineer		
INRAILED enclosed	nt	
INRIGGED with rowlocks on gunwhale	nt	
INSANELY crazily; deliriously		
INSANITY dementia; mania; lunacy		
INSCIENT ignorant; illiterate; unread		
INSCONCE ensconce; hide; lurk		
INSCRIBE dedicate; engrave; imprint		
INSCROLL write on a scroll		
INSEAMED marked by a seam		
INSECTED segmented		
INSECURE uncertain; hazardous		
INSERTED introduced; injected		
INSETTED implanted		
INSHADED tinted		
INSHRINE enshrine; dedicate		
INSIGNIA badges; emblems; tokens		
INSISTED persisted; maintained; urged		
INSITION ingraftment		
INSNARED entangled; caught; ginned		
INSNARER trapper		
INSOLATE dry in the sun		
INSOLENT contumacious; hubristic		
INSOMNIA sleeplessness	md	
INSOMUCH so that		

INSPHERE ensphere; englobe		
INSPIRED inhaled; animated		
INSPIRER spiritual leader		
INSPIRIT enhearten; infuse		
INSTABLE unstable; transient		
INSTANCE specify; occurrence; incident		
INSTANCY urgency; solicitation		
INSTATED established		
INSTINCT natural propensity		
INSTREAM to flow		
INSTRUCT edify; direct; enjoin; order		
INSTYLED entitled; named; yclept		
INSUCKEN milling restriction	lw	
INSULATE isolate; enisle		
INSULTED affronted; outraged		
INSULTER taunter; abuser; offender		
INSURANT policy holder		
INSURING assuring; underwriting		
INTAGLIO opposite to cameo		
INTARSIA pictorial inlay		
INTEGRAL whole; entire; complete		
INTENDED betrothed; meant; purposed		
INTENDER contemplator		
INTENTLY with fixed attention		
INTERACT theatrical interval		
INTER-COM inter-communication		
INTEREST concern; attention; discount		
INTERIOR inside; inward; inner		
INTERLAY insert		
INTERMIT suspend		
INTERMIX blend; commingle		
INTERNAL domestic; within; inside		
INTERNED confined; imprisoned		
INTERNEE arrested alien		
INTERPOL international criminal police		
INTERRED buried; inhumed; entombed		
INTERREX a regent; protector		
INTERTIE connecting piece		
INTERVAL gap; pause; interim		
INTER-WAR of period between wars		
INTEXINE pollen cover	bt	
INTIMACY familiarity; friendship		
INTIMATE near; close; declare		
INTIMITY inwardness		
INTONATE intone		
INTONING chanting		
INTRADOS lower surface of arch		
INTRENCH encroach; infringe; trespass		
INTREPID dauntless; doughty; daring		
INTRIGUE cabal; interest; conspiracy		
INTROMIT insert; admit		
INTRORSE facing inwards		
INTRUDED butted in; thrusted		
INTRUDER trespasser; interloper		
INTUBATE insert a tube		
INUNDANT overflowing; overwhelming		
INUNDATE flood; swamp; deluge		
INURBANE rude; uncouth; discourteous		
INURNING putting in an urn		
INUSTION a branding		
INVADING violating; raiding; entering		

INVARIED set; constant; uniform		
INVASION foray; attack; assault		
INVASIVE aggressive		
INVECKED ⎫ scalloped		
INVECTED ⎭		
INVECTED engrailed		hd
INVEIGLE entice; wheedle; decoy; lure		
INVEILED veiled		
INVENTED devised; created; fabricated		
INVENTOR innovator; contriver		
INVERTER conversion device		el
INVESTED arrayed; indued; beset		
INVESTOR buyer; purchaser		
INVITING attractive; alluring		
INVOCATE adjure; invoke; beseech		
INVOICED billed		
INVOKING conjuring; summoning		
INVOLUTE spiral		
INVOLVED complicated; complex		
INWALLED enclosed		
INWARDLY privily; secretly		
INWORKED inset		
IODAZIDE iodine azide		ch
IODIZING (iodine)		md
IODOFORM an antiseptic		md
IODYRITE iodide of silver		ch
IOLANTHE a fairy; an opera		mu
IONICIZE Grecianize		
IONIZING electrolysing		
IOTACISM excessive use of 'I'		
IREFULLY angrily; furiously		
IRENICAL tranquil; pacific		
IRENICON peace propaganda		
IRIDITIS eye inflammation		md
IRISATED like a rainbow		
IRISCOPE spectroscope		
IRISHISM Celtic expression, humorous		
IRISHMAN (Ireland)		
IRONBARK eucalyptus		bt
IRONCLAD plated		
IRON-CLAY yellow iron ore		mn
IRONGREY a colour		
IRONICAL satirical; sarcastic; derisive		
IRON-SAND firework mixture		mn
IRONSICK rusty and leaky		
IRONSIDE a Cromwellian		
IRONWARE ironmongery		
IRONWOOD tough timber		bt
IRONWORK smithery		
IRRIGATE supply with water; moisten		
IRRISION derision; banter		
IRRITANT annoying; exasperating		
IRRITATE gall; nettle; provoke		
IRRORATE as if dew-covered		bt
IRRUPTED burst in; invaded; raided		
ISABELLE yellowish grey		
ISAGOGIC introductory		
ISENGRIM a fabulous wolf		zo
ISLAMISM Mohammedanism		rl
ISLAMITE worshipper of Allah		rl
ISLAMIZE proselytize		rl

ISLANDED isolated
ISLANDER not an inlander
ISLESMAN (from the Hebrides)
ISOBARIC (equal barometric pressure)   mt
ISOCHEIM line indicating equal winter temperatures
ISOCHELA equal-jointed chela   zo
ISOCHORE gas pressure and temperature
ISOCORIA equal size of eye pupils
ISOCRYME line indicating equal winter temperatures
ISODICON short anthem   rl
ISODOMON ⎫ masonry composed of
ISODOMUM ⎭ uniform blocks
ISOGONAL equi-angular
ISOGONIC (equal magnetic angles)
ISOLATED solitary
ISOLOGUE like/unlike compound   ch
ISOMERIC ⎫ different properties   ch
ISONYMIC ⎭ of similar compounds
ISOPATHY homeopathy   md
ISOPLETH map showing weather constituents
ISOPRENE synthetic rubber   ch
ISOSTASY equal-pressure-caused equilibrium
ISOSTERE atmospheric volume line   mt
ISOTHERE (equal summer heat)
ISOTHERM line of equal heat
ISOTONIC having equal tones
ISOTOPIC of isotopes
ISSUABLE distributable
ISSUANCE delivery
ISTHMIAN Corinthian
ITALIOTE a Greek colonist in Italy
ITCH-MITE burrowing insect   zo
ITERANCE repetition
ITERATED repeated; recapitulated
ITHURIEL cherub; guardian angel
IVORY-NUT a palm-nut   bt

J

JABBERED gabbled; chattered
JABBERER wind-bag
JACKAROO greenhorn squatter (Aust.)
JACKETED having a paper cover
JACKFISH pike   zo
JACK-FLAG smaller than ensign   nt
JACK-FOOL perfect fool
JACK-KNIFE diving; sport
JACKWOOD jaca-tree   bt
JACKYARD a boom   nt
JACOBEAN (James I)
JACOBITE partisan of James II
JACQUARD loom mechanism   wv
JACULATE to throw; to dart
JAGGEDLY raggedly; unevenly
JAILBIRD old lag
JALOUSIE Venetian blind

JAMAICAN (Jamaica)
JAMBEAUS leggings
JAMBOREE rally; boisterous frolic
JAMPANEE chair carrier
JANGLING wrangling
JANICEPS 2-headed monstrosity   md
JANUFORM double-faced
JAPANESE of Japan
JAPANNED varnished; enamelled
JAPANNER a shoeblack
JAPAN-WAX lacquer from sumac tree berries
JAPHETIC Armenian alphabet
JAPONICA Japanese quince   bt
JARARAKA poisonous snake   zo
JAROSITE iron-potassium sulphate   mn
JASPONYX an onyx   mn
JAUNDICE bile-obstruction disorder   md
JAUNTIER more sprightly
JAUNTILY debonairly
JAUNTING an outing
JAVANESE an Indonesian
JAVELINA wild boar   zo
JAW-LEVER veterinary instrument
JAW-TOOTH a molar   pl
JEALOUSY green-eyed monster
JEANETTE coarse cloth   tx
JEBUSITE a Canaanite
JEHOVIST Hebrew Theologian   rl
JELLYBAG a strainer
JELUTONG pale Malayan hardwood   fr
JENTLING Danube chub   zo
JEOPARDY danger; peril; hazard; risk
JEREMIAD lamentation
JEROBOAM super champagne bottle
JERQUING customs searching   nt
JERRICAN 5 gallon (22 litres) petrol tin
JEST-BOOK collection of jokes
JESUITIC, JESUITRY craftiness, cunning
JET-BLACK deepest black
JET-CRAFT }
JET-PLANE } jet propelled aircraft
JETTISON throw overboard   nt
JETTYING projecting
JEWELLED set with gems
JEWELLER a craftsman with gems
JEWISHLY judaical
JEW'S-HARP small mouth instrument   mu
JICKAJOG a shake; a push
JIGGERED flabbergasted
JIGGLING wriggling; joggling
JIGMAKER a tool-maker
JINGLING tinkling; rhyming
JINGOISH super-patriotic
JINGOISM ultra-patriotism
JOBATION a tedious scolding
JOCKEYED jostled; outwitted; deluded
JOCOSELY facetiously; joyously
JOCOSITY sportiveness; fun
JOCUNDLY mirthfully; waggishly

JODHPURS riding breeches
JOGGLING shaking; jostling; elbowing
JOHANNES old Portugese gold coin   nm
JOIN-HAND connected script
JOINT-ILL umbilicus disease   vt
JOINTING finishing joints between timbers/bricks   bd
JOINT-OIL synovia
JOINTURE a settlement
JOISTING fitting with laths
JOKINGLY in jest; hilariously
JOLLIEST very merry and bright
JOLT-HEAD dunderhead
JONGLEUR wandering minstrel   mu
JORDANON faintly varied breeding race   bt
JOSTLING pushing; hustling; crowding
JOUNCING shaking; jolting (slang)
JOUSTING a tourney
JOVIALLY festively; blithely
JOVIALTY merriment; conviviality
JOYFULLY rapturously; gladly
JOYOUSLY blissfully; happily
JOYSTICK aeroplane control lever   ae
JUBILANT triumphant; exulting
JUBILATE celebrate; rejoice
JUDAICAL Jewish   rl, lw
JUDAIZED conformed to Mosaic law
JUDAIZER opponent of St Paul
JUDGMENT sentence; decree; award
JUDICIAL legal; legitimate; sagacious
JUGGLERY manual dexterity
JUGGLING conjuring; swindling
JUGO-SLAV Yugoslav
JULIENNE clear soup
JUMBLING confusing; mixing
JUMP-SEAT collapsible seat
JUNCTION union; coalition; coupling
JUNCTURE crisis; exigency; strait
JUNKETED feasted; caroused
JUNK-RING piston-packing
JUNONIAN queenly
JURASSIC geological period   gl
JURATORY comprising an oath
JURISTIC legal jurisdictive
JURYMAST temporary mast   nt
JUSTLING jostling; jolting
JUSTNESS equity; impartiality
JUVENILE young; puerile; adolescent

K

KAILWIFE cabbage-seller; a scold (Sc.)
KAILYARD kitchen-garden (Sc.)
KAKEMONO Japanese picture
KALA-AZAR black fever   md
KALAMDAN Persian writing case
KALAMKAR Indian printed cotton   tx

KALENDAR calendar; almanac	
KALERUNT cabbage stalk	bt
KALEVALA Finnish epic	
KALEYARD kitchen-garden	bt
KALINITE alum	mn
KALIYUGA Hindu mythological era	
KALOLOGY science of beauty	
KALOTYPE early photograph	
KAMADEVA Indian Eros	
KAMIKAZE suicide bomb; plane (Jap.)	
KANARESE language (Mysore, India)	
KANDAHAR East Indian wool	tx
KANGAROO a marsupial	zo
KANTIKOY religious dance	rl, mu
KARELIAN (Finno-Russian)	
KARYOTIN nuclear reticulum substance	cy
KASHMIRI people and language (Kashmir)	
KATABION katabolic-predominant organism	bl
KATAKANA Japanese script	
KAURI-GUM a resin (Aust.)	bt
KAYMAKAM Turkish Governor	
KECKLING binding rope	nt
KEDGEREE a breakfast-dish	
KEEL-BOAT type of yacht	nt
KEEL-HAUL (punishment)	nt
KEENNESS acuity; astuteness	
KEEPSAKE memento; relic	
KENETRON large vacuum diode	el
KENOTRON wireless valve	ro
KERASINE, KERATOSE horn	
KERATOMA skin tumour	md
KERCHIEF a head cover	
KERMESSE annual fair in Low Countries	
KERN-BABY harvest image	bt
KERNELLY full of seeds	bt
KEROSENE paraffin	mn
KETOXIME ketone reaction product	ch
KEYBLOCK printing	
KEYBOARD clavier	mu
KEY-BUGLE Kent bugle	mu
KEY-FRUIT ash, sycamore, etc.	bt
KEY-MONEY levy on a tenant	
KEYPLATE keyhole escutcheon	
KEYPUNCH punch-card recording system	cp
KEYSTONE main arch support	ar
KIBITZER critical observer (USA)	
KICKABLE suitable for booting	
KICK-DOWN switch	
KICKSHAW a fallal	
KID-GLOVE soft delicate glove	
KIEFEKIL meerschaum	mn
KIELBASA smoked Polish sausage	
KILL-CROP a changeling	
KILLDEER American plover	zo
KILLOGIE a kiln (Sc.)	
KILL-TIME a pastime	
KILN-HOLE mouth of kiln	
KILODYNE 1000 dynes	me
KILOGRAM 1000 grams	me

KILOWATT 1000 watts	me
KINDLESS unnatural; merciless	
KINDLIER more forbearing	
KINDLING animating; tinder	
KINDNESS benevolence; generosity	
KINEMICS gestural expression	
KINESICS gestural body movements	
KINETICS dynamics	
KINGBIRD American fly-catcher	zo
KING-CRAB tropical crab	zo
KINGFISH the opah	zo
KINGHOOD sovereignty	
KINGLESS republican	
KINGLIKE truly regal	
KINGLING ruler of petty state	
KINGPOST principal strut	
KINGSHIP kingcraft	
KINGWANA language	
KINGWOOD ebony (S. Amer.)	bt
KINKAJOU raccoon; honey-bear	zo
KINSFOLK kindred; relations	
KIPPERED cured	
KIRIKANE gold foil application (Jap.)	
KIRKYARD graveyard	rl
KIROUMBO tropical bird	zo
KISS-CURL a tempting lock	
KISTVAEN stone sepulchre	
KITEFOOT a tobacco plant	bt
KITTENED had a kitty litter	
KITTLISH ticklish	
KLYSTRON electron converter	
KNABBING gnawing	
KNACKISH knavish	
KNAPPING flint breaking	
KNAPSACK haversack; rucksack	
KNAPWEED bachelor's buttons	bt
KNEADING dough work	
KNEE-DEEP ⎫ nearly thigh high	
KNEE-HIGH ⎭	
KNEEHOLM knee-holly	bt
KNEELING kotowing	
KNEE-STOP organ lever	mu
KNELLING tolling	
KNICKERS knickerbockers	
KNIFE-BOY scullery lad	
KNIGHTED now Sir?	
KNIGHTLY courtly	
KNIT-BONE herb comfrey	bt
KNITTING uniting; interlacing	
KNITWEAR reticulated fabric	
KNOCKING rapping; hitting; motoring	
KNOCK-OUT K.O.; dealer's auction	
KNOLLING knelling	
KNOTLESS free from ties	
KNOTTIER more intricate	
KNOTTING securing; entangling	
KNOTWORK ornamental work	
KNOUTING scourging	
KNOWABLE ascertainable; scibile	
KNOW-ALLS wiseacres	
KNUCKLED yielded; jointed	

KOFTGARI } inlaying steel with gold
KOFTWORK }
KOHELETH Preacher (Solomon)   rl
KOHINOOR famous diamond   mn
KOHLRABI cole-turnip   bt
KOLINSKY Siberian mink   zo
KOMITAJI Balkan guerilla band
KONISTRA orchestra of a Greek theatre
KOORBASH } whip made from
KOURBASH }   rhino hide
KOTOWING making obeisance
KREASOTE creasote   ch
KREUTZER small Austrian copper coin nm
KUKUKUKU people (New Guinea)
KURVEYOR transport rider (S. Afr.)
KYANIZED cyanized   ch
KYLOSSIS club-foot   md
KYPHOSIS vertebral deformity   md

L

LABDANUM ladanum   ch
LABELLED directed
LABELLUM lower petal   bt
LABIALLY lipwise
LABIATED lipped
LABILITY quick emotional variations pc
LABOURED strove
LABOURER a toiler
LABSKAUS meat/vegetable stew (Scand.)
                                     ck
LABURNIC derived from laburnum
LABURÑUM flowering tree   bt
LACE-BARK bark of a tree   bt
LACE-BOOT (no buttons)
LACE-LEAF aquatic plant   bt
LACERATE tear
LACEWING an insect   zo
ŁACEWORK decoration
LACE-YOKE needlework
LACHESIS one of the Fates
LACING-IN attaching end-boards to book
  body
LACK-A-DAY sorrowful exclamation
LACKEYED valeted
LACONISM brevity; pithiness
LACROSSE a Canadian game
LACRYMAL tearful
LACTEOUS milk-like
LACTIFIC milk producing
LACTUCIC (lettuce)   bt
LACUNOSE pitted; furrowed
LADDERED (stockings)
LADLEFUL a measure
LADYBACK tandem cycle
LADYBIRD a helpful beetle   zo
LADY-FERN tall slender fern   bt
LADY-HELP distressed gentlewoman
LADYHOOD gentility
LADYLIKE well-bred; delicate
LADYLOVE a sweetheart

LADYSHIP a title
LAGTHING Norwegian upper house
LAICIZED opened to the laity
LAITANCE milky mortar scum   bd
LAKE-LIKE merely?
LAMANTIN the manatee   zo
LAMASERY Tibetan monastery   rl
LAMBDOID lambda-shaped (Gr.)
LAMBENCY play of light
LAMBLIKE gentle; meek
LAMBLING lambkin   zo
LAMBSKIN soft fleece
LAME-DUCK a bankrupt
LAMELLAR of thin plates
LAMENESS halting; crippledness
LAMENTED deeply regretted
LAMENTER deplorer; bewailer
LAMINARY in thin plates
LAMINATE in layers
LAMPHOLE sewer lighting shaft
LAMP-POST support for drunk
LANCEGAY a kind of spear
LANCELET primitive vertebrate   zo
LAND-CRAB land-dwelling crustacean   zo
LANDFALL landslip   nt
LAND-FISH fish out of water
LAND-GIRL wartime farm help
LAND-HERD a herd of animals   zo
LANDLADY mine hostess
LANDLESS no holding
LANDLINE overhead cable
LANDLOCK protect from wind and sea
LANDLORD mine host
LANDMARK notable event
LANDMINE parachuted bomb
LANDNAMA Domesday Book (Ice.)
LANDRAIL corncrake   zo
LAND-ROLL clod-crusher
LAND-SHIP a tank
LANDSLIP landslide
LANDSMAN cf. seaman
LAND-TURN land-breeze
LANDWARD rural
LANDWEHR German militia
LAND-WIND off-shore wind
LANGLAUF cross-country skiing (Ger.)
LANGRAGE grape shot
LANGSHAN black Chinese hen   zo
LANGSYNE time long past
LANGUAGE diction; vernacular
LANGUISH pine; droop; decline
LANIATED torn to pieces
LANKIEST leanest
LANKNESS length without breadth
LANNERET small falcon
LANOLINE wool fat
LANTHORN hornsided lantern
LAP-BOARD board used by tailors
LAPELLED with lapels
LAPIDARY stone-cutter
LAPIDATE pelt with stones

LAPIDIFY turn into stone	
LAPIDIST stone-worker	
LAPILLUS fragment of lava	mn
LAP-JOINT an overlapping joint	
LAPPETED with flaps	
LAPSABLE terminal; transient	
LAPSTONE (used by a shoemaker)	
LARBOARD port	nt
LARCENER a thief; pilferer	
LARDERER a store keeper	
LARGESSE liberality; generosity	
LARKSPUR a delphinium	bt
LARRIKIN Australian hooligan	
LARVATED masked	zo
LASER-RAY searing ray	md
LASH-DOWN secure firmly	nt
LASSLORN jilted	
LAST-FOLD last folded sheet in a book	
LATCH-KEY domestic open sesame	
LATENESS tardiness	
LATENTLY secretly; apparently not	
LATERITE brick-clay	mn
LATHERED soapy; larruped	
LATHWORK lath and plaster	
LATINISM Latin idiom	
LATINIST Latin scholar	
LATINITY purity of Latin style	
LATINIZE latinise	
LATITUDE width; scope; laxity	
LATTERLY more recently; lately	
LATTICED cross-barred	
LAUDABLE praiseworthy; honourable	
LAUDABLY commendably	
LAUDANUM an opiate	md
LAUGHING riant	
LAUGHTER convulsive merriment	
LAUNCHED hurled; began; initiated	
LAUREATE crowned with laurel	
LAVA-LIKE hard and full of holes	
LAVATION washing; purification	
LAVATORY a wash-house	
LAVENDER greyish blue	bt
LAVEROCK skylark	zo
LAVISHED spent; squandered	
LAVISHLY prodigally; wastefully	
LAWFULLY legally; justly; validly	
LAWGIVER a legislator; a Solon	lw
LAWMAKER an M.P.	
LAWYERLY verbose	
LAXATION relaxation; slackness	
LAXATIVE opening mixture	md
LAY-ABOUT lazy; good for nothing	
LAY-CLERK a responder	rl
LAY-ELDER Presbyterian elder	rl
LAYERING horticultural process	
LAYSTALL byre	
LAYSTOOL table for newly printed/clean paper	
LAZARIST R.C. missionary	rl
LAZARONE Neapolitan beggar	
LAZINESS inertness; slackness	

LAZULITE a blue stone	mn
LAZURITE lapis lazuli constituent	mn
LEACHING making an alkali	
LEAD-MILL lapidary's plate	
LEADSMAN a lead-swinger	nt
LEAF-LARD leaf-fat lard	
LEAFLESS destitute of leaves	
LEAFSCAR a mark	bt
LEAGUING confederating; coalescing	
LEANFACE narrow-width type	pr
LEANNESS thinness; gauntness	
LEAPFROG a game	
LEAP-YEAR a year of 366 days	
LEARNING scholarship; erudition	
LEASABLE able to be let	
LEASHING binding; securing	
LEATHERN made of leather	
LEATHERY tough	
LEAVENED modified; tempered	
LEAVINGS residue; relics	
LEBANESE a native of Lebanon	
LECANORA lichen; manna	bt
LECITHIN egg tissue	
LECTURED reprimanded; chided	
LECTURER an expositor	
LED-HORSE spare horse	
LEE-BOARD anti-drift device	nt
LEECHING doctoring	md
LEEFANGE sheet guide	nt
LEE-SHORE windward shore	nt
LEFT-HAND sinister	
LEFTWARD to the left	
LEFT-WING (politics)	
LEGACIES bequests; gifts	
LEGALISE authorise; sanction	
LEGALISM adherence to law	lw
LEGALIST stickler for law	
LEGALITY lawfulness	
LEGALIZE sanction; warrant	
LEGATARY legatee	lw
LEGATINE relating to a legate	
LEGATION an embassy	
LEG-BREAK (cricket)	
LEGERITY lightness	
LEGUMINA pods	bt
LEGUMINE nitrogenous proteid	bt
LEMONADE a soft drink	
LEMUROID, LEMURINE monkey-like	zo
LENDABLE loanable	
LENGTHEN extend; elongate; protract	
LENIENCE } mildness; clemency;	
LENIENCY } mercifulness; forbearance	
LENINISM, LENINIST follower of Lenin	
LENITIVE mitigating; sedative	
LENS-HOOD light-shield	pg
LENTANDO slowing up	mu
LENTICEL cell-formation	bt
LENTICLE lenslike mass	gl
LENT-LILY daffodil	bt
LEPEROUS leprous	md

LEPIDOID ganoid; scaly	**zo**	
LEPIDOTE with scalelike hairs	**bt, zo**	
LEPORINE like a hare	**zo**	
LESSENED diminished; decreased		
LETHARGY dullness; apathy; oblivion		
LETTERED learned; printed		
LEUCITIC containing volcanic ore	**mn**	
LEUCOSIS pallor; albinism	**md**	
LEVANTED decamped; welshed		
LEVANTER N. African wind		
LEVELLED flattened; raged; demolished		
LEVELLER ultra-republican, 1649		
LEVERAGE mechanical advantage		
LEVERING exerting pressure		
LEVIABLE taxable; imposable		
LEVIGATE to smooth; to polish		
LEVIRATE Hebrew marriage custom		
LEVITATE cause to float		
LEVITIES frivolities; flippancies		
LEVOLOSE fruit sugar		
LEWDNESS licentiousness		
LEWDSTER a profligate		
LEWISITE poison gas	**ch**	
LIBATION a drink-offering		
LIBATORY oblatory		
LIBELLED slandered; defamed		
LIBELLER lampooner; calumniator		
LIBERATE set free; emancipate		
LIBERIAN (Liberia)		
LIBRATED balanced		
LIBRETTO words of musical play		
LICENSED authorized; allowed		
LICENSEE holder of a license		
LICENSER licence issuer		
LICHENIC made from lichen	**bt**	
LICHENIN moss starch		
LICHGATE lychgate		
LICHWAKE likewake; death-watch		
LICKER-IN toothed carding roller	**tx**	
LICORICE liquorice	**bt**	
LIEGEMAN vassal; henchman	**nt**	
LIFEBELT ⎫ marine lifesaving		
LIFEBOAT ⎭ equipment		
LIFEBUOY floating navigation marker		
LIFEHOLD lease for life	**lw**	
LIFELESS dull; inanimate; extinct		
LIFELIKE as if living		
LIFELINE vital cord		
LIFELONG till death		
LIFE-PEER (not hereditary)		
LIFE-RAFT (for shipwreck)	**nt**	
LIFE-RATE (life insurance)		
LIFE-RENT rent during lifetime	**lw**	
LIFE-SIZE full scale		
LIFE-TIME an uncertain period		
LIFE-WORK reason for a career		
LIFTABLE capable of elevation		
LIGAMENT binder; tendon		
LIGASOID gaseous/liquid colloidal system		
	ps	
LIGATING binding; bandaging	**md**	

LIGATION a fastening	
LIGATURE bandage; band	**mu**
LIGHTFUL cheery; happy; radiant	
LIGHTING illuminating; kindling	
LIGHTISH not heavy; fickle	
LIGNEOUS wooden	
LIGNITIC (lignite; brown coal)	**mn**
LIGULATE straplike	
LIGURITE pea-green gem	**mn**
LIKEABLE pleasant enough	
LIKENESS resemblance; similarity	
LIKENING comparing	
LIKEWAKE lichwake; death-watch	
LIKEWISE also; moreover; besides	
LILACINE extract of lilac	**bt**
LILLIPUT miniature	
LILY-IRON harpoon for swordfish	
LILY-STAR feather-star	**bt**
LIMACOID like a slug	**zo**
LIMATION filing; polishing	
LIMATURE filings	
LIMA-WOOD Peruvian red-wood	**bt**
LIME-FREE clear of calcium	
LIME-KILN a furnace	
LIMERICK verse often perverse	
LIME-SINK a depression	
LIME-TREE linden tree	**bt**
LIME-TWIG a snare	
LIME-WASH whitewash	
LIMEWORT lychnis viscaria	**bt**
LIMITARY finite; bounded	
LIMITING confining; restricting	
LIMONITE haematite ore	**mn**
LINAMENT lint	**md**
LINARITE a lead compound	**mn**
LINCHPIN keeps the wheel on	
LINCTURE linctus; medicine	**md**
LINEALLY in a direct line	
LINEARLY directly	
LINE-FISH fish taken on a line	
LINELLAE filament system in sarcodina	**zo**
LINESMAN referee's assistant	
LING-BIRD meadow-pipit	**zo**
LINGERED lagged; delayed; tarried	
LINGERER dawdler; loiterer; dallier	
LINGERIE undies	
LINGUIST seldom tongue-tied?	
LINIMENT embrocation	
LINNAEUS eminent botanist (1707-78)	
LINOLEUM lino; floorcloth	
LINOTYPE type-setting machine	
LINSTOCK flame-holder	
LIONIZED heroized	
LIPAEMIA fatty blood	**md**
LIPARITE rhyolite; granitic lava rock	**gl**
LIPIODOL X-ray-opaque substance	
LIPO-GRAM (letter omission)	
LIPOSOME fatty/oily globule	**bt**
LIPSTICK a cosmetic	
LIQUABLE fusible; fluent	
LIQUATED liquified	

LIQUIDLY smoothly; fluidal
LIQUIDUS solidification temperature line   ch
LIQUORED in drink; tipsy
LIRIPOOP hood; trick; nincompoop
LIROCONE floury; powdery
LISTENED hearkened; attended; heard
LISTENER eavesdropper
LISTLESS languid; apathetic; torpid
LITERACY ability to read and write
LITERARY erudite; scholarly
LITERATE learned; studious
LITERATI men of letters
LITEROSE bookish
LITHARGE lead oxide   mn
LITHERLY mischievous; lazy
LITIGANT engaged in a lawsuit   lw
LITIGATE to go to law   lw
LITTERED scattered; strewn; deranged
LITTLE-GO examination (Camb.)
LITTORAL a coastal strip
LITURATE blurred; spotted
LITURGIC ritualistic   rl
LIVEABLE habitable; residential
LIVE-AXLE driving axle
LIVE-BAIT sometimes a worm
LIVELILY vivaciously; briskly; alertly
LIVELONG lasting; the orpine   bt
LIVENING cheering up; animating
LIVE-RAIL rail carrying current
LIVERIED in uniform
LIVERIES garbs; uniforms
LIVERISH bilious; testy   md
LIVE-WELL kind of aquarium
LIVE-WIRE human dynamo
LIVIDITY discolouration
LIVINGLY lively; energetically; agilely
LIXIVIAL residual   ch
LIXIVIUM lye; residuum   ch
LOAD-LINE Plimsoll's mark   nt
LOANABLE able to be lent
LOAN-WORD borrowed word
LOATHFUL abhorrent; detestable
LOATHING hating; antipathy
LOBBYING endeavouring to influence
LOBBYIST a journalist
LOBELINE monoacidic alkaloid   ch
LOBLOLLY gruel; lout; attendant
LOCALISM provincialism
LOCALITY situation; district; spot
LOCALIZE assign to a place
LOCATING positioning; fixing
LOCATION film rendezvous
LOCATIVE grammatical case
LOCKFAST firmly fastened
LOCK-GATE (on canal or river)
LOCKLESS without a lock
LOCK-SILL threshold of a lock
LOCKSMAN a turnkey
LOCKSPIT digging mark
LOCK-WEIR weir with lock

LOCO-FOCO lucifer; ultra-radical
LOCULATE } divided
LOCULOSE   internally
LOCULOUS } into cells   bt
LOCUTION diction; phrase
LOCUTORY place for conversation   rl
LODESMAN pilot   nt
LODESTAR pole-star
LODGINGS digs; accommodation
LODGMENT occupation; golf
LODICULE grass stamen scale   bt
LOG-BOARD rough log   nt
LOG-CABIN timber hut
LOG-CANOE dug-out   nt
LOG-GLASS timing device   nt
LOGICIAN one skilled in logic
LOGICIZE deduce from reasoning
LOGISTIC logical
LOGOGRAM puzzle in verse
LOGOTYPE twin letters in printing
LOG-SLATE recording slate   nt
LOITERED lingered; tarried
LOITERER an idler; flaneur
LOKWEAVE carpet-splice
LOLLARDY Lollard doctrine   rl
LOLLIPOP a sweet
LOLLOPED lounged; lurched
LOMENTUM branching fruit   bt
LOMONITE a zeolite   mn
LONDONER city slicker
LONENESS seclusion; solitude
LONESOME solitary
LONGBOAT big rowboat   nt
LONGERON main spar of aeroplane   ae
LONGEVAL long lived
LONG-FIRM swindling company
LONGHAND handwriting
LONG-LEGS daddy long-legs   zo
LONG-MOSS tillandsia   bt
LONG-SHIP a galley   nt
LONG-SLIP (cricket)
LONGSOME tiresome; tedious; irksome
LONG-SPUN protracted; extended
LONG-STOP (cricket)
LONG-TAIL not docked
LONG-TERM far seeing
LONGUEUR tedious patch, padding in lit.
LONGWAYS lengthways
LONGWISE in extenso
LONICERA honey-suckle genus   bt
LOOKER-ON spectator; observer
LOOM-GALE minor gale   mt
LOOP-HOLE an escape
LOOP-LINE alternative route
LOOSE-BOX a stall
LOOSENED undone; relaxed; slackened
LOOSENER a laxative   md
LOP-EARED with drooping ears
LOPOLITH lens-shaped igneous intrusion   gl
LOP-SIDED unbalanced; biased
LORD-LIKE haughty; imperious

LORDLING a would-be lord
LORDOSIS spinal curvature   md
LORD'S-DAY Sunday
LORDSHIP sway; dominion; control
LORICATE to incrust
LORIKEET Australian parrot   zo
LOSINGLY wastefully
LOTHARIO a libertine; a filly-buster
LOUDNESS uproar; clamour; resonance
LOUNGING reclining; lolling; idling
LOVEBIRD a budgerigar   zo
LOVECHILD bastard
LOVEKNOT a tangle
LOVELACE a libertine
LOVELESS passionless; frigid
LOVELIES beauteous damsels
LOVE-LIFE romance
LOVELILY delectably; enchantingly
LOVELOCK a manly curl
LOVELORN jilted
LOVE-NEST romantic abode
LOVESICK languishing
LOVESOME adorable
LOVESUIT courtship
LOVINGLY affectionately; fondly
LOWERING depressing; threatening
LOW-WATER at the ebb
LOYALIST patriot; faithful follower
LUBBERLY clumsily; maladroit
LUCIDITY clearness; luminosity
LUCKIEST most fortunate; happiest
LUCKLESS singularly unfortunate
LUCKY BAG ⎫ a bran pie
LUCKY DIP ⎭ with hidden gifts
LUCULENT translucent; lucid; clear
LUCULLUS an epicure
LUGARITE rare analcite-gabbro form   gl
LUKEWARM tepid
LUMBERED rumbled along
LUMBERER woodman
LUMINANT shining; radiant
LUMINARY a heavenly body
LUMINATE illuminate; brighten
LUMINOUS phosphorescent; lucent
LUMPFISH a sea fish   zo
LUNARIAN a moon observer
LUNATION a lunar month
LUNCHEON midday repast
LUNCHING eating in early afternoon
LUNGEING fencing; horse training
LUNGFISH queer fish   zo
LUNGLESS not breathing
LUNGWORT a lichen   bt
LUNIFORM moon-shaped
LUNULATE like a crescent
LUPERCAL Roman festival
LUPININE lupinus-seed alkaloid   ch
LUPININE a bitter extract   bt
LUPULONE soft hops resin   br
LURCHING stumbling; rolling; lurking
LUSCIOUS rich in flavour

LUSTIEST beefiest; heftiest; sexiest
LUSTRATE purify
LUSTRING silk cloth
LUSTROUS shining; luminous
LUSTWORT the sun-dew   bt
LUTANIST a lute player   mu
LUTATION sealing
LUTECIUM a metallic element   ch
LUTEOLIN yellow dye   bt
LUTETIAN of Paris
LUTHERAN Protestant   rl
LUTIDINE bone-oil/coal-tar constituent
LUXATING displacing
LUXATION dislocation
LUXMETER illuminance measurement device
LUXURIES unnecessary pleasures
LUXURIST an indulger
LYCHGATE lichgate   rl
LYCOPODE yellow powder   bt
LYMPHOID like lymph   md
LYNCHING mob law
LYNCH-LAW short-shrift
LYNX-EYED keen of vision
LYOLYSIS acid/base formation process   ch
LYRE-BIRD Australian bird   zo
LYRICISM lyric composition
LYSERGIC l.s.d. acid   ch
LYSOSOME sac of hydrolytic enzymes   bl
LYSOZYME bacteriolytic enzyme   bl

M

MACARIAN blessed
MACARISM a beatitude
MACARIZE to bless
MACARONI fop; food
MACAROON almond biscuit
MACASSAR hair oil
MACERATE harass; to steep; to rot
MACHINAL mechanical
MACHINED turned on a machine
MACHINER operative
MACKEREL scad; cloud pattern   zo
MACRANER large male ant   zo
MACROPOD long-legged   zo
MACROPUS kangaroo genus   zo
MACULATE to spot; to stain
MADDENED infuriated; incensed
MADHOUSE Bedlam; asylum
MADRIGAL pastoral ditty   mu
MAECENAS rich art patron
MAENADIC bacchanalian
MAESTOSO majestically   mu
MAFFLING a simpleton
MAGAZINE depot; store; periodical
MAGDALEN home for repentants
MAGICIAN wizard; marabout
MAGIRICS the culinary art

MAGISTER master; doctor	**md**	
MAGNADUR ceramic magnet/insulator material		
MAGNESIA a medicine	**md**	
MAGNESON magnesium reagent	**ch**	
MAGNETIC attractive; drawing		
MAGNIFIC splendid; majestic		
MAGNOLIA a flowering tree	**bt**	
MAGOT-PIE magpie	**zo**	
MAHADENA Hindu god, Siva	**rl**	
MAHARAJA Indian rajah		
MAHOGANY tropical tree	**bt**	
MAIDENLY modest; demure; bashful		
MAIDHOOD girlhood; virginity		
MAIEUTIC delivering; evolving		
MAILABLE postable		
MAIL BOAT a packet	**nt**	
MAIL-CART post wagon		
MAIL-CLAD armour-plated		
MAIL-DRAG mail-coach		
MAIN-BOOM ⎱ parts of sailing	**nt**	
MAIN-DECK ⎰ ship	**nt**	
MAINLAND continent		
MAINMAST ⎱ chief	**nt**	
MAINSAIL ⎰ rigging units	**nt**	
MAINSTAY chief support	**nt**	
MAINTAIN continue; assert; aver; hold		
MAINYARD part of rigging	**nt**	
MAJESTIC imperial; august; regal		
MAJOLICA pottery (Majorca)		
MAJORATE rank of major		
MAJORITY over 18		
MAKEBATE quarrel-maker		
MAKELESS matchless		
MAKIMONO Japanese picture		
MALACOID soft-bodied		
MALADIES disorders; ailments	**md**	
MALAGASH ⎱ relating to		
MALAGASY ⎰ Madagascar		
MALAMUTE Arctic sledge dog	**zo**	
MALAPERT saucy; impertinent; flippant		
MALAPROP of misuse of words		
MALARIAL (malaria)	**md**	
MALCHITE diorite rock	**gl**	
MAL-DE-MER sea-sickness	**md**	
MALE-FERN common lowland fern	**bt**	
MALEFICE evil deed; enchantment		
MALETOLT ⎱ illegal exaction	**lw**	
MALETOTE ⎰		
MALIGNED traduced; slandered		
MALIGNER defamer; reviler; abuser		
MALINGER feign illness		
MALLEATE to hammer		
MALLECHO villainy; mischief (Shak.)		
MALMROCK sandstone	**mn**	
MALODOUR a smell; stench		
MALT-DUST malt grains		
MALTHENE asphaltic bitumen constituent	**ch**	
MALT-KILN ⎱ comprise malt factory		
MALT-MILL ⎰		

MALTREAT abuse; hurt; harm; injure		
MALTSTER malt-maker		
MALT-WORM a tippler; weevil	**zo**	
MALUNION improper bone-knitting	**md**	
MAMALIGA maize-meal porridge	**ck**	
MAMBRINO source of Don Quixote's helmet		
MAMELUKE Circassian cavalry-man		
MAMMALIA suckers	**zo**	
MAMMARED stammered		
MAMMIFER a mammal	**zo**	
MAMMILLA a nipple	**md**	
MAMMODIS Indian muslin	**tx**	
MANACLED shackled; fettered		
MAN-CHILD a boy		
MAN-EATER cannibal; tiger	**zo**	
MANGANIN copper-base alloy		
MAN-HATER allergic to man		
MAN-HOURS labour measure		
MAN-OF-WAR warship	**nt**	
MAN-POWER male potential		
MAN-SIZED adult dimensions		
MAN-TO-MAN frank and confidential		
MANAGING controlling; contriving		
MANCIPLE a steward; purveyor		
MANDAEAN Babylonian sect		
MANDAMUS a writ	**lw**	
MANDARIN official; orange; language	**bt**	
MANDATOR commander; director		
MANDELIC bitter almond extract	**bt**	
MANDIBLE a jaw	**zo**	
MANDINGO tribe (South Sahara)		
MANDIOCA cassava; manioc	**bt**	
MANDOLIN a guitar	**mu**	
MANDORLA oval panel		
MANDRAKE white bryony	**bt**	
MANDRILL a baboon	**zo**	
MANELESS without a mane		
MANELIKE like a mane		
MANEQUIN manikin; artist's model		
MANFULLY boldly; courageously		
MANGABEY Malagasy monkey	**zo**	
MANGCORN mixed grain crop		
MANGLING calendering; mutilating		
MANGONEL a ballistic machine		
MANGROVE a tree	**bt**	
MANIACAL raving; frenzied; lunatic		
MANICATE hairy	**bt**	
MANICHEE a doctrinaire		
MANICURE hand treatment		
MANIFEST invoice of ship's cargo	**nt**	
MANIFEST evince; clear; obvious		
MANIFOLD multiplied; numerous		
MANNERLY of good address		
MANNIKIN manikin; dwarf		
MANNITOL hexahydric alcohol	**ch**	
MANOCYST receptive papilla in oomycetes	**bt**	
MANORIAL referring to a manor		
MANOSTAT pressure-constancy device	**eg**	
MANSUETE mild; gentle		

MANTELET small cloak	**MASSACRE** pogrom; carnage	
MANTIGER heraldic term	**MASSAGED** kneaded; rubbed	hd
MANTILLA lace veil (Sp.)	**MASS-BELL** sacring-bell	rl
MANTISSA decimal part of logarithm	**MASS-BOOK** R.C. missal	rl
MANTLING blushing; flushing; suffusing	**MASSETER** a jaw muscle	md
MANUALLY by hand	**MASSEUSE** a manipulator	md
MANUCODE bird of paradise zo	**MASSICOT** lead oxide	mn
MANURING fertilizing	**MASSORAH** Hebrew tradition	
MANUTYPE hand-painted	**MASTERED** conquered; overcame	
MAORI-HEN the weka zo	**MASTERLY** expertly; dexterously	
MAQUETTE mock-up model, sketch (Fr.)	**MASTHEAD** newspaper main title	nt
MARABOUT Indian stork zo	**MASTITIS** breast removal	md
MARABOUT Moslem priest or wizard rl	**MASTLESS** dismasted	
MARAGING steel-hardening heat treatment ml	**MASTODON** early mammoth	zo
	MASURIUM a metallic element	ch
MARASMUS emaciation	**MAT-GRASS** weavable reeds	bt
MARATHON long distance race	**MATADORE** bull-fighter; domino game	
MARAUDED roved; plundered; pillaged	**MATAMATA** S. Amer. river tortoise	zo
MARAUDER raider; bandit; outlaw	**MATCHBOX** chez Lucifer	
MARAVEDI small Spanish copper nm	**MATCHING** equalling; suiting	
MARBLING form of decor	**MATELOTE** fish/wine stew (Fr.)	ck
MARCANDO with precision mu	**MATERIAL** stuff; essential; relevant	
MARCHING bordering; foot slogging	**MATERIEL** equipment (Fr.)	
MARGARIC pearly	**MATERNAL** motherly	
MARGARIN ersatz butter	**MATESHIP** comradeship	
MARGARON a fatty substance	**MATHESIS** mathematics; learning	
MARGINAL in the margin	**MATHILDA** a tank	
MARGINED edged; bordered	**MATRONAL** motherly; sedate	
MARGRAVE German Count	**MATRONLY** elderly	
MARIGOLD orange flower bt	**MATTERED** signified; imported	
MARIGRAM tidal-height record sv	**MATTRESS** bed made of stuffed bag	
MARINADE pickled fish	**MATURANT** a cataplasm	md
MARINATE to preserve; to salt	**MATURATE** to poultice	md
MARITIME marine; naval; nautical	**MATURELY** deliberately; completely	
MARJORAM aromatic plant bt	**MATURING** ripening; mellowing	
MARKEDLY unmistakably; eminently	**MATURITY** readiness; fullness	
MARKETED sold; vended	**MAUNDRIL** a pick-axe	to
MARKSMAN crack shot	**MAUVEINE** synthetic dyestuff	ch
MARLINED twined with twine nt	**MAVERICK** unbranded animal	
MARLITIC (clay) mn	**MAXIM-GUN** single-barrelled machine gun	
MARMOSET American monkey zo	**MAXIMIST** a dealer in old saws	
MAROCAIN fine-rep dress fabric tx	**MAXIMIZE** raise to maximum	
MARONITE Jewish sect	**MAY-APPLE** N. American fruit	bt
MAROONED left on desert island	**MAY-BLOBS** marsh marigold	bt
MAROQUIN morocco leather	**MAY-BLOOM** hawthorn	bt
MARQUESS a marquis	**MAY-QUEEN** spring deity	
MARQUISE marchioness	**MAYORESS** wife of mayor	
MARRIAGE wedlock; espousal	**MAZARINE** deep blue	
MARRYING wedding; uniting	**MAZDEISM** Zoroastrianism	
MARSH-GAS methane ch	**MAZINESS** perplexity; haziness	
MARSH-HEN moorhen zo	**MAZOLOGY** a zoological science	zo
MARSH-TIT blackheaded tom-tit zo	**MEAGRELY** scantily; sparsely; meanly	
MARTAGON turk's cap lily bt	**MEAL-POCK** ⎫ beggar's meal-bag	
MARTELLO circular tower	**MEAL-POKE** ⎭	
MARTINET a disciplinarian	**MEALTIME** breakfast, lunch or dinner	
MARTYRED victimized	**MEALWORM** one infesting flour	zo
MARY-SOLE a flat-fish zo	**MEAN-BORN** of humble origin	
MARYGOLD marigold bt	**MEANNESS** sordidness; paltriness	
MARZIPAN a sweetmeat	**MEANTIME** meanwhile	
MASCARON face on door-knocker	**MEASURED** meted; ascertained; steady	
MASORITE a theologist	**MEASURER** computer; gauger	

MEAT-BALL rissole			**MENOLOGY** calendar of saints		
MEATLESS of vegetarian foods			**MENOPOME** mud-devil		zo
MEAT-RACK hooked storage facilities			**MENSURAL** measurable		
MEAT-SAFE protection against servants			**MENTALLY** intellectually		
MECARBAM chemical insecticide			**MEPHITIC** noxious; pestilential		
MECHANIC artisan			**MEPHITIS** an exhalation; miasma		
MECONATE, MECONINE	bt		**MERCABLE** saleable; vendible		
MECONIUM poppy-juice; opium			**MERCHAND** to traffic; to trade		
MEDALIST a prize winner			**MERCHANT** trader; dealer; monger		
MEDALLIC relating to medals			**MERCIFUL** humane; clement; lenient		
MEDDLING interfering; intruding			**MERCURIC** mercurial; sprightly		
MEDIATED intervened; reconciled			**MERICARP** seed carpel		bt
MEDIATOR an intercessor; arbitrator			**MERIDIAN** great circle; noon		
MEDICATE to doctor; to dose			**MERINGUE** a sweet		
MEDICEAN (Medici of Florence)			**MERIONES** Can. jumping mouse		zo
MEDICINE the curative art	md		**MERISTEM** formative tissue		
MEDIEVAL (Middle Ages)			**MERISTIC** segmented		zo
MEDIOCRE middling; ordinary			**MERITING** deserving; earning		
MEDITATE ruminate; muse; intend			**MEROGAMY** individualized-gamete union		
MEDULLAR pithy	bt				bt
MEDULLIN lilac cellulose	bt		**MEROSMIA** smell sense deficiency		md
MEEKENED became gentle			**MEROSOME** a segment; a somite		zo
MEEKNESS submissiveness; humility			**MEROXENE** biotite class		mn
MEETNESS fitness; propriety			**MEROZOON** protozoon fragment		zo
MEGALINE magnetic flux unit	el		**MERRYMAN** mountebank; jester		
MEGALITH stone monument			**MERSALYL** a diuretic		
MEGALOPS last larval stage in crabs	zo		**MERCYISM** rumination		
MEGAPODE mound bird	zo		**MESCALIN** alkaloid 'truth drug'		md
MEGATRON light-house valve			**MESDAMES** ladies		
MEGAVOLT million volts			**MESHWORK** network; reticulation		
MEGAWATT million watts			**MESITITE** a carbonate		mn
MEIONITE a silicate	mn		**MESMEREE** one mesmerized		
MEIOTAXY whorl development failure	bt		**MESMERIC** hypnotic		
MELAMINE organic compound	ch		**MESOCARP** central carpel		bt
MELANISM black coloration			**MESODERM** inner skin		md
MELANITE black garnet	mn		**MESOLITE** needlestone		mn
MELANOMA pigmented mole			**MESOMERE** muscle-plate zone in verte-		
MELANOUS dark-visaged			brates		zo
MELANURE sea-bream	zo		**MESOSOMA** abdomen division in arach-		
MELIBEAN alternately responsive			nida		zo
MELILITE complex mineral	mn		**MESOTRON** electron-directing device		
MELINITE a high explosive			**MESOTYPE** zeolitic mineral		mn
MELLIFIC honeyed			**MESOZOIC** Triassic period		gl
MELLOWED matured; ripened; enriched			**MESQUITE** African thorn-bush		bt
MELLOWLY sweetly; melodiously			**MESSIDOR** June 19th–July 18th (Fr.)		
MELODEON harmonium	mu		**MESSMATE** table companion		
MELODIST composer			**MESSROOM** forces' dining room		
MELODIZE render harmonious	mu		**MESSUAGE** premises and garden		
MEMBERED having limbs			**METACISM** excess of 'M'		
MEMBRANE tissue	bt, zo		**METACONE** cusp of mammal molar		zo
MEMORIAL relic; monument; memento			**METAIRIE** (produce sharing) Fr.		
MEMORIZE learn by heart			**METALLED** (roads); plated		
MEMPHIAN, MEMPHITE (Memphis)			**METALLIC** lustrous		
MEMSAHIB white lady (India)			**METALMAN** metal-worker		
MENACING threatening; intimidating			**METAMICT** glassy amorphous state		mn
MENDABLE repairable			**METAPHOR** allegory; image		
MENHADEN American herring	zo		**METASOMA** abdomen part in arachnida		
MENILITE brown opal	mn				zo
MENINGES brain membranes	md		**METASOME** mid-body of cyclops		zo
MENISCAL crescent-shaped			**METATOME** an architectural space		
MENISCUS type of lens			**METAYAGE** see metairie		

METAZOAN ⎫	multicellular	
METAZOIC ⎬	construction of an	
METAZOON ⎭	animal	zo
METECORN	a corn issue	
METEORIC	transient; dazzling; flashing	
METERAGE	measurement	
METEWAND ⎫	yard-stick	
METEYARD ⎭		me
METHANOL	methyl alcohol	ch
METHINKS	I think	
METHODIC	systematic; orderly	
METHYLAL	chemical solvent	
METHYLIC	(methyl)	ch
METHYSIS	drunkenness	md
METONYMY	a trope	
ME-TOOISM	alsoiology	
METOPISM	(frontal suture)	md
METOPRYL	anaesthetic	ch
METRICAL	rhythmic	
MEZEREON	aromatic shrub	bt
MIASMATA	nauseous exhalations	
MICRANER	small male ant	zo
MICROBAR	unit of pressure	ps
MICROBIC	microbial	zo
MICROZOA	animalculae	zo
MICRURGY	cell-study technique	bl
MIDDLING	mediocre; medium; average	
MIDNIGHT	24.00 hours	
MIDSHIPS	boat-centred	nt
MIGHTFUL	powerful; dynamic	
MIGHTILY	vigorously; potently	
MIGRAINE	the vapours	md
MIGRATED	left; moved	
MIGRATOR	emigrant; nomad; rover	
MILANESE	(Milan)	
MILDEWED	mouldy; musty; rusty	
MILDNESS	gentleness; blandness	
MILEPOST	milestone	
MILESIAN	early Irish race	
MILITANT	eager to fight; warring	
MILITARY	martial; soldierly; warlike	
MILITATE	oppose; contend; fight	
MILK-MAID	dairy-maid	
MILK-TREE	the messaranduba	bt
MILK-WALK	(a district)	
MILK-WARM	tepid	
MILK-WEED	the sow-thistle	bt
MILK-WORT	flowering plant	bt
MILKY-WAY	a galaxy	
MILLEPED	centipede	zo
MILL-HAND	factory operative	
MILLIARD	a thousand millions	
MILLIARE	thousandth of an are (Fr.)	
MILLIBAR	unit of barometric pressure	me
MILLIGAL	1000th of a gal	gp
MILLILUX	unit of illumination intensity	lt
MILLINER	bonnet-maker	
MILLIPED	milleped	zo
MILLPOND	mere quiescence?	
MILLRACE	actuating stream	
MILLTAIL	water past mill-wheel	

MILLWORK	mill machinery	
MILTONIC	(Milton)	
MIMETITE	lead compound	mn
MIMICKED	aped; took off; imitated	
MIMICKER	impersonator; mime	
MINATORY	menacing; threatening	
MINCE-PIE	fruit-filled tart	ck
MINDLESS	stupid; heedless	
MINGLING	mixing; blending	
MINIATED	illuminated	
MINIFIED	depreciated	
MINIMENT	muniment (obs.)	
MINIMIZE	treat slightingly	
MINISTER	servant; pastor; succour	
MINISTRY	agency; cabinet	
MINORITE	Franciscan friar	rl
MINORITY	the smaller number	
MINOTAUR	half man, half bull	
MINSTREL	ballad-monger	
MINTMARK	identification mark	
MINUTELY	particularly; exactly	
MINUTEST	smallest; tiniest	
MINUTIAE	small details	
MINUTING	recording; noting	
MIRE-CROW	black-headed gull	zo
MIREPOIX	vegetable bed for braised meats	
		ck
MIRINESS	muddiness; swampiness	
MIRRORED	reflected	
MIRTHFUL	festive; jocund; vivacious	
MISAIMED	ill-directed	
MISAPPLY	pervert; misuse; abuse	
MISARRAY	disarray; disorder	
MISBEGOT	shapeless (Shak.)	
MISBOUND	in wrong order	pr
MISCARRY	to fail; be abortive	
MISCELLA	oil/solvent solution	ch
MISCHIEF	injury; harm; hurt; trouble	
MISCHOSE	made wrong choice	
MISCIBLE	mixable	
MISCLAIM	claim in error	
MISCOUNT	reckon wrongly	
MISCREED	false creed	
MISCUING	(billiards)	
MISDATED	forgot what day it was	
MISDEALT	(cards)	
MISDOING	wronging; offending	
MISDOUBT	suspicion; irresolution	
MISDRAWN	badly drawn	
MISDREAD	regard with dread	
MISENTER	to enter wrongly	
MISENTRY	erroneous record	
MISERERE	51st Psalm	rl
MISFAITH	distrust; perfidy	
MISFEIGN	to disguise	
MISFIELD	cricket	
MISFIRED	did not go off	
MISGRAFF ⎫	to graft amiss	
MISGRAFT ⎭		
MISGUIDE	lead astray	
MISHEARD	didn't get it	

MISHMASH medley	
MISHNAIC (Jewish Oral Laws)	rl
MISHNOTH Jewish Oral Laws	lw
MISINFER deduce erroneously	
MISJUDGE misconstrue; mistake	
MISLABEL address incorrectly	
MISLAYER untidy person	
MISLETOE also mistletoe	bt
MISLIKED disapproved; disliked	
MISMATCH out-class	
MISNAMED wrong appellation	
MISNOMER incorrect appellation	
MISOGAMY hatred of marriage	
MISOGYNY hatred of women	
MISPLACE displace; mislay	
MISPLEAD win case for opponent	
MISPOINT punctuate improperly	
MISPRINT typographical error	
MISPRISE to mistake	
MISPRIZE slight; undervalue; belittle	
MISQUOTE cite erroneously	
MISRATED rated erroneously	
MISRULED governed badly	
MISSERVE serve unfaithfully	
MISSHAPE to deform	
MISSPEAK utter wrongly	
MISSPELL write wrong	
MISSPELT an error in orthography	
MISSPEND squander; misuse	
MISSPENT wasted; dissipated	
MISSTATE state falsely	
MISTAKEN in error; wrong; incorrect	
MISTEACH teach wrongly	
MISTHINK think ill of	
MISTIMED chronologically erroneous	
MISTITLE use wrong title	
MISTRAIN to educate amiss	
MISTRESS lady of the house	
MISTRIAL (jury fail to agree)	lw
MISTRUST want of confidence	
MISTRYST to deceive (Sc.)	
MISTUNED discordant	
MISTUTOR to instruct amiss	
MISUSAGE abuse; perversion	
MISUSING misapplying; profaning	
MISVOUCH to bear false witness	
MISWRITE write incorrectly	
MISYOKED mismatched	
MITCHELL hewn Purbeck stone	
MITHRAIC (Mithras)	
MITIGANT alleviating, lenitive	
MITIGATE lessen; allay; assuage	
MITTENED wearing mitts	
MITTIMUS a writ	lw
MIZZLING clearing off; drizzling	
MNEMONIC aiding the memory	
MOBILITY changeability; fickleness	
MOBILIZE gather resources	
MOBOCRAT demagogue	
MOCASSIN } leather shoe;	
MOCCASIN } venomous snake	zo

MOCKABLE ridiculous; derisive	
MODALISM Sabellian doctrine	
MODALIST theorist	
MODALITY logical custom	
MODELLED fashioned; designed	
MODELLER copyist; plastic planner	
MODERATE so-so; fair; pacify; mollify	
MODERATO at moderate pace	mu
MODESTLY decently; unobtrusively	
MODIFIED altered; varied; changed	
MODIFIER moderator	
MODIOLAR like a bushel measure	
MODIOLUS central pillar of cochlea	zo
MODISHLY foppishly; fashionable	
MODULATE regulate; harmonize	
MOFUSSIL rural districts (Hindu)	
MOHARRAM Mohammedan fast	rl
MOIDERED spent; toiled	
MOISTFUL damp; humid	
MOISTURE humidity	
MOLALITY } mole/solvent solution ratio	
MOLARITY }	ch
MOLASSES treacle	
MOLE-CAST a molehill	
MOLE-EYED having small eyes	
MOLE-HILL miniature mountain	
MOLE-SKIN strong cotton fustian	tx
MOLECULE group of atoms	ch
MOLESTED troubled; pestered	
MOLESTER an annoyer; harasser	
MOLINIST a Jesuit	rl
MOLLIENT assuaging; softening	
MOLLUSCA invertebrates	zo
MOLYBDIC (molybdenum)	ch
MOMENTLY every moment	
MOMENTUM impetus; impulsive weight	
MONACHAL monastic	rl
MONANDRY (one husband only)	
MONARCHO fantastic person (Shak.)	
MONARCHY a kingdom; an empire	
MONASTIC a monk	rl
MONAZITE a phosphate	mn
MONDAINE woman of fashion	
MONDAYNE mundane (obs.)	
MONETARY relating to money	
MONETIZE to coin bullion	
MONEYBOX cash-box	
MONGERED dealt in	
MONGOOSE mungoose	zo
MONIMENT monument; image (Spens.)	
MONISTIC single-minded	
MONITION a summons	lw
MONITIVE warning	
MONITORY cautionary	
MONITRIX woman instructor	
MONKEYED played about with	
MONKFISH angler-fish	zo
MONKHOOD monastic state	rl
MONK-SEAL kind of sea creature	zo
MONNIKER sobriquet; nickname	
MONOBATH developing/fixing solution	pg

MONOBLOC integral cylinder casting	au	
MONOCARP an annual plant	bt	
MONOCLED wearing an eye-glass		
MONOCRAT autocrat		
MONOCULE one-eyed animal	zo	
MONOCYTE uninuclear leucocyte	zo	
MONODIST writer of dirges		
MONODONT having a single tooth	zo	
MONOGAMY (one wife)		
MONOGERM seed-producing single seedling	bt	
MONOGONY asexual reproduction		
MONOGRAM interwoven initials		
MONOGYNY (one wife)		
MONOLITH stone monument		
MONOLOGY soliloquizing		
MONOLULU Epsom Downs tipster		
MONOMARK identification mark		
MONOMIAL expressed by one term		
MONOPODE single-footed		
MONOPOLY exclusive privilege		
MONORAIL single rail system		
MONOTINT picture in one colour		
MONOTONE unvaried tone		
MONOTONY dull uniformity; tedium		
MONOTYPE printing machine		
MONSIEUR a Frenchman		
MONTANIC mountainous		
MONTEITH punch-bowl; kerchief		
MONTEURS artificial flower makers		
MONTICLE hillock; molehill		
MONUMENT a memorial; cenotaph		
MOOCHING loitering		
MOONBEAM a lunar ray		
MOONCALF monster; dolt		
MOON-EYED purblind		
MOON-SAIL a small sail	nt	
MOON-TYPE embossed lettering		
MOON-YEAR lunar year		
MOONFACE a round face		
MOONFISH opposite of sunfish	zo	
MOONLESS dark		
MOONLING simpleton		
MOONSEED climbing plant	bt	
MOONSHEE Moslem linguist		
MOONWORT a fern	bt	
MOORCOCK red grouse	zo	
MOORFOWL moorcock	zo	
MOORGAME grouse	zo	
MOORHAWK marsh harrier	zo	
MOORLAND moreland; peaty soil		
MOORWHIN a genista	bt	
MOORWORT marsh andromeda	bt	
MOOT-CASE a moot-point		
MOOT-HALL judgment hall		
MOOT-HILL a rendezvous		
MOOTABLE debatable; doubtful		
MOPE-EYED myopic; purblind		
MOPISHLY gloomily; dejectedly		
MOQUETTE a carpet (Fr.)		
MORALIST virtuous man		

MORALITY ethics; virtue		
MORALIZE philosophize		
MORATORY delaying		
MORAVIAN (John Huss)		
MORBIDLY unhealthily		
MORBIFIC causing disease	md	
MORELAND moorland		
MOREOVER besides; also; likewise		
MORESQUE arabesque		
MORIBUND dying		
MORILLON grape; duck	bt, zo	
MORMYRUS Egyptian pike	zo	
MOROCCAN (Morocco)		
MOROLOGY foolish talk		
MOROSELY sullenly; sourly		
MOROXITE a phosphate	mn	
MORPHEAN sleepy; dreamy		
MORPHEUS god of sleep		
MORPHINE morphia	md	
MORTALLY fatally; deadly		
MORTARED (gun-fire; brickwork)		
MORTGAGE pledge	lw	
MORTISED jointed		
MORTLING morling; dead sheep	zo	
MORTMAIN inalienable property	lw	
MORTUARY charnel house; morgue		
MOSLINGS curried leather		
MOSQUITO an insect	zo	
MOSS-BACK a Rip van Winkle		
MOSS-CLAD mossy		
MOSS-PINK a phlox	bt	
MOSS-ROSE house plant	bt	
MOSS-RUSH bog plant	bt	
MOSSLAND peat-land		
MOTHBALL naphthalene; anti-moth		
MOTHERED adopted		
MOTHERLY parental; tender		
MOTILITY movement; mobility		
MOTIONAL emotional		
MOTIONED gestured; proposed		
MOTIONER a mover		
MOTIVATE actuate; impel; induce		
MOTIVITY power of energizing		
MOTOR-BUS coach		
MOTOR-CAR automobile		
MOTORIAL motory; giving motion		
MOTORING travelling by car		
MOTORISE equip with motors		
MOTORIST car driver		
MOTORMAN chauffeur		
MOTORWAY fast main road		
MOTTLING variegating		
MOUCHING slouching; skulking		
MOUFFLON wild sheep	zo	
MOULD-BOX box for casting		
MOULDING shaping; fashioning		
MOULINET drum of capstan		
MOULTING shedding feathers		
MOUNDING banking		
MOUNTAIN a light wine		
MOUNTANT photographic paste		

MOUNTIES R. Can. Mounted Police		**MUREXIDE** a crystal	mn
MOUNTING embellishment; ascending		**MURIATED** soaked in brine	
MOURNFUL lugubrious; grievous		**MURIATIC** hydrochloric	ch
MOURNING lamenting; sorrow		**MURICATE** prickly; thorny; spiky	
MOUSE-EAR a herb	bt	**MURIFORM** like a wall	
MOUSSAKA mince-stuffed aubergine (Gr.)		**MURKSOME** darksome; obscure	
	ck	**MURMURED** complained; repined	
MOUSSEUX sparkling frothy wine (Fr.)		**MURMURER** grumbler; grouser	
MOUTHFUL pithy statement		**MURRHINE** (fluor-spar)	mn
MOUTHING con molto espressione		**MUSCADEL** muscatel	bt
MOVABLES personal belongings; chattels,		**MUSCATEL** grape; wine	bt
furniture		**MUSCULAR** brawny; sturdy; powerful	
MOVELESS fixed; stationary		**MUSELESS** artless	
MOVEMENT agitation; crusade		**MUSHROOM** upstart; blewit	bt
MOVINGLY affectingly; eloquently		**MUSICALE** private recital	
MOWBURNT (hay)		**MUSICIAN** instrumentalist	mu
MUCCHERO rose and violet infusion		**MUSINGLY** in contemplative fashion	
MUCEDINE a fungus	bt	**MUSK-BALL** perfumed sachet	
MUCHNESS almost abundance		**MUSK-CAVY** a rodent	zo
MUCILAGE gum	bt	**MUSK-DEER** Cent. Asian ruminant	zo
MUCIVORA insects	zo	**MUSK-DUCK** Muscovy duck	zo
MUCK-HEAP midden		**MUSK-PEAR** ⎱ odiferous	bt
MUCK-HILL dung-hill		**MUSK-PLUM** ⎰ fruits	bt
MUCK-RAKE dig up dirt		**MUSK-ROSE** rambling rose	bt
MUCK-WEED white goosefoot	bt	**MUSK-WOOD** musky tree	bt
MUCK-WORM a miser; a grub	zo	**MUSKETRY** rifle-shooting	
MUCKERED made a muck of		**MUSLINET** coarse muslin	tx
MUCOCELE mucus accumulation	md	**MUSQUASH** musk-rat	zo
MUCOSITY mouldiness		**MUSQUITO** mosquito	zo
MUCULENT slimy; viscous		**MUSTACHE** moustache	
MUD-VALVE sediment valve		**MUSTAIBA** Brazilian hardwood	bt
MUDARINE an extract	bt	**MUSTERED** assembled; gathered	
MUDDLING confusing; deranging		**MUTACISM** mytacism	
MUDDYING miring		**MUTATION** discontinuous variation	
MUDGUARD a screen		**MUTCHKIN** pint (Sc.)	me
MUDSTONE argillaceous sedimentary rock	gl	**MUTENESS** dumbness	
MUFFLING deadening; shrouding		**MUTICATE** without a point	bt
MUG-HOUSE ale-house		**MUTICOUS** lacking defence structures	zo
MUHARRAM a Moslem month		**MUTILATE** maim; dismember	
MULBERRY a fruit-tree	bt	**MUTINEER** insurgent	
MULCHING fertilizing		**MUTINIED** rebelled; revolted; struck	
MULCTING fining; amercing		**MUTINOUS** seditious; unruly; turbulent	
MULE-DEER N. American deer	zo	**MUTTERED** mumbled; whispered	
MULETEER mule-driver		**MUTTERER** grumbler; grouser	
MULEWORT a fern	bt	**MUTUALLY** reciprocally	
MULISHLY obstinately; stubbornly		**MUZZLING** restraining; silencing	
MULTEITY multiplicity		**MYCELIUM** mushroom spawn	bt
MULTIFID many cleft		**MYCETOMA** a foot disease	md
MULTIPED with many feet		**MYCETOME** special insect organ	zo
MULTIPLE a factor; numerous		**MYCODERM** fungoid pellicc	md
MULTIPLY increase; augment; spread		**MYCOLOGY** study of fungi	
MUMBLING muttering		**MYELITIS** spinal disease	md
MUMMYING embalming		**MYLODONT** (extinct sloth)	zo
MUNCHING chewing; masticating		**MYLONITE** compact streaky rock	gl
MUNERARY donative		**MYOBLAST** embryonic-muscle cell	
MUNGOOSE mongoose	zo	**MYOGENIC** of spontaneous muscle con-	
MUNIMENT title-deed; stronghold		traction	
MUNITION military stores; equipment		**MYOGRAPH** recording machine	md
MURALLED painted on a wall		**MYOMANCY** divination by mice	
MURDERED assassinated, slain		**MYONOSUS** ⎱ muscular disease	
MURDERER a Cain		**MYOPATHY** ⎰	md

MYOPHORE muscle-connected structure
zo
MYOPLASM contractile part of muscle cell
cy
MYOSITIC ⎫
MYOSITIS ⎬ muscular inflammation
MYOSOTIS the forget-me-not bt
MYOTASIS muscular tension pl
MYRIAPOD centipede zo
MYRIARCH a commander
MYRICINE (bee's wax)
MYRMIDON desperate ruffian
MYRRHINE (myrrh) bt
MYRTENOL myrtle oil monoalcohol ch
MYSTICAL enigmatical; occult
MYSTIQUE reverence for cleverness/skills
MYTACISM excess of 'm' in speaking
MYTHICAL legendary; fabulous
MYTILITE fossil mussel zo
MYTILOID mussel-like
MYXOPODA protozoans zo

N

NACREOUS pearly; iridescent
NAIL-FILE manicurist's implement
NAILHEAD visible outer portion of nail
NAIL-HOLE surface depression after hammering
NAILWORT whitlow grass bt
NAINSOOK jaconet muslin tx
NAISSANT issuing hd
NAMEABLE identifiable
NAMELESS obscure; inglorious
NAMESAKE having identical name
NANOSOMA dwarfism md
NAPHTHOL coal-tar constituent ch
NAPIFORM turnip-shaped
NAPOLEON nap; 20 francs nm
NAPOLITE volcanic substance mn
NAPTALAM chemical weedkiller
NARCEINE opium extract md
NARCISSI flowers bt
NARCOSIS stupefaction; stupor md
NARCOTIC anodyne; sedative; opiate
NARGHILE hookah-pipe
NARICORN horny beak zo
NARIFORM beak-like
NARRATED recited; related; recounted
NARRATOR story-teller; historian
NARROWED contracted; cramped
NARROWER closer; nearer
NARROWLY nearly; barely; scarcely
NASALITY nosiness
NASALIZE enunciate nasally
NASCENCY growth; production
NASICORN horn-beaked zo
NASIFORM nose-shaped
NATALITY population's increase ability ec
NATANTES water-spiders zo
NATANTLY buoyantly

NATATION swimming
NATATORY of aquatic habits
NATHLESS nevertheless
NATHMORE never more
NATIONAL public; general; racial
NATIVELY by birth; naturally
NATIVITY birth; a horoscope
NATTERED chatted
NATTIEST neatest; smartest
NATURISM nature worship
NATURIST practiser of nudism
NAUMACHY a sea-fight
NAUPLIUS a shell-fish zo
NAUSCOPY ship-sighting
NAUSEANT disgusting; revolting
NAUSEATE to sicken
NAUSEOUS offensive; repulsive nt
NAUTICAL marine; maritime; naval
NAUTILUS cuttlefish; diving bell zo
NAVALISM sea power nt
NAVARCHY admiralship nt
NAVICERT naval permit nt
NAVICULA incense-boat
NAVIFORM art; boat-like nt
NAVIGATE voyage; cruise; steer; pilot nv
NAVY-BLUE dark blue nt
NAZARENE of Nazareth
NAZARITE ⎫ a sect of early
NAZIRITE ⎬ Christians rl
NAZIFIED corrupted in thought
NEALOGIC adolescent
NEARCTIC N. of N. America
NEARHAND nigh; nearly
NEARNESS propinquity; closeness
NEATHERD cow-herd
NEATNESS spick and span; dexterity
NEBULOSE ⎫ nebular; cloudy; hazy;
NEBULOUS ⎬ misty; obscure
NECKATEE kerchief; scarf
NECKBAND collar
NECKBEEF coarse flesh
NECKLACE rivière; dog-collar
NECKWEAR scarves; ties; collars
NECROPSY post-mortem
NECROSIS mortification; death md
NECROTIC moribund
NECTARED honeyed
NECTOPOD swimming appendage zo
NEED-FIRE fire by friction
NEEDLESS unnecessary; superfluous
NEEDLING embroidering; sewing
NEGATING denying; disclaiming
NEGATION denial; dementi
NEGATIVE right of veto; not
NEGATRON thermionic tube el
NEGLIGEE loose apparel
NEGRITOS pygmies (Malay)
NEGROISM peculiarity of negro speech
NEIGHING whinnying
NEMALINE fibrous
NEMALITE hydrate of magnesia mn

NEMATOID like a thread	
NEMERTEA worms	zo
NEMOROSE growing in groves	
NEMOROUS woody	
NENUPHAR water-lily	bt
NEOBLAST large amoeboid cell	zo
NEOCRACY rule by upstarts	
NEO-LATIN modern Latin	
NEOLOGIC (novel words)	
NEOMYCIN antibiotic	pm
NEONATAL of newborn infants	md
NEOPHRON genus of vultures	zo
NEOPHYTE novice; tyro; proselyte	
NEOPLASM new tissue	
NEPALESE a native of Nepal	
NEPENTHE drug causing oblivion	md
NEPHRITE jade	mn
NEPHROID kidney-shaped	
NEPHROMA kidney tumour	md
NEPIONIC of embryonic period	zo
NEPOTISM favouritism of family	
NEPOTIST favours relatives	
NERONIAN (Nero)	
NERVE-WAR cold war	
NESCIENT⎫ ignorant; unlettered;	
NESCIOUS⎭ unaware; agnostic	
NESISTOR bipolar-field-dependent transistor	
NESTLING young bird	zo
NETHINIM temple servants (Heb.)	
NETTLING irritating; provoking	
NEURALGY neuralgia	md
NEURITIS nerve inflammation	md
NEUROPIL brain nerve fibre maze	zo
NEUROSAL neurotic; temperamental	
NEUROSIS nervous disease	md
NEUROTIC highly strung	
NEUTRINO subatomic particle	nc
NEVADITE rhyolite, acid lava	gl
NEWBLOWN just blossoming	
NEWCOMER late arrival	
NEW-MODEL (Parliamentary Army)	
NEWS-HAWK a reporter	
NEWS-REEL topical film	
NEWS-ROOM reading room	
NEXTNESS proximity; propinquity	
NIBBLING biting bit by bit	
NIBELUNG mythical character	
NICENESS precision; discrimination	
NICKELIC of nickel	
NICKNACK a trifle, gewgaw	
NICKNAME a monniker; sobriquet	
NICOTINE tobacco constituent	ch
NIDERING rascal; coward	
NIDOROSE⎫ smelling of cookery	
NIDOROUS⎭	
NIDULANT⎫ nestling	
NIDULATE⎭	
NIELLURE metal-work	
NIFFNAFF a trifle; nicknack	
NIFLHEIM region of mist (Teutonic)	

NIGERIAN (Nigeria)	
NIGGLING finicking; trifling	
NIGHNESS nearness; proximity	
NIGHTCAP cap or drink; horsehood	
NIGHT-DOG nocturnal venatic hound	
NIGHT-FLY nocturnal moth	zo
NIGHT-HAG a witch	
NIGHT-JAR night-churr; goat-sucker	
NIGHT-MAN scavenger	
NIGHT-OWL who stays out late	zo
NIHILISM extreme doctrine	
NIHILIST Russian revolutionary	
NIHILITY nothingness	
NINE-EYES lampreys	zo
NINEFOLD 9 times	
NINEPINS skittles	
NINETEEN cardinal number	
NINEVITE of Nineveh	
NISBERRY naseberry; medlar	bt
NITIDOUS lustrous	bt
NITRATED (nitric acid)	ch
NITROGEN an inert gas	ch
NITROLIC with nitro oxine group on same atom	
NITROXYL halogen/metal-attached radical	
NOACHIAN (Noah); archaic; bygone	
NOBBLING doping; injuring; swindling	
NOBELIUM man-made element	ch
NOBILITY distinction; aristocracy	
NOBLEMAN a peer	
NOBLESSE the nobility	
NOCENTLY guiltily; culpably	
NOCTILIO bat-genus	zo
NOCTUARY night record	
NOCTURNE night scene	mu
NODECUSP a curve	
NODIFORM knotted	
NODOSITY an entanglement	
NODULOSE knotty; nodulous	
NOEMATIC⎫ intellectual;	
NOETICAL⎭ mental; thoughtful	
NOISETTE hazelnut entrée	ck
NOMADISM gipsy life	
NOMADIZE wander with flocks	
NOMARCHY provincial rule	
NOMINATE designate; name; appoint	
NOMISTIC lawful	
NOMOGENY life origin	
NOMOLOGY psychology	
NON-CLAIM failure to claim	lw
NON-CREEP smooth flow additive	ch
NON-ELECT not of the elect	
NON-JUROR (Jacobite clergy)	rl
NONMETAL negative-ion former	ch
NON-MORAL amoral	
NON-PARTY independent	
NON-RIGID limp	
NON-TOXIC not poisonous	md
NON-UNION (trades union)	
NONESUCH without parallel; paragon	
NONSENSE balderdash; inanity; trash	

NOONTIDE midday	**NUMERARY** not supernumerary
NORMALCY regularity; standard	**NUMERATE** to number; to tell
NORMALLY usually; ordinary	**NUMEROUS** many; manifold; frequent
NORSEMAN Scandinavian	**NUMMULAR** numismatic
NORTHERN of the north	**NUMSKULL** blockhead; dunce
NORTHING distance northward	**NUNCHEON** luncheon
NORTHMAN Scandinavian	**NUNDINAL** (market day)
NORWEYAN Norwegian (Shak.)	**NUPTIALS** a marriage
NOSE-DIVE a plunge	**NURIMONO** lacquer-ware (Jap.)
NOSE-LEAF a bat appendage zo	**NURSLING** an infant; child
NOSE-RING bull's ornament	**NURTURED** brought up; tended
NOSEBAND part of bridle	**NUT-BROWN** colour of ale
NOSELESS non-nasal	**NUT-SCREW** monkey wrench
NOSOLOGY ⎫ classification md	**NUTARIAN** nut-eater
NOSONOMY ⎭ of diseases	**NUTATION** nodding
NOTALGIA backache md	**NUTHATCH** small bird zo
NOTANDUM a memorandum	**NUTHOUSE** lunatic asylum
NOTARIAL clerical lw	**NUTMEGGY** like a nutmeg
NOTATION system of figures	**NUTRIENT** nourishing; alimental
NOTCHING nicking; scoring	**NUTSHELL** receptacle for small amount
NOTEBOOK jotting pad	**NUZZLING** nestling
NOTELESS insignificant; petty; trivial	**NYMPHAEA** water-lilies bt
NOTICING observing; remarking	**NYMPHEAN** ⎫ maidenly;
NOTIFIED made known; apprised	**NYMPHISH** ⎭ like a nymph
NOTIONAL fanciful; imaginative	**NYSTATIN** antifungal antibiotic
NOTORNIS coot, (extinct) NZ zo	
NOTTURNO emotional piece mu	
NOTWHEAT unbearded wheat bt	
NOUMENAL not phenomenal	**O**
NOUMENON a definite conception	
NOVATIAN puritanical sect rl	**OAK-APPLE** wen on oak tree bt
NOVATION debt transference lw	**OAK-PAPER** a wall paper
NOVELESE inferior-novel language style	**OAT-GRASS** sort of straw bt
NOVELISH resembling a novel	**OATHABLE** capable of being sworn
NOVELIST romancer; innovator	**OBDUCING** enveloping; covering
NOVELIZE to spin yarns	**OBDURACY** stubbornness; callousness
NOVEMBER eleventh month	**OBDURATE** harsh; hardened; inflexible
NOVENARY nine collectively	**OBEDIENT** dutiful; submissive
NOVERCAL like a step-mother	**OBEISANT** reverencing; respectful
NOVERINT a writ lw	**OBELIZED** marked as spurious, (†)
NOWADAYS in these days; at present	**OBERHAUS** upper house (Ger.)
NUBECULA cloudiness md	**OBITUARY** list of the dead
NUBILITY marriage	**OBJECTED** protested; interposed
NUBILOSE ⎫ cloudy; overcast	**OBJECTOR** opposer; heckler
NUBILOUS ⎭	**OBLATION** an offering; libation
NUCAMENT a catkin bt	**OBLATORY** donative; sacrificial
NUCELLUS nucleus of ovule bt	**OBLIGANT** bound by contract lw
NUCIFORM nut-like	**OBLIGATE** oblige; pledge; mortgage
NUCLEASE nucleic-acid-hydrolysis en-	**OBLIGATO** of special import mu
zyme ch	**OBLIGING** gratifying; constraining
NUCLEATE having a nucleus	**OBLIQUED** slanted
NUCLEOLE small nucleus	**OBLIQUUS** obliquely placed muscle zo
NUCLEOME protoplast's nuclear substance	**OBLIVION** forgetfulness; (nepenthe)
bl	**OBLONGUM** wing-vein cell coleoptera zo
NUDATION stripping area of plants bt	**OBSCURED** eclipsed; clouded; dimmed
NUDISTIC scantily attired	**OBSCURER** a concealer; hider
NUGATORY ineffectual; futile; bootless	**OBSERVED** saw; remarked; obeyed
NUISANCE pest; annoyance; bother	**OBSERVER** spectator; commentator
NUMBERED reckoned; computed	**OBSESSED** besieged; beset; haunted
NUMBERER counter; numerator	**OBSIDIAN** volcanic rock mn
NUMBNESS torpor; stupefaction	**OBSOLETE** discarded; archaic; effete
	OBSTACLE hindrance; barrier; check

OBSTRUCT block; clog; impede; choke		
OBTAINED got; won; earned; acquired		
OBTAINER procurer; achiever		
OBTECTED covered; hidden		
OBTEMPER to comply with (Sc.)	lw
OBTESTED besought; protested		
OBTRUDED interfered; ejected		
OBTRUDER intruder; gate-crasher		
OBTUNDED blunted; deadened		
OBTURATE to close up; seal; shut		
OBTUSELY stolidly; stupidly		
OBTUSION bluntness		
OBVERTED faced; confronted		
OBVIATED avoided; prevented		
OBVOLUTE wavy; enfolded	bt
OCCAMISM ⎱ doctrine of Occam	rl
OCCAMIST ⎰	
OCCASION create; event; incident		
OCCIDENT the west		
OCCLUDED absorbed; shut up		
OCCLUSOR a shutter; a valve		
OCCULTED concealed; eclipsed		
OCCULTLY secretly; reconditely		
OCCUPANT holder; tenant; resident		
OCCUPIED engaged; employed		
OCCUPIER inhabiter		
OCCURRED chanced; happened; befell		
OCEANIAN (Oceania)		
OCEANITE basaltic igneous rock	mn
OCELLARY ⎱ with spots like eyes	
OCELLATE ⎰	
OCHEROUS yellow		
OCHIDORE shore-crab	zo
OCHLESIS ⎱ illness due to	
OCHLETIC ⎰ overcrowding	md
OCHREATE sheathing	bt
OCHREOUS yellowish		
OCHROITE cerite	mn
OCTAPODY verse of 8 feet		
OCTARCHY government by 8		
OCTONARY referring to 8		
OCTOROON one-eighth negro blood		
OCTUPLET (eight notes)	mu
OCULARLY visibly; demonstrably		
ODIOUSLY hatefully; offensively		
ODOGRAPH distance and course meter		
ODOMETER mileage recorder		
ODONTIST dentist	md
ODONTOID toothlike		
ODONTOMA tooth tumour	md
OENANTHE water dropwort	bt
OENOLOGY study of wine		
OERLIKON light A.A. gun		
OESTROUS female reproductive cycle		
OFF-BREAK (cricket)		
OFF-PRINT a reprint		
OFF-SHOOT branch		
OFF-SHORE near the land		
OFF-STAGE off the record		
OFF-WHITE pale cream		
OFFENDED violated; affronted		

OFFENDER transgressor; delinquent		
OFFERING tendering; proposing		
OFFICIAL functional; authorized		
OFT-TIMES frequently; repeatedly		
OHMMETER (resistance)	me
OIL-FIELD oil well area		
OIL-FIRED boiler; furnace		
OIL-GLAND secreting gland	mc
OILING-IN pre-painting surface preparation		
OIL-PAPER transparent paper		
OIL-PRESS olive squeezer		
OILCLOTH linoleum		
OILINESS greasiness; lubricity		
OILSKINS weatherproof garments		
OILSTONE whetstone		
OINTMENT an unguent	me
OITICICA oil from nut tree (Brazil)	f
OLD-TIMER old-stager		
OLD-WORLD antiquated		
OLEANDER an evergreen	b
OLEASTER wild olive	b
OLEFIANT oil producing		
OLEOBROM developing process	ps
OLEOCYST oil-containing diverticulum	z
OLEOSOME cell fat inclusion	b
OLIBANUM frankincense	b
OLIPHANT elephant (obs.)	z
OLIVE-OIL perfect food	b
OLIVETAN a Benedictine		
OLYMPIAD period of 4 years		
OLYMPIAN godlike		
OLYMPICS games		
OMADHAUN madman (Irish)		
OMELETTE beaten-egg dish		
OMISSION oversight; failure; disregard		
OMISSIVE exclusive; neglectful		
OMITTING missing; skipping; dropping		
OMMATEUM compound eye	z
OMNIFORM of all shapes; protean		
OMOHYOID (shoulder-blade)	m
OMOIDEUM pterygoid bone	m
OMOPLATE shoulder-blade	m
OMPHALIC (navel)	m
OMPHALOS boss on a shield; hub		
ONCE-OVER comprehensive glance		
ONCIDIUM orchid genus	b
ONCOLOGY science of tumours	m
ONCOMING approach; advance		
ONCOTOMY cutting a tumour	m
ONE-HORSE poorly equipped		
ONE-SIDED partial; biased		
ONE-TRACK single interest or file		
ONISCOID like a woodlouse	z
ONLINESS loneliness		
ONLOOKER spectator; observer		
ONOFRITE a mercury salt	m
ONOMANCY divination		
ONRUSHES onsets		
ONTOGENY embryonic development		
ONTOLOGY metaphysics		

ONYCHIUM pulvillus in insect	zo	
ONYMATIC generic	zo	
OOGONIUM algae/fungi female sex organ		
	bt	
OOKINETE vermiform stage in protozoa		
	zo	
OOLOGIST collector of bird's eggs		
OOSPHERE an egg	zo	
OOTOCOUS oviparous	zo	
OPALESCE to be iridescent		
OPALIZED make like an opal		
OPEN-EYED watchful		
OPEN-WELL uncovered well	ar	
OPEN-WORK metal/lace pattern		
OPENCAST outcrop; surface coal	mn	
OPENNESS frankness; sincerity		
OPERA-HAT a gibus		
OPERATED performed; worked	md	
OPERATIC having to do with opera		
OPERATOR workman; artisan; hand		
OPERETTA short opera	mu	
OPHIDIAN reptilian	zo	
OPHIDION conger eel	zo	
OPHIURAN starfish	zo	
OPIFICER artificer		
OPINABLE conjecturable		
OPIUM-DEN Hong Kong night spot		
OPOPONAX a perfume; a gum	bt	
OPPILATE block up; obstruct		
OPPONENS muscle related to digits	zo	
OPPONENT foe; rival; antagonist		
OPPOSING resisting; withstanding		
OPPOSITE contrary; adverse; inimical		
OPPUGNED contested; fought		
OPPUGNER adversary; competitor		
OPTATIVE optional; elective; voluntary		
OPTICIAN spectacle-maker		
OPTIMACY the nobility		
OPTIMISM hopefulness		
OPTIMIST a sanguine person		
OPTIMIZE take a bright view		
OPTIONAL left to choice; discretional		
OPULENCE wealth; affluence; profusion		
OPULENCY riches; possessions		
OPUSCULE a small work		
ORACULAR portentous; ominous		
ORANGERY orange garden		
ORANGISM (William of Orange)		
ORANGITE thorium silicate	mn	
ORATORIO sacred musical drama		
ORATRESS a woman orator		
ORCADIAN (Orkney Islands)		
ORCHANET alkanet	bt	
ORCHESIS art of dancing		
ORDAINED bid; decreed; enjoined		
ORDAINER assignor; prescriber	rl	
ORDERING disposing; directing		
ORDINAND candidate for orders	rl	
ORDINANT a prelate	rl	
ORDINARY a dinner; usual; customary		
ORDINATE methodical; orderly		

ORDNANCE guns; cannon; artillery		
ORGANDIE figured muslin	tx	
ORGANIFY add organic matter		
ORGANISM living structure		
ORGANIST a player	mu	
ORGANIZE frame; constitute; construct		
ORICHALC imitation gold		
ORIENTAL Eastern		
ORIENTED lined up; on the beam		
ORIGINAL primitive; primeval; novel		
ORILLION a bastion		
ORINASAL mouth and nose sound		
ORNAMENT embellishment; decoration		
ORNATELY elaborately; in florid style		
ORNITHIC referring to birds	zo	
ORONASAL of mouth and nose	zo	
ORPHANCY orphanhood		
ORPHANED parentless		
ORPIMENT arsenic sulphide	ch	
ORTHICON type of camera tube	tv	
ORTHODOX true; conventional; correct		
ORTHOEPY correct pronunciation		
ORYCTICS fossils	mn	
ORYZENIN rice glutelin protein	ch	
OSCINIAN (singing birds)	zo	
OSCITANT drowsy; yawning		
OSCITATE to gape		
OSCULANT kissing		
OSCULATE to buss		
OSETROVA sturgeon; caviar	zo	
OSMAZOME meat extract		
OSNABURG coarse linen	tx	
OSOPHONE headphone for the deaf	ac	
OSSIANIC (Ossian)		
OSSIFIED turned into bone		
OSSOBUCO stew of veal with bone, wine (It.)		
OSTEITIS bone inflammation	md	
OSTEOZOA the vertebrata	md	
OSTERICK bistort plant	bt	
OSTINATO recurrent theme	mu	
OSTIOLAR cellular		
OSTRAKON engraved pottery shard (Gr.)		
OTAHEITE Malay apple (Pacific)		
OTOCONIA small concretions in mollusca		
	zo	
OTORRHEA discharge from ear	md	
OTOSCOPE ear examiner	md	
OTOSCOPY ear examination	md	
OUISTITI marmoset	zo	
OUTBLUSH outflush		
OUTBOARD type of boat motor		
OUTBOUND outward bound		
OUTBRAVE defy; dare; challenge		
OUTBREAK fray; riot; broil; revolt		
OUTBURST eruption; ebullition		
OUTCLASS excel; outvie; surpass		
OUTCROSS (cross-breeding)		
OUTDARED defied; flouted		
OUTDATED outmoded; old-fashioned		
OUTDOING surpassing; outstripping		

OUTDOORS not at home	**OUTVOICE** talk down
OUTDWELL outstay	**OUTVOTED** won election
OUTFACED braved	**OUTVOTER** imaginary elector
OUTFIELD (cricket)	**OUTWARDS** externally
OUTFLANK overlap	**OUTWATCH** peer superiorly
OUTFLASH outshine	**OUTWEARY** bore stiff
OUTFLING sharp retort	**OUTWEIGH** ⎫ exceed in value;
OUTFLOWN lost flying competition	**OUTWORTH** ⎭ offset; overbalance
OUTFLUSH sudden glow of heat	**OUTWOUND** extricated
OUTFROWN win brow-creasing contest	**OUTWREST** extort by violence
OUTGOING expenditure; outlay	**OVARIOLE** egg-tube in insects z
OUTGROWN become too constricting	**OVARIOUS** consisting of eggs z
OUTGUARD outpost	**OVEN-BIRD** a tree-creeper z
OUTGUIDE file marker for removed entries	**OVER-AGED** time expired
OUT-HEROD be bigger stinker	**OVERALLS** garments
OUTHOUSE shed; shack; shanty; barn	**OVERARCH** overhang
OUTLAWED beyond the pale	**OVERAWED** quelled; intimidated
OUTLAWRY exile; banishment	**OVERBEAR** overwhelm; domineer
OUTLEAPT jumped over	**OVERBLOW** cover with blossom
OUTLEARN excel in learning	**OVERBODY** embody excessively
OUTLINED delineated; sketched	**OVERBOIL** let kettle blow top
OUTLIVED outlasted	**OVERBOLD** impudent; presumptuous
OUTLYING far; remote; distant	**OVERBOWL** cricket
OUTMARCH walk until drop	**OVERBRIM** overflow
OUTMODED out of fashion	**OVERBROW** project
OUTPACED over-run	**OVERBULK** loom large
OUTPOINT win (sport)	**OVERBURN** burn with zeal
OUTPOWER overpower; vanquish	**OVERBUSY** officious
OUTRAGED insulted; maltreated	**OVERCAME** vanquished; subdued
OUTRANGE extend further	**OVERCAST** lowering; cloudy
OUTRAZED exterminated	**OVERCLOY** to surfeit
OUTREACH exceed; surpass	**OVERCOAT** winter topcoat
OUTREIGN sit on throne longer	**OVERCOLD** too cold
OUTRIDER mounted attendant	**OVERCOME** defeat
OUTRIGHT at once; utterly	**OVERCROW** to insult; exult; brag
OUTRIVAL excel; outvie; beat	**OVERDATE** post-date
OUTROPER kind of bailiff lw	**OVERDONE** exaggerated
OUTSCOLD upbraid excessively	**OVERDOSE** too many pills
OUTSCORN despise; disdain; contemn	**OVERDRAW** take too much from bank
OUTSHINE eclipse; overshadow	**OVERDREW** exaggerate in drawing
OUTSHONE outrivalled	**OVERFALL** tidal effect
OUTSIDER not a favourite	**OVERFAST** insufficiently slow
OUTSIGHT outlook	**OVERFEED** glut; cloy; satiate
OUTSKIRT border	**OVERFILL** flood
OUTSLEEP perchance to outdream	**OVERFISH** cf. underdog
OUTSLEPT snored longer than	**OVERFLOW** overrun; inundate; swamp
OUTSLIDE slide better than everyone else	**OVERFOLD** inverted strata
OUTSMART diddle; outwit; overreach	**OVERFOND** doting
OUTSPEAK speak boldly	**OVERFULL** too full
OUTSPENT over tired	**OVERGAZE** look over
OUTSPOKE bad English	**OVERGIVE** give lavishly
OUTSPORT outdo in sport	**OVERGROW** non-existent verb
OUTSTAND resist; withstand	**OVERHAIR** long outside hair
OUTSTARE look longer than	**OVERHAND** overarm
OUTSTOOD withstood	**OVERHANG** jut; impend
OUTSTRIP outrun; undress faster	**OVERHAUL** repair; overtake; examine
OUTSWEAR collect cursing prize	**OVERHEAD** aloft
OUTSWELL overflow	**OVERHEAR** eavesdrop
OUT-TO-OUT overall measurement	**OVERHEAT** scorch
OUTVALUE appraise too highly	**OVERJUMP** neglect; pass by
OUTVENOM opposite of invenom	**OVERKILL** excess of casualties (nuclear w

OVERKIND indulgent
OVERKING control lesser kings
OVERKNEE (above the knee)
OVERLADE overburdened
OVERLAID ⎫
OVERLAIN ⎬ smothered
OVERLAND cross-country
OVERLEAF on the next page
OVERLEAP skip
OVERLIVE survive
OVERLOAD encumber
OVERLOCK lock up too much
OVERLONG too long
OVERLOOK to slight; connive; condone
OVERLORD feudal superior
OVERMOST highest; topmost
OVERMUCH in excess
OVERNAME nickname; recount
OVERNEAT finicky
OVERNICE fastidious
OVERPAID given excessive wages
OVERPART overtask
OVERPASS disregard
OVERPAST gone; spent
OVERPEER to look down on; overlook
OVERPLAY gambling
OVERPLUS remainder; surplus
OVERRAKE to sweep over like a wave
OVERRATE esteem too highly
OVERREAD peruse (Shak.)
OVERRENT exact too high a rent
OVERRIDE trample; quash; annul
OVERRIPE passé; past the prime
OVERRULE prevail; repudiate; rescind
OVERSEAM a seam
OVERSEAS abroad
OVERSEEN observed; overlooked
OVERSEER superintendent; foreman
OVERSELL make excess profits
OVERSEWN sewn over the edge
OVERSHOE a galosh
OVERSHOT went too far
OVERSIDE overboard
OVERSIZE out-size
OVERSKIP leap-over; overtrip
OVERSLIP pass without notice
OVERSMAN overseer; umpire
OVERSOLD hyperpeddled
OVERSOUL divine principle
OVERSPIN cricket
OVERSTAY outstay
OVERSTEP exceed; transgress
OVERSWAY overrule
OVERTAKE pass
OVERTASK overtax; overtoil
OVERTILE imbrex   bd
OVERTILT upset
OVERTIME extra-pay hours
OVERTOIL overexert
OVERTONE harmonic   mu
OVERTRIP to trip along

OVERTURE offer; proposal; prelude
OVERTURN upset; invert; perturb
OVERVEIL to cover
OVERVIEW an inspection
OVERWASH glacial formation
OVERWEAR outdoor clothing
OVERWEEN to be conceited
OVERWIND (springs)
OVERWISE too clever
OVERWORK overtask
OVERWORN threadbare
OVERYEAR last year's
OVIPOSIT to lay eggs
OWL-GLASS malicious character (Ger.)
OWL-LIGHT dusk
OXIDABLE oxidisable
OXIDATOR he who oxidates   ch
OXIDIZED combined with oxygen
OXIDIZER oxidizing agent
OX-PECKER African bird   zo
OX-TONGUE a plant   bt
OXYGONAL having acute angles
OXYMORON bitter-sweet
OXYTOCIC causing muscle contraction   zo
OXYTOCIN pituitary hormone   pl
OZOKERIT waxen material
OZONIZED (ozone)
OZONIZER oxygen-to-ozone converter   ch

P

PABULARY alimentary
PABULOUS nourishing
PACHYOTE thick-eared
PACHYPOD thick-footed
PACIFIED calmed; lulled; assuaged
PACIFIER tranquillizer; conciliator
PACIFISM appeasement
PACIFIST peace-maker
PACK-LOAD load for an animal
PACK-MULE beast of burden   zo
PACKETED made into a parcel
PAD-CLOTH numnah
PADDLING propelling a boat
PADELION lady's mantle   bt
PADELOUP inlaid leather book decoration
PADISHAH Turkish title
PADUASOY corded silk
PAGANISH heathen
PAGANISM idolatry
PAGANIST paynim; infidel
PAGANIZE make give up true faith
PAGINATE to number the pages
PAGODITE pagoda-stone   mn
PAGURIAN (hermit-crabs)   zo
PAINLESS pangless
PAINTBOX box of colours
PAINTING a picture; limning
PAINTOUT test of pigment   pt
PAIR-WISE in pairs
PAITRICK a partridge (Sc.)   zo

PAKISTAN country in Asia		
PALAMATE web-footed	zo	
PALAMINO beige-coloured horse (Sp.)		
PALATIAL royal; magnificent; stately		
PALATINE with royal privileges		
PALE-EYED with bleached orbs		
PALE-FACE a white man		
PALEBUCK the oribi	zo	
PALENESS wanness		
PALESTRA wrestling school		
PALIFORM stake-shaped	bt	
PALILOGY repetition		
PALINODE recantation		
PALISADE a fortification		
PALL-MALL ancient croquet		
PALLIATE extenuate; mitigate; gloss		
PALLIDLY palely; wanly		
PALM-WINE fermented palm juice		
PALMETTE palm-leaf decor		
PALMETTO fan-palm; hat	bt	
PALMIPED web-footed	zo	
PALMITIN natural oil fat		
PALPABLE perceptible; evidently		
PALPABLY obviously; tangibly		
PALPACLE tentacle in siphonophora	zo	
PALPATED handled; felt		
PALPEBRA eyelid	pl	
PALPIFER lobe of maxilla	zo	
PALPLESS absence of palpi	zo	
PALPOCIL sense hairlet in coelenterata	zo	
PALSTAFF ⎱ Celtic stone axe		
PALSTAVE ⎰		
PALSYING paralyzing		
PALTERED shuffled; quibbled		
PALTERER dodger; prevaricator		
PALTRILY equivocately		
PALUDINE marshy		
PALUDISM malaria	md	
PALUDOSE boggy		
PAMAQUIN synthetic antimalarial drug	pm	
PAMPERED coddled; humoured		
PAMPERER over-indulgent person		
PAMPHLET a broadsheet; brochure		
PANAGHIA bishop's pendant	rl	
PANCAKED landed flat		
PANCARTE royal charter		
PANCHEON earthenware pan		
PANCREAS sweetbread	md	
PANDANUS (screw-pines)	bt	
PANDEMIC epidemic in an area		
PANDERED procured; ministered		
PANDOWDY apple-charlotte		
PANEGYRY eulogy; encomium; adulation		
PANEL-SAW a cutting tool	to	
PANELESS no glass		
PANELLED (walls; a jury)		
PANGAMIC of indiscriminate mating	zo	
PANGOLIN scaly ant-eater	zo	
PANICKED terrorized; affrighted		
PANICLED in clusters	bt	

PANIONIC (Ionian people)		
PANMIXIA cessation of natural selection	zo	
PANNIKEL brain-pan; skull		
PANNIKIN small vessel		
PANOPTIC all seeing		
PANORAMA extensive view		
PANOTYPE antique photograph		
PANSOPHY all wisdom		
PANTHEON complete mythology		
PANURGIC skilled in all craft		
PAPABILE suitable for papal/other office		
PAPALISM popery	r
PAPALIST an R.C.	r
PAPALIZE proselytize	r
PAPERBOY newsagent's delivery boy		
PAPERING decorating		
PAPILLAE nipples	ze	
PAPILLAR warty		
PAPISHER a papist	r
PAPISTIC popish	r
PAPPADAM Indian bread wafer	ck
PAPULOSE pimply		
PAPYRINE like paper		
PARABEMA Byzantine sacristy	r
PARABLED used a parable		
PARABOLA a conic section		
PARABOLE similitude		
PARACHOR molecular volume		
PARACONE molar cusp in mammals	ze
PARADIGM example; model		
PARADING displaying; flaunting		
PARADISE Heaven; Eden; Elysium		
PARAFFIN an oil	mn
PARAFORM fumigant; formaldehyde	ch
PARAGOGE literal addition		
PARAGRAM a pun		
PARAGULA region of insect head	ze
PARAKEET paroquet; small parrot	ze
PARAKITE tailless kite		
PARALLAX alternation; displacement		
PARALLEL side by side		
PARALOGY false reasoning		
PARALYZE benumb; deaden; unnerve		
PARAMERE an antimere	ze
PARAMOUR a lover; mistress		
PARANEMA paraphysis	b
PARANGON matchless jewel		
PARANOEA ⎱ chronic monomania;		
PARANOIA ⎰ hallucination	me
PARAPSID reptile skull condition	z
PARAPSIS (thorax)	z
PARAQUAT weedkiller toxic to humans	cl
PARASANG about 4 miles (Pers.)	m
PARASEVE Jewish Saturday night	r
PARASHOT an anti-parachutist		
PARASITE a sycophant; toady	z
PARASTAT gramophone record cleaner	a
PARAVAIL inferior; cf. paramount		
PARAVANE mine remover	r
PARAXIAL near to axis	p

PARCENER co-heir	lw		**PASTRIES** confectionery	
PARCHING scorching; drying			**PASTURED** grazed	
PARCLOSE screen	rl		**PATAGIUM** wing membrane	zo
PARDONED excused; absolved			**PATCH-BOX** collection of black spots	
PARDONER (papal indulgences)	rl		**PATCHERY** botchery	
PARENTAL affectionate; fatherly			**PATCHING** repairing; cobbling	
PARERGON subsidiary work			**PATELLAR** of the knee-cap	pl
PARGETED daubed; painted			**PATENTED** protected by law	
PARGETER plasterer			**PATENTEE** \ one to whom a patent	
PARHELIA mock suns			**PATENTER** / is granted	
PARIETAL partitional			**PATENTOR** issuer of a patent	
PARIETES organ/cavity walls	pl		**PATERERO** pederero; ancient gun	
PARISIAN (Paris)			**PATERNAL** fatherly; parental	
PARISITE a marble	mn		**PATHETIC** sad; grievous; emotional	
PARLANCE mode of speech			**PATHLESS** no beaten track	
PARLANDO articulation in singing	mu		**PATIENCE** cards; an opera	
PARLANTE crisp (piano playing)	mu		**PATOCOLE** forest-floor animal	ec
PARLAYED conferred; discussed			**PATONCEE** heraldic cross	hd
PARMESAN a cheese			**PATOXENE** accidental forest-floor animal	
PARODIED took off; burlesqued			**PATRONAL** condescending	
PARODIST caricaturist			**PATTENED** wearing clogs	
PARONYME similar sounding word			**PATTERED** (rain)	
PAROQUET small parrot; parakeet	zo		**PATTERER** cheap jack	
PAROSMIA smell sense abnormality	md		**PATTY-PAN** baking dish	
PAROUSIA second Advent	rl		**PATULOUS** spreading	
PAROXYSM fit; convulsion	md		**PAULDRON** a shoulder plate	
PARROTER copyist			**PAUNCHED** obese	
PARROTRY servile imitation			**PAVEMENT** footway; sidewalk	
PARRYING warding; frustrating			**PAVILION** large tent; canopy	
PARSONIC like a parson			**PAVISADO** galley defence	
PART-SONG glee	mu		**PAVONINE** like a peacock	
PARTAKEN consumed			**PAWNSHOP** usurer's	
PARTAKER sharer; partner			**PAYCLERK** employee charged with paying	
PARTERRE (flower beds, etc.)			**PAYSHEET** list of wages owed	
PARTHIAN (Parthia)			**PEACEFUL** placid; serene; pacific	
PARTIBLE divisible			**PEACHERY** a hothouse	
PARTIBUS marginal note	lw		**PEACHICK** young peafowl	zo
PARTICLE an atom; scrap; fragment			**PEACHING** divulging; informing	
PARTISAN votary; adherent; halberd			**PEAGREEN** a colour	
PARTNERS a framework	nt		**PEAK-LOAD** maximum activity	el
PART-TIME works for part of day only			**PEARL-ASH** potash	mn
PARTYISM party loyalty			**PEARL-EYE** cataract	md
PASCUAGE grazing			**PEARLIES** coster's buttons	
PASCUOUS growing in pastures			**PEARLING** diving for pearls	
PASHALIK pasha's jurisdiction			**PEARLITE** iron/steel microconstituent	ml
PASILALY universal speech			**PEARMAIN** an apple	bt
PASS-BOOK bank-book			**PEASECOD** pea-pod	bt
PASSABLE tolerable			**PEASTONE** limestone	mn
PASSABLY acceptably			**PEAT-MOOR** peat-bog	
PASSER-BY non-stop pedestrian			**PEAT-MOSS** sphagnum	bt
PASSERES perching birds	zo		**PEAT-REEK** peat smoke	
PASSLESS trackless			**PECCABLE** weak; frail; erring	
PASSOVER Jewish feast	rl		**PECCANCY** sinfulness; offence	
PASSPORT a permit			**PECTINAL** like a comb	
PASSWORD watchword; countersign			**PECTORAL** breast-plate	
PASTICHE imitation			**PECULATE** embezzle; steal; purloin	
PASTILLE medicated lozenge	md		**PECULIAR** odd; singular; unusual	
PASTORAL rustic			**PECULIUM** prerogative; privilege	
PASTORLY pastorlike; priestly			**PEDAGOGY** instruction	
PASTRAMI smoked/sun-dried seasoned			**PEDALIAN** referring to feet	
meat	ck		**PEDALIER** pedal keyboard	

PEDALITY foot measurement
PEDALLED worked by foot
PEDALLER cyclist
PEDANTIC finical; exact; precise
PEDANTRY priggishness; conceit
PEDDLERY hawking
PEDDLING retailing; trifling
PEDERERO paterero; swivel gun (Sp.)
PEDESTAL plinth; base
PEDIATRY childish diseases   md
PEDICURE foot treatment   md
PEDIGREE lineage; stock; genealogy
PEDIMENT portico decoration
PEDIPALP whip-scorpion   zo
PEDIREME a crustacean   zo
PEDOLOGY study of soil
PEDUNCLE stalk   bt
PEEK-A-BOO punching cards with identity code
PEEP-HOLE a chink
PEEP-O'-DAY dawn
PEEP-SHOW galanty-show
PEERLESS unrivalled; matchless
PEESWEEP peewit   zo
PEETWEET spotted sandpiper   zo
PEGAMOID imitation leather
PEGASEAN (Pegasus)
PEIGNOIR loose wrapper
PEINTURE special consistent use of paints
PEJORATE deteriorate
PEKINESE small pug-nosed dog   zo
PELAGIAN (deep sea)
PELARGIC stork-like
PELASGIC early Grecian
PELE-MELE in disorder
PELERINE a tippet or cape
PELL-MELL rapidly; confusedly
PELLAGRA acute anaemia   md
PELLICLE thin skin or crust
PELLUCID transparent; vitreous; clear
PELORISM abnormality   bt
PELT-WOOL wool from a hide
PELTATED shield-shaped
PEMMICAN dried meat/berry food   ck
PENALIZE handicap; punish
PENCHANT inclination; turn; bent
PENCRAFT penmanship
PENDENCE suspense
PENDENCY indecision
PENDULUM swinging weight
PENELOPE currasow-bird (S. Amer.)   zo
PENITENT contrite; repentant
PENKNIFE pocket-knife
PENNORTH a pennyworth
PENNY-DOG a kind of shark   zo
PENOLOGY prison management
PENSTOCK duct to waterwheel
PENT-ROOF single sloped roof
PENTACLE five-pointed star
PENTAFID cleft in five
PENTAGON five sided figure

PENTELIC (marble)   mn
PENTOSAN polysaccharide   ch
PENUMBRA partial shadow
PENWIPER rag for pen user
PENWOMAN authoress
PEOPLING populating
PEPERINO granular tufa   mn
PEPPERED hit with shot
PEPTOGEN digestive principle
PEPTONIC digestive
PEPYSIAN (Samuel Pepys)
PERACUTE very sharp or violent
PERCEIVE apprehend; discern; descry
PERCHING roosting
PERCLOSE screen; railing   hd
PERDENDO dying away   mu
PERDURED endured; lasted
PERFORCE of necessity; forcibly
PERFUMED scented; odoriferous
PERFUMER perfume seller
PERFUSED sprinkled; bedewed
PERIAGUA a canoe (Sp.)
PERIANAL region around anus   pl
PERIANTH floral envelope   bt
PERIBLEM portion of apical meristem   bt
PERICARP seed-vessel   bt
PERICOPE scriptural passage   rl
PERICYTE small-blood-vessel cell   md
PERIDERM outer bark   bt
PERIDIUM outer wall of fungus fruit-body   bt
PERIGEAL } (when moon's orbit is
PERIGEAN }   nearest to the earth)
PERIGONE perianth   bt
PERILLED endangered; risked
PERILOUS hazardous; risky; parlous
PERIODIC at stated intervals
PERIOTIC around inner ear
PERIPETY climax; solution
PERIPLUS circumnavigation
PERISARC chitinous layer in hydrozoa   zo
PERISCII polar people
PERISHED decayed; died; expired
PERISSAD (odd atomic valency)   ch
PERITRON special cathode-ray tube   el
PERJURED perfidious; forsworn
PERJURER false witness
PERKNITE coarse-grained igneous rock   gl
PERLITIC vitreous obsidian   mn
PERMEANT highly mobile animal   ec
PERMEATE penetrate; percolate; seep
PERMUTED exchanged; transmuted
PERNANCY rent in kind   lw
PERNETTI kiln support
PEROLENE heat exchange organic fluid   ch
PERONATE with thick-sheathed stipe   bt
PERONEAL (fibula)   md
PERONEUS fibula or leg muscle   zo
PERORATE declaim; harangue
PEROXIDE a bleacher   ch
PERRUQUE peruke; a wig

PERSICOT peach cordial		**PHONE-BOX** call-box	
PERSIMON date-plum	bt	**PHONETIC** vocal	
PERSONAL distinctive; individual		**PHORESIS** ion passage through membrane	
PERSPIRE sweat			pl
PERSUADE induce; sway; entice		**PHORMIUM** New Zealand flax	bt
PERTHITE potassium/sodium-felspar		**PHOSGENE** poisonous gas	ch
intergrowth		**PHOSPHAM** ammonia compound	
PERTNESS sauciness; flippancy		**PHOSPHOR** morning star; Venus	
PERTUSED punched		**PHOTOGEN** phosphorescent organ	zo
PERUSING reading; scrutinizing		**PHOTOPSY** an eye trouble	md
PERUVIAN (Peru)		**PHRASING** expressing; uttering	
PERUVINE Peruvian balsam	bt	**PHRYGIAN** a Montanist	
PERVADED permeated; diffused		**PHTHISIS** consumption	md
PERVERSE stubborn; vexatious		**PHYLARCH** Greek tribal leader	
PERVIOUS porous; permeable		**PHYLETIC** tribal	
PESSULUS osseus trachea band in birds		**PHYLITTE** clay slate	mn
	zo	**PHYLLARY** bract outside capitulum	bt
PESTERED plagued; harassed; worried		**PHYLLIUM** leaf insects	zo
PESTERER tormentor; teaser		**PHYLLODE** a form of leaf	
PESTLING pounding; abrading		**PHYLLODY** } leaf-like structure	
PETALINE (petal)	bt	**PHYLLOID** }	bt
PETALISM banishment; ostracism		**PHYLLOME** foliage	bt
PETALITE silicate of alumina	mn	**PHYSALIA** Portuguese man-of-war	
PETALODY stamen-to-petal transforma-		**PHYSALIS** Cape gooseberry	bt
tion	bt	**PHYSETER** sperm whale	zo
PETALOID petal-shaped	bt	**PHYSICAL** material; corporeal; tangible	
PETALOUS having petals	bt	**PHYSIQUE** bodily structure	
PETECHIA tiny haemorrhage spot	md	**PHYTOMER** phyton; plant unit	bt
PETERING calling at cards		**PHYTOSIS** vegetable parasites	bt
PETERMAN a fisherman		**PHYTOZOA** sea anemones, etc.	zo
PETIOLAR having a leaf-stalk	bt	**PIACULAR** atrociously bad	
PETITION supplication; ask; beseeching		**PIANETTE** small piano	mu
PETITION (of Right)		**PIASSABA** } Brazilian palm; fibre used	
PETITORY petitioning; craving		**PIASSAVA** } for ropes and brooms	bt
PETRIFIC turning to stone		**PIAZZIAN** like a piazza	
PETRONEL horse pistol		**PICARIAN** (woodpeckers)	zo
PETROSAL otic-fusion bone	zo	**PICAROON** small hooked pulling pole	fr
PETTIFOG quibble over details		**PICAROON** pirate; rogue	
PETULANT irritable; querulous; testy		**PICCADIL** high collar	
PETUNTSE china clay	mn	**PICIFORM** woodpecker type	zo
PETWORTH variety of marble	mn	**PICK-ME-UP** a cordial	
PEWTERER worker in pewter		**PICKEREL** pike; dunlin	zo
PEZIZOID like cup-shape apothecium	bt	**PICKETED** enclosed; guarded	
PHAKITIS eye inflammation	md	**PICKLING** preserving	
PHALANGE finger-bone	pl	**PICKLOCK** skeleton key	
PHANTASM spectre; chimera		**PICKWICK** a club	
PHANTASY airy speculation; fancy		**PICOTITE** a spinel	mn
PHARISEE formalist		**PICTURED** described; represented	
PHARMACY drug-store		**PIECENER** a piecer; joiner of threads	
PHEASANT a game bird	zo	**PIECRUST** tart pastry	
PHELLOID plant-surface cell crust	bt	**PIEDNESS** spotted diversity	
PHENGITE species of mica	mn	**PIEDROIT** pier without cap or base	bd
PHENOLIC plastic mould		**PIERCING** keen; shrill; acute	
PHIALIDE flask-shaped sterigma	bt	**PIERHEAD** jetty	
PHIALLED bottled		**PIERIDES** the nine Muses	
PHILABEG } the kilt		**PIFFLING** trifling; peddling	
PHILIBEG }		**PIG-FACED** swine-visaged	
PHILOMEL the nightingale	zo	**PIGEONED** fleeced; swindled	
PHLYCTEN nodule on conjunctiva	md	**PIGEONRY** pigeon loft	
PHOCENIC (dolphins)	zo	**PIGOTITE** aluminium compound	mn
PHONATED gurgled		**PIGSTIES** pig-pens	

PIG'S-WASH swill
PIKEHEAD head of a pike
PILASTER square column   ar
PILCHARD sea-fish   zo
PILE-WORK foundation of piles
PILE-WORM teredo; boring worm   zo
PILE-WORN threadbare
PILE-WORT celandine   bt
PILEATED capped
PILFERED filched; peculated
PILFERER purloiner; embezzler
PILIDIUM larval form of nemertea   zo
PILIFORM slender as a hair
PILING-UP petrol deposition in manifold   au
PILLAGED ransacked; looted
PILLAGER plunderer; rifler; robber
PILLARED columnar
PILLCORN oats   bt
PILLOWED cushioned
PILLWORT a plant   bt
PILOSELY hairily
PILOSITY hairiness
PILOTAGE pilot's fee
PILOTING directing; guiding; steering
PIMELITE aluminium silicate   mn
PIMPLING fuel can surface swelling   nc
PINACOID crystalline structure
PINAFORE apron
PINASTER the cluster-pine   bt
PINCE-NEZ eye-glasses
PINCHERS pincers; pliers
PINCHING nipping; being frugal
PINDAREE mogul freebooter
PINDARIC in the style of Pindar
PINE-CLAD crowned with pines
PINE-CONE fir-cone   bt
PINE-WOOD deal
PINE-WOOL fibrous substance
PING-PONG table tennis
PININGLY longingly; languishingly
PINIONED bound; shackled
PINK-EYED having small eyes
PINK-ROOT a vermifuge   bt
PINKSTER Whitsuntide; a pink flower
PINMAKER who makes pins   rl
PIN-MONEY an allowance
PINNACLE apex; acme; zenith; crown
PINNATED feathered
PINNIPED fin-footed; a seal   zo
PINOLEUM wood and canvas sunblind
PINPATCH periwinkle   bt
PINPOINT locate exactly
PINTABLE bagatelle gambling
PIN-WHEEL firework; clock part   hr
PINWHEEL revolving coloured wheel on stick
PIONNATE fungal spore layer   bt
PIPE-CASE pipe-holder
PIPE-CLAY a kaolin-like clay   mn
PIPE-FISH sea-horse type   zo

PIPE-LINE oil or water pipes
PIPE-RACK collection of pipes
PIPE-ROLL Great Roll of Exchequer
PIPE-TREE the lilac   bt
PIPE-WINE wine from the cask
PIPE-WORK a pipe-vein of ore   mn
PIPERINE extract of pepper   bt
PIPEWORT pepperwort   bt
PIQUANCY pungency; raciness
PIRATING infringing a copyright
PIRIFORM pearshaped
PISCATOR Izaak Walton; fisherman
PISCINAL (fishpond)
PISIFORM fishlike   zo
PISOLITE coarse oolite   mn
PISTACIA the pistachio-tree   bt
PISTOLET small pistol
PITCHING flinging; casting; lurching
PIT-FRAME framework round mine   mn
PITHECUS an ape   zo
PITHLESS lacking energy; sapless
PITIABLE sad; rueful; woeful; sorry
PITIABLY deplorably; movingly
PITILESS merciless; ruthless
PITTACAL a blue dye
PITTANCE dole; small allowance
PITUITAL (pituitary gland)   pl
PITYROID branlike
PIVOT-GUN swivel-gun
PIVOT-MAN key-man
PIVOTING moving around; hingeing
PIXY-RING fairy-ring
PLACABLE relenting; forgiving
PLACATED pacified; appeased
PLACEMAN office-holder
PLACENTA the afterbirth
PLACIDLY serenely; tranquilly; calmly
PLAGIARY literary theft
PLAGUILY pestiferously
PLAGUING tormenting; pestering
PLAINANT plaintiff   lw
PLAITING pleating; braiding
PLANCHED planked
PLANCHET disc; a blank
PLANETIC planetary; revolving
PLANGENT resounding; reverberating
PLANKING flooring; putting down
PLANKTON drifting organic life   zo
PLANLESS unsystematic; aimless
PLANNING scheming; plotting; devising
PLANTAIN banana-like fruit; a weed   bt
PLANTING inculcating; inserting
PLANTLET a small shrub   bt
PLANTULE embryo of a plant   bt
PLANULAR (embryo of hydrozoa)   zo
PLASHING dabbling; splashing
PLASHING hurdle-making process   bd
PLASMOID characteristic plasma section   ps
PLASTERY plasterwork   ar
PLASTRON breastplate

PLATBAND impost; lintel; projecting   **bd**
   moulding
PLATEFUL a meal
PLATELET constituent of blood   **md**
PLATFORM scheme of action
PLATINIC (platinum)   **ch**
PLATINUM metallic element   **ch**
PLATONIC philosophical
PLATTING plaiting; weaving
PLATYPUS duck bill   **zo**
PLATYSMA dermal musculature   **zo**
PLAUSIVE plausible
PLAY-DEBT gambling debt
PLAY-MARE hobby-horse
PLAYABLE dramatic
PLAYBILL programme
PLAYBOOK book of dramas
PLAYGOER stage fan
PLAYMATE sportive companion
PLAYSOME frolicsome; wanton
PLAYTIME recreation
PLEACHED interwoven; plaited; matted
PLEADING arguing; disputing
PLEASANT welcome; delectable
PLEASING grateful; charming
PLEASURE indulgence; gladness; joy
PLEATING folding
PLEBEIAN popular; vulgar; ignoble
PLECTRUM quill for lyre   **mu**
PLEDGING plighting; pawning
PLEIADES group of 7 stars
PLENARTY (benefice)   **rl**
PLEONASM verbosity
PLEONAST a sprouter; demagogue
PLESSITE entectic intergrowth in
   meteorites
PLETHORA superabundance; surfeit
PLEURISY lung inflammation   **md**
PLEXITIS nerve plexus inflammation   **md**
PLIANTLY easily bent; flexibly
PLICATED folded; involved; intricate
PLIGHTED betrothed
PLIGHTER one who pledges
PLIMMING becoming plump
PLIMSOLL rubber shoe; ship's load line
PLIOCENE a geological strata   **gl**
PLIOTRON hot-cathode vacuum tube   **el**
PLODDING slow but sure
PLOPPING dropping into water
PLOTTING contriving; planning
PLOUGHED furrowed; failed
PLOUGHER a husbandman
PLUCKILY courageously; valorously
PLUCKING stripping; (examinations)
PLUG-UGLY street ruffian
PLUGGING stopping; insistent
PLUM-CAKE Christmas cake
PLUM-DUFF a pudding
PLUMB-BOB (test for uprightness)
PLUMBAGO graphite   **mn**
PLUMBAGO blue or violet flower   **bt**

PLUMBEAN leaden; dull; heavy
PLUMBERY lead work
PLUMBING sounding
PLUMBISM lead poisoning   **md**
PLUMELET downy feather   **zo**
PLUMIPED feathered feet   **zo**
PLUMMING sinking a shaft
PLUMPEST fattest
PLUMPING going all out
PLUNGEON a sea-bird   **zo**
PLUNGING immersing; ducking
PLURALLY more than once
PLUTARCH a lively 2nd-century writer
PLUTONIC infernal; dark; igneous
PLUVIOUS rainy; pluvial; humid
POACHING stabbing; trespassing
POCHETTE a wallet
POCKETED filched; pouched
POCKMARK a scar   **md**
POCKWOOD a hard wood   **bt**
PODAGRAL ⎫ gouty   **md**
PODAGRIC ⎭
PODALGIA neuralgia in foot   **md**
PODARGUS genus of nocturnal birds
PODAUGER grooved auger   **to**
PODISMUS spasm of foot   **md**
PODOCARP stalk to a carpel   **bt**
POPODERM dermal layer of hoof   **zo**
PODOMERE limb segment in arthropoda **zo**
PODOSOMA leg-bearing segments in
   acarina   **zo**
POEMATIC poetical; lyric; metrical
POETICAL imaginative; rhyming
POETIZED versified
POIGNANT acutely painful; caustic
POIGNARD small dagger
POINDING distraining   **lw**
POINTING directing; aiming; indicating
POISONED corrupted; envenomed
POISONER who gives poison
POLARITY united opposites
POLARIZE magnetize
POLE-JUMP high-flying sport
POLE-STAR Polaris; a lode-star
POLEMAST (without a topmast)   **nt**
POLEMICS controversies
POLICIES lines of conduct; parks
POLICING maintaining order
POLISHED smooth; burnished
POLISHER shoe or furniture shiner
POLITELY courteously; urbanely
POLITICS art of government
POLITICO opportunist politician
POLL-ADZE blunt-headed adze   **to**
POLL-BOOK register of voters
POLL-EVIL bursa inflammation in horse **vt**
POLLICES thumbs or great toes   **pl**
POLLINAR covered with pollen   **bt**
POLLIWOG, POLLYWOG tadpole   **zo**
POLLSTER opinion taker
POLLUTED profaned; corrupted

POLLUTER defiler
POLOCYTE polar body zo
POLONIUM radio-active element
POLTROON coward; dastard; craven
POLYARCH of many-stranded stele bt
POLYAXON having many axes zo
POLYCARP gonad form in urochorda zo
POLYFOIL circular ornamentation
POLYGAMY plurality of wives
POLYGLOT in several languages
POLYGRAM many sided figure
POLYMERY whorl of many members bt
POLYOPIA multiple vision md
POLYPARY hard covering of polyps
POLYPIDE compound polyzoan zo
POLYPODE having many feet
POLYPODY a fern bt
POLYPOID ⎫ resembling polyps;
POLYPOUS ⎭ octopus type zo
POLYPOSE multi-pose portrait pg
POLYSOME cluster of ribosomes ch
POLYSOMY multiple-chromosome state cy
POLYTERM unit concept heading
POLYTYCH many-leaved ancient book
POLYTYPE cast of an engraving
POLYURIA excessive urine secretion md
POLYZOAN colony of polyzoa zo
POLYZOIC zoolatrous; sporozoic zo
POLYZOON barnacle type zo
POMANDER perfumed ball
POMIFORM like an apple
POMOLOGY apple culture bt
POMPEIAN (Pompeii)
POND-LILY inhabitant of lily-pond bt
POND-WEED aquatic plant bt
POND-WORT water-soldier plant bt
PONDERAL ascertained by weight
PONDERED meditated; thought
PONDERER cogitator; ruminator
PONTIFEX a Roman pontiff
PONTIFIC priestly; papal rl
PONTINAL bridging
PONY-SKIN soft hide
PONY-TAIL girl's hairstyle
POOH-POOH sneer at; deride
POOL-ROOM billiard-room
POONSPAR an Indian tree bt
POOR-JOHN salted hake
POOR-LAWS laws of long ago helping to
support paupers lw
POOR-RATE a tax
POORNESS poverty; indigency
POPE-JOAN a card game
POPELING a would-be pope rl
POPE'S-EYE fatty gland zo
POPESHIP popehood rl
POPINJAY parrot; coxcomb; fop
POPISHLY in popish style rl
POPLITIC (knee-joint or ham) md
POPPLING bubbling
POPPY-OIL slow-drying paint ingredient

POPULACE rabble; mob; masses
POPULATE propagate
POPULINE aspen bark extract bt
POPULOUS thronged; crowded; dense
PORIFERA the sponges zo
PORIFORM like a pore
PORISTIC porismatic; inferential
PORK-CHOP meat of pig
PORKLING young pig zo
POROCYTE tube-pierced cell in porifera zo
POROGAMY pollen-tube entry in micropyle
bt
POROSITY porousness
POROTYPE a reproduction
PORPHYRY igneous rock mn
PORPOISE sea-hog zo
PORRIDGE Scotch oat dish
PORTABLE easily carried
PORTERLY coarse; vulgar
PORTESSE a breviary rl
PORTFIRE an igniter
PORTHOLE opening in ship's side nv
PORTIERE doorway curtain
PORTLAND (stone; cement) mn
PORTLAST gunwale nt
PORTMOTE court held in port lw
PORTOISE gunwale nt
PORTOLAN charts of bearing & ports nv
PORTRAIT likeness; representation
PORT-ROPE rope for porthole lid
PORTUARY portable breviary rl
POSEIDON sea-god; Neptune
POSITRON sub-atomic particle
POSHTEEN sheepskin coat
POSINGLY so as to puzzle
POSITING postulating; affirming
POSITION spot; post; locality
POSITIVE actual; real; true
POSITRON radioisotope decay product nc
POSOLOGY science of quantity md
POSSIBLE feasible; likely
POSSIBLY practicably
POST-BILL placard
POST-CARD card sent by post
POST-DATE cf. antedate
POST-FACT a later occurrence
POST-FREE postage paid
POST-HORN curled instrument
POST-NATI born after a certain date
POST-NOTE promissory note
POST-OBIT payable after death
POST-PAID prepaid
POST-TIME hour of despatch
POST-TOWN mailville
POSTABLE mailable
POSTICHE counterfeit; coil of false hair;
wig
POSTIQUE added ornament
POSTLUDE conclusion mu
POSTMARK date stamp
POSTPONE defer; adjourn; shelve

POSTURAL postulatory	**PRECINCT** a close; enclosure	
POSTURED posed	**PRECIOUS** dear; prized; treasured	
POSTURER acrobat	**PRECLUDE** shut out; obviate; debar	
POTAMOUS living in streams	ec	**PRECURSE** a prognostication
POT-BELLY a paunch	**PREDABLE** raptorial; predacious	
POT-HOUSE drinking booth	**PREDATED** antedated	
POT-METAL lead and copper alloy	**PREDELLA** altar decoration; stool	rl
POT-PLANT (grown in a pot)	bt	**PREENING** tidying up; cleaning
POT-ROAST braised meat	**PREFACED** introduced by	
POT-STICK stirring stick	**PREFACER** preface writer	
POT-STILL malt whiskey	**PREFINED** limited beforehand	
POTATION drinking bout	**PREFIXED** anticipated; put before	
POTATOES edible tubers	bt	**PREGNANT** prolific; fertile; fraught
POTATORY draughty	**PREHNITE** silicate of alumina	mn
POTENTLY forcibly; powerfully	**PREJUDGE** condemn unheard	
POTHERED bothered; harassed	**PRELUDED** prefaced; started	
POTSHARD ⎫ broken piece of	**PRELUDER** prelude player	
POTSHARE ⎬ earthenware	**PREMIANT** incentive	
POTSHERD ⎭	**PREMIATE** to reward	
POTSTONE soapstone	mn	**PREMIERE** first performance
POTTERED dawdled	**PREMISED** introduced	
POTTERER desultory worker	**PREMISES** a messuage	lw
POTTOROO rat kangaroo	zo	**PREMOLAR** bicuspid tooth	md
POTULENT rather tipsy	**PREMORSE** ending abruptly	
POUCHING pocketing	**PRENASAL** in front of your nose	
POUCHONG black tea	bt	**PRENATAL** before birth
POULAINE long pointed shoe	**PRENOMEN** Christian name	
POULTICE a cataplasm	**PRENTICE** apprentice	
POUNCING sudden onset	**PREORDER** arrange beforehand	
POUNDAGE discount; taxation	**PREPARED** provided; planned; made	
POUNDING bruising; braying	**PREPARER** arranger	
POWDERED sprinkled	**PREPENSE** premeditated	
POWERFUL potent; puissant	**PRESAGED** foreboded; foretold	
POWERGAS coal-gas	**PRESAGER** seer; soothsayer	
POYOK-OIL W. African drying oil	pt	**PRESBYTE** a far-sighted person
PRACTICE performance; wont	**PRESCIND** cut off; distract	
PRACTICK skilful; deceitful	**PRESENCE** mien; demeanour; company	
PRACTISE to perpetrate; pursue	**PRESERVE** conserve; defend; keep	
PRACTIVE adept; dexterous	**PRESIDED** controlled; officiated	
PRAECIPE writ or instruction	lw	**PRESS-BED** collapsible bed
PRAEFECT magistrate	lw	**PRESS-BOX** reporter's box
PRAISING lauding; exalting; eulogizing	**PRESSING** urgent; importunate; vital	
PRANCING bounding; capering	**PRESSION** compression	
PRANDIAL concerning dinner	**PRESSMAN** journalist	
PRANGING crashing; bombing	ae	**PRESSURE** straits; urgency; stress
PRANKING displaying; gambolling	**PREST-MAN** an enlisted man	
PRANKISH freakish; impish	**PRESTIGE** reputation; fame; renown	
PRASITES type of wine	**PRESUMED** surmised; thought	
PRATIQUE clearance certificate	nt	**PRESUMER** conjecturer
PRATTLED babbled; chattered	**PRETENCE** cloak; mask; guise	
PRATTLER chatterbox	**PRETERIT** the past tense	
PRE-ELECT choose beforehand	**PRE-TRIAL** court case dry run	
PRE-ENTRY previous to joining	**PRETTIFY** beautify; adorn	
PRE-EXIST live before	**PRETTILY** neatly; daintily	
PREPUBIC in front of pubis	zo	**PREVIOUS** antecedent; prior; former
PRE-STUDY con; cogitate; ponder	**PREVISED** foreseen	
PREACHED proclaimed; exhorted	**PRICKING** inciting; spurring	
PREACHER pastor; divine; declarer	**PRICKLED** spiky	
PREAMBLE an introduction; preface	**PRIDEFUL** haughty; scornful	
PREBOUND (books) in a library binding	**PRIESTLY** sacerdotal	
PRECEDED anticipated; headed; led	**PRIGGERY** super-respectability	

PRIGGING larceny; pinching
PRIGGISH conceited; prim; affected
PRIGGISM coxcombry; pedantry
PRIMATES monkeys; archbishops   zo
PRIMEVAL antediluvian; pristine
PRIMMING decking; pranking
PRIMNESS formality; demureness
PRIMROSE a badge   bt
PRINCELY regal; stately; lavish
PRINCEPS the original
PRINCESS king's daughter
PRINCOCK a prig; coxcomb
PRINKING strutting; pranking
PRINTING typography
PRIORATE office of prior   rl
PRIORESS lady prior   rl
PRIORITY precedence
PRISMOID prismatic
PRISONED incarcerated; gaoled
PRISONER captive
PRISTINE original; ancient
PRIZEMAN a winner
PROATLAS bone between skull and vertebra   zo
PROBABLE credible; likely
PROBABLY maybe; peradventure
PROBATOR examiner; approver
PROCAINE crystalline solid   pm
PROCEEDS results; produce
PROCHEIN next; nearest   lw
PROCINCT complete preparation
PROCLAIM bruit; trumpet; blazon
PROCURED got; obtained; acquired
PROCURER a pander
PRODDING goading
PRODIGAL wasteful; reckless; lavish
PRODITOR traitor
PRODROME preliminary treatise
PRODUCED created; caused; made
PRODUCER generator; manufacturer
PROEMIAL introductory
PROFANED violated; debased
PROFANER blasphemer; desecrater
PROFILED outlined
PROFITED benefited; gained
PROFITER profiteer
PRO-FORMA advance checking for confirmation
PROFOUND deep; abysmal; occult
PROGGING begging food
PROGONAL of genital ridge portion   ■■
PROGRESS advancement; growth
PROHIBIT interdict; forbid; ban
PROLAPSE fall down
PROLIFIC productive; fertile; fecund
PROLIXLY at great length
PROLOGUE dramatic preface; poem
PROLONGE rope; rings and toggle
PROMETAL heat-resistant cast iron   ml
PROMISED guaranteed; engaged
PROMISEE assured person

PROMISER ⎫ assuror; warranter;
PROMISOR ⎭ pledger; stipulator
PROMOTED elevated; preferred
PROMOTEE advanced person
PROMOTER active agent
PROMPTED suggested
PROMPTER encourager; (theatre)
PROMPTLY readily; quickly
PROMULGE announce; publish
PRONATED bent
PRONATOR an arm muscle   md
PRONG-HOE a gardening tool
PRONOTUM prothorax notum in insects   zo
PRO-NYMPH a stage of insect life   zo
PROOFING testing; making waterproof
PROPANOL propyl alcohol   ch
PROPENOL allyl alcohol   ch
PROPENSE inclined; disposed
PROPERLY correctly; formally; exactly
PROPERTY quality; wealth; chattels
PROPHAGE inactive bacteriophage   bt
PROPHASE mitosis/meiosis early stage   cy
PROPHECY forecast; divination
PROPHESY to prognosticate; foretell
PROPHYLL bracteole   bt
PROPLASM mould; matrix
PROPOLIS beeswax
PROPOSAL suggestion; tender
PROPOSED intended; meant; planned
PROPOSER mover; instigator
PROPOUND advocate; enunciate
PROPPAGE support
PROPPING shoring up
PROPRIUM self-hood; egotism
PROPYLON temple gateway
PRORATED assessed
PROROGUE adjourn; defer; postpone
PROSAISM prose writing
PROSAIST prosy person
PROSEMAN writer of prose
PROSODUS canal in porifera   zo
PROSPECT aspect; outlook; survey
PROSPORY sporangia formation   bt
PROSTATE male gland near bladder   pl
PROSTYLE pillared portico
PROTASIS maxim; prologue
PROTATIC introductory
PROTEASE protein enzyme   ch
PROTEGEE a ward   ch
PROTEIDS, PROTEINS albuminoids   ch
PROTELES the aard-wolf   zo
PROTENSE extension (obs.)
PROTEOSE protein derivative   ch
PROTHECA coral calyx rudiment   zo
PROTISTA organisms   bt, zo
PROTOCOL treaty; draft agreement
PROTOPOD early abdominal phase in insects
PROTOSET mine rescue equipment   mn
PROTOZOA early life forms   zo

PROTRACT draw out; prolong; delay
PROTRUDE bulge; jut; project
PROVABLE demonstrable
PROVABLY verifiably
PROVIANT provender
PROVIDED if; supplied; yielded
PROVIDER furnisher; caterer
PROVINCE department; tract
PROVINED (vine culture)
PROVISOR purveyor; treasurer
PROVOKED exasperated; stung; vexed
PROVOKER inciter; annoyer; offender
PROWLING roving for prey; slinking
PROXIMAL adjoining; adjacent
PRUDENCE discretion; judiciousness
PRUINOSE ⎫
PRUINOUS ⎭ powdery; mealy
PRUNELLA self-heal plant   bt
PRUNELLO dried plum   bt
PRURIENT interested in the obscene
PRURITIS persistent severe itching   md
PRYINGLY inquisitively; curiously
PSALMIST inspired singer   rl
PSALMODY psalms collectively   rl
PSALTERY stringed instrument   mu
PSAMMITE sandstone   mn
PSELLISM stammering   md
PSITTACI the parrot tribe   zo
PSYCHICS mental phenomena
PSYCHISM spiritualism
PSYCHIST psychologist
PTEROMYS flying squirrel   zo
PTEROPOD class of molluscs   zo
PTEROTIC skull ear-wall bone   zo
PTERYLAE clump of feathers   zo
PTILINUM cephalic sac in dipters   zo
PTILOSIS plumage   zo
PTOMAINE organic poison   md
PTYALISM salivation   md
PUBCRAWL round of taverns
PUBLICAN collector of tribute
PUBLICLY open to all
PUCELAGE virginity
PUCKBALL puffball   bt
PUCKERED wrinkled; crinkled
PUDDLING clay/iron refining process   mn
PUDICITY modesty
PUFF-BALL lycoperdon   bt
PUFF-BIRD S. American bird   zo
PUFF-PUFF onomatopoeic locomotive
PUG-FACED monkey-faced
PUGGAREE scarf round helmet
PUGILISM the noble art
PUGILIST a pug; a boxer
PUISSANT powerful; forcible
PULEGONE terpene ketone in pennyroyal
    ch
PULINGLY fretfully; whiningly
PULLBACK a restraint
PULLOVER jersey; sweater
PULMONIC consumptive   md

PULPITER preacher   rl
PULSATOR vibrator
PULSIFIC throbbing
PULVINAR a cushion
PULVINUS swollen leaf base   bt
PUMICATE polish; make smooth
PUMP-DALE water trough
PUMP-ROOM mineral spring at spa
PUMP-WELL water pumped from well
PUNCHEON steel tool; large cask
PUNCHING perforating; striking
PUNCTATE pointed
PUNCTUAL punctilious; timely
PUNCTURE a hole; perforate; prick
PUNGENCE acridness
PUNGENCY keenness: acuteness
PUNINESS feebleness; frailty
PUNISHED chastised; penalized
PUNISHER disciplinarian
PUNITIVE punishing; penal
PUNITORY corrective
PUNTILLA lace-work
PUNTSMAN he who punts
PUPARIAL, PUPI- ⎫ a chrysalis;   zo
FORM, PUPARIUM ⎭ pupa
PUPATION incubation   zo
PUPILAGE wardship; minority
PUPILARY in statu pupillari
PUPILATE having a central spot
PUPIPARA viviparous insects   zo
PUPPETRY puppet-show; finery
PUPPYISH conceited
PUPPYISM affectation
PURBLIND dim-sighted
PURCHASE buy; procure; leverage
PURENESS purity; chastity
PURFLING embroidering
PURIFIED ceremonially cleansed
PURIFIER a refiner
PURIFORM resembling pus   md
PURISTIC scrupulously stylish
PURPARTY share of an estate   lw
PURPLING dyeing with purple
PURPLISH somewhat purple
PURPOSED resolved; meant; intended
PURPURIC madder-purple
PURSEFUL enough to fill a purse
PURSE-NET purse with strings
PURSLANE salad herb
PURSUANT conformably
PURSUING prosecuting; chasing
PURULENT suppurating   md
PURVEYED procured; retailed
PURVEYOR caterer
PUSEYISM tractarianism   rl
PUSEYITE high church doctrinaire   rl
PUSHBALL a great ball game
PUSHBIKE a cycle
PUSHCART barrow; handcart
PUSHOVER easy success
PUSHPULL amplifier   el

PUSS-MOTH large hairy moth	zo
PUSS-TAIL a bristle grass	bt
PUSSY-CAT willow-catkin	bt, zo
PUSTULAR pimpled	md
PUTATION computation; sum	
PUTATIVE reputed; alleged	
PUTCHOCK root used for incense	bt
PUT-TO-BED too late to add to printing	
PUTTYING fixing panes	
PUZZLING bewildering; perplexing	
PYCNOSIS staining-matter shrinkage	cy
PYELITIS kidney pelvis inflammation	md
PYOGENIC pus-producing	md
PYRAMOID of pyramid form	
PYRAZOLE heterocyclic compound	ch
PYRENOID refractive protein mass	bt
PYRENOUS globular; nucleiform	bt
PYREXIAL feverish	md
PYRIDINE organic compound	ch
PYRIFORM pear-shaped	
PYRITIZE turn into pyrites	
PYRITOUS like pyrites	mn
PYROGRAM mechanical firework	
PYROLOGY blowpipe analysis	
PYROSOMA luminous animalculae	zo
PYROSTAT a thermostat	
PYROTRON thermonuclear device	nc
PYROXENE augite	mn
PYROXYLE gun-cotton	ch
PYRRHOUS reddish	
PYTHONIC oracular	
PYXIDATE having a lid	bt
PYXIDIUM lidlike capsule	bt

Q

QUACKERY charlatanism; humbug	
QUACKING boasting	
QUACKISH somewhat bogus	
QUACKISM medical pretence	
QUACKLED almost choked	
QUADRANS Roman farthing	nm
QUADRANT quarter-circle	
QUADRATE square; to agree	
QUADRIGA four-horsed chariot	
QUADROON (quarter negro blood)	
QUADRUNE gritstone	mn
QUAESITA to be decided on later	
QUAESTOR treasurer	
QUAFFING swallowing; imbibing	
QUAGMIRE a bog; swamp	
QUAGMIRY yielding; boggy	
QUAILING flinching; blenching	
QUAINTER odder; stranger	
QUAINTLY whimsically; fancifully	
QUAKERLY soberly	
QUALMISH squeamish; queasy	
QUANDANG Australian peach	bt
QUANDARY dilemma; predicament	
QUANTIFY determine quantity	
QUANTITY measure; amount; bulk	

QUARRIED hewn	
QUARRIER quarryman	
QUARRIES arrows; panes of glass	
QUARTERN a gill; 4 lb (1.8 kg)	me
QUARTERS living places	
QUARTILE (a planet aspect)	
QUARTINE a seed covering	bt
QUASHING annulling; crushing	
QUASSINE } extract of quassia;	md
QUASSITE } a febrifuge	
QUATERON a quadroon	
QUATORZE a count in piquet	
QUATRAIN four line stanza	
QUAVERED quivered; shook; vibrated	
QUAVERER a warbler	
QUAY-WALL harbour-wall	
QUEASILY squeamishly	
QUEBRADA a ravine (Sp.)	
QUEEN-BEE ruler of hive	zo
QUEENDOM queenly state	
QUEENING playing the queen	
QUEENLET a petty queen	
QUEEREST quaintest; oddest	
QUEERING spoiling; disarranging	
QUEERISH rather strange	
QUELLERZ limonite	mn
QUELLING crushing; subduing; curbing	
QUENCHED extinguished	
QUENCHER a long drink	
QUENELLE forcemeat	
QUERCITE acorn extract	bt
QUERLING twirling	
QUERYING challenging; inquiring	
QUESTFUL adventurous	
QUESTING seeking; searching	
QUESTION interrogation; catechize	
QUESTMAN authorized inquirer	
QUEUEING lining up	
QUIBBLED evaded the question	
QUIBBLER prevaricator	
QUICKEST speediest; fastest	
QUICKIES quickly done films, drinks, etc.	
QUICKSET living plant	bt
QUIDDANY a mess of quinces	
QUIDDING food expulsion after chewing	vt
QUIDDITY captious question; quibble	
QUIDDLED wasted time; pottered	
QUIDDLER a trifler	
QUIDNUNC tattler; know-all	
QUIESCED silenced, subsided	
QUIETAGE tranquility	
QUIETEST calmest	
QUIETISE pacify	
QUIETISM placidness	
QUIETIST a mystic	
QUIETIVE sedative	
QUIETUDE rest; repose	
QUILLING crimping; goffering	
QUILL-NIB penpoint	
QUILTING quilted work	

QUINABLE interval of a fifth   mu
QUINCUNX plantation of 5 trees   fr
QUINTAIN balanced tilting beam
QUINTILE aspect of the planets
QUINTOLE five-stringed viol   mu
QUIPPING taunting; jesting
QUIPPISH sarcastic
QUIRINAL Italian Court
QUIRINUS defied Romulus
QUIRITES Roman citizens
QUIRKING twisting
QUIRKISH evasive
QUISLING traitor; betrayer
QUIT-RENT rent in lieu of service
QUITTING deserting; ratting
QUIXOTIC ⎫ romantic and absurd
QUIXOTRY ⎬   notions and actions
QUIZZERY ridicule
QUIZZIFY hoax; puzzle
QUIZZING bantering; chaffing
QUOTABLE citable
QUOTIENT how many times
QUOTIETY proportionate frequency

R

RABATINE turned-down collar
RABBETED grooved
RABBINIC Hebrew language, etc.
RABBITER rabbit catcher
RABBITRY enclosure for rabbits
RABELAIS indelicate satirist
RABIDITY raving madness; frenzy
RABIETIC maniacal; insane; demented
RACE-CARD record of runners
RACEGOER watcher of winners
RACEMOSE ⎫ in clusters   bt
RACEMOUS ⎬
RACEMULE small bunch   bt
RACHILLA leaf-rib   bt
RACHITIC rickety   md
RACHITIS rickets   md
RACINESS piquancy
RACK-RAIL toothed tail
RACK-RENT exorbitant rent
RACK-TAIL part of clock
RACK-WORK rack and pinion
RACKETED frolicked; clamoured
RACKETER a noisy person
RACLETTE cheese for melting; Swiss   ck
RACOVIAN Polish Socinian
RADARMAN radar petty officer R.N.
RADECHON mesh-grid storage tube   el
RADIALLY like spokes of a wheel
RADIANCE effulgence; lustre
RADIANCY brilliancy; glitter; sheen
RADIATED shone; sparkled
RADIATOR heating apparatus
RADICANT taking root
RADICATE to plant; emplant

RADICOSE having a large root   bt
RADICULE a small root   bt
RADIOING transmitting by wireless
RADIOLUS part of a feather   zo
RADULATE (rasping tongue)   zo
RAFFLING lottery for an article or
    articles
RAFT-DUCK black-headed duck   zo
RAFT-PORT (timber loading)   nt
RAFT-ROPE thickish piece of string
RAFTERED timbered
RAFTSMAN castaway
RAG-PAPER high-quality paper
RAG-WHEEL polishing wheel
RAGABASH ragamuffin
RAGGEDLY in tatters
RAGINGLY furiously; rabidly
RAGNAROK twilight of the gods
RAGSTONE impure limestone   mn
RAILHEAD a terminus
RAILLERY banter; chaff; ridicule
RAILROAD railway
RAINBAND band in solar spectrum
RAINBIRD Jamaican bird   zo
RAINCOAT waterproof
RAINDROP single drop of rain
RAINFALL shower
RAINLESS state of drought
RAINPOUR downpour
RAINTREE S. American tree   bt
RAIN-WASH gravity/rain soil creepage   gl
RAISINEE a confection
RAKEHELL a rip; debauchée
RAKISHLY set at an angle
RAKSHASA Hindu ghoul
RALLYING reuniting; gathering
RAMAYANA Indian epic poem
RAMBLING roaming; wandering
RAMBOOZE a cordial
RAMBUTAN Malayan fruit tree   bt
RAMENTUM brown scale on ferns   bt
RAMICOLE living on twigs   bt
RAMICORN horny sheath
RAMIFIED diverse
RAMIFORM like a branch
RAMPAGED romped; rioted; gambolled
RAMPANCY excessive prevalence
RAMPSMAN highwayman
RAMRODDY stiff
RAMSHORN an ammonite   mn
RAMULOUS ramulose; branching
RANARIUM frog aquarium   zo
RANCHERO cow-puncher
RANCHING cattle-raising
RANCHMAN stockbreeder
RANCIDLY fustily; mustily; sourly
RANDOMLY at a venture; fortuitously
RANGIFER a reindeer   zo
RANIFORM froglike   zo
RANKLING festering; smouldering
RANKNESS overgrowth; exuberance

RANSOMED redeemed; released	**REALNESS** actuality; verity; fact
RANSOMER liberator; indemnifier	**REANOINT** relubricate
RAPACITY greed; avarice; voracity	**REANSWER** reply again
RAPE-CAKE cattle fodder	**REAPPEAR** turn up again
RAPE-SEED (hence colza oil) **bt**	**REAR-LINE** behind the army
RAPHANIA ergotism; blight	**REAR-RANK** back line
RAPHANUS radish **bt**	**REARMING** re-equipping
RAPHIDES crystals in plants	**REARMOST** last; ultimate
RAPIDITY celerity; despatch; speed	**REARWARD** rearguard
RAPPAREE Irish robber; bandit	**REASCEND** climb again
RAPTORES birds of prey **zo**	**REASCENT** a further climb
RAPTURED ravished; ecstatic	**REASONED** argued; disputed
RAREFIED tenuous	**REASONER** debater
RARENESS infrequency; scarceness	**REASSERT** re-affirm
RARERIPE early ripe; untimely	**REASSESS** re-impose; revalue
RASCALLY knavish; roguish; dishonest	**REASSIGN** give different job to
RASHLING reckless fellow	**REASSURE** console; comfort
RASHNESS foolhardiness; unwariness	**REATTACH** refix
RASORIAL scratching	**REATTAIN** get again
RAT-GOOSE brent goose **zo**	**REAVOWED** said so again
RATAPLAN beat of drum	**REBATING** deducting from
RATCHETY jerky	**REBELLED** revolted; mutinied
RATCHING yarn-tightening process **wv**	**REBELLER** a rebel; insurgent
RATE-BOOK book of valuations	**REBELLOW** re-echo
RATEABLE assessable	**REBITING** re-engraving
RATHRIPE early ripe	**REBOILER** vessel at still bottom **ch**
RATIFIED confirmed; endorsed	**REBRACED** restrengthened
RATIFIER approver; authorizer	**REBUFFED** repulsed; snubbed
RATIONAL reasonable; judicious; sane	**REBUKING** chiding; carpeting
RATIONED on an allowance	**REBURIED** re-interred
RAT'S-BANE rat poison	**REBUTTAL** refutation; retort
RAT'S-TAIL tapering	**REBUTTED** confuted; refuted
RATSNAKE rat-killing snake **zo**	**REBUTTER** a legal reply **lw**
RATTINET a woollen stuff	**RECALLED** revoked; annulled; denied
RATTLING quick; lively; clattering	**RECANTED** retracted; abjured
RAVAGING despoiling; plundering	**RECAPTOR** one who retakes
RAVEHOOK ripping iron **to**	**RE-CASING** rebinding of book in original
RAVELLED entangled; untwisted	cover
RAVENING plundering; devouring	**RECEDING** retreating; ebbing
RAVENOUS starving; voracious	**RECEIVED** got; allowed; welcomed
RAVINGLY with fury; frantically	**RECEIVER** a recipient; receptionist **lw**
RAVISHED enchanted; charmed	**RECENTLY** lately
RAVISHER abductor	**RECESSED** dimpled; secluded
RAW-BONED gaunt	**RECESSES** niches; vacations
RAWLBOLT) nail or screw	**RECESSUS** a recess; a niche
RAWLPLUG / wall fixing system	**RECHARGE** attack anew; reload
REABSORB soak up again	**RECISION** cutting back; pruning
REACCESS fresh approach	**RECITING** rehearsing; relating
REACCUSE indict again	**RECKLESS** heedless; rash; headstrong
REACHING extending; attaining	**RECKLING** weakest in a litter **zo**
REACTANT substance involved in chem.	**RECKONED** considered; judged
reaction	**RECKONER** calculator; computer
REACTION counter-measure; recoil	**RECLINED** leant; lay; reposed
REACTIVE power to react	**RECLINER** a reclining dial
READABLE interesting	**RECLOSED** shut again
READABLY legibly	**RECLOTHE** provide new garments
READJUST reset	**RECOALED** refilled the bunkers
REAFFIRM state anew	**RECOILED** retreated; reacted
REAGENCY reflex influence	**RECOILER** flincher
REALIZED felt; understood	**RECOINED** minted afresh
REALLEGE assert again	**RECOLLET** Franciscan monk **rl**

RECOLOUR repaint		
RECOMMIT refer again; re-entrust		
RECONVEY transfer back		
RECORDED entered; minuted	lw	
RECORDER flageolet; judge	mu	
RECOUPED indemnified		
RECOURSE reference; resort; refuge		
RECOVERY convalescence; revival		
RECREANT craven; apostate		
RECREATE refresh; delight		
RECTIGON thermionic gas diode	el	
RECTORAL rectorial	rl	
RECUBANT recumbent		
RECUMBED reclined; reposed		
RECURRED remembered; repeated		
RECURVED bent back		
RECUSANT Elizabethan R.C.	rl	
RED-BELLY terrapin; char	zo	
RED-CEDAR pencil-wood	bt	
RED-CHALK reddle	mn	
RED-CORAL living coral	mn	
RED-CROSS humanitarian organization		
RED-EARTH reddish loam	mn	
RED-FACED florid; rubicund		
RED-METAL a copper alloy		
RED-SHIRT follower of Garibaldi		
RED-SHORT brittle		
RED-STAFF millstone trimmer		
REDACTOR editor		
REDARGUE to refute; disprove		
REDDENDA rent clauses	lw	
REDDENDO (vassal's duties)	lw	
REDDENED blushed; flushed		
REDEEMED ransomed; freed; retrieved		
REDEEMER liberator; saviour		
REDELESS unwise; ill-advised		
REDEMAND request again		
REDEMISE reconveyance	lw	
REDENTED indented		
REDEPLOY movement of army; industrial		
REDIGEST reduce to form again		
REDIRECT re-address		
REDITION return		
REDIVIDE re-allot		
REDNOSED nose red with cold		
REDOLENT aromatic; fragrant		
REDOUBLE a bridge call		
REDRIVEN herded back again		
REDSHANK red-legged sandpiper	zo	
REDUBBER old clothes merchant		
REDUCENT reducing		
REDUCING curtailing; abating		
REDUVIUS predacious bug	zo	
RE-DYEING recolouring		
RE-ECHOED reverberated; repeated		
REED-BAND clarionets, etc.	mu	
REED-BIRD bobolink	zo	
REED-MACE cat's tail	bt	
REED-PIPE an organ pipe	mu	
REED-STOP an organ stop	mu	
REED-WREN greater reedwarbler	zo	

REEDLESS no rush		
REEDLING bearded titmouse		zo
REEF-BAND strip of canvas		nt
REEF-KNOT secure flat knot		
REEF-LINE a rope		nt
REEL-LINE fishing line		
REEL-RALL topsy-turvy (Sc.)		
REEL-SEAT reel housing on rod		
REELABLE able to be wound		
RE-EMBARK get back in a boat		
RE-EMBODY reform into a body		
RE-EMERGE come out again		
RE-ENFORCE reinforce		
RE-ENLIST sign on again		
RE-EXPORT ship out again		
REFASTEN refix		
REFERRED attributed; assigned		
REFERRER enquirer		
REFIGURE present anew		
REFILLED replenished		
REFINERY purification plant		
REFINING purifying		
REFITTED re-equipped		
REFLEXED curved back		
REFLEXLY reactively		
REFLOWED ebbed		
REFLOWER bloom again		
REFLUENT flowing back		
REFOREST plan anew		
REFORGED kept signing false name		
REFORMED remodelled; restored		
REFORMER innovator		
REFRAMED traduced all over again		
REFREEZE make icebound again		
REFRINGE infringe		
REFUNDED reimbursed; repaid		
REFUNDER one who pays back again		
REFUSING declining; repudiating		
REFUTING gainsaying; rebutting		
REGAINED retrieved; recaptured		
REGALIAN regal; sovereign		
REGALING faring sumptuously		
REGALISM sovereignty		
REGALITY royalty		
REGARDED noticed; heeded; gazed		
REGARDER observer; watcher		
REGATHER recollect		
REGICIDE killer of a king		
REGILDED made golden once more		
REGIMENT organize; a military unit		
REGIONAL topographical		
REGIONIC local		
REGISTER record; chronicle; fit		
REGISTRY labour agency		
REGLETTE measuring tape scale		sv
REGNANCY predominance; supremacy		
REGORGED vomited		
REGRATED freshened; scraped		
REGRATER huckster; regrator		
REGROUND (razors); resharpened		
REGROWTH new growth		

REGULATE adjust; control; arrange
REGULIZE refine chemically
REHANDLE finger a 2nd time
REHASHED furnished up
REHEARSE recapitulate
RE-HEATED réchauffé
REHOUSED given new homes
REIGNING prevailing; governing
RE-IGNITE rekindle
REIMBODY re-incorporate
REIMPORT bring back
REIMPOSE retax
REINCITE reanimate
REINDEER the caribou   zo
REINFECT make sick again
REINFORM renotify
REINFUND pour in again
REINFUSE reanimate
REIN-HOOK bearing-rein hook
REINLESS unchecked
REINSERT put in again
REINSMAN accomplished driver
REINSURE make doubly certain
REINVENT create anew
REINVEST put money in again
REINVITE ask again
REISSUED put out again
REJECTED excluded; rebuffed
REJECTOR decliner; rejecter
REJOICED exulted; gloried; delighted
REJOICER reveller; merry-maker
REJOINED knit together; reunited
REJUDGED re-examined; reconsidered
REKINDLE arouse anew; relight
RELANDED came down twice
RELAPSED retrogressed
RELAPSER backslider
RELATING narrating; telling
RELATION connection; kinsman
RELATRIX female informant   lw
RELAXANT a loosener
RELAXING slackening; unbending
RELAYING transmit programmes   ro
RELEASED emancipated; freed
RELEASEE discharged person
RELEASER releasor; liberator
RELEGATE consign; transfer
RELESSEE releasee
RELESSOR releaser   lw
RELEVANT applicable; apt; pertinent
RELIABLE trustworthy; trusty; safe
RELIABLY dependably
RELIANCE confidence; trust
RELICTED left bare   lw
RELIEVED palliated; soothed; eased
RELIEVER mitigator; assuager
RELIGION faith
RELISHED appreciated
RELISTEN hear once more
RELIVING experiencing again
RELOADED ready to fire again

RELUCENT transparent; shining
RELUMINE rekindle
REMAINED left over; stopped
REMAKING rebuilding
REMANENT remaining
REMANNED provided with a new crew
REMARKED said; declared; mentioned
REMARKER commentator; observer
REMARQUE marginal etching
REMEDIAL curative; healing
REMEDIED repaired; rectified
REMEMBER recall; recollect
REMERCIE to thank (obs.)
REMIFORM oar-shaped
REMINDED brought to notice
REMINDER keepsake; souvenir
REMISING releasing   lw
REMISSLY negligently; slackly
REMITTAL surrender; remittance
REMITTED relaxed; forgave
REMITTEE consignee
REMITTER pardoner; remittor
REMOBOTH Syrian society
REMODIFY remodel
REMOLADE salad dressing
REMOLTEN remelted
REMOTELY faintly
REMOTION remoteness (obs.)
REMOVING dislodging; abstracting
REMURMUR complain again
RENAMING rechristening
RENDERED translated; gave
RENDERER supplier; assignor
RENDIBLE able to be torn
RENEGADE ⎫ quisling; apostate
RENEGADO ⎬ runagate; traitor;
RENEGATE ⎭ recreant; rebel
RENEGING revoking at cards
RENEWING renovating; rejuvenating
RENIDIFY build a new nest
RENIFORM kidney-shaped
RENIGATE renegade
RENITENT allergic; resistant
RENOUNCE disclaim; forsake; abjure
RENOVATE renew; repair; refresh
RENOWNED famous; eminent
RENOWNER swaggerer; braggart
RENTABLE leasable
RENTERER invisible mender
RENT-FREE living without paying rent
RENT-ROLL list of tenants
RENUMBER put new numbers on
RENVERSE inverted; reverse
REOBTAIN get again
REOCCUPY move back in
REOPENED no longer shut
REOPPOSE not capitulate
REORDAIN refrock the defrocked
REORIENT arising again
REPACIFY calm down again
REPAGULA egg-protection bodies   zo

REPAIRED redressed; went
REPAIRER restorer
REPARTEE witty retort; riposte
REPASSED went by twice
REPASTED fed
REPAYING refunding
REPEALED rescinded; annulled
REPEALER abrogator; revoker
REPEATED iterated; echoed
REPEATER a watch
REPELLED repulsed; checked; rebuffed
REPELLER deterrer; rejecter
REPENTED truly contrite; rued
REPEOPLE repopulate
REPERTOR a finder
REPERUSE read again
REPETEND recurring decimal
REPINING fretting; murmuring
REPLACED reinstated; restored
REPLACER a substitute
REPLEDGE swear again
REPLEVIN a legal action   lw
REPLUNGE dive again
REPLYING answering
REPOLISH shine up again
REPONING replacing   lw
REPORTED communicated; related
REPORTER announcer; journalist
REPOSING reclining; resting
REPOSURE repose; peace; tranquillity
REPOTTED (gardening)
REPOUSSE embossed
REPRIEVE respite; pardon; acquit
RE-PRIMER recapping machine
REPRISAL retaliation; revenge
REPROACH reprimand; upbraid
REPROVAL admonition; censure
REPROVED blamed; rebuked; chided
REPROVER reprehender
REPRUNED lopped again
REPTILIA snakes   zo
REPUBLIC democratic state
REPUGNED resisted; opposed
REPUGNER a rebel
REPULPIT restore a preacher
REPULSED checked; refused; rebuffed
REPULSER repeller
REPURIFY purify again
REPUTING esteeming
REQUIRED wanted; demanded; lacked
REQUIRER exactor; claimant
REQUITAL recompense; punishment
REQUITED reciprocated
REQUITER avenger
RE-RAILED got back on track
REREFIEF an under-fief (Sc.)   lw
REREWARD rear-guard
REROOFED given new roof
RESAILED sailed again
RESALUTE put hand to head again
RE-SCORED rearranged   mu

RESCRIBE rewrite
RESCRIPT edict; decree
RESCUING extricating; liberating
RESEARCH scientific enquiry
RESEATED given chair again
RESEIZED } legal seizure of   lw
RESEIZER } disseized property
RESEMBLE liken; compare; collate
RESENTED strongly objected; resisted
RESENTER an injured party
RESERVED shy; distant; unsociable
RESERVER withholder
RESETTER receiver of stolen goods
RESETTLE repopulate
RESHABAR dry wind in Kurdistan   mt
RESIANCE residence
RESIDENT politcal agent
RESIDUAL left over
RESIDUUM residue; surplus; excess
RESIGNED abdicated; relinquished
RESIGNEE he who gets resigned
RESIGNER renouncer; quitter
RESILING recoiling
RESINATA } Grecian white wine
RESINATE } of resinous flavour
RESINIFY } to make resinous
RESINISE }
RESISTED withstood; repelled; opposed
RESISTER opposer
RESISTOR non-conductor   el
RESMOOTH smooth again
RESOLDER solder again
RESOLUTE steadfast; staunch
RESOLVED melted; determined
RESOLVER solver
RESONANT resounding; sonorous
RESONATE re-echo; vibrate
RESORBED absorbed
RESORCIN crystalline phenol   ch
RESORTED betook; repaired; flew
RESORTER frequenter
RESOURCE expedient; means; device
RESOWING broadcasting again
RESPECTS compliments
RESPERSE disperse; sprinkle
RESPIRED inhaled
RESPITED postponed; reprieved
RESPOKEN repeated
RESPONSE answer; reply; rejoinder
RESTATED reaffirmed
REST-CURE convalescence
RESTLESS agitated; turbulent; uneasy
RESTORED returned; renewed; cured
RESTORER reviver; healer
RESTRAIN check; curb; suppress
RESTRICT limit; confine; hamper
RESTRIKE lay down work a second time
RESTRING tennis racket; violin
RESULTED caused; followed; ensued
RESUMING renewing; continuing
RESUMMON call again

RESUPINE lying on the back
RESURVEY review
RETAILED gossiped; peddled
RETAILER not a wholesale merchant
RETAILLE divided twice   hd
RETAINED detained; kept; withheld
RETAINER henchman; lackey; servant
RETAKING recapturing
RETARDED slowed up; delayed
RETARDER hinderer; obstructionist
RETENTOR retaining muscle   md
RETEPORE a coral   zo
RETICENT taciturn; reserved; quiet
RETICULE lady's workbag
RETIERCE heraldic arrangement   hd
RETIFERA the true limpet   zo
RETIFORM meshed; reticulated
RETINENE rhodopsin component   ch
RETINITE obsidian; amber   mn
RETINOID resin-like
RETINULA pigmented cells   zo
RETIRACY retirement
RETIRADE a retrenchment
RETIRING shy; unobtrusive; diffident
RETORTED rejoined; replied   hd
RETORTER responder
RETOSSED thrown back
RETRACED returned by same route
RETRAXIT loss of action   lw
RETRENCH curtail; economize
RETRIEVE recover; regain; rescue
RETROACT oppose
RETRORSE bent back
RETRUDED thrust back
RETRYING attempting again
RETUNDED blunted
RETURNED rendered; reverted
RETURNER remitter
REUNITED rejoined
REURGING pressing on again
REUSSITE magnesium compound   mn
REVALUED re-assessed
REVAMPED repatched
REVANCHE revenge (Fr.)
REVEALED disclosed; published
REVEALER betrayer; divulger
REVEHENT taking away
REVEILLE trumpet-call; dawn
REVELLED wantoned; feasted
REVELLER carouser
REVENANT returned from the dead; ghost
REVENGED requited; repaid
REVENGER vindicator
REVEREND respectful epithet
REVERENT submissive; humble
REVERING venerating; honouring
REVERIST a dreamer
REVERSAL complete change
REVERSED subverted; overthrew
REVERSER mortgager of land   lw
REVESTED reappointed

REVETTED faced with masonry
REVIEWAL a critique
REVIEWED revised; edited; surveyed
REVIEWER an inspector; critic
REVILING aspersing; maligning
REVISING checking; amending
REVISION re-examination
REVISORY correctional
REVIVIFY reanimate; revive
REVIVING renewing; rousing
REVOKING repealing; quashing
REVOLTED felt disgust
REVOLTED rebelled
REVOLTER guerilla; partisan
REVOLUTE rolled back
REVOLVED rotated; wheeled; circled
REVOLVER a firearm
REVULSOR h. and c. apparatus   md
REWARDED decorated; requited
REWARDER guerdon giver
REWORDED redrafted
RHABDITE rod-like structure   zo
RHABDOID spindle-shaped body   zo
RHABDOME lens supporter   md
RHAETIAN (Rhaetia)
RHAGADES fissures of the skin   md
RHAGODIA grapelike genus   bt
RHAMNOSE menthyl-pentose   ch
RHAPSODE rhapsodist
RHAPSODY rambling composition   mu
RHEOBASE minimal elect. response
    stimulus
RHEOCORD resistance wire
RHEOLOGY formation of matter   ps
RHEOSTAT (variable resistance)
RHEOTOME a switch
RHETORIC florid oratory
RHINIDAE sharks   zo
RHINITIS nasal inflammation   md
RHINODON immense shark   zo
RHIZANTH flowering root   bt
RHIZOGEN parasite plant   bt
RHIZOMYS genus of mole-rats   zo
RHIZOPOD locomotive protozoa   zo
RHODANIC roe-red colour   ch
RHODEINA goldfish   zo
RHODEOSE isomer of rhamnose   ch
RHODITES genus of gall-flies   zo
RHOEADIC (poppy extract)   ch
RHOMBOID quadrilateral figure
RHUMETER molten-metal impurity
    measurer   ml
RHONCHAL bronchial   md
RHONCHUS a râle   md
RHOPALIC a hexameter
RHO-THETA distance/bearing nav. system
    nv
RHUBARBY cathartic   md
RHYOLITE a quartz   mn
RHYTHMIC harmonious; metric; lilting
RHYTHMUS rhythm; cadence; verse

RIB-GRASS ribwort   **bt**
RIB-NOSED like a baboon
RIB-ROAST beat soundly
RIBALDRY ⎱ irreverent jesting;
RIBAUDRY ⎰ obscenity
RIBBONED striped; streaked
RIBOSOME nuclear source of protein
    synthesis
RICE-BIRD the bobolink   **zo**
RICE-DUST rice-meal
RICE-GLUE a cement
RICE-MEAL oriental flour
RICE-MILK milk with rice
RICE-SOUP congee
RICH-LEFT richly endowed
RICHNESS wealth; opulence; affluence
RICINIAE mites; ticks, etc.   **zo**
RICINIUM Roman mantle
RICKETLY shaky; weak; tottering
RICK-RACK openwork edging
RICKSHAW Indian or Chinese vehicle
RICOCHET rebound
RICOLITE ornamental stone   **mn**
RIDDANCE deliverance; release
RIDDLING perforating; sieving
RIDEABLE broken in
RIDICULE deride; lampoon; mock
RIFENESS prevalence
RIFFRAFF sweepings; refuse; rabble
RIFLEMAN modern musketeer
RIFLE-PIT short trench
RIGADOON lively dance
RIGATION irrigation
RIGHTFUL genuine; true; lawful
RIGHTING doing justice; rectifying
RIGIDITY stiffness
RIGORISM austerity
RIGORIST a martinet
RIGOROUS inflexible; severe; harsh
RILL-MARK corrugation
RIMIFORM having a rim
RIMOSITY roughness
RIMULOSE fissured
RINABOUT vagrant (Sc.)
RIND-CALL defect in timber
RING-BARK make a circular cut
RING-BILL ring-necked duck   **zo**
RINGBONE exostosis on horse foot bones
    vt
RING-DIAL portable sundial
RING-DOVE cushat; wood-pigeon   **zo**
RINGDOWN operator-signalling method **tc**
RING-GOAL a ball game
RING-LOCK a puzzle lock
RING-MAIL chain armour
RING-NECK ring-plover
RING-ROAD by-pass
RING-ROPE a cable rope   **nt**
RING-SIDE close to the scene
RING-TAIL hen-harrier   **zo**
RING-TIME time for marriage

RING-WALL ring fence
RINGWISE experienced (sport)
RINGWOMB incomplete cervix dilatation
    vt
RING-WORK mail construction
RING-WORM skin disease   **md**
RINGBOLT embedded ring
RINGBONE callus on pastern
RINGLETY with ringlets
RIOMETER ionosphere absorption mea-
    surer   **ps**
RIPARIAN riparial; riverbanks
RIPENESS maturity; mellowness
RIPPLING flax cleaning
RIPTOWEL reaping gratuity
RISE-BUSH a faggot
RISE-WOOD hedge cuttings
RISKIEST most reckless
RISORIAL ludicrous
RITENUTO restrained, slower tempo   **mu**
RITUALLY ceremoniously
RIVALISE compete
RIVALITY equality in rank
RIVALLED emulated; vied; matched
RIVER-BED a channel
RIVER-GOD tutelary deity
RIVER-HOG the capybara   **zo**
RIVER-MAN river-liver
RIVER-PIE water-ousel   **zo**
RIVERINE riparian
RIVETING clinching
RIVULOSE wavy; rivose
RIXATION brawl; quarrel
RIZZERED salted and sun-dried
ROAD-BOOK guide-book
ROAD-POST signpost
ROAD-WEED plantago   **bt**
ROAD-WORK highway repairs
ROADLESS unwayed
ROADSIDE footpath; wayside
ROADSMAN road repairer
ROADSTER coachdriver; cycle
ROAN-TREE rowan tree; mountain ash
ROASTING parching; bantering
ROBURITE an explosive
ROBUSTLY lustily; stoutly; sturdily
ROCAILLE scroll ornament
ROCCELLA dyers' lichen   **bt**
ROCK-ALUM alum stone   **mn**
ROCK-BIRD a pigeon   **zo**
ROCK-CAKE small, hard bun
ROCK-CIST a plant   **bt**
ROCK-COOK rock-fish   **zo**
ROCK-CORK asbestos   **mn**
ROCK-CRAB stony crustacean   **zo**
ROCK-DOVE pigeon nesting on rocks
ROCK-FIRE firework mixture
ROCK-FISH wrasse. bass, etc.   **zo**
ROCK-GOAT ibex   **zo**
ROCK-HAWK merlin   **zo**
ROCK-HEAD bed-rock   **mn**

ROCK-HEWN cut from rock	
ROCK-LARK rock-pipit	zo
ROCK-LILY (various types)	bt
ROCK-LING cod; haddock	zo
ROCK-MOSS lichen	bt
ROCK-ROSE member of rock garden	bt
ROCK-RUBY a garnet	mn
ROCK-SALT native salt	mn
ROCK-SEAL common seal	zo
ROCK-SOAP a kind of bole	mn
ROCK-WOOD ligniform asbestos	mn
ROCK-WORK a rockery	
ROCK-WREN stone-preferring bird	zo
ROCKAWAY American carriage	
ROCKETED shot away	
ROCKETER a high flier	
ROCKETRY science of rockets	
ROCKLESS destoned; without rocks	
RODENTIA rats; mice; squirrels	zo
RODOMONT vain boaster; braggart	
ROENTGEN unit of radiation	me
ROE-STONE oolite	mn
ROGAILLE decorative work with rocks, shells	
ROGATION litany; supplication	
ROGATORY interrogatory	
ROISTING blustering; bullying	
ROITELET kinglet; gold-crest	zo
ROLLBACK price legislation	
ROLL-CALL famous picture	
ROLY-POLY Swiss roll	
ROMANCED economized the truth	
ROMANCER tall tale teller	
ROMANESE Wallachian language	
ROMANIAN (Romania)	
ROMANISH Catholic	rl
ROMANIST R.C.	rl
ROMANIZE Latinize; convert	rl
ROMANSCH Swiss dialect	
ROMANTIC quixotic; fanciful	
ROME-SCOT Peter's pence	rl
ROMEWARD verging on Romanism	
RONCADOR Pacific fish	zo
RONDELET form of poem	
RONDELLE ladder rung	
ROOD-ARCH (over rood-screen)	
ROOD-BEAM mast supporting rood	
ROOD-LOFT gallery over screen	
ROOD-TREE Holy-rood; the cross	
ROODEBOK bush-buck	zo
ROOF-RACK automobile baggage holder	
ROOF-TREE a beam	
ROOFLESS vulnerable to rain	
ROOMSOME spacious	
ROOSTING perching; lodging	
ROOT-BEER dandelion ale	
ROOT-CROP (esculent roots)	
ROOT-FAST firmly rooted	
ROOT-FORM shape of a root	
ROOT-HAIR delicate filament	bt
ROOT-KNOT an abnormality	bt

ROOT-LEAF a leaf that roots	bt
ROOTLESS footloose	
ROPE-PUMP (by an endless rope)	
ROPE-RIPE fit to be hanged	
ROPE-WALK shed for spinning ropes	
ROPE-YARN manilla; hemp; sisal, etc.	
ROPINESS stringiness	
ROQUETED (croquet)	
RORIDULA sundew plants	bt
RORULENT dewy	
ROSARIAN a rose fancier	
ROSARIUM rose garden	
ROSASITE copper/zinc carbonate	mn
ROSE-BUSH source of roses	bt
ROSE-DROP rose-flavoured orange	bt
ROSEFISH redfish; Atlantic food fish	
ROSE-GALL an excrescence	
ROSE-HUED rosy	
ROSE-KNOT a rosette	
ROSE-PINK sentimental	
ROSE-RASH German measles	md
ROSE-ROOT herbaceous plant	bt
ROSE-TREE a standard rose	bt
ROSEWOOD Brazilian timber tree	bt
ROSE-WORM a caterpillar	zo
ROSE-YARD rose garden	
ROSELITE cobalt arseniate	mn
ROSEMARY aromatic plant	bt
ROSETTED having a rosette	
ROSINESS rubicundity	
ROSINING impelling; hustling	
ROSIN-OIL a lubricant	
ROSMARUS walruses, etc	zo
ROSOGLIO red wine of Malta	
ROSTRATE beaked	
ROSTROID like a rostrum	
ROSULATE having rosetted leaves	bt
ROSY-DROP a grog blossom	
ROSY-WAVE a moth	zo
ROT-GRASS butterwort	
ROT-STEEP cotton purification	
ROTALIAN } protozoan	zo
ROTALINE	
ROTALITE fossil rotalian	
ROTARIAN (Rotary Club)	
ROTATING spinning; turning	
ROTATION revolution; series	
ROTATIVE in succession	
ROTATORY circulatory	
ROTIFERA animalculae	zo
ROTIFORM wheel-shaped	
ROTTENLY putridly	
ROTTLERA dye yielding plant	bt
ROTURIER plebeian	
ROUGHAGE litter	
ROUGH-DRY not ironed	
ROUGH-HEW back formation from rough-hewn	
ROUGHING (ice-nails)	
ROUGHISH rather boisterous	
ROULEAUX bundles of fascines	

ROULETTE a game of chance
ROUND-ALL acrobatic feat
ROUND-ARM (bowling)
ROUND-TOP masthead platform   nt
ROUNDERS a game
ROUNDING encircling
ROUNDISH not quite spherical
ROUNDLET a small circle
ROUT-CAKE cake for parties
ROUTEING selecting a route
ROVINGLY wanderingly
ROWDY-DOW hubbub; uproar
ROWDYISH riotous; noisy
ROWDYISM turbulence; brawling
ROWELLED spurred
ROXBURGH a book-binding
ROYALISM liking for crowned heads
ROYALIST king-supporter
ROYALIZE turn into a king
RUBBISHY trashy
RUBECULA robin redbreast   zo
RUBEDITY ruddiness
RUBELLAN magnesia mica   mn
RUBEZAHL mountain imp (Ger.)
RUBIANIC madder-coloured
RUBICUND ruddy; florid
RUBIDIUM metallic element   ch
RUBIFORM like a ruby
RUBRICAL marked in red
RUBSTONE whetstone
RUBY-TAIL cuckoo-fly   zo
RUBY-WOOD red sandalwood   bt
RUCERVUS East Indian deer   zo
RUCKLING crumpling; creasing
RUCKSACK knapsack
RUDDLING marking with ochre
RUDENESS unmannerliness
RUDENTED ornamented
RUDIMENT first principle; embryo
RUEFULLY sorrowfully; regretfully
RUFFLING disturbing; agitating
RUFULOUS somewhat rufous
RUGBEIAN (Rugby)
RUGGEDLY jaggedly; unevenly
RUGOSELY wrinkly
RUGOSITY roughness
RUGULOUS creased; rumpled
RUINABLE of delicate virtue
RUINATED demolished
RULE-CASE a printing tray
RULE-WORK tabulation
RULINGLY dominantly
RUM-BARGE a warm drink
RUM-SHRUB an odd decoction
RUMANIAN (Romania)
RUMBLING noise from stomach
RUMINANT chewing the cud   zo
RUMINATE meditate; muse; ponder
RUMMAGED ransacked; rifled
RUMMAGER searcher
RUMOROUS vaguely heard

RUMOURED bruited; reported
RUMOURER a gossip; tattler
RUMPLESS having no tail
RUMPLING puckering; rimpling
RUNABOUT flivver; vagabond
RUNAGATE renegade; vagabond
RUNMAKER cricket
RUNNER-UP second
RUNOLOGY rune-craft
RUNRIDGE open-field husbandry
RUN-ROUND railway shunting
RUPICOLA cocks of the rock   zo
RURALISM country life
RURALIST country bumpkin
RURALITY ruralness
RURALIZE rusticate
RUSH-HOUR commuter-time
RUSH-LINE football
RUSH-TOAD the natterjack   zo
RUSHLIKE reedy; weak
RUST-MITE gall-mite   zo
RUSTICAL rustic; sylvan
RUSTLESS stainless
RUSTLING cattle lifting
RUTABAGA Swedish turnip; Swede   bt
RUTHLESS pitiless; barbarous
RUTILANT shining
RUTILATE emit rays of light
RYE-GRASS fodder grass   bt
RYOT-WARI } system of land
RYOT-WARY } tenure of India

S

SABAEISM star worship
SABBATIA gentian   bt
SABBATIC restful
SABBATON armoured boot
SABELINE sable type or skin   zo
SABINENE terpene derivative   ch
SABLIERE sand-pit
SABOTAGE wanton destruction
SABOTEUR a wrecker
SABOTIER a wearer of wooden shoes
SABULOSE growing in sandy places   bt
SABULOUS sandy; gritty
SACCATED pouched
SACCULAR baggy; saclike; vesiculate
SACCULUS a small sac or cyst   zo
SACELLUM makeshift altar   rl
SACKLESS quiet; simple (Sc.)
SACK-RACE race run in sack
SACREDLY divinely; holily
SACRISTY the vestry   rl
SADDENED mournful; downcast
SADDLERY horse furniture
SADDLING loading
SADDUCEE Jewish ritualist   rl
SADFACED gloomy; depressed

SAFENESS security; trustiness
SAFFRONY saffron coloured
SAFRANIN saffron dye ch
SAGACITY wisdom; shrewdness
SAGAMORE American Indian chief
SAGE-COCK American grouse zo
SAGE-ROSE an evergreen bt
SAGENESS sapience; sagacity; wisdom
SAGENITE crystals of rutile mn
SAGINATE pamper; fatten
SAGITTAL like an arrow
SAGO-PALM food-giving tree bt
SAGUINUS marmoset bt
SAHIB-LOG Europeans
SAIBLING the char zo
SAIKLESS sackless
SAIL-BOAT yacht nt
SAIL-FISH basking shark zo
SAIL-HOOP mast-hoop nt
SAIL-LOFT (where sails are made)
SAIL-PLAN layout of sails nt
SAIL-ROOM storage place for sails nt
SAIL-YARD spar for sails nt
SAILABLE navigable
SAILLESS steam-driven
SAINFOIN a fodder-plant bt
SAINTISH rather saintlike
SAINTISM sanctimoniousness
SALACITY lustfulness
SALAD-OIL olive-oil
SALADING salad vegetables bt
SALARIED receiving wages
SALE-ROOM auction room
SALE-WORK work carelessly done
SALEABLE marketable
SALEABLY vendibly
SALESMAN sometimes a drummer
SALICINE extract of willow bark
SALIENCE prominence
SALIFIED made into salt
SALINITY saltness
SALITRAL saltpetre mine
SALIVANT
SALIVARY
SALIVATE } referring to saliva md
SALIVOUS
SALLYING dashing out
SALMONET young salmon zo
SALOPIAN from Shropshire
SALPICON Spanish savoury dish
SALSILLA edible tuber bt
SALI-BUSH Australian plant bt
SALT-CAKE sulphate of soda mn
SALT-COTE salt-pit
SALT-FOOT (below the salt)
SALT-JUNK salted beef
SALT-LICK animals' rendezvous
SALT-MINE mine of rock salt
SALT-WELL salt spring
SALT-WORK salt factory
SALT-WORT (several species) bt

SALTLESS insipid; tasteless
SALTNESS salinity
SALUTARY beneficial
SALUTING greeting; hailing
SALVABLE rescuable
SALVAGED saved
SALVINIA genus of ferns bt
SAMARIUM spectroscopic metal ch
SAMAROID (winged fruit) bt
SAMAVEDA Veda with chants rl
SAMBUCUS honeysuckle type bt
SAMENESS monotony; similarity
SAMPHIRE a herb bt
SAMPLARY an example (obs.)
SAMPLING matching
SANATION a cure
SANATIVE healing
SANATORY curative; remedial
SANATRON valve circuit el
SANCTIFY make holy; hallow rl
SANCTION ratification; approve
SANCTITY holiness; godliness
SANDARIC N. Afr. resin for map varnishes
SAND-BALL pumice soap
SAND-BAND protecting band
SAND-BANK a shoal
SAND-BATH (used by chemists)
SAND-BEAR Indian badger zo
SAND-BIRD sandpiper zo
SAND-COCK redshank zo
SAND-CRAB the lady crab zo
SAND-DART a moth zo
SAND-DUNE a ridge of drifted sand
SAND-FISH dry land fish zo
SAND-FLAG a sandstone mn
SAND-FLEA chigoe or jigger zo
SAND-HEAT heat of sand-bath ch
SAND-HILL mound of sand
SAND-IRON a niblick
SAND-LARK a wading bird zo
SAND-MOLE S. African rodent zo
SAND-PEEP American stint zo
SAND-PUMP (rock drilling)
SAND-REED a shore grass bt
SAND-REEL a windlass
SAND-ROLL a casting
SAND-SHOT small shot
SAND-STAR starfish zo
SAND-TRAP sand eliminator
SAND-WASP the digger-wasp zo
SAND-WELD silica fusing
SAND-WORM lob-worm; lug-worm zo
SAND-WORT genus Arenia bt
SANDARAC realgar; resin mn, bt
SANDEVER } glass scum in state of
SANDIVER } fusion
SANDWICH to interpose; intrude
SANENESS sanity; mental equilibrium
SANGAREE W. Indian drink
SANGLANT bleeding
SANGLIER wild boar zo

SANGRAAL holy grail	rl		**SATURDAY** Jewish sabbath	
SANGREAL sangraal			**SATURNIA** a moth genus	zo
SANGUIFY to make blood			**SATURNIC** (lead poisoning)	
SANGUINE optimistic; hopeful			**SATYRIUM** orchid genus	bt
SANIDINE potassium feldspar	mn		**SAUCEBOX** impudent fellow	
SANITARY hygienic; healthful			**SAUCEPAN** cook-pot	
SANSERIF serifless type face	pr		**SAUCISSE** powder bag for use in mines	
SANSKRIT ancient Indian language			**SAURLESS** savourless; tasteless (Sc.)	
SANTALIC (sandal-wood)	bt		**SAURODON** fossil fish	mn
SANTALIN red dye			**SAURURUS** pepper plants	bt
SANTALUM sandal-wood genus	bt		**SAUTERNE** white wine	
SANTONIN wormwood	ch		**SAUTOIRE** heraldic ribbon	hd
SAP-GREEN yellow green			**SAVAGELY** barbarously; inhumanly	
SAPIDITY tastiness			**SAVAGERY** ferocity; brutality	
SAPIENCE wisdom; sagacity; intellect			**SAVAGING** maltreating	
SAPINDUS the soapberry	bt		**SAVANNAH** savanna; a treeless plain	
SAPI-UTAN wild ox, (Celebes)	zo		**SAVEABLE** rescuable; salvable	
SAPONIFY convert into soap			**SAVINGLY** thriftily; frugally	
SAPONINE soapwort extract			**SAVOURED** tasted	
SAPONITE hydrous silicate of magnesium			**SAVOURLY** well seasoned	
	mn		**SAVOYARD** Gilbert and Sullivan	
SAPOROUS tasty; piquant			**SAW-FLIES** boring insects	zo
SAPPHIRE blue, green or red gem	mn		**SAW-FRAME** blade holder	to
SAPREMIA blood poisoning	md		**SAW-GRASS** a marsh grass	bt
SAPROPEL stagnant water sediment	gl		**SAW-HORSE** cradle for sawing logs	
SAPSTAIN fungus-caused discoloration	fr		**SAW-TABLE** boring table	
SAPUCAIA Brazil nut-tree	bt		**SAW-WREST** a saw-set	
SARABAND Spanish dance			**SAWBONES** a surgeon	md
SARATOGA American travelling trunk			**SAXATILE** rock-inhabiting	
SARCELLE a teal	zo		**SAXICAVA** mollusc genus	zo
SARCENET sarsenet; woven silk			**SAXICOLA** the stone-chats	zo
SARCINIC fungoid	bt		**SAXICOLE** growing on rocks	bt
SARCITIS eye inflammation	md		**SAXONDOM** Anglo-Saxon world	
SARCOCOL gum Arabic	bt		**SAXONISM** a Saxon idiom	
SARCODIC protoplasmic; resembling flesh			**SAXONIST** Saxon scholar	
	zo		**SAXONITE** coarse-grained igneous rock	gl
SARCOSIS a tumour	md		**SCABBARD** sheath	
SARCOTIC generating flesh	md		**SCABBLED** rough hewn; scappled	
SARDELLE herring-like fish	zo		**SCABIOSA** teasel plants	bt
SARDONIC ironical; cynical			**SCABIOUS** scurfy; itchy	bt
SARDONYX variety of onyx	mn		**SCAB-MITE** a parasite	zo
SARGASSO sea of seaweed			**SCABROUS** rough; rugged	
SARPLIER packing cloth			**SCAFFOLD** temporary structure	
SARRASIN a portcullis			**SCALABLE** climbable; measurable	
SARRIZIN buckwheat	bt		**SCALARIA** ladder-shells	zo
SARSENET sarsenet; woven silk			**SCALAWAG** scallywag; scamp	
SASH-DOOR door having panes of glass			**SCALDING** injuring with boiling water	
SASSANID a Persian ruler			**SCALDINO** Italian brazier	
SASSOLIN native boracic acid	mn		**SCALENUM** scalene triangle	
SASSOROL rock-pigeon	zo		**SCALENUS** a muscle	pl
SATANISM devil worship			**SCALIOLA** imitation marble	
SATANITY devilry; diablery			**SCALLION** shallot; leek	bt
SATELESS insatiable			**SCALPING** selling tickets at surcharge	
SATHANAS Satan			**SCAMBLED** mauled; mangled	
SATIABLE appeasable			**SCAMBLER** gate-crasher	
SATIATED glutted; gratified			**SCAMMONY** convolvulus	bt
SATIRIST lampoonist; ironic writer			**SCAMPING** shirking; skimping	
SATIRIZE ridicule			**SCAMPISH** knavish; rascally	
SATRAPAL province of a satrap			**SCANDENT** climbing	
SATURANT saturating			**SCANDIUM** a metal	ch
SATURATE soak; drench			**SCANNING** scrutinizing; viewing	

SCANSION rhythm	
SCANTIES light attire	
SCANTILY meagrely; sparingly	
SCANTING stinting	
SCANTLED in small pieces	
SCANTLET a small pattern	
SCAPANUS shrew-moles	zo
SCAPHISM a Persian torture	
SCAPHITE fossil ammonite	mn
SCAPHIUM beetle genus	zo
SCAPHOID boat-shaped	
SCAPPLED rough hewn; scabbled	
SCAPULAR (shoulder-blade); scarf	
SCARABEE scarab; beetle	zo
SCARCELY hardly; barely	
SCARCITY dearth; rarity; lack	
SCARE-BUG a bugbear	
SCARFING uniting timber	
SCARF-PIN male decoration	
SCARIDAE parrot-fish	zo
SCARIOUS dry; scaly	
SCARITID (carabid beetles)	zo
SCARLESS unwounded; scatheless	
SCARN-BEE dung-beetle	zo
SCARPHED (a timber joint)	bd
SCARRING wounding; injuring	
SCATCHES stilts	
SCATHING bitterly severe; caustic	
SCATHOLD open pasture ground	
SCATLAND peat and pasture land	
SCATTERY dispersed	
SCAVENGE to collect refuse	
SCAWTITE calcium silicate/carbonate	mn
SCELERAT villain	
SCELIDES the hind-legs	zo
SCENARIO plan of a play	
SCENE-MAN scene shifter	
SCENICAL scenic; dramatic	
SCENT-BAG animal's pouch	zo
SCENT-BOX perfume pack	
SCENTFUL highly odoriferous	
SCEPTRAL regal	
SCEPTRED kingly	
SCHEDULE catalogue; inventory; list	
SCHELLUM rascal; rogue	
SCHEMING planning; intriguing	
SCHEMIST projector; astrologer	
SCHEROMA dryness of the eye	md
SCHIEDAM schnapps; gin	
SCHILLER bronze lustre	
SCHISTIC laminated; slaty	mn
SCHIZOID tendency to dementia	pc
SCHIZONT trophozoite ready to reproduce	zo
SCHLAGER duelling sword (Ger.)	
SCHMALTZ grease (Ger.); sentimental	
SCHMELZE enamel (Ger.)	
SCHNAPPS akvavit; firewater	
SCHOENUS a sedge genus	bt
SCHOLION ⎫ marginal note in	
SCHOLIUM ⎭ old classics	

SCHOOLED disciplined; trained	
SCHOONER large drinking glass	
SCHOONER fore-and-aft rigged ship	nt
SCHRADAN chemical insecticide	
SCIATICA neuralgia	md
SCIENTER knowingly; deliberately	
SCIENTLY fully aware	
SCILICET to wit; namely	
SCIMITAR curved sword	
SCINCOID pertaining to the skink	zo
SCIOGRAM radio photograph	
SCIOLISM superficiality	
SCIOLIST a know-all	
SCIOLOUS shallow; skin-deep	
SCIOPTIC (camera obscura)	
SCIRRHUS cancerous tumour	md
SCISSILE able to be cut	
SCISSION division	
SCISSORS acrobatic feat; forfex	to
SCISSURA fissure; cleft	
SCISSURE rupture division	
SCIURINE ⎫ rodent mammals,	zo
SCIUROID ⎭ squirrels, etc.	
SCLERITE hardened tissue	md
SCLEROID ossified	
SCLEROMA sclerosis	md
SCLEROUS bony	
SCOFFING deriding; taunting; jeering	
SCOFF-LAW contemptuous to law	
SCOLDING nagging; chiding; rating	
SCOLEINA earth-worms, etc.	zo
SCOLOPAX woodcock genus	zo
SCOLYTUS destructive beetle	zo
SCOMFISH to nauseate (Sc.)	
SCONTION inside quoin	bd
SCOONING skimming	
SCOOP-NET a hand-net	
SCOOPING ladling	
SCOOTING decamping	
SCOPARIA sweet bromweed	bt
SCOPEFUL with wide prospect	
SCOPIDAE African wading birds	zo
SCOPIPED having brushy feet	zo
SCORCHED parched; charred	
SCORCHER road-hog	
SCORDATO out of tune	mu
SCORIOUS ashy; clinkery	
SCORNFUL mocking; insolent	
SCORNING spurning; scouting	
SCORPION stingtail	zo
SCOT-FREE untaxed	
SCOTCHED wounded; blocked	
SCOTOPIC night vision	
SCOTSMAN Scot	
SCOTTICE in Scottish manner	
SCOTTIFY Caledonianise	
SCOTTISH Scots	
SCOURAGE refuse water	
SCOURGED chastised	
SCOURING scurrying; scrubbing	
SCOUTHER to scorn (Sc.)	

SCOUT-LAW Scout Code
SCOUTING rejecting; scorning
SCOWLING glowering; frowning
SCOWTHER a brief shower (Sc.)
SCRABBLE scribble; scrawl
SCRAGGED strangled; throttled
SCRAGGLY rough-looking
SCRAMBLE hurry; strife; clamber
SCRAN-BAG food sack   nt
SCRANNEL squeaking; slender; meagre
SCRAPING abrading; rasping
SCRAPPED discarded; fought
SCRAPPLE to grub about; scrabble
SCRATCHY ragged; sketchy
SCRATTLE to scuttle
SCRAWLED scribbled
SCRAWLER slovenly writer
SCREAMED yelled; cried; squalled
SCREAMER tropical bird   zo
SCREECHY shrill and harsh
SCREENED veiled; hidden; sieved
SCREEVER begging-letter writer
SCREW-KEY a spanner   to
SCREW-POD screw-bean   bt
SCREWING exacting; twisting; racking
SCRIBBET painter's pencil
SCRIBBLE scrawl; write
SCRIBING recording
SCRIBISM Jewish literature
SCRIGGLE wriggle
SCRIMPED stinted
SCRIMPLY miserly
SCRINIUM scroll/relic container
SCRIPTOR ancient book-copier, handwriter
SCRIVANO Italian clerk
SCRODDLE to variegate
SCROFULA the king's evil   md
SCROGGIE full of brushwood
SCROLLED convoluted
SCROOPED grated; cracked
SCROUGED squeezed
SCROUGER a whopper
SCROUNGE acquire by stealth; cadge
SCRUB-OAK stunted oak   bt
SCRUBBED scoured
SCRUBBER charlady
SCRUPLED hesitated; wavered
SCRUPLER demurrer; doubter
SCRUTINY close inquiry; search
SCUDDICK scuttock; a trifle; a shilling
SCUDDING speeding
SCUDDING pre-tanning hide treatment   le
SCUFFLED tussled
SCUFFLER brawler
SCULLERY room for washing dishes
SCULLING rowing
SCULLION dish-washer
SCULPSIT he engraved it
SCULPTOR image maker
SCUMBLED painted over
SCURRIED scampered; hastened

SCURRIES pony races
SCURRILE scurrilous
SCURVILY basely; shabbily
SCUTCHED separated
SCUTCHER hedger
SCUTELLA sea-urchin genus   zo
SCUTIFER shield-bearer
SCUTIPED having scaly shanks   zo
SCUTTLED ran; bolted; scampered
SCUTTLER ship-sinker
SCUTTOCK see scuddick
SCYELITE coarse-grained igneous rock   gl
SCYTHIAN (Scythia)
SCYTODES a genus of spiders   zo
SEA-ACORN a barnacle   zo
SEA-ADDER stickle-back   zo
SEA-APRON a seaweed   bt
SEA-ARROW flying squid   zo
SEA-BEACH seashore
SEA-BEAST a sea monster   zo
SEA-BELLS bindweed   bt
SEA-BOARD the coast
SEA-BORNE shipped
SEA-BRANT brent goose   zo
SEA-BREAM mackerel type   zo
SEA-CHART marine map
SEA-COAST seashore
SEA-CRAFT seamanship
SEA-DAISY the lady's cushion   bt
SEA-DEVIL ray; angel-fish   zo
SEA-DRAKE sea-crow   zo
SEA-EAGLE the osprey   zo
SEA-FIGHT marine engagement
SEA-FRONT shore promenade
SEA-FROTH foam
SEA-GATES (tidal basin)
SEA-GAUGE ship's draught
SEA-GOOSE a dolphin   zo
SEA-GRAPE glasswort   bt
SEA-GRASS the thrift   bt
SEA-GREEN marine colour
SEA-GROVE under-water grove
SEA-HEATH beach plant   bt
SEA-HOLLY the eryngo   bt
SEA-HORSE the walrus   zo
SEA-HOUND dog-fish   zo
SEA-JELLY sea-blubber
SEA-LEECH an annelid   zo
SEA-LEMON a doridoid mollusc   zo
SEA-LEVEL mean tide level
SEA-LOACH a gadoid fish   zo
SEA-LOUSE a parasite   zo
SEA-LUNGS a comb-jelly   zo
SEA-MARGE seashore
SEA-MELON sea-cucumber   zo
SEA-MOUSE the dunlin; a worm   zo
SEA-NYMPH an Oceanid
SEA-ONION a squill   bt
SEA-OTTER marine otter   zo
SEA-OXEYE seashore plant   bt
SEA-PEACH sea-squirt   zo

SEA-PERCH bass	zo
SEA-PIECE seascape	
SEA-PLANE hydroplane; floatplane	
SEA-PLANT a seaweed	bt
SEA-POWER strategic	
SEA-PURSE eggcase of skate	zo
SEA-QUAIL the turnstone	zo
SEA-QUAKE marine earthwake	
SEA-RAVEN cormorant	zo
SEA-REEVE customs officer	
SEA-ROBIN gurnard fish	zo
SEA-ROVER pirate; pirate ship	nt
SEA-SHARK man-eater shark	
SEA-SHRUB a sea-fan	zo
SEA-SNAIL the periwinkle	zo
SEA-SNAKE sea-serpent	zo
SEA-SNIPE sandpiper	zo
SEA-SQUID cuttlefish	zo
SEA-STICK herring cured at sea	
SEA-SWINE porpoise	zo
SEA-TENCH black sea-bream	zo
SEA-THONG cord-like seaweed	bt
SEA-TROUT saltwater trout	zo
SEA-WATER brine	
SEA-WOMAN mermaid	
SEA-WRACK coarse seaweed	
SEAFARER voyager; sailor	
SEAGOING deepwater line ship	
SEAL-PIPE a dip pipe	
SEAL-RING signet ring	
SEAL-SKIN pelt; fur	
SEAL-WORT Solomon's seal	bt
SEAMANLY seamanlike	
SEAMIEST most sordid	
SEAMLESS in one piece	
SEAM-RENT a tear at the seam	
SEAMSTER one who sews	
SEARCHED quested; probed; sought	
SEARCHER inquirer; examiner	
SEARNESS dryness; sereness	
SEARWOOD dry wood	
SEASCAPE sea-piece	
SEASHELL marine shell	zo
SEASHORE the beach	
SEASONAL not always available	
SEASONED matured; inured	
SEASONER a relish; strong flavouring	
SEAT-BACK loose cover	
SEAT-LOCK a catch	
SEAT-MILE transport statistic	
SEAT-RAIL a crosspiece	
SEAT-WORM pin-worm	zo
SEBESTAN } a tree with	bt
SEBESTEN } plumlike fruit	
SEBUNDEE Indian militia-man	
SECAMONE shrubby climber	bt
SECATEUR pruning shears	to
SECEDING withdrawing; retiring	
SECERNED secreted	
SECESHER a secessionist	
SECLUDED aside; shut off	

SECODONT with cutting teeth	zo
SECONDED aided; transferred	
SECONDER supporter; abettor	
SECRETED cloaked; concealed	
SECRETIN secretion-stimulating hormone	
	bc
SECRETLY privily; covertly	
SECTATOR an adherent	
SECTORAL in a sector	
SECTROID space between groins	bd
SECUNDUM acording to (Latin)	
SECURELY fast; safely	
SECURING acquiring; getting	
SECURITE an explosive	
SECURITY safety; surety; pledge	
SEDATELY calmly; seriously; soberly	
SEDATIVE tranquillizing; soothing	md
SEDERUNT court session (Sc.)	lw
SEDGE-HEN marsh-hen	zo
SEDILIUM chancel seat	rl
SEDIMENT lees; dregs; grounds	
SEDITION treason; mutiny; rebellion	
SEDUCING enticing; inveigling	
SEDUCTOR tempter; corrupter	
SEDULITY assiduity; diligence	
SEDULOUS industrious; busy	
SEED-BIRD water-wagtail	zo
SEED-CAKE caraway cake	
SEED-COAT husk	bt
SEED-CORN corn for sowing	bt
SEED-DOWN down on cotton, etc.	bt
SEED-FISH spawn; roe	zo
SEED-FOWL grain-fed bird	zo
SEED-GALL plant disease	
SEED-LEAF a cotyledon	bt
SEED-LEAP seed-basket	
SEED-LOBE seed-leaf	bt
SEED-PLOT a hot-bed	
SEED-TICK a parasite	zo
SEED-WOOL cotton-wool and seeds	
SEEDLESS pipless	
SEEDLING young plant	bt
SEEDSMAN dealer; sower	
SEEDTIME sowing season	
SEEDY-TOE a horse disease	vt
SEER-FISH seir-fish	zo
SEERSHIP (soothsaying)	
SEESAWED oscillated	
SEETHING boiling	
SEGREANT rampant and salient	hd
SEIDLITZ mineral water	mn
SEIGNEUR lord of the manor	
SEIGNIOR seigneur; feudal lord	
SEINE-NET long shallow net	oc
SEIR-FISH seer-fish	zo
SEIZABLE apprehendable	
SEIZLING the carp	zo
SEJUGOUS (six pairs of leaflets)	bt
SELADANG Malayan tapir; bison	zo
SELAMLIK men's quarters (Turk.)	
SELECTED chosen; culled; preferred	
SELECTOR picker	

SELENATE a selenic salt	ch	
SELENIDE a compound	ch	
SELENITE gypsum	mn	
SELENIUM a chemical element	ch	
SELF-BORN self-begotten		
SELF-ENDS endpaper leaves in books		
SELF-HEAL burnet saxifrage	bt	
SELF-HELP unaided effort		
SELFHOOD conscious personality		
SELFLESS unselfish		
SELF-LIKE indulgence		
SELF-LIKE twin		
SELF-LOVE self-seeking		
SELF-MADE independent		
SELFNESS egotism		
SELF-PITY sorriness for self		
SELFSAME identical; equivalent		
SELF-WILL obstinacy		
SELF-WISE self-conceit		
SELICTAR Turkish sword-bearer		
SELLABLE saleable; marketable		
SELVAGEE untwisted rope		
SELVEDGE woven border		
SEMANTIC significant; expressive		
SEMBLANT resembling; like		
SEMESTER period of six months		
SEMI-ACID half-acid		
SEMI-BULL a papal bull	rl	
SEMI-COPE outer monastic garment		
SEMI-DOME half-dome		
SEMI-FLEX to half bend		
SEMI-MUTE half deaf		
SEMI-NUDE barely clothed		
SEMI-OPAL half-opal	mn	
SEMI-OPEN sport		
SEMI-OVAL half-oval		
SEMI-PULP ground-wood impurities in paper		
SEMI-RING half-circle		
SEMINARY academy; college; school		
SEMINATE propagate; sow		
SEMINOLE American Indian tribe		
SEMIOTIC sign language		
SEMITAUR half-bull; half-man		
SEMITISM Hebrew idiom		
SEMITIST Hebrew scholar		
SEMITONE musical interval	mu	
SEMOLINA ⎫ granules of flour		
SEMILINO ⎭ manna; grits		
SEMPLICE simply	mu	
SEMPSTER seamstress		
SEMUNCIA Roman coin	nm	
SENARIUS verse of six feet		
SEND-DOWN expel; rusticate		
SENG-GUNG Java badger	zo	
SENGREEN the houseleek	bt	
SENILITY dotage; old age		
SENNIGHT a week		
SENONIAN geological formation	gl	
SENORITA Spanish young lady		
SENSEFUL judicious; rational		
SENSIBLE intelligent; wise; discreet		
SENSIBLY sagaciously; sanely		
SENSIFIC exciting		
SENSUISM sensuality		
SENSUIST amorist; materialist		
SENSUOUS aesthetic; voluptuous		
SENTENCE doom; maxim; clause		
SENTIENT perceptive		
SENTINEL sentry; watchman; warder		
SENTRIES watchers		
SENTRY-GO sentry duty		
SEPALINE (leaf of calyx)	bt	
SEPALODY ⎫ reversion of petals to	bt	
SEPALOID ⎭ sepals		
SEPALOUS sepaline		
SEPARATE sort; divorce; sever		
SEPDUMAG 2-magnetic-sound-track film	cn	
SEPDUOPT 2-optical-sound-track film	cn	
SEPIACEA cuttlefish	zo	
SEPIIDAE cephalopods	zo	
SEPIMENT hedge; boundary		
SEPTARIA turtle-stones	mn	
SEPTATED divided into cells	bt	
SEPTETTE (seven performers)	mu	
SEPTFOIL the tormentil	bt	
SEPTUARY group of seven		
SEPTULUM small cell	bt	
SEPTUPLE sevenfold		
SEQUENCE continuity; series		
SERAFILE serrefile		
SERAGLIO a harem		
SERAPHIC angelic; sublime		
SERAPHIM celestial being	rl	
SERAPIAS genus of orchids	bt	
SERENADE ⎫ open air musical		
SERENATA ⎭ composition	mu	
SERENELY tranquilly; calmly; placidly		
SERENEST calmest; most tranquil		
SERENISE glorify		
SERENITY peacefulness; quiet		
SERGEANT serjeant		
SERGETTE thin serge		
SERIALLY consecutively		
SERIATIM in regular order		
SERICATE silky; downy		
SERICITE potash mica	mn	
SERIFORM Chinese writing		
SERINGHI Indian viol	mu	
SERJEANT sergeant		
SERMONER preacher	rl	
SERMONET short address		
SERMONIC admonitive	rl	
SEROLOGY study of sera	md	
SEROSITY (exuding serum)	md	
SEROTINE species of bat	zo	
SERPETTE pruning knife (Fr.)	to	
SERPLATH 80 stone (Sc.)	me	
SERPOLET wild thyme	bt	
SERRANUS perch; bass	zo	
SERRATED notched; like a saw		
SERRATUS a thorax muscle	zo	
SERRIPED with serrated feet	zo	

SERVIENT subordinate; slavish; abject		
SERVIOUS obsequious; sycophantic		
SERVITOR waiter; henchman		
SESAMOID (toe bones)	md	
SESTERCE Roman 2d. coin	nm	
SESTETTE sextet	mu	
SESTOLET sextuplet	mu	
SET-ASIDE reserve(d)		
SET-PIECE stage scene		
SETIFORM bristly		
SETTLING colonizing; deciding; fixing		
SETULOSE prickly; spinate; spicate		
SEVERELY rigorously; strictly		
SEVERING disrupting; sundering		
SEVERITY harshness; austerity		
SEWELLEL mountain beaver	zo	
SEWER-GAS bad smell		
SEWERAGE drainage		
SEXAGENE angle of 60 degrees		
SEXANGLE a hexagon		
SEXTETTE sextet	mu	
SEXTUPLE sixfold		
SEXUALLY in a sexual way		
SFORZATO emphatically	mu	
SHABBIER more ragged		
SHABBILY despicably; meanly		
SHABRACK saddle-cloth		
SHACKING tramping; hibernating		
SHACKLED fettered; manacled		
SHAD-BIRD American snipe	zo	
SHAD-BUSH the June-berry	bt	
SHAD-FROG jumping frog	zo	
SHADDOCK grapefruit	bt	
SHADEFUL umbrageous		
SHADIEST most obscure		
SHADOWED followed; obscured		
SHAFTING (machinery)		
SHAGGING shredding		
SHAGREEN sharkskin		
SHAKE-OUT return to normal; economics		
SHALLOON woollen fabric	tx	
SHAMANIC magical		
SHAMBLES slaughter-house; ruin		
SHAMEFUL humiliating; heinous; base		
SHAMMING feigning; counterfeiting		
SHAMROCK Irish emblem	bt	
SHANGHAI kidnap		
SHANKING mishitting at golf		
SHANTIES sea songs; huts		
SHANTUNG coarse silk	tx	
SHAPABLE fashionable		
SHARP-CUT clearly defined		
SHARPING tricking		
SHARP-SET keen		
SHASHLIK grilled lamb on skewer	ck	
SHATTERY brittle; rickety		
SHAW-FOWL a wappenshaw fowl	zo	
SHEADING district, Isle of Man		
SHEALING shepherd's hut (Sc.)		
SHEARHOG shorn sheep	zo	
SHEARING clipping; shaving; fleecing		
SHEARMAN cloth-cutter		

SHEA-TREE butter tree		bt
SHEATHED encased; sheeted		
SHEAVING collecting; harvesting		
SHEDDING discarding; diffusing		
SHEELING shealing; shelter		
SHEEP-DIP sheep's health bath		
SHEEP-PEN an enclosure		
SHEEP-RUN tract of pasture		
SHEEPDOG a chaperon		zo
SHEEPFLY a parasite		zo
SHEEPISH diffident; bashful		
SHEER-LEG a spar		
SHEERING moving aside		
SHEET-FED separate-sheet printing		pr
SHEETING cloth for sheets		
SHEILING shealing; hut		
SHEKINAH Divine Aura		
SHELDUCK female sheldrake		zo
SHELL-GUN a cannon		
SHELL-ICE (no water below it)		
SHELLING bombarding; husking		
SHELTERY affording shelter		
SHELVING sloping; shelves		
SHEMITIC Semitic; (Shem)		
SHEPHERD a swain		
SHERATON furniture designer		
SHIELDED sheltered; screened		
SHIELDER protector		
SHIELING Highland hut; sheiling		
SHIFTILY deceitfully; evasively		
SHIFTING moving; varying; changing		
SHILLALY Irish blackthorn cudgel		
SHILLING a bob		nm
SHIMMING wedging		
SHIN-BONE the tibia		md
SHINGLED bobbed		
SHINGLES herpes		md
SHINNING climbing		
SHIPLESS without boats		
SHIPLOAD a full cargo		nt
SHIPMATE fellow seaman		
SHIPMENT embarkation		
SHIPPING freighting; seaborne craft		nt
SHIP-TIRE head-dress		
SHIP-WORM the teredo		zo
SHIPYARD building yard		nt
SHIREMAN sheriff		
SHIRKING evading; scamping		
SHIRTING material for shirts		tx
SHIVAREE mock serenade; charivari		
SHIVERED shattered; quaked; trembled		
SHOALING thronging		
SHOCK-DOG a poodle		zo
SHOCKING offensive; outrageous		
SHOEBILL whale-headed heron		zo
SHOEHORN footwear aid		
SHOELACE a latchet		
SHOELESS barefoot		
SHOGGING shaking; jogging		
SHOGUNAL (Japanese C. in C.)		
SHOOTING a game-preserve		
SHOP-BELL bell at shop door		

SHOPGIRL shop assistant	**SICK-ROOM** patients' room md
SHOPLIFT pilfer; rob a store	**SICKENED** languished; ailed; wearied
SHOPPING purchases	**SICKENER** a cause of disgust
SHOPWORN faded	**SICKLIED** pallid; wan
SHORLING newly shorn sheep zo	**SICKLILY** languidly
SHORTAGE deficiency; lack	**SICKNESS** malady; disease; illness
SHORT-AND the ampersand; &	**SICULIAN** early Sicilian
SHORT-CUT (tobacco); a quick way	**SIDE-ACHE** side stitch or pain
SHORT-LEG (cricket)	**SIDE-ARMS** sword or bayonet
SHORT-RIB a false rib md	**SIDEBAND** close frequencies ro
SHOT-BELT bandolier	**SIDE-BEAM** (above crank-shaft) au
SHOT-FREE Scot free; untaxed	**SIDE-COMB** ornamental comb
SHOT-HOLE hole for explosives	**SIDE-DISH** an entrée
SHOT-SILK iridescent silk	**SIDE-DRUM** assistant drum mu
SHOTTING loading with shot	**SIDELINE** subsidiary activity
SHOULDER carry; hump; a prominence	**SIDELING** sideways; sloping
SHOUTING cheering; crying; calling	**SIDE-LOCK** a curl
SHOW-BILL a showcard	**SIDELONG** obliquely
SHOW-CARD card of patterns	**SIDE-NOTE** marginal note
SHOW-CASE display case	**SIDEREAL** of interval between 2 transits
SHOW-DOWN cards on the table	as
SHOW-ROOM display salon	**SIDERITE** ironstone mn
SHOW-YARD (horses and cattle)	**SIDE-SEAT** seat not in front
SHOWERED bestowed liberally	**SIDE-SHOW** raree show at fair
SHRAPNEL a projectile	**SIDE-SLIP** a skid
SHREDDED cut into strips	**SIDESMAN** deputy churchwarden rl
SHREDDER machine for shredding	**SIDE-STEP** evade
SHREWDLY sagaciously; astutely	**SIDETONE** telephony
SHREWISH vixenish	**SIDE-VIEW** profile
SHRIEKED yelled; squealed; cried	**SIDEWALK** pavement
SHRIEKER screamer	**SIDEWAYS** crabwise
SHRIEVAL (sheriff)	**SIDE-WIND** undue influence
SHRILLED squeaked; piped	**SIDE-WIRE** wire staple stitching pr
SHRIMPED went fishing for shrimps	**SIEGE-GUN** heavy gun
SHRIMPER boat or catcher	**SIFFLEUR** whistler
SHRINING enshrining	**SIFFLING** whistling
SHRINKER a contractor?	**SIGATOKA** fungal banana disease bt
SHRIVING absolving; pardoning	**SIGHTING** spotting; aiming; viewing
SHROUDED veiled; hidden; screened	**SIGMATIC** (sigma)
SHROVING Shrove-tide festivity	**SIGNABLE** able to have a name written on
SHRUGGED uplifted	**SIGNALLY** eminently; notably
SHUCKING husking; stripping	**SIGNIEUR** seignior; feudal lord
SHUFFLED (cards); evaded	**SIGNLESS** making no sign
SHUFFLER palterer; quibbler	**SIGN-POST** modern milestone
SHUNNING avoiding; evading	**SIKYOTIC** plasma-fusing parasitic bt
SHUNPIKE a byroad	**SILENCED** stilled; hushed
SHUNTING switching railway cars	**SILENCER** (cars, guns, etc.)
SHUTDOWN closure	**SILENTLY** mutely; dumbly; taciturnly
SHUTTING fastening; barring	**SILICATE** silicon compound ch
SHWANPAN Chinese abacus	**SILICIDE** silicon-content compound ch
SIBERIAN of Siberia	**SILICIFY** make into silica
SIBERITE red tourmaline mn	**SILICITE** labradorite mn
SIBILANT hissing; buzzing	**SILICIUM** silicon ch
SIBILATE to hiss	**SILICOLE** plant on silica-rich soil bt
SIBILOUS sibilant	**SILICONE** organo-silicon compound ch
SIBYLLIC oracular; prophetic	**SILICULA, SILICULE** seed vessel bt
SICANIAN Sicilian	**SILK-MILL** cloth factory
SICELIOT a Greek in Sicily	**SILKENED** made glossy tx
SICILIAN (Sicily)	**SILK-REEL** spool for silk
SICK-CALL doctor's visit	**SILKWORM** source of silk zo
SICK-FLAG quarantine-flag nt	**SILLABUB** syllabub; a drink ck
SICK-LIST register of patients	**SILLADAR** Indian cavalryman

SILLY-HOW a caul	
SILPHIUM rosin-weed	bt
SILURIAN rock formation	mn
SILURIST a Silurian	
SILVANUS a forest-god	
SILVERLY like silver	
SIMARUBA quassia; bitterwood	bt
SIMILIZE compare; liken	
SIMMERED boiled gently	
SIMONIAC one guilty of simony	rl
SIMPERED smiled fatuously	
SIMPERER smirker	
SIMPLIFY make plain and easy	
SIMPLING gathering herbs	
SIMPLISM affected simplicity	
SIMPLIST herbalist	
SIMULANT like unto	
SIMULATE pretend; imitate; sham	
SIN-EATER (a Welsh custom)	
SINAITIC (Mount Sinai)	rl
SINAPISM mustard plaster	md
SINCIPUT the skull	pl
SINECURE salary for no work	
SINEWING strengthening	
SINEWOUS strong; vigorous	
SINFONIA a symphony	mu
SINFULLY unrighteously; naughtily	
SINGERIE monkeys represented as human	am
SING-SING a prison in USA	
SING-SONG community singing	
SINGABLE vocable	
SINGEING scorching; searing	
SINGLING selecting; picking	
SINGULAR peculiar; unique; quaint	
SINICISM a Chinese custom	
SINIGRIN black-mustard-seed glucoside	ch
SINISTER evil; unlucky; baneful	
SINK-HOLE a vent	
SINN-FEIN Irish home-ruler	
SINOLOGY Chinese lore	
SINOPHIL lover of China	
SINUATED insinuated; wound	
SINUSOID geometric curve	
SIPHONAL working on the siphon principle	
SIPHONED extracted to a lower level	
SIPHONET aphid cornicle	
SIPHONIC working on the siphon principle	
SIPYLITE niobite of erbium	ch
SIRENIZE entice; allure	
SIRIASIS sunstroke	md
SIRVENTE troubadour's song	
SISCOWET **SISKIWET** **SISKOWET** a variety of trout from Lake Superior	zo
SISTERLY affectionate; sororal	
SISYPHUS stone-roller	
SITOLOGY dietetics	md
SITTYBUS papyrus-roll title label	
SITUATED placed; located; sited	
SITZ-BATH hip-bath	
SIXPENCE a tanner	nm

SIXPENNY worth sixpence	
SIXTIETH ordinal number	
SIZEABLE of some bulk	
SIZINESS adhesiveness	
SIZING-UP estimation, rapid evaluation	
SIZZLING hissing; seething; frying	
SKEAN-DHU Highland dirk	
SKELETAL like a skeleton	
SKELETON outline; nucleus; cadre	
SKELLOCK squeal (Sc.)	
SKETCHED drafted; depicted; drew	
SKETCHER delineator	
SKEWBACK an abutment	
SKEWBALD piebald	
SKEWERED impaled	
SKIAGRAM X-ray photograph	md
SKIATRON type of cathode-ray tube	el
SKIDDING side-slipping	
SKILLESS maladroit; artless	
SKILLING outhouse; bay of a barn	
SKIM-MILK weightwatcher's drink	
SKIMMING scan superficially	
SKIMMITY a burlesque	
SKIMPING scamping; stinting	
SKIN-DEEP superficial	
SKINLESS flayed	
SKINNING flaying	
SKINTLED of irregularly laid brickwork	bd
SKIN-WOOL wool from dead sheep	
SKIPETAR an Albanian	
SKIP-JACK upstart; click-beetle	zo
SKIPPING leaping; bounding; hopping	
SKIRLING bagpipe music	mu
SKIRMISH contest; brush; fray	
SKIRTING bordering	
SKITTISH mettlesome; fickle	
SKITTLES ninepins	
SKUA-GULL the great skua	
SKULKING lurking; slinking	
SKULL-CAP the sinciput	
SKUNKISH like a skunk	zo
SKYLIGHT glazed hole in roof	
SKY-PILOT aviator; padre	rl
SKYSCAPE cloud painting	
SKY-SHADE lens; hood	pg
SLABBING cutting into slabs	
SLABLINE a running rope	nt
SLACKING relaxing; loosening	
SLAISTER slovenly work (Sc.)	
SLAMMING banging	
SLANGILY colloquially	
SLANGING vituperating	
SLANTING sloping; tilting; oblique	
SLAP-BANG violently	
SLAP-DASH carelessly; rashly	
SLAPJACK flapjack; pancake	
SLAPPING large; strong; spanking	
SLASHING showy; severe; gashing	
SLATE-AXE a seax	to
SLATTERN slovenly person	
SLAVERED dribbled	
SLAVERER driveller; idiot	

SLAVONIC (Czechs; Poles; etc.)	
SLEAVING separating	
SLEDDING sled-transport	
SLEDGING sleighing	
SLEEKING gliding; smoothing	
SLEEPFUL somnolent	
SLEEPILY drowsily	
SLEEPING dormant; slumbering	
SLEETING rain, snow and hail	
SLIDABLE capable of sliding	
SLIGHTED insulted; peeved	
SLIGHTLY slenderly; faintly; scantily	
SLIME-PIT pit of viscous mire	
SLIMMING banting; reducing; dieting	
SLIMNESS craftiness; artfulness	
SLINGING throwing; flinging; tossing	
SLINKING skulking; lurking; sneaking	
SLIP-DOCK slipway	nt
SLIP-KNOT sailor's device	
SLIPOVER sleeveless sweater	
SLIP-RAIL form of gate (Australian)	
SLIP-ROAD minor by-pass; siding	
SLIPPERY evasive; shifty; elusive	
SLIPPING tripping; erring; sliding	
SLIPSHOD down at heel	
SLIPSLOP jejune; trash; slovenly	
SLITHERY slimy; deceitful	
SLITTING splitting	
SLIVERED cut into strips	
SLOBBERY moist	
SLOGGING smiting	
SLOP-BOWL slop-basin	
SLOP-DASH weak cold tea	
SLOP-PAIL household bucket	
SLOPPING spilling	
SLOPSHOP (ready-made clothes) R.N.	
SLOPWORK slovenly work	
SLOTHFUL idle; dronish; dilatory	
SLOTTERY squalid; dirty	
SLOTTING grooving	
SLOUCHED bent; depressed	
SLOUGHED cast off	
SLOVENLY negligently; unkempt	
SLOVENRY slovenliness; disorder	
SLOWBACK lazy lubber	
SLOW-DOWN ca' canny; reduce capacity	
SLOWNESS tardiness; sluggishness	
SLOW-WORM limbless lizard	zo
SLUBBING twisting	
SLUG-HORN a trumpet	mu
SLUGGARD laggard; lounger; slacker	
SLUGGING slogging	
SLUGGISH slothful; inert	
SLUICING flushing	
SLUMBERY somnolent; soporous	
SLUMMING visiting slums	
SLUMPING falling heavily	
SLURGALL knitted-fabric fault	tx
SLURRIED smeared	
SLURRING disparaging	
SLUTTERY dirt and disorder	
SLUTTISH slatternly	

SLY-BOOTS a wag	
SLY-GOOSE the sheld-duck	zo
SMACKING tasting of; slapping	
SMALL-ALE (no hops)	
SMALLAGE wild celery	bt
SMALLEST minutest; tiniest	
SMALLISH on the small side	
SMALLPOX variola	md
SMALTINE } compound of cobalt	mn
SMALTITE } and arsenic	
SMARTING stinging; rankling	
SMASH-HIT popular song; musical	
SMASHING disrupting; shattering	
SMEARING daubing; begriming	
SMECTITE fuller's earth	mn
SMELLING redolent; scenting	
SMELTERY foundry	
SMELTING producing metal	
SMIRCHED soiled; clouded	
SMIRKING simpering	
SMITCHEL a particle	
SMITHERY a smiddy; a smithy	
SMITHING iron-working	
SMOCKING pleating	
SMOKABLE fumable	
SMOKE-BOX (steam locomotive)	
SMOKE-DRY cure; bloat	
SMOOTHED palliated; levelled	
SMOOTHEN to allay; mollify	
SMOOTHLY suavely; blandly	
SMORBROD open sandwich (Scand.)	
SMORZATO diminuendo	mu
SMOTHERY stifling; stuffy	
SMOULDER hangfire	
SMOULDRY slow burning	
SMUDGING blotting	
SMUG-BOAT smuggling boat	nv
SMUGGLED brought in illegally	
SMUGGLER an owler	
SMUGNESS self-satisfaction	
SMUTBALL a fungus	bt
SMUTCHED blacken with soot	
SMYTERIE many small people (Sc.)	
SNACK-BAR buffet	
SNAFFLED purloined; filched	
SNAGBOAT (removing snags)	nt
SNAGGING lopping trees	
SNAILERY small farm	
SNAKE-EEL sinuous fish	zo
SNAP-LINE chalked-string design marker	
	pt
SNAP-VOTE sudden vote	
SNAP-WEED balsams, etc.	bt
SNAPPING biting; breaking; cracking	
SNAPPISH short-tempered	
SNAPSHOT amateur photograph	
SNARLING entangling	
SNATCHED plucked; clutched; wrested	
SNATCHER grasper; grabber	
SNEAK-CUP insidious scoundrel	
SNEAKING telling; secret; slinking	
SNEERING taunting; jeering; mocking	

SNEEZING snuff	**SODA-LIME** soda and quicklime
SNICKING cutting; nicking	**SODALITE** a soda compound mn
SNIFFING indicating incredulity	**SODALITY** comradeship; association
SNIGGLED snared	**SODAMIDE** ammonia-sodium compound
SNIPPETY fragmentary	ch
SNIPPING shearing; clipping	**SODA-SALT** baking ingredient ch
SNIP-SNAP smart sharp dialogue	**SODDENED** saturated; drenched
SNITCHER handcuff; informer	**SOFTENED** mollified; melted; assuaged
SNIVELLY whining	**SOFTENER** mitigator; mollifier
SNOBBERY tuft-hunting	**SOFT-EYED** compassionate
SNOBBISH feeling superior	**SOFTLING** weakling
SNOBBISM aping gentility	**SOFTNESS** tenderness
SNOBLING a little snob	**SOFT-SHOE** light tap-dancing
SNOOPING furtive enquiry; prying	**SOFT-SOAP** flattery
SNOOZING dozing; drowsing	**SOFT-WOOD** sap-wood bt
SNORTING puffing	**SOILLESS** untarnished
SNOWBALL guelder-rose bt	**SOIL-PIPE** drain-pipe
SNOWBIRD American finch zo	**SOLACING** consoling; comforting
SNOWBOOT long boot; galosh	**SOLANDER** case for prints
SNOWCAPT crowned with snow	**SOLANINE** an alkaloid bt
SNOWCOLD cold as snow	**SOLANOID** potato-shaped md
SNOWDROP first sign of spring bt	**SOLARISM** solar myths
SNOW-EYES snow goggles	**SOLARIST** mythologist
SNOWFALL frozen precipitation	**SOLARIUM** sun-dial; sun-parlour
SNOWLIKE cold, white and soft	**SOLARIZE** injure by sun's rays
SNOWLINE line of perpetual snow	**SOLASTER** starfish zo
SNOWSHED railway protection	**SOLATIUM** compensation
SNOWSHOE wide framed shoe for walking	**SOLDANEL** blue moonwort bt
on snow	**SOLDERED** cemented
SNOWSLIP avalanche	**SOLDERER** a joiner of metals
SNOWSUIT winter garments	**SOLDIERY** the military
SNUBBING checking a rope	**SOLECISM** incongruity; impropriety
SNUBBISH petulant	**SOLECIST** ⎫ (breaches of manners
SNUB-NOSE short nose	**SOLECIZE** ⎭ or syntax)
SNUFFBOX collector's item	**SOLEMNLY** gravely; formally; staidly
SNUFFERS candle trimmers	**SOLENESS** singleness
SNUFFLED sniffed	**SOLENITE** fossil razor-shell mn
SNUFFLER one who snuffles	**SOLENOID** copper coil
SNUFFLES infantile breathing noise md	**SOLFAISM** ⎫ (singing by syllables) mu
SNUGGERY cosy quarters	**SOLFAIST** ⎭
SNUGGING lying close	**SOLIDIFY** harden; congeal; petrify
SNUGGLED cuddled	**SOLIDISM** ⎫ (medical theory of
SNUGNESS warmth and comfort	**SOLIDIST** ⎭ diseases) md
SO-CALLED soi-disant	**SOLIDITY** compactness
SOAPSUDS froth on soapy water	**SOLITARY** lonely; single; remote
SOAP-TEST (for hardness of water)	**SOLITUDE** isolation; seclusion
SOAP-TREE a Chilean tree bt	**SOLLERET** foot armour
SOAPWORK soap factory	**SOLONIAN** (Solon, a lawgiver) lw
SOAPWORT a genus of plants bt	**SOLSTICE** an ecliptic point
SOB-STORY false, pathetic tale	**SOLUTION** release; elucidation
SOB-STUFF synthetic emotion	**OOLUTIVE** loosening
SOBERIZE to calm down	**SOLVABLE** explainable; resolvable
SOBRANJE Bulgaria; Sobranye	**SOLVENCY** all debts payable
SOBRIETY dispassion; temperance	**SOMACTID** bony fin rod in fish zo
SOCIABLE companionable	**SOMATISM** a doctrine
SOCIABLY friendlily	**SOMATIST** materialist
SOCIALLY gregariously	**SOMATOME** homologous segment
SOCINIAN a polemic theologian	**SOMBRERO** broad-brimmed hat (S.
SOCKETED shanked	Amer.)
SOCMANRY feudal tenure lw	**SOMBROUS** gloomy; sombre; doleful
SOCRATIC (Socrates)	**SOMEBODY** more than a nobody

SOMEDEAL in some degree
SOMEGATE somewhere (Sc.)
SOMERSET sommersault
SOMESUCH similar
SOMETIME formerly; once
SOMEWHAT more or less
SOMEWHEN some time or other
SOMNIFIC inducing sleep; soporific
SON-IN-LAW daughter's husband
SONATINA short sonata   mu
SONG-BIRD warbler   zo
SONG-BOOK collection of songs   mu
SONGLESS not in good voice   mu
SONGSTER vocalist   mu
SONOBUOY underwater noise-fixing equipment
SONORITY resonance   mu
SONOROUS melodious; audible   mu
SOOTHING pleasing; calming; lulling
SOOTHSAY foretell; augur; predict
SOPHERIM Hebrew scribes
SOPITION lethargy
SOPOROUS drowsy; somnolent
SORALIUM group of soredia in lichen   bt
SORBITOL hexahydric alcohol   ch
SORBONNE University of Paris
SORCERER wizard; magician
SORDIDLY ignobly; basely; meanly
SOREDIUM a brood-bud   bt
SOREHEAD disgruntled person
SORENESS regret; rancour
SORICINE (shrew-mice)   zo
SORORISE be a sister to
SORORITY women's club (Amer. univ.)
SORPTION absorption, adsorption, etc.   ch
SORROWED grieved; lamented; wept
SORROWER mourner; repiner
SORTABLE befitting; suitable
SORTMENT assortment; distribution
SOTADEAN satirical and malicious
SOTERIAL about salvation
SOUCHONG black China tea
SOUGHING moaning; sighing
SOUL-BELL passing-bell   rl
SOULLESS dull; spiritless
SOUL-SCOT } requiem fee   rl
SOUL-SHOT }
SOUL-SICK morally diseased
SOUND-BOW part of a bell
SOUNDING swinging the lead
SOUR-BALL tart hard spherical sweet
SOURDINE a muffler; sordet   mu
SOUR-DOCK sorrel   bt
SOUR-EYED morose
SOURNESS tartness; asperity
SOUR-PUSS a kill-joy
SOUTHERN of the south
SOUTHING of star crossing meridian   as
SOUTHING towards the south
SOUVENIR memento; relic; keepsake
SOW-BREAD a tuber   bt

SOW-DRUNK beastly drunk
SOYA-BEAN protein/oil plant (Manchuria)
SOZZLING getting fuddled   [bt
SPACE-BAR typewriter gadget
SPACEMAN astronaut
SPACIOUS vast; roomy; ample; wide
SPADILLE } ace of spaces in
SPADILIO } ombre & quadrille
SPADROON double-handed sword
SPAGIRIC chemical
SPALLING stonework fragmentation
SPALPEEN scamp; rascal (Ir.)
SPANDREL } triangular space
SPANDRIL } beside an arch
SPANEMIA anaemia   md
SPANGLED glittering
SPANGLER sparkler
SPANIARD an Iberian
SPANKING dashing; slapping
SPANLESS immeasurable
SPAN-LONG 9 inches (22 cm)   me
SPANNING bridging; extending
SPAN-ROOF roof with eaves
SPAR-DECK the upper deck   nt
SPAR-HAWK sparrow-hawk   zo
SPAR-HUNG (with fluorspar)
SPARABLE shoe nail
SPARE RIB a piece of pork
SPARGING sprinkling
SPARKFUL lively; gay
SPARKING playing the gallant
SPARKISH well-dressed; airy
SPARKLER a diamond   mn
SPARKLET charge of gas
SPARLING a smelt   zo
SPARRING boxing
SPARSELY thinly; meagrely
SPARSILE scanty; infrequent
SPATHOSE } foliated or lamular   bt
SPATHOUS }
SPATHURA humming-birds   zo
SPAVINED (leg swelling)
SPAWLING slobbering
SPAWNING putting forth eggs
SPEAKING hailing; addressing
SPEARING lancing
SPEARMAN he who spears
SPECIFIC distinctive; peculiar
SPECIMEN sample; type; exemplar
SPECIOUS plausible; ostensible
SPECKING staining
SPECKLED variegated
SPECTANT expectant
SPECTRAL ghostly; spooky
SPECTRUM (colour bands)
SPECULAR reflective
SPECULUM a mirror
SPEEDFUL speedy; hasty; impetuous
SPEEDIER faster; quicker
SPEEDILY with rapidity
SPEEDWAY racing track

SPEKBOOM S. African shrub	bt	
SPELDING ⎱ dried haddock; or fish		
SPELDRIN ⎰ split and dried in		
SPELDRON the sun		
SPELLING charming		
SPEND-ALL spendthrift		
SPENDING exhausting; squandering		
SPERABLE hopeful		
SPERGULA spurry; sandweed	bt	
SPERM-OIL whale by-product		
SPHAGNUM bog-moss	bt	
SPHECIUS digger-wasps	zo	
SPHENOID wedge-shaped		
SPHERICS spherical geometry		
SPHEROID almost a sphere		
SPHEROME cell-inclusion causing oil globule		
SPHERULE small globe		
SPHRAGID ochreous clay	mn	
SPHYGMIC pulsative	md	
SPICATUM herring-bone work		
SPICCATO clearly	mu	
SPICE-BOX condiment-holder		
SPICEFUL aromatic		
SPICKNEL baldmoney plant	bt	
SPICULAR spiky; pointed		
SPICULUM small spike	bt	
SPIFFING delightful		
SPIGELIA worm-grass; pink-root	bt	
SPIKELET unit of grass inflorescence	bt	
SPILIKIN spillikin		
SPILLING upsetting; shedding		
SPILLWAY overflow		
SPILOTES a snake genus	zo	
SPINDLED tapering		
SPINIFEX porcupine grass	bt	
SPINITIS spinal fever	md	
SPINNERY spinning mill		
SPINNING whirling; twirling		
SPINSTER unmarried woman		
SPINSTRY spinning industry		
SPIRACLE ⎱ breathing-hole;		
SPIRICLE ⎰ pore	pl	
SPIRALLY whorled		
SPIRIFER fossil brachiopod	mn	
SPIRITED sprightly; alert		
SPIRITUS aspiration; breathing		
SPIRTING spurting; sprinting		
SPIT-CURL soap-lock		
SPITEFUL vindictive; malicious		
SPITFIRE fighting aircraft; irascible		
SPITTING piercing		
SPITTOON a cuspidor		
SPLASHED spattered		
SPLASHER a mud-guard		
SPLATTER to splash		
SPLAYING sloping		
SPLEENED angered		
SPLENDID lustrous; refulgent		
SPLENIAL splint-like bone	md	
SPLENIUM posterior bend of commissure	zo	

SPLENIUS a neck muscle	pl	
SPLICING joining; binding		
SPLINTER fragment; cleave		
SPLITTER separator		
SPLOTCHY unevenly daubed		
SPLUTTER a bustle; a stir		
SPOFFISH fussy; officious		
SPOILFUL wasteful; rapacious		
SPOILING marring; vitiating		
SPOLIARY Roman mortuary		
SPOLIATE plunder; pillage		
SPOLVERO perforation cartoon technique		
SPONDIAC (spondee)		
SPONDIAS hog-plums, etc.	bt	
SPONDYLE a vertebra	pl	
SPONGING cadging; sorning		
SPONSION sponsorship		
SPONTOON kind of halberd		
SPOOFING bluffing		
SPOOKISH ghostly		
SPOOLING winding on spools		
SPOONFUL a bite		
SPOONILY amorously		
SPOONING courting		
SPORADIC scattered; irregular		
SPOROSAC a gonophore	zo	
SPORTFUL frolicsome; jocose		
SPORTING generous		
SPORTING romping; displaying		
SPORTIVE wanton; hilarious		
SPOT-BALL billiards		
SPOTLESS pure; untainted		
SPOTTING observing		
SPOUTING orating; gushing		
SPRACHLE ⎱ to clamber up		
SPRACKLE ⎰ with difficulty		
SPRAGGED scotched up		
SPRAINED overstrained		
SPRAINTS dung of an otter		
SPRAWLED straggled; spread		
SPRAWLER lounger		
SPRAYING atomizing		
SPREADER extender		
SPRIGGED adorned with sprigs		
SPRINGAL catapult; youth		
SPRINGER arch support	zo	
SPRINKLE bedew; perfuse		
SPRINTED speeded; spurted		
SPRINTER racer		
SPROCKET a cog		
SPRUCELY neatly; tidily		
SPRUCIFY to smarten		
SPRUCING refurbishing		
SPRUNTED sprang; sprouted		
SPUILZIE to spoil (Sc.)		
SPUNYARN loosely twisted rope		
SPUR-GALL wound with a spur		
SPUR-GEAR gear wheels		
SPURIOUS bastard; faked		
SPURLESS without incentive		
SPURLING the smelt	zo	

SPURNING disdaining; scouting
SPURRIER spur-maker
SPURRING inciting
SPURRITE carbonate/silicate of calcium
SPURTING gushing
SPURTLED showered
SPY-CRAFT secret service
SPY-GLASS a telescope
SPY-MONEY pay to secret agent
SQUAB-PIE pigeon-pie
SQUABBED stuffed; crashed
SQUABBLE wrangle; brawl; printing
SQUADDED grouped
SQUADRON military grouping
SQUALENE symmetrical triterpine   ch
SQUALLED yelled; cried
SQUALLER screamer; informer
SQUALOID like a shark   zo
SQUAMATA reptile genus   zo
SQUAMATE } covered with scales; scaly
SQUAMOID }
SQUAMOSE } squamous;
SQUAMULA } a small scale   zo
SQUAMULE }
SQUANDER dissipate; lavish; fritter
SQUARELY evenly; quadrilaterally
SQUARING adjusting; regulating
SQUARISH not quite square
SQUARSON squire-parson   rl
SQUASHED compressed; squeezed
SQUASHER suppresser
SQUATTED cowered; crouched; sat
SQUATTER settler without title
SQUATTLE to squat down (Sc.)
SQUAWKED squalled
SQUAWMAN N. American Indian
SQUEAKED shrilled
SQUEAKER informer
SQUEALED squalled
SQUEEGEE rubber mop
SQUEEZED crushed; constricted
SQUEEZER playing card
SQUEGGER self-quenching circuit
SQUIBBED wrangled
SQUIGGLE squirm; wriggle
SQUILGEE squeegee
SQUINTED peered with narrowed/crossed eyes
SQUIREEN a petty squire
SQUIRELY gallantly
SQUIRING escorting
SQUIRMED wriggled
SQUIRREL plume-tailed rodent   zo
SQUIRTED ejected; gushed
SQUIRTER a syringe
STABBING piercing; thrusting
STABLING accommodation for horses
STABLISH establish
STACCATO abruptly   mu
STACKING piling
STADDLED supported

STAFFING providing personnel
STAFFMAN surveyor's assistant
STAG-EVIL horse disease   vt
STAGGARD 4-year-old stag   zo
STAGGERS giddiness
STAGHORN large fern   bt
STAGNANT motionless; inert
STAGNATE become dull
STAHLIAN } medical theory   md
STAHLISM }
STAINING sullying; discolouring
STAIR-ROD carpet retainer
STAIRWAY a staircase
STAKE-NET fishing net
STALKING approaching warily
STALLAGE stall rent
STALL-FED luxuriously nurtured
STALLING losing speed when flying
STALLION male horse   zo
STALLMAN stall-holder
STALWART resolute; sturdy; valiant
STAMENED having stamens   bt
STAMINAL constitutional; vigorous
STAMPEDE panic; rush; flight
STAMPING pounding; impressing
STANCHED staunched; stopped
STANCHEL next (Sc.)
STANCHER a tourniquet
STANCHLY steadily; staunchly
STAND-OFF (Rugby football)
STAND-PAT decline to budge
STANDARD banner; colours; fruit tree
STANDING rank; duration; status
STANHOPE dog-cart
STANK-HEN moorhen   zo
STANNANE tin hydride   ch
STANNARY tin mine
STANNATE a salt   ch
STANNINE a tin alloy
STANNITE sulphostannate of copper/iron
STANNOUS containing tin
STANZAIC (stanzas)
STAPELIA milkweed plants   bt
STAPLING sorting; binding
STAR-DUST cosmic dust
STARE-CAT over-inquisitive neighbour
STAR-FISH an echinoderm   zo
STAR-FORT angular redoubt
STAR-GAZE astronomise
STAR-LIKE stellate
STAR-NOSE N. American mole   zo
STAR-REED Peruvian plant   bt
STARCHED formal; stiff
STARCHER stiffener
STARCHLY rigidly; punctiliously
STARLESS lacking stars
STARLING ring of piles; bird   zo
STAROSTA Polish noble
STAROSTY life-estate
STARRING taking the lead
STARTERS introductory meal course   ck

STARTFUL skittish; jumpy
STARTING inventing; evoking
STARTISH nervous; fearful; scared
STARTLED affrighted; dumbfounded
STARTLER a shock; a rouser
STAR-TURN revue or circus act
STARVING famished; hungry
STARWEED star-shaped plant   bt
STARWORT aster genus   bt
STASIMON choral ode   rl
STATABLE declarable; affirmable
STATEDLY regularly
STATICAL in equilibrium; restful
STATUARY sculpture
STATURED full grown
STAYBAND mast hoop to take stay wires   nt
STAY-BOLT a holdfast
STAY-LACE corset cord
STAYSAIL part of rigging   nt
STEADIED supported; upheld
STEADILY constantly; firmly
STEADING farm out-houses
STEALING filching; purloining
STEALTHY clandestine; furtive; sly
STEAM-GUN steam-propelled firearm
STEAMING evaporating; reeking
STEAM-TUG steam-driven boat   nt
STEANING well-shaft lining
STEAPSIN fat-digesting enzyme   zo
STEARATE a fatty acid
STEARINE tallow; suet; etc.
STEATITE soapstone   mn
STEATOMA wen or tumour   md
STEELING hardening; bracing; nerving
STEEL-PEN a nib
STEENING well-shaft lining
STEEPING soaking; macerating
STEEPLED having a thick spire
STEERAGE third class at sea   nt
STEERING directing; piloting; guiding
STEEVELY stiffly (Sc.)
STEEVING stowing
STEINBOK African antelope   zo
STEINING process of well-lining   ce
STELLARY starry
STELLATE radiated
STELLION a lizard   zo
STELLITE zeolitic mineral   mn
STEM-HEAD top of stem
STEM-LEAF part of plant   bt
STEMLESS no stalk
STEMMING opposing; stopping
STENLOCH overgrown coalfish   zo
STENOSED contracted
STENOSIS constriction
STEP-DAME step-mother
STEP-GIRL doorstep cleaner
STEPPING pacing; walking
STEPWISE photocopying method
STERCOME faecal matter in sarcodina   zo

STEREOME mechanical plant tissue   bt
STERIGMA fungal-spore-bearing hypha   bt
STERLING genuine; pure; sound
STERNAGE steerage   nt
STERNITE part of an insect   zo
STERNWAY backward movement
STIBBLER clerical locum tenens   rl
STIBNITE antimony compound
STICCADO xylophone   mu
STICKING adhering; fixing; piercing
STICKJAW toffee
STICKLED interposed; obstructed
STICKLER purist over trifles
STIFF-BIT horse's bit
STIFFISH rather tight
STIFLING suffocating; muffling
STIGMATA sacred marks   rl
STILBENE S-diphenylethylene   ch
STILBITE zeolitic mineral   mn
STILBOID having stalked spore-head   bt
STILETTO small dagger; high heel
STILLAGE cask-storing platform   br
STILLING calming; distilling; ceramics
STILLION stand for a cask
STIMMUNG tone; atmosphere, mood (Ger.)
STIMULUS spur; incitement; goad
STING-RAY a fish   zo
STINGILY parsimoniously; miserly
STINGING pricking; wounding
STINKARD teledu; badger   zo
STINKPOT a grenade
STINTING limiting; pinching
STIPPLED dotted
STIPPLER engraver
STIPULAR } having pin-feathers;   zo
STIPULED } (leaf lobe)   bt
STIRLESS quiescent; still; dull
STIRRING rousing; exciting lively
STITCHED united; sewn
STITCHEL a hairy wool
STITCHER seamstress
STOCCADE } a thrust in fencing
STOCCADO }
STOCKADE palisaded defence
STOCKIER stouter built
STOCKILY thickset
STOCKING footwear; storing
STOCKISH stupid; blockish
STOCKIST a tradesman
STOCKMAN herdsman
STOCKPOT (gravy and soup)
STOICISM imperturbation
STOLIDLY impassively; obtusely
STOLZITE lead tungstate   mn
STOMATIC mouth medicine   md
STOMIDIA disc apertures in actinaria   zo
STONE-BOW (for shooting stones)
STONE-FLY a lure for trout   zo
STONE-OIL petroleum   mn
STONEPIT quarry

STOOGERY clownish fraudulence	**STRIGATE** striped; variegated	
STOOKING corn gathering	**STRIGGED** with fruit stalks removed	
STOOLING ramifying	**STRIGINE** owl-like	zo
STOOMING fermenting	**STRIGOPS** owl-parrots	zo
STOOPING condescending; bending	**STRIGOSE** \ bristly; setous	bt
STOP-BATH developing accessory pg	**STRIGOUS** / aciform; setiform	
STOP-COCK regulating valve	**STRIKING** impressive; forcible	
STOP-OVER intermediate landing	**STRINGED** (rackets; billiards)	mu
STOPPAGE a deduction of pay	**STRINGER** horizontal tie rod	
STOPPING a filling; checking	**STRINKLE** sprinkle sparingly	
STOPPLED corked	**STRIPING** making stripes	
STORABLE reservable	**STRIP-OFF** dismantling, undressing	
STORMILY angrily; tempestuously	**STRIPPED** deprived; naked; fleeced	
STORMING assaulting; ranting	**STRIPPER** pillager; peeler; husker	
STORYING narrating	**STROBILA** tape-worm	zo
STOVAINE an anaesthetic md	**STROBILE** hardened catkin	bt
STOWAWAY secret passenger nt	**STROKING** (rowing); caressing	
STOWDOWN arrange cargo	**STROLLED** sauntered; wandered	
STRADDLE bracket; striddle	**STROLLER** actor; vagrant	
STRAGGLE stray; digress; wander	**STROMBUS** wing-shells, etc.	zo
STRAIGHT direct; honest; upright	**STRONGLY** forcibly; mightily	
STRAINED stressed; exerted; taxed	**STRONTIA** strontium oxide	ch
STRAINER a filter; percolator	**STROPHIC** choral	
STRAITEN confine; perplex; constrict	**STROPPED** (razors)	
STRAITLY narrowly; closely	**STRUCKEN** struck	
STRAMASH a tumult (Sc.)	**STRUGGLE** wrestle; strive; contend	
STRAMMEL straw bt	**STRUMMED** vamped	mu
STRANDED driven ashore; aground	**STRUMOSE** with cushion-like swellings	bt
STRANGER odder; quainter; alien	**STRUMOUS** scrofulous	md
STRANGLE choke; suppress; smother	**STRUMPET** trollop; fly-by-night	
STRAP-OIL a thrashing	**STRUTHIO** ostrich genus	zo
STRAPPED secured; stropped	**STRUTTED** braced	
STRAPPER harness-maker	**STRUTTER** proud walker	
STRATEGY military art	**STUB-IRON** (used for gun-barrels)	
STRATIFY laminate	**STUB-NAIL** short thick nail	
STRATOSE of well-defined layers bt	**STUBBING** uprooting	
STRATULA thin rock layer	**STUBBLED** bristly	
STRAVAIG wander (Sc.)	**STUBBORN** refractory; wilful; perverse	
STRAW-HAT Panama headgear	**STUCCOED** plastered	
STRAYING roving; deviating; erring	**STUD-BOOK** pedigree book	
STREAKED variegated; striped	**STUD-FARM** (horse breeding)	
STREAKER dare-naked runner	**STUDBOLT** headless bolt	
STREAMED flowed; poured; gushed	**STUDDING** putting in studs	
STREAMER a pennant	**STUDIOUS** diligent; scholarly	
STRELITZ Muscovite militia-man	**STUD-MARE** breeding mare	zo
STRENGTH power; vigour; might	**STUDWORK** form of brickwork	
STREPENT noisy; strident	**STUDYING** conning; learning	
STREPERA crow-shrikes zo	**STUFFING** cramming; taxidermy	
STREPHON love-sick swain	**STULTIFY** deaden; dull the mind	
STRESSED emphasized; accented	**STUMBLED** tripped; lurched	
STRETCHY elastic	**STUMBLER** blunderer	
STREWING scattering; broadcasting	**STUMMING** fermenting	
STRIATED furrowed; streaked	**STUMPING** (cricket); nonplussing	
STRIATUM brain ganglion md	**STUNDISM** \ (Russian dissenters)	
STRICKEN afflicted; smitten; struck	**STUNDIST** /	
STRICKLE a template	**STUNNING** dazing; marvellous	
STRICTLY exactly; literally; severely	**STUNSAIL** studding-sail	nt
STRIDDEN strode	**STUNTING** dwarfing; performing	
STRIDDLE straddle; bracket	**STUPEOUS** with matted hair	zo, bt
STRIDENT harsh; grating; creaking	**STUPIDLY** doltishly; senselessly	
STRIDING bestriding; stalking	**STUPRATE** to ravish	

STURDILY stoutly; stalwartly			**SUBTEPID** lukewarm	
STURGEON caviare fish	zo		**SUBTITLE** secondary title	
STURNOID (starlings)	zo		**SUBTLETY** cunning; artfulness	
SUASIBLE persuasible			**SUBTONIC** leading note of scale	mu
SUBACRID pungent			**SUBTOPIA** suburban ideal	
SUBACUTE slightly blunt; dull			**SUBTRACT** withdraw; deduct; take	
SUB-AGENT an underling			**SUBTRIBE** section of a tribe	
SUBAHDAR Indian captain			**SUBTRIST** somewhat sad	
SUBCHORD way-measuring chord length			**SUBTUTOR** under-master	
		sv	**SUBULATE** awl-shaped	
SUB-CLASS subdivision			**SUBURBAN** subregional	
SUBCOSTA primary wing vein in insects			**SUBURBIA** the suburbs	
		zo	**SUBVENED** relieved; subsidized	
SUBCRUST layer between pavement and			**SUBZONAL** below the belt	
foundation			**SUCCINCT** concise; compact; terse	
SUBDUING overpowering; mastering			**SUCCINIC** derived from amber	
SUBDUPLE ratio of one to two			**SUCCUBUS** night demon	
SUBDURAL under dura mater	zo		**SUCHLIKE** in such manner; similar	
SUB-ENTRY subdivision			**SUCHWISE** in like manner	
SUB-EQUAL nearly equal			**SUCKENER** a tenant (Sc.)	
SUBERATE compound derived from cork			**SUCKERED** with suckers removed	
SUBERECT half upright, half nodding			**SUCKLING** unweaned child	
SUBERINE compound derived from cork			**SUDAMINA** sweating fever	md
SUBEROSE somewhat gnawed	bt		**SUDANESE** (Sudan)	
SUBEROUS corky			**SUDARIUM** sweat/face cloth; sweating	
SUB-FLORA floral division	bt		room	
SUBGALEA parastipes in insects	zo		**SUDATION** perspiration	
SUB-GENUS subdivision			**SUDATORY** connected with sweating	
SUB-GIANT bright star	as		**SUDDENLY** hastily; abruptly; quickly	
SUB-GRADE lower division			**SUFFERED** underwent; allowed; bore	
SUB-GROUP subsidiary part			**SUFFERER** victim; martyr	
SUB-HUMAN almost human			**SUFFICED** satisfied; was adequate	
SUBHYOID under the tongue	md		**SUFFIONI** volcanic fumes	
SUB-IMAGO a state of change	zo		**SUFFIXED** added; subjoined; appended	
SUBIMAGO stage in mayfly life history	zo		**SUFFLATE** inflate; blow up	
SUB-INDEX index within an index			**SUFFRAGE** vote; prayers; intercession	
SUBLATED taken away			**SUFFRAGO** hock joint	vt
SUB-LEASE an underlet			**SUFFUSED** permeated; overspread	
SUBLIMED exalted			**SUFISTIC** (Moslem pantheism)	rl
SUBLUNAR under the moon			**SUGARING** sweetening	
SUBMERGE plunge; drown; flood			**SUICIDAL** self-destructive	
SUBMERSE duck; douse; dive			**SUITABLE** appropriate; convenient	
SUBNASAL under your nose			**SUITABLY** fittingly; aptly	
SUBNODAL below a node	bt		**SUITCASE** portable oblong bag	
SUBORDER subdivision; sub-genus			**SUKIYAKI** Jap. meat/vegetable dish	ck
SUBORNED bribed; lead astray			**SULCATED** grooved; furrowed	
SUBORNER perjurer; false witness			**SULCULUS** siphonoglyph of anthozoa	zo
SUBOVATE almost egg-shaped			**SULFOTEP** chemical insecticide	
SUBPOENA writ of attendance	lw		**SULLENLY** morosely; gloomily	
SUBPOLAR adjacent to polar sea			**SULLYING** smirching	
SUBPRESS die set, punch & die unit	eg		**SULPHATE** ⎫	
SUBPRIOR prior's deputy			**SULPHIDE** ⎬ sulphur compounds	ch
SUBRIGID fairly stiff			**SULPHITE** ⎭	
SUBSERVE help forward; promote			**SULPHONE** hexavalent sulphur compound	
SUBSIDED sank; abated; waned				ch
SUBSOLAR under the sun			**SULPHURY** containing sulphur	
SUBSONIC slower than sound			**SULTANIC** despotic	
SUBSTAGE microscopic device			**SULTANRY** Sultan's dominion	
SUBSTYLE line on sundial			**SUMERIAN** (Babylonian)	
SUBSUMED logically included			**SUMMERED** passed summer	
SUBTENSE chord of an arc			**SUMMONED** bid; cited; arraigned	

SUMMONER invoker; prosecutor	**SURVIVED** outlasted; endured; outlived
SUMPITAN Malay blow-pipe gun	**SURVIVOR** who lives through
SUN-BLIND window-shade	**SUSPENSE** uncertainty; indecision
SUNBURNT tanned; bronzed	**SUSPIRAL** breathing-hole
SUNBURST dazzling gleam	**SUSPIRED** sighed
SUNCRACK a fissure	**SUSURRUS** whispering; muttering; rustling
SUNDERED parted; severed; broken	**SUZERAIN** paramount ruler
SUNDRIED dehydrated	**SWABBING** mopping
SUNDRIES miscellanea; odds and ends	**SWADDLED** swathed; wrapped
SUNLIGHT illumination from Helios	**SWADDLER** a Methodist (nickname) rl
SUNNITES orthodox Moslems rl	**SWADESHI** Indian boycott
SUNPRINT photograph	**SWAGGING** sagging
SUNPROOF fadeless	**SWAGSHOP** where trash is sold
SUNSHADE a parasol	**SWAINING** lovemaking; courting
SUNSHINE illumination	**SWAINISH** boorish; rustic
SUNSHINY sunny	**SWAMPING** overwhelming; inundating
SUNSTONE feldspar mn	**SWAMP-OAK** semi-tropical tree bt
SUPERADD increase the total	**SWAMP-ORE** bog-ore mn
SUPERBLY magnificently; gorgeously	**SWAN-HERD** tender of swans
SUPERHET (wireless oscillations) ro	**SWAN-LIKE** as a swan
SUPERIOR head of a monastery rl	**SWAN-MARK** identification mark
SUPERMAN an admirable Crichton	**SWAN-NECK** curved
SUPERNAL celestial; heavenly	**SWANNERY** (Abbotsbury) zo
SUPERTAX a gross imposition	**SWAN-SHOT** buck-shot
SUPINATE bring palm upward	**SWAN-SKIN** soft flannel
SUPINELY inertly; languidly	**SWAN-SONG** last act or appearance
SUPPLANT displace by intrigue	**SWANKING** bragging
SUPPLIAL provision; provenance	**SWAPPING** bartering
SUPPLIED bestowed; furnished; gave	**SWARDING** turfing
SUPPLIER contributor; provider	**SWARMING** thronging; crowding
SUPPOSAL supposition; conjecture	**SWARTISH** tawny; swarthy
SUPPOSED assumed; opined; imagined	**SWASHING** splashing
SUPPOSER surmiser; thinker; fancier	**SWASHWAY** navigable channel nv
SUPPRESS quell; check; smother	**SWASTIKA** Nazi emblem; triskele
SURBASED (pedestal moulding)	**SWATHING** wrapping; binding
SURCEASE cessation	**SWATTING** killing flies
SURCULUS a botanical sucker bt	**SWEALING** melting; singeing
SURENESS certainty; infallibility	**SWEARING** profaneness; avowing
SURETIES sponsors	**SWEATILY** laboriously
SURF-BIRD plover; sandpiper zo	**SWEATING** toiling; extorting
SURF-BOAT shallow-draught boat nt	**SWEAT-OUT** plastic defect due to moisture
SURF-DUCK the scoter zo	**SWEEPING** comprehensive; extensive
SURFACED smoothed	**SWEEP-NET** fishing gear
SURGICAL chirurgical md	**SWEEP-SAW** curved-cut saw to
SURICATE the meercat zo	**SWEET-BAY** the tree laurel bt
SURMISAL surmise; assumption	**SWEET-GUM** a gum tree bt
SURMISED took for granted	**SWEETING** sweet apple bt
SURMISER conjecturer; supposer	**SWEETISH** rather sweet
SURMOUNT overcome; surpass; scale	**SWEET-OIL** olive oil
SURMULOT brown rat zo	**SWEET-PEA** attractive flower bt
SURNAMED having as family name	**SWEET-SOP** an evergreen shrub bt
SURPLICE linen vestment rl	**SWELLDOM** fashionable world
SURPRISE shock; bewilder; astound	**SWELLING** bombastic; dilating
SURREBUT rebut a rebuttal lw	**SWELLISH** foppish
SURRENAL above the kidneys pl	**SWELL-MOB** thieving gang
SURROUND encircle; hem; beset; loop	**SWERVING** deviating; diverging
SURSOLID fifth power ma	**SWIFTEST** fastest; fleetest
SURVEYAL review; scrutiny; prospect	**SWIFTLET** (bird's nest soup) zo
SURVEYED scrutinized; scanned	**SWIGGING** quaffing; drinking
SURVEYOR inspector; land measurer	**SWILLING** rinsing; toping
SURVIVAL an outliving; relic	**SWIMMING** dizziness

SWIMSUIT bathing costume
SWINDLED defrauded; cheated
SWINDLER sharper; trickster
SWINE-OAT a coarse oat — bt
SWINE-POX disease of pigs — vt
SWINE-STY a pig-sty
SWINGING vibrating; dangling
SWINGLED flailed
SWINKING drudging; moiling; toiling
SWIRLING twirling; gyrating; eddying
SWISHING birching
SWITCHED shunted; bypassed
SWITCHEL treacle beer
SWOONING a syncope — md
SWOOPING descending; rushing
SWOPPING exchanging
SWORD-ARM right arm
SWORD-CUT a wound
SWORD-LAW violence
SWOTTING studying hard
SYBARITE a voluptuary
SYBOTISM pig culture
SYCAMINE mulberry tree — bt
SYCAMORE species of maple — bt
SYCONIUM figlike fruit — bt
SYENITIC (syenite) — mn
SYLLABIC in syllables
SYLLABLE to utter
SYLLABUB sillabub; a drink
SYLLABUS an abstract; summary
SYLPHISH, SYLPHINE fairy like
SYMBATIC of partly-like polymorphism types
SYMBOLIC emblematic; representative
SYMMETRY harmony; regularity
SYMMORPH similar notion
SYMPATHY fellow-feeling; affinity
SYMPHILE guest species among insects
SYMPHONY unison of sound — mu
SYMPHYLA an insect genus — zo
SYMPLAST multinucleate cell variety — cy
SYMPLOCE rhetorical repetition
SYNACRAL (common vertex)
SYNALGIA sympathetic pain — md
SYNANCIA fish genus — zo
SYNAPSID reptile skull condition — zo
SYNAPTIC of nerve-cell contact — zo
SYNAPTON model imitating living matter — bl
SYNARCHY joint rule
SYNASTRY stellar coincidence
SYNCLINE geological basin
SYNCOPAL (alteration in
SYNCOPIC rhythm) — mu
SYNDESIS fusion of chromosomes — cy
SYNDETIC linking together
SYNDROME concurrence
SYNECHIA an eye-disease — md
SYNEDRAL (angularity)
SYNERGIC working together — zo
SYNGRAPH signed deed — lw

SYNOCHAL feverish — md
SYNODIST (synod) — rl
SYNOMOSY sworn brotherhood
SYNONYME alternative word with
SYNONYMY similar meaning
SYNOPSIS abstract; short outline
SYNOPTIC comprehensive
SYNOVIAL (synovia) — md
SYNTAXIS syntax; grammar
SYNTEXIS emaciation — md
SYNTONIC intense sharp — mu
SYNTONIN acid albumin — md
SYPHERED flush jointed
SYRIARCH a chief priest — rl
SYRIGMUS noises in the ear — md
SYSTASIS political union
SYSTEMIC pertaining to the system — md
SYSTOLIC contractive
SYZYGANT (quadratic function)

T

TABARDER a herald
TABASHIR mostly silica — mn
TABBINET damask-like fabric — tx
TABBY-CAT a mouser — zo
TABBYING watered fabric process — tx
TABITUDE emaciation; atrophy — md
TABLEAUX pictures (Fr.)
TABLEDEX co-ordinate book index for computers
TABLE-CUT flat-faced
TABLEFUL filling a table
TABLEMAT plate underlay
TABOOING prohibiting; banning
TABORINE tambourine — mu
TABORING drumming — mu
TABORITE extreme Hussite — rl
TABOURET embroidery frame — tx
TABULATE enumerate; catalogue
TAC-AU-TAC (fencing)
TACAHOUT a leaf gall — bt
TACHISME spilling, smearing painting technique — pt
TACITRON type of thyratron — el
TACITURN mute; reticent; silent
TACKLING harnessing; dealing with
TACKMARK dot(s) used in 'work & turn' system — pr
TACKSMAN tenant (Sc.)
TACTICAL strategic
TACTLESS insensitive; indiscreet
TAENIDIA thickenings of eudotrachea — zo
TAENIOID ribbonlike
TAFFRAIL tatereel; stern-rail — nt
TAGILITE copper phosphate — ch
TAGMOSIS grouping of somites — zo
TAIGLING entangling
TAILBAND decorative back-cover band — pr
TAIL-BOOM an aeroplane spar
TAILCOAT formal jacket

TAIL-EDGE lower edge
TAILGATE trombone technique   mu
TAILINGS mining refuse
TAILLESS Manx; without end
TAILORED cut to figure
TAILRACE (mill stream)
TAILROPE guide-rope
TAINTING corrupting; sullying
TAINTURE taint; stain; blot
TAKE-OVER acquire control
TAKER-OFF mimic; quantity surveyor
TAKINGLY captivatingly; winningly
TALANDIC of rhythmic changes in cell   cy
TALAPOIN Buddhist monk   rl
TALENTED accomplished; gifted
TALESMAN a juror
TALISMAN charm; amulet
TALKABLE conversable
TALK-DOWN landing technique   ae, ro
TALLNESS height; loftiness
TALLOWED fattened
TALLOWER tallow-chandler
TALLYING recording; agreeing
TALLYMAN pedlar
TALMUDIC (the Talmud)   rl
TAMANDUA
TAMANOIR } arboreal ant-eater   zo
TAMARACK American larch   bt
TAMARIND tropical tree   bt
TAMARISK evergreen shrub   bt
TAMEABLE submissive; docile
TAMELESS intractable; wild
TAMENESS dullness; monotony
TAMPERED interfered; machinated
TAMPERER meddler; schemer; plotter
TANAISTE deputy premier (Irish)
TAN-BALLS (refuse bark)
TAN-HOUSE tan-bark store
TAN-STOVE used for tan-bark
TANGENCY, TANGENCE a state of contact
TANGIBLE tactile; positive; corporeal
TANGIBLY palpably; obviously
TANGLING complicating; matting
TANISTRY Irish land tenure   lw
TANNABLE able to be cured   le
TANNADAR Indian policeman
TANTALUM metallic element   ch
TANTALUS spirit-stand
TANTICLE stickleback   zo
TANTRISM Indian doctrine
TANTRIST a devotee
TANZIMAT Turkish reform bill
TAPADERA leather stirrup guard
TAP-DANCE toe-tapping dance
TAPE-LINE tape measure
TAPERING slightly conical; pointed
TAPESTRY woven work
TAPEWORM a parasite   zo
TAPIROID like the tapirs   zo
TARA-FERN bracken (NZ)   bt

TAR-BLACK coal-tar product for earthed posts
TARBOOSH a fez
TARGETED armed with a buckler
TARGUMIC (Bible in Aramaic)   rl
TARIFFED dutiable; taxed
TARLATAN muslin; tarletan   tx
TARPEIAN (Roman rock)
TARRAGON savoury herb   bt
TARRYING awaiting; loitering; halting
TARSIPED kangaroo-footed   zo
TARSIPES small marsupial   zo
TARTARIC (Tartar)
TARTARIN potash   ch
TARTARUM tartar compound
TARTARUS sunless abyss
TARTNESS sharpness; piquancy
TARTRATE a tartar salt   ch
TARTUFFE a hypocrite
TARVIATE of tar/stone surfacings   ce
TAR-WATER an infusion   md
TASKWORK piece-work
TASTABLE savoury; palatable
TASTE-BUD sensory bud on tongue
TASTEFUL discriminative; elegant
TATTERED in rags; rent
TATTLERY idle gossip
TATTLING chatting; prattling
TATTOOER, TATTOOED skin artist
TAUNTING deriding; flouting; reviling
TAUROCOL bull's glue
TAUTENED tightened; stretched
TAUTNESS strain; tenseness
TAVERNER inn-keeper; Boniface
TAWDRILY gaudily; garishly; flashily
TAXATION imposition; levy; toll
TAXIARCH Greek commander
TAXIRANK cab queue
TAXODIUM swamp-cyprus   bt
TAXOLOGY, TAXONOMY classification
TAXPAYER one liable for taxation
TEA-BOARD tea-tray
TEA-BREAK refreshment pause (industrial)
TEA-CADDY small tea box
TEA-CHEST box of tea
TEA-TOWEL towel for drying dishes
TEA-FIGHT a bun-worry
TEA-HOUSE oriental pleasure dome
TEA-PARTY (Boston 1773)
TEA-PLANT source of tea   bt
TEA-SPOON kitchen measurement
TEA-TABLE where tea is served
TEACHING instructing; enlightening
TEAMSTER waggoner; drayman
TEAMWISE harnessed together
TEAMWORK co-operation
TEARDROP a tear
TEAR-DUCT lachrymal duct   md
TEARLESS unfeeling
TEATHING fertilizing
TECHNICS doctrine of arts

TECTARIA shellfish	zo	
TECTONIC constructive		
TEEN-AGER youngster		
TEETHING dentition		
TEETOTAL dry; total abstinence		
TEETOTUM small top		
TEGUMENT the skin	pl	
TEGUMERE portion of tegumant in somite	zo	
TELARIAN web-spinner	zo	
TELEBLEM membrane of hyphae in agarics	bt	
TELECAST televised		
TELECINE TV cine film projector		
TELEFILM television film		
TELEGONY hereditary influence		
TELEGRAM a wire		
TELEOSIS purposive development	bl	
TELESTIC ending		
TELETRON TV cathode ray tube		
TELETYPE teleprint (Telex)		
TELEVIEW watch television programmes	tv	
TELEVISE to broadcast	tv	
TELLTALE sneak; revealer; indicator		
TELLURAL earthy		
TELLURIC (tellurium)	ch	
TELONISM last letters of author's name; pseudonym		
TELOOGOO Dravidian dialect		
TELOTYPE printed telegram		
TEMERITY rashness; audacity		
TEMEROUS reckless; bold; foolhardy		
TEMPERED toughened; moderated		
TEMPLATE a pattern; a jig		
TEMPORAL secular; transient		
TEMPTING alluring; inveigling		
TENACITY adhesiveness; cohesion		
TENAILLE a rampart		
TENANTED occupied; dwelt		
TENANTRY the tenants		
TENDANCE attendance; care; attention		
TENDENCY bias; drift; inclination		
TENDERED offered; estimated		
TENDERLY leniently; gently; softly		
TENEBRAE R.C. service	rl	
TENEMENT a flat or house-block		
TENESMUS ineffectual evacuation straining		
TENONING mortising		
TENON-SAW metal-backed saw	to	
TENORIST a tenor	mu	
TENORITE oxide of copper	mn	
TENOTOMY tendon-cutting	md	
TENSIBLE tensile; ductile		
TENTACLE a feeler	zo	
TENTERED stretched		
TENTILLA branches of a tentacle	zo	
TENTWORK embroidery		
TENTWORT a fern	bt	
TEOCALLI Mexican temple		
TEPEFIED warmed up		

TEPHRITE andesite	mn	
TEPIDITY lukewarmness		
TERAPHIM Hebrew idols		
TERATISM being a foetal monstrosity		
TERATOMA foetal tumour		
TEREBENE (turpentine)	ch	
TEREDINE teredo, boring worm	zo	
TERGETIC dorsal	zo	
TERMATIC an artery	md	
TERMINAL binding screw		
TERMINER a determination	lw	
TERMINUS the end of a line		
TERMLESS boundless		
TERRACED having or being in terraces		
TERRAPIN tortoise	zo	
TERRAZZO mosaic in cement; terrace	bd	
TERRIBLE formidable; dire; gruesome		
TERRIBLY frightfully; awfully		
TERRIFIC horrific; dreadful		
TERTIARY third in order		
TERTIATE triplicate		
TERYLENE man-made cloth	tx	
TERZETTO a trio	mu	
TESSELLA ⎫ small tiles for paving		
TESSERAE ⎭		
TESSERAL tesselated		
TESSULAR like dice		
TEST-CASE sample	lw	
TEST-TUBE glass tube	ch	
TESTABLE bequeathable; devisable		
TESTACEA animals with shells	zo	
TESTACEL a little shell	zo	
TESTAMUR a certificate		
TESTATOR will-maker; devisor	lw	
TESTICLE male gonad	zo	
TETANIZE cause spasms	md	
TETANOID convulsive		
TETCHILY peevishly; testily		
TETHERED restricted; tied; fastened		
TETRADIC fourfold	ch	
TETRAGON quadrangle		
TETRALIN organic solvent	ch	
TETRAPLA Bible in four versions	rl	
TETRAPOD four-footed		
TETRARCH Roman governor		
TETRARCH with 4 xylem strands	bt	
TETRAXON having 4 axes	zo	
TETRONAL hypnotic/sedative drug	pm	
TEUTONIC Germanic		
TEXT-BOOK a manual		
TEXT-HAND large script		
TEXTRINE textile	tx, wv	
TEXT-TYPE type for bookprinting	pr	
TEXTUARY authoritative		
TEXTUIST text reciter	rl	
THALAMIA layers of cells	bt	
THALAMUS an inner room; brain	md	
THALLIUM metallic element	ch	
THANEDOM thane's jurisdiction		
THANKFUL grateful; beholden		
THANKING acknowledging gratefully		

THATCHED covered with straw	**THRALDOM** slavery; bondage
THATCHER a craftsman	**THRANITE** trireme rower
THEARCHY theocracy rl	**THRAPPLE** windpipe; thropple zo
THEBAINE variety of morphine pm	**THRASHED** drubbed
THEETSEE black varnish bt	**THRASHER** fox-shark; thrush zo
THEIFORM like tea	**THRAWART** obstinate (Sc.)
THEMATIC dissertative	**THREADED** strung
THEOCRAT divine ruler	**THREADEN** made of thread
THEODICY a philosophy	**THREADER** shuttle-worker
THEOGONY (genesis of the gods)	**THREAPED** contradicted (Sc.)
THEOLOGY divinity rl	**THREATEN** menace; intimidate
THEORIES speculations; hypothesis	**THREE-PLY** threefold; triple; treble
THEORIST conjecturer	**THRENODY, THRENODE** sad song mu
THEORIZE postulate	**THRESHED** beat out grain; discussed
THEOSOPH inspired person	**THRESHEL** a flail
THERBLIG division of movement	**THRESHER** mocking-bird zo
THEREFOR for that purpose	**THRESTLE** three-legged stool
THEREOUT therefrom	**THRIDACE** lettuce juice
THERIACA an opiate md	**THRILLED** agitated; stirred; excited
THERMION ion from incandescent matter	**THRILLER** a gripping story; curdler
ps	**THRIVING** flourishing; prospering
THERMITE incendiary mixture ch	**THROBBED** pulsated; beat; palpitated
THESPIAN barnstormer; trouper	**THROMBIN** blood clotting enzyme md
THEURGIC magical	**THROMBUS** blood-clot md
THEWLESS weak; frail; feeble	**THRONGED** crowded; flocked
THIAMINE vitamin B-1	**THRONING** enthroning
THIAMIDE amide compound ch	**THROPPLE** windpipe; thrapple zo
THIAZINE heterocyclic compound ch	**THROSTLE** missel thrush zo
THIAZOLE pyridine-like liquid ch	**THROTTLE** garrotte; strangle; stifle
THICKEST densest; closest	**THROWING** casting; hurling; slinging
THICKISH rather thick	**THROW-OUT** rejected product
THICKNEE the stone curlew zo	**THRUMMED** strummed
THICKSET closely planted	**THRUMMER** vamper mu
THIEVERY larceny	**THRUSTED** intruded; drove; pushed
THIEVING purloining; filching	**THRUSTER** reckless rider
THIEVISH sly; stealthy	**THUDDING** reverberating
THIGGING begging	**THUGGERY** ⎫ brutality; violence;
THINGAMY thingumabob	**THUGGISM** ⎭ criminal assault
THINKING ruminating; cogitating	**THUMBING** fingering
THINNESS attenuation; emaciation	**THUMB-NUT** screwed by hand
THINNEST lankiest; leanest	**THUMBPOT** small flower pot
THINNING reducing; diminishing	**THUMPING** enormous
THINNISH meagre; spare	**THUNDERY** gloomy; frowning
THIO-ACID hydroxyl-replaced acid ch	**THURIBLE** incense censer rl
THIOCTIC lipoic acid	**THURIFER** incense bearer rl
THIOPHEN coal-tar constituent ch	**THURSDAY** one of weekdays
THIOPHIL with affinity for sulphur ch	**THUSWISE** like so
THIOUREA thiocarbamide; bismuth re-	**THWACKED** thumped; belaboured
agent ch	**THWARTED** frustrated; balked
THIRLAGE milling rights lw	**THWARTER** obstructionist
THIRSTED craved; yearned; longed	**THYRSOID** (Bacchus's ivied staff)
THIRTEEN the baker's dozen	**TIBIALIS** tibial muscle md
THISNESS individuality	**TICK-BEAN** horse bean
THLIPSIS compression md	**TICK-SEED** coreopsis bt
THOLE-PIN rowlock	**TICK-SHOP** (goods on credit)
THOMEANS Malabar Christians rl	**TICK-TACK** signalling system (racing)
THORACIC (thorax) zo	**TICK-TICK, TICK-TOCK** watch or clock
THORNBUT turbot zo	**TICKETED** labelled
THORNSET beset with thorns bt	**TICKLING** titillation
THOROUGH complete; perfect	**TICKLISH** critical; risky
THOUSAND M; mille	**TIDEGATE, TIDE-LOCK** dock

TIDELESS not rising/falling
TIDEMARK H.W.M. or L.W.M.
TIDEMILL sea-operated mill
TIDESMAN customs officer
TIDE-WAVE tidal wave
TIDINESS neatness; trimness
TIED-DOWN involved; restricted
TIGELLUM first bud on a stem   bt
TIGELLUS an internode   bt
TIGER-CAT margay; ocelot   zo
TIGERISH ferocious
TIGERISM voracity
TIGHT-WAD a miser
TILE-KILN tile factory
TILLABLE arable; cultivable
TILLERED produced offshoots
TILT-BOAT boat with roof   nt
TILT-YARD tilting yard
TIMBERED wooded
TIME-BALL time signal
TIME-BILL time-table
TIME-BOMB explodes by time-fuse
TIME-BOOK works record
TIME-CARD a register
TIME-FUSE time-fuze
TIMELESS untimely
TIME-WORK rate of pay
TIMEWORN decayed; weatherbeaten
TIMIDITY fearfulness; shyness
TIMONEER helmsman   nt
TIMONIST misanthrope
TIMOROSO hesitatingly; timidly   mu
TIMOROUS fearful; pusillanimous
TINCTURE tinge; solution   md
TINE-TARE the vetch   bt
TINEWALD, TYNEWALD Manx Parliament
TINGEING colouring
TINGLING thrilling
TINGLISH sensation
TING-TANG two-note clock   hr
TINKERED botched
TINKERLY clumsily
TINKLING clinking
TINNITUS ringing in the ears   md
TINPLATE covered in tin
TINSELLY tawdry
TINSMITH tin worker
TINSTONE cassiterite   mn
TINSTUFF tin ore   mn
TINTAMAR confused noise
TINTLESS colourless
TIPPED-IN inserted by use of gum   pr
TIPPLING toping; soaking steadily
TIPSTAFF court officer   lw
TIPULARY (crane-flies)   zo
TIRELESS inexhaustible
TIRESOME tedious; fretful
TIRONIAN (Roman shorthand)
TIRRIVIE tantrum (Sc.)
TISSUING interweaving

TIT-TAT-TO a game; criss-cross
TITANESS giantess
TITANIAN (titanium)   ch
TITANITE sphene   mn
TITHABLE subject to tithes   rl
TITHONIC actinic
TITIVATE tidy up
TITLE-CUT title-page woodcut decoration   pr
TITMOUSE a small bird   zo
TITRATED solution added from burette   ch
TITTERED giggled
TITTEREL whimbrel; curlew   zo
TITTERER sniggerer
TITTUPPY frisky; lively
TITUBANT stumbling
TITUBATE stagger
TITULARY nominal; titular
TIVERING marking sheep
TOAD-FISH the sapo   zo
TOAD-FLAX snapdragon   bt
TOAD-PIPE a horsetail   bt
TOAD-SPIT cuckoo-spit
TOADYING fawning
TOADYISH sycophantic
TOADYISM obsequiousness
TOBOGGAN toboggin; taboggin
TOCOLOGY obstetrics   md
TODDLING strolling aimlessly
TOGETHER in unison
TOHU-BOHU desolation, confusion, chaos (Heb.)
TOILETTE ceremonial wear
TOILLESS workless
TOILSOME arduous; laborious
TOILWORN fatigued; tired; weary
TOKOLOGY tocology   md
TOKONOMA flower alcove in a house (Jap.)
TOLBOOTH a toll-booth
TOLERANT forbearing; liberal
TOLERATE suffer; brook
TOLL-DISH (used in mills)   me
TOLL-GATE where tolls collected
TOLLETAN of Toledo
TOLTECAN early Mexican
TOM-NODDY puffin; a dolt   zo
TOMAHAWK war hatchet
TOMALLEY lobster-liver   zo
TOMATOES love apples   bt
TOMBLESS no tomb
TOMENTUM a downy covering   md
TOMMY-BAR small lever
TOMMY-GUN a handy weapon
TOMMY-ROT balderdash; nonsense
TOMOGRAM X-Ray photograph   md
TOMORROW the following day
TOMUNDAR Baluchi chief
TONALITE igneous rock   mn
TONALITY pitch   mu
TONE-DEAF unmusical

TONELESS unmusical	
TONGUING barking; licking	
TONICITY healthiness	md
TONSILAR (tonsils)	md
TONSURED clerical; shaven	rl
TOONWOOD Indian red wood	bt
TOOTHFUL a short drink	
TOOTH-KEY forceps	md
TOOTLING playing the flute	mu
TOP-BOOTS longish boots	
TOP-DRESS to manure	
TOP-HEAVY tipsy; ill-proportioned	
TOP-LEVEL, TOPNOTCH excellent	
TOP-LOFTY bombastic	
TOPOTYPE specimen from original locality	zo
TOP-PROUD very proud	
TOP-SHELL a mollusc	zo
TOP-STONE a finial	
TOPARCHY small state control	
TOPAZINE (topaz)	mn
TOPOLOGY an aid to memory	
TOPONOMY } topical terminology	
TOPONYMY }	
TOPPLING falling	
TOR-OUZEL the ring-ousel	zo
TORCHERE ornamental lampstand	
TORCHING night fishing	
TORCULAR a tourniquet	md
TOREADOR bullfighter	
TOREUTES artist in metal	
TOREUTIC chased metal-work	
TORMINAL colicky	md
TORNADIC (tornadoes); very stormy	
TORNARIA larval form of balanoglossida	zo
TOROIDAL like an anchor-ring	
TOROSITY muscularity	
TORPIDLY apathetically; dully	
TORQUATE collared	
TORSHENT youngest child (USA)	
TORTILLA maize cake; omelette (Sp.)	
TORTIOUS injurious	lw
TORTOISE terrapin	zo
TORTUOSE } twisted; winding;	
TORTUOUS } wreathed; deceitful	
TORTURED agonized; racked	
TORTURER tormentor	
TORULOID } somewhat cylindrical	
TORULOSE }	
TOTALITY full amount; sum	
TOTALIZE to add up	
TOTEMISM symbolism	
TOTITIVE (no common factor)	
TOTTERED reeled; staggered	
TOUCHILY peevishly; petulantly	
TOUCHING concerning; pathetic	
TOUCHPAN priming pan	
TOUGHEST most stubborn	
TOUGHISH stiffish; leathery	
TOURELLE slender tower	

TOURNURE turn; contour; curve	
TOUSLING ruffling; rumpling	
TOWARDLY toward; docile; tractile	
TOWERING soaring; mounting	
TOWN-HALL council offices	
TOWNLAND a township	
TOWNLESS without a town	
TOWNSHIP a municipality	
TOWNSMAN urbanite	
TOWN-TALK local gossip	
TOXAEMIA blood-poisoning	md
TOXICANT poisonous	
TOXICITY poisonousness	
TOYISHLY playfully	
TRACHEAL } (windpipe)	pl
TRACHEAN }	
TRACHOMA eye disease	md
TRACHYTE volcanic rock	mn
TRACKAGE towing; traction	
TRACKING spooring; trailing	
TRACKMAN (railroad track)	
TRACKWAY path or open road	
TRACTATE a treatise; a tract	
TRACTILE ductile; tractable	
TRACTION attraction; towage; hauling	
TRACTIVE pulling	
TRACTORY tractive	
TRACTRIX geometrical curve	
TRADEFUL commercial	
TRADITOR traitor; quisling; renegade	
TRADUCED defamed; slandered	
TRADUCER calumniator; libeller	
TRAGICAL calamitous; disastrous	
TRAGOPAN Chinese pheasant	zo
TRAGSITZ suspended alpine rescue stretcher	
TRAILING hauling; dragging	
TRAIL-NET a trawl	
TRAINING drilling; schooling	
TRAIN-OIL railway lubricant	
TRAIPSED gadded about	
TRAMPING trudging; hiking	
TRAMPLED trod under foot	
TRAMPLER grape-treader	
TRAMROAD tramway	
TRANCING sleeping; dreaming	
TRANGRAM a knick-knack	
TRANQUIL placid; calm; serene	
TRANSACT negotiate; conduct; enact	
TRANSECT belt of vegetation for study	bt
TRANSEPT cross-aisle	rl
TRANSFER make over; exchange	
TRANSFIX penetrate; perforate; impale	
TRANSHIP change conveyance	
TRANSIRE customs pass	
TRANSMEW transmute (obs.)	
TRANSMIT despatch; forward; remit	
TRANSUDE to sweat	
TRANSVAR power-transfer coupler	tc
TRAP-BALL an old game	
TRAP-DOOR door in the floor	

TRAP-FALL a trap		
TRAP-TUFA ⎰ rock of volcanic		
TRAP-TUFF ⎱ origin	mn	
TRAPESED traipsed; tramped		
TRAPEZIA trapeziums		
TRAPPEAN (traprock)	mn	
TRAPPING snaring		
TRAPPIST Cistercian monk	rl	
TRAPPOUS like traprock	mn	
TRASHERY rubbish; balderdash		
TRASHILY in a rubbishy way		
TRASLING freshwater perch	zo	
TRAVERSE thwart; obstruct		
TRAVESTY a burlesque; parody		
TRAWLING fishing		
TRAY-TRIP a draughts game		
TREACLED (moth catching)		
TREADING trampling; pacing; stepping		
TREADLED pedalled		
TREADLER bicyclist		
TREASURE preserve; hoard; garner		
TREASURY a repository		
TREATING entertaining; dealing		
TREATISE written discourse; essay		
TREBLING doing 3-fold		
TRECENTO 14th Century in Italian art		
TREE-CALF leather binding		
TREE-CRAB (lives on coco-nuts)	zo	
TREE-DOVE Indian pigeon	zo	
TREE-FERN tropical fern	bt	
TREE-FROG many species	zo	
TREELESS lacking forest cover		
TREE-NAIL long wooden pin		
TREKKING migrating		
TREMANDO tremulously	mu	
TREMATIC of gill-clefts	zo	
TREMBLED quivered; shook; quaked		
TREMBLER vibrator; oscillator		
TREMLELA jelly-like fungi	bt	
TRENCHED encroached; furrowed		
TRENCHER wooden-platter		
TRENDING inclining; tending		
TREPHINE cutting tool	md	
TREPHONE cell-breakdown substance	bl	
TREPTION environment-change response	cy	
TRESPASS sin; intrude; transgress		
TRESSURE heraldic border	hd	
TREVETTE loop-pile wire knife	tx	
TREWSMAN (wearing trews)		
TRIADIST composer of triads		
TRIALISM (body, soul and spirit)		
TRIALITY threeness		
TRIANGLE flogging frame; 3-sided figure		
TRIAPSAL having three apses		
TRIARCHY rule of three		
TRIARIAN of the third rank		
TRIASSIC geological formation	mn	
TRIASTER mitobic figure	cy	
TRIAXIAL having three axes		
TRIAZOLE heterocyclic compound	ch	

TRIBASIC with 3 hydrogen atoms	ch	
TRIBELET a small tribe		
TRIBONYX genus of water-hens	zo	
TRIBRACH three short syllables		
TRIBUNAL court of justice		
TRIBUTED contributed		
TRIBUTER piece-work miner		
TRICHINA parasitic worm	md	
TRICHITE hairlike fibre	mn	
TRICHODA hairy infusoria	zo	
TRICHOID hairlike	zo	
TRICHOMA hair disease	md	
TRICHOME hairy outgrowth	bt	
TRICHORD three-stringed lyre	mu	
TRICKERY chicanery; deception		
TRICKILY artfully; cunningly		
TRICKING duping; gulling		
TRICKLED oozed; percolated		
TRICKLET small rill		
TRICKSEY wily; pretty		
TRICOLOR flag of France		
TRICORNE 3-cornered hat		
TRICTRAC variety of backgammon		
TRICYCLE 3-wheeled bicycle		
TRIDACNA genus of molluscs	zo
TRIFLING toying; trivial; paltry		
TRIGAMMA wing-vein feature in lepidop-		
tera	zo
TRIGENIC controlled by 3 genes	gn	
TRIGGING stopping; skidding		
TRIGLOID gurnard genus	zo
TRIGLYPH Doric ornamentation		
TRIGNESS trimness; neatness		
TRIGONAL ⎰ triangular		
TRIGONIC ⎱		
TRIGONON a triangle		
TRIGRAPH a triphthong		
TRILEMMA (three alternatives)		
TRILLING quavering; warbling	mu
TRILLION million³ (GB) million² (USA)		
TRILLIUM a lily genus	bt
TRILOBED trilobate	bt
TRIMARAN 3-hulled vessel	nt	
TRIMERIC of 3 times molecular weight	ch	
TRIMETER (versification)		
TRIMMING decorating; adjusting		
TRIMNESS neatness; tidiness		
TRIMURTI Hindu Trinity	rl
TRINGINE ⎰ genus of sandpipers		
TRINGOID ⎱	zo
TRINODAL treble-jointed		
TRIODION Greek prayer-book	rl
TRIOLEIN fatty oil		
TRIP-BOOK (fishing records)		
TRIPEMAN tripeseller		
TRIPHANE spodumene	mn
TRIPLANE an aeroplane		
TRIPLING trebling		
TRIPLITE a phosphate	mn
TRIPLOID with triple chromosomes	cy
TRIPODAL tripedal; three-footed		

TRIPPANT heraldic trotting	hd		**TRUNNION** gun support	
TRIPPING lapsing; dancing; felling			**TRUSSING** binding; fastening	
TRIP-SLIP tram ticket (USA)			**TRUSTFUL** confiding; trusty	
TRIPTANE trimethyl butane			**TRUSTILY** faithfully; staunchly	
TRIPTOTE having 3 cases only			**TRUSTING** relying on; believing	
TRIPTYCH painted screen	rl		**TRY-HOUSE** oil refinery	
TRIP-WIRE obstacle; brake	nt		**TRYPTONE** pancreatic ferment	md
TRISEMIC iambic			**TRYSTING** rendezvousing; meeting	
TRISKELE swastika			**TUB-WHEEL** flat water-wheel	
TRISOMIC of 3-chromosome type	cy		**TUBE-FORM** tubular	
TRISTFUL sorrowful; dejected; doleful			**TUBERCLE** tumour	md
TRITICAL trite; common; hackneyed			**TUBEROSE** Mexican lily	bt
TRITICUM wheat, etc.	bt		**TUBEROUS** knobbed	
TRIUMVIR one of three (Rome)			**TUBE-WELL** artesian well	
TRIUNITY trinity			**TUBICOLE** caddis-worm	zo
TRIVALVE with three valves			**TUBIFORM** tubular	
TROCHAIC (verse)			**TUBIPORE** a coral	zo
TROCHITE sea-urchin's joint	zo		**TUB-SIZED** dipped and strengthened	
TROCHLEA a cartilage	md		(handmade paper)	pp
TROCHOID cycloid			**TUBULATE** formed of tubes	
TROILITE nonmagnetic iron sulphide	mn		**TUCKAHOE** edible fungus	bt
TROLLING singing; spinning			**TUCKSHOP** sweet-shop	
TROLLOPY slatternly			**TUCOTUCO** small rodent	zo
TROMBLON fire-arm support			**TUG-OF-WAR** rope sport	
TROMBONE a brass musical wind			**TUG-PLANE** (gliders)	ae
instrument	mu		**TUKUTUKU** tucotuco; rodent (SA)	zo
TROOPIAL American starling	zo		**TULA-WORK** niello-work	
TROOPING collecting; parading			**TUMBLING** falling; tripping	
TROPHESY indigestion	md		**TUMEFIED** swollen; distended	
TROPHIES emblems of victory			**TUMIDITY** bombast; pomposity	
TROPICAL figurative; fervid			**TUMOURED** distended; enlarged	
TROT-COSY head covering (Sc.)			**TUMP-LINE** carrying strap	
TROTTEUR walking skirt, shoe			**TUMULATE** make a barrow	
TROTTING walking quickly			**TUMULOSE** tumulous; many mounds	
TROTTOIR side-walk (Fr.)			**TUN-BELLY** pot-belly	
TROUBLED incommoded; vexed			**TUNELESS** unharmonious; unmusical	
TROUBLER disturber; pest			**TUNGSTEN** same as wolfram	ch
TROUNCED thrashed; castigated			**TUNGSTIC** (tungsten)	ch
TROUPIAL American song-bird	zo		**TUNICARY** ascidian; sea-squirt	zo
TROUSERS trowsers			**TUNICATE** coated; a mollusc	zo
TROUTING fishing for trout			**TUNING-IN** adjusting to listen	ro
TROUTLET small trout	zo		**TUNISIAN** (Tunis)	
TROUVERE French lyric poets			**TURANIAN** family of languages	
TROWSERS trousers			**TURANOSE** disaccharide	ch
TRUANTLY lazily; evasively			**TURBANED** wearing a turban	
TRUCKAGE cost of conveyance			**TURBIDLY** disorderly; opaquely	
TRUCKING bartering; hawking			**TURBINAL** scroll-like bone	md
TRUCKLED cringed; yielded; stooped			**TURBO-JET** gas engine	ae
TRUCKLER servile agent			**TURCOMAN** ⎫	
TRUDGEON a swimming stroke			**TURKOMAN** ⎬ a Turk of central Asia	
TRUDGING foot-slogging			**TURF-CLAD** grassy	
TRUE-BLUE faithful partisan			**TURF-MOSS** boggy land	
TRUE-BORN ⎫			**TURGIDLY** pompously; grandiosely	
TRUE-BRED ⎬ not a mongrel			**TURLOUGH** shallow pool (Irish)	
TRUE-LOVE sweetheart; a herb	bt		**TURMERIC** yellow dye	bt
TRUENESS honesty; accuracy; veracity			**TURNAGRA** thrush (NZ)	zo
TRUMPERY rubbish; trash; trifling			**TURNCOAT** renegade	
TRUMPING ruffing			**TURNCOCK** water-man	
TRUNCATE lopped			**TURNDOWN** fold down; reject	
TRUNDLED rolled; bowled; revolved			**TURNMARK** logline mark	nt
TRUNKFUL enough to fill a trunk			**TURNOVER** a pasty	

TURNPIKE toll-gate; a road
TURN-SICK giddy
TURN-SKIN a were-wolf
TURNSOLE sunflower   bt
TURNSPIT kitchen-boy
TURRETED having little towers
TUSSOCKY tufty
TUTELAGE guardianship; charge; care
TUTELARY protective
TUTORAGE instruction
TUTORESS governess
TUTORIAL educational
TUTORING teaching
TUTORISM education; coaching
TWADDLED gabbled
TWADDLER tattler; chatter-box
TWANGING making plucked-wire noise
TWANGLED twanged
TWATTLED prattled
TWATTLER a gossip
TWEAKING twisting
TWEEDLED fiddled
TWEELING twilling
TWEEZERS forceps   to
TWELVEMO 4 times folded for 12 leaves   pr
TWENTYMO paper folded into 20 leaves   pr
TWIDDLED twisted
TWIDDLER thumb-twirler
TWIGGING understanding
TWILIGHT dusk
TWILLING weaving
TWINBATH 2-solution processing method   pr
TWIN-BORN contemporaneous
TWINGING twitching
TWINKLED sparkled
TWINKLER a star
TWINLING twin lamb   zo
TWINPLEX radio-telegraph system   tc
TWINWIRE paper-holding system for offset   pr
TWIRLING revolving; whirling
TWISTING writhing; contorting
TWITCHED jerked; snatched
TWITCHER convulsive mover
TWITTING upbraiding; taunting
TWO-EDGED double-cutting
TWO-FACED false; double-dealing
TWO-LAYER twin-ply paper/board
TWOPENNY cheap; worthless
TWO-PIECE costume; suit
TYCHONIC astronomic; (Tycho Brahe)
TYMPANIC like a drum
TYMPANUM ear-drum   md
TYNEWALD Manx Parliament
TYPE-CAST single-character actor
TYPE-HIGH standard height
TYPHLOPS earthworms, etc.   zo
TYPHONIC cyclonic

TYPIFIED exemplified; symbolized
TYPIFIER prototype
TYPOLITE fossil footstep   mn
TYPOLOGY symbolism
TYPORAMA facsimile
TYRAMINE amino-ethyl benzene   ch
TYROCINY pupilage
TYROLEAN, TYROLESE (Tyrol)
TYROLITE Tyrol sandstone   mn
TYRONISM apprenticeship
TYRRANIC despotic; autocratic
TYRTAEAN (warlike verse)
TZAREVNA } Empress of Russia;
TZARITSA } Tsarina

U

UBIQUITY omnipresence
UDOMETER rain gauge
UGLIFIED made hideous
UGLINESS repulsiveness; unsightliness
UINTAITE variety of natural asphalt   mn
ULTERIOR remote; hidden; indirect
ULTIMATA plural of ultimatum
ULTIMATE furthest; final; eventual
ULTIMITY last consequence
ULTRAISM extreme views
ULTRAIST extremist
ULULATED howled; yowled; lamented
UMBELLAR form of inflorescence   bt
UMBONATE having a boss
UMBRATIC shadowy; shady; obscure
UMBRELLA a gamp
UMBRETTE African heron   zo
UMBRIERE vizor of helmet
UMPIRAGE arbitration; adjudication
UMQUHILE formerly (Sc.)
UNABASED not degraded; unashamed
UNABATED undiminished; persistent
UNACHING free from pain
UNACTIVE inactive; inert; torpid
UNADMIRE view with tolerance
UNADORED unloved; unvenerated
UNAFRAID bold; valiant; undaunted
UNAIMING purposeless; random
UNALLIED alone; separate; isolated
UNAMAZED composed; unruffled
UNAMUSED not entertained; bored
UNANCHOR let loose
UNANELED unshriven; unanointed
UNARGUED not disputed
UNARTFUL simple; artless; naive
UNATONED not expiated
UNATTIRE disrobe; undress
UNAVOWED unconfessed; secret
UNAWARES suddenly; unexpectedly
UNBACKED unaided; unassisted
UNBAGGED trouserless; let loose
UNBANDED disbanded; disembodied
UNBANNED permitted; unrestricted
UNBARBED unshaven; pointless

UNBARKED stripped of bark
UNBARRED unfastened; opened
UNBATHED untubbed
UNBEATEN untrodden; undefeated
UNBEDDED uprooted
UNBEFOOL undeceive
UNBEHELD not visible
UNBELIEF incredulity; scepticism
UNBENIGN malignant; malevolent
UNBEREFT not bereaved; unspoiled
UNBESEEM to be unworthy
UNBIASED impartial; unprejudiced
UNBIDDEN spontaneous; unsolicited
UNBISHOP deprive of a bishopric   rl
UNBITTED unbridled; uncurbed   nt
UNBLAMED uncensured; unrebuked
UNBLOODY not cruel
UNBODIED incorporeal
UNBODING not expecting; unforeseeing
UNBOILED raw
UNBOLTED unfastened; unbarred
UNBONNET remove the hat; uncap
UNBOOTED stripped of boots
UNBOUGHT not bribed; incorrupt
UNBOYISH sedate; unchildish
UNBRACED relaxed; unsupported
UNBREECH debag
UNBREWED pure; genuine
UNBRIBED not corrupt
UNBRIDLE free from restraint
UNBROKEN inviolate; continuous
UNBUCKLE unfasten; unclasp
UNBUDDED not yet in bud
UNBUNDLE unpack
UNBUOYED not lifted   nt
UNBURDEN disclose; reveal
UNBURIED uninterred
UNBURNED uncharred
UNBURROW to ferret out
UNBUSIED idle; unemployed
UNBUTTON unfasten
UNCAGING releasing; liberating
UNCALLED not awakened
UNCANDID reserved; cautious
UNCAPPED unbonneted
UNCARTED unloaded
UNCASING disengaging; unpacking
UNCAUGHT still free
UNCAUSED no reason for
UNCHANCE misfortune
UNCHANCY uncanny; dangerous
UNCHARGE unload
UNCHASTE impure; lewd
UNCHEERY dull; gloomy
UNCHEWED not masticated
UNCHIDED unrebuked
UNCHURCH excommunicate   rl
UNCIATIM ounce by ounce
UNCIFORM hook-shaped
UNCINATA marine worms   zo
UNCINATE hooked

UNCLENCH } to open the hand
UNCLINCH }
UNCLEWED unwound   nt
UNCLOSED open; ajar
UNCLOTHE undress
UNCLOUDY clear
UNCLUTCH declutch
UNCOATED dejacketed
UNCOIFED headdressless; unkempt
UNCOILED unwound
UNCOINED not minted
UNCOMBED unkempt
UNCOMELY lacking grace
UNCOMMON odd; rare; strange
UNCOOPED set free
UNCORDED unbound
UNCORKED ready to pour
UNCOSTLY inexpensive
UNCOUPLE disconnect
UNCOWLED unveiled
UNCREATE kill
UNCTUOUS greasy; oily; fulsome
UNCULLED unpicked
UNCURBED licentious; loose; unbridled
UNCURLED straightened
UNCURSED not execrated
UNDAMPED free to vibrate
UNDASHED undaunted; undismayed
UNDAZZLE undaze
UNDECENT indecent (obs.)
UNDECKED not adorned   nt
UNDEEDED not noteworthy
UNDEFIED unchallenged
UNDEFINE make indefinite
UNDENTED smooth
UNDERACT perform inadequately
UNDER-AGE immature
UNDERAID help secretly
UNDERARM (bowling)
UNDERBID offer less
UNDERBUD opposite of overbud
UNDERBUY cut the price
UNDERCUT the tenderloin
UNDERDID economized effort
UNDER-DOG weaker contestant
UNDERFED on short commons
UNDERLAP extend below
UNDERLAY foundation
UNDERLET sublet
UNDERLIE below the surface
UNDER-LIP to lip insufficiently
UNDERMAN (insufficient crew)   nt
UNDERPAY remunerate inadequately
UNDERPIN support
UNDERRAN opposite of overran
UNDERRUN to run insufficiently
UNDERSAY minimize
UNDERSET a contrary current
UNDERSKY lower sky
UNDERTOW tidal current
UNDEVOUT irreligious; unholy

UNDIMMED untarnished	**UNGALLED** unhurt	
UNDINTED undented	**UNGEARED** unharnessed	
UNDIPPED dry	**UNGENIAL** uncongenial; cold	
UNDIVINE secular	**UNGENTLE** rude; rough	
UNDOCKED (tails) **nt**	**UNGENTLY** harshly; unkindly	
UNDOCTOR cf. undentist, unsurgeon	**UNGIFTED** without talent	
UNDOUBLE unfold	**UNGILDED** plain	
UNDRAPED nude	**UNGILLED** (free fish from net)	
UNDREAM unimagined	**UNGIRDED** beltless; unenclosed	
UNDRIVEN not propelled	**UNGIVING** rigid	
UNDROSSY free from impurity	**UNGLAZED** paneless	
UNDULANT wavy	**UNGLOVED** barehanded	
UNDULATE vibrate	**UNGLUING** ungumming	
UNDULOUS undulating	**UNGOADED** not harassed; unurged	
UNEARNED free	**UNGORGED** not sated	
UNEASILY restlessly	**UNGOTTEN** not gained	
UNEDIBLE inedible	**UNGOWNED** unrobed	
UNELATED not puffed up	**UNGRACED** awkward	
UNENDING everlasting; ceaseless	**UNGROUND** not milled	
UNENVIED viewed with complacency	**UNGUICAL** (snail, claw, hoof) **zo**	
UNERRING certain; sure; exact	**UNGUIDED** unregulated	
UNESPIED not observed	**UNGUILTY** innocent	
UNEVENLY ruggedly; unequally	**UNGULATA** hoofed mammals **zo**	
UNEXEMPT liable	**UNGULATE** having hoofs **zo**	
UNEXPERT unskilled	**UNGUMMED** unstuck	
UNFABLED real; true	**UNHACKED** not notched	
UNFADING everlasting; constant	**UNHAIRED** scalped	
UNFAIRLY dishonestly; falsely	**UNHALLOW** profane	
UNFALLEN still standing	**UNHANDED** let go	
UNFASTEN open; let loose	**UNHANGED** not dependent	
UNFAULTY free from blemish	**UNHARMED** scatheless; immune	
UNFEARED not held in awe	**UNHASPED** unlatched	
UNFELLOW to dissociate	**UNHEADED** beheaded	
UNFENCED not enclosed; open	**UNHEATED** cold	
UNFETTER unchain; unshackle	**UNHEDGED** hedgeless	
UNFILIAL undutiful	**UNHEEDED** disregarded	
UNFILLED empty	**UNHEIRED** without an heir	
UNFILMED not photographed	**UNHELMED** rudderless	
UNFIXING detaching	**UNHELMET** deprive of a helmet	
UNFLATED deflated	**UNHELPED** unassisted	
UNFLAWED flawless; faultless	**UNHEPPEN** clumsy; maladroit	
UNFLESHY skinny	**UNHEROIC** timid; shrinking	
UNFLOWER deflower	**UNHINGED** unsettled	
UNFLUENT tongue-tied	**UNHIVING** unhousing	
UNFOILED not baffled	**UNHONEST** dishonest (obs.)	
UNFOLDED deployed; disclosed	**UNHOODED** bareheaded	
UNFOOTED untrodden	**UNHOOKED** unfastened	
UNFORCED easy; natural	**UNHOOPED** hoopless	
UNFORGED not yet made	**UNHORNED** uncuckolded	
UNFORMAL informal; unconventional	**UNHORSED** dismounted	
UNFORMED shapeless	**UNHOUSED** dislodged	
UNFOUGHT uncontested	**UNHUNTED** unsought	
UNFOULED clean; unsullied	**UNHUSKED** still in shell	
UNFRAMED frameless	**UNIAXIAL** having a single axis	
UNFRIEND an enemy	**UNIBASAL** having a single base **ch**	
UNFROZEN uncongealed	**UNICYCLE** acrobat's cycle	
UNFRUGAL prodigal; lavish; wasteful	**UNIDEAED** thoughtless	
UNFUELED unfuelled	**UNIFYING** uniting; merging	
UNFUNDED floating	**UNILOBAR** } having one lobe **bt**	
UNFURLED displayed	**UNILOBED** }	
UNGAINLY uncouth; clumsy	**UNIMBUED** not saturated	

UNINURED not hardened	**UNMILKED** fat-uddered
UNINVITE cancel invitation	**UNMILLED** unground
UNIONISM combination; alliance	**UNMINDED** forgotten
UNIONIST confederate; conservative	**UNMINGLE** sort out
UNIONITE lime silicate mn	**UNMISSED** good riddance
UNIPOLAR of one-process nerve cells zo	**UNMOANED** not lamented
UNIQUELY peculiarly; exceptionally	**UNMODISH** out of fashion
UNIQUITY singularity	**UNMOORED** cast off
UNISONAL harmonious	**UN-MOSAIC** contrary to Mosaic law
UNITEDLY jointly; concertedly	**UNMOVING** motionless; impassive
UNITIZED treated as a unit	**UNMUDDLE** co-ordinate
UNIVALVE a mollusc zo	**UNMUFFLE** (drums)
UNIVERSE the world	**UNMUZZLE** take muzzle off of
UNIVOCAL unanimous	**UNNAPPED** smooth cloth tx
UNJOINED uncoupled	**UNNATIVE** unnatural
UNJOYFUL dull; mirthless; downcast	**UNNEEDED** superfluous
UNJOYOUS gloomy; melancholy; glum	**UNNERVED** frightened
UNJUDGED awaiting verdict	**UNNETTED** still flying/swimming around
UNJUSTLY prejudicially; unfairly	**UNNIMBED** without a nimbus
UNKENNED unknown	**UNNOOKED** guileless; straightforward
UNKENNEL release	**UNNOTIFY** cancel
UNKINDLY unfriendly; harshly	**UNOPENED** closed
UNKINGED deposed	**UNPACKED** taken out of wrappings
UNKINGLY non-regal	**UNPACKER** parcel-opener
UNLACING unloosing	**UNPAINED** not hurting
UNLADING unloading	**UNPAIRED** singly
UNLAPPED unwrapped	**UNPANGED** without remorse
UNLARDED not intermixed	**UNPARTED** together
UNLASHED unfastened	**UNPATHED** trackless
UNLAVISH sparse; frugal	**UNPAWNED** not pledged
UNLAWFUL illegal; illicit	**UNPEELED** with skin intact
UNLAYING untwisting	**UNPEGGED** not stabilized
UNLEARNT forgotten	**UNPENNED** released
UNLICKED ungainly; awkward	**UNPEOPLE** depopulate
UNLIKELY improbable; risky	**UNPICKED** not selected
UNLIMBER get into action	**UNPINION** imaginary verb
UNLINEAL not in succession	**UNPINKED** not pierced
UNLINING emptying	**UNPINNED** loose
UNLINKED disconnected	**UNPITIED** not felt sorry for
UNLIVELY cheerless; listless	**UNPLACED** not in the first three
UNLOADED discharged	**UNPLIANT** stubborn; stiff; rigid
UNLOCKED open	**UNPLUMED** plucked
UNLOOKED unheeded	**UNPOETIC** prosaic
UNLOOSED slackened	**UNPOISED** out of balance
UNLOOSEN set free	**UNPOISON** detoxidify
UNLORDED not raised to peerage	**UNPOLISH** make rough
UNLORDLY commonly	**UNPOLITE** unmannerly; impolite
UNLOVELY unpleasing; hideous	**UNPOLLED** not voted
UNLOVING passionless	**UNPOSTED** not stuck up
UNMAIMED sound	**UNPRAISE** crab; criticize
UNMAKING destroying	**UNPRAYED** impossible participle
UNMANNED disheartened	**UNPREACH** recant
UNMANTLE unrobe	**UNPRETTY** plain
UNMAPPED uncharted	**UNPRICED** priceless
UNMARKED unobserved	**UNPRIEST** unfrock rl
UNMARRED unsullied	**UNPRINCE** cf. unqueen, unduke
UNMARTYR debunk	**UNPRISON** release
UNMASKED exposed; unveiled	**UNPRIZED** not valued
UNMEDDLE unmuddle	**UNPROPER** improper
UNMEETLY improperly	**UNPROVED** untested
UNMELTED undissolved	**UNPROVED** run wild

UNPUCKER uncrease	**UNSMOOTH** rough
UNPURGED unpurified	**UNSOAPED** unwashed
UNRACKED unharassed	**UNSOCIAL** reserved
UNRAISED low	**UNSOCKET** dislocate
UNRANGED in disorder	**UNSOILED** clean
UNREALLY illusively	**UNSOLDER** make unstuck
UNREAPED not harvested	**UNSOLEMN** gay
UNREASON lack of sense	**UNSOLVED** enigmatic
UNREELED unwound	**UNSONCIE** unlucky (Sc.)
UNREINED unbridled	**UNSONSIE**
UNREPAID not requited	**UNSORTED** mixed
UNREPAIR in disrepair	**UNSOUGHT** not looked for
UNRIDDLE solve; unravel; decipher	**UNSOULED** spiritless
UNRIFLED not ransacked	**UNSOURED** sweet
UNRIGGED dismantled	**UNSPARED** victimized
UNRIPPED torn	**UNSPEEDY** deliberate
UNROBING undressing	**UNSPHERE** remove spheres from
UNROLLED spread out	**UNSPIKED** with barbs removed
UNROOFED topless	**UNSPOILT** natural
UNROOTED uprooted	**UNSPOKEN** untold
UNROUTED still grouped	**UNSPRUNG** ready-set trap
UNRUFFLE plume	**UNSTABLE** inconsistant; irresolute
UNRUINED intact	**UNSTARCH** destiffen
UNRUMPLE smooth	**UNSTATED** not mentioned
UNSADDLE remove saddle from	**UNSTAYED** unrestrained
UNSAFELY perilously	**UNSTEADY** vacillating
UNSAFETY danger; hazard	**UNSTITCH** unsew
UNSALTED fresh	**UNSTORED** not warehoused
UNSAPPED not undermined	**UNSTRING** take strings off of
UNSATING not filling	**UNSTRUCK** not impressed
UNSAYING recanting	**UNSTRUNG** relaxed; loosed
UNSCARED not alarmed; unruffled	**UNSUCKED** full, erect
UNSEALED still open	**UNSUITED** unbecoming
UNSEAMED ripped open	**UNSUNNED** pale
UNSEARED uncharred	**UNSURELY** unsafely
UNSEASON mistime (obs.)	**UNSWATHE** unwrap
UNSEATED unhorsed	**UNSWAYED** unbiased
UNSECRET not trusty	**UNTACKED** disjoined
UNSECURE inseeure	**UNTACKLE** unhitch
UNSEEDED not sown	**UNTALKED** unspoken
UNSEEING blind	**UNTANGLE** unravel
UNSEEMLY unbecoming	**UNTANNED** pale
UNSEIZED not grabbed	**UNTAPPED** unbroached
UNSERVED not waited on	**UNTASKED** jobless
UNSETTLE unhinge; disturb	**UNTASTED** virginal
UNSEXUAL not hot	**UNTAUGHT** illiterate
UNSHADED lit	**UNTENANT** evict
UNSHAKEN firm	**UNTENDED** neglected
UNSHAMED unabashed	**UNTENDER** unsympathetic
UNSHAPEN formless	**UNTENTED** uncared for (Sc.)
UNSHARED whole	**UNTESTED** unproved
UNSHAVED unbarbed	**UNTETHER** untie
UNSHAVEN unshorn	**UNTHAWED** frozen
UNSHELVE take away (from) shelves	**UNTHORNY** smooth
UNSHROUD unveil	**UNTHREAD** disentangle
UNSHRUNK full-size	**UNTHRIFT** a prodigal
UNSIFTED not examined	**UNTHRONE** dethrone
UNSINGED unseared	**UNTHROWN** still in saddle
UNSLAKED unquenched	**UNTIDILY** disorderly
UNSLUICE open a sluice	**UNTILING** unroofing
UNSMOKED fresh	**UNTILLED** fallow

UNTIMELY premature	**UPMAKING** filling pieces	nt
UNTINGED uncoloured	**UPPERCUT** boxing blow	
UNTIRING unwearied	**UPPER-TEN** the aristocracy	
UNTITHED 10% not paid	rl	**UP-PLOUGH** plough up	
UNTITLED common	**UPRAISED** lifted	
UNTOMBED disenterred	**UPRIDGED** in ridges	
UNTONGUE to silence	**UPRISING** insurrection	
UNTOWARD perverse; froward	**UPROOTED** eradicated	
UNTRACED untracked	**UPROUSED** awoken	
UNTRADED inexperienced	**UPSNATCH** clutch	
UNTRUCED without truce	**UPSTAIRS** among the gentry	
UNTRUISM a fallacy	**UPSTAYED** upheld	
UNTRUSTY unfaithful	**UPSTREAM** against the current	
UNTUCKED unfolded	**UPSTROKE** alternates with downstroke	
UNTUFTED tuftless	**UPTHRUST** upheaval	
UNTUNING disordering	**UPTOSSED** upchucked	
UNTURFED stripped of turf	**UPTURNED** inverted	
UNTURNED straight	**UPWAFTED** borne aloft	
UNTWINED untwisted	**UPWARDLY** upwards	
UNVAILED untipped	**URALITIC** (uralite)	mn
UNVALUED not prized	**URBANISM** town planning	
UNVARIED monotonous	**URBANITY** suaveness; courteousness	
UNVASSAL free; emancipate	**URBANIZE** derusticate	
UNVEILED disclosed	**URCEOLUS** floral envelope	bt
UNVEILER revealer	**URETHANE** ethyl carbamate	ch
UNVENTED unuttered	**URGENTLY** momentously; pressingly	
UNVERSED unskilled	**UROBILIN** bile/urine pigment	
UNVIRTUE evil; sin; vice	**UROCHORD** (sea-squirt)	zo
UNVIZARD dehelmet	**UROCHROA** humming-birds	zo
UNVOICED not spoken; mute	**UROCISSA** Asiatic magpie	zo
UNWAITED unattended	**URODAEUM** urinary duct in cloaca	zo
UNWALLED not enclosed	**UROESTON** a tail bone	zo
UNWARILY rash; reckless	**UROMERIC** (tail-piece)	zo
UNWARMED unexcited	**UROSCOPY** urine examination	md
UNWARNED unadmonished	**UROSTEGE** a snake's scale	zo
UNWARPED flat	nt	**UROSTYLE** lengthy tail	zo
UNWASHED dirty	**URSIFORM** like a bear	zo
UNWASTED made use of	**URSULINE** a nun, (St Ursula)	rl
UNWEANED unalienated	**URTICANT** irritating, stinging	zo
UNWEDDED unwed	**URTICATE** to sting; cause a rash	
UNWEEDED overgrown	**USEFULLY** advantageously	
UNWIELDY ponderous	**USHERDOM** schoolmastery	
UNWILFUL docile; pliant	**USHERING** heralding; introducing	
UNWILLED involuntary	**USTILAGO** genus of fungi	bt
UNWINDED not blown	**USTULATE** scorched	
UNWISDOM folly; fatuity	**USUFRUCT** temporary possession	lw
UNWISELY irrationally	**USURIOUS** at high interest	
UNWONTED unusual	**USURPING** arrogating; assuming	
UNWOODED treeless	**UTILIZED** employed; used	
UNWORDED silent	**UTOPIAST** (Utopia)	
UNWORMED with worms removed	**UTRIFORM** bottle-shaped	
UNWORTHY undeserving	**UTTEREST** furthest; remotest	
UNYOKING relieving	**UTTERING** disclosing; issuing	
UPCAUGHT caught up	**UXORIOUS** wife-loving	
UPCOILED coiled		
UPCOMING impending; ascending		
UPCURLED frizzed up		
UPHEAVAL earthquake		
UPHEAVED lifted up; raised	**VACATING** quitting; annulling	
UPHOLDER partisan	**VACATION** intermission; recess; holiday	
UPLIFTED exalted	**VACCINAL** pertaining to vaccine	md

V

VACCINIA cow-pox   **md**
VAGABOND vagrant; nomad; wanderer
VAGANTES itinerant clerics   **rl**
VAGARIES whims; caprices; crotchets
VAGILITY power of movement   **ec**
VAGINANT sheathing   **bt**
VAGINATE sheathed   **bt**
VAGINULA sheath of seta in bryophyta **bt**
VAGOTOMY division of vagus nerves   **md**
VAGRANCY nomadism; itinerance
VAINNESS vanity; conceit; inanity
VALENCED decorated; draped
VALENTIA woven material   **tx**
VALERIAN all-heal, medicinal plant   **bt**
VALETING personal attendance
VALHALLA hall of heroes
VALIANCE bravery; intrepidity
VALIANCY courageousness; chivalry
VALIDATE confirm; legalize
VALIDITY soundness; justness
VALKYRIA the Valkyries
VALLANCY large wig
VALLATED cup-shaped; circumvallated
VALORIZE make a currency reform
VALOROUS intrepid; bold; heroic
VALUABLE precious; costly; expensive
VALUATOR appraiser; assessor
VALVELET small valve
VALVULAR containing valves
VAMBRACE arm-armour
VAMOOSED decamped; skedaddled
VAMPIRIC extortionative
VAMPLATE hand-guard of lance
VANADATE vanadium salt   **ch**
VANADIUM metallic element   **ch**
VANADOUS of divalent vanadium   **ch**
VANDALIC Hunnish; barbarous; savage
VANDYKED indented; notched
VANGUARD forefront; front line
VANILLIC flavoured with vanilla
VANILLIN compound from vanilla pods **ck**
VANISHED disappeared; dissolved
VANISHER absconder
VANQUISH overpower; rout; subdue
VAPIDITY insipidity
VAPORIZE turn into gas
VAPOROSE unsubstantial; gaseous
VAPOROUS unreal; steamy
VAPOURED evaporated; peevish
VAPOURER boaster; vaunter; braggart
VAQUERIA cattle ranch
VARANOID lizardlike   **zo**
VARGUENO writing table (Sp.)
VARIABLE mutable; fickle; mercurial
VARIABLY changeably; fitfully
VARIANCE discord; strife; dispute
VARIANCE average of deviation squares
  (statistics)
VARIATED altered; variegated
VARIATIM variations; in different ways
VARICORN a horned beetle   **zo**

VARICOSE } permanently dilated   **md**
VARICOUS }
VARIETAL mutative; subgeneric
VARIFORM protean; diverse
VARIOLAR pox-marked   **md**
VARIORUM commentated edition
VARISTOR 2-electrode semi-conductor   **el**
VARLETRY the rabble; the crowd
VARTABED Armenian priest   **rl**
VASALIUM vascular tissue   **md**
VASCULAR vessels; ducts, etc.   **md**
VASCULUM specimen-box   **bt**
VASELINE petroleum jelly   **mn**
VASIFORM like a duct   **md**
VASSALED enslaved
VASSALRY bondage; feudal system
VASTNESS immensity; spaciousness
VATERITE polymorph of calcium
  carbonate   **mn**
VATICIDE murder of a prophet
VAT-SIZED with sizing added to pulp   **pp**
VAULTAGE arched work
VAULTING leaping; bounding
VAUNTERY boastfulness; arrogance
VAUNTFUL ostentatious; swaggering
VAUNTING bragging; crowing
VAUNTLAY (hound movement)
VAVASORY (land tenure)   **lw**
VAVASOUR feudal tenant
VEALSKIN a skin-disease   **md**
VEDANTIC (Hindu philosophy)   **rl**
VEGETATE to sprout; (secluded life)
VEGETIVE a vegetable (Shak.)   **bt**
VEHEMENT impetuous; ardent
VEILLESS open to view; undisguised
VEINLESS lack of venation   **bt**
VELARIUM awning; canopy
VELATION mystery; concealment
VELATURA picture glazing (It.)
VELLEITY volition; inclination
VELLOPED heraldic wattles   **hd**
VELOCITY swiftness; rapidity; rate
VELODYNE tachogenerator   **el**
VELOGRID a grid in a wireless valve   **ro**
VELVERET ersatz velvet
VELVETED like velvet
VENALITY mercenariness; corruptness
VENATION veins as a whole   **bt, zo**
VENATION hunting; pursuit of game
VENDETTA a blood feud; vengeance
VENDEUSE saleswoman, shop assistant
VENDIBLE marketable; disposable
VENDIBLY saleably
VENEERED overlaid; disguised
VENENATE poisonous; poisoned; toxic
VENERATE esteem; respect; revere
VENETIAN (Venice)
VENGEFUL vindictive; retributive
VENIABLE pardonable
VENIALLY excusably; trivially
VENOMING poisoning

VENOMOUS venemous; poisonous	
VENOSITY full-bloodedness	
VENOUSLY veined	
VENT-HOLE air-hole	
VENTOUSE vacuum-traction birth	**md**
VENT-PLUG barrel-peg	
VENTURED hazarded; dared	
VENTURER speculator; adventurer	
VERACITY truth; truthfulness	
VERANDAH covered balcony	
VERATRIC hellebore extract	**ch**
VERATRUM hellebore, etc.	**bt**
VERBALLY orally; by word of mouth	
VERBATIM word for word	
VERBIAGE verbosity; prolixity	
VERDANCY greenness	
VERDERER forest-keeper	
VERDITER green pigment	
VERGENCY border; verge	
VERGETTE heraldic pallet	**hd**
VERIFIED confirmed; authenticated	
VERIFIER corroborator	
VERJUICE sour juice	
VERMINLY verminously	
VERMOUTH absinthe; wormwood	
VERNICLE miraculous imprint	
VERONESE (Verona)	
VERONICA speedwell plants	**bt**
VERRUGAS Peruvian skin disease	**md**
VERSABLE reversible	
VERSELET ⎫ brief ode	
VERSICLE ⎭	
VERTEBRA segment of the spine	**pl**
VERTICAL upright; erect; perpendicular	
VERTICES summits; apices; zeniths	
VERTICIL a whorl	**bt**
VESICANT blistering	
VESICATE to blister	
VESICULA a pustule	**md**
VESPIARY wasp's nest	
VESTIARY a wardrobe	
VESTMENT garment; robe; dress	**rl**
VESTUARY vestiary	
VESTURAL (robe; clothing)	
VESTURER vestment keeper	**rl**
VESUVIAN fusee; fuzee	
VEXATION affliction; torment; worry	
VEXILLAR feathery	**zo**
VEXILLUM a banner; Roman standard	
VEXINGLY provokingly; annoyingly	
VIAMETER an odometer	**me**
VIATICUM Eucharist	**rl**
VIBRATED quivered; oscillated	
VIBRATOR a trembler; buzzer	
VIBRISSA whisker; bristle	
VIBROGEN cellular tissue	**bt**
VIBRONIC electronic vibrations	**el**
VIBURNUM guelder-rose	**bt**
VICARAGE vicar's house	**rl**
VICARIAL substituted	
VICARIAN deputy	

VICARIUS a vicar	**rl**
VICE-DEAN a canon	**rl**
VICE-KING regent; viceroy	
VICENARY based on twenty	
VICHYITE (Vichy)	
VICINAGE ⎫ neighbourhood;	
VICINITY ⎭ proximity	
VICTORIA a vehicle	
VICTRESS woman conqueror; victrix	
VICTUALS provisions; sustenance	
VIDENDUM thing to be seen	
VIETMINH people of Vietnam	
VIEWABLE able to be seen	
VIEWLESS vistaless	
VIEWSOME panoramic	
VIGILANT circumspect; alert; wakeful	
VIGNERON wine-grower (Fr.)	
VIGNETTE character sketch	
VIGAROSO forcibly	**mu**
VIGOROUS lusty; powerful; virile	
VILENESS baseness; depravity; vice	
VILIFIED slandered; defamed; decried	
VILIFIER traducer; maligner	
VILIPEND disparage; calumniate	
VILLADOM suburban villas	
VILLAGER dweller in village	
VILLAINY depravity; fraud; rascality	
VILLATIC (village)	
VILLITIS coronet inflammation in horse	**vt**
VINCIBLE conquerable; surmountable	
VINCULUM bond of union; link; chain	
VINE-CLAD covered with vines	
VINE-GALL vine disease	
VINE-GRUB a parasite	**zo**
VINE-LAND grape acreage	
VINEYARD grape plantation	**bt**
VINOLOGY art of wine making	
VINOSITY wine flavour	
VINTAGER grape gatherer	
VINTNERY the wine trade	
VINYLITE plastic glass	
VIOLABLE transgressive	
VIOLATOR ravisher; debaucher	
VIOLENCE brute force	
VIPERINE venomous	**zo**
VIPERISH malignant	
VIPEROUS treacherous	
VIREMENT bookkeeping transfer	
VIRGINAL early form of spinet	**mu**
VIRGINIA tobacco; creeper	**bt**
VIRIDIAN bluish-green colour	
VIRIDINE green variety of andalusite	**mn**
VIRIDITY verdure; greenness	
VIRILISM male characteristics in woman	
VIRILITY manhood; energy; manliness	
VIROLOGY virus diseases	**md**
VIRTUOSE expert in art	
VIRTUOSO connoisseur; expert	
VIRTUOUS upright; moral; chaste	
VIRULENT bitter in enmity; toxic	
VISCACHA pampas hare	**zo**

VISCERAL abdominal	md	**VOTARIST** adherent; votary; zealot	
VISCOUNT a title		**VOTIVELY** by way of vow	
VISIGOTH Spanish Goth		**VOUCHING** warranting; backing	
VISIONAL illusory; chimerical		**VOUSSOIR** arch stone	
VISITANT guest; frequenter		**VOWELISM** use of vowels	
VISITING inspecting; haunting; calling		**VOWELIST** user of vowels	
VITALISM ⎱ (hypothetical vital		**VOWELLED** with vowels	
VITALIST ⎰ principle)		**VOYAGEUR** Canadian boatman	
VITALITY vigour; life; energy		**VRAICING** gathering seaweed (Ch. Is.)	
VITALIZE animate; quicken		**VULCANIC** volcanic	
VITELLIN a protein in egg		**VULGARLY** commonly; boorishly	
VITELLUS the yolk of an egg		**VULSELLA** forceps	md
VITIATED impaired; spoilt; debased			
VITIATOR a pervert			
VITICIDE a vine pest	zo		
VITILIGO patchy skin depigmentation	md	**W**	
VITREOUS glassy		**WABBLING** wobbling	
VITULINE (veal)		**WADDLING** walking like a duck	
VIVA-VOCE orally		**WAESUCKS** alas (Sc.)	
VIVACITY sprightliness; liveliness		**WAFERING** sealing	
VIVARIUM small zoo	zo	**WAGE-FUND** (a theory)	
VIVIDITY vividness; clarity; lucidity		**WAGE-WORK** paid work	
VIVIFIED quickened; enlivened		**WAGELESS** unpaid	
VIVIPARY manner of bud/seed production		**WAGERING** betting; laying; staking	
	bt	**WAGGLING** swaying	
VIVISECT operate on the living	md	**WAGGONER** wagoner	
VIXENISH quarrelsome; snappish		**WAGGONET** wagonette	
VIZERATE viziership		**WAGONAGE** cost of transport	
VOCALIST singer	mu	**WAGONFUL** load	
VOCALITY utterableness		**WAGONING** carting	
VOCALIZE voice; articulate		**WAGON-LIT** sleeping car (Fr.)	
VOCATION profession; calling; pursuit		**WAILMENT** lamentation	
VOCATIVE (invocation); a case		**WAINBOTE** timber for carts	
VOGESITE hornblende-lamprophyre	mn	**WAINROPE** cart-rope	
VOIDABLE able to be annulled		**WAINSCOT** panelling	
VOIDANCE evasion; annulment		**WAIT-A-BIT** (various shrubs)	bt
VOIDNESS nullity; emptiness		**WAITRESS** a female waiter	
VOIGTITE form of mica	mn	**WAKENING** rousing; stimulating	
VOLATILE lively; gay; capricious		**WAKERIFE** wakeful (Sc.)	
VOLCANIC eruptive		**WALDHORN** hunting horn (Ger.)	mu
VOLITANT able to fly		**WALHALLA** Valhalla	
VOLITION freewill; choice; purpose		**WALKABLE** able to be walked	
VOLITIVE wishful		**WALK-MILL** fulling mill	
VOLLEYED (tennis)		**WALK-OVER** easy victory	
VOLPLANE glide		**WALLAROO** large kangaroo	
VOLSUNGS Norse legendary race		**WALL-EYED** glaring; fierce	
VOLTAISM galvanism		**WALL-GAME** Eton football	
VOLTZITE zinc sulphide	mn	**WALL-KNOT** Turk's head	nt
VOLULITE petrified shell	mn	**WALL-MOSS** stonecrop	bt
VOLUMIST an author		**WALL-NEWT** lizard; gecko	zo
VOLUTION convolution; spiral		**WALL-TREE** fruit tree	bt
VOLVULUS stoppage	md	**WALL-WORT** dwarf-elder	bt
VOMITING ejecting		**WALLOPED** thrashed	
VOMITION sickness	md	**WALLOPER** a slogger	
VOMITIVE vomitory		**WALLOWED** floundered; weltered	
VOMITORY an emetic	md	**WALLOWER** groveller	
VORACITY rapacity; greed		**WALLSEND** house coal	mn
VORTEXES whirlpools; vortices		**WALTZING** dancing	
VORTICAL turning		**WAMBLING** rumbling	
VORTICES eddies; maelstroms		**WANDERED** strayed; roamed	
VOTARESS lady devotee		**WANDERER** rambler; nomad	
		WANDEROO langur monkey	zo

WANGLING winning by craft
WANTLESS fully satisfied; abundant
WANTONED frolicked
WANTONLY sportively; capriciously
WAPPENED tearful
WAPPERED blinked
WARBLING quavering; trilling
WAR-DANCE tribal ceremony
WARDCORN castle guard
WARDENRY warden's district
WARDMOTE court of inquiry
WARDROBE clothes closet
WARD-ROOM mess-room   nt
WARDSHIP guardianship
WARE-ROOM show-room
WARFARER combatant
WARFARIN anticoagulant and rodenticide   ch
WAR-FIELD battle-field
WAR-HORSE a charger   zo
WARINESS alertness; craftiness
WARMNESS warmth; ardour
WARPAINT battle make up
WAR-PLANE fighting aircraft
WAR-PLUME plume de guerre
WARPROOF valorous
WARRAGAL the dingo   zo
WARRANTY authority
WARRENER warren keeper
WARRISON healing (obs.)
WARTLESS unbumped
WARTWEED ⎫ spurge used for
WARTWORT ⎭   curing warts   bt
WAR-WEARY tired of fighting
WAR-WHOOP a war-cry
WASHABLE non-shrink
WASHAWAY a breach
WASHBALL soap-ball
WASHBOWL washbasin
WASH-COAT pre-treatment primer   pt
WASH-DIRT process   mn
WASH-ROOM ablution room
WASP-BITE wasp-sting
WASTEFUL prodigal; improvident
WATCHBOX sentry box
WATCHDOG a guardian   zo
WATCHFUL vigilant; alert; wary
WATCHING wakefulness; vigil
WATCH-KEY antique implement
WATCHMAN a look-out; custodian
WATERAGE transport dues
WATER-BED bed filled with water
WATERBUG various types   zo
WATERCAN yellow waterlily   bt
WATER-DOG water spaniel   zo
WATERFLY aquatic insect   zo
WATER-FOX the carp   zo
WATER-GAS illuminating gas
WATER-GOD Neptune
WATER-HEN moorhen   zo
WATER-ICE a confection

WATERING diluting; irrigating
WATERISH insipid; moist; damp
WATERLOG saturate
WATERMAN ferryman; turncock
WATER-POA species of grass   bt
WATERPOT watering can
WATER-RAM hydraulic ram
WATER-RAT water vole   zo
WATER-RUG water spaniel   zo
WATER-TAP spigot
WATERWAY a canal
WATT-HOUR measure of work   me
WATTLING plaiting; hurdling
WAVEBAND group of wave-lengths
WAVEFORM characteristic of radio wave
WAVELESS calm; undisturbed; serene
WAVELIKE undulating; rippling
WAVE-LINE stream-line
WAVE-LOAF a wave-offering
WAVERING tottering; vacillating
WAVEROUS fluctuating; unsteady
WAVE-TRAP maritime hazard
WAVEWORN of coastal rocks
WAVINESS unsteadiness
WAXCLOTH oil-cloth
WAXLIGHT a taper
WAX-PAPER stencil paper
WAX-PLANT honeywort   bt
WAXWORKS an exhibition
WAY-BOARD thin stratum   mn
WAYBREAD common plaintain   bt
WAYFARER traveller; pedestrian
WAYGOING departing
WAYGOOSE a printer's festivity
WAYLAYER intercepter; lurker
WAYLEAVE right of way
WAYMAKER a precursor
WAY-SHAFT an engine shaft
WAYTHORN buckthorn   bt
WAY-TRAIN slow train
WAYWISER pedometer
WEAKENED debilitated; enfeebled
WEAKENER enervator
WEAK-EYED needing glasses
WEAKLING delicate creature
WEAKNESS feebleness; frailty
WEANLING newly weaned
WEAPONED armed
WEARABLE fit to be worn
WEARIFUL wearisome; tedious
WEARYING tiring; fatiguing
WEED-HOOK garden tool
WEEDLESS well weeded
WEEVILED infested with weevils   zo
WEIGHAGE a toll
WEIGHING balancing; pondering
WEIGH-OUT (horse racing)
WEIGHTED given due weight
WEISSITE iolite   mn
WELCOMED greeted; hailed; saluted
WELCOMER polite host; receptionist

WELDABLE fusable	**WHIFFLER** prevaricator
WELD-IRON wrought iron	**WHIGGERY** ⎫
WELDMENT welded assembly **eg**	**WHIGGISH** ⎬ Liberalism
WELLADAY alas; alackaday	**WHIGGISM** ⎭
WELLAWAY welladay	**WHIM-WHAM** a gadget
WELL-BOAT fishing boat **nt**	**WHIMBREL** wimbrel; curlew **zo**
WELL-BORN of noble birth	**WHIMSIES** notions; caprices; fancies
WELL-BRED of good stock	**WHINCHAT** singing bird **zo**
WELLCURB ring of masonry	**WHINNIED** neighed
WELLDECK open-deck **nt**	**WHINNOCK** a milk-pail
WELLDOER a benefactor	**WHINYARD** sword; dirk
WELL-HEAD source of a spring	**WHIPCORD** string; material
WELL-HOLE (flight of stairs)	**WHIPHAND** advantage over; control
WELL-KEPT carefully tended	**WHIPLASH** crack of whip
WELL-KNIT compact; sturdy	**WHIPPING** lashing; castigating
WELLNIGH nearly; almost	**WHIPSTER** whippersnapper
WELL-READ learned; scholarly	**WHIPTAIL** slender tail
WELL-SEEN experienced; skilful	**WHIRLBAT** cestus
WELL-TO-DO prosperous; affluent	**WHIRLING** gyrating; rotating
WELLSIAN (H. G. Wells)	**WHIRRING** spinning; twirling; turning
WELL-WORN threadbare; shabby	**WHISKERS** (Dundreary)
WELSHING absconding	**WHISKING** brushing; seizing
WELSHMAN a man of Wales	**WHISTLED** piped **mu**
WELTERED wallowed; floundered	**WHISTLER** broken-winded horse **zo**
WEREGILD compensation for homicide	**WHITE-ANT** a termite **zo**
WEREWOLF a changeling **zo**	**WHITE-ARM** arme blanche
WESLEYAN (John Wesley) **rl**	**WHITE-BOY** Irish white-shirt
WESTERLY in westward direction	**WHITE-HOT** hotter than red-hot
WESTWARD toward the west	**WHITE-LIE** an evasion
WET-NURSE breast-giver	**WHITE-MAN** a true and trusty man
WET-ON-WET short-interval	**WHITENED** blanched
spray-painting	**WHITENER** bleacher
WHACKING astounding; a beating	**WHITE-OUT** open space in display texts
WHALEMAN Jonah	**WHITEPOT** a confection
WHALE-OIL oil from blubber of whale	**WHITLING** sea trout; bull trout **zo**
WHANGHEE bamboo cane **bt**	**WHITSOUR** summer apple **bt**
WHANGING whacking	**WHITSTER** a whitener
WHARFAGE dock dues	**WHITTLED** pared; cut; trimmed
WHARFING wharves	**WHITTRET** the weasel **zo**
WHATEVER anything which	**WHIZZING** speeding
WHEATEAR fallowfinch **zo**	**WHODUNIT** a crime novel
WHEAT-EEL a wheat disease **zo**	**WHOMEVER** whomsoever
WHEAT-FLY a pest **zo**	**WHOOPING** yelling; hooting
WHEEDLED coaxed; cajoled; inveigled	**WHOPPING** beating; colossal
WHEEDLER sycophant; fawner; toady	**WHURRING** pronounced word
WHEELMAN (cycling)	**WICKEDLY** heinously; atrociously
WHEEL-ORE bournonite **mn**	**WICKERED** made of osiers
WHEEL-TAX carriage tax	**WIDE-EYED** afraid; gullible
WHEELAGE a toll	**WIDELINE** vertical mark in papermaking
WHEELING cycling; turning; twirling	**WIDENESS** breadth; width **[pp**
WHEELMAN cyclist	**WIDENING** extending; broadening
WHEEZILY asthmatically	**WIDOWING** bereaving
WHEEZING breathing heavily	**WIELDING** brandishing; plying
WHELMING overburdening; crushing	**WIFEHOOD** wivehood
WHELPING littering	**WIFELESS** unmarried
WHENEVER at any time that	**WIFELIKE** wifely
WHEREOUT out of which	**WIG-BLOCK** wigmaker's block
WHEREVER to whatever place	**WIGGLING** wriggling
WHETTING sharpening	**WIGMAKER** perukist
WHEY-FACE pale face	**WILD BOAR** Richard III's mascot; hog **zo**
WHIFFING puffing	**WILD-BORN** not born indoors

WILD-DUCK mallard and others	zo		**WITHDREW** retreated; departed	
WILD-FIRE sheet lightning			**WITHERED** faded; shrunk; drooped	
WILD-FOWL untamed birds	zo		**WITHE-ROD** American shrub	bt
WILD-LAND uncultivated soil			**WITHHELD** kept back; detained	
WILD-WOOD forest			**WITHHOLD** restrain; reserve	
WILDERED bewildered (obs.)			**WITHWIND** bindweed	bt
WILDNESS savageness; recklessness			**WITTOLLY** complacently	
WILFULLY obstinately; deliberately			**WIVEHOOD** wifehood	
WILINESS craftiness; artfulness			**WIVELESS** wifeless	
WILLOWED full of willows	bt		**WIZARDLY** magically	
WILLYARD wilful; shy (Sc.)			**WIZARDRY** sorcery; necromancy	
WIMBLING boring			**WIZENING** withering	
WIMPLING rippling			**WOAD-MILL** dye extracting mill	
WINCHMAN windlass operator			**WOBEGONE** woebegone; calamitous	
WIND-BAND (wind instruments)	mu		**WOEFULLY** sorrowfully; tragically	
WIND-PUMP small windmill			**WOLF-FISH** catfish	zo
WIND-RODE riding at anchor	nt		**WOLF-SKIN** outer layer of wolf	
WIND-ROSE a diagram			**WOMANISH** effeminate	
WIND-SEED wind-carried seed	bt		**WOMMERAH** stick for spear-throwing	
WINDBILL guarantee			**WONDERED** speculated; marvelled	
WINDERED fanned			**WONDERER** conjecturer; ponderer	
WINDFALL (fruit; legacy)	bt		**WONDROUS** marvellous; miraculous	
WIND-GALL puffy swelling			**WONTLESS** unaccustomed; unused	
WINDLASS a winch; capstan	nt		**WOOD-ACID** acetic acid	ch
WINDLESS calm; winded			**WOODBIND** ⎰ wild honeysuckle	bt
WINDMILL swimming stroke			**WOODBINE** ⎱	
WINDOWED fenestrated			**WOOD-BIRD** forest denizen	zo
WINDPIPE the trachea	pl		**WOODCHAT** shrike; woodpecker	zo
WINDSAIL ventilating funnel	nt		**WOOD-COAL** charcoal; lignite	mn
WINDWARD toward the wind			**WOODCOCK** bird allied to snipe	zo
WINE-CASK barrel for wine			**WOOD-DOVE** stockdove	zo
WINELESS undrunk			**WOOD-EVIL** cattle disease	
WINE-RACK wine bottle storage unit			**WOOD-HOLE** woodstore	
WINESKIN bag for wine			**WOOD-IBIS** tantalus; stork	zo
WING-CASE horny cover	zo		**WOOD-KERN** Irish outlaw	
WINGLESS apterous	zo		**WOODLAND** forest land	
WING-SHOT flying shot			**WOODLARK** forest bird	zo
WINNOWED sifted			**WOODLESS** treeless	
WINNOWER chaff remover			**WOOD-LICE** millepeds	zo
WINTERED hibernated			**WOOD-LILY** lily of the valley	bt
WINTERLY cheerless			**WOODLOCK** to stop	nt
WIREDRAW to make wire			**WOOD-MITE** a beetle	zo
WIRE-HEEL a foot disease			**WOODMOTE** forest court	lw
WIRELESS radio			**WOODNOTE** bird call	
WIREMARK horizontal mark in papermaking	pp		**WOOD-OPAL** silicified wood	mn
			WOOD-PULP cellulose	
WIREROPE tightrope; circus stay			**WOODROCK** asbestos	mn
WIRESIDE underside of paper	pp		**WOODROOF** ⎰ a plant	bt
WIRE-WORM a centipede	zo		**WOODRUFF** ⎱	
WIRE-WOVE (glazed writing paper)	pp		**WOOD-SEAR** ⎰ cuckoo-spit;	
WIRINESS toughness			**WOOD-SEER** ⎱ an insect;	zo
WISEACRE a simpleton			**WOOD-SERE** ⎰ a season	
WISELING wiseacre			**WOOD-SHED** store for wood	
WISERITE manganese carbonate	mn		**WOODSKIN** Guyana canoe	
WISHBONE merrythought			**WOODSMAN** a woodcutter	
WISH-WASH weak drink			**WOOD-SOOT** charcoal soot	
WISTARIA a climbing plant	bt		**WOOD-TICK** death-watch beetle	zo
WITCH-ELM variety of elm tree	bt		**WOOD-VINE** clematis	bt
WITCHERY fascination; sorcery			**WOODWALE** ⎰ golden oriole;	zo
WITCHING enchanting; charming			**WOODWALL** ⎱ green woodpecker	zo
WITHDRAW retire; recall; retract			**WOODWARD** forest keeper	

WOODWORK carpentry
WOOD-WORM a grub _zo_
WOOD-WREN willow-warbler _zo_
WOOINGLY enticingly
WOOLBALL roll of yarn
WOOLDING binding _nt_
WOOL-DYED dyed in the wool
WOOLFELL skin with wool on it
WOOL-MILL cloth factory
WOOLPACK 240 lb. of wool
WOOLSACK Lord Chancellor's seat
WOOLWARD wearing wool
WOOLWORK knitting, etc.
WORD-BOOK a vocabulary
WORDLESS silent; dumb; mute
WORD-PLAY punning; repartee
WORKABLE feasible
WORKADAY prosaic; ordinary
WORKBOOK duties of staff for the day
WORKCARD report on work, defects, results
WORKFOLK toilers
WORKGIRL female employee
WORKMARK title letter and catalogue number _pr_
WORKROOM crafts workplace
WORKSHOP tool workroom
WORM-BORE damage by worms to books, furniture
WORMCAST thrown by worms
WORMGEAR gear wheels, etc.
WORM-HOLE track of woodworm
WORMLIKE vermicular _zo_
WORMSEED santonica _bt_
WORMWOOD absinthe; vermouth _bt_
WORRICOW hobgoblin
WORRYING harassing; fretting; chafing
WORSENED deteriorated
WORSTING besting; defeating
WORTHILY deservedly; meritoriously
WORTHITE silica compound _mn_
WOUNDILY excessively
WOUNDING injuring
WRACKFUL ruinous; destructive
WRACKING gathering seaweed
WRANGLED brawled; bickered
WRANGLER disputant
WRANNOCK the wren _zo_
WRAPPAGE a wrapper
WRAPPING enclosing; muffling
WRATHFUL irate; incensed; wroth
WRATHILY indignantly; furiously
WRAULING caterwauling
WREAKFUL revengeful; angry
WREAKING inflicting; punishing
WREATHED garlanded; festooned
WREATHEN entwined
WRECKAGE debris
WRECKFUL causing ruin
WRECKING sabotaging; destroying
WRENCHED twisted; strained; wrung

WRESTING extorting; forcing; usurped
WRESTLED strove; grappled
WRESTLER sturdy struggler
WRETCHED miserable; paltry; sorry
WRICKING spraining; straining
WRIGGLED squirmed
WRIGGLER shuffler
WRIGHTIA tropical climber _bt_
WRINGING twisting; squeezing
WRINKLED furrowed; creased; rumpled
WRISTLET wrist-band
WRIST-PIN connecting pin
WRITE-OFF total loss
WRITHING wriggling; squirming
WRITHLED wrinkled
WRONGFUL injurious; unjust; unfair
WRONGING violating; maltreating
WRONGOUS illegal (Sc.)
WURTZITE sulphide of zinc _mn_

X

XANTHATE a salt _ch_
XANTHEIN yellow colour
XANTHENE chemical dye
XANTHIAN from Xanthus
XANTHINE yellow dye
XANTHITE yellow idocrase _mn_
XANTHIUM a plant _bt_
XANTHOMA skin disease _md_
XANTHOUS yellowish
XANTHURA American jay _zo_
XANTIPPE termagant; wife of Socrates
XENOGAMY cross-fertilisation _bt_
XENOLITE aluminium silicate _mn_
XENOPHYA foreign particles _zo_
XENOTIME yttrium phosphate _mn_
XENURINE armadillo-like _zo_
XERANSIS dryness _md_
XERANTIC exsiccant _md_
XEROCOLE animal living in dry place _ec_
XEROSERE dry-land succession _bt_
XESTURGY process of polishing
XILINOUS of cotton _tx_
XIPHIOID like a swordfish _zo_
XYLOCARP hard woody fruit _bt_
XYLOIDIN starch/nitric acid explosive
XYLONITE form of celluloid
XYLOTYPE wood engraving; print

Y

YACHTING ice, ocean, or lake pastime
YAHOOING howling and yelping
YAMMERED lamented; whined
YANOLITE axinite _mn_
YAPPEDGE overlapping book cover
YARDLAND usually 30 acres (12 hectares) _me_
YARDWAND yardstick _me_
YARWHELP bar-tailed godwit _zo_

YATAGHAN long Turkish dagger	
YEANLING eanling; a lamb	zo
YEAR-BOOK voluminous annual	
YEARLING one year old animal	zo
YEARLONG twelve months	
YEARNFUL mournful; distressing	
YEARNING longing; craving; desirous	
YELDRING \ yowley; yorling;	zo
YELDROCK / the yellow-bunting	zo
YELLOWED dyed yellow	
YEOMANLY sturdily; staunchly	
YEOMANRY volunteer cavalry	
YESTREEN last evening (Sc.)	
YIELDING bearing; affording	
YODELLED sang falsetto	
YOGEEISM abstract meditation	
YOICKING shouting encouragingly	
YOKELESS unrestrained	
YOKEMATE an associate; a partner	
YOKE-TOED pair-toed	
YOKOHOMA a breed of fowls	zo
YONDMOST farthest; uttermost	
YOUNGEST most youthful	
YOUNGISH somewhat juvenile	
YOURSELF reflexive pronoun	
YOUTHFUL boyish; puerile; fresh	
YTTERBIA oxide of ytterium	ch
YTTERITE gadolinite	mn
YTTRIOUS containing yttrium	ch
YUGOSLAV Jugo-Slav	
YULETIDE Christmas; Noel	rl

Z

ZALOPHUS seal genus	zo
ZAMBOMBA Spanish instrument	mu
ZAMINDAR zemindar; tax-collector	
ZAMPOGNO Italian bagpipe	mu
ZANTIOTE native of Zante	
ZARATITE nickel compound	mn
ZARZUELA Spanish operetta	
ZEALLESS slack; apathetic	
ZEALOTRY fanaticism; fervour; ardour	
ZECCHINO sequin (Venice)	nm
ZEGIDINE silver drinking cup (Hung.)	
ZELANIAN (New Zealand)	
ZEMINDAR Indian tax collector	
ZENITHAL culminating; crowning	
ZEOLITIC (felspar)	mn
ZEPPELIN airship	

ZERUMBET East Indian drug	bt
ZETICULA a small room	
ZIBELINE like a sable	zo
ZIGGURAT Sumerian temple	
ZINCKIFY cover with zinc	
ZINGIBER ginger, etc.	bt
ZINNOBER vermilion pigment	
ZIONWARD heavenward	
ZIPHIOID like a swordfish	zo
ZIRCONIA zirconium oxide	mn
ZIZYPHUS jujube tree	bt
ZOANTHUS sea-anemone	zo
ZODIACAL (zodiac)	
ZOETROPE early form of cinema	
ZOIATRIA veterinary surgery	
ZOLOTNIK Russian weight	me
ZONATION occurrence in bands	bt
ZONELESS beltless	
ZOOBLAST animal cell	zo
ZOOCHEMY animal chemistry	ch
ZOOECIUM wall/chamber of polyzoan individual	zo
ZOOGENIC generative	
ZOOGLOEA colony of bacteria	md
ZOOGRAFT grafting tissue	md
ZOOLATER animal worshipper	
ZOOLATRY animal worship	
ZOOLITIC (fossilized animals)	mn
ZOOMANCY divination	
ZOOMETRY animal mensuration	
ZOOMORPH animal in decorative art	
ZOONITIC articulated	zo
ZOONOMIA animal physiology	
ZOOPHAGA carnivorous animals	zo
ZOOPHILY love of animals	
ZOOPHYTE plantlike animal	zo
ZOOSCOPY seeing snakes, etc.	md
ZOOSPERM male seed-cell	md
ZOOSPORE animated spore	bt
ZOOTOMIC (vivisection)	md
ZOOT-SUIT long coat and tight trousers	
ZOPILOTE turkey-buzzard	zo
ZUCCHINI green squash, marrow (It.)	ck
ZWIEBACK biscuit rusk	ck
ZYGADITE aluminium compound	mn
ZYGODONT (molar teeth)	md
ZYGONEMA zygotene phase of meiosis	cy
ZYGOTENE 2nd stage of meiotic prophase	cy
ZYMOLOGY study of fermentation	

GENERAL INFORMATION

WEIGHTS AND MEASURES

With some approximate English equivalents

Two Letters

LI	2115 feet	China
OZ	ounces	Britain
RI	$2\frac{1}{2}$ miles	Japan
TO	4 gallons	Japan

Three Letters

AAM	30-35 gallons	E. Indies
ARE	120 square yards	Univ.
AUM	31 Imp. gallons	S. Africa
CAB	3 pints	Hebrew
CHO	$5\frac{1}{4}$ chains	Japan
COR	$8\frac{1}{4}$ bushels	Hebrew
CWT	a hundredweight	Britain
DWT	a pennyweight	Britain
ELL	(Eng.) 45 inches	Britain
ELL	(Scot.) 37 inches	Britain
FOU	a bushel	Scotland
GUZ	33 inches	E. Indies
HIN	6 quarts	Hebrew
KEN	2 yards	Japan
KIN	$1\frac{1}{2}$ lb	Japan
LOG	$\frac{3}{4}$ pint	Hebrew
LUX	unit of light	Univ.
NIU	1 inch	Thailand
OKA	3 lb	Egypt
OKE	$2\frac{3}{4}$ lb	Turkey
PIN	half a firkin	Britain
RAI	$\frac{1}{3}$ acre	Thailand
RIO	ounce	Japan
ROD	$5\frac{1}{2}$ yards	Britain
SEN	44 yards	Thailand
SHO	$\frac{1}{4}$ peck	Japan
SUN	1 inch	Japan
TAN	133 lb	China
TOD	2 stone	Britain
TON	20 cwt.	Britain
TUN	252 gallons	Britain
WAH	80 inches	Thailand
WEY	13 stone	Britain

Four Letters

ACRE	4840 square yards	Britain
BALE	10 reams	Britain
BATH	6 gallons	Hebrew
BUTT	108 gallons	Britain
CH'IH	1 foot	China
COSS	about $1\frac{3}{4}$ miles	India
CRAN	about 750 herrings	Britain
DRAH	22 inches	Morocco
DRAM	1/16 oz	Britain
EPHA	a bushel	Hebrew
FOOT	12 inches	Britain
FUNT	1 lb	U.S.S.R.

GILL	$\frac{1}{4}$ pint	Britain
GRAM	15.4323 grains	Univ.
HAND	(horses) 4 inches	Britain
HIDE	120 acres	Britain
INCH		Britain
KELA	$\frac{1}{2}$ bushel	Egypt
KILO	2.205 lb	Univ.
KNOT	6080 feet	Britain
KOKU	5 bushels	Japan
KOSS	2000 yards	India
KWAN	8 lb	Japan
LAKH	100,000 rupees	India
LAST	12 inches	Britain
LINK	8 inches	Britain
MILE	1760 yards	Britain
MILE	2240 yards	Ireland
MOIO	$2\frac{3}{4}$ quarts	Portugal
MUDD	1 bushel	Morocco
NAIL	$2\frac{1}{4}$ inches	Britain
NATR	2 lb	Ethiopia
OKET	1 oz avoirdupois	Ethiopia
PAAL	$1\frac{1}{2}$ metres	Indonesia
PACK	240 lb	Britain
PECK	2 gallons	Britain
PINT	4 gills	Britain
PIPE	126 gallons	Britain
POLE	$16\frac{1}{2}$ feet	Britain
POOD	36 lb	U.S.S.R.
REAM	20 quires	Britain
REED	152 inches	Hebrew
ROOD	$\frac{1}{4}$ acre	Britain
ROTL	1 lb	Egypt
SACK	2 weys	Britain
SAWK	20 inches	Thailand
SEAH	14 pints	Hebrew
SEAM	(glass) 24 stone	Britain
SEER	2 lb	India
SKOT	low-intensity lighting	Univ.
TAEL	1 oz	China
TOLA	180 grains	India
TS'UN	1 inch	China
VARA	32 inches	Honduras
YARD	3 feet	Britain

Five Letters

ANKER	$7\frac{1}{2}$ gallons	S. Africa
ARDEB	5 bushels	Egypt
BAHAR	$3\frac{1}{2}$ cwt	E. India
CABLE	100 fathoms	Britain
CANDY	500 lb	India
CANEH	6 cubits	Hebrew
CANNA	2 yards	Malta
CARAT	200 milligrams	France
CATTY	1 lb	China
CAWNY	1 acre	India

CHAIN 22 yards	Britain	**FIRKIN** 9 gallons	Britain
CHANG 3 lb	Thailand	**GALLON** 4 quarts	Britain
CHANG 12 feet	China	**KANTAR** 100 lb	Ethiopia
CHEKI 509 lb	Turkey	**MICRON** millionth part of a metre	France
CHIEN 1 lb	China	**MUSCAL** 1½ drams	Turkey
CLOVE 7 lb	Britain	**NOGGIN** small cup, ¼ pint	Britain
COOMB 4 bushels	Britain	**POTTLE** 4 pints	Britain
CUBIT 18 inches	Britain	**ROTOLO** 1¾ lb	Malta
EPHAH a bushel	Hebrew	**SCHENE** 7½ miles	Egypt
GRAIN 1/24 pennyweight	Britain	**SHTOFF** 1 quart	U.S.S.R.
GROSS 12 dozen	Britain	**SIEMEN** electrical conduction	
HOMER 8 bushels	Hebrew	**TALBOT** luminous energy	
KANEH 6 cubits	Hebrew	**TIERCE** 42 gallons	Britain
KILEH 1 bushel	Turkey	**VISHAM** 3 lb	India
LIANG an ounce	China	**YOJANA** about 5 miles	India
LIBRA 1 lb	Malta & Brazil		
LIPPY half a gallon	Scotland		
LITRE	Univ.	**Seven Letters**	
LIVRE 1 lb	Greece	**BRACCIO** a cubit	Italy
MAUND 82 lb	India	**CALORIE** unit of heat	Univ.
METRE	Univ.	**CENTNER** 1 cwt	Germany
OCQUE 3 lb	Greece	**CHALDER** 96 bushels	Britain
OKIEH 1 oz	Egypt	**DECIARE** $\frac{1}{10}$th are	France
OUNCE	Britain	**DECIBEL** unit of noise	Britain
PARAH 15 gallons	China	**DIOPTER** optical measure	Greece
PECUL 133 lb	China	**DRACHMA** silver coin	Greece
PERCH pole, 5½ yards	Britain	**FURLONG** 220 yards	Britain
PICUL 133 lb	China	**HECTARE** 100 ares	Univ.
PIEDE 11 inches	Malta	**MEGA-ERG** a million ergs	Greece
POUND	Britain	**MILLIER** 1000 kilos	France
QIRAT 209 square yards	Egypt	**POUNDAL** unit of force	Britain
QUART	Britain	**QUANTAR** 99 lb	Egypt
QUIRE 24 sheets	Britain	**QUARTER** 28 lb	Britain
SAJEN 7 feet	U.S.S.R.	**QUINTAL** 1 cwt	France
SHAKU 12 inches	Japan	**ROTTOLO** a weight	Mid. East
STERE cubic metre	France	**SCRUPLE** 20 grains	Britain
STONE 14 lb	Britain	**THERMIE** unit of heat/calory	France
TSUBO 4 square yards	Japan	**THORLAND** unit of illumination	
UNGUL 1 inch	India	**VIRGATE** a quarter of a hide	Britain
VEDRO 3 gallons	U.S.S.R.		
VERST 1166 yards; 2/3 mile	U.S.S.R.	**Eight Letters**	
YOJAN about 5 miles	E. Indies	**CENTIARE** a square metre	France
		CENTIBAR meteorological meas.	France
Six Letters		**CHALDRON** 25 cwt of coal	France
ARROBA 32 lb	Brazil	**DECAGRAM** 10 grams	Univ.
ARSHIN (cloth) 27 inches	Turkey	**DECIGRAM** $\frac{1}{10}$th gram	Univ.
BANDLE 2 feet	Rep. of Ire.	**FOOT-RULE** a 12 inch measure	Britain
BARREL 36 gallon cask	Britain	**HOGSHEAD** a large cask	France
BATMAN 17 lb	Turkey	**KILODYNE** 1000 dynes	France
BUNDLE 2 reams	Britain	**KILOGRAM** 1000 grams	Univ.
BUSHEL 8 gallons	Britain	**KILOWATT** 1000 watts	Univ.
CANDIE 500 lb	India	**MUTCHKIN** about a pint	Scotland
CANTAR 124 lb	Turkey	**PARASANG** about 4 miles	Iran
CENTAL 100 lb	N. America	**PUNCHEON** a large cask	France
CHOPIN a quart	Scotland	**QUADRANT** an arc of 90°	France
DECARE 1000 square metres	France	**QUARTERN** a gill; 4 lb	Britain
DJERIB 2½ acres	Turkey	**SERPLATH** 80 stone	Scotland
ENDAZE 25½ inches	Turkey	**YARDLAND** usually 30 acres	Britain
FANEGA 11 bushels	Costa Rica	**YARDWAND** yardstick	Britain
FATHOM 6 feet	Britain	**ZOLOTNIK** unit of weight	U.S.S.R.
FEDDAN 1 acre	Egypt		

COINS AND MONIES: ANCIENT AND MODERN

Two Letters
AS a bronze Roman coin

Three Letters
BOB a shilling
COB Spanish
DAM Indian copper coin
ECU French five-franc piece
FEN Chinese
FIL Iraqui, Jordanian
KIP Laotian
LAT Latvian
LEU Romanian
LEV Bulgarian
MIL proposed coin, 1/1000
ORE Scandinavian
PIE Pakistani, Nepali
PYA Burmese
REE Portuguese money
REI of account
SEN Japanese, Indonesian
SOL old French halfpenny, Peruvian
SOU French five-centime piece
WON Korean
YEN Japanese

Four Letters
ANNA Pakistani
AURA Icelandic
BANI Romanian
BAHT Thai
BEKA ½ Shekel Hebrew
BUCK American dollar
CASH small Eastern coin
CENT (various countries)
CHIP a counter; a sovereign
DAWM dam; Indian copper coin
DIME American 10-cent piece
DOIT Dutch half-farthing
DONG N. Vietnamese
GELD ancient tribute
HWAN Korean
JOEY 4d. piece (Joseph Hume)
KRAN Persian
KYAT Burmese
LAKH 100,000 rupees
LIRA Italian, Turkish
LIRE plural of lira (Italian)
MARK German
MERK Scottish 13s. 4d.
MITE a very small coin
OBOL Charon's ferry fee, 1½d.
PARA Yugoslav, Turkish
PESO Filipino
PICE the fourth of an anna
PULS Afghani
QUID a sovereign
RAND S. African
REAL the fourth of a peseta
RIAL Iranian
RIEL Cambodian

RYAL gold coin; the rose noble
TAEL Chinese
YUAN Chinese

Five Letters
ANGEL old English gold coin
AUREI Roman gold coins
BELGA a Belgian coin
BETSO small Venetian coin
BRASS money colloquially
COLON Costa Rican
CROWN five-shilling piece
DARIC gold coin of Darius
DINAR Serbian, Iranian, Jordanian
DUCAT Italian, gold or silver
EAGLE 10-dollar gold coin
FRANC French, Swiss, Belgian
GROAT silver 4d. piece
KRONA Scandinavian
LEPTA Greek
LIARD old French farthing
LIBRA Peruvian
LITAS Lithuanian
LIVRE old French franc
LOCHO Venezuelan
LOUIS 20-franc piece
MEDIO Venezuelan
MOHUR 15-rupee gold coin
MONGO Mongolian
NOBLE old English coin, 6/8d.
PENCE plural of penny
PENNI Finnish
PENNY English copper coin
POUND 100 pence
QURSH Arabian
RIYAL Sudanese
RUPEE Indian
SAUDI Arabian gold sovereign
SCUDI plural of scudo
SCUDO Italian
SEMIS half a Roman as
SOLDI plural of soldo
SOLDO Italian halfpenny (former)
STICA small Saxon coin
STYCA styca; Saxon coin
SUCRE Ecuadorean
TICAL Thai
TICCY S. African 3d. piece
ZLOTY Polish

Six Letters
AMANIA Afghani
AUREUS Roman gold coin
BALBOA Panamanian
BAUBEE ⎫
BAWBEE ⎬ Scottish halfpenny
BEZANT Byzantine gold coin
BUKSHA Yemeni
CONDOR Chilean

COPANG Japanese gold coin
COPPER one penny
DECIME a tenth of a franc
DIRHAM Moroccan
DOBLON Chilean
DOLLAR (various countries)
ESCUDO Portuguese
FILLER Hungarian
FLORIN silver 2-shilling piece
FORINT Hungarian
GOURDE Haitian
GROSZY Polish
GUINEA 21 shillings
GULDEN Dutch, Hungarian
HELLER Austrian
KOPECK Russian
KORUNA Czech
KURUSH Turkish
LEPTON Greek
MARKKA Finnish
NICKEL 5-cent piece, USA
OBOLUS obol; ancient Greek coin
PAGODA Indian gold coin
PESETA Spanish
PRUTAH Indonesian
RAPPEN Swiss
ROUBLE Russian
SATANG Thai
SEQUIN Venetian gold coin
SHEKEL Jewish half crown
SOMALO Somali
SOVRAN poetical sovereign
STATER Greek gold or silver coin
TALARI Abyssinian
TALENT Hebrew
TANNER sixpence
TESTER Henry VIII shilling
THALER German
TICKEY S. African 3d. piece
TOMAUN Persian gold coin
ZECHIN sequin; Venetian coin

Seven Letters
AFGHANI (100 puls) Afghani
ANGELOT a Louis XI gold coin
ANGOLAR Angolan escudo

BOLIVAR S. American
CAROLUS gold coin of Charles I
CENTAVO S. American
CENTIME one-hundreth of a franc
CORDOBA Nicaraguan
CRUSADO Portuguese
DENARII pence
DRACHMA Greek
GUARANI Paraguayan
GUILDER Dutch florin
JACOBUS gold coin of James I
LEMPIRA Brazilian
MANILLA W. African copper coin
MILREIS Brazilian
MOIDORE old Portuguese coin
PFENNIG German copper coin
PIASTRE Egyptian
PISTOLE old Spanish gold coin
QUARTER quarter of a dollar
QUETZAL Guatemalan
QUINTAR Albanian
SEXTANS ancient Roman bronze coin
TESTOON old Italian silver coin
TESTRIL tester; a sixpence
TUGHRIK Mongolian

Eight Letters
AMBROSIN Milanese coin
CRUZEIRO Brazilian
DENARIUS Roman silver coin
DOUBLOON 2 pistoles (Spanish)
DUCATOON Venetian silver coin
FARTHING a quarter of a penny
FLORENCE Edward III gold florin
GROSCHEN Austrian
HALFMARK old English coin, 6s. 8d.
JOHANNES old Portuguese coin
KREUTZER Austrian copper coin
LOUIS-D'OR 20-franc gold piece
MARAVEDI small Spanish copper coin
NAPOLEON French 20-franc gold coin
QUADRANS Roman copper coin
SESTERCE Roman silver coin
SHILLING English, 12 pence (d.)
SIXPENCE English silver coin
STOTINKA Bulgarian

DISTINCTIVE GROUP PHRASEOLOGY

Terms of the Chase
NYE of pheasants
RAG of colts
BEVY of roes or quails
CAST of hawks
CETE of badgers
DOWN of hares
DULE of turtles
FALL of woodcock
GANG of elks

HERD of cranes, curlew, deer
LEPE of leopards
NEST of rabbits
PACE of asses
PACK of hounds
ROUT of wolves
SORD of mallards
SUTE of mallards
STUD of mares
TEAM of oxen

WISP of snipe
BROOD of hens
CHARM of goldfinches
COVEY of partridges
DOYLT of tame swine
DROVE of kine
FLOCK of sheep
PLUMP of wild fowl
PRIDE of lions
SEDGE of herons
SHOAL of fish
SIEGE of herons
SKEIN of geese (flying)
SKULK of foxes
SLOTH of bears
SWARM of bees
TRIBE of goats
TROOP of monkeys
WATCH of nightingales
BARREN of mules
COLONY of gulls
COVERT of coots
DESERT of lapwings
GAGGLE of geese
HARRAS of horses
FLIGHT of doves
KENNEL of raches
KINDLE of kittens
LABOUR of moles
LITTER of whelps
MUSTER of peacocks
SCHOOL of porpoises
SPRING of teal
BADLING of ducks
CLOWDER of cats
COMPANY of widgeon
DOPPING of sheldrake
FESNYING of ferrets
BUILDING of rooks
RICHESSE of martens
SOUNDER of swine
SINGULAR of boars
COWARDICE of curs
BADELYNGE of ducks
SHREWDNESS of apes
CHATTERING of choughs
MURMURATION of starlings
EXALTATION of larks
CONGREGATION of plovers

Miscellaneous
BLAST of hunters

BLUSH of boys
LYING of pardoners
SKULK of friars
STALK of foresters
STATE of princes
MELODY of harpers
RAYFUL of knaves
DRAUGHT of butlers
POVERTY of pipers
FIGHTING of beggars
MORBIDITY of majors
SAFEGUARD of porters
WANDERING of tinkers
DISGUISING of tailors
SIMPLICITY of subalterns
SUBTILNE of sergeants
OBSERVANCE of hermits
DRUNKENSHIP of cobblers
SUPERFLUITY of nuns
MALAPERTNESS of pedlars
INCREDIBILITY of cockolds

Modern
BAND of musicians
NEST of machine guns
PARK of artillery
GANG of thieves
ROPE of pearls
TUFT of grass
CASTE of flower pots
CLUMP of trees
CROWD of people
FLEET of cars
HORDE of savages
POSSE of savages
SHEAF of corn
SKEIN of silk
STAND of arms
TRUSS of hay
BUDGET of papers
FLIGHT of aeroplanes
GALAXY of beauty
PUNNET of strawberries
TROUPE of actors
CLUSTER of stars
COMPANY of actors
SEQUENCE of cards
COMMUNITY of saints
GATHERING of the clans

THE CHEMICAL ELEMENTS

Name	Symbol	Name	Symbol	Name	Symbol
ALUMINIUM	Al.	HOLMIUM	Ho.	PRASEODYMIUM	Pr.
ANTIMONY	Sb.	HYDROGEN (gas)	H.	RADIUM	Ra.
ARGON (gas)	A.	ILLINIUM	Il.	RHENIUM	Re.
ARSENIC	As.	INDIUM	In.	RHODIUM	Rh.
BARIUM	Ba.	IODINE	I.	RUBIDIUM	Rb.
BERYLLIUM	Be.	IRIDIUM	Ir.	RUTHENIUM	Ru.
BISMUTH	Bi.	IRON	Fe.	SAMARIUM	Sm.
BORON	B.	KRYPTON (gas)	Kr.	SCANDIUM	Sc.
BROMINE	Br.	LANTHANUM	La.	SELENIUM	Se.
CADMIUM	Cd.	LEAD	Pb.	SILICON	Si.
CAESIUM	Cs.	LITHIUM	Li.	SILVER	Ag.
CALCIUM	Ca.	LUTETIUM	Lu.	SODIUM	Na.
CARBON	C.	MAGNESIUM	Mg.	STRONTIUM	Sr.
CERIUM	Ce.	MANGANESE	Mn.	SULPHUR	S.
CHLORINE (gas)	Cl.	MASURIUM	Ma.	TANTALUM	Ta.
CHROMIUM	Cr.	MERCURY	Hg.	TELLURIUM	Te.
COBALT	Co.	MOLYBDENUM	Mo.	TERBIUM	Tb.
COLUMBIUM	Cb.	NEODYMIUM	Nd.	THALLIUM	Tl.
COPPER	Cu.	NEON (gas)	Ne.	THORIUM	Th.
DYSPROSIUM	Dy.	NEOYTTERBIUM	Yb.	THULIUM	Tm.
ERBIUM	Er.	NEUTRON (gas)	Nu.	TIN	Sn.
EUROPIUM	Eu.	NICKEL	Ni.	TITANIUM	Ti.
FLUORINE (gas)	F.	NIOBIUM	Nb.	TUNGSTEN	W.
GADOLINIUM	Gd.	NITROGEN (gas)	N.	URANIUM	U.
GALLIUM	Ga.	OSMIUM	Os.	VANADIUM	V.
GERMANIUM	Ge.	OXYGEN (gas)	O.	WOLFRAM	W.
GLUCINUM	Gl.	PALLADIUM	Pd.	XENON (gas)	Xe.
GOLD	Au.	PHOSPHORUS	P.	YTTERBIUM	Yb.
HAFNIUM	Hf.	PLATINUM	Pt.	YTTRIUM	Y.
HELIUM (gas)	He.	POTASSIUM	K.	ZINC	Zn.
				ZIRCONIUM	Zr.

GASEOUS EMANATIONS

ACTINIUM from Thorium   **NITON** from Radium
IONIUM from Uranium   **POLONIUM** from Radium

THE SEVEN SENSES

SIGHT   SMELL
HEARING   UNDERSTANDING
FEELING   SPEECH
TASTE

THE SIGNS OF THE ZODIAC

Spring		*Autumn*	
ARIES Ram	(1)	LIBRA Balance	(7)
TAURUS Bull	(2)	SCORPIO Scorpion	(8)
GEMINI Twins	(3)	SAGITTARIUS Archer	(9)
Summer		*Winter*	
CANCER Crab	(4)	CAPRICORNUS Goat	(10)
LEO Lion	(5)	AQUARIUS Water Carrier	(11)
VIRGO Virgin	(6)	PISCES Fishes	(12)

THE NINE MUSES

CALLIOPE	Epic Song	ERATO	Erotic Poetry
CLIO	History	TERPSICHORE	Dance
EUTERPE	Lyric Poetry	POLYHYMNIA	Hymns
MELPOMENE	Tragedy	URANIA	Astronomy
THALIA	Comedy		

THE GREEK FATES

CLOTHO	spins the thread of life	The Spinner
LACHESIS	controls its destiny	The Disposer of Lots
ATROPOS	cuts it off	The Inflexible One

THE FURIES

Avenging deities—Erinyes—sent from Tartarus to avenge wrong and punish crime.

ALECTO
MEGAERA
TISIPHONE

THE HARPIES

(Malignant monsters with birds' wings and claws who snatched away the souls of the dead.)

AELLO
OCYPETE
CELAENO or PODARGE

THE PLANETS AND THEIR SATELLITES

MARS	SATURN	URANUS
Deimos	Rhea	Ariel
Phobos	Dione	Titania
	Mimas	Oberon
	Titan	Umbriel
EARTH	Phoebe	Miranda
Luna	Tethys	
	Janus	JUPITER
VENUS	Iapetus	Io
	Hyperion	Europa
NEPTUNE	Enceladus	Callisto
Triton		Ganymede
Nereid		
	PLUTO	MERCURY

THE BOOKS OF THE APOCRYPHA

ESDRAS
TOBIT
JUDITH
ESTHER
THE WISDOM OF SOLOMON
ECCLESIATICUS
BARUCH
EPISTLE OF JEREMY
SONG OF THE THREE HOLY CHILDREN
HISTORY OF SUSANNA
BEL AND THE DRAGON
THE PRAYER OF MANASSES
MACCABEES

ALPHABETS

Greek

ALPHA	NU
BETA	XI
GAMMA	OMICRON
DELTA	PI
EPSILON	RHO
ZETA	SIGMA
ETA	TAU
THETA	UPSILON
IOTA	PHI
KAPPA	CHI
LAMBDA	PSI
MU	OMEGA

Hebrew

ALEPH	LAMED
BETH	MEM
GIMEL	NUN
DALETH	SAMECH or SAMEKH
HE	AIN or AYIN
VAU	PE
ZAIN or ZAYIN	TZADDI or ZADE
CHETH or HETH	KOPH
TETH	RESH
JOD or YOD	SCHIN or SHIN
CAPH or KAPH	TAU

THE SEVEN WONDERS OF THE WORLD

1 The **PYRAMIDS** of Egypt   2 The **HANGING GARDENS** of Babylon
3 The **TOMB** of **MAUSOLOS**   4 The **TEMPLE** of **DIANA** at Ephesus
5 The **COLOSSUS** at Rhodes   6 The **STATUE** of **ZEUS** by Phidias
7 The **PHAROS** of Egypt, or The **PALACE** of **CYRUS** cemented with gold

MONTHS OF THE JEWISH YEAR

TISHRI	NISAN or ABIB
HESHVAN	IYAR
KISLEV	SIVAN
TEBET	TAMMUS
SHEBAT	AB
ADAR or VEADAR	ELUL

FRENCH REVOLUTIONARY CALENDAR

FRENCH REPUBLIC 1794

VENDEMIAIRE	Vintage	Sept.	FLOREAL	Blossom	Apr.
BRUMAIRE	Fog	Oct.	PRAIRAL	Pasture	May
FRIMAIRE	Sleet	Nov.	MESSIDOR	Harvest	June
NIVOSE	Snow	Dec.	THERMIDOR }	Heat	July
PLUVIOSE	Rain	Jan.	FERVIDOR }		
VENTOSE	Wind	Feb.	FRUCTIDOR	Fruit	Aug.
GERMINAL	Seed	Mar.			

THE STATES OF AMERICA

ALABAMA	Ala.	FLORIDA	Fla.
ALASKA	Alas.	GEORGIA	Ga.
ARIZONA	Ariz.	HAWAII	No official abbreviation
ARKANSAS	Ark.	IDAHO	Id., Ida.
CALIFORNIA	Cal.	ILLINOIS	Ill.
COLORADO	Colo.	INDIANA	Ind.
COLUMBIA (District)	D.C.	IOWA	Ia.
CONNECTICUT	Conn.	KANSAS	Kan.
DELAWARE	Del.	KENTUCKY	Ky., Ken.

LOUISIANA	La.	OHIO	O.
MAINE	Me.	OKLAHOMA	Okla.
MARYLAND	Md.	OREGON	Ore., Oreg.
MASSACHUSETTS	Mass.	PENNSYLVANIA	Penn.
MICHIGAN	Mich.	RHODE ISLAND	R.I.
MINNESOTA	Minn.	SOUTH CAROLINA	S.C.
MISSISSIPPI	Miss.	SOUTH DAKOTA	S.Dak.
MISSOURI	Mo.	TENNESSEE	Tenn.
MONTANA	Mont.	TEXAS	Tex.
NEBRASKA	Neb.	UTAH	Ut.
NEVADA	Nev.	VERMONT	Vt.
NEW HAMPSHIRE	N.H.	VIRGINIA	Va.
NEW JERSEY	N.J.	WASHINGTON	Wash.
NEW MEXICO	N.M.	WEST VIRGINIA	W.Va.
NEW YORK	N.Y.	WISCONSIN	Wis.
NORTH CAROLINA	N.C.	WYOMING	Wyo.
NORTH DAKOTA	N.D.		

BRITISH PRIME MINISTERS

From 1770

Lord NORTH	Lord ABERDEEN	H. H. ASQUITH**
Lord ROCKINGHAM	Lord PALMERSTON	David LLOYD GEORGE
Lord SHELBURNE	Lord DERBY	A. BONAR LAW
Duke of PORTLAND	Lord PALMERSTON	Stanley BALDWIN
William PITT	Lord John RUSSELL	J. R. MACDONALD
Henry ADDINGTON	Lord DERBY	Stanley BALDWIN
William PITT	Benjamin DISRAELI	J. R. MACDONALD**
Lord GRENVILLE	W. E. GLADSTONE	Stanley BALDWIN**
Duke of PORTLAND	Benjamin DISRAELI	Neville CHAMBERLAIN**
Spencer PERCEVAL	Lord BEACONSFIELD	W. Spencer CHURCHILL**
Lord LIVERPOOL	W. E. GLADSTONE	Clement ATTLEE**
George CANNING	Lord SALISBURY	Sir W. CHURCHILL
Lord GODERICH	W. E. GLADSTONE	Sir Anthony EDEN
Duke of WELLINGTON	Lord SALISBURY	Harold MACMILLAN**
Lord GREY	W. E. GLADSTONE	Sir Alec DOUGLAS-HOME
Lord MELBOURNE	Lord ROSEBERY	Harold WILSON**
Sir Robert PEEL	Lord SALISBURY	Edward HEATH
Lord MELBOURNE	A. J. BALFOUR	Harold WILSON**
Sir Robert PEEL	Sir H. CAMPBELL-	James CALLAGHAN
Lord John RUSSELL	BANNERMAN	Margaret THATCHER
Lord DERBY		

** Signifies the number of consecutive terms of office.

PRESIDENTS OF THE UNITED STATES

George WASHINGTON		William TAFT
John ADAMS	James BUCHANAN	Woodrow WILSON
Thom. JEFFERSON	Abraham LINCOLN	Warren HARDING
James MADISON	Andrew JOHNSON	Calvin COOLRIDGE
James MONROE	Ulysses GRANT	Herbert HOOVER
John Quincy ADAMS	Rutherford HAYES	F. D. ROOSEVELT
Andrew JACKSON	James GARFIELD	Harry TRUMAN
Martin van BUREN	Chester ARTHUR	Dwight D. EISENHOWER
William HARRISON	Grover CLEVELAND	John F. KENNEDY
John TYLER	Benjamin HARRISON	Lyndon B. JOHNSON
James Knox POLK	Grover CLEVELAND	Richard M. NIXON
Zachary TAYLOR	William McKINLEY	Gerald R. FORD
Millard FILLMORE	Theodore ROOSEVELT	James E. CARTER

COUNTIES OF THE BRITISH ISLES

England and Wales

3

MON •

4

AVON
BEDS
CAMS
GLAM •
GLOS
KENT
OXON
TYNE &
  WEAR

5

BERKS
BUCKS
CARDS •
CARMS •
CLWYD
DERBY
DEVON
DYFED
ESSEX
FLINT •
GWENT
HANTS
HERTS
HUNTS
LANCS
LEICS
LINCS
NOTTS
PEMBS •
POWYS
SALOP
WILTS
WORCS
YORKS

6

BRECON •
DORSET
DURHAM
LONDON
OXFORD
RADNOR •
STAFFS
DURHAM
SURREY
SUSSEX

7

BEDFORD
CUMBRIA
DENBIGH •
GWYNEDD
LINCOLN
NORFOLK
RUTLAND •
SUFFOLK
WARWICK

8

ANGLESEY •
CARDIGAN •
CHESHIRE
CORNWALL
HEREFORD
HERTFORD
MONMOUTH •
PEMBROKE •
SOMERSET
STAFFORD

Scotland

3

AYR •

4

BUTE •
FIFE
ROSS •

5

ANGUS •
BANFF •
ELGIN •
MORAY •
NAIRN •
PERTH •

6

ARGYLL •
FORFAR •
LANARK •
ORKNEY

7

BERWICK •
BORDERS
CENTRAL
KINROSS •
LOTHIAN
PEEBLES •
RENFREW •
SELKIRK •
TAYSIDE
WIGTOWN •

8

ABERDEEN •
AYRSHIRE •
CROMARTY •
DUMFRIES &
  GALLOWAY
GRAMPIAN
HIGHLAND
ROXBURGH •
STIRLING •

Ireland

4

CORK †
DOWN
LEIX †
MAYO †

5

CAVAN †
CLARE †
KERRY †
LOUTH †
MEATH †
SLIGO †

6

ANTRIM
ARMAGH
CARLOW †
DUBLIN †
GALWAY †
OFFALY †
TYRONE
ULSTER (P)

7

DONEGAL †
KILDARE †
LEITRIM †
MUNSTER (P) †
WEXFORD †
WICKLOW †

8

KILKENNY †
LAOIGHIS
LEINSTER (P) †
LIMERICK †
LONGFORD †
MONAGHAN †

* Counties which no longer exist after local government reorganization in 1974.
† Counties of the Republic of Ireland.

PREFIXES

Two Letters

AB	AM	CO	EC	EU	OB	RE
AC	AT	DE	EM	EX	OC	SE
AD	BE	DI	EN	IL	OF	TO
AG	BI	DO	EP	IM	ON	UN
AL	BY	DU	ES	IN	OP	UP

Three Letters

ABS	BIO	DIA	FOR	MON	PAR	SUB
AMB	BIS	DIS	HOM	NEG	PER	SUR
ANA	CAT	DIF	MAL	NON	POR	SYN
ANT	COL	DYS	MEN	OFF	PRE	TOM
APH	CON	EPH	MET	OUT	PRO	TRA
APO	COR	EPI	MIS	PAN	RED	TRI

Four Letters

ALLO	BENE	ENDO	HOLO	META	PERI	SEMI
AMBI	BULL	FORE	HOME	METH	POLY	SINE
ANTE	CATA	GAIN	HOMO	MONO	POST	TELE
ANTI	CATH	HEMI	HYPH	MULT	POUR	VICE
ARCH	DEMI	HEPT	HYPO	OVER	PROS	WITH
AUTO	DINO	HEXA	MALE	PARA	PROT	

Five Letters

AFTER	ENTER	HORSE	INTRO	PENTA	QUASI	TETRA
AMPHI	EXTRA	HYPER	JUXTA	PROTO	RETRO	TRANS
ARCHE	FORTH	INTER	MULTI	QUADR	SUPER	ULTRA
ARCHI	HEPTA	INTRA	PANTO	QUART	SUPRA	UNDER

Six Letters

CIRCUM	CONTRA	CONTRO	HETERO	PRETER
PSEUDO	SUBTER			

The PREFIXES and SUFFIXES may be found useful when coping with anagrams of lengthy words.

SUFFIXES

Two Letters

AC	CY	EN	EY	IE	ON	SY
AL	ED	ER	FY	LE	OR	TH
AN	EE	ES	IC	LY	RY	TY
AR	EL	ET	ID			

Three Letters

ACY	ASM	ERY	ILE	ITE	OID	TER
ADE	ATE	ESE	INE	IVE	ORY	TOR
AGE	BLE	ESS	ING	IZE	OSE	TRE
AIN	CLE	EST	ION	KIN	OUR	ULE
ANE	DOM	FUL	ISE	LET	OUS	URE
ANT	EER	ICS	ISH	NCE	PLE	WAY
ARD	EHE	IDE	ISM	NCY	RED	YER
ARY	ERN	IER	IST	OCK	RIC	YSM

Four Letters

ABLE	EREL	HERD	LESS	MONY	TEEN	WARD
ANCE	ERLY	HOOD	LIKE	MOST	THER	WAYS
ANCY	ETTE	IBLE	LING	NESS	TION	WIFE
CULE	FAST	ICLE	LITE	SHIP	TORY	WISE
ENCE	FOLD	IQUE	LOGY	SION	TRIX	
ENCY	FULL	ITIS	LONG	SOME	TUDE	
EOUS	HEAD	LENT	MENT	STIR	UBLE	

Five Letters

ASTER	ATIVE	CRAFT	LENCE	OLOGY	RIGHT	SCOPY
ATION	ATORY	GRAPH	METER	PATHY	SCOPE	STEAD

Six Letters

ACEOUS	ACIOUS	ANEOUS	ESCENT	FEROUS	GRAPHY
MONGER					

PRONOUNS AND POSSESSIVE ADJECTIVES

Two Letters

HE	IT	ME	MY	US	WE	YE

Three Letters

HER	HIS	ONE	SHE	THY	YOU	WHO
HIM	ITS	OUR	ANY			

Four Letters

HERS	NONE	OURS	THEE	THEY	THOU	WHOM
MINE	ONES	THAT	THEM	THIS	WHAT	YOUR
SOME						

Five Letters

THEIR	THESE	THOSE	THINE	WHOSE	WHICH	YOURS

Six Letters

ITSELF	MYSELF	THEIRS	NOBODY	ANYONE